Entertainment Law
(Second Edition)
Document Supplement

MELVIN SIMENSKY
(First and Second Editions)
Member of New York Bar
Member of the firm of
Hall, Dickler, Kent, Friedman & Wood LLP

THOMAS D. SELZ
(First and Second Editions)
Member of New York Bar
Member of the firm of
Frankfurt, Garbus, Klein & Selz, P.C.

BARBARA BURNETT
Professor of Law
Syracuse University
College of Law

ROBERT C. LIND
Professor of Law
Southwestern University School of Law

CHARLES A. PALMER
Professor of Law
Thomas M. Cooley Law School

MATTHEW BENDER

ISBN#: 0-8205-4260-1

Editorial Offices
744 Broad Street, Newark, NJ 07102 (973) 820-2000
201 Mission St., San Francisco, CA 94105-1831 (415) 908-3200
701 East Water Street, Charlottesville, VA 22902-7587 (434) 972-7600
www.lexis.com

(Pub.166)

DEDICATIONS

To my sons, Daniel and
Nicholas, in the hope
that they will always
know the joys of learning

Thomas D. Selz

For Brenda, Adam and Joanna

Melvin Simensky

To the memory of my
mother and father, Robert
and Gertrude Palmer.
Their kind encouragement
of this project and many
others will forever be
appreciated.

Charles A. Palmer

To my husband, Cass.

Barbara Burnett

To my better half, Ellen Hurley

Robert C. Lind

PREFACE

This Document Supplement contains material that is to be used in conjunction with the Entertainment Law (Second Edition) casebook and is important to any study of entertainment law. It is a compilation of many of the basic contracts and statutes that are used in the practice of entertainment law. The entertainment business is built on relationships. Those relationships often have a contractual basis, obtained through collective bargaining or through individual negotiations.

The Document Supplement contains selected provisions of the Directors Guild of America Basic Agreement, the Producer-Screen Actors Guild Codified Basic Agreement and the Writers Guild of America Theatrical and Television Minimum Basic Agreement. We have also included forty-eight full-length individual agreements used in the television, motion picture, music, print publishing and live theater branches of the entertainment industry, as well as multimedia and infomercial contracts. In addition, we have compiled federal and state statutes, relevant to the practice of entertainment law, that are involved in the areas of copyright, trademark, dilution, contracts, talent agencies and right of publicity.

The material contained in the Document Supplement has been integrated into the readings, questions and hypotheticals presented in the Entertainment Law (Second Edition) casebook. By using the Document Supplement, students will have the opportunity to analyze judicial decisions, business situations and hypothetical problems with the assistance of the most current agreements employed by the entertainment industry.

Many of the agreements contained in this Document Supplement were provided by well-established entertainment companies and organizations that use the agreements in their transactions. Most of the unattributed documents were taken from ENTERTAINMENT INDUSTRY CONTRACTS, edited by Donald Farber and published by Matthew Bender. This multi-volume treatise is respected, not only for its outstanding selection of contracts, but also for its accompanying commentaries regarding the various provisions found in each contract. It is highly recommended that anyone teaching an entertainment law course have access to this useful treatise.

ACKNOWLEDGMENTS

The compilation and editing of these materials was a massive undertaking made possible only through the efforts of loyal research assistants who came to know the meaning of publication deadlines. So it is with great appreciation that the authors recognize these students: Tim Griggs, Charles Steenveld, Aaron Bartz, Jason Rosenbaum, Sara Avakian, Jeff Feinberg, Wendy Jaffe, Daron Case, Monica Penichet, Sonja Sonnenburg, Anelise Herman, Jeremy Kenik, Kerwin Miller, Helen Quan, Kristi Gasaway, Elaine Goldman, Donald Ornelas, Adam Reisner, Joyce Li, Irena Kopelev, Arezou Kohan, Christine Renten, Rachel Roth, Marc Miles, Douglas Rothschild, Todd Whiteley and Bret Chapman.

A number of attorneys helped to insure that the materials contained in this Document Supplement were accurate and up-to-date. The authors extend their gratitude to: Joseph De Marco, Alan Feldstein, Roni Mueller, Michael Blaha, Wayne Levin, Michelle Kucsma Klein, Kent Klavens, Michael Fuller, Larry Verbit, Keith Blau, David Besbris, Mark De Vitre, Bruce Lazarus, Carol Lombardini, Elliott Williams, Doreen Braverman, Vicki Shapiro, Howard Fabrick, Paula Katz, Gary Roth, Robert Cohen and Ellen Hurley.

The staff and administration of the Southwestern University School of Law is largely responsible for providing the logistical and economic means by which this Document Supplement was completed. The staff of the Southwestern University School of Law library was outstanding in providing material and assistance. Special thanks go to its Director, Linda Whisman, Carole Weiner, Dennis Ladd, David McFadden, Sharrel Gerlach, LeVont Crockett and Tom Hall. The staff of the Southwestern University School of Law faculty support center provided unerring logistical support. Our appreciation goes to its Director, Jeannie Nicholson, Martha Fink and Margaret Soh. The financial and scheduling support given to this project by Southwestern University School of law made its timely completion possible. The authors thank Dean Leigh Taylor, Assistant Dean Doreen Heyer, Catherine Carpenter and Julia Mason.

Several organizations and companies were willing to provide assistance and permission to use many of the documents students will find useful in learning about the entertainment industry. These include: Alliance of Motion Picture & Television Producers; Directors Guild of America; Screen Actors Guild; Writers Guild of America; Actors' Equity Association; Fox Searchlight; Twentieth Century Fox Film Corporation; Philips Media and the law firm of Hall, Dickler, Kent, Friedman & Wood. Other individuals who were also instrumental in the production of this work include Lolita Peralta and Guy Pace. Lastly, the authors wish to express their appreciation to our editors who toiled throughout the process of completing this manuscript, Clark Kimball, Barbara Post and Ed Berger.

TABLE OF CONTENTS

TABLE OF CONTENTS

COLLECTIVE BARGAINING AGREEMENTS

COLLECTIVE BARGAINING AGREEMENTS

Form 1
DIRECTORS GUILD OF AMERICA, INC.
1993 BASIC AGREEMENT (As Amended 1996)*

SYNOPSIS

---

* Reprinted with the permission of the Directors Guild of America and the Alliance of Motion Picture and Television Producers.

ARTICLE 1

* * *

Section 1-200   DEFINITIONS

1-201   Definition of "Motion Picture" and "Motion Picture Industry"

The phrase "motion picture" and the phrase "motion picture industry," wherever used in this BA, shall be deemed to mean the production of all types of motion pictures on film or tape or transferred from tape to film or film to tape, or otherwise, of any gauge or size or type, whether for public or private showings as theatrical, television, videodiscs/videocassettes, supplemental markets, industrial, religious, educational, commercial, documentary or government motion pictures, and whether produced by means of motion picture cameras, electronic cameras or devices, tape devices or any combination thereof, or other means, methods or devices now known or yet to be devised, in connection with which any Employee renders services.

Notwithstanding the foregoing, this BA does not apply to:

(1)   non-entertainment motion pictures produced primarily for the basic cable market;

(2)   entertainment motion pictures produced primarily for the basic cable market except to the extent set forth in Paragraph 1-102(b); and

(3)   motion pictures described in Paragraph 20-905 except to the extent set forth in that Paragraph.

The direction of second units and staged talent tests for a role in a motion picture are within the jurisdiction of the Guild.

1-202   Theatrical Motion Pictures and Free Television Motion Pictures

The term "Television Motion Pictures" or "Television Films" or "Free Television Films," as used herein, is deemed to mean and refer only to motion pictures produced primarily for "Free Television" exhibition. Motion pictures produced primarily for exhibition in theaters or any other place where a charge, by any method, is paid by the viewing audience are subject to the provisions herein relating to "Theatrical Motion Pictures."

1-203   Basic Cable

The term "basic cable," as distinguished from pay television or free television, refers to that type of exhibition which is commonly understood in the industry today to be basic cable exhibition.

1-204 The following provisions of this BA which are applicable to free television motion pictures are also applicable to motion pictures of the type covered by Article 20, except to the extent provided in Article 20.

1-205 Definition of Network

The term "network," as used in this Basic Agreement, means ABC, CBS and NBC or any other entity which qualifies as a "network" under Section 73.662(f) of the rules of the Federal Communications Commission, unless the FCC determines that such entity is not a "network" for purposes of such Section.

Section 1-300 DEFINITIONS OF EMPLOYEES RECOGNIZED

1-301 Director

A Director is one who directs the production of motion pictures, as the word "direct" is commonly used in the motion picture industry. The fact that the Director may also render services as a Producer and/or Writer or in any other capacity shall not take him or her out of the classification as a Director, with reference to any work he or she performs as a Director, and during the period of such work.

1-302 Unit Production Manager

A Unit Production Manager is one who is assigned by the Employer as a Unit Production Manager of one or more motion pictures, as the term "Unit Production Manager" is customarily used and understood in the motion picture industry. Subject to the provisions of Paragraph 13-202, a Unit Production Manager (hereinafter referred to as "UPM" and collectively referred to as "UPMs") niay be assigned to work concurrently on one or more productions, whether theatrical and/or television. No UPM need be employed in those instances specifically set forth in Paragraph 13-202.

After a picture is approved for production, there shall be no delegating to other employees (except First Assistant Directors when no UPM is assigned to the production involved) the duties of UPMs. It is an element of good faith of, and part of the consideration for, this BA that no Employer will make a general rearrangement of duties among such categories, change classifications of employment for such categories, employ persons not covered by this BA or delegate the duties ordinarily performed by UPMs to persons other than First Assistant Directors acting in the dual capacity of UPMs or to *bona fide* Producers for the purpose of eliminating UPMs who otherwise would have been employed hereunder. There shall be no restriction on delegation of duties ordinarily performed by UPMs when a UPM and a First Assistant Director both are assigned to the production.

The UPM, under the supervision of the Employer, is required to coordinate, facilitate and oversee the preparation of the production unit or units (to the extent herein provided) assigned to him or her, all off-set logistics, day-to-day production decisions, locations, budget schedules and personnel. Without limitation, among the duties which the Employer must assign to the UPM or First Assistant are the supervision of or participation in the following:

1. Prepare breakdown and preliminary shooting schedule.

2. Prepare or coordinate the budget.

3. Oversee preliminary search and survey of all locations and the completion of business arrangements for the same.

4. Assist in the preparation of the production to insure continuing efficiency.

5. Supervise completion of the Production Report for each day's work, showing work covered and the status of the production, and arrange for the distribution of that report in line with the company's requirement.

6. Coordinate arrangements for the transportation and housing of cast, crew and staff.

7. Oversee the securing of releases and negotiate for locations and personnel.

8. Maintain a liaison with local authorities regarding locations and the operation of the company.

Subject to the following paragraph, the foregoing description of the UPM's duties is not intended, nor shall it be construed, either to enlarge or diminish the duties of UPMs, First and Second Assistant Directors or other personnel as such duties are presently and were heretofore customarily performed in the motion picture industry.

Notwithstanding any other provision of this paragraph 1-302, an Employer may not assign the duties of a Unit Production Manager to Extra Player Coordinators, Production Assistants, or persons in positions in which the assigned duty has not been customarily performed in the motion picture industry. There shall be no alteration of job titles to evade or subvert the provisions of this Paragraph 1-302.

1-303 First Assistant Director

A First Assistant Director is one who is assigned by the Employer as the first assistant to the Director.

The First Assistant Director, alone or in conjunction with the UPM, organizes preproduction, including organizing the crew, securing equipment, breaking down the script, preparing the stripboard and a shooting schedule. During production, he assists the Director with respect to on-set production details, coordinates and supervises crew and cast activities and facilitates an organized flow of production activity. The First Assistant Director may be assigned responsibilities of the UPM. His or her prime responsibility is to service and assist the Director. Without limitation, among the duties which the Employer must assign to the First Assistant Director or UPM are the supervision of or participation in the following:

1. Prepare breakdown and stripboard; prepare shooting schedule keeping the same within time limitations imposed by budget, cast availability and the requirement of complete coverage of the script.

2. If delegated by UPM or in his or her absence, oversee the search, survey and management of locations and ascertain the specific requirements of those locations as they might affect the production. The First Assistant Director must be sent to each location site sufficiently prior to the commencement of photography to adequately perform his or her duties.

3. Check weather reports.

4. Prepare day out of day schedules for talent employment and determine cast and crew calls.

5. Supervise the preparation of the call sheet for the cast and crew.

6. Direct background action and supervise crowd control.

7. May be required to secure minor contracts, extra releases, and on occasion to obtain execution of contracts by talent.

8. Supervise the functioning of the shooting set and crew.

Subject to the following paragraph, the foregoing description of the First Assistant Director's duties is not intended, nor shall it be construed, either to enlarge or diminish the duties of UPM, First and Second Assistant Directors or other personnel as such duties are presently and were heretofore customarily performed in the motion picture industry.

Notwithstanding any other provision of this paragraph 1-303, an Employer may not assign the duties of a First Assistant Director to Extra Player Coordinators, Production Assistants, or persons in positions in which the assigned duty has not been customarily performed in the motion picture industry. There shall be no alteration of job titles to evade or subvert the provisions of this Paragraph 1-303.

1-304 Second Assistant Director

The Second Assistant Director is one who is assigned by the Employer as an assistant to the First Assistant Director in conducting the business of the set or the location site.

The term "Second Assistant Director" includes Key Second Assistant Directors, Second Assistant Directors and Additional Second Assistant Directors.

Without limitation, among the duties which the Employer must assign the Second Assistant Director are the supervision of or participation in the following:

1. Prepare the call sheets, handle extras' requisitions, and other required documents for approval by the First Assistant Director, the Unit Production Manager and/or the production office.

2. Prepare the daily production report and end of day paper work.

3. Distribute scripts and script changes (after shooting has started) to cast and crew.

4. Distribute call sheets to cast and crew.

5. Distribute, collect, and approve extra vouchers, placing adjustments as directed by the First Assistant Director on the vouchers.

6. Communicate advance scheduling to cast and crew.

7. Aid in the scouting, surveying and managing of locations.

8. Facilitate transportation of equipment and personnel.

9. May be required to secure execution of minor cast contracts, extra releases, and on occasion to secure execution of contracts by talent. (May also be delegated to First Assistant Director and Unit Production Manager.)

10. Coordinate with production staff so that all elements, including cast, crew and extras, are ready at the beginning of the day, and supervise the wrap in the studio and on location (local and distant).

11. Schedule food, lodging and other facilities.

12. Sign cast members in and out.

13. Maintain liaison between Unit Production Manager and/or the production office and the First Assistant Director on the set.

14. Assist the First Assistant Director in the direction and placement of background action and in the supervision of crowd control.

15. Perform crowd control in New York and Los Angeles except where the work is customarily performed by police officers or is performed by security personnel of a facility at which the photography takes place and which requires or customarily provides this service; provided, however, persons not covered by this BA may perform such work if at least two Additional Second Assistant Directors are employed in addition to a Key Second Assistant Director and Second Assistant Director or two Key Second Assistant Directors.

16. Supervise and direct the work of any Trainee or Intern assigned to the picture.

17. May assist in the proper distribution and documentation of mileage money by the Producer's appointed representative.

Subject to the following paragraph, the foregoing description of the Second Assistant Director's duties is not intended, nor shall it be construed, either to enlarge or diminish the duties of UPM, First and Second Assistant Directors or other personnel as such duties are presently and were heretofore customarily performed in the motion picture industry.

Notwithstanding any other provision of this Paragraph 1-304, an Employer may not assign the duties of a Second Assistant Director to Extra Player Coordinators, Production Assistants, or persons in positions in which the assigned duty has not been customarily performed in the motion picture industry. There shall be no alteration of job titles to evade or subvert the provisions of this Paragraph 1-304.

* * *

ARTICLE 2

Disputes

Section 2-100 MATTERS SUBJECT TO GRIEVANCE AND ARBITRATION

2-101 Arbitrability

The following matters shall be subject to arbitration: All grievances, disputes or controversies over the interpretation or application of the BA and, in addition, all grievances, disputes or controversies over the interpretation or application of any Employee's personal services contract or deal memo with respect to (1) credit provisions, (2) cutting rights provisions, (3) preview rights provisions, (4) creative rights provisions (including, without limitation, all consultation and/or approval rights of any kind relating to any motion picture), (5) money claims for unpaid compensation seeking $450,000 or less, (6) cash per diem payments for Employees only; provided, however, that grievances, disputes or controversies over the interpretation or application of any personal service contract or deal memo shall not be arbitrable if they relate to (a) perquisites such as per diem (except as provided above), travel arrangements, secretarial services and the like, (b) compensation measured by net or gross proceeds, or (c) other provisions not referred to in (1) through (6) hereinabove.

The Arbitrator shall determine any dispute as to the arbitrability of any matter hereunder.

2-102 Limitation on Arbitrator's Power

The Arbitrator shall not have the power to vary, alter, modify or amend any of the terms of the BA or of any deal memo or personal service contract in making a decision or award.

2-103 Defenses, Setoffs and Counterclaims

(a) In any grievance or arbitration concerning a claim for unpaid compensation under an Employee's deal memo or personal service contract, the Employer may assert any and all defenses, counterclaims and setoffs, including any defenses based on a claim of suspension or termination.

(b) In any grievance or arbitration concerning a claim for unpaid minimum compensation under the BA only, the Employer may, but need not, assert any and all defenses including any defense based on a claim of suspension or termination and may, but need not, assert any setoff or counterclaim not exceeding the amount claimed by the Guild. It is expressly agreed that any award by the Arbitrator concerning the matter at issue in such arbitration shall not be binding, res judicata or serve as collateral estoppel upon either the Employer or Employee in any separate arbitration or court proceeding brought by the Employer or Employee, except that (i) the amount of any award and the amount of any setoff or counterclaim shall be credited against any liability of Employer to Employee or vice versa and (ii) Employer may not assert any claim, counterclaim or setoff against Employee in any subsequent arbitration or court proceeding if such matter was asserted in the arbitration, except to the extent the amount exceeds the amount claimed by the Guild in the arbitration.

Section 2-200 GRIEVANCE PROCEDURE

2-201 Time Limits

The Guild or an Employer may file a grievance over any matter subject to the disputes procedure of this Article 2; provided, however, that a joint filing by the Guild and the Employee shall be required if the grievance relates to arbitrable matters in the personal service contract or deal memo in excess of BA minimums, and provided further, however, that any grievance must be filed on or before the earlier of:

(a) Twelve (12) months following the date on which the facts upon which the claim is based were discovered by the party bringing the grievance or arbitration proceeding; or

(b) (i) Four (4) years following the date on which the event in dispute occurred in cases involving pension and health contributions, residual compensation or other contingent or deferred compensation; or

(ii) Two (2) years following the date on which the event in dispute occurred in all other cases.

2-202 Grievance Notice

The grievance shall be in writing, state the essential facts of the claim and refer to the contractual provisions alleged to have been breached.

2-203   Grievance Meeting

Within ten (10) working days after the filing of the grievance, an authorized representative of the Guild and an authorized representative of the Employer shall meet and attempt to settle the dispute or difference.

Section 2-300   ARBITRATION PROCEDURE

2-301   Parties

In any grievance or arbitration hereunder, only the Guild and the Employer shall be parties, except that in any grievance or arbitration involving claims for unpaid compensation under, or other arbitrable violations of, a personal service contract or deal memo, the Employee involved and the Employee's loanout company, if any, shall also be parties.

2-302   Demand for Arbitration

If the dispute or difference is not settled at the meeting described in Paragraph 2-203 above, or if the other party refuses or fails to meet, the party aggrieved (hereinafter "claimant") may deliver to the other party (hereinafter "respondent") a written demand for arbitration which shall set forth the basis of the dispute, the material facts, the position of the claimant, and the relief sought. Such demand must be served not later than sixty (60) days after the filing of the grievance. The arbitration shall proceed as described in the Arbitration Procedure set forth below.

2-303   Respondent's Statement of Its Position

The respondent shall promptly, within five (5) business days following receipt of the demand for arbitration, inform the claimant (the Guild in the case of a joint filing) of its representative and serve a written statement of its position.

2-304   Selection of the Arbitrator

(a)   Within ten (10) business days following service of the demand for arbitration, or within such additional time as the parties mutually agree upon, the parties will attempt to mutually agree upon an Arbitrator. If the parties do not mutually agree upon an Arbitrator, the Arbitrator next in rotation on an Employer-by-Employer basis from the following list of persons shall be automatically assigned to the arbitration. The parties' mutual selection of an Arbitrator shall not affect the rotation of Arbitrators.

LOS ANGELES	NEW YORK
HERMIONE BROWN	JAMES V. ALTIERI
THOMAS CHRISTOPHER	MAURICE C. BENEWITZ
ROGER DAVIS	MILTON FRIEDMAN
DIXON DERN	WALTER GELHORN
WILLIAM EATON	DANIEL HOUSE
GERRY FELLMAN	MATHEW KELLY
JOSEPH GENTILE	GEORGE NICOLAU
SAM KAGEL*	JESSE SIMONS
MICHAEL RAPPAPORT	JANET SPENCER
SOL ROSENTHAL	ARTHUR STARK
ARTHUR ROSETT	
MURRAY SCHWARTZ	
CHARLES SILVERBERG	
MYRON D. SLOBODIEN	

Other Arbitrators may be added from time to time by mutual agreement between the Guild and the Employer.

*Not available for Expedited Arbitrations

(b) From July 1, 1993 to and including January 1, 1995, the Arbitrator shall be selected in rotation on an Employer-by-Employer basis starting from the top of the list down, and during the remainder of the term of this BA, the Arbitrator shall be selected in rotation on the same basis starting from the bottom of the list up.

(c) If no person on the list is available to hear the dispute, an Arbitrator shall be mutually selected by the Guild and the Employer. If they fail to agree, the Federal Mediation and Conciliation Service shall select the Arbitrator.

(d) If more than one Employer is named as a respondent in any arbitration complaint, the Arbitrator selected shall be the one next in line from the list of the Employer most recently a party to any arbitration.

(e) During the ten (10) business days or additional time mentioned in subparagraph (a) above, the claimant(s) and the respondent(s) shall each have the right to exercise one (1) peremptory challenge of one of the two Arbitrators whose names are next in order on the list immediately following the name of the Arbitrator last selected.

(f) If the Arbitrator selected cannot serve, a substitute shall be selected in accordance with the procedure set forth in subparagraphs (a), (b), (c) and (d), except the parties need not attempt to mutually agree on the substitute Arbitrator.

2-305 Situs of Arbitration

All arbitrations shall be in Los Angeles, absent agreement by the parties, except that they shall be in New York if the personal service agreement out of which the dispute arose was negotiated, entered into and production was based in New York and a majority of the witnesses required for the arbitration hearing reside regularly in and around the New York area. Any dispute as to where the arbitration should be held shall be determined by an Arbitrator in Los Angeles selected according to the method set forth herein. If the Arbitrator determines that Los Angeles is the proper situs for the arbitration, he or she shall hear the merits thereof, provided he or she is available.

Arbitrations held in Los Angeles will alternate on an Employer-by-Employer basis between the Guild's Offices and, at the election of the Employer, the AMPTP's offices, if available, or the Employer's offices, if in Los Angeles. The party providing the hearing room shall do so at no cost to the other.

2-306 Notification to Arbitrator

The claimant(s) shall notify the Arbitrator of his or her selection in writing with a copy to each respondent and at the same time furnish the Arbitrator with a copy of the BA, a copy of the demand for arbitration and the name, address and telephone number of the person who will represent the claimant(s) in the arbitration hearing.

2-307 Hearing

(a) Upon receipt of the demand for arbitration, the Arbitrator shall forthwith set the date for the arbitration hearing after contacting the parties' representatives for their available dates. If possible, the date for the hearing shall be within 15 to 30 days after the demand for the arbitration. The Arbitrator shall notify the parties of the time and place of the arbitration hearing.

(b) The arbitration hearing shall take place on the scheduled date. If either party fails to appear, the Arbitrator is specifically authorized and empowered to hear the matter on the evidence of the appearing party and enter an award based on such evidence.

(c) Each party shall bear the costs of presenting its own case. The fees of the Arbitrator and the hearing shall be allocated by the Arbitrator in his or her sound discretion.

(d) All hearings and deliberations conducted pursuant to the grievance and arbitration provisions of this Article 2 shall be closed to the public. Only authorized representatives of the Guild and Employer or witnesses called by the Arbitrator or by either party may attend.

(e)   All written communication to and from the Arbitrator or writings filed in connection with the arbitration proceedings and all testimony and arguments at the arbitration shall be privileged.

2-308 Exchange of Information

The parties will cooperate in the exchange of information reasonably in advance of the hearing date regarding the expected utilization of documents and physical evidence. Not later than thirty (30) days prior to the arbitration hearing, either party may make a written request to the other to produce, on a date not earlier than five (5) days before the hearing, documentary evidence of the type producible pursuant to a subpoena duces tecum. The documents must be produced on the date requested, but the other party may object to the production of the documents to the same extent as though the documents were subpoenaed. Any such objection shall be considered by the Arbitrator at the hearing.

The introduction of documents or physical evidence shall not be precluded because they were not exchanged in advance of the hearing.

2-309 Award

The award of the Arbitrator shall be promptly furnished to the parties in writing and shall be final and binding on the Guild, the Employee and the Employer. An arbitration award interpreting any of the terms of this BA thereafter shall be binding upon the Guild and the Employer; provided, however, that in any subsequent arbitration between the Guild and the Employer involving an interpretation of the same term or terms of the BA, the Arbitrator may determine whether or not, as a result of the different combination of facts, the prior arbitration award is relevant or determinative of the issue in such subsequent arbitration.

Section 2-400 EXPEDITED ARBITRATION PROCEDURE

2-401 Notwithstanding any other provision of the BA, any personal service contract or any deal memo, the following Expedited Arbitration Procedure shall be followed if, in the opinion of a party, a grievance will become moot or damages will be increased by reason of delay if processed through the above Grievance and Arbitration Procedure.

(a)   A Notice of Expedited Arbitration (so labeled by the claimant) shall be reduced to writing and given to the respondent and the first available Arbitrator listed in subparagraph 2-304(a) who can hear the matter within two business days following the filing of the Notice of Expedited Arbitration. The Notice of Expedited Arbitration shall include the name, address and telephone number of the claimant's representative(s) and the name of the person who represents the respondent. A copy of the BA and any applicable available personal service contract and/or deal memo shall be given to the Expedited Arbitrator along with the Notice of Expedited Arbitration.

(b) Upon receipt of the Notice of Expedited Arbitration, the Arbitrator shall, by telephone or telegraph, notify the parties of the time and place of the Expedited Arbitration hearing.

(c) An Expedited Arbitration hearing shall not be continued, absent agreement of the parties, except upon proof of good cause by the party requesting such continuance. The unavailability of any witness shall not constitute good cause unless the witness' testimony is relevant to the issues in the arbitration and could not be received by means consistent with fundamental fairness which do not require the witness' presence at the hearing.

(d) Paragraphs 2-101, 2-102, 2-103, 2-201, 2-301, 2-304(b) through (d), 2-305, 2-307(b) through (e) and 2-309 of this Article 2 shall be applicable to this Expedited Arbitration Procedure, except that:

    (i) the Expedited Arbitration hearing shall be commenced not later than on the second business day next following receipt of the Notice of Expedited Arbitration;

    (ii) the Arbitrator's written award shall be issued within two (2) business days from the end of the Expedited Arbitration hearing, but failure to meet the deadline shall not oust the Arbitrator of jurisdiction;

    (iii) the award shall be served on the parties by messenger; and

    (iv) the same list of Arbitrators for non-expedited arbitrations shall apply to Expedited Arbitrations, but the rotation shall be separate.

(e) Nothing contained in this Expedited Arbitration Procedure shall preclude the parties from discussing the settlement of the Expedited Arbitration, except that such discussion shall not delay the Expedited Arbitration Procedure.

(f) The failure of the claimant to serve the Notice of Expedited Arbitration within ten (10) business days following the date on which the facts upon which the claim is based were discovered by the party bringing the Expedited Arbitration shall constitute a waiver of the right to this Expedited Arbitration Procedure. If two or more claims are submitted to Expedited Arbitration and the Expedited Arbitration Procedure has been waived or is inapplicable to one or more claims, the same Arbitrator may determine the claims not subject to Expedited Arbitration, provided that such non-Expedited Arbitration claim or claims shall be determined in accordance with the regular Arbitration proceedings, unless the parties agree otherwise.

(g)   Any party to an arbitration hereunder may, if the circumstances herein-above set forth exist, require that the arbitration be conducted as an expedited arbitration by serving appropriate notice to that effect.

(h)   If the Expedited Arbitration involves multiple disputes or controversies, the Expedited Arbitrator may, upon the request of a party, bifurcate or separate such disputes or controversies and render separate awards, each of which shall be deemed final.

Section 2-500   ARBITRAL REMEDIES

2-501   Authority of Arbitrator

The Arbitrator shall have the authority to grant or award one or more of money damages, orders to withdraw, cancel, change or re-do advertising material already issued or prepared, or to require Employer to change or re-do any film titles, or to order back pay or reinstatement, or to order any other reasonable relief the Arbitrator deems appropriate in the circumstances, whether relating to credit on the screen or in advertising or any other arbitrable matter, in the event the Arbitrator finds a breach of the BA or of those provisions of the personal service contract or the deal memo which are subject to arbitration pursuant to the provisions of Paragraph 2-101 hereof.

2-502   Consideration for Determining Remedies

In determining the appropriate remedy, the Arbitrator shall take into account such evidence as may be adduced by the claimant of similar prior violations by the respondent. The Arbitrator shall also take into account evidence of failure on the part of the claimant to notify the respondent promptly of the violation, and evidence of inadvertent breach.

2-503   Compliance with Arbitrator's Award

Should the Arbitrator issue an award which in whole or part is not self-executing, and a party fails to comply with such award, the party aggrieved thereby may, but need not, submit the matter to the Arbitrator who issued the award.

Section 2-600   COURT PROCEEDINGS

2-601   Arbitration Exclusive Remedy

Arbitration hereunder shall be the exclusive remedy in connection with claims for violation by the Employee, Guild or the Employer of the provisions of the BA and of the arbitrable provisions of any personal service contract or deal memo other than claims for compensation.

2-602   Claims for Compensation

(a)   The Employee shall have the right, prior to commencement of an arbitration by any party entitled thereto, to commence action in any court of competent jurisdiction with respect to unpaid compensation in any amount, and in any event regarding the non-arbitrable portions of Employee's personal service contract. Upon the filing of such action, the further operation of the procedures and remedies described in this Article 2 shall cease to apply to such dispute. The Guild shall have the right, but not the obligation, to be party in any such action in court.

(b)   The Guild shall have the right to take to grievance and arbitration any claim by the Guild of an Employer's breach of the BA, including a failure to pay minimum compensation, regardless of whether or not such claimed breach may also involve a breach by the Company of its contract with the Employee. Such proceeding shall not affect the right of the Employee to pursue remedies at law or in equity, except as limited by the provisions of the BA.

(c)   If the Employee and the Guild make a claim for unpaid compensation in an arbitration proceeding, then to the extent of any unpaid non-contingent compensation in excess of $450,000, collection of such excess from the Employer shall be deemed waived. No Employee shall have the right to commence court proceedings to collect any unpaid compensation for which claim has been made in arbitration, including, but not limited to, compensation in excess of the jurisdictional amount of $450,000.

2-603   Petition to Confirm, Vacate or Modify Award

(a)   Nothing in the BA shall preclude any court of competent jurisdiction from confirming, setting aside or modifying any award hereunder in accordance with applicable law.

(b)   Service of a petition to confirm, set aside or modify an arbitration award hereunder may be served by certified or registered mail, return receipt requested.

Section 2-700   WITHDRAWAL OF SERVICES

2-701   Notwithstanding any provision of any personal service contract, deal memo or of the BA to the contrary, it shall not be a violation thereof for the Guild or any Employee (at the direction of the Guild) to withhold services from the Employer if the Employer fails or refuses to abide by the final award of any Arbitrator for any reason whatsoever.

* * *

ARTICLE 4

Directors' Freelance Contracts

4-101 Cost of Motion Picture As Basis of Salary

The cost of a motion picture as estimated by the Employer in good faith at the time of the commencement of principal photography shall be the cost of such motion picture for the purpose of the schedule set forth in Paragraph 3-101. For the purpose of this clause, any deferment of "direct" production costs shall be deemed to be a part of production costs. When the Director believes the budget is not accurate and it affects salary, the matter may be submitted through the Grievance and Arbitration Procedure.

* * *

4-108 Deal Memorandum

Following the oral confirmation between Employer and a Freelance Director (or the Director's agent) of the rate of compensation and the starting date for a proposed employment of the Director, the Employer will deliver a "deal memorandum" to the Guild and to the Director (Or the Director's agent) prior to his or her employment. Such "deal memorandum" shall set forth at least the information contained in Exhibit "C-3" attached hereto. The "deal memorandum" submitted may contain further terms in addition to those specified in such Exhibit "C-3," including part or all of the terms of the employment contract.

With respect to any motion picture, including a multipart closed-end series but excluding an episode of a television series or serial, Employer shall submit to the Director the then available top sheet of the budget at the same time it delivers the Director's Deal Memorandum.

In no event is any Director to commence services before delivery of the "deal memorandum" to the Guild, except in cases of *bona fide* emergency. If such services commence prior to delivery of the "deal memorandum" to the Guild, the Guild may notify Employer to forthwith deliver such "deal memorandum" to the Guild. If Employer fails to deliver the "deal memorandum" within twenty-four (24) hours after such notice, the Guild may order the Director to withhold services until a "deal memorandum" is delivered to the Guild. The Employer may require Director to sign a copy of the "deal memorandum" prior to permitting the Director to commence services.

Upon commencement of principal photography of a theatrical motion picture, or of a television motion picture 90 minutes or longer, Employer shall furnish to the Director and to the Guild an addendum to the Director's deal memorandum containing the following information, to the extent that such information is then known to the Employer: the dates scheduled for start and finish of the Director's cut; the dates for special photography and processes, if any; the date for delivery of the answer print; and date of release (for theatrical films) or date of network broadcast (if applicable). Employer shall notify the Director and the Guild as soon as practicable in the event of a change in the post-production schedule. After January 1, 1994, the Creative Rights standing Committee shall examine the utility of these obligations.

4-109 Personal Services Agreement

Following the "deal memorandum," the Employer will, as soon as practicable, deliver to the Director a proposed written contract of employment of the Director. Such contract shall clearly set forth the Director's weekly salary rate.

4-110 Prohibition Against Credits and Offsets

Overscale cannot be used to credit or offset in any manner any payments required to be made to the Director.

The only exception to the prohibition against crediting or offset of monies in excess of scale is the right of Employer to negotiate with the Director to credit or offset residuals against monies in excess of 200% of scale. However, the foregoing exception shall not be applicable to any residual or other additional compensation required to be paid under Article 20 of this BA.

No prepayment of residuals will be permitted unless set forth in the "deal memorandum" in the specific amounts which are to be prepaid. Residual compensation shall not otherwise be prepaid. Any prepayment of residual compensation shall be sent to the Director in care of the Guild and not combined with the other payments for his or her services.

4-111 Development Services

(a) If a Director, at the request of Employer, renders services in supervising development of a screenplay (as distinguished from reviewing or commenting upon a completed or substantially-completed screenplay) with the option to direct and if such option is not exercised or if the Director is replaced or the motion picture is abandoned, the Director shall receive a minimum of $25,611 ($26,635 effective July 1, 1994 and $27,701 effective July 1, 1995) at the time a picture based on such screenplay is produced, if at all, so long as one or more of the writers supervised by such Director in development is accorded writing credit. Payments made to the Director in connection with development shall apply towards the minimum of $25,611 ($26,635 effective July 1, 1994 and $27,701 effective July 1, 1995).

(b) If a Director, at the request of an Employer, renders services in supervising development of a teleplay (as distinguished from reviewing or commenting upon a completed or substantially-completed teleplay) for a prime-time dramatic program of 90 minutes or longer with the option to direct and if such option is not exercised or if he or she is replaced or the production is abandoned, he or she shall receive a minimum of $19,209 ($19,977 effective July 1, 1994 and $20,776 effective July 1, 1995) at the time a television program based on such teleplay is produced, if at all, provided one or more of the writers supervised by such Director in development is accorded writing credit and provided further, the Company realizes revenues from the production. Payments made to the Director in connection with development shall apply towards the minimum of $19,209 ($19,977 effective July 1, 1994 and $20,776 effective July 1, 1995).

* * *

ARTICLE 6

Suspension and Termination of Director.

6-101   Except as expressly provided in this Article, the provisions of this BA with reference to the obligation of the Employer to furnish employment for the respective "guarantee" periods specified, or to provide for payment of salary in aggregate amounts herein specified, shall, of course, be subject to any and all rights of suspension and/or termination which the Employer may have by contract or otherwise in the event of any incapacity or default of the Director or, in the case of any interference, suspension or postponement of production by reason of strikes, acts of God, governmental action, regulations or decrees, casualties, or any other causes provided for in the so-called "force majeure" clause of such Director's contract of employment or the force majeure provisions of this BA. No suspension or termination of Director's services shall be permitted or effected by Employer under such force majeure clause or provisions unless the entire cast and the Director of Photography of the picture are likewise suspended or terminated, as the case may be. Subject to such rights of suspension and/or termination, the obligation of the Employer upon entering into a contract for the employment of a Freelance Director to furnish employment during any of the foregoing "guarantee" periods of employment shall be wholly satisfied by the payment of the agreed salary for the applicable minimum period. With respect to only theatrical motion pictures, or television films 61 minutes or more in length, the illness or incapacity for one week or less of a member of the cast or any other person in connection with the picture shall not be considered "force majeure." With respect to television motion pictures: If the Director is employed on a film under 61 minutes in length, and he is suspended by reason of illness or incapacity of a member of the cast or any other person connected with the picture, then the Director may forthwith terminate the employment, but if such termination occurs, the Employer may thereafter employ the same or another Director to fulfill the remaining portion of the guaranteed period of employment. The Employer further agrees that if, despite such suspension, the star of the picture or the Director of Photography is paid in whole or in part with respect to such picture, then the Director will be paid in the same *pro rata* amount as the star or the Director of Photography is paid. If there is a difference in the proportionate amount paid to the star and the Director of Photography, then the higher proportionate amount shall be paid to the Director. The foregoing provision shall not apply to the continuation of payments to a term player or Director of Photography who is carried by the Employer under the provisions of a term contract.

* * *

6-105 Payment To and Mitigation By Discharged Employees

If a Director is removed from a motion picture, the Employer shall forthwith deliver to the Guild for the Director all remaining unpaid non-deferred, non-contingent compensation as provided by the personal services agreement or deal memo.

If Employer disputes its obligation to pay said compensation to the Director, the amount in dispute shall be deposited with a mutually acceptable bank or other third party designated by an Arbitrator. Such escrow agent shall distribute the amount deposited, together with interest accumulated, if any, according to the provisions of any settlement agreement or, if the dispute is not settled, according to the award of an Arbitrator or judgment of a court of law.

If the Director is employed by third parties during the remaining period during which the Director was guaranteed employment in the motion picture, Employer shall be entitled to an offset of the compensation arising from such new employment for such remaining portion of the guaranteed period against the compensation remaining unpaid under the earlier agreement. Under the described circumstances, the Guild guarantees repayment from the Director to the extent herein provided. Employer agrees that the Director shall have no obligation to mitigate damages arising from his or her removal and that the only obligation of the Director in such event will be to repay or offset sums as herein set forth if the Director, in his or her sole discretion, actually accepts employment during the remaining guaranteed period of the motion picture.

* * *

ARTICLE 7

Directors' Minimum Conditions — Preparation, Production and Postproduction

Section 7-100   PREAMBLE

7-101   The Director's professional function is unique, and requires his or her participation in all creative phases of the film-making process, including but not limited to all creative aspects of sound and picture.

The Director works directly with all of the elements which constitute the variegated texture of a unit of film entertainment or information.

The Director's function is to contribute to all of the creative elements of a film and to participate in molding and integrating them into one cohesive dramatic and aesthetic whole.

No one may direct, as the term direct is generally known in the motion picture industry, except the Director assigned to the picture.

Section 7-200   DISCLOSURE AND CONSULTATION WITH RESPECT TO COMMITMENTS

7-201   Disclosure Before Assignment

Prior to the employment of the Director, or in the case of a Director employed under a term contract or multiple picture contract or under option, prior to his assignment to a picture, Employer shall inform him or her of the following in relation to the picture in question:

(a)   the names of artistic and creative personnel already employed;

(b)   all existing film contemplated to be used;

(c)   any rights of script approval or cast approval contractually reserved to any person other than the Employer and the individual Producer;

(d)   the top sheet (summary) of any Theatrical Budget or a Television Pattern Budget (as the case may be) which has been established and any limitations thereof, in any. The Director shall use his or her best efforts to conform with such budget. The Director shall have the responsibility and opportunity to express his or her opinion with respect to the practicability of the budget; and

(e)   the story on which the motion picture is based and the script, if any exists shall be made available to the Director.

It is the intention hereof that Employer shall make full and complete disclosure to the Director of all of the existing artistic and creative commitments with respect to the picture for which the Director is to be employed prior to his or her actual employment, or prior to his or her assignment to the picture if previously employed or optioned without such an assignment.

It is recognized that Directors frequently accept an assignment based upon the Employer's representation as to the budget and shooting schedule of a motion picture. It is therefore agreed that after the Director's assignment to a theatrical motion picture or a television motion picture 90 minutes or longer, the Employer shall not in bad faith or capriciously reduce the budget or the shooting schedule.

7-202 Consultation After Assignment

Subject to other specific provisions hereof, between the time the Director is employed (or in the case of a Director employed under a term contract or multiple picture contract or under option, after his or her assignment to the picture), and until the time he or she delivers the Director's Cut, he or she shall be informed as soon as practicable of any proposal concerning and, if reasonably available, shall participate in all decisions with respect to: (a) any changes in the elements of which he or she has been previously notified, or proposed casting and the employment of other artistic or creative personnel, and of any rights or approval thereafter granted to third parties; (b) all creative elements in the production of the film, including but not restricted to the script and any revision thereof, casting, employment of artistic and creative personnel, location selection, set design and construction; preproduction, shooting and postproduction scheduling; (c) in no case will any creative decision be made regarding the preparation, production, and postproduction of a motion picture without the consultation of the Director. The Director's advice and suggestions shall be considered in good faith.

7-203 Consultation Regarding UPM

With respect to theatrical motion pictures and non-episodic television programs, Director will have the right of consultation with respect to assignment of a UPM assigned after the Director is assigned. The final decision with respect to assignment of the UPM shall remain with the Employer.

7-204 Selection of First Assistant Director

The Director shall have the right, subject to the terms of Articles 14 and 15, to select the First Assistant Director on any theatrical motion picture and any non-series television motion picture 90 minutes or longer, provided that such selection must be consistent with the budget of the motion picture and the First Assistant Director selected is not guilty of any criminal conduct. The Director may replace the First Assistant Director provided that such action does not adversely affect the budget of the motion picture. The Employer shall have the right for just cause to discharge a First Assistant Director selected in accordance with this Paragraph 7-204 and a substitute First Assistant Director shall be selected pursuant to this Paragraph.

7-205   Second Unit Director

In the event second unit work shall be contemplated, the Director shall be given an opportunity to consult with the individual Producer and participate in considerations as to the person to be engaged to direct such second unit work. In the event of disagreement between the Employer and the Director as to the choice of the person to be engaged as Second Unit Director, the Employer shall submit to the Director a list of three (3) qualified individuals any one of whom would be approved as Second Unit Director and the Director shall be obligated to approve one of such three persons.

The Director shall be given the opportunity to consult with the Second Unit Director with respect to the manner in which the second unit work is to be performed and may delegate the supervision of the assemblage of second unit photography to the Second Unit Director.

7-206   Individual With Final Cutting Authority

The individual having final cutting authority over the motion picture shall be designated in the Director's Deal Memorandum. In the event such individual ceases to be employed by Employer, the individual named by the Employer to succeed the designated individual shall be a person of equivalent rank. The successor's name shall be deemed incorporated into the Director's Deal Memorandum. If the Employer has not named any such person, then the Employer shall submit to the Director names of three (3) individuals, any of whom would be acceptable to the Employer as the person to have the final cutting authority over the motion picture. The Director shall select one individual from the three (3) proposed names, and the name of the individual selected shall be deemed to have been incorporated into the Director's Deal Memorandum. Employer shall not be deemed to have breached this provision for a reasonable time following the end of employment of the individual originally designated in the Deal Memorandum. During this period, Employer may designate any individual who may temporarily perform all or some of the former employee's functions in exercising final cutting authority.

*   *   *

Section 7-300   PREPARATION

7-301   Literary Material

When the Director is assigned, at his or her request, any existing script or outline in whatever form intended for the production of the motion picture shall be immediately delivered to him or her. Any changes or additions in such script shall be submitted to the Director promptly and before such changes or additions are made available for general distribution. The individual Producer or other appropriate person will confer with the Director to discuss and consider the Director's suggestions and opinions with respect to such changes or additions and will confer with the Director to discuss and consider any script changes or revisions which the Director recommends.

7-302 Delivery of Shooting Script

In episodic television, the Employer shall deliver the completed shooting script to the Director not later than one day prior to the commencement of the Director's preparation period. For each day the delivery of the completed shooting script is delayed, an additional day shall be added to the Director's preparation period.

A "completed shooting script" is defined as that script (not necessarily the final shooting script) which the Employer intends to use for photography of a motion picture, subject to changes such as acting, technical and/or staging problems or those with respect to weather or other emergencies.

The Guild shall grant an automatic and unconditional waiver on an episodic basis for each episode for which the Employer sends the Guild a written request therefor, before it fails to deliver the script as required, only for those series in the second year of production whose first year of production consisted of thirteen (13) or fewer episodes.

7-303 Stunts

Any stunt sequence mentioned in the shooting script delivered to the Director (whether or not a waiver of Paragraph 7-302 was granted) may not be increased in magnitude or in degree of difficulty, nor may a stunt sequence be added to such script or later increased in magnitude or degree of difficulty, without the Director's consent to the change. Such consent will not be unreasonably withheld. The Employer may diminish the magnitude of a stunt sequence in the shooting script or eliminate it entirely without the consent of the Director.

7-304 Television Preparation Time

With respect to a motion picture (excluding pilots) which is produced for Network Prime Time or is governed by Article 20 and of a type generally produced for Network Prime Time, the Director shall be afforded actual preparation time of no less than three (3) days for a one-half hour program, seven (7) days for an hour program and fifteen (15) days for a two-hour or longer program.

7-305   Inclusion of Director's Name on Episodic Television Scripts

With respect to episodic television motion pictures, the Director's name shall appear on the title page of each script distributed after he/she is assigned. The omission of the Director's name shall not, however, be subject to grievance and arbitration under Article 2 of this Agreement.

Section 7-400   PRODUCTION

7-401   Dailies

Consistent with the orderly progress of photography, the Director shall see the dailies of each day's photography at a reasonable time. No one shall be present at the screenings of such dailies except those persons designated by the individual Producer, the Employer, or the Director, and all such persons shall have a reasonable purpose for attending such dailies. The Editor assigned to the picture shall be present at all such screenings at the studio.

Dailies for a television film may be in the form of videocassettes.

While the Director is on distant location, and when it is required that the Director be provided with distant location viewing facilities pursuant to Paragraph 7-402 below, the Employer will ship the dailies of each day's photography within twenty-four (24) hours (excluding Saturdays, Sundays, and holidays) after synchronization of picture and track by the Editor or someone else under his or her supervision. Failure to ship dailies of more than three (3) aggregate days' photography shall constitute a breach of this obligation, unless excused by a force majeure.

7-402   Distant Location Viewing Facilities

With respect to theatrical motion pictures, anthology television motion pictures and pilot films, when the company and the Director are scheduled for distant location of four (4) or more consecutive days of shooting, if requested by the Director not less than five (5) days, if practicable, prior to the departure for the distant location, the Director will be provided with interlocking sound and picture projection facilities or their equivalent (for example, kemtable type of viewing device or cassette viewing equipment) for viewing dailies on such distant location.

7-403   Private Office and Parking

The Employer will provide the Director with a private office at the studio, and a private facility on the set or immediately adjacent thereto at the studio but not at the same time. On distant location where private facilities are provided to others on the set or immediately adjacent thereto, a private facility shall also be provided the Director on the set or immediately adjacent thereto.

(a) For purposes of this Section, an "office" shall be a room with a door which can be shut, adequate ventilation, a telephone, a desk and desk chair, room for no less than two additional persons and good lighting. Sanitary facilities shall be in a reasonable proximity to said office.

b) When the Employee utilizes an office in his or her home in connection with an employment agreement with the Employer, such utilization by the Employee shall be deemed to be at the request of and for the convenience of the Employer. Employer acknowledges that Employees are frequently required to perform services hereunder at their home.

(c) Employer shall use its best efforts to provide reasonable parking space at no charge for all Employees while they are rendering services in production, pre-production and postproduction covered by this BA.

(d) Upon the Director's request, the Employer shall provide the Director private transportation during the period of photography to and from local locations, provided such transportation does not increase Employer's costs.

* * *

Section 7-500 EDITING AND POSTPRODUCTION

7-501 Responsibility of Director

The Director shall be responsible for the presentation of his or her cut of the motion picture (herein referred to as the "Director's Cut") and it is understood that his or her assignment is not complete until he or she has presented the Director's Cut to the Employer, subject to the terms and conditions of this BA, as soon as possible within the time period hereinafter provided for.

Subject to 7–505(g)(ii), no one other than the Director may supervise the editing of the first cut of the film following completion of the editor's assembly, but if the Director refuses to, or due to incapacity, cannot supervise the first cut, the Employer may assign another person to edit the film. Within one day following such an assignment, the Employer shall send the Guild written notice thereof.

7-502 "Hotline"

Any Director who has completed 90% but less than 100% of the scheduled principal photography of a theatrical motion picture or television motion picture 90 minutes or more in length cannot be replaced, except for cause, until the following procedure (herein referred to as "hotline") has taken place: (a) The Employer shall give the Director and the Guild prompt notice of its intention to so replace the Director; and (b) the available parties shall immediately jointly discuss the matter (the Employer is to be represented in such discussion by the person designated in the deal memo, or a higher ranking executive); and (c) if the parties are unable to resolve the matter, the decision of the Employer shall be final.

7-503   Vesting of Postproduction Rights

Notwithstanding the provisions of Paragraph 7-502, a Director who is replaced after directing 90% but less than 100% of the scheduled principal photography of any motion picture shall be the Director of the film entitled to all the postproduction creative rights set forth in this Article 7, unless (a) the Director was primarily responsible for causing the motion picture to be "over budget" or (b) the substituting Director was required to direct more than 10% of all principal photography for the picture. Reshooting initial photography due to faulty negative caused by technical problems shall not be included in the computation of the 10%. The Employer may not schedule additional photography to avoid the express intent of this provision and has the burden of proving the necessity of such additional photography.

7-504   No Interference with Director's Cut

No one shall be allowed to interfere with the Director of the film during the period of the Director's Cut. There shall be no "cutting behind" the Director as that term is commonly understood in the motion picture industry. The term "cutting behind" means any editing prohibited by the terms of this BA, including editing by electronic means. When a release date must be met in an emergency, the Director's cutting time may be reduced to an amount of time equal to one-half the actual time period available to cutting.

7-505   Preparation of Director's Cut

The Director shall prepare the Director's Cut of the film for presentation to the individual Producer and to the person designated in the Director's deal memo as having final cutting authority, in the ordinary course of business, over the motion picture. The Director shall diligently and continuously render his or her services in connection with the preparation of the Director's Cut and shall remain reasonably available on the premises during such period.

In pursuance thereof, the following procedure shall be followed:

(a)   The Director shall see the assembled sequences as soon as the Editor has assembled them in accordance with the Director's instructions during the photography of the picture, provided this will not delay the time and preparation of the assemblage of the sequences. If the Director does not give such directions, the Editor may proceed with the assemblage of the sequences without them. The Director shall then make whatever changes he or she deems necessary. As to television, such changes shall be made by the Director working with the Editor and in consultation with the individual Producer. The Editor will make no further changes except under the Director's instructions until the completion of the Director's Cut.

(b)   The Director's Cut shall be accomplished within the following time periods:

Theatrical Motion Pictures

(i)   Within ten weeks after the close of principal photography or within a period of time after the close of principal photography equal to one day of editing time for each two days of originally scheduled photography (as such schedule may have been increased or decreased by mutual agreement between the Director and the Employer), whichever is greater.

(ii) With respect to a low budget film (as defined in Paragraph 3–101), within six weeks after the close of principal photography or within a period of time after the close of principal photography equal to one day of editing time for each one day of originally scheduled photography (as such schedule may have been increased or decreased by mutual agreement between the Director and the Employer), whichever is greater.

Television Motion Pictures

(iii) As to television motion pictures having a running time of 30 minutes or less, within one (1) day plus time and the opportunity to make changes, if necessary, but not to exceed one (1) more day.

(iv) As to television motion pictures having a running time of 60 minutes or less, but more than 30 minutes, within four (4) days.

(v)   As to television motion pictures having a running time of 90 minutes or less, but more than 60 minutes, within fifteen (15) days.

(vi) As to television motion pictures having a running time of 120 minutes or less, but more than 90 minutes, within twenty (20) days.

(vii) As to television motion pictures having a running time of more than 2 hours, twenty (20) days, plus five (5) days for each additional hour in excess of 2 hours.

(c)   If the assemblage of the film is not completed at the close of principal photography, the above time periods shall not commence to run until such assemblage is completed, unless delay in the completion of the assembly of the film beyond the close of principal photography is caused by the Director.

For the purpose of this Paragraph 7-505, the word "promptly" shall be defined as four (4) business days after close of principal photography in the case of a half-hour television program. Employer shall use reasonable efforts to cause the assembly to be delivered as soon as possible following close of principal photography and before the fourth (4th) or sixth (6th) business day, whichever is applicable. If the assembly is not promptly completed and made available, then, when it is completed, Employer shall hold it available for Director's first availability up to two (2) calendar weeks to permit the Director to prepare the Director's cut.

No one (other than the Editor and Editor's immediate staff) shall view the completed assembly before the Director or, if the Director so requests, for twenty-four (24) hours after the Director's initial viewing. The Director may not exhibit the film to anyone else without approval of the Employer.

(d) When the Director's Cut is ready, the Director shall screen such cut for the individual Producer and for the person, if any, designated in the Director's deal memo as having final cutting authority over the motion picture. During the screenings of the Director's Cut for the individual Producer and the person, if any, so designated in the deal memorandum, the Director shall be entitled to make recommendations for further changes in following cuts.

(e) At the Director's request, the Director's Cut of a theatrical motion picture shall, at Employer's election, be previewed before a public audience or be screened before a private audience which shall consist of no fewer than 100 persons, exclusive of relatives or employees of the Employer. For the purpose of such preview or screening, the Director shall have the right to include tracked music and effects in the Director's Cut. Employer shall grant the Director access to the music and effects, if any, in its library and shall provide the Director no less than one day of dubbing to incorporate music and effects into the Director's Cut. In the event the Director requests such a showing, such preview or screening shall be deemed to be the delivery of the Director's Cut.

(f) The following procedures are intended to implement the provisions of Paragraphs 7-505 and 7-507 relating to cutting time for Directors of television films and represent no substantive change in the Director's rights and obligations as contained in said Paragraphs.

The Director and the Editor will view the Editor's assembly in a projection room and on a moviola or other similar device and the Editor will note all the Director's instructions. The Editor will then implement all the instructions. The Director and Editor will again view the material in a projection room, and the Editor will note and implement any further instructions.

(g)   The following rules apply to television films 60 minutes or less:

   (i)   The Director's Cut may be no more than approximately one minute over or under the planned broadcast time. Upon Employer's request, photography in the editor's assembly not used in the Director's Cut shall be maintained separately.

   (ii)   If the Director does not start the Director's Cut within 24 hours after he or she receives notice that the editor's assembly is or will be complete, Employer may assign any other person to supervise editing of the first cut of the film following completion of the editor's assembly. Any time the Employer assigns a person other than the Director to supervise editing of such first cut, Employer shall send the Guild written notice thereof not later than one day following the assignment.

   (iii)   If Employers' costs increase because of the provisions of this subparagraph (g), the AMPTP may terminate such provisions not earlier than January 1, 1995, provided the AMPTP sends the Guild sixty (60) days written notice advising the Guild that this subparagraph (g) is terminated and provided representatives of the AMPTP and the Guild meet within the sixty (60) days in a good faith attempt to resolve the Employers' problems.

7-506   Right to be Present and to Consult

The Director shall have the right, subject only to his or her availability, to be present at all times and to consult with the Employer throughout the entire postproduction period in connection with the picture. The Director must be notified of the date, time and place of each postproduction operation. The Director shall be afforded a reasonable opportunity, subject to his or her availability, to screen and discuss the last version of the film before negative cutting or dubbing, whichever occurs first.

A postproduction locale will not be selected for the purpose of depriving the Director of his or her postproduction rights. The Director shall be informed of the intended postproduction locale in his or her deal memo. When the postproduction locale is at a distant location (i.e., where the Director is required to remain away from home and be lodged overnight), the Employer will pay for Director's transportation, meals and accommodations while the Director is rendering postproduction services.

7-507   Delivery Date for Television Film

(a)   Notwithstanding anything to the contrary in this Article 7, it is understood and agreed that with respect to television motion pictures, the Director's editing privileges herein set forth may not be exercised when the preparation of any television film for a projected delivery date does not permit the expenditure of any or all of the time which would be required by the exercise of the Director's cutting rights.

(b) Nothing in this Paragraph 7-507 permits reduction of the period of the Director's cut resulting from the practice of "warehousing," as this term was used by the negotiators.

* * *

7-509 <u>Editing Theatrical Motion Pictures</u>

(a) This Paragraph 7-509 applies only to theatrical motion pictures which are subject to this BA and the principal photography of which commenced during the term of this BA.

(b) Employer recognizes that it is desirable for theatrical motion pictures to be telecast without abridgment except as required by Network Broadcast Standards and Practices. To this end, Employer will endeavor to license films for network telecasting with no abridgment other than for the aforementioned Broadcast Standards and Practices reasons. In any event, Employer agrees that the Director, if available, shall be accorded the first opportunity to make such cuts as are required if a film is required to be abridged for network telecast. In the event the Director of such picture is deceased, the Guild will appoint a Director of comparable stature and ability to discharge such functions who will be deemed substituted for the original Director in all respects under this Paragraph 7-509. Such "Director abridging cut" shall be done for the Employer at no additional cost, and subject to its approval. It is the intention of the foregoing that in the first instance and as far as practicable, the abridgment, if any, of theatrical motion pictures shall be accomplished by the Employer, with the participation of the Director, as aforementioned, and not by the network acquiring telecasting rights in the theatrical motion pictures.

(c) If a motion picture is licensed by Employer for United States network free television or for United States nation network pay television exhibition under a contract which provides that the network may edit the motion picture for such exhibition, the Employer agrees to obligate the network or the distributor to consult with the Director of such motion picture with regard to such editing done by the network, subject to the following conditions:

    (i) The Employer or the distributor shall notify the Director in writing, at Director's last address known to Employer or the distributor, that such motion picture has been so licensed and is to be edited for such exhibition by the network. A copy of such notice shall be mailed to the Guild. If the Director wishes to be consulted by the network or the distributor with reference to such editing, the Director shall, within five (5) business days after service of such notice, notify the Employer and the distributor in writing that the Director so desires to be consulted. Upon service of such notice by the Director, the Employer or the distributor shall notify the network that the Director wishes to be consulted with reference to such editing. The Employer shall obligate the network or the distributor to give the Director who has served such notice reasonable notice of the time and place at which the network or the distributor will consult with the Director with reference to such editing. If the Director reports at the time and place so designated, the network or the distributor shall then be obligated to consult with the Director and in such consultations, the Director may express his or her views with regard to the editing of the motion picture for such network television exhibition. As between the Director and the network and the distributor, however, the final decision as to such editing shall rest with the network and the distributor. The requirement of consultation with the Director, as set forth above, shall not apply when no editing is done by the network or in any case in which the exigencies of time do not permit, or if the Director does not make himself or herself available at the time and place designated as aforesaid.

(ii)   The Director's services in connection with consultations shall be provided at the time and place specified in the notice at no cost to the network or Employer or the distributor.

(iii)   The consultation rights of this Paragraph 7-509 shall apply to all editing of a theatrical motion picture released for such network exhibition. For this purpose only, the word "editing" includes placement of or changes in commercial breaks, interruptions, and promotional announcements.

(d) If a motion picture is licensed by Employer for United States syndication and Employer edits such motion picture at its own facilities, the Director, if available, shall have the right to edit the motion picture if no additional costs are thereby incurred.

(e) If the Employer desires to have new footage shot and added to the motion picture beyond the theatrical version, the Director (subject to reasonable availability) shall be offered employment to shoot such new footage as and to the extent required by Employer at a daily compensation rate no less than one-half of the Director's initial daily compensation rate on the motion picture.

(f)   Employer agrees not to license or edit or authorize any licensee to edit feature length theatrical motion pictures in versions of less than two hours duration or the length of the picture as released for general theatrical exhibition, whichever is lesser, (except for Standards and Practices requirements) for in-flight use as defined in subparagraph 18-102 (b) (e.g., to avoid 45-minute versions of motion pictures previously licensed as theatrical films for use on Continental Airlines).

In the event of any inconsistencies between the provisions of this subparagraph and the balance of Paragraph 7-509, then the provisions of this subparagraph shall control.

(g)   The provisions of this Paragraph 7-509 shall also apply if a theatrical motion picture is licensed by Employer for domestic videodisc/ videocassette distribution.

7-510 Edition of Motion Picture for Foreign Television Exhibition

If a motion picture originally produced for television is sold or licensed for foreign exhibition and Employer requires additional shooting, the Director (subject to reasonable availability) shall supervise any editing of the English language version at no additional compensation, and shall be offered employment to shoot any such additional footage at a daily compensation rate equal to the Director's initial daily compensation rate on the motion picture.

*   *   *

7-513 Right of Consultation

The Employer shall consult with the Director with respect to coloring, time compression and expansion, changes in the exhibition of the aspect ratio (e.g., "planning and scanning") and changes to allow exhibition in three dimensions made to a theatrical motion picture after delivery of the answer print. The Director's services in connection with such consultation shall be provided at no cost to the network or Employer or distributor.

*   *   *

7-515 Motion Picture Rating

If the Employer decides to appeal the rating given to a theatrical motion picture by the Classification and Rating Administration of the Motion Picture Association of America, the Director has the right to participate fully in the proceedings before CARA's Appeals Board. If changes are required to achieve the desired rating, the Director shall have the right to make the changes.

Section 7-700 PREVIEWS

7-701 With respect to theatrical motion pictures, the Employer will give the Director of the film five (5) business days advance notice, if possible, of the time and place of all previews (excluding press previews) at his or her last known address. If the Director cannot be reached, the Guild must be notified. The Employer will also give the Director reasonable advance notice of the time and place of the first trade-press preview which is held in either Los Angeles or in New York.

7-702 If the first preview (excluding press previews) is held outside of Los Angeles or Orange Counties, California, the Employer must provide the Director of the film, if he or she is available and has to travel to attend such preview, with first-class transportation and lodging, from the place where the Director is then located in the United States to the place of such preview.

* * *

7-704 With respect to all theatrical motion pictures covered by this BA, Employer will guarantee at least one public or private showing. The choice of the public preview or private showing shall be within the discretion of the Employer; provided, however, that if a private showing is chosen by the Employer it shall be with an audience of sufficient size and diversity to obtain adequate audience reaction.

* * *

Section 7-1000 ADDITIONAL SCENES AND/OR RETAKES

7-1001 If the Director completes 100% of the scheduled principal photography, he or she shall be entitled to direct any additional scenes and/or retakes to be photographed, subject only to his or her availability. If the Director of the film is not available, he or she shall be accorded the opportunity to consult with the substituting Director about such photography.

Section 7-1100 LOOPING AND NARRATION

* * *

7-1103 Should the Director of the film be unavailable to attend such looping or narration recordings, as above provided, the Employer shall consult with the Director, if he or she is available, as to what person is available and fitted to direct such loopings and narrations. The final decision in the selection of such person (who may, but need not be, a person subject to this BA) shall remain with the Employer, but the Director of the film shall be given the opportunity, if practicable, to explain to such person his or her ideas as to the content and qualities of the work to be done.

Section 7-1200 THE DUBBING OF SOUND AND MUSIC

7-1201 The Director of the film, if available, shall participate in the spotting and dubbing of sound and music, provided that such participation does not necessarily increase costs.

Section 7-1300 FOREIGN VERSION

7-1301 Each Director shall have the right to a Director's Cut of the foreign version of any motion picture by a single Director (as distinguished from a combination of different films by different Directors) which is produced to be and is initially exhibited as such on television in the United States and which is then released theatrically in foreign countries. The Director shall not have such a right to such cut if the foreign version cut of such motion picture is made outside the United States or if such foreign version cut is done in the United States for foreign local acceptance.

If the motion picture as so exhibited is not recut for its foreign theatrical release, this provision shall not be applicable.

Section 7-1400 REPLACEMENT OF DIRECTOR

7-401 No person assigned to or performing in a particular motion picture before the Director is replaced can replace the Director. The Director may be replaced only by a person who has never been assigned to or performed in the particular picture and who has theretofore directed a feature motion picture or not less than 90 minutes of television programming, which has been exhibited in the United States, regardless of where produced. None of the above conditions shall apply in the case of a *bona fide* emergency, in which event a person employed on the shooting company may direct for a period not in excess of five (5) shooting days pending arrival of a substitute Director. In the event the Employer claims such an emergency exists, Employer shall give the Guild notice of such emergency as soon as practical. If the Guild, within 72 hours after receipt of notice from the Employer, disputes the existance of such an emergency, then within 24 hours after the Guild notifies the Employer of such dispute an authorized representative of the Guild and the Employer shall meet in a good faith attempt to settle or resolve the issue of whether there was an emergency. If the Guild does not give such notice to the Employer within such 72 hour period, the claimed emergency shall be deemed to be a *bona fide* emergency.

In the event the parties fail to meet or otherwise fail to settle or resolve the dispute as to whether there was such an emergency, then, within 24 hours of the last time period referred to above, only said dispute as to whether there was an emergency shall be submitted directly to Expedited Arbitration in accordance with the Expedited Arbitration procedure set forth in Section 2-400.

Section 7-1500   GENERAL PROVISIONS

7-1501   Employer's Decision Final

The Employer's decision in all business and creative matters shall be final, but this provision shall not release the Employer or the Director from their respective obligations hereunder.

* * *

7-1503   No Retaliation

The Employer shall not discriminate or retaliate against a Director because the Director exercises or asserts his or her rights under this Article 7.

7-1504   Attendance at Casting Sessions

In order to provide the most creative environment possible for the Director and actor(s) in casting sessions, no one shall be present at casting sessions except those persons designated by the individual Producer, the Employer or the Director and all such persons shall have a reasonable purpose for attending.

7-1505   Electronic Transmissions

No images or sounds may be transmitted electronically from the stage or control booth without first informing the Director. Any instances of non-disclosed transmission shall be presented to the Creative Rights Standing Committee. The Employer shall use its best efforts to identify those places or persons that have access to such transmissions.

* * *

ARTICLE 8

Directors' Credits

Section 8-100   GENERAL PROVISIONS

8-101   Guild to Determine Controversy Over Credits

Should more than one Director do work on a motion picture, the Guild and all such Directors (other than Directors of second units) shall be notified in writing as to the directorial credit intended to be given. Should any such Director be dissatisfied with such determination, he or she may immediately appeal to the Guild and likewise notify the Employer in writing that he or she is so doing. The Guild may then determine the issue. Except as herein provided, the Employer agrees to be bound by such determination as to credits. If the Guild should fail to reach a decision and notify the Employer within fourteen (14) days in the case of a theatrical motion picture, and seven (7) days in the case of a television motion picture (such time to run from receipt by the Guild of the print of the film), the Employer shall determine the issue and its determination shall be final. In the event that the Guild's determination as to credit is given at too late a date to permit the giving of screen or advertising credit as indicated by the Guild, then credit shall be given in any bulletin to be issued by the Guild or in such other bulletin as may be mutually agreed upon. In no event shall an Employer be obligated to delay the preparation or issuance of advertising matter or the release of any motion picture pending proceedings for the determination of credits.

8-102   Form of Director's Credit

The form of the Director's credit on screen, paid advertising, phonograph records, books, tapes, videodiscs, videocassettes and the containers thereof, when and as required, shall be "Directed by . . . ." The words "Directed by" on screen shall be at least one-half the size of type used to accord credit to the Director's name.

Should a Director other than the Director, or one of the Directors, receiving credit on the motion picture have the same first and last name, the Guild shall determine whether or not such Director's credit must include his or her middle name, if any, or middle initial. The Directors involved shall be bound by such determination and the Employer shall also be bound, if notified thereof by the Guild in writing within a reasonable time before prints with the main titles are prepared but shall not be bound with respect to advertising, publicity or other material prepared prior to such notice.

8-104 Better Conditions

The foregoing provisions relating to credits are minimum provisions, and any Director shall have the right to negotiate for any credit in excess of minimum. It is the policy of the Employers to affirm the traditional right of each individual and management to negotiate freely for conditions above the minimum, including all forms of special credits. Subject only to present collective bargaining agreements, each Employer intends to exercise control over granting of any special credits above the minimums on screen and in paid advertising.

Section 8-200 CREDIT FOR DIRECTORS OF THEATRICAL MOTION PICTURES

8-201 Screen Credit

The Director of the film shall be accorded credit on all positive prints and all videodiscs/videocassettes of the film in size of type not less than 50% of the size in which the title of the motion picture is displayed or of the largest size in which credit is accorded to any other person, whichever is greater. No other credit shall appear on the card which accords credit to the Director of the film. Such credit shall be on the last title card appearing prior to principal photography. If more than one Director is given such credit, in accordance with the provisions of Paragraph 6-101, then such 50% may be reduced to 30% for each. The Employer shall furnish to the Guild copies of the main and end titles as soon as the same are prepared in final form but before the print are made, for the purpose of checking compliance with the credit provisions of this BA. After such copies are furnished, there can be no changes relating to the term Director, Direction or any derivation thereof, without first giving the Guild notice of such proposed changes or elimination.

8-202 Visibility of Director's Name

Because the Employer pledges to use its best efforts to improve the visibility of the Director's name in publicity, the Guild agrees to the following provision in Paragraph 8-203 relating to paid advertising. The provisions of Paragraph 8-203 shall be effective from July 1, 1993 to January 1, 1995 and thereafter unless and until the Guild gives the AMPTP six (6) months written notice advising the AMPTP that Article 8 hereof is terminated. In the case of such notice, the Employer shall be bound thereafter by the provisions of Articles 8 And 12 of the DGA Basic Agreement of 1976. The Guild shall have the right to serve such notice any time during the term of this BA after January 1, 1995.

8-203   Credits on Paid Advertising

The Employer shall accord credit for direction of a motion picture on all paid advertising issued or prepared by the Employer in the continental United States and prepared subsequent to final determination of directorial credit in the manner herein provided, it being understood that in such advertising prepared or issued prior to such final determination the Employer shall include such credit for direction as the Employer may in good faith believe to be proper, and if this varies from the credits as finally determined, then it will not be used subsequent to such determination, to the extent not theretofore distributed.

Copies of theme credits as determined, with respect to motion pictures covered hereunder, shall be sent to all of the Employer's foreign sales and distribution offices, if any.

The foregoing obligations of Employer are subject to the following:

a.   Size and Location of Credit

Except as stated otherwise in this Section 8-200, the location of the Director's credit shall be discretionary with the Employer, and the size of type of the Director's credit shall be no less than 15% of the size of type used for the title of the motion picture, but in no event less than the size and style of type for any credit accorded any persons other than actors.

b.   Title of Motion Picture

The name of any person in the title of the motion picture shall be considered a credit, except for (i) a name which forms part of the name of a corporate Employer in existence prior to the execution date of this agreement or (ii) a name which is part of the film's title if such name reflects the content of the film and is not a form of possessory credit.

c.   "One Sheets"

The Director shall receive credit on all "one sheets."

d.   Outdoor-Type Advertising

Employer need not accord credit to the Director on an outdoor-type advertisement (including "24 sheets"), provided the advertisement contains no more than the title of the motion picture, key art (which may include likenesses or photographs of no more than two starring actors), logos, the motion picture's rating and copyright notice and copy of no more than 25 words (which may not include reviews or the name of any person, whether or not connected with the production).

If the advertisement does not meet the foregoing requirements, the Director's credit must be included in a size of type no less than 35% the size of type used for the title or of any individual credit, whichever is larger. If the name of the Writer or Producer appears in a presentation credit in addition to his or her other credit, the Director's credit must be boxed. If the advertisement contains five (5) or more personal credits (or mentions), the Director's credit shall be boxed. If the advertisement contains six (6) or more personal credits (or mentions), the Director shall also be accorded an additional credit above the title in the form "A Film By" which shall be not smaller in size of type than the "Directed By" credit. For the purpose of calculating the number of personal credits hereunder, credit to two starring actors, and no more than two actors, shall be deemed one personal credit. Hyphenated credits (e.g., "Produced and Written by") count as separate credits.

e.   "Trade Paper" Advertising

The Director shall receive credit in size of type not less than 30% the size of type used for the title of the motion picture in any United States motion picture industry trade paper advertisement.

f.   Advertising in Newspapers, Magazines and Other Periodicals

Employer need not accord credit to the Director in an advertisement of 250 lines or less (or the equivalent in the Standard Advertising Unit system) in newspapers, magazines and other periodicals (excluding "trade papers"), provided that the advertisement mentions no person (excluding only the names of reviewers) other than two starring actors. For the purpose of calculating the size of the advertisement, theater listings shall be excluded.

Employer need not accord credit to the Director in an advertisement of more than 250 lines but not more than 1,200 lines (or the equivalent in the Standard Advertising Unit system) (approximately 1/8 to 1/2 page; 2/3 of a page in tabloid size papers) in newspapers, magazines and other periodicals (excluding "trade papers") provided that the advertisement does not include: (1) more than 35 words of copy (including reviews); (2) likenesses or photographs of more than three (3) starring actors; (3) any corporate name or logo; and/or (4) the name of any person other than reviewers and two starring actors. The Guild will not unreasonably deny Employer's request that the provisions of this subparagraph be waived as to an advertisement which includes likenesses or photographs of more than three (3) starring actors, but otherwise does not require credit to the Director. For the purpose of calculating the size of the advertisement, theater listings shall be excluded. If the Employer places such advertising without the Director's credit, the Employer shall box the Director's credit in all subsequent advertisements in which the Director's credit is required. Unless specifically negotiated in a subsequent collective bargaining agreement, the provisions of this paragraph shall automatically terminate, without notice, on June 30, 1996.

Employer need not accord credit to the Director in any advertisement which contains no more than the title of the motion picture, logos, key art (which may include likenesses or photographs of no more than two starring actors) the motion picture's rating and copyright notice and copy of no more than 25 words (which may not include reviews or the name of any person). The Guild will not unreasonably deny Employer's request that the provisions of this subparagraph be waived as to an advertisement which includes likenesses or photographs of more than two starring actors but otherwise does not require credit to the Director.

Notwithstanding the foregoing provisions of this subparagraph f., with respect to any theatrical advertising campaign in Los Angeles and/or New York utilizing advertisements larger than 10 column inches (or the equivalent in the Standard Advertising Unit system) in which the Director is not accorded credit pursuant to the preceding unnumbered paragraphs, the Director shall be accorded credit in advertisements on one weekend day (Friday, Saturday or Sunday) for three consecutive weeks, provided the motion picture is in distribution in such cities during such weekends.

g. Exceptions

  (i)   subject to the provisions of (ii) below, none of the foregoing obligations under this Paragraph 8-203 shall apply:

    (1) to group advertising, *i.e.,* more than one motion picture is advertised;

    (2) to so-called "teaser" advertising, as that term is used in the motion picture industry;

    (3) to "trailer" advertising, as that term is used in the motion picture industry. Notwithstanding the foregoing, if credit is given for film or camera process (such as Panavision, Technicolor or DeLuxe), or if the individual producer or writer is mentioned, then the Director's name shall be mentioned; and

    (4) to other advertising on the screen, radio, or television, not to exceed one (1) minute.

  (ii) None of the exceptions under (i) above shall apply and the name of the Director shall also be mentioned if the name of any person other than two starring actors is mentioned, in any of the advertising listed above, with the exception only of congratulatory advertising or award advertising where no one is mentioned other than the person being congratulated or mentioned for the award.

8-204 Publicity

In any formal publicity released by the Employer, whenever the name of the picture is mentioned, the name of the Director, when known, shall also be mentioned.

8-205 Publicity Tours

The Employer, at its expense, shall send the Director of any motion picture on any domestic publicity tour, provided the Director is available and provided actors are also sent.

8-206 Phonograph Records, Books and Tapes

The Director shall be given credit on any book, phonograph record or tape identified with a motion picture hereunder or the container thereof, if credit is accorded to any other person who rendered services or performed in connection with the picture on which such book, record or tape is based. This Paragraph is applicable only to books, phonograph records, or tapes which the Employer distributes or licenses for distribution.

* * *

8-210 Submission of Press Books and Advertising to Guild

All press books and paid advertising campaign material prepared by or under the supervision of the Employer or the Employer's distributor for use in the United States and Canada shall be submitted to the Guild for approval of Director's credit prior to public release thereof. At any time Employer or such distributor prepares advertising campaign material previously submitted, copies thereof shall likewise be submitted to the Guild if there is a change in the form, size or style of Director's credit prior to distribution thereof. Employer is not required to submit advertising which has the same credits, copy and artwork as a previously submitted advertisement, provided it is proportionate in size and the size and use of the advertisement does not invoke different credit requirements. Failure of the Guild to notify Employer or distributor within two (2) business days after receipt of any such material that it disapproves the form, size or style of Director's credit shall be deemed a waiver. In the event there are *bona fide* exigencies of time which interfere with the above procedure, Employer shall discuss the matter with a responsible officer of the Guild who may impose reasonable alternate conditions to those herein set forth.

8-211 Pseudonym

If a Director wishes to use a pseudonym in substitution of the Director's name on the screen, advertising, publicity and any other material in which credit, in any form whatsoever, is given for direction of the motion picture, the Director may invoke the following procedure:

(a)   the Director may notify Employer and the Guild of his or her desire to use a pseudonym no later than 72 hours (three business days) following the Director's first viewing of the version of the film the Employer intends to release,

(b)   the Directors' Council of the Guild, utilizing the same stringent criteria it has used in the past, may grant the Director permission to use a pseudonym and in such case the Guild shall notify the Employer within 48 hours (two business days) following the Director's notice to the Employer, and

(c)   if Employer is unwilling to grant such request, a Panel comprised of an equal number of Guild and AMPTP representatives (including at least one AMPTP representative and one Guild representative serving on the Creative Rights Negotiating Subcommittee which negotiated this provision) may determine by majority vote that Employer shall use a pseudonym.

The Panel may also determine that the Director waives the right to receive contingent compensation, including residuals, should the Director or the Guild elect to demand that the Employer comply with the Panel's decision requiring the Employer to use a pseudonym. The decision of the Panel shall be final, and shall have the same status as an arbitration award.

By invoking the foregoing procedure, the Director is deemed to have agreed to refrain from publicly discussing the request for a pseudonym. As a condition for using a pseudonym, the Director must refrain from publicly criticizing the film.

* * *

Section 8-300   CREDIT FOR DIRECTORS OF TELEVISION FILMS

8-301   Screen Credit

The Director shall be given credit in the form "directed by" on all television films, including such films released on videodiscs and videocassettes, on a separate card which shall be the last title card before the first scene of the picture or the first title card following the last scene of the picture. However, in the case of split credits where credit is given to any person before the first scene of the picture, the Director shall be given the last solo credit card before the first scene of the picture. For purpose of this clause, the credits of the established stars playing a continuing role in the series, or of well-established stars in the motion picture industry, or of a *bona fide* producing company credit shall not be considered credits of a person. (A loanout company shall not be considered a *bona fide* producing company.) No commercial or other material shall intervene between the Director's credit card and the picture.

* * *

8-303   Size of Director's Screen Credit

The Director's name on the screen shall be no less than forty percent (40%) of the episode or series title, whichever is larger.

8-304   Visibility of Director's Screen Credit

The Director's credit shall be in such contrast to the background and/or such color as to be clearly visible, and shall be of not less than two seconds in the clear for television films of less than two hours in duration; and not less than three seconds in the clear for television films of two hours duration or longer. In no event shall credit accorded to Director be displayed for a cumulative time less than the "produced by" credit.

8-305   Submission of Proposed Screen Credit Format to Guild

Employer shall submit to the Guild the proposed format for the final screen credit for each television episodic and anthology series (as distinguished from each segment), together with changes in such format of credits, before prints are prepared. This provision likewise applies to each television special.

8-306   Advertising Credit

In all paid advertising, other than night-strip advertisements, of a non-series television film 90 minutes or longer, licensed by Employer to a national free television network, the Employer agrees to obligate the network to give the Director credit if the advertisement appears in a "TV Guide-type" or newspaper advertisement one-half page or larger. The obligation to give a Director credit under this subparagraph shall be no greater than it would be if the advertisement were prepared under the control of or at the direction of Employer.

In all paid advertising of a television film prepared under the control of or at the direction of Employer the Director shall be accorded credit in the largest size in which any person other than actors is accorded credit. Notwithstanding the preceding sentence, if the advertising relates solely to a television series directed by more than one Director and produced by one producer, then Employer shall not be obligated to accord credit to the Directors by reason of the fact that one producer who is the producer of the entire series is accorded credit.

Except for the foregoing provisions of this Section 8-300, Director's credits in connection with television films shall be governed by the provisions of Paragraphs 8-202 and 8-203.

* * *

8-311   Pseudonym

The Director of a television film 90 minutes or longer (excluding an episode of an episodic series or serial) shall be entitled to request the use of a pseudonym pursuant and subject to the provisions of Paragraph 8-211.

* * *

ARTICLE 10

Minimum Salaries and Working Conditions of Directors Employed on AFree TV Pictures

10-101   Minimum Salaries

The minimum salaries and working conditions of employment set forth in the following schedules and footnotes shall apply to Directors employed in the making of "free" television films:

Network Prime Time Shows**

Length	7/1/93	7/1/94	7/1/95	* Guaranteed Days (shooting/Prep)*** *****	
1/2 hour	$13,786	$14,338	$14,911	7	(4/3)
1 hour	23,411	24,348	25,322	15	(8/7)
1-1/2 hours	39,019	40,579	42,203	25	(13/12)
2 hours	65,548	68,170	70,897	42	(27/15)

The rate applicable to all such services shall be that in effect on the starting date of employment.

For a double length episode of an episodic series or serial, Director may be employed at 200% of minimum and 200% of the guaranteed days appearing in the schedule above. For Network Prime Time programs in excess of 2 hours, the minimum and guaranteed days shall be computed at the two hour rate plus *pro rata* of the 1 hour schedule; and the additional days may be allocated between shooting and preparation time at Employer's discretion. For other than Network Prime Time programs, the following schedule shall apply, but in the event of the production of programs in excess of 2 hours, minimum and guaranteed days shall be computed *pro rata*.

Non-Network or Network Non-Prime Time Shows**

Type of employment/ Length of film	7/1/93	7/1/94	7/1/95	*Guaranteed Days (Shooting/Prep) ***
Term Contract 20 out of 26 weeks or multiples thereof	$ 4,678 weekly	$ 4,865 weekly	$ 5,060 weekly	No Guarantee
Trailers and Promos	$ 4,678 weekly or $ 1,170 daily	$ 4,865 weekly or $ 1,217 daily	$ 5,060 weekly or $ 1,265 daily	Section 10-110
7 Minutes and Under	$ 1,170	$ 1,217	$ 1,265	1 day (for each additional film on such day - $1,066, increased to $1,109 effective July 1, 1994, and increased to $1,153 effective July 1, 1995)
8-15 Minutes	$ 5,619	$ 5,844	$ 6,078	6 days (3/3). May do 2 films during guaranteed period without additional pay. For third and each subsequent film, an additional 3 days *pro rata* compensation, for which Employer shall be entitled to an additional 3 consecutive days per film.
16 - 30 Minutes	$ 5,619	$ 5,844	$ 6,078	6 days (3/3)
1 Hour	$11,235	$11,685	$12,152	12 days (6/6)
90 Minutes	$16,857	$17,532	$18,233	18 days (9/9)
2 Hours	$22,476	$23,376	$24,311	24 days (12/12)

Second Unit ****

The rate applicable to all such services shall be that in effect on the starting date of employment.

The *daily pro rata salary* shall be computed by dividing the minimum guarantee per show by the number of days guaranteed for such show.

The *weekly salary* shall be computed by multiplying the applicable daily pro rata salary by 5 days.

The *salary for daily* employment, where permissible, shall be 1/4 of such weekly salary.

Directors employed under term contract who, during such term, direct a Network Prime Time show(s) shall be adjusted to the Network Prime Time Show rate for the period of time spent in directing such show(s); provided, however, that Employer shall be entitled to offset against such adjustment all compensation paid under such term contract for the period of time the Director is not assigned to direct any motion picture hereunder.

The rates for "Network Prime Time Shows" shall be applicable to all television motion pictures hereunder, the network initial broadcast of which either begins or ends in Network Prime Time. There shall be excepted from the foregoing a television motion picture scheduled for non-Prime Time Network broadcast which appears all or in part in network prime time due to last minute rescheduling beyond the control of the network such as national emergency or disaster.

If a television motion picture originally produced for non-Prime Time Network broadcast is initially broadcast on non-Network Prime Time and is then broadcast in Network Prime Time as aforesaid, either for its first or second rerun, the Director's salary shall be adjusted to the applicable Network Prime Time show rate. There shall be no such salary adjustment if such picture is first broadcast in Network Prime Time in its third or any subsequent rerun. If a television motion picture is produced for non-Prime Time Network broadcast under a budget equivalent to that of a similar type of television motion picture produced within the last three years for Network Prime Time broadcast, the Director's salary shall be paid at the applicable Network Prime Time show rate.

* *Guaranteed Period of Employment*. In the event of a change or substitution of a Director for reasons other than the incapacity of the Director, the substituting Director shall only be guaranteed the unexpired portion of the previous Director's guarantee, at not less than double minimum compensation for the work performed. However, there shall be no compounding of premium pay to such substituting Director for work performed on a holiday or for the sixth or seventh day worked in the Director's workweek.

In the event that a Director is replaced by reason of his or her own incapacity, the substituting Director shall only be guaranteed the greater of the number of guaranteed shooting days remaining under Paragraph 10-101 or the number of days actually remaining on the shooting schedule at the time such substituting Director begins the assignment. In addition, the substituting Director shall be guaranteed payment for prep time as follows: the guaranteed prep time shall bear the same relation to the number of days remaining on the shooting schedule at the time the substituting Director begins the assignment as the maximum preparation days provided in Paragraph 10-101 for a motion picture of that type bears to the maximum number of shooting days provided in Paragraph 10-101 for a motion picture of that type.

** *The pro rata minimum weekly salary* shall be based on the one-hour show rate. (See Paragraph 10-102, "Compensation for Fractional Week," below.)

*** *Sixth and seventh days worked in the Director's workweek appl. against guarantee*. Additional pay for the sixth day worked in the Director's workweek in the studio and for the seventh day worked in the Director's workweek and holidays worked shall be in accordance with Paragraph 4-107 above. Work on such days shall be defined, and counted as such, only when photographing is in progress under the supervision of the Director, or when the Director travels or prepares pursuant to the Employer's written instructions and direction.

**** *Second Unit Directors* will be compensated at the weekly rate applicable to the program for which he or she is employed (including programs defined in Paragraph 10-103), or on a daily basis at one-fourth the applicable weekly rate for each day so employed. Preparation time shall be determined in accordance with Paragraph 4-102 of this BA.

***** *Guaranteed Days (Shooting/Prep) Time*. Total guaranteed days shown are the maximum allowed for the applicable rate. The first number in the parenthesis indicates the maximum number of shooting days allowed within the total number of guaranteed days.

10-102 Compensation for Fractional Week

In computing compensation to be paid any freelance Director employed on a weekly basis for any period less than a week following the guaranteed period of employment, the weekly salary shall be prorated and for this purpose the rate per day shall be one-fifth (1/5) of the Director's weekly rate.

10-103 Pilot and Spinoff Films

(a) In connection with pilots or spinoff episodes for Network Prime Time, the Director shall be paid the following compensation and receive the following guarantees:

Length	7/1/93	7/1/94	7/1/95	Maximum Guaranteed Days
1/2 hour	$39,019	$40,579	$42,203	14
1 hour	52,022	54,103	56,267	24

1-1/2 hours	65,026	67,627	70,332	34
2 hours	91,040	94,681	98,468	50

For each additional hour over 2 hours, the applicable Network Prime Time minimum rate based on the hour rate or fractions thereof will be payable.

Days in excess of maximum will be prorated to actual salary but in no event at a rate of less than $1,633 ($1,698 effective July 1, 1994 and $1,766 effective July 1, 1995) per day.

For non-network or network other than prime time pilots and spinoffs, the applicable amount will 60% of the applicable Network Prime Time amount follows:

Length	7/1/93	7/1/94	7/1/95
1/2 hour	$23,411	$24,348	$25,322
1 hour	31,214	32,462	33,761
1-1/2 hours	39,016	40,576	42,199
2 hours	54,624	56,809	59,081

(b) De Facto Pilot If a television series is produced based upon characters in a television program not originally intended as a pilot or a spinoff episode, the Director of such program shall be paid the difference between the compensation originally paid to said Director for such program and the applicable pilot fee set forth above. The payment of such difference shall be made promptly after a new series containing such new characters is ordered only one such payment shall be made for any new series. The Guild will determine allocation if there is more than one Director entitled to the payment.

When a theatrical motion picture is used as a pilot for the sale of a television series (when no actual television pilot is produced), the Director of such theatrical motion picture, upon receipt by the Employer of the firm written license order for such series, is entitled to additional compensation as above set forth. If more than one theatrical motion picture is involved, only the Director of the first theatrical motion picture shall be so entitled. This provision shall not apply when such Director is paid the minimum theatrical rate plus double the minimum television rate for the actual series length. If the Director was paid in excess of theatrical minimum but less than the theatrical plus double such minimum television rate, then he or she shall be paid the difference between the amount set forth and the amount actually paid.

(c) Series Without Pilot In connection with the first produced film of an open-ended series which is ordered without a pilot, minimum shall be 150% of scale.

(d) Series Bonus If an open-ended series is sold subsequent to the production of a pilot film in any of the forms above, or if such series is based on a theatrical motion picture, then the Director of the spinoff or pilot or of the film introducing the character(s) shall be entitled to an additional aggregate series bonus payment for each production year as follows:

	7/1/94	7/1/95	7/1/96
1/2 hour -	$1,921	$1,998	$2,078
1 hour -	$3,842	$3,995	$4,155
90 minutes or longer -	$5,122	$5,327	$5,540

Payment is to be made within 5 days after firm order for production.

10-104 Interchange of Assignment --Theatrical --Television

With respect to Directors, there may be complete interchange of assignment between production of theatrical films and television films. Whenever such interchange takes place, such Director shall receive not less than the respective minimum pay and working conditions pertaining to theatrical motion pictures or television motion pictures, whichever is applicable to the assignment on which the Director is employed at the time in question.

10-105 Other Provisions

For the provisions relating to "Travel," "Compensation on Recall for Particular Services" (however, the weekly rate shall be prorated in the manner provided in Paragraph 10-102, entitled "Compensation for Fractional Week"), "Holidays, Sixth and Seventh Days Worked in the Director's Workweek," "Deal Memorandum," "Personal Services Agreement," and "Prohibition Against Credits and Offsets," see Paragraphs 4-104, 4-105, 4-107, and 4-108 through 4-110, respectively. For "Directors' Minimum Conditions --Preparation, Production and Post-production," see Article 7.

10-106 Daily Employment

No Director shall be employed on a daily basis except in case of second units, trailers, promos, lead-ins, government, industrial, educational motion pictures, and talent tests, the type of services described in Paragraph 4-105, changes in photoplay, pictures 7 minutes or less in length, bridging or shooting added scenes for television films for theatrical release or bridging or shooting added scenes for theatrical motion pictures for television release. In each such case, the Director may be employed on a daily basis.

10-107 Adjustment of Term Directors

Directors employed under term contract who, during such term, direct a Network Prime Time show(s) shall be adjusted to the Network Prime Time show rate for the period of time spent in directing such show(s); provided, however, that Employer shall be entitled to offset against such adjustment all compensation paid under such term contract for the period of time the Director is not assigned to direct any motion picture hereunder.

10-108 Preparation Allowance Time

With respect to a single television picture where preparation time is allowed by the Employer, it shall be allowed before principal photography and the

Director shall receive full salary for all days the Director is engaged in preparation at the Employer's direction. Once principal photography commences, shooting days shall be consecutive.

Except as specifically prohibited below, all preparation shall apply toward fulfillment of Employer's obligation on a Director's "guaranteed employment period." With respect to a single television picture, only preparation days which are consecutive with shooting days shall be applied against Employer's obligations for the guaranteed employment period, except that with respect to: (a) for 8-15 minute and 16-30 minute television films, one non-consecutive day, subject to the Director's availability, prior to commencement of consecutive employment may be applied against Employer's obligation for the guaranteed employment period; (b) for 31-60 minute television films, two such non-consecutive days, subject to the Director's availability, may be so applied.

10-109   Order of Shooting or Preparation of Consecutive Films at Employer's Discretion

When a Director has been employed for the making of two or more television films consecutively and Employer has complied with the applicable guarantees as set forth in Paragraph 10-101 above, then Employer may require such Director to work on more than one film during any period of his or her employment; the order of shooting, rehearsal, cutting and preparation being at the Employer's discretion.

Employer may cumulate both payments and time on a multi-part closed-end (mini) series and continuing story on any series as well as continuous employment on two episodes of one or more open-end series.

10-110   Trailers and Promos

(a)   Trailers and promos are divided into two classes: (1) integrated and (2) all others. An "integrated trailer or promo" is one designed to be shown only with the entertainment film or films of the series directed in whole or in part by the Director during his or her term of employment.

Integrated trailers and/or promos may be made without extra pay to the Director on any shooting day, or on any additional shooting day for which the Director is paid an additional day's compensation.

Other trailers and promos may be made without limitation or restriction on the kind or number of such, provided the Director is specifically employed by the week, by the day, or under a term contract, under the terms of the applicable minimum salary schedule set forth in Paragraph 10-101 above.

(b)   If a term Director is on salary for any purpose, trailers and promos may be made by such Director on any day during the period he or she is on salary, without extra pay to the Director.

(c)   In the event a Director is called specifically and only for the purpose of making trailers and/or promos, the Director shall receive the minimum salary (daily, weekly or term) provided for in the applicable minimum salary schedule in Paragraph 10-101 above, prorated on the basis of the applicable one hour rate.

(d)   There shall be no limitation on the number of trailers and/or promos a Director may shoot in a day.

(e)   If a Director is called specifically and only to do trailers, and/or promos, one day of preparation time shall be provided regardless of the length of employment or number of shooting days; provided, however, if the Director is called for a single day's employment, and the shooting of trailers and/or promos takes five hours or less, then the preparation reguirement shall be included in the same day and only one day's compensation shall be paid.

(f)   The inclusion of trailers or promos herein is not intended to change the present practice of making trailers or promos.

10-111   Options --Notice to Director

Whenever the Employer exercises an option for an additional term under a term contract, the Director shall be given at least 30 days' advance written notice.

10-112   Multiple Picture Commitments

Commitments for a Director to direct more than ten one-half or five one-hour films within any consecutive 26-week period will not be permitted without the written consent of the Guild unless the Director's salary for the total number of films involved is at least $65,266 ($67,877 effective July 1, 1994 and $70,592 effective July 1, 1995). Any multiple picture commitment entered into prior to January 1, 1978 is governed by the 1973 BA.

10-113   Director Rest Period

In connection with television productions, in the event the time elapsing between company wrap on one day and the time the Director is required to be on the set on the following day or the call of the Director of Photography on the following day, whichever is later, is less than 11 hours, then Employer shall make a contribution to the Directors Guild of America Educational and Benevolent Foundation in the sum of $750 for each such incursion into the rest period of the Director, but no payment shall be due hereunder unless payment for forced call is in fact made to the Director of Photography of the picture.

ARTICLE 11

Additional Compensation to Directors for "Free" Television Films

Section 11-100   ADDITIONAL COMPENSATION FOR RERUNS AND FOREIGN TELECASTS

11-101   Additional Compensation for Reruns

The salary paid to the Director for his or her services in a television motion picture shall constitute payment in full for the telecasting of such motion picture once in each city in the United States and Canada in which any television broadcasting stations are now located and once in each city in the United States, its territories and possessions, and Canada in which any television broadcasting stations are hereafter for the first time established.

(a)　A television motion picture which has been telecast not more than once in any city in the United States and Canada is in its first run. A television motion picture which has been telecast more than once, but not more than twice, in any city in the United States, its territories and possessions, and Canada, is in its second run. A similar test applies in determining when a television motion picture is in its third and succeeding runs.

(b)　If the Employer desires to telecast any television motion picture for more than one run in the United States, its territories and possessions, and Canada, the employment contract of each Director engaged therein shall contain a separate provision for additional compensation for reruns, which shall not be less than the amounts set forth in the applicable provisions of subparagraphs (i) through (iii) below:

(i)　**Network Prime Time – Domestic Reruns**

Length	7/1/93	7/1/94	7/1/95
1/2 hour	$ 7,744	$ 8,015	$ 8,295
1 hour	14,655	15,094	15,623
1-1/2 hours	21,661	22,528	23,429
2 hours*	28,609	29,754	30,944

* Over 2 hours, residuals will be computed *pro rata* based on the applicable 1 hour rate.

(ii)　**Base for Network Non-Prime Time and Syndication Residuals**

Length	7/1/93	7/1/94	7/1/95
7 minutes and under	$ 1,432	$ 1,489	$ 1,549
8-15 minutes	2,990	3,110	3,234
16-30 minutes	7,412	7,709	8,017
1 hour	13,396	13,932	14,489
1-1/2 hours	19,377	20,152	20,958

| 2 hours* | 25,359 | 26,374 | 27,429 |

* Over 2 hours, residuals will be computed *pro rata* based on the applicable 1 hour rate.

(iii) **Percentage of above Base Rate* Payable for Domestic Residuals other than Network Prime Time**

* (referred to in subparagraph (b) above)

	Network	Non Network
2nd Run	50%	40%
3rd Run	40%	30%
4th Run	25%	25%
5th Run	25%	25%
6th Run	25%	25%
7th Run	15%	15%
8th Run	15%	15%
9th Run	15%	15%
10th Run	15%	15%
11th Run	10%	10%
12th Run	10%	10%
13th Run and each subsequent Run in perpetuity	5%	5%

(iv) (1)Notwithstanding the provisions of subparagraphs (b) (ii) and (iii) above, the Employer shall pay the following to the Director of an episode of a one (1) hour network prime time dramatic television series, whether covered under this or a prior Basic Agreement, which has not previously been exhibited in syndication, for reuse of such episode in syndication:

(A) Two and six-tenths percent (2.6%) of the "Employer's gross" received for exhibitions in syndication until such time as the "Employer's gross" received therefrom exceeds the sum of $400,000.

(B) Thereafter, one and three-quarters percent (1.75%) of the "Employer's gross" received for exhibition(s) in syndication.

However, payments made pursuant to this provision shall not exceed one hundred fifty percent (150%) of the "fixed residual schedule" set forth in subparagraphs (b) and (iii) above. Similarly, such payments shall not be less than fifty percent (50%) of such "fixed residual schedule" for such exhibitions, except in the case of series licensed only in markets representing less than one-third of all United States television households.

(2) For the purposes of this Paragraph 11-101(b)(iv), the term "Employer's gross" shall have the same meaning as it does in Article 18 with respect to pay television exhibition of a free television film.

(3) Payments due and payable hereunder shall be sent to the Guild within the time and in the manner required by the first, fourth and fifth paragraphs of Paragraph 18-106.

The provisions of this Article 11 are not applicable to commercials or the "bridging" or shooting of added scenes for theatrical films for television release, or to second units, trailers or promos, for which there are no rerun payments.

(c) The Employer shall pay as provided herein for each respective rerun, not later than four months after the first telecast of the respective rerun in any city in the United States or Canada, or upon the completion of the telecasting of the respective rerun in 70 cities in the United States and Canada, whichever occurs earlier. However, in the event any rerun is telecast on a television network, the Employer shall make the appropriate rerun payment not later than 30 days after the telecast of such rerun.

(d) The telecasting of a picture over a television network shall mean the telecast of such picture over the network facilities of NBC, CBS, ABC or any other entity which qualifies as a "network" under Section 73.662(f) of the rules of the Federal Communications Commission, unless the FCC determines that such entity is not a "network" for purposes of such Section, except (i) pictures telecast on any single regional network presently established and (ii) pictures telecast on any single regional network which may hereafter be established and which does not include New York, Chicago or Los Angeles.

(e) The above formula is a minimum formula and nothing herein shall preclude any Director from bargaining for better terms with respect to such reruns.

(f) Whenever a payment is due under the foregoing provisions of this paragraph 11-101 for telecasts, after the effective date of this Agreement, of a television motion picture in a language or languages other than English, then in lieu of such payment the payment due the Director(s) of such television motion picture shall be an aggregate amount equal to 1.2% of the Employer's "accountable receipts," as defined in Article 18, from the distribution Of such television motion picture for such telecasts.

Such payment shall not affect the Employer's obligation to make the applicable rerun payments for telecasts of a motion picture in English.

This subparagraph will apply to all television motion pictures produced on or after July 1, 1971.

11-102   Foreign Telecasting Payments

(a) If the Employer desires to telecast any television motion picture in any part of the world outside the United States and Canada, the Employer shall pay additional compensation for such foreign telecasting of not less than 15% of the applicable "base amount" in effect on the date of commencement of principal photography, not later than 30 days after the Employer obtains knowledge of the first foreign telecast.

(b) When the Distributor's Foreign Gross, as defined herein, of any such television motion picture has exceeded $7,000 for a one-half hour picture, $13,000 for a one-hour picture, or $18,000 if such picture is one and one-half hours or more in length, the Director shall be entitled to the additional payment of not less than 10% of the applicable "base amount" in effect on the date of commencement of principal photography, not later than thirty (30) days after such Gross has been so exceeded.

(c) When the Distributor's Foreign Gross of any such television motion picture has exceeded $10,000 for a one-half hour picture, $18,000 for a one-hour picture, or $24,000 if such picture is one and one-half hours Or more in length, the Director shall be entitled to the additional payment of not less than 10% of the applicable "base amount" in effect on the date of the commencement of principal photography, not later than thirty (30) days after such Gross has been so exceeded.

(d) The "base amounts" referred to and the applicable payments under subparagraphs (a), (b) and (c) above are as follows:

Effective Dates

7/1/93 Length of Program	7/1/94 Residual Base- % and Amount	7/1/95 Residual Base- % and Amount	Residual Base- % and Amount
7 minutes and under	1,432 15% - 215 10% - 143	1,489 15% - 223 10% - 149	1,549 15% - 232 10% - 155
8-15 minutes	2,990 15% - 449 10% - 299	3,110 15% - 467 10% - 311	3,234 15% - 485 10% - 323
16 - 30 minutes	7,412 15% -1,112 10% - 741	7,709 15% - 1,156 10% - 771	8,017 15% - 1,203 10% - 802
31-60 minutes	13,396 15% - 2,009 10% - 1,340	13,932 15% - 2,090 10% - 1,393	14,489 15% - 2,173 10% - 1,449
61-90 minutes	19,377 15% - 2,907 10% - 1,938	20,152 15% - 3,023 10% - 2,015	20,958 15% - 3,144 10% - 2,096
91-120 minutes*	25,359 15% - 3,804 10% - 2,536	26,374 15% - 3,956 10% - 2,637	27,429 15% - 4,114 10% - 2,743

* Over 120 minutes, prorate payment based on 1 hour rate.

(e)   After the Director has received a total of the amounts specified in subparagraphs (a), (b) and (c) above with respect to any picture, no further sums shall be payable for foreign telecasting of such picture.

(f)   Notwithstanding the foregoing, for those one-hour network prime time dramatic television series referred to in 11-101(b) (iv) above, foreign residuals shall be calculated as follows:

    (i)   For such period as subparagraph (f) (ii) below does not apply, the 15%, 10% and 10% of the applicable base amount referred to in subparagraphs (a) through (e) above shall be collapsed into a single payment of 35% of the applicable base amount payable not later than thirty (30) days after the Employer obtains knowledge of the first foreign telecast and in no event later than six (6) months after the first foreign telecast;

    (ii)   The Guild, at its option, shall have a one-time right to elect that payment of foreign telecasting payment be calculated at 1.2% of Distributor's Foreign Gross to the Director; provided, however, in no event shall such payment be more than one hundred thirty percent (130%) of the amount that would otherwise be due under subparagraphs (a) through (e) above nor shall such payment be less than eighty-five percent (85%) of the amount that would otherwise be due under such subparagraphs.

           In the event the Guild elects that foreign telecasting payments be calculated pursuant to this subparagraph (ii), only those episodes produced after the date of the Guild's election shall be subject to this calculation.

(g)   The term "foreign telecasting," as used herein, shall mean any telecast (whether simultaneous or delayed) outside the United States, its territories and possessions, and Canada other than a telecast on any of the following regularly affiliated stations of a United States television network as a part of the United States network television telecast: XEW-TV or XEQ-TV or XHTV or XHGC-TV, Mexico City; and ZBM, Pembroke, Bermuda, for CBS and NBC; and any network affiliate in Tijuana; and ZBF, Hamilton, Bermuda, for ABC.

(h)   As used herein, the term "Distributor's Foreign Gross" shall mean, with respect to any television motion picture, the absolute gross income realized by the distributor of such picture for the foreign telecasting thereof and including, in the case of a "foreign territorial sale" by any such distributor, the income realized from such sale by such distributor but not the income realized by the "purchaser" or "licensee." The phrase "absolute gross income" shall not include:

    (i)   Sums realized or held by the way of deposits or security, until and unless earned, other than such sums as are non-returnable.

    (ii)   Sums required to be paid or withheld as taxes, in the nature of turnover taxes, sales taxes or similar taxes based on the actual receipts of the picture or on any monies to be remitted to or by the distributor, but there shall not be excluded from Distributor's Foreign Gross any net income, franchise tax or excess profit tax or similar tax payable by the distributor on its net income or for the privilege of doing business.

    (iii)   Frozen foreign currency until the distributor shall have either the right to use such foreign currency in or to transmit such foreign currency from the country or territory where it is frozen. In the event such currency may be utilized or transmitted as aforesaid, it shall be deemed to have been converted to United States dollars at the prevailing free market rate of exchange at the time such right to use or transmit accrues.

Distributor's Foreign Gross realized in foreign currency in any reporting period required hereunder shall be deemed to be converted to United States dollars at the prevailing free market rate of exchange at the close of such reporting period.

If any transaction involving any picture subject to a foreign telecast payment under this BA shall also include motion pictures, broadcast time, broadcast facilities or material (including commercial or advertising material) which are not subject to such payment, there shall be a reasonable allocation between the television motion pictures which are subject to foreign telecast payment and such other pictures, time, facilities or material, and only the sums properly allocable to pictures which are subject to a foreign telecast payment shall be included in the Distributor's Foreign Gross.

(iv) The above formula for foreign telecasting is a minimum formula, and nothing herein shall preclude any Director from bargaining for better terms with respect to such foreign telecasting.

11-103 Method of Payment; Guild Access to Records

All payments of additional compensation for reruns or foreign telecasts shall be made promptly by check, payable to the order of the Director entitled thereto, and shall be delivered to the Guild for forwarding to such Director, and compliance herewith shall constitute payment to Director. The Employer shall accompany such checks with a statement of the title and production date of the film and the "run" or "runs" for which such payment is made. The Employer shall keep or have access (a) to complete records showing all cities in the United States and Canada in which all television motion pictures subject to this BA have been telecast and the number of telecasts in each such city, the television stations on which telecast, and the dates thereof; and (b) to records reflecting all pertinent gross sums collected from TV exhibition outside of the United States and Canada. The Guild shall have the right at all reasonable times to inspect such records and at its cost make copies of such records. If Employer fails to pay such additional compensation when due and payable, such delinquent payment shall bear interest at the rate of one and one-half percent (1-1/2%) per month commencing to accrue from the date of such delinquency.

11-104 Reports of Foreign Telecasting

With respect to each television motion picture which is distributed for foreign telecasting, Employer shall furnish reports to the Guild showing Distributor's Foreign Gross derived from such motion picture until:

(a)   Such picture has been withdrawn from distribution for foreign telecasting, or

(b)   The Director of such picture has received the full additional payments for such foreign telecasting to which he or she is entitled pursuant to Paragraph 11-102 above.

11-105 Television Motion Pictures and Contracts to Which Provisions Hereof Are Applicable

The provisions hereof shall apply to all existing employment contracts in effect on July 1, 1993, as well as future contracts and employments for television motion pictures on which principal photography was commenced on or after July 1, 1993.

11-106 Responsibility for Residuals—Television Distributor's Liability and Employer's Liability

(a)   If a signatory Employer produces a television motion picture of which it is not the distributor and enters into a distribution agreement with a distributor who is not a signatory to this BA, Employer shall forthwith, upon entering into such distribution agreement, obtain from the distributor and deliver to the Guild a separate written agreement, herein called "Television Distributor's Assumption Agreement," made expressly for the benefit of the Guild as representative of the Director involved, by which such distributor agrees to assume and pay all fees and payments which become payable by reason of distribution under such distribution agreement as and when the same become due.

In the event of the expiration or termination of any such distribution agreement, the obligation of Employer to obtain and deliver to the Guild such Television Distributor's Assumption Agreement shall apply as well to any subsequent distribution agreement entered into by Employer with a non-signatory, and Employer shall obtain and deliver an executed Television Distributor's Assumption Agreement within ten days after the execution of each subsequent distribution agreement.

Such Television Distributor's Assumption Agreement shall be in substantially the form of Exhibit "A" hereto attached.

(b)   If a signatory Employer becomes a distributor of a motion picture which was produced by another Employer hereunder, such signatory Employer shall be automatically bound by all of the terms and provisions of the Television Distributor's Assumption Agreement, Exhibit "A," with respect to all fees and payments which become payable by reason of distribution under such distribution agreement, to the same effect and extent as though it has signed the Television Distributor's Assumption

Agreement, Exhibit "A," with respect to such motion picture. The provisions of this subparagraph (b) shall be likewise applicable to each signatory Employer which subsequently becomes a distributor of such motion picture with respect to all fees and sums which become payable by reason of the distribution of such motion picture by such subsequent distributor.

(c)   If a signatory Employer is not the actual producer of a television motion picture which was produced by a Guild signatory, but acquires title thereto by purchase, assignment, transfer, voluntary or involuntary, or by foreclosure of a chattel mortgage or security agreement or at a pledgee's sale, such signatory Employer shall be obligated to make the payments herein provided which become due thereafter when such picture is rerun on television or released for foreign telecasting or for theatrical exhibition, by or for the account of such signatory Employer.

(d)   In the event any television motion picture is sold under foreclosure of any security agreement or chattel mortgage thereon or at a pledgee's sale or other involuntary sale, Employer shall nevertheless continue to be liable for all rerun fees, fees for foreign telecasting and for theatrical exhibition which become due and payable by reason of any further distribution of such motion picture, except as hereinbelow in this subparagraph otherwise provided. Employer may obtain from the purchaser at any such foreclosure or other involuntary sale an Assumption Agreement substantially in the form of Exhibit "B," attached hereto, made expressly for the benefit of the Guild as representative of the Directors involved by which such purchaser agrees to make the applicable payments when such motion picture is subsequently rerun on television or released for foreign telecasting or for theatrical exhibition. Upon delivery of such Assumption Agreement to the Guild and on condition that the Guild approves, in writing, the financial responsibility of such purchaser, Employer shall not be liable for said payments which shall thereafter become due and payable by reason of any further distribution of such motion picture.

The Guild agrees that it will not unreasonably withhold its approval of the financial responsibility of any such purchaser, assignee or transferee, it being further agreed that if the Guild, within twenty-one (21) days of receipt of notice of any such involuntary or foreclosure sale, has not advised the Employer that it disapproves the financial responsibility of such purchaser, the Guild will be deemed to have approved the financial responsibility thereof. In the event the Guild advises the Employer within such 21 day period that it disapproves the financial responsibility of any such purchaser, and the Employer disputes such disapproval, the Employer shall have the right, at its election, to cause to be immediately submitted to grievance or arbitration, pursuant to the grievance or arbitration provisions hereof, the issue of whether the Guild has unreasonably withheld the approval of the financial responsibility of such purchaser.

(e)   In the event a television motion picture is sold under foreclosure or other involuntary sale, should a signatory Employer distribute any such television motion picture for the mortgagee, pledgee, security holder or purchaser at such sale, such signatory Employer shall be bound for the period of such distribution to pay the return fees, fees for foreign telecasting and for theatrical exhibition thereafter payable with respect to the further distribution of such television motion picture.

(f)   It is expressly understood that except as otherwise provided in subparagraphs (d) and (g) hereof, Employer shall not be relieved of liability under this Article to make the payments of rerun fees, fees for foreign telecasting and for theatrical exhibition with respect to all motion pictures produced under this BA by it. Irrespective of the assumption of such liability by any other person, firm or corporation.

(g)   If Employer dissolves and if a distributor assumes all of the obligations of the Employer for the payment of rerun fees, fees for foreign telecasting and for theatrical exhibition. And the financial responsibility of the distributor is approved by the Guild in its discretion, the Employer shall thereupon be released of any obligation with respect to any payments due hereunder.

(h)   No television network, station, sponsor or advertising agency shall be required to execute any Television Distributor's Assumption Agreement or Buyer's Assumption Agreement or shall be bound by the automatic provisions of subparagraph (b) above, unless it is the distributor of such television motion picture or the buyer of the Employer's television rights in such motion picture, as the case may be.

11-107 Responsibility for Residuals—Buyer's Liability and Employer's Liability

(a)   If the Employer shall sell, assign, or transfer its right to the motion picture on free television (as distinguished from a distribution agreement), Employer may obtain from the buyer a separate agreement, herein called "Buyer's Assumption Agreement," made expressly for the benefit of the Guild, as representative of the Director involved. Such agreement shall be in substantially the form of Exhibit "B" hereto attached.

* * *

Section 11-108   Basic Cable Exhibition

11-108   Upon release, on or after July 1, 1993, to basic cable or free television motion pictures, as to which free television residuals would otherwise be payable, Employer shall pay to the Director thereof the following percentage of the Employer's gross receipts obtained therefrom: With respect to free television motion pictures produced prior to July 1, 1984, said percentage shall be 2.5%; with respect to free television motion pictures produced after July 1, 1984, said percentage shall be 2%. For the purpose of this provision, the term "basic cable" means one or more basic cable systems which do not meet the definition of pay television as set forth in the BA and wherein the release on basic cable is a separate release and not part of a free television broadcast. The definition of Employer's gross is the same as it is in Article 18 with respect to pay television exhibition of a free television film.

Payments due and payable hereunder shall be sent to the Guild by check payable to the Director. Reports shall be furnished to the Guild in the manner required by the first and fourth paragraphs of Paragraph 18-106.

Section 11-200   ADDITIONAL COMPENSATION FOR THEATRICAL EXHIBITION

11-201   Additional compensation shall immediately accrue and be payable to the Director of a television film when such film is used for theatrical exhibition as follows (excepting the "bridging" of television films for theatrical release, trailers, promos or second units, for which there will be no additional compensation):

If a television film is exhibited theatrically outside of the United States and Canada, then upon the release of such television film for theatrical exhibition the Director shall be paid an amount equal to one hundred percent (100%) of the applicable theatrical minimum. If such film is released theatrically in the United States or Canada, the Director shall be paid one hundred fifty percent (150%) of such applicable theatrical minimum; provided, however, that the maximum payment under the provisions of this paragraph 11-201 for theatrical release of a television film shall be one hundred fifty percent (150%) of applicable theatrical minimum.

The foregoing shall not apply to the incidental use of a television excerpt (as that term is generally used in the industry) in a theatrical exhibition. The following provisions shall apply to use of such a television excerpt:

(a)   For use of such an excerpt in a theatrical motion picture the following payments will be made:

(i)   Excerpt less than 30 seconds, $387;

(ii)   Excerpt 30 seconds to 2 minutes, $774 per excerpt;

(iii) Excerpt over 2 minutes, $774 plus $310 for each additional minute or fraction thereof.

(b)   The provisions of this paragraph 11-201 relating to the use of excerpts apply to the use after July 1, 1993 of any excerpt from a television motion picture, whenever produced.

(c)   The actual production company which produces the program or motion picture containing the excerpt requiring payment is obligated to make the payment, provided the company is signatory to this BA. Employer shall otherwise remain liable for the payment due.

(d)   If two or more Directors are entitled to share any payment, the Guild shall determine the allocation among the Directors.

(e)   If an excerpt is used in a local program and the program is broadcast in no more than one market, the payment for such use shall be fifty percent (50%) of the amount provided in this Paragraph 11-201. If the program is broadcast later in another market, the Director shall be paid the remaining fifty percent (50%).

* * *

ARTICLE 17

Miscellaneous Provisions

* * *

17-123 Morals Clause

Employer agrees that it shall not include or enforce any so-called "Morals Clause," as the term is commonly understood in the motion picture and television industries, in any contract of employment or deal memo for the services of an Employee.

* * *

ARTICLE 18

Supplemental Markets — Theatrical and Free Television Motion Pictures

18-101 Motion Pictures Covered

The provisions of this Article 18 relate and apply only to theatrical and free television motion pictures which are:

(a) produced by the employer or within the provisions of paragraph 18-113;

(b) the principal photography of which commenced on or after July 1, 1993, which motion pictures are, either during the term hereof or at any time thereafter, released in supplemental markets (as defined below); and

(c) produced by Employer with Directors, UPMS and First and Key Second Assistant Directors employed by Employer under the terms of this BA or in the employ of the actual producer as described in paragraph 18-113 (to which employment the provisions of the paragraph apply).

Such a motion picture is sometimes herein called "Such picture."

18-102 Definitions

The term "Supplemental Markets," as used in this BA means only: The exhibition of motion pictures by means of cassettes (to the limited extent provided in subparagraph (a) of this paragraph 18-102) or pay television as those terms are hereafter defined in this paragraph 18-102 and the exhibition of television motion pictures on any commercial carrier such as commercial airlines, trains, ships and buses (referred to herein as "in-flight").

(a) Cassettes: For the purposes of this Article 18, a cassette is any audio-visual device, including without limitation, cassette, cartridge, phono-gram or other similar audio-visual device now known or hereafter devised, containing a motion picture (recorded on film, discs, tapes or other material) and designed for replay through a television receiver or comparable device. The sale or rental of cassettes for replay through a television receiver or comparable device in the home or in closed-circuit use such as in hotel rooms constitutes "Supplemental Markets."

(b) Pay Television: The term "pay television," as used in this Article, shall mean exhibition on a home-type television screen by means of a telecast, cable, closed circuit, satellite to home or CATV when a majority of licensed systems meet the following tests:

(i)   a separate channel is provided for which the subscriber pays a separate fee (which fee is a substantial charge relative to other charges made to the subscriber) for that channel;

and/or

(ii) the subscriber pays for the motion picture or motion pictures selected (except that a motion picture or motion pictures selected for which only a token charge is made shall not be considered pay television);

and/or

(iii) the subscriber pays a fee for an encoded telecast, which fee is a substantial charge relative to other fees paid for encoded telecasts.

The foregoing tests cover those types of services and systems which exist in the industry today and are commonly understood in the industry today to be pay television services or systems.

The term "pay television," as used in this Article 18, shall also include the exhibition of motion pictures through a television receiver or comparable device by means of telecast, cable, closed circuit, satellite or CATV for which the viewing audience (whether by the individual viewer or by the hotel, motel, hospital or other accommodation where the viewer is) pays to receive the program by making a separate payment for such specific program. Exhibition in theaters or comparable places by such means is theatrical exhibition and shall not be considered pay television.

The term "Supplemental Markets" does not include the exhibition of a motion picture by cassette or otherwise over a television broadcast station in free television, or in theatrical exhibition (and, for this purpose, "theatrical exhibition" includes what has previously been considered to be the educational market), the exhibition of theatrical motion pictures on any commercial carrier (referred to herein as "in flight") such as commercial airlines, trains, ships and buses, and other uses which have been traditionally considered theatrical exhibition of theatrical motion pictures. Wherever reference is made in this Article 18 to pay television, such reference shall be deemed to include only those uses of motion pictures as to which a charge is actually made to the subscriber (which may be a hotel, motel or other accommodation) for the program viewed, or where the subscriber or viewer has the option, for a payment, to receive special programming over one or more special channels. Subject to paragraph 11-108, the exhibition of motion pictures made for theatrical or free television exhibition on "basic cable" is considered free television exhibition as distinguished from "Supplemental Markets" exhibition.

With respect to theatrical motion pictures, the Employer has agreed to the inclusion of pay television in the "Supplemental Markets" because under the present pattern of distribution of theatrical motion pictures, pay television is supplemental to the primary market. The Employer reserves the right in future negotiations to contend that the pattern of release has changed so that pay television is no longer a Supplemental Market" but constitutes or is a part of the primary market of distribution of theatrical motion pictures, and that therefore no additional payment pursuant to this Article should be made with respect to the release of theatrical motion pictures (including those covered by this BA) in said markets. The Guild reserves the right to contend in future negotiations that the method of employment and payment provided for in this BA is applicable and appropriate to employment directly for motion pictures intended primarily for release on pay television or cassettes, and that the provisions of this BA with respect to all kinds of "Supplemental Markets," whether they are or have become primary markets or not, shall be improved for the benefit of Employees hereunder for said markets. Nothing herein shall limit the scope of negotiations on said subjects.

18-103   Supplemental Market Distribution Other Than By Cassettes

The following provisions of this Paragraph 18-103 apply to the distribution of any "Such Picture" in "Supplemental Markets" other than by means of cassettes as defined in subparagraph 18-102(a):

(a)   Percentage Payment: Employer shall pay additional compensation of one and 2/10 percent (1.2%) of the Employer's accountable receipts from the distribution of Such Picture. Such payment is to be divided as follows: 1/2 of such amount to be paid to the Director; 1/3 of such amount to be paid to the Directors Guild of America-Producer Pension Plan (herein referred to as the "Pension Plan"); and a *pro rata* share of 1/6 of such amount to be paid to the UPM, the First Assistant Director and the Key Second Assistant Director employed on such motion picture (such portion of such 1/6 *pro rata* share to be based upon their respective minimum schedule wage rate hereunder). If more than one Director, UPM, First Assistant Director or Key Second Assistant Director renders services in connection with Such Picture, the allocations of their respective portion of the *pro rata* shares shall be determined by the Guild and the Employees shall be bound by such determination.

(b)   Definition of "Employer's Gross"

The term "Employer's gross," as used herein, means the worldwide total gross receipts derived by the distributor of Such Picture (who may be the Employer or a distributor licensed by the Employer) from licensing the right to exhibit Such Picture in Supplemental Markets other than by means of cassettes; provided, however, that in the case of any Such Picture which is produced outside of the United States, if Such Picture is subject to this BA and if such production is under an arrangement (herein referred to as a "foreign production deal") pursuant to which a foreign producer or distributor provides or guarantees any of the financing for the production of Such Picture or furnishes any other consideration for such production and a foreign distributor acquires one or more foreign territories for the distribution of Such Picture in Supplemental Markets, then no monies from any such distribution in any such foreign territory shall be included in Employer's gross except to the extent such foreign producer or foreign distributor is obligated to account to Employer or to the distributor of Such Picture for such monies, and except for gross receipts received by such foreign distributor from such distribution in the United Kingdom.

If the distributor of Such Picture does not distribute Such Picture directly in Supplemental Markets, but employs a subdistributor to so distribute Such Picture, then the "Employer's gross" shall be the worldwide total gross receipts derived by such subdistributor from licensing the right to exhibit Such Picture in Supplemental Markets. In case of an outright sale of the Supplemental Markets distribution rights, for the entire world, or any territory or country, the income derived by the seller from such sale, but not the income realized by the purchaser or licensee of such rights, shall be the "Employer's gross." If any such outright sale shall include Supplemental Markets exhibition rights and other rights, then (but only for the purpose of the computation required hereunder) the Employer shall allocate to the Supplemental Markets exhibition rights a fair and reasonable portion of the sales price which shall, for the purpose hereof, be the "Employer's gross." In reaching this determination, Employer may consider the current market value of Supplemental Markets exhibition rights in comparable motion pictures.

If the Guild shall contend that the amount so allocated was not fair and reasonable, such claim may be determined by submission to arbitration as herein provided; and in the event the Arbitrator shall find that such allocation was not reasonable and fair, he or she shall determine the fair and reasonable amount to be allocated. If the outright sale includes Supplemental Markets distribution rights to more than one motion picture, Employer shall likewise allocate to each Such Picture a fair and reasonable portion of the sales price of the Supplemental Market rights; and if the Guild contends that such allocation is not fair and reasonable, the question may be determined by submission to arbitration as above provided. If the Arbitrator shall find that such allocation was not fair and reasonable, the Arbitrator shall determine the fair and reasonable amount to be so allocated to each Such Picture. Nothing with respect to the price received on the outright sale of only supplemental markets distribution rights in a single Such Picture shall be subject to arbitration except that, in the event of a dispute, there may be arbitrated the question of whether the price reported by the Employer to the Guild as having been received by the Employer on such outright sale is less than the amount actually received by the Employer on such outright sale.

The "Employer's gross" shall not include sums required to be paid or withheld as taxes, in the nature of turnover taxes, sales taxes or similar taxes based on the actual receipts of such motion picture or on any monies to be remitted to or by the Employer, but there shall not be excluded from Employer's gross any net income tax, franchise tax or excess profit tax or similar tax payable by the Employer or such Distributor on its net income or for the privilege of doing business.

(c) Definition of "Accountable Receipts"

The term "accountable receipts," as used herein, means one hundred percent (100%) of the "Employer's gross."

(d) Employer's obligation shall accrue hereunder only after Employer's gross is received by Employer, but as to foreign receipts such obligation shall accrue only when such receipts can be freely converted to U.S. dollars and are remitted to the United States, and until such time no frozen foreign receipts shall be included in Employer's gross. Payment of amounts accruing hereunder shall be made quarterly on the basis of quarterly statements, as hereinafter provided. Upon request, and if permitted by the authorities of a foreign country, the Employer will transfer to the Pension Plan and to any Director, UPM, First or Second Assistant Director, in the currency of such foreign country, its or his or her share, if any, of frozen foreign receipts in such country, provided the recipient will bear any costs involved; and such transfer shall be deemed to be payment of an equivalent number of U.S. dollars at the then current free market rate for blocked funds of that category as determined by the Employer. Concurrently with such transfer, the recipient will pay to the Employer in U.S. dollars the total amount the Employer is required to withhold from such payment under all applicable laws. If the Employer utilizes frozen foreign currencies derived from exhibition of Such Picture in Supplemental Markets by conversion thereof to properties that may be freely exported and turned to account, the amount so utilized by the Employer shall be deemed to have been converted to U.S. dollars at the then current free market rate for blocked funds of that category determined as above provided. Frozen foreign receipts from Supplemental Markets shall be deemed to be released on a "first-in, first-out basis," unless the authorities of the foreign country involved designate a specific period that would render such basis inapplicable. Such released funds shall be allocated between Such Picture and other motion pictures distributed by the distributor in Supplemental Markets in the same ratio that receipts derived from the distribution of Such Picture in Supplemental Markets within the foreign country bear to the total receipts derived from the distribution of Such picture and all other motion pictures in Supplemental Markets within the foreign country during the applicable period, unless the authorities of the foreign country involved require another method of allocation, in which case such other method shall be used. Foreign receipts shall be accounted for in U.S. dollars at the rate of exchange at which such receipts are actually converted and remitted, and should any discounts, taxes, duties or charges be imposed in connection with the receipt or remittance of foreign funds, only so much of such funds as remain thereafter shall be included in accountable receipts. Employer shall not be responsible for loss or diminution of foreign receipts as a result of any matter or thing not reasonably within the control of the Employer. The Guild, the Pension Plan and the Employees shall be bound by any arrangements made in good faith by the Employer or for its account, with respect to the deposit or remittance of foreign revenue. Frozen foreign receipts shall not be considered trust funds and the Employer may freely commingle the same with other funds of the Employer. No sums received by way of deposits or security need be included in Employer's gross until earned, but when the Employer is paid a non-returnable advance by a distributor, such advance shall be included in the Employer's gross.

(e)   Allocation of License or Sales Fee

If any license or outright sale of exhibition rights to Such Picture in Supplemental Markets includes as a part thereof any filmed commercial or advertising material, the Employer shall be permitted to allocate a reasonable amount (in accordance with then current standard charges in the industry) to such commercial or advertising material, and the amount so allocated shall not be included in Employer's gross hereunder.

18-104   Supplemental Market Distribution on Cassette

The following provisions of this Paragraph 18-104 apply to the distribution in Supplemental Markets of any Such Picture by means of cassettes as defined in subparagraph 18-102(a):

(a)   Percentage Payment

Employer shall pay additional compensation of one and five-tenths percent (1.5%) of the "Employer's gross," as defined below, until the Employer's gross equals one million dollars ($1,000,000). Thereafter, Employer shall pay one and eight-tenths percent (1.8%) of "Employer's gross" in excess of $1,000,000. Such percentage payments are to be divided as follows:

(i)   until the Employer's gross equals $1,000,000, 1% thereof shall be paid to the Director, 0.3% thereof shall be paid to the Pension Plan and 0.2% thereof shall be paid to the UPM, the First Assistant Director and the Key Second Assistant Director.

(ii)   after the Employer's gross exceeds $1,000,000, 1.2% thereof shall be paid to the Director, 0.36% thereof shall be paid to the Pension

Plan and 0.24% thereof shall be paid to the UPM, the First Assistant Director and the Key Second Assistant Director.

(iii)   the portion of the 1.5% and 1.8% percentage payment due the UPM, First Assistant Director and Key Second Assistant Director shall be divided among them in *pro rata* shares based upon their respective minimum wage rate hereunder. If more than one Director, UPM, First Assistant Director or Key Second Assistant Director renders services in connection with Such Picture, the allocations of their respective portion of the *pro rata* shares shall be determined by the Guild and the Employees shall be bound by such determination.

(b)   Definition of Employer's Gross

If the Employer is the Distributor or the Distributor is owned by or affiliated with the Employer, the Employer's gross derived from the distribution of Such Picture by "cassettes" shall be 20% of the worldwide wholesale receipts derived by the Distributor. In such cases, if the Distributor is also the retailer, a reasonable allocation of the retail gross receipts shall be made as between the Distributor as distributor and the Distributor as retailer, and 20% of the former only shall be deemed to be "Employer's gross." The reasonableness of such allocation shall be subject to arbitration, and in such arbitration, generally prevailing trade practices in the cassette industry with respect to dealings between non-related companies shall be relevant evidence. Such worldwide wholesale receipts shall not include:

(i)   Rebates, credits or repayments for cassettes returned (and in this connection the Employer shall have the right to set up a reasonable reserve for returns);

(ii)   Sums required to be paid or withheld as taxes, in the nature of turnover taxes, sales taxes or similar taxes based on the actual receipts of such motion picture or on any monies to be remitted to or by the Employer, but there shall not be excluded from Employer's gross any net income tax, franchise tax or excess profit tax or similar tax payable by the Employer or such Distributor on its net income or for the privilege of doing business;

(iii)   In the case of any Such Picture which is produced outside of the United States, if Such picture is subject to this BA and if such production is under an arrangement (herein referred to as a "foreign production deal") pursuant to which a foreign producer or distributor provides or guarantees any of the financing for the production of Such Picture or furnishes any other consideration for such production and a foreign distributor acquires one or more foreign territories for the distribution of Such Picture in Supplemental Markets, monies from any such distribution in any such foreign territory except to the extent such foreign producer or foreign distributor is obligated to account to Employer or to the distributor of Such Picture for such monies, and except for gross receipts received by such foreign distributor from such distribution in the United Kingdom.

If the Distributor is not the Employer and is not owned by or affiliated with the Employer, the "Employer's gross" shall be 100% of the fees received by the Employer from licensing the right to distribute Such Picture by cassettes.

(c) Employer's obligation shall accrue hereunder only after Employer's gross is received by Employer, but as to foreign receipts such obligation shall accrue only when such receipts can be freely converted to U.S. dollars and are remitted to the United States, and until such time no frozen foreign receipts shall be included in Employer's gross. Payment of amounts accruing hereunder shall be made quarterly on the basis of quarterly statements, as hereinafter provided. Upon request, and if permitted by the authorities of a foreign country, the Employer will transfer to the Pension Plan and to any Director, UPM, First or Second Assistant Director, in the currency of such foreign country, its or his or her share, if any, of frozen foreign receipts in such country, provided the recipient will bear any costs involved; and such transfer shall be deemed to be payment of an equivalent number of U.S. dollars at the then current free market rate for blocked funds of that category as determined by the Employer. Concurrently with such transfer, the recipient will pay to the Employer in U.S. dollars the total amount the Employer is required to withhold from such payment under all applicable laws. If the Employer utilizes frozen foreign currencies derived from exhibition of Such Picture in Supplemental Markets by conversion thereof to properties that may be freely exported and turned to account, the amount so utilized by the Employer shall be deemed to have been converted to U.S. dollars at the then current free market rate for blocked funds of that category determined as above provided. Frozen foreign receipts from Supplemental Markets shall be deemed to be released on a "first-in, first-out basis," unless the authorities of the foreign country involved designate a specific period that would render such basis inapplicable. Such released funds shall be allocated between Such picture and other motion pictures distributed by the distributor in Supplemental Markets in the same ratio that receipts derived from the distribution of Such Picture in Supplemental Markets within the foreign country bear to the total receipts derived from the distribution of Such Picture and all other motion pictures in Supplemental Markets within the foreign country during the applicable period, unless the authorities of the foreign country involved require another method of allocation, in which case such other method shall be used. Foreign receipts shall be accounted for in U.S. dollars at the rate of exchange at which such receipts are actually converted and remitted, and should any discounts, taxes, duties or charges be imposed in connection with the receipt or remittance of foreign funds, only so much of such funds as remain thereafter shall be included in Employer's gross. Employer shall not be responsible for loss or diminution of foreign receipts as a result of any matter or thing not reasonably within the control of the Employer. The Guild, the Pension Plan and the Employees shall be bound by any arrangements made in good faith by the Employer or for its account, with respect to the deposit or remittance of foreign revenue. Frozen foreign receipts shall not be considered trust funds and the Employer may freely commingle the same with other funds of the Employer. No sums received by way of deposits or security need be included in Employer's gross until earned, but when the Employer is paid a non-returnable advance by a distributor, such advance shall be included in the Employer's gross.

(d)   Allocation of License or Sales Fee

If any license or outright sale of exhibition rights to Such Picture in Supplemental Markets includes as a part thereof any filmed commercial or advertising material, the Employer shall be permitted to allocate a reasonable amount (in accordance with then current standard charges in the industry) to such commercial or advertising material, and the amount so allocated shall not be included in Employer's gross hereunder.

* * *

ARTICLE 19

Theatrical Motion Pictures the Principal Photography of Which Commences after July 1, 1990 * and Released to Free Television

19-101   Motion Pictures Covered

As to all theatrical motion pictures the principal photography of which commenced prior to May 1, 1960, the Guild does not and will not make any claim for compensation for the exhibition of such motion pictures on television.

The provisions of this Article relate and apply only to theatrical motion pictures:

(a)   produced by the Employer or within the provisions of Paragraph 19-111;

(b)   the principal photography of which commenced between July 1, 1993 and June 30, 1996, inclusive, which motion pictures are, either during the term hereof or at any time thereafter, released to free television; and

(c)   produced by Employer with Directors employed by Employer under the terms of this BA or in the employ of the actual producer as described in Paragraph 19-111 (to which employment the provisions of this Article apply).

19-102   Percentage of Accountable Receipts Payable

As to each such motion picture, the Employer will pay (i) to the Directors Guild of America-Producer Pension Plan (herein referred to as the Pension Plan) an amount equal to one percent (1%) of the Employer's accountable receipts from the distribution of such motion picture on free television, computed as hereinafter provided, and (ii) one percent (1%) of such accountable receipts to be paid the Director of the motion picture on a *pro rata* allocation to each Director when there is more than one Director. In the latter case, in the event of any controversy as to the *pro rata* allocation of such 1%, the amount allocable to each Director shall be resolved by the Guild and each

---

* Note: With respect to theatrical motion pictures the principal photography of which commenced after April 30, 1960, and (i) prior to May 1, 1968, see the Directors Guild Basic Agreements of 1960 and 1964; (ii) between May 1, 1968 and May 1, 1973, see the Directors Guild Basic Agreement of 1968, as amended April 1, 1972; (iii) between May 1, 1973 and December 31, 1977, see the Directors Guild Basic Agreement of 1973; (iv) between January 1, 1978 and June 30, 1981, see the Directors Guild Basic Agreement of 1978; (v) between July 1, 1981 and June 30, 1984, see the Directors Guild of America Basic Agreement of 1981; (vi) between July 1, 1984 and June 30, 1987, see the Directors Guild Basic Agreement of 1984; (vii) between July 1, 1987 and June 30, 1990, see the Directors Guild Basic Agreement of 1987; and (viii) between July 1, 1990 and June 30, 1993, see the Directors Guild Basic Agreement of 1990.

individual Director involved shall be bound thereby. The payment of the 1% to be paid to the Director or Directors shall be sent to the Guild for forwarding to such Director or Directors and compliance therewith shall constitute payment to the Director. Such 2% payment is hereinafter referred to as the "percentage payment." These payments are not subject to Health and Welfare or Pension contributions. The above is subject to the following conditions:

19-103 Definition of "Employer's Gross"

The term "Employer's Gross," as used herein, means the worldwide total gross receipts derived by the distributor of such motion picture (who may be the Employer or a distributor licensed by the Employer) from licensing the right to exhibit the motion picture on free television but shall not include:

(a) Sums realized or held by way of deposit as security, until and unless earned, other than such sums as are non-returnable;

(b) Sums required to be paid or withheld as taxes, in the nature of turnover taxes, sales taxes or similar taxes based on the actual receipts of such motion picture or on any monies to be remitted to or by the Employer or such other distributor, but there shall not be excluded from Distributor's gross receipts any net income tax, franchise tax or excess profit tax or similar tax payable by the Employer or such Distributor on its net income or for the privilege of doing business.

(c) Frozen foreign currency until the Employer shall either have the right to freely use such foreign currency or Employer or Distributor has the right to transmit to the United States to Employer or Distributor such foreign currency from the country or territory where it is frozen. If such currency may be utilized or transmitted as aforesaid, it shall be deemed to have been converted to United States dollars at the rate of exchange at which such currency was actually transmitted to the United States as aforesaid, or if not actually transmitted, then at the prevailing free market rate of exchange at the time such right to use or to transmit occurs.

Such gross income realized in foreign currency in any reporting period required hereunder shall be deemed to be converted to United States dollars at the prevailing market rate of exchange at the close of such reporting period, except that when such gross income has actually been transmitted to the United States, it shall be deemed converted to United States at the rate of exchange at which such foreign currency was actually so transmitted.

Frozen foreign currency shall be deemed to be unblocked on the basis of "first-in, first-out" unless otherwise allocated by local foreign fiscal authorities. Allocation of such unblocked funds as between revenue which serves as the basis of determining payments hereunder and other revenue, shall be on a proportional basis, subject to different earmarking by local foreign fiscal authorities.

If the Distributor of the motion picture does not distribute the motion picture directly to free television, but employs a subdistributor to so distribute the motion picture, then the Employer's gross shall be the worldwide total gross receipts derived by such subdistributor from licensing the right to exhibit the motion picture on free television.

In case of an outright sale of the free television distribution rights, for the entire world, or any territory or country, the income derived by the seller from such sale, but not the income realized by the purchaser or licensee of such rights, shall be the Employer's gross. If any such outright sale shall include free television exhibition rights and other rights, then (but only for the purpose of the computation required hereunder), the Employer shall allocate to the free television exhibition rights a fair and reasonable portion of the sales price which shall, for the purpose hereof, be the Employer's gross. In reaching such determination Employer may consider the current market value of free television exhibition rights in comparable motion pictures.

If the Guild shall contend that the amount so allocated was not fair and reasonable, such claim may be submitted to arbitration as herein provided; and in the event the Arbitrator shall find that such allocation was not reasonable and fair, the Arbitrator shall determine the fair and reasonable amount to be so allocated.

If the outright sale includes free television distribution rights to more than one motion picture, Employer shall likewise allocate to each motion picture a fair and reasonable portion of the sales price of the free television rights; and if the Guild contends that such allocation is not fair and reasonable, the question may be determined by submission to arbitration as above provided. If the Arbitrator shall find that such allocation was not fair and reasonable, he or she shall determine the fair and reasonable amount to be so allocated to each motion picture. Nothing with respect to the price received on the outright sale of only free television distribution rights in a single motion picture shall be subject to arbitration except that in the event of a dispute, there may be arbitrated the question of whether the price reported by the Employer to the Guild as having been received by the Employer on such outright sale is less than the amount actually received by the Employer on such outright sale. Sums paid to any advertising agency in connection with any exhibition of a motion picture on free television shall not be included in Employer's gross.

19-104   Definition of "Accountable Receipts"

The term "accountable receipts," as used herein, means the balance of the Employer's gross after deducting an arbitrary forty percent (40%) of the Employer's gross for distribution fees and expenses; except that in the case of an outright sale of free television distribution rights, there shall be deducted only an arbitrary ten percent (10%) of the Employer's gross for sales commissions and expenses of sale.

* * *

19-109   Crediting

If a participating Director's employment agreement with the Employer requires that the Director's compensation shall be based, in whole or in part, upon, or measured by a percentage of the gross receipts or revenues derived from the distribution of the motion picture, any payment due hereunder shall be credited *pro rata* against such percentage compensation. When all or a part of a Director's compensation is a specified sum of money, including what is commonly known and referred to as a "deferment," such specified sum of money may not be credited against amounts payable by the Employer hereunder.

* * *

ARTICLE 20

Minimum Salaries and Residual Compensation for Directors of Motion Pictures Produced Mainly for the Pay Television and Videodisc/Videocassette Market

Section 20-100   APPLICABILITY OF THIS ARTICLE

20-101   Covered Motion Pictures

This Article is applicable to the employment of Directors for motion pictures produced mainly for the "pay television" and/or the "videodisc/videocassette" market, as the quoted terms are defined below, except that the following types of motion pictures produced mainly for such market are covered only by Paragraph 20-905 of this Article 20: industrial and religious motion pictures, commercials, advertising shorts and trailers, educational, informational and instructional motion pictures and documentaries. A motion picture to which this Article is applicable is referred to herein as a "covered motion picture," but such term does not include motion pictures covered only by Paragraph 20-905.

20-102   Videodisc/Videocassette

The term "videodisc/videocassette," as used in this Article, shall mean disc, cassette, cartridge and/or other device serving a similar function which is sold or rented for play on a home-type television screen in the home.

20-103   Pay Television

The term "pay television," as used in this Article, shall mean exhibition on a home-type television screen by means of a telecast, cable, closed circuit, satellite to home or CATV when a majority of licensed systems meet the following tests:

(a)   a separate channel is provided for which the subscriber pays a separate fee (which fee is a substantial charge relative to other charges made to the subscriber) for that channel;

and/or

(b)   the subscriber pays for the motion picture or motion pictures selected (except that a motion picture or motion pictures selected for which only a token charge is made shall not be considered pay television);

and/or

(c)   the subscriber pays a fee for an encoded telecast, which fee is a substantial charge relative to other fees paid for encoded telecasts.

The foregoing tests cover those types of services and systems which exist in the industry today and are commonly understood in the industry today to be pay television services or systems.

20-104   Service and Subscribers

The term "service," as used in this Article, refers to a television service, such as HBO or Showtime, which licenses systems to exhibit motion pictures on a pay television basis; in addition, the term "service" includes systems which have been licensed to exhibit the motion picture on a pay television basis other than through such a service. For the purposes of this Article 20, the term "subscribers" includes only pay television subscribers to services which make payments for the pay television exhibition of the covered motion picture (a) to the Employer, (b) to those acting pursuant to authority derived from the Employer or (c) to an entity authorized by law to receive payment for the Employer. Only paying subscribers are counted in determining the number of subscribers for any purpose under this Article 20.

* * *

Section 20-200   DIRECTORS' MINIMUM SALARIES

20-201   Initial Minimum

The initial minimum salary applicable to a Director employed in the making of a covered motion picture shall be determined in accordance with the provisions of this Section 20-200.

(a)   "Network Prime Time"

The initial minimum salary for a covered motion picture of a type generally produced for network prime time television shall be as follows:

(i)   Less than one and one-half million (1,500,000) subscribers — 50% of the applicable free television minimum. (This minimum is also applicable if there are no license agreements for the pay television exhibition of the motion picture at the time the Director is employed.)

(ii)   One and one-half million (1,500,000) subscribers or more but less than two million (2,000,000) subscribers — 70% of the applicable free television minimum.

(iii)   Two million (2,000,000) subscribers or more but less than three million (3,000,000) subscribers — 80% of the applicable free television minimum.

(iv)   Three million (3,000,000) subscribers or more — 100% of the applicable free television minimum.

The foregoing references to "applicable free television minimum" are to the minimum salary set forth in the BA for a "Network Prime Time Show" of the same length. The number of subscribers is determined, as of the time the Director is employed, by the number of subscribers to all services which have contracted for the pay television exhibition of the motion picture other than on a pay per view basis, plus the number of subscribers, if any, who have contracted to view the program on a pay per view basis.

(b)   "Non-Network or Network Non-Prime Time" — Other Than Local Distribution

The initial minimum salary for a covered motion picture of a type not generally produced for network prime time shall be 100% of the minimum salary set forth in the BA for a "Non-Network or Network Non-Prime Time Show" of the same length unless the motion picture is intended for local pay television distribution only.

If such minimum is higher than the minimum would be if it had been computed pursuant to subparagraph (a) above, then the applicable minimum shall be computed in accordance with subparagraph (a), using the Network Prime Time rate and the applicable number of subscribers.

(c)   Local Distribution

If the program is intended for local pay television distribution only, then the initial minimum salary shall be determined in accordance with the schedule set forth in subparagraph (a) above except that the references to "applicable free television minimum" shall be to the minimum salary set forth in the BA for a "Non-Network or Network Non-Prime Time Show" of the same length. The term "local distribution," as used in this Article, means exhibition in no more than two markets.

20-202   Adjustments of Initial Minimum

If the Employer has paid the Director less than 100% of the applicable free television initial minimum salary, the Employer shall pay adjustments in the Director's initial salary according to the terms of this paragraph 20-202. Nothing in this BA shall be interpreted to prevent the prepayment of adjustments in the initial minimum.

If videodisc or videocassettes of a motion picture are released for sale or rental to consumers prior to the commencement of the term of a pay television license, the initial minimum salary shall be adjusted to 100% of the applicable free television minimum.

If a motion picture intended only for local pay television distribution at the time the Director is employed is distributed in more than two markets, the initial minimum salary shall be adjusted to the amount which would have been applicable had the motion picture not been intended for local distribution.

The Director's initial minimum salary shall also be adjusted if the number of subscribers increases to a level requiring a greater percentage under paragraph 20-201. For example, if the number of subscribers was less than 1-1/2 million (1,500,000) at the time the Director was employed and the Employer paid the Director 50% of the applicable free television minimum, the Employer must pay an adjustment to make the Director's salary 70% of the applicable free television minimum if the number of subscribers later increases to 1-1/2 million (1,500,000) (i.e., the Employer must pay an additional 20% of such minimum).

For the purpose of determining if an adjustment in initial minimum salary is due and the amount of such adjustment, the number of subscribers previously counted for purposes of initial compensation and adjustments in initial compensation shall have added to it: (i) the number of subscribers to services which contract for the first time to exhibit the motion picture on pay television, other than pay per view, after the Director was employed; (ii) any increases in the number of subscribers at the beginning or end of a service's subsequent exhibition years (but not a service's first exhibition year); and (iii) the number of subscribers who paid to view the program on a pay per view basis to the extent that such number is in excess of the number who had contracted for such viewing at the time the Director was employed.

A pay per view subscriber is counted each time the subscriber pays to view the program. If a pay per view subscriber who pays for the program once is thereby given the right to view the program more than once, or at any one of several alternate times, the subscriber is counted only one time.

If an adjustment in minimum compensation required by this Paragraph increases the applicable initial minimum compensation to an amount exceeding the initial compensation which the Director received, payment of such excess shall be made within thirty (30) days following the end of the calendar quarter during which the adjustment became due. Payment shall be by check payable to the order of the Director entitled thereto (or the Director's loanout Company) and shall be delivered to the Guild for forwarding to such Director and compliance herewith shall constitute payment to the Director.

Section 20-300 RESIDUAL COMPENSATION FOR PAY TELEVISION AND VIDEODISC/VIDEOCASSETTE EXHIBITION

The various methods of computing residual compensation for pay television and videodisc/videocassette exhibition are set forth in the following Sections:

(a) Section 20-400, pay television exhibition excluding (i) pay per view and (ii) sports and non-staged event programs;

(b) Section 20-500, pay television exhibition (including pay per view) of sports and non-staged event programs;

(c) Section 20-600, pay per view exhibition other than sports and non-staged event programs;

(d) Section 20-700, videodiscs/videocassettes.

Exhibit C-1

EXHIBIT "C-1" (UPMs and ASST. DIRECTORS)

FORM FOR

WEEK TO WEEK OR DAILY DEAL MEMORANDUM

_____

Date

_____

Name

     _____ Unit Production Manager
     _____ First Assistant Director
     _____ Key Second Asst. Director
     _____ Additional Second Asst. Director

This will confirm our agreement to employ you for a <u>theatrical, television</u> (cross one out) motion picture film tentatively entitled_____ to befilmed <u>in the studio, on distant location, combination</u> (cross one out) . Your starting date for such employment shall be_____. Your salary shall be _____ for a guaranteed period of <u>one week</u>, <u>one day</u> (cross one out) and shall be prorated thereafter.

_____

Signatory Company

By_____

Exhibit C-2

EXHIBIT "C-2" (UPMs and ASST. DIRECTORS)

FORM FOR

TERM DEAL MEMORANDUM

_____

Date

_____

Name

—— Unit Production Manager
—— First Assistant Director
—— Key Second Asst. Director
—— Additional Second Asst. Director

This will confirm our agreement to employ you for a <u>theatrical, television</u> (cross one out) motion picture film tentatively entitled _____
to be filmed <u>in the studio, on distant location, combination</u> (cross one out). Your starting date for such employment shall be on or about _____. Your salary shall be $_____ for a guaranteed period of _____ weeks and shall be prorated thereafter at the rate of $_____ per <u>day, week</u> (cross one out).

This employment agreement shall be subject to termination in the event of any incapacity or default of the Employee or in the case of any suspension or postponement of production by reason of strikes, acts of God, governmental action, regulations, or decrees, or for any other customary "force majeure" reason. Other terms: (<u>e.g.,</u> suspension, per diem, etc.)

_____

Signatory Company

By_____

Exhibit C-3

EXHIBIT "C-3" DIRECTOR DEAL

MEMORANDUM

This confirms your engagement as Director of the picture(s) named below as follows:

Name _____   SS#_____

Address _____   Tel.#_____

Salary $_____ ____ per week   Additional time: $ _____ per week

                 ____ per day   ____ per day

Start date on or about: _____

Check one: Theatrical _____ Free Television _____

                Pay Television and Videodiscs/Videocassettes _____

Guaranteed period: _____ _____ *Pro rata*

Current Title of Picture(s): _____

Series Title (TV) _____

Length of Program (TV): _____

Theatrical Film Budget (check one):

_____ A. Under $500,000

_____ B. Between $500,000 and $1,500,000

_____ C. Over $1,500,000

Free Television: Network Prime Time _____

                  Other than Network Prime Time _____

Pay Television:

Number of subscribers to the pay television services to which the program is licensed at the time of employment:

       _____ Less than 1,500,000   _____ 1,500,000 or over but less than 2,000,000

       _____ 2,000,000 or more   _____ 3,000,000 or more
              but less than
              3,000,000

       Is the budget $5,000,000 or more? Yes _____ No _____

The individual having final cutting authority over the film is: _____

(insert name)

Other conditions (including credit above minimum):_____
_____
_____

You hereby authorize your Employer, _____ to deduct from the salary payable to you the amount specified in the Directors Guild of America Basic Agreement as the employee's contribution to the Directors Guild of America-Producer Pension Plan. The Employer will pay the amount so deducted directly to the Pension Plan on your behalf.

THE UNDERSIGNED RESERVES THE RIGHT TO DISCHARGE THE EMPLOYEE AT ANY TIME SUBJECT <u>ONLY</u> TO THE OBLIGATION TO PAY THE BALANCE OF ANY COMPENSATION DUE, TO THE EXTENT REQUIRED BY THE 1993 DGA BASIC AGREEMENT, TO WHICH THIS EMPLOYMENT IS SUBJECT.

Accepted and Agreed: Employer:_____

Employee: _____   By: _____

Date: _____   Date:_____

PRODUCER-
SCREEN ACTORS GUILD
CODIFIED BASIC AGREEMENT
OF 1995

Form 2

SCREEN ACTORS GUILD

<u>CODIFIED BASIC AGREEMENT OF 1995</u>

———

SYNOPSIS

THIS AGREEMENT is made by and between **SCREEN ACTORS GUILD, INC.,** a California non-profit corporation, hereinafter called the "Union" or "SAG," and the **ALLIANCE OF MOTION PICTURE & TELEVISION PRODUCERS,** hereinafter also referred to as the "AMPTP" or "Alliance," acting on behalf of Producers who have authorized said Alliance to act on their behalf, a list of which is attached hereto as Exhibit A, all of which constitute a multi-employer bargaining unit, each hereinafter called "Producer" and collectively referred to as "Producers."

WITNESSETH:

In consideration of the mutual agreements hereinafter contained, it is agreed as follows:

GENERAL PROVISIONS

1. RECOGNITION AND SCOPE OF AGREEMENT

A. Recognition

The Union is recognized by Producer as the exclusive collective bargaining agent for performers in the production of motion pictures in the motion picture industry within the territorial limits of the United States of America. The term "performer" means those persons covered by the terms of this Agreement and includes performers, professional singers, stunt performers, airplane and helicopter pilots, dancers employed on theatrical motion pictures, stunt coordinators, puppeteers and body doubles. Extra performers are not considered "performers."

The Union is also recognized by Producer as the exclusive bargaining agent for extra performers covered by the terms of this Agreement and employed in the production of motion pictures in the motion picture industry in the Hawaii, Las Vegas, Los Angeles, New York, San Diego and San Francisco Zones, as defined in Schedule X, Part I and Schedule X, Part II.

The term "motion pictures," as used herein and in all prior Agreements between the parties, means and includes, and has always meant and included, motion pictures whether made on or by film, tape or otherwise, and whether produced by means of motion picture cameras, electronic cameras or devices, tape devices or any combination of the foregoing or any other means, methods or devices now used or which may hereafter be adopted.

The Union is recognized by the Producer as the exclusive bargaining agent for all extra performers employed in the production of motion pictures in the zones defined in subparagraphs C.(1) through C.(10) hereof. This Agreements covers the employment of such extra performers in the zones as defined in subparagraphs C.(1) through C.(10) hereof. Producer agrees that the terms of this Agreement will apply outside such zones in the event Producer moves the site of production in order to avoid the economic cost of employing extra performers within such zones. The term "extra performer" means all persons performing extra work as the term "extra player" is defined in the certification of representatives dated April 2, 1946, in the matter of RKO Radio Pictures, Inc., Case No. 21-R-3206, before the National Labor Relations Board including all classifications listed in Schedule J, within the zones of jurisdiction as defined in subsections C.(1) through C.(10) of this Section 1.

B. Scope

(1) When Producer has its base of production in the United States or any commonwealth, territory or possession of the United States, the Basic Contract shall apply, excluding the Union Security provisions in Alaska or any commonwealth, territory or possession of the United States until the Union establishes a Branch in such area.

(2) When Producer has its base of production as provided in (1) above and goes on location in Canada, the Basic Contract, excluding the Union Security provisions, shall apply to all performers hired by Producer at such location.

(3) When Producer employs a performer in the United States and transports him anywhere outside of the United States for a motion picture, the terms of the Basic Contract shall apply.

(4) Only the provisions of Schedule X, Part I shall apply to the employment of extra performers in the Los Angeles, Las Vegas, San Diego, San Francisco and Hawaii Zones. Only the provisions of Schedule X, Part II shall apply to extra performers employed in the New York Zone.

*   *   *

2. UNION SECURITY

A.   Every performer hereafter employed by any Producer, whether by contract or otherwise, or who acts before the camera, or who makes sound track within the Union's jurisdiction, for any Producer, shall be a member of the Union in good standing. As defined and applied in this Section, the term "member of the Union in good standing" means a person who offers to pay (and, if the Union accepts the offer, pays) union initiation fees and dues as financial obligations in accordance with the requirements of the National Labor Relations Act.

B.   Each Producer shall give the Union full opportunity to check performance by such Producer of its agreement under this Section including access to sets, but the Union's checking shall be done in such a manner as not to interfere with production. The Union agrees that it will accept as a member of the Union any performer the Producer wishes to employ, but the Union may refuse such admission or, if it sees fit, admit on terms, performers suspended or expelled by the Union or by any branch of the Associated Actors and Artistes of America or by any other performers' union. Nothing herein shall limit the right of the Union to discipline, suspend or expel a member or to refuse to re-admit him. The Union agrees, however, that if it suspends or expels a member who is under contract to a Producer, or if a member resigns, the suspension, expulsion or resignation shall not affect the performer's obligation to perform any existing contract or contracts with such Producer or such Producer's right to demand performance, unless the Producer otherwise consents. Subject to the qualifications hereinafter set forth, the Producer agrees that in every future contract it enters into with a performer, the performer shall agree that the performer shall be a member of the Union in good standing and shall remain so for the duration of the contract. Any non-member of the Union and any suspended or expelled member whom the Producer may be lawfully entitled to employ under this Agreement shall be paid the same minimum salary and shall be given the same working conditions as are provided in this Agreement. No breach by a member of the Union of his obligation to the Union shall give such member a defense to any Producer's right to enforce an existing contract against such member.

C.   The foregoing subsections A. and B., requiring as a condition of employment membership in the Union, shall not apply until on or after the thirtieth day following the beginning of such employment or the effective date of this Agreement, whichever is the later; the Union and the Producers interpret this sentence to mean that membership in the Union cannot be required of any performer by a Producer as a condition of employment until thirty (30) days after his first employment as a performer in the motion picture industry; "first employment" meaning the first employment as a performer in the motion picture industry on or after August 10, 1948. The foregoing sentence shall be deemed inoperative if any of the following events shall occur: (a) if the Labor Management Relations Act of 1947 is repealed; or (b) if the provision of such Act to which the foregoing sentence has reference is repealed or modified so the foregoing sentence is unnecessary to comply with such Act; or (c) if such Act or such provision is held unconstitutional by the Supreme Court of the United States. The Producer shall not be held to have violated this paragraph if it employs a performer who is not a member of the Union in good standing, if the Producer has reasonable grounds for believing that membership in the Union was not available to such performer on the same terms and conditions generally applicable to other members, or if the Producer has reasonable grounds for believing that membership in the Union was denied to such performer or such performer's membership in the Union was terminated for reasons other than the failure of the performer to tender the periodic dues and the initiation fee uniformly required as a condition of acquiring or retaining membership in the Union; provided, however, the Producer shall not be deemed to have such reasonable grounds for believing until he has made inquiry of the Union as to the facts. The preceding sentence shall be deemed inoperative if any of the following events shall occur: (a) if the Labor Management Relations Act of 1947 is repealed; or (b) if the provision of such Act to which the preceding sentence has reference is repealed or modified so the preceding sentence is unnecessary to comply with such Act;

or (c) if such Act or such provision is held unconstitutional by the Supreme Court of the United States.

D.   The Producer agrees to report to the Union in writing within fifteen (15) days of the first employment of a non-member of the Union, (or within twenty-five (25) days of the first employment of a non-member of the Union on an overnight location), giving the non-member's name, Social Security Number and his first date of employment. An inquiry by any Producer to the Union as to the first date on which a performer has been employed in the industry shall be answered by the Union, and its answer shall bind the Union, and the Producer, if it acts in good faith, shall not be liable for acting on such answer, but the Producer who failed to report shall be liable to the Union for such failure to report. The inquiry provided for in the preceding sentence may be made before, on or one (1) business day after the date of employment.

E.   The interpretation contained in the first sentence of subsection C. of this Section 2 has been approved by an advisory opinion of the General Counsel of the National Labor Relations Board. If such approval of such sentence is changed by a ruling of such General Counsel, then the new ruling of such general counsel shall prevail, until the same is overruled by the Board or a court of competent jurisdiction. If the Board or a court of competent jurisdiction shall change said ruling in a proceeding in which the Union is a party, then the new ruling or opinion shall prevail, until the same is reversed by a court of competent jurisdiction.

F.   The Producer shall pay to the Union as liquidated damages for each employment of a performer in violation of the provisions of this Section 2 the sum of $500, it being agreed that the actual damages suffered by the Union for such breach would be incapable of ascertainment.

G.   The Union agrees that it will not impose unreasonable dues or assessments. If Producer claims a violation by the Union of the provisions of this subsection G., such question shall be handled by conciliation and, if necessary, by arbitration in accordance with the provisions of Section 9 hereof. It is the intention of the parties to prevent the Union from closing its books so as to prevent any person who wishes to action in pictures from joining the Union. Nothing in the preceding sentence shall limit the right of the Union to discipline or suspend or expel a member or to refuse to re-admit him.

H.   It is agreed that children under four (4) years of age are not subject to the Union Security provisions of this Agreement.

I.   Whenever any Producer is entitled hereunder to a permit or waiver from the Union, the Union agrees to issue the same without cost.

J.   Any breach of the provisions of this Section shall be subject to arbitration between the Union and the Producer under Section 9 of these General Provisions.

* * *

4. THEATRICAL MOTION PICTURES, THE PRINCIPAL PHOTOGRAPHY OF WHICH COMMENCED BETWEEN JANUARY 31, 1960 AND JULY 21, 1980 RELEASED TO FREE TELEVISION

Theatrical motion pictures produced under a prior Producer-Screen Actors Guild Codified Basic Agreement, the principal photography of which commenced between January 31, 1960 and July 21, 1980 and which are released to free television, shall be governed by the provisions relating to additional compensation payable to performers for exhibition of theatrical motion pictures on free television of the applicable Codified Basic Agreement under which such pictures were produced.

5. TELEVISION EXHIBITION OF THEATRICAL MOTION PICTURES, THE PRINCIPAL PHOTOGRAPHY OF WHICH COMMENCED AFTER OCTOBER 6, 1980 *

A. With respect to theatrical motion pictures, the principal photography of which commenced after October 6, 1980 and released to free television anywhere in the world, Producer agrees to pay to SAG a deferred compensation, for rateable distribution to the performers appearing in such pictures, equal to six percent (6%) of the worldwide total gross receipts from the distribution of such pictures on free television, after deducting a flat amount of forty percent (40%) of such total gross receipts for distribution fees and expenses. Said compensation shall include pension and health contributions. Such pension and health contributions shall be at the rate provided in and subject to the ceiling and other provisions of Section 32 hereof or of the "Pension and Health Plans" provision of the Agreement under which such picture was produced, whichever is applicable.

When the Producer does not itself so distribute such picture, but effects its distribution through another distributor, the percentage paid shall be based on such distributor's gross receipts from such distribution of such picture on free television, after deducting said flat amount of forty percent (40%) from such total gross receipts, payable only after they are received by the Producer, and after such forty percent (40%) deduction. Where Producer is paid advances by a distributor, the above percentage shall likewise be payable on the amount of such advances. Where Producer sells outright the right to exhibit on free television, SAG shall be paid promptly the above percentage on the gross amounts actually received by Producer for such free television exhibition rights, after deducting a flat amount of ten percent (10%) of such gross amounts so received by Producer from such outright sale of free television exhibition rights, for sales commission and expenses of sale.

---

* [footnote omitted]

If any such outright sale shall include both free television exhibition rights and other rights with respect to one or more pictures, the Producer shall allocate, to the free television exhibition rights covered by such sale, a fair and reasonable portion of the sale price (but only for the purpose of determining the percentage payment due hereunder) based on the sale of free television exhibition rights in comparable pictures. If SAG shall be contend that the amount so allocated in any such outright sale for free television exhibition rights was not fair and reasonable as aforesaid, then such claim shall be submitted to arbitration as herein provided. In the event the arbitrator shall find that such allocation was not reasonable and fair as aforesaid, he/she shall determine the fair and reasonable amount to be so allocated. Where the sale is of the free television exhibition rights only in a group of pictures, Producer shall likewise make an allocation of a portion of the sale price to each picture. If SAG contends that allocation is not fair and reasonable, the matter may be similarly submitted to arbitration, as above provided. In the event the arbitrator shall find that such allocation was not reasonable and fair, as aforesaid, he/she shall determine the fair and reasonable amount to be so allocated.

The provisions of the preceding paragraph shall not apply to any sale of free television exhibition rights only in a single picture.

The term "performer" means those persons covered by this Agreement and includes performers, professional singers, stunt performers, airplane and helicopter pilots, dancers, stunt coordinators and puppeteers, but excludes body doubles. [footnotes omitted]

B.   Distribution Formula

The amount received by Screen Actors Guild under the formula set forth in Paragraph A. above shall be distributed as follows:

Units will be assigned to performers entitled to participate as follows:

(1)   Time Units

With respect to each performer, units for time worked shall be computed as follows:

Each day = one-fifth (1/5) unit

Each week = one (1) unit

No more than five (5) time units may be credited to any performer.

(2)   Salary Units

With respect to each performer, units for total compensation received from the film shall be credited as follows:

(a) Day Performer: Each multiple of daily scale equals one-fifth (1/5) unit. A fraction of daily scale, when more than one-half (1/2), shall be credited as another one-fifth (1/5) unit.

(b) All Other Performers: Each multiple of weekly scale equals one (1) unit. A fraction of a multiple, when more than one-half (1/2) of weekly scale, shall be credited as another weekly unit.

(c) No more than ten (10) salary units may be credited to any performer.

(3) Computation

Each performer shall be credited with the sum of time and salary units as computed above, and each performer will receive that rateable proportion of the monies as the performer's number of units bears to the total number of units for the entire cast.

C. With respect to such pictures made outside of the United States, when part of the cast is composed of performers subject to this Agreement and part of the cast of performers is not subject to this Agreement, then sums payable hereunder shall be prorated based on the proportion which the salaries and the time worked payable to the performers subject to this Agreement bear to the total performers' salaries and time worked for the picture. If records reflecting time worked are not reasonably available, then the aforementioned proration may be based on salaries alone.

D. Application to Pictures Initially Released Theatrically

The provisions of this Section 5 regarding additional compensation for free television exhibition apply only to a theatrical motion picture which is exhibited on free television after it has had a *bona fide* theatrical release. Such motion picture exhibited on free television that has not had a *bona fide* theatrical release shall be governed by the Screen Actors Guild Television Agreement then in effect, but only with respect to the provisions relating to additional compensation for reruns and foreign telecasts, or as may otherwise be agreed upon between the Producer and the Union.

The provisions of this Section 5 shall not apply to the televising of trailers or advertising a motion picture by shots, etc., substantially in the nature of a trailer, subject to the limitations provided in Section 18 hereof.

* * *

5.2 SUPPLEMENTAL MARKETS EXHIBITION OF THEATRICAL MOTION PICTURES, THE PRINCIPAL PHOTOGRAPHY OF WHICH COMMENCED AFTER OCTOBER 6, 1980 *

A. Schedule of Payments

With respect to each theatrical motion picture produced under a prior Screen Actors Guild Codified Basic Agreement, the principal photography of which commenced after October 6, 1980 but prior to July 1, 1984, which is released

---

* [footnote omitted]

by Producer for exhibition in Supplemental Markets anywhere in the world, Producer agrees to pay to Screen Actors Guild, for rateable distribution to the performers appearing in said pictures, deferred compensation equal to three and six-tenths percent (3.6%) of the "Distributor's gross receipts," as defined herein.

With respect to each theatrical motion picture produced under a prior Producer-Screen Actors Guild Codified Basic Agreement or hereunder, the principal photography of which commenced on or after July 1, 1984, which is released by Producer for exhibition in Supplemental Markets anywhere in the world, Producer agrees to pay to Screen Actors Guild, for rateable distribution to the performers appearing in said pictures, deferred compensation equal to:

(1) From the distribution of such pictures to "Pay Television," as defined herein, three and six-tenths percent (3.6%) of "Distributor's gross receipts," as defined herein; and

(2) From the distribution of such pictures on "cassettes," as defined herein, four and five-tenths percent (4.5%) of the first one million dollars ($1,000,000) of "Distributor's gross receipts," and five and four-tenths percent (5.4%) of "Distributor's gross receipts" thereafter.

The foregoing amounts shall include pension and health contributions. Such contributions shall be at the rate provided in and subject to the ceiling and other provisions of Section 34 hereof or the "Pension and Health Plans" provision of the Agreement under which the picture was produced, whichever is applicable.

The term "performer" means those persons covered by this Agreement and includes performers, professional singers, stunt performers, airplane and helicopter pilots, dancers, stunt coordinators and puppeteers, but excludes extra performers and body doubles. The provisions of this Section 5.2 shall not apply with respect to any performer in connection with use in Supplemental Markets if no part of the performer's performance is used in the film as released in Supplemental Markets. [footnotes omitted]

B.   Distribution Formula

The amount received by Screen Actors Guild under the formula set forth in Paragraph A. above shall be distributed as follows:

Units will be assigned to performers entitled to participate as follows:

(1) Time Units

With respect to each performer, units for the time worked shall be computed as follows:

Each day = one-fifth (1/5) unit

Each week = one (1) unit

No more than five (5) time units may be credited to any performer.

(2) Salary Units

With respect to each performer, units for total compensation received from the film shall be credited as follows:

(a) Day Performer: Each multiple of daily scale equals one-fifth (1/5) unit. A fraction of daily scale when more than one-half (1/2) shall be credited as another one-fifth (1/5) unit.

(b) All Other Performers: Each multiple of weekly scale equals one (1) unit. A fraction of a multiple, when more than one-half (1/2) of weekly scale, shall be credited as another weekly unit.

(c) No more than ten (10) salary units may be credited to any performer.

(3) Computation

Each performer shall be credited with the sum of time and salary units as computed above, and each performer will receive that rateable proportion of the monies as the performer's number of units bears to the total number of units for the entire cast.

C.   With respect to such pictures made outside of the United States, where part of the cast is composed of performers subject to this Agreement and part of the cast of performers is not subject to this Agreement, then sums payable hereunder shall be prorated based on the proportion which the salaries and the time worked payable to the performers subject to this Agreement bear to the total performers' salaries and time worked for the picture. If records reflecting time worked are not reasonably available, then the aforementioned proration may be based on salaries alone.

D.   Definition of Supplemental Markets

The term "Supplemental Markets," as used in this Agreement, means: The exhibition of theatrical motion pictures by means of cassettes (to the limited extent provided in paragraph (I) of this subsection D.), or Pay Television, as those terms are hereafter defined in this subsection D.

(1) Cassettes

For the purposes of this Section, a cassette is any audio-visual device, including, without limitation, cassette, cartridge, phonogram or other similar audio-visual device now known or hereafter devised, containing a theatrical motion picture (recorded on film, disc, tapes or other material) and designed for replay through a television receiver or comparable device. The sale or rental of cassettes for replay through a television receiver or comparable device in the home or in closed-circuit use, such as in hotel rooms, constitutes "Supplemental Markets" for the purposes of this provision, insofar as cassettes are concerned.

(2) Pay Television

The term "pay television," as used in this Section, shall mean exhibition of theatrical motion pictures on a television screen by means of telecast, cable, closed-circuit, satellite to home or CATV, for which substantially all systems to which the program is licensed meet the following tests:

(a)   a separate channel is provided for which the subscriber pays a separate fee (which fee is a major charge relative to other charges made to the subscriber) for that channel;

and/or

(b)   the subscriber pays for the motion picture or motion pictures selected (except that a motion picture or motion pictures selected for which only a token charge is made shall not be considered pay television);

and/or

(c)   the subscriber pays a fee for an encoded telecast, which fee is a major charge relative to other fees paid for encoded telecasts.

The foregoing tests cover those types of services and systems which exist in the industry today and are commonly understood in the industry today to be pay television services or systems.

The term "pay television," as used in this Section shall also include the exhibition of theatrical motion pictures through a television receiver or comparable device by means of a telecast, cable, closed-circuit, satellite or CATV for which the viewing audience (whether by the individual viewer or by the hotel, motel, hospital or other accommodation where the viewer is) pays to receive the program by making a separate payment for such specific program. Exhibition in theatres or comparable places by such means is theatrical exhibition and shall not be considered pay television.

The term "Supplemental Markets" does not include the exhibition of a theatrical motion picture by cassette or otherwise over a television broadcast station or in theatrical exhibition and, for this purpose, "theatrical exhibition" includes the educational market, the exhibition of theatrical motion pictures on any commercial carrier (referred to herein as "in-flight"), such as commercial airlines, trains, ships and buses, and other uses which have been traditionally considered theatrical exhibition of theatrical motion pictures, other than the specific home use hereinabove defined as "Supplemental Markets" for cassettes.

Wherever reference is made in this Section to Pay Television, such reference shall be deemed to include only those uses of theatrical motion pictures as to which a charge is actually made to the subscriber for the program viewed, or where the subscriber has the option, by additional payment, to receive special programming over one or more special channels. Where no program charge or special channel charge is made to the subscriber in addition to the general charge, the transmission of theatrical motion pictures by the CATV or television facility, including programming originated by the CATV or television facility, is free television exhibition for the purposes of this Agreement, and such exhibition shall not be considered Supplemental Markets exhibition.

The Producers have agreed to the inclusion of Pay Television in the "Supplemental Markets" because, under the present pattern of distribution of theatrical motion pictures, Pay Television is supplemental to the primary theatrical market. The Producers reserve the right in future negotiations to contend that the pattern of release has changed so that Pay Television is no longer a Supplemental Market but constitutes or is a part of the primary market of distribution of theatrical motion pictures, and that therefore no additional payment should be made with respect to the release of theatrical motion pictures (including those covered by this Agreement) in said markets. Nothing herein shall limit the scope of negotiations on said subject.

E. Definition of Distributor's Gross Receipts

(1) In applying the formula set forth in subsection A. of Section 5.2, Distributor's gross receipts from the Supplemental Markets (if applicable) shall be included in the formula at one hundred percent (100%) of the Distributor's gross received from Supplemental Markets after June 30, 1979.

(2) For purposes of calculating Supplemental Market fees due under this Section 5.2 arising from the distribution of theatrical motion pictures to "Pay Television," as defined above, the term "Distributor's gross receipts" shall mean the worldwide total gross receipts derived by the distributor (who may be the Producer or a distributor licensed by the Producer) from licensing the right to exhibit such picture on "pay television," as defined above; provided, however, that in the case of any such picture which is produced outside of the United States, if such picture is subject to this Agreement and if such production is under an arrangement (herein referred to as a "foreign production deal") pursuant to which a foreign producer or distributor provides or guarantees any of the financing for the production of such picture or furnishes any other consideration for such production and a foreign distributor acquires one or more foreign territories for the distribution of such picture in Supplemental Markets, then no monies from any such distribution in any such foreign territory shall be included in "Distributor's gross receipts" except to the extent such foreign producer or foreign distributor is obligated to account to Producer or to the distributor of such picture for such monies, and except for gross receipts received by such foreign distributor from such distribution in the United Kingdom.

If the distributor of such picture does not distribute such picture directly in Supplemental Markets, but employs a sub-distributor to so distribute such picture, then the "Distributor's gross receipts" shall be the worldwide total gross receipts derived by such sub-distributor from licensing the right to exhibit such picture in Supplemental Markets. In case of an outright sale of the Supplemental Markets distribution rights for the entire world, or any territory or country, the income realized by the purchaser or licensee of such rights, shall be the "Distributor's gross receipts." If any such outright sale shall include Supplemental Markets exhibition rights and other rights, then (but only for the purpose of the computation required hereunder) the Producer shall allocate to the supplemental Markets exhibition rights a fair and reasonable portion of the sales price which shall, for the purpose hereof, be the "Distributor's gross receipts." In reaching this determination, Producer may consider the current market value of Supplemental Markets or exhibition rights in comparable motion pictures.

If the Union shall contend that the amount so allocated was not fair and reasonable, such claim may be determined by submission to arbitration as herein provided; and in the event the Arbitrator shall find that such allocation was not reasonable and fair, he or she shall determine the fair and reasonable amount to be allocated. If the outright sale includes Supplemental Markets distribution rights to more than one (1) motion picture, Producer shall likewise allocate to each such picture a fair and reasonable portion of the sales price of the Supplemental Market; and if the Union contends that such allocation is not fair and reasonable, the question may be determined by submission to arbitration as provided herein. If the Arbitrator shall find that such allocation was not fair and reasonable, the Arbitration shall determine the fair and reasonable amount to be so allocated to each such picture. Nothing with respect to the price received on the outright sale of only Supplemental Markets distribution rights in a single such picture shall be subject to arbitration except that, in the event of a dispute, there may be arbitrated the question of whether the price reported by the Producer to the Guild as having been received by the Producer on such outright sale is less than the amount actually received by the Producer on such outright sale.

(3) For purposes of calculating Supplemental Markets fees under this Section 5.2, arising from the distribution of theatrical motion pictures on "cassettes," as defined above, the term "Distributor's gross receipts" is defined as follows:

(a) If the Producer is the Distributor or the Distributor is owned by or affiliated with the Producer, the "Distributor's gross receipts" derived from the distribution of such picture by "cassettes" shall be twenty percent (20%) of the worldwide wholesale receipts derived by the Distributor. In such cases, if the Distributor is also the retailer, a reasonable allocation of the retail gross receipts shall be made as between the Distributor as distributor and the Distributor as retailer, and twenty percent (20%) of the former only shall be deemed to be "Distributor's gross receipts." The reasonableness of such allocation shall be subject to arbitration and, in such arbitration, generally prevailing trade practices in the cassette industry with respect to dealings between non-related companies shall be relevant evidence.

(b) If the Distributor is not the Producer and is not owned by or affiliated with the Producer, the "Distributor's gross receipts" shall be one hundred percent (100%) of the fees received by the Producer from licensing the right to distribute such picture by cassette.

(c) In the case of any such picture which is produced outside of the United States, if such picture is subject to this Agreement and if such production is under an arrangement (herein referred to as a "foreign production deal") pursuant to which a foreign producer or distributor provides or guarantees any of the financing for the production of such picture or furnishes any other consideration for such production and a foreign distributor acquires one or more foreign territories for the distribution of such picture in Supplemental Markets, then no monies from any such distribution in any foreign territory shall be included in "Distributor's gross receipts" except to the extent such foreign producer or foreign distributor is obligated to account to Producer or to the distributor of such picture for such monies, and except for gross receipts received by such foreign distributor from such distribution in the United Kingdom.

(d) In case of an outright sale of the Supplemental Markets distribution rights for the entire world, or any territory or country, the income derived by the seller from such sale, but not the income realized by the purchaser for licensee of such rights, shall be the "Distributor's gross receipts." If any such outright sale shall include Supplemental Markets exhibition rights and other rights, then (but only for the purpose of the computation required hereunder) the Producer shall allocate to the Supplemental Markets exhibition rights a fair and reasonable portion of the sales price which shall, for the purpose hereof, be the "Distributor's gross receipts." In reaching this determination, Producer may consider the current market value of Supplemental Markets or exhibition rights in comparable motion pictures.

(4) The "Distributor's gross receipts," as that term is used herein, shall not include:

(a) Sums realized or held by way of deposit as security, until and unless earned, other than such sums as are non-returnable;

(b) Rebates, credits or repayments for cassettes returned (and, in this connection, the Producer shall have the right to set up a reasonable reserve for returns);

(c) Sums required to be paid or withheld as taxes, in the nature of turnover taxes, sales taxes or similar taxes based on the actual receipts of such motion picture or on any monies to be remitted to or by the Producer or such other distributor, but there shall not be excluded from

"Distributor's gross receipts" any net income tax, franchise tax, or excess profit tax or similar tax payable by the Producer or such Distributor on its net income or for the privilege of doing business;

(d)   Frozen foreign currency until the Producer shall either have the right to freely use such foreign currency or Producer or Distributor has the right to transmit to the United States to Producer or Distributor such foreign currency from the country or territory where it is frozen. If such currency may be utilized or transmitted as aforesaid, it shall be deemed to have been converted to United States dollars at the rate of exchange at which such currency was actually transmitted to the United States as aforesaid or, if not actually transmitted, then at the prevailing free market rate of exchange at the time such right to use or to transmit occurs.

(5) Such gross income realized in foreign currency in any reporting period required hereunder shall be deemed to be converted to United States dollars at the prevailing market rate of exchange at the close of such reporting period, except that where such gross income has actually been transmitted to the United States, it shall be deemed converted to United States dollars at the rate of exchange at which such foreign currency was actually so transmitted.

Frozen foreign currency shall be deemed to be unblocked on the basis of "first-in, first-out," unless otherwise allocated by local foreign fiscal authorities. Allocation of such unblocked funds, as between revenue which serves as the basis of determining payments hereunder and other revenue shall be on a proportional basis, subject to different earmarking by local foreign fiscal authorities.

(6) If any agreement for distribution on free television or (if applicable) in Supplemental Markets or for such foreign territorial sale includes more than one motion picture, the Producer shall allocate a portion of the monies payable under such agreement to each motion picture covered by such agreement. If any distribution agreement or foreign territorial sale agreement includes any two (2) or more of free television rights, Supplemental Markets rights and other rights, the Producer shall allocate a portion of the monies payable under such agreement to each of the rights covered by such agreement. Such allocations shall be for the purpose of determining payments due hereunder, shall be made in good faith and, if so made, shall be binding and conclusive for purposes of this Agreement. If the Union contends that such allocation has not been made in good faith, then such claim shall be submitted to arbitration under Section 9 hereof.

For determination as to the proper allocation, the provisions of this Section 5.2 E. (6) shall not apply to any such agreement relating only to the free television exhibition rights or to Supplemental Markets rights in a single motion picture.

* * *

J. Reopening Rights

If the member companies of the Alliance of Motion Picture & Television Producers make a "better deal" with the Directors Guild of America, Inc., or the Writers Guild of America, West, Inc., with reference to payments for the release to "Supplemental Markets" of theatrical motion pictures, the principal photography of which commenced prior to July 1, 1971, the Union shall have the right to reopen this Agreement with respect to that subject (*i.e.,* payment for the release of such theatrical motion pictures to the Supplemental Markets) or to accept the "better deal" on that subject. Any dispute as to whether or not a "better deal" has been made on that subject with either of said Unions shall be subject to arbitration pursuant to Section 9 hereof. In the event that no agreement is reached in such negotiations within a period of thirty (30) days after such reopening, either the Union or the Alliance, on behalf of all its members, may, upon a thirty (30) day written notice to the other party, terminate this Agreement.

* * *

6. RESPONSIBILITY FOR PAYMENTS

With respect to all theatrical motion pictures produced hereunder or under a prior Producer-Screen Actors Guild Codified Basic Agreement, the principal photography of which commenced on or after October 6, 1980 and which are released to free television or which are released to Supplemental Markets, to the extent those motion pictures are not subject to a Distributor's Assumption Agreement executed before July 1, 1995, the following provisions shall be applicable:

A. Distributor's Assumption Agreement — Television and Supplemental Markets

Prior to the commencement of principal photography of each such motion picture in which one or more performers covered by this or any prior Agreement renders services, if the Producer is not also the Distributor of such motion picture on free television or in Supplemental Markets (as applicable), Producer shall obtain from the Distributor having such free television distribution rights or Supplemental Markets distribution rights (as applicable) and deliver to SAG a separate written agreement herein called "Distributor's Assumption Agreement," made expressly for the benefit of SAG as representative of the performers involved, by which such Distributor agrees to assume and pay the amounts payable hereunder by reason of the exhibition of such motion picture on free television or in Supplemental Markets (as applicable), when and as the same become due.

In the event such Distributor is a signatory Producer, he shall be deemed automatically bound to such Distributor's Assumption Agreement and delivery and execution of said Assumption Agreement shall not be necessary.

Such agreement shall be substantially in the following form:

DISTRIBUTOR'S ASSUMPTION AGREEMENT

In consideration of the execution of a DISTRIBUTION AGREEMENT between _____, Producer, and the undersigned Distributor, Distributor agrees that the motion picture presently entitled _____
(the "Picture") is subject to the Producer-Screen Actors Guild Codified Basic Agreement of 1995, 1989, 1986, 1983 or 1980 (strike those which are not applicable) ("Basic Agreement") covering theatrical motion pictures and particularly to the provisions of (strike those of the following clauses (1) , (2) or (3) which are not applicable):

(1) Section 5 thereof, pertaining to additional compensation payable to performers when theatrical motion pictures, the principal photography of which commenced after October 6, 1980 and which are covered by said Section, are released to free television, and Section 34 pertaining to applicable pension and health contributions, if any are required;

(2) Sections 5.1 thereof, pertaining to additional compensation payable to performer when theatrical motion pictures, the principal photography of which commenced after June 30, 1971 but prior to July 21, 1980 and which are covered by said Section, are released in Supplemental Markets and Section 34 pertaining to applicable pension and health contributions, if any are required;

(3) Section 5.2 thereof, pertaining to additional compensation payable to performers when theatrical motion pictures, the principal photography of which commenced after October 6, 1980 and which are covered by said Section, are released in Supplemental Markets and Section 34 pertaining to applicable pension and health contributions, if any are required.

Distributor is distributing or licensing the Picture for distribution (select one)

_____ in perpetuity (*i.e.*, for the period of copyright and any renewals thereof)

_____ for a limited term of _____years in the following territories and media (indicate those that are applicable):

Territory:

_____ Domestic (the U.S. and Canada, and their respective possessions and territories)

_____ Foreign (the world excluding the U.S. and Canada and their respective possessions and territories)

_____ Other (please describe):

Media:

———— All

———— Home Video

———— Pay Television

———— Free Television

———— Other (please describe):

———— See description, attached hereto as Exhibit "A" and incorporated herein by reference.

Distributor hereby agrees, expressly for the benefit of the Screen Actors Guild, herein called SAG, as representative of the performers whose services are included in the Picture, when the Picture is telecast on free television or exhibited in Supplemental Markets (as applicable), to make the additional compensation payment required thereby, if any, and the pension and health contributions required thereby, if any, with respect to the territories, media and term referred to above as provided in the applicable Sections referred to hereinabove (all such payments are collectively hereinafter referred to as "Residuals"). Distributor, for and on behalf of the Producer, shall make all Social Security, withholding, unemployment insurance and disability insurance payments required by law with respect to the additional compensation referred to in the preceding sentence.

It is expressly understood that the rights of Distributor to license the Picture for exhibition on free television or in Supplemental Markets (as applicable), or to exhibit or cause or permit the Picture to be exhibited on free television or in Supplemental Markets (as applicable), shall be subject to and conditioned upon the prompt payment of Residuals with respect to the territories, media and term referred to above in accordance with said applicable Sections. It is agreed that SAG, in addition to all other remedies, shall be entitled to injunctive relief against Distributor in the event such payments are not made.

To the extent that Producer has executed a security agreement and financing statement in SAG's favor in the Picture and related collateral as defined in the SAG-Producer Security Agreement ("SAG Security Interest"), Distributor agrees and acknowledges that Distributor's rights in the Picture acquired pursuant to the Distribution Agreement (to the extent those rights are included in the collateral covered by the Security Agreement) are subject and subordinate to the SAG Security Interest. SAG agrees that so long as Residuals with respect to the Picture for the territories, media and term referred to above are timely paid in accordance with said applicable Sections that SAG will not exercise any rights under the SAG Security Interest which would in any way interfere with the rights of the Distributor to distribute the Picture and receive all revenues from such distribution.

SAG further agrees that if it exercises its rights as a secured party, it will dispose of collateral which encompasses any of Distributor's rights or interests in, or physical items relating to, the Picture, only to a transferee which agrees in writing to be bound by SAG's obligations under this Assumption Agreement.

Within a reasonable time after the expiration of each calendar quarter, but not exceeding sixty (60) days, Distributor will furnish or cause to be furnished to SAG a written report showing the gross receipts during the preceding quarter from the distribution of the Picture by Distributor on free television or in Supplemental Markets (as applicable), with respect to which Distributor is required to make payments hereunder, (whether distributed by the Distributor or through another Distributor), and showing the date of the first exhibition on television or in Supplemental Markets (as applicable), and whether such exhibition was on network television and, if so, whether in prime time.

Distributor shall also make available for inspection by SAG all Distributor's statements delivered to Producer insofar as they relate to such gross receipts. SAG shall have the right at reasonable times and on reasonable notice to examine the books and records of Distributor as to such gross receipts pertaining to such distribution on free television or in Supplemental Markets (as applicable) of the Picture. If Distributor shall fail to make such payments as and when due and payable, Distributor shall pay late payment damages as specified in Section 5, 5.1 or 5.2, whichever is applicable, of the Basic Agreement.

In the event of any sale, assignment or transfer of Distributor's distribution or exhibition rights in the Picture, Distributor shall remain liable for the Residuals unless Distributor obtains an executed Distributor's Assumption Agreement from such purchaser, assignee or transferee and SAG approves in writing the financial responsibility of the party obtaining such rights. SAG agrees that it will not unreasonably withhold its approval of the financial responsibility of any such purchaser, assignee or transferee. In the event SAG is notified that such purchaser, assignee or transferee is a Qualified Distributor, then the financial responsibility of such purchaser, assignee or transferee shall be deemed automatically approved on the date SAG receives written notice of the assumption of obligations hereunder by the Qualified Distributor. Nothing herein shall release Producer of its obligations under the Basic Agreement or any other agreement between Producer and SAG.

If SAG does not approve in writing the financial responsibility of the party obtaining such rights, this DISTRIBUTOR'S ASSUMPTION AGREEMENT shall remain effective and binding upon Distributor, and Distributor shall be obligated to pay Residuals which accrue during the term for those territories and media for which it was granted distribution rights and all extensions and renewals. Such obligations shall be subject to Section 6.C. of the Basic Agreement. The Distributor shall have the right, at its election, to cause to be immediately submitted to arbitration, pursuant to the provisions of Section 9 hereof, the issue of whether SAG has unreasonably withheld the approval of the financial responsibility of such purchaser, assignee or transferee for payments due hereunder.

Distributor and SAG hereby agree that all disputes based upon, arising out of or relating to this Assumption Agreement, other than SAG's entitlement to injunctive or other equitable relief, shall be submitted to final and binding arbitration in accordance with the arbitration provisions contained in the Basic Agreement. Notwithstanding the foregoing, Distributor agrees and acknowledges that SAG is not precluded by this or any other provision of this Assumption Agreement from obtaining from a court injunctive relief or any other legal remedy at any time prior to arbitration or issuance of an arbitration award. The right to obtain in injunctive relief from a court shall be applicable whether an arbitration proceeding has or has not been initiated, and further, without limitation, shall be applicable in conjunction with a proceeding to confirm and enforce an arbitration award against Distributor.

THIS DISTRIBUTOR'S ASSUMPTION AGREEMENT SHALL BE GOVERNED BY AND CONSTRUED IN ACCORDANCE WITH THE LAWS OF THE STATE OF CALIFORNIA AND THE UNITED STATES, AS THE SAME WOULD BE APPLIED BY A FEDERAL COURT IN CALIFORNIA WITHOUT REGARD TO PRINCIPLES OF CONFLICTS OF LAW. SAG and Distributor agree that any arbitration or legal action or proceeding brought to interpret or enforce the provisions of this Distributor's Assumption Agreement (including and action to compel arbitration or a petition to vacate an arbitration award) shall be held or brought in Los Angeles County, California, and Distributor irrevocably submits to the jurisdiction of the federal and state courts therein. Notwithstanding the foregoing, SAG at its option may bring a legal action or proceeding outside California under the following circumstances: (a) if Distributor has no principal place of business in California; or (b) whether or not Distributor has a principal place of business in California, to enforce or execute upon an arbitration award or court order or judgment, in any jurisdiction in which Distributor's assets are located (and Distributor irrevocably submits to the jurisdiction of the courts of such places for purposes of such execution or enforcement). Distributor consents to service of process by personal delivery or by certified or registered mail, return receipt requested, to Distributor's general counsel or to Distributor's representative identified below or by first class mail to Distributor when Distributor has not designated a representative or a general counsel, or by any other method permitted by law.

Date _____   _____
                                 ("Distributor")

                                 Address: _____
                                 _____

By: _____

_____

Please print name

Title _____

Distributor's Representative or General
Counsel:

_____

An inadvertent failure on the part of any such Distributor to comply with any of the reporting provisions of this subsection A. shall in no event constitute a default by the Producer or such Distributor or a breach of this Agreement, provided that such failure is cured promptly after notice in writing thereof from the Screen Actors Guild.

In the event of the expiration or termination of any distribution agreement, the obligation of Producer to obtain and deliver to SAG such Distributor's Assumption Agreement shall apply as well to any subsequent distribution agreement entered into by Producer, and Producer shall obtain and deliver an executed Distributor's Assumption Agreement within ten (10) days after the execution of each such subsequent distribution agreement.

With respect to any such motion picture produced hereunder, SAG, prior to the commencement of principal photography of such motion picture, may require such financial assurances from Producer as it deems advisable to insure performance of Producer's obligations to pay the Residuals, including without limitation, the execution of security agreements, guarantees or other protective agreements, subject, however, to the following:

If SAG shall require financial assurances from the Producer in the form of a security agreement for a security interest in the Picture, so long as the Residuals are timely paid with respect to all territories, media and term acquired by the Distributor in accordance with Section 5, 5.1 and/or 5.2 of the Basic Agreement, as applicable, SAG shall not exercise any rights under such security agreement which would in any way interfere with the rights of the Distributor to distribute the Picture and receive all revenues from such distribution, provided that such Distributor has executed and delivered a Distributor's Assumption Agreement to SAG and is in compliance with the terms thereof.

If any "Qualified Distributor" assumes in perpetuity under the Distributor's Assumption Agreement the obligation to pay the Residuals for all territories and media with respect to the Picture or guarantees in a written form satisfactory to SAG all of such obligations thereunder, SAG will release and cause to be discharged of record all such security interests, liens, charges or encumbrances entered into by or obtained from such Producer and will not require further financial assurances from such Producer; provided, however, the Producer's primary liability as a Producer shall not be released thereby.

If any "Qualified Distributor" acquires rights to distribute the Picture in specific territories and media (but not all territories and media) in perpetuity, and thereby has assumed responsibility for the payment of Residuals for such territories and media so acquires pursuant to the Distributor's Assumption Agreement or guarantees in a written form satisfactory to SAG all of such obligations thereunder, then if the Producer has granted or thereafter grants a security interest in favor of SAG in the Picture and related collateral as defined in the SAG Security Agreement, SAG: (i) agrees to modify the definition of the collateral in the SAG Security Agreement to exclude those territories and media acquired by such Qualified Distributor; and (ii) acknowledges Distributor's continuing rights of full, unlimited but non-exclusive access to and use of any and all physical items and elements relating to the Picture.

If any "Qualified Distributor" acquires rights to distribute the Picture in specific territories and media for a limited period of time, and thereby has assumed responsibility for the payment of Residuals for such term and in such territories and media pursuant to the Distributor's Assumption Agreement or guarantees in a written from satisfactory to SAG all of such obligations thereunder, then any security agreement or security interest obtained by SAG from the Producer in connection with the Picture shall remain in effect, but SAG agrees: (i) to modify the definition of the collateral in the SAG Security Agreement to exclude those territories and media for the term of the rights acquired by Distributor, including renewals and extensions; and (ii) acknowledges Distributor's continuing rights of full, unlimited but non-exclusive access to and use of any and all physical items and elements relating to the Picture.

In addition to those distributors who have been deemed "Qualified" by SAG due to their past bargaining relationship and/or Residuals payment history, the term "Qualified Distributor" shall mean a Distributor who satisfies the requirements set forth in Paragraphs A. and B. below:

A. Distributor has the financial history, liquidity, net earnings before interest, taxes and amortization, assets, and net worth to establish its present and future ability to pay Residuals arising from the exploitation of the SAG Pictures being distributed.

B. The Distributor has been in business for five (5) or more years and has a history of prompt and proper payment or Residuals pursuant to SAG contracts in five (5) consecutive years immediately prior to seeking Qualified Distributor status.

A Qualified Distributor must agree to assume Residuals obligations, or guarantee the payment of Residuals in accordance with the Qualified Distributor's Letter of Agreement, for each Picture produced under a SAG collective bargaining agreement for the territories, media and term for which it has distribution rights and must execute the Qualified Distributor's Agreement.

In the event of a dispute as to qualifications of an applicant for Qualified Distributor status of an applicant for Qualified Distributor status, Producer shall provide such financial assurances as SAG may deem appropriate, which may include, but are not limited to, a security interest in the Picture and related collateral, in which case Distributor shall acknowledge same. Said security interest shall remain effective unless and until it is established by agreement or in an arbitration, pursuant to the arbitration provisions contained in the Basic Agreement, that the applicant Distributor meets the aforementioned requirements for qualification. Such applicant shall have the burden of proof that it satisfies the aforementioned requirements for qualification in any arbitration and shall, upon SAG's request, furnish to SAG all relevant financial or corporate information relating thereto as SAG may reasonably require.

Any information submitted to SAG in order to determine whether a Distributor is entitled to status as a Qualified Distributor shall, at the Distributor's discretion, be subject to reasonable confidentiality arrangements.

In the event that a Qualified Distributor, after notice and a reasonable opportunity to cure, generally fails to report and/or pay Residuals when they are due or generally fails to pay obligations to creditors when they become due or in the event a petition is filed under the Bankruptcy Code by or against a Qualified Distributor, SAG shall have the right to terminate the Distributor's Qualified Distributor status. The Distributor shall have the right to invoke the arbitration procedures described above to challenge such termination. Pending the resolution of such challenge, the Qualified Distributor's status shall be considered terminated. SAG agrees that it will not terminate a Qualified Distributor's status when there is a *bona fide* dispute as to whether Residuals are due, or a *bona fide* dispute as to the amount of Residuals due to SAG, if the Distributor has otherwise timely reported and paid Residuals. In addition to the above, if a SAG audit conducted pursuant to the Codified Basic Agreement or other financial information discloses that the Qualified Distributor no longer meets the aforementioned standards for qualification, SAG may initiate an arbitration pursuant to the Basic Agreement to terminate the Qualified Distributor's status.

B. Buyer's Assumption Agreement

If the Producer shall sell, transfer or assign its rights to exhibit on free television any of the motion pictures produced hereunder or under a prior Producer-Screen Actors Guild Codified Basic Agreement, the principal photography of which commenced on or after October 6, 1980, or its rights to distribute in Supplemental Markets any of the motion pictures produced hereunder or under a prior Producer-Screen Actors Guild Codified Basic Agreement, the principal photography of which commenced on or after October 6, 1980, in which one (1) or more performers coved by the Basic Agreement renders services, to the extent those motion pictures are not subject to a Buyer's Assumption Agreement executed before July 1, 1995, it shall obtain from such buyer, transferee or assignee a separate agreement, made expressly for the benefit of Screen Actors Guild as representative of the performers involved, requiring such buyer, transferee or assignee to comply with the provisions of this Agreement with respect to additional compensation to performers and pension and health contributions by reason of the exhibition of such motion pictures in Supplemental Markets (as applicable), when and as the same become due. Such agreement shall be in substantially the following form:

BUYER'S ASSUMPTION AGREEMENT

For valuable consideration, the undersigned

_____

(INSERT NAME OF BUYER, TRANSFEREE OR ASSIGNEE)

(hereinafter referred to as "Buyer") hereby agrees with

_____

(INSERT NAME OF PRODUCER)

that all motion picture covered by this agreement ("the Picture") identified in the attached Exhibit "A" is subject to the Producer-Screen Actors Guild Codified Basic Agreement of 1995, 1992, 1989, 1986, 1983 or 1980 (strike those which are not applicable) (hereinafter "Basic Agreement") covering theatrical motion pictures and particularly to the provisions of (strike those of the following clauses (1), (2) or (3) which are not applicable):

(1) Section 5 thereof, pertaining to additional compensation payable to performers when theatrical motion pictures, the principal photography of which commenced after October 6, 1980 and which are covered by said Section, are released to free television and Section 34 pertaining to applicable pension and health contributions;

(2) Section 5.1 thereof, pertaining to additional compensation payable to performer when theatrical motion pictures, the principal photography of which commenced after June 30, 1971 but prior to July 21, 1980, and which are covered by said Section, are released in Supplemental Markets and Section 34 pertaining to applicable pension and health contributions.

(3) Section 5.2 thereof, pertaining to additional compensation payable to performers when theatrical motion pictures, the principal photography of which

commenced after October 6, 1980 and which are covered by said Section, are released in Supplemental Markets and Section 34 pertaining to applicable pension and health contributions.

Buyer is purchasing rights in the following territories and media (indicate those that are applicable):

Territory:

_____ Domestic (the U.S. and Canada, and their respective possessions and territories)

_____ Foreign (the world excluding the U.S. and Canada and their respective possessions and territories)

_____ Other (please describe):

Media:

_____ All

_____ Home Video

_____ Pay Television

_____ Free Television

_____ Other (please describe):

_____ See description, attached hereto as Exhibit "A" and incorporated herein by reference.

Buyer hereby agrees, expressly for the benefit of the Screen Actors Guild, hereinafter called SAG, as representative of the performers whose services are included in the Picture when telecast or when exhibited in Supplemental Markets (as applicable), to assume and be bound by Producer's obligation thereunder to make the additional compensation payments required thereby, if any, with respect to the territories and media referred to above and the pension and health contributions required thereby, if any, as provided in the applicable Section(s) referred to hereinabove (all such payments are collectively hereinafter referred to as "Residuals"). Buyer, for and on behalf of the Producer, shall make all Social Security, withholding, unemployment insurance and disability insurance payments required by law with respect to the additional compensation referred to in the preceding sentence.

It is expressly understood that the right of Buyer to license the Picture for exhibition on free television or in Supplemental Markets (as applicable), or to exhibit or cause or permit the Picture to be exhibited on free television or in Supplemental Markets (as applicable), shall be subject to and conditioned upon the prompt payment of Residuals with respect to the territories and media referred to above in accordance with said applicable Section(s). It is agreed that SAG, in addition to all other remedies, shall be entitled to injunctive relief against Buyer in event such payments are not made.

To the extent that Producer has executed a security agreement and financing statement in SAG's favor in the Picture and related collateral as defined in the SAG-Producer Security Agreement ("SAG Security Interest"), Buyer agrees and acknowledges that Buyer's rights to the Picture acquired pursuant to the Purchase Agreement (to the extent those rights are included in the collateral covered by the Security Agreement) are subject and subordinate to the SAG Security Interest. Buyer further agrees to execute a security agreement, mortgage of copyright, UCC-1, and other UCC documentation and any other document required under the Basic Agreement or necessary or desirable in SAG's discretion to continue the SAG Security Interest. SAG agrees that so long as Residuals with respect to the Picture for all the territories and media referred to above are timely paid in accordance with said applicable Section(s), that SAG will not exercise any rights under the SAG Security Interest which would in any way interfere with the rights of the Buyer to distribute the Picture and receive all revenues from such distribution.

SAG further agrees that if it exercises its rights as a secured party, it will dispose of collateral which encompasses any of Buyer's rights or interests in, or physical items relating to, the Picture, only to a transferee which agrees in writing to be bound by SAG's obligations under this Assumption Agreement.

Within a reasonable time after the expiration of each calendar quarter, but not exceeding sixty (60) days, Buyer will furnish or cause to be furnished to SAG a written report showing the gross receipts during the preceding quarter from the distribution of the Picture by Buyer on free television or in Supplemental Markets (as applicable) with respect to which Buyer is required to make payments hereunder (whether distributed by Buyer or through another Distributor), and showing the date of the first exhibition on television or in Supplemental Markets (as applicable), and whether such exhibition was on network television and, if so, whether in prime time.

Buyer shall also make available for inspection by SAG all distributor's statements delivered to Buyer insofar as they relate to such gross receipts. SAG shall have the right at reasonable times to examine the books and records of Buyer as to such gross receipts pertaining to such distribution on free television or in Supplemental Markets (as applicable) of the Picture. If Buyer shall fail to make such payments as and when due and payable, Buyer shall pay late payment damages as specified in Section 5, 5.1 or 5.2, whichever is applicable, of the Basic Agreement.

In the event of any sale, assignment or transfer of Buyer's distribution or exhibition rights in the Picture, Buyer shall remain liable for the Residuals, with respect to the territories, media and term referred to above, unless Buyer obtains an executed Buyer's Assumption Agreement and other documents required by SAG from such purchaser, assignee or transferee and SAG approves in writing the financial responsibility of the party obtaining such rights. SAG agrees that it will not unreasonably withhold its approval of the financial responsibility of any such purchaser, assignee or transferee. Nothing herein shall release the Producer of its obligations under any other agreement between Producer and SAG relating to the Picture, unless the Producer has been relieved of liability pursuant to the provisions of this Section 6.B.

If SAG does not approve in writing the financial responsibility of the party obtaining such rights, this Buyer's Assumption Agreement shall remain effective and binding upon Buyer.

Buyer and SAG hereby agree that all disputes based upon, arising out of or relating to this Assumption Agreement, other than SAG's entitlement to injunctive or other equitable relief, shall be submitted to final and binding arbitration in accordance with the arbitration provisions contained in the Basic Agreement. Notwithstanding the foregoing, Buyer agrees and acknowledges that SAG is not precluded by this or any other provision of this Assumption Agreement from obtaining from a court injunctive relief or any other legal remedy at any time prior to arbitration or issuance of an arbitration award. The right to obtain injunctive relief from a court shall be applicable whether an arbitration proceeding has or has not been initiated, and further, without limitation, shall be applicable in conjunction with a proceeding to confirm and enforce an arbitration award against Buyer.

THIS BUYER'S ASSUMPTION AGREEMENT SHALL BE GOVERNED BY AND CONSTRUED IN ACCORDANCE WITH THE LAWS OF THE STATE OF CALIFORNIA AND THE UNITED STATES, AS THE SAME WOULD BE APPLIED BY A FEDERAL COURT IN CALIFORNIA WITHOUT REGARD TO PRINCIPLES OF CONFLICTS OF LAW. SAG and Buyer agree that any arbitration or legal action or proceeding brought to interpret or enforce the provisions of this Buyer's Assumption Agreement (including and action to compel arbitration or a petition to vacate an arbitration award) shall be held or brought in Los Angeles County, California, and Distributor irrevocably submits to the jurisdiction of the federal and state courts therein. Notwithstanding the foregoing, SAG at its option may bring a legal action or proceeding outside California under the following circumstances: (a) if Buyer has no principal place of business in California; or (b) whether or not Buyer has a principal place of business in California, to enforce or execute upon an arbitration award or court order or judgment, in any jurisdiction in which Buyer's assets are located (and Buyer irrevocably submits to the jurisdiction of the courts of such places for purposes of such execution or enforcement). Buyer consents to service of process by personal delivery or by certified or registered mail, return receipt requested, to Buyer's general counsel or to Buyer's representative identified below or by first class mail to Buyer when Buyer has not designated a representative or a general counsel, or by any other method permitted by law.

DATE _____

BUYER _____

ADDRESS _____

BY _____

BUYER'S REPRESENTATIVE OR GENERAL COUNSEL _____

The Producer agrees to deliver to SAG an executed copy of the above referred to Buyer's Assumption Agreement within thirty (30) days after the sale, assignment or transfer of such motion picture, with the name and address of the purchaser or assignee.

Any inadvertent failure on the part of the Buyer to comply with any of the reporting provisions of this subsection B. shall in no event constitute a default by the Producer or such Buyer or a breach of this Agreement, provided that such failure is cured promptly after notice in writing thereof from the Screen Actors Guild.

Upon delivery of such Buyer's Assumption Agreement and other documents from Buyer required under this Assumption Agreement and on condition that SAG approves in writing the financial responsibility of the purchaser, assignee or transferee, Producer shall not be further liable for the keeping of any such records, or for the payment of Residuals in accordance with said applicable Section, it being agreed that the purchaser, assignee or transferee shall solely be liable therefor.

SAG agrees that it will not unreasonably withhold its approval of the financial responsibility of any such purchaser, assignee or transferee, it being further agreed that if SAG, within twenty-one (21) days of receipt of written notice of any such sale, assignment or transfer has not advised the Producer that it disapproves the financial responsibility of such purchaser, assignee or transferee, SAG will be deemed to have approved the financial responsibility thereof. If any such purchaser, assignee or transferee is a Qualified Buyer, then the financial responsibility of such purchaser, assignee or transferee shall be deemed automatically approved. In the event SAG advises the Producer within such twenty-one (21) day period that it disapproves the financial responsibility of any such purchaser, assignee or transferee and the Producer disputes such disapproval, the Producer shall have the right, at its election, to cause to be immediately submitted to arbitration, pursuant to the provisions of Section 9 hereof, the issue of whether SAG has unreasonably withheld the approval of the financial responsibility of such purchaser, assignee or transferee for payments due hereunder.

To the extent that Producer has granted a security interest in favor of SAG in the Picture and related collateral as defined in any SAG Security Agreement, Buyer's rights in the Picture acquired pursuant to the Purchase Agreement shall be subject to the following:

So long as the Buyer timely pays Residuals for the Picture with respect to all territories and media in which Buyer has distribution rights in accordance with Section 5, 5.1 and/or 5.2 of the Basic Agreement, as applicable, SAG shall not exercise any rights under such security agreement which would in any way interfere with the rights of the Buyer to distribute the Picture and receive all revenues from such distribution, provided that such Buyer has executed and delivered a Buyer's Assumption Agreement to SAG and is in compliance with the terms thereof.

If any "Qualified Buyer" assumes in perpetuity under the Buyer's Assumption Agreement the obligation to pay the Residuals for all territories and media with respect to the Picture or guarantees in a written form satisfactory to SAG all of such obligations thereunder, SAG will release and cause to be discharged of record all such security interests, liens, charges or encumbrances entered into or obtained from such Producer and will not require further financial assurances from such Producer.

If any "Qualified Buyer" acquires rights to distribute the Picture in specific territories and media (but not all territories and media) in perpetuity, and thereby has assumed responsibility for the payment of Residuals for such territories and media so acquired pursuant to the Buyer's Assumption Agreement or guarantees in a written from satisfactory to SAG all of such obligations thereunder, then if the Producer has granted a security interest in favor of SAG in the Picture and related collateral as defined in the SAG Security Agreement, SAG: (i) agrees to modify the definition of the collateral in the SAG Security Agreement to exclude those territories and media acquired by such Qualified Buyer; and (ii) acknowledges Buyer's continuing rights of full, unlimited but non-exclusive access to and use of any and all physical items and elements relating to the Picture.

In addition to those buyers who have been deemed "Qualified" by SAG due to their past bargaining relationship and/or Residuals payment history, the term "Qualified Buyer" shall mean a Buyer who satisfies the requirements set forth in Paragraphs A. and B. below:

A. Buyer has the financial history, liquidity, net earnings before interest, taxes and amortization, assets, and net worth to establish its present and future ability to pay Residuals arising from the exploitation of the SAG Pictures being distributed.

B. The Buyer has been in business for five (5) or more years and has a history of prompt and proper payment or Residuals pursuant to SAG contracts in five (5) consecutive years immediately prior to seeking Qualified Distributor status.

A Qualified Buyer must agree to assume Residuals obligations, or guarantee the payment of Residuals in accordance with the Qualified Buyer's Letter of Agreement, for each Picture produced under a SAG collective bargaining agreement for the territories, media and term for which it has distribution rights and must execute the Qualified Buyer's Agreement.

In the event of a dispute as to qualifications of an applicant for Qualified Buyer status of an applicant for Qualified Buyer status, Producer shall provide such financial assurances as SAG may deem appropriate, which may include, but are not limited to, a security interest in the Picture and related collateral, in which case Buyer shall acknowledge same. Said security interest shall remain effective unless and until it is established by agreement or in an arbitration, pursuant to the arbitration provisions contained in the Basic Agreement, that the applicant Buyer meets the aforementioned requirements for qualification. Such applicant shall have the burden of proof that it satisfies the aforementioned requirements for qualification in any arbitration and shall, upon SAG's request, furnish to SAG all relevant financial or corporate information relating thereto as SAG may reasonably require.

Any information submitted to SAG in order to determine whether a Buyer is entitled to status as a Qualified Buyer shall, at the Buyer's discretion, be subject to reasonable confidentiality arrangements.

In the event that a Qualified Buyer, after notice and a reasonable opportunity to cure, generally fails to report and/or pay Residuals when they are due or generally fails to pay obligations to creditors when they become due or in the event a petition is filed under the Bankruptcy Code by or against a Qualified Buyer, SAG shall have the right to terminate the Buyer's Qualified Buyer status. The Buyer shall have the right to invoke the arbitration procedures described above to challenge such termination. Pending the resolution of such challenge, the Qualified Buyer's status shall be considered terminated. SAG agrees that it will not terminate a Qualified Buyer's status when there is a *bona fide* dispute over whether Residuals are due to SAG, or a *bona fide* dispute as to the amount of Residuals due to SAG, if the Buyer has otherwise timely reported and paid Residuals. In addition to the above, if a SAG audit conducted pursuant to the Codified Basic Agreement or other financial information discloses that the Qualified Buyer no longer meets the aforementioned standards for qualification, SAG may initiate an arbitration pursuant to the Basic Agreement to terminate the Qualified Buyer's status.

C. Distributor's Liability

With respect to any such motion picture, the principal photography of which commenced on or after October 6, 1980 in which one (1) or more performers covered by the Basic Agreement renders services, the following provisions shall be applicable to the Distributor of such motion picture for telecasting on free television or (if applicable) for distribution in Supplemental Markets:

When the Distributor has provided or guaranteed any of the financing for the production of such motion picture, the Distributor shall be obligated to pay all

Residuals which accrue under Section 5, 5.1 or 5.2 (as applicable) during the term and in the territories and media for which it was granted distribution rights, including renewals and extensions, notwithstanding the termination of such distribution agreement or any foreclosure of a chattel mortgage, security agreement, pledge or lien on such motion picture. In the case of foreclosure, should such mortgagee, pledge or security holder or a third party, who is neither the Producer nor Distributor, acquire title to such motion picture and execute the Buyer's Assumption Agreement and other documents customarily required by SAG and, upon condition that SAG, at its discretion, approves in writing such purchaser's financial responsibility, then, when the Distributor ceases to be the Distributor of such motion picture for telecasting on free television or (if applicable) for distribution in Supplemental Markets, the Distributor shall thereupon be released from any and all further obligations under said Section 5, 5.1 or 5.2, as the case may be, with respect to such motion picture. Should any third party (other than in connection with any such foreclosure) acquire the rights of such Distributor to the distribution of such motion picture on free television or (if applicable) in Supplemental Markets and execute a Distributor's Assumption Agreement pursuant to which it is liable in perpetuity to make the payments under said Section 5., 5.1 or 5.2, as the case may be, then, upon condition that SAG, in its discretion, approves such third party's financial responsibility, such Distributor shall thereupon be released from any and all further obligations under said Section 5, 5.1 or 5.2, as the case may be, with respect to such motion picture. In any event, such Distributor shall not be liable for the payment of any television fees or Supplemental Markets use payments or pension and health contributions based on monies received by a foreign distributor under a "foreign production deal," as defined in section 5.1, 5.2 E. (2) and 5.2 E.(3)(c), with respect to which such foreign distributor or independent producer is not obligated to account to such Distributor.

D. Acquisition of Title by Producer

If Producer was not the actual producer of such picture which was produced by a Union signatory, but acquired title thereto by purchase, assignment, transfer, voluntary or involuntary, or by foreclosure of a chattel mortgage or security agreement or a pledge's sale, Producer shall nevertheless be obligated to make the payments herein provided when such picture is exhibited on free television or (if applicable) in Supplemental Markets, unless such payment required hereunder has already been paid.

E. Financing-Distribution Agreement by Producer

The obligation of the signatory Producer hereunder with respect to the payments provided for in Section 5 or 5.2, as the case may be, shall also apply to motion pictures, the principal photography of which commenced on or after October 6, 1980 and in which performers covered by the Basic Agreement render services, produced by an independent producer under a contract between the signatory Producer and such independent producer for the production of such motion picture, and for the financing and distribution thereof by the signatory Producer. However, such signatory Producer shall not be liable for the payment of any television fees, Supplemental Markets use payments, or pension and health contributions, if any are required, based on monies received by a foreign distributor under a foreign production deal, as defined in Section 5.2 E.(2) and 5.2 E.(3)(c) with respect to which such foreign distributor or such independent producer is not obligated to account to such signatory Producer; nor shall such signatory Producer be obligated to obtain any Distributor's Assumption Agreement from any foreign distributor referred to in said Section 5.2 E.(2) and 5.2 E.(3)(c) except if such foreign distributor is obligated to account to such signatory Producer pursuant to Section 5.2 E.(2) and 5.2 E.(3)(c) with respect to monies as therein provided.

F. Producer Liability

It is expressly understood and agreed that Producer shall in all events remain bound hereunder to make the payments due by reason of the exhibition of each picture on free television or (if applicable) in Supplemental Markets, irrespective of the assumption of such liability by any other person, firm or company, as hereinabove provided, except as otherwise expressly provided in this Agreement.

G. Failure to Deliver Assumption Agreement

The failure of Producer to obtain and deliver an executed assumption agreement, as provided in Section 6.A. and 6.B. hereof, shall be deemed a substantial breach of this Agreement.

H. Producer's Dissolution

If Producer dissolves and is no longer in the business of producing motion pictures and if a Distributor assumes all of the obligations of the Producer under Section 5 or 5.2, whichever is applicable, and the financial responsibility of the Distributor is approved by the Union in its discretion, then Producer shall thereupon be released of any obligation with respect to any payments due hereunder.

I. Network and Television Stations

No television network, station, sponsor or advertising agency shall be required to execute any Distributor's Assumption Agreement under Section 6.A. hereof or Buyer's Assumption Agreement under Section 6.B., except if it is the distributor of such motion picture on free television or (if applicable) in Supplemental Markets or the buyer of the Producer's free television rights or (if applicable) Supplemental Markets rights in such motion picture.

J. Notice to Union

On written request by the Union, Producer shall promptly notify the Union, in writing, whether it has entered into a distribution or a financing and distribution agreement with an independent producer with respect to a particular motion picture or pictures.

* * *

9. ARBITRATION

Disputes shall be arbitrable only as hereinafter in this Section set forth.

A. Disputes involving or relating to injunctive relief are not arbitrable.

B. Disputes involving or relating to the right of termination of a performer's individual employment contract are not arbitrable (1) except with respect to day performers, stunt performers, stunt coordinators, airplane pilots, singers, dancers employed on theatrical motion pictures, puppeteers, body doubles and freelance performers whose guaranteed compensation is less than $50,000 per picture, and (2) except as provided in subsection C.(4)(a) below.

C. Individual Disputes between Performer and Producer

Subject to the provisions of subsections A. and B. above, only the following disputes between a performer and Producer are arbitrable:

(1) As to a day performer, stunt performer, stunt coordinator, airplane pilot, singer, dancer employed on a theatrical motion picture, puppeteer, body double or either a freelance performer or a multiple-picture performer whose guaranteed compensation is less than $50,000 per picture, the issue of whether a contract was entered into and any dispute involving the interpretation, performance, non-performance or an alleged breach of a term or condition of the performer's contract, including claims for compensation at scale or overscale, and all disputes arising under the applicable terms of the collective bargaining agreement relating to such performer;

(2) As to a contract performer receiving a weekly rate of compensation up to and including $4,000 per week, any dispute arising under the applicable terms of the collective bargaining agreement relating to such performer and any dispute arising under the performer's individual employment contract concerning the payment of compensation at scale or overscale;

(3) As to all performers not expressly covered in (1) and (2) above, and except as provided in paragraph (4)(a) of this subsection C., only disputes arising under the applicable terms of the collective bargaining agreement shall be arbitrable. Except as provided in said paragraph (4)(a), disputes arising under the individual employment contract of such performers including claims for compensation therein provided, shall not be arbitrable;

(4)   With respect to contract performers receiving $4,000 per week or less, multiple-picture performers guaranteed less than $50,000 per picture, and freelance performers guaranteed less than $50,000 for the picture, the following provisions shall apply where a dispute as to any such performer arising under his individual employment contract or the collective bargaining agreement involves both a claim of compensation and the issue of termination:

(a)   When the Producer claims to have terminated or seeks a termination of the performer's individual employment contract: (i) if the total amount of money claimed by the performer is under $75,000, the entire dispute shall be arbitrable, it being agreed that the performer's entire claim shall be presented in a single arbitration; (ii) if the total amount of money claimed by the performer is $75,000 or over, the dispute shall not be arbitrable, in whole or in part.

(b)   When the performer claims to have terminated or seeks a termination of his individual employment contract, the dispute shall not be arbitrable, in whole or in part.

(c)   If either party claims to have terminated or seeks a termination of the performer's individual employment contract, such party shall so notify the other, in writing, at any time prior to the expiration of the ten (10) days following delivery of the written statement of grievance provided for in subsection E.(3) of this Section.

* * *

11.   AGREEMENT AND SCHEDULES INCORPORATED IN PERFORMER'S CONTRACT—WAIVERS

A. There are attached hereto and made a part of this collective bargaining agreement the following Schedules of wage scales and working conditions:

Schedule A — Day Performers.

Schedule B — Television freelance performers whose weekly guaranteed salary is $4,000 or less per week and who are guaranteed less than $28,500 per television picture and theatrical freelance performers whose weekly guaranteed salary is $4,500 or less per week and who are guaranteed less than $45,000 per theatrical picture.

Schedule C — Television freelance performers whose weekly guaranteed salary is more than $4,000 per week and who are guaranteed less than $28,500 per television picture and theatrical freelance performers whose weekly guaranteed salary is more than $4,500 per week and who are guaranteed less than $45,000 per theatrical picture.

Schedule D — Television multiple picture performers receiving $4,000 or less per week and guaranteed less than $28,500 per television picture and theatrical motion picture performers receiving $4,500 or less per week and guaranteed less than $45,000 per theatrical picture.

Schedule E — Television contract performers whose weekly guaranteed salary is $4,000 or less per week and theatrical contract performers whose weekly guaranteed salary is $4,500 or less per week.

Schedule F — Television contract performers whose weekly guaranteed salary is in excess of $4,000 per week and theatrical contract performers whose weekly guaranteed salary is in excess of $4,500 per week; television multiple picture performers receiving more than $4,000 per week or who are guaranteed $28,500 or more per television picture; theatrical multiple picture performers receiving more than $4,500 per week or who are guaranteed $45,000 or more per theatrical picture; performers employed under television "deal contracts," or otherwise, who are guaranteed $28,500 or more per television picture; performers employed under theatrical "deal contracts," or otherwise, who are guaranteed $45,000 or more per theatrical picture; performers employed in multi-part closed-end pictures receiving more than $4,000 per week and who are guaranteed $34,000 or more for the multi-part picture.

Schedule G-I — Professional singers employed by the day.

Schedule G-II — Professional singers employed by the week on television at $4,000 or less per week and professional singers employed by the week on theatrical productions at $4,500 or less per week.

Schedule H, Part I — Stunt performers employed by the day.

Schedule H, Part II — Stunt performers employed by the week on television at $4,000 or less per week and stunt performers employed by the week on theatrical productions at $4,500 or less per week.

Schedule H, Part III — Stunt performers employed by the week on television at more than $4,000 per week and stunt performers employed by the week on theatrical productions at more than $4,500 per week.

Schedule I — Airplane pilots.

Schedule J — Dancers employed on theatrical motion pictures.

Schedule K, Part I — Stunt coordinators employed by the day at less than the "flat deal" minimum.

Schedule K, Part II — Stunt coordinators employed by the week at less than the "flat deal" minimum.

Schedule K, Part III — Stunt coordinators employed under "flat deal" contracts.

Schedule X, Part I — Extra performers employed in the Los Angeles, San Diego, San Francisco, Las Vegas and Hawaii Zones.

<u>Schedule X, Part II</u> — Extra performers employed in the New York Zone.

The salary Schedule under which a performer is originally employed shall not be changed merely because a change occurs in the money break tests of the salary Schedules during such performer's employment.

Individual employment contracts, entered into under a preceding collective bargaining agreement, which continue during the term of this Agreement, shall be subject to the Schedules of Wage Scales under said preceding collective bargaining agreement.

B. The applicable provisions of this Agreement and the provisions contained in the appropriate Schedule shall be deemed incorporated in the individual contract of employment between Producer and each performer; the Producer, the Union and the individual performer shall be bound thereby. Each class of performer is intended to be covered by the appropriate Schedule; if the classification of any performer is not expressly included in one of such Schedules, he shall receive the working conditions and minimums most nearly applicable to him.

C. Producer agrees that no waiver by any performer of any term of this Agreement, including the appropriate Schedule, shall be requested of the performer or be effective unless the consent of the Union is first had and obtained. Such consent may be oral, but the Union agrees that all oral waivers will be confirmed by it in writing. The Union further agrees that, upon being notified by any Producer that a company is going on location, it will appoint a deputy to be with the company is going on location, with full power to grant waivers. The Union further agrees that it will maintain a twenty-four hour (24) service at Los Angeles, California, for the giving of waivers in accordance with the provisions of this subsection.

D. Whenever the Producer is entitled to a permit or a waiver from the Union, the Union agrees to issue the same without cost.

* * *

18. TRAILERS AND PROMOTIONAL FILMS

A. <u>Trailers</u>

(1) Full day performer rates shall be paid to performers employed in each trailer, with right of Producer to use on television and in theatres. Producer shall have the right to make a "teaser" trailer in addition to the full-length trailer for theatrical use only.

(2) The foregoing shall not apply to a performer who appears as a star or featured performer in a theatrical motion picture or to a term contract performer who, during his employment period, performs in a trailer or trailers for such

motion picture. The foregoing provisions as to term contract performers shall not be used to willfully subvert the provision of this Section.

(3) No additional compensation shall be payable for the use of any portion of a motion picture, or for the use of scenes photographed simultaneously with a separate camera (behind-the-scenes shots), utilized as a trailer.

(4) The above provisions refer to trailers to be used for theatrical exhibition, television exhibition or a combination of both.

(5) Any trailer when exhibited over television shall be limited to either 400 feet of 35mm film containing not less than two scenes or 200 feet of 35mm film containing only one scene.

(6) Editing

Changes may be made only in the tag ending of a trailer to show time and place of exhibition of the advertised picture, and performer shall be paid a premium rate of twenty-five percent (25%) for each tag made beyond the first.

(7) A performer employed to perform services in connection with the production of a television trailer for advertising a theatrical motion picture made outside of the geographic scope of this Agreement, or by a party who was not a signatory hereto, shall be paid for such services in accordance with the provisions of the current applicable Screen Actors Guild Commercials Contract.

The foregoing shall not apply to a star, featured performer or term contract performer who was employed under the Basic Agreement to perform services in the motion picture, in which case the foregoing provisions of this Section 18.A. shall apply.

B. Thirty (30) Minutes (or less) Promotional Films for Theatrical and Television Motion Pictures

(1) Performers receiving $25,000 or more for the motion picture: Compensation to such performers for appearing in such promotional films shall be a matter of individual bargaining. The performer may agree to make such promotional films, or to permit the use of any portion of the motion picture or of behind-the-scenes shots in such promotional films, without compensation.

(2) Term contract performers acting in such promotional films during their employment under such contracts or appearing in any portion of the motion picture or in behind-the-scenes shots used in such promotional films made during the term of such contracts: Compensation for such services, or for such use of film clips or of behind-the-scenes shots shall be a matter of individual bargaining. The performer may agree to make such promotional films during the term contract employment or to permit the use of such film clips and behind-the-scenes shots in such promotional films made during the term of such employment without compensation.

(3) All other performers appearing in such promotional films, or who appear in any portion of the motion picture or in behind-the-scenes shots used in such promotional films: At the time of employment, Producer may bargain with performer for such services or behind-the-scenes shots in such promotional films but the minimum compensation payable shall be day performer minimum scale. For the use of film clips from the motion picture being promoted, Producer shall pay the day performer minimum scale to performers appearing in such clips without the need for individual bargaining, provided the length of such clips is either four hundred (400) feet of 35mm film containing not less than two (2) scenes or two hundred (200) feet of 35mm film containing only one (1) scene. As to film clips which exceed such limits, Producer shall bargain with performer at the time of use and the minimum compensation payable shall be the day performer minimum scale.

(4) Such promotional films may not be combined to make "specials."

(5) If the Producer does not obtain permission of the performer where required by the provisions of this subsection B., or if more than one (1) performer is involved and one (1) of them does not agree, the provisions of subsections B. and C. of Section 22 hereof shall apply.

* * *

20. PROHIBITION AGAINST CREDITING

No compensation paid to a performer for his services in excess of the minimum may be credited against overtime, penalties or any other compensation otherwise due the performer.

* * *

22. REUSE OF PHOTOGRAPHY OR SOUND TRACK

A. No part of the photography or sound track of a performer shall be used other than in the picture for which he was employed, without separately bargaining with the performer and reaching an agreement regarding such use. The foregoing requirement of separate bargaining hereafter applies to reuse of photography or sound track in other pictures, television, theatrical or other, or the use in any other field or medium. Bargaining shall occur prior to the time such reuse is made, but performer may not agree to such reuse at the time of original employment. The foregoing shall apply only if the performer is recognizable and, as to stunts, only if the stunt is identifiable. See subsection F. of this Section. No reuse may be made of nude photography without the performer's written consent.

The day performer rate shall be the minimum for purposes of the bargaining referred to above with respect to such use of such material in any motion picture other than the one for which performer was employed. As to any other use of photography or sound track referred to above, the bargaining shall be subject to the minimum wages and residuals provided for in the collective bargaining agreement, if any, applicable in the field in which the photography or sound track is used, unless compensation for such other use is already provided by this Agreement.

The provisions of this subsection A. shall not limit Producer's right to use photography or sound track in exploiting the picture, or in trailers, promotion films thirty (30) minutes (or less) in length for theatrical and television motion pictures, or in advertising, as provided in this Agreement.

The Union may, in its discretion, grant waivers of the requirements of this Section with respect to the reuse of photography and sound track in public service, educational and like programs and will follow a liberal policy in granting such waivers.

B. If Producer fails to separately negotiate as provided in subsection A. hereof, the performer shall be entitled to damages for such unauthorized use, equivalent to three (3) times the amount originally paid the performer for the number of days of work covered by the material used. If the Producer is unable to find the performer, it shall notify SAG, and if SAG is unable to find the performer within a reasonable time, the Producer may use the photography or sound track without penalty.

C. If Producer and the performer negotiate for such use and are unable to reach an agreement, and all performers involved have agreed to compensation for such use except a single performer who, Producer claims, is unreasonably refusing to accept an equitable sum, Producer may submit the matter to SAG's Board of Directors for determination and both Producer and performer shall be bound by the determination so made, if the material is used. In all other cases where Producer and the performer are unable to reach an agreement, Producer shall be prohibited from making such reuse of the material, and in case of violation, or in a case in which the Producer fails to obtain the performer's written consent to reuse nude photography, the performer shall be entitled, at his option, to either accept damages as provided in subsection B. hereof, or to arbitrate his claim hereunder, or to take legal proceedings in a court of competent jurisdiction.

D. If the performer is employed under a term contract and the use occurs during the time he is still under contract with Producer, the performer shall not be entitled to additional compensation; but if such reuse occurs at a time when the performer is no longer under contract with Producer, the provisions of subsections A., B. and C., hereof shall apply.

E. Neither Producer nor SAG waive their respective claims with respect to the reuse of photography of performers employed under "deal contracts."

F. Notwithstanding the foregoing, the reuse of stunt work is subject to the following:

(1) With respect to any stunt which was contained in any theatrical motion picture, the production of which commenced prior to February 1, 1956, the Producer may reuse the photography containing such stunt in other theatrical motion pictures without limitation or any liability for additional compensation.

(2) With respect to any stunt which was contained in any theatrical motion picture, the production of which commenced prior to August 1, 1948, the Producer may reuse the photography containing such stunts in any television motion picture without limitation or additional compensation.

(3) With respect to any stunt which was photographed but not used in the motion picture for which it was made, the Producer may use such stunt once in another theatrical motion picture without limitation or additional compensation.

(4) Producer shall have the right to reuse photography or sound track of identifiable stunts which would otherwise be subject to an obligation to bargain prior to being reused (including stunts in motion pictures which were produced under prior SAG Agreements which restricted the reuse of such photography or soundtracks) in the media specified below upon payment of the day performer minimum or, if a different amount is specified below, upon payment of the amount so specified to the stunt performer(s) appearing in the footage. It is not necessary for the Producer to bargain with the stunt performer before reusing the stunt footage.

The foregoing shall apply with respect to the use of stunt footage in:

(i) other theatrical motion pictures, free television motion pictures, motion pictures made for the pay television/videocassette market, and motion pictures made for basic cable;

(ii) commercials, but the required payment shall be the applicable commercial session fee and residuals. As to commercial tie-ins, the following shall apply:

(A) commercial tie-in advertising of a motion picture which is available for sale at the same point of purchase as the other product being advertised shall be considered to "exploit the motion picture" and, thus, may be done without negotiation or payment; and

(B) tag line-type advertising (brief tag or mention of a different product appended to or included in a commercial promoting motion picture) shall be considered to "exploit the motion picture" and, thus, may be done without negotiation or payment.

(iii) standard openings and closing of television shows, but payment must be made on the same basis as is required under Exhibit A of the SAG Television Agreement for performers;

(iv) theme parks (other than uses that are promotional or exploit the motion picture, for which no bargaining or payment is required) for a period of five years. (If a longer term of use is desired, an additional payment of then-current day performer minimum would be required for each subsequent five year period.) In the alternative, Producer may obtain such rights in perpetuity upon payment to the stunt performer(s) appearing in the footage of a sum equal to three (3) times the then-current day performer minimum.

(v) in games and interactive videos.

Payment as provided above shall be made for each "excerpt" of photography or sound track which is reused. However, more than one excerpt of stunt photography or sound track may be reused upon payment of a single day performer minimum payment in the following circumstances: (1) if the reused stunts were performed by the same stunt performer in a single day; or (2) if a stunt sequence is intercut with live action as part of a scene which includes footage on a television screen, movie theater screen or other similar viewing device.

In the event that the Producer fails to issue payment to the stunt performer within thirty (30) business days from the exhibition of the permitted reuse, the stunt performer shall be entitled to late payments as provided under Section 31.B. (2) of this Agreement.

(5) The provisions of subsections A., B., C., D. and E. above shall apply to the reuse of stunt footage in:

(i) music videos other than those which promote, advertise or exploit the motion picture from which the footage was taken. (Stunt footage may continue to be used without bargaining or payment in music videos which promote, advertise or exploit the picture from which the footage is taken, so long as the use meets the contractual criteria for which bargaining is unnecessary.)

(ii) "compilation" stunt programs (i.e., shows comprised substantially of stunt footage).

G. The above provision for payments for reuse of stunts shall only apply to stunt performers the Union can identify and establish as having performed the stunt in question. The Producer may rely upon the Union's designation of any stunt performer as the person who performed such stunt and payment by the Producer to such stunt performer shall be final and conclusive and shall relieve the Producer or any further obligations for the reuse or rerun of such stunt as herein provided.

H. Producer will not publicly exhibit nor license for public exhibition blooper reels without the appropriate consent of the recognizable performer(s) involved, including individual voice-overs.

I. The late payment provisions of Section 31.B.(2) herein shall apply to reuse of photography payments, except that the time for payment shall be thirty (30) business days from exhibition.

J. The provisions of this Section shall not limit the Producer's right to use or authorize the use of clips from theatrical pictures, without bargaining or making additional payment: (1) within regularly-scheduled news programs; and in connection with other news and review purposes under the same circumstances as in the past; and (2) in Oscar Award programs.

With respect to uses which would otherwise require payment pursuant to this Section 22, a star performer may, at the time of use, waive payment for the use of theatrical film clips containing such performer's voice or likeness, it being understood that such waiver shall not affect other performers entitled to payment hereunder.

K. Both the Guild and the Networks expressly reserve their respective positions concerning the use of footage, including stunt footage, in network promotional announcements containing tie-ins (e.g., CBS promotionals with K-Mart tie-in which promote the fall season program line-up).

L. This Section 22 is not applicable to stunt coordinators, except as it applies to stunt performer work performed by a stunt coordinator under a "flat deal" contract.

*   *   *

25. SCREEN CREDITS

A. Producer agrees that a cast of characters on at least one (1) card will be placed at the end of each theatrical feature motion picture, naming the performer and the role portrayed. All credits on this card shall be in the same size and style of type, with the arrangement, number and selection of performers listed to be at the sole discretion of the Producer. All such credits shall be in a readily readable color, size and speed. The Union will not unreasonably withhold waivers in connection with the foregoing. Any performer identified by name and role elsewhere in the picture need not be listed in the cast of characters at the end of the picture.

Producer shall send the Guild a copy of the complete version of the closing credits of each theatrical motion picture covered hereunder upon completion of the answer print of such picture.

B. Feature Motion Pictures

In all feature motion pictures with a cast of fifty (50) or less, all performers shall receive credit. In all other feature motion pictures, not less than fifty (50) shall be listed in the cast of characters required at the end of each feature motion picture in connection with theatrical exhibition, excluding performers identified elsewhere in the picture. Stunt performers need not be identified by role. The Union, and only the Union, may seek to arbitrate an alleged violation of this subsection B. pursuant to the arbitration procedures set forth in this Section 25.C.(3).

C. Billing

(1) Producer shall honor individually-negotiated billing for the screen as to placement, size and description as agreed upon in performer's individual contract.

(2) In its distribution and licensing agreements with exhibitors, distributors, broadcasters, etc., Producer will include a provision prohibiting the licensee from eliminating or changing the billing as it appears on the positive prints of the motion picture.

(3) Disputes as to whether agreed-upon screen credit has been accorded shall be arbitrable. A panel of arbitrators for this purpose shall be agreed upon. A single arbitrator shall hear and determine the dispute. The cost of such arbitrator shall be shared equally by the Union and Producer. The decision and award shall be in writing and shall be final and binding on the parties and performers involved.

(4) The provisions hereof shall not apply to Schedule F performers or when termination of a contract is involved as provided by Section 9.C.(4)(b) of the arbitration provisions.

(5) Liquidated Damages

As to Schedule A and B performers, if a breach occurs and the facts are not in dispute or if breach is found by an arbitrator, damages in the following amounts shall be payable:

(a) In the case of a day performer, his daily rate, but not in excess of the amount payable under (c) of this subparagraph (5).

(b) In the case of a three (3) day performer in television, his three (3) day rate, but not in excess of the amount payable under (c) of this subparagraph 5.

(c) In the case of a weekly freelance performer, his weekly rate (not exceeding the limits of Schedule B). Such liquidated damages shall be the exclusive remedy for such performers.

(6) As to all other performers subject to the provisions hereof, the arbitrator shall have the authority to award appropriate relief consisting of damages, correction of prints subject to subparagraph (7) below, or both.

(7) Correction of Prints

(a) Theatrical Motion Pictures

Correction of prints may be awarded by the arbitrator, in his discretion, if Producer received notice of the claimed breach in sufficient time to make such correction before release. If correction is awarded, Producer shall be obligated to make such corrections as soon as is practical, consistent with existing distribution commitments and, in any event, before any reissue. For this purpose, television release of the film shall be considered a reissue.

(b) Television Motion Pictures

Correction of television prints with respect to the first broadcast or first rerun may be awarded by the arbitrator if Producer received notice of the alleged breach in sufficient time to make the necessary correction for the applicable run.

(8) Inadvertent oversight by Producer shall not be a defense to any claim of breach hereunder, but may be considered with respect to the issue of appropriate relief.

(9) All claims must be filed within one (1) year after the first theatrical release of a theatrical film or within one (1) year of the first television broadcast of a television film.

D. The foregoing provisions of this Section do not apply to body doubles.

* * *

28. INJURIES TO PERSONS OR PROPERTY DURING PERFORMANCE; SAFETY

* * *

B. Protection of Performers; Safety

It shall be the policy of the parties to this Agreement that performers employed hereunder shall, to the extent possible, not be placed in circumstances hazardous or dangerous to the individual. In furtherance of this policy, it is agreed:

(1) When Producer requires script or non-script stunts or stunt–related activity of a performer, an individual qualified by training and/or experience in the planning, setting up and/or performance of the type of stunt involved shall be engaged and present on the set. No performer without such requisite training and/or experience shall be required to perform a stunt or stunt–related activity without an opportunity for

prior consultation by the performer with such individual. The foregoing provisions of this paragraph (1) shall not apply to a stunt performer who both plans and performs a stunt which does not involve other performers.

(2)   No performer shall be required to work with an animal which a reasonable person would regard as dangerous in the circumstances, unless an animal handler or trainer qualified by training and/or experience is present.

(3)   No performer shall be rigged with any type of explosive charge of any nature whatsoever without the use of a qualified special effects person.

(4)   The performer's consent shall be a requisite precondition to performing stunts or other hazardous activity. The performer's consent shall be limited to the stunt or activity described to the performer at the time consent was given. In the case of a minor, written consent to perform a stunt must be given by the minor's parent or guardian.

Violation of this provision shall be subject to liquidated damages in the amount of $900.

* * *

29. LOAN-OUTS

Where Producer "borrows" a performer, whether from a domestic or foreign company, and whether or not the lending company is a signatory to a Screen Actors Guild collective bargaining agreement, and such performer is used by Producer within the jurisdiction of this Agreement, Producer guarantees to the Union that the performer who is so borrowed shall receive the same working conditions as provided herein, except the Union Security provisions; provided, however, that the Union Security provisions shall apply where the lending company is a signatory to a Screen Actors Guild collective bargaining agreement (whether such lending company is a domestic or foreign corporation) and the performer is used by the borrowing Producer within the jurisdiction of this Agreement; provided further, that the obligation to make the payment of pension and health contributions shall be subject to Section 34.K. Producer shall give reasonable advance written notice to the Union, prior to the commencement of the term of the loan-out when Producer borrows a performer from a company, foreign or domestic, which is not a signatory to a Screen Actors Guild collective bargaining agreement, to render services within the jurisdiction of this Agreement.

30. PRODUCTION STAFF

A. Persons employed as members of Producer's casting or production staff will neither be engaged nor utilized as performers in any pictures on which they also render any services on Producer's casting or production staff without the express consent of the Union.

B. The only exceptions shall be the following:

(1)   animal handlers (appearing in a scene in which they handle animals);

(2)   performer/directors, performer/writers, or performer/producers engaged in written contract as such prior to the commencement of principal photography of a motion picture;

(3)   in an "emergency" on location. "Emergency" is defined as a situation, on location, in which a member of the cast cannot perform because of unavailability for any reason.

C. Violations of the foregoing shall require payment of liquidated damages, as follows:

Day Performers:	$400.00
Three-Day Performers:	$500.00
Freelance Performers:	$700.00

* * *

43. NUDITY

A. The Producer's representative will notify the performer (or his representative) of any nudity or sex acts expected in the role (if known by management at the time) prior to the first interview or audition. The performer shall also have prior notification of any interview or audition requiring nudity and shall have the absolute right to have a person of the performer's choice present at that audition. Total nudity shall not be required at such auditions or interviews; the performer shall be permitted to wear "pasties" and a G-string or its equivalent.

B. During any production involving nudity or sex scenes, the set shall be closed to all persons having no business purpose in connection with the production.

C. No still photography of nudity or sex acts will be authorized by the Producer to be made without the prior written consent of the performer.

D. The appearance of a performer in a nude or sex scene or the doubling of a performer in such a scene shall be conditioned upon his or her prior written consent. Such consent may be obtained by letter or other writing prior to a commitment or written contract being made or executed. Such consent must include a general description as to the extent of the nudity and the type of physical contact required in the scene. If a performer has agreed to appear in such scenes and then withdraws his or her consent, Producer shall have the right to double, but consent may not be withdrawn as to film already photographed. Producer shall also have the right to double children of tender years (infants) in nude scenes (not in sex scenes).

* * *

48. FAVORED NATIONS CLAUSE

If, during the term of this Agreement, any union through its collective bargaining agreement negotiated with the Alliance of Motion Picture & Television Producers obtains a "Cost of Living Escalation Clause" with respect to minimum rates, then, in such event, the Union will be entitled to the benefits of such clause commencing with the third year of this collective bargaining Agreement.

* * *

50. EMPLOYMENT OF MINORS

A. Preamble

(1) The Producers and Union, recognizing the special situation that arises when minor children are employed, have formulated the following provisions in addition to those contained in other Sections of this Agreement to ensure that:

(a) The environment in which the performance is to be produced is proper for the minor;

(b) The conditions of employment are not detrimental to the health, morals and safety of the minor; and

(c) The minor's education will not be neglected or hampered by his or her participation in such performance.

(2) Engagement

Upon employment of any minor, Producer shall notify the minor's parent or guardian of the terms and conditions of employment, including the name of the Producer, place and duration of location work, if any, and special abilities required.

Upon the employment of any minor in any areas outside of California, Producer shall notify the Union of such employment and the area where such employment will take place.

B. It is recognized that when minors are employed in the State of California or taken from the state of California pursuant to a contractual arrangement made in the State of California, the applicable California laws and regulations shall regulate such employment.

When minors are hired and employed within states other than California, the Producer shall be required to determine and comply with the prevailing law governing and defining minors. In addition to these legal requirements for minors not employed in the State of California or not taken from the State of California pursuant to a contractual arrangement made in the State of California, the Producer and the Union agree to the following provisions of Section 50 herein for the employment of minors:

C. Definition of Minor

The term "minor," as used herein, means any performer under the age of eighteen (18) years, except that it shall not include any such performer if: (1) the performer has satisfied the compulsory education laws of the state governing the performer's employment; (2) the performer is married; (3) the performer is a member of the armed forces; or (4) the performer is legally emancipated.

D. Education

(1) (a) If a minor is guaranteed three (3) or more consecutive days of employment, Producer agrees to employ a teacher, from the first day of such employment, whenever the minor is engaged on any day during which the primary or secondary school regularly attended by the minor is in session. The same shall apply where the Producer's production schedule for a given production plans for scenes to be photographed with the minor on three (3) or more consecutive days. Where the minor is employed in scenes planned on the production schedules for only two (2) consecutive days and it is subsequently determined that additional calls will be necessary, Producer shall use its best efforts to provide a teacher on the third consecutive day of such employment, or at the latest, on the fourth consecutive day of such employment and thereafter.

(b) On any day a minor is employed but is not otherwise entitled to have a teacher, the minor shall nevertheless be taught if the primary or secondary school such minor regularly attends is in session and Producer has employed a teacher to instruct another performer engaged on the same production.

(c) If Producer employs a minor for post-production work, no teacher need be provided if the minor's call for such work is after the minor's regular school has been dismissed for the day.

(d) Producer shall provide schooling as required by this Agreement during Producer's workweek for the production.

(2) Such teacher shall have proper teaching credentials appropriate to the level of education required (i.e., primary or secondary level) from Washington D.C. or any state within the United States, but need not be credentialed by or a resident of the state wherein the minor's employment occurs unless otherwise required by law.

(3) The teacher's remuneration shall be paid by Producer.

(4) Producer shall provide a ratio of not more than twenty (20) minors per teacher, except that up to twenty (20) minors may be taught per teacher if the minors are in not more than two (2) grade levels.

(5) A teacher may not serve more than one (1) production in any one (1) day, except in an emergency and except as provided in subsection D.(1)(c) above.

(6) If the minor's regular instruction is primarily in a language other than English, teaching in that language will be provided whenever feasible.

(7) However, on any day that the minor is not required to report to the set, the minor may attend his or her regular school, but Producer shall not count more than three (3) hours of the hours attended per day at the minor's regular school as school time for purposes of this Agreement. If the minor's parent or guardian does not choose to have the minor attend regular school on such day, Producer may elect to either teach the minor on the set or in the minor's home or in the home of the teacher employed by Producer, but only if there are no other minors present in the home who are not also being taught by the teacher.

(8) Producer agrees to provide a school facility, such as a schoolhouse, classroom, trailer schoolhouse or other schooling area, which closely approximates the basic requirements for classrooms, especially with respect to adequate lighting, heating, desks and chairs. Stationary buses or cars are not adequate school facilities unless used exclusively for the minors during instruction. A moving car or bus shall never be used as a school facility; minors must not be taught while being transported to or from local locations.

(9) Producer shall provide schooling equipment and supplies. However, the minor's parent or guardian must, if permitted by the minor's regular school, secure school assignments and the minor's school books for use at the place of employment.

(10) No one shall be allowed in an area being utilized by Producer as a school facility except the teacher and those minors being taught.

(11) The teacher shall determine the required number of hours to be devoted to instruction during a day, but the minor must be taught an average of at least three (3) hours per day, no period of less than twenty (20) minutes duration being acceptable as school time. The maximum number of hours that may be set aside for the minor's instruction in any one (1) day shall be as follows: for kindergarten, four (4) hours; for grades one (1) through six (6), five (5) hours; and for grades seven (7) through twelve (12), six (6) hours.

(12) Producer shall require the teacher to prepare a written report for such minor covering attendance, grades, etc. The reports shall be given to the minor's parents or guardian to deliver to the minor's regular school at the end of each assignment or at such intervals as required by such school.

E. Supervision

(1) On days when the minor's regular school is in session, Producer must require the minor to report to the teacher immediately upon arrival at the place

of employment. When school is in session, the teacher has primary responsibility for the education and supervision of the minor.

(2) Presence of the teacher does not relieve parents, however, of the responsibility of caring for their own children. A parent or guardian must be present at all time while a minor is working, and shall have the right, subject to filming requirements, to be within sight and sound of the minor, except as restricted herein by subsection D.(10).

(3) When a parent is working at the minor's place of employment but not at the scene of employment, either the other parent or a guardian must be present with the minor.

(4) A guardian, as that term is used in this Section, must be at least eighteen (18) years of age, have the written permission of the minor's parent(s) to act as a guardian, and show sufficient maturity to be approved by Producer (and teacher, if teacher is present).

(5) No minor may be sent to wardrobe, make-up, hairdressing, or employed in any manner unless under the general supervision of a teacher, parent or guardian.

(6) If Producer engages any minor under the age of fourteen (14), Producer must designate one (1) individual on each set to coordinate all matters relating to the welfare of the minor and shall notify the minor's parent or guardian and teacher, when one is present, of the name of such individual.

(7) Parents and guardians are not permitted to bring other minors not engaged by Producer to the place of employment without Producer's specific permission.

F. Working Hours

(1) Minors less than six (6) years of age are permitted at the place of employment for six (6) hours (excluding meal periods, but including school time, if any).

(2) Minors who have reached the age of six (6) years but who have not attained the age of nine (9) years may be permitted at the place of employment for eight (8) hours (excluding meal periods but including school time).

(3) Minors who have reached the age of nine (9) years but who have not attained the age of sixteen (16) years may be permitted at the place of employment for nine (9) hours (excluding meal periods, but including school time).

(4) Minors who have reached the age of sixteen (16) years but who have not attained the age of eighteen (18) years may be permitted at the place for employment for ten (10) hours (excluding meal periods, but including school time).

(5) The work day for a minor shall begin no earlier than 5:00 a.m. and shall end no later than 10:00 p.m. on evenings preceding school days. On evenings preceding non-school days, the minor's work day shall end no later than 12:30 a.m. on the morning of the non-school day.

(6) If a minor is at location, the minor must leave location as soon as reasonably possible following the end of his or her working day, and may not be held for transportation.

(7) Interviews and fittings for children who are attending school shall be held outside of school hours. Such interviews and fittings shall be held not later than 9:00 a.m.

At least two (2) adults shall be present at all times during a fitting.

(8) A minor shall not work more than six (6) consecutive days. However, for this purpose, a day of school only or travel only shall not be counted as one of said consecutive days.

(9) Producer shall set the first call at the beginning of the minor's employment and dismissal on the last day of the minor's employment so as to ensure that the minor will have a twelve (12) hours rest period prior to and at the end of the employment. For example, if a minor's last day of employment is Wednesday, and the minor will be attending school at 8:30 a.m. on Thursday, the minor must be dismissed by 8:30 p.m. on Wednesday.

* * *

55. STUNT COORDINATORS

This Agreement covers stunt coordinators performing stunt coordinating work, whether or not other services are rendered under this Agreement. However, the addition of the stunt coordinator classification to those covered under the Agreement is not intended, nor shall it be construed, either to require the employment of stunt coordinators in circumstances in which persons other than stunt coordinators are presently or have heretofore performed the functions of stunt coordinators nor to diminish the employment of stunt coordinators by assigning stunt coordinating work to persons in positions in which such work has not customarily been performed.

56. BODY DOUBLES

Body doubles employed in scenes requiring nudity or conduct of a sexual nature shall be principal performers, except that the provisions relating to residuals, screen credit, consecutive employment and preference of employment shall not apply to such persons.

* * *

SCHEDULE A

DAY PERFORMERS

1. DAY PERFORMER — DEFINITION

A day performer is a performer employed by the day, other than an extra performer, stunt performer, stunt coordinator, professional singer, dancer employed on a theatrical motion picture or airplane pilot.

2. MINIMUM WAGE — SINGLE ROLE

The day performer rate provided herein shall cover only single role in a specified picture.

The minimum wage for a day performer shall be $522.00 for the period July 1, 1995 through June 30, 1996; $540.00 for the period July 1, 1996 through June 30, 1997; and $559.00 for the period July 1, 1997 through June 30, 1998.

3. SCHEDULE A INCLUDED IN INDIVIDUAL CONTRACTS

The conditions in this Schedule shall govern the employment of all day performers and shall become a part of the contract with the day performer.

4. ENGAGEMENT

A. A day performer shall be considered definitely engaged in any of the following events:

(1) When the performer is given written notice of acceptance;

(2) When a former contract signed by Producer is delivered to the performer or when an unsigned contract is delivered by Producer to performer and is executed by performer as so delivered and returned to Producer;

(3) When a script is delivered to the performer by Producer; however, this does not include the delivery of a script for a test, audition or interview nor the submission of a script for the purpose of permitting the performer to determine if he desires the engagement;

(4) When a performer is fitted for work; this shall not apply to wardrobe tests; and

(5) When the performer is given a verbal call by Producer or an authorized company representative, which is accepted;

(6) When the performer is actually called by the Producer and agrees to report on the commencement date for which the call is given; however,

until noon of the day preceding such commencement date, either the Producer or the performer may cancel such employment. If the Producer is unable to reach the performer personally, either by telephone or otherwise, notice of such cancellation may be given to the performer by telegraph, in which event the time when such telegram is given by the Producer to the telegraph company, addressed to the performer at his address last known to the Producer, shall be the time of such cancellation.

B. To the extent that the agreement reached between the Producer and the performer can be reflected on the form required by the collective bargaining agreement (see Exhibit II attached) plus Producer's standard riders to be filed with the Union, Producer shall deliver a copy of such contract to the performer not later than the first day of performer's employment. Where the agreement cannot be so reflected, Producer shall deliver a copy of such contract to the performer not later than the first day of performer's employment or four (4) business days after such agreement has been reached, whichever is later.

When Producer chooses to deliver a copy of a contract to the performer on the set, an extra copy for retention by the performer shall be provided.

W-4 forms shall be presented to performer no later than the first day of employment. A W-4 form may be given to performer on the set on the first day of employment.

W-4 forms shall be available on every set. It shall be the performer's responsibility to return a completed W-4 form to Producer in a timely manner. It is understood that where a performer fails to do so, there shall be no retroactive adjustments to the withholding required by law. W-4 forms shall be attached to day performer and three (3) day performer contracts.

C. Liquidated damages in the amounts provided in section 31.B. of the General Provisions hereof for late payments shall be payable until a written contract is delivered to the performer.

D. Neither auditions nor interviews shall constitute an engagement.

E. When a performer is engaged and not used for any reason other than his default, illness, or other incapacity, he shall be entitled to one (1) day of salary or his guarantee, whichever is greater. If the performer who is selected is unavailable when called to render actual services, he shall not be entitled to a day of pay.

If a performer has been engaged and his services pursuant to such engagement have not commenced, he may accept (but is not obligated so to do) a substitute engagement in the same photoplay, in which event he shall be paid only for the substitute engagement, but not less than his original rate of pay and guarantee; provided, however, that if he has received a definite starting date, the substitute engagement must have the same starting date.

A day performer who is replaced in a photoplay for reasons other than his default, illness or other incapacity, after commencement of his services pursuant to his engagement and before the completion of his engagement, shall receive his guarantee, or one (1) day of salary in addition to payment for services rendered to that time, whichever is greater.

If a day performer has completed his performance in the picture, including the recording, and his voice is not satisfactory to the Producer and Producer re-dubs the entire sound track of the day performer, such re-dubbing shall not be a replacement.

In the event that a performer is replaced in the role, the performer, or performer's agent, shall be notified of this fact at the time of the replacement.

F. A copy of the "booking slip" shall be provided to performer no later than the day next preceding the first day of performer's employment.

(1) Definition of Booking Slip. A booking slip is a document containing a designation of the role, salary and number of days of guaranteed employment.

(2) If performer is engaged after 6:00 p.m. on the day prior to the first day of performer's employment, the booking slip will be included with the script provided to performer. However, if the script was provided to performer prior to such date and hour, Producer need not provide such booking slip.

(3) The foregoing requirements for delivery of a booking slip shall not apply if performer's contract has previously been delivered to performer or performer's agent.

* * *

6. CONSECUTIVE DAYS OF EMPLOYMENT

A. Employment of the day performer shall be for consecutive days from the beginning of the engagement, any seventh day in the workweek, holiday and studio sixth day excepted, unless the performer's services are required on such seventh day in the workweek, holiday or studio sixth day. The Producer shall have the right to terminate such engagement at any time. Except as provided in the next sentence, performers engaged by the day may be recalled by Producer for any purpose, other than those hereinafter in Section 28 referred to, after a lapse of fourteen (14) days, as the case may be, without payment for the intervening time, if at the time of performer's original employment, performer is given a firm start date for such subsequent call. Performers engaged by the day on episodic television series (including pilots) at a salary of at least two (2) times the day performer minimum may be recalled once without payment for the intervening time, if at the time of performer's original employment, performer is given a firm start date for such subsequent call. (The preceding sentence shall not apply to any performer who meets the definition of a "major role performer.")

With respect to any performer recalled by Producer as a freelance performer, Producer and performer may agree that performer shall be recalled on or after such recall date. For purposes of this provision, "on or after" shall mean the time on the date specified or a time within twenty-four (24) hours thereafter. When a performer is recalled on a freelance basis, the recall date may be advanced subject to performer's availability; except, however, Producer may not recall performer sooner than ten (10) or fourteen (14) days, as the case may be, without being obligated to pay for such intervening time.

If, within fourteen (14) days after termination of performer's engagement, Producer recalls performer for any purpose other than those hereinafter in Section 28 referred to, the performer's compensation shall nevertheless be paid for the intervening period between the date of such earlier termination and the date of recall; provided, however, that if at any time when the Producer attempts to recall the performer, the performer is ill or otherwise incapacitated, or is employed, or is committed to other employment, or for any other reason is unavailable, then the Producer's obligation to pay compensation for such intervening time shall terminate when the Producer so attempts to recall the performer. Furthermore, if, during such intervening period, the performer is ill or is otherwise incapacitated or employed, no compensation shall accrue to the performer during such period of illness, incapacity or employment. With respect to day performers, if a firm date for recall is not given and if the performer is recalled subsequent to fourteen (14) days after termination, compensation shall be paid to the performer for the intervening period between the date of such earlier termination and the date of recall. The Producer shall be entitled to avoid payment for intervening time with respect to a recall subsequent to two (2) weeks after earlier termination only once for the same performer in the same photoplay.

The foregoing consecutive employment provisions do not apply:

(1)   to body doubles, except that body doubles shall be paid for intervening days on an overnight location when required to remain at such location by the Producer; and

(2)   to days off during a break of two (2) weeks, which breaks includes the Christmas and New Year's holidays.

B. Neither tests, auditions, fittings, publicity stills, pre-production stills, nor pre-recordings, after employment but before the starting day of such employment, shall start the consecutive days of employment of day performers.

Rehearsal shall not start the consecutive days of employment under the circumstances described in Section 21.E. of this Schedule A.

* * *

36. USE OF "DOUBLE"

The provisions of Section 36 of Schedule B shall apply to day performers employed at or above a salary of $750.00 per day.

* * *

SCHEDULE B

TELEVISION FREELANCE PERFORMERS WHOSE WEEKLY GUARANTEED SALARY IS $4,000 OR LESS PER WEEK AND WHO ARE GUARANTEED LESS THAN $28,500 PER TELEVISION PICTURE AND THEATRICAL FREELANCE PERFORMERS WHOSE WEEKLY GUARANTEED SALARY IS $4,500 OR LESS PER WEEK AND WHO ARE GUARANTEED LESS THAN $45,000 PER THEATRICAL PICTURE

1. DEFINITION

A television freelance performer is a performer employed for a specific television motion picture in a designated role on a weekly basis at a salary of $4,000 or less per week but no less than $1,813 per week ($1,876 per week for the period July 1, 1996 through June 30, 1997 and $1,942 per week for the period July 1, 1997 through June 30, 1998) and who is guaranteed less than $28,500 per television picture. A theatrical freelance performer is a performer employed for a specific theatrical motion picture in a designated role on a weekly basis at a salary of $4,500 or less per week but no less than $1,813 per week ($1,876 per week for the period July 1, 1996 through June 30, 1997 and $1,942 per week for the period July 1, 1997 through June 30, 1998) and who is guaranteed less than $45,000 per theatrical picture.

2. SCHEDULE B INCLUDED IN INDIVIDUAL CONTRACTS

It is agreed that the conditions of this Schedule shall govern the employment of freelance performers and shall become a part of the contract with the freelance performer.

3. MINIMUM CONTRACT — REQUIRED PROVISIONS

The minimum freelance contract shall be as follows:

SCREEN ACTORS GUILD, INC. MINIMUM FREELANCE CONTRACT

Continuous Employment — Weekly Basis — Weekly Salary — One (1) Week Minimum Employment

THIS AGREEMENT is made this _____ day of _____, 19 _____, between _____, hereinafter called "Producer," and _____, hereinafter called "performer."

WITNESSETH:

1. *Photoplay, Role, Salary, and Guarantee.* Producer hereby engages performer to render service as such in the role of _____, in a photoplay, the working title of which is now _____, at the salary of $_____ ($_____per week). Performer accepts such engagement upon the terms herein specified. Producer guarantees that it will furnish performer not less than _____weeks of employment. (If this blank is not filled in, the guarantee shall be one (1) week.)

2. *Term.* The term of employment hereunder shall begin on _____, on or about _____, and shall continue thereafter until the completion of the photography and recordation of said role. [footnote omitted]

3. *Basic Contract.* All provisions of the collective bargaining agreement between Screen Actors Guild, Inc. and Producer relating to theatrical motion pictures which are applicable to the employment of the performer hereunder shall be deemed incorporated herein.

4. *Performer's Address.* All notices which the Producer is required or may desire to give to the performer may be given either by mailing the same addressed to the performer at _____, _____, or such notice may be given to the performer personally, either orally or in writing.

5. *Performer's Telephone.* The performer must keep the Producer's casting office or the assistant director of said photoplay advised as to where the performer may be reached by telephone without unreasonable delay. The current telephone number of the performer is (_____)_____.

6. *Motion Picture and Television Fund.* The performer (does) (does not) hereby authorize the Producer to deduct from the compensation hereinabove specified an amount equal to _____ percent of each installment of compensation due the performer hereunder, and to pay the amount so deducted to the Motion Picture and Television Fund.

7. *Furnishing of Wardrobe.* The (performer) (Producer) agrees to furnish all modern wardrobe and wearing apparel reasonably necessary for the portrayal of

said role; it being agreed, however, that should so-called "character" or "period" costumes be required, the Producer shall supply the same.

8. *Arbitration of Disputes.* Should any dispute or controversy arise between the parties hereto with reference to this contract, or the employment herein provided for, such dispute or controversy shall be settled and determined by conciliation and arbitration in accordance with the conciliation and arbitration provisions of the collective bargaining agreement between the Producer and Screen Actors Guild relating to theatrical motion pictures, and such provisions are hereby referred to and by such reference incorporated herein and made a part of this Agreement with the same effect as though the same were set forth herein in detail.

9. *Next Starting Date.* The starting date of performer's next engagement is _____.

10. The performer may not waive any provision of this contract without the written consent of Screen Actors Guild, Inc.

11. Producer makes the material representation that either it is presently a signatory to the Screen Actors Guild collective bargaining agreement covering the employment contracted for herein or that the above referred to photoplay is covered by such collective bargaining agreement under the provisions of Section 24 of the General Provisions of the Producer-Screen Actors Guild Codified Basic Agreement of 1995.

IN WITNESS WHEREOF, the parties have executed this agreement on the day and year first above written.

PRODUCER _____

PERFORMER _____

BY _____

4. STARTING DATE

A. The phrase "on or about," as used in a freelance performer's contract, shall allow a latitude of twenty-four (24) hours, exclusive of Saturdays, Sundays and holidays, either prior to or after the date specified in the contract, as the commencement of the term thereof.

B. If a freelance contract is delivered to the performer at least seven (7) days before the starting date, the "on or about" clause may be used. If a contract is delivered to a performer less than seven (7) days before the specified starting date, a definite starting date must be specified and the "on or about" clause shall not be used. To illustrate: If the starting date of a performer is on the eighth day of the month, and the contract is delivered to the performer on the first day of the month, the "on or about" clause may be used, but if the contract is delivered to the performer on the second day of the month, the "on or about" clause may not be used.

C. In any case where it is impracticable or impossible to fix any definite starting date of any performer to be employed under a freelance contract because of such performer's activities on the stage or in radio or otherwise in the amusement business (except motion pictures), the Union agrees to waive the requirement of a definite starting date in such freelance contract, provided that such freelance contract contains a reasonable provision for the fixing of the starting date thereof and notice thereof. Any dispute between the Union and any Producer with respect to the issuance of any such waiver shall be determined by arbitration under Section 9 of the General Provisions hereof.

D. In the event a performer is engaged in accordance with Section 6.B. hereof, but a start date has not yet been provided to the performer by the Producer, performer may terminate such engagement in order to accept conflicting *bona fide* employment by a third party; subject, however, to the performer first giving Producer the following minimum period during which Producer may specify a start date which then becomes binding, which conflicts with the proffered third party employment:

    (1)   If performer informs Producer before noon of a business day, by the end of the same day; or

    (2)   If performer informs Producer at any other time, by noon of the next business day.

5. MINIMUM SALARY — GUARANTEE

The minimum salary for a freelance performer shall be $1,813 per week for the period July 1, 1995 through June 30, 1996; $1,876 per week for the period July 1, 1996 through June 30, 1997; and $1,942 per week for the period July 1, 1997 through June 30, 1998.

One (1) picture employment for a freelance performer shall guarantee at least one (1) week of employment. The guarantee provided in this paragraph shall be subject to the rights of suspension and termination granted to the Producer by the provisions of Sections 40, 41 and 42 of this Schedule B.

* * *

15. WORK TIME

A. The provisions of this Section shall apply only to television freelance performers whose weekly guaranteed salary is $4,000 or less per week and who are guaranteed less than $28,500 per television picture and to freelance performers whose weekly guaranteed salary is $4,500 or less per week and who are guaranteed less than $45,000 per theatrical picture.

B. For the purpose of ascertaining and computing hours of work, the rest period and overtime, the period from the time the performer is required to and does report, as directed, until the time such performer is finally dismissed for the day, shall constituted work time, continuously and without interruption, except as follows:

(1)   Allowable meal periods, as provided by in Section 17;

(2)   Tests, auditions, wardrobe tests and interviews, as provided by Section 19;

(3)   Fittings, as provided by Section 20;

(4)   Story, song and production conferences, to the extent provided in Section 21;

(5)   Study of lines or script, to the extent provided by Section 22;

(6)   Interviews for publicity purposes, as provided by Section 23;

(7)   Publicity stills, to the extent provided by Section 24;

(8)   Make-up, hairdress and wardrobe, to the extent provided by Section 16;

(9)   Travel time, to the extent provided by Section 44.

C. Any period during which the performer fails or refuses or is unable because of disability to render services, and any period during which the performer at his own request is excused from rendering services, shall not be work time for any purpose.

D. After the freelance performer has been employed and after the starting date of such employment, none of the provisions of this Section shall break the continuous days of employment of such freelance performer, except as provided in subsection C. above and in Section 25.D. of this Schedule B.

The foregoing consecutive employment provisions do not apply:

(1)   to body doubles, except that body doubles shall be paid for intervening days on an overnight location when required to remain at such location by the Producer; and

(2)   to days off during a break of up to two (2) weeks, which break includes the Christmas and New Year's holidays.

* * *

21.   STORY, SONG AND PRODUCTION CONFERENCES

Story, song and production conferences on any day on which the performer is not otherwise working shall not be counted as work time for any purpose. This provision shall not be construed to interrupt the continuous employment of a freelance performer.

22. STUDY OF LINES OR SCRIPT

Study of lines or script, except during the period between reporting and dismissal, shall not be counted as work time for any purpose.

23. PUBLICITY INTERVIEWS

Publicity interviews held at a time mutually satisfactory to the performer and the Producer shall not be work time for any purpose unless held on a day on which the performer is otherwise working for the Producer. Such interviews for publicity purposes held on any day on which the performer is otherwise working for the Producer shall not be counted as work time if held after the performer's dismissal for the day, if such interview is held at a time mutually satisfactory to the performer and the Producer. If the interview is held during a meal period, it shall not be deemed to constitute a violation thereof.

24. PUBLICITY STILLS

A. If the Producer should desire the services of a freelance performer for making publicity stills, either before the commencement of his term of employment or after the expiration thereof, the performer shall render such services without compensation for one (1) day, as and when requested by the Producer, unless the performer is otherwise employed, but if otherwise employed, the performer will cooperate to the fullest extent in the making of such publicity stills.

B. Publicity stills, after employment but before the starting date of such employment, shall not start the consecutive days of employment of a freelance performer.

25. REHEARSAL TIME

A. The reading of lines, acting, singing or dancing, in preparation for the performer's performance, in the presence and under the supervision of a representative of Producer, constitute a rehearsal. Rehearsals shall be counted as work time.

B. Auditions, tests, interviews, make-up and wardrobe tests do not constitute rehearsals.

C. The Union agrees to freely grant waivers for the training of a performer in a particular skill such as horseback riding, fencing, etc. Compensation, if any, shall be agreed to between the performer and the Producer, subject to the approval of the Union.

D. Neither tests, auditions, fittings, publicity stills, pre-production stills, pre-recordings nor training under subsection C. above, after employment but before the starting date of such employment, shall start the employment period of such performer. Compensation, if any, for any of such services shall be as otherwise provided in this Schedule.

* * *

30. RETAKES, ADDED SCENES, LOOPING, ETC.

A. If, after the expiration of the term provided by the freelance contract, the Producer should desire the services of the performer in making retakes, or in making added scenes or sound track, or in making any process shots, transparencies or trick shots, or in making trailers, or in making any change or changes in said photoplay, or in making any foreign version or versions of said photoplay, then, and in either of said events, the performer agrees to render such services in connection therewith as and when the Producer may request, unless the performer is otherwise employed, but if otherwise employed, the performer will cooperate to the fullest extent. If commenced within four (4) months after the expiration of the term hereof, such services shall be at the same rate of compensation as set forth in the performer's contract, except that compensation for such services shall be paid only for the days on which the performer is actually so employed, and except also that the applicable conditions governing the employment of day performers under the Basic Agreement shall apply to the computation of time in connection with such services. It is agreed, however, that if, prior to the commencement of the rendition of such services, the Producer shall have agreed in writing to guarantee the performer at least one (1) week or work or one (1) week of compensation in connection therewith, then, and in that event, such services shall be upon the same terms and at the same rate of compensation as elsewhere in this Schedule set forth, such compensation to be paid from the time when the performer's services are first rendered in connection therewith, until the completion of the performer's services connection therewith.

Performer may be recalled to loop (record sound track) after completion of principal photography at one-half (1/2) of the performer's pro rata daily salary for a four (4) hour looping session. If the session exceeds four (4) hours, a full day's pro rata salary shall be payable.

B. The performer's contract shall not include guarantees for looping, retakes, added scenes, process transparencies, trick shots, trailers, changes or foreign versions (subject to availability) outside the period of consecutive employment.

C. Close-ups

The Union will freely grant waivers of continuous employment for the making of close-ups made after the completion of the Director's first rough cut of the photoplay, so that the performer shall be paid only for the day or days upon which he renders such services.

31. OVERLAPPING ENGAGEMENT

In any case where the engagement of a performer under a freelance contract extends into or overlaps any other engagement of such performer as a freelance performer or day performer

(1)   because of any unanticipated delay in production or *bona fide* mistake, or

(2)   because of any failure of such performer to disclose his other engagements at the time of accepting any engagement, or

(3)   in any case in which, as an accommodation to such performer, such performer is permitted to work concurrently in two (2) pictures,

it is agreed as follows: For any day or days on which such performer renders his services for the Producer of the picture in which he has first rendered his services, he shall receive compensation from such first Producer. For any day or days on which such performer renders services for the Producer of the second picture in which he has rendered his services, he shall be compensated by the Producer of such second picture. For any day or days on which the performer does not render his services either for the first Producer or for the second Producer, he shall be compensated by the second Producer, unless the first and second Producers agree between themselves (and notice thereof is given to the performer) that compensation for such additional day or days shall be paid by the first Producer. The compensation to be paid by the first Producer shall be paid at the rate specified in the performer's contract with the first Producer, and the compensation to be paid by the second Producer shall be at the rate specified in the performer's contract with the second Producer; provided, however, that if the rate paid by the first Producer is less than the rate specified in the performer's contract with the second Producer, the difference shall be paid by the second Producer and, provided further, that for any day or days on which the performer does not render services either for the first or for the second Producer, he shall be compensated at the rate of compensation which is the higher of the two. This Section does not affect such performer's right to receive compensation from both Producers where the performer, while employed by one Producer, makes retakes, added scenes, etc., for the other Producer after the expiration of his term of employment with such other Producer, in any case where the performer is otherwise entitled thereto. Nothing in this Section contained shall be deemed or construed in any way to limit or prejudice any right or remedy of any Producer, either with respect to any of the contingencies hereinbefore specified or otherwise. Freelance performers may be required to state on their contracts the starting date of their next engagement by inserting such date in the following statement, which may be endorsed or printed on such contracts:

"The starting date of the performer's next engagement is _____."

* * *

35. DEFINITION OF ROLE

The term "role," as used in the Minimum Contract for Freelance Performers, shall be deemed to refer to said role as written at the time the freelance contract is entered into, or as it may from time to time thereafter be rewritten or lengthened or shortened by the Producer in the exercise of its sole discretion and judgment.

36. USE OF "DOUBLE"

A. The Producer agrees that it will not "dub" or use a "double" in lieu of the performer, except under the following circumstances:

(1) When necessary to expeditiously meet the requirements of foreign exhibition;

(2) When necessary to expeditiously meet censorship requirements, both foreign and domestic;

(3) When, in the opinion of the Producer, the failure to use a double for the performance of hazardous acts might result in physical injury to the performer;

(4) When the performer is not available; and

(5) When the performer fails or is unable to meet certain requirements of the role, such as singing or the rendition of instrumental music or other similar services requiring special talent or ability other than that possessed by the performer.

The performer does hereby agree that under either or any of the conditions hereinabove in subparagraphs (1) to (5), both inclusive, of this Section set forth, the Producer shall have the right to double and/or dub not only the acts, poses, plays and appearances of the performer, but also the voice of the performer, and all instrumental, musical and other sound effects to be produced by the performer, to such extent as may be required by the Producer.

B. Pre-production

Upon the application of Producer, the Union agrees to liberally grant waivers so that there will be no continuous employment for a freelance performer where that performer is doubled in pre-production. The Union may require, as a condition of the issuance of such a waiver, one day of pay to the performer for each day that the performer is doubled.

In order to encourage the use of principals in pre-production, the Union will liberally grant waivers to permit principals to appear in pre-production shots, without commencing their consecutive employment until principal photography actually commences. This provision shall apply only to Hollywood-based domestic production of theatrical motion pictures and features made primarily for first exhibition on television.

37. RIGHT TO NAME OR CHARACTER

No Producer shall, after the termination of the performer's employment, prevent such performer from continuing the use of any stage or screen name used by such performer. The name of a role owned or created by the Producer, such as Tarzan or Charlie Chan, belongs to the Producer and not to the performer.

38. STUDIO RULES

The performer agrees to be prompt in appearing for work as required by the Producer, to perform services hereunder in a conscientious and painstaking manner and in accordance with the reasonable instructions of the Producer, and to abide by the reasonable studio rules and regulations of the Producer. The Producer shall have the exclusive right to the services of the performer during the term hereof, and the performer agrees that during the term hereof the performer will not render any services of any kind to or for any person, firm or corporation other than the Producer without first obtaining the express written consent of the Producer.

39. RIGHTS GRANTED TO PRODUCER

The term "photoplay," as used in said freelance contract, shall be deemed to include motion pictures produced and/or exhibited with sound and voice recording, reproducing and/or transmitting devices, radio devices, and all other improvements and devices, including television, which are now or may hereafter be used in connection with the production and/or exhibition and/or transmission of any present or future kind of motion picture production. The Producer shall have the right to photograph and/or otherwise produce, reproduce, transmit, exhibit, distribute and exploit in connection with the said photoplay any and all of the performer's acts, poses, plays and appearances of any and all kinds hereunder, and shall further have the right to record, reproduce, transmit, exhibit, distribute and exploit in connection with said photoplay the performer's voice and all instrumental, musical and other sound effects produced by the performer in connection with such acts, poses, plays and appearances. The Producer shall likewise have the right to use and give publicity to the performer's name and likeness, photographic or otherwise, and to recordations and reproductions of the performer's voice and all instrumental, musical and other sound effects produced by the performer hereunder, in connection with the advertising and exploitation of said photoplay. The rights of this Section granted to the Producer shall inure to the benefit not only of the Producer, but also to the benefit of all persons who may hereafter acquire from the Producer any right to distribute, transmit, exhibit, advertise or exploit said photoplay.

The grant of rights provided herein shall not be deemed to include:

A. Merchandising rights unless separately bargained for with the performer;

B. The photograph or likeness of the performer in books commercially published for sale to the public, unless the prior written consent of the performer is obtained;

C. The right to feature the photograph or likeness of the performer on the album or jacket cover of commercial phonograph or tape recordings which would indicate that the performer's performance is included in the recording, when in fact the performer's performance is not included in such recording, unless the prior written consent of the performer is obtained.

40. GENERAL RIGHT OF TERMINATION

A. The Producer may terminate the performer's employment at any time, either prior to the commencement of production of said photoplay or during the course of production.

B. If the Producer elects to terminate the performer's employment under the freelance contract prior to the commencement of the term thereof, the Producer shall be obligated to pay the performer compensation during the minimum guaranteed period provided for in said freelance contract, but if the performer receives other employment during such period, the compensation received by the performer from such other employment shall be applied in reduction of the Producer's liability.

C. If the Producer elects to terminate the performer's employment at any time after the commencement of the term of said freelance contract, the Producer shall be obligated to pay the performer such balance, if any, as is then unpaid for services theretofore rendered by the performer, and also one (1) week of compensation, upon the payment of which the Producer shall be discharged of and from all liability whatsoever thereunder, subject, however, to the provisions of paragraph 1 of the freelance contract and Sections 41 and 42 hereof.

D. In the event that a performer is replaced in the role, the performer, or the performer's agent, shall be notified of this fact at the time of the replacement.

41. ILLNESS OF PERFORMER (SUSPENSION OF SALARY AND TERMINATION)

The Producer need pay no salary during any period that the performer is incapacitated, by illness or otherwise, from performing the required services under a freelance contract and, in the event of such illness or incapacity, the Producer, at its option, may terminate such employment without further liability.

42. EMERGENCY SUSPENSION OR TERMINATION

If the production of the photoplay specified in the freelance contract be necessarily prevented, suspended or postponed during the course of production by reason of fire, accident, strike, riot, act of God or of the public enemy, or by any executive or judicial order, or postponed by reason of the illness of any other member of the cast or of the director, one-half (1/2) salary shall be paid the performer for the first three (3) weeks of prevention, suspension or postponement. It shall be the duty of the Producer during the first week of any prevention, suspension or postponement to notify the performer in writing whether the Producer will entirely discontinue the production or further suspend or postpone it and, in the latter event, the Producer shall pay the performer one-half (1/2) salary during such further suspended or postponed period. At the end of three (3) weeks from the date on which the Producer has stopped production, the performer may terminate said employment if the performer so elects, unless the Producer continues thereafter to pay the performer full weekly compensation. If the production of said photoplay is prevented, suspended or postponed for any reason hereinabove in this Section provided, then and in that event the Producer may terminate said employment at any time after the commencement of such prevention, suspension or postponement. If the Producer elects to terminate said employment by reason of the illness of any other member of the case or of the director, then the Producer shall be obligated to pay the performer such balance, if any, as is then unpaid for services theretofore rendered by the performer, and also one (1) week of compensation, upon the payment of which the Producer shall be discharged of and from all liability whatsoever thereunder. If such termination be based on the happening of any other cause hereinabove in this Section set forth, then the Producer shall be obligated to pay the performer only such balance, if any, as is then unpaid for services theretofore rendered by the performer and, upon the payment of such unpaid balance, if any, the Producer shall be discharged of and from all liability whatsoever thereunder.

Where the production is suspended as a result of illness of another member of the cast or the director, and such suspension continues for five (5) days or more, the suspension may be effective as of the beginning of the event of illness, but if the duration is less than five (5) days, the suspension is not effective.

43. RESUMED PRODUCTION AFTER TERMINATION

If the Producer elects to terminate a performer's employment under a freelance contract pursuant to its right to do so for any cause hereinabove in Section 42 specified, and if, at any time more than three (3) weeks after such termination, the Producer shall desire to resume the production of said photoplay, the Producer shall notify the performer of its election to resume production and, in such event, the performer agrees to render his services in connection with such resumed production as and when the Producer may request, unless the performer is otherwise employed, but if otherwise employed, the performer will cooperate to the fullest extent in trying to make his services available for the Producer in connection with such resumed production. If production is resumed within six (6) months from the date of termination, the performer's compensation shall be at the same rate as that hereinabove specified and shall be payable only from the date of commencement of the performer's services in such resumed production.

* * *

SCHEDULE C

TELEVISION FREELANCE PERFORMERS WHOSE WEEKLY GUARANTEED SALARY IS MORE THAN $4,000 PER WEEK AND WHO ARE GUARANTEED LESS THAN $28,500 PER TELEVISION PICTURE AND THEATRICAL FREELANCE PERFORMERS WHOSE WEEKLY GUARANTEED SALARY IS MORE THAN $4,500 PER WEEK AND WHO ARE GUARANTEED LESS THAN $45,000 PER THEATRICAL PICTURE

1. DEFINITION

For the purposes of this Schedule C, the words "freelance performer" shall be defined as follows: For televison productions, a freelance performer is a performer employed for a specific picture in a designated role, on a weekly basis, at a salary of more than $4,000 per week and whose guarantee is less than $28,500 per television picture; for theatrical productions, a freelance performer is a performer employed for a specific picture in a designated role, on a weekly basis, at a salary of more than $4,500 per week and whose guarantee is less than $45,000 per theatrical picture.

* * *

15. WORK TIME FOR PURPOSES OF OVERTIME

A. For the purpose of ascertaining and computing hours of work, the rest period and overtime, the period from the time the performer is required to and does report, as directed, until the time such performer is finally dismissed for the day, shall constituted work time, continuously and without interruption, except as follows:

(1)   Allowable meal periods, as provided by in Section 17;

(2)   Tests, auditions, wardrobe tests and interviews;

(3)   Fittings, as provided by Section 19;

(4)   Story, song and production conferences, to the extent provided in Section 20;

(5)   Study of lines or script, to the extent provided by Section 21;

(6)   Interviews for publicity purposes, as provided by Section 22;

(7)   Publicity stills, to the extent provided by Section 23;

(8)   Make-up, hairdress and wardrobe, to the extent provided by Section 16;

(9)   Travel time, to the extent provided by Section 41.

B. Any period during which the performer fails or refuses or is unable because of disability to render services, and any period during which the performer at his own request is excused from rendering services, shall not be work time for any purpose.

C. After the freelance performer has been employed and after the starting date of such employment, none of the provisions of this Section shall break the continuous days of employment of such freelance performer, except as provided in subsection B. above and in Section 25.D. of this Schedule C.

The foregoing consecutive employment provisions do not apply:

(1)   to body doubles, except that body doubles shall be paid for intervening days on an overnight location when required to remain at such location by the Producer; and

(2)   to days off during a break of up to two (2) weeks, which break includes the Christmas and New Year's holidays.

* * *

20. STORY, SONG AND PRODUCTION CONFERENCES

Story, song and production conferences on any day on which the performer is not otherwise working shall not be counted as work time for any purpose. This provision shall not be construed to interrupt the continuous employment of a freelance performer.

21. STUDY OF LINES OR SCRIPT

Study of lines or script, except during the period between reporting and dismissal, shall not be counted as work time for any purpose.

22. PUBLICITY INTERVIEWS

Publicity interviews held at a time mutually satisfactory to the performer and the Producer shall not be work time for any purpose unless held on a day on which the performer is otherwise working for the Producer. Such interviews for publicity purposes held on any day on which the performer is otherwise working for the Producer shall not be counted as work time if held after the performer's dismissal for the day, if such interview is held at a time mutually satisfactory to performer and Producer. If the interview is held during a meal period, it shall not be deemed to constitute a violation thereof.

23. PUBLICITY STILLS

A. If the Producer should desire the services of a freelance performer for making publicity stills, either before the commencement of his term of employment or after the expiration thereof, the performer shall render such services without compensation for one (1) day, as and when requested by the Producer, unless the performer is otherwise employed, but if otherwise employed, the performer will cooperate to the fullest extent in the making of such publicity stills.

B. Publicity stills, after employment but before the starting date of such employment, shall not start the consecutive days of employment of a freelance performer.

24. REHEARSAL TIME

A. The reading of lines, acting, singing or dancing, in preparation for the performer's performance, in the presence and under the supervision of a representative of Producer, constitutes a rehearsal. Rehearsals shall be counted as work time.

B. Auditions, tests, interviews, make-up and wardrobe tests do not constitute rehearsals.

C. The Union agrees to freely grant waivers for the training of a performer in a particular skill such as horseback riding, fencing, etc. Compensation, if any, shall be agreed to between the performer and the Producer, subject to the approval of the Union.

D. Neither tests, auditions, fittings, publicity stills, pre-production stills, pre-recordings nor training under subsection C. above, after employment but before the starting date of such employment, shall start the employment period of such performer. Compensation, if any, for any of such services shall be as otherwise provided in this Schedule.

Rehearsal time shall not start the consecutive days of employment for a performer employed under this Schedule who is engaged for a long-form television motion picture or a theatrical motion picture, subject to the following:

(1)   The performer must be paid for rehearsal at the same rate as photography (*pro rata* of the weekly salary, but not less than day performer minimum per day, when rehearsing for less than a week);

(2)   The performer must be generally available for rehearsal, as distinguished from professionally available;

(3)   The performer must be given an "on or about" start date; and

(4)   Consecutive employment applies during the rehearsal period.

* * *

27.   RETAKES, ADDED SCENES, LOOPING, ETC.

A. If, after the expiration of the term provided by the freelance contract, the Producer should desire the services of the performer in making retakes, or in making added scenes or sound track, or in making any process shots, transparencies or trick shots, or in making trailers, or in making any change or changes in said photoplay, or in making any foreign version or versions of said photoplay, then and in either of said events, the performer agrees to render such services in connection therewith as and when the Producer may request, unless the performer is otherwise employed, but if otherwise employed, the performer will cooperate to the fullest extent. If commenced within four (4) months after the expiration of the term hereof, such services shall be at the same rate of compensation as set forth in the performer's contract, except that compensation for such services shall be paid only for the days on which the performer is actually so employed, and except also that the applicable conditions governing the employment of day performers under the Basic Agreement shall apply to the computation of time in connection with such services. It is agreed, however, that if, prior to the commencement of the rendition of such services, the Producer shall have agreed in writing to guarantee the performer at least one (1) week of work or one (1) week of compensation in connection therewith, then and in that event, such services shall be upon the same terms and at the same rate of compensation as elsewhere in this Schedule set forth, such compensation to be paid from the time when the performer's services are first rendered in connection therewith until the completion of the performer's services in connection therewith.

Performer may be recalled to loop (record sound track) after completion of principal photography at one-half (1/2) of the performer's pro rata daily salary for a four (4) hour looping session. If the session exceeds four (4) hours, a full day of pro rate salary shall be payable.

B. The performer's contract shall not include guarantees for looping, retakes, added scenes, process transparencies, trick shots, trailers, changes or foreign versions (subject to availability) outside the prior of consecutive employment.

C. Close-ups

The Union will freely grant waivers of continuous employment for the making of close-ups made after the completion of the Director's first rough cut of the photoplay, so that the performer shall be paid only for the day or days upon which he renders such services.

28. OVERLAPPING ENGAGEMENT

In any case where the engagement of a performer under a freelance contract extends into or overlaps any other engagement of such performer as a freelance performer or day performer

    (1)   because of any unanticipated delay in production or *bona fide* mistake, or

    (2)   because of any failure of such performer to disclose his other engagements at the time of accepting any engagement, or

    (3)   in any in which, as an accommodation to such performer, such performer is permitted to work concurrently in two (2) pictures,

it is agreed as follows: For any day or days in which such performer renders his services for the Producer of the picture in which he has first rendered his services, he shall receive compensation from such first Producer. For any day or days in which such performer renders services for the Producer of the second picture in which he has rendered his services, he shall be compensated by the Producer of such second picture. For any day or days on which the performer does not render his services either for the first Producer or for the second Producer, he shall be compensated by the second Producer, unless the first and second Producer agree between themselves (and notice thereof is given to the performer) that compensation for such additional day or days shall be paid by the first Producer. The compensation to be paid by the first Producer shall be paid at the rate specified in the performer's contract with the first Producer, and the compensation to be paid by the second Producer shall be at the rate specified in the performer's contract with the second Producer; provided, however, that if the rate paid by the first Producer is less than the rate specified in the performer's contract with the second Producer, the difference shall be paid by the second Producer and, provided further, that for any day or days on which the performer does not render services either for the first or for the second Producer, he shall be compensated at the rate of compensation which is the higher of the two. This Section does not affect such performer's right to receive compensation from both Producers when the performer, while employed by one Producer, makes retakes, added scenes, etc., for the other Producer after the expiration of his term of employment with such other Producer, in any case in which the performer is otherwise entitled thereto. Nothing in this Section contained shall be deemed or construed in any way to limit or prejudice any right or remedy of any Producer, either with respect to any of the contingencies hereinbefore specified or otherwise. Freelance performers may be required to state on their contracts the starting date of their next engagement by inserting such date in the following statement, which may be endorsed or printed on such contracts:

    "The starting date of the performer's next engagement
    is _____."

29. PRE-RECORDINGS AND PRE-PRODUCTION STILLS

Section 24 of this Schedule provides that neither prerecordings nor preproduction stills, after employment but before the starting date of such employment, shall start the consecutive days of employment of a freelance performer. It is agreed that such a performer shall be paid for the day or days on which he renders services in connection with pre-recordings and pre-production stills.

30. REPORTING PRIOR TO COMMENCEMENT OF EMPLOYMENT

A performer residing outside of the County of Los Angeles shall not be required to report for tests or wardrobe earlier than ten (10) days prior to the commencement of his employment except where Producer agrees to pay reasonable compensation for the excess time over the ten (10) day period.

31. DAMAGE TO WARDROBE

Any loss of or damage to costumes, wardrobe and other property furnished by the performer necessarily arising through the performance of the performer's services, or through lack of due care on the part of the Producer, shall be paid for by the Producer to the performer. All costumes, wardrobe and other property furnished by the Producer shall belong to the Producer and be returned promptly to it and any loss of or damage thereto arising through lack of due care on the part of the performer, or not necessarily arising through the performance of the performer's services, shall be paid for by the performer to the Producer. Any loss of or damage to wardrobe, for which either party hereto may be liable, shall be computed on the basis of depreciation schedules to be furnished from time to time by the American Appraisal Company.

32. DEFINITION OF ROLE

The term "role," as used in the Minimum Contract for Freelance Performers, shall be deemed to refer to said role as written at the time the freelance contract is entered into, or as it may from time to time thereafter be rewritten or lengthened or shortened by the Producer in the exercise of its sole discretion and judgment.

33. USE OF "DOUBLE"

A. The Producer agrees that it will not "dub" or use a "double" in lieu of the performer, except under the following circumstances:

    (1)   When necessary to expeditiously meet the requirements of foreign exhibition;

    (2)   When necessary to expeditiously meet censorship requirements, both foreign and domestic;

(3)   When, in the opinion of the Producer, the failure to use a double for the performance of hazardous acts might result in physical injury to the performer;

(4)   When the performer is not available; and

(5)   When the performer fails or is unable to meet certain requirements of the role, such as singing or the rendition of instrumental music or other similar services requiring special talent or ability other than that possessed by the performer.

The performer does hereby agree that under either or any of the conditions hereinabove in subparagraphs (1) to (5), both inclusive, of this Section set forth, the Producer shall have the right to double and/or dub not only the acts, poses, plays and appearances of the performer, but also the voice of the performer, and all instrumental, musical and other sound effects to be produced by the performer, to such extent as may be required by the Producer.

B. Pre-production

Upon the application of Producer, the Union agrees to liberally grant waivers so that there will be no continuous employment for a freelance performer where that performer is doubled in pre-production. The Union may require, as a condition of the issuance of such a waiver, one day of pay to the performer for each day that the performer is doubled.

In order to encourage the use of principals in pre-production, the Union will liberally grant waivers to permit principals to appear in pre-production shots without commencing their consecutive employment until principal photography actually commences. This provision shall apply only to Hollywood-based domestic production of theatrical motion pictures and features made primarily for first exhibition on television.

34.   RIGHT TO NAME OR CHARACTER

No Producer shall, after the termination of the performer's employment, prevent such performer from continuing the use of any stage or screen name used by such performer. The name of a role owned or created by the Producer, such as Tarzan or Charlie Chan, belongs to the Producer and not to the performer.

35.   STUDIO RULES

The performer agrees to be prompt in appearing for work as required by the Producer, to perform services hereunder in a conscientious and painstaking manner and in accordance with the reasonable instructions of the Producer, and to abide by the reasonable studio rules and regulations of the Producer. The Producer shall have the exclusive right to the services of the performer during the term hereof, and the performer agrees that during the term hereof the performer will not render any services of any kind to or for any person, firm or corporation other than the Producer without first obtaining the express written consent of the Producer.

36. RIGHTS GRANTED TO PRODUCER

The term "photoplay," as used in said freelance contract, shall be deemed to include motion pictures produced and/or exhibited with sound and voice recording, reproducing and/or transmitting devices, radio devices, and all other improvements and devices, including television, which are now or may hereafter be used in connection with the production and/or exhibition and/or transmission of any present or future kind of motion picture production. The Producer shall have the right to photograph and/or otherwise produce, reproduce, transmit, exhibit, distribute and exploit in connection with the said photoplay any and all of the performer's acts, poses, plays and appearances of any and all kinds hereunder and shall further have the right to record, reproduce, transmit, exhibit, distribute and exploit in connection with said photoplay the performer's voice and all instrumental, musical and other sound effects produced by the performer in connection with such acts, poses, plays and appearances. The Producer shall likewise have the right to use and give publicity to the performer's name and likeness, photographic or otherwise, and to recordations and reproductions of the performer's voice and all instrumental, musical and other sound effects produced by the performer hereunder, in connection with the advertising and exploitation of said photoplay. The rights of this Section granted to the Producer shall inure to the benefit not only of the Producer, but also to the benefit of all persons who may hereafter acquire from the Producer any right to distribute, transmit, exhibit, advertise or exploit said photoplay.

The grant of rights provided herein shall not be deemed to include:

A. Merchandising rights unless separately bargained for with the performer;

B. The photograph or likeness of the performer in books commercially published for sale to the public, unless the prior written consent of the performer is obtained;

C. The right to feature the photograph or likeness of the performer on the album or jacket cover of commercial phonograph or tape recordings which would indicate that the performer's performance is included in the recording when in fact the performer's performance is not included in such recording, unless the prior written consent of the performer is obtained.

37. GENERAL RIGHT OF TERMINATION

A. The Producer may terminate the performer's employment at any time, either prior to the commencement of production of said photoplay or during the course of production.

B. If the Producer elects to terminate the performer's employment under the freelance contract prior to the commencement of the term thereof, the Producer shall be obligated to pay the performer compensation during the minimum guaranteed period provided for in said freelance contract, but if the performer receives other employment during such period, the compensation received by the performer from such other employment shall be applied in reduction of the Producer's liability.

C. If the Producer elects to terminate the performer's employment at any time after the commencement of the term of said freelance contract, the Producer shall be obligated to pay the performer such balance, if any, as is then unpaid for services theretofore rendered by the performer, and also one (1) week of compensation, upon the payment of which the Producer shall be discharged of and from all liability whatsoever thereunder, subject, however, to the provisions of paragraph 1 of the freelance contract and Sections 38 and 39 hereof.

D. In the event that a performer is replaced in the role, the performer, or performer's agent, shall be notified of this fact at the time of the replacement.

38. ILLNESS OF PERFORMER (SUSPENSION OF SALARY AND TERMINATION)

The Producer need pay no salary during any period that the performer is incapacitated, by illness or otherwise, from performing the required services under a freelance contract, and in the event of such illness or incapacity, the Producer, at its option, may terminate such employment without further liability.

39. EMERGENCY SUSPENSION OR TERMINATION

If the production of the photoplay specified in the freelance contract be necessarily prevented, suspended or postponed during the course of production, by reason of fire, accident, strike, riot, act of God or of the public enemy, or by any executive or judicial order, or postponed by reason of the illness of any other member of the cast or of the director, one-half (1/2) salary shall be paid the performer for the first three (3) weeks of prevention, suspension or postponement. It shall be the duty of the Producer during the first week of any prevention, suspension or postponement to notify the performer in writing whether the Producer will entirely discontinue the production or further suspend or postpone it and, in the latter event, the Producer shall pay the performer half salary during such further suspended or postponed period. At the end of three (3) weeks from the date on which the Producer has stopped production, the performer may terminate said employment if the performer so elects, unless the Producer continues thereafter to pay the performer full weekly compensation. If the production of said photoplay is prevented, suspended or postponed for any reason hereinabove in this Section provided, then and in that event, the Producer may terminate said employment at any time after the commencement of such prevention, suspension or postponement. If the Producer elects to terminate said employment by reason of the illness of any other member of the cast or of the director, then the Producer shall be obligated to pay the performer such balance, if any, as is then unpaid for services theretofore rendered by the performer, and also one (1) week of compensation, upon the payment of which the Producer shall be discharged of and from all liability whatsoever thereunder. If such termination be based on the happening of any other cause hereinabove in this Section set forth, then the Producer shall be obligated to pay the performer only such balance, if any, as is then unpaid for services theretofore performer and, upon the payment of such unpaid balance, if any, the Producer shall be discharged of and from all liability whatsoever thereunder.

When the production is suspended as a result of illness of another member of the cast or the director, and such suspension continues for five (5) days or more, the suspension may be effective as of the beginning of the event of illness, but if the duration is less than five (5) days, the suspension is not effective.

40. RESUMED PRODUCTION AFTER TERMINATION

If the Producer elects to terminate a performer's employment under a freelance contract pursuant to its right to do so for any cause hereinabove in Section 39 specified, and if, at any time more than three (3) weeks after such termination, the Producer shall desire to resume the production of said photoplay, the Producer shall notify the performer of its election to resume production and, in such event, the performer agrees to render his services in connection with such resumed production as and when the Producer may request, unless the performer is otherwise employed, but if otherwise employed, the performer will cooperate to the fullest extent in trying to make his services available for the Producer in connection with such resumed production. If production is resumed within six (6) months from the date of termination, the performer's compensation shall be at the same rate as that hereinabove specified and shall be payable only from the date of commencement of the performer's services in such resumed production.

* * *

SCHEDULE D

MULTIPLE PICTURE PERFORMERS RECEIVING $4,000 OR LESS PER WEEK AND GUARANTEED LESS THAN $28,500 PER TELEVISION PICTURE OR RECEIVING $4,500 OR LESS PER WEEK AND GUARANTEED LESS THAN $45,000 PER THEATRICAL PICTURE

1. DEFINITION

A multiple picture performer, for the purposes of this Schedule D, is a performer who is employed for two (2) or more pictures per year, whose contract with respect to services in the production of motion pictures is non-exclusive, and, in addition, (A) whose compensation for any television motion picture is at the rate of $4,000 or less per week or equivalent compensation on a picture or other basis, and who is guaranteed less than $28,500 per television picture; and (B) whose compensation for any theatrical motion picture is at the rate of $4,500 or less per week or equivalent compensation on a picture or other basis, and who is guaranteed less than $45,000 per theatrical picture. A multiple picture performer contract may be for a period of years, provided that the contract calls for at least two (2) pictures in any yearly period.

2. MINIMUM COMPENSATION

The minimum salary for a multiple picture performer shall be $1,813 per week for the period July 1, 1995 through June 30, 1996; $1,876 per week for period July 1, 1996 through June 30, 1997 and $1,942 per week for the period July 1, 1997 through June 30, 1998.

* * *

3. INCORPORATION OF SCHEDULE B – EXCEPTIONS

Reference is made to Schedule B of this Agreement; each of the provisions of Schedule B is incorporated in this Schedule except:

(1) Sections 1, 2, and 3:

(2) The requirement to designate the role, the photoplay, and the starting date: and

(3) Section 42, "Emergency Suspension or Termination," and Section 43, "Resumed Production after Termination," when the multiple picture performer is guaranteed $10,000 or more for his services in a photoplay.

* * *

SCHEDULE E

CONTRACT PERFORMERS WHOSE WEEKLY GUARANTEED SALARY IS $4,000 OR LESS PER WEEK FOR TELEVISION MOTION PICTURES OR WHOSE WEEKLY GUARANTEED SALARY IS $4,500 OR LESS PER WEEK FOR THEATRICAL MOTION PICTURES

1. DEFINITION

A contract performer is a performer employed under a contract for television motion pictures or theatrical motion pictures or both (in which latter case such contracts are sometimes referred to as "combination term contracts"), which contract is for a term of at least ten (10) out of thirteen (13) weeks and which may not specify any role, picture or series, unless otherwise requested by the performer and approved by the Union. The Union agrees it will liberally grant waivers in the event of such request. The Producer and the performer may agree on any overall term of hiring in excess of ten (10) guaranteed weeks, provided that the guaranteed number of weeks is in the same proportion to the overall period as "ten (10) out of thirteen (13)."

2. CLASSIFICATIONS OF CONTRACT PERFORMERS — TERM CONTRACT

A. When a performer is employed for two (2) or more pictures per year or other specified period (hereinafter referred to as the "employment period") and the contract is exclusive with respect to his services in the production of motion pictures, the performer shall be classified, for the purpose of this Agreement, as a "term contract performer" and his classification as a term contract performer with respect to "hours" shall be determined in accordance with the following formula:

The total guaranteed compensation of the performer shall be divided by the proportionate number of weeks in the employment period that forty (40) bears to fifty-two (52). For example: if the employment period is one year, the guaranteed compensation shall be divided by forty (40) weeks; if the employment period is six (6) months, the guaranteed compensation shall be divided by twenty (20) weeks, etc. If the resulting figure reflects a compensation of more than $4,000 per week for television motion pictures or more than $4,500 per week for theatrical motion pictures, the provisions of Schedule F shall apply to the employment. If the resulting figure is $4,000 per week or less for television motion pictures or $4,500 per week or less for theatrical motion pictures, the provisions of Schedule E shall apply to the employment.

When a performer who, under the above formula, has been classified so as to receive the provisions of Schedule E receives compensation in addition to his minimum guaranteed compensation, which additional compensation, when added to his total minimum guaranteed compensation and divided by the said proportionate number of weeks in the employment period, would raise the performer above the $4,000 breaking point for television motion pictures or above the $4,500 breaking point for theatrical motion pictures, then such performer, from that time forward, shall receive the provisions of Schedule F instead of Schedule E for the balance of the employment period in question. The so-called "breaking point" for a performer whose employment period is one (1) year shall be $100,000; for an employment period of six (6) months, $50,000; for an employment period of three (3) months, $25,000, etc.

B. The employment period of ten (10) out of thirteen (13) weeks may not be used in the same term contract except during the first year; thereafter, the contract shall guarantee a minimum period of employment of twenty (20) out of twenty-six (26) weeks. This subsection is subject to Section 12(c) of the 1995 Screen Actors Guild Television Agreement.

3. SCHEDULE E INCLUDED IN INDIVIDUAL CONTRACTS

It is agreed that the terms, conditions and exceptions of this Schedule shall become a part of the contract of a contract performer while he is receiving $4,000 or less per week for a television motion picture or is receiving $4,500 or less per week for a theatrical motion picture.

W-4 forms shall be presented to performer no later than the first day of employment. A W-4 form may be given to performer on the set on the first day of employment.

W-4 forms shall be available on every set. It shall be the performer's responsibility to return a completed W-4 form to Producer in a timely manner. It is understood that where a performer fails to do so, there shall be retroactive adjustments to the withholding required by law.

4. MINIMUM SALARY OF CONTRACT PERFORMERS

The minimum weekly salary for contract performers, other than "beginners," is as follows:

If performer is guaranteed ten (10) but no more than nineteen (19) weeks — $1,556.00 for the period July 1, 1995 through June 30, 1996; $1,610.00 for the period July 1, 1996 through June 30, 1997; and $1,666.00 for the period July 1, 1997 through June 30, 1998.

If performer is guaranteed twenty (20) or more weeks — $1,294.00 per week for the period July 1, 1995 through June 30, 1996; $1,339.00 for the period July 1, 1996 through June 30, 1997; and $1,386.00 for the period July 1, 1997 through June 30, 1998.

5. COMBINATION TERM CONTRACTS

A. Performer employed under a combination term contract and used in a television series in a continuing role:

    (1)   If a performer is used in a continuing role in a one-half (1/2) hour television series, he shall be adjusted for the duration of such services to the series contract salaries and applicable rerun, theatrical, Supplemental Market, basic cable and foreign telecast rates.

    (2)   If performer is used in a continuing role in a one (1) hour or one-and-one-half (1-1/2) hour television series, he shall be adjusted for the duration of such services to the weekly freelance salary rate and applicable rerun, theatrical, Supplemental Market, basic cable and foreign telecast rates, it being understood in this connection that such adjustment shall not result, with respect to his services in any episode in such series, in his receiving less than a week of freelance salary.

    (3)   If Producer uses the performer in a greater number of episodes than the number of weeks of employment guaranteed under this subsection A., or in a combination of this provision and subsection B. below, the performer shall be paid the weekly freelance salary and applicable rerun, theatrical, Supplemental Market, basic cable and foreign telecast rates for each additional episode in which his services are used. If the performer is employed beyond the guaranteed period of employment, he shall be paid an amount equal to the weekly freelance salary for each additional week or episode, whichever is the greater.

B. Performer employed under a combination term contract and used in a television episode, but not a continuing role:

    (1)   A term performer who is guaranteed a minimum of twenty (20) out of twenty-six (26) weeks, who works in a television episodes or episodes, but who does not have a continuing role in a series, shall not be used in more than fifteen (15) television episodes during such period. If he is used in more than fifteen (15) such episodes, he shall be paid an additional week of salary and applicable rerun, theatrical, Supplemental Market, basic cable and foreign telecast rates for each such additional episode.

    (2)   A term performer who is guaranteed a minimum of ten (10) out of thirteen (13) weeks, who works in a television episode or episodes but who does not have a continuing role in a series, if used in more than seven (7) such episodes, shall be paid an additional week of salary and applicable rerun, theatrical, Supplemental Market, basic cable and foreign telecast rates for each such additional episode.

(3)   If such performer is used beyond the guaranteed period of employment, he shall be paid an amount equal to his weekly salary for each additional week or episode, whichever is greater.

(4)   For all such term performers who do not appear in a continuing role, the applicable rerun, theatrical, Supplemental Market, basic cable and foreign telecast rates per episode shall be based on the applicable weekly rate.

C. Applicable television weekly freelance salary, series contract salary, rerun, theatrical, Supplemental, basic cable and foreign telecast rates referred to above are those rates provided by the applicable Screen Actors Guild Television Agreement in effect when such services were rendered in such television films.

D. When a term contract performer is assigned to regular employment in television and Producer avails himself of the layoff rights provided for term contract performers, Producer may not also exercise its hiatus rights provided in the collective bargaining agreement covering the employment of term contract performers in television.

E. A separate clause shall be inserted in all combination term contracts, specifying separate compensation for services, reruns, theatrical exhibition, Supplemental Market, basic cable use and foreign telecasting of television motion pictures for each contract term or option period.

F. No advance payments may be made for reruns or theatrical or foreign telecast rights nor may overscale salary be credited against any sums due the performer under the contract. As to term contracts in existence on February 1, 1960 providing for advances against reruns, no such advances may be applied against reruns, except reruns of episodes made within the contract period or option term during which such advances were made.

G. Other Conditions for Combination Term Contracts

(1) If a performer employed under a combination term contract performs, in any single employment week during such term, services in rehearsals or recordings or before the camera, in both a television motion picture film and a theatrical motion picture film hereunder, such performer shall receive, as additional compensation for such week, an amount not less than the applicable weekly term contract minimum.

(2) If a performer under a combination term contract renders services in any single employment week in principal photography in either a television motion picture or a theatrical motion picture and also renders services in such week in retakes, added scenes, sound track, process shots, transparencies, trick shots, trailers, changes or foreign versions of the photoplay (hereinafter referred to as "retakes, etc."), in the other field, such performer shall be paid, in addition to his weekly term contract salary, one-fifth (1/5) of the minimum term contract weekly rates for each day on which he renders services on such retakes, etc.

(3) If the performer renders services in any week in both a television motion picture and a theatrical motion picture, he shall be paid as in this subsection G. provided, even though he is also placed on layoff at any time during such week.

(4) If a performer who is on layoff is recalled for retakes, etc., in either television motion pictures or theatrical motion pictures, or both, he shall he paid one-fifth (1/5) of the minimum term contract weekly rates for each day in each field on which he renders such services.

(5) If a performer renders services in either a television motion picture or a theatrical motion picture in any week and also renders services in retakes, etc. in the same week in the other field, and is placed on layoff prior to the end of such week, he shall be paid, in addition to the weekly salary due, an amount equal to one-fifth (1/5) of the minimum term contract weekly rates for each day on which he renders services in such retakes, etc.

(6) When a performer employed under a combination term contract renders services in any week in both theatrical motion pictures and television motion pictures, for the purpose of determining whether Schedule E or Schedule F applies and making the computations therein, the performer's weekly salary for such week shall be deemed to be his aggregate weekly salary, as herein provided.

6. BEGINNERS

A. Definition

A "beginner" is defined as:

(1) A person under the age of thirty (30) with no professional experience as a performer prior to a date twelve (12) months before the commencement of the term of his employment and, for such person, chorus work or extra work, even though he was adjusted as an extra performer for speaking lines, shall not constitute professional experience as a performer; or

(2) A person thirty (30) years of age or over who has had no professional experience as a performer prior to the commencement of the term of his employment and, for such person, chorus work or extra work shall constitute professional experience as a performer.

For the purpose of the foregoing definitions, little theatre work shall not be considered to be professional experience as a performer.

(3) A person employed as a beginner under a term employment contract shall not, for the purpose of the minimum compensation provisions of this paragraph, continue to be a beginner under such

employment contract after the expiration of twelve (12) months from the commencement of the term of such employment contract. If a person has been employed as a beginner under a term employment contract, such person may not, after the expiration of twelve (12) months from the date of the commencement of the term of such employment contract, be again employed as a beginner by the same or any other Producer unless a waiver is obtained from the Union.

B. Minimum Salary

For the first six (6) months — $697.00 per week for the period July 1, 1995 through June 30, 1996; $721.00 per week for the period July 1, 1996 through June 30, 1997; and $746.00 per week for the period July 1, 1997 through June 30, 1998.

For the second six (6) months — $780.00 per week for the period July 1, 1995 through June 30, 1996; $807.00 per week for the period July 1, 1996 through June 30, 1997; and $835.00 per week for the period July 1, 1997 through June 30, 1998.

C. Employment in Television or Theatrical Pictures

A beginner used by Producer in a television motion picture shall be adjusted to the non-beginner's applicable term contract rates and adjustments, if any, herein provided, for the time he performs such services in such television motion picture and to the applicable rerun, theatrical and foreign telecast rates.

If Producer uses a beginner in a theatrical motion picture produced by Producer, or in which Producer has a financial interest, the performer shall remain a beginner.

D. Loan-outs

A beginner loaned-out to a television Producer for a television motion picture in which Producer has no financial interest shall he paid the television freelance rate during the time he performs such services and applicable rerun, theatrical and foreign telecast rates. When he returns to Producer, he returns as a beginner.

A beginner who is loaned-out to a television Producer for a television motion picture in which Producer has a financial interest shall be paid at the weekly rate specified in Section 4 of this Schedule for the time he performs such services and applicable rerun, theatrical and foreign telecast rates. When he returns to Producer, he returns as a beginner.

A beginner loaned-out for a theatrical motion picture remains a beginner during such services.

* * *

17. TESTS AND AUDITIONS

Tests and auditions before the employment of contract performers shall not be counted as work time for any purpose. Tests and auditions after the employment of contract performers shall be work time. Tests and auditions which occur during the consecutive layoff period of any contract performer shall be deemed to break such layoff period unless a waiver is obtained from the Union. Option test agreements are not to be construed as contracts to employ.

18. STUDY OF LINES OR SCRIPT

Study of lines or script, except during the period between reporting and dismissal shall not be counted as work time for any purpose.

19. STORY, SONG AND PRODUCTION CONFERENCES

Story, song and production conferences on any day on which the performer is not otherwise working shall not be counted as work time for any purpose, except that if the same occur at the request of the Producer during the consecutive layoff period of any contract performer, such layoff period shall be deemed broken thereby. The submission of a script to a contract performer, at the studio or elsewhere, during his layoff, shall not be deemed to break the same.

20. PUBLICITY INTERVIEWS

Publicity interviews held at a time mutually satisfactory to the performer and the Producer shall not be work time for any purpose unless held on a day on which the performer is otherwise working for the Producer. Such interviews for publicity purposes held on any day on which the performer is otherwise working for the Producer shall not be counted as work time if held after the performer's dismissal for the day, if such interview is held at a time mutually satisfactory to the performer and the Producer. If the interview is held during a meal period, it shall not be deemed to constitute a violation thereof.

Interviews for publicity purposes, including those held at the studio, shall not be deemed to break the layoff.

21. PUBLICITY STILLS

Services rendered by any performer covered by this Schedule in connection with publicity stills shall be work time, except where such services are rendered for a period not exceeding eight (8) hours on a day in which such performer is not otherwise working, in which case such services shall not be counted as work time for any purpose, except as provided in the next sentence. If a performer is on layoff and is called and reports for publicity stills, the same shall break the consecutive layoff and the day upon which the performer renders such services shall not be considered layoff.

22. RETAKES, ADDED SCENES AND CHANGES

Services rendered by a contract performer in retakes after completion of ordinary photography of the performer's role, and in added scenes and changes after the completion of the ordinary photography of the picture, when such services are rendered on the same day on which such performer works in a different picture, whether at the same or a different studio, shall not he counted as work time for the purpose of computing the overtime, if any, worked by such performer in excess of ten (10) hours during such day; but this provision shall not be applied by a Producer to the same contract performer with respect to more than three (3) days in any week or with respect to more than six (6) weeks in any year. Such services shall be counted as work time for the purpose of computing the overtime, if any, worked by such performer in excess of forty-eight (48) hours during the week in which such services are rendered, but to the extent that the weekly overtime for such week is caused by such services, it shall be computed on the basis of straight time instead of on the basis of time-and-one-half. Where the period intervening between the time of such performer's dismissal for the day in connection with the picture in which he is then currently employed and the time such performer is requested to and does report for retakes, added scenes or changes, as aforesaid, is two (2) hours or more, such intervening time shall not be counted as work time for any purpose. In special cases, the Union may, by waiver, give its consent to the application of the provisions of this Section to added scenes and changes made by contract performers after the completion of ordinary photography of the role and before the completion of ordinary photography of the picture.

The performer's contract shall not include guarantees for looping, retakes, added scenes, process transparencies, trick shots, trailers, changes or foreign versions (subject to availability) outside the period of consecutive employment.

23. TOURS AND PERSONAL APPEARANCES

A. If a performer agrees in his contract to make tours or personal appearances and he is simultaneously working in a picture, all hours spent in connection therewith shall be work time for all purposes.

B. As to all performers under this Schedule, if the performer is not working in a picture, he shall receive a day of pay at straight time for each day, including travel days, in which he is engaged in tours or personal appearances.

C. First-class transportation and reasonable expenses shall be paid to all performers on tours and personal appearances.

D. Producers shall cooperate to ensure that performers on tour and personal appearances are allowed adequate rest periods.

E. One personal appearance of any such performer requested by the Producer in connection with the opening of any picture in which such performer has performed, one rehearsal in connection therewith and any period immediately prior thereto which otherwise would not be work time, shall not be work time for any purpose. Personal appearances requested of any such performer by the Producer in connection with any benefit approved by the Theatre Authority, Inc., so long as the same has the sanction of the Union, or by any similar agency substituted therefor which at the time has the sanction of the Union, rehearsal in connection therewith and any period immediately prior thereto which otherwise would not be work time, shall not be work time for any purpose.

24. REHEARSAL TIME

A. The reading of lines, acting, singing or dancing, in preparation for the performer's performance, in the presence and under the supervision of a representative of Producer, constitutes a rehearsal. Rehearsals shall be counted as work time.

B. Auditions, tests, interviews, make-up and wardrobe tests do not constitute rehearsals.

C. The Union agrees to freely grant waivers the training of a performer in a particular skill such a horseback riding, fencing, etc. Compensation, if any, shall be agreed to between the performer and the Producer, subject to the approval of the Union.

D. Neither tests, auditions, fittings, publicity stills, pre-production stills, pre-recording nor training under subsection C. above, after employment but before the starting date of such employment, shall start the employment period of such performer. Compensation, if any, for any of such services shall be as otherwise provided in this Schedule.

Rehearsal shall not start the consecutive days of employment for a performer employed under this Schedule who is engaged for a long-form television motion picture or a theatrical motion picture, subject to the following:

(1) The performer must be paid for rehearsal at the same rate as photography (*pro rata* of the weekly salary, but not less than day performer minimum per day, when rehearsing for less than a week);

(2) The performer must be generally available for rehearsal, as distinguished from professionally available;

(3) The performer must be given an "on or about" start date; and

(4) Consecutive employment applies during the rehearsal period.

* * *

27. RIGHT TO NAME OR CHARACTER

No Producer shall, after the termination of the performer's employment, prevent such performer from continuing the use of any stage or screen name used by such performer. The name of a role owned or created by the Producer, such as Tarzan or Charlie Chan, belongs to the Producer and not to the performer.

28. "ACT OF GOD" CLAUSE — SUSPENSION OF PERFORMER

A. This Section shall only apply to "beginners" and to contract performers receiving no more than the minimum salaries provided herein.

B. The suspension period specified in the "Act of God" clause of a performer's individual contract shall be limited to four (4) weeks; however, Producer retains the right to continue such suspension, from week to week, for an additional period of eight (8) weeks, provided Producer pays to such performer one-half (1/2) salary for such additional period.

*   *   *

33. COMMERCIALS

A. All commercials shall be bargained for separately by the performer and Producer under the terms of the industry-wide Screen Actors Guild Commercials Contract in effect at the time of such bargaining.

B. Employment agreements in effect on July 1, 1995 shall be excluded from the foregoing provision and shall be governed by the Television Agreement in effect when such employment contract was entered into.

* * *

SCHEDULE F

CONTRACT PERFORMERS WHOSE WEEKLY SALARY IS IN EXCESS OF $4,000 PER WEEK FOR TELEVISION MOTION PICTURES OR IN EXCESS OF $4,500 PER WEEK FOR THEATRICAL MOTION PICTURES; MULTIPLE PICTURE PERFORMERS RECEIVING MORE THAN $4,000 PER WEEK OR WHO ARE GUARANTEED $28,500 OR MORE PER TELEVISION PICTURE OR RECEIVING MORE THAN $4,500 PER WEEK OR WHO ARE GUARANTEED $45,000 OR MORE PER THEATRICAL MOTION PICTURE; PERFORMERS EMPLOYED UNDER "DEAL CONTRACTS," OR OTHERWISE, WHO ARE GUARANTEED $28,500 OR MORE PER TELEVISION PICTURE OR WHO ARE GUARANTEED $45,000 OR MORE PER THEATRICAL MOTION PICTURE; PERFORMERS EMPLOYED IN MULTI-PART CLOSED-END PICTURES RECEIVING MORE THAN $4,000 PER WEEK AND WHO ARE GUARANTEED $34,000 OR MORE FOR THE MULTI-PART PICTURE

1. DEFINITIONS

A. Contract Performer

For the purpose of this Schedule F, a contract performer is a performer employed under a contract at a salary in excess of $4,000 per week for television motion pictures or in excess of $4,500 per week for theatrical motion pictures or both (in which latter case such contracts are sometimes referred to as "combination term contracts"), which contract is for a term of at least ten (10) out of thirteen (13) weeks and which may not specify any role, picture or series, unless otherwise requested by the performer and approved by the Union. The Union agrees it will liberally grant waivers in the event of such request. The Producer and the performer may agree on any overall term of hiring in excess of ten (10) guaranteed weeks, provided that the guaranteed number of weeks is in the same proportion to the overall period as "ten (10) out of thirteen (13)."

When a performer is employed for two (2) or more pictures per year or other specified period (hereinafter referred to as the "employment period") and the contract is exclusive with respect to his services in the production of motion pictures, the performer shall be classified, for the purposes of this Agreement, as a "contract performer" and his classification as a contract performer with respect to "hours" shall be determined in accordance with the following formula:

The total guaranteed compensation of the performer shall be divided by the proportionate number of weeks in the employment period that forty (40) bears to fifty-two (52). For example: If the employment period is one (1) year, the guaranteed compensation shall be divided by forty (40) weeks; if the employment period is six (6) months, the guaranteed compensation shall be divided by twenty (20) weeks, etc. If the resulting figure reflects a compensation of more than $4,000 per week for television motion pictures or more than $4,500 per week for theatrical motion pictures, the provisions of Schedule F shall apply to the employment. If the resulting figure is $4,000 or less per week for television motion pictures or $4,500 or less per week for theatrical motion pictures, the provisions of Schedule E shall apply to the employment.

When a performer who, under the above formula, has been classified so as to receive the provisions of Schedule E receives compensation in addition to his minimum guaranteed compensation, which additional compensation when added to his total minimum guaranteed compensation and divided by the said proportionate number of weeks in the employment period would raise the performer above the $4,000 breaking point for television motion pictures or above the $4,500 breaking point for theatrical motion pictures, then such performer, from that time forward, shall receive the provision of Schedule F instead of Schedule E for the balance of the employment period in question. The so-called "breaking point" for a performer whose employment period is one (1) year shall be $100,000; for an employment period of six (6) months, $50,000; for an employment period of three (3) months, $25,000, etc.

B. Multiple Picture Performer

A multiple picture performer, for the purpose of this Schedule F, is a performer who is employed for two (2) or more pictures per year, whose contract with respect to services in the production of motion pictures is non-exclusive, and in addition:

whose compensation for televison motion pictures is more than $4,000 per week or equivalent compensation on a picture or other basis, or who is guaranteed $28,500 or more per televison picture; or whose compensation for theatrical motion pictures is more than $4,500 per week or equivalent compensation on a picture or other basis, or who is guaranteed $45,000 or more per theatrical picture.

A multiple picture contract may be for a period of years, provided that the contract calls for at least two (2) pictures in any yearly period.

C. Deal Performer

A deal performer is a performer who is employed for one (1) or more pictures at a guaranteed salary of $28,500 or more per television or at a guaranteed salary of $45,000 or more per theatrical motion picture.

2. COMBINATION TERM CONTRACTS

A. Performer employed under a combination term contract and used in a television series in a continuing role:

(1) If a performer is used in a continuing role in a one-half (1/2) hour television series, he shall be adjusted, for the duration of such services, to the series contract salaries and applicable rerun, theatrical, Supplemental Market, basic cable and foreign telecast rates under the Television Agreement then in effect.

(2) If performer is used in a continuing role in a one (1) hour or one-and-one-half (1-1/2) hour television series, he shall be adjusted, for the duration of such services, to the weekly freelance salary rate and applicable rerun, theatrical, Supplemental Market, basic cable and foreign telecast rates, it being understood in this connection that such adjustment shall not result, with respect to his services in any episode in such series, in his receiving less than a week of freelance salary.

(3) If Producer uses the performer in a greater number of episodes than the number of weeks of employment guaranteed under this subsection A., or in a combination of this provision and subsection B. below, the performer shall be paid the weekly freelance salary and applicable rerun, theatrical, Supplemental Market, basic cable and foreign telecast rates for each additional episode in which his services are used. If the performer is employed beyond the guaranteed period of employment, he shall be paid an amount equal to the weekly freelance salary for each additional week or episode, whichever is the greater.

B. Performer employed under a combination term contract and used in a television episode but not in a continuing role:

(1) A term performer who is guaranteed a minimum of twenty (20) out of twenty-six (26) weeks, who works in a television episode or episodes, but who does not have a continuing role in a series, shall not be used in more than fifteen (15) television episodes during such period. If he is used in more than fifteen (15) such episodes, he shall be paid an additional week of salary and applicable rerun, theatrical, Supplemental Market, basic cable and foreign telecast rates for each such additional episode.

(2) A term performer who is guaranteed a minimum of ten (10) out of thirteen (13) weeks, who works in a television episode or episodes, but who does not have a continuing role in a series, if used in more than seven (7) such episodes, shall be paid an additional week of salary and applicable rerun, theatrical and foreign telecast rates for each such additional episode.

(3)   If such performer is used beyond the guaranteed period of employment, he shall be paid an amount equal to his weekly salary for each
additional week or episode, whichever is greater.

(4)   For all such term performers who do not appear in a continuing role,
the applicable rerun, theatrical, Supplemental Market, basic cable and
foreign telecast rates per episode shall be based on the applicable
weekly rate.

C. Applicable television weekly freelance, series contract, rerun, theatrical,
Supplemental Market, basic cable and foreign telecast rates referred to above
are those rates provided by the applicable Screen Actors Guild Television
Agreement in effect when such services were rendered in such television film.

D. Where a term contract performer is assigned to regular employment in
television and Producer avails himself of the layoff rights provided for term
contract performers, Producer may not also exercise its hiatus rights provided
in the television collective bargaining agreement covering the employment of
term contract performers in television.

E. A separate clause shall be inserted in all combination term contracts,
specifying separate compensation for services, reruns, theatrical exhibition,
Supplemental Market use, basic cable release and foreign telecasting of television
motion pictures for each contract term or option period.

F. No advance payments may be made for reruns or theatrical rights or foreign
telecast rights, nor may overscale salary be credited against any sums due the
performer under the contract. As to term contracts in existence on February 1,
1960 providing for advances against reruns, no such advances may be applied
against reruns except reruns of episodes made within the contract period or option
term during which such advances were made.

G. Other Conditions for Combination Term Contracts

(1) If a performer employed under a combination term contract performers,
in any single employment week during such term, services in rehearsals or
recordings or before the camera, in both a television motion picture film and
a theatrical motion picture film hereunder, such performer shall receive, as
additional compensation for such week, an amount not less than the applicable
weekly term contract minimum.

(2) If a performer under a combination term contract renders services in any
single employment week in principal photography in either a television motion
picture or a theatrical motion picture and also renders services in such week in
retakes, added scenes, sound track, process shots, transparencies, trick shots,
trailers, changes or foreign versions of the photoplay (hereinafter referred to as
"retakes, etc."), in the other field, such performer shall be paid, in addition to
his weekly term contract salary, one-fifth (1/5) of the minimum term contract
weekly rates for each day on which he renders services on such retakes, etc.

(3) If the performer renders services in any week in both a television motion picture and a theatrical motion picture, he shall be paid as in this subsection G. provided, even though he is also placed on layoff at any time during such week.

(4) If a performer who is on layoff is recalled for retakes, etc., in either television motion pictures or theatrical motion pictures, or both, he shall be paid one-fifth (1/5) of the minimum term contract weekly rates, for each day in each field on which he renders such services.

(5) If a performer renders services in either a television motion picture or a theatrical motion picture in any week and also renders services in retakes, etc., in the same week in the other field, and is placed on layoff prior to the end of such week, he shall be paid, in addition to the weekly salary due, an amount equal to one-fifth (1/5) of the minimum term contract weekly rates for each day on which he renders services in such retakes, etc.

(6) When a performer employed under a combination term contract renders services in any week in both theatrical motion pictures and television motion pictures, for the purpose of determining whether Schedule E or Schedule F applies, and making the computations therein, the performer's weekly salary for such week shall be deemed to be his aggregate weekly salary, as herein provided.

(7) If the performer received more than $4,200 per week for television motion pictures or more than $4,500 per week for theatrical motion pictures, he may agree to apply any sum he received in excess of $4,200 per week or $4,500 per week, respectively, toward such additional compensation provided in this subsection G.

* * *

13. TOURS AND PERSONAL APPEARANCES

A. As to all term contract performers under this Schedule F, if the performer is not working in a picture, he shall receive a day of pay at straight time for each day, including travel days, in which he is engaged in tours or personal appearances.

B. First-class transportation and reasonable expenses shall be paid to all performers on tours and personal appearances.

C. Producer shall cooperate to ensure that performers on tour and personal appearances are allowed adequate rest periods.

D. One personal appearance of any such performer requested by the Producer in connection with the opening of any picture in which such performer has performed, one rehearsal in connection therewith and any period immediately prior thereto which otherwise would not be work time, shall not be work time for any purpose. Personal appearances requested of any such performer by the Producer in connection with any benefit approved by the Theatre Authority, Inc., so long as the same has the sanction of the Union, or by any similar agency substituted therefor which at the time has the sanction of the Union, rehearsal in connection therewith and any period immediately prior thereto which otherwise would not be work time, shall not be work time for any purpose.

14. RIGHT TO NAME OR CHARACTER

No Producer shall, after the termination of the performer's employment, prevent such performer from continuing the use of any stage or screen name used by such performer. The name of a role owned or created by the Producer, such as Tarzan or Charlie Chan, belongs to the Producer and not to the performer.

* * *

19. COMMERCIALS

A. All commercials shall be bargained for separately by the performer and Producer under the terms of the industry-wide Screen Actors Guild Commercials Contract in effect at the time of such bargaining.

B. Employment agreements in effect on July 1, 1995 shall be excluded from the foregoing provision and shall be governed by the Television Agreement in effect when such employment contract was entered into.

* * *

21. APPLICABLE PROVISIONS OF SCHEDULE F INCLUDED IN INDIVIDUAL CONTRACTS

The respective provisions and exceptions of this Schedule shall become a part of the individual contract of the performer to whose classification such provisions and exceptions apply.

W-4 forms shall be presented to performer no later than the first day of employment. A W-4 form may be given to performer on the set on the first day of employment.

W-4 forms shall be available on every set. It shall be the performer's responsibility to return a completed W-4 form to Producer in a timely manner. It is understood that where a performer fails to do so, there shall be no retroactive adjustments to the withholding required by law.

22. REPLACEMENT OF PERFORMER

In the event that a performer is replaced in the role, the performer, or performer's agent, shall be notified of this fact at the time of the replacement.

23. INTERVIEWS AND AUDITIONS

A. A performer shall not be kept waiting for an interview or audition for more than one (1) hour after the time scheduled for the interview or audition. The type of interview or audition referred to is an interview or audition for a specific picture, not a general or get-acquainted type of interview. If the performer is more than five (5) minutes late, the above rule shall not be applicable. It is not the intent of this provision to limit the duration of the interview or audition itself. If a performer is detained for more than the permitted period, he shall be compensated for the excess time he is required to wait at his straight time hourly rate in one-half (1/2) hour units. If no salary has been agreed upon before the interview or audition, and if the performer and Producer cannot agree on the applicable salary, the salary rate at which such performer shall be compensated for such excess time shall be determined by conciliation and, if conciliation fails, by arbitration in accordance with the applicable provisions of the Basic Agreement. However, claims for violation of this subsection A. must be filed by the Screen Actors Guild not later than fifteen (15) days after the date of the alleged violation.

B. If parking space is not provided or readily available, Producer will validate or reimburse parking costs incurred by performers in connection with interviews.

C. The latest version of the script will be made accessible to the performer in the casting office twenty-four (24) hours in advance of a scheduled reading or immediately after the scheduling of the interview, whichever last occurs.

D. For scheduled interviews (other than general or get-acquainted type interviews) and auditions conducted and confirmed by the casting office (or, if Producer has no casting office, in the office of Producer's casting representative), sign-in sheets shall be required at the place where the performer is first directed to report. Copies of such sheets shall be kept by Producer for thirty (30) days and, during that time, such sheets will be made available to the Union upon request. The sign-in sheet shall indicate whether parking was provided.

Sign-in sheets for scheduled interviews and auditions shall include the following information: performer's name; social security number; name of role; performer's agent (if any); whether the interview or audition was videotaped; whether parking was provided; whether the script was available; actual calls; waiting time; and performer's initials.

E. A person authorized to effectively recommend selection shall be present at any second or subsequent interview/audition for a specific role.

F. If a performer who has been individually interviewed or auditioned for a specific role desires to have the videotape of such interview or audition erased, the Producer will do so upon written request of the performer. If two (2) or more performers are so interviewed or auditioned together on the same videotape, the Producer will erase such tape upon the written request of all such performers. In either case, the erasure will take place after completion of the casting process.

WRITERS GUILD OF AMERICA
1995 THEATRICAL AND TELEVISION
BASIC AGREEMENT

Form 3

WRITERS GUILD OF AMERICA *
1995 THEATRICAL AND TELEVISION BASIC AGREEMENT *

SYNOPSIS

---

* Reprinted with the permission of the Writers Guild of America and the Alliance of Motion Picture & Television Producers.

* Bracketed headings, supplied by the authors, do not appear in the original Agreement.

* * *

ARTICLE 1 — DEFINITIONS

The following terms or words used herein shall have the following meaning:

A. GENERAL

    1.   The term *"television motion picture"* (sometimes referred to in this Basic Agreement as "television film") means the entertainment portion of motion pictures, whether made on or by film, tape or otherwise and whether produced by means of motion picture cameras, electronic cameras or devices or any combination of the foregoing or any other means, methods or devices, now used or which may hereafter be

adopted for the recordation of motion pictures produced primarily for exhibition by free television. The preamble to this Basic Agreement and the provisions cited in the preamble determine the extent to which the provisions of the Basic Agreement which are applicable to television motion pictures are also applicable to pay television and basic cable.

2. The term *"theatrical motion picture"* means motion pictures and photoplays, whether made on or by film, tape or otherwise and whether produced by means of motion picture cameras, electronic cameras, or devices or any combination of the foregoing or any other means, methods or devices now used or which may be hereafter adopted for the recordation of motion pictures produced primarily for exhibition in a theater or similar location in which a fee or admission charge is paid by the viewing audience, for exhibition in another market covered by this Basic Agreement.

3. The term *"basic cable,"* as distinguished from pay television or free television, refers to that type of exhibition which is commonly understood in the industry today to be basic cable exhibition.

4. The terms *"pay television"* and "video disc/video cassette" are defined in Article 51 and in Appendix B of this Basic Agreement.

5. The term *"literary material"* shall be deemed to include stories, adaptations, treatments, original treatment, scenarios, continuities, teleplays, screenplays, dialogue, scripts, sketches, plot, outlines, narrative synopses, routines, and narrations, and, for use in the production of television film, formats.

6. The term *"radio rights"* means the right to broadcast by radio for aural reception only and unaccompanied by any recordation, transmission or broadcast intended for visual reception.

7. *"Week-to-week employment."* Employment of a writer on a week-to-week basis is employment which, except for such restriction as may herein elsewhere be contained, may be terminated by the Company or writer at any time.

8. The term *"public domain"* refers to literary material which is not subject to copyright protection in the United States.

9. A *"member of the Guild in good standing"* is defined as a member of the Guild who has tendered the initiation fee and periodic dues uniformly required as a condition of acquiring or retaining membership.

10. The term *"writer"* shall not be deemed to include any corporate or impersonal purveyor of literary material or rights therein.

11. Other than as provided in Article 14 hereof, this Basic Agreement shall not nor is it intended to cover the employment of Producers, Directors, Story Supervisors, Composers, Lyricist, or other persons employed in a *bona fide* non-writing capacity except to the extent that such employment consists of writing services covered under this Article 1, section B.1.(a)(2) or section C.1.(a), nor the employment of Story Analysts, at any time prior to the expiration of this Basic Agreement, in the synopsizing of literary material, as referred to in subparagraph 1(f) of the wage scales and working conditions of the current agreement between "Producer and I.A.T.S.E. & M.P.T.A.A.C. and Local #854 thereof."

12. It is understood that this Basic Agreement shall not, nor is it intended to, cover contracts for the purchase of literary material (a) which literary material at the time of purchase is published or exploited in any manner or by any medium whatever, or (b) with a person who is not a professional writer as defined in Article 1.B.1.b. or 1.C.1.b. hereof, whichever of said subparagraphs of Article 1 is applicable.

12.1 The term "*network*," as used in this Agreement, means ABC, CBS and NBC or any other entity which qualifies as a "network" under Section 73.662(f) of the rules of the Federal Communications Commission, unless the FCC determines that such entity is not a "network" for the purposes of such Section.

13. Other terms not expressly defined in this Basic Agreement are used in their present commonly understood meaning in the theatrical motion picture and television motion picture industry in the State of California.

* * *

B. THEATRICAL

1. Writer and Professional Writer

   a. A "*writer*" is a person who is:

   (1) employed by the Company to write literary material as defined herein, where the Company has the right by contract to direct the performance of personal services in writing or preparing such material or in making revisions, modifications or changes therein; or,

   (2) employed by Company, who performs services (at Company's direction or with its consent) in writing or preparing such literary material or making revisions, modifications, or changes in such literary material regardless of whether such

services are described or required in his/her contract of employment; provided, however, that any writing services described below performed by Producers, Directors, Story Supervisors (other than as provided in Article 14 hereof), Composers, Lyricist, or other employees, shall not be subject to this Basic Agreement and such services shall not constitute such person a writer hereunder:

(a)   Cutting for time

(b)   Bridging material necessitated by cutting for time

(c)   Changes in Technical or stage directions

(d)   Assignment of lines to other existing characters occasioned by cast changes

(e)   Changes necessary to obtain continuity acceptance or legal clearance

(f)   Casual minor adjustments in dialogue or narration made prior to or during the period of principal photography

(g)   Such changes in the course of production as are made necessary by unforeseen contingencies (e.g., the elements, accidents to performers, etc.)

(h)   Instructions, directions, or suggestions, whether oral or written, made to writer regarding story or screenplay

In addition to the foregoing in the case of a person who at the time he/she performs services has not received at least two (2) screen credits for story or screenplay or both, as determined pursuant to the Theatrical Schedule A of this Basic Agreement, or Schedule A of prior Theatrical Basic Agreements, within a period of ten (10) years (or has not received at least one (1) of such credits within a period of five (5) years) immediately prior to the rendition of such services, and who is employed solely in the capacity of the *bona fide* producer of a motion picture and whose employment does not include the requirement that he perform writing services, then, such person may, in addition to the above, perform the following writing services: make changes in dialogue, narration or action, but not including significant changes in plot, and such services by such person shall not be subject to this Basic Agreement. If such person does make significant changes in plot, story line or interrelationship of character, then such services by such person shall be subject to this Basic Agreement, except Article 6 hereof.

In addition to the foregoing, in the case of a person who at the time he/she performs services has received at least two (2) such screen credits within such ten-year period (and with at least one (1) of such credits within such five-year period) immediately prior to the rendition of the capacity of the *bona fide* producer of a motion picture, and whose employment does not include the requirement that he/she perform writing services, then, if such person shall perform writing services in addition to those described in (a) through (h) above, such services by such person shall be subject to this Basic Agreement.

In addition to the foregoing, in the case of a person who at the time he/she performs services is employed solely in the capacity of the director of a motion picture, and whose employment does not include the requirement that he/she perform writing services, then such person may, in addition to the above, perform the following writing services: make changes in dialogue, narration or action, but not including significant changes in plot, story line or interrelationship of characters, and such services by such person shall not be subject to this Basic Agreement.

If such person does make significant changes in plot, story line or interrelationship of characters, then such services by such person shall be subject to this Basic Agreement, except Article 6 hereof.

In any event, if any producer or director shall receive screen credit pursuant to the provisions of the Theatrical Schedule A and the Guild's credit rules relating to the writing contribution necessary for such credit, then the provisions of paragraph 9. of Article 6 hereof shall apply with respect to such person.

With respect to a person employed solely as a producer-director, on the motion pictures which he/she directs the director paragraph above shall apply and on the motion pictures which he/she does not direct, the producer paragraphs above shall apply.

As used above, "*producer*" shall also include the *bona fide* executive producer of said motion picture if such executive producer is of the same industry stature and has responsibilities and functions similar to those held or exercised by the following executive producers during 1977: Samuel Arkoff, Ron Miller and Marvin Mirisch.

With respect to signatory Companies, no services of any kind of any executive of the same industry stature and with responsibilities and functions similar to those held by or exercised by the following executives during 1977: Cardon Walker, Alan Ladd, Jr., John Calley, and Daniel Melnick, shall be covered by any provisions of this Basic Agreement, except that if any such executive shall receive screen credit pursuant to the provisions of the Theatrical Schedule A and the Guild's credit rules relating to the writing contribution necessary for such credit, then the provisions of paragraph 9. of Article 6 of this Basic Agreement shall apply with respect to such person.

b. The term *"professional writer"* means a person who on or after May 2, 1995, sells, licenses or options to a Company the ownership of or rights to use literary material written by such writer, for use in the production of a motion picture, which literary material had not prior to such sale or option been published or exploited in any manner or by any medium whatever, and who at such time:

(1) has received employment for a total of thirteen (13) weeks, which need not be consecutive, as a motion picture and/or television writer, or radio writer for dramatic programs; or

(2) has received credit on the screen as a writer for a television or theatrical motion picture; or

(3) has received credit for three (3) original stories or one (1) teleplay for a program one-half hour or more in length in the field of live television; or

(4) has received credit for three (3) radio scripts for dramatic radio programs one-half hour or more in length; or

(5) has received credit for one (1) professionally produced play on the legitimate stage, or one (1) published novel.

The Company may rely on the statement of the writer with respect to whether or not the material had therefore been published or otherwise exploited.

2. The term *"treatment"* means an adaptation of a story, book, play or other literary, dramatic or dramatico-musical material for motion picture purposes in a form suitable for use as the basis of a screenplay.

   The term *"original treatment"* means an original story written for motion picture purposes in a form suitable for use as the basis of a screenplay.

3. The term *"screenplay"* means the final script with individual scenes, full dialogue and camera setups.

4. The term *"first draft screenplay"* means a first complete draft of any script in continuity form, including full dialogue.

5. The term *"story"* means literary or dramatic material indicating the characterization of the principal characters and containing sequences and action suitable for use in, or representing a substantial contribution to, a final script.

6. The term *"shorts"* or *"short subjects,"* for the purposes of this Basic Agreement, are defined as motion pictures which when released are 3,600 lineal feet or less in length, other than motion pictures known as cartoons, newsreels, trailers, travelogues, commercials or news and sports commentaries and motion pictures intended primarily for exhibition by free television, if such motion pictures are originally made and originally distributed as such.

7. The term *"rewrite"* means the writing of significant changes in plot, story line, or interrelationship of characters in a screenplay. *"Polish,"* as used herein, means the writing of changes in dialogue, narration or action, but not including a rewrite.

8. Merchandising Rights - The term *"merchandising rights"* means the right to manufacture and to sell or otherwise dispose of any object or thing first described in literary material written by the writer pursuant to an employment agreement subject to this Basic Agreement, entered into on or after May 2, 1995, or acquired from a professional writer; provided such object or thing is fully described in such literary material and by such description appears to be unique and original. Merchandising rights include the right of publication in publications of the generic type described as "photo novels" or "photo albums."

   The writer shall have no merchandising rights. However, if the Company exploits the merchandising rights (as defined above) in any such literary material, Company shall pay to such writer an amount equal to five percent (5%) of absolute gross, that is, monies remitted by the manufacturer on account of the exploitation of the subject merchandising rights. The provisions of this subparagraph 8. are also applicable to a writer who is not entitled to Separation of Rights.

9. The term *"interactive rights"* means the right:

   a. to reuse a theatrical motion picture, in whole or in substantial part, in an interactive program, as provided in Article 64.B.1.;

   b. to utilize excerpts from a theatrical motion picture in an interactive program, as provided in Article 64.B.2.; and

   c. to produce an interactive program based upon literary material for a theatrical motion picture written by a writer pursuant to an employment agreement (to which employment the provisions of this Basic Agreement or any prior MBA containing a separation of rights provision applies) or acquired by the Company from a professional writer (to which acquisition the provision of this Basic Agreement or any prior MBA containing a separation of rights provision applies), which interactive program meets the requirements of Article 64.C.1.

   The writer shall have no interactive rights. However, if the interactive rights are licensed as provided in Article 64.B.1., B.2., C.1., D.1.a. or D.2.a., Company shall make payment to the writer in accordance with such provisions.

C. TELEVISION

1. Writer and Professional Writer

   a. A *"writer"* is a person who:

      (i) engaged by the Company to write literary material as defined herein (including making changes or revisions in literary material), where the Company has the right by contract to direct the performance of personal services in writing or preparing such material or in making revisions, modifications or changes therein; or

      (ii) engaged by Company who performs services (at Company's direction or with its consent) in writing or preparing such literary material or making revisions, modifications, or changes in such material regardless of whether such services are described or required in his/her contract of employment.

      A writer is a creative and professional person who performs a unique and indispensable function in relation to the production of motion pictures. It is an element of good faith, and part of the consideration of this Agreement, that no Company will use any of the following provisions of this paragraph with the purpose or intent of circumventing the employment of writers. Accordingly, it is agreed that the following services performed by an employee who is not employed as a writer shall not be subject to this Agreement and such services shall not constitute such a person a writer hereunder:

(a)   Cutting for time

(b)   Bridging material necessitated by cutting for time

(c)   Changes in technical or stage directions

(d)   Assignment of lines to other existing characters occasioned by cast changes

(e)   Changes necessary to obtain continuity acceptance or legal clearance

(f)   Casual minor adjustments in dialogue or narration made prior to or during the period of principal photography

(g)   Such changes in the course of production as are made necessary by unforeseen contingencies (e.g., the elements, accidents to performers, etc.)

(h)   Instructions, directions or suggestions, whether oral or written, made to a writer regarding story or teleplay

In addition to the foregoing, if a person is employed solely in the capacity of the *bona fide* executive producer or a producer of a specific television program and his/her employment agreement does not include the requirement that he/she perform writing services, and if said person has not been employed as a writer at least twice since June 1, 1966, and if said person nevertheless renders writing services (other than those specified in (a) through (h) above, then his/her employment as a writer shall be subject to this Basic Agreement, except that Article 6 and Article 14 of this Basic Agreement shall not be applicable if he/she performs no more than the following writing services on not more than three (3) programs in any one (1) production season (not more than one (1) of which may be a program in a mini-series, which for this purpose is a series of not more than eight episodes in the production season): changes in dialogue, narration or action, but not including significant changes in plot, story line or interrelationship of characters. If such person makes significant changes in plot, story line or interrelationship of characters, such person shall be subject to Articles 6 and 14 of this Basic Agreement.

In determining whether a person has been employed as a writer since June 1, 1966, for the purposes of this subparagraph, (I) each separate occasion, if any, for which he/she has declared earnings to the Guild for services as a writer performed on a particular theatrical motion picture or television project since June 1, 1966, and (ii) each occasion, if any, on which he/she has been listed as a participating writer in relation to a screen authorship credit determination pursuant to a collective bargaining with the Guild with respect to services performed as a writer since June 1, 1966, shall be conclusively counted as an employment as a writer. The exception provided for in this subparagraph shall not be valid in a particular case unless the Company obtains from the individual a warranty in writing that he/she has not been employed as a writer at least twice since June 1, 1966. If the Guild should question whether the exception applies, whether relating to employment by the Company or by another signatory, the Company shall cooperate in making available to the Guild any evidence in its possession or control which may be relevant to the inquiry. Said exception shall not apply to a writer if such writer has been previously employed as a writer also employed in additional capacities as provided in said Article 14.

With respect to signatory Companies, no services of any kind of any executive of the same industry stature and with responsibilities and functions similar to those held by or exercised by the following executives during the 1977-78 broadcast season: Larry White at Columbia Pictures Industries, Inc., Allan Shayne at Warner Bros. Inc., Sy Salkowitz at Twentieth Century-Fox Film Corp., and Ron Miller at Walt Disney Productions, shall be covered by any provisions of the Basic Agreement, except that if any such executive shall receive screen credit pursuant to the provisions of Television Schedule A and the Guild's credit rules relating to the writing contribution necessary for such credit, then the provisions of Article 6, paragraph 9. shall apply with respect to such person.

In addition to the foregoing, in the case of a person who at the time he/she performs services is employed solely in the capacity of the director of a specific television program, and whose employment does not include the requirement that he/she perform writing services, then, such person may, in addition to (a) through (h) above, perform the following writing services: make changes in dialogue, narration or action, but not including significant changes in plot, story line or interrelationship of characters, and such services by such person shall not be subject to this Basic Agreement. If such person does make significant changes in plot, story line or interrelationship of characters, then such services by such person shall be subject to this Basic Agreement, except Article 6 hereof.

In any event, if any director shall with respect to the particular program receive screen credit pursuant to the provisions of Schedule A and the Guild's credit rules relating to the writing contribution necessary for such credit, then the provisions of Article 6, paragraph 9. shall apply with respect to such person. A writer who renders services as a director on a particular episode shall be deemed to be a director as to such episode.

b.   A *"professional writer"* means any person who has (a) received employment for a total of thirteen (13) weeks as a television, motion picture or radio writer, or (b) has received credit on the screen as a writer for a television or theatrical motion picture, or (c) has received credit for three (3) original stories or one (1) teleplay for a program one-half hour or more in length in the field of live television, or (d) has received credit for three (3) radio scripts for radio programs one-half hour or more in length, or (e) has received credit for one (1) professionally produced play on the legitimate stage or one (1) published novel.

2.   The term *"teleplay"* means the final script with individual scenes, full dialogue or monologue (including narration in connection therewith), and camera setups if required; provided, however, that if the Company desires any script to consist in part of suggested or indicated dialogue (so that an actor portraying a role may extemporize therefrom) such suggested or indicated dialogue shall be deemed to satisfy the requirement of "full dialogue or monologue."

The term *"rewrite"* means the writing of significant changes in plot, story line or interrelationship of characters in a teleplay.

The term *"polish"* means the writing of changes in dialogue, narration or action, but not including a rewrite.

A *"back-up script"* is a story and/or teleplay for a proposed episodic series for which a writer is employed prior to the exploitation of the television sequel rights for such proposed series, other than a pilot script.

A *"pilot script"* is a story and/or teleplay intended to be used for the production of a pilot film for a proposed serial or episodic series and setting forth the framework intended to be repeated in the subsequent episodes, including the setting, theme and premise of the proposed serial or series and its central running characters. A story and/or teleplay may be a "pilot script" whether or not there is a separate format for the proposed serial or series and regardless of whether it is written for broadcast as a unit of a unit series or as a one-time program. The foregoing definition of pilot script also may apply to a story and /or teleplay intended to be used for the production of a pilot film for a proposed unit series which does not have central running characters, but which story and/or teleplay does set forth the context and continuing framework intended to be repeated in subsequent units. including the central premises, themes, setting (local, time, etc.), flavor, mood, style and attitude of the proposed unit series.

Nothing herein shall be construed to require that a pilot be produced for any such serial or series nor that a pilot script must be written for any such serial or series.

3. The term *"first draft teleplay"* means a first complete draft of any script in continuity form, including the full dialogue.

4. The term *"story"* means a story indicating the characterization of the principal characters and containing sequences and action suitable for use in or representing a substantial contribution to a final script; provided, however, that the writer shall not be obligated to insert dialogue therein (except to the extent necessary to show characterization) or to prepare the story in the form of a step outline.

5. A *"national radio network broadcast"* means a broadcast carried simultaneously by a station or stations in excess of the stations comprising a regional radio network. A *"regional radio network"* means a network maintained by a network company for regional coverage as distinguished from national or transcontinental coverage.

6. The term *"dramatic rights"* means the right of presentation in dramatic form on the speaking stage with living actors appearing and performing in the immediate presence of an audience, without any recordation, transmission, or broadcast thereof intended for aural or visual reception at places away from the place of performance; except that the dramatic rights shall include the right to broadcast directly by television such live presentation without any kinescope or other recording thereof, subject to restriction concerning the time when such broadcasts may be made as hereinafter provided.

7.   The term *"publication rights"* means the right to publication of the work in book form or in magazine or periodical form, including serial publication.

8.   *"Series sequel rights"* means the right to use the leading character or characters of a work participating in a substantially different story in an "episodic series" or "serial" type television program or radio program.

     "MOW sequel rights" means the right to use the leading character or characters of a work participating in a substantially different story in a program, ninety (90) minutes or longer, which is ordered subsequent to the broadcast of the "first MOW," as defined in Article 16.B.2.b., and is other than an exploitation of the "series sequel rights".

9.   The term *"single unit"* means a television program intended for broadcast as a single show, broadcast or program, and not as a part of a unit series or episodic series.

10. The term *"unit series"* means a series of programs each of which contains a separate complete story, without a character or characters common to each of the programs in the series but held together by the same title, trade name or mark of identifying device or personality common to all the programs in the series.

11. *"Episodic series"* means a series of programs each of which contains a separate complete story with a character or characters common to each of the programs in the series, provided, however, that such series shall still remain an episodic series even though a two-three-four-or five-multi-part story is utilized in the series.

     With regard to "literary material" for an "episodic series," extricable material shall consist of the plot of such material, and such original characters and characterizations which are distinctive and identifiable and which are the sole original creation of the writer, but shall not include the names of the characters.

12. The term *"serial"* means a series of programs in which generally the same characters carry on a continuing narrative.

13. The term *"established serial or episodic series"* means a serial or episodic series based upon material that has been published or exploited in any manner or by any medium whatsoever, or based upon a story in the public domain or owned by the Company.

14. **Merchandising Rights**

     a.   The term *"merchandising rights"* with regard to any established serial or episodic series, or any unit series or one-time television program to which separated rights do not apply, means the right to manufacture and to sell or otherwise dispose of any object or thing first described in literary material written by the writer, provided such object or thing is fully described therein and by such description appears to be unique and original.

b.   With regard to writers entitled to separation of rights, merchandising rights shall mean the exclusive right to grant to manufacturers or others the right to refer, in conjunction with the marketing or exploitation of objects or things, to the series in which the writer's separation of rights exists or to characters of such series, but such objects or things shall not include:

(1)   The television motion picture itself or any part of the television motion picture;

(2)   Music composed for or identified with such series or with any episode of such series, including any form of exploitation of music, such as records or publishing;

(3)   Objects or things furnished by a manufacturer or other person or company for use in or in connection with such series or any episode of such series, where the Company receives no revenue from the marketing of such objects or things (for example, a motorcycle manufacturer furnishes motorcycles to the Company for photography in a series dealing with motorcyclists in exchange for the right granted to the manufacturer to refer to the series or to characters of the series in conjunction with the marketing and exploitation of its motorcycles);

(4)   Objects or things manufactured or sold by any sponsor of such series, where the right to refer to such series or characters of such series in conjunction with the marketing of such objects or things is obtained by the sponsor as part of the initial agreement for the sponsorship of the series, and the Company receives no revenue from the marketing of such objects or things (as distinguished from the revenue received by the Company for the series itself); but the sponsor or sponsors of the series, as distinguished from the companies advertising in "spot" commercials;

(5)   Objects or things which, in the reasonable judgment of the Company, it would be harmful to the Company, network, sponsor or series to identify with such series or with characters of such series.

To effectuate the purposes of the foregoing provisions the writer shall, prior to granting any license hereunder, notify the Company in writing of the proposed license and the object or thing which is to be the subject of the license, at least ten (10) business days before granting the license, so as to give the Company the opportunity to give appropriate notice to the writer. If the Company notifies the writer that any proposes license is in violation of any of the foregoing provisions of this subparagraph 14., the Company shall concurrently send a copy of such notice to the Guild. Within one (1) business day after receipt of such notice the Guild may submit the dispute to arbitration, for which purpose the "quick arbitration" provisions of subparagraph 26. of Theatrical Schedule A shall be used (but for this purpose a special panel of arbitrators shall be selected by the parties as promptly as possible following the execution of this Agreement). With respect to subparagraph (5), the arbitrator's authority shall be limited to deciding whether the Company's judgment was reasonable. The reserved merchandising rights do not include the right to use or license the use of:

(i)   The name or likeness of any person;

(ii) Any proper name, trademark, service mark, trade name, or literary or artistic character (except public domain characters) existing and first exploited independently of such series.

The Company does not warrant or represent that it has or will have the right to use the title of the series or of any episode of the series in merchandising deals. In the event that a writer of a particular episode is entitled to a merchandising rights payment which would otherwise be due the writer entitled to separation of rights in the series. The definition of "merchandising rights" as it applies to writers entitled to separation of rights shall be without prejudice to the respective position of the parties hereto as to the meaning of the term in previous collective bargaining agreements.

14.1   The term *"interactive rights"* means the right:

a.   to reuse a television motion picture, in whole or in substantial part, in an interactive program, as provided in Article 64.B.1.;

b.   to utilize excerpts from a television motion picture in an interactive program, as provided in Article 64.B.2.; and

c.   to produce an interactive program based upon literary material for a television motion picture written by a writer pursuant to an employment agreement (to which employment the provisions of this Basic Agreement or any prior MBA containing a separation of rights provision applies) or acquired by the company from a professional writer (to which acquisition the provisions of this Basic Agreement or any prior MBA containing a separation of rights provision applies), which interactive program meets the requirements of Article 64.C.2., subject to the following:

(1)   When separation of rights does not apply to such literary material, but the writer(s) describes an object or thing or introduces a character as provided in Article 64.C.2.a. or b., such writer shall have no interactive rights. However, if the Company exploits the interactive rights as provided in Article 64.C.2., D.1.b. or D.2.b., Company shall make payment to such writer in accordance with such provisions.

(2)   The interactive rights described in this subparagraph c. are reserved to the writer(s) entitled to separation of rights pursuant to Article 16.B.3.a. (subject to Article 16.B.3.d. or e. and 16.B.5.)

With respect to subparagraphs a. and b. above, the writer shall have no interactive rights. However, if the Company exploits either of such rights as provided in Article 64.B., D.1.b. or D.2.b. (Subject to subparagraph c.(2) above), Company shall make payment to the write[r] in accordance with such provision.

15.   A *"routine"* means a self-contained dramatic unit constituting fifty percent (50%) or less of the entertainment portion of a comedy-variety program; provided that such routine is either (a) an adaptation of material previously used in television or any other medium; or (b) original and written to fit the special talents and personality of the particular actor or actors in the program involved.

16.   The term *"simulcast"* means the broadcast of a single performance of a program by radio and television, whether or not the radio and television broadcast are made at the same time, provided that the original broadcasts by radio and television take place within twenty-one (21) days of each other.

17.   Writers of *"variety and audience participation programs"* shall be deemed included under all the provisions of this Basic Agreement, to the same extent as writers of dramatic programs, despite the fact that only "story" and "teleplay" are hereinafter referred to.

18.   The term *"weekly unit of television films"* means the number of television films of a particular series of variety (including comedy-variety), quiz or audience participation programs prepared by the same writer or writers for initial broadcast within one (1) week.

19.   The term *"format"* means a written presentation consisting of the following:

   (a)   As to a serial or episodic series, such format sets forth the framework within which the central running characters will operate and which framework is intended to be repeated in each episode; the setting, theme, premise or general story line of the proposed serial or episodic series; and the central running characters which are distinct and identifiable, including detailed characterizations and the interplay of such characters. It also may include one or more suggested story lines for individual episodes.

   (b)   As to a multi-part series telling a complete story such as *"Rich Man, Poor Man"* (Book I) or *"Roots"* or a prime time serial, such as *"Executive Suite,"* such format as described in (a) above shall be called a *"bible"* if, in addition and at the request or upon the instructions of the Company, it contains all of the following characteristics and requirements:

      (i)   It is in much greater detail than a traditional format, and includes the context, framework, and central premises, themes and progression of the multi-part series or serial.

      (ii)   It sets forth a detailed overall story development for the multi-part series or for the first broadcast season of the serial (or such lesser period as may be contracted for with the writer) and includes detailed story lines for (A) all of the projected episodes of the multi-part series or (B) most of the projected episodes for the first broadcast season of the serial (or such lesser period as may be contracted for with the writer).

      (iii) The characters must be not only distinct and identifiable, but must be set forth with detailed descriptions and characterizations.

   (c)   Except as to minimum compensation and reversion pursuant to Article 16.B.2.a., a *"bible"* is a format for all other purposes of this Agreement, including but not limited to other applicable provisions of Article 16.B.

   (d)   As to a unit (anthology) series, a format means a written presentation consisting of the following: a detailed description of the concept of the proposed series: the context and continuing framework intended to be repeated in each episode; and the central premises, themes, setting (locale, time, etc.), flavor, mood, style and attitude of the proposed series; and it may include suggested story lines for several of the projected episodes.

20. The term *"narration"* means material used (typically off camera) to explain or relate sequences or action (excluding promos or trailers).

21. *Narrative Synopsis:* An outline of a story owned by a writer, which is prepared for the purpose of determining the suitability of the story for teleplay purposes, which outline shall indicate characters and plot line but need not be sufficiently developed to meet the definition of a story.

ARTICLE 2 — TERM AND EFFECTIVE DATE OF AGREEMENT

A. GENERAL

1. The term of this Basic Agreement shall commence on May 2, 1995, and shall continue to and include May 1, 1998.

2. With respect to all employment agreements with writers in effect on May 2, 1995, the terms of this Basic Agreement relating to minimum compensation and to rights in material shall apply only to services performed and literary material written under such employment contracts where the date of actual employment (i.e., the commitment date) was on or after May 2, 1995, except as specifically otherwise provided herein in Article 2, section B. or Section C.

3. With respect to literary material acquired from professional writers (as described herein) the terms of this Basic Agreement relating to minimum compensation and rights in material acquired from such professional writers on or after May 2, 1995.

4. Company or Guild may by written notice to the other served not earlier than ninety (90) days, nor later than sixty (60) days, prior to the expiration date of this Basic Agreement signify its desire to negotiate a new collective bargaining agreement which shall become effective upon a date determined by mutual agreement between the Company and the Guild. Such notice shall set forth in detail the proposals or recommendations of the party serving such notice. If such notice is served, the parties hereto agree to commence negotiations covering the proposals or recommendations set forth therein, and the proposals and recommendations of the party receiving such notice, within thirty (30) days after the receipt of such notice and to continue such negotiations diligently and in good faith, it being understood and agreed that the existing Basic Agreement shall continue in full force and effect until the termination date above provided.

5. For the second year of this Basic Agreement (May 2, 1996 to and including May 1, 1997), there are increases of three percent (3%) in the network prime time rates, four percent (4%) in the rates for breakdowns for non-prime time serials and three and one-half percent

(3.5%) in the rates for the provisions set forth in Paragraph 2.d. of the 1995 WGA-Network Memorandum of Agreement, because the Trustees of the Health fund determined that no additional contribution was needed to maintain the level of benefits existing on May 1. For the third year of this Basic Agreement (May 2, 1997 to and including May 1, 1998), there are increases of three percent (3%) in the network prime time rates, four and one-half percent (4.5%) in the rates for breakdowns for non-prime time serials, and three and one-half percent (3.5%) in the rates for the provisions set forth in paragraph 2.d. of the 1995 WGA-Network Memorandum of Agreement, because the Trustees of the Health Fund determined that no additional contribution was needed to maintain the level of benefits existing on May 1, 1995.

6. [Appeared as Article 2.A.5. in predecessor Basic Agreements.] Nothing herein contained shall be deemed to modify or affect the terms or conditions of any existing contract which are more favorable to the writer than the terms and conditions of this Basic Agreement.

B. THEATRICAL

1. With respect to all theatrical employment agreements with writers under term or deal contracts which were in effect on May 2, 1995, the new minimum compensations, conditions and Theatrical Schedule A as herein contained shall not in any manner be applicable for the period prior to, nor effective until:

    (a) in the case of a term contract, the effective date of the exercise of the next option which occurs after May 2, 1995, for the renewal of the employment period, or six (6) months after the effective date of the commencement of the current employment period, whichever occurs first, but in no event prior to May 2, 1995.

    (b) in the case of a deal contract, the effective date of the next step of such a deal contract which commences after May 2, 1995.

2. Any contractual obligation by Company, in effect on December 12, 1966, to give credit for source material or story, in connection with a photoplay, shall not in any manner be affected by the provisions of the Theatrical Schedule A contained herein.

C. TELEVISION

1. With respect to television employment agreements with writers on a term or week-to-week contract basis in effect on May 2, 1995, the terms of this Basic Agreement relating to rights in material shall apply only to literary material written pursuant to assignments made on or after May 2, 1995.

2. Notwithstanding any other provisions of this Article, the terms of this Basic Agreement relating to rights in material shall not apply to literary material written pursuant to any agreement in effect on May 2, 1995, if the granting or reserving of such rights, as herein provided, would conflict with any contractual obligation of the Company to any third party entered into prior to the effective date of this Basic Agreement; provided that the Company does not have a right to require the removal or elimination of the conflict created by such contractual obligation to the third party.

ARTICLE 3 — WORK LISTS, LOAN-OUTS AND RECOGNITION

A. GENERAL

* * *

2. Loan-Out Agreements

In the event the Company borrows the services of a writer from a loan-out company, then the Company shall not acquire such writer's services on terms less advantageous to the loan-out company than if the Company had employed an individual to write the material pursuant to the terms of this basic agreement.

Borrowing a writer's services through a loan-out company will not in any manner deprive the writer of any benefits of this Agreement to which the writer would have been entitled had he/she been employed directly by the Company, provided that the Company (as distinguished from the loan-out company) shall be responsible for such benefits only to the extent that they are within the control of the Company. Such benefits to which the writer is entitled from the Company shall include but not be limited to credits, compensation for television licensing of theatrical motion pictures, residuals with respect to television motion pictures, residuals with respect to television motion pictures, and separation of rights, if applicable.

With respect to compensation, and other payments which may be due under this Basic Agreement, the Company shall pay the loan-out company or the writer at least minimum, but is not responsible for payment by the loan-out company to the writer. With respect to grievance and arbitration, claims by the loan-out company against the Company for unpaid compensation for writing services under the loan-out agreement shall be subject to grievance and arbitration to the same extent as though the transaction had been an employment contract. With respect to pension and health, the agreement between the Company and the loan-out company shall provide that the Company shall make pension and health contributions directly to the Plans on behalf of the loan-out company. In no event shall the Company be obligated to make larger contributions than it would have been obligated to make had it employed the borrowed writer directly. *"Loan-out company,"* for the purposes of the foregoing and for the purposes of Article 12 of this Basic Agreement, means a company controlled by the writer.

B. RECOGNITION (THEATRICAL)

1. The Company hereby recognizes the Guild as the exclusive representative for the purposes of collective bargaining for all writers in the motion picture industry.

2. The provisions of this Basic Agreement (other than the provisions of Article 6, Guild Shop; Article 17, Pension Plan and Health Fund) to the extent the same are applicable, shall apply to professional writers. The Company each week shall send the Guild a list of the names of the writers, professional and non-professional, from whom the Company acquired literary material which had not been previously published or exploited in any manner or by any medium, provided that failure on the part of the Company to furnish any such list shall not constitute a default by the Company or a breach of this Basic Agreement unless the Company fails to deliver such list within forty-eight (48) hours after receiving the Guild's written request to do so.

C. RECOGNITION (TELEVISION)

1. The Company hereby recognizes the Guild as the exclusive representative for the purposes of collective bargaining of all writers engaged by the Company as employees for the purpose of preparing literary material for the entertainment portion of motion pictures produced primarily for exhibition over television.

2. If a professional writer sells or licenses to the Company the ownership of or rights to use literary material written by such writer, for use in the production of a television film, then upon condition that such literary material had not prior to such sale or license been published or exploited in any manner or by any medium whatsoever, Company agrees that the provisions of this Basic Agreement (other than the provisions of Article 6 and Article 17) to the extent the same are applicable, shall be effective to determine the rights of such professional writer and the obligations of the Company with respect to such literary material. The Company may rely on the statement of the writer with respect to whether or not the material had theretofore been published or otherwise exploited. The Company each week shall send

the Guild a list of the names of the writers from whom the Company acquired literary material which had not been previously published or exploited in any manner or by any medium, provided that failure on the part of the Company to furnish any such list shall not constitute a default by the Company or a breach of this Basic Agreement unless the Company fails to deliver such list within forty-eight (48) hours after receiving from the Guild a written request to do so.

ARTICLE 4 — PARTIES BOUND BY THIS BASIC AGREEMENT

A. GENERAL

1. With regard to a partnership signatory, all general partners are personally bound.

2. With regard to any entity which becomes bound by this Basic Agreement by reason of this section, said entity will upon request of the Guild execute necessary documentation, but will be deemed signatory even without doing so.

3. With respect to a theatrical or television motion picture covered hereunder which is financed fifty percent (50%) or more by the Company (or fifty percent (50%) or more owned subsidiary of the Company), Company will obtain a warranty from the actual employer or purchaser that writer was paid all compensation for writing services theretofore due. Upon request of the Guild, Company will provide the Guild with a certified copy of such warranty provision.

4. In the event the Company borrows a writer (whose employment had he/she been employed directly by the Company would have been covered by this Basic Agreement), whether from a domestic or foreign company, the Company shall, within ten (10) days after the execution of the agreement covering the loan-out transaction, give the Guild a written notice of the transaction, including the name of the lending company. An inadvertent failure by the Company to give such notice shall not be deemed to be a breech of this Basic Agreement.

B. THEATRICAL

1. This Basic Agreement shall be binding upon the Company and its subsidiaries in which it has a fifty percent (50%) or more financial interest and all parties who by reason of mergers, consolidations, reorganizations, sale, assignment or the like shall succeed to or become entitled to a substantial part of the business of a signatory.

2. With respect to a motion picture produced by an independent producer under a contract with the Company for the financing and distribution of such motion picture, if Company gives the Guild notice within ten

(10) days following agreement between Company and independent producer with respect to such contract that such motion picture is not covered by this Basic Agreement, then Company shall not be obligated with respect to such picture except as otherwise provided in Article 15. If the Company does not give the Guild such notice, then Company shall be obligated under this Basic Agreement (and no other collective bargaining agreement with the Guild shall be applicable) with respect to such motion picture. The provisions of this subparagraph 2. apply only to (i) a writer whose employment, had he/she been employed directly by Company in connection with such motion picture, would have been covered by this Basic Agreement; and (ii) a professional writer where the sale, license or option of the literary material involved, had it been made directly to Company in connection with the motion picture involved, would have been covered by this Basic Agreement.

3.   Company agrees to notify the Guild within seven (7) days after it executes an agreement with any person, firm or corporation (not covered by the provisions of the preceding subparagraphs 1. and 2. of this Article), for the use of its studio for the production of a theatrical motion picture. Company further agrees to notify the Guild within fourteen (14) days after it executes an agreement in the County of Los Angeles, California, with any person, firm or corporation (not covered by the provisions of the preceding subparagraphs 1. and 2. of this Article) for the production, distribution or release of a theatrical motion picture where Company's studio is not used for the production of such picture; such notice to the Guild shall contain the name and address of such person, firm or corporation as well as the name of the person who signed the agreement on behalf of such person, firm or corporation. An inadvertent failure on the part of the Company to comply with the provisions of this paragraph shall in no event constitute a default by the Company or a breach of this Basic Agreement.

C.   TELEVISION

1.   Company agrees to cause any subsidiary company, owned or controlled by it, which shall hereafter engage in the production of television motion pictures, to become a signatory to this Basic Agreement prior to its employment of any writer employed to prepare any material for use in such motion pictures.

2.   With respect to a television motion picture produced by a non-signatory independent producer under a contract with Company for the financing, production and distribution of such television motion

picture, if Company gives the Guild written notice not later than ten (10) days following agreement between Company and independent producer with respect to such contract that this motion picture is not to be covered by this Basic Agreement, then Company shall not be obligated hereunder with respect to it.

a.   If Company does not give the Guild such notice, then Company shall be obligated hereunder with respect to such television motion picture.

b.   This provision is subject to Article 5., "Geographical Application."

ARTICLE 5 — GEOGRAPHICAL APPLICATION OF THIS BASIC AGREEMENT (GENERAL)

Notwithstanding anything to the contrary contained herein, this Basic Agreement shall apply to writers only in the specific instances set forth below regardless of where the contract of employment or acquisition, as the case may be, is signed:

1.   As to a writer or professional writer who lives in the United States, if a deal is made in the United States to employ such writer to render his/her services or if an acquisition deal is made in the United States with such professional writer, and if at the time such deal is made such writer or professional writer is present in the United States, regardless of where the services are rendered; provided further, however, that if such writer or professional writer is a permanent resident of the United States but is temporarily abroad, and if the deal is made by his/her agent, attorney or other representative (including the Guild acting on the writer's behalf) who is in the United States at the time the deal is made, such deal shall be within the scope and coverage of this subparagraph 1., even if such deal is made by such representative in communication by telephone, mail or cable with a representative of the Company, whether such deal is made by representative in communication by telephone, mail or cable with a representative of the Company, whether such representative of the Company is in the United States or abroad.

2.   As to a writer or professional writer who lives in the United States and is transported abroad by Company, if a deal is made to employ such writer to render his/her services or if an acquisition deal is made with such professional writer while the writer or professional writer is abroad as a result of being so transported.

3.   As to an employee whose writing services are required or requested by the Company to be performed and are performed in the United States under the supervision and direction of the Company.

4. "A writer or professional writer who lives in the United States," as such phrase is used in subparagraphs 1. and 2. above, does not include either of the following:

    a. A person who lives outside the United States (other than for a temporary visit) even though he/she may at any given time be temporarily in the United States; or

    b. A person who lives outside of the United States (other than for a temporary visit) whether or not he/she has retained his/her domicile in the United States.

5. A "deal is made" within the meaning of both subparagraphs 1. and 2. above when agreement is reached by the Company and the writer as to the money terms.

ARTICLE 6 — GUILD SHOP (GENERAL)

1. Except as provided below, in both theatrical and television motion pictures each writer employed by Company on the effective date of this Basic Agreement who is then a member of the Guild in good standing shall remain a member in good standing, and each writer so employed who is not a member shall, on or before the thirtieth day following the effective date of this Basic Agreement, become and remain a member of the Guild in good standing. Each writer employed hereunder by Company after the effective date of this Basic Agreement shall not later than the thirtieth day following the beginning of his/her first employment, as hereinafter defined, in the motion picture and television industry, become and remain a member of the Guild in good standing.

    The term *"first employment"* as referred to above shall mean the first such employment to which the provisions of this Basic Agreement apply as a writer for a motion picture by an employer in the motion picture and television industry, on or after the effective date of this Basic Agreement.

2. The provisions of subparagraph 1. of this Article 6 shall not apply:

    a. If a writer is not a member of the Guild at the time of his/her employment and although required by the provisions of his/her employment agreement to do so, fails or refuses to become a member of the Guild in good standing within the thirty (30) days above-mentioned, provided that within fifteen (15) days after written notice thereof from the Guild to the Company, the Company shall either terminate such employment or shall pay or cause to be paid the initiation fees and dues of the writer in the manner, within the time, and subject to the provisions of subparagraph 5.b. hereof relating to the payment of dues. If the Company elects to and does pay such initiation fees and dues, such writer shall be deemed to be a member of the Guild in good standing, but only for the period necessary to permit him/her to complete the performance of his/her services in connection with the then current assignment. The Company may use this exception only once for any particular person.

b. To a writer whom the Company is required to employ as a condition of the sale, license or option of material, provided that within fifteen (15) days after written notice from the Guild to the Company that such writer is not a member of the Guild in good standing, the Company shall either terminate such employment, or shall pay or cause to be paid the initiation fees and dues that the writer would otherwise be required to pay hereunder during such employment, in the manner, within the time, and subject to the provisions of subparagraph 5.b. hereof relating to the payment of dues. However, the writers employed by the Company within the exception provided for in this subparagraph b. shall not exceed ten percent (10%) of the total number of writers in the employ of the Company. For the purpose of such computation, if the Company has in its employ at any time less than ten (10) writers, then one (1) of such writers so employed may fall within this exception. Promptly following the employment of any writer claimed by the Company to be within this exception, the Company will notify the Guild in writing of the name of the writer employed, the date of the employment agreement and the fact that the Company claims that such writer is an exception hereunder. For the purpose of such computation, a writer who is employed under an exclusive contract by a Company shall be regarded as being employed by the Company at all times during the term of such contract, including periods during which the writer may be on layoff and periods during which such contract may be suspended by reason of illness or default of the writer or otherwise. The writer shall be regarded as continuing in the employ of the Company by which he/she is employed regardless of the fact that his/her services may be loaned to another Company.

3. The term "dues," as used herein, shall not include fines or initiation fees.

4. Promptly after request by any person designated by the Company, the Guild will admit such person to membership in the Guild upon terms and conditions not more burdensome to such person than those then

applicable to other applicants. Membership shall be effective as of the date of such request. Guild agrees that during the term it will not impose any unreasonable initiation fee as a condition to admission to membership, and agrees that during the term hereof it will not impose upon its members any obligation to pay dues that does not uniformly apply to all members of the Guild.

It is agreed that the Guild shall not close its membership books or otherwise prevent any person who wishes to become or remain a writer from becoming a member of the Guild, but on the contrary (subject to the provisions hereof relating to waivers as to members suspended or expelled) will make available the privileges of membership to any and all writers employed by the Company. The Guild will reinstate or readmit to membership any writer who applies for reinstatement or readmission, after being declared to be not in good standing or after suspension, expulsion, or resignation for any reason whatsoever, provided the writer will apply for such reinstatement or readmission and with such application tender to the Guild unpaid dues permitted by law, and upon such tender the Company may employ or continue to employ such writer. Instead of readmitting or reinstating such writer, the Guild may, at its option, grant to the Company a waiver as to such writer, in which event, for the purpose of determining the Company's compliance with the provisions of this Article 6, such writers shall not be considered as being employed by the Company.

5. If, during any time that a writer is employed by the Company under a contract of employment, such writer is or becomes a member of the Guild in good standing and if such writer shall subsequently and before his/her employment under such contract terminates, cease to be a member of the Guild in good standing then:

   a. If such writer has ceased or shall cease to be a member for any reason other than his/her failure to pay dues, such writer shall, for the purposes of this Basic Agreement, be deemed to remain a member of the Guild in good standing throughout the writer's employment under said contract of employment as the same may be extended or renewed pursuant to any provisions or options therein contained.

   b. It he/she has ceased or shall cease to be a member in good standing by reason of his/her failure *to* pay dues, and if the Guild gives the Company written notice of that fact within three (3) business days after such writer is first named on the weekly list provided for in Article 3.A. 1. of this Basic Agreement (in the case in which he/she has ceased to be a member in good standing prior to such employment), such writer shall, for the purposes of this Basic Agreement, be deemed to remain a member in good standing for a period of fifteen (15) days after written notice that he/she has ceased to be a member in good standing for failure to pay dues, from the Guild to such writer and to the Company, and if, prior to the expiration of said fifteen (15) day period, payment of said dues in fact due and owing and specified in said notice shall be made by the writer or the Company, then, for the purposes of this Basic Agreement, such writer shalt not lose his/her status as a member in good standing. To the extent that it may be lawful for the Company to do so, the Company may require, as a condition of employment, that any writer become and/or remain a member of the Guild in good standing, and may also require such written consent or consents as may be necessary so that, if the Company elects, it may pay to the Guild any dues of any writer and the Company shall have the right, insofar as its obligations to the Guild and to any writer under the terms and provisions of this Basic Agreement are concerned, if it elects, to deduct the amount of such dues from any compensation then or thereafter due or to become due to the writer. If, prior to the expiration of said fifteen (15) day period, payment of said dues in fact due and owing as specified in said notice shall not be made, the Company shall terminate the employment of such writer.

Every personal service contract of employment shall provide that if the writer fails or refuses to become or remain a member of the Guild in good standing, as above provided, the Company shall have the right at any time thereafter to terminate such employment agreement with such writer.

If the Company is required or directed by any decision of a court of competent jurisdiction or any proper governmental authority to refund to any writer, in whatsoever form the same may be recovered, any dues deducted and paid to the Guild by the Company under the provisions of subparagraph b. of this paragraph 5., the Guild agrees to repay to the Company the amount of such dues so refunded. The Guild will cooperate with the Company in obtaining the necessary authorizations from writers for the payment and deduction of dues in the manner provided in subparagraph b. above.

Notwithstanding anything to the contrary in paragraph 2. of this Article 6 or in this paragraph 5., if the payment of initiation fees or dues (in the case of paragraph 2.), or if the payment of dues (in the case of this paragraph 5.), or the deduction thereof from the compensation of the writer, is or shall become contrary to law, or any statute, or is declared by any court of competent jurisdiction in the State of

California or by any Federal Court or the National Labor Relations Board or its General Counsel, or by any other board or individual having jurisdiction over the matter, to be in violation of any applicable law or statute and if by reason thereof the Company fails to deduct and pay to the Guild such initiation fees or dues, as the case may be, as aforesaid, and shall notify the Guild thereof in writing within the fifteen (15) days after any notice from the Guild above-mentioned then although such initiation fees or dues, as the case may be, are not paid within the fifteen (15) day period, for the purposes of this Basic Agreement such writer shall, nevertheless, be deemed to remain a member of the Guild in good standing throughout the term of the writer's assignment.

6.   The Guild will facilitate employment of its members by the Company and will at all reasonable times promptly furnish to the Company in writing information concerning the status of any of its members, and the Company shalt be entitled to rely upon such information so furnished by the Guild.

7.   The Guild represents and warrants that discipline, resignation, admission, reinstatement readmission and all other matters relating to membership status will at all times during the term hereof be within the exclusive jurisdiction of the Guild; and the Guild agrees that it will exercise such jurisdiction subject to and in accordance with the provisions and intent of this Article 6 and of any other applicable provisions of this Basic Agreement.

8.   It is understood that the provisions of this Article 6 shall never under any circumstances be so construed during the term of this Basic Agreement as to constitute or permit what is known as a "closed shop" or construed in any manner that will at any time deprive the Company of its right to employ or continue the employment of a writer who is not a member of the Guild in good standing, or who does not become a member of the Guild in good standing within the period prescribed in subparagraph 1. of this Article 6 if the Company has reasonable grounds for believing that such a membership was not available to such writer on the same terms and conditions generally applicable to other like members of the Guild, or if the Company has reasonable grounds for believing that membership in the Guild was denied, deferred, suspended or terminated for reasons other than the failure of such person to tender the applicable periodic dues uniformly required as a condition for acquiring or retaining membership in the Guild.

9.   If a person who has not been listed by the Company as a writer in accordance with the provisions of Article 3 hereof shall receive, or

shall have been entitled to receive, a writing credit in the form of "Story by," "Written by," "Screenplay by," or "Teleplay by," and if the period during which the person performed his services in the writing of the literary material has exceeded a period of thirty (30) days from the commencement of such services, then within fifteen (15) days after receipt of written notice from the Guild to the Company, the writer or the Company shall pay or cause to be paid the initiation fee, if any, and the dues which otherwise would have been payable to the Guild and such person shall be deemed to have been a member of the Guild in good standing during the time that he/she was so performing his/her services as a writer. For such purpose, the person receiving or entitled to such credit or the Company may apportion on a reasonable basis, salary payable to such person during the period he/she was employed as a writer.

10. When the Company has failed to include a writer employed by the Company on the list of names of writers to be sent to the Guild under Article 3 of this Basic Agreement and when such writer's performance of writer's services has continued for more than thirty (30) days after the beginning of his/her first employment, then within fifteen (15) days after receipt of written notice thereof from the Guild to the Company, the writer or the Company shall pay or cause to be paid (in the manner, within the time, and subject to the provisions of subparagraph 5.b. hereof, relating to the payment of dues) the initiation fee, if any, and the dues payable to the Guild for the period during which such writer was employed by the Company after such thirty (30) day period. Upon such payment, such writer shall be deemed to have been a member of the Guild in good standing during the time that he/she was so performing his/her services as a writer. The provisions of this paragraph shall not apply in the event the Guild gives the Company such notice prior to the expiration of such period of thirty (30) days.

11. In relation to investigations by the Guild of compliance with the provisions of this Agreement, the Guild through its authorized representatives shall have access to the Company's premises at reasonable times during normal business hours for the purpose Agreement, provided that such interviews shall not interfere with the normal conduct of the Company's business.

* * *

ARTICLE 8 — CREDITS FOR SCREEN AUTHORSHIP (GENERAL)

The Company agrees that credits for screen authorship shall be given only pursuant to the terms of and in the manner prescribed in the applicable Schedule A attached hereto and by this reference incorporated herein, with respect to credits for screen authorship finally determined during the term hereof, and with respect to credits for screen authorship finally determined after the expiration of the term hereof involving material written during the term hereof or during the term of a prior collective bargaining agreement between the Company and the Guild; provided, however, that any such credits determined during the term of a successor collective bargaining agreement between the Company and the Guild shall be determined pursuant to the terms of such successor collective bargaining agreement.

ARTICLE 9 — MINIMUM TERMS (GENERAL)

The terms of this Basic Agreement are minimum terms; nothing herein contained shall prevent any writer from negotiating and contracting with any Company for better terms for the benefit of such writer than are here provided, excepting only credits for screen authorship, which may be given only pursuant to the terms and in the manner prescribed in Article 8. The Guild only shall have the right to waive any of the provisions of this Basic Agreement on behalf of or with respect to any individual writer.

ARTICLE 10 — GRIEVANCE AND ARBITRATION

A. MATTERS SUBJECT TO GRIEVANCE AND ARBITRATION (GENERAL)

Except as otherwise specifically provided in this Article or elsewhere in this Basic Agreement, the following matters shall be submitted to grievance and thereafter to arbitration as hereinafter provided, and no other matters shall be submitted to grievance or arbitration:

1. Any dispute between the Guild and the Company concerning the interpretation of any of the terms of this Basic Agreement and the application and effect of such terms as determined by an interpretation thereof.

2. Any alleged breach of any of the terms or provisions of this Basic Agreement by the Guild or the Company.

3. Any claim by the Guild and a writer, on the one hand, against the Company, on the other hand, for unpaid compensation under the writer's individual employment agreement or loan-out agreement with the Company, or for payment under a purchase agreement with the Company in the case of a professional writer, excluding, however, any claim not related to the writer's services as a writer or not related to the sale of literary material. (Claims for compensation or payment

under an employment, loan-out or purchase agreement shall be referred to hereafter as **"compensation claims"** or **"claims for compensation."**) Notwithstanding the foregoing, the grievance committee and arbitrator shall not have jurisdiction to render an award for compensation or payment exceeding the sum of three hundred fifty thousand dollars ($350,000.00) for a theatrical or television employment or purchase. (Said amounts are herein referred to as the *"jurisdictional maximum."*) If a compensation claim exceeds the jurisdictional maximum, the claim may nevertheless be submitted to grievance and/or arbitration, but by such submission the Guild and writer waive any award exceeding the jurisdictional maximum and shall have no further claim or right with respect to any amount in excess of the jurisdictional maximum. A claim for compensation cannot be split nor may more than one (1) grievance or arbitration proceeding be brought for the purpose of avoiding the jurisdictional maximum.

4.   In any grievance or arbitration proceeding with respect to a claim for compensation brought under Section 3. of this Article 10.A., the Company may, but need not, assert any and all defenses, including defenses based on an alleged right of suspension or termination, and any counterclaim or setoff (hereinafter referred to as *"cross-claim"*). A cross-claim is either mandatory or permissive. A mandatory cross-claim is one arising out of or related to the pending claim for unpaid compensation. A permissive cross-claim is any other cross-claim by the Company against the writer. Provided that the Company has obtained knowledge of the facts upon which the cross-claim is based, the Company shall assert any and all mandatory cross-claims in any arbitration proceeding involving a compensation claim. If the amount claimed by the Company in a cross-claim exceeds the jurisdictional maximum of three hundred fifty thousand dollars ($350,000.00), the Company shall have the option of submitting such cross-claim to grievance and (whether or not submitted to grievance) to arbitration or to institute an action at law or in equity with respect to such cross-claim. The Company may, but need not, assert any permissive cross-claim.

5.   Any claim of overpayment by a Company under Article 11.A.9. of this Basic Agreement.[2]

B. LIMITATION OF MATTERS SUBJECT TO GRIEVANCE AND ARBITRATION

1.   Except as otherwise provided in this Basic Agreement, disputes under individual employment agreements, and loan-out agreements and

---

[2] Articles 10.A.5. and 11A.9. replace Article 13.C. of the 1973 Basic Agreement.

under purchase agreements with professional writers, involving (i) Company's rights of suspension and termination, (ii) Company's right to seek or obtain injunctive relief or specific performance, (iii) any of the warranties or grants of rights made by the writer, or (iv) any of the rights of the Company to any literary material, shall not be subject to grievance or arbitration (except as provided to the contrary in Article 16), and the Company reserves all of its legal and equitable rights and remedies with respect thereto. Any decision in grievance or award in arbitration purporting to determine or affect any of the aforementioned matters shall, to that extent, be of no force or effect whatsoever; provided, however, that if the Company asserts in any grievance or arbitration any defense or cross-claim involving or based upon the alleged exercise of a right of suspension or termination, the same shall be determined in such grievance and arbitration proceeding.

2.   The grievance committee and the arbitrator shall have jurisdiction to determine only such disputes as are submitted for grievance or arbitration under this Basic Agreement, subject to the limitations upon the powers of said grievance committee and arbitrator under this Basic Agreement. Neither the grievance committee nor the arbitrator shall have the power or jurisdiction to reform, amend or extend the express terms and provisions of this Basic Agreement or of any employment, loan-out agreement or purchase agreement.

C. MATTERS SUBJECT TO ARBITRATION BUT NOT GRIEVANCE

Notwithstanding anything elsewhere contained in this Article 10, the following matters shall be submitted to arbitration but not to grievance:

1.   Any dispute as to whether the arbitrator has jurisdiction or whether any matter is arbitrable, provided, however, that the arbitrator may not order an arbitration of any matter not arbitrable as provided above.

2.   Any dispute concerning the credit provisions of this Basic Agreement. Such disputes are subject to the procedures set forth in Article 11.E. of this Basic Agreement.

3.   Any dispute concerning separation of rights under the provisions of subparagraph 6. of Article 16.A. of this Basic Agreement.

4.   Any dispute concerning allocation of receipts under Section 15.A.3.a of this Basic Agreement.

D. REFUSAL TO ARBITRATE

A failure or refusal by any party to go to grievance on a matter subject to grievance or to arbitrate an arbitrable matter, including disputes as to jurisdiction and arbitrability pursuant to this Article 10, is a substantial breach of this Basic Agreement. A failure or refusal by any party to go to grievance on a matter subject to grievance or to arbitrate an arbitrable matter shall not limit, impair or divest the jurisdiction and powers of the grievance committee or arbitrator provided notice of grievance or arbitration has been served as provided herein. Grievance and arbitration may proceed despite the failure of a party to appear and the grievance committee or arbitrator may enter an award against such party.

E. REFERENCES

All references in Articles 10, 11, and 12 to individual employment agreements, loan-out agreements or purchase agreements only refer to such agreements as are subject to this Basic Agreement.

ARTICLE 11 — GRIEVANCE AND ARBITRATION RULES AND PROCEDURES

A. GENERAL RULES

Unless otherwise provided in this Article 11 or elsewhere in this Basic Agreement, the rules and procedures for grievance and arbitration shall be as follows:

    1.   Parties

        a.   In any grievance or arbitration concerning any claim by a writer for compensation under Article 10.A.3., the Guild and the writer involved shall be jointly a party and may be represented by joint counsel. In any grievance or arbitration concerning such a claim by any loan-out company, the loan-out company also shall be jointly a party and may be represented by joint counsel. The claim shall be initiated by the Guild on behalf of the writer and the loan-out company, if any.

        b.   Except as provided in subparagraph a. above, only the Company and the Guild shall be parties.

        c.   [Renumbered Article 11.B.3. and deleted here.]

        d.   The party commencing a claim in grievance or arbitration is sometimes referred to herein as complainant. The party against whom such grievance or arbitration is commenced is sometimes referred to herein as respondent. Use of such terms in the singular shall be deemed to include the plural.

        e.   The grievance and arbitration provisions shall apply to disputes with respect to purchase agreements with professional writers to the same extent but no greater than they are applicable to disputes involving employed writers.

        f.   As used in Articles 10, 11 and 12 of this Basic Agreement, the term "writer" shall be deemed to include the plural, the writer's loan-out company if any (as defined in Article 3 of this Basic Agreement) and, in the case of a purchase agreement, a professional writer (as defined in Article 1 of this Basic Agreement).

2. **Time Limits**

    a. Proceedings for grievance (or arbitration, to the extent a party is required to initiate arbitration without invoking a grievance proceeding) of a claim relating to actual or alleged television employment or purchase shall be commenced no later than two (2) years after the party bringing the grievance or arbitration proceeding (whether it is the Company, Guild or the writer) has obtained knowledge of the facts upon which the claim is based. Proceedings for grievance (or arbitration, to the extent a party is required to initiate arbitration without invoking a grievance proceeding) of a claim relating to actual or alleged theatrical employment or purchase shall be commenced no later than eighteen (18) months after the party bringing the grievance or arbitration proceeding (whether it is the Company, Guild or the writer) has obtained knowledge of the facts upon which the claim is based.

    b. In any event, grievance and arbitration proceedings shall commence not later than four (4) years after the occurrence of the facts upon which the claim is based. An arbitration may be commenced prior to initiation or conclusion of a grievance proceeding, if it reasonably appears that the grievance proceeding will not be concluded in sufficient time to permit the arbitration proceeding to be commenced in time.

    c. With respect to separation of rights in television literary material, Company may accelerate the applicable limitation of time by serving notice on the Guild, after the literary material is completed, that the writer concerned does not have separation of rights in such material and by furnishing with such notice copies of all literary material and contracts upon which the Company's position in such notice is based. The Guild must respond within ninety (90) days from the date such notice is received or the claim to separation of rights is waived on behalf of the writer and the Guild.

    d. If grievance or arbitration proceedings are not commenced within the applicable time period specified in this Article 11, such claim shall be deemed to be waived. All time limits provided in Article 11 may be extended by mutual agreement of the parties to the dispute.

    e.   It is the intent of the Guild and the Company that all arbitration awards should be rendered within sixty (60) days following the close of the arbitration hearing or submission of post-hearing briefs, whichever is later. However, the arbitrator's failure to render an award within such period shall not deprive him/her of jurisdiction over the dispute or render the award invalid because it is made thereafter.

3. Place of Hearing

Except as otherwise provided in this paragraph, all arbitrations shall be in Los Angeles, absent agreement of the parties. At the election of Writers Guild of America, East, the arbitration shall be in New York if a majority of the witnesses required for the arbitration hearing reside regularly in and around the New York area; provided, however, if any Company which is a party to the arbitration has its headquarters for the production of motion pictures in California, such arbitration shall be held in Los Angeles. Any dispute as to where the arbitration should be held shall be determined by an arbitrator in Los Angeles, selected in accordance with the procedures set forth in Article 11.C.2., and said arbitrator shall be disqualified from hearing the merits of the dispute. Said arbitrator shall take testimony by telephone from distant witnesses when requested to do so by either party. If the arbitrator determines that the arbitration shall be heard in New York, the arbitrator assigned to hear the merits of the dispute shall be selected from the New York list of arbitrators set forth in Article 11.C.2.

The selection of the situs of the hearing room within the appropriate city shall be by mutual agreement of the Company and the Guild. If there is no such agreement, those parties will alternate in selecting the hearing room, with the party making the selection supplying the room at no charge to the other.

4. Award

The grievance committee and the arbitrator may make any appropriate award permitted herein. Such award shall be in writing and shall be limited as provided in this Basic Agreement. Subject to the provisions of this Basic Agreement, the award shall be final and binding upon the parties to the proceeding, whether participating in the proceeding or not, and in any grievance or arbitration proceeding in which the writer involved is not a party. Any interpretation of this Basic Agreement made in such award shall be final and binding on such writer.

5. Costs

Each party shall pay the costs of its representatives on the grievance committee. The fee and expenses of the arbitrator shall be shared equally, unless otherwise provided by the arbitrator. The arbitrator may require a court reporter and a transcript, and if so required, the cost thereof shall be shared equally. All other costs and expenses of grievance and arbitration shall be borne by the party incurring the same.

6. Notices

a. All written notices referred to in this Article 11 commencing a grievance or arbitration or alleging a cross-claim shall be sent by registered or certified mail or by personal delivery and shall set forth the particulars thereof. If the moving party is unable to effect service in this manner, service then may be effected by first class mail, postage prepaid, to the address for service last designated in writing by the Company, together with publication in *Daily Variety, The Hollywood Reporter, The Los Angeles Times* and *The New York Times.* All other written notices may be served by first class mail, postage prepaid, unless otherwise specifically provided herein.

b. All notices sent by the Guild to the Company shall be sent to the address designated by the Company in writing to the Guild at the time Company becomes signatory to the Basic Agreement. Should Company change its address for the purpose of receiving notices relating to grievance or arbitration, the Company shall notify the Executive Director of Writers Guild of America, West, Inc. and the Executive Director of Writers Guild of America, East, Inc. of such new address, which shall then be substituted for the prior address.

c. Unless otherwise designated by Company in a written notice to the Guild, all notices sent by the Guild to the Company shall be addressed to the attention of an officer of the Company, or to its Labor Relations Department. If the Company maintains an office in Los Angeles, California or its vicinity, all such notices shall be sent to said office.

d. A petition to confirm, modify or vacate, as the case may be, an arbitration award in any court of competent jurisdiction shall be served upon the respondent by registered or certified mail or by personal delivery. If the petitioner is unable to effect service in this manner, service then may be effected by first class mail, postage prepaid, to the address for service last designated in writing by the Company, together with publication in *Daily Variety, The Hollywood Reporter, The Los Angeles Times* and *The New York Times.*

7. Conduct of Proceedings

Except as set forth elsewhere herein, the grievance committee and the arbitrator shall adopt such rules of procedure and shall conduct proceedings in such manner as they shall determine to be proper; provided, however, that each party to any grievance or arbitration shall be afforded a reasonable opportunity to present evidence and argument before the grievance committee and the arbitrator.

All hearings, deliberations and proceedings of the arbitrator and the grievance committee shall be closed to the public and shall be absolutely privileged. Only interested parties, their representatives and witnesses may attend. All communications to and from the arbitrator or the grievance committee shall likewise be absolutely privileged. Unless the Company objects, the arbitrator will send a copy of the award to the AMPTP, ABC, CBS and NBC. The Guild shall have access to those awards.

8. Claims for Compensation, Cross-Claims and Defenses

Subparagraphs a. through e. of this Section 8. relate to compensation claims, cross-claims and defenses covered by Articles 10.A.3. and 10.A.4. of this Basic Agreement.

a. The grievance committee and arbitrator shall have no jurisdiction to determine or affect any claim relating to services in connection with any theatrical or television motion picture other than the theatrical or television motion picture as to which the compensation claim is asserted unless a defense or cross-claim is asserted with respect to another theatrical or television motion picture.

b. A decision made or award rendered in grievance or arbitration of a claim for compensation shall be limited to deciding or awarding what compensation, if any, is due the writer from the Company and what amount, if any, is due the Company from the writer on account of any cross-claim asserted by the Company in such grievance or arbitration.

c. If a claim for compensation under Article 10.A.3. of this Basic Agreement is submitted to grievance or arbitration, any claim of a breach of this Basic Agreement arising out of or connected with said claim must, to the extent permitted by the Basic Agreement, be submitted for grievance and arbitration together with the claim for compensation, provided that the Guild or the writer has obtained knowledge of the facts upon which said claim of breach is based. Failure to so submit such claim shall constitute a waiver of any and all rights to assert such claim thereafter.

d. The institution of any action in court by the Company shall not stay an arbitration proceeding brought by the Guild and writer for compensation, nor shall any such grievance or arbitration proceeding stay any action instituted by the Company upon any matter Company is not required to submit to grievance or arbitration as a defense or cross-claim, whether or not such action is instituted prior to the submission of the compensation claim to grievance or arbitration.

e. Cross-claims must be submitted to grievance or arbitration by serving written notice on the complainant, by certified or registered mail, setting forth the particulars thereof.

9. Overpayments

If the Company claims that it has made an overpayment to a writer of any compensation provided for in this Basic Agreement or in any prior collective bargaining agreement between the Company and the Guild (i.e., minimum compensation, residuals and other compensation provided for in this Basic Agreement or any other such collective bargaining agreement (hereinafter called "MBA compensation")) or of any compensation provided for in an employment or loan-out contract with a writer or an option agreement subject to the MBA or a purchase agreement with a professional writer not in excess of the applicable jurisdictional maximum of three hundred fifty thousand dollars ($350,000.00) as set forth in Article 10.A.3. above (hereinafter called "arbitrable overscale compensation"), and if the Company desires to offset such payment against other compensation payable to such writer, the Company shall advise the Guild thereof in writing setting forth the particulars of such claim of overpayment. If the Guild requests that the question of whether the Company has overpaid MBA compensation or arbitrable overscale compensation to the writer be submitted to grievance and arbitration, such request shall be made within seven (7) days after such notice from the Company to the Guild. If the Guild does not make a timely request, the Company may proceed with the offset, subject to all of the legal rights and remedies of the writer. If the Guild does make a timely request, then pending the outcome of such grievance and arbitration, the Company agrees that it will not apply the offset, but will pay the amount it desires to apply as an offset to the Guild. The Guild shall then promptly deposit the amount so paid in a separate interest-bearing trust account until it is determined in such grievance and arbitration proceeding whether there was in fact an overpayment of MBA compensation or arbitrable overscale compensation, as the case may be. The grievance and arbitration shall involve only the question of whether there was in fact an overpayment of such compensation and the amount thereof, and if it is determined that there was in fact an overpayment of such compensation, the right of offset is recognized. Upon conclusion of the arbitration, the payments into such account, together with applicable interest, shall be paid to the Company or to the writer in accordance with the arbitration decision. The parties shall cooperate in obtaining a speedy determination of the grievance and arbitration. As to any claimed right of offset with respect to any alleged overpayments of monies other than MBA compensation or arbitrable overscale compensation, the Guild and the Company reserve their respective rights and contentions.

10. Withdrawal of Services

Notwithstanding any provision of any personal service contract (including a memorandum agreement) or of the MBA to the contrary, it shall not be a violation thereof for the Guild or any employee (at the direction of the Guild) to withhold services from the Company if the Company fails or refuses to abide by the final award of an arbitrator for any reason whatsoever.

11. . Any grievance and/or arbitration concerning a dispute arising under a prior MBA or a writer's individual employment agreement, loan-out agreement, option agreement or purchase agreement subject to a prior MBA shall be subject to the following grievance and arbitration rules and procedures as set forth in the MBA in effect at the time the grievance or arbitration is initiated:

(a) The lists of arbitrators;

(b) The method of selecting an arbitrator;

(c) A party's unilateral right to waive second step grievance;

(d) Use of a sole disinterested arbitrator rather than a tripartite arbitration panel;

(e) Respondent's written statement of position. prior to an arbitration hearing; and

(f) Methods of effecting service of grievance notices, arbitration claims, cross-claims and notices, and petitions to confirm, modify or vacate an arbitration award.

The parties agree that the provisions of this Article 11.A.11. shall not be construed to render a dispute subject to grievance and/or arbitration hereunder if that dispute was not subject to grievance and/or arbitration under such prior MBA. The parties further agree that to the extent a claim of overpayment as described in Article 11.A.9. of this Agreement or a "cross-claim" may lie, the provisions of this Article 11.A.11. also shall apply.

B. GRIEVANCE

1. Step One - Informal Conference

a. Prior to submitting to grievance any matter properly a subject thereof, an authorized representative of the Guild and an authorized representative of the Company will meet in a good faith attempt to settle the dispute. If the representatives of the parties shall fail to settle the dispute within fourteen (14) days after the matter is first brought to the attention of the respondent, then the dispute may be referred to Step Two Grievance.

2. Step Two - Grievance

a. Commencement of grievance

Complainant shall set out the nature of its claim in writing, and serve a copy ("grievance notice") thereof upon respondent by certified or registered mail. Respondent may, but need not, reply in writing, setting forth its position. The parties shall attempt to agree upon a mutually satisfactory date to convene a grievance committee and hold a grievance hearing, but if no mutually agreeable date is chosen, respondent may within five (5) days after receipt of the grievance notice designate by written notice to complainant a date upon which the grievance committee shall convene to hold the grievance hearing. Such date shall be no earlier than fifteen (15) nor later than thirty (30) days after receipt of the grievance notice. If respondent fails or refuses to designate such a date, complainant may designate the date for such meeting, such date to be not earlier than fifteen (15) nor later than thirty (30) days after service of the grievance notice.

b. Grievance committee

The grievance committee shall consist of three (3) representatives chosen by respondent and three (3) representatives chosen by complainant. Either party shall have the right to designate a substitute for any of its representatives. The committee will, by majority vote, select its chairman. By mutual agreement, the grievance committee may consist of two (2) representatives chosen by respondent and two (2) representatives chosen by complainant.

c. Grievance hearing

The grievance committee thus designated shall meet upon the date selected pursuant to the procedure described above, and shall consider and attempt to resolve the dispute brought before it. The hearing shall be conducted in an orderly fashion, but rules of evidence and technicalities of procedure shall not be controlling. It is the intent of this Basic Agreement that the committee members shall use their good faith, best judgment and common sense, as persons experienced in the motion picture and television industry, in attempting to resolve the dispute brought before it. No matter shall be considered by the grievance committee unless a quorum is present. A quorum shall consist of six (6) members. If any four (4) members of the committee shall agree on a decision, such decision shall be final and binding upon the parties to the proceedings and any interpretation of this Basic Agreement made in such decision shall also be binding upon the writer or writers involved. If no decision is agreed upon, then in any subsequent arbitration or other proceeding, no reference shall be made to the grievance proceeding or to any statements or discussions therein, or to the failure of the grievance committee to settle the dispute.

    d.   Unresolved grievance

If either party fails to designate its representatives within ten (10) days after notice of grievance is served, or if the Committee shall fail to meet and commence hearings on the date selected in accordance with the procedures described above, or if four (4) members of the committee shall fail to concur in a decision, or if a grievance hearing is waived by one (1) of the parties hereto, or in any event if the dispute has not been settled by the committee or otherwise within forty-five (45) days after the mailing of the grievance notice, then either party may submit such matter to arbitration.

    3.   Waiver of Grievance Steps

[Article 11.A.1.c. in predecessor Agreements.] Either party may, by written notice to the other party, waive grievance. In such event, the dispute shall be submitted directly to arbitration.

C. ARBITRATION

    1.   Initiation of Proceedings

A dispute which is subject to grievance proceedings shall not be subject to arbitration, except as provided in Section B.2.d. or Section B.3. of this Article 11. An arbitration shall be initiated by complainant by written notice, setting forth the particulars of the claim, to be sent to respondent in accord with the procedures described in Article 11.A.6.a. of this Basic Agreement. Respondent will provide complainant with a written statement of its position not later than ten (10) days prior to the date of the hearing.

    2.   Selection of Arbitrator

a.   The arbitrator shall be a disinterested person. The parties shall in good faith attempt to mutually agree upon an arbitrator within ten (10) business days after respondent's receipt of the arbitration notice. Should the parties fail to so agree, the arbitrator shall be selected by the "Strike Process" as follows:

(1)   The arbitrators listed in Article 11.C.2.c shall constitute the lists of arbitrators.

(2)   On a Company-by-Company basis, the Guild and the Company shall alternate on a case-by-case basis in first striking a name from the applicable list of arbitrators (Los Angeles or New York). Thereafter, the other party shall "strike" a name from the list. The parties shall continue to alternate in striking names from the list, until one (1) arbitrator's name remains.

(3)   The arbitrator whose name remains (after the Strike Process is completed) shall be the arbitrator.

(4)   The "Strike Process" shall commence within two (2) business days following completion of the ten (10) business day period referred to in 2.a. above and must conclude no later than three (3) business days following completion of the ten (10) day period referred to in Section 2.a. above.

(5)   In the event that one of the parties fails to participate in the Strike Process, or fails to strike in order and/or timely, the other party may thereupon select the arbitrator to hear the matter.

a.   [Deleted]

b.   If more than one Company is a party, then the Company which is the real party in interest shall participate in the striking process with the Guild. In the event that such Companies cannot agree on which of them is the real party in interest, then such Companies shall determine by lot which Company shall participate in the striking process with the Guild.

c.   The authorized lists of arbitrators approved by the parties hereto are as follows:

LOS ANGELES

Sara Adler	Michael Rappaport
Tom Christopher	Lionel Richman
Dixon Dern	Sol Rosenthal
Gerry L. Feilman	Murray Schwartz
Edna Francis	Myron Slobodien

Joe Gentile	Robert Steinberg
Frederic A. Horowitz	Louis Zigman
Edgar A. Jones, Jr.	

NEW YORK

Stanley Aiges	George Nicolau
James Altieri	Eva Robins
Daniel Collins	Milton Rubin
Dr. Clara H. Friedman	Eric J. Schmertz
Milton Friedman	Arthur Stark
Walter Gellhorn	

Additional names may be added from time to time during the term of the contract by mutual agreement of the parties, provided that each panel shall consist of an odd number of arbitrators at all times.

3. Substitution of Arbitrators

If the arbitrator selected cannot serve, a substitute shall be selected in accordance with subparagraph 2. above.

4. Notice of Hearing

The arbitrator or, at his/her request, one of the parties shall give written notice to the parties of the time and place of the arbitration hearing. In fixing such date, the arbitrator shall consult the parties and shall consider the time reasonably necessary for the parties to prepare their cases.

5. Exchange of Information

The parties will cooperate in the exchange of information prior to the hearing regarding the expected utilization of documents and witnesses, including the exchange of lists of witnesses and copies of documents to be utilized. Such utilization shall not be precluded because such exchange did not take place.

6. Hearing

a. The arbitrator may, upon a showing of good cause, continue the hearing.

b. The arbitration shall take place as noticed or continued regardless of whether one (1) or more of the parties fails to participate.

D. ARBITRATION OF DISPUTES WHICH INVOLVE QUESTIONS OF JURISDICTION OR ARBITRABILITY

An objection to jurisdiction or arbitrability shall first be determined by the arbitrator prior to proceeding with a hearing on the merits. If the arbitrator determines that there is jurisdiction and that the dispute is arbitrable, the arbitrator shall proceed to a decision on the merits; provided, however, that the party contesting arbitration or jurisdiction shall not by proceeding to a determination of the merits of such arbitration be deemed to have waived its position that the dispute is not arbitrable or that the arbitrator does not have jurisdiction. If the arbitrator rules he has no jurisdiction over the dispute or that the dispute is not arbitrable, then each party is relieved of its obligation to further delay taking any action at law or in equity which it may desire to take.

E. ARBITRATION OF DISPUTES CONCERNING CREDIT PROVISIONS

A dispute concerning the credit provisions of this Basic Agreement shall be submitted to an expedited arbitration proceeding governed by the following rules:

1. The Guild shall act on behalf of itself and the writer.

2. Within twenty-four (24) hours after the Guild serves written notice upon the Company concerning a dispute involving a credit provision, an authorized representative of the Guild and an authorized representative of the Company will make a good faith attempt to settle or resolve the dispute.

3. In the event the parties shall fail to meet or shall otherwise fail to settle or resolve the dispute within twenty-four (24) hours after the twenty-four (24) hours provided in subparagraph 2. above, the dispute shall be submitted to arbitration to be commenced not later than five (5) business days after the service of the written notice provided for in subparagraph 2. above.

4. The dispute shall be submitted to a sole neutral arbitrator mutually selected from the authorized list of arbitrators approved by the parties hereto as follows:

LOS ANGELES

Sara Adler	Melvin Lennard
Tom Christopher	Michael Rappaport
Dixon Dern	Sol Rosenthal
Gerry L. Feilman	Murray Schwartz
Edna Francis	Myron Slobodien
Frederic A. Horowitz	Louis Zigman
Edgar A. Jones, Jr.	

NEW YORK

Stanley Aiges	George Nicolau
James Altieri	Eva Robins
Daniel Collins	Milton Rubin
Dr. Clara H. Friedman	Eric J. Schmertz
Milton Friedman	Arthur Stark
Walter Gellhorn	

> Additional names may be added from time to time during the term of the contract by mutual agreement of the parties, provided that each panel shall consist of an odd number of arbitrators at all times.

In the event the parties are unable, within forty-eight (48) hours (not including weekends or holidays) after respondent's receipt of the written notice provided for in subparagraph 2. above, to agree upon an arbitrator from the above list or otherwise, the arbitrator shall be selected by use of the following "strike process":

(i) The arbitrators listed in this Article 11.E.4. shall constitute the lists of arbitrators.

(ii) Thereafter, the other party shall "strike" a name from the list. The parties shall continue to alternate in striking names from the list until one arbitrator's name remains.

(iii) The arbitrator whose name remains (after the strike process is completed) shall be the arbitrator, so long as the arbitrator is a disinterested person.

(iv) The "strike process" shall commence within twenty-four (24) hours (not including weekends or holidays) after the period for mutual agreement has expired and shall be completed within forty-eight (48) hours (not including weekends or holidays) after the period for mutual agreement has expired.

(v) If one of the parties fails to participate in the strike process, or fails to strike in order and/or timely, the other party may thereupon select a neutral arbitrator to hear the matter.

(vi) If more than one Company is a party, then the Company which is the real party in interest shall participate in the strike process with the Guild. In the event that such Companies cannot agree on which of them is the real party in interest, then such Companies shall determine by lot which Company shall participate in the strike process with the Guild.

5. Notwithstanding anything in this Basic Agreement to the contrary, the arbitrator shall have jurisdiction and power to award damages, to order the Company to withdraw, cancel, change, or re-do advertising materials already issued or prepared, to require the Company to re-do any film titles, and to order any other reasonable relief the arbitrator deems appropriate in the circumstances whether relating to credit on the screen, advertising or otherwise. Any award rendered by the arbitrator shall be binding on the parties and upon the writer.

6. Any or all time limits set forth herein may be waived by the mutual consent of the parties.

7.   To the extent not inconsistent herewith, all other provisions of the Basic Agreement relating to arbitrations shall be applicable.

F. EQUAL STATUS OF PARTIES

It is understood that the Companies and the Guild are parties of equal status under this Agreement and in the administration of the arbitration processes throughout this Agreement. The equal status of the parties in the administration of the arbitration process shall be recognized in matters involving the determination of the availability of arbitrators, the selection of hearing dates, the retention of stenographic reporters, and insofar as applicable in all communications with the arbitrators.

Arbitration claims, cross-claims and notices shall carry the caption "WRITERS GUILD OF AMERICA - PRODUCERS ARBITRATION TRIBUNAL."

ARTICLE 12 — COURT PROCEEDINGS

A. DISPUTES CONCERNING CREDITS

Nothing in this Basic Agreement shall limit the rights of the Guild or any writer to assert any and all appropriate legal and equitable rights and remedies to which the Guild or such writer is entitled in courts of competent jurisdiction with regard to an alleged breach of Article 8 and Schedule A of this Basic Agreement with respect to writing credit; subject, however, to the following conditions and limitations:

1.   The Guild and the writer shall be bound by any court proceedings instituted by the Guild.

2.   If the Guild or the writer commences any proceedings in court with respect to any such alleged breach prior to the submission of the dispute to the arbitration hereunder, then neither the Guild nor the writer may submit such dispute to arbitration and no arbitrator shall have jurisdiction to consider the alleged breach of such credit provision.

3.   If the Guild or the Company commences an arbitration proceeding hereunder with respect to any such alleged breach prior to the submission of the dispute to a court, then neither the Guild nor the writer shall thereafter commence any proceeding in court with respect to such alleged breach.

4.   Any permissible court proceeding referred to in this Section A. must be commenced by the Guild or the writer, if at all, within the applicable time limits specified in subparagraph 2. of Article 11.A.

B. DISPUTES CONCERNING COMPENSATION

With respect to a compensation claim which is arbitrable pursuant to the provisions of this Basic Agreement, the writer, at his/her option, need not proceed by grievance and arbitration, but instead may institute an action at law or in equity with respect to such claim prior to submission of such claim to grievance or arbitration; provided, however, that for compensation claims of three hundred fifty thousand dollars ($350,000.00) or less for theatrical or television employment or purchase, the writer must submit such claim to grievance and arbitration pursuant to Article 10 and 11 of this Basic Agreement and failure to so proceed by grievance and arbitration shall constitute waiver by the writer as to such compensation claim.

C. Nothing in this Basic Agreement shall impair, affect or limit the right of the Company, the Guild or any writer to assert and exercise any and all appropriate legal or equitable rights or remedies to which such Company, Guild or writer is entitled in any court of competent jurisdiction as to any dispute which is not subject to grievance or arbitration pursuant to this Basic Agreement. The rights of the parties to assert and exercise legal or equitable rights or remedies as to disputes which are subject to grievance or arbitration are as more particularly defined in this Basic Agreement.

D. The Guild shall have the right to take to grievance and arbitration a claim of the Guild of a breach by the Company of any of the terms or provisions of this Basic Agreement, claimed breach may also involve a breach by the Company of its contract with the writer and such proceeding shall not affect the right of the writer to pursue his/her own remedies at law or in equity, except as limited by the provisions of this Basic Agreement.

E. Nothing in this Basic Agreement shall preclude any court of competent jurisdiction form confirming, setting aside or modifying any grievance or arbitration award hereunder in any proceeding brought for such purpose in accordance with applicable law.

ARTICLE 13 — COMPENSATION

A. THEATRICAL

Company agrees that the minimum basic compensation to be paid a writer who is employed for a feature length photoplay on a so-called flat deal basis shall be as herein set forth.

For the purpose of this Article 13.A.1.a., "High Budget" photoplay shall be a photoplay the cost of which equals or exceeds two million five hundred thousand dollars ($2,500,000.00); a photoplay the cost of which is less than two million five hundred thousand dollars ($2,500,000.00) shall be referred to as a "Low Budget" photoplay.

The Company may option to purchase or license from a professional writer literary material, which would be covered by this Basic Agreement, for a period of eighteen (18) months upon payment of ten percent (10%) of the applicable minimum compensation for such literary material. Company may renew or extend such option for subsequent eighteen (18) month periods upon payment of an additional ten percent (10%) of the applicable minimum compensation for such literary material for each such eighteen (18) month period. Notwithstanding anything in this Basic Agreement to the contrary, the option payment(s) shall be credited against the purchase price or other compensation payable to the writer.

1. a. Minimum Compensation

FLAT DEAL SCREEN MINIMUMS

HIGH BUDGET

		5/2/95- 5/1/96	Effective 5/2/96- 5/1/97	5/2/97- 5/1/98
(a)	Screenplay including treatment	$64,207	$66,454	$69,112
(b)	Screenplay excluding treatment	44,399	45,953	47,791
(c)	Final Draft Screenplay or Rewrite	19,736	20,427	21,244
(d)	Polish	9,867	10,212	10,620
(e)	First Draft of Screenplay (alone or with option for Final Screenplay):			
	First Draft Screenplay	29,603	30,639	31,865
	Final Draft Screenplay	19,736	20,427	21,244
(f)	Treatment	19,736	20,427	21,244
(g)	Original Treatment	29,603	30,639	31,865
(h)	Story	19,736	20,427	21,244
(i)	Additional Compensation Screenplay -No Assigned Material	9,867	10,212	10,620

FLAT DEAL SCREEN MINIMUMS

LOW BUDGET

		5/2/95- 5/1/96	Effective 5/2/96- 5/1/97	5/2/97- 5/1/98
(a)	Screenplay including treatment	$34,528	$35,736	$37,165
(b)	Screenplay excluding treatment	21,575	22,330	23,224
(c)	Final Draft Screenplay	12,946	13,399	13,935
(d)	Polish	6,476	6,703	6,971
(e)	First Draft of Screenplay (alone or with option for Final Draft Screenplay):			
	First Draft Screenplay	15,538	16,082	16,725
(f)	Treatment	12,946	13,399	13,935
(g)	Original Treatment	17,877	18,503	19,243
(h)	Story	12,946	13,399	13,935
(i)	Additional Compensation Screenplay -No Assigned Material	4,937	5,110	5,314

NOTE: The minimum for a screen writer shall be not less than the "appropriate" television minimum, consistent with the particular literary element and the length of the motion picture.

  b. Discount – New Writers

   Company may employ a writer who has not been previously employed as a writer under any Guild MBA in television or theatrical motion pictures or radio dramatic programs on a flat deal basis at not less than seventy-five percent (75%) of the applicable minimum compensation set forth in this subparagraph 1. If such writer receives any writing credit on the theatrical motion picture for which he/she was so employed, his/her compensation will be adjusted to one hundred percent (100%) of the applicable minimum compensation. Such payment will be made within ten percent (10%) business days after determination of final writing credit.

  c. Additional Payment – No Assigned Material

   When Company employs a writer to write a screenplay on a flat deal basis at the minimum basic compensation provided in this Article 13.A., unless Company in good faith furnished such writer a novel, play, treatment, original treatment, or story upon which the screenplay is to be based or from which it is to be adapted, such writer shall be paid an additional amount as described in subparagraph 1. above. The assigned material shall be specifically identified in the notice of employment and contract; if not then known, the writer and the Guild shall be furnished with such identification when it is available.

   Any dispute as to whether or not Company has so furnished such writer a novel, play, treatment, original treatment, or story shall be subject to automatic arbitration by the Guild arbitration committee (referred to in Theatrical Schedule A); provided, however, that in the event Company or the writer does not accept the decision of such Guild arbitration committee, such party shall notify the Guild and the other party, in writing, of its position and such dispute shall thereupon be subject to the grievance and arbitration provisions of Articles 10, 11 and 12 of this Basic Agreement.

 2. Narration by a writer other than any writer of screenplay or story and screenplay.

  Minimums for narration are based on status of film assembly and nature of previously written material as follows:

Nature of Material Written prior to Employment of Narration writer	Film Assembled in Story Sequence	Film Footage Not Assembled in Story Sequence
None	Applicable Screenplay excluding Treatment Minimum	Applicable Screenplay including Treatment Minimum
Story Only	Applicable Screenplay excluding Treatment Minimum	Applicable Screenplay excluding Treatment Minimum
Story and Screenplay	Per Rate Schedule A	Per Rate Schedule A

Rate Schedule A	5/2/95-5/1/96	Effective 5/2/96-5/1/97	5/2/97-5/1/98
Two minutes or less	$ 604	$ 625	$ 650
Over two minutes through five minutes	2,135	2,210	2,298
Over five minutes	applicable polish minimum		

Aggregate sound track running in minutes of narration written by writer hired pursuant hereto.

Narration writer may be hired on a week-to-week basis.

There is no separation of rights for narration.

3. Initial Payment

    The company shall use its best efforts to issue to the writer (or his/her designated representative), for the writer's signature, a written document memorializing the agreement reached between the Company and the writer within ten (10) business days after agreement is reached on the major deal points of a writing assignment (e.g., agreement on initial compensation, including bonus, if any, and number of drafts) for a theatrical motion picture (twelve (12) business days in the case of either a term writing agreement or an agreement for both writing and non-writing services), but in no event later than the earlier of: (a) fifteen (15) business days after agreement is reached on the major deal points of the writing assignment, or (b) the time period required by Article 19.

    With respect to any employment under this Article 13.A. on a flat deal basis, the Company will pay to the writer, not later than the next regular payday in the week following the day the company instructs the writer to commence his/her services, a single advance amount (to be applied against the first compensation which otherwise would be due to the writer) at least equal to the greater of (a) ten percent (10%) of the writer's agreed compensation which otherwise would be due to the writer upon delivery of the first required material, or (b) one week's compensation at the weekly rate for term employment for 14 out of 14 weeks.

4. Maximum Period of Employment

With respect to writers employed at the minimum basic compensation provided for in this Article 13.A. to write a story, treatment, original treatment, first draft screenplay, final draft screenplay, screenplay, or rewrite, the Company shall not require the writer to render services beyond that period of weeks (and fractions thereof) obtained by dividing such applicable minimum basic compensation set forth above in (a) through (i), as the case may be, by the minimum weekly compensation provided for in Article 13.A., subparagraph 15. hereof, for writers employed on a weekly basis.

In the event that the same writer is employed to write any combination of those items set forth above in (a) through (i), such time periods shall be cumulative.

If the writer is required by written notice from the Company to render his/her services beyond such time period, he/she shall be entitled to the specified compensation on delivery and to the minimum weekly compensation to which such writer would be entitled if employed on a weekly basis, as hereinafter in subparagraph 15. of Article 13.A. provided, for services rendered after the expiration of such period.

5. Computation of Writer's Period of Employment

In computing the duration of a writer's employment under this Article 13.A. there shall be excluded the following:

a. Any time during which the writer's employment agreement was suspended by reason of any breach or default on the part of the writer;

b. Any time during which the writer's employment agreement was suspended by reason of any of the causes specified in the *"force majeure"* clause of such writer's employment agreement;

c. Except as hereinafter provided, waiting time which occurs during or after the writer's employment;

Any excess waiting time shall be included in computing the duration of the writer's employment.

However, excess waiting time after the expiration of the duration of the writer's employment shall not be included in computing the duration of the writer's employment unless the writer holds himself/herself available for the Company's further instructions pursuant to the Company s written notice to the writer so to hold himself/herself available after the expiration of the writer's employment.

Any time during which the writer shall make revisions called for by the Company shall be included in computing the duration of the writer's employment.

6. Waiting Time

The waiting time to be excluded in computing the duration of the writer's employment shall not exceed three (3) days following delivery of material, and such waiting time shall not be compensable. In the event that the same writer is employed to write any combination of story, treatment or original treatment, first draft screenplay, final draft screenplay or screenplay, such waiting time shall be cumulative. "Excessive waiting time" as used in this Article 13.A. means waiting time in excess of the waiting to be excluded as provided in this subparagraph 6. If the writer is called into conference on any day or instructed to perform any services on any day, such day may not be included in waiting time. Sundays and holidays generally recognized in the motion picture industry shall be excluded in computing waiting time.

7. Extension of Employment Period

If the employment agreement under this Article 13.A. for a treatment on a flat deal basis contains any option for additional literary material, and the Company wishes the writer to change, revise or complete his/her assignment after the expiration of the maximum allotted employment period under this Article, the company may postpone the time for exercise of such option by notifying the writer that it elects to continue the employment of the writer on a week-to-week basis commencing upon the expiration of the employment period then expiring at the minimum weekly compensation prescribed in subparagraph 15. hereof, but without any minimum guaranteed period of employment. The Company must notify the writer to this effect promptly upon the expiration of such maximum allotted employment period. Such employment shall continue until further notice from the company, and the waiting time shall commence upon such termination of the employment, If the Company thereafter exercises any option, and the maximum allotted employment period under this Article 13.A. for which the Company would be entitled to the writer s services under such option shall exceed the period during which the writer performed his/her services (excluding time for which the writer was compensated on a week-to-week basis and excluding waiting time), then the Company shall be entitled to credit against the amount due under such option, an amount equal to the minimum weekly compensation specified in subparagraph 15. herein for the period of such excess. Such credit shall not exceed the amount actually paid to the writer for services performed on a week-to-week basis.

8.   Failure to Deliver Material Within Allotted Time Period

If the writer has not completed and delivered to the Company the material within the maximum allotted employment period provided for in this Article 13.A., or any shorter period specified in the individual writer's employment agreement, then the Company may exercise the succeeding option and require the writer to complete such material within the succeeding option period. If the writer has not completed and delivered to the Company the material within such maximum allotted employment period, or such shorter period specified in the individual writer's employment agreement, and if the failure of the writer so to complete and deliver such material was not caused by any instructions or directions on the part of the Company, then and at any time thereafter and prior to the delivery of such material, the Company may terminate the writer's employment agreement, and the Company shall not be obligated to make any further or additional payment thereunder. For purposes of determining whether to terminate such contract, the Company may require the writer to deliver for inspection any material then written and compliance with such requirement shall not constitute delivery for the purpose above mentioned without the written consent of the Company. The Company shall retain title to and ownership of any material theretofore delivered for which payment was made by the Company, subject to the provisions of Article 16.A.

9.   Teams

Every writer shall receive no less than the applicable minimum except that if a *bona fide* team of no more than two (2) writers offers, prior to employment on the script in question, to collaborate, the team as a unit shall receive in the aggregate not less than the applicable minimum compensation.

10.   Week-to-Week, Term, Flat Deal

The Company may employ a writer on a week-to-week or term basis to write a story, treatment, original treatment, first draft screenplay, final screenplay, screenplay, or rewrite. At any time thereafter, Company may employ such writer or any other writer on a flat deal basis to write any such material in accordance with the provisions of this Article 13.A. If Company employs a writer on a flat deal basis to write any such material, at anytime thereafter Company may employ such writer or any other writer to write any such material on a week-to-week basis or term basis. If the Company imposes the condition that such material must be completed and delivered by a specified date, and the writer accepts the employment upon such conditions and completes and delivers the material to the Company in compliance with such condition, then such employment shall be deemed to be employment on a flat deal basis and the writer shall be entitled to the applicable flat deal minimums provided in this Article 13.A. for the work involved. If the Company employs two (2) writers as a team on a week-to-week basis to write a story, treatment, original treatment, first draft screenplay, final screenplay, screenplay or rewrite and imposes the conditions that such material must be completed and delivered by a specified date, and if the period by which the writers are to complete and deliver the material under their employment agreement is less than one-half of the applicable maximum period of employment for the work involved as provided in this Article 13.A., the Company shall only be obligated to pay to each such writer one-half of the amount payable to one (1) writer employed on a flat deal basis for the work involved; but if the period by which the writers are to complete and deliver the material under their employment agreement is more than one-half of the applicable maximum period of employment for the work involved provided in this Article, the Company shall not be obligated by this Article 13.A. to pay any additional amount to such writers. For example, if a team of writers is employed on a week-to-week basis during the period May 2, 1995 through May 1, 1996 to write a "screenplay, including treatment" for a High Budget photoplay (for which the flat deal minimum is sixty-four thousand two hundred seven dollars ($64,207.00)) and a date later than ten (10) weeks after the commencement of such employment is specified in the employment agreement for completion and delivery of such final screenplay, then if such final screenplay is completed and delivered within such time, the Company need only pay each writer the thirty-two thousand one hundred three dollars and fifty cents ($32,103.50) received as weekly salary. In the event of a dispute as to whether the Company has imposed such a specified date of completion and delivery, such dispute shall be subject to grievance and arbitration pursuant to the provisions of Articles 10, 11 and 12 hereof.

11. Applicable Deal Minimum Compensation

When Company hereafter employs one or more writers on a flat deal basis for the minimum basic compensation as above provided, then regardless of the exercise of any option, if a motion picture is actually produced by Company from the screenplay so written under such deal basis, the compensation (hereinafter called "applicable minimum deal compensation" paid to the writer or writers who participated in the writing under such flat deal shall be not less than the applicable "Flat Deal Screen Minimums" set forth in Article 13.A., subparagraph 1.a. above. In the event an amount at least equal to such applicable minimum deal compensation has not been paid to such writer or writers by the time screen credits for such motion picture have been finally determined, then Company shall pay to the writer or writers receiving screen credit for such motion picture, within thirty (30) days after such screen credit has been finally determined, the difference between all of the compensation theretofore paid to the writer or writers employed by Company on such flat deal basis in connection with such photoplay, on the one hand, and the applicable minimum deal compensation provided, on the other hand. A writer or writers employed at the minimum week-to-week compensation to write a treatment and also a screenplay for a motion picture which is produced by Company shall be compensated at not less than the applicable minimum basic compensation provided for in this Article 13.A., and shall be considered as employed on a flat deal basis at such minimum compensation for purposes of subparagraph 1.c. of this Article. No writer employed on a term basis shall be entitled to additional compensation by reason of the provisions of this Article 13.A.

When a planned Low Budget theatrical motion picture is produced as a High Budget theatrical motion picture for reasons other than *force majeure* (including but not limited to disability, illness or inclement weather) or labor cost escalations undetermined at commencement of production, the Company shall pay any necessary increase in the applicable minimum deal compensation within thirty (30) days after Company knows that the cost of the motion picture has increased or will increase past the High Budget break figure, and in any event within thirty (30) days after delivery of the answer print of said motion picture.

12. Inapplicability of Provisions

The provisions of this Article 13.A. shall not apply to writers employed at compensation in excess of the applicable minimum specified in this Article except as hereinafter provided. However, even though the total compensation shall exceed such minimums, the amount payable for the writing of the story, treatment, original treatment, first draft screenplay, final screenplay, screenplay or rewrite shall be not less than the minimum for such individual work as above designated. The provisions of paragraphs 4., 5. and 6. of this Article 13.A. shall be applicable to writer employed at compensation not exceeding twice the applicable minimum compensation except that the three (3) day waiting period in paragraph 6. shall be two (2) weeks for the above-scale writer covered by this sentence. The provisions of paragraph 8., paragraph 14. and the last two paragraphs of paragraph 15. of this Article 13.A. are applicable to all employment agreements regardless of compensation.

The provisions of this Article 13.A. shall not apply to any short or short subject, except that the Company agrees that any such agreement made by the company with any writer employed on a similar basis with respect to a short or short subject shall guarantee such writer an aggregate compensation for services rendered in the writing and preparation of such material which shall be not less than a sum equal to the minimum weekly compensation to which such writer would be entitled if employed on a weekly compensation basis, as provided in subparagraph 15. hereof, multiplied by the number of weeks (plus any fraction of a week) during which the writer actually and continuously performed such services, it being understood that the Company may terminate the employment of such writer at the time the writer becomes entitled to additional compensation by reason of the provisions of this paragraph or at any time thereafter.

13. Purchases

a. The applicable minimums for purchases of licenses subject to this Agreement from a professional writer shall be the flat deal minimum for the appropriate budget as determined by the Company in good faith; provided, however, that if a motion picture is produced based upon the story, treatment or screenplay, as the case may be, and if such motion picture is a High Budget photoplay, and if the purchase price or license fee paid for the acquisition or license was less than the applicable minimum for the respective type of work (story, treatment or screenplay, as the case may be) for such class of motion picture, *i.e.*, High Budget, pursuant to Article 13.A.1., an additional payment shall be made to the professional writer in an amount such that such writer shall have received in the aggregate an amount equal to such higher applicable minimum.

b. [Deleted]

14. Payment of Compensation Under Deal Contract

Company will use its best efforts to pay writers employed to write on a deal basis not less than the applicable minimum within forty-eight (48) hours after the delivery of a completed story, treatment or original treatment, first draft screenplay or final draft screenplay, as the case may be, but in no event shall any such payment be made later than seven (7) days after delivery of such material. Payment shall not be contingent upon the acceptance or approval by the Company of the material so delivered. Company shall include in writer's deal memorandum or personal service contract: a) the place where and the name(s) or function of the person(s) to whom delivery of such material is to be made, and b) the name(s) of the person(s) authorized to request rewrites of said material. Company shall give writer written notice of any change in the name(s) of the person(s) to whom delivery is to be made and/or the name(s) of the person(s) authorized to request rewrites.

Company will pay interest of one and one-half percent (1.5%) per month when any initial compensation payment is due and not paid as provided. If the Company has failed to make such payment because the executed contract was not delivered by the writer to the Company, then no such interest is due. If the contract is not so delivered by the writer because of a dispute as to the terms of the contract and the Company shall be held to be wrong, the above-described interest payment shall be applicable.

15. Minimum Weekly Compensation

Every writer employed on a week-to-week or term basis shall receive a salary at the rate of not less than the amount a week specified below for the respective period designated:

At the Rate of Per Week

Term Contracts	5/2/95- 5/1/96	5/2/96- 5/1/97	5/2/97- 5/1/98
40 out of 52 weeks	$2,531	$2,620	$2,725
20 out of 26 weeks	2,754	2,850	2,964
14 out of 14 weeks	2,982	3,086	3,209
Week-to-Week	3,211	3,323	3,456

Every week-to-week or term contract shall specify the exact compensation for each full week of services rendered or to be rendered thereunder.

If any writer under a week-to-week or term contract shall render services after the expiration of the guaranteed period of employment, then, for purposes only of prorating days worked in a partial workweek (*i.e.*, less than six (6) days), at the end of such employment, the writer shall receive one-fifth (1/5) of the weekly rate for each day worked during such partial workweek, after the expiration of the guaranteed period.

Company may employ a writer who has not been previously employed as a writer under any Guild MBA in television or theatrical motion pictures or radio dramatic or comedic programs on a week-to-week or term basis for a period not to exceed fourteen (14) consecutive weeks at seventy-five percent (75%) of the minimum weekly compensation as provided in this paragraph 15.

16.   Theatrical Motion Picture Released on Free Television

If a theatrical motion picture is released on free television before it has had a *bona fide* theatrical release (determined as provided in Article 15.A.3.j. of this Basic Agreement), the compensation of the writer or writers who have received screen authorship credit for such motion picture shall be adjusted so that it shall be no less than the appropriate television minimum compensation or the appropriate theatrical minimum compensation, whichever is higher.

17.   Remakes

The Company's right to remake a theatrical film shall be subject to the following:

a.   If a credited writer's material is used for a remake and no writer is employed to rewrite, adapt or revise such material for the remake, the Company will pay such writer(s) the applicable minimum compensation for the intended medium of the remake (but this provision shall not be construed as affecting the rule that a *bona fide* team shall be considered a unit). In addition, the writer will be entitled to receive payment in accordance with Article 15.A. with respect to a theatrical remake licensed to free television, Article 15.B. with respect to reruns or foreign telecast of a television remake, and Article 51 with respect to a theatrical or free television remake released in Supplemental Markets.

b.   If a writer is employed to rewrite, adapt or revise such literary material for the remake, then the credited writer(s) of the original material shall also be participant(s) in the credit determination and if accorded credit shall accordingly be entitled to the portion of applicable minimum compensation for the intended medium of the remake equal to the proportion of credit awarded pursuant to subparagraph (1) below (but this provision shall not be construed as affecting the rule that a *bona fide* team shall be considered a unit). In addition, the writer will be entitled to share in any additional compensation in accordance with Article 15.A. with respect to a theatrical remake licensed to free television, Article 15.B. with respect to reruns or foreign telecast of a television remake, and Article 51 with respect to a theatrical or free television remake released in Supplemental Markets. The writer's portion of such additional compensation shall be equal to the portion of credit awarded pursuant to subparagraph (1) below.

c.   With respect to a television remake of a theatrical film, the phrase "applicable minimum compensation" in subparagraphs a. and b. of this paragraph 17. means the applicable rate provided for in Article 13.B.7.a., b. or e. of this Agreement.

In a credit arbitration concerning such remake the arbiters shall determine the following issues:

(1)   the contribution made by the writer(s) of the original material expressed as a percentage of the whole, and

(2)   the form of credit to be accorded such writer(s), which credit may include a credit in the nature of a source material credit, such as "Based on a Screenplay by . . ."

The foregoing provisions shall apply to material written during the term of this Agreement upon which a remake is based.

18.   Script Annotations

If the Company is to require one or more script annotations, it shall so inform the writer at the time of the negotiation of the writing assignment, or option or acquisition of literary material, unless from the nature of the project the Company's need for the annotation(s) is not reasonably known at the outset. In the latter case, the Company shall inform the writer than an annotation is needed when the Company knows, or reasonably should have known, of it.

If the Company uses written guidelines or standards describing the type of information to be included in an annotation for a fact-based project or a project inspired by fact, such guidelines or standards shall be furnished to the writer when the Company first informs the writer that an annotation is needed.

B.   TELEVISION

1.   Minimum Basic Compensation

a.   Options

When the Company options to purchase or license from a professional writer literary material, which would be covered under this

Basic Agreement, Company shall pay five percent (5%) of the applicable minimum compensation for such literary material for the first period of up to one hundred eighty (180) days, and an additional ten percent (10%) of the applicable minimum compensation for each subsequent period of up to one hundred eighty (180) days.

Notwithstanding anything in this Basic Agreement to the contrary, the option payment(s) shall be credited against the purchase price or other compensation payable to the writer.

The foregoing paragraph shall not apply to arrangements under which the consideration for the agreement is the Company's good faith effort to effectuate network or other buyer/licensee interest or otherwise obtain a development commitment for the material.

* * *

2. "High Budget" Films

For the purposes of this schedule, "High Budget" television motion pictures are those for which the negative costs equal or exceed the following amounts:

15 minutes or less	$150,000
30 minutes or less (but more than 15 minutes)	$215,000
60 minutes or less (but more than 30 minutes)	$300,000
75 minutes or less (but more than 60 minutes)	$400,000
90 minutes or less (but more than 75 minutes)	$500,000
120 minutes or less (but more than 90 minutes)	$900,000
For each additional 30 minutes or less, an additional	$300,000

However, in the case of non-prime time network films, "High Budget" films shall be films the negative costs of which equal or exceed the following amounts:

15 minutes or less	$60,000
30 minutes or less (but more than 15 minutes)	$100,000
60 minutes or less (but more than 30 minutes)	$200,000
75 minutes or less (but more than 60 minutes)	$260,000
90 minutes or less (but more than 75 minutes)	$340,000
120 minutes or less (but more than 90 minutes)	$450,000
For each additional 30 minutes or less, an additional	$125,000

3. "Low Budget" Films

    For the purpose of this schedule, "Low Budget" television motion pictures are those for which the negative cost is less than the amounts indicated above.

*   *   *

5. Story Claim By Production Executive

    If Company shall claim that a writer has been assigned to write a teleplay based upon a story composed or created by a production executive, the story and teleplay shall be subject to an automatic arbitration pursuant to the provisions of Television Schedule A hereof, and if the arbitrators shall accord both the story and teleplay credit to the writer, then the combined story and teleplay minimum above provided for shall apply to the material so written, provided that Company may appeal any such credit determination to arbitration pursuant to Articles 10, 11, and 12 hereof.

*   *   *

7. Schedule of Minimum Compensation

    a. **Story** (For all television films except (i) network prime time and Fox Broadcasting Company ("FBC") prime time programs of the types covered by d. below and (ii) serials which are covered by e.(1) or e.(3) below)

High Budget

Program Length in Minutes	5/2/92- 5/1/96	5/2/96- 5/1/97	5/2/97- 5/1/98
15 or less	$1,770	$1,832	$1,905
30 or less (but more than 15)	3,242	3,355	3,489
60 or less (but more than 30)	5,877	6,093	6,337
75 or less (but more than 60)	8,382	8,675	9,022
90 or less (but more than 75)	8,849	9,159	9,525
120 or less (but more than 90)	11,594	12,000	12,480

Low Budget

Program Length in Minutes	5/2/92- 5/1/96	5/2/96- 5/1/97	5/2/97- 5/1/98
15 or less	$1,506	$1,559	$1,621
30 or less (but more than 15)	2,505	2,593	2,697
60 or less (but more than 30)	4,738	4,904	5,100
75 or less (but more than 60)	6,750	6,986	7,265
90 or less (but more than 75)	7,224	7,477	7,776
120 or less (but more than 90)	9,544	9,878	10,273

b.   **Teleplay** (For all television films except (i) network prime time
      and FBC prime time programs of the types covered by d. below
      and (ii) serials which are covered by e.(1) or e.(3) below)

High Budget

Program Length in Minutes	5/2/92- 5/1/96	5/2/96- 5/1/97	5/2/97- 5/1/98
15 or less	$3,242	$3,355	$3,489
30 or less (but more than 15)	5,262	5,446	5,664
60 or less (but more than 30)	10,197	10,554	10,976
75 or less (but more than 60)	14,840	15,359	15,973
90 or less (but more than 75)	15,684	16,233	16,882
120 or less (but more than 90)	20,803	21,531	22,392

Low Budget

Program Length in Minutes	5/2/92- 5/1/96	5/2/96- 5/1/97	5/2/97- 5/1/98
15 or less	$2,359	$2,442	$2,540
30 or less (but more than 15)	4,056	4,198	4,366
60 or less (but more than 30)	7,733	8,004	8,324
75 or less (but more than 60)	11,160	11,551	12,013
90 or less (but more than 75)	11,841	12,255	12,745
120 or less (but more than 90)	15,670	16,218	16,867

c.   **Story and Teleplay** when the same writer prepares both ("bargain
      rates") (For all television films except (i) network prime time and
      FBC prime time programs of the types covered by d. below and
      (ii) serials which are covered by e.(1) or e.(3) below)

High Budget

Program Length in Minutes	5/2/92- 5/1/96	5/2/96- 5/1/97	5/2/97- 5/1/98
15 or less	$4,421	$4,576	$4,759
30 or less (but more than 15)	8,099	8,382	8,717

60 or less (but more than 30)	14,720	15,235	15,844
75 or less (but more than 60)	20,980	21,714	22,583
90 or less (but more than 75)	22,121	22,895	23,811
120 or less (but more than 90)	28,991	30,006	31,206

Low Budget

Program Length in Minutes	5/2/92- 5/1/96	5/2/96- 5/1/97	5/2/97- 5/1/98
15 or less	$3,756	$3,887	$4,042
30 or less (but more than 15)	6,258	6,477	6,736
60 or less (but more than 30)	11,854	12,269	12,760
75 or less (but more than 60)	17,170	17,771	18,482
90 or less (but more than 75)	18,065	18,697	19,445
120 or less (but more than 90)	23,862	24,697	25,685

For programs in excess of one hundred twenty (120) minutes, compensation is based on the one hundred twenty (120) minute or less minimum (shown above) plus, for each additional thirty (30) minutes or less the following additional payments:

High Budget	5/2/95- 5/1/96	5/2/96- 5/1/97	5/2/97- 5/1/98
Story	$2,746	$2,842	$2,956
Teleplay	5,118	5,297	5,509
Story and Teleplay	6,868	7,108	7,392
Low Budget			
Story	$2,316	$2,397	$2,493
Teleplay	3,816	3,950	4,108
Story and Teleplay	5,802	6,005	6,245

The minimums set forth in the above schedules constitute the writer's minimum compensation for the purposes of Article 15.B.

The category of minimums provided for in subparagraph c. of this paragraph 7. (The so-called "bargain rate") is applicable only when the employment is for story and teleplay, not when the employment is for story with option for teleplay.

cc. **Story with options**

If company engages a writer to write a story with an option to have the writer write a teleplay, the Company must exercise such option, if at all, within fourteen (14) days after delivery of the final story.

d. **Network Prime Time and Fox Broadcasting Company ("FBC") Prime Time**

(For all network prime time and FBC prime time episodic series, one-time shows, unit series shows, once-per-week network prime time serials, and anthology programs. This paragraph d. is not applicable to programs covered by Appendix A and other non-dramatic programs (e.g. Wild Kingdom and travelogues). The rates set forth in this paragraph d. are not to be utilized for the purpose of Article 15.B. of this Agreement.)

(i) **Story**

Program length in Minutes	Effective		
	5/2/95- 5/1/96	5/2/96- 5/1/97	5/2/97- 5/1/98
15 or less	$2,843	$2,928	$3,016
30 or less (but more than 15)	5,209	5,365	5,526
45 or less (but more than 30)	7,188	7,404	7,626
60 or less (but more than 45)	9,169	9,444	9,727
90 or less (but more than 60)	12,250	12,618	12,997
For Serials and Episodic Programs 120 or less (but more than 90)	16,362	16,853	17,359
For other than Serials and Episodic Programs 120 or less (but more than 90)	17,857	18,393	18,945

(ii) **Teleplay**

Program length in Minutes	Effective		
	5/2/95- 5/1/96	5/2/96- 5/1/97	5/2/97- 5/1/98
15 or less	$6,902	$7,109	$7,322
30 or less (but more than 15)	11,209	11,545	11,891
45 or less (but more than 30)	11,854	12,210	12,576
60 or less (but more than 45)	15,120	15,574	16,041
90 or less (but more than 60)	21,785	22,439	23,112
For Serials and Episodic Programs 120 or less (but more than 90)	27,953	28,792	29,656
For other than Serials and Episodic Programs 120 or less (but more than 90)	30,503	31,418	32,361

(iii) **Story and Teleplay** when the same writer prepares both ("bargain rates")

Program length in Minutes	Effective		
	5/2/95- 5/1/96	5/2/96- 5/1/97	5/2/97- 5/1/98
15 or less	$8,539	$8,795	$9,059
30 or less (but more than 15)	15,627	16,096	16,579
45 or less (but more than 30)	18,015	18,555	19,112
60 or less (but more than 45)	22,984	23,674	24,384
90 or less (but more than 60)	32,338	33,308	34,307

For Serials and Episodic Programs 120 or less (but more than 90)	42,546	43,822	45,137
For other than Serials and Episodic Programs 120 or less (but more than 90)	46,505	47,900	49,337

For programs in excess of one hundred twenty (120) minutes, compensation is based on the one hundred twenty (120) minute or less minimum (shown herein) plus, for each additional thirty (30) minutes or less, the following additional payments:

Story	$2,746	$2,828	$2,913
Teleplay	5,118	5,272	5,430
Story and Teleplay	6,868	7,074	7,286

dd. **Segment Rate**

Writers who are employed to write segments for use on programs meeting the requirements of this section may, at the option of the Company, be paid in accordance with this section rather than in accordance with the otherwise applicable provisions of this Agreement. In order to utilize this section, the Company (i) must apply this section to all writers employed on the program or, in the case of a program series, the individual episode; and (ii) must inform such writers no later than the time of assignment to the program that this section is being utilized. As to any single dramatic program or any program of a dramatic television series thirty (30) minutes or more in length which consists of self-contained segments of various lengths (whether or not such segments are intercut within each program), the aggregate minimum compensation shall be one hundred seventy-five percent (175%) of the applicable minimum compensation for story and teleplay set forth in subparagraphs c. and d. Writers employed to write segments for use in such programs shall be compensated at the following rates:

Total Length of Program in Minutes	Length of Segment in Minutes	Segment Compensation as Percentage of Aggregate Minimum Compensation
30 or less	3 or less	10%
	5 or less	15%
	10 or less (over 5)	30%
	15 or less (over 10)	40%
60or less (But more than 30)	8 or less	16-2/3%
	15 or less (over 8)	20%
	20 or less over 15)	25%
	30 or less (over 20)	40%
90or less (But more than 60)	8 or less	10%
	15 or less (over 8)	12-1/2%
	20 or less (over 15)	16-2/3%
	30 or less (over 20)	27-1/2%
	60 or less (over 30)	40%
120 or less (But more than 90)	8 or less	8-1/3%
	15 or less (over 8)	10%
	20 or less (over 15)	12-1/2%
	30 or less (over 20)	20%
	60 or less (over 30)	30%

Should the total minimum compensation payable to the writers of the segments pursuant to the schedule immediately above be less than the aggregate minimum compensation specified above, the difference shall be distributed among the segment writers in proportion to the segment compensation set forth above. In said distribution, the Company may credit to an individual writer any overscale payment paid to such writer.

With respect to such programs, the following provision will be incorporated into appropriate sections of the MBA:

1. The applicable minimums for rewrites shall be twenty-five percent (25%) of the segment minimum as determined in accordance with the above formula.

2. Separation of rights shall apply to each segment excluding only those elements (continuing characters, etc.) which are part of the continuing series format.

3. Any story for which no teleplay is written during the same production season will revert to the writer.

4. The minimum compensation as computed above for each writer shall be the basis for calculation of all rerun, foreign telecast and theatrical exhibition payments required under the Basic Agreement.

5. Writing credits are to be given for each individual segment, identified by segment title, with a single card devoted to each segment.

e. **Serials**

   (1) Employment and purchase of literary material for serials produced for broadcast three, four, five, six or seven times per week other than prime time is treated in Appendix A. (See Appendix A, Article 13.)

   (2) The minimum compensation for stories and/or teleplays, rewrites and polishes for episodes of a once-a-week network prime time serial shall be the corresponding minimums for stories and/or teleplays, rewrites and polishes for episodes of network prime time episodic series.

   (3) As to serials other than those described in subparagraphs e.(1) and (2) above, there is to be no differentiation between stories and teleplays for compensation purposes and minimum compensation for writing such material for such serials shall be as follows:

Program Length in Minutes	5/2/92- 5/1/96	5/2/96- 5/1/97	5/2/97- 5/1/98
15 or less	$3,049	$3,156	$3,282
30 or less	5,076	5,254	5,464
60 or less	9,645	9,983	10,382
90 or less	13,782	14,264	14,835

For programs in excess of ninety (90) minutes, compensation is based on the ninety (90) minute or less minimum shown herein, plus for each additional thirty (30) minutes or less, the difference between the appropriate ninety (90) minute compensation and the sixty (60) minute compensation.

* * *

g. **Plot Outline -Narrative Synopsis of Story**

Company may request writer to prepare a narrative synopsis of reasonable length (herein designated as an "outline") of a story owned by writer in order to determine its suitability for television purposes. The minimum compensation for the preparation of such outline shall be:

Program Length in Minutes	5/2/95- 5/1/96	5/2/96- 5/1/97	5/2/97- 5/1/98
15 Minutes or less	$885	$916	$953
30 Minutes or less	1,474	1,526	1,587
60 minutes or less	2,797	2,895	3,011
75 minutes or less	3,649	3,777	3,928
90 minutes or less	4,134	4,279	4,450
120 minutes or less	5,450	5,641	5,867

Company shall, within fourteen (14) days from time of delivery of such outline, notify writer of its election to acquire such outline and employ writer to prepare a teleplay based thereon. If Company shall so elect, the agreed compensation paid for the outline shall be deemed an advance against the applicable minimum compensation for such story with an option for teleplay, which option shall be deemed exercised, and writer shall receive the difference, if any. If Company shall elect not to proceed, it shall return the outline to the writer not later than the end of such fourteen (14) day period and writer shall be entitled to retain the above applicable minimum for the outline and shall own all right, title and interest in the literary material contained in such outline, except to the extent that the outline was prepared for an episodic series or serial type film and program format and/or characters belonging to the Company were incorporated in the material written by the writer.

Company shall sign and deliver to writer, on the date of hiring, a slip stating it has employed the writer to prepare an outline of such material and that the conditions of such employment are upon terms not less favorable than those provided by this subparagraph g.

h. **Compensation for Rewrites and Polishes**

Company shall pay not less than the following minimum compensation with respect to rewrites and polishes:

(1) **Rewrites**

High Budget – Non-serial pictures and serials described in 13.B.7.e.(2)

Program Length in Minutes	5/2/95-5/1/96	5/2/96-5/1/97	5/2/97-5/1/98
15 or less	$1,909	$1,976	$2,055
30 or less	3,188	3,300	3,432
45 or less	4,609	4,770	4,961
60 or less	6,031	6,242	6,492
75 or less	8,464	8,760	9,110
90 or less	8,883	9,194	9,562
120 or less	11,734	12,145	12,631

Low Budget — Non-serial pictures and serials described in 13.B.7.e.(2)

Program Length in Minutes	5/2/95-5/1/96	5/2/96-5/1/97	5/2/97-5/1/98
15 or less	$1,398	$1,447	$1,505
30 or less	2,394	2,478	2,577
60 or less	4,564	4,724	4,913
75 or less	6,343	6,565	6,828
90 or less	6,738	6,974	7,253
120 or less	8,904	9,216	9,585

Teleplays for serials described in 13.B.7.e.(3)

Program Length in Minutes	5/2/95-5/1/96	5/2/96-5/1/97	5/2/97-5/1/98
15 or less	$1,521	$1,574	$1,637
30 or less	2,540	2,629	2,734
60 or less	4,816	4,985	5,184

(2) **Polishes**

High Budget – Non serial pictures and serials described in 13.B.7.e.(2)

Program Length in Minutes	5/2/95-5/1/96	5/2/96-5/1/97	5/2/97-5/1/98
15 or less	$955	$988	$1,028
30 or less	1,591	1,647	1,713
45 or less	2,301	2,382	2,477
60 or less	3,019	3,125	3,250
75 or less	4,226	4,374	4,549
90 or less	4,439	4,594	4,778
120 or less	5,866	6,071	6,314

Low Budget – Non-serial pictures and serials described in 13.B.7.e.(2)

Program Length in Minutes	5/2/95-5/1/96	5/2/96-5/1/97	5/2/97-5/1/98
15 or less	$696	$720	$749
30 or less	1,193	1,235	1,284
60 or less	2,280	2,360	2,454
75 or less	3,171	3,282	3,413
90 or less	3,371	3,489	3,629
120 or less	4,455	4,611	4,795

Teleplays for serials described in 13.B.7.e.(3)

Program Length in Minutes	5/2/95-5/1/96	5/2/96-5/1/97	5/2/97-5/1/98
15 or less	$763	$790	$822
30 or less	1,276	1,321	1,374
60 or less	2,413	2,497	2,597

* * *

m. (1) **Format**

Minimum basic compensation for a format shall be:

5/2/95-5/1/96	$6,126
5/2/96-5/1/97	6,340
5/2/97-5/1/98	6,594

If a story, or stories, are included in a purchased format and the story is used, the applicable minimum for such story or stories shall apply. If such story or stories are not used no story minimum would apply.

If a writer is employed to write a format and a story or stories are included, at the direction of Company, the applicable story minimum shall apply.

At the time of purchase or hire, Company shall submit to writer any formats in control of the Company relating to the project for which writer has been engaged. The writer shall be obligated to read, initial and date such format.

(2) **Bible**

Minimum basic compensation for a network, prime time bible shall be:

5/2/95-5/1/96	$30,974
5/2/96-5/1/97	32,058
5/2/97-5/1/98	33,340

plus ten percent (10%) thereof for each detailed storyline in excess of six (6) ordered by the Company in connection therewith. With respect to a non-network and/or non-prime time bible for a multi-part closed end series, the minimum basic compensation shall be twenty percent (20%) less than set forth above. The writer of the bible shall be entitled to the applicable story payment (including the additional compensation set forth in Article 13.B.7.d.(i), if applicable) for each segment or episode of the multi-part program or prime-time serial for which he/she receives story credit. Ten percent (10%) of the applicable minimum for a bible may be credited against such payment for each story. Notwithstanding the foregoing, should the Company separately pay the full story and teleplay minimum to the bible writer or any other writer, the story payment (including the additional compensation set forth in Article 13.B.7.d.(i), if applicable) otherwise due to the bible writer under this subparagraph shall not be required.

(3)   **Rewrite or Polish of Format or Bible**

Minimum basic compensation for rewrite of a format shall be fifty percent (50%) of the applicable minimum set forth above. Minimum basic compensation for a polish of a format shall be twenty-five percent (25%) of the applicable minimum set forth above.

Minimum basic compensation for a rewrite or polish of a bible shall be:

	Rewrite	Polish
5/2/95-5/1/96	$15,488	$7,743
5/2/96-5/1/97	16,030	8,014
5/2/97-5/1/98	16,671	8,335

provided, however, that where the writer rewrites or polishes more than six (6) story lines in the bible, the minimum basic compensation shall be increased as follows (for rewrite or polish, as the case may be) for each such story line in excess of six (6):

	Rewrite	Polish
5/2/95-5/1/96	$1,548	$776
5/2/96-5/1/97	1,602	803
5/2/97-5/1/98	1,666	835

With respect to rewriting or polishing a non-network and/or non-prime time bible, the minimum basic compensation shall be twenty percent (20%) less than set forth above.

* * *

r.   **Pilot Scripts, Back-up Scripts and Spin-offs**

Pilot Script

A writer employed to write a pilot story or a pilot story and teleplay shall receive for said pilot story or pilot story and teleplay an amount equal to one hundred fifty percent (150%) of the applicable minimum initial basic compensation (including the rates set forth in Article 13.B.7.d. where applicable) set forth in this Article 13.B. for a pilot story or pilot story and teleplay, but this provision shall not be construed to increase said writer's rights or minimum compensation for any other purpose under this Basic Agreement, such as, but not limited to, reruns and theatrical uses.

If a writer was paid less than the amount set forth herein by reason of the fact that Company did not intend that the material would be used in a pilot film at the time the writer was engaged or material acquired by the Company, but the Company nevertheless actually exploits the television series sequel rights to such material without making a pilot, then such writer shall be paid the amount by which the applicable pilot fee set forth above exceeds the compensation originally paid to such writer for such material.

Back-up Script

A writer employed to write a back-up script shall receive for said story and/or teleplay an amount equal to one hundred fifteen percent (115%) of the applicable minimum initial basic compensation (including the rates set forth in Article 13.B.7.d., if applicable) set forth in this Article 13.B. for a story and/or teleplay, but this provision shall not be construed to increase said writer's minimum compensation for any other purpose under this Basic Agreement, such as but not limited to, reruns and theatrical uses.

Spin-off

When the Company knows prior to engaging a writer to write a story or story and teleplay for an episode of a series that such episode is intended to be used as a spin-off, the Company shall also advise the writer at the time of the initial interview. If Company does not have such knowledge but thereafter broadcasts one or more programs in a new television series based upon such episode, then if the initial compensation paid such writer for such episode was less than one hundred fifty percent (150%) of WGA minimum initial basic compensation therefore Company shall pay writer the difference between such one hundred fifty percent (150%) and writer's initial compensation, but this provision shall not be construed to increase the writer's basic compensation for any other purposes under this Basic Agreement, such as, but not limited to, reruns and theatrical use. Such payment need not be made when the new television series is based primarily on either a public domain format or public domain character or characters used in the spin-off episode.

* * *

ARTICLE 14 — WRITERS ALSO EMPLOYED IN ADDITIONAL CAPACITIES (TELEVISION)

A. DEFINITION

The parties acknowledge that it is customary in the television industry to employ persons to render services as writers under the terms of this Basic Agreement, and the same persons to render services in other capacities which are not subject to this Basic Agreement. For the purposes of this Article 14, a person employed as a writer (as defined in Article 1.C.1.a. of this Basic Agreement) and also as an executive producer, producer, associate producer or story editor (as such terms are customarily used and understood in the television industry) is referred to as a "writer also employed in additional capacities," or "such person" or "such writer." Because of the difficulty of ascertaining the amount, duration, nature and extent of the services rendered by such person as a writer, and for the purpose of avoiding disputes concerning those matters and concerning the extent of such person's contributions as a writer to the programs with respect to which he/she renders his/her services, the parties agree that the duration or term of such person's employment as a writer in relation to a particular series, during a particular production season, shall be no less than the duration or term of his/her employment in the additional capacity in relation to such series, during such production season (except as provided in paragraphs C. and I. of this Article 14), and that such person shall be employed as a writer in relation to such series, during such production season only in accordance with the provisions of this Article 14.

B. · CONTRACTS OF EMPLOYMENT

The contract of employment of a writer also employed in additional capacities may cover both the employment as a writer and the employment in additional capacities, or there may be a separate contract covering the employment as a writer and a separate contract covering the employment in additional capacities, provided that in the latter case (*i.e.*, when there are separate contracts) separate compensation shall be provided for the services as a writer from the services in additional capacities, and such separately stated compensation for such person's services as a writer shall not be less than the appropriate minimum compensation for a writer also employed in additional capacities as provided in paragraph K. of this Article 14. Similarly, where the employment as a writer and in additional capacities is covered by the same contract, and the compensation as a writer is segregated from the compensation for the additional services, such compensation as a writer shall not be less than the appropriate minimum compensation for a writer also employed in additional capacities as provided in said paragraph K. When the contract of employment of a writer also employed in additional capacities under such contract does not segregate his/her compensation as a writer from his/her compensation for his/her additional services, the Company shall have the right to allocate to his/her services as a writer not less than the appropriate minimum compensation for a writer also employed in additional capacities as provided in said paragraph K. Except as provided in the immediately preceding sentence, none of the compensation due such person for his/her services in a capacity or capacities other than as a writer shall be offset or credited against any compensation due such person for his/her services as a writer.

C. FORMS OF EMPLOYMENT

A writer also employed in additional capacities may be employed as a writer only on a week-to-week or term basis, (which employment may be exclusive), at no less than the appropriate minimum compensation provided in paragraph K. of this Article 14 and subject to all of the provisions of this Basic Agreement; provided, however, that if the Company employs two (2) such persons, then the Company may employ other individuals (referred to in this Article 14 for convenience as "additional writers") as writers also employed in additional capacities, in relation to the respective series, and such additional writers may be employed as writers on a week-to-week, term or freelance basis, and the duration or term of their employment need not be coterminous with the duration or term of their employment in additional capacities.

D. AMOUNT, NATURE AND EXTENT OF SERVICES

Because of the difficulty of determining the amount, nature and extent of the services as a writer performed by a writer also employed in additional capacities and his/her contribution as a writer to any specific program of a series, it is agreed that, for the purposes of paragraph G. of this Article 14, such writer (other than the additional writers referred to in paragraph C. of this Article 14) shall be deemed to have performed services as a writer on each program of the series for which he/she is employed for which writing is done during the respective production season; provided, however, that if the employment of such writer has been suspended for cause, or terminated for cause (and for this purpose, any termination of employment of a writer employed on a week-to-week basis shall be deemed to be termination for cause), the number of programs of the respective series for which such writer shall be compensated pursuant to said paragraph G. shall be proportionately reduced. In the case of suspension, the reduction shall be in the proportion that the length of the suspension bears to the overall period of employment of such writer during the respective production season; in the case of termination, the reduction shall be in the proportion that the length of the period from the date of termination to the completion of principal photography of the series during such production season bears to the period from the commencement of such person's employment as a writer during such production season to the date at completion of principal photography of the series during such production season. If such calculation results in a fraction, no payment shall be made with respect to a fraction of less than fifty percent (50%), and full payment of one (1) program fee shall be made with respect to a fraction of fifty percent (50%) or more. An additional writer (as such is referred to in paragraph C. above) who is employed on a week-to-week, term or freelance basis, need not be deemed to have performed services on each program of the series for which he/she is employed but shall be entitled to a program fee (or to a share thereof) pursuant to paragraph G. for each program for which he/she did render writing services during his/her employment. The Company shall notify the term or week-to-week writer that he/she is an additional writer at the time of his/her employment, or (as to a writer already employed) when he/she is assigned as an additional writer.

E.   WHAT MINIMUM COMPENSATION COVERS

(1)   All writing services rendered by a writer also employed in additional capacities up to and including rewrites shall be deemed to be compensated by the minimum compensation provided for such writer pursuant to paragraph K. of this Article 14.

(2)   All formats, stories and teleplays written by such writers during their employment as writers also employed in additional capacities shall be separately compensated, without any offset, credit or allocation of any kind against or by any other compensation of any kind due said individual. Notwithstanding the foregoing, with respect to any writer hereunder who is guaranteed compensation of at least one hundred thousand dollars ($100,000.00) for up to fifty-two (52) weeks of employment for both writing and non-writing services, the Company shall have the right to credit such compensation freely against the compensation which otherwise would be due to said writer for the writing of any literary material during such employment (but not against residuals or the program fees provided for in paragraph G. below) or for non-writing services. In the event of such crediting, the applicable minimum compensation for writing services set forth in paragraph K. below shall be credited at no less than one hundred ten percent (110%) thereof, and the compensation for the writing of stories and teleplays for non-pilot one-time programs ninety (90) minutes or longer shall be credited at no less than one hundred fifty percent (150%) of the applicable minimum therefor (but this provision shall not be construed to increase the writer's compensation for any other purpose under this Basic Agreement, such as, but not limited to reruns and theatrical uses). In such event, the base amount upon which the Company shall compute pension and health contributions with respect to such employment shall be one hundred eighty-five thousand six hundred forty-four dollars ($185,644.00) for the period May 2, 1995 through May 1, 1996; effective May 2, 1996, the base amount will increase to two hundred two thousand dollars ($202,000.00). If the period of guaranteed employment is longer than fifty-two (52) weeks, the applicable base amount for computation of contributions referred to above shall be increased proportionately. If the period of guaranteed

employment is shorter than fifty-two (52) weeks, the applicable base amount for computation of contributions shall be decreased proportionately. As to contracts in effect on March 1, 1985, the Company may elect to pay pension and health contributions according to the formula set forth above or according to the formula in the 1981 MBA.

(3) **Writers Not Considered to be "Writers Also Employed in Additional Capacities"**

In any case in which a writer is employed to write one or more formats, stories or teleplays, or any combination (with or without options) of formats, stories or teleplays, on a freelance basis, concurrently with his/her employment as a producer, executive producer, associate producer or story editor, and whether or not such freelance employment is entered into at the same time as he/she enters into his/her employment in such other capacity or at a different time or times, such person shall not, by reason of such freelance employment, be deemed to be a "writer also employed in additional capacities" for any of the purposes of this Article 14, and this Article 14 shall in no way apply to such employment, notwithstanding anything to the contrary in this Article 14.

F. **(1)** **Becoming a "Writer Also Employed in Additional Capacities" after Initial Employment**

If an individual is initially employed as an executive producer. producer, associate producer or story editor, but not as a writer, so that at the time of such employment such individual is not a "writer also employed in additional capacities" as defined in paragraph A. of this Article 14, but if during such employment such individual, with the knowledge and consent of the Company, performs services as a writer for the series for which he/she is employed in such additional capacity, such individual shall, from the time he/she starts to perform such services as a writer, be deemed to be employed as a "writer also employed in additional capacities" for the purposes of this Article 14, except that: (a) if such writing services are limited to those described in subparagraphs (a) to (h), inclusive, of Article 1 C.i.a. of this Basic Agreement and to those described in paragraph E.(3) of this Article 14; or (b) if such person is not a "writer," by reason of the provisions of the third paragraph of said Article 1 C.1 a. (immediately following said subparagraph (h)) and such writing does not qualify him/her as a "writer," then in any of said excepted cases, such employment of such individual shall not be subject to this paragraph F. With respect to contracts in existence on the date of execution of this Agreement, providing for employment as an executive producer, producer, associate producer or story editor, but not for employment as a writer, and which do not contain an express provision that the employee shall not render services as a writer, or is not employed to render services as a writer, such contracts shall be deemed to include such a provision for the purposes of this paragraph F., if the Company serves written notice on such person to the effect that such person shall not render services as a writer (other than the excepted services referred to above in this subparagraph (1) and in paragraph E.(3) of this Article 14).

(2)   **Duration of Services**

A person who becomes a writer also employed in additional capacities pursuant to subparagraph (1) of this paragraph F. shall continue to be employed as a writer in connection with the respective series on a term contract basis for a period coterminous with the remainder of the duration or term of his/her employment in the other capacity or capacities in relation to such series during the respective production season or until the completion of principal photography of all programs of such series produced during such production season, whichever is the earlier, subject to the following provisions of this paragraph F and to the provisions of paragraph I. of this Article 14. In such case, the Company shall have the right to allocate to his/her services as a writer no less than the appropriate minimum compensation for a writer also employed in additional capacities as provided in paragraph K. of this Article 14.

(3)   Notwithstanding anything to the contrary in this paragraph F., if such person is an "additional writer," as defined in paragraph C. of this Article 14, then such person shall be deemed to be employed as a writer and also in additional capacities, pursuant to this paragraph F., only during the period during which he/she performs services as a writer, and such employment may be on a week-to-week, term or freelance basis.

(4)   **Substitute Writer**

Any writer employed on a term basis pursuant to this paragraph F. may be replaced by the Company with another writer at any time during such term, provided that: (a) the substitute writer may not be replaced during the term of his/her employment as a writer during the respective production season, except for cause; (b) the rate of compensation payable to such substitute writer for writing shall be no less than the appropriate minimum rate of compensation provided for in paragraph K. of this Article 14, or the rate paid to the replaced writer for writing, whichever is higher; (c) the term of employment of the substitute writer shall be no less than the remainder of the term of employment of the replaced writer during the respective production season. Subparagraph (a) of this subparagraph (4) is to be interpreted as meaning that the Company shall pay the writer's compensation but shall not be obligated to use such writer's services as a writer, and may employ other writers to perform such services. This subparagraph (4) does not apply to any "additional writer" referred to in subparagraph (3) of this paragraph F.

(5)   The Company specifically represents to the Guild that it is not the intention of the Company to use any of the provisions of this Article 14 in such manner as to evade the purpose and intent of this Article 14. Specifically, the Company expressly represents that it is not its intention to, and agrees that it will not, use the provisions of subparagraphs E.(3) or F.(1) for the purpose of avoiding its obligations under this Article 14 regarding the coterminous employment of a writer also employed in additional capacities. Accordingly, when a person is employed as an executive producer, producer, associate producer or story editor with no intention that such person is to perform services as a writer, including rewrites and polishes (other than the excepted writing services referred to in subparagraphs F.(3) and F.(1) of this Article 14), and provided that his/her contract of employment for such other capacity or capacities provides that such person shall not render services as a writer, or is not employed to render services as a writer (other than the excepted writing services referred to in subparagraphs E.(3) and F.(1)):

   (a)   If such person, without the Company's knowledge and consent, nevertheless does perform services as a writer on the series for which he/she is employed in the other capacity or capacities (other than the excepted writing services referred to in subparagraphs E.(3) and F.(1)), then promptly after the Company or the Guild becomes aware of that fact, it shall notify the other party, and said parties shall jointly and cooperatively take appropriate steps designed to prevent such person from further performing unauthorized writing services. If the Guild believes that the Company knows of and condones such person's unauthorized writing, or that it was originally the intent of the Company and its employee to evade the provisions of this Article 14, the Guild may bring the matter to arbitration (but not to grievance) pursuant to Articles 10 and 11 of this Basic Agreement. If the arbitrator rules in favor of the Guild, the arbitrator shall have the power to make a monetary award to the Guild, no part of which shall be paid or otherwise applied to the benefit of the writer, directly or indirectly. In determining the amount of such award, if any is granted, the arbitrator may consider, among other things, the amount of the minimum compensation which would have been paid to such writer had he/she initially been employed for the particular series during the particular production season as a writer and in additional capacities pursuant to this Article 14.

(b) If such person, with the Company's knowledge and consent (and the fact of said knowledge or consent is not disputed by the Company), nevertheless does any rewriting or polishing, then such person shall be deemed to be a term writer pursuant to Article 14.B. retroactively from the commencement of his/her employment by the Company on the particular series during the respective production season.

(c) If his/her contract of employment does not include a provision that such person shall not render services as a writer, or is not employed to render services as a writer (other than the excepted writing services referred to in subparagraphs E.(3) and F.(1)), and if such person nevertheless does any rewriting or polishing, then such person shall be deemed to be a term writer pursuant to Article 14.B. retroactively from the commencement of his/her employment by the Company on the particular series during the respective production season.

G. PROGRAM FEES

Each person whose employment as a writer is governed by this Article 14, whether such employment is on a week-to-week, term or freelance basis (including the "additional writers" defined in paragraph C. of this Article 14) shall be paid a program fee for each program of a series produced for network prime time exhibition for which such writer performed services as a writer pursuant to this Article 14 (or is deemed to have performed services as a writer, as provided in paragraph D. of this Article 14), in the following amount:

Program Fees	5/2/95- 5/1/96	Effective 5/2/96- 5/1/97	5/2/97- 5/1/98
30-minute Program	$602	$623	$648
60-minute Program	800	828	861
90-minute Program or longer	1,000	1,035	1,076

Provided, however, that in no event for a particular program need the Company pay total program fees in an amount which exceeds three (3) times the applicable rate. If more than three (3) writers (a team is deemed to be one (1) writer) are entitled to receive program fees for the same program, a total sum of three (3) times the applicable rate shall be divided equally among them. Program fees may not be prepaid nor may they be offset or credited against or by any other compensation of any kind due the respective writers and must be paid not later than the first regular payroll date following completion of principal photography of the respective program. Program fees shall not be included in "applicable minimum compensation" for the purposes of Article 1 5.B. of this Basic Agreement, but shall be included in "initial compensation" for the purposes of Article 17 of this Basic Agreement.

H. SUSPENSION, TERMINATION AND/OR OFFSET

Nothing in this Article 14 shall be interpreted as precluding the Company from exercising rights of suspension for cause or termination for cause under individual employment contracts, nor from exercising rights of offset, if any, in relation to an indebtedness of the writer to the Company pursuant to law, subject, however, to the provisions of Article 11 A.9. of this Basic Agreement.

I. HIATUS PERIODS

For the purposes of this paragraph I., the following periods will be referred to as "writing hiatus" periods:

> (a) With respect to a writer also employed in additional capacities (except one who becomes such a writer pursuant to paragraph F. of this Article 14 and except a story editor), the period between the date of commencement of his/her employment in a particular production season until the occurrence of the earliest of the following:
>
> > (i) Services as a writer are performed by any writer on the respective series during such production season;
> >
> > (ii) A commitment is made with a writer (other than as a writer also employed in additional capacities) for such series during such production season;
> >
> > (iii) A story conference is held with a writer for such series during such production season;
> >
> > (iv) Principal photography of a program of such series is started during such production season; and the period following the completion of principal photography of the last program of such series produced during such production season until the termination of such person's employment during such production season.
>
> (b) With respect to a writer also employed in additional capacities (including one so employed pursuant to paragraph F. of this Article 14 but not including a story editor), if in a particular production season principal photography of all of the programs of the respective series theretofore ordered by the network has been completed, the period between such date of completion until the occurrence of the earliest of the following after the start of such period:

(i)   Services as a writer are performed by any writer on the respective series during such production season;

(ii)   A commitment is made with a writer (other than as a writer also employed in additional capacities) for such series during such production season;

(iii)   A story conference is held with a writer for such series during such production season;

(iv)   Principal photography of a program of such series is started during such production season, provided that such period continues for at least fourteen (14) consecutive days.

The Company may suspend the employment of such person as a writer during any writer hiatus period, both as to services as a writer and compensation as a writer; provided, however, that such person's overall compensation shall be allocated by the Company so that there shall be no reduction in the overall compensation of such person by reason of such suspension, and provided further that the re-allocated payments are subject to contributions to an industry pension plan.

J.   For the purposes of this Article 14, one-time programs including but not limited to a movie-of-the-week, and development deals for specific television programs, shall each separately, be considered to be a "series," and the employment of an individual as a writer and in additional capacities for such a show or deal shall be governed by this Article 14; the writer also employed in additional capacities on such show or program shall receive the program fee regardless of whether such writer receives or shares in a "Written by" credit. Payment of the program fee for such show or program shall not be payable before the screen authorship credits are finally determined. If there are one or more periods of suspension of writing services between the various steps of a development deal or of a project for a show (for example, between format and screenplay, or between teleplay and production), the employment as writer of the individual employed as a writer and in other capacities may be suspended as to services and compensation during such periods of suspension.

K. MINIMUM COMPENSATION

The minimum compensation for week-to-week and term employment for writers also employed in additional capacities shall be the following:

Rate per week

	Effective		
	5/2/95- 5/1/96	5/2/96- 5/1/97	5/2/97- 5/1/98
(1) Week-to-week & Term Employment up to and including 9 weeks	$4,804	$4,972	$5,171
(2) Term employment 10 through 19 weeks	4,004	4,144	4,310
(3) Term employment 20 weeks or over	3,602	3,728	3,877

L. (1) Submission of Contracts to Guild

When the employment of a writer also employed in additional capacities is covered by a single contract, a copy of the entire contract shall be submitted to the Guild as provided in Article 19.C. 1. of this Basic Agreement. When such employment is covered by separate contracts, the Company shall, concurrently with the delivery to the Guild of a copy of the writer's employment contract pursuant to said Article 19.C.1., deliver to the Guild a copy of those provisions of the contract governing the additional services which define or specify the term of employment.

(2) Weekly Work Lists

The weekly list provided for in Article 3.A.1. of this Basic Agreement shall indicate the type of employment as a writer (week-to-week, term or freelance), the series for which the person is employed as a writer, whether the writer is also employed in additional capacities and, if so, in what additional capacities.

Such list shall also include the names of persons, if any, who perform services as writers during the respective week (other than services described in subparagraphs (a) to (h), inclusive, of Article 1 .C.1. of this Basic Agreement), but who are not "writers" because of the provisions of the third paragraph of said Article 1 C.1.a. (immediately following subparagraphs (a) through (h). If such a person is included, the list shall state that he/she is excepted as a "writer" pursuant to Article 1 .C.1 a. of this Basic Agreement.

Apart from the mere listing of names, as required by Article 3.A.1., any information once given in the report pursuant to this paragraph L.(2) need not be repeated in subsequent reports unless there is a change in the information previously given.

M. BETTER TERMS

Nothing contained in this Article 14, including the rights of the Company to allocate compensation and to terminate or suspend employment as a writer as above set forth, shall prevent any such writer from negotiating and contracting with the Company for better terms for the benefit of such writer than are provided in this Article 14. Only the Guild shall have the right to waive any of the provisions of this Article 14 on behalf of or with respect to such writer.

ARTICLE 15 — TELEVISION EXHIBITION

A. THEATRICAL

1. **Pre-1960 Motion Pictures**

    As to all motion pictures, the principal photography of which commenced prior to June 13, 1960, the Guild agrees that it does not and will not, either during the term of this Basic Agreement or at any time thereafter, make any claim for compensation for or with respect to the exhibition of such motion pictures on television.

2. The provisions of this subparagraph 2. relate and apply only to theatrical motion pictures as defined in Article 1.A.2.:

    a. produced by the Company or within the provisions of subparagraph 3.h.(4) of this Article 15.A.; and

    b. The principal photography of which commenced on or after May 2, 1995, which motion pictures are, either during the term hereof or at any time thereafter, released to free television; and

    c. based upon a story or screenplay written by writer while in the employ of the Company or in the employ of the actual producing Company as described in subparagraph 3.h.(4) of this Article 15.A. (To which Article 5 hereof) or acquired by the Company (or such actual producing Company) from a professional writer (to which acquisition the provisions of the Basic Agreement apply as provided in Article 5 hereof), which writer or professional writer receives screen credit for the authorship of such story or screenplay, as provided in Theatrical Schedule A.

3. **Payment**

    As to each such theatrical motion picture referred to in subparagraph 2. above (herein sometimes called "Such Picture"), except as provided in Article 64, the Company will pay to each participating writer (as such term is hereinafter defined) as additional compensation, a pro rata share of two percent (2) (hereinafter referred to as the "percentage payment") of the Company's accountable receipts from the distribution of Such Picture on free television, computed as hereinafter provided and subject to the following conditions:

a.   The term *"Producer's gross,"* as used herein, means the worldwide total gross receipts derived by the distributor of Such Picture (who may be the Company or a distributor licensed by the Company) from licensing the right to exhibit Such Picture on free television; provided, however, that in the case of any Such Picture which is produced outside of the United States, if Such Picture is subject to this Basic Agreement and if such production is under an arrangement (herein referred to as a "foreign production deal") pursuant to which a foreign producer or distributor provides or guarantees any of the financing for the production of Such Picture or furnishes any other consideration for such production and a foreign distributor acquires one of more foreign territories for the distribution of Such Picture on free television, then no monies from any such distribution in any such foreign territory shall be included in Producer's gross except to the extent such foreign producer or foreign distributor is obligated to account to Company or to the distributor of Such Picture for such monies, and except for gross receipts received by such foreign distributor from such distribution in the United Kingdom.

If the distributor of Such Picture does not distribute Such Picture directly to free television, but employs a subdistributor to so distribute Such Picture, then the "Producer's gross" shall be the worldwide total gross receipts derived by such subdistributor from licensing to television. In case of an outright sale of the free television distribution rights, for the entire world, or any territory or country, the income derived by the seller from such sale, but not the income realized by the purchaser or licensee of such rights, shall be the "Producer's gross." If any such outright sale shall include free television exhibition rights and other rights, then (but only for the purpose of the computation required hereunder) the Company shall allocate to the free television exhibition rights a fair and reasonable portion of the sales price which shall, for the purpose hereof, be the "Producer's gross." In reaching such determination Company may consider the current market value of free television exhibition rights in comparable motion pictures.

If the Guild shall contend that the amount so allocated was not fair and reasonable, such claim may be determined by submission to arbitration as herein provided. If the arbitrator shall find that such allocation was not reasonable and fair, he/she shall determine the fair and reasonable amount to be so allocated. If the outright sale includes free television distribution rights to more than one motion picture, Company shall likewise allocate to each Such Picture a fair and reasonable amount to be so allocated. If the outright sale includes free television distribution rights to more than one motion picture, Company shall likewise allocate to each Such Picture a fair and reasonable portion of the sales price of the free television rights. If the Guild contends that such allocation is not fair and reasonable, the question may be determined by submission to arbitration as above provided. If the arbitrator shall find that such allocation was not fair and reasonable, he/she shall determine the fair and reasonable amount to be so allocated to each Such Picture. Nothing with respect to the price received on the outright sale of only free television distribution rights in a single Such Picture shall be subject to arbitration except that in the event of a dispute, there may be arbitrated the question of whether the price reported by the Company to the Guild as having been received by the Company on such outright sale is less than the amount actually received by the Company on such outright sale. Sums paid to any advertising agency in connection with any exhibition of any Such Picture on free television shall not be included in Producer's gross.

Guild's right to elect. The parties further agree with reference to Article 15.A.3.: If in the upcoming negotiations with SAG and DGA, the Company agrees to modify the basic substantive provisions regarding licensing of theatrical motion pictures for exhibition on free television, Company will so notify the Guild and accord it the opportunity to elect that this subparagraph be modified in the same manner, as of the date on which the Guild so notifies the Company. Adjustments which statistically maintain the relative allocations of proceeds derived from post-1960 theatrical motion pictures licensed to television among SAG, DGA and WGA as established in 1960 (i.e., the ratio of 6, 2 and 2 of accountable receipts respectively) will not activate this provision, but an increase in the relative allocations to SAG, or DGA in such proceeds will activate this provision, with any such increase to be accorded proportionately to WGA. Upon request the Guild shall be provided with the statistics upon which the adjustments have been made, and the Guild's right to activate this provision shall be arbitrable. The Guild shall give notice of its election within sixty (60) days after receipt of the Company's notice or after being provided with the statistics referred to, whichever is later. The election shall be limited to accepting the entire agreement reached with SAG or DGA on licensing theatrical motion pictures for exhibition on free television, and only such entire agreement, but with appropriate equivalent adjustment for writers for provisions peculiar to actors or directors, as the case may be.

b. **"Accountable Receipts"**

The term **"accountable receipts,"** as used herein, means the balance of the Producer's gross after deducting an arbitrary forty percent (40%) of the Producer's gross for distribution fees and expenses; except that in the case of an outright sale of free television distribution rights, there shall be deducted only an arbitrary ten percent (10%) of the Producer's gross for sales and commissions and expenses of sale.

c. **When Payment Obligation Accrues**

Company's obligation shall accrue hereunder only after accountable receipts are received by Company but as to foreign receipts such obligation shall accrue only when such receipts can be freely converted to U.S. dollars and are remitted to the United States, and until such time no frozen foreign receipts shall be included in accountable receipts. Payment of amounts accruing hereunder shall be made quarterly on the basis of quarterly statements, as hereinafter provided. Upon request, and if permitted by the authorities of a foreign country, the Company will transfer to any writer, in the currency of such foreign country, his/her share, if any, of frozen foreign receipts in such country, provided the writer will bear any costs involved; and such transfer shall be deemed to be payment to the writer of an equivalent number of U.S. Dollars at the then current free market rate for blocked funds of that category as determined by the Company. Concurrently with such transfer the writer will pay to the Company in U.S. dollars the total amount the Company is required to withhold from such payment under all applicable laws. If the Company utilizes frozen foreign currencies derived from exhibition of Such Picture on free television by conversion thereof to properties that may be freely exported and turned to account, the amount so utilized by the company shall be deemed to have been converted to U.S. dollars at the then current free market rate for blocked funds of that category determined as above provided. Frozen foreign receipts from free television shall be deemed to be released on a first-in, first-out basis, unless the authorities of the foreign country involved designate a specific period that would render such basis inapplicable. Such released funds shall be allocated between Such

Picture and other motion pictures distributed by the distributor on free television in the same ratio that receipts, derived from the distribution of Such Picture on free television within the foreign country, bear to the total receipts derived from the distribution of Such Picture and all other motion pictures on free television within the foreign country during the applicable period, unless the authorities of the foreign country, during the applicable period, unless the authorities of the foreign country involved require another method of allocation, in which case such other method of allocation, in which case such other method shall be used. Foreign receipts shall be accounted for in U.S. dollars at the rate of exchange at which such receipts are actually converted and remitted, and should any discounts, taxes, duties or charges be imposed in connection with the receipt or remittance of foreign funds, only so much of such funds as remain thereafter shall be included in accountable receipts. Company shall not be responsible for loss or diminution of foreign receipts as a result of any matter or thing not reasonably within the control of the Company. The Guild and the writers shall be bound by any arrangements made in good faith by the Company or for its account, with respect to the deposit or remittance of foreign revenue. Frozen foreign receipts shall not be considered trust funds and the Company may freely commingle the same with other funds of the Company. No sums received by way of deposits or security need be included in Producer's gross until earned, but when the company is paid a nonreturnable advance by a distributor, such advance shall be included in the Producer's gross.

Such Picture is *"available"* when the first of the following occurs:

(1) The product first may be exhibited or otherwise exploited by a specified method of distribution and in a territory under the terms of the applicable license or distribution agreement, or

(2) It first may be sold or rented by a retailer under the terms of the applicable license or distribution agreement.

Such Picture is *"identifiable"* when the Company first knows or reasonably should have known that a given motion picture is covered by a particular license or distribution agreement for its exploitation in the applicable market.

The amount of the advance payment is *"ascertainable"* if:

(1) the advance is for one motion picture, means of exhibition, and territory, or

(2)   the total amount of the advance is for more than one motion picture, means of exhibition and/or territory, in which case the Company shall fairly and reasonably allocate such advance among the licensed motion pictures, exhibition markets and/or territorial markets. As each of these pictures become identifiable and available, the allocated portion of the non-returnable advance is to be included in "Producer's gross" for that quarter. The Company shall notify the Guild of its allocation when the report of "Producer's gross," which includes the advance, is to be filed. The Guild has the right to challenge in an MBA arbitration a failure to allocate or any allocation that it contends is not fair and reasonable.

If Such Picture is available in any territory or by any means of exhibition is ascertainable, but the Company does not provide the WGA with the information required by the MBA and applicable law, then the advance shall be deemed includable in "accountable receipts" no later than six (6) months after the Company receives it.

An advance received by a Company's parent, subsidiary or any other related or affiliated entity or successor-in-interest, or by any other entity to which the advance payment is directed by the Company or license or distribution agreement, shall be considered as an advance payment received by the Company.

A *"non-returnable advance"* is to be included in "accountable receipts" when Such Picture is "available" and "identifiable" and the amount of the advance payment is "ascertainable."

d.   If any license or outright sale of exhibition rights to Such Picture on free television includes as a part thereof any recorded commercial or advertising material, the Company shall be permitted to allocate a reasonable amount (in accordance with then current standard charges in the industry) to such commercial or advertising material, and the amount so allocated shall not be included in Producer's gross hereunder.

e.   The term *"participating writer"* as used herein, means a writer who, while in the employ of the Company or in the employ of the actual producing Company of Such Picture as described in subparagraph 3.h.(4) above (to which employment the provisions of this Basic Agreement apply), or a professional writer from whom the Company (or such actual producer) acquired literary material (to which acquisition the provisions of this Basic Agreement apply), participated in the writing of and received credit pursuant to the Theatrical Schedule A hereof for the writing of the story or screenplay upon which Such Picture was based. If Such Picture is a remake of a prior motion picture, and if any of the writers of the prior motion picture receive writing credit for the remake, such writers shall be deemed to be "participating writers" for the purposes of this Article 15.A., but then only if their employment as writers for the prior motion picture, or if the purchase of literary material from them for the prior motion picture, was covered by and subject to a collective bargaining agreement with the Guild.

The "*pro rata* share" payable to each participating writer shall be as follows:

(1)   If the participating writer or writers receive "Written by" credit, one hundred percent (100%) thereof shall be payable to the credited writer or writers receiving "Written by" credit.

(2)   If the participating writer or writers receive either story or screen story credit, or screenplay credit, but not both, one hundred percent (100%) thereof shall be payable to the credited participating writer or writers receiving story or screen story, or screenplay credit, as the case may be; provided, however, that if the individual employment contract or purchase agreement with the other writer(s) (i.e., those who are not subject to this Basic Agreement) provides, for payment to such writer or writers of the additional compensation provided for in this Article 15.A., such writer or writers shall receive the share which would have been payable had such writer or writers been participating writers as provided in subparagraph (3) below.

(3)   If the participating writer or writers receive both "Story by" or "Screen Story by" and screenplay credit, seventy five percent (75%) thereof shall be payable to the credited screenplay writer or writers, and twenty-five percent (25%) thereof to the credited story or screen story writer or writers. In the event there is a minor credit, such as adaptation, the writer or writers receiving such minor credit shall be paid ten percent (10%) thereof which sum shall be deducted from the screenplay writer's share.

Any participating writers receiving the same screen credit referred to above shall share equally in such percentage amount specified.

If there are one or more participating writers who receive screenplay credit and no credit is given for story or screen story, then the *pro rata* share which would have been payable to a participating writer had he/she received such story or screen story credit shall, subject to the provisions of the next following paragraph, be paid to the participating writers who receive such screenplay credit. The provisions of the immediately preceding sentence shall also apply with respect to the determination under the Producer-Writers Guild Theatrical Basic Agreements of 1960, 1963, 1970 and 1973 of "*pro rata* shares" payable to participating writers as therein defined.

If the writer's services in Such Picture are performed for the Company on a loan-out basis, then for the purposes of this Article 15.A. the Company shall be deemed to be the employer, and the lender shall not have any responsibility hereunder with respect to Such Picture.

f. **Time and Manner of Payment**

If the picture is licensed for network exhibition, payment with respect to the gross receipts from such license shall be made as follows:

(i)   If under the terms of the license there is no possibility that the picture can or may be dropped out of the license, payment must be made within thirty (30) days after receipt of payment from the network with respect to Such Picture.

(ii) If there is a possibility that Such Picture can or may be dropped out of such license, then payment with respect to Such Picture shall be made within thirty (30) days after exhibition of Such Picture on television pursuant to such license, but not earlier than thirty (30) days after receipt of payment from the network with respect to Such Picture.

Payment shall be accompanied with a written report of the license fee payable for Such Picture pursuant to the license and of the amount paid by the network for Such Picture.

With respect to exhibition of the picture on free television other than pursuant to a license for network exhibition, the following provisions of this subparagraph f. shall apply:

Within a reasonable time after the expiration of each calendar or fiscal quarter, but not exceeding sixty (60) days, Company will furnish or cause to be furnished to the Guild a written report showing the Producer's gross during the preceding quarter from the distribution of each Such Picture by Company on free television with respect to which Company is required to make payments hereunder (whether distributed by the Company or through another distributor).

Concurrently with the furnishing of each such report, the Company will make the payments shown to be due by such report. All payments shall be made by check payable to the order of the writers entitled thereto, and shall be delivered to the Guild for forwarding to such writers, and compliance herewith shall constitute payment to the writers.

No such reports need be furnished with respect to any period during which there was no such Producer's gross. The Company shall make available for inspection by the Guild all distributor's statements and exhibitor's statements which are available to the Company insofar as they relate to such Producer's gross, and all the financial terms of contracts pertaining to such Producer's gross, and the Guild shall have the right, at reasonable times, to examine the books and records of the Company as to such distribution of any Such Picture, at whatever place or places such records are customarily kept by the Company. If the Guild requests that it be informed of the license fee paid under a license for the free television exhibition of the picture, or if the Guild requests that it be sent an extract of the financial terms of such license, and if such information is not extensive in nature, the Company will forward such information or extract without making it necessary for the Guild to send a representative to the offices of the Company. In general, the Company will cooperate in furnishing such information to the Guild by mail or telephone, where doing so is not unreasonable or burdensome. If more than one picture is licensed in a single license agreement, the Company shall inform the Guild, at its request, of the identity of the pictures covered by the license, and shall make available for inspection by the Guild in the office where such license agreement is customarily kept a copy of the terms of such license showing the titles of the pictures licensed under such agreement and the license fee for each Such Picture. Company agrees to cooperate in responding to reasonable inquiries from the Guild as to whether any Such Picture is currently being distributed for telecasting on free television. An inadvertent failure to comply with the reporting provisions paragraph f. shall not constitute a default by the Company hereunder, provided such failure is cured promptly after notice thereof from the Guild is received by the Company.

Company shall make all social security, withholding, unemployment insurance, and disability insurance payments required by law with respect to the additional compensation provided for in this Article 15.A.

If the Company shall fail to make any payment provided for in this Article 15.A. to be made to the writer when and as the same becomes due and payable, it shall bear interest at the rate of one and one-half percent (1.5%) per month on the unpaid balance thereof commencing to accrue on the earlier of: (i) seven (7) days after notice in writing to Company from the Guild of such delinquency, or (ii) sixty (60) days after such payment becomes due and payable.

The compensation payable under this Article 15.A. shall be excluded from the gross compensation upon which Company contributions are to be made to the Pension Plan.

g. **Crediting**

If a participating writer's employment agreement with the Company requires that the writer's compensation shall be based, in whole or in part, upon, or measured by, a percentage of the gross receipts derived from the distribution of Such Picture, then such percentage compensation shall be credited against any amounts payable to the writer hereunder, and likewise any payment due to the writer hereunder shall be credited against such percentage compensation. When all or part of a writer's compensation is a specified sum of money, commonly known and referred to as a "deferment," such deferment may not be credited against amounts payable by the Company to such writer hereunder.

h. With respect to all Such Pictures, the following provisions shall be applicable:

(1) Television Distributor's Assumption Agreement: Prior to the commencement of principal photography of each Such Picture, if the company is not also the distributor on free television of Such Picture, Company shall obtain from the distributor having such free television distribution rights and deliver to Guild, a separate written agreement herein called "TELEVISION DISTRIBUTOR'S ASSUMPTION AGREEMENT," made expressly for the benefit of Guild as representative of the writers involved, by which such distributor agrees to assume and pay the amounts payable hereunder by reason of the exhibition of Such Picture on free television, when and as the same become due. Such agreement shall be substantially in the following form:

"TELEVISION DISTRIBUTOR'S ASSUMPTION AGREE-MENT[8]

In consideration of the execution of a DISTRIBUTION AGREEMENT between _____ Company, and the undersigned Distributor, Distributor agrees that the motion picture presently entitled is subject to the 1995 Writers Guild of America Theatrical and Television Basic Agreement — ABC, CBS, and NBC (hereinafter "Basic Agreement") and particularly to the provisions of Article 15.A. thereof, pertaining to additional compensation payable to writers when theatrical motion pictures are released to free television, and Distributor hereby agrees expressly for the benefit of the Writers Guild of America, West, Inc., and the Writers Guild of America, East, Inc., herein called WGA, as representative of the writers whose services are included in such motion picture when telecast to make the additional compensation payment required thereby when such motion picture is exhibited on free television. Distributor for and on behalf of the Company shall make all social security, with-holding, unemployment insurance and disability insurance payments required by law with respect to the additional compensation referred to in the preceding sentence.

It is expressly understood that the right of Distributor to license such motion picture for exhibition on free television, or to exhibit or cause or permit such motion picture to be exhibited on free television, shall be subject to and conditioned upon the prompt payment of such additional compensation, in accordance with Article 15.A. of the Basic Agreement. It is agreed that WGA, in addition to all other remedies, shall be entitled to injunctive relief against Distributor in the event such payments are not made.

Prompt payment:

(a)   Network exhibition

If the picture is licensed for network exhibition, payment with respect to the gross receipts from such license shall be made as follows:

---

[8] The parties agree that all Assumption Agreements shall include the applicable credit obligations of the WGA collective bargaining agreement, if any, governing the writer's employment and/or the acquisition of the literary material which is the subject matter of the Assumption Agreement. In addition, the parties shall refer the various forms of Assumption Agreements to a legal committee for simplification and unification without otherwise effecting any substantive changes. The term Assumption Agreements, as used in this paragraph, means those Assumption Agreements required by the Basic Agreement.

(i)   If under the terms of the license there is no possibility that the picture can or may be dropped out of the license, payment must be made within thirty (30) days after receipt of payment from the network with respect to Such Picture.

(ii) If there is a possibility that Such Picture can or may be dropped out of such license, then payment with respect to Such Picture shall be made within thirty (30) days after exhibition of Such Picture on television pursuant to such license, but not earlier than thirty (30) days after receipt of payment from the network with respect to Such Picture.

Payment shall be accompanied with a written report of the license fee payable for Such Picture pursuant to the license and of the amount paid by the network for Such Picture.

(b)   Other free television exhibition

With respect to exhibition of the picture on free television other than pursuant to a license for network exhibition, the following provisions shall apply: Within a reasonable time after the expiration of each calendar or fiscal quarter, but not exceeding sixty (60) days, Distributor will furnish or cause to be furnished to WGA a written report showing the Producer's gross (as defined in Article 15.A. of the Basic Agreement) during the preceding quarter from the distribution of Such Picture by Distributor on free television with respect to which Distributor is required to make payments hereunder (whether distributed by the Distributor or through another distributor licensed by Distributor). Such report shall be accompanied by such payments as may be due.

Distributor shall also make available for inspection by WGA all Distributor's statements delivered to Company insofar as they relate to Producer's gross. WGA shall have the right at reasonable times and on reasonable notice to examine the books and records of Distributor as to Producers gross. If Distributor shall fail to make such payments as and when due and payable, they shall bear interest at the rate of one and one-half percent (1.5%) per month on the unpaid balance thereof commencing to accrue on the earlier of: (i) seven (7) days after notice in writing from WGA of such delinquency, or (ii) sixty (60) days after such payment becomes due and payable.

This DISTRIBUTOR'S ASSUMPTION AGREEMENT shall remain effective and binding upon Distributor as long as it remains the Distributor of such motion picture on free television, and thereafter in perpetuity only if it has provided or guaranteed any of the financing for the production of such motion picture, in accordance with and subject to the provisions of paragraph h.(3)(i) of Article 15.A.3 of the Basic Agreement.

When there is more than one distributor, the provisions of such paragraph h.(3)(iii) of Article 15.A.3. of the Basic Agreement shall apply to each distributor which neither provides nor guarantees any of the financing for the production of such motion picture.

The Distributor has, has not (strike whichever is inapplicable) provided or guaranteed financing for production of such motion picture.

Date: _____
             Distributor

By _____

Address:"

An inadvertent failure on the part of any such distributor to comply with any of the reporting provisions of this paragraph h.(1) shall in no event constitute a default by the Company or such distributor or breach of this Basic Agreement, provided that such failure is cured promptly after notice in writing thereof from the Guild.

In the event of the expiration or termination of any distribution agreement, the obligation of Company to obtain and deliver to the Guild such TELEVISION DISTRIBUTOR'S ASSUMPTION AGREEMENT shall apply as well to any subsequent distribution agreement entered into by Company and Company shall obtain and deliver an executed TELEVISION DISTRIBUTOR'S ASSUMPTION AGREEMENT within ten (10) days after the execution of each of such subsequent distribution agreements.

If, with respect to any Such Picture, distributor is not liable in perpetuity to pay the television fees provided for hereunder, or if there is no distribution agreement made by Company with respect to any Such Picture granting television distribution rights to the distributor, then the Guild, prior to the commencement of principal photography of Such Picture, may require such further financial assurances from Company as it deems advisable to insure performance of Company's obligations to pay the television fees provided for herein, including without limitation the execution of security agreements, guarantees, or other protective agreements. If any member company of the Alliance of Motion Picture & Television Producers, Inc., becomes liable in perpetuity under a TELEVISION DISTRIBUTOR'S ASSUMPTION AGREEMENT to pay the television fees provided for hereunder with respect to Such Picture, the Guild will release and cause to be discharged of record all such security agreements entered into or obtained by or from Company; provided, however, that Company's primary liability shall not be released thereby.

(2) Buyer's Assumption Agreement:

If the Company shall sell, transfer or assign its rights to exhibit on free television any Such Picture, it shall obtain from such buyer, transferee or assignee, a separate agreement made expressly for the benefit of the Guild as representative of the writers involved, requiring such buyer, transferee or assignee to comply with the provisions of this Basic Agreement with respect to additional compensation to writers by reason of the exhibition of Such Picture on free television, when and as the same become due. Such agreement shall be substantially in the following form:

"BUYER'S ASSUMPTION AGREEMENT[9]

For a valuable consideration, the undersigned _____ (insert name of Buyer, transferee or assignee) (hereinafter referred to as "Buyer") hereby agrees with _____ (insert name of Company) that all motion pictures covered by this agreement, a list of which is appended hereto, are subject to the 1995 Writers Guild of America Theatrical and Television Basic

---

[9] See footnote 8 . . . accompanying Article 15.A.3.h.(1).

Agreement — ABC, CBS and NBC (hereinafter "Basic Agreement") and particularly to the provisions of Article 15.A. thereof, pertaining to additional compensation payable to writers when theatrical motion pictures are released to free television and Buyer hereby agrees expressly for the benefit of the Writers Guild of America, West, Inc., and Writers Guild of America, East, Inc., hereinafter called WGA, as representative of the writers whose services are included in each such motion picture when telecast, to assume and be bound by Company's obligation thereunder to make the additional compensation payments required thereby when each such motion picture is exhibited on free television. Buyer for and on behalf of the Company shall make all social security, withholding, unemployment insurance, and disability insurance payments required by law with respect to the additional compensation referred to in the preceding sentence.

It is expressly understood that the right of the Buyer to license each such motion picture for exhibition on free television, or to exhibit or cause or permit such motion picture to be exhibited on free television, shall be subject to and conditioned upon the prompt payment of such additional compensation, in accordance with Article 15.A. of the Basic Agreement. It is agreed that WGA, in addition to all other remedies, shall be entitled to injunctive relief against Buyer in event such payments are not made.

Prompt payment:

(a)   Network exhibition

If the picture is licensed for network exhibition, payment with respect to the gross receipts from such license shall be made as follows:

(i)   If under the terms of the license there is no possibility that the picture can or may be dropped out of the license, payment must be made within thirty (30) days after receipt of payment from the network with respect to Such Picture.

(ii)   If there is a possibility that Such Picture can or may be dropped out of such license, then payment with respect to Such Picture shall be made within thirty (30) days after exhibition of Such Picture on television pursuant to such license, but not earlier than thirty (30) days after receipt of payment from the network with respect to Such Picture.

Payment shall be accompanied with a written report of the license fee payable for Such Picture pursuant to the license and of the amount paid by the network for Such Picture.

(b)   Other free television exhibition

With respect to exhibition of the picture on free television other than pursuant to a license for network exhibition, the following provisions shall apply: Within a reasonable time after the expiration of each calendar or fiscal quarter, but not exceeding sixty (60) days, Buyer will furnish or cause to be furnished to WGA a written report showing the "Producer's gross" (as defined in Article 15.A. of the Basic Agreement) during the preceding quarter from the distribution of Such Pictures by Buyer on free television with respect to which Buyer is required to make payments hereunder (whether distributed by Buyer or through another distributor licensed by Buyer). Such report shall be accompanied by such payments as may be due.

Buyer shall also make available for inspection by WGA all Distributor's statements delivered to Buyer insofar as they relate to Producer's gross. WGA shall have the right at reasonable times to examine the books and records of Buyer as to Producer's gross. If buyer shall fail to make such payments as and when due and payable, they shall bear interest at the rate of one and one-half percent (1.5%) per month on the unpaid balance thereof commencing to accrue on the earlier of: (i) seven (7) days after notice in writing from WGA of such delinquency, or (ii) sixty (60) days after such payment becomes due and payable.

When there is more than one Buyer, the provisions of paragraph h.(3)(iii) of Article 15.A.3. of the Basic Agreement shall apply to each Buyer.

_____

BUYER

Date: _____

By   _____

Address:"

The Company agrees to deliver to the Guild an executed copy of the above referred to Buyer's Assumption Agreement within thirty (30) days after the sale, assignment or transfer of Such Picture, with the name and address of the purchaser or assignee.

Any inadvertent failure on the part of the Buyer to comply with any of the reporting provisions of this subparagraph (2) shall in no event constitute a default by the Company or such Buyer or a breach of this agreement, provided that such failure is cured promptly after notice in writing thereof from the Guild.

Upon delivery of such Buyer's Assumption Agreement and on condition that the Guild approves in writing the financial responsibility of the purchaser, assignee, or transferee, Company shall not be further liable for the keeping of any such records, or for the payment of such additional compensation for the exhibition of any Such Pictures on free television, it being agreed that the purchaser, assignee, or transferee, shall solely be liable therefor.

The Guild agrees that it will not unreasonably withhold its approval of the financial responsibility of any such purchaser, assignee or transferee, it being further agreed that if the Guild, within twenty-one (21) days of receipt of written notice of any such sale, assignment or transfer has not advised the Company that it disapproves the financial responsibility of such purchaser, assignee or transferee, the Guild will be deemed to have approved the financial responsibility thereof. In the event the Guild advises the Company within such twenty-one (21) day period that it disapproves the financial responsibility of any such purchaser, assignee or transferee and the Company disputes such disapproval, the Company shall have the right, at its election, to cause to be immediately submitted to arbitration, as herein provided, the issue of whether the Guild has unreasonably withheld the approval of the financial responsibility of such purchaser, assignee or transferee for payments due hereunder.

(3)   Television Distributor's Liability:

With respect to any Such Picture, the following provision shall be applicable to the distributor of Such Picture for telecasting on free television:

(i)   When the distributor has provided or guaranteed any of the financing for the production of Such Picture, the obligations of the distributor under this Article 15.A. shall continue in perpetuity notwithstanding the expiration or termination of such distribution agreement, or any foreclosure of a chattel mortgage, security agreement, pledge, or lien on Such Picture. In the case of foreclosure, should such mortgagee, pledgee or security holder or a third party, who is neither the Company or distributor, acquire title to Such Picture and execute the Buyer's Assumption Agreement, and upon condition that the Guild, in its discretion, approves such purchaser's financial responsibility, then when the distributor ceases to be the distributor of Such Picture for the telecasting on free television, the distributor shall thereupon be released from any and all further obligations under this Article 15.A. with respect to Such Picture. Should any third party (other than in connection with any such foreclosure) acquire the rights of such distributor to the distribution of Such Picture on free television and execute a Television Distributor's Assumption Agreement pursuant to which it is liable in perpetuity to make the payments under this Article 15.A., then upon condition that the Guild in its discretion approves such third party's financial responsibility, such distributor shall thereupon be released from any and all further obligations under this Article 15.A. with respect to Such Picture. However, such distributor shall not be liable for the payment of any television fees based on monies received by a foreign distributor under a "foreign production deal" as defined in subparagraph 3.a of this Article 15.A. with respect to which such foreign distributor or independent producer is not obligated to account to such distributor.

(ii) When the distributor of Such Picture does not provide or guarantee any of the financing of Such Picture, the Television Distributor's Assumption Agreement shall be binding upon the distributor only as long as it is the distributor of Such Picture on free television.

(iii) When there is more than one distributor or buyer of Such Picture on free television, the liability of any such distributor or buyer, which neither provides nor guarantees any of the financing for the production of Such

Picture, for the payment of television fees under this
Article 15.A. shall be applicable only to such portion of
Producer's gross as is derived by distributor or buyer as
the case may be.

The distributor or buyer as used in this subparagraph (iii)
refers to a distributor or buyer, as the case may be, under
any distribution or sale agreement, as the case may be,
with Company, as distinguished from an agreement
between such distributor or buyer and its subdistributor.

(4) Acquisition of Title by Company:

If Company was not the actual producer of Such Picture
which was produced by a signatory Company but acquired
title thereto by purchase, assignment, transfer, voluntary or
involuntary, or by foreclosure of a chattel mortgage or
security agreement or a pledgee's sale, Company shall nevertheless be obligated to make the payments herein provided
when Such Picture is exhibited on free television, unless such
payment required hereunder has already been paid.

(5) Financing-Distribution Agreement by Company:

The obligation of the signatory Company hereunder with
respect to the payments provided for in this Article 15.A. shall
also apply to any Such Pictures produced by an independent
producer under a contract between the signatory Company
and such independent producer for the production of such
motion picture, and for the financing and distribution thereof
by the signatory Company. However, such signatory Company shall not be liable for the payment of any television fees
based on monies received by a foreign distributor under a
foreign production deal as defined in paragraph a. of this
subparagraph 3., with respect to which such foreign distributor or such independent producer is not obligated to account
to such signatory Company. Nor shall such signatory Company be obligated to obtain any Television Distributor's
Assumption Agreement from any foreign distributor referred
to in paragraph a. of this subparagraph 3. except if such
foreign distributor is obligated to account to such signatory
Company pursuant to subparagraph (a) of this paragraph 3.
with respect to monies as therein provided.

(6) Company Liability:

It is expressly understood and agreed that Company shall in
all events remain bound hereunder to make the payments due

by reason of the exhibition of each Such Picture on free television, irrespective of the assumption of such liability by any other person, firm or company as hereinabove provided, except as otherwise expressly provided in this Basic Agreement.

(7) Failure to Deliver Assumption Agreement:

The failure of Company to obtain and deliver an executed assumption agreement as provided in paragraphs h.(1) and h.(2) and subparagraph (i) of this Article 15.A.3. shall be deemed a substantial breach of this Basic Agreement.

(8) Company's Dissolution:

If Company dissolves and is no longer in the business of producing motion pictures and if a distributor assumes all of the obligations of the Company under this Article 15.A. and the financial responsibility of the distributor is approved by the Guild in its discretion, the Company shall thereupon be released of any obligation with respect to any payments due hereunder; provided that if the distributor which assumes all of the obligations of the Company is a member company of the Alliance of Motion Picture & Television Producers, Inc., or if any such member company is permanently liable to pay the television fees provided for in this Article 15.A. with respect to the motion pictures for which the Company is liable to make such payment of television fees, then the financial responsibility of such distributor shall be responsibility of such distributor shall be conclusively deemed approved and such Company shall be released of any obligation with respect to any such payments.

(9) Networks and Television Stations:

No television network, station, sponsor or advertising agency shall be required to execute any Television Distributor's Assumption Agreement, or Buyer's Assumption Agreement, or a Literary Material Assumption Agreement, except, if it is the distributor of Such Picture on free television or the buyer of the Company's free television rights in Such Picture, as the case may be.

i. If the Company shall sell, transfer, assign or otherwise dispose of its rights in any story or screenplay (to which the provisions of this Article 15.A.3. apply, or may apply) prior to the production of a motion picture based thereon, to any person or company (hereinafter referred to as the "Buyer") other than a person or company with headquarter outside the United States, the Company shall obtain from the Buyer a separate agreement in substantially the following form:

"LITERARY MATERIAL ASSUMPTION AGREEMENT[10]

_____ agrees (hereinafter referred to as the "Buyer") with _____ (Company) that the story, screenplay or story and screenplay covered by this agreement is subject to the 1995 Writers Guild of America Theatrical and Television Basic Agreement — ABC, CBS and NBC (herein the "Basic Agreement") and particularly to the provisions of Article 15.A.3. thereof pertaining to additional payments to writers on release of a theatrical motion picture based thereon to free television (but excluding paragraph h. of said Article 15.A.3.), and the said Buyer hereby agrees, expressly for the benefit of the Writers Guild of America, West, Inc., and Writers Guild of America, East, Inc. (herein referred to as the Guild), as representatives of the writers involved, to abide by and perform the provisions of said Basic Agreement and make the additional payments required thereunder, as aforesaid. For the purpose of applying such provisions of said Basic Agreement, the writer or writers of such material shall be treated in all respects as though the said material were written by such writer or writers while in the employ of the Buyer.

It is expressly understood and agreed that the rights of the Buyer to exhibit or license the exhibition of any motion picture based upon said material shall be subject to and conditioned upon the payment to the writer or writers involved of additional compensation, if any, required under subparagraph 3. (except paragraph h. thereof) of said Article 15.A. of said Basic Agreement, and it is agreed that the Guild shall be entitled to injunctive relief and damages against Buyer in the event such payments are not made.

If the Buyer shall sell, transfer, assign or otherwise dispose of its rights in such material to any person or company with headquarters in the United States, it may obtain from the party acquiring such rights a separate agreement in the same form (including this sentence) as this agreement, and will notify the Guild thereof, together with the name and address of the transferee, and deliver to the Guild a copy of such assumption agreement; it being the intent hereof that the obligations herein set forth shall be continuing obligations on the part of such

---

[10] See footnote 8 . . . accompanying Article 15.A.3.h.(1).

subsequent owners, of such material, so headquartered in the United States.

_____

BUYER

Date: _____

By _____

Address:"

The Company agrees to give notice to the Guild of such sale, transfer or assignment of the nature above mentioned, with the name and address of the Buyer, and to deliver to the Guild an executed copy of such assumption agreement. An inadvertent failure on the part of the Company to comply with any of the provisions of this paragraph i. shall in no event constitute a default by the Company hereunder or a breach of this Basic Agreement, provided that such a failure is cured promptly after notice thereof from the Guild.

Upon delivery of such assumption agreement, Company, or any subsequent owner obtaining the execution of such an assumption agreement, shall not be further liable to the Guild or any writer for the keeping of any such records or the payment of such additional compensation, or for compliance with credit obligation insofar as they relate to the broadcast of Such Picture on free television; and the Guild agrees to look exclusively to the party last executing such an assumption agreement for the keeping of such records, payment and compliance with credit obligations. If a company with headquarters outside the United States is a subsidiary of the Company, or the Company is the distributor of Such Picture for such a company, then for the purposes of this paragraph i. such company shall be deemed to be headquartered only in the United States.

j. Anything to the contrary herein notwithstanding, it is agreed that the provisions of this subparagraph 3. apply only if Such Picture is first exhibited on free television after Such Picture has had a *bona fide* theatrical release. For such purpose Such Picture may be regarded as having had a *bona fide* theatrical release even though such release has not been fully completed, or shall not have been withdrawn from its theatrical release, and even though Such Picture may have been released theatrically only domestically or theatrically only in foreign countries or territories. If Such Picture is exhibited on free television prior to the time that it has had a *bona fide* theatrical release, then the release of Such Picture to free television shall be governed by the provisions of the Basic Agreement then in effect between the parties hereto, but only with respect to the provisions thereof relating to additional compensation for television reruns on free television.

The provisions of this subparagraph 3. shall not apply to the televising or exhibition of trailers or advertising a motion picture by shots, etc., substantially in the nature of a trailer, or to the use of stock shots, or to the televising or exhibition of excerpts from theatrical motion pictures for news or review purposes. Except as modified by Article 15.B.10.e., for any other use of excerpts from Such Picture, in television programs (and, for this purpose, the term "television programs" includes programs made for free television, pay television, video discs/video cassettes and basic cable) including television programs which consist substantially of excerpts from theatrical motion pictures, or for any other use of excerpts from Such Picture, the principal photography of which commenced on or after May 2, 1995, in another theatrical motion picture, the Company shall pay the following aggregate one-time-only sum to the writers determined by the Guild to be entitled to such compensation and prorated as determined by the Guild:

		5/2/95- 5/1/98
(a)	thirty (30) Seconds or less of excerpts	$154
(b)	over thirty (30) seconds but not over two (2) minutes of excerpts	465
(c)	over two (2) minutes of excerpts:	
	for the first two (2) minutes	465
	for each minute or portion thereof in excess of two (2) minutes	154

If an excerpt is used in a local program and the program is broadcast in no more than one market, the payment for such use shall be sixty percent (60%) of the amount provided in this Article 15.A.3.j. If the program is broadcast later in another market, the writer(s) shall be paid the remaining forty percent (40%).

The use of an excerpt from a television motion picture in an interactive program shall be governed by the provisions of Article 64.

No compensation shall be payable pursuant to this subparagraph j. to a writer of a motion picture from which an excerpt is derived if such writer writes material for and receives writing credit on the program or motion picture into which such except is inserted.

jj. Notwithstanding any other provision of this Agreement, if the writer

    (1) first describes in literary material an object or thing which is fully described in such literary material and by such description appears to be unique and original; and/or,

    (2) introduces a character and the characterization of such character is fully developed and fully described in the material written by the writer and from such development and description the character appears to be unique and the principal creation of the writer,

and an interactive program is based upon such object, thing or character, the writer will be paid as provided in Article 64.

k. Notwithstanding the sooner termination of this Agreement, the parties hereto agree that the terms and conditions of this subparagraph 3. shall apply and remain in full force and effect, and without change, to Such Pictures produced by the Company, the principal photography of which commenced between May 2, 1995 and May 1, 1998, both dates inclusive, regardless of when (either during or at any time after the expiration of the term of this Basic Agreement or of such period) Such Pictures are released to free television, and regardless of the terms or provisions of any Basic Agreement which is a modification, extension, or renewal of, or substitution for this Basic Agreement.

4. Small Accountings - With regard to all television licensing payments required under this Article 15.A., the Company may accrue such payments until the aggregate is equal to fifty dollars ($50), at which time the payment provision of the appropriate subparagraph shall be effective, except that in any event all accrued amounts of less than fifty dollars ($50) due to the writer shall be paid no later than thirty (30) days following the close of the calendar year in which accrued. Nothing herein shall relieve the Company of its obligation to make the accounting reports required elsewhere herein.

5. At the request of the Guild, the Company authorizes any networks, as defined in Article 1.A.12.1., as well as any television station to advise the Guild of the fact that a payment was or was not made by the network or station for, and the date of any previous telecast of, a theatrical motion picture specified in the Guild's request.

6. In the event that a Company liable for the payments required hereunder shall license a motion picture to television stations owned or controlled by it, or to a network owned or controlled by it, the "accountable receipts" shall be comparable to the accountable receipts paid to

distributors by comparable stations or comparable networks, as the case may be, for comparable telecasts of comparable motion pictures in comparable markets and the accountable receipts paid to Company by comparable stations or comparable networks, as the case may be, for the comparable telecast of such motion picture in comparable markets.

7. The Company shall notify the Guild in writing, to the attention of the Residuals Administrator at its Los Angeles, California office, of any and all English language changes made by the Company in the title of any theatrical motion picture subject to this Agreement released to free television, within thirty (30) days of said change of title.

ARTICLE 15 — TELEVISION EXHIBITION RERUNS & FOREIGN TELECAST OF TV MOTION PICTURES

B. TELEVISION

1. United States and Canada

   a. The minimum compensation above provided for in Article 13.B. shall constitute payment in full for each telecasting of such motion picture once in each city in the United States and Canada in which any television broadcasting station is now located and once in each city in the United States and Canada in which any television broadcasting station is hereafter for the first time established.

   b. Rerun Formula, Free Television, in the United States and Canada

      (1) A television motion picture which has been telecast not more than once in any city in the United States and Canada is in its first run. A television motion picture which has been telecast more than once, but not more than twice, in any city in the United States and Canada, is in its second run. A similar test applies in determining when a television motion picture is in its third and succeeding runs.

      (2) In the event a television motion picture based upon literary material to which this Basic Agreement applies is telecast for more than one (1) run in any city in the United States or Canada, the writer or writers who receive story and/or teleplay screen credit therefor shall be paid additional compensation which, in the aggregate, shall not be less than the following amounts (if more than one writer shares a story or teleplay credit then all of the writers sharing each credit shall be considered a unit and shall participate equally in and receive in the aggregate the rerun payments applicable thereto, and when adaptation credit is accorded, the writer

or writers receiving such credit shall be paid ten percent (10%) thereof, which sum shall be deducted from the share of the teleplay writer(s)).

(a) Reruns over television network in prime time:

With respect to any television motion picture the credited writer(s) of which commenced writing services on or after May 2, 1995, the additional compensation payable for the second or any subsequent run which includes telecasting of said motion picture over a television network in prime time shall be not less than 100% of the writer's applicable minimum compensation.

(b) Reruns over Fox Broadcasting Company ("FBC") in prime time:

With respect to any television motion picture rerun on FBC on or after May 2, 1995, the additional compensation payable for the second or any subsequent run which includes telecasting of said motion picture over FBC in prime time shall be not less than the applicable amount set forth below:

(i) For the second run, not less than 50% effective May 2, 1995 (55% effective May 2, 1996) of the writer's applicable minimum compensation;

(ii) For the third run, not less than 37.5% of the writer's applicable minimum compensation;

(iii) For the fourth run, not less than 31.5% effective May 2, 1995 (34.375% effective May 2, 1996) of the writer's applicable minimum compensation;

(iv) For the fifth run, not less than 31.25% effective May 2, 1995 (34.375% effective May 2, 1996) of the writer's applicable minimum compensation;

(v) For the sixth run, not less than 31.25% effective May 2, 1995 (34.375% effective May 2, 1996) of the writer's applicable minimum compensation;

(vi) For the seventh run, not less than 18.75% effective May 2, 1995 (20.625% effective May 2, 1996) of the writer's applicable minimum compensation;

(vii) For the eighth run, not less than 18.75% effective May 2, 1995 (20.625% effective May 2, 1996) of the writer's applicable minimum compensation;

(viii) For the ninth run, not less than 18.75% effective May 2, 1995 (20.625% effective May 2, 1996) of the writer's applicable minimum compensation;

(ix) For the tenth run, not less than 18.75% effective May 2, 1995 (20.625% effective May 2, 1996) of the writer's applicable minimum compensation;

(x) For the eleventh run, not less than 12.50% effective May 2, 1995 (13.75% effective May 2, 1996) of the writer's applicable minimum compensation;

(xi) For the twelfth run, not less than 12.50% effective May 2, 1995 (13.75% effective May 2, 1996) of the writer's applicable minimum compensation;

(xii) For the thirteenth run and each and every run thereafter, not less than 6.25% effective May 2, 1995 (6.875% effective May 2, 1996) of the writer's applicable minimum compensation (paid separately for each such run).

(c) Other reruns: [11]

(i) For the second run, not less than 50% of the writer's applicable minimum compensation if such second run includes the telecasting of such motion picture over a television network, otherwise such payment shall be not less than 40% of the writer's applicable minimum compensation;

(ii) For the third run, not less than 40% of the writer's applicable minimum compensation if such third run includes the telecasting of such motion picture over a television network, otherwise such payment shall be not less than 30% of the writer's applicable minimum compensation;

(iii) For the fourth run, not less than 25% of the writer's applicable minimum compensation;

(iv) For the fifth run, not less than 25% of the writer's applicable minimum compensation;

(v) For the sixth run, not less than 25% of the writer's applicable minimum compensation;

---

11 [These provisions were Article 15.B.1.b.(2)(b) in predecessor Basic Agreements.] See Sideletter [to Article 15.b.1.b.(2)(c), *infra*] for special provisions governing certain reruns of certain one-hour network prime time dramatic series.

(vi)   For the seventh run, not less than 15% of the writer's applicable minimum compensation;

(vii)   For the eighth run, not less than 15% of the writer's applicable minimum compensation;

(viii) For the ninth run, not less than 15% of the writer's applicable minimum compensation;

(ix)   For the tenth run, not less than 15% of the writer's applicable minimum compensation;

(x)   For the eleventh run, not less than 10% of the writer's applicable minimum compensation;

(xi)   For the twelfth run, not less than 10% of the writer's applicable minimum compensation;

(xii)   For the thirteenth run and each and every run thereafter, not less than 5% of the writer's applicable minimum compensation (paid separately for each such run).

(3)   The **"applicable minimum compensation"** is the minimum salary or amount required to be paid, under the provisions of this Basic Agreement, for the type of story or teleplay involved; provided, however, that for purposes of this Article 15.B., the minimum compensation figures which are set forth in Article 13.B.7.a., b., and c. shall be the "applicable minimum compensation" for programs covered by Article 13.B.7.d.

When the writer has been employed to write a story with option for teleplay, the "applicable minimum compensation" for the story is the minimum set forth in Article 13.B.7.a. The rate applicable to story and teleplay under Article 13.B.7.c. is the "applicable minimum compensation" only in the case of employment under a contract providing for a commitment for both the story and the teleplay.

(4)   If a writer or writers are entitled to the applicable minimum payments per episode required to be made on account of exploitation of the television series sequel rights and/or MOW sequel rights (as provided in Article 16.B.2.a. or b.) or on account of exploitation of character rights (as provided in subparagraph h. of Article 15.B.14.), and if an episode for which such a payment is required is telecast for more than one (1) run in any city in the United States or Canada, the writer or writers entitled to such payments shall be paid

additional compensation calculated as provided in subparagraph (2) above, and for such purpose the "applicable minimum compensation" is such applicable minimum payment.

(5)   The Company shall pay as provided herein for each respective rerun, not later than four (4) months after the first telecast of the respective rerun in any city in the United States or Canada. However, in the event any rerun is telecast on a television network (or on a regional television network) the Company shall make the appropriate rerun payment not later than thirty (30) days after the telecast of such rerun.

(6)   The term "**television network**," as used in this paragraph shall mean the network facilities of the American Broadcasting Company, CBS Inc., the National Broadcasting Company or any other entity which qualifies as a "network" under Section 73.662(f) of the rules of the Federal Communications Commission, unless the FCC determines that such entity is not a "network" for purposes of such Section, except in the case (i) when television motion pictures are telecast on any single regional network presently established, and (ii) when television motion pictures are telecast on any single regional network which may hereafter be established and which does not include New York, Chicago or Los Angeles.

c.   (1) For broadcasts in the domestic market after March 1, 1981, in a language other than English, released other than as part of free television licensing, the credited writer(s) shall be paid an aggregate amount equal to two percent (2%) of the Company's "accountable receipts," as defined in Article 51, from the sale or license of such television motion picture for such broadcasts rather than the otherwise required rerun payment.

(2)   The provisions of subparagraph (1) above will apply to all television motion pictures produced on or after July 1, 1971.

d.   The use of a television motion picture, in whole or in substantial part, in an interactive program shall be governed by the provisions of Article 64.

2.   Foreign Telecasting Formula

a.   In the event such television motion picture is telecast in any part of the world outside the United States and Canada, the writers referred to in Article 15.B.1.b.(2) and (4) above shall be paid additional compensation for such foreign telecasting as follows:

(1)   initial payment of not less than fifteen percent (15%) of their applicable minimum compensation payable not later than

thirty (30) days after the Company obtains knowledge of the first foreign telecast, and in no event later than six (6) months after the first foreign telecast;

(2)   Ten percent (10%) of the applicable minimum when the Distributor's Foreign Gross exceeds seven thousand dollars ($7,000.00) for half-hour pictures, thirteen thousand dollars ($13,000.00) for one-hour pictures, or eighteen thousand dollars ($18,000.00) for pictures in excess of one hour in length. Such payment to be made no later than thirty (30) days after such gross has been so exceeded; and

(3)   a final payment of ten percent (10%) of the applicable minimum compensation when the Distributor's Foreign Gross exceeds ten thousand dollars ($10,000.00) for half-hour pictures, eighteen thousand dollars ($18,000.00) for one-hour pictures, or twenty-four thousand dollars ($24,000.00) for pictures in excess of one hour in length. Such payments to be made no later than thirty (30) days after such gross has been so exceeded.

aa.   Notwithstanding the provisions of subparagraph a. above, the following shall apply to one-hour network prime time dramatic series covered under the sideletter waiving the provisions of Article 15.B.1.b.(2)(c):

(i)   For such period of time as subparagraph (ii) below does not apply, the fifteen percent (15%), ten percent (10%) and ten percent (10%) of applicable minimum compensation payments provided in Article 15.B.2.a.(1), (2) and (3), respectively, shall be collapsed into a single payment of thirty-five percent (35%) of applicable minimum compensation, payable not later than thirty (30) days after the Company obtains knowledge of the first foreign telecast, and in no event later than six (6) months after the first foreign telecast.

(ii)   At any time while the limited waiver of domestic residuals for one-hour network prime time dramatic programs is in effect, the Guild, at its option, shall have a one-time right to elect payment of foreign telecasting monies on the following basis:

(A)   For each episode of a one-hour prime time series covered under such limited waiver, the principal photography of which commences after the date of the Guild's election to proceed under this Article 15.B.2.aa (ii), Company shall pay one and 2/10 percent (1.2%) of Distributor's

Foreign Gross to the writer or writers who receive story and/or teleplay screen credit therefor; provided, however, in no event shall such payment be more than one hundred thirty percent (130%) of the amount that would otherwise be due under subparagraph aa.(i) above, nor shall such payment be less than eighty-five percent (85%) of the amount that would otherwise be due under subparagraph aa.(i) above.

(B)   This Article 15.B.2.aa.(ii) shall automatically terminate if the limited waiver for domestic free television residuals for one-hour network prime time series is terminated. In that event, the provisions of subparagraph aa.(i) shall apply to episodes of one-hour network prime time dramatic series, the principal photography of which commenced on or after the effective date of the termination of the limited waiver.

(C)   1. In order that the Guild may make an informed election under (A), above, the Guild may request from the Companies, no more than once in each calendar year during the term of this Agreement, the anticipated foreign sales revenues for each network prime time dramatic one-hour series that is covered or is eligible for coverage under the waiver sideletter.

       2. The Companies shall, as soon as practicable after receipt of such request, but in no event more than ninety (90) days thereafter, provide the Guild with the information requested in the form of a chart(s) and/or summary(ies), which shows the level of anticipated foreign sales revenues, arranged in twenty-five thousand dollar ($25,000.00) increments, for each such series, but which do(es) not disclose the identity of the series or the Company, and instead designates each series as "A," "B" and so on.

       3. Each Company signatory hereto shall cooperate fully and promptly in providing the requisite information so that the Guild has a full understanding of the overall picture of present and future foreign residuals for such one-hour series, as provided for herein, so as to be able to make an informed election under (A), above.

       4. If, after receipt of the information requested, the Guild elects to have foreign residuals paid under

subparagraph (ii)(A) above, the Guild may send an independent auditor(s) selected by the Guild in its sole and undeterred discretion, to audit fully the books and records of each Company as to the information described in subparagraphs 1., 2. and 3 above. Such auditor(s) shall have full access to the books and records of each Company, as needed, within Los Angeles County within sixty (60) days of the Guild's notice to the Company of the intent to audit. The auditor(s) shall be instructed not to disclose to the Guild the identity of series designated "A," "B" and "C" and so on and shall not do so. Copies of the auditor's written report, if any, shall be sent simultaneously to the Company. If there is a material variance between the auditor's report and the information supplied to the Guild by the Company, then the Guild shall have the right, in its sole discretion and within a reasonable time, to rescind its election to have foreign residuals paid under the provisions of subparagraph (A) above.

b.   After the writer has received a total of thirty-five percent (35%) of his/her applicable minimum compensation with respect to any television film, no further sums shall be payable by reason of the Distributor's Foreign Gross received thereafter.

c.   The term *"foreign telecasting,"* as used herein, shall mean any telecast (whether simultaneous or delayed) outside the United States, its territories and possessions, and Canada, other than a telecast on any of the following regularly affiliated stations of a United States television network as a part of the United States network television telecast: XH-TV, Mexico City; ZBM, Pembroke, Bermuda, for CBS; XEW-TV or XEQ-TV or XH-TV or XHGC, Mexico City, and ZBM, Pembroke, Bermuda for NBC; and XE-TV, Tijuana; and ZFB, Hamilton, Bermuda, for ABC.

d.   As used herein, the term *"Distributor's Foreign Gross"* shall mean, with respect to any television film, the absolute gross income realized by the distributor of Such Picture from the foreign telecasting thereof and including, in the case of a "foreign territorial sale" by any such distributor, the income realized from such sale by such distributor but not the income realized by the "purchaser" or "licensee." The phrase "absolute gross income" shall not include:

(1)   Sums realized or held by the way of deposits or security, until and unless earned, other than such sums as are non-returnable.

"[S]uch sums as are non-returnable" are to be included in the "Distributor's Foreign Gross" when such television motion picture is "available" and "identifiable" and the amount of the non-returnable sum is "ascertainable."

Such television motion picture is "available" when the first of the following occurs:

(i)   The product first may be exhibited or otherwise exploited by a specified method of distribution and in a territory under the terms of the applicable license or distribution agreement, or

(ii)   It first may be sold or rented by a retailer under the terms of the applicable license or distribution agreement.

Such television motion picture is "identifiable" when the Company first knows or reasonably should have known that a given television motion picture is covered by a particular license or distribution agreement for its exploitation in the applicable market.

The amount of the non-returnable sum is "ascertainable" if:

(i)   the non-returnable sum is for one television motion picture, means of exhibition, and territory, or

(ii)   the total amount of the non-returnable sum is for more than one motion picture, means of exhibition and/or territory, in which case the Company shall fairly and reasonably allocate such sum among the licensed motion pictures, exhibition markets and/or territorial markets. As each of these pictures becomes identifiable and available, the allocated portion of the non-returnable sum is to be included in the Distributor's Foreign Gross for that quarter. The Company shall notify the Guild of its allocation when the report of Distributor's Foreign Gross, which includes the non-returnable sum, is to be filed. The Guild has the right to challenge in an MBA arbitration a failure to allocate or any allocation that it contends is not fair and reasonable.

If such television motion picture is available in any territory or by any means of exhibition, and is identifiable and the amount of the non-returnable sum is ascertainable, but the Company does not provide the WGA with the information required by the MBA and applicable law, then the non-returnable sum shall be deemed includable in Distributor's Foreign Gross no later than six (6) months after the Company receives it.

A non-returnable sum received by a Company's parent, subsidiary or any other related or affiliated entity or successor-in-interest, or by any other entity to which the payment is directed by the Company or license or distribution agreement, shall be considered as a non-returnable sum received by the Company.

(2) Sums required to be paid or withheld as taxes, in the nature of turnover taxes, sale taxes or similar taxes based on the actual receipts of the television film or on any monies to be remitted to or by the distributor, but there shall not be excluded from Distributor's Foreign Gross any net income, franchise tax or excess profit taxes or similar tax payable by the distributor on its net income or for the privilege of doing business.

(3) Frozen foreign currency until the distributor shall have either the right to use such foreign currency in or to transmit such foreign currency from the country or territory where it is frozen. In the event such currency may be utilized or transmitted as aforesaid, it shall be deemed to have been converted to United States dollars at the prevailing free market rate of exchange at the time such right to use or transmit accrues.

Distributors's Foreign Gross realized in foreign currency in any reporting period required hereunder shall be deemed to be converted to United States dollars at the prevailing free market rate of exchange at the close of such reporting period.

e. If any transaction involving any television motion picture subject to a foreign telecast payment under this Basic Agreement shall also include motion pictures, broadcast time, broadcast facilities or material (including commercial or advertising material) which are not subject to such payment, there shall be a reasonable allocation between the televison motion pictures which are subject to a foreign telecast payment and such other pictures, time, facilities or material, and only the sums properly allocable to pictures which are subject to a foreign telecast payment shall be included in Distributor's Foreign Gross.

* * *

5.   The Company shall keep or have access to (i) complete records showing all cities in the United States and Canada in which all television motion pictures subject to this Basic Agreement have been telecast and the number of telecasts in each such city, the television station on which telecast, and the dates thereof, and (ii) complete records showing Distributor's Foreign Gross for such televison motion pictures to the extent that such records are pertinent to the computation of payments for foreign telecasting. Company shall also keep or have access to such records as are necessary for the computation of additional compensation for reruns and foreign telecasts for so long as such rerun or foreign telecast payments may be due or payable. The Guild shall have the right, at all reasonable times, to inspect such records. The undersigned shall give the Guild prompt written notice of the date on which each television motion picture covered hereby is first telecast in any city in the United States and Canada for the second run and for each subsequent run thereafter.

6.   With respect to each television motion picture which is distributed for foreign telecasting, Company shall furnish reports to the Guild and the Alliance of Motion Picture & Television Producers, Inc., showing Distributor's Foreign Gross derived from such television motion picture until:

a.   such television motion picture has been withdrawn from distribution for foreign telecasting, or

b.   all of the credited writers of such televison motion picture have received the full additional payments for such foreign telecasting to which they are entitled pursuant to subparagraph 2. above.

Such reports shall be rendered to the Guild on a quarterly basis during the first three (3) years in which any such television motion picture is distributed for foreign telecasting, on a semi-annual basis for the next two (2) years and on an annual basis thereafter. Company agrees to cooperate in responding to reasonable requests from the Guild as to whether any television motion picture is currently being distributed for foreign telecasting.

An inadvertent failure on the part of the Company to comply with the reporting provision of this section shall in no event constitute a default by the Company or a breach of this Basic Agreement, provided such failure is cured promptly after notice thereof from the Guild.

7.   If a writer's individual employment contract contains a provision giving such writer a percentage or other participation in the receipts,

revenues or profits of a television motion picture, such payment may be credited against the minimum additional compensation for reruns and foreign telecast or either provided herein, but writer, in any event, shall be entitled to be paid out not less than such minimum additional compensation for reruns, and foreign telecast, or either, as the case may be, and any payment on account thereof shall likewise be credited against such participation; provided that amounts received by writer as a percentage or other participation in the receipts, revenues or profits of the television motion picture may not be credited against the minimum additional compensation for reruns or foreign telecasts until writer has received as compensation from all sources an amount equal to twice the applicable minimum compensation.

8. Television Assumption Agreement (footnote omitted)

If producer shall sell, transfer, assign or otherwise dispose of its television rights in any television motion picture or any literary material covered hereby, it shall obtain from such buyer a separate agreement made expressly for the benefit of Guild as representative of the writers entitled to additional compensation under this Article 15.B. requiring such buyer to comply with the provisions of this Basic Agreement with respect to such additional compensation to such writers for reruns and foreign telecasting or either, of such motion picture, and the credit provisions of Television Schedule A hereof. Such agreement shall be substantially in the following form:

"The undersigned _____ (insert name of Buyer) (hereinafter referred to as 'Buyer') hereby agrees with _____ (insert name of Company) that all television motion pictures (based upon literary material being acquired hereunder) covered by this Agreement are subject to the 1995 Writers Guild of America-Alliance of Motion Picture & Television Producers Theatrical and Television Basic Agreement (herein Basic Agreement) and particularly to the provisions thereof pertaining to the payment of additional compensation to writers for reruns and foreign telecasting of such television motion pictures, and Television Schedule A relating to screen credit, and said Buyer hereby agrees, expressly for the benefit of the Writers Guild of America, West, Inc., and Writers Guild of America, East, Inc., as representative of such employees involved, to abide by and perform the provision of said Basic Agreement and make the additional compensation payments required thereby and to cause the requisite screen and advertising credits to be given. Buyer for and on behalf of the Company shall make all Social Security, withholding, Unemployment Insurance and Disability Insurance payments required by law with respect to the additional compensation referred to in the preceding sentence. Buyer further agrees for and on behalf of the Company to make all appropriate contributions to the Producer-Writers Guild of America Pension Plan and the Writers Guild Industry Health Fund required under the above-mentioned Basic Agreement with respect to such additional compensation. It is expressly understood and agreed that the rights of Buyer to telecast such motion picture shall be subject to and conditioned upon the prompt payment to such writers involved of additional compensation for reruns and foreign telecasting of said television motion picture as provided in said Basic Agreement and his/her abiding by the credits provisions of such Schedule A, and it is agreed that Guild shall be entitled to injunctive relief and damages against Buyer in the event such payments are not made or such credit be not given.

The Buyer agrees to keep or have access to (i) complete records showing all cities in the United States and Canada in which all television motion pictures covered by this Assumption Agreement have been telecast and the number of telecasts in each such city, the television stations on which telecast, and the dates thereof, and (ii) complete records showing Distributor's Foreign Gross for such films to the extent that such records are pertinent to the computation of payments for foreign telecasting. Writers Guild of America shall have the right at all reasonable times to inspect such records. The Buyer shall also keep or have access to such records as are necessary for the computation of additional compensation for reruns and foreign telecasting for so long as such rerun or foreign telecasting payments may be due or payable. The Buyer shall give Writers Guild of America prompt written notice of the date on which each motion picture covered hereby is first telecast in any city in the United States or Canada, for the second run and for each subsequent run thereafter. With respect to each television motion picture which is distributed for foreign telecasting, the Buyer shall furnish reports to the Writers Guild of America showing Distributor s Foreign Gross derived from such motion picture until (i) such motion picture has been withdrawn from distribution for foreign telecasting have received the full additional payments for such foreign telecasting to which they are entitled pursuant to subparagraph 2. of Article 15.B. of the Basic Agreement. Such reports shall be rendered to the Guild on a quarterly basis during the first three (3) years in which any such motion picture is distributed for foreign telecasting, on a semi-annual basis for the next two (2) years and on an annual basis thereafter. The Buyer agrees to cooperate in responding to reasonable requests from the Guild as to whether any motion picture is currently being distributed for foreign telecasting. An inadvertent failure to comply with said requirement of notice shall not constitute a default by the Buyer hereunder, provided said failure is cured promptly after notice thereof from Writers Guild of America.

<hr>

BUYER

Date: _____

By _____

Address:"

Company agrees to give notice to the Guild within thirty (30) days of each sale, assignment or transfer of a television motion picture or literary material which is subject to this Basic Agreement, with the name and address of the purchaser, assignee, or transferee, and to deliver to the Guild an executed copy of the above referred to the Television Assumption Agreement together with a complete list of writers receiving screen credit for such television motion picture including social security numbers and rerun salary information. Failure to comply with this requirement shall be deemed a substantial breach of this Basic Agreement. An inadvertent failure on the part of the Company to comply with any of the provisions of this paragraph shall in no event constitute a default by the company or a breach of this Basic Agreement provided that such failure is cured promptly after notice thereof from the Writers Guild of America.

Upon delivery of such Television Assumption Agreement and on condition that the Guild approves in writing the financial responsibility of the purchaser, assignee or transferee, Company shall not be further liable for the keeping of any such records to the Guild or writer or for the payment of such additional compensation for reruns or foreign telecasting of for contributions to the Producer-Writers Guild of America Pension Plan, or to the Writers Guild-Industry Health Fund, or for credit, which are required in connection therewith, it being agreed that the purchaser, assignee or transferee shall solely be liable therefor.

The Guild agrees that it will not unreasonably withhold its approval of the financial responsibility of any such purchaser, assignee or transferee, it being further agreed that if the guild within twenty-one (21) days of receipt of notice of any such sale, assignment or transfer has not advised the Company that it disapproves the financial responsibility of such purchaser, assignee or transferee, the Guild will be deemed to have approved the financial responsibility thereof. In the event the Guild advises the Company within such twenty-one (21) day period that it disapproves the financial responsibility of any such purchaser, assignee or transferee and the Company disputes such disapproval, the Company shall have the right, at its election, to cause to be immediately submitted to arbitration, pursuant to the provisions of Articles 10, 11, and 12 hereof, the issue of whether the guild has unreasonably withheld the approval of the financial responsibility of such purchaser, assignee or transferee.

9. Continuance of Company's Responsibility

No television network, station, sponsor, or advertising agency which is not the producer of a television motion picture shall be liable for payment of such additional compensation unless it becomes the owner of the Company's television rights therein. It is expressly understood and agreed that the mandatory assumption agreement provisions of subparagraph 8. Above shall not be deemed to apply to distribution agreements under which the company licenses a distributor to distribute television motion pictures. However, Company may, if it wishes, obtain an assumption agreement from any such distributor or other licensee of television motion pictures, but the obtaining of any such assumption agreement shall in no event relieve the Company from the obligation to keep records hereunder or from the obligation to make payment of additional compensation for reruns or foreign telecasts and should company obtain any such assumption agreement from any such distributor, such distributor or licensee and Company may, if Company wishes, be made jointly and severally liable for the keeping of such records and for making of any such rerun and foreign telecast payments, except that such distributor shall not be liable for such payments or record keeping other than such obligations which arise from telecasts made under the distribution agreement of such distributor.

10. Use of excerpts

The use of an excerpt from a television motion picture shall be deemed a run or foreign telecast of such motion picture hereunder, except in the following circumstances:

a.   When used for promotional, trailer, news or review purposes; provided, however, that the length of such excerpt(s) shall not exceed four hundred (400) feet of 35mm film containing not less than two (2) scenes or two hundred (200) feet of 35mm film containing one (1) scene, or the equivalent in running time of the foregoing if 16mm film or video tape is used. For purposes of this subparagraph, a "**promotional**" use of an excerpt shall be for the purpose of advertising or publicizing the specific program or serial or series from which the excerpt is taken.

b. When used as a so-called "stock shot" (as customarily understood in the industry - *i.e.*, shots excluding dialogue or identifiable characters).

c. When used for purposes of recapping the story to date in the context of a serial, multi-part program, episodic series, unit series or anthology; provided, however, that if such recap shall exceed ninety (90) seconds in length when used on a program up to and including sixty (60) minutes in total length, or exceed one hundred twenty (120) seconds in length when used on a program in excess of sixty (60) minutes in total length, Company shall pay to the credited writer(s) of the program(s) from which the excerpts in the recap were taken an aggregate one-time-only sum equal to one hundred sixty-four dollars ($164.00) (effective May 2, 1996, one hundred seventy-four ($174.00)) for each minute or portion thereof by which the recap exceeds such length limitation; and provided, further, that no such recap shall exceed (without being deemed a run or foreign telecast as set forth above) four hundred (400) feet of 35mm film containing not less than two (2) scenes or two hundred (200) feet of 35mm film containing one (1) scene, or the equivalent in running time of the foregoing if 16mm film or video tape is used.

d. When used as a flashback in the context of multi-part series, episodic series, unit or anthology series or a one-time show or a prime time serial; provided however, that if such flashback shall exceed thirty (30) seconds in length, Company shall pay to the credited writer(s) of the program(s) from which the excerpts in the flashback were taken an aggregate, one-time-only sum equal to one hundred sixty-four dollars ($164.00) (effective May 2, 1996, one hundred seventy-four ($174.00)) for each minute or portion thereof by which the flashback exceeds such length limitation; and provided, further, that no such flashback shall exceed (without being deemed a run or foreign telecast as set forth above), four hundred (400) feet of 35mm film containing not less than two (2) scenes or two hundred (200) feet of 35mm film containing one (1) scene, or the equivalent in running time of the foregoing if 16mm film or video tape is used. For purposes of this subparagraph, a "*flashback*" use of an excerpt shall be for the purpose of informing viewers of past developments to explain or advance the current story being told.

dd.   For any use on television of excerpts not within the exceptions provided for in subparagraphs a. through d. above nor subparagraph e. below, or if such excerpts are otherwise within subparagraphs c. and d., but the aggregate running time of such excerpts from a single program exceeds the maximum applicable footage lengths, the Company shall pay the following aggregate one-time-only sum to the write or writers determined by the Guild to be entitled to such compensation and prorated as determined by the Guild:

	5/2/95- 5/1/96	5/2/96- 5/1/98
(1) ten (10) seconds or less of excerpts	$291	$308
(2) over ten (10) seconds but not more than two (2) minutes of excerpts	$879	$932
(3) over two (2) minutes but not more than ten (10) minutes of excerpts:		
for the first two (2) minutes	$879	$932
for each minute or portion thereof excess of two (2) minutes	$145	$154

or the applicable rerun fee; whichever is less.

(4)   Over ten (10) minutes of excerpts from such program - the applicable rerun fee.

In no event shall less than two hundred ninety-one dollars ($291.00) (effective May 2, 1996, three hundred eight dollars ($308.00)) be paid for the use of excerpts from a single program.

In addition, if ten percent (10%) (15% in the case of a thirty (30) minute program) or more but fifty percent (50%) or less of the running time of a program is comprised of excerpts from television motion pictures, or from theatrical and television motion pictures, and including excerpts used as flashbacks, Company shall pay for the use of such excerpts pursuant to Article 15.A.3.j. (if applicable) and this subparagraph dd. For the purposes of this subparagraph and subparagraph e. below, the "running time" of a program excludes commercials, title sequences and a recap up to and including 400 feet of 35mm film or equivalent.

e.   For "compilation" television programs utilizing excerpts from television motion pictures, or from theatrical and television motion pictures, the Company will pay, for such use, to the credited writer(s) of the excerpted material, prorated as determined by the Guild, an aggregate one-time-only sum equal to two and one-half (2-1/2) times the applicable thirty (30) minute minimum (and for this purpose, minimum is deemed to be the story and teleplay minimum set forth in Article 13.B.7.d. if the compilation is for network prime time) for each thirty (30) minutes of overall program length in which compilations are used. Exhibition of excerpts from television motion pictures in such compilation television programs shall not be deemed reruns or other use of the television motion pictures from which the excerpts are taken and the payments pursuant to this subparagraph relating to compilation shall not reduce or affect any other payments which may become due to the writer for the use of the television motion pictures from which such excerpts are taken. Payments pursuant to this subparagraph to the writers of the theatrical excerpts shall be in lieu of the excerpt payments set forth in Article 15.A.3.j.

For purposes of this subparagraph, a *"compilation"* television program is a program the running time of which is comprised of more than fifty percent (50%) of excerpts, including excerpts used as flashbacks.

If such compilation television includes excerpts which are not from "MBA-covered" programs, then the amount of time of the non-covered excerpts shall be subtracted from the running time of the entire program; and,

(1) If the MBA-covered excerpts are more than fifty percent (50%) of the remainder, the Company shall pay the compilation rate for such program pursuant to this Article 15.B.10.e. For purposes of calculating the appropriate compilation rate, the length of the program shall be determined based on the length of the remainder of the program utilizing the program lengths delineated in Article 13.B.7. In no event may the calculation be based on less than fifty percent (50%) of the length of the entire program; or,

(2) If fifty percent (50%) or less of the remainder of the program is MBA-covered excerpts, Articles 15.A.3.j. and 15.B.10.dd. will apply.

For the purposes of this subparagraph, the term "MBA-covered" includes excerpts from programs written pursuant to a WGA-PBS Agreement.

This compilation provision shall be applicable to excerpts derived from any television programs and any theatrical motion pictures utilizing literary material subject to any Guild collective bargaining agreement, prior or current, excluding only literary material the rights to which have reverted to the writer (for example, under the 1968 WGA Television Freelance MBA with the networks). Use of excerpts from programs to which such reversion of rights has occurred shall be subject to individual negotiation with the writers involved. When the Guild determines its allocation of payments for a compilation program, the allocation will be made as if the writers to whom rights had reverted were entitled to share in the allocation and thereafter funds to which those writers would have been entitled will be repaid to the Company by the Guild within thirty (30) days of the time within which the Company pays the Guild the lump sum allocation. If there is a dispute as to whether rights have reverted, the Guild, if it is aware of such dispute prior to making such payment, will hold the amount applicable to such dispute in escrow in a trust account pending the resolution of such dispute.

In the case of such dispute, the writer may elect to submit the matter to arbitration under the procedures set forth in Article 11.C. in lieu of any other remedy. The only parties to such arbitration shall be the writer and the Company. If the arbitrator rules that the rights in dispute have reverted, and if the excerpt is used, the writer will be entitled to a total of twice the amount he/she would have received (pursuant to the Guild's allocation) if the rights had not reverted. The foregoing shall be the sole damages or other relief available to the wrier if arbitration is elected. Any amount paid from the escrow account referred to above shall be deducted from the amount due from the Company.

f.   The production company which actually produces the program containing excerpts requiring payment shall be obligated to make such payment, but if such company is not signatory to this Basic Agreement, Company shall remain liable for payments due hereunder.

ff. If an excerpt from a free television motion picture is used on pay television or video discs/video cassettes, as such terms are used in Appendix B, or basic cable as defined in Appendix C, such use shall be treated in the same manner as though the excerpt were used on free television.

The use of an excerpt from a television motion picture in an interactive program shall be governed by the provisions of Article 64.

g. Except for payments required to be made pursuant to subparagraph e. above, no compensation shall be payable pursuant to this paragraph 10. to a writer of a television motion picture from which an excerpt is derived if such writer writes material for and receives writing credit on the program into which such excerpt is inserted. If two (2) or more writers are entitled to share the additional compensation provided for in subparagraph c., d., or dd. above, the Guild shall determine the allocation among said writers.

h. If an excerpt is used in a local program and the program is broadcast in no more than one (1) market, the payment for such use shall be sixty percent (60%) of the amount provided in this Article 15.B.10. If the program is broadcast later in another market, the writer(s) shall be paid the remaining forty percent (40%).

i. If writers entitled to payments under Article 15.B.10. of this Basic Agreement cannot be identified by name, the Company shall pay the required amount in full to the Guild to be distributed by the Guild to all the credited writer(s) of the television motion picture(s) from which the excerpted material was taken. The Company shall use its best efforts to provide the Guild with sufficient information to insure that the number of credited writers to whom such payments are distributed is as low as possible.

* * *

13. Additional Compensation for Theatrical Exhibition

In the event a television motion picture, based upon literary material to which this Basic Agreement applies, is exhibited theatrically, the writer or writers employed thereon who receive story and teleplay screen credit therefor shall be paid additional compensation as follows:

(i) If the television motion picture is exhibited theatrically outside of the United States, an amount which in the aggregate shall not be less than the total minimum compensation applicable to such literary material as specified in Article 13.B.7.a., b., c. and e. of the Basic Agreement, or not less than the total minimum compensation applicable to such literary material as specified in Article 13.A.1. hereof, whichever is greater;

(ii) If the television motion picture is exhibited theatrically in the United States, or both in the United States and in a foreign country or territory, an amount which in the aggregate is not less than one hundred fifty percent (150%) of the total minimum compensation applicable to such literary material as specified in Article

13.B.7.a., b., c. and e. of the Basic Agreement, or not less than the total minimum compensation applicable to such literary material as specified in Article 13.A.1. hereof, whichever is greater.

There is to be no duplication of the payments provided for in (i) and (ii) above; *i.e.*, if the initial theatrical release of the television motion picture takes place outside of the United States and payment is made pursuant to (i) above, then upon the subsequent theatrical release of the television motion picture in the United States, the amount payable to the writer will be the difference between the amount provided for in (i) above and the amount provided for in (ii) above, and conversely, if the initial theatrical release of the television motion picture takes place in the United States and payment is made pursuant to (ii) above, then no additional compensation will be payable if the television motion picture is subsequently released theatrically outside of the United States. For the purposes of (i) and (ii) above, if two (2) or more television motion pictures are combined for theatrical release, the applicable minimum provided for in Article 13.A.1. shall be the minimum applicable to one (1) theatrical motion picture of the cost of the combined television motion pictures. Such additional compensation shall be paid regardless of whether such motion picture is exhibited alone or as a part of or in combination with other motion pictures; and if such motion picture is combined with other television motion pictures, the additional compensation for such theatrical release shall be not less than the total minimum compensation applicable to the writing of all such television motion pictures or parts thereof which have been so combined. If more than one writer shares the story or teleplay credit, then all of the writers sharing each credit shall be considered a unit and shall participate equally and receive in the aggregate the theatrical exhibition payment applicable thereto, except that in the case of a comedy variety program the Guild shall determine the proportions in which such participating writers will share the theatrical exhibition payment, will notify the Company thereof and Company will make payments accordingly.

a. Such additional compensation for theatrical exhibition shall be payable whenever such television motion picture (in whole or in substantial part) is placed in any theatrical exhibition.

b. All payments of such additional compensation for theatrical exhibition shall be made promptly by check payable to the order of the writer entitled thereto, and if not paid to the writer at the time of employment shall be delivered up to Guild for forwarding to such writer, and compliance herewith shall constitute payment to the writer.

c. The Company, at its option, may make the additional payment for theatrical exhibition at the time of the employment of the writer or at any time prior to the time the same is due (but only if the agreement between the Company and the writer with respect thereto is set forth in the writer's individual contract); provided that only such part of the compensation initially paid to the writer as shall exceed the applicable minimum compensation may be applied in prepayment of additional compensation for theatrical exhibition.

Any exhibition of a motion picture, other than through the medium of free television or as covered by Article 51 (Supplemental Markets), shall constitute a theatrical exhibition and (subject to the provisions of Appendix C) payment for such theatrical exhibition shall be as herein provided, except that this shall not apply to showings where no fee or admission charge is paid by the viewing audience.

If the Company licenses or grants to any third party the right to place in the theatrical exhibition a television motion picture produced after March 1, 1981, which exhibition is to be before a viewing audience which pays no fee or admission charge to view the same, Company will pay to the writer(s) entitled to story and/or teleplay credit an amount equal in the aggregate to five percent (5%) of the gross amounts received by Company derived therefrom; provided, however, the sums paid to the writer(s) hereunder shall in no event exceed the applicable amount otherwise payable to such writer(s) under the provisions of paragraph 13. had there been a fee or admission charge paid by the viewing audience. Where Company licenses or grants any such right to a subsidiary or other related entity, the gross amounts referred to in the preceding sentence shall be the amounts specifically paid to the Company subject to there having been good faith bargaining between the Company and such subsidiary or related entity. Company shall account to the writer(s) entitled to payments hereunder on no less than an annual basis; provided that no accounting need be made for any twelve (12) month period following the twelve (12) month period during which the Company received no gross amounts with respect thereto. There shall be no duplication of the payments provided for in this subparagraph, and the payments provided for in any other provision of paragraph 13. That is, any payment made under this subparagraph shall be credited against any payment which may become due the writer(s) under all other provisions of paragraph 13. Conversely, payment is made to the writer(s) under the provisions of paragraph 13. other than under this subparagraph, then no further sum shall be payable under this subparagraph.

d. With respect to a television motion picture or multi-part program whose aggregate length as initially broadcast on television is more than four (4) hours and which is exhibited theatrically in condensed form, for purposes of this paragraph 13. the total minimum compensation applicable to such literary material as specified in Article 13.B.7.a., b., c., and e. shall be specially determined as follows:

(1) If said motion picture is exhibited theatrically outside of the United States, said minimum shall be based on the actual length of the motion picture in its condensed, theatrical-release form but not less than four (4) times the applicable sixty (60) minute minimum;

(2) If said motion picture is exhibited theatrically in the United States, or both in the United States and in a foreign country or territory, said minimum shall be based on the actual length of the motion picture in its condensed, theatrical release form, but no less than the sum of (a) four (4) times the applicable sixty (60) minute minimum plus (b) one-half of the difference between (i) the minimum applicable to the program in its initially broadcast length and (ii) four (4) times the applicable sixty (60) minute minimum.

The provisions set forth above in paragraph 13. relating to non-duplication of payments shall also apply to the foregoing special provisions.

e. If the Company shall sell, transfer, assign or otherwise dispose of its theatrical exhibition rights in any television motion picture, it shall obtain from the buyer a separate agreement in substantially the form prescribed with respect to reruns, requiring the buyer to comply with the provision of this Basic Agreement with respect to additional compensation payable to the writer for theatrical exhibition of the motion picture; and upon obtaining such agreement Company shall not be further liable to the Guild or writer for the payment of additional compensation for theatrical exhibition.

f. The excerpting of so-called "stock shots" by Company from television motion picture for transposition to and use in otherwise separately produced theatrical motion picture shall not be deemed to be an exercise of the theatrical exhibition rights by Company within the meaning of this paragraph 13. For any other use of excerpts from a television motion picture in a theatrical motion picture, the Company shall pay the following aggregate one-time-only sum to the writer or writers determined by the Guild to be entitled to such compensation and prorated as determined by the Guild:

	5/2/95- 5/1/96	5/2/96- 5/1/98
(a) thirty (30) seconds or less of excerpts	$366	$388
(b) over thirty (30) seconds but not over two (2) minutes of excerpts	$730	$774
(c) over two (2) minutes of excerpts: for the first two (2) minutes	$730	$774
for each minute or portion thereof in excess of two (2) minutes	$291	$308

g. If Company shall produce a motion picture budgeted at one hundred twenty-five thousand dollars ($125,000.00) or more intended primarily for television release and it shall thereafter release such motion picture theatrically in any country in the world, Company shall pay to writer any amount by which the established flat deal theatrical motion picture minimum for such motion picture at the time of its production shall exceed the total of the minimum applicable compensation and minimum theatrical exhibition payments required to be made hereunder. The established flat deal theatrical motion picture minimum shall be the compensation set forth in Article 13.A. hereof.

14. **Additional Compensation for Certain Use of Material to Which Separated Rights Do Not Apply**

Except as hereinbelow specifically provided, the Company shall have the right to use the literary material written for a serial, episodic series, unit series, or one-time television program in any field or medium whatsoever without any obligation to pay to the writer(s) thereof additional compensation. Additional compensation shall be paid to the writer of a story or (subject to the next sentence hereof) teleplay or story and teleplay for an established serial or episodic series, or for a unit series or one-time television program to which separated rights do not apply (and when specific use is made of the writer's material, rather than, for example, the source material only), as provided in this subparagraph 14., provided that the terms of this Basic Agreement relating to rights in material apply to such story, teleplay or story and teleplay as provided in Article 2 of this Basic Agreement. If such a teleplay be based upon a story in the public domain or upon a story owned by the Company, the writer of such teleplay shall not be entitled to any payments under the provisions of this subparagraph 14., except as provided in subparagraph 1. below. A writer employed to rewrite or polish a teleplay written by another person shall not be entitled to any payments under this subparagraph 14. If more than one writer qualifies for additional compensation under this subparagraph 14., the Guild shall determine the division of such additional compensation among them.

Such additional compensation shall be as follows:

a. If Company produces a theatrical motion picture based upon such material, it will pay to the writer whichever is the greater of (1), (2) or (3) below:

(1) Effective

5/2/95-5/1/96	$5,542
5/2/96-5/1/97	$5,736
5/2/97-5/1/98	$5,965

(2) Two percent (2%) of the above-the-line costs (excluding all theatrical script writing costs and deducting from the above-the-line costs the following arbitrary amount representing the value of the underlying rights):

Effective

5/2/95-5/1/96	$4,874
5/2/96-5/1/97	$5,045
5/2/97-5/1/98	$5,247

(3) the applicable minimum compensation for a screenplay under the then current Basic Agreement

b. If Company licenses or grants to any third party the right to use the material as the basis for a theatrical motion picture, it shall require such third party to agree in writing to pay to the writer the greater of 14.a.(1) or (2) above, and such undertaking by the third party will relieve the Company of any obligations to the writer in connection with such license or grant.

c. If Company produces a radio program based upon such material, it will pay to the writer the following:

Effective	For Each National Radio Network Broadcast	For Each Regional Radio Network Broadcast	Unlimited Right to Use In Syndication Any Transcription Made of a Program
5/2/95-5/1/96	$277	$183	$183
5/2/96-5/1/97	287	189	189
5/2/97-5/1/98	298	197	197

d. If the Company licenses or grants to any third party the right to use the material as the basis for a radio program, Company will pay to the writer an amount equal to fifty percent (50%) of Company net receipts therefrom. The net receipts to the Company shall be computed by deducting from the gross amounts paid to the Company on account of such license or sale of the radio rights all royalties, license fees or participations which the Company is contractually obligated to pay by reason of the license or grant of the radio rights, together with agents' commissions, if any, on the license or grant of such radio rights.

e. If Company exercises the dramatic rights in such material by producing a play on the speaking stage, it will pay to the writer an amount equal to one percent (1%) of the gross box office receipts of the play.

f. If the Company licenses or grants to any third party the right to use the dramatic rights in the material, Company will pay to the writer an amount equal to twenty-five percent (25%) of the gross receipts derived by the Company from the license or sale of such rights.

g. If the Company licenses or grants to any third party or exercises itself the publication rights to such material (other than publication rights customarily granted for advertising or publicizing the exploitation of any other rights in the material), Company will pay to the writer an amount equal to twenty-five percent (25%) of the Company's net receipts derived therefrom.

If the Company licenses or grants to any third party, or exercises itself, the right to produce or reproduce such material on phonograph records, cartridges, compact devices or any other devices which are audio only, Company will pay to the writer or writers as a group an amount equal to that fraction of twenty-five percent (25%) of the Company's net receipts derived from the licensing, grant or use of the literary material which is equal to the fraction of the overall material in the applicable audio device which such material constitutes. Notwithstanding the foregoing, if such material constitutes more than fifty percent (50%) of the overall material in the applicable audio device, the Company will pay the writer or writers as a group an amount equal to twenty-five percent (25%) of the Company's net receipts derived therefrom. For purposes of this subparagraph g., the Company's net receipts in each instance shall be computed by deducting from the gross amounts paid to the Company or its licensing agent, whether affiliated or otherwise, with respect to the licensing, grant or use of such material, all costs, expenses and charges incident thereto, including a distribution or servicing fee by the Company (which will include any and all subdistribution or subservicing fees), which fee shall be reasonably in accordance with customary distribution or servicing fees charged in the industry. When Company licenses or grants any such rights to a subsidiary or other related entity, the gross amounts referred to in the preceding sentence shall be the amounts specifically paid to the Company for such license, grant or use, subject to there having been good faith bargaining between the Company and such subsidiary or related entity. Company shall account to the writer(s) entitled to payments under this subparagraph g. on no less than an annual basis; provided that no accounting need be made for any twelve (12) month period following the twelve (12) month period during which the Company received no gross amounts with respect to the applicable audio device.

h. Character payments

(1)   a. If the writer introduces a new character in the serial or episodic series, and the characterization of such character is fully developed and fully described in the material written by the writer, and from such development and description the character appears to be unique and the principal creation of the writer, and if the Company uses such character as the central character with a continuing role in a new and different serial or episodic type free television series, the Company will pay to the writer the sum specified in the following table for each episode of such new and different series produced and broadcast, provided that such writer shall be entitled only to sixty percent (60%) of said amount for fifteen (15) minute episodes but shall be entitled to one hundred ninety percent (190%) of said amount for sixty (60) minute episodes and two hundred fifty percent (250%) of said amount for ninety (90) minute or longer episodes. Said applicable amount shall be paid in the same manner as provided in subparagraph 1. of Article 16.B. with respect to television series sequel rights

and rerun payments will be made in accordance with Article 15.B., the "applicable minimum compensation" for such purpose being said applicable amount.

For such characters in literary material written hereunder by writer during

5/2/95-5/1/96	$1,149
5/2/96-5/1/97	$1,189
5/2/97-5/1/98	$1,237

The character payments provided by this subparagraph (1) shall not apply if any writer, including the creator of the character, is entitled under Article 16.B. to separation of rights in the new and different serial or episodic series. However, if separation of rights does exist in the new and different serial or episodic series and the writer who previously introduced the central character is not a participant in such separated rights, said writer alternatively shall be paid with respect to each episode of the new serial or series in which the character appears the lesser character payment which now applies to a principal character used in subsequent episodes of the same series in which it is introduced.

b. If the writer introduces a new character in the serial or episodic series, and the characterization of such character is fully developed and fully described in the material written by the writer, and from such development and description the character appears to be unique and the principal creation of the writer, and if the Company uses such character as the central character with a continuing role in a new and different serial or episodic type series produced pursuant to Appendix B of this Basic Agreement, the Company will pay to the writer the following amounts as a one-time payment for each episode of such new and different series produced and broadcast:

Program Length in Minutes	5/2/95-5/1/96	5/2/96-5/1/97	5/2/97-5/1/98
15 or less	$675	$699	$727
30 or less (but more than 15)	1,347	1,394	1,450
60 or less (but more than 30)	2,022	2,093	2,177
90 or more	2,696	2,790	2,902

Said applicable amount shall satisfy all obligations of the Company to such writer, and no additional sum or sums shall be payable by reason of any use of such episodes.

The character payments provided by this subparagraph (1)b. shall not apply if any writer, including the creator of the character, is entitled under Article 16.B. to separation of rights in the new and different serial or episodic series. However, if separation of rights does exist in the new and different serial or episodic series produced pursuant to Appendix B and if the writer who previously introduced the central character is not a participant in such separated rights, said writer alternatively shall be paid with respect to each episode of the new serial or series in which the character appears the lesser character payment which now applies to a principal character used in subsequent episodes of the same series in which it is introduced.

(2) If a writer for an established episodic series creates a principal character who is distinct and identifiable, and is fully developed and fully described in the material written by the writer, and from such development and description the character appears to be unique and other than generic and the principal creation of the writer, the Company will pay such writer the sum specified in the following table for each subsequent episode of such series in which the character appears.

For such characters in literary material written hereunder by writer during

5/2/95-5/1/96	$328
5/2/96-5/1/97	339
5/2/97-5/1/98	353

The character shall not be deemed unique, as required by the foregoing, if the character is played by an actor who plays himself or herself, or plays an established alter ego.

Company shall be liable for no more than four (4) such payments (or no more than an amount equal to four (4) such payments) for characters on any one (1) episode, unit or program and the writer(s) of the pilot script for any such series shall not be eligible for such payments at all with respect to characters in such pilot script subsequently used in episodes of the series.

Uses of a character in separate episodes of a multi-part closed-end series shall not constitute the use of the character in a new and different episode for the purposes of this Agreement, if the writer who created the character is a participating writer on the subsequent episode.

The character payment provided for by this subparagraph (2) are not subject to rerun payments.

(3) Payments for use of a character which meets the criteria of this Article 15.B.14.h., but which is introduced in a unit of a unit series or a one-time free television program to which separation of rights does not apply, shall also be made as follows:

(a) If used as the central character with a continuing role in a new and different serial or episodic series to which separation of rights does not apply, the same character payment as provided in the applicable table in subparagraph (1) above; or

(b) If used as a principal character in a new and different unit of a unit series or in a new and different one-time television program, to which separation of rights does not apply, the same character payment as provided in the table in subparagraph (2) above.

(3.1) Payments for use of a character which meets the criteria of Article 15.B.14.h. but which is introduced in a unit of a unit series or a one-time program produced pursuant to Appendix B of this Basic Agreement to which program or series separation of rights does not apply, also shall be made as follows:

(a) If used as the central character with a continuing role in a new and different serial or episodic series produced pursuant to Appendix B, to which separation of rights does not apply, the same character payment as provided in the table in subparagraph (1)b., above, or

(b) If used as a principal character in a new and different unit of a unit series or in a new and different one-time program produced pursuant to Appendix B to which separation of rights does not apply, the same character payment as provided in the table in subparagraph (2) above.

(3.2) If a writer introduces a new character in a serial or episodic series, and the characterization of such character is fully developed and fully described in the material written by the writer, and from such development and description the character appears to be unique and the principal creation of the writer, and if the Company uses such character as a principal character in a theatrical motion picture, the Company will make the following one-time-only payment to such writer for each theatrical motion picture in which such character is used:

5/2/95-5/1/96	$5,877
5/2/96-5/1/97	6,083
5/2/97-5/1/98	6,326

The character payments provided by this subparagraph (3.2) shall not apply:

a.   if the creator of the character is also the writer of the screenplay containing such character; or

b.   if the creator of the character is entitled to separation of rights under Article 16.B. in the serial or episodic series from which the character was taken.

The foregoing payment shall be made within thirty (30) days after release of such theatrical motion picture.

(4)   A dispute between writers as to who created such a character shall be determined by the Guild in accordance with its credit arbitration proceedings.

(5)   If the Company licenses or grants to any third party the right to use such a new character in the manner described in this subparagraph h., the Company will require such third party to agree in writing to pay to the writer the amounts hereinabove provided, and such undertaking by the third party will relieve the Company of any obligations to the writer in connection with such license or grant.

i.   In the event that such a teleplay is used for a live television broadcast, and no writer is employed to rewrite, adapt or revise such teleplay for the live broadcast, the provisions of Article 13.B.7.o. shall apply.

j.   In the event that a writer is employed to rewrite, adapt or revise such material for a live television broadcast, and such rewritten, adapted or revised material shall be used for a live television broadcast, the provisions of Article 13.B.7.o. shall apply.

k.   [Deleted.]

l.   The writer of a teleplay based upon a story in the public domain shall be entitled to payments under the foregoing provisions of this subparagraph 14. if such teleplay is substantially used by Company in any field or medium referred to in said provisions and such public domain story was suggested by the writer in a written proposal made to Company by the writer and the use in question otherwise meets the conditions set forth in this subparagraph 14. In addition:

(1) If such a teleplay is used for the production of a free television motion picture which is the pilot of an episodic series or serial which is an established series or serial by virtue of being based upon such public domain story, the writer thereof shall be entitled to a payment in the amount specified in the following table for each episode in such series or serial which is thereafter produced and broadcast substantially utilizing the writer's creative treatment embodied in such teleplay; provided, however, that said writer shall be entitled only to sixty percent (60%) of said amount for fifteen (15) minute television motion pictures, but shall be entitled to one hundred ninety percent (190%) of said amount for sixty (60) minute television motion pictures and two hundred fifty percent (250%) of said amount for ninety (90) minute or longer television motion pictures.

For such teleplay written hereunder by writer during

5/2/95-5/1/96	$1,149
5/2/96-5/1/97	1,189
5/2/97-5/1/98	1,237

Except as provided in subparagraphs 1. and 2. of this Article 15.B., the applicable payment referred to in the preceding sentence shall satisfy all obligations of the Company to the writer, and no additional sum or sums shall be payable by reason of any use of such episode; or

(2) If such teleplay is used for the production pursuant to Appendix B of this Basic Agreement of a program which is the pilot of an episodic series or serial which is an established series or serial by virtue of being based upon such public domain story, the writer thereof shall be entitled to a one-time payment of the following for each episode in such series or serial which is thereafter produced pursuant to Appendix B and broadcast and which substantially utilizes the writer's creative treatment embodied in such teleplay:

Program Length in Minutes	5/2/95-5/1/96	5/2/96-5/1/97	5/2/97-5/1/98
15 or less	$675	$699	$727
30 or less (but more than 15)	1,347	1,394	1,450
60 or less (but more than 30)	2,022	2,093	2,177
90 or more	2,696	2,790	2,902

The applicable payment referred to in the preceding sentence shall satisfy all obligations of the Company to the writer and no additional sum or sums shall be payable by reason of any use of such episode.

Nothing in subparagraphs (1) or (2) above shall give to the writer any rights to payment under this subparagraph 14. with respect to any use by the Company of the public domain material itself as distinct from the use of the writer's teleplay based thereon, nor impair the Company's right to deal with such public domain material freely without obligation to the writer or anyone. The question of whether the writer suggested and furnished such public domain story and the question of whether the Company substantially used the writer's said creative treatment in subsequent episodes or in another field or medium entitling the writer to a payment hereunder shall be subject to the grievance and arbitration provisions of Articles 10, 11, and 12 herein. A decision under such procedures as provided in said Articles 10, 11, and 12 shall be binding upon the Company, the Guild and the individual writer or writers involved. The only and maximum remedy under such procedures shall be the applicable minimum additional payment as provided in these subparagraphs (1) and (2).

m. If the Company licenses or grants to any third party the merchandising rights to such material (as described in Article 1), Company will pay to writer an amount equal to five percent (5%) of Company's net receipts (as net receipts are defined in paragraph g. of this subparagraph 14.) derived from such merchandising rights. Comic books, magazine publications, comic strips, cutouts, and other activity books shall be deemed to be included as merchandising rights.

n. Notwithstanding any other provision of this Agreement, if the writer

(1) first describes in literary material an object or thing which is fully described in such literary material and by such description appears to be unique and original; and/or,

(2) introduces a character and the characterization of such character is fully developed and fully described in the material
written by the writer and from such development and description the character appears to be unique and the principal
creation of the writer,

and an interactive program is based upon such object, thing or
character, the writer will be paid as provided in Article 64.

o. Company shall give notice to Guild on completion of arrangement
for uses under this subparagraph 14. [footnote omitted]

* * *

ARTICLE 16 — SEPARATION OF RIGHTS

A. THEATRICAL

1. Definitions

For the purpose of this Section A., Theatrical, the following terms
or words used herein shall have the following meanings:

a. The term *"dramatic rights"* means the right of presentation in
dramatic form on the speaking stage with living actors appearing
and performing in the immediate presence of an audience, without
any recordation, transmission or broadcast thereof intended for
or permitting concurrent or future aural, or visual and aural,
reception or reproduction at places away from the auditorium or
other place of performance.

b. The term *"publication rights"* includes the right of publication
in all writing forms and all writing media, excluding only comic
books, comic strips and newspaper comics.

The provisions of this paragraph shall apply only to material
subject to this Basic Agreement and acquired after the effective
date hereof under contracts subject to and entered into after the
effective date of this Basic Agreement.

c. The term *"sequel"* as used with reference to a particular motion
picture, means a new theatrical motion picture in which the
principal characters of the first theatrical motion picture participate in an entirely new and different story.

d. The term *"assigned material"* means all material in writing or
any other fixed form, of every nature that the Company has
furnished the writer (or to which the Company has directed the
writer) upon which material the Company intends the story (or
story and screenplay) to be based or from which it is to be, in

whole or in part, adapted. The term *"assigned material"* may include public domain material or a character or characters proposed for use in the story (or story and screenplay).

2. Initial Qualification

The Company agrees that if a writer, while in the employ of the Company, writes an original story (or original story and screenplay), including a complete and developed plot and character development, he/she shall be initially qualified for separation of rights hereunder. A writer shall be deemed to have written a complete and developed plot and character development if he/she does so himself/herself or if the product of the work of such writer and writers previously (but after June 13, 1960) employed hereunder together constitute such a complete and developed plot and character development. Company also agrees that if it purchases from a professional writer such a story (or story and screenplay) written by such person, such person shall be initially qualified for separation of rights hereunder. If at the time of the transfer of rights to the material so purchased there is in existence a valid agreement for the publication or dramatic production of such material, then for the purpose of this Article 16.A. such material shall be deemed to have been published or exploited.

With respect to a writer employed by the Company, if there is assigned material then:

a. If the employment agreement (or written assignment delivered by the Company to the writer, in the case of a term contract, week-to-week contract, or multiple picture type employment) designates as the assigned material upon which the motion picture is to be based, or from which it is to be adapted, a story contained in a book, magazine, screenplay, play or other dramatic composition, treatment or story in any other form, then the writer, or any other writer working thereon, shall not be qualified for separation of rights unless:

   (1) With the knowledge and prior or subsequent consent of the Company the writer departed from the story contained in such assigned material and created an original story (or original story and screenplay) of the nature first described in this subparagraph 2., to the extent that there is no longer any substantial similarity between such story written by the writer and such story contained in the assigned material; or

   (2) The assigned material designated in the employment agreement or written assignment was not actually available to the writer, and the writer creates a story (or story and screenplay) of the nature first described in this subparagraph 2.

If the writer makes either of such contentions and the Company and writer cannot agree thereon, either the writer or the Company may submit the issue to arbitration and if it is determined by arbitration that the facts were as described in (1) or (2) above, then such writer shall be initially qualified for separation of rights hereunder.

b. If a character or characters furnished by the Company is intended by the Company to be a principal character in the motion picture, and if such character was taken from material, of any nature, theretofore published or exploited in any manner or by any medium, and if such character is used in the screenplay as a principal character, then the writer shall not be qualified for separation of rights hereunder. If, however, any such character furnished by the Company as aforesaid was a minor character in previously published or otherwise exploited material, and with the prior or subsequent consent of the Company was converted by the writer into a principal character in the story (or story and screenplay) of the nature above described in this subparagraph 2., written by the writer, and if no minor character as furnished by the Company (as distinguished from such character or characters as developed by the writer) constitutes a substantial contribution to the final screenplay, and if no principal character furnished by the Company remains a principal character in the motion picture, then such writer shall be initially qualified for separation of rights hereunder. If such character or characters furnished by the Company were not taken from material theretofore published or exploited any manner or by any medium, and if the writer were otherwise qualified for separation of rights hereunder, the writer shall not be deprived of such separation of rights, unless Company constitutes a substantial contribution to the final screenplay, in which latter event such writer shall not be qualified for separation of rights hereunder.

3. **Final Qualification**

If it is determined, in the manner provided in Theatrical Schedule A attached hereto, that the writer of the story (or story and screenplay), initially qualified for separation of rights as above provided, is entitled to receive "Story by" or "Written by" or "Screen Story by" credit, he/she shall be entitled to separation of rights in the following areas:

a. **Publication Rights.** Publication rights throughout the world in the "separable material," as hereinafter defined, shall be licensed exclusively to the writer on a royalty-free basis both for the original term of copyright and for any extensions and renewals thereof, without the necessity for the execution by the Company of any further instrument, except as expressly provided below and subject to the provision of subparagraph 7.e hereof and to the following:

(1)   No publication rights may be exercised by the writer prior to the expiration of three (3) years from date of the employment contract (or the date of the assignment of the writer in the case of a term contract, week-to-week contract or multiple picture type employment) or three (3) years from the date of acquisition in case the material is purchased, or prior to the expiration of six (6) months following the general release of the motion picture or one (1) year following commencement of principal photography, whichever shall first occur. Notwithstanding the foregoing provisions of this subparagraph (1), the time restriction on the exercise by the writer of hardcover publication rights shall not extend beyond the commencement of the general release of the motion picture.

(2)   The Company shall be entitled to and shall own the exclusive right to make, publish and copyright or cause to made, published and copyrighted in the name of the Company or its nominee, serially or otherwise, in any and all languages and throughout the world, synopses, summaries, resumes, adaptations, stories and fictionalized versions of and excerpts from any screenplay or photoplay, in any form and in any publication media (with or without illustrations) for the purpose of advertising, publicity or exploitation, of the motion picture based on such material, provided that any single photo-novel publication may not exceed 5,000 words in length or 7,500 words in length for any other single publication.

(3)   If a Company desires to publish, or cause to be published, a "paperback" type of novelization for the purpose of publicizing or exploiting such motion picture, the Company shall have the right to do so (and without being subject to any limitation on the number of words) if it follows either of the following procedures:

(i) Regular Procedure

(a) Publication shall not take place earlier than six (6) months prior to the initial scheduled release date of the motion picture. The Company shall give written notice to the Guild and to the writer(s) entitled to separation of rights, specifying Company's desire for such publication and the names of at least three (3) publishers (not more than one of which may be affiliated with Company) who are acceptable to the Company.

(b) The Company may also submit to such writer(s) a proposed arrangement for publication which may include the right to publish, novelization by any person, and the use of the "art work" referred to below ("a package proposal").

(c) If the qualifying "Story by," "Screen Story by" or "Written by" credit is shared by more than one writer, said writers shall determine which writer shall have the right to negotiate with the publisher for the right to publish and for the services of one of said writers for novelization. If the writers cannot reach agreement, the Guild will determine which of such writers shall have the right to negotiate the right to publish and which of such writers is to write the novelization.

(d) In any event the Company shall be notified by the Guild within ten (10) days of the Company's giving notice of the name of the writer(s) who shall negotiate (the "negotiating writer") and the name of the writer(s) who will write the novelization. If the negotiating writer(s) approves the package proposal, publication may proceed on that basis.

(e) In the event that an agreement reached by the negotiating writer(s) shall result in a deal for both rights and services, two-thirds (2/3) of all monies payable shall be for the right to publish and one-third (1/3) shall be for services.

(f) A publication agreement entered into by the negotiating writer(s) shall provide that the Company shall control the time of publication and the time and locale of release. The Company shall retain the exclusive right to arrange for and to keep as its sole property, payment for any legends, advertising material, stills and any other elements furnished by the Company (hereinafter "art work"), but not title and logo.

(g) The publisher selected by the writer shall have the right to use the title and logo (but not including the likeness of characters except as provided below) of the motion picture for use in connection with or on the novelization and the Company shall be paid for such use twenty-five percent (25%) of the monies paid for publication rights. Except as provided in the preceding sentence, all payments for the right to publish shall be made to and retained by the writer(s). The publisher shall have the right, in connection with or on the novelization, to use the likeness of a character or characters appearing in the motion picture only where all of the following conditions are present: (i) such likeness is an inextricable part of the logo; (ii) the Company has the right to authorize such use; and (iii) no additional payments will be required of Company as a result of such use.

(h) If the Guild does not give the notice referred to in (d) above within the aforementioned ten (10) day period, or if the writer(s) does not elect to write the novelization or if the writer does not consummate a publication agreement with a publisher within thirty (30) days after the notice referred to in (a) above, then the Company shall have the right, on such terms as it may elect, to cause the novelization to be published by such publisher as it may elect. If the compensation to be paid the person writing such novelization exceeds that offered by a publishing company for the services of a writer(s) with separated rights who was selected to write such novelization pursuant to this subparagraph, then such writer will be given an opportunity to write the novelization for such increased compensation.

(i) Copyright in any novelization written pursuant to this subparagraph (3) shall be taken and remain in the name of the Company or its nominee.

(ii)   Expedited procedure

(a)   The Company may request the Guild at any time to specify the "negotiating writer" and the writer(s) who will write the novelization. If at the time of the Company's request the credits are not determined and there has been more than one participating writer, the Guild will expeditiously determine the writer entitled to "preliminary separation of rights" in accordance with the provision of Theatrical Schedule A.

If at the time of the Company's request there is only one participating writer, then such writer will be named by the Guild as the negotiating writer and the writer who will write the novelization.

(b)   The negotiating writer will have the right to negotiate with the publisher(s) named by the Company for publication of the novelization.

If the Company names only a publisher which is an affiliate or subsidiary of the Company, such publisher will promptly make a proposal to the writer for the publication of the novelization. The writer will have a period of thirty (30) days to negotiate with another publisher of commensurate status in the publishing industry. If writer obtains a better proposal from the other publisher, he/she will offer it to the Company-named publisher on a first refusal basis. If the Company-named publisher does not meet the terms within five (5) business days, the writer may proceed with a publication agreement with the other publisher.

(c)   If the negotiating writer enters into a publication agreement and thereafter the Guild determines that any other writer has an interest in the separation of rights, the negotiating writer shall be required to share the proceeds of such publication in such proportion as determined by the Guild and all the participating writers shall be bound by the Guild's determination.

(d)   If the negotiating writer does not enter into a publication agreement within the thirty (30) day period, the Company may cause the novelization to be published and the payments which would be due the negotiating writer will be paid to the Guild for the account of the writer or writers ultimately determined by the Guild to be entitled to separated rights.

(e)   At Company's election, the publication may take place earlier than six (6) months prior to the initial scheduled release date of the motion picture; provided, however, that such publication must be for the purpose of publicizing or exploiting the motion picture, and provided, further, that principal photography of the motion picture must be commenced prior to the actual publication date.

If Company elects the expedited procedure in (ii) above, and the negotiating writer enters into a publication agreement pursuant thereto, in all other respects the provisions of the regular procedure in (i) above shall apply, including Company's sole control of licensing of the "art work," except for title and logo.

If the negotiating writer does not enter into the publication agreement within the applicable aforementioned period, the Company will nevertheless pay or cause to be paid to the writer, if any, entitled to separation of rights, a three thousand five hundred dollar ($3,500.00) advance against an amount equal to thirty-five percent (35%) of the Company's adjusted gross receipts from the publisher with respect to such publication. Adjusted gross receipts are the total receipts received by the Company from the publisher with respect to such publication less only (A) the actual monies paid for the writing of such novelization (but for the purpose hereof deduction of such monies shall not be greater than an amount reasonably in accordance with customary amounts paid by the established publishing companies for the paperback novelization of motion picture screenplays), and (B) the sum of seven thousand dollars ($7,000.00) which shall be deemed to be, for this purpose only, the cost of the art work. The term "novelization" as used in the preceding sentence means a novelization which is based upon the separable material and utilizing the separable material in a manner which would constitute a copyright infringement of such separable material of the writer if the writer were the sole copyright owner thereof. At the request of Company in case of conflict between the time periods delineated hereinabove, and the release schedule of the picture, the Guild will give reasonable waivers to reduce the applicable period for negotiation by the negotiating writer.

(4) If the writer exercises any of the publication rights, and on each occasion that the writer exercises the publication rights licensed to him/her hereunder, copyright in the published work shall be taken and remain in the name of the Company or its nominee; writer shall cause the publisher to comply with all necessary copyright formalities; and the Company shall have, and is hereby granted all rights of every nature in and to the published work, including the right to extend or renew the copyright, except for such rights, if any, as may have been expressly reserved by the writer under and pursuant to his/her employment agreement or in the agreement for the purchase of unpublished and unexploited material from a Guild member, and excepting also the publication rights and dramatic rights therein, to the extent that publication and dramatic rights are licensed to and permitted to be used by the writer under all the terms and provisions of this Article 16.A. If the writer arranges for the publication of a novel or short story, as permitted hereunder, all royalties and other monies received by such writer under the publication agreement between the publisher and the writer shall be the sole property of the writer.

(5) If the writer exercises any publication rights licensed him/her hereunder, the writer shall have the right to make his/her own arrangements of republication of the novel or short story, as permitted hereunder, and shall have exclusive control of all matters relating to such publication, except as expressly provided in subparagraph (4) above and this subparagraph (5) in connection with such exercise. As soon as practical after the writer has the same, but in any event within a reasonable period prior to the publication thereof, the writer will submit to the Company a copy or proof of the work in the form in which it is to be published together with a reasonably detailed statement of the manner in which the publication will be made. The writer will not use the title of the motion picture as the title of his/her published work without the prior written consent of the Company; and if the Company requests the writer to use the title of the motion picture as the title of his/her published work, the writer agrees to do so. If prior to the release of the motion picture by the

Company it is determined that the writer is entitled to separation of rights, in the manner hereinafter provided, and if prior to such release the writer exercises any publication rights licensed hereunder, the Company may, but shall not be required to, use the title of the published work or any translation or adaptation thereof as the title of the motion picture.

(6) The term **"publication rights,"** for purposes of this Article 16.A. only, includes the right to publish a script in whole or in substantial part. The Company and, subsequent to the time periods set for in this Article 16.A.3.a.(1), the writer, each shall have the non-exclusive right to publish less than a substantial portion or portions of a script.

b. **Dramatic Rights**. If the Company does not exploit or cause to be exploited the dramatic rights in the story, screenplay or motion picture at any time prior to two (2) years following the general release of the motion picture in a *bona fide* dramatic production intended to exploit such dramatic rights, or if the company does not commence the principal photography of the motion picture within five (5) years (plus the aggregate of periods, not to exceed six (6) months, that commencement of photography is postponed by "force majeure" type contingencies occurring within the last six (6) months of the five (5) year period) following the date of the employment contract (or the date of the written assignment in the case of a term contract, week-to-week contract or multiple picture type employment) or the date of acquisition if the material is purchased, then in either such event the Company shall lose its rights to exploit the dramatic rights, and thereafter the separable material shall be licensed exclusively to the writer on a royalty-free basis both for the original term of copyright and any extension or renewals thereof without the necessity for the execution by the Company of any further instrument, except as expressly provided below and subject to the provisions of subparagraph 7.e. hereof and to the following:

(1) If the writer exercises the dramatic rights licensed to him/her hereunder, the Company shall be the copyright proprietor of the dramatic work and, if the dramatic work is registered for statutory copyright, copyright therein shall be taken and remain in the name of the Company or its nominee. Whether or not writer registers the dramatic work for statutory copyright, the Company shall acquire all rights of every nature in and to the dramatic work, including the right to extend

and renew the copyright, except for such rights, if any, as may have been expressly reserved by the writer under and pursuant to his/her employment agreement or in the agreement for the purchase of unpublished and unexploited material from a Guild member and except for the publication rights and dramatic rights therein (but only to the extent that such publication rights and dramatic rights are licensed to and permitted to be used by the writer under all of the terms and provisions of this Article 16.A.) and except for such musical compositions interpolated in the dramatic work (but not contained in whole or in part in the story, screenplay, or motion picture nor acquired in whole or in part from the Company), which neither contributes to nor forms a part of the story line of the dramatic work. With respect to the musical compositions in which the Company acquires rights under the preceding sentence, nothing contained in such sentence shall be construed to grant to Company any rights in any such musical compositions which are greater than the maximum rights therein at any time acquired or controlled by the writer.

(2) If the Company, within the period above mentioned, exploits the dramatic rights, the Company will pay or cause to be paid to the writer sums equal to fifty percent (50%) of the minimum amounts payable to an "Author" under the terms of the Minimum Basic Production Contract recommended by the Dramatists Guild of the Authors League of America, Inc., in effect upon the commencement of the dramatic performance; unless the writer is the "Author" of the dramatic work in which case the writer shall only be entitled to the minimum amounts payable pursuant to such Minimum Basic Production Contract in effect when the writing services as such "Author" of the dramatic work are performed. Subject to the provisions hereinafter contained in this subparagraph (2), "minimum amounts" as used in this subparagraph (2), mean and include only the minimum percentage of gross box office receipts payable to an "Author" by a "Producer" under such Minimum Basic Production Contract, or would otherwise be payable to such "Author," as aforesaid, except by reason of the deferment thereof because of prepayment against such percentages. For purposes of this subparagraph (2) there shall not be offset against the minimum percentages of such gross box office receipts otherwise payable to such "Author" by such "Producer" under such Minimum Basic Production

Contract payments set forth in "THIRD (a)" or "FOURTH (a)" of the Minimum Basic Production Contract now in effect (or comparable payments set forth in any Minimum Basic Production Contract hereafter in effect) which such "Producer" may have made thereunder to such "Author"; nor shall any percentages of any such payments be payable hereunder to the writer. Where, under such Minimum Basic Production Contract, the "Producer" elects to pay to the "Author" (as an alternative to the payment of the percentage of the gross weekly box office receipts) monies under "THIRD (c)(i)" or "THIRD (d)(i)" of such Minimum Basic Production Contract for non-musical plays now in effect or under "THIRD (c)(i)" of such Minimum Basic Production Contract for musical now in effect, or elects to make comparable alternative payments under any Minimum Basic Production Contract hereafter in effect, then for purposes of this subparagraph (2) "minimum amounts" shall mean and include only such alternative payments at the minimum rates therefor set forth in such Minimum Basic Production Contract to the extent that such alternative payments are made thereunder in lieu of such percentage of the gross weekly box office receipts. In the case of a musical play where the person who has written the book therefor has not also written the music and lyrics, such "minimum amounts" mean and include only a fraction of such minimum percentages of such gross box office receipts or such alternative payments at such minimum rates therefor, as the case may be. Such fraction shall be the same as the fraction of gross box office receipts or alternative payments, as the case may be, to which the person who has written the book is entitled under such person's agreement with such one or more persons who has or have written the music and lyrics for such musical play.

(3)   If the writer exercises the dramatic rights licensed to him/her hereunder, he/she will, prior to the first performance of the dramatic work, submit to the Company a copy thereof, and the writer will not, without the consent of the Company, use the title of the motion picture or the story or screenplay, as the case may be, as the title of the dramatic work. If the Company requests the writer to do so, the writer agrees to use the title of the motion picture as the title of the dramatic work. If prior to the release of the motion picture by the Company it is determined that the writer is entitled to separation of rights, in the manner hereinafter provided, and

if prior to such release the writer exercises any dramatic rights licensed hereunder, the Company may, but shall not be required to, use the title of the dramatic work or any translation or adaptation thereof as the title of the motion picture.

(4) If the writer shall exploit the dramatic rights licensed to him/her hereunder, and shall require financing from any source, the writer shall first offer the Company the opportunity to provide such financing by a written notice to the Company, setting forth in detail the terms and conditions upon which the writer proposes to obtain such financing. Within thirty (30) days after receipt of such notice, the Company may notify the writer that it elects to provide all or any part of such required financing upon the terms set forth in the writer's notice. If within such period the Company notifies the writer that it does not elect to provide such financing, or fails within the thirty (30) day period to respond to the writer's notice, then the writer may obtain the required financing elsewhere, but the writer agrees that he/she will not offer to any lender or investor terms or conditions more favorable in any respect to such lender or investor than those set forth in writer's notice to the Company, without again notifying the Company of such more favorable terms or conditions, and permitting the Company a period of thirty (30) days within which to accept or reject the writer's proposal, in the manner above provided. The provisions of this subparagraph shall apply in each instance in which the writer makes any change in any term or condition of his/her financing offer more favorable to the lender or investor than those set forth in the writer's last notice to the Company.

c. With respect to a screenplay sold or licensed to Company by a professional writer (as defined in Article 1.B.1.b.) to which separation of rights applies, the Company shall offer the first writer the opportunity to perform the first rewrite services at not less than the applicable minimum compensation for a rewrite. (If such writer is unable to perform such services or waives his/her right, the Company may engage another writer.) If the writer performs the rewrite and Company thereafter contemplates replacing the original writer, a senior production executive who has read the material shall discuss with the writer the Company's view and give the writer a reasonable opportunity to discuss continuing to perform services on the project.

In addition, the Company shall offer such writer the opportunity to perform one (1) additional set of revisions, if any are required by the Company, because of a changed or new element (*e.g.*, director or principal performer) assigned to the development or production of the writer's screenplay. The Company's obligation to make such an offer shall exist for a period of two (2) years after delivery of the writer's first or final set of revisions, whichever occurs later. However, this obligation does not arise if the Company engaged another writer to make revisions to the screenplay before the first changed or new element was assigned to the project. If the first writer is unable to perform such services or waives his/her right, the Company may engage another writer.

With respect to a screenplay written under employment by a writer who has separation of rights therein, if the Company contemplates replacing such writer, a senior production executive who has read the material shall discuss with the writer the Company's view and give the writer a reasonable opportunity to discuss continuing to perform services on the project.

Disputes as to whether Company has complied with the discussion requirements in the first and/or third unnumbered paragraphs of this subparagraph c. may be submitted to the "Hot Line" dispute resolution procedure in Article 48.

d. With respect to an option of a screenplay written by a professional writer (as defined in Article 1.B.1.b.) to which separation of rights applies, the writer of the optioned material shall be entitled, during the option period, to perform the first rewrite of such material unless such writer is unavailable or waives this requirement in writing in a separate document or in the writer's deal letter/ memorandum. If such writer performs such rewrite, the provisions of Article 16.A.3.c shall be deemed satisfied.

e. The Producer or creative executive will consult with the writer regarding each set of revisions requested of the writer by the Company.

4. Separable Material

Separable material, in which a writer or writers entitled thereto shall have separation of rights hereunder, refers to those portions or elements of the story (or story and screenplay) which are the original creation of such writer or writers. Separable material shall not include any assigned material or source material, and nothing herein contained shall be interpreted or construed as granting to the writer any rights of any nature in or to such material. The writer agrees that he/she will not make, or permit to be made, any use of any separable material that would infringe upon the copyright (either common law or statutory) or any other rights of the copyright proprietor or other proprietor of any literary, dramatic or musical material. With respect to public domain material incorporated in the writer's story (or story and screenplay), nothing herein contained shall impair the Company's right to use or deal in or with such material at any time, in any manner or to any extent, without the necessity for the writer's consent, and without any obligation to the writer. A writer who writes or contributes to the writing of a screenplay based upon or adapted from an original story created by another person, which person is entitled to separation of rights hereunder, and which writer would otherwise be entitled hereunder to separation of rights in such story and screenplay had he/she written such story, shall not be entitled to any separation of rights; but under such circumstances such other person who has created such story shall have the same rights in such story and screenplay as though such screenplay were originated and created by him/her. The writer employed to rewrite or polish a screenplay written by another person shall not have any separation of rights hereunder, and material originated or created by such writer shall be separable material available to the writer entitled to separation of rights with respect to such screenplay.

Only if the writer is employed, subject to this Agreement, to write a story and such writer becomes entitled to separation of rights hereunder, then if a person other than such writer is employed subject to this Agreement to write a screenplay based on such story, the Guild shall have the right to determine the screenplay writer's proportionate participation, if any, in the distribution of the proceeds or payments, if any, from the separated rights provided for in this Article, including sequel payments (as distinguished from any compensation for additional services to be rendered). However, such distribution shall not entitle such screenplay writer to any separation of rights. Provided the Company has complied with the relevant provision of this Basic Agreement relating to such payments, payments made by Company to a writer in reliance on such a determination made by the Guild shall be deemed to have been made to the writer entitled thereto, insofar as the Company is concerned, and as to such payments Company shall have no liability to any other writer under this provision. The Guild shall notify the Company in writing of any rules, standards or formula utilized by the Guild in determining participation, if any, in the distribution of such proceeds, and also shall advise the Company in writing of the screenplay writer's proportionate participation, if any, in such distribution of such proceeds. Neither the contracts with the writers nor the names of the writers shall be disclosed to the Guild Arbitration Committee, if any, making such determination.

5.   **Sequel Payments and Interactive Payments**

a.   Notwithstanding the fact that the writer is entitled to separation
of rights hereunder, he/she shall have no sequel rights in or to
the motion picture or the separable material; however, on each
occasion that the Company produces a theatrical motion picture
which is a sequel to a theatrical motion picture as to which a writer
has been granted separation of rights hereunder, the Company will
pay to the writer an amount equal to twenty-five percent (25%)
of the fixed compensation paid to the writer under employment
for his/her writing services in the writing of the story (or story
and screenplay) involved or of the fixed payment initially made
to such writer will be apportioned in accordance with the Company's normal accounting procedure, but in no event shall the
payment made to any term writer on account of the production
of a motion picture sequel exceed the sum of twenty thousand
dollars ($20,000.00).

b.   If the writer is entitled to separation of rights under this Article
and if the separable material contained a character or characters
which are used as the basis for a television series or a one-time
television program produced primarily for broadcast over "free"
television, the Company will pay to the writer an amount equal
to the applicable sequel payments as provided in Article 16.B.2.a.
or b. for each episode of such television series or the one-time
television program so produced and broadcast, either live or by
film. All of the foregoing is subject to the following conditions:

(1)   If the writer's contract provides for any television royalties
and residuals or any payment based on profits or any other
revenue derived from the television series or one-time television program, the payments to be made under this subparagraph 5.b. can be recouped from or offset against such
payments based on such royalties, residuals, profits or other
revenue.

(2)   Rerun payments shall be payable under this paragraph b. only
as to separable material acquired by Company from a writer
pursuant to an agreement with Company entered into on or
after December 13, 1966. Such rerun payments shall be equal
in amount to those applicable payments specified in Article
15.B.1.b.(4).

(3)   As to any television series or one-time television program
for which a television sequel payment is otherwise payable
to a writer under the Basic Agreement, or any other collective

bargaining agreement to which this Basic Agreement is a successor, no payment shall be payable under this subparagraph 5.b.

(4) If more than one writer is entitled to payment under this subparagraph 5.b. with respect to the television series or one-time television program involved, then all such writers shall be considered as a unit and shall share equally in such payment.

(5) The provisions of this subparagraph 5.b. shall apply only to material subject to this Basic Agreement and acquired after the effective date hereof under contracts subject to and entered into after the effective date of this Basic Agreement.

c. If the writer is entitled to separation of rights under this Article and if the separable material contained a character or characters which are used as the basis for a program produced pursuant to Appendix B. of this Basic Agreement, the Company will pay to the writer a one-time payment of

Program Length in Minutes	5/2/95- 5/1/96	5/2/96- 5/1/97	5/2/97- 5/1/98
15 or less	$675	$699	$727
30 or less (but more than 15)	1,347	1,394	1,450
60 or less (but more than 30)	2,022	2,093	2,177
90 or more	2,696	2,790	2,902

for each program so produced and broadcast. All of the foregoing is subject to the following conditions:

(1) If the writers contract provides for any royalties or residuals or any payment based on profits or any other revenue derived from such Appendix B program, the payments to be made under this subparagraph 5.c. can be recouped from or offset against such payments based on such royalties, residuals, profits or other revenue.

(2) As to any such Appendix B program for which a sequel payment is otherwise payable to a writer pursuant to this agreement or its successor, no payment shall be payable under this subparagraph 5.c.

(3) If more than one writer is entitled to payment under this subparagraph 5.c. with respect to the appendix B. program involved, then all such writers shall be considered as a unit and shall share equally in such payment.

(4) The provisions of this subparagraph 5.c. shall apply only to material subject to this Basic Agreement and acquired after

the effective date hereof under contracts subject to and entered into after the effective date of this Basic Agreement.

d. Notwithstanding the fact that the writer is entitled to separation of rights hereunder, he/she shall have no interactive rights in or to the motion picture or the separable material; however, on each occasion that the Company produces an interactive program based upon the theatrical motion picture as to which a writer has been granted separation of rights hereunder, the Company will pay the writer as provided in Article 64.

6. Arbitration

a. If the writer who receives "Story by" or "Written by" or "Screen Story by" credit pursuant to Theatrical Schedule A. hereof shall contend that he/she is qualified for separation of rights under one of the exceptions stated in subparagraphs 2.a. and b. of this Article 16.A., the Guild shall, within ninety (90) days after the determination of "Story by" or "Written by" or "Screen Story by" credit, pursuant to such Schedule A hereof, serve written notice of such writer's contention on the Company together with a list of the credits as finally determined. If the Guild fails to give timely notice of any such writer's contention as set forth above, the Guild and such writer shall be deemed to have waived any and all claims with respect to separation of rights in the material which was the subject of such credit determination.

Company may dispute such contention by giving the Guild written notice to such effect no later than twenty (20) days after the actual receipt by Company of the notice referred to in the preceding sentence. Company's notice shall be accompanied by a copy of the assigned material and shall set forth in reasonable detail the basis of Company's contention. If Company does not so timely dispute such contention, then the writer shall be conclusively deemed to have separation of rights in the separable material as defined in subparagraph 4. of this Article 16.A. If the Company does so timely dispute such contention, the Guild may, within sixty (60) days thereafter, give written notice to Company that it disputes Company's contention (setting forth the basis of its position in reasonable detail) or institute arbitration proceedings for the settlement of the dispute under the provisions of Articles 10, 11 and 12 hereof.

If the Guild fails to so notify the Company or to institute arbitration proceedings within the periods above mentioned, such writer shall be deemed to have waived, and shall not be entitled to, any separation or rights with respect to the story (or story and screenplay) involved; provided, however, that if there is such an arbitration proceeding, as above provided, involving a situation where more than one writer receives credit as aforesaid, and if in such arbitration proceedings it is determined that a writer is entitled to separation of rights under this Article 16.A., the provisions of 7.b. below shall be applicable and no writer who is to be regarded as a tenant in common thereunder, shall be deemed to have made any waiver under this sentence. If the writer and the Company agree, in writing, that the writer is entitled to separation of rights, then the writer shall be entitled to such separation of rights, as so agreed upon, subject to the provisions of 7.b. below. Any action or waiver by the Guild under this provision shall also bind the writer or writers involved. These provisions shall apply only where the screen credits are determined on or after June 16, 1970.

b. If, prior to the commencement of principal photography of any motion picture and prior to the determination of credits as provided in subparagraph 3. hereof, a writer shall contend that he/she is the author of separable material, and would at the time such contention is made be entitled to exercise publication or dramatic rights, but for the fact that there has been no determination of credits, such writer may obtain a determination that he/she is entitled to separation of rights by following the procedure set forth in this subparagraph 6.b. The writer shall notify the Company in writing of his/her contention and in such written notice the writer shall designate the particular right or rights intended to be exercised and shall further set forth, in reasonable detail, a description of those portions or elements of the story (or story and screenplay) claimed to be separable material pursuant to the provisions of this Article 16.A. If the writer and the Company are unable to agree thereon within the (10) days after receipt by the Company of the aforesaid notice from the writer, then the writer may within seven (7) days after the expiration of said ten (10) day period institute arbitration proceedings for the settlement of the dispute under the provisions of Articles 10, 11 and 12 hereof.

If the writer institutes such arbitration proceedings, the issue to be determined by arbitration shall be whether the material designated in writer's notice is separable material and whether the writer is entitled to separation of rights therein. The arbitrator shall be guided in such determination by the provisions of this Article

16.A. and the standards set forth in Theatrical Schedule A. hereof for the proper use of the credits "Written by," "Story by" and "Screen Story by." If the motion picture is thereafter produced, such determination in arbitration shall not affect any determination of credits made pursuant to the provisions of such Schedule A attached hereto. After such an arbitration is instituted and upon request of the Guild, Company shall furnish or make available to the Guild the names of all participating writers and the material contributed by such participating writers in connection with the story or story and screenplay in issue.

A determination, by agreement or arbitration under the provisions of this subparagraph 6.b., that any writer or writers are entitled to separation of rights with respect to any material shall be binding upon all other writers theretofore contributing to the writing of such material, and such determination shall supersede the provisions of the first paragraph of subparagraph 3. and 7.b. hereof with respect to material; but such determination shall not affect the rights, if any, of any other writer subsequently contributing to the writing of such material, under the provisions of subparagraph 3. and 7.b. hereof.

c.   If at any time Company desires to determine whether any person (hereinafter at times referred to as the "claimant") claims separation of rights hereunder, Company may, by written notice to the claimant, request from such person a statement as to whether or not such claimant claims such separation of rights in respect of a designated story (or story and screenplay). If Company sends such a written notice to the claimant, then Company shall also send a copy of such notice to the Guild. Within twenty (20) days after receipt by the Guild of such notice, such claimant and the Guild shall each notify the Company in writing either that it is the position of such claimant and the Guild, respectively, that such claimant is not entitled to separation of rights or that it is the position of such claimant and the Guild, respectively that such claimant is entitled to separation of rights, in which latter case claimant or the Guild shall further set forth, in such detail as is reasonably possible, a description of those portions or elements of the story (or story and screenplay) claimed to be separable material pursuant to the provisions of this Article 16.A. Such claimant shall be deemed to have waived, and shall not be entitled to any separation of rights with respect to the story (or story and screenplay) involved, if any one of the following occurs:

(1)   If both such claimant and the Guild notify the Company in writing that such claimant is not entitled to separation of rights; or

(2)   If the Guild notifies the Company in writing that such claimant is not entitled to separation of rights and such claimant does not, within such twenty (20) day period after receipt of such notice by the Guild from Company, serve written notice on the Company that such claimant is entitled to separation of rights, which notice contains the above-mentioned descriptions; or

(3)   If within such twenty (20) day period, neither the Guild nor such claimant serves such written notice upon the Company that such claimant is entitled to separation of rights, which notice contains the above-mentioned description.

If separation of rights has not been waived as aforesaid, then at any time after the Company has made such request but no later than twenty (20) days after the Company receives such notice claiming separation of rights as aforesaid from such claimant or the Guild, whichever is last received, the Company may institute arbitration proceedings under the provisions of Articles 10, 11 and 12 hereof for the determination of whether, and the extent to which, such claimant is entitled to separation of rights. If the Company institutes such arbitration proceedings and if such claimant does not, within five (5) days after the receipt of written notice from the Company of the name of the arbitrator, who shall be selected by mutual agreement within three (3) business days or, if no mutual agreement is reached within such time, through use of the striking procedures within two (2) business days thereafter, serve written notice on Company that such claimant claims separation of rights and setting in such notice, in such detail as is reasonably possible, a description of those portions or elements of the story (or story and screenplay) claimed to be separable material pursuant to the provisions of this Article 16.A., such claimant shall be deemed to have waived, and shall not be entitled to any separation of rights with respect to the story (or story and screenplay) involved. If at the time of such submission to arbitration there has been no determination of credits as provided in subparagraph 3. above, then the issue to be determined by arbitration shall be, and with the same effect, as set forth in subparagraph 6.b. above. The Company may make any request under this subparagraph 6.c. or institute arbitration proceedings under this subparagraph 6.c. against one or more persons either at the same time or at different times, as Company may from time to time determine. If separation of rights has not been waived as aforesaid, the contents of any notice served or sent under this subparagraph 6.c. by the Company, the Guild or such claimant, shall not preclude any party to such arbitration proceeding from raising therein any matter relevant to such determination of separation of rights.

d. No grievance under Articles 10, 11 and 12 hereof shall be required either as a condition precedent to any arbitration proceedings under this subparagraph 6. or otherwise under this subparagraph 6.

7. Miscellaneous

a. **Acquisition of Rights by Company**. If at any time prior to the disposition or exploitation by the writer of publication or dramatic rights in separable materials, as permitted herein, and either before or after the Company has acquired or employed the writer to write such material, Company shall wish to acquire either or both of such rights, it shall so notify the writer and the Guild. The Guild agrees that within fourteen (14) days after such notice, a paid negotiator, whose fees and expenses shall be paid by the Guild, shall meet with the Company for the purpose of negotiating a purchase price for the rights sought to be acquired by the Company. It is agreed that the negotiator will promptly thereafter quote a price at which the desired rights may be acquired by the Company. Company shall have the right to acquire the rights in question for the quoted price within thirty (30) days after Company receives such quotation. If the Company shall fail to purchase the rights in question at the price quoted by such negotiator, the writer may thereafter sell such rights to any other person, firm or corporation at any price; provided that, if the Company has acquired, or employed the writer to write, such material, the writer shall first give the Company fourteen (14) days written notice thereof, within which time Company may acquire such rights at such price as has been offered to writer in good faith by such other person, firm or corporation. If a negotiator is not made available within the fourteen (14) day period first above mentioned, the Company may negotiate directly with the writer or his representatives.

b. **Writer Teams**. If two (2) or more writers collaborate in or separately contribute to the writing of a story (or story and screenplay) which satisfies the requirements for separation of rights under the provisions of subparagraph 2. hereof, and it is determined that such writers are entitled to share a credit specified in subparagraph 3.1 such writers shall be regarded as equal tenants in common in the rights herein granted with respect to the separable material, and the separable material written by each of such writers shall be included in the separable material so owned in common by all of such writers.

c.   **Application to Contracts**. If any employment contract, or any contract for the acquisition of literary material, was entered into prior to the date of the commencement of the term of this Basic Agreement, then the writer or writers that were parties to any such contract shall not be entitled to any separation of rights under the provisions of this Article 16.A.

d.   **Execution of Instruments**. The Company and the writer will, upon request of the other, duly execute, acknowledge and deliver to the other any and all assignments or other instruments which may be reasonably necessary or desirable to effectuate the intent and purposes of this Basic Agreement or to evidence and establish the rights herein agreed to be licensed or granted; provided that such obligation on the part of the Company shall be deemed satisfied if any such assignment or other instrument is in the form of a license by the Company to the writer without warranties.

e.   **Successors and Assigns**. The provisions of this Article 16.A. shall be binding upon and shall inure to the benefit of the successors, assigns, heirs, executors, administrators and legal representatives of the Company and the writers entitled to separation of rights hereunder. The writer will not cause, allow or sanction any publication or dramatization of the separable material, or any part thereof, or any arraingement, translation or revision thereof to be made in any part of the world or in any language without first granting to, reserving or securing for the Company, without further consideration, all of the rights, licenses and privileges reserved to the Company pursuant to subparagraphs 3.a.(2), (3), (4) and (5) or subparagraphs 3.b.(1), (3) and (4); and, in any grants, assignments or licenses hereafter made or entered into by writer concerning the separable material, the writer will expressly except and reserve such rights to the Company. The writer will deliver to the Company an executed copy of any such grant, assignment or license promptly following the execution thereof.

f.   **Notices**. All notices which the company is required or may desire to serve upon a writer, a claimant, or the Guild, under the provisions of this Article 16.A., shall be addressed to such writer, claimant or the Guild, at the Guild's office in either Los Angeles,

California or New York, New York; all notices which a writer, a claimant or the Guild is required or may desire to serve upon the Company under the provisions of this Article 16.A. shall be addressed to the Company at its headquarters for the production of theatrical films in California, at the address it has designated for service of process pursuant to Article 41. Such notices may be served by registered mail or telegram. Any notice so mailed, postage prepaid, shall be conclusively deemed to have been received on the second day following deposit if posted within the State of California, or on the fifth day following such deposit if posted from a place outside the State of California but within the continental United States, or on the tenth day following such deposit if posted from a place outside the continental United States. Any notice delivered to a telegraph office, toll prepaid, shall be conclusively deemed to have been received upon the day following such delivery. Notwithstanding the foregoing there shall be no presumption of receipt during the period of any strike or work stoppage in the Unites States mail system.

8. **Writer's Right to Reacquire Literary Material**

    The provisions of this subparagraph 8. apply only to literary material (i) which is original, i.e., not based on any pre-existing material, and (ii) which has not been exploited in any medium.

    a. With respect to literary material acquired by Company subject to the terms of the 1970 or 1973 WGA agreement, if the writer who has written the same desires to purchase Company's right, title and interest therein, the Guild, on behalf of such writer, may notify Company in writing of such desire. Within ninety (90) days following receipt of such written notice, Company shall notify the Guild of the terms and conditions, including the price at which it will sell its right, title and interest in such literary material; provided, however, that Company may instead notify the Guild that the literary material does not meet one or more of the conditions precedent specified in the first sentence of this subparagraph 8. or that the literary material is in active development at the time of the Company's notification to the Guild. If the Company proceeds in accordance with the foregoing proviso and the Guild disputes the factual basis upon which the Company relies for so proceeding, such dispute shall be subject to the grievance and arbitration provisions of this Agreement. However, the Company's decision regarding the terms and conditions of sale shall not be subject to challenge by the Guild or by the writer on any grounds whatsoever whether in arbitration or otherwise.

The purchase price designated by Company shall not be in excess of the total direct costs previously incurred by Company in relation only to such literary material, including payments for the acquisition of the literary material and for writing services connected therewith (including writing services in relation to treatments and screenplays based thereon), and fringe benefit costs in relation thereto, such as pension and health fund payments and social security payments, but exclusive of overhead and exclusive of costs of any other kind (e.g., costs relating to proposed production other than writing costs.)

Within thirty (30) days following notice from the Company of the terms and conditions on which it will sell its right, title and interest in such literary material, including the purchase price, the Guild, on behalf of the writer, may serve written notice of acceptance of such terms and conditions and immediately following service of such notice the parties shall proceed to close the transaction. Failure to effect such purchase in accordance with the procedure specified by the foregoing provisions shall result in the forfeiture of writer's right to purchase such material. At any time before receipt of notice of acceptance of the terms and conditions of sale, Company may dispose of such literary material or of any rights therein or with respect thereto or may itself commence active development of such material, and in either such event the writer shall no longer have the right to acquire Company's right, title or interest in such material.

b. In addition to the foregoing, but with respect only to literary material acquired by a Company on and after March 2, 1977 but prior to March 2, 1981, the writer may reacquire with the procedures set forth below, if production of a theatrical or television motion picture based on the literary material has not commenced upon expiration of the following applicable time period:

(1) If, during the five (5) year period after (i) the Company's purchase or license of the literary material (if written by a professional writer), or (ii) completion of the writer's services rendered in connection with the literary material, the Company has not had additional writing services rendered thereon or otherwise actively developed the literary material, and if, further, upon expiration of said five (5) year period, the Company is not engaged in negotiations for the sale or license of the literary material to a third party, then upon expiration of said five (5) year period; or

(2)   If, upon expiration of the five (5) year period referred to in subparagraph (1) above, the Company is engaged in negotiations for the sale or license of the literary material to a third party but has not also had additional writing services rendered thereon or otherwise actively developed the literary material, and if said negotiations do not result in a sale or license thereof, then upon the conclusion of said negotiations; or

(3)   If neither subparagraph (1) or (2) above applies, then upon expiration of the seven (7) year period after (i) the Company's purchase or license of the literary material (if written by a professional writer), or (ii) completion of the writer's services rendered in connection with the literary material.

If the writer does reacquire such literary material, such reacquisition is subject to all existing commitments, such as security interest, participations, options, turnaround rights, employment rights, etc.

At any time during the two (2) year period immediately following expiration of the applicable time period set forth above, the Guild may give the written notice provided in the second sentence of this paragraph 8. (hereafter "Guild's notice"), and within ninety (90) days thereafter Company shall give the written notice provided in the third sentence of this paragraph 8. (hereafter "Company's notice") stating the terms and conditions on which it will sell its right, title and interest in such literary material, including the purchase price. Upon the giving of Company's notice, the literary property shall be deemed literary material which the Company has decided it will not exploit in any medium in the future. The purchase price designated by Company shall not be in excess of the total direct costs previously incurred by Company in relation only to such literary material as set forth in the sixth sentence of paragraph 8.a. above. Within one hundred twenty (120) days of the giving of the Company's notice (during which period the Company shall not exploit, produce, sell or dispose of said material to any third person), the Guild, on behalf of the writer, may serve written notice of acceptance of such terms and conditions and immediately following service of such notice the parties shall proceed to close the transaction. Failure to effect such purchase in accordance with the procedure specified by the foregoing provisions by the end of such two (2) year period (i.e., the years commencing after the expiration of the applicable time period set forth above) shall result in the forfeiture of writer's right to purchase such material any time thereafter under any provision of this paragraph 8. Within said two (2) year period the Guild on behalf of the writer may repeat the Guild's notice one or more times. All of the procedures and rights above described with respect to the first giving of the Guild's notice shall apply to the first such repeat notice. All of said procedures and rights shall also apply to the second and any subsequent repeat notices except that the Company shall not exploit, produce, sell or dispose of said material to any third person during any period between the giving of the Guild's second (or subsequent) repeat notice and the expiration of one hundred twenty (120) days following the giving of the Company's respective notice.

Furthermore, if Company had previously granted some other person or company the right or option to acquire such material or any rights therein, the writer of such literary material shall not have the right to purchase the same so long as such other right remains outstanding. In the event that more than one writer is involved in the writing of such literary material the Guild shall have the sole responsibility to determine which of such writers has the right to purchase as provided herein and all interested writers shall be bound by the decision of the Guild.

c.   In addition to the foregoing, but with respect only to literary material acquired by Company on or after March 2, 1981 but prior to March 8, 1988, the writer may reacquire such literary material on the terms set forth below upon expiration of the five (5) year period following the later of (i) the Company's purchase or license of the covered literary material, or (ii) completion of the writer's services rendered in connection with the literary material. The writer may reacquire such literary material pursuant to this paragraph only if it is not in active development at the time that the procedures for reacquiring the literary material are instituted.

Examples of active development for the purpose of this paragraph are:

(i)   Employment of a writer to rewrite the literary material;

(ii)   Employment of a director, major actor or other key above-the-line element on a pay-or-play basis for a motion picture based upon the literary material;

(iii)   A production designer, production manager or other supervisor is in active preparation for the production of the motion picture;

(iv)   A unit production manager or other person is engaged to prepare a budget for the motion picture; or

(v)   Production has commenced upon a theatrical or television motion picture based on the literary material.

If the writer does reacquire such literary material, such reacquisition is subject to all existing commitments, such as security interests, participations, options, turnaround rights, employment rights, etc.

Furthermore, if Company had previously granted some other person or company the right or option to acquire such material or any rights therein, the writer of such literary material shall not have the right to purchase the same so long as such other right remains outstanding. In the event that more than one writer is involved in the writing of such literary material, the Guild shall have the sole responsibility to determine which of such writers has the right to purchase as provided herein and all interested writers shall be bound by the decision of the Guild.

The writer shall reacquire the literary material pursuant to the foregoing paragraphs upon payment to the Company of all compensation actually paid by the Company to the writer for services in connection with the literary material, or for the purchase or license of the literary material in the case of a professional writer. The writer shall obligate the acquiring company to reimburse the Company for any other direct cost previously incurred by the Company in relation to such literary material (as described in the second subparagraph 8.a)) out of the first revenue after production costs have been recovered. The document by which the writer reacquires the literary material shall contain a provision setting forth the obligations referred to in the preceding sentence.

d.   **Reacquisition under the 1988 Basic Agreement, the 1992 Extension Agreement and the 1995 Basic Agreement.**

With respect only to literary material acquired by Company on or after August 8, 1988, the writer may reacquire such literary material pursuant to the terms set forth below upon expiration of the five (5) year period following the later of (i) the company's purchase or license of the covered literary material, or (ii) completion of the writer's services rendered in connection with the literary material, if such literary material is not in active development. Examples of active development for the purpose of this paragraph are included in subparagraph c. above. If the writer does reacquire such literary material, such reacquisition is subject to existing commitments, such as security interest, participations, turnaround rights and employment rights.

Procedures for Reacquisition

(i) At any time during the two (2) year period immediately following expiration of the Company's five (5) year period within which to actively develop the material, the writer may notify the Company in writing of the writer's intent to reacquire the material. The writer shall include in such notice the address(es) where further correspondence and notices relating to reacquisition of the material shall be sent.

(ii) If the material is not in active development at that time Company received writer's notice of intent to reacquire, then, within sixty (60) days following receipt of such notice, Company shall have the right to place the material into active development. However, during such sixty (60) day period, the material will be deemed to be placed into active development only if, during such period, Company employs a writer to rewrite the literary material or Company employs a director or major actor on a pay-or-play basis for a motion picture based upon the literary material.

(iii) Within sixty (60) days following receipt of writer's notice of intent to reacquire, Company shall give the writer and the Guild written notice of the terms and conditions (which shall not include a so-called "change elements" clause, i.e., a right of first and/or last refusal or provisions which have the same effect) upon which it will sell its right, title and interest in the literary material, and the price of the material as set forth in this subparagraph d., and the encumbrances and/or commitments, if any (such as security interest, participations, employment rights, future options and/or future turnaround rights) that were attached to the literary material at the time the Company received the writer's notice of intent to reacquire the literary material.

(iv) In the alternative, the Company may notify the writer and the Guild that the literary material does not meet one or more of the conditions precedent specified in the first sentence of this subparagraph 8. or that the literary material is in active development at the time of the Company's notification to the writer or that the literary material has been sold or is under option or is in turnaround to a third party. If the Company advises the writer that the literary material has been sold to a third party, the Company shall include in its written notice the identity of the third party and the date of such sale. If the Company advises the writer that the literary material is in active development, or is under option, or is in turnaround, at the time of the Company's notification to the writer, the two (2) year period for reacquisition, or any time remaining on it, shall be tolled during the period of such active development, option or turnaround and until the writer receives notice from the Company that the script is no longer in active development, or under option or in turnaround. In such event, the Company shall include in its written notice the expiration date of any option or turnaround right. Should any such option or turnaround right be exercised by a third party, the Company shall promptly notify the writer and the Guild.

(v)   In the event the literary material is in active development at the time of the Company's receipt of the writer's notice of intent to reacquire and the Company later ceases to actively develop the material, and/or if the Company places the material into active development within the sixty (60) day period following writer's notice of intent to reacquire the material, and the Company later cease to actively develop the material, Company shall notify the writer and the Guild promptly in writing that the material is no longer in active development. If, within thirty (30) days after receipt of such written notice from the Company, the writer advises the Company in writing that he/she desires to reacquire the material in accordance with his/her earlier notice, then the Company shall give the writer and the Guild the written notice of the terms and conditions, purchase price, encumbrances and/or commitments as described above within sixty (60) days after receipt of the writer's most recent notice to reacquire. In such event, Company shall have no right to place the material into active development during this latter sixty (60) day period, or thereafter during the writer's period for reacquisition. If the writer provides written notice of intent to reacquire more than thirty (30) days after writer's receipt of Company's notice that active development of the material has ceased, then the procedures contained within the first four subparagraphs of this "Procedures for Reacquisition" section shall apply for the remainder of the writer's period for reacquisition.

(vi)   If the Company proceeds in accordance with subparagraph (iv) of this "Procedures for Reacquisition" section and the Guild or the writer disputes the factual basis upon which the Company relies for so proceeding, such dispute shall be subject to the grievance and arbitration provisions of Articles 10, 11 and 12 of this Agreement. However, the Company's decision regarding the terms and conditions of the sale, as distinguished from the purchase price, shall not be subject to challenge by the Guild or the writer on any grounds whatsoever, whether in arbitration or otherwise. Notwithstanding the preceding sentence, disputes as to whether the terms and conditions of the reacquisition sale conform to the express provisions of this Article 16.A.8.d. shall be subject to the grievance and arbitration provisions of Articles 10, 11 and 12 of this Agreement.

(vii)   The writer shall reacquire such literary material if writer tenders the purchase price within six (6) months after writer's receipt of the Company's notice. The Company shall not further encumber the literary material during such six (6) month period by entering into new agreements or commitments, such as options, turnarounds, security interests, participations and employment rights or actively develop or sell the literary material. In the event the writer fails to make the payment within such six (6) month period, the writer may reinstitute the procedure for reacquisition at any time remaining in the two (2) year period referred to above, it being understood that such procedures need only be commenced, and not completed, within the two (2) year period.

Rights and Procedures for Reacquisition of Material That Has Been Sold or Optioned.

If the Company sells or options the literary material prior to the expiration of the writer's period to reacquire such material from the Company, then such writer's rights to reacquire shall be extended on the following basis and the Company, the writer and the buyer, where applicable, shall be subject to the following procedures in regard thereto:

(i)   If the Company sells the literary material to another person or company, it shall obligate the acquiring person or company (hereinafter referred to as "the buyer") in a written agreement to comply with the provisions of this subparagraph 8.d. Said written agreement shall further obligate the buyer(s) in subsequent sales transactions to comply with the provisions of this subparagraph 8.d. The buyer(s) shall have five (5) years from the date of its/their agreement with the Company for such sale to place the material into active development (as described in subparagraph 8.c. above). The writer shall have the right to reacquire the literary material from the buyer upon the expiration of such five (5) year period in accordance with the procedures set forth in this subparagraph 8.d.

(ii)   If the literary material or any rights therein are placed under option or into turnaround during the period when the Company may actively develop the material, the Company's active development period shall be tolled while such material is under option or in turnaround or for eighteen (18) months, whichever is shorter. Only the first such option or turnaround granted by the Company shall toll the Company's active development period.

(iii) If an option is exercised, the buyer shall have five (5) years from the effective date of the option agreement to put the literary material into active development (as described in subparagraph 8.c. above). Thereafter, the writer shall have the right to reacquire the literary material from the buyer in accordance with the procedures set forth in this subparagraph 8.d.

(iv)   If an option is not exercised and the Company's period of active development, as provided in this subparagraph 8.d., has ended, and the writer's notice of intent to reacquire was received during the time the literary material was under option, the writer may, without further notice to Company, reacquire such material in accordance with the provisions of this subparagraph 8.d. In such event, Company will be deemed to have received the writer's notice of reacquisition on the date of expiration of the option period, irrespective of the date it was actually received.

Payment.

(i)   The writer shall reacquire the literary material pursuant to this subparagraph 8.d. upon payment to the Company (or the buyer, if applicable) of all compensation actually paid by the Company (or the buyer, if applicable) to the writer for services in connection with the literary material and/or for the purchase or license of the literary material from the writer or Company. It is understood that the purchase price, as set forth in the preceding sentence, is the sole monetary consideration due from the writer to the Company to reacquire the literary material; in no event will the writer be obligated to pay more than the amount specified in the preceding sentence (e.g., in the form of profit participations to the Company).

(ii) If the writer reacquires the literary material from the Company (or buyer, if applicable) and the writer thereafter sells or licenses the literary material to a third party, the writer shall obligate such third party to reimburse the Company (or buyer, if applicable), upon the commencement of principal photography, for any other direct cost previously incurred by the Company (or buyer, if applicable) in relation to such literary material (as described in the second paragraph of subparagraph 8.a.) plus interest thereon. The document by which the writer reacquires the literary material shall contain a provision setting forth the obligations referred to in the preceding sentence.

Procedure if More Than One Writer Desires to Reacquire the Literary Material. In the event that more than one writer is involved in the writing of such literary material, the Guild shall have the sole responsibility to determine which of such writers has the right to purchase as provided herein and all interested writers shall be bound by the decisions of the Guild.

Special Notice and Receipt Provisions Applicable to Reacquisition. All notices which the Company is required or may desire to serve upon a writer pursuant to the provisions of this Article 16.A.8.d. shall be addressed to such writer at the address(es) specified by the writer in his or her first notice to the Company, as provided in subparagraph (i) under "Procedures for Reacquisition" above. Company shall direct correspondence and notices hereunder to the writer at such address(es), notwithstanding any contrary provisions for the giving of notice in the writer's deal memorandum or personal service agreement and by so doing shall be deemed to have fulfilled the notice requirements hereunder, as provided herein, notwithstanding any contrary notice provision in the writer's deal memorandum or personal service agreement. The writer may, by notice to the Company, amend such address(es) and, after receipt of an amendment, the Company shall use such amended address(es) for purposes of this Article 16.A.8.d.

All notices which the Company is required or may desire to serve upon the Guild pursuant to the provisions of this Article 16.A.8.d. shall be addressed to the Guild either at its principal office in Los Angeles County, California, or New York, New York.

All notices which a writer or the Guild is required or may desire to serve upon the Company (or the buyer(s)) pursuant to the provisions of this Article 16.A.8.d. shall be addressed to the Company at its headquarters for the production of motion pictures in California or to the buyer at its headquarters in Los Angeles County or to such other address provided by the buyer to the writer and the Guild.

Such notices may be served by registered mail or telegram. Any notice so mailed, postage prepaid, shall be conclusively deemed to have been received (i) on the fifth day following deposit if mailed within the State of California to an addressee within the State of California; or (ii) on the tenth day following such deposit in the continental United States if mailed to an addressee in a state within the continental United States different from the state of deposit; or (iii) on the twentieth day following deposit if mailed in the continental United States to an addressee outside of the continental United States or if mailed outside of the continental United States to an addressee within the continental United States. Any notice delivered to a telegraph office, toll prepaid, shall be conclusively deemed to have been received upon the day following such delivery. Notwithstanding the foregoing, there shall be no presumption of receipt by mail during the period of any strike or work stoppage in the United States mail system.

For purposes of the foregoing, time computations relating to notices to or from the writer shall be determined by the address of the writer, not the Guild, regardless of the fact that the Guild may be required to be copied on notices given by the writer.

B. TELEVISION

1. General Qualifications

a. Company agrees that separation of rights as provided in subparagraphs 2. and 3. inclusive of this Article 16.B. shall be accorded to the writer of a format, story, or story and teleplay for any television motion picture (other than one of an established serial or episodic series) provided that the terms of this Agreement relating to rights in material apply to such format, story or story and teleplay as provided in Article 2 hereof. If at the time of the transfer of rights to the material so purchased there is in existence a valid agreement for the publication or dramatic production of such material, then for the purpose of this Article 16.B. such material shall be deemed to have been published or exploited. It is agreed as to an established serial or episodic series the Company shall own all of the rights in the material of any nature or description whatever including, but not limited to, the right to use the same in any field or medium whatever without obligation to the writer except as provided in subparagraph 14. of Article 15.B.

with respect to additional payments to be made for specific uses. The Guild shall determine which of the writers (considered as a single entity) shall have separation of rights or the proportion in which each shall share in such separation of rights. In that regard the Guild shall establish a set of rules for the determination of the separation of rights as between such writers. The Company is to be supplied with a copy of such rules. Neither the contracts with the writers nor the names of the writers shall be disclosed to the Guild Arbitration Committee.

b. A writer who contributes to the writing of a teleplay based upon or adapted from a story or format created and written by another person shall not have any separation of rights and shall retain no interest of any character whatsoever in the teleplay. If such a teleplay be based upon a story in the public domain, or upon a story owned by the Company, the Company shall own all rights in the material of every nature and description whatsoever, and the writer shall retain no interest of any character in such material; provided, however, that if such teleplay is based upon a story in the public domain which was suggested and furnished by the writer of such teleplay, then: (i) if such teleplay was written for a television motion picture of an established serial or episodic series, the writer shall be entitled to the payments referred to in said subparagraph 1. of Article 15.B.14.; or (ii) if such teleplay was written for a television motion picture (other than one of an established serial or episodic series) and such teleplay otherwise meets the conditions set forth in said subparagraph 1., the writer thereof shall be entitled to the payments referred to in said subparagraph 1. in the same manner as if said television motion picture were one of an established serial or episodic series. It is agreed, however, that if Company shall employ a writer to write a teleplay based upon or adapted from a story to which the provisions of this Agreement (including the separation of rights provisions) apply, the writer of such teleplay shall retain no interest of any character in such teleplay, the writer of the story shall have the same rights in the teleplay as he/she reserved with the same respect to the story, and the Company shall have the same rights in the teleplay as were granted to it in the story for the same period of time for which the Company has been granted rights in the story, as herein provided. A writer employed to rewrite or polish a teleplay written by another person shall not have any separation of rights hereunder.

c. Notwithstanding the fact that the Company shall own all rights in literary material included in episodic series or serial type television motion pictures to which the provisions of this Basic Agreement apply, the Company agrees that it will not, without the prior consent of the Guild, use any such literary material in the production of a theatrical motion picture or a live television or radio broadcast prior to use of such material in the production of a television motion picture; and the Guild agrees that it will not unreasonably withhold such consent.

d. If a serial or episodic series (herein called "new serial or new episodic series") is based upon an episode which is a "spin-off" from an existing serial or episodic series, the writer(s) of the format and/or the story or story and teleplay of such spin-off episode may be entitled to separation of rights in the new serial or new episodic series, subject to the provisions of Article 1.C.13.

2. **Television Rights.** Company shall own the exclusive television rights in the literary material to which the provisions of this Article 16.B. apply for a period of thirty (30) months from the date of delivery of the material or after date of acquisition if such material is not in active development except that a four (4) year period shall apply (i) to material in active development (which includes pitches to buyers, e.g., networks), and (ii) to non-topical material intended for a program of more than sixty (60) minutes in length. Thereafter, Company and writer shall each have a non-exclusive right to utilize and exploit the television rights in the material. Such non-exclusive rights on the part of the Company shall be deemed to include the right to continue to exploit and exhibit forever the television motion picture and to remake the picture for television purposes without additional compensation, except to the extent required under the provisions hereof relating to additional compensation for reruns on television, foreign telecast and theatrical exhibition. Such exclusive television rights shall not include television sequel rights, except as otherwise hereinafter provided.

a. Company shall have the exclusive right to commence the exploitation of the television sequel rights within the following period:

(i) within thirty (30) months from the delivery of the story or story and teleplay (to which the separation of rights provisions of this Article 16.B. apply) if the material is not in active development, or within four (4) years from the delivery of the story or story and teleplay (to which the separation of rights provisions of this Article 16.B. apply) if the material is in active development or if it is non-topical material intended for a program of more than sixty (60) minutes in length; or

(ii)   if a motion picture based thereon is broadcast within the thirty (30) month period specified in (i) above, then within three (3) years from the date of broadcast; or

(iii) if a second pilot is made, then within four (4) years from the delivery of the story or story and teleplay (to which the separation of rights provisions of this Article 16.B. apply), or within three (3) years from the release of said pilot, whichever shall be earlier.

If Company shall so exploit such rights it shall pay to the writer for each episode produced the following sum:

For such literary material written by or purchased from writer hereunder, during

5/2/95-5/1/96	$1,149
5/2/96-5/1/97	1,189
5/2/97-5/2/98	1,237

provided that such writer shall be entitled only to sixty percent (60%) of said amount for fifteen (15) minute episodes but shall be entitled to one hundred ninety percent (190%) of said amount for sixty (60) minute episodes and two hundred fifty percent (250%) of said amount for ninety (90) minute or longer episodes. For the purpose of this provision, an episode shall be deemed "produced" when production (including post-production) of such episode has been completed. Except as provided in Article 15.B.1.b. and Article 15.B.2. hereof, the payment of said applicable amount shall satisfy all obligations of the Company to the writer, and no additional sum or sums shall be payable, by reason of any use of such episodes. If the story or story and teleplay was written by more than one writer all such writers shall be considered as a unit and shall share equally such sequel payments.

In the event and only in such event that Company does not commence such exploitation within said period of time, such sequel rights in the story or story and teleplay and in the format, if any, shall revert to the writer or writers entitled to separation of rights, and Company will have no further interest therein.

The Company shall be deemed to have commenced the exploitation of the television sequel rights when it has obtained a firm commitment for the production, broadcasting or distribution in syndication of a program involving the exploitation of such sequel rights.

Nothing in this subparagraph 2.a. shall be construed to preclude the Company from producing a second pilot during the exclusive period provided for therein or from exhibiting such additional pilot during or after said period, provided that a deal is made with the writer of the first pilot to write a story and teleplay for the second pilot at a compensation not less than that paid him/her for the first pilot. The production and release of a second pilot shall not constitute exploitation of the television sequel rights within the meaning of this subparagraph 2.a.

Rights acquired in a format revert to the writer(s) unless, within eighteen (18) months after delivery of the format, the Company engages the writer or another writer to write a story and teleplay based on said format. Rights acquired in a bible revert to the writer unless within twenty-four (24) months after delivery of the bible, the Company engages the writer or another writer to write a story and teleplay based on such bible. If either reversion occurs, only the material supplied by the writer reverts. It does not include anything furnished by Company.

When there is such a reversion and thereafter the writer sells such format and a series is produced from such format, then after the time the format is exploited the Company shall be reimbursed by the writer (to the extent that the writer had received payment on such resale for such format) for the amount paid by Company to such writer for the format in excess of minimum.

In those instances where, at the time of the writer's request hereunder, Company has not produced a television motion picture based on the writer's separated rights material and the television series sequel rights and MOW sequel rights , as described in Article 16.B.2.b. below, have reverted to the writer, such writer may reacquire from the Company the Company's non-exclusive television rights in accordance with the following: Writer shall have the right to reacquire such material upon payment to the Company of all compensation actually paid by the Company to the writer for services in connection with the literary material and/or for the purchase or license of the literary material in the case of a professional writer. The writer shall obligate the acquiring company to reimburse the Company for any other direct cost previously incurred by the Company in relation to such literary material out of the first revenue after production costs have been recovered. The document by which the writer reacquires the literary material shall contain a provision setting forth the obligations referred to in the preceding sentence. For purposes of this provision, "any other direct cost" shall include payments for literary material and writing services connected therewith (including writing services in relation to formats and stories and teleplays based thereon), and fringe benefit costs in relations thereto, such as pension and health fund payments and social security payments, but exclusive of overhead and exclusive of costs of any other kind (e.g., costs relating to proposed production other than writing costs). If the writer does reacquire such literary material, such reacquisition is subject to all existing commitments, such as network agreements, security interest, participations, options, turnaround rights, etc. Transfers of the literary material to third parties shall not cut off the writer's right to reacquire the literary material, and the writer may reacquire the literary material from the acquiring company if the literary material is not in active development (as described in Article 16.A.8.c.) eighteen (18) months following the acquiring company's purchase or option of the literary material.

If the Company grants an option in the literary material, the optionee shall have a maximum of eighteen (18) months from commencement of the option to exercise such option.

In the event that more than one writer is involved in the writing of such literary material, the Guild shall have the sole responsibility to determine which of such writers has the right to purchase as provided herein and all interested writers shall be bound by the decision of the Guild.

b.   The "*first MOW*," for purposes of this Section, is a television motion picture, ninety (90) minutes or longer, to which the separation of rights provisions of this Article 16.B. apply. "*MOW sequels*" are programs, ninety (90) minutes or longer, which are ordered subsequent to the broadcast of the first MOW and are other than an exploitation of the series sequel rights.

The Company shall have the exclusive right to commence the exploitation of the television MOW sequel rights within the following period:

(i)   within thirty (30) months from the delivery of the story or story and teleplay (to which the separation of rights provisions of this Article 16.B. apply) if the material is not in active development, or within four (4) years from the delivery of the story or story and teleplay (to which the separation of rights provisions of this Article 16.B. apply) if the material is in active development or if it is non-topical material; or

(ii)   if a motion picture is based thereon is broadcast within the thirty (30) month period specified in (i) above, then within three (3) years from the date of broadcast.

In no event shall the exploitation of the MOW sequel rights be deemed the exploitation of the television series sequel rights (as described in Article 16.B.2.a., above).

In the event the Company, prior to the exploitation of the series sequel rights of the first MOW,

(1)   obtains a firm commitment for the production, broadcasting or distribution in syndication of an MOW sequel within the period of exclusivity provided in subparagraph b.(i) or (ii), above, and such MOW sequel is broadcast within six (6) months after the end of the exclusivity period, or

(2)   broadcasts an MOW sequel within the period of exclusivity provided in subparagraph b.(i) or (ii), above, and less than eighteen (18) months is left in the period of exclusivity at the time of the broadcast of such MOW sequel,

the period of exclusivity for the commencement of the exploitation of the series sequel rights and/or the further exploitation of the MOW sequel rights will be extended to eighteen (18) months from the date of broadcast of the MOW sequel. If an additional MOW sequel is broadcast within the period of exclusivity (including extensions), the Company will have an additional eighteen (18) months from the date of broadcast of the subsequent MOW sequel during which time it may produce and broadcast yet another MOW sequel and/or commence exploitation of the series sequel rights. Such extensions shall continue under the same terms as described herein. If an MOW sequel is produced but not broadcast prior to the expiration of the six (6) month period referred to above or any other period of exclusivity, the Company will nevertheless have the exclusive right to broadcast such MOW sell revert to the writer. Upon exploitation, within the time periods set forth above, of the series sequel rights of the first MOW, the Company shall have the right to exploit thereafter in perpetuity such series sequel rights (including MOWs ninety (90) minutes or longer).

The writer(s) of the first MOW must be offered the opportunity to write the first MOW sequel at no less than he/she was paid to write the first MOW, subject to the writer's availability within a period reasonably proximate to the date on which writing services are to commence. As to any MOW sequel beyond the first sequel, the writer(s) of the first MOW must be offered the opportunity to write such MOW sequel at not less than the amount he/she was paid to write the immediately preceding MOW sequel unless the writer(s) did not receive sole teleplay credit (pursuant to Television Schedule A) on the immediately preceding MOW sequel. The requirement set forth in the preceding sentence is also subject to the writer's availability within a period reasonably proximate to the date on which writing services are to commence.

For the right to produce each MOW sequel, the Company shall pay the writer(s) four (4) times the television series sequel payment provided in Article 16.B.2.a., above. As to any MOW sequel after the first sequel, if the writer(s) is not employed by the Company due to the fact that he/she did not receive sole teleplay credit on the immediately preceding MOW sequel, and was not offered the opportunity to write such MOW sequel, the writer(s) will be paid, for that MOW sequel only, an amount not less than two (2) times the MOW sequel payment otherwise due. Payment of the amount provided in the preceding sentences shall be due when production of the MOW sequel (including post-production) is completed. Except as provided in Articles 15.B.1.b., 15.B.2., 51 and 58, the payment of said applicable amount shall satisfy all obligations of the Company to the writer(s) , and no additional sum or sums shall be payable by reason of any use of such MOW sequel. Article 15.B.1.b. and 15.B.2. payments shall be based on the applicable sequel payments as provided in this Agreement. Article 51 and 58 residuals will be payable to the writer(s) entitled to such sequel residual payments at an additional twenty-five percent (25%) of the applicable minimum residual payable to the credited writer(s) of the MOW sequel. If the story or story and teleplay was written by more than one writer, all such writers shall be considered as a unit and shall share equally in such sequel payments and sequel residual payments.

In the event and only in the event that the Company does not commence exploitation of the MOW or series sequel rights within said period of time, such MOW sequel rights shall revert to the writer or writers entitled to separation of rights, and Company will have no further interest therein.

The Company shall be deemed to have commenced the exploitation of the television MOW sequel rights when it has obtained a firm commitment for the production, broadcasting or distribution in syndication of a television motion picture involving the exploitation of the MOW sequel rights.

In the event that more than one writer is involved in the writing of such literary material, the Guild shall have the sole responsibility to determine which of such writers has the MOW sequel rights and all interested writers shall be bound by the decision of the Guild.

3. **Other Rights**

a. Writer shall retain all other rights (hereinafter referred to as the "**reserved rights**") not expressly referred to in subparagraph 2. of this Article 16.B. including but not limited to dramatic, theatrical motion picture, publication, merchandising rights, radio rights, live television rights, interactive rights as provided in Article 1.C.14.1.c.(2) and television sequel rights (other than the sequel rights mentioned in subparagraph 2. of this Article 16.B.), and Company shall only have the limited interest in such rights as hereinafter described.

b. With reference to certain reserved rights in a format, story or story and teleplay, the writer shall have no right to and will not use, or grant, license or otherwise dispose of to any third party or parties the right to use the following rights:

(1) The live television rights until a date three and one-half (3 1/2) years after the first broadcast of the television motion picture, or a date five (5) years after the delivery of the story and teleplay, whichever shall be earlier.

(2) The right to broadcast directly by television a live dramatic presentation of the material, in the exercise of the reserved dramatic rights, until a date three and one-half (3 1/2) years after the first broadcast of the television motion picture, or a date (5) years after the delivery of the story or story and teleplay, whichever shall be earlier.

(3) The right to release a theatrical motion picture based upon the format, story or story and teleplay until one (1) year after the first broadcast of the television motion picture or a date two (2) years after the delivery of the story or story and teleplay, whichever shall be earlier.

(4) The right to broadcast by radio any program based upon or adapted from the format, story or story and teleplay until three (3) years after the first broadcast of the television motion picture or a date four (4) years after the delivery of the story or story and teleplay, whichever shall be earlier.

(5) The right to use the leading character or characters in a substantially different story in an "interactive program," other

than in the nature of a game, until after the expiration of the Company's exclusive right to commence the exploitation of the television sequel rights as set forth in Article 16.B.2. or until six (6) months after the date of the last broadcast of the series, if such rights have been exploited.

c.   If during the four (4) year period mentioned in subparagraph 2. above, the writer desires to sell, license or otherwise dispose of any of the reserved rights, other than dramatic or publication rights, the Company shall have a right of first refusal thereof as follows: At such time as writer shall receive from a third party a *bona fide* offer, and the writer desires to sell, license or otherwise dispose of the rights involved on the terms of such offer, writer will, by written notice to the Company, advise the Company of the rights involved and of such terms. Within seven (7) days (excluding non-business days as provided in Article 43) after receipt of such notice, Company may, by written notice to the writer, elect to purchase, license or otherwise acquire the rights involved on the terms set forth in writer's notice, in which case Company and writer will enter into an agreement upon such terms. If within the seven (7) day period Company notifies the writer that it does not elect to exercise its right of first refusal, or fails to give writer any written notice, the writer shall be free to enter into an agreement with such third party, but may not do so on terms more favorable to the third party than those set forth in the notice to the Company without again submitting the more favorable terms to the Company for first refusal, as herein provided. The right of first refusal herein granted shall apply to television sequel rights if the same shall revert to the writer prior to the expiration of said four (4) year period.

d.   If at any time prior to the disposition or exploitation of such rights (as permitted herein) by writer, Company shall wish to acquire any of the reserved rights (including dramatic or publication rights) Guild shall meet with Company for the purpose of negotiating a purchase price for the rights sought to be acquired by Company. It is agreed that the Guild will quote a price at which the rights desired to be acquired by the Company may be purchased. Company shall then have the right to acquire the rights in question for the price agreed upon as a result of such negotiations within thirty (30) days from the completion thereof. If Company shall fail to purchase at the lowest price offered by Guild, writer may thereafter sell such rights to any other person, firm or corporation at any price; provided, however, that he/she first give Company fourteen (14) days written notice thereof within which time Company may acquire such rights at such price as has been offered to writer in good faith by such other person, firm or corporation.

If at any time the Company wishes (i) to secure protection against a competitive use for which no period of non-competitive use is prescribed in subparagraph 3.b. above, or (ii) to extend any period of non-competitive use prescribed in subparagraph 3.c. above, or (iii) to extend the four (4) year period of the right of first refusal prescribed in subparagraph 3.c. above, or (iv) to secure a right of first refusal on reserved dramatic or publication rights, it will negotiate therefor through the Guild.

It is understood that in acquiring any reserved right, the Company may designate related or subsidiary rights that it wishes to acquire and negative covenants concerning the use of competing rights that it wishes to secure; and the Guild will include such related and subsidiary rights and negative covenants in the price quoted for the reserved right acquired. For example, if the Company desires to acquire the dramatic rights it may include limited publication, radio and television rights for advertising and publicizing the play, and may also require the writer to agree that he/she will not use or license or grant to others the right to use his/her reserved live and film television rights. In such case the Guild shall have the right to grant the subsidiary rights and impose the negative covenants requested, and will quote a price to the Company which shall include such subsidiary rights and negative covenants.

e. Company has the right to negotiate directly with the writer to acquire the theatrical rights, publication rights, and merchandising rights and interactive rights as provided in Article 1.C.14.1.c.(2), and each of them, notwithstanding any provisions of subparagraphs d. and f. of this Article 16.B.3. or either of them, pertaining to negotiation with the Guild for compensation on no less than the following basis:

(1) Theatrical Rights - The Company shall pay two and one-half percent (2-1/2%) of the *bona fide* budgeted direct cost (and overhead or other indirect cost shall be excluded except to the extent it exceeds twenty-five percent (25%) of direct cost), or twenty thousand dollars ($20,000.00), whichever is greater, for theatrical rights. The above shall apply to each theatrical remake and sequel. If such two and one-half (2-1/2%) is greater than twenty thousand dollars ($20,000.00),

the excess shall be paid not later than sixty (60) days from the delivery of the answer print.

(2)   (a) Publication and Merchandising Rights and each of them - The Company shall pay six percent (6%) of absolute gross (that is, monies remitted by the manufacturer or the publisher, as the case may be), as derived from licensing, for the publication and merchandising rights. Comic books, magazine publications, comic strips, cutouts, and other activity books shall be deemed to be included as merchandising rights.

(b)   Interactive Rights - The Company shall pay the appropriate percentage of "Applicable Gross," as provided in Article 64.C. or 64.D. of this agreement, for the interactive program rights described in Article 1.D.14.1.c.(2).

(3)   In the event the Company fails to commence exploitation of any of the four (4) rights stated in subparagraphs (1) and (2) above within four (4) years from the date of delivery of literary material or three (3) years from the exhibition of the first motion picture of the series or serial in which separation of rights obtains, whichever is shorter, then any rights as to which Company has failed to commence exploitation shall revert to the writer. The payment of the above-described twenty thousand dollars ($20,000.00) payment for the theatrical rights shall constitute exploitation of such right. Nevertheless, the Company has the right of first refusal as provided in this Article 16.B.3.d. There shall be no crediting of any initial compensation against the above-described payments.

f.   In regard to the reserved theatrical motion picture rights in any material to which the separation of rights provisions of this Article 16.B. apply, if the writer commences the production of a theatrical motion picture based thereon, or has sold, licensed or otherwise disposed of the theatrical motion picture rights in such material (as permitted herein) and shall notify the Company thereof in writing, then, unless prior to receipt of such notice Company has commenced the production of a television motion picture which is a remake of the television motion picture initially based upon such material, the Company will not thereafter exercise or sell, license or otherwise dispose of the television remake rights in such material. If the Company acquires the theatrical motion picture rights in such material prior to the time the writer has commenced the production of a television motion picture based thereon, or has sold, licensed or otherwise disposed of his/her non-exclusive television rights in such material, the writer will not thereafter exercise or sell, license or otherwise dispose of his/her non-exclusive television rights in such material. For the purpose of determining whether the Company has commenced the production of a remake or the writer has commenced the production of a theatrical or television motion picture, the party shall be deemed to have commenced the production of the motion picture involved if such party has expended a substantial sum or has undertaken a binding contractual commitment requiring such party to expend a substantial sum for any item of production cost customarily incurred in connection with the production of a motion picture of the type involved; provided, however, that if principal photography of such motion picture shall not be commenced within one (1) year after such item of production cost has been incurred, then for the purpose of determining the rights of such parties hereunder the commencement of production of such motion picture shall be deemed not to have occurred. A dispute as to whether a substantial sum has been expended or committed, or as to abandonment, may be submitted to arbitration hereunder.

It is acknowledged that the reserved theatrical motion picture rights in material to which the separation of rights provisions of this Article 16.B. apply include the right to use the story or teleplay as the basis for a motion picture produced primarily for exhibition by pay television and, accordingly, unless the Company has acquired the theatrical motion picture rights, it may not make such use of the story or teleplay.

g. Company will inform the writer of the name of the person from whom the Company acquired rights with respect to the underlying property and Company without limiting its right to do the same agrees that the writer has the right to make a separate agreement with the owner of the underlying property as to such rights in such property as are reserved by the owner in his/her dealings with the Company.

h. With respect to a teleplay for ninety (90) minute or longer television motion picture sold or licensed to the Company by a professional writer (as defined in Article 1.C.1.b.) who has separation of rights therein, Company shall offer to such writer the opportunity to perform the first rewrite at not less than the applicable minimum compensation for a rewrite, unless time constraints render such assignment impractical (e.g., the start date of principal photography precludes compliance). If the writer is unable to perform such services or waives his/her right, the

Company may engage another writer. If the writer performs such rewrite and Company thereafter contemplates replacing such writer, a creative executive or producer who has read the material and who has decision-making authority on behalf of the Company shall discuss the Company's view and give the writer a reasonable opportunity to discuss continuing to perform services on the project. Disputes as to whether time constraints render such assignment impractical may be submitted to the "Hot Line" dispute resolution procedure in Article 48.

With respect to a teleplay for a ninety (90) minute or longer television motion picture written under employment by a writer who has separation of rights therein, if the Company contemplates replacing such writer, a creative executive or producer who has read the material and who has decision-making authority on behalf of the company shall discuss the Company's view and give the writer a reasonable opportunity to discuss continuing to perform services on the project.

Disputes as to whether Company has complied with the discussion requirements in the first and/or second unnumbered paragraphs of this subparagraph c. may be submitted to the "Hot Line" dispute resolution procedure in Article 48.

i. With respect to an option of a story and teleplay written by a professional writer (as defined in Article 1.C.1.b.) to which separation of rights applies, the writer of the optioned material shall be entitled, during the option period, to perform the first rewrite of such material, unless such writer is unavailable or waives this requirement in writing in a separate memorandum. If such writer performs such rewrite, the provisions of Article 16.B.3.h. shall be deemed satisfied.

j. The Producer or a creative executive will consult with the writer regarding each set of revisions requested of the writer by the Company.

4. Sketches and Routines

Notwithstanding the foregoing provisions of this Article 16.B., but subject to the rights to buyout as specified in subparagraph 3.e. above, with respect to any sketch or routine included in a comedy-variety type television motion picture, Company shall receive only the right to use and exploit the television motion picture in any manner, and in perpetuity, and to remake the motion picture (but only if the motion picture is remade substantially in its entirety); provided that the writer or writers of such sketches or routines shall have no right to, and will not use or grant, license or otherwise dispose of the right to use the television rights in such sketches or routines until a date one (1) year after the first broadcast of Company's television motion picture or a date two (2) years after delivery of the script of such material, whichever shall be earlier; and provided further that notwithstanding anything herein contained to the contrary, Company shall be free to use, in any manner, all or any part of any routine or sketch written by a writer hereunder so long as such use, if it were made by another without authorization from the writer, would not violate any rights of the writer.

Notwithstanding the restrictions hereinabove set forth in this Article 16.B.4., if a writer creates a segment of a comedy-variety program consisting of a self-contained dramatic plot, and characters and characterizations which are distinctive and identifiable and the principal creation of the writer, and where such segment is fully developed and fully described in the material written by the writer, then such writer shall be entitled to a sequel payment equal to fifty percent (50%) [seventy-five percent (75%) in the case of a network, prime time, once a week or less program] of the episodic sequel payment for a thirty (30) minute episode for each program of the series in which such segment is used after the termination of the writer's employment on such series, it being understood that such sequel payments are not due for programs written during such writer's employment. A dispute between writers as to who created such a segment shall be determined by the Guild in accordance with its credit arbitration procedures.

5. **Upset Price**

Notwithstanding any of these provisions of this Article 16.b. or of any other provisions of this Basic Agreement, in the event Company pays not less than the following "upset price" to each writer or team of writers entitled to separated rights for the writing or acquisition of a format or a format, story and teleplay or a story and teleplay as to which separation of rights applies, the Company may bargain freely with the writers concerned with respect to separation of rights subject to the payment of minimum sequel payments. Such upset price shall be as follows for each writer or team of writers as defined in Article 13:

UPSET PRICE

Initial Compensation of At Least

	Effective		
	5/2/95- 5/1/96	5/2/96- 5/1/97	5/2/97- 5/1/98
Format only (if by a writer other than the writer of story and teleplay)	$24,507	$25,365	$26,380
Story only (other than by the writer of the teleplay)			
15 minutes or less	8,526	8,824	9,177
30 minutes or less (more than 15)	15,170	15,701	16,329
45 minutes or less (more than 30)	21,559	22,314	23,207
60 minutes or less (more than 30)	26,709	27,644	28,750
90 minutes or less (more than 75)	36,755	38,041	39,563
More than 90 minutes	36,755	38,041	39,563
Story & Teleplay (other than by the writer of the format)			
15 minutes or less	$25,614	$26,510	27,570
30 minutes or less (more than 15)	45,523	47,116	49,001
45 minutes or less (more than 30)	54,040	55,931	58,168
60 minutes or less (more than 30)	66,942	69,285	72,056
90 minutes or less (more than 75)	97,008	100,403	104,419
More than 90 minutes	97,008	100,403	104,419
Format, Story & Teleplay by one Writer			
15 minutes or less	$25,614	$26,510	27,570
30 minutes or less (more than 15)	45,523	47,116	49,001
45 minutes or less (more than 30)	54,040	55,931	58,168
60 minutes or less (more than 30)	66,942	69,285	72,056
90 minutes or less (more than 75)	97,008	100,403	104,419
More than 90 minutes	97,008	100,403	104,419
Bible	61,948	64,116	66,681

When the upset price has been paid, the rights acquired after negotiation, permitted by payment of the upset price, shall be set forth in a separate contract.

The separate agreement for acquisition of the reserved rights shall state a separate consideration (other than the consideration for the original employment or purchase). Only the amount of initial compensation shall be used in determining whether the upset price has been reached, and with respect to week-to-week or term writers, compensation may be allocated toward the upset price if the writer receives in excess of $3,526 per week (effective May 2, 1996 through May 1, 1997, $3,649; effective May 2, 1997 through May 1, 1998, $3,795).

6. **Adapter's Royalty**

The credited writer or writers of a pilot story (if applicable) and teleplay to which separation of rights does not attach, which teleplay is the basis of a serial or episodic series, shall receive as a group a royalty equal to seventy-five percent (75%) of the corresponding sequel payment for each episode produced of said serial or episodic series, but no residuals.

7. **Extricable Material**

With regard to an episodic series program, other than the initial program or the pilot of such series, the story writer shall have a non-exclusive right to the television use of the extricable material commencing one (1) year after production of the series is discontinued. The writer shall further have similar rights to use extricable material in a theatrical motion picture provided that after production of the series is discontinued he/she gives the Company eighteen (18) months written notice of such intention and provided further that prior to completion of such eighteen (18) month period the Company does not use such material in a theatrical motion picture, or sell, license or otherwise dispose of theatrical motion picture rights in such material.

8. **Continuing Rights and Obligations**

The provisions of this Article 16.B. shall be binding upon and shall inure to the benefit of the heirs, next of kin, executors, administrators, legal representatives, successors and assigns of the Company and the writer.

* * *

ARTICLE 19 — USE AND DELIVERY OF STANDARD FORM CONTRACTS

A. GENERAL

If the Company borrows a writer from a loan-out company (as defined in Article 3 hereof), the Company will provide to the Guild a copy of its contract with the loan-out company for such services. The Guild agrees that the contract and information so furnished shall be deemed confidential and shall not be furnished or communicated to any person, firm or corporation not directly concerned.

When the writer utilizes an office in his/her home in connection with an employment agreement with the Company, such utilization by the writer shall be deemed to be at the request of and for the convenience of the employer.

B. THEATRICAL

1. The Company agrees that from and after the effective date hereof, Company will submit to the writer or his/her agent a written contract setting forth the terms of the writer's employment in the following cases:

   a. In a simple week-to-week contract, the contract will be submitted to the writer or his/her agent within two (2) weeks after his/her employment; or

   b. In a simple deal contract, the contract will be submitted to the writer or his/her agent within three (3) weeks after his/her employment.

   c. A simple contract is defined as a one (1) picture contract or a week-to-week contract in which there are no provisions for percentages, participation or deferments and in which there are no options for additional pictures.

2. It is understood that there may be other provisions or factors with respect to which the submission of a complete and definite contract within the time periods specified in subparagraphs 1 a. and b. above may be impractical. In any such case, the Company may request a waiver from the Guild of the requirements of this Article 19.B.1 a. or b., and the Guild will not unreasonably withhold the granting of such waiver. The fact that a deal contract provides for writing to be done in stages, for example, first draft screenplay followed by final draft screenplay, does not prevent it from being a simple contract.

3. As to all other contracts, the Company agrees that from and after the effective date hereof, upon the employment of any writer, such writer shall be tendered, within a reasonable length of time, a written contract setting forth the terms of the employment. Employment contracts shall contain nothing contradictory to any of the provisions of this Basic Agreement.

4. Upon the full execution of a written contract, not less than two (2) copies thereof shall be delivered to the writer or his/her agent and either or both of such copies shall be executed by the Company, and if both of such copies are not executed by the Company, the copy not so executed shall be accurately conformed by an officer or employee of the Company who shall place upon any such conformed copy his/her signature or initials in form sufficient to identify such officer or employee.

5. Within one (1) week after the final execution of an employment contract between a Company and writer, then if such contract is subject

to this Basic Agreement, the Company will deliver to the Guild a properly conformed copy of such employment contract.

Within one (1) week after receipt by Company of the executed contract referred to below, Company will also send to the Guild: (a) excerpts from contracts of employment with persons employed primarily in non-writing capacities (*i.e.,* producers, directors, etc.) if such contracts contain a right to require writing services subject to this Basic Agreement, which excerpts shall include all of the provisions therein relating to such writing services, and (b) copies of separate contracts for such writing services which are entered into with persons employed in non-writing capacities together with such portions of their contracts for non-writing services which relate to their compensation for such writing services.

6. In an acquisition contract with a professional writer, Company will include a statement that such contract is subject to the provisions of this Basic Agreement to the extent provided in Article 3.6.2. (other than the provisions of Article 6, Guild Shop, and Article 17, Pension Plan and Health Fund) of this Basic Agreement to the extent the same are applicable. Company will tender such acquisition contract to the professional writer within thirty (30) days (or forty (40) days if contract is to be executed outside the State of California) after agreement with respect to the acquisition of the material has been reached, and will send a copy thereof to the Guild within one (1) week after execution thereof by the professional writer.

An inadvertent failure by the Company to furnish a copy of an acquisition contract with a professional writer executed outside of California or a copy of a contract referred to above shall not constitute a breach of this Basic Agreement.

C. TELEVISION

1. Company agrees that from and after the effective date hereof, upon the employment of any writer under the television provisions of this Basic Agreement, it shall tender the writer a contract setting forth all of the terms of the writer's employment, including all of the provisions set forth in Television Schedule B attached hereto and made part hereof (except that in the case of writers on term employment or under week-to-week contract, said terms shall reflect that the agreement is not a freelance television writer's contract and shall be changed accordingly). None of the terms or conditions of any employment contract shall be less favorable to the writer than, or inconsistent with, or violative of, the applicable terms and conditions contained in this Basic Agreement. Company agrees to tender such contract to the writer

within ten (10) days following the commencement of his/her employment, and agrees to send to Guild a copy of the executed contract of employment within one (1) week after receipt by Company of such executed contract The Company further agrees that if a copy shall not be so sent to the Guild, the Guild shall have the right to require the writer to refuse to continue rendering services for the Company until a copy shall be so sent to the Guild and the writer's compliance with such directive from the Guild shall not constitute a breach of his/her individual contract with the Company. In the event that the Guild gives notice in writing to the Company that such contract contains provision(s) less favorable to the writer, or inconsistent with, or violative of, the applicable terms and conditions contained in this Basic Agreement and in the further event that Company fails to make the change so requested within a period of fifteen (15) days from and after receipt of Guild's written notice, the difference or controversy may be submitted by either Company or Guild to grievance and arbitration and the finding of the arbitration panel shall be final and conclusive upon the parties hereto.

2. If Company purchases from a non-professional writer literary material which would otherwise be subject to this Basic Agreement, as provided in Article 3.C.2. hereof, it will notify the Guild of the name of such non-professional writer from whom such material is purchased.

3. If Company acquires from a professional writer literary material subject to this Basic Agreement, to the extent provided in Article 3.C.2. hereof, it will include in the acquisition agreement a statement that such agreement is subject to the provisions of this Basic Agreement to the extent provided in Article 3.C.2. Company will tender such acquisition contract to the writer within ten (10) days (or twenty (20) days if contract is to be executed outside the State of California) after agreement with respect to the acquisition of the material has been reached, and will send a copy thereof to the Guild within one (1) week after execution thereof by the writer.

    An inadvertent failure by the Company to furnish a copy of an acquisition contract with a professional writer executed outside of California or a copy of a contract referred to immediately above or the name of a non-professional writer referred to above shall not constitute a breach of this Basic Agreement.[14]

---

[14] See Article 14.L. concerning tarnishing of contracts.

Note: A total redraft of Article 19, for the purposes of generally simplifying procedures and clarification, will be assigned to a joint legal committee, consisting of counsel appointed by WGA and counsel appointed by the companies. Recommendations of the joint committee shall be referred back to the parties for consideration. Revisions agreed upon by the parties shall be included in the MSA. Pending completion of the redraft, Article 19, as provided above, remains in effect.

ARTICLE 20 — SPECULATIVE WRITING

A. THEATRICAL

1. The company and the guild agree that there shall be no speculative writing, nor shall either party condone it as a practice. As used herein, the term "speculative writing" has reference to any agreement covered hereunder which is entered into between the Company and any writer whereby the writer shall write material, payment for which is contingent upon the acceptance or approval of the Company or upon the occurrence of any other event such as obtaining financing, or whereby the writer shall, at the request of the Company, engage in rewriting or revising any material submitted under the terms of this Basic Agreement and compensation for the writer's services in connection with such material is contingent upon the acceptance or approval of the Company, or upon the occurrence of any other event such as obtaining financing. Company shall not request a writer to write and submit literary material, other than a submission contemplated by Article 3.B.2. of this Basic Agreement, unless the Company first makes commitment with the writer for the writing of at least a story or treatment. If the Company does so make a prohibited request, the writer shall not write and submit such material.

2. The Company and the Guild recognize that there is possibly an area wherein the proper and constructive exchange of ideas and criticism between a writer and a Company may be claimed by the Guild to be speculative writing. Whenever the Guild feels that speculative writing has occurred, the case will be referred to grievance and arbitration and the Company's intent as determined by the facts shall be an important factor in the consideration. It is understood in this connection that nothing is this Article shall limit Company from discussing with any writer any ideas suggested by such writer, or discussing with any writer any ideas or any material suggested by the Company in order to determine the writer's thoughts and reactions with respect to any such idea or other material to determine the writer's suitability for an assignment.

B. TELEVISION

1. The Company and the Guild agree that there shall be no speculative writing, nor shall either party condone it as practice. As used herein, the term "speculative writing" has reference to any agreement entered into between the Company and any writer whereby the writer shall write material, payment for which is contingent upon the acceptance or approval of the Company, or whereby the writer shall, at the request

of the Company, engage in rewriting or revising any material submitted under the terms of this Basic Agreement and compensation for the writer's services in connection with such material is contingent upon the acceptance or approval of the Company. Company shall not request a writer to write and submit literary material, other than a submission contemplated by Article 3.C.2. of this Basic Agreement unless the Company first makes a commitment with the writer for the writing of at least a story. If the Company makes such a prohibited request, the writer shall not write and submit the requested material.

2. The Company and Guild recognize that there is possibly an area wherein the proper and constructive exchange of ideas and criticism between a writer and a Company may be claimed by the Guild to be speculative writing. Whenever the Guild feels that speculative writing has occurred, the case will be referred to grievance and arbitration and the Company's intent as determined by the facts shall be an important factor in the consideration. It is understood in this connection that nothing in this Article shall limit the submission of original stories or prevent the Company from discussing with any writer any ideas or any material suggested by the Company in order to determine the writer's thoughts and reactions with respect to any such idea or other material to determine the writer's suitability for an assignment, provided, however, that any such discussion relating to an assignment shall be subject to the provisions of subparagraph 3. hereof.

3. (a) A writer's initial interview with the Company concerning employment in connection with an assignment may only be with (i) a person who is empowered to make, subject to the negotiation of mutually acceptable terms and conditions, the final creative decision to engage a writer for an assignment, or (ii) a person designated by the Company to interview writers with regard to the particular program; except that a writer's initial interview with the Company at the Company's request concerning employment in connection with an assignment for an episodic series may only be with a producer or other person who is empowered to make the final creative decision to engage a writer for an assignment.

(b) Unless a commitment was made by the Company in such initial interview, a second interview by the writer with the Company concerning the same assignment may only be with a person who without reference to or consultation with any other person, firm or corporation, including but not limited to, network or sponsor, is empowered to make, subject to the negotiation of mutually acceptable terms and conditions, the final decision to engage a writer for an assignment. In no event may a third interview by the writer with the Company take place concerning such assignment, nor may the Company request the writer to render any writing services, unless there has first been a business meeting between the writer, his/her agent, or representative, with the business affairs executive or other executive of the Company charged with responsibility for negotiating the terms and conditions of a proposed employment contract between the writer and the Company and such terms and conditions have in fact been agreed upon. However, if a time emergency does not permit such business meeting to precede such interview, such business meeting may take place after such third interview if there has been agreement prior thereto as to the monies to be paid the writer.

For the purpose of this subparagraph 3., an interview shall not be deemed to include (i) a telephone request by Company addressed either to the agent or the writer solely for information concerning the writer's availability for employment or as to his/her credits, or (ii) an appointment solicited by the writer, the purpose of which is to inform Company of the writer's availability for employment or as to his/her credits, or (iii) motion picture screenings. It is expressly understood that the writer may in no event be required to deliver any material written by him/her until all the terms and conditions relating to his/her employment in connection with such material have been agreed upon.

(c) If in the first interview the writer gives a story, then a second meeting at the request of the Company concerning that story shall constitute a story commitment at minimum compensation.

(d) If at the request of the Company the writer gives a story, either by telephone or in person or otherwise, then a meeting on that story at the request of the Company is a commitment. The parties hereto agree that the use of a telephone call, initiated by an authorized representative of the Company, as a method of circumventing a meeting in person to discuss the story is a violation of the provisions of the next sentence.

(e) (i) With respect to an episodic series or once-per-week serial for which more than six (6) episodes, excluding the pilot, have been ordered, Company shall have the option of interviewing not less than one (1) freelance writer for each story commitment which is unassigned at the time of the network program order for a given broadcast season.

For each such interview, Company shall inform the writer at the beginning of the interview of all storylines then in work, provided that if a storyline is confidential due to marketing or other considerations, e.g., a "cliffhanger," etc., Company is not required to inform the writer of such storyline.

The number of such interviews may be reduced by one (1) for each freelance assignment made. It is understood that the requirement for such interview shall not be deemed to imply in any way a commitment for employment.

Company shall furnish the Guild, upon request, written reports containing the name of the Company, the name of the particular series, the date of and number of episodes in the network order, the number of story commitments in the network order, the names of the freelance writers interviewed, the dates of such interviews, and the names of all freelance writers employed by Company as a result of such interviews.

In the event the Company records an interview with the writer, the Company shall furnish a copy or transcription of such recording to such writer.

(ii) In the alternative, in connection with a particular episodic series, Company shall employ freelance writers who have not been employed on such series in the previous broadcast season, to write not less than two (2) stories with option for teleplay in the case of an initial network program order of thirteen (13) episodes or three (3) stories with option for teleplay, one (1) of which must be exercised, in the case of a network program order of twenty-two (22) or more episodes of each such series during a given broadcast season. In connection with once-per-week serials, Company shall have the alternative right to commit to one (1) teleplay per season for each such serial.

(iii) Company shall elect either paragraph (e)(i) or (e)(ii) above for each broadcast season of a series. However, if Company elects paragraph (e)(i) above and does not generate the levels of freelance employment specified in paragraph (e)(ii) above, then Company must comply with paragraph (e)(ii) in the subsequent season of such series. Paragraph (e)(i) would thereafter be available only if the levels of employment specified in paragraph (e)(ii) were fulfilled in the immediately prior season of such series.

(iv) The foregoing access provisions under this Article 20.B.3. are not applicable to programs produced under Appendix B of this Agreement.

(f) During the 1988 negotiations, the Guild raised concerns about increasing employment for freelance writers by strengthening the provisions of the existing contract with respect to such employment.

According to the statistics provided by the Guild, on most series, freelance writers have, in fact, been employed at the levels proposed by the Guild.

In recognition of the Guild's desire to encourage Companies to continue to employ freelance writers at those levels during the term of this Agreement, the parties have agreed as follows: In the event the Guild finds that a particular Company is not employing freelance writers at those levels, the Company, upon request of the Guild, will participate in a meeting with the Guild to discuss the Guild's concerns. The Company will invite the persons responsible for making script assignments on the series in question to such meeting.

4. Company shall furnish in writing to the Guild, as to each program and series and serial, the names of all persons empowered to make a commitment with the writers; such notification shall be binding on Company. Any changes must be furnished to the Guild in writing, but shall be effective only after receipt by the Guild.

5. Each writer called in to an interview for an episodic series or once-per-week serial shall be provided with a format, including character descriptions and brief synopses, of all storylines previously produced for the current season.

* * *

ARTICLE 28 — WARRANTY AND INDEMNIFICATION (GENERAL)

1. Company and writer may in any individual contract of employment include provisions for warranties of originality and no violation of rights of third parties, indemnification against judgments, damages, costs and expenses including attorneys fees in connection with suits relating to the literary material or the use of the literary material supplied by the writer or the use thereof by Company; provided, however, that the writer shall in no event

   a. be required by contract to waive his/her right to defend himself/herself against a claim by Company for costs, damages or losses arising out of settlements, stipulations for entry of judgment or other similar agreements to resolve disputes, not consented to by the writer, unless the writer agrees to such waiver in a separate writing signed by the writer, and Company reserves all of the rights it may otherwise have against the writer;

b. be required to warrant or indemnify with respect to any claim that his/her literary material defamed or invaded the privacy or publicity of any person or entity unless the writer knowingly used the name, likeness, characteristics or personality of such person or entity or should have known, in the exercise of reasonable prudence, that such person would or might claim that his/her name, likeness, characteristics or personality was used in such material;

c. be required to warrant or indemnify with respect to any material other than that furnished by the writer;

d. be required to warrant or indemnify with respect to third party defamation, invasion of privacy or publicity claims, when the writer is requested by the Company to prepare literary materials which are based in whole or in part on any actual individual, whether living or dead, provided writer accurately provides all information reasonably requested by Company for the purpose of permitting the Company to evaluate the risks involved in the use of the material supplied by writer.

2. The Company shall indemnify such writer against any and all damages, costs and expenses, including attorneys' fees, and shall relieve the writer of all liability in connection with any claim or action respecting:

a. material supplied to the writer by the Company for incorporation into the writer's work or incorporated in the writer's work by employees, agents having actual, apparent or ostensible authority or officers of the Company other than the writer;

b. changes in the writer's literary material made by the writer at the Company's request or direction; or

c. material other than that furnished to the Company by the writer.

3. The Company and the writer, upon the presentation of any such claim to either of them or the institution of any such action naming either or both of them as defendants, shall promptly notify the other of the presentation of any such claim or the institution of any such action giving such other party full details thereof. The pendency of any such claim or action shall not relieve the Company of its obligation to pay to the employee any monies due to the writer with respect to the literary material contributed by the employee.

The Company shall name or cover the writer (including writers employed via loan-out companies) as additional insured on its errors and omissions policies respecting theatrical and televisions motion pictures.

4. The indemnified party shall cooperate (without being required to incur any costs or expenses) in the defense of any claim for which indemnification is provided in this Article.

* * *

ARTICLE 42 — POSTING BONDS (GENERAL)

Posting of Bonds - The Guild reserves the right, in the event it determines that a particular Company is not reliable or financially responsible, to require the posting in advance of an adequate bond, cash or other security.

The Company acknowledges the Guild's right to instruct its members to withhold their services from any Company that has failed to post a bond when required to do so in accordance with the foregoing paragraph.

For the coverage of initial compensation an escrow account may be utilized in lieu of the foregoing bonding provision.

* * *

ARTICLE 48 — PROFESSIONAL STATUS OF WRITERS: WRITER PARTICIPATION IN THE PRODUCTION PROCESS (GENERAL)

Preamble

During the negotiations for the 1988 MBA, the Company reaffirmed with emphasis the creative significance of writers as set forth herein.

It is mutually recognized that the writer of the screenplay or teleplay, by reason of his/her unique knowledge of the material and creative abilities, can contribute to the translation of the screenplay or teleplay to the screen by participating in other stages of production, including but not limited to discussions with the producer and director during preparation, production and after preview, in relation to changes in the screenplay or teleplay and in the motion picture. It is the policy of the Company to encourage such participation. With respect to discussions not covered under subparagraph A. below, if the writer of the screenplay or teleplay notifies the Company he/she wishes to participate in such discussions, Company shall in good faith invite such participation to such extent as may be feasible under the circumstances, it being understood that the Company shall have the right to determine who shall or shall not be present at a particular conference.

A.   By way of implementation of the foregoing, the following shall apply with respect to theatrical motion pictures, television pilots, movies-of-the-week and multi-part closed-end series: The Company recognizes that the writer has a unique vision of the motion picture and, therefore, Company agrees:

1.   if the director has not been engaged, to arrange a pre-production meeting between the producer and the writer (a participating writer of the Company's choice) so that the writer has the opportunity for a meaningful discussion of the translation of his/her vision to the screen;

2.   upon the assignment of a director, the producer will arrange such a meeting, and will invite and encourage the director to participate; and

3.   if an authorized representative of the Company believes that enhanced participation by the writer will benefit the production process, the Company will facilitate the writer's participation.

Disputes that arise under Article 48.A.1. shall be arbitrable under Articles 10 and 11 of this Agreement only after resort to the "hot line" procedure described below in Article 48.E.

Disputes that arise under Article 48.A.2. or 48.A.3. are not subject to grievance or arbitration, but may be subject to resolution under the "hot line" procedure described below in Article 48.E. or may be referred to the Committee described below in Article 48.F.

B. **THEATRICAL**

1.   **Affirmations.** Company affirms that writers play an integral role in the filmmaking process and that it is the Company's policy to involve writers in that process as much as possible, including viewing the motion picture prior to its completion, as provided below.

2.   **General Right — Writer's Viewing Period.** Each participating writer shall have the right to a "Writer's Viewing Period" during which time the writer shall have the right to see a cut of the film.

It is understood that the creative process differs on each motion picture and that different viewing times may be dictated by different circumstances on each production.

Therefore, the scheduling of the "Writer's Viewing Period" shall be at the sole discretion of the Company, except that Company shall ensure that each participating writer is given an opportunity to see a cut of the motion picture sufficient time so that any editing suggestions made by the writer concerning the film, if approved, could be reasonably and effectively implemented.

In unusual circumstances, waivers of the foregoing, if requested, will not be unreasonably denied.

3. **MBA Committee.** Issues pertaining to this provision will be reviewed each year in the Committee on the Professional Status of Writers and on an *ad hoc* basis if requested by the Company or the WGA.

4. **Sneak Previews.** Company shall give each credited writer five (5) days notice, if possible, of the time and place of the first sneak preview, if any, to be held in Los Angeles County and shall invite each credited writer to such preview. Provided, however, that any inadvertent failure on the part of the Company to extend the writers such invitation shall not be deemed to be a breach of this Basic Agreement or a default on the part of the Company. Information concerning the time and place of any sneak preview shall be confidential.

5. **Video cassette.** The Company shall furnish the credited writer(s) of the motion picture, at no cost to such writer(s), a copy of the video cassette version of the theatrical motion picture, provided it is manufactured for sale on video cassettes.

6. **Sideletters to Article 48.B. of the 1995 MBA.** The Companies acknowledge that the Guild and companies represented by the AMPTP in negotiations for the 1995 WGA-AMPTP MBA included two Sideletters to Article 48B. Of such Agreement. The Guild and the Companies agree that these two Sideletters, which are found at the end of this MBA, would be relevant to the interpretation and application of language new to Article 48.B. of the 1995 MBA.

C. TELEVISION

For movies-of-the-week and multi-part closed-end series, Company shall invite all participating writers to view the "Director's cut" within forty-eight (48) hours following the Company's viewing. In the event that, in lieu of a viewing, the Company is provided with a videocassette copy of the cut, the Company shall simultaneously furnish a videocassette copy of the cut to the writer(s). In an emergency situation which renders such viewing impracticable, and when no videocassette copy of the cut is available, the viewing will be scheduled as soon as practicable, but not later than the next viewing of a cut. If, thereafter, the

Company calls a discussion meeting by telephone or in person regarding the cut, the most recent participating writer shall be invited to participate in such discussion; in any event, the producer shall remain available to receive the writers' comments.

For television pilots, the Company shall invite all participating writers to view the final director's cut or a subsequent cut prior to the final cut of the motion picture.

It is understood that the viewing of the cut must be sufficient time for the writers to offer editing suggestions which, if approved, could be effectively implemented.

For television pilots, movies-of-the-week, and multi-part closed-end series, Company shall give each credited writer five (5) days notice, if possible, of the first sneak preview, if any, of any television pilot, movie-of-the-week or multi-part closed-end series, to be held in Los Angeles County and shall invite each credited writer to such preview.

Provided, however, that any inadvertent failure on the part of the Company to extend the writers such invitation shall not be deemed to be a breach of this Basic Agreement or a default on the part of the Company. Information concerning the time and place of any sneak preview shall be confidential. As to other television motion pictures, the Company shall designate an employee who, upon request, shall inform the following writers of the time and place of the showing of a cut and the answer print:

1. Prior to the final determination of credits, as in Television Schedule A attached hereto provided, all writers who have participated in the writing of the story and final teleplay;

2. After the final determination of the screen credits, as in said Schedule A provided, only those writers who have been accorded story and teleplay credit.

D. In any event, where exigencies of the time do not permit (e.g., where a delivery date precludes compliance), the provisions of subparagraphs B. and C. above shall not apply.

As a means of drawing attention to the requirements of subparagraphs B. and C. above, the Companies agrees to issue a bulletin highlighting the Company's obligations under these provisions and to provide a copy to the Guild.

E. **"Hot Line Dispute Resolution":** Before resort to grievance or arbitration for claims under this Article 48, the WGA will contact a representative of the Companies designated for this purpose to attempt in good faith a prompt resolution of the dispute. The Companies will notify the Executive Directors of the Guild of the designated representative and one or more designated substitutes in the event of unavailability, such initial notice to be given within thirty (30) days following ratification of this Agreement and annually thereafter. Except as provided above, the WGA will not be precluded from filing a grievance or arbitration claim if use of the "hot line" procedure does not resolve the dispute within seven (7) days after the WGA's initial contact with the designated representative.

F. Committee on the Professional Status of Writers: The "Committee on the Professional Status of Writers" will meet at least twice a year, at the call of the WGA or the AMPTP and/or ABC, CBS and NBC. At such meetings, any subject that the Committee members wish to discuss relating to the professional status of writers will be a suitable subject for discussion and study, including appropriate recommendations of solutions to problems that may arise. In connection with the foregoing, the Committee will review and study the subject of coverages on a periodic basis. [footnote omitted]

G. Authorized Expenses: Participation by the writer as provided in this Article 48 shall be voluntary and without compensation and shall not require any additional cost to the Company, other than reimbursement of the writer under Article 21 for expenses specifically authorized by the Company in connection with such participation.

H. Campaign For Greater Appreciation of the Role of the Writer: The Company is committed to a campaign for greater appreciation of the writer's role in the creation of theatrical and television motion pictures.

The campaign will include measures to be agreed upon to develop greater visibility for writers in the promotion and marketing of motion pictures. Among these measures are:

Companies agree to facilitate meetings as follows:

    (1) between the Guild and each Company's marketing division for the purpose of discussing ways in which they can develop marketing strategies which will both enhance awareness of the importance of writers and effectively promote the Company's motion pictures; and

    (2) between the Guild and retail video distributors of the Guild's choosing for the purpose of advising them of the value of writing credits in the promotion of their product.

If an industry-wide labor-management cooperative committee is established, pursuant to Section 6(b) of the Labor Management Cooperation Act, 29 U.S.C. 175a, for the creation of writer publicity and promotion, the Companies agree to participate in such committee, subject to the concurrence of other representatives to the committee. Such participation shall include monetary contributions by the Companies of their proportionate share, to be matched by the WGA and other management representative, to a WGA-supervised fund. A representative of the Companies shall serve as a consultant to the fund. The Companies shall be consulted on the use of the monies. The Companies agree to cooperate, for example, in providing access to films and scripts for a Guild-coordinated campaign at colleges and film schools to broaden recognition of the writer's role in motion pictures.

I. Interim Agreement of the Parties Regarding Possessive Credits

The WGA and the Companies have agreed to the following Interim Agreement:

Theatrical Provisions

1. The parties agree to meet on a tripartite basis with the Directors Guild of America to attempt to reach an industry-wide agreement regarding possessive credits. The parties also agree that the issue of credits in advertising will be reviewed in the tripartite setting.

2. The Company will not enter into any agreement with any guild, craft, union or labor organization which mandates a possessive credit, except that any possessive credit requirement contained in a collective bargaining agreement in effect on May 2, 1995 may continue in effect.

3. In addition to the meetings specified in Article 48.F. above, the Committee on the Professional Status of Writers agrees to meet annually for the purpose of reviewing progress in diminishing the use of possessive credits. Among the issues to be reviewed shall be the incidence of possessive credits on theatrical motion pictures as well as the incidence of granting of possessive credits in individual negotiations over the prior year. The Company will supply to the Committee on the Professional Status of Writers all information necessary for such review.

4. Each Company intends to exercise control over granting of possessive credits above the minimums. If meaningful progress in diminishing the use of possessive credits has not been made within four (4) years from the effective date of this Agreement, the Company will enter into good faith negotiations with the guild regarding one or more of the following methods to balance the according of possessive credits to directors:

    a. Company issuance of separate publicity solely for the benefit of the writer;

    b. Company contributions to a WGA fund for writer publicity;

    c.   The right of a writer to negotiate for a special credit to balance the giving of a possessive credit. Such special credit to the writer shall be accorded in the event the writer receives sole writing credit;

    d.   Any other methods the parties mutually agree upon.

5.   Subject to extension, amendment or other agreement (in the CAC, the MBA Committee on the Professional Status of Writers, or otherwise), the provisions of this Interim Agreement shall remain in effect until the earlier of the expiration of the successor collective bargaining agreement to the 1995 WGA MBA or until a tripartite resolution, as contemplated herein, has been reached.

Television Provisions

As to television, the Guild recognizes the Company's current rights and responsibilities in regard to the use of possessive credits. The company recognizes the Guild's concerns regarding possessive credits and agrees to exercise its rights, and meet its responsibilities, in a manner consistent with its past practice.

* * *

ARTICLE 51 — SUPPLEMENTAL MARKETS

1.   The provisions of this Article 51 relate and apply only to motion pictures as defined in Article 1.A.1. and 1.A.2.:

    a.   produced by the Company or within the provisions of subparagraph 3.h.(4), of this Article 51, and

    b.   the principal photography of which commenced on or after May 2, 1995, which motion pictures are, either during the term hereof or at any time thereafter, released in Supplemental Markets (as defined below), and

    c.   based upon a story or screenplay (the word "screenplay" shall be deemed to include teleplay, for the purposes of this Article) written by a writer while in the employ of the Company or in the employ of the actual producing Company as described in subparagraph 3.h(4) of this Article 51 (to which employment the provisions of this Basic Agreement apply as provided in Article 5 hereof) or acquired by the Company (or such actual producing Company) from a professional writer (to which acquisition the provisions of this Basic Agreement apply as provided in Article 5 hereof), which writer or professional writer received or receives screen credit for authorship of such story or screenplay, as provided in the appropriate Theatrical or Television schedule A, as the case may be.

2. DEFINITIONS. The term "Supplemental Markets," as used in this Agreement means only: The exhibition of motion pictures by means of cassettes (to the limited extent provided in this subparagraph 2.a.), pay-type CATV, or pay television, as those terms are hereafter defined in this subparagraph 2. and the exhibition of television motion pictures on any commercial carrier such as commercial airlines, trains, ships, and buses (referred to herein as "in-flight").

a. The term "video disc/video cassette," as used in this Article 51, shall mean disc, cassette, cartridge and/or other device serving a similar function which is sold or rented for play on a home-type television screen in the home or in closed circuit use such as in hotel rooms.

b. The term "pay television" or "pay-type CATV" as used in this Article 51, shall mean exhibition on a home-type television screen by means of telecast, cable, closed circuit, satellite to home or CATV where substantially all licensed systems meet the following tests:

   (i) A separate channel is provided for which the subscriber pays a separate fee (which fee is a substantial charge relative to other charges made to the subscriber) for that channel;

   and/or

   (ii) The subscriber pays for the program or programs selected (except that a program or programs selected for which only a token charge is made shall not be considered pay television);

   and/or

   (iii) The subscriber pays a fee for an encoded telecast, which fee is a substantial charge relative to other fees paid for encoded telecasts.

   The foregoing tests cover those systems which exist in the industry today and are commonly understood in the industry today to be pay television systems.

The term "Supplemental Markets" does not include the exhibition of a motion picture by cassette or otherwise over a television broadcast station in free television, or in theatrical exhibition, and for this purpose "theatrical exhibition" includes what has previously been considered to be the educational market, the exhibition of theatrical motion pictures on any commercial carrier (referred to herein as "in-flight"), such as commercial airlines, trains, ships and buses, and other uses which have been traditionally considered theatrical exhibition of theatrical motion pictures. Whenever reference is made in this Agreement to pay-type CATV or pay television, such reference shall be deemed to include only those uses of motion pictures as to which a charge is actually made to the subscriber (which may be a hotel, motel or other accommodation) for the program viewed, or where the subscriber or viewer has the option, for a payment, to receive special programming over one or more special channels.

With respect to theatrical motion pictures, the Company has agreed to the inclusion of pay-type CATV and pay television in the "Supplemental Markets" because under the present pattern of distribution of theatrical motion pictures, pay-type CATV and pay television are supplemental to the primary market. The Company reserves the right in future negotiations to contend that the pattern of release has changed so that pay-type CATV and/or pay television are no longer a "Supplemental Market" but constitute or are a part of the primary market of distribution of theatrical motion pictures, and that therefore no additional payment pursuant to this Article should be made with respect to the release of theatrical motion pictures (including those covered by this Agreement) in said markets. The Guild reserves the right to contend in future negotiations that the method of employment and payment provided for in this Basic Agreement for writers of motion pictures are applicable and appropriate to employment and payment to writers of literary materials written directly for motion pictures intended primarily for release on pay-type CATV, pay television or cassettes, and that the provisions of this Agreement with respect to all kinds of "Supplemental markets," whether they are or have become primary markets or not, shall be improved for the benefit of the writers of literary materials for said markets. Nothing herein shall limit the scope of negotiations on said subjects.

3. a. (i) As to each such motion picture referred to in 1. above, (herein sometimes called "Such Picture"), the Company will pay to each participating writer (as defined in Article 51.3.e.) as additional compensation, a *pro rata* share of one and two-tenths percent (1.2%) (hereinafter referred to as the "percentage payment") of the Company's accountable receipts from the distribution of Such Picture to pay-type CATV or pay television (as defined in this Article 51), computed as hereinafter provided and subject to the following conditions:

The term "Producer's gross," as used herein, means the worldwide total gross receipts derived by the distributor of

Such Picture (who may be the Company or a distributor licensed by the Company) from licensing the right to exhibit Such Picture on pay-type CATV of pay television (as defined in Article 51 of this Basic Agreement). The Producer's gross shall not include sums required to be paid or withheld as taxes, in the nature of turnover taxes, sales taxes or similar taxes based on the actual receipts of such monies to be remitted to or by the Producer but there shall not be excluded from Producer's gross any net income tax, franchise tax or excess profit tax or similar tax payable by the Producer or such Distributor on its net income or for the privilege of doing business.

The term "accountable receipts" as used herein, means one hundred percent (100%) of the "Producers gross."

If the distributor of Such Picture does not distribute Such Picture directly on pay-type CATV or pay television as defined in Article 51 of this Basic Agreement, but employs a subdistributor to so distribute Such Picture, then the "Producer's gross" shall be the monies defined above in this Article 51.3.a.(i) derived by such subdistributor from licensing the right to exhibit Such Picture on pay-type CATV or pay television.

(ii)   As to each Such Picture, the Company will pay to each participating writer (as defined in Article 51.3.e. of this Basic Agreement) as additional compensation, a *pro rata* share of one and five-tenths percent (1.5%) (hereinafter referred to as the "percentage payment") of the "Producer's gross," as defined below, derived from the distribution of Such Picture on video discs or video cassettes until the Producer's gross equals one million dollars ($1,000,000.00). Thereafter, the Company shall pay a *pro rata* share of one and eight-tenths percent (1.8%) of the Producer's gross, in excess of one million dollars ($1,000,000.00) derived from distribution of each Such Picture on video discs or video cassettes.

If the Company is the Distributor or the Distributor is owned by or affiliated with the Company, the "Producer's gross" derived from the distribution of Such Picture on video discs or video cassettes shall be twenty percent (20%) of the worldwide wholesale receipts derived by the Distributor. In such cases, if the Distributor is also the retailer, a reasonable allocation of the retail gross receipts shall be made as between the Distributor as distributor and the Distributor as retailer, and twenty percent (20%) of the former only shall be deemed to be "Producer's gross." The reasonableness of such allocation shall be subject to arbitration and, in such arbitration, generally prevailing trade practices in the video disc and video cassette industry with respect to dealings between non-related companies shall be relevant evidence. Such worldwide wholesale receipts shall not include:

(a)   Rebates, credits or repayments for cassettes returned (and in this connection the Producer shall have the right to set up a reasonable reserve for returns);

(b)   Sums required to be paid or withheld as taxes, in the nature of turnover taxes, sales taxes or similar taxes based on the actual receipts of such motion picture or on any monies to be remitted to or by the Producer but there shall not be excluded from Producer's gross any net income tax, franchise tax or excess profit tax or similar tax payable by the Producer or such Distributor on its net income or for the privilege of doing business.

If the Distributor is not the Company and is not owned by or affiliated with the Company, the term "Producer's gross" shall be one hundred percent (100%) of the fees received by the Company from licensing the right to distribute each Such Picture on video discs or video cassettes.

(iii)   Provided, however, with respect to Article 51.3.a.(i) and (ii) above, that in the case of any Such Picture which is produced outside of the United States, if Such Picture is subject to this Basic Agreement and if such production is under an arrangement (herein referred to as a "foreign production deal") pursuant to which a foreign producer or distributor provides or guarantees any of the financing for the production of Such Picture or furnishes any other consideration for such production and a foreign distributor acquires one or more foreign territories for the distribution of Such Picture in Supplemental Markets, then no monies from any such distribution in any such foreign territory shall be included in Producer's gross except to the extent such foreign producer or foreign distributor is obligated to account to Company or to the distributor of Such Picture for such monies, and except for gross receipts received by such foreign distributor from such distribution in the United Kingdom.

In case of an outright sale of the Supplemental Markets distribution rights, for the entire world, or any territory or country, the income derived by the seller from such sale, but not the income realized by the purchaser or licensee of such rights, shall be the "Producer's gross."

If any such outright sale shall include Supplemental Markets exhibition rights and other rights, then (but only for the purpose of the computation required hereunder) the Company shall allocate to the Supplemental Markets exhibition rights a fair and reasonable portion of the sales price which shall, for the purpose hereof, be the "Producer's gross." In reaching such determination Company may consider the current market value of Supplemental Markets exhibition rights in comparable motion pictures. If the Guild shall contend that the amount so allocated was not fair and reasonable, such claim may be determined by submission to arbitration as herein provided; and in the event the arbitrator shall find that such allocation was not reasonable and fair, the arbitrator shall determine the fair and reasonable amount to be so allocated. If the outright sale includes Supplemental Markets distribution rights to more than one motion picture, Company shall likewise allocate to each Such Picture a fair and reasonable portion of the sales price of the Supplemental Markets rights; and if the Guild contends that such allocation is not fair and reasonable, the question may be determined by submission to arbitration as above provided. If the arbitrator shall find that such allocation was not fair and reasonable, the arbitrator shall determine the fair and reasonable amount to be so allocated to each such Picture. Nothing with respect to the price received on the outright sale of only Supplemental Markets distribution rights in a single Such Picture shall be subject to arbitration except that, in the event of a dispute, there may be arbitrated the question of whether the price reported by the Company to the Guild as having been received by the Company on such outright sale is less than the amount actually received by the Company on such outright sale.

(iv) If Such Picture, in whole or in substantial part, is used in an interactive program, the provisions of Article 64 shall apply.

b. [Inserted as the next to last unnumbered paragraph of Article 51.3.a.(i).]

c.   Company's obligation shall accrue hereunder only after Producer's gross is received by Company but as to foreign receipts such obligation shall accrue only when such receipts can be freely converted to U.S. dollars and are remitted to the United States, and until such time no frozen foreign receipts shall be included in Producer's gross. Payment of amounts accruing hereunder shall be made quarterly on the basis of quarterly statements, as hereinafter provided.

Upon request, and if permitted by the authorities of a foreign, country, the Company will transfer to any writer, in the currency of such foreign country, his/her share, if any, of frozen foreign receipts in such country, provided the writer will bear any costs involved; and such transfer shall be deemed to be payment to the writer of an equivalent number of U.S. dollars at the then current free market rate for blocked funds of that category as determined by the Company. Concurrently with such transfer the writer will pay to the Company in U.S. dollars the total amount the Company is required to withhold from such payment under all applicable laws. If the Company utilizes frozen foreign currencies derived from exhibition of Such Picture in Supplemental Markets by conversion thereof to properties that may be freely exported and turned to account, the amount so utilized by the Company shall be deemed to have been converted to U.S. dollars at the then current free market rate for blocked funds of that category determined as above provided. Frozen foreign receipts from Supplemental Markets shall be deemed to be released on a first-in-first-out basis, unless the authorities of the foreign country involved designate a specific period that would render such basis inapplicable. Such released funds shall be allocated between Such Picture and other motion pictures distributed by the distributor in Supplemental Markets in the same ratio that receipts, derived from the distribution of Such Picture in Supplemental Markets within the foreign country, bear to the total receipts derived from the distribution of Such Picture and all other motion pictures in Supplemental Markets within the foreign country, during the applicable period, unless the authorities of the foreign country involved require another method of allocation, in which case such other method shall be used. Foreign receipts shall be accounted for in U.S. dollars at the rate of exchange at which such receipts are actually converted and remitted, and should any discounts, taxes, duties or charges be imposed in connection with the receipt or remittance of foreign funds, only so much of such funds as remain thereafter shall be included in accountable receipts.

Company shall not be responsible for loss or diminution of foreign receipts as a result of any matter of thing not reasonably within the control of the Company. The Guild and the writers shall be bound by any arrangements made in good faith by the deposit or remittance of foreign revenue. Frozen foreign receipts shall not be considered trust funds and the Company may freely commingle the same with other funds of the Company. No sums received by way of deposits or security need be included in Producer's gross until earned, but when the Company is paid a non-returnable advance by a distributor, such advance shall be included in the Producer's gross.

A "non-returnable advance" is to be included in "Producer's gross" when Such Picture is "available" and "identifiable" and the amount of the advance payment is "ascertainable."

Such Picture is "available" when the first of the following occurs:

(1)   The product first may be exhibited or otherwise exploited by a specified method of distribution and in a territory under the terms of the applicable license or distribution agreement, or

(2)   It first may be sold or rented by a retailer under the terms of the applicable license or distribution agreement.

Such Picture is "identifiable" when the Company first knows or reasonably should have known that a given motion picture is covered by a particular license or distribution agreement for its exploitation in the applicable market.

The amount of the advance payment is "ascertainable" if:

(1)   the advance is for one motion picture, means of exhibition, and territory, or

(2)   the total amount of the advance is for more than one motion picture, means of exhibition and/or territory, in which case the Company shall fairly and reasonably allocate such advance among the licensed motion pictures, exhibition markets and/or territorial markets. As each of these pictures becomes identifiable and available, the allocated portion of the non-returnable advance is to be included in Producer's gross for that quarter. The Company shall notify the Guild of its allocation when the report of "Producer's gross," which includes the advance, is to be filed. The Guild has the right to challenge in an MBA arbitration a failure to allocate or any allocation that it contends is not fair and reasonable.

If Such Picture is available in any territory or by any means of exhibition, and is identifiable and the amount of the advance is ascertainable, but the Company does not provide the WGA with the information required by the MBA and applicable law, then the advance shall be deemed includable in "Producer's gross" no later than six months after the Company receives it.

An advance received by a Company's parent, subsidiary or any other related or affiliated entity or successor-in-interest, or by any other entity to which the advance payment is directed by the Company or license or distribution agreement, shall be considered as an advance payment received by the Company.

d.   If any license or outright sale of exhibition rights to Such Picture in Supplemental Markets includes as a part thereof any recorded commercial or advertising material, the Company shall be permitted to allocate a reasonable amount (in accordance with then current standard charges in the industry) to such commercial or advertising material, and the amount so allocated shall not be included in Producer's gross hereunder.

e.   The term "participating writer," as used herein, means a writer who, while in the employ of the Company or in the employ of the actual Producing Company of Such Picture as described in this subparagraph 3.h.(4) (to which employment the provisions of this Basic Agreement apply), or a professional writer from whom the Company (or such actual producer) acquired literary material (to which acquisition the provisions of this Basic Agreement apply), participated in the writing of and received credit pursuant to Theatrical Schedule A hereof, as the case may be, for the writing of the story or screenplay, or story and teleplay, as the case may be, upon which Such Picture was based. If Such Picture is a remake of a prior motion picture, and if any of the writers of the prior motion picture receive writing credit for the remake, such writers shall be deemed to be "participating writers" for the purposes of this subparagraph e., but only if their employment as writers for the prior motion picture, or if the purchase of literary material from them for the prior motion picture, was covered by and subject to a collective bargaining agreement with the Guild. The *pro rata* share" payable to each participating writer shall be as follows:

Seventy-five percent (75%) thereof shall be payable to the credited screenplay writer or writers and twenty-five percent thereof shall be payable to the credited story or screen story writer or writers. In the event there is a minor credit, such as adaptation, the writer or writers receiving such minor credit shall be paid ten percent (10%) thereof which sum shall be deducted from the screenplay or teleplay writers' share. The writer or writers receiving a "Written by" credit shall be entitled to one hundred percent (100%) of the monies.

Any participating writers receiving the same screen credit referred to above shall share equally in such percentage amount specified.

If there are one or more participating writers who receive screenplay or teleplay credit and no credit is given for story or screen story, then the *pro rata* share which would have been payable to a participating writer had he/she received such story or screen story credit shall, subject to the provisions of the next following paragraph, be paid to the participating writers who receive such screenplay or teleplay credit.

If the writer's services in Such Picture are performed for the Company on a loan-out basis, then for the purposes of this Article the Company shall be deemed to be the employer, and the lender shall not have any responsibility hereunder with respect to Such Picture. With respect to any Such Picture, if there are one or more participating writers who receive credit as aforesaid and one or more writers who perform services in connection with the writing of the story or teleplay or screenplay and receive screen credit in connection with Such Picture, but who are not subject to this Basic Agreement, then that portion of the applicable percentage payment as defined in this Article 51 which would otherwise have been payable to such one or more writers not subject to this Basic Agreement may be retained by Company, and the Company shall not be obligated to pay such portion to any such participating writer receiving credit as aforesaid.

f.   Within a reasonable time after the expiration or each calendar or fiscal quarter, but not exceeding sixty (60) days, Company will furnish or cause to be furnished to the Guild a written report showing the Producer's gross during the preceding quarter from the distribution of each Such Picture by Company in Supplemental Markets with respect to which Company is required to make payments hereunder (whether distributed by the Company or through another distributor). The quarterly reports required in this Article 51.3.f. shall separately set forth the Producer's gross from distribution of each Such Picture on video discs or video cassettes and the Producer's gross from distribution of each Such Picture on video discs or video cassettes and the Producer's gross from distribution of each Such Picture on pay-type CATV and/or pay television.

Concurrently with the furnishing of each quarterly report, the Company will make the payments shown to be due by such report. All payments shall be made by check payable to the order of the writers entitled thereto, and shall be delivered to the Guild for forwarding to such writers; and compliance herewith shall constitute payment to the writers.

No such reports need be furnished with respect to any period during which there was no such Producer's gross. The Company shall make available for inspection by the Guild all distributor's statements and exhibitor's statements which are available to the Company insofar as they relate to such Producer's gross, and all the financial terms of contracts pertaining to such Producer's gross, and the Guild shall have the right at reasonable times, to examine the books and records of the Company as to such Producer's gross and the Guild shall have the right, at reasonable times, to examine the books and records of the Company as to such Producer's gross pertaining to such distribution of any Such Picture, at whatever place or places such records are customarily kept by the Company. If the Guild requests that it be informed of the license fee paid under a license for the exhibition of Such Picture in Supplemental Markets, or if the Guild requests that it be sent an extract of the financial terms of such a license, and if such information is not extensive in nature, the Company will forward such information or extract without making it necessary for the Guild to send a representative to the offices of the Company. In general, the Company will cooperate in furnishing such information to the Guild by mail or telephone, where doing so is not unreasonable or burdensome. If more than one picture is licensed in a single license agreement, the Company shall inform the Guild at its request, of the identity of the pictures covered by the license, and shall make available to inspection by the Guild in the office where such license agreement is customarily kept a copy of the terms of such license showing the titles of the pictures licensed under such agreement and the license fee for each Such Picture. Company agrees to cooperate in responding to reasonable inquiries from the Guild as to whether any Such Picture is currently being distributed for telecasting on pay television or in any other supplemental Market as herein defined. An inadvertent failure to comply with the reporting provisions of this subparagraph f. shall not constitute a default by the Company hereunder, provided such failure is cured promptly after notice thereof from the Guild is received by the Company.

Company shall make all social security, withholding, unemployment insurance, and disability insurance payments required by law with respect to the additional compensation provided for in this Article 51.

If the Company shall fail to make any payment provided for in this Article 51 to be made to the writer when and as the same becomes due and payable, it shall bear interest at the rate of one and one-half percent (1 1/2 %) per month on the unpaid balance thereof commencing to accrue on the earlier of: (i) seven (7) days after notice in writing to Company from the Guild of such delinquency, or (ii) sixty (60) days after such payment becomes due and payable.

The compensation payable under this Article 51 shall be excluded from the gross compensation upon which the Company contributions are to be made to the Pension Plan.

g.   If participating writer's employment agreement with the Company requires that the writer's compensation shall be based, in whole or in part, upon, or measured by, a percentage of the gross receipts derived from the distribution of Such Picture, then such percentage compensation shall be credited against any amounts payable to the writer hereunder, and likewise any payment due to the writer hereunder shall be credited against such percentage compensation. Where all or part of a writer's compensation is a specified sum of money, commonly known and referred to as a "deferment," such deferment may not be credited against amounts payable by the Company to such writer hereunder.

h.   With respect to all Such Pictures, the following provisions shall be applicable:

(1)   Distributor's Assumption Agreement:

Prior to the commencement of principal photography of each Such Picture, if the Company is not also the distributor in Supplemental Markets of Such Picture, Company shall obtain from the distributor having such Supplemental Markets distribution rights and deliver to Guild, a separate written agreement herein called "DISTRIBUTOR'S ASSUMPTION AGREEMENT," made expressly for the benefit of Guild as representative of the writers involved, by which such distributor agrees to assume and pay the amounts payable hereunder by reason of the exhibition of Such Picture in Supplemental Markets, when and as the same become due. Such agreement shall be substantially in the following form:

"DISTRIBUTOR'S ASSUMPTION AGREEMENT" [19]

In consideration of the execution of a DISTRIBUTION AGREEMENT between _____ insert name of Company) and the undersigned Distributor, Distributor agrees that the motion picture, presently entitled _____, is subject to the Writers Guild of America-Alliance of Motion Picture & Television Producers Theatrical and Television Basic Agreement of 1995 (hereinafter 'Basic Agreement') and particularly to the provisions of Article 51 thereof, pertaining to additional compensation payable to writers when motion pictures are released in Supplemental Markets, and Distributor hereby agrees expressly for the benefit of the Writers Guild of America, west, Inc., and Writers Guild of America, East, Inc., herein called WGA, as representative of the writers whose services are included in such motion picture as released in Supplemental Markets, to make the additional compensation payment required thereby when such motion picture is exhibited in Supplemental Markets. Distributor for and on behalf of the Company shall make all social security, withholding, unemployment insurance and disability insurance payments required by law with respect to the additional compensation referred to in the preceding sentence.

It is expressly understood that the right of Distributor to license such motion picture for exhibition in Supplemental Markets, or to exhibit or cause or permit such motion picture to be exhibited in Supplemental Markets, shall be subject to and conditioned upon the prompt payment of such additional compensation, in accordance with Article 51 of the Basic Agreement. It is agreed that WGA, in addition to all other remedies, shall be entitled to injunctive relief against Distributor in the event such payments are not made.

Within a reasonable time after the expiration of each calendar of fiscal quarter, but not exceeding sixty (60) days, Distributor will furnish or cause to be furnished to WGA a written report showing the Producer's gross (as defined in Article 51 of the Basic Agreement) during the preceding quarter from

---

[19] See footnote 8 . . . accompanying Article 15.A.3.h.(i).

the distribution of Such Picture by Distributor in Supplemental Markets with respect to which Distributor is required to make payments hereunder (whether distributed by the Distributor or through another distributor licensed by Distributor). Each report shall be in the format described in Article 51.3.f. of this Basic Agreement. Such report shall be accompanied by such payments as may be due.

Distributor shall also make available for inspection by WGA all Distributor's statements delivered to Company insofar as they relate to Producer's gross. WGA shall have the right at reasonable times and on reasonable notices to examine the books and records of Distributor as to Producer's gross. If Distributor shall fail to make such payments as and when due and payable, they shall bear interest at the rate of one and one-half percent (1 1/2%) per month on the unpaid balance thereof commencing to accrue on the earlier of (i) seven (7) days after notice in writing to Company or Distributor from WGA of such delinquency, or (ii) sixty (60) days after such payment becomes due and payable.

This DISTRIBUTOR'S ASSUMPTION AGREEMENT shall remain effective and binding upon Distributor as long as it remains the Distributor of such motion picture in Supplemental Markets, and thereafter in perpetuity only if it has provided or guaranteed any of the financing for the production of such motion picture, in accordance with and subject to the provisions of Article 51.3.h(3)(i) of the Basic Agreement.

When there is more than one distributor, the provisions of Article 51.3.h.(3)(iii) of the Basic Agreement shall apply to each distributor which neither provides nor guarantees any of the financing for the production of such motion picture.

The Distributor has, has not (strike whichever is inapplicable) provided or guaranteed financing for production of such motion picture.

Date:

_____

DISTRIBUTOR

By_____

Address:"

An inadvertent failure on the part of any such Distributor to Comply with any of the reporting provisions of this subparagraph h.(1) shall in no event constitute a default by the

Company or such Distributor or breach of this Basic Agreement, provided that such failure is cured promptly after notice in writing thereof from the Guild.

In the event of the expiration or termination of any distribution agreement, the obligation of Company to obtain and deliver to the Guild such DISTRIBUTOR'S ASSUMPTION AGREEMENT shall apply as well to any subsequent distribution agreement entered into by Company, and Company shall obtain and deliver an executed DISTRIBUTOR'S ASSUMPTION AGREEMENT within ten (10) days after the execution of each such subsequent distribution agreement.

If, with respect to any Such Picture, Distributor is not liable in perpetuity to pay the Supplemental Markets fees provided for hereunder, or if there is no distribution agreement made by Company with respect to any Such Picture granting Supplemental Market distribution rights to the Distributor, then the Guild, prior to the commencement of principal photography of Such Picture, may require such further financial assurances from Company as it deems advisable to insure performance of Company's obligations to pay the Supplemental Markets fees provided for herein, including, without limitation, the execution of security agreements, guarantees, or other protective agreements. If any member or company of the Alliance of Motion Picture & Television Producers, Inc., becomes liable in perpetuity under a DISTRIBUTOR'S ASSUMPTION AGREEMENT to pay the Supplemental Markets fees provided for hereunder with respect to Such Picture, the Guild will release and cause to be discharged of record all such security agreements, guarantees or other protective agreements entered into or obtained by or from Company, provided, however, that Company's primary liability shall not be released thereby.

(2) Buyer's Assumption Agreement.

If the Company shall sell, transfer or assign its rights to exhibit in Supplemental Markets any Such Picture, it shall obtain from such buyer, transferee or assignee a separate agreement made expressly for the benefit of the Guild as representative of the writers involved, requiring such buyer, transferee or assignee to comply with the provisions of the Basic Agreement with respect to additional compensation to writers by reason of the exhibition of Such Picture in

Supplemental Markets, when and as the same become due. Such agreement shall be substantially in the following form:

"BUYER'S ASSUMPTION AGREEMENT"[20]

For a valuable consideration, the undersigned _____ (insert name of Buyer, transferee or assignee) (hereinafter referred to as 'Buyer') hereby agrees with _____ (insert name of Company) that all motion pictures covered by this agreement, a list of which is appended hereto, are subject to the Writers Guild of America-Alliance of Motion Picture & Television Producers Theatrical and Television Basic Agreement of 1995 (hereinafter 'Basic Agreement') and particularly to the provisions of Article 51 thereof, pertaining to additional compensation payable to writers when motion pictures are released to Supplemental Markets, and Buyer hereby agrees expressly for the benefit of the Writers Guild of America, west, Inc., and Writers Guild of America, East, Inc., hereinafter called WGA, as representative of the writers whose services are included in each such motion picture when telecast, to assume and be bound by Company's obligation thereunder to make the additional compensation payments required thereby when each such motion picture is exhibited in Supplemental Markets. Buyer for and on behalf of the Company shall make all social security, withholding, unemployment insurance, and disability insurance payments required by law with respect to the additional compensation referred to in the preceding sentence.

It is expressly understood that the right of the Buyer to license each such motion picture of exhibition in Supplemental Markets, or to exhibit or cause or permit such motion picture to be exhibited in Supplemental Markets, shall be subject to and conditioned upon the prompt payment of such additional compensation, in accordance with Article 51 of the Basic Agreement. It is agreed that WGA, in addition to all other remedies, shall be entitled to injunctive relief against Buyer in event such payments are not made.

---

[20] See footnote 8 . . . accompanying Article 15.A.3.h.(1).

Within a reasonable time after the expiration of each calendar or fiscal quarter, but not exceeding sixty (60) days, Buyer will furnish or cause to be furnished to WGA a written report showing the 'Producer's gross' (as defined in Article 51 of the Basic Agreement) during the preceding quarter from the distribution of Such Picture by Buyer in Supplemental Markets with respect to which Buyer is required to make payments hereunder (whether distributed by Buyer or through another distributor licensed by Buyer). Each report shall be in the format described in Article 51.3.f. of this Basic Agreement. Such report shall be accompanied by such payments as may be due.

Buyer shall also make available for inspection by WGA all Distributor's statements delivered to Buyer insofar as they relate to Producer's gross. WGA shall have the right at reasonable times to examine the books and records of Buyer as to Producer's gross.

If Buyer shall fail to make such payments as and when due and payable, they shall bear interest at the rate of one and one-half percent (1 1/2%) per month on the unpaid balance thereof commencing to accrue on the earlier of (i) seven (7) days after notice in writing to Company or Distributor from WGA of such delinquency, or (ii) sixty (60) days after such payment becomes due and payable.

Where there is more than one buyer, the provisions of Article 51.3.h.(3)(iii) of the Basic Agreement shall apply to each Buyer.

               BUYER

Date:

      By _____

Address:"

The Company agrees to deliver to the Guild an executed copy of the above referred to Buyer's Assumption Agreement within thirty (30) days after the sale, assignment or transfer of Such Picture, with the name and address of the purchaser or assignee.

Any inadvertent failure on the part of the Buyer to comply with any of the reporting provisions of this subparagraph (2) shall in no event constitute a default by the Company or such

Buyer or a breach of this agreement, provided that such failure is cured promptly after notice in writing thereof from the Guild.

Upon delivery of such Buyer's Assumption Agreement and on condition that the Guild approves in writing the financial responsibility of the purchaser, assignee, or transferee, Company shall not be further liable for the keeping of any such records, or for the payment of such additional compensation for the exhibition of any Such Pictures in Supplemental Markets, it being agreed that the purchaser, assignee, or transferee, shall solely be liable therefór.

The Guild agrees that it will not unreasonably withhold its approval of the financial responsibility of any such purchaser, assignee or transferee, it being further agreed that if the Guild, within twenty-one (21) days of receipt of written notice of any such sale, assignment or transfer has not advised the Company that it disapproves the financial responsibility of such purchaser, assignee or transferee, the Guild will be deemed to have approved the financial responsibility thereof. In the event the Guild advises the Company within such twenty-one (21) day period that it disapproves the financial responsibility of any such purchaser, assignee or transferee and the Company disputes such disapproval, the Company shall have the right, at its election, to cause to be immediately submitted to arbitration, as herein provided, the issue of whether the Guild has unreasonably withheld the approval of the financial responsibility of such purchaser, assignee or transferee for payments due hereunder.

(3)   Distributor's Liability:

With respect to any Such Picture, the following provisions shall be applicable to the Distributor of Such Picture in Supplemental Markets:

(i)   Where the Distributor has provided or guaranteed any of the financing for the production of Such Picture, the obligations of the Distributor under this Article 51 shall continue in perpetuity notwithstanding the expiration or termination of such distribution agreement, or any foreclosure of a chattel mortgage, security agreement, pledge, or lien on Such Picture. In the case of foreclosure, should such mortgagee, pledgee or security holder or third party, who is neither the Company nor Distributor, acquire title to Such Picture and execute the Buyer's

Assumption Agreement, and upon condition that the Guild, in its discretion, approves such purchaser's financial responsibility, then, when the Distributor ceases to be the distributor of Such Picture in Supplemental Markets, the Distributor shall thereupon be released from any and all further obligations under this Article 51 with respect to Such Picture. Should any third party (other than in connection with any such foreclosure) acquire the rights of such Distributor to the distribution of Such Picture in Supplemental Markets and execute a Distributor's Assumption Agreement pursuant to which it is liable in perpetuity to make the payments under this Article 51, then, upon condition that the Guild in its discretion approves such third party's financial responsibility, such Distributor shall thereupon be released from any and all further obligations under this Article 51 with respect to Such Picture.

However, such Distributor shall not be liable for the payment of any Supplemental Market fees based on monies received by a foreign distributor under a "foreign production deal" as defined in this Article 51.3.a. with respect to which such foreign distributor or independent producer is not obligated to account to such Distributor.

(ii)   When the Distributor of Such Picture does not provide or guarantee any of the financing of Such Picture, the Distributor's Assumption Agreement shall be binding upon the Distributor only as long as it is the distributor of Such Picture in Supplemental Markets.

(iii)   When there is more than one Distributor or Buyer of Such Picture in Supplemental Markets, the liability of any such Distributor or Buyer, which neither provides nor guarantees any of the financing for the production of Such Picture, for the payment of Supplemental Market fees under this Article 51, shall be applicable only to such portion of Producer's gross as is derived by Distributor or Buyer as the case may be.

The Distributor or Buyer as used in this subparagraph (iii) refers to a distributor or buyer, as the case may be, under any distribution or sale agreement, as the case may be, with Company, as distinguished from an agreement between such Distributor or Buyer and its subdistributor.

(4)   Acquisition of Title by Company:

If Company was not the actual producer of Such Picture which was produced by a signatory Company but acquired title thereto by purchase, assignment, transfer, voluntary or involuntary, or by foreclosure of a chattel or mortgage or security agreement or a pledgee's sale, Company shall nevertheless be obligated to make the payments herein provided when Such Picture is exhibited in Supplemental Markets, unless such payment required hereunder has already been paid.

(5)   Financing-Distribution Agreement by Company:

The obligation of the signatory Company hereunder with respect to the payments provided for in this Article 51 shall also apply to any Such Pictures produced by an independent producer under a contract between the signatory Company and such independent producer for the production of such motion picture, and for the financing and distribution thereof by the signatory Company. However, such signatory Company shall not be liable for the payment of any Supplemental Market fees based on monies received by a foreign distributor under a foreign production deal as defined in this subparagraph 3.a., with respect to which such foreign distributor or such independent producer is not obligated to account to such signatory Company. Nor shall such signatory Company be obligated to obtain any Distributor's Assumption Agreement from any foreign distributor referred to in this subparagraph 3.a. except if such foreign distributor is obligated to account to such signatory Company pursuant to this subparagraph 3.(1) with respect to monies as therein provided.

(6)   Company's Liability:

It is expressly understood and agreed that Company shall in all events remain bound hereunder to make the payments due by reason of the exhibition of each Such Picture in Supplement Markets, irrespective of the assumption of such liability by any other person, firm or company as hereinabove provided, except as otherwise expressly provided in this Basic Agreement.

(7)   Failure to Deliver Assumption Agreement:

The failure of Company to obtain and deliver an executed assumption agreement as provided in paragraph h.(1) and h.(2) and subparagraph (i) of this Article 51.3 shall be deemed a substantial breach of this Basic Agreement.

(8)   Company's Dissolution:

If Company dissolves and is no longer in the business of producing motion pictures and if a distributor assumes all of the obligations of the Company under this Article 51 and the financial responsibility of the distributor is approved by the Guild in its discretion, the Company shall thereupon be released of any obligation with respect to any payments due hereunder; provided that if the distributor which assumes all of the obligations of the Company is a member company of the Alliance of Motion Picture & Television Producers, Inc., or if any such member company is permanently liable to pay the Supplemental market fees provided for in this Article 51 with respect to the motion pictures for which the Company is liable to make such payment of Supplemental Market fees, then the financial responsibility of such distributor shall be conclusively deemed approved and such Company shall be released of any obligation with respect to any such payments.

(9)   Networks and Television Stations:

No television network, station, sponsor or advertising agency shall be required to execute any Distributor's Assumption Agreement, or Buyer's Assumption Agreement, or a Literary Material Assumption Agreement, except if it is the distributor of Such Picture in Supplemental Markets or the buyer of the Company's Supplemental Markets rights in Such Picture, as the case may be.

i.   If the Company shall sell, transfer, assign or otherwise dispose of its rights in any story, screenplay or teleplay (to which the provisions of this Article 51.3 apply, or may apply) prior to the production of a motion picture based thereon, to any person or company (hereinafter referred to as the "Buyer") other than a person or company with headquarters outside the United States, the Company shall obtain from the Buyer separate agreement in substantially the following form:

"LITERARY MATERIAL ASSUMPTION AGREEMENT"[21]

_____ (hereinafter referred to as the 'Buyer') agrees with _____ (Company) that the story, screenplay, story and screenplay or story and

---

[21] See footnote 8 . . . accompanying Article 15.A.3.h.(1).

teleplay covered by this Agreement is subject to the Writers Guild of America-Alliance of Motion Picture & Television Producers Theatrical and Television Basic Agreement of 1995 (herein the 'Basic Agreement'), and particularly to the provisions of Article 51.3 thereof pertaining to additional payments to writers on release of a motion picture based thereon in the Supplemental Markets (but excluding paragraph h. of said Article 51.3), and the said Buyer hereby agrees, expressly for the benefit of the Writers Guild of America, west, Inc., and Writers Guild of America, East, Inc., (herein referred to as 'the Guild') as representatives of the writers involved, to abide by and perform the provisions of said Basic Agreement and make the additional payments required thereunder, as aforesaid. For the purpose of applying such provisions of said Basic Agreement, the writer or writers of such material shall be treated in all respects as though the said material were written by such writer or writers while in the employ of the Buyer.

It is expressly understood and agreed that the rights of the Buyer to exhibit or license the exhibition of any motion picture based upon said material shall be subject to and conditioned upon the payment to the writer or writers involved of additional compensation, if any, required under subparagraph 3. (except paragraph h. thereof) of said Article 51.3. of said Basic Agreement, and it is agreed that the damages against Buyer in the event such payments are not made.

If the Buyer shall sell, transfer, assign or otherwise dispose of its rights in such material to any person or company with headquarters in the United States, it may obtain from the party acquiring such rights a separate agreement in the same form (including this sentence) as this agreement, and will notify the Guild thereof, together with the name and address of the transferee, and deliver to the Guild a copy of such assumption agreement; it being the intent hereof that the obligations herein set forth shall be continuing obligations on the part of such subsequent owners of such material, so headquartered in the United States.

_____

BUYER

Date:

By _____

Address:"

The Company agrees to give notice to the Guild of such sale, transfer or assignment of the nature above mentioned, with the name and address of the Buyer, and to deliver to the Guild an executed copy of such assumption agreement. An inadvertent failure on the part of the Company to comply with any of the provisions of this subparagraph i. shall in no event constitute a default by the Company hereunder or a breach of this Basic Agreement, provided that such failure is cured promptly after notice thereof from the Guild.

Upon delivery of such assumption agreement, Company, or any subsequent owner obtaining the execution of such an assumption agreement, shall not be further liable to the Guild or any writer for the keeping of any such records or the payment of such additional compensation, or for compliance with credit obligations insofar as they relate to the exhibition of Such Picture in Supplemental Markets; and the Guild agrees to look exclusively to the party last executing such an assumption agreement for the keeping of such records, payment and compliance with credit obligations. If a company with headquarters outside the United States is a subsidiary of the Company, or the Company is the distributor of Such Picture for such a company, then for the purposes of this subparagraph i. such company shall be deemed to be head-quartered only in the United States. The provisions of this subparagraph 3. shall not apply to Supplemental Markets of trailers or advertising a motion picture by shots, etc., substantially in the nature of a trailer, or to the use of stock shots.

j.   Notwithstanding the sooner termination of this Agreement, the parties hereto agree that the terms and conditions of this subparagraph 3. shall apply and remain in full force and effect, and without change, to Such Pictures produced by the Company, the principal photography of which commenced between May 2, 1995 and May 1, 1998, both dates inclusive, regardless of when (either during or at any time after the expiration of the term of this Basic Agreement or of such period) Such Pictures are released in Supplemental Markets, and regardless of the terms or provisions of any Basic Agreement which is a modification, extension, or renewal of, or substitution for this Basic Agreement, subject, however, to the provisions of the provisions of the third paragraph of this Article 51.2

4.   If in the upcoming negotiations with SAG and DGA, the Company agrees to modify the basic substantive provisions regarding Supplemental Markets, Company will so advise the Guild and accord it the

opportunity to elect that this Article be modified in the same manner, as of the date on which the Guild so notifies the Company. Adjustments which statistically maintain the relative allocations of proceeds derived from Supplemental Markets among SAG, DGA and WGA as established in existing collective bargaining agreements will not activate this provision, but an increase in the relative allocations to SAG or DGA in such proceeds will activate this provision, with any such increase to be accorded proportionately to WGA. Upon request the Guild shall be provided with the statistics upon which the adjustments have been made, and the Guild's right to activate this provision shall be arbitrable. The Guild shall give notice of its election within sixty (60) days after receipt of the Company's notice or after being provided with the statistics referred to, whichever is later. The election shall be limited to accepting the entire agreement reached with SAG or DGA on Supplemental Markets, and only such entire agreement, but with appropriate equivalent adjustment for writers for provisions peculiar to actors or directors as the case may be.

* * *

ARTICLE 57 — PAY TELEVISION AND VIDEO DISC/VIDEO CASSETTE PRODUCTION

Employment of writers and acquisition of literary material by the Company for the pay television and/or video disc/video cassette markets shall be governed by the provisions of Appendix B attached hereto.

ARTICLE 58 — RELEASE OF FREE TELEVISION PROGRAMMING AND THEATRICAL MOTION PICTURES TO BASIC CABLE

Except as provided in the following paragraph, the exhibition on basic cable of television motion pictures shall be considered free television exhibition as distinguished from "Supplemental Markets" exhibition.

Upon release, on or after May 2, 1995, to basic cable of product initially produced for free television, as to which free television residuals would otherwise be payable, Company shall pay, in the aggregate, to the credited writer or writers the following percentage of the Company's accountable receipts obtained therefrom: With respect to free television motion pictures produced prior to July 1, 1984, said percentage shall be two and one-half percent (2-1/2%); with respect to free television motion pictures produced after July 1, 1984, said percentage shall be two percent (2%). For the purpose of this provision, the term "basic cable" means one or more basic cable systems which do not meet the definition of pay television as set forth in this Agreement and wherein the release on basic cable is a separate release and not part of a free television broadcast.

Upon release, on or after May 2, 1995, to basic cable, of product initially produced for theatrical release, the Company shall pay to the credited writer or writers aggregate compensation of 1.2% of the Company's accountable receipts obtained therefrom.

The term "[u]pon release" in the preceding two paragraphs means that the theatrical or television motion picture product is "available," which is when it first may be exhibited on Basic Cable pursuant to the terms of a license or distribution agreement.

Residual payments for the release to basic cable of television programs made under the W.A. Royalty Plan, which appeared as Exhibit A-1 to the 1960 Writers Guild of America Television Film Basic Agreement, which are due on or after October 1, 1994 shall be made to the credited writer(s) thereof in accordance with the provisions of Article 58 of the applicable MBA. It is agreed that the MBA in effect at the time of the first release of a Royalty Plan program to basic cable after March 1, 1985 shall be the "applicable MBA" for purposes of such payments. The parties further agree that when Royalty Plan programs are released to either domestic or foreign basic cable, the Company's accountable receipts therefrom are fully reportable and residuals are payable in perpetuity at the rate set forth in Article 58 of the applicable MBA. The provisions of this paragraph amend the WGA Royalty Plan and prior MBAs.

* * *

ARTICLE 64 — REUSE OF MBA-COVERED MATERIAL IN INTERACTIVE PROGRAMS

A. Definitions and Coverage

1. **Definition of interactive program.** An "interactive program" is a non-linear program that allows the individual viewer/user(s) to control and/or manipulate in real time the output of the program elements via an interactive device. A "non-linear" program is a program in which the material embodied therein is intended to be viewed by the viewer/user(s) in such order selected by the viewer/user(s) and which does not have a predetermined "beginning" and "end" (although it may have an opening "default" menu or resting position from which selection of the order of viewing is determined by the viewer/user(s)), as opposed to a "linear" program in which the material embodied therein is intended to be viewed (in its entirety or in segments) in a predetermined order, but such material may be accessed randomly by the viewer/user(s). Such capability of random access shall not affect the status of such program as a "linear" program.

2. **Definition of interactive device.** An "interactive device" is a device which is necessary in order to control and/or manipulate an interactive program. An interactive device may thus be a locally-operated device (i.e., a single device that both reads the data from the storage medium and permits the viewer/user(s) to control and/or manipulate the interactive program) or a remotely-operated device (i.e., a device that reads the data from the storage medium at a centrally-based location but which enables the viewer/user(s) to control and/or manipulate the interactive program from a remote location via wired or wireless transmission).

3. **Interactive rights license.**

   a. **Definition of interactive rights.** See Articles 1.B.9. and 1.C.14.1.

   b. **Definition of interactive rights licensee.** An "interactive rights licensee" is the entity that first exploits, directly or indirectly, the interactive rights (such as by developing, producing or publishing an interactive program or performing similar functions, but not by reselling only).

   An entity which both resells interactive rights and adds value to those rights by developing, producing, publishing or performing similar functions may qualify as an interactive rights licensee if the value thus added constitutes exploitation of the rights by making a substantial creative and/or technical contribution to the development, production or publication of the interactive program.

   c. **Definition of interactive rights licensor; definition of interactive rights license.** An "interactive rights licensor" is an entity that grants a license for interactive rights to an "interactive rights licensee." An "interactive rights license" or an "interactive rights license agreement" includes a license (written or oral) or other permission to exploit interactive rights of, or granted by, an interactive rights licensor.

4. **Applicable gross.** "Applicable Gross" is the aggregate of all monies remitted by the interactive rights licensee to the interactive rights licensor in respect of a license of interactive rights, subject to the following:

   a. **Unaffiliated licensee.** If the interactive rights licensee is not an affiliated entity of the interactive rights licensor, then the Applicable Gross shall be the monies actually received by the interactive rights licensor in respect of the license of interactive rights.

   b. **Affiliated licensee.** If the interactive rights licensee is an affiliated entity of the interactive rights licensor, then the Applicable Gross shall be the monies actually received by the interactive rights licensor in respect of the license of interactive rights, provided the monies actually received by the interactive rights licensor in respect of the license of interactive rights are not less than the fair market value of the interactive rights. If such monies are less than the fair market value, then the Applicable Gross shall be the fair market value of the interactive rights.

c.   **Licensor as producer, et al.** If the interactive rights licensor is also the producer, developer, publisher and/or distributor of the interactive program, then the Applicable Gross shall be the fair market value of the interactive rights.

d.   **Selling or reselling.** No monies attributable to the functions of selling or reselling of the interactive rights, or earned thereby, shall be deducted from, or otherwise used to reduce, the Applicable Gross.

e.   **Licensor as investor.** If the interactive rights licensor invests in the production, development, publication and/or distribution of the interactive program or in the entity which performs such functions, any monies which are a recoupment of such investment by the interactive rights licensor shall be included in the Applicable Gross. Monies received by way of investment recoupment shall be separate from monies received for the licensing of the interactive rights so long as the Applicable Gross, as reported to the Guild, is the fair market value of the interactive rights.

f.   **Fair market value of the interactive rights.** The fair market value of the interactive rights shall be determined by ascertaining the monies which would have been paid by an unaffiliated licensee to an interactive rights licensor for the license of the interactive rights.

g.   **Licensing of multiple rights/multiple pictures.** If, as part of the same or related transaction(s) for the license of interactive rights, other rights (e.g., theatrical exhibition and/or television distribution rights) are licensed, then a fair and reasonable allocation of the aggregate monies remitted shall be made in respect of the interactive rights. No deductions or expenses or other costs related to the license of other rights shall be deducted from this allocation and this allocation shall be the Applicable Gross.

Similarly, when interactive rights to more than one motion picture are licensed as part of the same or related transaction(s), a fair and reasonable allocation of the aggregate monies remitted shall be made in respect of the interactive rights to each motion picture.

If, as part of the same or related transaction(s), excerpts exempt from payment and excerpts requiring payment pursuant to Article 64.B.2. below are licensed, a fair and reasonable allocation of the aggregate monies remitted shall be made in respect of the exempt and non-exempt excerpts. The amount so allocated to the non-exempt excerpts shall be no less than the fair market value of the interactive rights for those excerpts.

h. Title, Logo, Art Work, Sound Effects and/or Music Soundtrack.

(1) No Payment For License of Only Title, Logo, Art Work, Sound Effects and/or Music Soundtrack.

No payment is required when the only element(s) of the motion picture used in an interactive program is (are) the title and/or logo and/or art work and/or sound effects and/or music soundtrack.

(2) No Deduction Permitted for Title, Logo, Art Work, etc- Used in an Interactive Program

The payment provisions hereunder encompass all elements of the motion picture, including title, logo, art work and accompanying sound track, and no deduction may be made from the Applicable Gross for the use of such elements.

5. Coverage — General

This Article 64 covers reuse of covered material in interactive programs (including arcade games, wherever located) which are viewed/used on a home-type television screen or computer monitor and distributed by means of a cartridge, disc or any other similar device or by any means of television exhibition, including but not limited to, pay television, free television and basic cable.

B. Reuse of Covered Motion Pictures, In Whole or In Part

1. Whole or substantial part. The reuse of a covered theatrical or television motion picture, in whole or in substantial part, in an interactive program shall require an aggregate payment by the Company to the credited writer(s) equal to one and two-tenths percent (1.2%) of the Applicable Gross attributable to the licensing of such motion picture or substantial portion(s) thereof. These reuse provisions apply to all motion pictures covered by the Supplemental Markets provisions of any Guild collective bargaining agreement. This provision shall take effect on May 2, 1995, but is subject to contractual commitments with individual writers which are entered into prior to that date.

2. **Excerpts.** The use of excerpt(s) from a covered theatrical or television motion picture in an interactive program shall require an aggregate payment by the Company to the credited writer(s) equal to two percent (2%) of the Applicable Gross attributable to the licensing of such excerpt(s). This provision shall apply to all motion pictures covered by the excerpt provisions of any WGA MBA. This provision shall take effect on May 2, 1995, but is subject to contractual commitments with individual writers which are entered into prior to that date.

    The "flashback" and "recap" exceptions in Article 15.B.10.c. and d. shall not apply to this Article 64. The provisions of Articles 15.A.3.j., 15.B.10.a. and b. shall apply when the excerpt is used as a "stock shot," for review purposes or in a trailer. In addition, if the Guild and the Companies reach agreement on a definition of "news" and/or "promotional" uses, these exception(s) also will apply to this Article 64.

3. **Allocation of payments to credited writers.** Allocation of payments under this Section B. shall be made to writers who received writing credit pursuant to a credits schedule of a WGA Basic Agreement as follows:

"Written by" credit	— one hundred percent (100%) of the monies
"Screenplay by" or "Teleplay by"	— seventy-five (75%) of the monies
"Story by," "Screen Story by" or "Television Story by"	— twenty-five percent (25%) of the monies
Minor credits, such as "Adaptation by"	— ten percent (10%) of the monies, to be deducted from the share of the writer(s) receiving "Screenplay by" or "Teleplay by"

    Any writers receiving the same writing credit shall share equally in the percentage amount specified in this Section B.

    When there is no credit given for story, screen story or television story, then the *pro rata* share otherwise payable to a writer receiving such credit shall be paid to the writer(s) accorded screenplay or teleplay credit.

    When a covered motion picture is a remake of a prior motion picture, any writers of the prior motion picture who receive writing credit for the remake shall also be entitled to share in payments under this Section B., but only if their employment as writers for the prior motion picture, or the purchase of their literary material for the prior motion picture, was covered by a collective bargaining agreement with the Guild.

For purposes of Article 64.B., the Company is deemed to have been the employer of a writer whose services were performed for the Company on a loan-out basis. The lender shall not have any responsibility under Article 64,B. with respect to a covered motion picture. If there are one or more writers who receive credit under a WGA Basic Agreement and one or more writers who perform writing services in connection with the writing of the story or teleplay or screenplay and receive screen credit in connection with a covered motion picture, but who are not subject to this Basic Agreement, then that portion of the applicable percentage payment as defined in this Article 64 which would otherwise have been payable to such one or more writers not subject to this Basic Agreement may be retained by Company, and the Company shall not be obligated to pay such portion to any such writer receiving credit as aforesaid.

4. **No duplication of payments under Sections B.1. and B.2.** Whenever a motion picture is reused, in whole or in substantial part, in an interactive program, together with excerpts from the same motion picture, payment shall be made to the writer(s) of such motion picture in accordance with Section B.1., above.

C. Interactive Programs Based Upon Literary Material

1. **Theatrical.** When an interactive program is based upon literary material covered by the theatrical provisions of any MBA, as provided in Section C.3. below, an aggregate payment equal to one and one-half percent (1-1/2%) of the Applicable Gross attributable to the licensing of such literary material shall be made by the Company to the writer(s) with separation of rights and to the writer(s) who nevertheless

    a. first describes in literary material an object or thing which is fully described in such literary material and by such description appears to be unique and original; and/or

    b. introduces a character and the characterization of such character is fully developed and fully described in the material written by the writer and from such development and description the character appears to be unique and the principal creation of the writer,

    provided that such interactive program is based upon such object, thing and/or character(s).

    When different writers are entitled to payments pursuant to this Section C.1. for literary material from the same theatrical motion picture in an interactive program, the writers shall share in the payment required. The Guild shall determine the allocation among the writers.

2. **Television.** When an interactive program is based upon literary material covered by the television provisions of any MBA as provided in Section C.3. below, an aggregate payment equal to three percent (3%) of the Applicable Gross attributable to the licensing of such literary material shall be made by the Company to the writer(s) with separation of rights (subject to the provisions of Articles 16.B.3. and B.5. and corresponding provisions of prior MBAs) and to the writer(s) who nevertheless

   a. first describes in literary material an object or thing which is fully described in such literary material and by such description appears to be unique and original; and/or

   b. introduces a character and the characterization of such character is fully developed and fully described in the material written by the writer and from such development and description the character appears to be unique and the principal creation of the writer,

   provided that such interactive program is based upon such object, thing and/or character(s).

   When different writers are entitled to payments pursuant to this Section C.2. for literary material from the same television motion picture in an interactive program, the writers shall share in the payment required. The Guild shall determine the allocation among the writers.

3. The reuse provisions of this Section C. shall apply to literary material covered by any MBA providing for Separation of Rights. The provisions of this Section C. shall take effect on May 2, 1995, but are subject to contractual commitments with individual writers which are entered into prior to that date.

D. **Combination Payments for Reuses Described in Article 64.B. and C.**

1. **Combination of Motion Picture (whole or substantial part) and Literary Material Rights.**

   a. **Theatrical.** If a covered theatrical motion picture is used in whole or in substantial part in an interactive program, as provided in Article 64.B.1 above, and such interactive program is also based on literary material written in connection with the same covered motion picture, as provided in Article 64.C.1. above, the Company shall pay an aggregate payment of two percent (2%) of the Applicable Gross attributable to both the licensing of the motion picture or a substantial portion thereof and the licensing of the literary material upon which the interactive program is based.

Such payment shall be allocated as follows: one percent (1%) shall be paid to the writer(s) entitled to payments under Article 64.B.1. and one percent (1%) shall be paid to the writer(s) entitled to payments under Article 64.C.1.

b. **Television.** If a covered television motion picture is used in whole or in substantial part in an interactive program, as provided in Article 64.B.1. above, and such interactive program is also based on literary material written in connection with the same covered motion picture, as provided in Article 64.C.2. above, the Company shall pay an aggregate payment of three percent (3%) of the Applicable Gross attributable to both the licensing of the motion picture or a substantial portion thereof and the licensing of the literary material upon which the interactive program is based. Such payment shall be allocated as follows: one and one-half percent (1-1/2%) shall be paid to the writer(s) entitled to payments under Article 64.B.1. and one and one-half percent (1-1/2%) shall be paid to the writer(s) entitled to payments under Article 64.C.2.

2. **Combination of Excerpts and Literary Material Rights.**

a. **Theatrical.** If excerpts from a theatrical motion picture are used in an interactive program, as provided in Article 64.B.2. above, and such interactive program is also based on literary material written in connection with the same covered theatrical motion picture, as provided in Article 64.C.1. above, the Company shall pay an aggregate payment of two percent (2%) of the Applicable Gross attributable to both the licensing of excerpts and the licensing of the literary material upon which the interactive program is based. Such payment shall be allocated as follows: one percent (1%) shall be paid to the writer(s) entitled to payments under Article 64.B.2. and one percent (1%) shall be paid to the writer(s) entitled to payments under Article 64.C.1.

b. **Television.** If excerpts from a television motion picture are used in an interactive program, as provided in Article 64.B.2. above, and such interactive program is also based on literary material written in connection with the same covered television motion picture, as provided in Article 64.C.2. above, the Company shall pay an aggregate payment of three percent (3.0%) of the Applicable Gross attributable to both the licensing of excerpts and the licensing of the literary material upon which the interactive program is based. Such payment shall be allocated as follows: one and one-half percent (1-1/2%) shall be paid to the writer(s) entitled to payments under Article 64.B.2. and one and one-half percent (1-1/2%) shall be paid to the writer(s) entitled to payments under Article 64.C.2.

3. When different writers are entitled to payments for the use of literary material pursuant to this Section D. for the same motion picture in an interactive program, the writers shall share in the payment required. The Guild shall determine the allocation among the writers.

E. Reporting and Assumption Agreements

1. Reporting and payment

Company's obligation shall accrue hereunder only after Applicable Gross is received by Licensor but as to foreign receipts such obligation shall accrue only when such receipts can be freely converted to U.S. dollars and are remitted to the United States, and until such time no frozen foreign receipts shall be included in Applicable Gross. Payment of amounts accruing hereunder shall be made quarterly on the basis of quarterly statements, as hereinafter provided.

Upon request, and if permitted by the authorities of a foreign country, the Company (or Licensor, if applicable) will transfer to any writer, in the currency of such foreign Country, his/her share, if any, of frozen foreign receipts in such Country, provided the writer will bear any costs involved; and such transfer shall be deemed to be payment to the writer of an equivalent number of U.S. dollars at the then-current free market rate for blocked funds of that category as determined by the Company (or Licensor, if applicable). Concurrently with such transfer the writer will pay to the Company (or Licensor, if applicable) in U.S. dollars the total amount the Company (or Licensor, if applicable) is required to withhold from such payment under all applicable laws. If the Company (or Licensor, if applicable) utilizes frozen foreign currencies derived from the license of interactive rights, as provided herein, by conversion thereof to properties that may be freely exported and turned to account, the amount so utilized by the Company (or Licensor, if applicable) shall be deemed to have been converted to U.S. dollars at the then-current free market rate for blocked funds of that category determined as above provided. Frozen foreign receipts from the license of interactive rights, as provided herein, shall be deemed to be released on a first-in first-out basis, unless the authorities of the foreign country involved designate a specific period that would render such basis inapplicable. Such released funds shall be allocated between the license of interactive rights, as provided herein, and other licenses of interactive rights granted by the licensor in the same ratio that receipts derived from the license of interactive rights, as provided herein, within the foreign country, bear to the total receipts derived from the license of interactive rights, as provided herein, and all other licenses of interactive rights within the foreign country, during the applicable period, unless the authorities of the foreign country involved require another method of allocation, in which case such other method shall be used.

Foreign receipts shall be accounted for in U.S. dollars at the rate of exchange at which such receipts are actually converted and remitted, and should any discounts, taxes, duties or charges be imposed in connection with the receipt or remittance of foreign funds, only so much of such funds as remain thereafter shall be included in Applicable Gross. Company (or Licensor, if applicable) shall not be responsible for loss or diminution of foreign receipts as a result of any matter or thing not reasonably within the control of the Company (or Licensor, if applicable). The Guild and the writers shall be bound by any arrangements made in good faith by the Company (or Licensor, if applicable), or for its account, with respect to the deposit or remittance of foreign revenue. Frozen foreign receipts shall not be considered trust funds and the Company (or Licensor, if applicable) may freely commingle the same with other funds of the Company (or Licensor, if applicable). No sums received by way of deposits or security need be included in Applicable Gross until earned, but when the Licensor is paid a non-returnable advance for interactive rights by a licensee, such advance shall be included in the Applicable Gross. A "non-returnable advance" is to be included in Applicable Gross when interactive rights, as provided herein, are "available" and "identifiable" and the amount of the advance payment is "ascertainable."

Interactive rights are "available" when the rights first may be exploited under the terms of the applicable license agreement.

Interactive rights are "identifiable" when the Company first knows or reasonably should have known that the interactive rights to a given motion picture and/or literary material are covered by a particular license.

The amount of the advance payment is "ascertainable" if:

(a)   the advance is for interactive rights to one motion picture and/or literary material for one motion picture and territory, or

(b)   the total amount of the advance is for multiple rights or interactive rights to multiple motion pictures and/or territories, in which case a fair and reasonable allocation of such advance shall be made among the licensed rights in accordance with Section A.3. of this Article 64. As each of these interactive rights becomes identifiable and available, the allocated portion of the non-returnable advance is to be included in Applicable Gross for that quarter. The Company shall notify the Guild of its allocation when the report of Applicable Gross, which includes the advance, is to be filed. The Guild has the right to challenge in an MBA arbitration a failure to allocate or any allocation that it contends is not fair and reasonable.

If interactive rights are available and identifiable and the amount of the advance is ascertainable, but the Company does not provide the WGA with the information required by the MBA and applicable law, then the advance shall be deemed includable in Applicable Gross no later than six months after the licensor receives it.

An advance received by a Licensor's parent, subsidiary or any other related or affiliated entity or successor-in-interest, or by any other entity to which the advance payment is directed by the licensor or license agreement, shall be considered as an advance payment received by the licensor.

Within a reasonable time after the expiration of each calendar or fiscal quarter, but not exceeding sixty (60) days, the Company will furnish or cause to be furnished to the Guild a written report showing the Applicable Gross during the preceding quarter from the licensing of interactive rights, as provided herein, with respect to which Company is required to make payments under this Article 64. These quarterly reports shall (1) separately set forth the Applicable Gross from licensing interactive rights under Articles 64.B.1, 64.B.2., 64.C., 64.D.1 and 64.D.2. and (2) state whether the Applicable Gross used is monies received by the Licensor or fair market value.

Concurrently with the furnishing of each quarterly report, the Company will make the payments shown to be due by such report. All payments shall be made by check payable to the order of the writers entitled thereto, and shall be delivered to the Guild for forwarding to such writers. Compliance herewith shall constitute payment to the writers.

No such reports need be furnished with respect to any period during which there was no Applicable Gross.

An inadvertent failure to comply with the reporting provisions of this Article 64.E. shall not constitute a default by the Company under this Agreement, provided such failure is cured promptly after notice from the Guild is received by the Company.

The Company shall make available for inspection by the Guild all licensing statements which are available to the Company insofar as they relate to Applicable Gross, and all the financial terms of contracts pertaining to such Applicable Gross. The Guild shall have the right, at reasonable times, to examine the books and records of the Company as to such Applicable Gross, pertaining to such licensing of interactive rights, at whatever place or places such records are customarily kept by the Company. If the Guild requests that it be informed of the license fee paid under an interactive rights licensing agreement, or if the Guild requests that it be sent an extract of the financial terms of such a license, and if such information is not extensive in nature, the Company will forward such information or extract without making it necessary for the Guild to send a representative to the Company's offices. In general, the Company will cooperate in furnishing such information to the Guild by mail or telephone, where doing so is not unreasonable or burdensome.

When interactive rights to more than one picture are licensed in a single license agreement, the Company shall inform the Guild, at its request, of the identity of the motion pictures, the interactive rights to which are covered by the license, and shall make available to inspection by the Guild in the office where such license agreement is customarily kept a copy of the terms of such license showing the titles of the motion pictures and/or literary material, the interactive rights to which are covered by the license, and the license fee for each. The Company agrees to cooperate in responding to reasonable inquiries from the Guild as to whether the interactive rights to any motion picture or literary material, as provided herein, are currently being licensed.

Company shall make all social security, withholding, unemployment insurance, and disability insurance payments required by law with respect to the additional compensation provided for in this Article 64.

If the Company shall fail to make any payment provided for in this Article 64 to the writer when and as the same becomes due and payable, it shall bear interest at the rate of one and one-half percent (1-1/2%) per month on the unpaid balance thereof commencing to accrue on the earlier of: (a) seven (7) days after notice in writing to Company from the Guild of such delinquency, or (b) sixty (60) days after such payment becomes due and payable.

The compensation payable under this Article 64 shall be excluded from the gross compensation upon which the Company's contributions are to be made to the Pension and Health Plans.

2. Crediting

If a writer's employment agreement with the Company requires that the writer's compensation shall be based, in whole or in part, upon, or measured by, a percentage of the gross receipts derived from the licensing of interactive rights, then such percentage compensation shall be credited against any amounts payable to the writer hereunder, and likewise any payment due to the writer hereunder shall be credited against such percentage compensation. Where all or a part of a writer's compensation is a specified sum of money, commonly known and referred to as a "deferment," such deferment may not be credited against amounts payable by the Company to such writer hereunder.

3. Assumption Agreements

With respect to the interactive rights in any literary material or motion picture for which payment is due under this Article 64, the following provisions of subparagraphs 3.a., b. and c. shall apply. When subparagraph 3.a. below applies, the term "licensor/licensee" indicates that the Company (or Licensor, if applicable) must choose either "licensor" or "licensee" as the appropriate term for each Assumption Agreement. There is no obligation under subparagraphs 3.a. or 3.c. for a Company to obtain an assumption agreement when the Company either does not own the interactive rights, the Company is the licensor of the interactive rights, or the Company exploits the interactive rights (*i.e.*, the Company meets the definition of licensee in Article 64.A.3.b.).

a. Licensor/Licensee's Assumption Agreement

Prior to the commencement of principal photography of each motion picture, the reuse of which is governed by Article 64, if the Company (or Licensor, if applicable) is not also the licensor/licensee of the interactive rights to such literary material and/or motion picture, the Company (or Licensor, if applicable) shall obtain from the licensor/licensee having such rights and deliver to Guild a separate written agreement entitled "Licensor/Licensee's Assumption Agreement." This Assumption Agreement shall be made expressly for the benefit of the Guild as representative of the writers involved, by which such licensor/licensee agrees to assume and pay the amounts payable under this Article 64 when and as the same become due. Such agreement shall be substantially in the following form:

"Licensor/Licensee's Assumption Agreement"[22]

In consideration of the execution of a license agreement between _____ (insert name of the Company (or Licensor, if applicable)) and the undersigned licensor/licensee, licensor/licensee agrees that the motion picture, presently entitled

---

[22] See Sideletter to Article 64 — Applicable Credits Provisions at page 391.

_____, and/or the literary material therefor are subject to a Writers Guild of America Basic Agreement (referred to as 'Basic Agreement'), including applicable credits provisions, if any, and particularly to the provisions of Article 64 of the 1995 WGA Theatrical and Television Basic Agreement — ABC, CBS and NBC ('1995 WGA MBA'), pertaining to additional compensation payable to writers when interactive rights are licensed. Licensor/licensee hereby agrees expressly for the benefit of the Writers Guild of America, west, Inc., and Writers Guild of America, East, Inc., (collectively 'the WGA'), as representative of the writers whose services are included in such motion picture and/or literary material, to make the additional compensation payments required by Article 64 when interactive rights are licensed. Licensor/licensee, for and on behalf of the Company (or Licensor, if applicable), shall make all social security, withholding, unemployment insurance and disability insurance payments required by law with respect to the additional compensation referred to in the preceding sentence.

It is expressly understood that the licensor/licensee's right to exploit such interactive rights, or to cause or permit such rights to be exploited, shall be subject to and conditioned upon the prompt payment of the additional compensation required by Article 64 of the 1995 WGA MBA. It is agreed that the WGA, in addition to all other remedies, shall be entitled to injunctive relief against the licensor/licensee if such payments are not made.

Within a reasonable time after the expiration of each calendar or fiscal quarter, but not exceeding sixty (60) days, the licensor/licensee will furnish or cause to be furnished to the WGA a written report showing the Applicable Gross (as defined in Article 64 of the 1995 WGA MBA) during the preceding quarter from licensor/licensee's licensing of interactive rights, whether such license is by the licensor/licensee or through another licensor/licensee licensed by licensor/licensee. Each report shall be in the format described in Article 64.E.1. of the 1995 WGA MBA. Such report shall be accompanied by such payments as may be due.

Licensor/licensee shall also make available for the WGA's inspection all licensor/licensee's statements delivered to the Company (or Licensor, if applicable) insofar as they relate to Applicable Gross. The WGA shall have the right at reasonable times and on reasonable notice to examine the books and records of the licensor/licensee as to Applicable Gross. If the licensor/licensee shall fail to make such payments as and when due and payable, they shall bear interest at the rate of one and one-half percent (1-1/2%) per month on the unpaid balance thereof, commencing to accrue on the earlier of (a) seven (7) days after the Guild gives written notice of the delinquency to the Company, or (b) sixty (60) days after such payment becomes due and payable.

This Licensor/Licensee's Assumption Agreement shall remain effective and binding upon licensor/licensee as long as it remains the licensor/licensee of the interactive rights and thereafter in perpetuity only if it has provided or guaranteed any of the financing for the production of such covered motion picture, in accordance with and subject to the provisions of Article 64.E.3.b.(i) of the 1995 WGA MBA.

When there is more than one licensor/licensee, the provisions of Article 64.E.3.b.(iii) of the 1995 WGA MBA shall apply to each licensor/licensee which neither provides nor guarantees any of the financing for the production of such motion picture.

The licensor/licensee has [has not] (strike whichever is inapplicable) provided or guaranteed financing for production of such motion picture.

Date: _____

Licensor/licensee:

[insert business address of licensor/licensee]

SIGNED: _____ "

An inadvertent failure on the part of any such licensor/licensee to comply with any of the reporting provisions of Article 64.E.3.a. shall in no event constitute a default by the Company (or Licensor, if applicable) or such licensor/licensee or a breach of the 1995 WGA MBA, provided that such failure is cured promptly after notice in writing thereof from the Guild.

In the event of the expiration or termination of any license agreement for interactive rights, the Company's (or Licensor's, if applicable) obligation to obtain and deliver a Licensor/Licensee's Assumption Agreement to the Guild shall apply as well to any subsequent license agreement for interactive rights entered into by Company (or Licensor, if applicable). The Company (or Licensor, if applicable) shall obtain and deliver an executed Licensor/Licensee's Assumption Agreement within ten (10) days after the execution of each such subsequent license agreement.

If, with respect to any motion picture described in this Article 64.B.1. or 2. or any motion picture based upon any literary material described in Article 64.C.3., licensor/licensee is not liable in perpetuity for the Article 64 payments under the 1995 WGA MBA, or if the Company (or Licensor, if applicable) does not have a license agreement with the licensor/licensee for interactive rights, then the Guild, prior to commencement of principal photography of the motion picture, may require such further financial assurances from the Company (or Licensor, if applicable) as it deems advisable to insure performance of Company's (or Licensor's, if applicable) obligations to pay the Article 64 fees provided herein, including, without limitation, the execution of security agreements, guarantees, or other protective agreements. If ABC, CBS or NBC becomes liable in perpetuity under a Licensor/Licensee's Assumption Agreement to pay the Article 64 fees provided for hereunder, the Guild will release and cause to be discharged of record all such security agreements, guarantees or other protective agreements entered into or obtained by or from the Company (or Licensor, if applicable), provided, however, that the Company's (or Licensor's, if applicable) primary liability shall not be released thereby.

b.   Licensor/Licensee's Liability

With respect to the interactive rights in any literary material and/or motion picture for which payment is or may become due under this Article 64, the following provisions shall be applicable to the interactive rights licensor or licensee:

(i)   When the Licensor/Licensee has provided or guaranteed any of the financing for the production of a motion picture, the reuse of which is governed by Article 64, the obligations of the Licensor/Licensee under this Article 64 shall continue in perpetuity notwithstanding the expiration or termination of its interactive rights license agreement, or any foreclosure of a chattel mortgage, security agreement, pledge, or lien on such motion picture and/or the literary material upon which it is based. In the case of foreclosure, should such mortgagee, pledgee or security holder or a third party, who is neither the Company nor Licensor/Licensee, acquire title to the literary material and/or motion picture and execute the Buyer's Assumption Agreement (see Article 64.E.3.c. below), and upon condition that the Guild, in its discretion, approves such purchaser's financial responsibility, then, when the Licensor/Licensee ceases to be the licensor/licensee of such interactive rights, the Licensor/Licensee shall thereupon be released from any and all further obligations under this

Article 64 with respect to the literary material and/or motion picture. Should any third party (other than in connection with any such foreclosure) acquire the interactive rights of the Licensor/Licensee and execute a Licensor/Licensee's Assumption Agreement pursuant to which it is liable in perpetuity to make the payments under this Article 64, then, upon condition that the Guild in its discretion approves such third party's financial responsibility, such Licensor/Licensee shall thereupon be released from any and all further obligations under this Article 64 with respect to the interactive rights so acquired. However, such Licensor/Licensee shall not be liable for the payment of any Article 64 reuse payments based on monies received by a foreign distributor under a "foreign production deal" as defined in Article 51.3.a. of this Basic Agreement with respect to which such foreign distributor or independent producer is not obligated to account to such Licensor/Licensee.

(ii)   When the Licensor/Licensee does not provide or guarantee any of the financing for the production of a motion picture whose reuse is governed by Article 64, the Licensor/Licensee's Assumption Agreement shall be binding upon the Licensor/Licensee only as long as it has the interactive rights.

(iii)   When there is more than one Licensor/Licensee or Buyer[23] of literary material and/or a motion picture, the reuse of which is governed by Article 64, the liability of any such Licensor/Licensee or Buyer, which neither provides nor guarantees any of the financing for the production of such motion picture whose reuse is governed by Article 64, for reuse payments under this Article 64, shall be applicable only to such portion of Applicable Gross as is derived by the Licensor/Licensee or Buyer, as the case may be.

c. **Buyer's Assumption Agreement**

If the Company (or Licensor, if applicable) shall sell, transfer or assign its interactive rights in any covered motion picture and/or literary material, it shall obtain from such buyer, transferee or assignee (each may be referred to as "Buyer") a separate agreement made expressly for the benefit of the Guild as representative of the writers involved, requiring such Buyer to comply with the provisions of this Basic Agreement with respect to additional

---

[23] See Article 64.E.3.c. below for the definition of "Buyer" and provisions concerning "Buyer's Assumption Agreement."

compensation payable to writers under Article 64 when and as the same become due, and applicable credits provisions, if any.[24] Such agreement shall be substantially in the following form:

"BUYER'S ASSUMPTION AGREEMENT"

For a valuable consideration, the undersigned _____ (insert name of Buyer) (hereinafter referred to as 'Buyer') hereby agrees with _____ (insert name of Company (or Licensor, if applicable)) that all motion pictures and/or literary material, the interactive rights to which are covered by this agreement, a list of which is appended hereto, are subject to a Writers Guild of America Theatrical and Television Basic Agreement (hereinafter 'Basic Agreement') and particularly to the provisions of Article 64 of the 1995 WGA MBA, pertaining to additional compensation payable to writers when interactive rights to such motion pictures and/or literary material are licensed, and Buyer hereby agrees expressly for the benefit of the Writers Guild of America, west, Inc., and the Writers Guild of America, East, Inc., (hereinafter called 'WGA'), as representative of the writers whose services are included in such motion pictures and/or literary material, to assume and be bound by Company's (or Licensor's, if applicable) obligation hereunder to make the additional compensation payments required thereby when interactive rights to such motion pictures and/or literary material are licensed. Buyer for and on behalf of the Company (or Licensor, if applicable) shall make all social security, withholding, unemployment insurance, and disability insurance payments required by law with respect to the additional compensation referred to in the preceding sentence.

It is expressly understood that the right of the Buyer to license such interactive rights shall be subject to and conditioned upon the prompt payment of such additional compensation, in accordance with Article 64 of the 1995 WGA MBA. It is agreed that the WGA, in addition to all other remedies, shall be entitled to injunctive relief against Buyer in the event that such payments are not made.

Within a reasonable time after the expiration of each calendar or fiscal quarter, but not exceeding sixty (60) days, Buyer will furnish or cause to be furnished to the WGA a written report showing the Applicable Gross (as defined in Article 64 of the

---

[24] See Sideletter to Article 64 — Applicable Credits Provisions . . . .

1995 WGA MBA) during the preceding quarter from the Buyer's licensing of interactive rights with respect to which Buyer is required to make payments hereunder. Each report shall be in the format described in Article 64.E.1. of the 1995 WGA MBA. Such report shall be accompanied by such payments as may be due.

Buyer shall also make available for the WGA's inspection all licensor/licensee's [strike whichever is inapplicable] statements delivered to Buyer insofar as they relate to Applicable Gross. The WGA shall have the right at reasonable times to examine the books and records of Buyer as to Applicable Gross.

If Buyer shall fail to make such payments as and when due and payable, they shall bear interest at the rate of one and one-half percent (1-1/2%) per month on the unpaid balance thereof, commencing to accrue on the earlier of (i) seven (7) days after notice in writing to Buyer from WGA of such delinquency, or (ii) sixty (60) days after such payment becomes due and payable.

When there is more than one buyer, the provisions of Article 64.E.3.c. of the 1995 WGA MBA shall apply to each Buyer.

BUYER

Date:

By: _____

Address:"

The Company (or Licensor, if applicable) agrees to deliver to the Guild an executed copy of the above referred to Buyer's Assumption Agreement within thirty (30) days after the sale, assignment or transfer of the interactive rights to a covered motion picture and/or literary material, with the name and address of the purchaser, assignee or transferee.

Any inadvertent failure on the part of the Buyer to comply with any of the reporting provisions of Article 64.E.1. or Buyer's Assumption Agreement shall in no event constitute a default by the Company (or Licensor, if applicable) or such Buyer or a breach of this Agreement, provided that such failure is cured promptly after notice in writing thereof from the Guild.

Upon delivery of such Buyer's Assumption Agreement and on condition that the Guild approves in writing the financial responsibility of the purchaser, assignee, or transferee, Company (or Licensor, if applicable) shall not be further liable for the keeping of any such records, or for the payment of such additional compensation for the licensing of interactive rights, it being agreed that the purchaser, assignee, or transferee shall solely be liable therefor.

The Guild agrees that it will not unreasonably withhold its approval of the financial responsibility of any such purchaser, assignee or transferee, it being further agreed that if the Guild, within twenty-one (21) days of receipt of written notice of any such sale, assignment or transfer, has not advised the Company (or Licensor, if applicable) that it disapproves the financial responsibility of such purchaser, assignee, or transferee, the Guild will be deemed to have approved the financial responsibility thereof. In the event the Guild advises the Company (or Licensor, if applicable) within such twenty-one (21) day period that it disapproves the financial responsibility of any such purchaser, assignee, or transferee, and the Company (or Licensor, if applicable) disputes such disapproval, the Company (or Licensor, if applicable) shall have the right, at its election, to cause to be immediately submitted to arbitration, as herein provided, the issue of whether the Guild has unreasonably withheld the approval of the financial responsibility of such purchaser, assignee, or transferee for payments due hereunder.

4. Acquisition of Title by Company

If the Company (or Licensor, if applicable) was not the actual producer of a motion picture described in this Article 64.B.1. or 2. which was produced by a signatory Company, or if the Company (or Licensor, if applicable) was not the actual producer of a motion picture based upon literary material described in this Article 64.C.3. which was produced by a signatory Company, but acquired title thereto by purchase, assignment, transfer, voluntary or involuntary, or by foreclosure of a chattel mortgage or security agreement or a pledgee's sale, Company (or Licensor, if applicable) shall nevertheless be obligated to make the payments herein provided when the interactive rights to such picture are licensed, unless such payment required hereunder has already been paid.

5. Financing-Distribution Agreement by Company

The obligation of the signatory Company (or Licensor, if applicable) hereunder with respect to the payments provided for in this Article 64 shall also apply to any covered motion picture produced by an independent producer under a contract between the signatory Company (or Licensor, if applicable) and such independent producer for the production of such motion picture, and for the financing and distribution thereof by the signatory Company (or Licensor, if applicable).

However, such signatory Company (or Licensor, if applicable) shall not be liable for any Article 64 payments based on monies received by a foreign distributor under a "foreign production deal" as defined in Article 51.3.a.(iii) of this Agreement, with respect to which such foreign distributor or such independent producer is not obligated to account to such signatory Company (or Licensor, if applicable). Nor shall such signatory Company (or Licensor, if applicable) be obligated to obtain an assumption agreement from any foreign distributor referred to in this Article 64.E. except if such foreign distributor is obligated to account to such signatory Company (or Licensor, if applicable) with respect to Article 64 monies as therein provided.

6. Company's Liability

It is expressly understood and agreed that the Company (or Licensor, if applicable) shall in all events remain bound hereunder to make the Article 64 payments due by reason of the licensing of interactive rights, irrespective of the assumption of such liability by any other person, firm or company as hereinabove provided, except as otherwise expressly provided in this Basic Agreement.

7. Failure to Deliver Assumption Agreement

The Company's (or Licensor's, if applicable) failure to obtain and deliver an executed assumption agreement as provided in this Section E. shall be deemed a substantial breach of this Basic Agreement.

8. Company's Dissolution

If Company (or Licensor, if applicable) dissolves and is no longer in the business of producing motion pictures, and if a licensor/licensee assumes all of the obligations of the Company (or Licensor, if applicable) under this Article 64, and the financial responsibility of the licensor/licensee is approved by the Guild in its discretion, the Company (or Licensor, if applicable) shall thereupon be released of any obligation with respect to any payments due hereunder; provided that if the licensor/licensee which assumes all of the obligations of the Company (or Licensor, if applicable) is ABC, CBS or NBC, or if ABC, CBS or NBC is permanently liable to pay the interactive rights fees provided for in this Article 64 with respect to the interactive rights for which the Company (or Licensor, if applicable) is liable to make such payment of Article 64 fees, then the financial responsibility of such licensor/licensee shall be conclusively deemed approved and such Company (or Licensor, if applicable) shall be released of any obligation with respect to any such payments.

F.   The reuse of covered motion pictures or literary material in interactive programs shall be governed exclusively by Article 64. The provisions of the MBA relating to payments based upon uses of literary material are superseded by these provisions only with respect to the use of literary material in interactive programs. Article 64 does not apply to literary material the rights to which have reverted to the writer (for example, under the 1968 WGA Television Freelance MBA with the networks).

G. Recognition of Experimental Nature of Article; Cooperation

1. Acknowledgments

The Guild and the Companies acknowledge that it is difficult to reach agreement on new or different terms and conditions in the Basic Agreement covering markets or areas of exploitation which are in the early stages of development. The market for reuse of MBA-covered material in interactive programs is in its infancy.

The Guild and the Companies have agreed to this Article 64 with the knowledge that distribution patterns for interactive programs not fully known, anticipated or appreciated at the time of the 1995 negotiations may well arise during the term of this Agreement or later.

2. Cooperative Covenant

The parties shall cooperate in good faith to resolve issues attributable to the factors acknowledged in paragraph 1. above, including the settlement of disputes concerning contract interpretation. To assist in accomplishing the foregoing and to facilitate successful negotiations in the future (including in the CAC), the Guild and the Companies will cooperate by sharing information, upon request, about the market for interactive programming, subject to appropriate protection for proprietary information.

H. Interactive Media Committee

The parties agree to establish a joint Interactive Media Committee, composed of representatives from the Companies and the WGA, to discuss issues related to the appropriateness and/or administration of these provisions and any other issues related to interactive media that any party wishes to discuss. The Committee shall meet at least once every six (6) months at the call of either the Guild or one of the Companies. The Committee may invite entities not signatory to a WGA MBA to participate in its activities. The Committee may make recommendations to the CAC regarding any suggested mid-term amendments to these provisions.

* * *

THEATRICAL SCHEDULE A

THEATRICAL CREDITS

1. Credit shall be given on the screen for the screenplay authorship of feature-length motion pictures and shall be worded "Screenplay by." The term "screenplay" means the final script (as represented on the screen) with individual scenes and full dialogue, together with such prior treatment, basic adaptation, continuity, scenario, dialogue, and added dialogue as shall be used in and represent substantial contributions to the final script.

    In the exceptional case where a writer has contributed to the development of the final screenplay but is not given screenplay credit hereunder, credit in the form "Adaptation by" may be given, but such credit shall be subject to automatic credit arbitration as provided in subparagraph 18. of this Schedule A. In the event the credit arbitration determines such credit appropriate, "Adaptation by" credit shall be given on the screen.

    The credits specified in this Schedule A (such as "Screenplay by," "Story by," "Written by," etc.) shall not be varied or embellished in any manner whatsoever without prior approval by the Guild.

    In its distribution and licensing agreements with both theatrical exhibitors and broadcasters, the Company will include a provision prohibiting the license from eliminating or changing the writing credits as they appear on the positive prints of the motion picture.

    Subject to contractual commitments which may exist on May 1, 1995, a writer who is entitled to credit on the screen and who has been paid, or is guaranteed payment of less than two hundred thousand dollars ($200,000.00) for his/her services or literary materials relating to the particular motion picture shall have the right to have credit given to him/her on the screen, advertising or otherwise, in a reasonable pseudonymous name. The writer shall exercise his/her said right within five (5) days after the final determination of credits under this Schedule A. (None of the writer's rights including but not limited to compensation of any kind shall be affected by the use of said pseudonymous name.)

    The term "story," as used throughout this Schedule A, means all writing representing a contribution distinct from screenplay and consisting of basic narrative, idea, theme or outline indicating character development and action. The term "source material" means all material upon which the screenplay is based other than story as hereinabove defined, including other material on which the story is based. Credit shall be given on the screen for story authorship of feature-length motion pictures to the extent and in the forms provided in the following subparagraphs a. to e., inclusive.

a. When the screenplay is based upon a story and upon no other source material, screen credit for story authorship shall be given to the screen writer, and shall be worded, "Story by," if the story was written under employment of the Company or is an unpublished and unexploited story purchased from a professional writer.

b. Subject to contractual commitments of the Company which may exist on March 1, 1977, when the screenplay is based upon source material whose acquisition is not covered by this Basic Agreement, screen credit for story authorship shall not be given in the form "Story by" but may be given by the Company to the source material author and may be worded "From a Story by" or "Based on a Story by" or other appropriate wording indicating the form in which it is acquired.

c. When the screenplay is based upon both story and source material and the story is substantially new or different from the source material, credit for story authorship shall be worded "Screen Story by," which credit shall be subject to automatic credit arbitration as provided in subparagraph 18. of Schedule A. The Company shall not thereby be limited from giving credit to the author of source material provided such credit shall indicate the form in which it is acquired. The following examples are illustrative and are not intended to cover all situations: "From a Play by," "From a Novel by," "From a Saturday Evening Post Story by," "From a Series of Articles by," "From an Unpublished Story by," "Based on a Story by," "Earnest Hemmingway's Old Man and the Sea," or other appropriate wording indicating the form in which it is acquired.

"Based Upon a Screenplay by" is appropriate source material credit in cases in which literary material is acquired or writers are employed under circumstances in which the credit provisions of this Basic Agreement do not apply, and under contracts whereby purchaser or employer agrees to give writing credits, and if Company takes over the employment contract or acquires the material written under such contract, and subsequently employs, in relation to such material, a writer subject to this Basic Agreement.

Notwithstanding anything in Article 1.A.12. or Article 1.B.1.b. and 1.C.1.b. to the contrary, where a Company buys literary material and there is a commitment for publication or exploitation of that material, Company may agree to give appropriate source material credit permissible under this subparagraph 2.c.

d. When the screenplay is based upon a sequel story written by an employed writer, story credit for such sequel shall be given in the form "Story by." The writer entitled to separation of rights in a theatrical motion picture shall receive credit in the form "Based on Characters Created by" on each theatrical sequel; for purpose of placement and size on the screen, such credit shall be deemed a source material credit under paragraph 8. of this Theatrical Schedule A. Where there are no separated rights, the author of the source material upon which such sequel is based may be given credit "Based Upon Characters Created by" or other appropriate form of credit. The foregoing provisions of this subparagraph d. shall not apply where there is a contrary contractual commitment entered into prior to March 2, 1977.

In the case of a remake, credit to the writer(s) of a prior motion picture upon which the remake is based (in whole or in part) may be in the form of "Based Upon a Screenplay by . . ." The preceding sentence shall not apply if it conflicts with contractual commitments entered into prior to March 2, 1981, if said commitments were valid at the time the contractual commitments were made.

The Company may engage any person to write any source material (including, but not limited to, the source material referred to in subparagraph c. above) as an independent contractor, and may guarantee source material credit to such person as above provided.

Prior to a writer's acceptance of employment in connection with a designated motion picture, or at the time of assignment of a then employed writer to a designated motion picture, the Company shall notify the writer in writing of any then existing contractual obligation to give credit for source material in connection with such motion picture. The same must be given to a writer if the agreement to give source material credit is made while the writer is rendering his/her services. Notice shall include the wording of the source material credit if known to the Company. The Company shall not be thereby limited from making subsequent contractual obligations to give source material credit, as above provided, in connection with such photoplay. Neither the existence of any form of credit obligation nor the giving of any such credit information shall relieve a writer from his/her obligation to render services and otherwise perform as provided in his/her employment agreement. A Company which furnishes a writer hereunder with inaccurate or incorrect credit information shall not be deemed to be in breach of this Basic Agreement or its employment agreement with such writer, if the Company at the time of giving such credit information believes in good faith such information is correct.

The Company shall be deemed to be contractually obligated in any of the cases above mentioned if the Company in good faith considers itself so obligated.

Nothing herein contained shall limit the Company from using and purchasing source material, from entering into agreements to give source material credit therefor, as above provided, or from carrying out such credit obligations as may be therein provided.

3.   Screen credit on motion pictures on which one or more writers or teams has written both the story and the screenplay shall be worded "Written by."

If a writer is entitled to "Written by" credit on a motion picture which he/she also produces or directs, unless the writer objects nothing herein shall prevent according credit on the screen and/or in paid advertising in the following forms:

"Written and Produced by _____," or

"Written and Directed by _____," or

"Written, Produced, and Directed by _____."

4.   Screen credit for screenplay will not be shared by more than two (2) writers, except that in unusual cases, and solely as the result of arbitration, the names of three (3) writers or the names of writers constituting two (2) writing teams may be used. A writing team is two (2) writers who have been assigned at about the same time to the same script and who work together for approximately the same length of time on the script. The intention and spirit of the award of credits being to emphasize the prestige and importance of the screenplay achievement, the one (1), two (2) or at most three (3) writers, or two (2) teams, chiefly responsible for the completed work will be the only screen writers to receive screenplay credit. Story credit will not be shared by more than two (2) writers.

5.   The limitation on the number of credits provided for in subparagraph 4. shall apply to all feature-length motion pictures except episodic pictures (such as *"Tales of Manhattan"* and *"If I Had a Million"*) and revues. A revue is a feature-length motion picture in which the

story is subordinate to specialties, musical numbers or sketches, and in connection with which star or featured billing is given to the actors, singers, dancers, or musicians appearing in these separate specialties, musical numbers or sketches.

6. Unless the story and/or screenplay writing is done entirely without any other writer, no designation of tentative story or screenplay credit to a production executive shall become final or effective unless approved by a credit arbitration as herein provided, in accordance with the Guild rules for determination of such credit.

7. When more than one writer has participated in the authorship of a motion picture, then all participants will have the right to agree unanimously, among themselves, as to which of them shall receive writing credits on the screen, provided that (a) the form of credit agreed upon is in accordance with the terms of this Schedule A; (b) the agreement is reached in advance of arbitration; and (c) the form of such credit is not suggested or directed by the Company. If such unanimous agreement is communicated to the Company before a final determination of credits hereunder, the Company will accept such designation of credits, and such agreed credits shall become final hereunder. The Company will confirm such agreed credits by sending notice thereof to all participants and the Guild, in the manner hereinafter provided in subparagraphs 11. and 12. hereof.

In any case in which a foreign law or government regulation applicable to the employment of a writer requires credit to be given, Company shall furnish the Guild with a copy of such law or governmental regulation together with the tentative notice of credit and the Guild agrees that credits determined shall include the minimum credit necessary to comply with such legal requirements.

8. Writing credits as finally determined hereunder shall appear on the screen. If the writing credits appear in the main titles, they shall appear on a title card immediately preceding the card on which appears credit to the director of the motion picture, provided such writing credits shall not be more than the second personal credit prior to the beginning of the motion picture. If there are no personal names or portions of personal names whatsoever in the main titles, except as part of the name of an entity, which name or portion of the personal name does not appear in any other capacity on the motion picture, then the writing credits as finally determined hereunder may appear as the first credit in the end titles or immediately following the card on which appears the credit to the director and the writing credits may not appear in a position later than the second credit in the end titles after the body of the motion picture. Notwithstanding the foregoing, if the director

is also the only person receiving "Produced by" credit on the motion picture, the credit to the director may be combined in the form "Produced and Directed by" or "Directed and Produced by" on a single card.[footnote omitted] Writing credit shall appear on a separate card, except that where the sole credited writer of the screenplay is also the author of the source material, the source material credit may appear on the same card immediately below the "Screenplay by" credit. [footnote omitted]

Source material credits (if they appear on the screen) and writing credits finally determined hereunder shall, subject to the foregoing, appear only in the following manner:

a. On one (1) title card on which there appear only writing and source material credits.

b. On separate title cards on each of which there may appear any one (1) or more of such credits, and no other credits.

c. On the main title card of the motion picture on which there may appear any one (1) or more of such credits together with other credits.

Screen credit for the writer of the screenplay shall be accorded in the same style and size of type as that used to accord screen credit to the individual producer or director of the motion picture, whichever is larger.

Whenever source material credit appears on the same title card as the "Screenplay by" credit appears on the same title card as the "Screenplay by" credit as described above, the screenplay must be the initial credit and must occupy not less than fifty percent (50%) of the credit card in type at least as large in all respects as that accorded the source material credit.

Wherever story credit, but no source material credit, appears on the same title card as the screenplay credit, the story credit and screenplay credit shall be in the same size type, the screenplay credit shall be in the initial credit and shall occupy the top fifty percent (50%) of the card, and the story credit shall occupy the bottom fifty percent (50%) of the card, except that the requirements of this sentence shall not apply where there is a contrary contractual commitment entered into prior to March 2, 1977. The Company shall have the right to place the source material credit on another card so long as such other card is not inserted between the screenplay credit and the director's credit. The foregoing provisions of this subparagraph and the preceding subparagraph shall not be applicable to contract commitments entered into prior to December 13, 1963 which contain terms contrary thereto.

With regard to on-screen credits, the words "Written by," "Screenplay by," "Story by," "Adaptation by," or "Screen Story by" shall be at least one-half of the size of the type used for the name(s) of the writer(s).

9. A writer who has participated in the writing of a screenplay, or a writer who has been employed by the Company on the story and/or screenplay, or who has sold or licensed literary material subject to this Basic Agreement, shall, for the purpose of this Basic Agreement, be considered a participant. As a participant, the writer shall be entitled to participate in the procedure for the determination of screen credits. In addition, in the case of a remake, any writer who has received credit under this Agreement or a predecessor agreement to this Agreement, for story or screenplay or teleplay in connection with a prior version of the motion picture previously produced for theatrical release, for free television or basic cable exhibition or for pay television or the video cassette/video disc market shall also be considered a participant. The preceding sentence shall not apply if it conflicts with contractual commitments entered into prior to March 2, 1981.

10. Prior to the final determination of screen credits, as provided herein, the work of participants not receiving screen credit may be publicized by the Company. After such a determination of screen credits only persons receiving screen credits or source material credit may be so publicized.

11. Before the writing credits for a motion picture are finally determined and as soon as practicable following completion of principal photography of such motion picture, the Company will send to each participant, or to the current agent of a participant if that participant so elects and to the Guild concurrently a written notice which will state the Company's choice of credit on a tentative basis, together with the names of all participants, their addresses last known to the Company, and if a participant is then also a director or producer of the motion picture the notice will so indicate. A copy of the final shooting script (or if such script is not available, the latest revised script available) will be sent with the notice of tentative credits to each of the participating writers, or to the current agent of a participant if that participant so elects. Where the Company deems its record of participants incomplete, it may comply with the foregoing by giving notice to each writer whose name and address are furnished by the Guild within five (5) days after the Company's request for such information, in addition to giving notice to each participant shown on its own records.

If there is confusion as to the identity of a participating writer listed on the Company's notice of tentative credits because two or more writers have the same first and last name, the Company shall, upon request of the Guild, furnish to the Guild such writer's social security number, if known to the Company, or the employer identification number of such writer's loan-out company.

The Company shall on such notice of tentative credits, for the information of the Guild and participants, state the form of any source material credit which Company intends to use in connection with the motion picture. Such credits shall not be subject to the provisions for protest and arbitration as hereinafter provided, but the Guild shall have the right to object to the form of such a credit.

Notice of tentative credits shall be in the following form, which form has been approved by the Guild:

NOTICE OF TENTATIVE WRITING CREDITS - THEATRICAL

To: Writers Guild of America, West, Inc., 7000 West Third Street, Los Angeles, California 90048, or to Writers Guild of America, East, Inc., 555 West 57 Street, New York, New York 10019

   AND

All Participating Writer(s) (or to the current agent, if a participant so elects)

NAME(S) OF PARTICIPATING   ADDRESS(ES)
WRITER(S)

_____   _____
_____   _____
_____   _____

TITLE OF MOTION PICTURE: _____

EXECUTIVE PRODUCER: _____

PRODUCER: _____

DIRECTOR: _____

OTHER PRODUCTION EXECUTIVE(S), AND THEIR TITLE(S), IF PARTIC-IPATING WRITER(S): _____

Writing credits on this production are tentatively determined as follows:

ON SCREEN: _____

ON SCREEN, SOURCE MATERIAL CREDIT, IF ANY: _____
_____

ON SCREEN AND/OR IN ADVERTISING, presentation and production credit, IF ANY: _____

SOURCE MATERIAL upon which the motion picture is based, IF ANY:
_____

The final shooting script is being sent to all participating writers with the notice of tentative writing credits.

The above tentative writing credits will become final unless a protest is communicated to the undersigned not later than 6:00 pm _____

_____   _____
(Company)   By:
                                            Name:_____
                                            Address:_____
Date: _____   Telephone No.:_____

   At the Company's request, the Guild may, but shall not be obligated to, make a determination of screen credits and shall so notify the participants. When a Guild determination is so made, it shall be considered a final determination.

At the request of the Guild made to the Company on commencement of principal photography of such motion picture, the Company shall furnish the Guild with a list of all persons who, to the best of the Company's knowledge, are or were participants (see subparagraph 9. above) with respect to such motion picture. If thereafter any other writer is engaged by Company to render writing services in or in connection with such motion picture during the principal photography thereof, the Company will promptly notify the Guild of that fact. If the motion picture involved is a remake of an earlier motion picture produced by Company, the list of writers to be supplied by the Company pursuant to this paragraph shall include the name of any writer employed by the Company to render writing services with respect to the most recent prior production by Company of such earlier motion picture and who received screen credit for such writing services.

A casual or inadvertent failure by the Company to forward the notices, list, names or other information to the Guild or person specified at the times or places designated pursuant to this subparagraph 11. shall not be deemed to be a breach of this Basic Agreement.

12.   The notice specified in subparagraph 11. hereof will be sent by telegraph to writers outside of the Los Angeles area or by telegram, messenger or special delivery mail to writers in such area. In case of remakes the Company shall not be under any obligation to send any notice to any writer contributing to the screenplay or story of the original production unless such writer received screen credit in connection with such original production.

Notices may be sent by mail, telegram or personal delivery as above provided. If the notices are mailed, registered or certified mail shall be used, with return receipt requested; the failure of the addressee to sign or return the receipt shall not invalidate the notice.

13.   The Company will keep the final determination of screen credits open until a time specified in the notice by the Company, but such time will not be earlier than 6:00 p.m. of the tenth business day following the next day after the dispatch of the notice above specified; provided, however, that if in the good faith judgment of the Company there is an emergency requiring earlier determination and the Company so states in its notice, such time may be no earlier than 6:00 p.m. of the fifth business day following the next day after the dispatch of the notice above specified. In the event of an emergency and on company's request, the Guild may reduce such "fifth business day" period. The Guild agrees to cooperate as fully as possible in considering such requests.

If within the time specified, a written protest of the tentative credits has not been delivered to the Company from any participants or from the Guild, the tentative credits shall become final. Every protest, including that of the Guild, shall state the grounds or basis therefor in the notice thereof. The Guild agrees not to use its right of protest indiscriminately.

14.   Notwithstanding the foregoing, if an arbitration has been conducted pursuant to the Basic Agreement to determine preliminary separation of rights, and if no additional writing is done thereafter, then the credits determined in the preliminary separation of rights arbitration shall become the final writing credits without the need for an additional credits arbitration. The Company nonetheless is required to submit a notice of tentative writing credits concurrently to the Guild, to each participating writer or to the current agent of each participating writer pursuant to paragraph 11. of this Schedule A.

Upon receipt of a protest, the Company shall notify the participants and the Guild by telegraph informing them of the name of the protesting party and the new time set for final determination.

If a unanimous designation of credits as provided for in subparagraph 7. hereof or a request for arbitration as hereinafter provided is not communicated to the Company within the time limit set for the final determination of credits, the Company may make the tentative credits final.

Any notice specified in the foregoing paragraphs shall, unless a specified form of service thereof is otherwise provided for herein, be sent by the Company by telegraphing, mailing or delivering the same to the last known address of the writer or may be delivered to the writer personally. If the notices are mailed, registered or certified mail shall be used with return receipt requested; the failure of the addressee to sign or return the receipt shall not invalidate the notice.

Unless a unanimous agreement has been reached in accordance with subparagraph 7. hereof, any participant or the Guild may, within the period provided for in subparagraph 13. hereof, file, with the Company at its studio and the Guild at its Los Angeles or New York office, a written request for arbitration of credits. In any case where automatic credit arbitration is required under this Schedule A the Guild will be deemed to have made a written request for arbitration of credits, at the time the Company submits the notice of tentative credits and, in such case Company will immediately make available to the Guild the material as provided for under this subparagraph.

The Guild through its arbitration committee shall make and advise the Company of its decision within the limitations of this Schedule

A. Said decision shall be made and advised within twenty-one (21) business days of the requests referred to in the immediately preceding paragraph; if in the good faith judgment of the Company there is an emergency requiring earlier decision and the Company so notifies the Guild, said decision shall be made and advised within ten (10) business days of the request referred to in the immediately preceding paragraph. If the arbitration committee does not render a decision within said period, as the same may have been extended by the Company, the Company may make the tentative credits final, provided the terms and provisions of this subparagraph 18. have been fully complied with by the Company.

In the event of an emergency and upon the Company's request that time for arbitration be shortened, the Guild agrees to cooperate as fully as possible. If the material is voluminous or complex, or if other circumstances beyond the control of the Guild necessitate a longer period in order to render a fair decision, and the Guild requests an extension of time for arbitration, the Company agrees to cooperate as fully as possible. The Company will not unreasonably deny the Guild's request for an extension of time. Agreement for extensions of time shall be in writing and shall specify the new date by which the Company will be advised of the arbitration decision.

Prior to the rendition of the decision a special committee of writers may make such investigations and conduct such hearings as may seem advisable to it. Immediately upon receipt of said request for arbitration, the Company shall make available to Guild three (3) copies of the script, and three (3) copies of all available material written by the participants and three (3) copies of all available source material. In addition, the Company shall cooperate with the arbitration committee to arrive at a just determination by furnishing all available information relative to the arbitration. Upon request of the arbitration committee, the Company shall provide the committee with a copy of the cutting continuity if it is available at the time of arbitration. If no final shooting script is available, Company will provide the Guild with a video cassette or print of the motion picture.

The decision of the Guild arbitration committee, and any Policy Review Board established by the Guild in connection therewith, with respect to writing credits, insofar as it is rendered within the limitations of this Schedule A, shall be final, and the Company will accept and follow the designation of screen credits contained in such decision and all writers shall be bound thereby.

19. The decision of the Guild arbitration committee may be published in such media as the Guild may determine. No writer or Company shall

be entitled to collect damages or shall be entitled to injunctive relief as a result of any decision of the Committee with regard to credits. In signing any contract incorporating by reference or otherwise all or part of this Basic Agreement, any writer or Company specifically waives all rights or claims against the Guild and/or its arbiter or any of them under the laws of libel or slander or otherwise with regard to proceedings before the Guild arbitration committee and any full and fair publication of the findings and/or decisions of such committee. The Guild and any writer signing any contract incorporating by reference or otherwise or referring to this Schedule A, and any writer consenting to the procedure set forth in this Schedule A, shall not have any rights or claims of any nature against an Company growing out of or concerning any action of the Guild or its arbiters or any of them, or any determination or credits in the manner provided in this Schedule A, and all such rights or claims are hereby specifically waived.

20.   In the event that, after the screen credits are determined as hereinabove provided, material changes are made in the literary material, either the Company or a participant and the Guild jointly may reopen credit determination by making a claim to the Guild or Company, as the case may be, within forty-eight (48) hours after completion of the writing work claimed to justify the revision of credits, in which case the procedure for determining such revised credits will be the same as that provided for the original determination of credits.

The Company agrees to make revisions in advertising material previously forwarded to the processor or publisher to reflect such redetermined credits, provided that: (a) such revisions can physically and mechanically be made prior to the closing date of such processor or publisher and at the reasonable expense; and (b) the processor or publisher has not yet commenced work on that part of the material which the change would affect.

21.   No writer shall claim credit for any participation in the screen authorship of any motion picture for which the credits are to be determined by the procedure herein provided prior to the time when such credits have in fact actually been so determined, and no writer shall claim credits contrary to such determination.

22.   (1)   In any publicity issued or released prior to the final determination of credits as herein provided, the Company may include such screenplay or screenplay and story credits as the Company may in good faith believe to be a fair and truthful statement of authorship. After such final determination of credits, the Company shall not issue or release any publicity which shall state screenplay or screenplay and story authorship contrary to such determination.

No casual or inadvertent breach of the foregoing shall be deemed to constitute a breach by the Company.

(2) Writing credit, but not necessarily in the form specified in this Schedule A, shall be included in publicity releases issued by the Company relating to the picture when the producer and the director are mentioned, whether in the form of a "production" or "presentation" credit or otherwise, except where such release is restricted to information about such individual or individuals. The writing credit shall also be included in all other publicity and promotional matter, including screening invitations issued by the Company, where the credit of the producer or director is included whether in the form of a "production" or "presentation" credit or otherwise. Prior to a final determination of credits the Company shall include those credits which it in good faith believes to be a fair and truthful statement of authorship.

(3) If the Company has submitted the Notice of Tentative Writing Credits to the Guild within ten (10) business days after completion of principal photography, and if there is a good faith emergency which requires the Company to print the cover or sleeve of a sound track album, cassette or compact disc prior to the final determination of writing credits, then Company may include thereon the name of the writer whom the Company in good faith believes to be the writer of the motion picture. After the final determination of credits, the Company shall not print any such covers or sleeves which do not comply with subparagraph (16) of this paragraph 22.

(4) If the Company has submitted the Notice of Tentative Writing Credits to the Guild within ten (10) business days after completion of principal photography, and if there is a good faith emergency which requires the Company to print the cover, jacket or title page of any novel prior to the final determination of writing credits, then Company may include thereon such writing credit(s) as the Company may in good faith believe to be a fair and truthful statement of authorship, rather than the credits as finally determined. After the final determination of credits, the Company shall not print any such covers, jackets or title pages which do not comply with subparagraph (13) of this paragraph 22.

(5) Screenplay or screenplay and story credit in accordance with the final determination of such credit will be given on any paid advertising issued anywhere in the world, provided such advertising is prepared by the Company in the Continental United States and is controlled by the Company where such advertisement is

used; it being understood that in such advertising prepared prior to final determination of screenplay and story credits, the Company shall include such screenplay and or screenplay and story credit as the Company may in good faith believe to be a fair and truthful statement of authorship. After final determination of credits, the Company shall not prepare for issuance any advertising which shall state screenplay or screenplay and story authorship contrary to such final determination.

(6) Where there is only a single writer on a project and if a paid advertisement is issued in which that writer would have received credit hereunder had there been a final determination of credit at that time, then such writer shall be given credit in such advertisement in accordance with the credit requirements of this Schedule A.

(7) In forms of advertising covered hereunder the names of the individual writers accorded screenplay or screenplay and story credit for the motion picture will appear in the same size and style of type as that in which the name of either the individual producer or the director of the motion picture shall appear in such advertising, whichever is larger. Provided, however, that:

a. If three (3) or more writers share screenplay credit, then the Company shall not be required to use, for the advertising credit to which such three (3) or more writers are entitled, an area in excess of the minimum area that would be occupied by the names of the first two (2) of such writers, if only such first two (2) writers were entitled to share screenplay credit; it being understood that for such propose the Company may diminish height of the type in which the names of the three (3) or more writers appear in addition to narrowing from side to side the names of such three (3) or more writers; it being further understood that for the purpose of determining which of the writers are the first two (2), the order in which such writers appear in the notification of the Guild's determination reached in its credit arbitration proceedings shall control; and

b. Where a writer entitled to screenplay credit is also entitled to credit as the director and/or producer of the motion picture, then the name of such writer need only be mentioned once in such advertising, provided, however, that he/she receives credit as a writer; provided further that the order of credit as between writer, producer and director shall be the same as the order with respect to which such credits are given on the screen; and

c.   In giving such credit on twenty-four (24) sheets, the names of the individual writers shall in no event appear in type less than three and one-half (3 1/2) inches in height, or if the screenplay or story credit is shared by more than two (2), in type less than two and one-half (2 1/2) inches in height; and

d.   In giving such credit in forms of advertising covered hereunder, other than on twenty-four (24) sheets the names of the individual writers shall in no event appear in type of a height less than fifteen percent (15%) of the height of type used for the title of the motion picture, or if there are two (2) titles of the motion picture, the larger title. The Company may seek a waiver of the double billing provision, in particular cases such as the *"Beau Geste"* ads and the Guild will not unreasonably withhold such waivers.

e.   Writing credits shall be given as provided herein in advertising which features a quotation(s) from a review(s) of the motion picture if the name of an individual producer or director appears in any of the quotations; provided, however, if the name of individual producer or director in the quotation(s) shall be in the same size and style of type as the remainder of the quotation(s), then the writing credit need not conform in size or style of type to the name in the quotation but shall otherwise conform in size and style of type as provided in this paragraph 22.

(8)   In all cases the location of the credit accorded to any writer under this subparagraph 22. shall be discretionary with the Company.

(9)   Where the title of the motion picture is in letters of varying sizes, the percentage above referred to shall be based on not less than the average size of all the letters in such title.

(10)   The foregoing obligation to accord credit in paid advertising shall be limited to story, screenplay, or screen story, adaptation and written by credits and shall not apply:

a.   To so-called "teaser" advertising, except that if a "Produced by" or "Directed by" credit is included, the writing credit shall also be included.

b.   To advertisements less that four (4) column inches in size, but if such advertising contains a "Produced by" or "Directed by" credit, the writing credit shall also be included.

c.   To radio or the audio portion of television advertising.

     d.   Where credit is given neither to the individual producer nor director of the motion picture.

     e.   To special advertising relating only to the source material on which the picture is based, or author thereof, any member or members of the cast, the director, individual producer, or other personnel concerned in its production, or similar matters.

(11)   In any case in which there would be an obligation to accord an advertising credit to a writer if credit were given to the producer or the director, such obligation shall also exist if credit is given to the executive producer as an individual.

(12)   Advertising shall be deemed to have been prepared hereunder when the Company has forwarded the finished copy therefor to the processor or publisher. The Company agrees, however, to revise advertising prepared prior to the final determination of credits so as to show the screenplay or screenplay and story credit as finally determined, if such revision can physically and mechanically be made prior to the closing date of such processor or publisher and at reasonable expense, and provided the processor or publisher has not yet commenced work on that part of the material which the change would affect.

(13)   The Company shall require that all writing credits as they appear on the screen appear in any published version of the whole or substantial part of a picture script, and in any novel based on the screenplay, provided that with respect to any novel based on such screenplay the credit shall indicate that such novel is based on such screenplay. Such writing credit shall appear on the title page in the same size and style of type used for the writer of the novel. If the name of the writer of the novel appears on the cover, the "Screenplay by" or "Written by" credit shall also appear on the cover in the same size and style of type as the writer of the novel, provided, however, that the writing credit need not so appear if the writer of the screenplay is the writer of the novel. The contract with the publisher shall provide that this provision is for the express benefit of the writer and the Guild, and that the publisher will comply with such requirements. But the failure of a publisher to comply with any of such requirements shall not constitute a breach by the Company.

(14)   In connection with the radio or television broadcast of a half-hour or more in length, the whole or nearly the whole of the entertainment portion of which consists of the adaptation of a screenplay

or substantial part thereof, the screenplay or screenplay and story credit as it appears on the screen shall be given either orally or visually.

(15) Where the major writing contribution to a motion picture is in the form of narration, credit for such narration shall be given and worded in the following form: "Narration Written by." When a narration credit is given in lieu of a screenplay credit on any subject to all of the rights and limitations as are provided in this subparagraph 22. with respect to screenplay credit.

(16) If hereafter the Company distributes or licenses the distribution of a souvenir program or theatrical program of a motion picture hereunder, or a phonograph record or phonograph album made from the sound track of a motion picture hereunder, and the individual producer or director of such picture is named in his/her capacity as such in such program or on the liner, cover or jacket of such album or records, then the writer shall also be named. The size of such credit as specified under this Schedule A shall be related to the size of the title as it is used in the listing of credit for such picture on such program, liner, cover or jacket. If Company includes the director or individual producer credits in any catalogue or sales brochure it issues to the public, the applicable writer's credit will also be included.

(17) If in giving credits with relation to a product, the Company gives a "Produced by" and also a "Directed by" credit, then Company shall require the writers' credits to be given in accordance with the provisions of this Schedule A. The failure of a third party to comply with such requirement shall not constitute a breach by Company.

(18) Where the Company supplies written handouts to reviewers and critics it will list writing credits, if they have theretofore been determined.

(19) No casual or inadvertent breach of any of the foregoing shall be deemed to constitute a default, or a breach by the Company of this Basic Agreement.

(20) The Guild agrees to discuss with the Companies its policy regarding issuance of waivers for the inclusion of names of corporate employers in paid advertisements.

23. In connection with "sneak" previews before the first general release of a motion picture in the United States, the Company shall give such screenplay or screenplay and story credits as the Company may in good faith believe to be a fair and truthful statement of authorship,

but it shalt be the obligation of the Company in good faith to have such credit determined prior to such sneak previews; and there shall be no other preview or theatrical showings of any kind, except sneak previews, until correct writing credit has been determined as herein provided and included in the main title.

24. The provisions of this Schedule A shall govern the determination of writing credits for shorts (as defined in the Basic Agreement) based upon written scripts, except that:

    a. Such writing credits shall appear in forms selected by the Company. In this connection, the Company agrees to use forms of credit which represent a fair and truthful statement of authorship.

    b. The location of screen credit shall be discretionary with the Company and such credit may appear on a card with other credits.

    c. The right of protest shall be limited to participants. Protests shall be directed only to improper or untruthful statements of the facts of authorship, rather than to the form in which such authorship is stated.

    d. If a written protest of the tentative credits is received by the Company from a participant within the time specified in subparagraph 13. hereof, the Company will withhold the final determination of credits until a time to be specified by the Company which time will not be earlier than forty-eight (48) hours, exclusive of Sundays and holidays, after the scripts are delivered to the Guild office in Los Angeles, or forty-eight (48) hours after the Guild is notified that the scripts are available at the Company's studio, whichever is earlier. In the event of an emergency and on the Company's request, the Guild may grant a reduction of such forty-eight (48) hour period. The Guild agrees to cooperate as fully as possible in considering such requests.

    e. The period of time specified in subparagraph 18. shall be three (3) business days in place of twenty-one (21) business days, and the arbitration decision shall not affect the form of the writing credit.

    f. The provisions of subparagraph 22. requiring the giving of advertising credit shall not apply to shorts, but if such writing credits are advertised, they shalt be a fair and truthful statement of authorship.

25. In connection with the sale, assignment or licensing of any literary material or rights therein, which material is subject to the credit provisions of this Schedule, Company shall obtain an acknowledgment

in writing that the purchaser, assignee or licensee, as the case may be will abide by all of the obligations incurred to writers by Company under the terms and provisions of this Schedule A. Upon the execution of such an acknowledgment, Company shall be considered to have fully complied hereunder and thereupon shall be relieved of all obligations under this Schedule A, with respect to such material or rights therein, as the case may be.

26.   a.   (i)   Company will submit to the office of the Guild, 7000 West Third Street, Los Angeles California 90048, attention of its Executive Director . . . a copy of the initial and subsequent campaign advertising material, and any changes in that material made either for the initial release or for a reissue, prior to the issuance or distribution of such advertising material. If at the time of such submission, the Company has the copy of the souvenir program, theatrical program, liner, cover or jacket referred to in subparagraph 22. above or the copy of the title and cover page of the novelization referred to in subparagraph 22 above the Company will also furnish such copy to the Guild at such time. If the exigencies of time so require, Company may comply with the above by submitting such advertising material to the office of Writers Guild of America East, Inc., 556 West 57th Street, New York, New York 10019, attention of its Executive Director. If within twenty-four (24) hours after such submission in Los Angeles or if within thirty-six (36) hours after such submission in New York the Guild protests by telegram, delivered (collect if desired) to the Company, that such advertising material does not conform to the provisions of this Schedule A, subparagraph 22. above, then the Guild may, within twenty-four (24) hours after making such protest, submit the dispute to arbitration under this subparagraph 26. The arbitrator shall make his/her decision and deliver it to the respective offices of the Company and Guild within twenty-four (24) hours after such submission to arbitration.

(ii)   Notwithstanding anything in this paragraph 26. to the contrary, if exigencies of time exist such that it is not possible to include, in a timely fashion, any quotation(s) from a review(s) of the motion picture in the advertising material submitted to the Guild, then the Company need not include such quotation(s) in its submission to the Guild, but shall indicate where the quotation(s) shall appear in the advertising.

When the quotation(s) is available, the Company shall resubmit to the Guild the advertising material, including the quotation(s) used. In the event that the Company inadvertently fails to resubmit such advertising material to the Guild, but such advertising material otherwise comports with the requirements of Theatrical Schedule A, then the Company shall not be deemed to have violated the Agreement by reason of such inadvertent failure to resubmit the advertising material.

(iii) The arbitrator shall be selected in accordance with the following procedure. Within twenty-four (24) hours following the Company's receipt of the arbitration claim, the parties shall select a disinterested arbitrator either by mutual agreement or, failing such mutual agreement, by use of the following "strike process:"

(a) The arbitrators listed in this paragraph 26.a. shall constitute the list of arbitrators.

(b) On a Company-by-Company basis, the Guild and the Company shall alternate on a case-by-case basis in first striking a name from the list of arbitrators. Thereafter, the other party shall "strike" a name from the list. The parties shall continue to alternate in striking names from the list until one arbitrator's name remains.

(c) The arbitrator whose name remains (after the strike process is completed) shall be the arbitrator.

(d) In the event that one of the parties fails to participate in the strike process, or fails to strike in order and/or timely, the other party may thereupon select the arbitrator to hear the matter.

(e) If more than one Company is a party, then the Company which is the real party in interest shall participate in the strike process with the Guild.

In the event that such Companies cannot agree on which of them is the real party in interest, then such Companies shall determine by lot which Company shall participate in the strike process with the Guild.

The initial panel of arbitrators is:

LOS ANGELES

Sara Adler	Melvin Lennard
Tom Christopher	Michael Rappaport
Dixon Dern	Sol Rosenthal
Gerry L. Fellman	Murray Schwartz
Frederic R. Horowitz	Myron Slobodien
Edna Francis	Louis Zigman
Edgar A. Jones, Jr.	

NEW YORK

Stanley Aiges	George Nicolau
James Altieri	Eva Robins
Daniel Collins	Milton Rubin
Dr. Clara H. Friedman	Eric J. Schmertz
Milton Friedman	Arthur Stark
Walter Gelthorn	

Additional names may be added from time to time during the term of the contract by mutual agreement of the parties.

(iv) The situs of arbitration proceedings shall be Los Angeles, California, unless the parties mutually agree to New York, New York or some other situs.

If the parties agree to New York, New York, the arbitrator shall be selected from the New York list of arbitrators set forth in this subparagraph 26.a. The cost of such arbitration shall be borne equally by the Company and the Guild.

(v) If the arbitrator decides that the Guild's protest is valid, he/she must designate in what respect such advertising material does not conform to the provisions of this Schedule A, subparagraph 22. above. This shall be the limit of the arbitrator's authority. The decision of the arbitrator shall be binding upon the Company, the Guild, and the writer or writers involved. Company shall not issue any such advertising material which would violate such decision.

(vi) It is hereby agreed that if the arbitrator in any arbitration under the provisions of this subparagraph 26. does not make his/her decision and deliver it to the respective offices of the Company and Guild within twenty-four (24) hours after the dispute has been submitted to him/her under this subparagraph 26., then, at any time thereafter prior to the making and delivering of such decision, either the Guild or the

Company may elect to remove the dispute from such arbitrator and resubmit it to the next arbitrator in rotation If so resubmitted, such next arbitrator in rotation shall make his/her decision and deliver it to the respective offices of the Company and Guild within twenty-four (24) hours after such resubmission. The aforesaid election and resubmission shall be exercised and effected by written notice by the Guild or the Company, as the case may be, to the other party. If the first arbitrator shall make and deliver his/her decision after the expiration of twenty-four (24) hours after the dispute has been submitted to him/her and prior to the resubmission of the dispute to the next arbitrator in rotation as aforesaid, such decision shall have the same effect as though it had been made and delivered by the first arbitrator within twenty-four (24) hours after the original submission of the dispute to him/her.

(vii)   If the Guild fails to submit its protest in the manner and within the time period specified above, or if the Guild fails to submit the dispute to arbitration in the manner and within the time period specified above, then in either of such events the Guild shall be conclusively deemed to have approved such advertising material and such approval shall be binding upon the Guild and the writer or writers involved. The Company shall not issue or distribute any advertising material prior to the expiration of the period within which the Guild may protest nor in the event of a protest by Guild (submitted in the manner and within the time period specified above) prior to the expiration of (i) seventy-two (72) hours after such advertising material has first been submitted as aforesaid by Company to the Guild in Los Angeles, or (ii) eighty-four (84) hours after such advertising material has first been submitted as aforesaid by Company to the Guild in New York, as the case may be.

In determining any twenty-four (24) or thirty-six (36) hour period referred to above in this subparagraph 26.a., there shall be excluded Saturdays, Sundays, and the six (6) holidays recognized in the motion picture industry, to wit: New Year's Day, Memorial Day, Fourth of July, Labor Day, Thanksgiving and Christmas.

Time is of the essence as to all of the provisions of this subparagraph 26.

      b.   Company will forward, whenever practical, by air mail, to the Guild, to the attention of its Executive Director, a copy of each of its press books immediately upon its publication and before its general distribution. The present address of the Guild is 7000 West Third Street, Los Angeles, California 90048.

Such press books shall conform to the provisions of this Schedule A, subparagraph 22., above.

The Guild shall send a written answer to the Company immediately upon receipt of the Company's press book. If Company does not receive such an answer from the Guild within six (6) days from the time the Company has sent the press book to the Guild, the Guild shall be considered to have approved the press book, and such approval shall be binding upon the Guild and the writer or writers involved.

If within such six (6) days the Guild should protest to the Company that any advertising contained in such press book, neither previously approved as part of initial advertising material nor as part of subsequent advertising material, does not conform with the advertising provisions quoted above, the Guild and the Company shall appoint a joint committee which shall immediately determine the validity of the Guild's protest. If the committee determines it is a valid protest, it may specify the corrections, if any, necessary to conform the advertising with the above-mentioned advertising provisions.

27.   If the Company shall sell or license the so-called stage presentation rights to a screenplay with respect to which a writer has received a "Written by," Story by," or "Screen Story by" screen credit, then Company shall provide in the contract of sale or in the license that the writer shall be accorded appropriate credit reflecting such screen credit in (1) the program for the stage presentation based upon such screenplay, (2) newspaper advertising of one-half page or larger for the Broadway showings of such stage presentation, and (3) billboards and lobby displays for such stage presentations, but only if general credits are also accorded in such programs, newspaper advertising, lobby displays, and billboards, *e.g.*, director credit, stage play writer credit, producer credit, choreographer credit, and the like. The failure of the purchaser or licensee of the stage presentation rights to comply with such contractual requirements shalt not constitute a breach of this Agreement by the Company.

28. a.   Notwithstanding any other provision of this Schedule A, but subject to the provisions of subparagraph 28.d. below, if the

individual producer or director is accorded a "production" or "presentation" type of credit, such as "A Sam Jones Production" or "A Sam Jones Picture" or "A Sam Jones Presentation" or "A Sam Jones Film," on the screen (wherever such credit may appear on the screen other than in the position where such individual producer or director credit would normally appear pursuant to this Schedule A), such "production or presentation" type of credit may be accorded in a different style and/or a different size (whether larger or smaller) of type than used to accord credit to the writer of the screenplay, subject to the following:

(1) If such "production" or "presentation" type credit on the screen is in such different style or different size of type, it shall not be placed on the screen between the card according credit to the writer of the screenplay and the card according credit to the director of the motion picture; and

(2) Such writer shall receive credit in size of type not less than fifty percent (50%) of the size of type used for such "production" or "presentation" credit.

b. Subject only to the provisions expressly relating thereto contained in this subparagraph 28. and in Article 48.I., the matter of "production" or "presentation" type credit shall not be governed by this Basic Agreement, it being agreed that the Company may accord such "production" or "presentation" type credit as it may see fit.

c. [Deleted.]

d. When a "production" or "presentation" type of credit is given by the Company in advertising:

(1) The writing credit(s) in such advertising shall be in the same size of type as the size of the type of the "production" or "presentation" credit if such a credit is accorded to the producer or the director of the picture, and not less than one hundred percent (100%) of the size of the type of the largest "production" or "presentation" credit if two (2) or more persons receive such "production" or "presentation" credit, and not less than the size specified in (2) below. in all cases, such credit will be given in the same style of type as the credit of the individual receiving the largest "production" or "presentation" credit. The provisions of this subparagraph (1) shall not apply when a "production" or "presentation" credit is given to a writer (alone or with one or more other persons) and such writer receives sole writing credit for the respective motion picture.

(2)   When a single "presentation" or "production" credit is accorded, the writing credits shall be in size of type not less than twenty percent (20%) of the size of the type of the main title, as such title appears in the advertising involved. When more than one (1) presentation" or "production" credit is accorded, the size of the writing credits shall be increased by an additional five percent (5%) of the main title for each such additional "production" or "presentation" credit (*e.g.*, a total of twenty-five percent (25%) for two (2), thirty percent (30%) for three (3), etc.) For the purposes of this paragraph, if two (2) or more names are used on one (1) line in one (1) "presentation" or "production" credit, such will count as one (1) "presentation" or "production" credit (e.g., "A John Jones-Bob Brown Presentation;" but not "A John Jones Production of a Bob Brown Presentation").

(3)   The credit accorded to the author of the source material is not subject to the restrictions of this paragraph 28.d. and shall not be considered a "production" or "presentation" credit.

(4)   The provisions of this paragraph 28.d. shall not apply: (i) to impersonal corporate "presentation" or "production" credits when the corporate name is wholly impersonal, such as "Columbia Pictures Corp. presents," and shall further not apply to the names of any distributing company, whether or not impersonal, including Walt Disney Productions; and (ii) advertisements less than four (4) column inches in size, teasers and special advertising.

The Guild agrees to discuss with the Companies its policy with respect to issuance of waivers for the inclusion of names of corporate Employers in paid advertisements.

Notwithstanding anything to the contrary set forth above in subparagraph 22.(2) or in this subparagraph 28.d., both inclusive, all credit requirements of contracts in existence on the effective date of this Agreement which conflict with any of the provisions of said paragraphs shall control, and such contracts may be performed in accordance with their terms without regard to the provisions of said paragraphs. All advertising and publicity contained in copy prepared prior to the effective date of this Agreement which conforms to the applicable requirements of the 1992 WGA Extension Agreement may continue to be used.

29.   On the request of either party for modification of this Schedule A on the ground of hardship in the application of any of its provisions, the

other party agrees to meet and negotiate with respect to changes to eliminate such claimed hardships.

30.   When used in this Schedule A, the term "writer" or "employed writer" shall have the same meaning as provided in Article 1.B.1.a. of the Basic Agreement.

TELEVISION SCHEDULE A

TELEVISION CREDITS

1.   Credit shall be given on the screen for the authorship of stories and teleplays and shall be worded "Teleplay by," or "Story by," or "Written by" (for story and teleplay). The term "teleplay" means the script as produced on the television screen or as shown in its final form, by whatever means the medium may employ. In the exceptional case where a writer has contributed to the development of the final teleplay but is not given teleplay credit hereunder, credit in the form "Adaptation by" may be given, but such credit shall be subject to automatic credit arbitration as provided in subparagraph 17. of Television Schedule A. The credits specified in this Schedule A (such as "Teleplay by," "Story by," "Written by," etc.) shall not be varied or embellished in any manner whatsoever without prior approval by the Guild.

If a writer is entitled to "Written by" credit on a television motion picture which he/she also produces or directs, unless the writer objects, nothing herein shall prevent according credit on the screen and/or in paid advertising in the following forms:

"Written and Produced by_____," or

"Written and Directed by_____," or

"Written, Produced, and Directed by_____."

Subject to contractual commitments which may exist on May 1, 1995, a writer who is entitled to credit on the screen and who has been paid, or has been guaranteed payment of less than three (3) times the applicable minimum provided for in this Agreement, including the minimums set forth in Article 13.B.7.d. where applicable, for his/her writing services or literary materials relating to the particular teleplay, shall have the right to have credit given to him/her on the screen, advertising or otherwise in a reasonable pseudonymous name. The writer shall exercise such right within the time he/she may give written notice of protest as provided in paragraph 13. of this Schedule A; provided, however, that in the event of a timely protest by any participating writer, the time to exercise his or her right to use a pseudonym shall be extended to twenty-four (24) hours after the Guild's credit determination, but in no event later than the applicable time periods set forth in paragraph 14. of Television Schedule A. (None of the writer's rights, including but not limited to compensation of any kind, shall be affected by the use of said pseudonymous name.)

2. The term "story" means all writing written substantially in whole by a writer or writers as hereinbefore defined, representing a contribution distinct from teleplay and consisting of basic narrative, idea, theme or outline indicating character development and action. The term "source material" means all material upon which a teleplay is based other than the story, as hereinabove defined, including other material on which the story is based. Credit shall be given for story authorship of teleplays to the extent and in the forms provided in the following subparagraphs a. to e. inclusive:

    a. When a teleplay is based upon story and upon no other source material, credit for story authorship shall be given to the television writer and shall be worded, "Story by."

    b. When the teleplay is based upon source material, no story authorship credit may be given to the television writer (except pursuant to subparagraphs c. and d. below) but, subject to contractual commitments in effect on June 19, 1960 with source material authors, the source material author may not be given "Story by" credit, it being understood and agreed, however, that the Company may give to the source material author any appropriate credit other than the two words "Story by," and that the credit given to source material authors may include, but shall not be limited to, the source material credits referred to in subparagraph c. below.

    c. When the teleplay is based upon both story and source material and the story is substantially new or different from the source material credit for story authorship shall be worded, "Television Story by," which credit shall be subject to automatic credit arbitration as provided in subparagraph 17. of this Schedule A. The foregoing shall not limit the Company in giving credit to the author of source material provided such credit shall indicate the form in which it was acquired, such as, for example, "From a Play by," "From a Novel by," "From a Radio Play by," "From a Saturday Evening Post Story by," "From a Series of Articles by," "From an Unpublished Story by," "Based Upon a Short Story by," or other appropriate wording.

    Notwithstanding anything in Article 1.A.12. or Articles 1.B.1.b. and 1.C.1.b. to the contrary, where a Company buys literary material and there is a commitment for publication or exploitation of that material, Company may agree to give appropriate source material credit permissible under this subparagraph 2.c.

d.   Where the teleplay for a television motion picture (other than an MOW sequel to a "first MOW," as defined in Article 16.B.2.b., in which a writer(s) has separation of rights) is based upon a sequel story, credit for such sequel story shall be given in the form "Story by" and the author of the source material upon which such sequel is based may be given credit, "Based Upon Characters Created by," or other appropriate form of credit. If the source material is in the form of a format or characters, then the source material credit may be given in the following forms: "From the Format by," or "Characters Created by." In the case of a remake, credit to the writer(s) of a prior motion picture upon which the remake is based (in whole or in part) may be in the form of "Based upon a Teleplay by."

When the teleplay for an MOW sequel is based upon a sequel story, credit for such sequel story shall be given in the form "Story by" and the writer(s) entitled to separation of rights in the first MOW on which the MOW sequel is based shall be given credit in the form, "Based on Characters Created by" on each MOW sequel to the first MOW. For the purpose of placement and size on the screen, such credit shall be deemed a source material credit under paragraph 7 of this Television Schedule A. However, when Company exploits the series sequel rights of such first MOW, the provision of paragraph 23 of this Television Schedule A ("Created by" credit) shall apply in lieu of the foregoing obligation to accord credit in the form, "Based on Characters Created by."

e.   Upon the written request of a writer made prior to his/her acceptance of employment in connection with a designated program or upon the written request of a then employed writer at the time of his/her assignment to a designated program, the Company shall notify him/her in writing of any then existing contractual obligations to give credit for source material in connection with such program. The Company shall not thereby be limited from making subsequent contractual obligations to give source material credit as above provided in connection with such program. Neither the existence of any form of credit obligation nor the giving of any such credit information shall relieve a writer from his/her obligation to render services and otherwise perform as provided in his/her employment agreement. A Company which furnishes a writer hereunder with inaccurate or incorrect information shall not be deemed to be in breach of this Basic Agreement or its employment agreement with such writer if the company at the time of giving such credit information believes in good faith such information is correct.

The Company shall be deemed to be contractually obligated in any of the cases above-mentioned if the Company in good faith considers itself so obligated. Nothing herein contained shall limit the Company from using and purchasing source material, from entering into agreements to give source material credit therefor, as above provided, and from carrying out such credit obligations as may be therein provided.

In the case of a variety or audience participation program for which a writer has contributed material and is not otherwise entitled to be included in the "Written by" credit customarily shared by such writers, additional credit may be given for such material in the form "Special Material by." Writers of variety and audience participation shows shall be deemed included under all the provisions of this Schedule A, the same as writers of dramatic programs despite the fact that only "story" and "teleplay" are hereinafter referred to, and when credits for variety or audience participation shows are involved hereunder the terms "Written by" and "Special Material by" shall be deemed included whenever the terms "Story by" and "Teleplay by" appear.

3. Screen credit for teleplay will not be shared by more than two (2) writers, except that in unusual cases, and solely as the result of Guild arbitration provided hereunder, the names of three (3) writers or the names of two (2) writing teams may be used. A writing team for the purpose of this Schedule A. only shall be deemed to be two (2) writers (excluding production executives) who have been assigned at about the same time to the same script and who work together for approximately the same length of time on the script. The same limitation shall apply to screen credit for story authorship by writers hereunder.

4. The limitation as to the number of writer receiving credit provided for in subparagraph 3. shall apply to all teleplays except multiple-story teleplays, revues, variety and audience participation shows.

5. Unless the writing of the story and/or teleplay is done entirely without any other writer, no story or teleplay credit to a production executive shall become final or effective unless approved by a credit arbitration as herein provided, in accordance with the Guild rules for the determination of such credit. Such credit arbitration, however, shall

be without prejudice to the Company's position in any arbitration relating to payment pursuant to Article 13.B.7.c. A production executive for the purpose hereof shall be defined as any employee of Company customarily hired for or engaging in activities considered part of the managerial phase of Company's business activities. If Company shall claim that a writer has been assigned to write a teleplay based upon a story composed or created by a production executive, the story and teleplay shall be subject to an automatic arbitration pursuant to the provisions of this Schedule A.

6. When more than one (1) writer has participated in the authorship of a story and/or teleplay, then all participants will have the right to agree unanimously among themselves as to which of them shall receive writing credits on the television screen, provided that the form of credit agreed upon shall be in accordance with the terms of this Credits Schedule, and provided further the agreement is reached in advance of arbitration and the form of such credit is not suggested or directed by the Company. If such unanimous agreement is communicated to the Company before the final determination of credits hereunder, the Company will accept such designation of credits, and such agreed credits shall become final hereunder. The Company will confirm such agreed credits by sending notice thereof to all participants and to the Guild in the manner provided in this Schedule, subparagraphs 10.-11. In no case shall a writer grant to another writer, or accept for himself/herself, credit which is not properly earned.

7. Writing credit, required under the provisions of this Schedule A and as finally determined hereunder, shall appear on a separate card or cards on the television screen subject to the following conditions:

a. Writing credit (other than source material credit) may appear on the same card on which appears the title of the particular episode, but in no event in size of type less than thirty percent (30%) of the size of the title; or

b. Writing credit, including source material credit, if given, may appear on a separate card or cards immediately following the title card of the particular episode; or

c. Writing credit, including source material credit, may appear immediately prior to or following immediately after the director's credit. Writing credits placed pursuant to this subparagraph c. shall not be more than the second personal credit prior to the beginning or subsequent to the ending of the teleplay as the case may be. For this purpose, however, if source material credit appears on a separate card from the other writing credits these two separate cards immediately succeeding each other shall count as one credit. Commercials or a credit to the production company shall not be deemed to be a "personal credit" for the purposes of this provision.

d. Credit for Anthology Series. With respect to anthology series only, the Company shall give the writing credits in either of the positions set forth in a. or b. above unless the initial sponsor of the series having the right to do so pursuant to its agreement with the Company requires the Company to refrain from placing the credit in either of such positions. In such case, however, the Company shall place the writing credits as provided in c. above.

e. The credit given to a television writer or writers pursuant to this Schedule A shall precede (but need not immediately precede) source material credit except that

   (1) the obligation imposed by this sentence should be subject to contractual commitments, heretofore or hereafter entered into by the Company with any source material author, requiring that source material credit precede television writing credit;

   (2) the Company shall in any event have the right to give precedence to source material credit if the source material author's name has marquee value.

For purposes of illustration, a few examples of names having marquee value are: Kathleen Norris, Paddy Chayefsky, Ernest Hemingway, Erle Stanley Gardner, George Axelrod, Ogden Nash and John Van Druten.

If roller-type credits are used, the Company in lieu of the use of separate card shall set the writing credits in such fashion that when they are centered on the screen, no other credit shall be visible. Source material credit may be given on the same card on which other writing credits appear provided that writing credit (other than source material credit) shall be the first credit appearing on such card and provided further that the source material credit shall not occupy more than forty percent (40%) of the space on such card and is not displayed more prominently than the other writing credits appearing thereon; provided, however, that this provision shall be subject to and not affect any individual personal service agreements in effect on March 18, 1957. In no event, however, shall source material credit be included on the card on which the other writing credits appear with the title of the particular episode.

Teleplay credit shall precede story credit, it being understood that if both are on the same card, teleplay credit shall be the first credit and both credits shall be in the same style and size.

8.   A Company shall not enter in to any contract to give credit to any writer or writers hereunder for reasons of the writer's prestige or for any reasons other than earned credit, and writing credit for any writer or writers shall be assigned solely on the basis of actual contribution to the story or teleplay as determined in the event of question by the credits arbitration machinery of the Guild.

9.   [Deleted.]

10.   A writer who has participated in the writing of the teleplay or of the story (other than source material) with respect thereto, and, in the case of a remake, any writer who has received credit under this Agreement or under a predecessor Agreement to this Agreement for either story (other than source material) or teleplay or screenplay in connection with a prior version of the motion picture previously produced for theatrical release, for free or basic cable television exhibition or for Supplemental Markets, shall, for the purpose of this Basic Agreement, be considered a participant. As a participant, the writer shall be entitled to participate in the procedure for determination of writing credits. The Guild shall cooperate with the Company when requested relating to the writers of the prior version(s) of the motion picture. This paragraph shall not apply if it conflicts with contractual commitments entered in prior to March 2, 1981, if said commitments were valid at the time the contractual commitment was made.

11.   Before the writing credits are finally determined, the Company will send concurrently to each participant and to the Guild written notice, which will state the Company's choice of credits on a tentative basis, together with the names of all participants and their addresses last known to the Company. Said notice will be sent as soon as practicable following completion of principal photography. Where the Company deems its record of participants incomplete, it may comply with the foregoing by giving notice to each writer whose name and address are furnished by the Guild within two (2) days after the Company's request for such information, in addition to giving notice to each participant shown in its own records.

If there is confusion as to the identity of a participating writer listed on the Company's notice of tentative credits because two or more writers have the same first and last name, then Company shall, upon request of the Guild, furnish to the Guild such writer's social security number, if known to the Company, or the employer identification number of such writer's loan-out company.

The Company shall on such notice of tentative credits, for the information of the guild and participants, state the form of any source material credit which the Company intends to use in connection with the motion picture. Such credits shall not be subject to protest and arbitration as hereinafter provided but the Guild shall have the right to object to the form of such credit.

At the Company's request, the Guild may, but shall not be obligated to, make a tentative determination of screen credits and send out the notice.

12. The notice specified in subparagraph 11. hereof will be sent by telegram to writers outside of the Los Angeles or New York area, depending on the place of production, or by telegram, messenger or special delivery mail to writers in such areas. No notice will be sent to writers outside of the United States or writers who have not filed a forwarding address with the Company. In case of remakes the Company shall not be under any obligation to send any notice to any writer contributing to the teleplay or story of the original production, unless the writer has received credit.

Notices may be sent by mail, telegram or personal delivery as above provided. If notices are mailed, registered or certified mail shall be used, with return receipt requested; the failure of the addressee to sign or return the receipt shall not invalidate the notice.

13. The Company will keep the final determination of screen credits open until a time specified in the notice by the Company but such time will not be earlier than 6:00 p.m. of the fifth business day following the next day after the dispatch of the notice above specified; provided, however, that if in the good faith judgment of the Company there is an emergency requiring earlier determination and the Company so states in its notice, such time will not be earlier than 6:00 p.m. of the next business day following the next day after the dispatch of the notice above specified. If within the time specified, a written protest of the tentative credits has not been delivered to the Company from any participant or from the Guild, the tentative credits shall become final. Every protest, including that of the Guild, shall state the grounds or basis therefor in the notice thereof. The Guild agrees not to use its right of protest indiscriminately.

14. If a written protest of the tentative credits is received by the Company from a participant or the Guild within said period, the Company will withhold final determination of credits until a time to be specified by the Company, which time will not be earlier than eight (8) business days after the Company delivers to the Guild all of the scripts involved; provided, however, that if, in the good faith judgment of the Company, there is an emergency requiring earlier determination and the Company

so states in its notice, said time may be no earlier than one hundred forty-four (144) hours after the Company delivers to the Guild all of the scripts involved, except that if all the scripts are delivered to the Guild on a Friday before twelve noon, the time shall be no earlier than one hundred twenty (120) hours after the time the Company delivers to the Guild all the scripts involved.

In any case where the Guild's arbitration committee is required to read more than four (4) scripts pursuant to a protest hereunder, the Company shall be required to add to the eight (8) business days, one hundred forty-four (144) hours or one hundred twenty (120) hours above provided a period of twenty-four (24) hours for each additional script or fraction thereof.

If the material is voluminous or complex, or if other circumstances beyond the control of the Guild necessitate a longer period in order to render a fair decision, and the Guild requests an extension of time for arbitration, the Company agrees to cooperate wherever practicable. The Company will not unreasonably deny the Guild's request for an extension of time. Agreements for extension of time shall be in writing and shall specify the new date by which the Company will be advised of the arbitration decision.

15. Upon receipt of a protest, the Company will deliver three (3) copies of the final script and three (3) copies of all material written by the participants and three (3) copies of all available source material to the Guild offices in Los Angeles or New York and the Company shall notify the participants and the Guild by telegram informing them of the name of the protesting party and the new time set for final determination.

16. Any notice specified in the foregoing paragraphs shall, unless a specified form of service thereof is otherwise provided for herein, be sent by the Company by telegraphing, mailing or delivering the same to the last known address of the writer or may be delivered to the writer personally, and to the Guild at the last known address of the Guild in Los Angeles or New York.

17. Unless a unanimous agreement has been reached in accordance with subparagraph 6. hereof, any participant or the Guild may, within the period provided for in subparagraph 13. hereof, file with the Company at its studio and the Guild at its Los Angeles or New York office, as the case may be, a written request for arbitration of credits. In any case where automatic credit arbitration is required under this Schedule A, the Guild will be deemed to have made a written request for arbitration of credits at the time the Company submits the notice of

tentative credits and in such case the Company will immediately make available to the Guild the material as provided for under subparagraph 15. of this Schedule A. The Guild through its arbitration committee shall, within the time limit specified by the Company, make and advise the Company of its decision within the limitations of this Schedule A. In the event the decision of the arbitration committee is not rendered within said period, as the same may have been extended by the Company, the Company may make the tentative credits final, provided the terms and provisions of this Schedule have been fully complied with by the Company.

Prior to the rendition of the decision, a special committee of writers may make such investigations and conduct such hearings as may seem advisable to it. The Company shall cooperate with the arbitration committee to arrive at a just determination by furnishing all available information relative to that arbitration. Upon request of the arbitration committee, the Company shall provide the committee with a copy of the cutting continuity if it is available at the time of arbitration.

The decision of the Guild arbitration committee with respect to writing credits, including any Policy Review Board established in connection therewith, insofar as it is rendered within the limitations of this paragraph, shall be final, and the Company will accept and follow the designation of screen credits contained in such decision and all writers shall be bound thereby.

If the matter is referred to a Policy Review Board of the Guild, the Guild shall have an additional five (5) business days within which to render its credit arbitration decision; provided, however, that if in the good faith judgment of the Company there is an emergency and the Company so states in its notice, the Guild's time shall not be extended except as provided in paragraph 14.

18.   The decision of the Guild arbitration committee may be published in such media as the Guild may determine. No writer or Company shall be entitled to collect damages or shall be entitled to injunctive relief as a result of any decision of the committee with regard to credits. In signing any contract incorporating by reference or otherwise all or part of this Basic Agreement, any writer or Company specifically waives all rights or claims against the Guild and/or its arbiters or any of them under the laws of libel or slander or otherwise with regard to proceedings before the Guild arbitration committee and any full and fair publication of the findings and/or decisions of such committee. The Guild and any writer signing any contract incorporating by reference or otherwise referring to this subparagraph, or any writer consenting to the procedure set forth in this subparagraph, shall not

have any rights or claims of any nature against any Company growing out of or concerning any action of the Guild or its arbiters or any of them, or any determination of credits in the manner provided in this subparagraph, and all such rights or claims are hereby specifically waived.

19. In the event that after the screen credits are determined as hereinabove provided, material changes are made in the script, either the Company or a participant and the Guild jointly may reopen the credit determination by making a claim to the Guild or Company as the case may be, within forty-eight (48) hours after completion of the writing claimed to justify the revision of credits, in which case the procedure for determining such revised credits will be the same as that provided for the original determination of credits.

The Company agrees to make revisions in advertising material previously forwarded to the processor or publisher to reflect such redetermined credits, provided that such revisions can physically and mechanically be made prior to the closing date of such processor or publisher and at reasonable expense and provided the processor or publisher has not yet commenced work on that part of the material which the change would affect.

20. No writer shall claim credit for any participation in the screen authorship of any teleplay or story for which the credits are to be determined by the procedure herein provided for prior to the time when such credits have in fact been actually been so determined, and no writer shall claim credits contrary to such determination.

21. Writing credit for movies-of-the-week and television special such a mini-series, multi-part series and "long form" television programs (but not necessarily in the form specified in Schedule A), shall be included in publicity releases issued by the Company relating to the television motion picture when the producer and the director are mentioned, whether in the form of a "production" or "presentation" credit or otherwise, except where such release is restricted to information about such individual or individuals. Prior to a final determination of credits the Company shall include those credits which it in good faith believes to be a fair and truthful statement of authorship.

With reference to credits in advertising which is contracted for by the Company and which is more than eight (8) column inches in size, if the name of the individual producer or director (or executive producer as an individual) is included, the name of the writer shall be included and the writer shall receive parity as to size and style of type with the director, producer and executive producer. In connection with an anthology or episodic series, or serial, if advertising credit is given to a producer or director (or an executive producer as an individual) only in connection with advertising the entire series, the writer shall be given credit in such advertising when the number of scripts contributed by such writer shall equal the number of programs produced or directed by the producer, director or executive producer receiving such advertising credit. If spoken credits are accorded to the producer or director (or executive producer as an individual) they shall also be accorded to the writer. Oral self-identification by a producer or director or executive producer shall not be deemed to be a spoken credit for the purpose hereof.

With regard to advertising in Los Angeles or New York trade publications for a television series, or any individual episode of a series, if credit is given to a director, producer or executive producer with reference to the series, the writer(s) entitled to "Created by" or "Developed by" credits shall receive parity of credit with such executive producer, producer or director.

The foregoing provisions of this Paragraph 21 shall not apply to congratulatory or award advertising in which no one is mentioned other than the person(s) being congratulated for a nomination or award.

The following shall govern advertising relating to consideration of an award (e.g., "For Your Consideration . . ." advertisements): If either the director or the producer (or the executive producer as an individual) is named in such advertising together with any other person, then Company shall be obligated to accord credit to the writer(s) in such advertisement in accordance with the second paragraph of Paragraph 21. However, if such an advertisement is placed for a single television motion picture in which no one is named other than the executive producer(s) alone or with starring actors, then the forgoing obligation to accord credit to the writer(s) shall not apply.

In the event that the Company licenses or grants to any third party the right to make any of the uses of serial or episodic series material specified in Article 15.B.14., it shall use its best efforts, in contracting with such third party to accord to the writer or writers of such material credit therefor which is appropriate to the field or medium for which such material is licensed. If Company itself uses such material pursuant to Article 15.B.14.a. or e., it will accord appropriate credit to such writer or writers in connection therewith, but in the event of any dispute concerning the appropriateness of such credit the Company's decision shall be final.

The Company shall require that all writing credits as they appear on the screen appear in any published version of the whole or substantial part of a teleplay. The credit on a novel based on a teleplay shall indicate that the novel is based on that teleplay. Such writing credit shall appear on the title page in the same size and style of type used for the writer of the novel. If the name of the writer of the novel appears on the cover, the "Teleplay by" or "Written by" credit shall also appear on the cover in the same size and style of type as the writer of the novel, provided, however, that the writing credit need not so appear if the writer of the teleplay is the writer of the novel. The contract with the publisher shall provide that this credits provision is for the express benefit of the writer and the Guild, and that the publisher will comply with such requirements. But the failure of a publisher to comply with any of such requirements shall not constitute a breach by the Company.

Nothing contained in this subparagraph 21. shall be deemed to affect, limit or modify the provisions of Article 15.B.8. of this Basic Agreement, it being the intent that a "Buyer" executing an assumption agreement under subparagraph 8. shall in all respects be in the same position as the "Seller."

No casual or inadvertent breach of any of the foregoing shall be deemed to constitute a default or breach by the Company of this Basic Agreement.

The Guild agrees to discuss with the Companies its policy regarding issuance of waivers for the inclusion of names of corporate employers in paid advertisements.

22. No commercial or advertising material, audio or visual, shall appear on or above the writer's card either as background or otherwise. The following uses of a sponsor's name, mark, slogan, product or package shall not be deemed to involve an appearance of "commercial or advertising matter:"

a. Such use as a part of or in direct conjunction with the title of the program or program series, (as in *"Dupont Show of The Month," "GE Theatre," "US Steel Hour"*);

b. Such use as an integral part of draperies, sets, or props appearing under a superimposition of credits where such draperies, sets or props were used in the entertainment portion of the program (as in various types of variety, comedy-variety and audience participation programs);

c. The superimposition of a crawl or roller-type credit over a still or moving photograph of a sponsor's product on a set or sets used in the entertainment portion of the program where the use, demonstration, or exhibition of such product was integrated with the entertainment portion of the program;

d.   Such use as a part of the playing or singing of the sponsor's musical theme.

Anything in this subparagraph 22. to the contrary notwithstanding, it is understood and agreed that on any particular program the writer will be given parity of treatment with the director insofar as the appearance of commercial or advertising matter on their respective cards is concerned.

23.   A credit on the screen in the form "Created by" shall be given on each episode of an episodic series or serial to the writer where such writer has separated rights and is entitled to sequel payments for such episode under Article 16.B.2.a. Such credit ("Created by") shall be on a separate card and shall be contiguous to a writing credit, or, if the writer(s) entitled to the "Created by" credit gives (give) written approval, such credit may be placed on a single card immediately following the main cast of actors in the main titles. The Company may contract to give such credit to any person, but such contract shall provide that in the event another writer is determined to be entitled to such credit, as above provided, that writer shall be given the "Created by" credit and the person whose contract provided for such credit may be given a "Developed by" credit or other similar credit. If the contract was executed prior to June 16, 1966 providing for such "Created by" credit, such credit may be given notwithstanding the above provisions. In the event no one is entitled to such separation of rights or in the case of anthology episodes, nothing herein shall prevent, or require, the giving by the Company of a "Created by" credit.

a.   A writer entitled to "Created by" credit shall be given appropriate source material credit in hard cover or paperback book publications arising out of the series. The contract with the publisher shall provide that this provision is for the express benefit of the writer and the Guild, but the failure of a publisher to comply with such requirement shall not constitute a breach by the Company.

b.   With regard to any episodic series or serial in which a writer subject to this Basic Agreement has separated rights, is entitled to sequel payments under Article 16.B.2.a. and receives a "Created by" credit, if the Company desires to grant a "Developed by" credit, such credit may only be given for writing and shall be subject to a Guild arbitration to determine its appropriateness. The guild's decision in this regard shall be final.

c. A "Developed by" or "Developed for Television by" or any like credit may be given only to a person who has contributed to the writing of the program, series or episode involved; provided, however, that any such credit provided for in any contract in existence on March 2, 1981 may be given whether or not it satisfies the requirements of this subparagraph c.

24. A credit entitled "Narration Written by" or Narration by" shall be in accordance with the chart immediately following paragraph 31. of this Television Schedule A.

25. Notice of tentative credits shall be in the following form, which form has been approved by the Guild:

NOTICE OF TENTATIVE WRITING CREDITS

TO: Writer Guild of America, west, Inc., 8955 Beverly Boulevard, West Hollywood, California 90048 [or to Writers Guild of America, East, Inc., 555 West 57th Street, New York, New York 10019] and participating writers.

NAMES OF PARTICIPATING   ADDRESSES
WRITERS
_____   _____
_____   _____

Title of Episode:_____   Production #_____
    (indicate if pilot)

Series Title:_____

Producing Company:_____

Executive Producer:_____

Producer:_____   Assoc. Producer:_____
Director:_____   Story Editor
                                          (or Consultant):_____

Other Production Executives, if Participating Writers:_____

Writing credits on this episode are tentatively determined as follows:

ON SCREEN:

Source material credit ON THIS EPISODE (on separate card, unless otherwise indicated), if any:

Continuing source material or Created By credit APPEARING ON ALL EPISODES OF SERIES (on separate card, unless otherwise indicated), if any:

The above tentative credits will become final unless a protest or request to read the final script is communicated to the undersigned not later than 6:00 p.m. _____.

_____
(Company)

By:_____

26.   a.   Where the Company supplies publicity material to newspapers, trade papers or periodicals prior to the final determination of credits as herein provided, the Company may include such credits for writing as the Company in good faith believes to be a fair and truthful statement of authorship. After notification of the final determination of credits, the Company shall not issue or release any publicity which shall state authorship contrary to such determination. No casual or inadvertent breach of the foregoing shall be deemed to constitute a breach by the Company.

       b.   Where the Company supplies material to newspapers and periodicals, such as *TV Guide*, for listing programs, it will list writing credits if they have theretofore been determined.

27.   When the Company has failed to provide credit on the screen in accordance with final credit determination it shall correct each print before such print is retelecast and place a full-page advertisement in either DAILY VARIETY or the HOLLYWOOD REPORTER specifically crediting the writer. Such remedies shall be in addition to any claim the individual writer may have for damages by reason of such failure to provide proper credit.

28.   Each writing credit card required hereunder shall appear on the screen a minimum of two (2) seconds, or the length of the producer's or director's credit, whichever is shown longer.

29.   If by reason of method of assignment of the writer or other circumstances in connection with a program or series, the provisions of this Schedule A are inappropriate, either the Guild or the Company may raise the question of such inappropriateness and the mutual agreement reached by them with respect to the credit to be given, if any, shall be binding and conclusive on these parties and the writers.

30.   A writer also employed in the additional capacity of a story editor for any episodic series or serial shall receive as story editor on a separate card. Any form or credit for such person other than "story editor," "story consultant," or "story supervisor," cannot be used without Guild approval. Credit for such story editor shall not be deemed to be a credit for screen authorship, within the meaning of Article 8 of this Basic Agreement, or within the scope of paragraphs 1. to 29., both inclusive, of this Television Schedule A, for any purpose whatsoever, including but not limited to the procedure for determining credits for screen authorship. Any person entitled to such credit (whether in the forms stated, or otherwise) under any contract in existence on the effective date of this Agreement may be given such

credit as required by such contract, whether or not it satisfies or is consistent with the provisions of this paragraph 30.

31.   At the Company's election, in the case of the theatrical exhibition of a television motion picture, the word "screenplay" may be substituted for "teleplay," the phrase "screen story" may be substituted for "Television story" and the writing credits on screen, in advertising and publicity may otherwise comply in all respects with the provisions of Theatrical Schedule A.

* * *

TELEVISION SCHEDULE B

STANDARD FORM FREELANCE TELEVISION WRITER'S EMPLOYMENT CONTRACT

Agreement entered into at_____, this_____day of_____19_____, between_____; hereinafter called "Company" and_____, hereinafter called "Writer."

WITNESSETH:

1.   Company hereby employs the Writer to render services in the writing, composition, preparation and revision of the literary material described in subparagraph 2. hereof, hereinafter for convenience referred to as the "work." The Writer accepts such employment and agrees to render his/her services hereunder and devote his/her best talents, efforts and abilities in accordance with the instructions, control and directions of the Company.

2.   **FORM OF WORK:**

(   ) Plot outline (based on_____).

(   ) Story (based on_____).

(   ) Story and teleplay (based on_____).

(   ) Teleplay (based on_____).

(   ) Rewrite (of_____).

(   ) Polish (of_____).

(   ) Other material (described as_____).

3.   **DELIVERY:**

If the Writer has agreed to complete and deliver the work, and/or any changes and revisions, within a certain period or periods of time, then such agreement will be expressed in this paragraph as follows:

4. RIGHT TO OFFSET:

With respect to Writer's warranties and indemnification agreement, the Company and the Writer agree that upon the presentation of any claim or the institution of any action involving a breach of warranty, the party receiving notice thereof will promptly notify the other party in regard thereto. Company agrees that the pendency of any such claim or action shall not relieve the Company of its obligation to pay the Writer any monies due hereunder, and the Company will not have the right to withhold such monies until it has sustained a loss or suffered an adverse judgment of decree by reason of such claim or action.

5. COMPENSATION:

As full compensation for all services to be rendered hereunder, the rights granted to the Company with respect to the work, and the undertakings and agreements assumed by the Writer, and upon condition that the Writer shall fully perform such undertakings and agreements, Company will pay the Writer the following amounts:

a. Compensation for services $_____
b. Advance for television reruns $_____
c. Advance for theatrical use $_____

No amounts may be inserted in b. or c. above unless the amount set forth in a. above is at least twice the applicable minimum compensation set forth in the 1995 WGA Theatrical and Television Basic Agreement for the type of services to be rendered hereunder.

If the assignment is for story and teleplay or teleplay, the following amounts of the compensation set forth in a. above will be paid in accordance with the provisions of Article 13.B. of said Basic Agreement.

(1) $_____ following delivery of story.

(2) $_____ following delivery of first draft teleplay.

(3) $_____ following delivery of final draft teleplay.

In the event Writer receives screen credit on the television motion picture based on the above work and said motion picture is exhibited theatrically, Company shall pay to the Writer the additional sum of $_____ as provided in Article 15.B.13. of the Basic Agreement.

6. MINIMUM BASIC AGREEMENT:

The parties acknowledge that this contract is subject to all of the terms and provisions of the Basic Agreement and to the extent that the terms and provisions of said Basic Agreement are more advantageous to Writer than the terms hereof, the terms of said Basic Agreement shall supersede and replace the less advantageous terms of this agreement. Writer is an employee as defined by said Basic Agreement and Company has the right to control and direct the services to be performed.

7. GUILD MEMBERSHIP:

To the extent that it may be lawful for the Company to require the Writer to do so, Writer agrees to become and/or remain a member of Writers Guild of America in good standing as required by the provisions of said Basic Agreement. If Writer fails or refuses to become or remain a member of said Guild in good standing, as required in the preceding sentence, the Company shall have the right at any time thereafter to terminate this agreement with the Writer.

IN WITNESS WHEREOF, the parties hereto have duly executed this agreement on the day and year first above written.

By_____

     Company

_____

     Writer

(The foregoing Freelance Television Writer's Contract may contain any other provisions acceptable to both Writer and Company and not less favorable to, inconsistent with or violative of any of the terms or provisions of the Basic Agreement above mentioned.)

* * *

(WGA Stationery)

SIDELETTER B

As of August 8, 1968;
Revised as of May 2, 1992;
Revised as of May 2, 1995

Alliance of Motion Picture & Television Producers, Inc.
15503 Ventura Boulevard
Encino, California 91436

Ladies and Gentlemen:

The Guild agrees that the provisions of Article 42 of the WGA-AMPTP Theatrical
and Television Basic Agreement of 1995 shall not apply to member companies
(including future member companies) of the Alliance of Motion Picture &
Television Producers, unless any such company files for bankruptcy or fails to
honor an award rendered in grievance or arbitration which award has been finally
confirmed in court. In either such event, the exemption provided by this letter
shall terminate, effective immediately, as to such company.

Very truly yours,

WRITERS GUILD OF AMERICA, WEST, INC.
on behalf of itself and its affiliate
WRITERS GUILD OF AMERICA, EAST, INC.

By: /s/ Brian Walton
Brian Walton
Executive Director

On behalf of the respective
signatory companies represented by
THE ALLIANCE OF MOTION PICTURE &
TELEVISION PRODUCERS, INC.

By: /s/J. Nicholas Counter III
J. Nicholas Counter III

*   *   *

APPENDIX B

PRODUCTION FOR THE PAY TELEVISION AND THE VIDEO DISC/VIDEO CASSETTE MARKETS

A. Introduction and Scope

This Appendix B is applicable to the employment of writers and the acquisition of literary material for all programs, except as otherwise provided below, produced principally for the pay television and/or video disc/video cassette markets. (The terms "writer" and "literary material" are as defined in Article 1.A. and 1.C. of the MBA or, when applicable, Appendix A.) The provisions of Appendix A which modify the Basic Agreement shall, as to material for programs covered by Appendix A, be deemed part of the Basic Agreement for purposes of this Appendix B. The following types of programs are excluded from the coverage of Appendix B: sporting events, cartoons, industrial and religious programs, other informational programs not covered by the Basic Agreement, commercials, advertising shorts, trailers, and travelogues. Educational and instructional programs are excluded except when produced for the home video disc/video cassette market and, in any event, such programs are excluded when written and performed by the same person. Programs to which this Appendix B are applicable are hereinafter referred to as "covered programs."

B. Definitions

1. The term **"video disc/video cassette,"** as used in this Appendix B, shall mean disc, cassette, cartridge and/or other device serving a similar function which is sold or rented for play on a home-type television screen in the home.

2. The term **"pay television,"** as used in this Appendix B, shall mean exhibition on a home-type television screen by means of telecast, cable, closed circuit, satellite to home or CATV where substantially all licensed systems meet the following tests:

   (a) A separate channel is provided for which the subscriber pays a separate fee (which fee is a substantial charge relative to other charges made to the subscriber) for that channel

        and/or

   (b) The subscriber pays for the program or programs selected (except that a program or programs selected for which only a token charge is made shall not be considered pay television)

        and/or

    (c)   The subscriber pays a fee for an encoded telecast, which fee is a substantial charge relative to other fees paid for encoded telecasts.

The foregoing tests cover those systems which exist in the industry today and are commonly understood in the industry today to be pay television systems.

3.   If a different definition of pay television is negotiated by the Companies with SAG or DGA during the term of this Agreement, Companies will promptly notify the Guild of such definition and the Guild may, upon thirty (30) days written notice, substitute in its entirety such new definition for the pay television definition set forth in paragraph B.2. of this Appendix B.

4.   The terms "film" and "tape" shall be understood as they are commonly understood in the industry today. Should a different method of recordation develop which, in the judgment of either party to this Agreement, differs from both film and tape, such party may notify the other that it wishes to bargain concerning the Recoupable Amount, herein "break amount," for such method of recordation. The parties agree to commence such negotiations within thirty (30) days of receipt of such notice. If no agreement is reached within sixty (60) days after bargaining has commenced, the Guild may upon written notice to Company, instruct its members to refuse to render services with respect to programs using such method of recordation.

C. Initial Compensation

1.   The minimum initial compensation for a writer employed for a covered program, other than for an educational or instructional program, shall be the same as the applicable minimum initial compensation set forth in Article 13.B. or Article 14 or Appendix A for the program category involved. When the program is of a type generally produced for other than prime time network television, the rate for such other type program shall be applicable. Notwithstanding the foregoing provisions of this subparagraph 1., the second paragraph of Article 13.B.7.r. shall not apply to covered programs.

2.   The minimum initial compensation set forth in subparagraph 1. above, or the initial agreed compensation in the case of a covered educational or instructional program for the video disc/video cassette market, shall constitute payment in full for any use in pay television and/or on video disc/video cassettes until the Company's Receipts, as defined in Section D. below, exceed the following break amounts.

    (a) For dramatic programs of a type generally produced for prime time network television:

Program Length	Break Amount 5/2/95 through 5/1/98	
	Film	Tape
15 minutes or less	$ 423,465	$ 338,772
30 minutes or less (more than 15)	846,930	677,544
45 minutes or less (more than 30)	1,270,395	1,016,316
60 minutes or less (more than 45)	1,693,860	1,355,088
90 minutes or less (more than 60)	2,540,790	2,032,632
120 minutes or less (more than 90)	3,387,720	2,710,176
Each additional 30 minutes or portion thereof	846,930	677,544

(b)   For programs other than those covered by (a) above: When the applicable minimum initial compensation for a program differs from the applicable minimum initial compensation for a program of comparable length covered by (a) above, the break amount during the term of this Basic Agreement for a given program shall bear the same relationship to the break amount for a program of the type produced for network prime time of comparable length as the applicable minimum for story and teleplay (or the equivalent) for such program bears to the applicable minimum for story and teleplay for a prime time network program of comparable length. The break amounts for each type of program referred to in this paragraph (b) are computed in accordance with the following formula:

Applicable minimum initial compensation
for story and teleplay (or equivalent) for   Break amount for program
program covered by subparagraph (b)   =   covered by subparagraph (b)
Applicable minimum initial compensation   Break amount for program
by subparagraph (a)   covered by subparagraph (a)

Notwithstanding the foregoing, in no event shall the break amount for a program covered under this subparagraph (b) exceed the break amount applicable to such program which was in effect during the last period of the 1981 Basic Agreement.

(c)   Break amounts for material to which Appendix A applies shall be computed in accordance with the foregoing formula, using one or more of the following rules where applicable:

(1)   Aggregate Minimums

(i)   When an aggregate minimum initial compensation applies (e.g., to comedy-variety programs produced pursuant to a minimum variety show commitment, or to serials for other than prime time broadcast five (5) times per week) the aggregate applicable minimum initial compensation for such programs (prorated where the aggregate applies to more than one program) shall be used to compute the applicable break amount for such program. Said aggregate applicable minimum shall include any additional minimum initial compensation applicable to writing services on such program, viz., for sketches and lyrics.

(ii) If more than one writer is employed on a comedy-variety program broadcast once per week or less which is not subject to a minimum variety show commitment, the break amount shall be computed in the aggregate pursuant to (i) above as though such commitment applied, *i.e.*, shall be increased by fifty percent (50%) for the first additional writer and an additional twenty-five percent (25%) for each writer thereafter.

(2) Discounts. If one or more discounts apply pursuant to any of the provisions of Appendix A to reduce the applicable minimum initial compensation, the applicable break amount shall be reduced by the same percentage(s) as the percentage discount(s) permitted under Appendix A.

(3) Applicable Time Period. Where the Producer has used the "applicable time period" concept pursuant to Article 13 of Appendix A in determining the writer's compensation, the applicable break amount is that which applies to a program length equal to that of the applicable time period.

(d) [Deleted.]

(e) [Deleted.]

(f) In applying the formula in (b) above to covered educational and instructional programs for the video disc/video cassette market, the initial agreed compensation paid shall be utilized.

D. Additional Compensation (Residuals)

In addition to initial compensation, for uses of a covered program in the pay television and/or video disc/video cassette markets, the Company shall pay as additional compensation (hereafter "residuals") to the credited writer(s) an aggregate total of two percent (2%) of the "Company's Receipts" which exceed the applicable break amount. In no event shall the Company be required under the provisions of this Section D. to pay more than a total of two percent (2%) of the "Company's Receipts" to the writers. Such residuals shall be subject to Pension Plan and Health Fund contributions pursuant to Article 17. Company's Receipts consist of:

(1) For pay television, the Company's accountable receipts from the distribution of the program for exhibition according to Article 51.3. (Pay television networks such as HBO and Showtime are not deemed to be distributors for this purpose. However, license or other fees paid to the Company for the right to exhibit the program by such pay television networks shall be included in Company's accountable receipts.)

(2) For the video disc/video cassette market, the fee or other payment actually received by the Company as producer from "net unit sales" as defined below and from the licensing of covered programs for rental.

   (a) The term "disc" as used in this Section shall refer to both video disc and video cassettes. The term "unit" shall refer to the disc or aggregate discs in each package released by the Company for sale or rental. "Net unit sales" shall mean sales of units which are released by the Company or its distributor for sale and are not returned.

   (b) It is recognized that some Companies hereunder may act both as producers and as distributors of disc units in covered sales and/or rentals. In such a case, the payment set forth above shall be based on either (i) the fee or other payment received by the subsidiary, division or other department of the Company which serves as the production branch, as distinguished from the subsidiary, division or other department of the Company which serves as the distribution branch, or (ii) when no separate subsidiary, division, or other department serves as the production branch, a reasonable allocation of the gross receipts of the Company from covered sales and/or rentals attributable solely to fees or other payments which would be made to a production subsidiary, division or other department of the Company if one existed, or would be made to an outside producer. The reasonableness of such allocation in (ii) above, or of the fee or other payment received by the production subsidiary, division, or other department in (i) above, shall be determined by it license fee payments to outside producers for comparable disc units, or in the absence of such practice, by generally prevailing trade practice in the disc industry.

(3) The Company shall have the same rights under this Appendix B as it has in free television to credit or offset against residuals monies paid or payable for profit or other participations or as overscale

compensation. Any monies paid to writer in excess of double minimum which are used to credit or offset against residual monies shall
be specifically identified in the writer's contract as to amount and as
to the specific use (e.g., residuals for pay television or disc, compensation for free television reruns) for which such money is allocated.

E. Distribution Formula

The residuals payable under Section D. hereof shall be remitted by the
Company to the Guild on a quarterly basis according to the provisions of
Article 51.3.f. Said monies shall be distributed by the Guild to the writer(s)
entitled to share in such residuals in accordance with the method set forth in
Article 51.3.e., except that the proportional distribution shall be in the ratio
of two (2) for the teleplay to one (1) for the story.

F. Release in Other Media

1. Free Television – If a covered program is broadcast on Free Television, the Company shall pay to the credited writer(s) for the first such
   broadcast the applicable second run fee under Article 15.B. (or under
   Appendix A, where applicable) for such broadcast, and any subsequent
   broadcasts of such program shall be governed by that rerun formula;
   provided, that with respect to telecasts outside the United States and
   Canada, the foreign telecasting formula in Article 15.B.2. (or in
   Appendix A, where applicable) shall apply in lieu of the forgoing.

2. Theatrical Exhibition – If a covered program is released in theatrical
   exhibition, the Company shall be obligated to pay to the credited
   writer(s) the applicable minimum compensation set forth in Article
   13.A.

3. Basic Cable – If a covered program is licensed for exhibition on
   domestic basic cable (other than as part of domestic free television
   licensing), the Company shall be obligated to pay to the credited
   writer(s) two percent (2%) (plus pension and health contributions) of
   the Company's accountable receipts, in accordance with Article
   51.3.a.(i).

4. Supplemental Markets – If a program produced under these provisions is licensed for exhibition in other Supplemental Markets (such
   as "in-flight"), Company shall pay in accordance with Article 51.

G. Separation of Rights

The provisions of Article 16.B. and, as to programs covered by Appendix A,
the provisions of Appendix A which modify Article 16.B., shall include the
pay television and/or video disc/video cassette market and shall apply to writers
employed under this Appendix B, and said Article 16.B. shall be redrafted

accordingly. (*E.g.*, whether a writer is employed for free television, pay television and/or video disc/video cassette markets, the Company's television rights under 16.B.2. shall include both free and pay television/video disc/video cassette rights and the writer's reserved rights under 16.B.3. shall apply to both free and pay television/video disc/video cassette materials).

It is understood that residual sequel payments are not applicable for exhibition in the pay television and/or video disc/video cassette markets.

The "upset price" for covered programs shall be determined in accordance with the following formula in lieu of the amounts set forth in Article 16.B.5.:

Format	= 4 times minimum
Story	= 3 times minimum
Story and Teleplay	= 3 times minimum
Format, Story and Teleplay	= 3 times the Story and Teleplay minimum
Bible	= 2 times minimum

With respect to a program of ninety (90) minutes or longer, the minimum for purposes of determining the upset price is the applicable ninety (90) minute minimum.

The premium for a pilot as set forth in Article 13.B.7.r. is not part of the minimum for the purpose of calculating the upset price.

H. Other Provisions

1. [Deleted.]

2. In addition to the Articles (as modified) already referred to in this Appendix B, the other Articles of the Basic Agreement (as modified by Appendix A, where applicable) insofar as they refer to television production shall also apply to programs produced under these provisions, provided that throughout the Articles "program" or "motion picture" shall ordinarily be substituted for "film" and "exhibition or release" ordinarily substituted for "broadcast."

I. Use of Excerpts

It is the intent of the parties that excerpts from programs covered by this Appendix B used on free television, pay television, video disc/video cassettes or basic cable shall be paid for in the same manner and to the same extent as is provi ded for free television excerpts under Article 15.B.10. of this Agreement. However, it is recognized that the concepts of "run," "rerun" and "foreign telecast" have no application to the use of excerpts from such programs. Accordingly, except for the provisions of Article 15.B.10.ff., the provisions of Article 15.B.10.a. through i. of this Agreement shall be deemed incorporated herein by reference, making appropriate deletions where the terms "run," "rerun" or "foreign telecast" are used.

APPENDIX C
PROGRAMS MADE FOR BASIC CABLE TELEVISION

1. The term "basic cable" as distinguished from pay television or free television, refers to that type of exhibition which is commonly understood in the industry today to be basic cable exhibition.

2. The rates and other conditions of employment or for the acquisition of literary material from a professional writer applicable to programs made for basic cable shall be as follows:

    a. The following shall apply except with respect to high budget dramatic programs, as defined in subparagraph 2.b. below:

        (1) The Company may elect, with respect to all other programs, including Appendix A programs, to apply the provisions of subparagraph 2.b. to the employment of a writer. Otherwise, either the Guild or Company may notify the other that it wishes to bargain concerning rates and other conditions of employment to be applicable to the employment of writers or the acquisition of literary material for programs of the types heretofore traditionally produced for free television pursuant to any WGA Basic Agreement, produced primarily for the basic cable market. The parties agree to commence such negotiations within thirty (30) days of receipt of such notice. If no agreement is reached within sixty (60) days after bargaining has commenced, the Guild may, upon written notice to Company, instruct its members to refuse to render services with respect to such programs.

        (2) The employment of a writer for such an entertainment program (herein "Program") produced within the metropolitan areas of Los Angeles or New York, or of a writer hired within such areas for a Program to be produced within the United States, shall be subject to: (a) the Guild Shop provisions of this Agreement; (b) Article 17, the Pension Plan and Health Fund provisions of this Agreement; provided that in no event shall the Company be required to make pension and health contributions in an amount greater than would be required if the Program were made for free television; and (c) the requirement that the Company tender a written contract of employment to the writer within ten (10) days following the commencement of his or her employment and the requirement that the Company send to the Guild a copy of any writer's executed contract for employment on a Program within one (1) week after receipt by Company of

such executed contract, until such time as the Guild instructs its members to refuse to render services with respect to such programs produced pursuant to subparagraph 2.a.(1) above; provided, however, that with respect to material written to be part of such a Program, this subparagraph 2.a.(2) shall apply to continuity material only when such material is written to be a part of a Program originally produced for exhibition on basic cable (as distinguished from a program originally produced for exhibition in another medium).

b. With respect to the terms and conditions for the employment of writers and the acquisition of literary material from professional writers (as defined in Article 1.C.1.b.) for "high budget" dramatic programs and other programs to which Company has elected to apply this subparagraph 2.b., Company shall elect whether the provisions of subparagraphs (1), (2) or (3) below shall apply. For purposes of this Appendix C, "high budget" programs shall mean programs the negative costs of which equal or exceed the following amounts:

15 minute program	$ 150,000
30 minute program	285,000
60 minute program	530,000
90 minute program	850,000
120 minute program	1,250,000

(1) Except as otherwise provided herein, all terms and conditions of the 1995 Writers Guild of America Theatrical and Television Basic Agreement and all amendments and modifications thereto, that are applicable to a dramatic program produced for first run syndicated free television and other programs to which Company has elected to apply this subparagraph 2.b. shall apply to such employment or acquisition. If the program is exhibited more than once on the basic cable service for which it was primarily produced, or on any other basic cable service, then residuals shall be paid for each run thereafter as follows (commonly referred to as **"the Sanchez formula"**):

2nd run	14.4% of applicable minimum
3rd run	10.8% of applicable minimum
4th run	9.0% of applicable minimum
5th run	9.0% of applicable minimum
6th run	5.0% of applicable minimum
7th run	3.0% of applicable minimum

8th run	3.0% of applicable minimum
9th run	3.0% of applicable minimum
10th run	3.0% of applicable minimum
11th run	2.0% of applicable minimum
12th run	2.0% of applicable minimum
Each subsequent run	1.0% of applicable minimum

In such event, Company shall pay residuals for the second through fifth runs even if the program is not actually exhibited that many times. The residual payments for the third, fourth and fifth runs shall be made at the same time the residual payment is due for the second run. If the program is thereafter exhibited a third, fourth or fifth time, no additional payment shall be due for these runs. Such prepayment of residuals for the third, fourth or fifth run shall not constitute a violation of Article 15.B.3. of the MBA. Residuals for the sixth run and all runs thereafter will be triggered if, and only if, the program is actually run that many times.

Payment of any of the foregoing residuals shall include full residual payments for the first license agreement in Canada, whether it be for exhibition on a basic cable, pay television or free television service (which may not exceed five (5) years, except that the Guild shall not unreasonably withhold a waiver of the five (5) year limitation in the event of an outright sale, rather than a license of the program).

If the program is exhibited on syndicated free television (except for the first Canadian license, if it is for free television exhibition), residuals shall be paid for each run thereon as follows:

1st run	40.0% of applicable minimum
2nd run	30.0% of applicable minimum
3rd run	25.0% of applicable minimum
4th run	25.0% of applicable minimum
5th run	25.0% of applicable minimum
6th run	15.0% of applicable minimum
7th run	15.0% of applicable minimum
8th run	15.0% of applicable minimum
9th run	10.0% of applicable minimum
10th run	9.7% of applicable minimum
11th run	10.0% of applicable minimum
Each subsequent run	5.0% of applicable minimum

If the program is exhibited on network free television in the United States residuals shall be paid in accordance with the applicable network rerun provisions in Article 15.B.1.b.(2)(a) or (b).

Notwithstanding anything in this Agreement to the contrary, if the program has been exhibited ten (10) or more times on a basic cable service or if the program is part of a series that comprises sixty-six (66) or fewer episodes, and thereafter such program is run on free television, the credited writer(s) shall be paid for such runs pursuant to Article 58, in lieu of any payment that would otherwise be due.

-OR -

(2)   Except as otherwise provided herein, all terms and conditions of the 1995 Writers Guild of America Theatrical and Television Basic Agreement, and all amendments and modifications thereto, that are applicable to a program produced for first run syndicated free television shall apply to such employment or acquisition.

Additional minimum compensation shall be paid to the credited writer(s) in the form of a reuse fee. For dramatic programs, the fee (commonly referred to as **"the Hitchcock formula"**) shall be equal to the difference between the applicable minimum initial compensation due for such program had it been produced for network prime time and the other than network prime time minimum. Twenty-five percent (25%) of such fee shall be paid to the credited story writer(s) and seventy-five percent (75%) to the credited teleplay writer(s). A writer who receives "Written by" credit shall receive one hundred percent (100%) of such fee. For other programs, the fee shall be equal to seventy percent (70%) of the applicable minimum for such program. The reuse fee shall be payable upon initial exhibition of the program on any United States basic cable service or upon initial exhibition under the first Canadian license. Such fee shall cover use of the program for an initial cycle of no more than twelve (12) runs within five (5) years on such basic cable service and use of such program in Canada under the terms of the first license agreement, which may not exceed five (5) years (except that the Guild shall not unreasonably withhold a waiver of the five (5) year limitation in the event of an outright sale, rather than a license, of the program), entered into by the Company with a Canadian broadcast service (which, in this context, may be any free television, pay television or basic cable service). Such fee shall be sent to the Guild's Residuals Department, by check made payable to the writer(s). Such payment may not be made prior to the determination of credit nor later than thirty (30) days after the initial exhibition.

If a program is reused beyond the initial basic cable cycle and/or the initial Canadian television cycle, then such additional reuse shall be treated and paid for in the same manner as reuse of a program made for free television.

Notwithstanding anything in this Agreement to the contrary, if the program has been exhibited ten (10) or more times on a basic cable service or if the program is part of a series that comprises sixty-six (66) or fewer episodes, and thereafter such program is run on free television, the credited writer(s) shall be paid for such runs pursuant to Article 58, in lieu of any payment that would otherwise be due.

-OR-

(3)   In lieu of subparagraphs b.(1) or (2) above, the Company may, at its election, notify the Guild that it wishes to bargain in good faith with respect to an analogous formula to apply to high budget dramatic programs and other programs covered by this subparagraph 2.b. The parties agree to commence such negotiations within thirty (30) days of receipt of such notice. If no agreement is reached within sixty (60) days after such bargaining has commenced, the Guild may, upon written notice to the Company instruct its members to refuse to render services with respect to such programs.

* * *

SIDELETTER TO ARTICLE 15.B.1.b.(2)(c)

As of August 8, 1988
Revised as of May 2, 1992
and May 2,1995

J. Nicholas Counter III	American Broadcasting Companies, Inc.
President	
Alliance of Motion Picture	CBS Inc.
& Television Producers	
15503 Ventura Boulevard	National Broadcasting Company, Inc. and
Encino, California 91436	NBC Studios, Inc.

Re: Waiver re Domestic Free Television Residuals
        for One-Hour Network Prime Time Dramatic Series

Ladies and Gentlemen:

A. Revenues Contracted For: The Writers Guild of America hereby grants a limited waiver from the provisions of Article 15.B.1.b.(2)(c) of the 1995 WGA

MBA, and the comparable provisions of all prior MBAs, to all Companies signatory hereto with regard to residuals payable pursuant thereto ("fixed residual payments") to the credited writer(s) of episodes of one-hour network prime time dramatic series, which series have not been exhibited in syndication prior to March 1, 1988.

Residuals for episodes of such series shall be computed by multiplying the fixed residual amount otherwise due by a ratio, the numerator of which is the revenue contracted for by the distributor, as may be adjusted below, and the denominator of which is six hundred fifty thousand dollars ($650,000.00). As subsequent payments are made for any episode, appropriate payments or credits shall be made to bring earlier residual payments into conformity with any increase or decrease in the multiplier. In no event, however, shall any payment made pursuant to this limited waiver exceed one hundred fifty percent (150%) of the fixed residual payment otherwise due. Similarly, any such payment shall not be less than fifty percent (50%) of the fixed residual payment otherwise due, except in the case of series licensed only in markets representing fewer than one-third of all United States television households.

B. Combination Sales: If a series qualifying hereunder is sold in combination with any other series or other program, the Company shall allocate to each episode of the series qualifying hereunder a fair and reasonable portion of the revenues contracted for and shall include such amount in the numerator referred to above. The Company shall notify the Guild when a series qualifying hereunder is sold in combination with another series or program and in such notice identify the other series or program involved. If the Guild contends that the amounts so allocated were not fair and reasonable, such claim may be determined by submission to arbitration and the arbitrator shall have the authority to determine the fair and reasonable amount to be so allocated.

C. Barter Syndication: If any series qualifying hereunder is syndicated with advertising time withheld by the distributor (*i.e.*, barter syndication), the fair market value of the amount allocated to the "barter" portion of the deal shall be included in the numerator referred to above. The Company shall notify the Guild when a series qualifying hereunder is syndicated in any barter arrangement. If the Guild contends that the amount so allocated does not represent the fair market value of the "barter," such claim may be determined by submission to arbitration and the arbitrator shall have the authority to determine the fair market value to be so allocated.

D. Reporting:

1. The Company shall make the foregoing payments within the time period set forth in Article 15.8.1 .b.(5) and in the manner required by Article 1 5.B.4. Simultaneously with each payment due hereunder, the Company shall submit to the Guild a statement showing

per-episode market-by-market[43] revenue amounts used to compute the multiplier for the episode. In calculating the numerator of each multiplier, tine revenue contracted for by the distributor shall be adjusted by the Company to take into account uncollected revenues, to the extent that such are evidenced by bankruptcy, contract restructuring (including amendments and cancellations), reorganizations or accounts that are more than 270 days delinquent. In its statement to the Guild, the Company shalt notify the Guild of any such adjustment and the basis therefor.

2. If the Company excludes any amounts not collected with respect to contracts with any party whose debts have been discharged or whose contracts have been modified in a bankruptcy or reorganization proceeding, the Company shall notify the Guild of the exclusion, and upon request, shall promptly provide the Guild with copies of court documents, including those which substantiate the discharge, reorganization or contract modification.

3. Upon collection of any revenues previously treated as "uncollected" under this section D., the Company shall add such collected revenues back into the numerator of the multiplier. Any increased amounts shall be due with the next payment otherwise required hereunder, but in no event later than four (4) months from recovery or collection of such revenue by the Company. In its statement to the Guild, the Company shall notify the Guild of the amounts of such a collection and the basis therefor.

4. In any dispute over a decrease in the numerator alleged to have been made under this section D., the burden of proof shall be on the Company to establish that such decrease comports with the terms and conditions hereof.

5. The Company affirms its obligations under Article 1 5.B.5. and Article 53. Upon written request of the Guild, the Company shall promptly send to the Guild copies of those parts of the contracts showing the financial terms relevant to the determination of the accuracy of the payments to be made hereunder.[44] The Company shall also, upon

---

[43] The Guild agrees to maintain such information on a strictly confidential basis. The regular practice required by this Agreement is for the Company to send the Guild the market-by-market information in the statement; however, it is recognized that in certain limited instances, the Company may have business reasons, unrelated to compliance with this Basic Agreement, for believing that the inclusion in the written statement of specific market revenues contracted for, or some of them (as distinguished from the total revenues contracted for), may not be appropriate. In such instances, the Company will meet promptly to provide such figures in a confidential setting, limited to appropriate executives of the Guild and the Company.

[44] The Guild agrees to maintain such information on a strictly confidential basis. It is recognized

request of the Guild, provide the Guild promptly with access to any and all documents or records reasonably necessary to confirm compliance with the foregoing terms and conditions and, thereafter, upon written request of the Guild, the Company shall provide the Guild with copies of such documents and records. If the Company in good faith contends that any of such documents or records are proprietary and/or confidential, the Guild shall in good faith seek to address appropriate Company concerns. The Company may withhold copies pending an agreement with the Guild on how the Guild shall maintain appropriate confidentiality. If such an agreement is not reached, the Company may withhold such documents pending action by an arbitrator.

E. Termination of Waiver: If the Guild desires to terminate this limited waiver, it may, once during the term of this Agreement, so advise the AMPTP, ABC, CBS and NBC not later than June 1 of any year of this Agreement in such event, the parties shall promptly submit the issue of whether the economics of the off-network domestic syndication market for one-hour dramatic programs produced for network prime time have recovered sufficiently to justify the expiration of this limited waiver to a neutral fact-finder for an expeditious determination. The neutral fact-finder, who shall be chosen by mutual agreement of the parties or, absent such agreement of the parties, from a panel of arbitrators of the American Arbitration Association (AAA) in accordance with AAA rules, shall issue his/her findings in writing prior to the commencement of the fall television season.

The parties hereto agree that such written findings constitute an arbitration award for the purpose of proceedings to enforce, modify or vacate an arbitration award in any court of competent jurisdiction.

In the event the neutral fact-finder determines that the syndication market has recovered sufficiently to justify the expiration of the limited waiver, the Guild shall have the option to terminate this limited waiver as to the next fall television season and, in lieu thereof, to reinstate the fixed residual formula, as provided in Article 15.8.1.b.(2)(b). In the event the Guild elects to terminate the waiver, such election shall apply to series premiering on a network in the fall season(s) following the Guild's request for fact-finding.

---

that in certain limited instances the company may have business reasons, unrelated to compliance with this Basic Agreement, for believing that sending copies of financial terms of certain contracts to the Guild may not be appropriate. In such instances, the company may confer with the Guild to explain its concerns. The Guild shall in good faith consider the company's concerns and, if it concurs with the Company, it shall so indicate in writing and the Company shall not be required to send such items.

Very truly yours,

WRITERS GUILD OF AMERICA, WEST, INC.
on behalf of itself and its affiliate
WRITERS GUILD OF AMERICA, EAST, INC.

By: */s/* Brian Walton
Brian Walton
Executive Director, WGAw

ACCEPTED AND AGREED:

The respective signatory companies represented by the

ALLIANCE OF MOTION PICTURE & TELEVISION PRODUCERS, INC.

By: */s/* J. Nicholas Counter III
J. Nicholas Counter III, President

AMERICAN BROADCASTING
COMPANIES, INC.,
a wholly-owned subsidiary of
Capital Cities/ABC, Inc.

By: */s/* Robert Key
Vice President, Labor Contracts

CBS INC.
By: */s/* John McLean
Vice President, Labor Contracts

NATIONAL BROADCASTING
COMPANY, INC., and NBC
STUDIOS, INC.
By: */s/* Bernard Gehan
Vice President, Labor Relations

* * *

ARTICLE 64 — REUSE OF MBA-COVERED MATERIAL IN INTERACTIVE PROGRAMS SIDELETTER REGARDING CREDITS

As of March 28, 1995

The following credit requirements shall apply when motion pictures and/or literary material as described in Article 64 are reused in interactive programs:

(1)   If the reuse is of the whole or a substantial part of a theatrical or television motion picture which can be viewed in a linear fashion and is governed by Article 64.B.1. or 64.D.1., all writing credits[45] of the

---

[45] The WGA reserves its position that the television credits, "Created by," "Developed by" and "Developed for Television by" are "writing credits," as that term is used in the MBA. The Companies reserve their position to the contrary.

motion picture as they appeared on the screen shall appear in the interactive program. If such reuse is of a television motion picture on which a "Created by" credit was required pursuant to the terms of this or any prior MBA, then the "Created by" credit, as it appeared on the screen, also shall appear in the interactive program. It such reuse is of a television motion picture on which a "Developed by" credit was given pursuant to the terms of this or any prior MBA, then the Company shall obligate the licensee (which may include the Company) to accord "Developed by" credit, as it appeared on the screen or in the form "Developed for Television by" in the interactive program.

(2)   If the interactive program includes publication of the script of a theatrical or television motion picture, in whole or in substantial part, or a novelization of any such script, and such reuse is governed by Article 64.C. [literary material], 64.D.1. [combination of motion picture and literary material] or 64.D.2. [combination of excerpts and literary material], all writing credits of such theatrical or television motion picture as they appeared on the screen shall appear in the interactive program. If such publication is of a teleplay on which a "Created by" credit was required pursuant to the terms of this or any prior MBA, then the writer entitled to such credit shall be given appropriate source material credit in interactive program publications arising out of the series. With respect to any novelization based on the screenplay or teleplay, the credits shall indicate that such novelization is based on such screenplay or teleplay. Such writing credit shall appear on the "title page," or on the equivalent thereof, in the same size and style of type used for the writer of the novelization. If the name of the writer of the novelization appears on the "cover," or on the equivalent thereof, the "Screenplay by" or "Teleplay by" or "Written by" credit shall also appear on the "cover," or on the equivalent thereof, in the same size and style of type as the writer of the novelization; provided, however, that the writing credit need not so appear if the writer of the screenplay or teleplay is the writer of the novelization. The contract with the publisher shall provide that this provision is for the express benefit of the writer and the Guild, and that the publisher will comply with such requirements. However, the failure of a publisher to comply with any of such requirements shall not constitute a breach by the Company.

No casual or inadvertent breach of any of the foregoing in this paragraph (2) shall be deemed to constitute a default or a breach by the Company of this Basic Agreement.

(3)   If the reuse is governed by Article 64.6.2. [excerpts], 64.C. [literary material], 64.0.1. [combination of motion picture and literary material]

(and the reuse is not included in paragraphs (1) or (2) above), or 64.0.2. [combination of excerpts and literary material], (and the reuse does not include publication of the script or novelization), then the WGA reserves its position that the credits provisions of the MBA would apply and the Companies reserve their position to the contrary.

(4)   If the reuse is of the whole or a substantial part of a theatrical or television motion picture which can be viewed in a linear fashion and is governed by Article 64.B.1. or 64.D.1., then the WGA reserves its position that the provisions of the MBA governing credits in advertising and publicity also would apply and the Companies reserve their position to the contrary.

(5)   With respect to the instances described above in paragraph (3) only, the WGA and the Companies agree that the issues of whether or not writing credits provisions of the MBA should apply and. if so, in what form and manner the writing credits should be accorded, shall be referred to the Interactive Media Committee. Disputes as to whether credits are required to be accorded in the instances described in paragraph (4) above shall be subject to the Hot Line procedure under Article 48.E, except that if they are not resolved within the time specified, they shall be referred to the Interactive Media Committee, rather than to grievance/arbitration, for resolution. Only disputes under paragraphs (1) and (2) above shall be subject to grievance and/or arbitration under Articles 10, 11 and 12.

(6)   Favored nations. If one or more of the Companies reaches an agreement with any guild, craft, union or labor organization which includes mandatory credit(s) to be accorded on interactive programs, the Company(ies) will notify the WGA of such agreement(s) within five (5) business days and afford the WGA an opportunity to accept the same provision(s) applicable to writer's credits for the reuse of motion pictures and/or literary material governed by Article 64.

*   *   *

MOTION PICTURE AND TELEVISION AGREEMENTS

Form 4

Pilot Teleplay Deal Memo

NETWORK LETTERHEAD

(DATE)

(PRODUCER'S NAME AND ADDRESS)

Gentlemen:

You and we have agreed and do agree as follows respecting the development of a pilot teleplay, television pilot program and/or series of programs in color, on videotape or film, presently titled (TITLE) intended for network broadcast.

Clause 1. PILOT STORY AND TELEPLAY COMMISSION: We have authorized you to commission a one-hour pilot story and teleplay (hereinafter together referred to as the "Basic Property") written by (NAME) (the "Writer") as the basis for the pilot and series. You shall obtain from the Writer the maximum rights permissible for the fees agreed upon between us under the applicable guild agreement. You warrant that you shall have obtained all necessary rights in the Basic Property, and that our use thereof hereunder will not violate the rights of any third party.

Clause 2. COMPENSATION: We shall reimburse you for your direct auditable, out-of-pocket costs incurred pursuant to clause 1 above, but not exceeding $ (AMOUNT) plus applicable Guild Pension and Health and Welfare payments actually made on the story and teleplay, plus the additional sum of $ (AMOUNT) as a bonus for the Writer if we order production of the pilot.

Clause 3. DELIVERY SCHEDULE: (a) Delivery of all materials hereunder shall be made by you pursuant to the following schedule:

(DELIVERY SCHEDULE)

(b) Upon your delivery to us of the first draft story and teleplay, you shall designate a production entity (NAME OF PRODUCTION COMPANY) ("Contractor"), which entity shall be subject to our approval, for the production of a pilot and/or series of programs based on the Basic Property. You shall ensure by the terms of your agreement with Contractor that Contractor shall comply with all of the terms of this agreement and with any agreements you and we might enter into pursuant to Clauses 4 and 5 hereof.

Clause 4. NEGOTIATIONS IN GOOD FAITH: Upon your delivery to us of the first revised story and teleplay you and/or Contractor and we shall negotiate in good faith with respect to the terms and conditions for the production of a pilot and/or series of programs based on the Basic Property. At no time prior to or during a ONE-YEAR (1) period commencing with the delivery to us of the first revised story and teleplay (the "Holding Period") shall you and/or Contractor discuss with any third party the exploitation of the Basic Property or any substantial element thereof in any media in the United States, its territories and possessions.

Clause 5.   FIRST NEGOTIATION/LAST REFUSAL: If by the end of the Holding Period you and/or Contractor and we have not reached agreement as to such terms and conditions, then for SIX (6) months thereafter, you and/or Contractor shall not, without first complying strictly with the following procedure, enter into any agreement with any third party for the Basic Property to be used as the basis for a television program or programs on terms and conditions which are different from or equal to those in the last offer to us by you and/or Contractor during the Holding Period (the "Third Party Offer").

You and/or Contractor shall give us notice of the terms and conditions of the Third Party Offer, and we may enter into an agreement with you and/or Contractor thereon by giving you and/or Contractor notice to such effect within TEN (10) business days following receipt by us of your and/or Contractor's notice. In such agreement, we need accept only those terms and conditions from such Third Party Offer which relate solely to the production and broadcast of one or more programs based on the Basic Property and which are readily reducible to payment of a determinable sum of money.

Clause 6.   REVERSION OF RIGHTS: If you and/or Contractor and we fail to enter into an agreement under both clauses 4 and 5 hereof or if we give you and/or Contractor notice at any time that we do not desire to acquire broadcast rights hereunder in the Basic Property, then all rights we acquired in the Basic Property hereunder shall revert to you and/or Contractor free and clear of any obligation to us, but if you and/or Contractor at any time make, or permit or authorize to be made any disposition or exploitation of the Basic Property or any substantial elements thereof, then we shall be entitled to recoup all monies paid to you and/or Contractor by us hereunder which monies shall be due and payable within THIRTY (30) days thereafter.

Clause 7.   WRITTEN NOTICE: Notices must be in writing, mailed (registered or certified mail), telefaxed or hand-delivered to the party concerned, effective as of the date so sent, at the address specified in the first page hereof, or at such other address as may be subsequently designated in writing by such party.

If the foregoing reflects your agreement, please sign in the space provided below.

Very truly yours,

NETWORK By: _____ Title: _____

ACCEPTED AND AGREED:
PRODUCER By: _____ Title: _____

Form 5

Television Writer Deal Memo

Inter-Office Memo

To:

Subject:

From:

Date:

We have concluded an agreement with _____ Fed. ID#_____ ("Company") furnishing the services of _____ (herein collectively "Artist"), _____, Los Angeles. CA, 90005; Phone:_____; SS#_____ c/o _____ AGENCY,_____, Beverly Hills, CA 90210 in connection with a one-half hour pilot script and proposed one-half hour series entitled "_____" as follows:

I. PILOT

A. <u>Pilot Writing Fee</u>: $_____ / (story, first draft, two [2] sets of revisions and a polish) payable 10% upon commencement of services; 20% upon delivery of story; 40% upon delivery of first draft and 30% upon delivery of the final draft. Additionally, if the pilot script is produced for which Artist received sole "written by" credit thereon, then Artist shall receive an additional $_____.

B. <u>Pilot Services: Fees</u>: If Artist receives sole "written by" credit on the pilot then he shall be "locked" as "Executive Producer" for a fee of $_____(reducible to $_____ if the network requires another "show runner"). If Artist shares "written by" credit, then [PRODUCTION COMPANY] shall have the option to engage Artist's services as set forth above.

II. SERIES

A. <u>Series Sales Bonus</u>: $_____ for sole "created by" credit reducible to $_____ for shared "created by" credit. The series sales bonus is further reducible for an order of less than twelve (12) episodes (excluding the pilot) (but at least six) and increased on a pro-rata basis for a subsequent order up-to a ceiling of $_____(or $_____ for shared "created by" credit). The applicable bonus, if any, shall be paid upon completion of production of the first episode ordered.

B. <u>Series Services Fees</u>: If Artist receives sole "written by" credit on the pilot and renders all Executive Producer services thereon, and thereafter a series is ordered for which Artist receives sole "created by" credit, then Artist will be locked to Executive Produce the series for two years at

$_____$ per episode (reducible to $\$_____$ if the network requires another "show runner") and 5% over the applicable fee for any subsequent year(s). [PRODUCTION COMPANY] shall have two additional subsequent options which shall be exercisable by June 15 of the applicable contract year. In any year Artist's option is not exercised as Executive Producer and the network orders the series, Artist will be locked as "nonexclusive" executive consultant for one additional year for each year of service Artist rendered as Executive Producer if actual services as executive consultant are rendered at $\$_____$ per episode.

C. Contingent Compensation: If Artist receives sole pilot "written by" credit and sole "created by" credit on the series and renders all executive producer services as required by [PRODUCTION COMPANY], then Artist shall receive 10% of 100% of "Adjusted Gross" against 20% of 100% of "Defined Proceeds" vesting as follows: 25% upon production of the pilot for sole "written by" credit (reducible by one-half [½] for shared "written by" credit); 25% upon completion of executive producing services on the pilot; 25% upon completion of executive producing services for the first year of the series; and 25% upon completion of executive producing series for the second year of the series.

D. Royalties: For 12 or more episodes, if Artist receives sole "created by" credit on the series, $\$_____$ reducible $\$_____$ for shared "created by" credit; 100/5 reruns (U.S. domestic territory only).

III. OTHER TERMS:

A. Credit: Writing credit shall be per WGA. If actually produces pilot and during the series, then "Executive Producer" on a separate card, main titles or opening Act I credits, all other matters including position at [PRODUCTION COMPANY's] sole discretion.

B. Publicity: Artist shall not issue or authorize the issuance of any publicity with respect to this agreement, Artist's services or the project with which Artist is involved without first obtaining [PRODUCTION COMPANY's] prior written consent.

C. Sequel/Remakes: 50%/33⅓% of writing fee only reducible by one-half for shared credit.

D. Spinoffs: 50%/25% of the royalties set forth above; reducible by one-half for shared credit.

E. First Look/First Negotiations: During any period(s) when Artist is rendering services for [PRODUCTION COMPANY] (including any period during which [PRODUCTION COMPANY] retains an option for Artist's Services) pursuant to the provisions of this Agreement, [PRODUCTION COMPANY] shall have a right to first look/first negotiation with respect to any concepts, presentations, formats or scripts for television series or movie-for-television ("Concepts") developed, created or owned by Artist. [PRODUCTION COMPANY] shall have 15 business days following presentation of each such Concept, to enter into good faith negotiations with Artist with respect to development thereof. If [PRODUCTION COMPANY] does not enter into negotiations during such period, or is unable to finalize an acceptable deal, Artist shall be free to take such Concept elsewhere but may not render any series producing services in connection therewith (i.e., if Artist receives sole "written by" credit on a third party pilot Script, Artist may render pilot producing Services on said pilot in second position to his services on the Series on a "non-interfering basis"). Artist agrees to keep [PRODUCTION COMPANY] apprised of any third party services at all times.

F.   Standard Terms: All other terms and conditions shall be those standard in [PRODUCTION COMPANY's] agreements of this nature.

Please have an attorney prepare an agreement and send to _____ at the _____ Agency.

Form 6

Television Writer Agreement

Agreement dated as of December 18, 1995 between _____ ("_____") and _____ ("Company") ("Agreement") for the services of _____ ("Artist") in connection with a proposed pilot for a possible series presently entitled "_____" ("Pilot" and "Series", respectively) to be based on Artist's original idea or concept ("Idea").

1. *WRITING SERVICES; FEES*:

Artist shall write a one-half (½) hour Pilot script (including story, first draft teleplay, two (2) sets of revisions and a polish), based upon the Idea. For Artist's writing services, Company shall be entitled to receive _____ ($_____), plus applicable fringe, payable as follows:

   (a)   Ten percent (10%) upon commencement of services;

   (b)   Twenty percent (20%) upon delivery of story;

   (c)   Forty percent (40%) upon delivery of first draft teleplay;

   (d)   Ten percent (10%) upon delivery of first set of revisions;

   (e)   Ten percent (10%) upon delivery of second set of revisions; and

   (f)   Ten percent (10%) upon delivery of the final draft teleplay.

If the Pilot script is produced and Artist receives sole "written by" credit thereon, Company shall receive an additional _____ ($_____).

2. *DELIVERY*:

In accordance with the terms of this Agreement, all writing shall be delivered to _____, to the attention of _____, when reasonably required by _____ to enable _____ to review such writing and meet the network requirements for delivery. Artist shall attend all rehearsals, program conferences and any other meetings at which Artist's presence is required by _____. Except as set forth in paragraph 2 above, Artist shall not render any services in connection with the Pilot which are subject to the WGA Basic Agreement without _____'s prior written consent.

3. *REUSES*:

If _____ produces a Pilot based on Artist's script, Artist shall receive the applicable WGA minimums for all reuses of the Pilot, including, but not limited to, all domestic reruns, theatrical exhibition, foreign telecasting and supplemental market uses.

4. *PILOT*:

If a Pilot is produced based on a script written by Artist and Artist receives sole Pilot "written by" credit thereon, Artist shall be locked to render executive producer services on the Pilot for which Company shall receive the sum of ($_____), reducible to ($_____) should the network require an additional "showrunner" executive producer. If Artist shares "written by" credit, _____ shall have the option to engage Artist as executive producer as set forth herein.

5. *SERIES*:

(a) If a Series (herein defined as an aggregate of twelve (12) or more episodes excluding the Pilot) based on the Pilot is produced and Artist receives sole "created by" Series credit, Company shall receive a Series sales bonus of ($_____), payable upon completion of photography of the first episode. Such bonus shall be reducible to ($_____) for shared "created by" writing credit. Such bonus shall be further reducible on a pro-rata basis if less than twelve (12) episodes of the Series (excluding the Pilot) are produced but no less than six (6) are produced. If additional episodes are produced beyond an initial order of six (6), Company shall be paid on a pro-rata basis for each additional episode produced to a ceiling of twelve (12) episodes.

(b) If a Series of twelve (12) episodes (or more) is produced and Artist receives sole "created by" credit, Company shall be entitled to a royalty of ($_____) per one-half (½) hour episode (excluding the Pilot), reducible to ($_____) if Artist shares "created by" credit with a subsequent writer(s). Said royalty payments shall apply against all WGA minimum sequel, character and so-called adapter's royalty payments. Any royalty shall be paid upon completion of principal photography of each episode. Artist also shall be entitled to receive twenty percent (20%) of the applicable episodic royalty (or WGA minimum, whichever is greater) for each of the first five (5) re-runs of said episodes on "free television" in the U.S. broadcast territory.

(c) If the Series is produced and Artist receives sole Pilot "written by" credit and sole Series "created by" credit and renders executive producer services on the Pilot, Artist shall be locked to render exclusive services as an Executive Producer during the first two (2) years of the Series. Company shall be paid the sum of ($_____) per episode (reducible to ($_____) if the network requires another executive producer/"showrunner") for such services for the first two (2) Series years with a five percent (5%) cumulative annual increases for subsequent season(s). _____ shall have two (2) annual options for Artist's services as Executive Producer following the second year of the Series. Such options must be exercised by June 15 of the applicable contract year. In any year Artist's option is not exercised as executive producer and the network orders the Series, Artist shall be locked as "non-exclusive" executive consultant for one (1) additional year for each year Artist rendered services as Executive Producer, at

($_____) per episode, provided actual services as executive consultant are rendered.

6. *CREDIT*:

Artist shall receive writing credit as determined by the WGA. If Artist renders Executive Producer services on the Pilot and/or Series, Artist shall receive screen credit as "Executive Producer" on a separate card in the main titles or opening Act I credits. Artist shall receive an "Executive Consultant" credit in the end titles for all episodes in which Artist renders such services. All other matters relating to such credit shall be at _____'s sole discretion.

No omission, misplacement, nor casual or inadvertent failure to grant such credit(s) shall be deemed a breach of this Agreement by _____. Company and Artist hereby expressly recognize that in the event of a breach of _____'s obligations under this paragraph, the damage, if any, caused to Company or Artist thereby is not irreparable or otherwise sufficient to entitle Artist or Company to injunctive or other equitable relief and Artist or Company shall only be entitled to money damages. Upon written notification to _____ by Artist or Company of such a breach, _____ agrees to use good faith efforts to prospectively cure such breach on future program materials.

7. *FIRST LOOK*:

During any period(s) when Artist is rendering services for _____ (including any period during which _____ retains an option for Artist's services) pursuant to the provisions of this Agreement, _____ shall have a right of first look/first negotiation with respect to any concepts, presentations, formats or scripts for television series or movies-for-television ("Concept") developed, created or owned by Lender or Artist. _____ shall have fifteen (15) business days following presentation of each such Concept to enter into good faith negotiations with Lender with respect to development thereof. If _____ does not enter into negotiations within such period or the parties are unable to finalize an acceptable deal, Lender and Artist shall be free to take Concept elsewhere, but may not render any series producing services in connection therewith. Artist agrees to keep _____ apprised of any third party services at all times during Artist's term of service hereunder.

8. *CONTINGENT COMPENSATION*:

If the Series is produced and Artist receives sole "written by" credit on the Pilot and sole "created by" series credit and renders all executive producer services as required by _____, Company shall be entitled to receive (_____%) of one hundred percent (100%) of Adjusted Gross against (_____%) of one hundred percent (100%) of Defined Proceeds, vesting as follows: (_____%) upon production of the Pilot for sole "written by" credit (reducible by one-half (½) for shared "written by" credit); (_____%) upon completion of executive producing services on the Pilot; (_____%) upon completion of executive producing services for the first year of the Series; and (_____%) upon completion of executive producing services of the second year of the Series. Adjusted Gross and Defined Proceeds are defined in accordance with _____'s standard definitions attached hereto as Exhibits "A" and "B", respectively, the language of which definitions _____ agrees to negotiate in good faith, except that the distribution fees, interest and overhead shall remain unchanged and with the understanding that such negotiations shall not affect the rights acquired by _____ under this Agreement.

9. *SERIES SPINOFFS/GENERIC AND PLANTED*:

With respect to each spinoff series produced which is derived from the Original Series for which Artist created both the Original Series and the character being spun-off and also for which Artist received sole Series "created by" credit (i.e., a "Generic Spinoff"), Company shall receive fifty percent (50%) of the Episodic Royalty set forth above. Company shall receive twenty-five percent (25%) of the Episodic Royalty set forth above with respect to such spinoff Series if Artist created the Original Series (i.e., Artist received sole "created by" credit thereon), but the character spun-off was created by a third party (i.e., a "Planted Spinoff").

10. *SEQUELS AND REMAKES*:

If Artist receives sole "written by" credit on the Pilot, should _____ produce any sequel(s) or remake(s) of the original Series, _____ shall have the right to go forward with such sequel or remake but first shall offer Artist the opportunity to write such sequel or remake with terms to be negotiated in good faith with a floor of this Agreement. If the parties are unable to reach an agreement _____ shall pay to Artist fifty percent (50%) or thirty-three and one-third percent (33⅓%), respectively, of the writing fee set forth above for each such sequel or remake. Should Artist share "written by" credit on the Pilot, such payments shall be reduced by one-half (½).

11. *WARRANTIES AND REPRESENTATIONS; INDEMNITIES:*

(a) Company represents and warrants (i) that it has a valid subsisting exclusive agreement with Artist under which Artist is obligated to render Artist's services for Company for at least the full term of this Agreement; (ii) Company has the right to enter into this Agreement with _____ to furnish Artist's services and to grant to _____ all of the rights as herein set forth; (iii) that all of the results and proceeds of Artist's services hereunder, including, without limitation, all ideas, suggestions, themes, plots, stories, characterizations, dialogue, titles and other material, whether in writing or not in writing, created or contributed by Artist (hereafter collectively called the "Work") shall be wholly original with Artist or in the public domain and shall not violate the right of privacy or publicity of, or constitute a defamation against, any person or entity; (iv) that the Work will not infringe upon or violate the copyright or common law rights or any other rights of any person or entity; (v) that Company is a corporation duly organized and existing under the laws of Company's state or country of incorporation; (vi) that Company is a bona fide corporate business entity established for a valid business purpose within the meaning of the tax laws of the United States; (vii) that, if Company was incorporated outside of the United States, Company is not engaged in any trade or business in the United States, Company does not have a "permanent establishment" in the United States, as such term is defined in the tax treaty between the United States and the country of incorporation, and Company does not have any agent in the United States who has, or habitually exercises, general authority to negotiate and conclude contracts on behalf of Company; and (viii) that Company shall fulfill all of the responsibilities of the employer of Artist and shall fully discharge all of such obligations as required by any and all laws, regulations, and orders now or hereafter enforced, including but not limited to, those which may require the deduction or withholding of money for taxes or otherwise from any of the sums payable to Artist and the payment of all required fringe payments resulting from Company's employment of Artist (including FICA, SUI, FUTA).

(b) Company and Artist agree to indemnify, defend (if _____ so requests) and hold harmless _____, its parent, affiliates, subsidiaries, successors and assigns and licensees, sponsors and advertisers of works produced pursuant hereto and the officers, directors, employees, representatives and agents of each of the foregoing (collectively "_____ Parties") from and against all damages, claims, costs, and expenses, including reasonable attorneys' fees which the _____ Parties may sustain or incur by reason of any breach or alleged breach of any agreement, representation or warranty made by Company or Artist in this Agreement or arising out of or in any way connected with (a) any claim for compensation by Artist; (b) any failure on Company's part to make or pay the required deductions or withholdings, or both, from the compensation payable to Artist by Company; or (c) any failure on Company's part to discharge the obligations as the employer of Artist. _____ agrees that it will defend and hold Company and Artist harmless from and against all damages, claims, costs and expenses, including reasonable attorneys' fees, suffered and incurred by Company or Artist arising out of material supplied to Company or Artist by _____ for incorporation into the Work or the alteration by _____ of the Work. _____, Company and Artist agree that upon the presentation of any claim or the institution of any action involving a breach of warranty, the party receiving notice thereof will promptly notify the other party with respect thereto. This paragraph 11 is subject to and shall be deemed modified if and only to the extent necessary to conform to the provisions of Article 28 of the Writers Guild of America Basic Agreement ("MBA").

12. *GUILD MEMBERSHIP*:

To the extent that such requirement may be lawful, during the term hereof Artist shall be and remain a member in good standing of the Guild or Union, if any, which covers the services performed by Artist hereunder, and if Artist fails or refuses to meet such requirement, _____ shall have the right at any time thereafter to terminate this Agreement. With regard to the services of Artist as are rendered under the coverage of any collective bargaining agreement, _____ shall be entitled to the maximum rights permitted thereunder for the minimum required payment. If Artist renders services hereunder as a writer also employed in additional capacities pursuant to the MBA, then from the amounts paid to Company hereunder there shall be deemed to be allocated to Artist's services as a writer the appropriate minimum compensation for a writer also employed in additional capacities as specified in the MBA.

13. *FEDERAL COMMUNICATIONS ACT*:

Company acknowledges that Company and Artist are familiar with the requirements of Section 508 of the Federal Communications Act and that Company and Artist are aware that a violation of any of the provisions thereof constitutes a criminal offense. Company and Artist represent and warrant that Company and Artist have not violated, and will not violate, any of the provisions of such Section and that Company and Artist have not done, and will not do, any act which would require disclosure pursuant to such Section.

14. *PUBLICITY*:

Company grants to _____ the perpetual right to use and license others to use Artist's name, photographs, likeness and biography in marketing, advertising, publishing or otherwise exploiting the Work or any portion thereof in any medium including, without limitation, any television program produced from or utilizing the Work and any television series of which such program may be a part. _____ may not use Artist's name, likeness or biography in the form of a direct product or service endorsement. Company and Artist shall not issue or authorize the issuance of any publicity with respect to the services to be rendered hereunder and other matters referred to herein without first obtaining _____'s written consent. Notwithstanding the foregoing, Artist may make incidental reference to Artist's services hereunder, in interviews or similar situations, provided that such reference is not derogatory and the subject matter thereof is not considered by _____ to be confidential in nature.

15. *CONTROLS*:

_____ shall have all final business, financial and creative controls.

16. *PAY OR PLAY*:

Nothing contained in this Agreement shall require _____ to utilize the services of Artist or to produce or broadcast any television program or to make any use whatsoever of the results and proceeds of Artist's services. _____ shall have the absolute right to terminate Artist's services at any time, and in such event or in the event that _____ elects not to use Artist's services pursuant to this paragraph, _____ shall have fully discharged its obligations hereunder by paying Company the compensation then vested and due hereunder. _____ shall have no liability for any other claim or claims of any nature, including, without limiting the generality of the foregoing, consequential or special damages as a result of _____'s exercise of its rights pursuant to this paragraph.

17. *NOTICES*:

All notices which _____ is required or may desire to serve upon Company or Artist in connection with this Agreement may be served by delivery to Company personally, in writing or orally, or by sending such notice to Company by mail, telex, cable or electronic facsimile at: _____

or such other address as Company may hereafter designate in writing. All notices which Company or Artist may desire to serve upon _____ may be served by sending such notice to _____ by mail, telex, cable or electronic facsimile, at: _____

or at such other address as _____ may hereafter designate in writing. The date of mailing of any such notice or the date such notice is sent by telex, cable or electronic facsimile, as the case may be, shall be deemed the date of the service of such notice. If the date by which any such notice is to be made occurs on a Saturday, Sunday, national holiday or a day on which the business operations of the party serving the notice are not open for a full business day ("Closed Day"), then such date shall be extended without notice until the end of business on the first day thereafter which is not a Saturday, Sunday, national holiday or Closed Day.

18. *IMMIGRATION REFORM AND CONTROL ACT*:

As a condition of Company's engagement hereunder, if requested, Company and Artist will furnish to _____ all documentation that will satisfy the requirements of the IMMIGRATION REFORM AND CONTROL ACT OF 1986. If Company or Artist fails to provide the required documentation within the prescribed time limits, this Agreement and all contractual obligations hereunder are subject to termination upon notice from _____.

19. *GRANT OF RIGHTS:*

(a) Company and Artist agree that the Work is and shall be deemed to be a work made for hire for _____ within the scope of Artist's employment hereunder. If for any reason it is determined that the Work is not a work prepared by Artist within the scope of employment, then Company and Artist agree that the Work is and shall be deemed to be a work made for hire for _____, specially ordered or commissioned for use as a part of a motion picture or other audiovisual work and (subject to the provisions of the MBA) that _____ is and shall be considered the author and, at all stages, the sole and exclusive owner of the Work and all right, title and interest therein (the "Rights"). The Rights shall include without limitation all copyrights, neighboring rights, trademarks and any and all other ownership and exploitation rights now or hereafter recognized in all territories and jurisdictions throughout the universe in perpetuity in all media, markets and languages and in any manner now known or hereafter devised. If under any applicable law the fact that the Work is a work made for hire is not effective to place authorship and ownership of the Work and all rights therein in _____, then to the fullest extent allowable and for the full term of protection accorded to _____ or Artist under such applicable law, Company and Artist hereby assign and transfer to _____ the Rights and, in connection therewith, all right, title and interest of Company and Artist in all projects and matters which embody all or part of the Work.

(b) Company and Artist hereby grant _____ the right to add to, take from, translate, or otherwise modify the Work including the title or titles thereof, in any manner _____ may in its discretion determine. To the fullest extent allowable under any applicable law, Company and Artist hereby irrevocably waive or assign to _____ Artist's so-called "moral rights" or "*droit moral*". Company and Artist expressly acknowledge that many parties will contribute to the projects and matters that will embody all or part of the Work. Accordingly, if under any applicable law the above waiver or assignment by Company or Artist of "moral rights" or "*droit moral*" is not effective, then Company and Artist agree to exercise such rights in a manner which recognizes the contribution of and will not have a material adverse effect upon such other parties.

(c) _____ shall have the maximum rights, benefits and privileges permitted by all collective bargaining agreements applicable to the services rendered by Artist hereunder. If Artist is or shall become entitled to Separation of Rights in the Work or any portion thereof, then Artist and Company grant to _____ the reserved theatrical, publication and merchandising rights in and to the Work or such portion thereof, subject to payment to Artist of the minimum compensation specified in the MBA; provided, however, if _____ shall acquire Separation of Rights in the Work or such portion thereof pursuant to a separate so-called "upset price agreement", then _____ shall not be obligated to compensate Artist pursuant to the foregoing.

(d) Without limiting the foregoing, Company hereby grants to _____ all rights which it may have in and to the Work as Artist's general employer. _____ shall be entitled to any investment tax credit, deduction and other credits or benefits in connection with all projects and matters which embody all or part of the Work. Company and Artist will upon request execute, acknowledge and deliver to _____ all documents which _____ may deem necessary to evidence and effectuate any of _____'s rights under this Agreement and Company and Artist hereby irrevocably appoint _____ as Company's and Artist's attorney-in-fact with full authority to execute, verify, acknowledge and deliver any such instruments which Company or Artist shall fail or refuse to execute, verify, acknowledge or deliver. This appointment shall be a power coupled with an interest.

(e) All rights granted and agreed to be granted to _____ hereunder shall be irrevocably vested in _____ and shall not be subject to recission by Company or Artist for any cause whatsoever. The termination, suspension or expiration of this Agreement for any reason whatsoever shall not affect _____'s ownership of the Work or projects or matters which embody all or part of the Work, notwithstanding any other provision contained within this Agreement.

20. *SUSPENSION/TERMINATION*:

_____ shall have the right to suspend the running of time and Company's compensation under this Agreement or terminate this Agreement, or both, in the event that: (a) Artist shall be disabled from performing hereunder by reason of Artist's illness or other incapacity; or (b) _____'s normal business operations are materially hampered, interrupted or interfered with by reason of an event of force majeure or by virtue of any disruptive event which is beyond _____'s control or a labor dispute, strike or lockout ("Producer Disability"), or (c) Artist shall at any time fail or refuse to perform or comply with any of Artist's material obligations or required services hereunder, which failure or refusal, if curable, is not cured within a reasonable time after notification of its occurrence. _____ may exercise said right of termination at any time during any suspension hereof. _____ may by notice to Company withdraw any suspension, in which event Artist shall resume services hereunder on the date specified in said notice. _____ shall have the right (exercisable at any time) to extend the term of this Agreement (and postpone option periods and related option exercise dates) for a period equal to all or any part of any suspension, or _____ may reduce the term of this Agreement by a period of time equal to the aggregate length of all periods of suspension or any part thereof. If a suspension due to a "Producer Disability" (other than a suspension arising out of a labor dispute) shall exceed eight (8) weeks then Company shall thereafter have the right to terminate this Agreement by written notice to _____; provided however that _____ may reestablish the operation of this Agreement by recommencing payments to Company within one (1) week of _____'s receipt of said written notice from Company and the operation hereof if so reestablished shall not thereafter be suspended because of the same Producer Disability. If

Artist or Company claims that Artist is disabled from performing by reason of Artist's illness or incapacity, then _____ may have Artist examined by a physician of _____'s choice, in which event a physician designated by Artist may also be present at Artist's expense. If this Agreement is terminated pursuant to any of the provisions of this paragraph, _____ shall be released from and relieved of all further obligations and liabilities to Company and Artist, other than _____'s obligation to pay Company (subject to _____'s rights under this Agreement and at law) such compensation, if any, as may be due and payable to Company hereunder at the time of such termination.

21. *GENERAL PROVISIONS*:

(a) No waiver by any party hereto of any failure of the other party to fulfill any term of this Agreement shall be deemed to be a waiver of any preceding or succeeding failure to fulfill the same or other term or terms.

(b) Neither the termination nor expiration of this Agreement shall relieve Company, Artist or _____ of their respective obligations pursuant to any warranty or representation made hereunder.

(c) This Agreement constitutes the entire understanding between Company and _____ concerning the subject matter hereof, supersedes all prior written or oral agreements pertaining hereto and cannot be modified, except by an instrument in writing signed by Artist, Company and _____.

(d) _____ may assign this Agreement or any of its rights hereunder to any third party and this Agreement shall inure to the benefit of _____, its successors and assigns. In the event of any such assignment, _____ shall remain secondarily liable to Company for its obligations hereunder unless such assignment is to a major supplier of television motion pictures, a major distributor or syndicator or any financially responsible party that assumes _____'s executory obligations in writing. Neither Company nor Artist may assign this Agreement.

(e) This Agreement shall be construed and enforced in accordance with the law of the State of California applicable to contracts negotiated, executed and wholly performed within the State of California. The venue for any action or proceeding arising from or based upon this Agreement shall be the appropriate state and federal courts located in the County of Los Angeles in the State of California. Accordingly, Company and _____ agree that any such action or proceeding shall be commenced in and determined by those courts.

(f) _____'s rights and remedies shall be cumulative, and the exercise by _____ of one or more of such rights or remedies shall not preclude _____'s exercise of any other right or remedy under this Agreement, at law, or in equity.

(g) The headings contained herein are for reference only and are not intended to influence the interpretation of any provision.

(h) This Agreement may be executed in one or more counterparts, all of which together shall constitute one and the same instrument.

AGREED TO AND ACCEPTED:

By: _____

Title: _____

Dated: _____

The undersigned, hereby acknowledge that Artists have read and are familiar with each and every term and provision of the above agreement. The undersigned acknowledge that the agreement is of substantial benefit to Artists and in consideration of, and as an inducement to, _____ entering into the agreement, the undersigned hereby agree to perform the services for _____ as specified in the agreement. The undersigned further agree to look solely to _____ Productions, Inc. for the payment of any and all compensation due for the services rendered by the undersigned under the above agreement. Furthermore, the undersigned acknowledge that _____ would not have entered into the agreement without this endorsement and approval.

AGREED TO AND ACCEPTED:

_____

_____

Date of Execution _____

_____

TELEVISION PRODUCTION COMPANY

By: _____

Its Vice President

Exhibit "A"

ADJUSTED GROSS DEFINITION

Exhibit to agreement between _____ Television Production, a Division of _____ Entertainment Company ("_____") and ("Participant") dated December 18, 1995 ("Agreement") with respect to the television program or programs now entitled "_____"(herein referred to, individually or collectively as the context of the Agreement may require, as the "Program").

I. *DEFINITIONS*:

A. "Adjusted Gross" means the excess, if any, remaining after deducting from Gross Receipts the aggregate of the following in the following order of priority: An amount equal to ten percent (10%) of all Gross Receipts as a sales overhead fee, Distribution Expenses, Production Costs, and interest thereon, all contingent deferments and other contingent amounts approved by _____ which are not advanced or guaranteed. If, pursuant to the Agreement, Participant receives advances of Participant's share of Adjusted Gross, such advances shall be applied against and in reduction of Participant's share of Adjusted Gross.

B. "Gross Receipts" means all money received by _____ as consideration for the right to broadcast, exhibit or distribute the Program in any manner; barter revenue, net of agency commission; and all money recovered in litigation relating to any such rights but not including: (i) refunds, credits, discounts and adjustments; (ii) advance payments which have not been earned, unless they are non-returnable advances; and (iii) money held as deposits and subject to a refund.

1. If the Program is licensed or otherwise distributed in the Videogram market (*e.g.*, videocassettes, videodiscs and similar audio-visual devices) then there shall be included in Gross Receipts an amount equal to twenty percent (20%) of the gross wholesale rental income therefrom and gross wholesale sales income therefrom, less a reasonable allowance for returns.

2. There shall also be included in Gross Receipts a sum equal to one hundred percent (100%) of "_____'s share" of mechanical reproduction and performance fees and all other royalties, fees or income received in United States currency by _____ with respect to music and lyrics written specifically for and synchronized in the Program, to the extent _____ is vested with rights therein and in the receipts therefrom, and provided Participant is not entitled to receive composers' or lyricists' royalties with respect to such music and lyrics. "_____'s share" of mechanical reproduction and performance fees and all other fees,

royalties or income shall be the full amount paid under licenses, less the composers' share thereof and less an administration fee of twenty-five percent (25%). No distribution fees shall be charged on amounts included in Gross Receipts pursuant hereto. _____ will also include in Gross Receipts, without Distribution Fees, an amount equal to fifty percent (50%) of all gross license fees received by the licensor from Merchandising, less royalties and participations payable to third parties.

3. Gross Receipts are _____'s sole and exclusive property, and are not trust funds or otherwise held by _____ for Participant's benefit. _____'s obligations to make payments to Participant is that of a debtor only. Participant shall not own any interest in the Program, Gross Receipts, or Adjusted Gross or have any lien or other claim thereon.

C. "Distribution Expenses" means all costs and expenses incurred by _____ in connection with the distribution, advertising and exploitation of the Program or which are customarily treated as distribution expenses in the television industry, specifically including, but not limited to, the following:

1. Print costs, which includes the cost of release prints, dubbed negatives, soundtracks, tapes, cartridges, cassettes, film-to-tape transfers, and any and all other duplicating material and facilities, together with reels, cans, containers, and the costs of inspecting, repairing, and renovating, packing, storing, shipping and insuring the Program.

2. All costs of advertising, publicizing, exploiting and promoting the Program.

3. All costs of accommodating the Program for various distribution uses, including retitling, removing commercial material, dubbing for foreign distribution, theatrical distribution or otherwise altering or editing the Program.

4. All taxes (however denominated) assessed upon the negatives, duplicate negatives, prints, tapes or other materials relating to the Program, or upon the use or distribution thereof, or upon revenues derived therefrom or the remittance thereof; all sums paid or accrued on account of duties, customs and imposts, costs of acquiring permits, "contingents", and any similar authority to secure the entry, licensing, televising or other use of the Program in any country. The deductible amount of any sums referred to herein shall not be affected by the manner in which the same are treated by _____ in its own income, franchise, excess profits or other tax returns.

5. All royalties and similar payments to manufacturers of equipment, cartridges, cassettes and the like which are not included in Production Costs; all payments (including fringe benefits and payroll taxes) pursuant

to collective bargaining agreements or other agreements by reason of any exhibition of the Program or the exercise of any rights therein; and all agency fees and commissions payable by _____.

6. All costs and expenses resulting from claims and lawsuits involving the Program or any element thereof, including, but not limited to, the underlying rights therein, and protection therefrom, including errors and omissions insurance premiums, costs of copyright search and registration and investigation and defense. To the extent that any such claim or lawsuit is Participant's responsibility, the cost thereof shall be borne entirely by Participant and in such event shall not be deducted under this sub-paragraph.

7. All costs of collecting Gross Receipts and transmitting the same to the United States, including attorneys' fees, auditing and checking costs, and costs of contesting taxes, charges and other expenses. Such costs shall also include fees and charges incurred by efforts to prevent unauthorized exhibitions of the Program and collecting damages for copyright or other infringements as well as any fees, assessments, dues or other amounts payable to any trade association (such as, for example, the AMPTP) concerned with such matters on an industry basis, pro-rated on a reasonable basis to the Program.

D. "Production Costs" means the aggregate of all direct costs incurred by _____ for or in connection with the production of the Program, calculated according to the standard accounting practices now or hereafter employed by _____ for programs owned, financed, or distributed by _____. Direct costs shall include, without limitation, all items customarily reflected on _____'s production budget, whether such items are furnished by _____ or others. Production Costs shall also include: (i) a charge for _____'s overhead costs computed at fifteen percent (15%) of the Production Costs, exclusive of interest, and (ii) an executive supervisory fee of Fifty Thousand Dollars ($50,000) for each one (1) hour of length of each Program produced (ratably adjusted if more or less than one (1) hour is produced). Interest will be charged on the Production Costs at a rate which is one and one-half percent (1-1/2%) per annum above the prime commercial rate of First National Bank of Boston from time to time in effect. Such interest shall be recouped before principal. Should _____ advance or guarantee any portion of Participant's or any third party's share of the Adjusted Gross or contingent deferments, interest and overhead on the amount so advanced or guaranteed shall be included in Production Costs and the principal amount advanced or guaranteed to third parties shall be also included in Production Costs hereunder until such time as it is recovered from the share of Adjusted Gross or contingent deferments against which it applies.

E.   "_____" includes _____, _____, and _____. The term shall not include: any other person, firm, or corporation distributing the Program or exploiting subsidiary rights therein; exhibitors or others who may actually exhibit the Program to the public; radio or television broadcasters; cable operators; manufacturers, wholesalers, or retailers of videograms; book, magazine or music publishers; phonograph record producers or distributors; and manufacturers, distributors, wholesalers, retailers or operators of any type of merchandise, goods, services or theme park or other attractions, whether or not any of the foregoing are affiliated with _____.

F.   "United States" means the United States, its territories and possessions and Bermuda, but excluding Spanish-speaking Puerto Rico and the Canal Zone.

G.   "Merchandising" means licensing the use of the trademarks, trade names, service marks and copyrights in connection with the manufacture, distribution and sale of articles of merchandise involving characters or other elements which make reference to or are based upon the Program; but shall not include phonograph records, tapes, discs, printed publications of literary material, music or lyrics.

II. *ACCOUNTINGS AND PAYMENTS*:

A.   Accounting Unit. The Program shall be included in a single accounting unit for the determination of Adjusted Gross. Losses incurred with respect to any accounting period shall be carried forward and applied against subsequent Adjusted Gross, and also carried back to apply against Adjusted Gross in a prior accounting period. Gross Receipts from all sources of income shall be accounted for together so that a deficit incurred with respect to a given source may be offset against Adjusted Gross derived from another source. Should _____ make any overpayments to Participant for any reason, _____ shall have the right to deduct and retain an amount equal to any such overpayment from any sums that may thereafter become due or payable by _____ to the Participant under this or any other contract for _____'s own account, or may demand repayment from the Participant, in which event the Participant agrees to pay the same upon demand.

B.   Accounting Statements. _____ will render to Participant summary statements showing the computation of Adjusted Gross, if any, hereunder in accordance with its established accounting procedures, as such may be modified from time to time. If the Program is produced for initial broadcast on a U.S. national television network, then the initial statement shall be rendered after the close of the calendar quarter in which occurs the end of the broadcast year in which the Program is first exhibited; or if the

Program is produced for other than on a U.S. national television network, then the initial statement shall be rendered after the end of the fiscal quarter in which Gross Receipts are first received. Such quarterly statements shall continue until one year after the first-run broadcast of the last episode of the Program. Thereafter, such statements will be rendered at least annually after the end of the respective fiscal years, except that quarterly statements shall be rendered for two years commencing when and if the Program goes into syndication in the United States. No statements need be rendered for periods in which no Gross Receipts are generated. If _____ incurs any costs or receives any receipts in respect of matters pertaining to the Program together with other matters, a portion of such costs or receipts shall be allocated to the Program in accordance with _____'s usual and customary accounting procedures. If _____ reasonably anticipates retroactive wage adjustments, guild residuals, uninsured claims or other reasonably anticipated costs, expenses, or losses relating to the Program, which, if and when incurred, would be properly deductible hereunder, _____ may set up appropriate reserves therefor. Each statement shall be deemed final and conclusive unless an objection is made in writing, stating the basis thereof, and delivered to _____ within twenty-four (24) months from the rendition of such statement. Any such objection shall be deemed waived unless Participant initiates an action with respect thereto within six (6) months from the date such objection is sent. As a courtesy to Participant, _____ may include cumulative figures in any earnings or other statement, in which event the time within which Participant may commence any audit or make any objection with respect to a given statement shall not be extended as a result thereof.

C.   Payments. _____ shall pay all money due Participant pursuant to any such statement concurrently with the rendering of such statement, subject to all laws and regulations requiring the withholding of taxes. However, if _____ shall have received any attachments, garnishments, orders to withhold, notices of assignment, or conflicting claims to any money payable to Participant hereunder, or shall be aware of any facts which may result therein, _____ may withhold payment to Participant in whole or in part until such matters are resolved to _____'s satisfaction. No receipts shall be included in Gross Receipts or any statements hereunder unless and until such sums shall have been received by _____ in U.S. dollars in the United States, or used by _____, in which event they shall be included at the official or unofficial rate of exchange (as _____ may elect) prevailing at time of use. As to foreign revenues not included in statements, as aforesaid, _____ shall, at the request and expense of Participant (subject to all limitations affecting such transactions) deposit into a bank designated by Participant in the country involved, or pay to any other party designated by Participant in such country, such part thereof as would have been payable to Participant hereunder. Such deposits or payments to or for Participant shall constitute due remittance to Participant, and _____ shall have no further interest therein or responsibility therefor. In no event shall _____ be obligated to apply receipts not actually received by _____ in U.S. dollars in the United States to the recoupment of any cost deductible by _____ hereunder which was incurred in U.S. dollars.

D. Examination of Books. Participant may cause _____'s books and records of account relating to the Programs to be examined at Participant's expense, to the extent that they have not become incontestable, by a firm of certified public accountants who regularly audit companies in the motion picture and television business, subject to _____'s right of approval, to be exercised reasonably. _____ preapproves Sills & Adelman; Gelfand, Rennert & Feldman; Breslauer, Jacobson, Rutman & Sherman; Nigro, Karlin & Segal; and Phil Hacker & Co. Such examination may be conducted no more than once each calendar year during normal business hours in such a manner as not to interfere with the normal conduct of _____'s business and each such examination shall relate only to transactions concerning the Program occurring since the last preceding inspection, if any, or during the preceding twenty-four (24) months, whichever is shorter. No examination shall continue beyond thirty (30) days from its inception.

E. Commingling Funds. Any Gross Receipts, Adjusted Gross, working capital, reserve funds, deferred payments or other sums received or held by _____ may be commingled with _____'s general fund and Participant shall not have any right to interest therein nor any right to participate in any profit or other income derived by _____ from use of the sums so received or held.

III. *OBLIGATION TO EXPLOIT:*

Nothing shall be deemed to obligate _____ to distribute, exhibit or otherwise exploit the Program. _____ may do so or refrain therefrom as it may decide in its own absolute discretion, and if it elects to distribute, exhibit or otherwise exploit the Program the manner in which it does so shall not subject it to any liability to Participant. _____ makes no representation or warranty as to the amount of Adjusted Gross or that any Adjusted Gross will be realized.

IV. *MISCELLANEOUS:*

A. Participant shall have the right to sell, assign, transfer or hypothecate all or any part of its interest, if any, in and to the Program and all or any part of the monies which are or may become payable to Participant hereunder; provided that any such assignment shall be subject to all pertinent laws, governmental regulations and the rights of _____ hereunder. If at any time more than three (3) parties shall be entitled to receive payments which, under the terms hereof, are to be paid to or for the account of Participant, _____ may, at its option, require that all such parties execute and deliver an agreement in _____'s usual form appointing a disbursing agent for all such parties.

B. In the event Participant shall propose to sell, assign or transfer all or any part of its interest, if any, in and to the Program, or all or any part of the monies which are or may become payable to Participant hereunder, other than by way of a bona fide merger, consolidation, third party acquisition of Participant, bona fide gift, bequest or devise, _____ shall have a right of first refusal to acquire the same, which right _____ may exercise within ten (10) days after receipt of written notice from Participant specifying the prices and other terms and conditions upon which Participant proposes to make such sale, transfer or assignment. Should _____ fail to exercise such right of first refusal, then Participant shall not sell, transfer or assign such interest or monies or any part thereof to any third party upon terms and conditions more favorable to such third party than those set forth in said written notice without again giving _____ the opportunity to exercise said right of first refusal in accordance with the foregoing procedure.

Exhibit "B"

DEFINED PROCEEDS DEFINITION

Exhibit to agreement between _____ ("_____") and ("Participant") dated _____ ("Agreement") with respect to the television program or programs now entitled "_____" (herein referred to, individually or collectively as the context of the Agreement may require, as the "Program").

II. *DEFINITIONS*:

A. "Defined Proceeds" means the excess, if any, remaining after deducting from Gross Receipts the aggregate of the following in the following order of priority: Distribution Fees, Distribution Expenses, Production Costs, and interest thereon, all contingent deferments and other contingent amounts approved by _____ which are not advanced or guaranteed. If, pursuant to the Agreement, Participant receives advances of Participant's share of Defined Proceeds, such advances shall be applied against and in reduction of Participant's share of Defined Proceeds.

B. "Gross Receipts" means all money received by _____ as consideration for the right to broadcast, exhibit or distribute the Program in any manner; barter revenue, net of agency commission; and all money recovered in litigation relating to any such rights but not including: (i) refunds, credits, discounts and adjustments; (ii) advance payments which have not been earned, unless they are non-returnable advances; and (iii) money held as deposits and subject to a refund.

1. If the Program is licensed or otherwise distributed in the Videogram market (*e.g.*, videocassettes, videodiscs and similar audio-visual devices) then there shall be included in Gross Receipts an amount equal to twenty percent (20%) of the gross wholesale rental income therefrom and gross wholesale sales income therefrom, less a reasonable allowance for returns.

2. There shall also be included in Gross Receipts a sum equal to one hundred percent (100%) of "_____'s share" of mechanical reproduction and performance fees and all other royalties, fees or income received in United States currency by _____ with respect to music and lyrics written specifically for and synchronized in the Program, to the extent _____ is vested with rights therein and in the receipts therefrom, and provided Participant is not entitled to receive composers' or lyricists' royalties with respect to such music and lyrics. "_____'s share" of mechanical reproduction and performance fees and all other fees, royalties or income shall be the full amount paid under licenses, less the composers' share thereof and less an administration fee of twenty five percent (25%). No distribution fees shall be charged on amounts

included in Gross Receipts pursuant hereto. _____ will also include in Gross Receipts, without Distribution Fees, an amount equal to fifty percent (50%) of all gross license fees received by the licensor from Merchandising, less royalties and participations payable to third parties.

3. Gross Receipts are _____'s sole and exclusive property, and are not trust funds or otherwise held by _____ for Participant's benefit. _____'s obligations to make payments to Participant is that of a debtor only. Participant shall not own any interest in the Program, Gross Receipts, or Defined Proceeds or have any lien or other claim thereon.

C. "Distribution Fees" means the following percentage of Gross Receipts:

1. Ten percent (10%) for licenses to the ABC, CBS or NBC television network authorizing the initial broadcast of the Program, including repeats thereunder, in prime time;

2. Twenty percent (20%) for licenses to the ABC, CBS or NBC television network, other than these referred to in subparagraph 1 above, including, but not limited to, any non-prime time stripping of the Program;

3. Forty percent (40%) for all licenses to telecast the Program in the United States, other than those referred to in subparagraphs 1 and 2 above;

4. Thirty percent (30%) for all licenses to telecast the Program on the entire CBC or CTV networks in Canada.

5. Forty-five percent (45%) for all licenses to telecast the Program outside of the United States, other than those referred to in paragraph 4 above.

6. Thirty percent (30%) from Videogram exploitation of the Program in the United States.

7. Forty percent (40%) from Videogram exploitation of the Program outside of the United States.

8. Forty percent (40%) for any other uses of the Program or the material contained therein whether in the United States or elsewhere.

D. "Distribution Expenses" means all costs and expenses incurred by _____ in connection with the distribution, advertising and exploitation of the Program or which are customarily treated as distribution expenses in the television industry, specifically including, but not limited to, the following:

1. Print costs, which includes the cost of release prints, dubbed negatives, soundtracks, tapes, cartridges, cassettes, film-to-tape transfers, and any and all other duplicating material and facilities, together with reels, cans, containers, and the costs of inspecting, repairing, and renovating, packing, storing, shipping and insuring the Program.

2. All costs of advertising, publicizing, exploiting and promoting the Program.

3. All costs of accommodating the Program for various distribution uses, including retitling, removing commercial material, dubbing for foreign distribution, theatrical distribution or otherwise altering or editing the Program.

4. All taxes (however denominated) assessed upon the negatives, duplicate negatives, prints, tapes or other materials relating to the Program, or upon the use or distribution thereof, or upon revenues derived therefrom or the remittance thereof; all sums paid or accrued on account of duties, customs and imposts, costs of acquiring permits, "contingents", and any similar authority to secure the entry, licensing, televising or other use of the Program in any country. The deductible amount of any sums referred to herein shall not be affected by the manner in which the same are treated by _____ in its own income, franchise, excess profits or other tax returns.

5. All royalties and similar payments to manufacturers of equipment, cartridges, cassettes and the like which are not included in Production Costs; all payments (including fringe benefits and payroll taxes) pursuant to collective bargaining agreements or other agreements by reason of any exhibition of the Program or the exercise of any rights therein; and all agency fees and commissions payable by _____.

6. All costs and expenses resulting from claims and lawsuits involving the Program or any element thereof, including, but not limited to, the underlying rights therein, and protection therefrom, including errors and omissions insurance premiums, costs of copyright search and registration and investigation and defense. To the extent that any such claim or lawsuit is Participant's responsibility, the cost thereof shall be borne entirely by Participant and in such event shall not be deducted under this sub-paragraph.

7. All costs of collecting Gross Receipts and transmitting the same to the United States, including attorneys' fees, auditing and checking costs, and costs of contesting taxes, charges and other expenses. Such costs shall also include fees and charges incurred by efforts to prevent unauthorized exhibitions of the Program and collecting damages for copyright or other infringements as well as any fees, assessments, dues or other amounts payable to any trade association (such as, for example, the AMPTP) concerned with such matters on an industry basis, pro-rated on a reasonable basis to the Program.

E. "Production Costs" means the aggregate of all direct costs incurred by _____ for or in connection with the production of the Program, calculated according to the standard accounting practices now or hereafter employed by _____ for programs owned, financed, or distributed by

_____. Direct costs shall include, without limitation, all items customarily reflected on _____'s production budget, whether such items are furnished by _____ or others. Production Costs shall also include: (i) a charge for _____'s overhead costs computed at fifteen percent (15%) of the Production Costs, exclusive of interest, and (ii) an executive supervisory fee of ($_____) for each one (1) hour of length of each Program produced (ratably adjusted if more or less than one (1) hour is produced). Interest will be charged on the Production Costs at a rate which is one and one-half percent (1-1/2%) per annum above the prime commercial rate of First National Bank of Boston from time to time in effect. Such interest shall be recouped before principal. Should _____ advance or guarantee any portion of Participant's or any third party's share of the Defined Proceeds or contingent deferments, interest and overhead on the amount so advanced or guaranteed shall be included in Production Costs and the principal amount advanced or guaranteed to third parties shall be also included in Production Costs hereunder until such time as it is recovered from the share of Defined Proceeds against which it applies.

F. "_____" includes _____, _____, and _____. The term shall not include: any other person, firm, or corporation distributing the Program or exploiting subsidiary rights therein; exhibitors or others who may actually exhibit the Program to the public; radio or television broadcasters; cable operators; manufacturers, wholesalers, or retailers of Videograms; book, magazine or music publishers; phonograph record producers or distributors; and manufacturers, distributors, wholesalers, retailers or operators of any type of merchandise, goods, services or theme park or other attractions, whether or not any of the foregoing are affiliated with _____.

G. "United States" means the United States, its territories and possessions and Bermuda, but excluding Spanish-speaking Puerto Rico and the Canal Zone.

H. "Merchandising" means licensing the use of the trademarks, trade names, service marks and copyrights in connection with the manufacture, distribution and sale of articles of merchandise involving characters or other elements which make reference to or are based upon the Program; but shall not include phonograph records, tapes, discs, printed publications of literary material, music or lyrics.

II. *ACCOUNTINGS AND PAYMENTS*:

A. Accounting Unit. The Program shall be included in a single accounting unit for the determination of Defined Proceeds. Losses incurred with respect to any accounting period shall be carried forward and applied against subsequent Defined Proceeds, and also carried back to apply against Defined Proceeds in a prior accounting period. Gross Receipts from all sources of income shall be accounted for together so that a deficit incurred with respect to a given source may be offset against Defined Proceeds derived from another source. Should _____ make any overpayments to Participant for any reason, _____ shall have the right to deduct and retain an amount equal to any such overpayment from any sums that may thereafter become due or payable by _____ to the Participant under this or any other contract for _____'s own account, or may demand repayment from the Participant, in which event the Participant agrees to pay the same upon demand.

B. <u>Accounting Statements</u>. _____ will render to Participant summary statements showing the computation of Defined Proceeds, if any, hereunder in accordance with its established accounting procedures, as such may be modified from time to time. If the Program is produced for initial broadcast on a U.S. national television network, then the initial statement shall be rendered after the close of the calendar quarter in which occurs the end of the broadcast year in which the Program is first exhibited; or if the Program is produced for other than on a U.S. national television network, then the initial statement shall be rendered after the end of the fiscal quarter in which Gross Receipts are first received. Such quarterly statements shall continue until one year after the first-run broadcast of the last episode of the Program. Thereafter, such statements will be rendered at least annually after the end of the respective fiscal years, except that quarterly statements shall be rendered for two years commencing when and if the Program goes into syndication in the United States. No statements need be rendered for periods in which no Gross Receipts are generated. If _____ incurs any costs or receives any receipts in respect of matters pertaining to the Program together with other matters, a portion of such costs or receipts shall be allocated to the Program in accordance with _____'s usual and customary accounting procedures. If _____ reasonably anticipates retroactive wage adjustments, guild residuals, uninsured claims or other reasonably anticipated costs, expenses, or losses relating to the Program, which, if and when incurred, would be properly deductible hereunder, _____ may set up appropriate reserves therefor. Each statement shall be deemed final and conclusive unless an objection is made in writing, stating the basis thereof, and delivered to _____ within twenty-four (24) months from the rendition of such statement. Any such objection shall be deemed waived unless Participant initiates an action with respect thereto within six (6) months from the date such objection is sent. As a courtesy to Participant, _____ may include cumulative figures in any earnings or other statement, in which event the time within which Participant may commence any audit or make any objection with respect to a given statement shall not be extended as a result thereof.

C.   <u>Payments</u>. _____ shall pay all money due Participant pursuant to any such statement concurrently with the rendering of such statement, subject to all laws and regulations requiring the withholding of taxes. However, if _____ shall have received any attachments, garnishments, orders to withhold, notices of assignment, or conflicting claims to any money payable to Participant hereunder, or shall be aware of any facts which may result therein, _____ may withhold payment to Participant in whole or in part until such matters are resolved to _____'s satisfaction. No receipts shall be included in Gross Receipts or any statements hereunder unless and until such sums shall have been received by _____ in U.S. dollars in the United States, or used by _____, in which event they shall be included at the official or unofficial rate of exchange (as _____ may elect) prevailing at time of use. As to foreign revenues not included in statements, as aforesaid, _____ shall, at the request and expense of Participant (subject to all limitations affecting such transactions) deposit into a bank designated by Participant in the country involved, or pay to any other party designated by Participant in such country, such part thereof as would have been payable to Participant hereunder. Such deposits or payments to or for Participant shall constitute due remittance to Participant, and _____ shall have no further interest therein or responsibility therefor. In no event shall _____ be obligated to apply receipts not actually received by _____ in U.S. dollars in the United States to the recoupment of any cost deductible by _____ hereunder which was incurred in U.S. dollars.

D.   <u>Examination of Books</u>. Participant may cause _____'s books and records of account relating to the Programs to be examined at Participant's expense, to the extent that they have not become incontestable, by a firm of certified public accountants who regularly audit companies in the motion picture and television business, subject to _____'s right of approval, to be exercised reasonably. _____ preapproves _____. Such examination may be conducted no more than once each calendar year during normal business hours in such a manner as not to interfere with the normal conduct of _____'s business and each such examination shall relate only to transactions concerning the Program occurring since the last preceding inspection, if any, or during the preceding twenty-four (24) months, whichever is shorter. No examination shall continue beyond thirty (30) days from its inception.

E.   <u>Commingling Funds</u>. Any Gross Receipts, Defined Proceeds, working capital, reserve funds, deferred payments or other sums received or held by _____ may be commingled with _____'s general fund and Participant shall not have any right to interest therein nor any right to participate in any profit or other income derived by _____ from use of the sums so received or held.

III. *OBLIGATION TO EXPLOIT*:

Nothing shall be deemed to obligate _____ to distribute, exhibit or otherwise exploit the Program. _____ may do so or refrain therefrom as it may decide in its own absolute discretion, and if it elects to distribute, exhibit or otherwise exploit the Program the manner in which it does so shall not subject it to any liability to Participant. _____ makes no representation or warranty as to the amount of Defined Proceeds or that any Defined Proceeds will be realized.

IV. *MISCELLANEOUS*:

A. Participant shall have the right to sell, assign, transfer or hypothecate all or any part of its interest, if any, in and to the Program and all or any part of the monies which are or may become payable to Participant hereunder; provided that any such assignment shall be subject to all pertinent laws, governmental regulations and the rights of _____ hereunder. If at any time more than 3 parties shall be entitled to receive payments which, under the terms hereof, are to be paid to or for the account of Participant, _____ may, at its option, require that all such parties execute and deliver an agreement in _____'s usual form appointing a disbursing agent for all such parties.

B. In the event Participant shall propose to sell, assign or transfer all or any part of its interest, if any, in and to the Program, or all or any part of the monies which are or may become payable to Participant hereunder, other than by way of a bona fide merger, consolidation, third party acquisition of Participant, bona fide gift, bequest or devise, _____ shall have a right of first refusal to acquire the same, which right _____ may exercise within 10 days after receipt of written notice from Participant specifying the prices and other terms and conditions upon which Participant proposes to make such sale, transfer or assignment. Should _____ fail to exercise such right of first refusal, then Participant shall not sell, transfer or assign such interest or monies or any part thereof to any third party upon terms and conditions more favorable to such third party than those set forth in said written notice without again giving _____ the opportunity to exercise said right of first refusal in accordance with the foregoing procedure.

Exhibit "C"

UPSET PRICE AGREEMENT

(Loanout)

Gentlemen:

In consideration of our payment to you of $ _____ and compensation equal to the "upset price" specified in the applicable _____ and _____ ("_____") you hereby sell, grant, transfer and assign exclusively and perpetually to us, our successors, licensees and assigns, all rights in and to the literary material written by _____("Writer") pursuant to the loanout agreement (loanout agreement") between us dated _____, in all media, worldwide. Said rights will include, without limitation, all rights reserved to you and Writer pursuant to the WGA Agreement, theatrical motion picture, radio, dramatic stage, publication, phonograph record, merchandising and sequel and remake rights, and all other now or hereafter existing rights (except those we acquire under the loanout agreement) of every kind and character whatsoever pertaining to said literary material, whether or not said rights are now known or recognized or contemplated, and the complete and unconditional and unencumbered title in and to said literary material, and the copyright(s) thereof, for all purposes.

Very truly yours,

By: _____
Its Vice President

AGREED:

By: _____
Its: _____

Form 7

Negative Pickup Distribution Agreement

Agreement dated as of (DATE) between (NAME OF PRODUCTION COM-PANY) ("Production Company"), a (NAME OF STATE) corporation, (AD-DRESS OF PRODUCTION COMPANY) and (NAME OF PURCHASING/DISTRIBUTING COMPANY) ("Distributor"), a (NAME OF STATE) corporation, (ADDRESS OF PURCHASING/DISTRIBUTING COMPANY).

Clause 1.

DEFINITIONS:

(a) Picture: The term "Picture" refers to the feature-length, theatrical motion picture described in Schedule "A" hereof.

(b) Territory: Distributor's exclusive distribution "Territory" shall be unlimited and shall include the entire universe unless specified otherwise in Schedule "A" hereof.

(c) Distribution Term: The period of time during which Distributor may exercise the rights granted herein ("Distribution Term") with respect to each country or place of the Territory shall commence on the date hereof and be perpetual, unless specified otherwise in Schedule "A" hereof.

(d) Consideration: The consideration for all rights granted herein is set forth in Schedule "A" hereof.

Clause 2.

RIGHTS GRANTED:

(a) Grant: Production Company hereby grants to Distributor throughout the Territory [the sole and exclusive right and license to release, distribute, exploit, market, issue, reissue and otherwise dispose of and use all or any part of the Picture and Trailers thereof, and excerpts and clips therefrom in any and all languages and versions, including dubbed, subtitled and narrated versions, using any methods or devices of exhibition or exploitation media now or hereafter known or conceived.]

(i) to release, exploit, advertise, distribute, exhibit, license, sell and perform the Picture and Trailers thereof, in 35mm, 16mm, 8mm and other sizes, gauges, forms (including tapes, discs, records and videocassettes) and media (including without limitation CD-I, CD-ROM, interactive and multi-media) and in connection therewith to reproduce the Picture and/or the sound and music synchronized or recorded in or with the Picture;

(ii) to exhibit, project, perform and reproduce the Picture by television, whether free, pay, closed circuit, CATV, pay-per-view or otherwise; any such television exhibition may be before, during and/or after, and in addition to or instead of, the exhibition of the Picture in theatres in all or any part of any country; and

(iii) to broadcast, transmit or reproduce, separately from other portions of the Picture the visual portion, sound or music contained in the Picture, or excerpts, dramatizations or summaries of such visual portion, sound or music, or any part or combination of all or any part of the foregoing.

Without limiting the generality of the foregoing, the rights granted to Distributor shall include the sole and exclusive right throughout the Territory and during the entire Distribution Term:

(i) Titles: To select, designate or change the title or titles by which the Picture is or may be known or identified;

(ii) Music and Lyrics: To use and perform any and all music, lyrics and musical compositions contained in the Picture and/or recorded in the soundtrack thereof in connection with the distribution, exhibition, advertising, publicizing and exploiting of the Picture;

(iii) Versions: To make such dubbed and titled versions of the Picture, and the Trailers thereof, including without limitation, cut-in, synchronized and superimposed versions in any and all languages for use in such parts of the Territory as Distributor may deem advisable.

(iv) Editing: To make such changes, alterations, cuts, additional, interpolations, deletions and eliminations into and from the Picture and the Trailer [subject to consultation with Production Company [and/or Director]] [as Distributor may deem necessary or desirable, or as its licensees may deem necessary or desirable] for the effective marketing, distribution, exploitation or other use of the Picture. [Production Company agrees that any such consultation right shall not conflict with or otherwise impede or delay distribution of the Picture.]

(v) Advertising and Publicity: To publicize, advertise and exploit the Picture throughout the Territory during the Distribution Term and to cause or permit others so to do, including without limitation, the exclusive right in the Territory for the purpose of advertising, publicizing and exploiting the Picture to:

(A) Literary Material: Publish and to license and authorize others to publish in any language and in such forms as Distributor may deem advisable, synopses, summaries, adaptations, novelizations, resumes and stories of and excerpts from the Picture and from any literary or dramatic material included in the Picture or upon which the Picture is based in book form and in newspapers, magazines, trade periodicals, booklets, press books and any other periodicals and in all other media of advertising and publicity whatsoever not exceeding 7,500 words in length taken from the original material;

(B) <u>Radio and Television</u>: Broadcast by radio and television for advertising purposes and to license and authorize others to so broadcast, in any language, any parts or portions of the Picture (not to exceed (E.G., THREE (3)) minutes in length for any part or portion) and any literary or dramatic material included in the Picture or upon which the Picture was based alone or in conjunction with other literary, dramatic or music material; and

(C) <u>Names and Likenesses</u>: [Subject to the terms and conditions of Production Company's Agreement with (name of e.g., principal actor or director),] use, license and authorize others to use the name, physical likeness and voice (and any simulation or reproduction of any thereof) of any party rendering services in connection with the Picture for the purpose of advertising, publicizing or exploiting the Picture or Distributor, including commercial tie-ins.

(vi) <u>Use of Name and Trademarks</u>: To use Distributor's name and trademark and/or the name and trademark of any of Distributor's licensees on the positive prints of the Picture and in Trailers thereof, and in all advertising and publicity relating thereto, in such a manner, position, form and substance as Distributor or its licensees may elect.

(vii) <u>Commercials</u>: To permit commercial messages to be exhibited [during and] after the exhibition of the Picture.

(viii) <u>Trailers</u>: To cause Trailers and/or Teasers of the Picture and prints thereof and of the Picture to be manufactured, exhibited and distributed by every means, medium, process, method and device now or hereafter known.

(b) <u>Grant of Other Rights</u>: Production Company hereby grants to Distributor throughout the Territory the sole and exclusive right, license and privilege to exercise all Literary Publishing Rights, Live Television Rights, Merchandising Rights, Music Publishing Rights, Soundtrack Recording Rights, Radio Rights, Additional Motion Picture Rights, Remake Rights and Sequel Motion Picture Rights subject to the terms and conditions of the agreements pursuant to which Production Company acquired the foregoing rights with respect to the literary, dramatic and/or musical material used by Production Company in connection with the Picture. Production Company agrees that at the request of Distributor, Production Company will execute and deliver to Distributor for recordation purposes a separate document pursuant to which Production Company confirms the transfer and assignment to Distributor of the aforesaid rights.

(c) <u>Rights Free and Clear</u>: The foregoing is granted by Production Company to Distributor without qualification and free and clear from any and all restrictions, claims, encumbrances or defects of any nature and Production Company agrees that it will not commit or omit to perform any act by which any of said rights, licenses, privileges and interests could or will be encumbered, diminished or impaired, and that Production Company will pay or discharge, and will hold

Distributor harmless from, any and all claims that additional payments are due anyone by reason of the distribution, exhibition, telecasting, or rerunning of the Picture or the receipt of proceeds therefrom. Production Company further agrees that during the Distribution Term with respect to each country or place, Production Company shall neither exercise itself nor grant to any third party the rights granted to Distributor pursuant to the terms hereof.

Clause 3.

DELIVERY: Delivery of the Picture shall consist of delivery by Production Company at its expense to Distributor, at such place as Distributor shall designate, the following:

(a) Laboratory Access Letter: A Laboratory Access Letter in the form attached as Exhibit "1" shall be signed concurrently with this Agreement by Production Company and a laboratory selected by [Production Company] [Distributor], which recites that the laboratory has received and is holding in its possession for Production Company's account the elements of the Picture, such as a first generation interpositive master or internegative of the Picture together with the Music & Effects Track suitable for the manufacture of (STATE QUALITY OF PRINTS, E.G., COMMERCIALLY ACCEPTABLE FIRST-CLASS) positive release prints of the original and dubbed versions of the Picture and the Trailer and that such laboratory will manufacture and deliver positive release prints of the Picture and the Trailer to Distributor upon its order.

(b) Delivery Schedule: The materials and items specified in Exhibit "2" attached hereto.

(c) Credits: [Subject to the statements of credits which Production Company is obligated to accord pursuant to written agreement, Distributor shall have the right to determine all screen and advertising credits in and in connection with the Picture.] (OR) [The Picture and any negatives thereof delivered to Distributor, shall contain all required screen credits in conformity with all contractual specifications.] (OR) [Distributor shall comply with the statement of credits in Exhibit "2".] All claims, actions and causes of action arising as a result of [the failure of Production Company to deliver such statement to Distributor or as a result of compliance with such statement by Distributor or as a result of any error in such notice] [the credits appearing on the Picture and negative thereof] shall be deemed to be claims, actions and causes of action with respect to which Distributor is to be indemnified by Production Company.

(c)(i) [No casual or inadvertent failure by Distributor or any of its subdistributors or licensees to comply with the statement of credits shall constitute a breach of this Agreement. Production Company shall not be entitled to assert any claim or cause of action of any kind against Distributor because of the failure or alleged failure by Distributor or any of its subdistributors or licensees to comply with the statement of credits unless and until Production Company has given Distributor written notice of such failure or alleged failure and Distributor after receipt of such written notice fails to comply with such notice [on a prospective basis with respect to film and advertising materials not yet created and/or delivered]. In order to avoid any delay in the release schedule, the distributor will require that injunctive relief, which may otherwise be available, is waived by the production company.]

Clause 4.

PRODUCTION COMPANY'S WARRANTIES AND REPRESENTATIONS: Production Company represents and warrants to and agrees with Distributor, its successors, licensees and assigns as follows with respect to the Picture:

(a) Quality: The Picture is [(OR) when delivered will be] completely finished, fully edited and titled in first-class condition and fully synchronized with language dialogue, sound and music and in all respects ready and of a quality, both artistic and technical, adequate for general theatrical release and commercial public exhibition.

(b) Content: The Picture consists [(OR) will consist] of a continuous and connected series of scenes, telling or presenting a story, free from any [E.G., ANY OBSCENE, VULGAR, SALACIOUS, CONTROVERSIAL OR PARTI- SAN POLITICAL MATTERS] and suitable for exhibition to [E.G., THE GENERAL PUBLIC].

(c) Unrestricted Right to Grant: Production Company is the sole and absolute owner of the Picture, the copyright pertaining thereto and all rights associated with or relating to the distribution, exhibition and exploitation thereof, and has the absolute right to grant to and vest in Distributor, all the rights, licenses and privileges granted to Distributor under this Agreement and Production Company has not heretofore sold, assigned, licensed, granted, encumbered or utilized the Picture or any of the literary or musical properties used therein in any way that may affect or impair the rights, licenses and privileges granted to Distributor hereunder and Production Company will not sell, assign, license, grant or encumber or utilize the rights, licenses and privileges granted to Distributor hereunder.

(d) Discharge of Obligation: All the following have been fully paid or discharged or will be fully paid and discharged by Production Company or by persons other than Distributor:

(i) All claims and rights of owners of copyright in literary, dramatic and musical rights and other property and/or rights in and to all stories, plays, scripts, scenarios, themes, incidents, plots, characters, dialogue, music, words and other material of any nature whatsoever appearing, used or recorded in the Picture;

(ii) All claims and rights of owners of inventions and patent rights with respect to the recording of any and all dialogue, music and other sound effects recorded in the Picture and with respect to the use of all equipment, apparatus, appliances and other materials used in the photographing, recording or otherwise in the manufacture of the Picture;

(iii) All claims and rights with respect to the use, distribution, exhibition, performance and exploitation of the Picture and any music contained therein throughout the Territory, and

(iv) All payments or claims for exhibition or re-running or reissue of the Picture in all media throughout the Territory, if the Picture has been previously issued or released.

(e) No Infringement: Neither the Picture nor any part thereof, nor any materials contained therein or synchronized therewith, nor the title thereof, nor the exercise of any right, license or privilege herein granted, violates or will violate or infringes or will infringe any trademark, trade name, contract, agreement, copyright (whether common law or statutory), patent, literary, artistic, dramatic, personal, private, civil or property right or right of privacy or "moral rights of authors" or any other right whatsoever of or slanders or libels any person, firm, corporation or association whatsoever. In connection therewith, Production Company shall supply Distributor with a script clearance in a form acceptable to Distributor.

[(f) No Advertising Matter: The Picture does not contain any advertising matter for which compensation, direct or indirect, has been or will be received by Production Company or to its knowledge by any other person, firm, corporation or association.]

(g) No Impairment of Rights Granted: There are and will be no agreements, commitments or arrangements whatever with any person, firm, corporation or association that may in any manner or to any extent affect Distributor's rights hereunder or Distributor's share of the proceeds of the Picture. Production Company has not and will not itself, or pursuant to authority granted to any other Party, exercise any right or take any action which might tend to derogate from, impair or compete with the rights, licenses and privileges herein granted or purported to be granted to Distributor.

(h) Contracts: All contracts with artists and personnel, for studio hire, purchases, licenses and laboratory contracts and all other obligations and undertakings of whatsoever kind connected with the production of the Picture have been made and entered into by Production Company or Production Company's predecessor in title and by no other party and no obligation shall be imposed upon Distributor to which Distributor has not previously agreed thereunder and Production Company shall indemnify and hold Distributor harmless from any expense and liability thereunder. [All such contracts are in the form customarily in use in the Motion Picture industry and are consistent with the provisions of this Agreement, particularly with reference to the warranties made by Production Company and the rights acquired by Distributor hereunder.] [Said contracts shall not, without Distributor's prior written consent, be terminated, cancelled, modified or rescinded in any manner which would adversely affect Distributor's rights hereunder.]

[(i) <u>All Considerations Paid</u>: All the considerations provided to be paid under each and all the agreements, licenses or other documents relating to the production of the Picture have been paid in full, or otherwise discharged in full, and there is no existing, outstanding obligation whatsoever, either present or future, under any of said contracts, agreements, assignments or other documents, unless disclosed in Schedule "A".]

(j) <u>Full Performance</u>: All the terms, covenants and conditions provided to be kept or performed by Production Company or Production Company's predecessor in title under each and all of the contracts, licenses or other documents relating to the production of the Picture have been kept and performed and will hereafter be kept and performed by Production Company and there is no existing breach or other act of default by Production Company under any of said agreements, licenses or other documents, nor will there by any such breach or default during the Term of this Agreement.

[(k) <u>No Release/No Banning</u>: Neither the Picture nor any part thereof has been released, distributed or exhibited in any media whatsoever in the Territory, nor has it been banned by censors of or refused import permits for any portion of the Territory.]

(l) <u>Valid Copyright</u>: The copyright in the Picture and the literary, dramatic and musical material upon which it is based or which is contained in the Picture have not heretofore been [and will not hereafter be] transferred by Production Company to any third party and will be valid and subsisting during the Distribution Term with respect to each country or place of the Territory and no part of any thereof is in the public domain. [Upon delivery of the Picture to Distributor, Production Company will own and be able to convey to Distributor all copyrights in the Picture throughout the world for the full period of copyright and all extensions and renewals thereof.]

[(m) <u>Peaceful Enjoyment</u>: Distributor will quietly and peacefully enjoy and possess each and all the rights, licenses and privileges herein granted or purported to be granted to Distributor throughout the Distribution Term with respect to each country or place of the Territory without hindrance on the part of any third party.]

[(n) <u>Guild-Union-Performing Rights Society-Participation Payments</u>: Any payments required to be made to any performing rights society or to any body or group representing authors, composers, musicians, artists, and other participants in the production of the Picture, publishers or other persons having legal or contractual rights of any kind to participate in the receipts of the Picture or to payments of any kind as a result of the distribution or exhibition of the Picture and any taxes thereon or on the payment thereof will be made by Production Company or by the exhibitors and need not be paid by the Distributor.]

(o) Music Performing Rights: The Performing rights to all musical compositions contained in the Picture are: (i) controlled by the American Society of Composers, Authors and Publishers (ASCAP), Broadcast Music, Inc. (BMI) or similar organizations in other countries such as the Japanese Society of Rights of Authors and Composers (JASEAC), the Performing Rights Society Ltd. (PRS), the Society of European Stage Authors and Composers (SESAC), the Societe des Auteurs Compositeurs Et Editeurs de Musique (SACEM), Gesellschraft für Misikalische Auffuhrungs und Mechanische Vervielfaltigungsrechte (GEMA) or their affiliates, or (ii) in the public domain in the Territory or (iii) controlled by Production Company to the extent required for the purposes of this Agreement and Production Company similarly controls or has licenses for any necessary synchronization and recording rights.

[(p) Publicity Restrictions: Production Company shall not issue any publicity relating to the Picture without Distributor's prior consent. However, subject to Distributor's control of all such publicity, Production Company shall cooperate fully with Distributor in connection with all such publicity, including any publicity interviews (such as with performers) relating to the Picture.

(q) Authority Relative to this Agreement: Production Company has taken all action necessary to duly and validly authorize its signature and performance of this Agreement and the grant of the rights, licenses and privileges herein granted and agreed to be granted. [If a corporation, the person signing on behalf of the corporation represents and warrants that he or she has full authority and power to execute this agreement on behalf of the corporation and bind it to this agreement.]

[(r) Financial Condition: Production Company is not presently involved in financial difficulties as evidenced by its not having admitted its inability to pay its debts generally as they become due or otherwise not having acknowledged its insolvency or by its not having filed or consented to a petition in bankruptcy or for reorganization or for the adoption of an arrangement under the Federal Bankruptcy Act (or under any similar law of the United States or any other jurisdiction, which relates to insolvency or reorganization of companies or to the modification or alteration of the rights of creditors) or by its not being involved in any bankruptcy, liquidation, or other similar proceeding relating to Production Company or its assets, whether pursuant to statute or general rule of law, nor does Production Company presently contemplate any such proceeding, or have any reason to believe that any such proceeding will be brought against it or its assets.]

(s) Litigation: [To Production Company's knowledge] there is no litigation, proceeding or claim pending or threatened against Production Company which may materially adversely affect Production Company's exclusive rights in and to the Picture, the copyright pertaining thereto and the rights, licenses and privileges granted to Distributor hereunder.

[(t) <u>MPAA Rating</u>: The Picture is eligible to receive or has received, a Production Code Seal from the MPAA of [SPECIFY E.G., "G", "PG", "PG-13", "NC-17", OR "R"], or an equivalent mark of approval or rating, (i) by any similarly constituted authority which may succeed it; or (ii) by the respective authority in the event of a change in its rating system.]

Clause 5.

<u>INDEMNITY</u>: Production Company does hereby and shall at all times indemnify and hold harmless Distributor, its subdistributors and licensees, its and their officers, directors and employees, and its and their exhibitors, licensees and assignees, of and from any and all charges, claims, damages, costs, judgments, decrees, losses, expenses (including reasonable attorneys' fees), penalties, demands, liabilities and causes of action, whether or not groundless, of any kind or nature whatsoever by reason of, based upon, relating to, or arising out of a breach or claim of breach or failure of any of the covenants, agreements, representations or warranties of Production Company hereunder or by reason of any claims, actions or proceedings asserted or instituted, relating to or arising out of any such breach or failure or conduct or activity resulting in a breach or claim of breach. All rights and remedies hereunder shall be cumulative and shall not interfere with or prevent the exercise of any other right or remedy which may be available to Distributor. Upon notice from Distributor of any such claim, demand or action being advanced or commenced, Production Company agrees to adjust, settle, or defend the same at the sole cost of Production Company. [If Production Company shall fail [promptly] to do so, Distributor shall have the right and is hereby authorized and empowered by Production Company to appear by its attorneys in any such claim, demand or action, to adjust, settle, compromise, litigate, contest, satisfy judgments and take any other action necessary or desirable for the disposition of such claim, demand or action.] [In any such case, Production Company, within FIFTEEN (15) days after demand therefor by Distributor, shall fully reimburse Distributor for all such payments and expenses, including reasonable attorneys' fees. If Production Company shall fail to so reimburse Distributor, then, without waiving its right to otherwise enforce such reimbursement, Distributor shall have the right to deduct the same amount of such payments and expenses, or any part thereof, from any amounts accruing under this Agreement or any other agreement, to or for the account of Production Company.]

Clause 6.

<u>RESIDUALS AND ROYALTIES</u>: On condition Production Company shall have delivered to Distributor all documentation described in Exhibit "2" needed by

Distributor for such purpose, Distributor agrees to make the residual and other additional or supplemental payments required to be made thereafter by reason of the distribution or other exploitation of the Picture by Distributor in the Territory pursuant to the terms of any applicable collective bargaining agreement to which Distributor is a party [, it being understood that such payments shall constitute a recoupable distribution expense]. However, Production Company shall be responsible for any residual and other additional or supplemental payments required to be made by reason of the distribution or other exploitation of the Picture other than by Distributor in the Territory. In addition, Distributor shall pay to the person(s) engaged by Production Company to compose the music and lyrics for the Picture any royalties to which such person(s) is/are entitled, by reason of the use of such music and lyrics as provided herein, pursuant to the terms of the agreement relating to the services of such person(s) provided that such royalties are not in excess of the usual and customary royalties payable to such person(s) by reason of such use.

Clause 7.

OWNERSHIP OF THE PICTURE:

   (a) Copyright: During the entire Distribution Term and throughout the Territory, the Picture and all rights therein (including the right to enforce the copyright and to recover damages on account of infringement of said copyright, regardless of the date of such infringement) shall be owned solely by (and Production Company hereby assigns them to) Distributor and Production Company shall have no ownership or other interest therein.

   (b) Music: Without limiting the provisions of Subclause 7(a) it is agreed that Distributor or its designee shall be the sole [owner] [licensee] of the publication rights in all original music (including lyrics) composed or acquired for use in or in connection with the Picture. Production Company shall obtain such publication rights for Distributor or its designee.

   (c) Hypothecation: Distributor shall have the right to hypothecate its interest in the Picture and all or any rights therein; however, no such hypothecation shall release Distributor from its obligations hereunder, including the obligation to make any payment to which Production Company may become entitled hereunder.

   (d) Copyright Notice:

   (1) Production Company agrees that the main title of the Picture, as delivered to Distributor, shall include a copyright notice in conformity with the laws of the United States and the Universal Copyright Convention relating to the form and content of copyright notices, designating Distributor as copyright proprietor. The Picture shall also contain the following legend, such legend to appear on the film located on the end title at or near the cast of characters:

"THIS MOTION PICTURE IS PROTECTED UNDER LAWS OF THE UNITED STATES AND OTHER COUNTRIES. UNAUTHORIZED DUPLICATION, DISTRIBUTION OR EXHIBITION MAY RESULT IN CIVIL LIABILITY AND CRIMINAL PROSECUTION."

(2) Distributor [shall] [may take such steps (if any) to] register the copyright in the Picture in the United States Copyright Office, or to obtain or register the copyright in any other country, as it customarily takes with respect to its own pictures. Distributor does not represent, warrant or agree that any steps which it may take shall be such that valid copyright will result, and Distributor shall have no responsibility or liability in connection with taking any such steps or obtaining or maintaining valid copyright.

(e) <u>Prints and Physical Properties</u>:

(1) Distributor may cause negatives, prints, trailers and other physical properties (including tapes, discs and cassettes) relating to the Picture to be made, transported and stored. Distributor shall own all such items, and have exclusive rights and access to their possession and control, together with the right to dispose of or destroy any such items (except for the original negative, unless a substitute means of reproducing the Picture has been preserved). Production Company agrees to execute a Laboratory Access Letter in the form attached hereto as Exhibit "1"

(2) If Production Company so requests in writing during the period of (E.G., 30 DAYS) after the expiration (if any) of the Distribution Term, Distributor shall notify Production Company of all [negatives and] prints of the Picture then in existence and in Distributor's possession or control, and the location of each. Within (E.G., 30 DAYS) after the service of Distributor's notice, Production Company may notify Distributor of the disposition it wishes to be made of any or all of such [negatives or] prints, in which event Distributor shall make the requested disposition, on condition that Production Company prepays the cost of such disposition. If and to the extent that Production Company fails to request disposition of any such [negatives or] prints, within (E.G., 30 DAYS) after the service of Distributor's notice (whether or not Distributor's notice was requested by Production Company under the first sentence of this clause), Distributor may dispose of or destroy them, or store them at Production Company's expense.

(f) <u>Advertising Accessories</u>: Distributor may cause the manufacture and distribution of advertising accessories in connection with the Picture. Any income derived by Distributor from such advertising accessories shall belong to Distributor. Distributor shall not be obligated to make any accounting or payment to Production Company therefor. [Any loss from or expenses of such licensing shall be borne by Distributor, and no part thereof shall be chargeable to the Picture. However, where Distributor buys and furnishes any such advertising accessories to exhibitors or others without charge for use in connection with the Picture, the cost thereof shall be deductible as a distribution expense.]

(g) Film Library: Distributor may retain and use such portions of the Picture, as Distributor may desire, for the purpose of including them in Distributor's stock shot, process shot, sound effects and music libraries. Distributor shall own all items so included and may use and permit others to use them, without accounting or payment to Production Company. Distributor agrees to indemnify Production Company against any claims (including claims for compensation) brought against Production Company arising out of such use of film materials.

(h) Investment Tax Credit: Distributor shall, as between Distributor and Production Company, be entitled to claim an investment tax credit or similar benefit pursuant to any present or future law on costs incurred by Distributor (including all costs incurred in connection with the manufacture of prints of the Picture) and for such purpose, Production Company shall:

(i) execute and deliver to Distributor prior to a date which is [E.G., 90 DAYS] after the delivery of the picture hereunder a statement, in the form supplied to Production Company by Distributor, for use by Distributor in connection with any tax return in which an investment tax credit or similar benefit is claimed and otherwise satisfactory to Distributor, which statement shall:

(A) be addressed to the District Director of Internal Revenue Service;

(B) state that Production Company has not, prior to the date upon which this agreement was executed by Production Company, placed the Picture in service within the meaning of the Internal Revenue Code and/or said regulations;

(C) specify the nature and purchase price of any part of the Picture sold (within the meaning of the Internal Revenue Code and/or applicable Treasury Regulations) prior to the date of execution of this agreement; and

(D) describe (to the best of Production Company's knowledge) with respect to the Picture the nature and amount of each item qualifying as United States production costs within the meaning of the Internal Revenue Code and/or applicable Treasury Regulations; and

(ii) execute and deliver to Distributor (and/or to the Internal Revenue Service, if Distributor shall so direct) such additional documents (including additional copies of said statement) supplied by Distributor as Distributor may reasonably require, and otherwise cooperate with Distributor, in order to assist Distributor in obtaining the maximum benefit of said credit.

Clause 8.

DISTRIBUTION AND EXPLOITATION OF THE PICTURE: [Except as otherwise specified herein,] Distributor shall have the complete, exclusive and unqualified control of the distribution, exhibition, exploitation, marketing, reissuing, sale and other disposition of the Picture and all versions thereof, directly or by any subsidiary, affiliate, or other party in the media, granted to Distributor hereunder throughout the Territory during the Distribution Term with respect to each country or place [, in accordance with such sales methods, plans, patterns, programs, policies, terms and conditions as Distributor in its sole business judgment may determine proper or expedient.] [The decision of Distributor in all such matters shall be final and conclusive.] [Distributor shall use reasonable efforts in accordance with its business practices to distribute the Picture to an extent commensurate with its relative merit and marketability, as determined by Distributor in good faith from time to time.] The enumeration of the following rights of distribution and exploitation shall in no way limit the generality or effect of the foregoing:

(a) Terms: Distributor [shall, at all times, have full control in its sole and absolute discretion over] [may determine] the manner and terms upon which the Picture shall be marketed, distributed, licensed, exhibited, exploited or otherwise disposed of, and all matters pertaining thereto [and the decision of Distributor in all such matters shall be final and conclusive]. [Production Company shall have no interest or control whatsoever in or over the manner or extent to which Distributor or its subdistributors or licensees shall exploit the Picture, nor with reference to the terms and provisions of any licenses granted by Distributor to third parties nor as to the insufficiency of proceeds from the Picture.]

(b) Refrain from Distribution, Exhibition or Exploitation: Distributor may [in it sole discretion] refrain from the release, distribution, re-issue or exhibition of the Picture at any time, in any country, place or location of the Territory, in any media, or in any form as Distributor [in its sole business judgment exercised in good faith] may determine. [Production Company acknowledges that there is no obligation to exploit the Soundtrack Recording Rights or Music Publishing Rights or Merchandising Rights or Literary Publishing Rights, it being agreed that Distributor may elect to exercise any or all of said rights as Distributor in its sole business judgment may determine.]

(c) "Outright Sales": Distributor may make Outright Sales of the Picture [as Distributor in its sole business judgment may determine], [whether or not Distributor maintains its own distributing organization in the country, place or location of the Territory involved].

(d) Contracts and Settlements: Distributor may distribute the Picture under existing or future franchise or license contracts, which contracts may relate to the Picture separately or to the Picture and one or more other Motion Pictures distributed by or through Distributor. Distributor may, in the exercise of its sole business judgment, [exercised in good faith,] make, alter or cancel contracts with exhibitors, subdistributors and other licensees and adjust and settle disputes, make allowances and adjustments and give credits with respect thereto.

(e) <u>Means of Release</u>: Distributor may exhibit or cause the Picture to be exhibited in theatres or other places owned, controlled, leased or managed by Distributor. Distributor may enter into any agreement or arrangement with [a] [any other] major distributor for the distribution by such [other] major distributor of all or a substantial portion of Distributor's Theatrical Motion Pictures. Distributor may also enter into any agreement or arrangement with [a] [any other] major distributor or any other party for the handling of the shipping and inspection activities of Distributor's exchanges or the handling of other facilities in connection with the distribution of Motion Picture.

(f) <u>Time of Release</u>: The initial release of the Picture in any part of the Territory shall commence on [specify date][such date or dates as distributor or its subdistributors or licensees in their respective sole judgment and discretion may determine]. [Such releases shall be subject to the requirements of censorship boards or other governmental authorities, the availability of playing time in key cities, the securing of the requisite number of motion picture copies, and delays caused by reason of events of Force Majeure or by reason of any cause beyond the control of Distributor or its subdistributors or licensees.] [If any claim or action is made or instituted against Distributor or any of its subdistributors or licenses as to the Picture, Distributor or such subdistributors or licensees shall have the right to postpone the release of the Picture (if it has not then been released) or to suspend further distribution thereof (if it has been released) until such time as such claim or action shall have been settled or disposed of to the satisfaction of Distributor or such subdistributors or licensees [, and for such time thereafter as may be reasonably necessary in the judgment of Distributor or of such subdistributor or licensee to commence or resume distribution].]

(g) <u>Duration of Release</u>: Distribution of the Picture shall be continued in the Territory or any part thereof in which it is released by Distributor or its licensees only for [specify period] [so long as Distributor or its subdistributors or licensees may deem desirable in the exercise of their sole discretion]. [Distributor shall not be obligated to reissue the Picture at any time in the Territory but may do so from time to time as it may deem desirable.]

[(h) <u>Withdrawal of the Picture</u>: If Distributor or its subdistributors or licensees (in good faith) deem it inadvisable or unprofitable to distribute, exhibit or exploit the Picture in the Territory or any part thereof, Distributor or its subdistributors or licensees shall have the right to withhold or withdraw the Picture from such Territory or any part thereof.]

[(i) <u>Banning of Release</u>: If by reason of any law, embargo, decree, regulation or other restriction of any agency or governmental body, the number or type of motion pictures that Distributor is permitted to distribute in the Territory or any part thereof is limited, then Distributor may in its absolute discretion determine which motion pictures then distributed by Distributor will be distributed in the Territory or any part thereof, and Distributor shall not be liable to Production

Company in any manner or to any extent in the event the Picture is not distributed in the Territory or any part thereof by reason of any such determination.]

(j) <u>Collections</u>: Distributor shall [, in the exercise of its sole business judgment, determine the extent to] [in good faith] audit, check or verify the computation of any payments [and] [or to] press for the collection of any monies due from distribution of the Picture. [There shall be no responsibility or liability to Production Company for failure to audit, check, or verify or to collect any monies payable.]

(k) <u>Advertising</u>: Distributor shall not be obligated to expend any minimum or maximum amount with respect to the advertising and publicizing of the Picture. Distributor, in the [good faith] exercise of its sole business judgment, shall determine the amount of the advertising and publicizing budget and the extent of the advertising and publicizing campaign.

[(l) <u>Expenses</u>: Distributor may incur any expenses which Distributor, in the [good faith] exercise of its sole business judgment, deems appropriate with respect to the Picture or the exercise of any of Distributor's rights hereunder.]

[(m) <u>No Preferential Treatment</u>: Anything herein contained to the contrary notwithstanding, Production Company agrees that nothing herein shall require Distributor to prefer the Picture over any other motion picture produced or distributed by Distributor or shall restrict or limit in any way Distributor's full right to distribute other motion pictures of any nature or description whether similar or dissimilar to the Picture.]

Clause 9.

<u>DEALING WITH SUBSIDIARIES AND AFFILIATES</u>: Nothing herein contained shall limit or restrict Distributor's dealing with, or licensing any of its rights hereunder to, any affiliate or any of its subsidiaries or divisions. In each such transaction, Distributor's only obligation is to use good faith, which shall conclusively be deemed to exist if the transaction is on terms comparable to those in effect in similar transactions in the motion picture industry, (i) between unrelated parties; or (ii) between Distributor (or the respective other related party to the transaction) and unrelated parties.]

Clause 10.

<u>LABORATORY WORK</u>: All laboratory work in connection with the distribution of the Picture, and the exercise of any of Distributor's rights hereunder, shall be performed by such laboratory or laboratories as Distributor may select. Distributor may select a laboratory owned or controlled by Distributor or any of Distributor's affiliates, in which event the rates charged by such laboratory shall be the same as those then charged by it with respect to Distributor's own pictures produced primarily for theatrical exhibition.][Production Company

agrees to cause all film material to be promptly delivered to the laboratory selected by Distributor.]

Clause 11.

<u>INSURANCE</u>: Production Company agrees to maintain the following insurance policies as customarily maintained by production companies of feature-length theatrical motion pictures in the United States:

   (i)   cast insurance;

  (ii)   negative film insurance;

 (iii)   extra expense insurance;

 (iv)   producer's errors and omissions;

  (v)   comprehensive general and automobile liability;

 (vi)   third party property damage;

 (vii)   miscellaneous equipment floater;

(viii)   props, sets and wardrobe all-risk floater; and

 (ix)   workers' compensation or equivalent employer's liability.

All such insurance shall be placed with (SPECIFY NAME OF COMPANY).

The policy of Production Company's errors and omissions insurance referred to in (iv) above shall, (a) have limits of liability of not less than (E.G., $1,000,000/ $3,000,000), (b) pursuant to its terms provide primary errors and omissions coverage and not contributory coverage, notwithstanding any other errors and omissions insurance which Production Company and/or Distributor may obtain or maintain, and (c) be maintained in full force and effect by Production Company, at Production Company's sole cost and expense, for a period of not less than (E.G., THREE YEARS) following initial theatrical release of the Picture in the Territory, it being understood that in the event of cancellation or nonrenewal of said policy of Production Company's errors and omissions insurance, Production Company shall obtain and maintain a substitute policy therefore (and promptly deliver to Distributor evidence of the maintenance of such substitute policy), the terms of which substitute policy shall be in accordance with the provisions of this clause. Without limiting the foregoing provisions, (a) the comprehensive general and automobile liability insurance referred to in (v) above and the third party property damage insurance referred to in (vi) above shall each have limits of liability of not less than (E.G., $1,000,000) and (b) subject to the foregoing provisions of this clause, all of the aforesaid insurance shall have such limits of liability, be subject to such deductions and exclusions, and be maintained during such periods, as may be customary in the motion picture industry with respect thereto. Production Company shall cause Distributor to be added as a named insured, as its interest may appear, under the insurance policies referred to above in (i) through (viii), inclusive, and shall, as soon as practicable provide Distributor with written evidence satisfactory to Distributor of the maintenance of such insurance policies and of the provisions thereof (including evidence that Distributor has been named as a named insured).

Clause 12.

FURTHER DOCUMENTS: Production Company shall execute and deliver to Distributor, promptly upon the request of Distributor therefor, any other instruments or documents considered by Distributor to be necessary or desirable to evidence, effectuate or confirm this Agreement, or any of the terms and conditions hereof. If Production Company fails to execute and deliver any such document promptly on Distributor's written request, Distributor may do so as Production Company's attorney-in-fact, and Distributor is hereby irrevocably appointed to do so as Production Company's attorney-in-fact.

Clause 13.

WAIVER: No waiver of any breach of any provision of this Agreement shall constitute a waiver of any other breach of the same or any other provision hereof, and no waiver shall be effective unless made in writing signed by the party against whom the waiver is asserted.

Clause 14.

RELATIONSHIP OF PARTIES: Nothing herein contained shall be construed so as to create a joint venture or partnership between the parties hereto [nor a third party beneficiary relationship as to any third party]. Neither of the parties hereto shall hold itself out contrary to the terms of this provision, by advertising or otherwise nor shall Distributor or Production Company be bound or become liable because of any representations, actions or omissions of the other.

Clause 15.

ASSIGNMENT: Distributor may assign this Agreement to and/or may distribute the Picture through any of its subsidiaries, parents or affiliated corporations or any agent, instrumentality or other means determined by Distributor [provided that Distributor shall not thereby be relieved of the fulfillment of any of its obligations to Production Company hereunder]. [This Agreement shall be otherwise nonassignable.] [Production Company may assign the right to receive payment hereunder to any third party; provided, however, that Production Company shall not be permitted to assign any of its obligations hereunder.]

Clause 16.

NOTICES: All notices from Production Company or Distributor to the other, with respect to this Agreement, shall be given in writing by mailing or telegraphing the notice prepaid, return receipt requested, and addressed to Distributor or Production Company, as appropriate, at the address set forth in the preamble hereof. A courtesy copy of any notice to Production Company shall be sent to (NAME AND ADDRESS OF ATTORNEY), and a courtesy copy of any notice to Distributor shall be sent to (NAME AND ADDRESS OF ATTORNEY). Distributor or Production Company may change such addressed by written notice to the other at the address stated in the preamble hereof.

Clause 17.

GOVERNING LAW: This Agreement shall be governed by the laws of the State of [NAME OF STATE], without giving effect to the principles of conflict of laws thereof.

Clause 18.

CAPTIONS: The captions of the various clauses and sections of the Agreement are intended to be used solely for convenience of reference and are not intended and shall not be deemed for any purpose whatsoever to modify or explain or to be used as an aid in the construction of any of the provisions hereof.

Clause 19.

AMENDMENTS IN WRITING: This Agreement cannot be amended, modified or changed in any way whatsoever excepting only by a written instrument duly signed by authorized officers of Production Company and Distributor.

Clause 20.

ENTIRE AGREEMENT: This Agreement, which is comprised of the general terms above ("Main Agreement") and the attached Schedule and Exhibits, represents the entire agreement between the parties hereto with respect to the subject matter hereof, and this Agreement supersedes all previous representations, understandings or agreements, oral or written, between the parties with respect to the subject matter hereof.

By signing in the spaces provided below, the parties hereto have agreed to all the terms and conditions of this Agreement.

_____
("Distributor")

By _____

Its _____

("Production Company")

By _____

Its _____

Form 8

Pay Cable Television Production and License Agreement

THIS AGREEMENT, dated as of FEBRUARY 15, 1986, (the "Agreement"), is between PRODUCTIONS, INC. ("Producer"), A NEW YORK CORPORA- TION, AND CABLE PROGRAM SERVICE ("CPS").

Clause 1. PROGRAM:

(a) Producer shall produce and deliver to CPS ONE (1) television program approximately THIRTY (30) minutes in length (the "First Program"). The First Program shall be a program forming part of the series entitled "(TITLE)" (the "Series"). If CPS exercises the option to order one Optional Program pursuant to Clause 5, below, Producer shall produce and deliver to CPS such Optional Program. (The First Program and the Optional Program shall be referred to herein from time to time as a "Program"). The Program shall be of at least the same quality and have at least the same production standards as domestic network television programming currently being produced, taking into account the budget and format of the Program.

(b) Throughout the development and production of each Program, Producer shall consult regularly with CPS with respect to the format and content of, and the production and post-production techniques used in connection with such Program. Without limiting the generality of the foregoing:

(i) Prior to commencing production of each Program, Producer shall submit in writing, for CPS's approval in CPS's sole discretion, all major elements of such Program, including without limitation, the executive producer, director, line producer, lighting director, director of photography, writer, editor, art director, music coordinator, composer, unit production manager, casting director, performers, and any substitutes for elements previously approved.

(ii) As between Producer and CPS, CPS shall have the sole right to approve all stages of the production and post-production of each Program, including without limitation the following: (A) the shooting script of each Program (each, a "Script") and the final budget for each program (each, a "Budget"), (B) the final production and delivery schedule (upon final approval by CPS, each, a "Schedule"), specifying in addition to the dates set forth below, the number of rehearsal days, shooting days, the locations, the delivery dates for rough cuts and fine cuts, the Delivery Date (as hereinafter defined), the format and production and post-production techniques of such Program and such other items as are customarily included in a Schedule, (C) selected footage, (D) the rough cut, (E) the fine cut and (F) the completed Program. The Schedule for the First Program shall contain, without limitation, the following schedule:

A. On or before MARCH 1, 1986 Producer shall deliver the Budget and Schedule;

B. On or before MAY 15, 1986 Producer shall deliver to CPS the rough cut;

C. On or before JUNE 15, 1986 Producer shall deliver to CPS the fine cut; and

D. On or before JUNE 30, 1986 (the "Delivery Date" for the First Program), Producer shall deliver the Videotape (as hereinafter defined).

Within TEN (10) business days of each such delivery to CPS of any materials for any Program, CPS shall notify Producer whether CPS approves such materials. Producer shall make such changes and edits requested by CPS in such materials.

(iii) Producer shall consult with CPS concerning the length of each Program significantly in advance of delivery of the Videotape thereof to CPS. After delivery of each Videotape to CPS, CPS may title such Program, edit such Program and make such changes in such Program as CPS, in its sole discretion, deems appropriate. Producer shall deliver the selected footage, rough cut, and fine cut of each Program to CPS on three-quarter inch (¾") NTSC videotape cassettes. Producer shall retain all original production and master tapes, and the three (3) track master for each Program, containing separate music, dialogue and sound-effects tracks, and shall make such materials available to CPS upon request for CPS' use pursuant to this Agreement for as long as CPS retains any rights in each Program.

(c) On or before any Delivery Date, Producer shall deliver to a laboratory designated by CPS (the "Laboratory") TWO (2) videotapes, each such videotape meeting the technical standards set forth in Exhibit II hereto (collectively, the "Videotape"). TWO (2) weeks prior to each Delivery Date, Producer shall contact CPS for specific instructions for the delivery of such Videotape. Each Videotape shall be held in the name of Producer for the sole purpose of preparing at CPS' expense and for CPS' use hereunder, such videotapes or videocassettes of the Program thereof (collectively, for each Program, "Video Reproductions") as CPS requires pursuant to this Agreement. Producer shall direct the Laboratory to prepare and immediately release to CPS, on videotape and videocassette stock supplied and owned by CPS, such Video Reproductions. CPS is not granted the right to own or exhibit any Videotape. If any Videotape of any program delivered to the Laboratory is not, in CPS's sole judgment, of acceptable technical quality, CPS shall have the right to require Producer to deliver additional Videotapes of the Program thereof to the Laboratory until CPS has approved such Videotape. Timely delivery of the Videotape for each Program meeting the technical standards of quality set forth in this Agreement is of the essence.

(d) All costs (including, without limitation, shipping and forwarding charges and insurance) of transporting any Videotape shall be borne by Producer. Once received by CPS, all costs of transporting and preparing any Video Reproductions shall be borne by CPS.

(e)   (i) Producer shall use its best efforts to obtain music performing rights ("Performing Rights") for all musical compositions contained in each Program ("Compositions"). Producer shall deliver to CPS not later than the Delivery Date of each Program a music cue sheet setting forth with respect to each Composition its title, running time, composer, publisher and performing right society, as well as a fee quote for each Performing Right (for each Program, the "Music Cue Sheet"). If, in CPS's sole discretion, the fee for any composition is deemed reasonable, CPS shall have the right to require Producer to promptly obtain the Performing Right therefor. CPS shall reimburse Producer for any Performing Right so obtained within TEN (10) days after receipt of copies of the license agreement therefor.

(ii) If Producer, after using best efforts, is unable to obtain fee quotes for any Composition, Producer shall so notify CPS not later than THIRTY (30) days prior to delivery of the Program thereof; such notice shall also set forth (A) the names of persons or entities contacted by Producer to acquire the Performing Rights and (B) the reasons for their refusal to negotiate for the acquisition of such Performing Rights (for any Program, each, a "Memorandum of Best Efforts").

(iii) If (A) the fee quotes set forth in any Music Cue Sheet for any Program are deemed unreasonable by CPS in its sole discretion and CPS does not require Producer to obtain Performing Rights, or (B) Producer shall have delivered to CPS the Memorandum of Best Efforts for such Program, Producer shall have no further obligation with respect to obtaining such Performing Rights, subject to the representations and warranties set forth in Subclause 12(c), below.

Clause 2.   DISTRIBUTION AND EXHIBITION:

(a) As between Producer and CPS, CPS is hereby granted the irrevocable, sole and exclusive right to distribute, transmit, display, exhibit, exploit, project, license, simulcast and perform each Program, or any portion thereof (collectively "distribute" or "distribution", as applicable) by any and all means, uses and media, including without limitation, distribution by means of Non-Standard Television, Standard Television, and for Ancillary Uses (each, as hereinafter defined) throughout the universe (the "Territory") during the term of the copyright in each Program (the "Copyright Term").

(b) During the Copyright Term, CPS shall have the right to distribute, or to cause to be distributed, each Program without limitation as to the number of exhibitions or Exhibition Days (as hereinafter defined).

(c) CPS may distribute or cause the distribution of each Program pursuant to the rights granted to it herein on such terms and conditions as CPS may elect in its sole discretion and without obtaining any approvals or consents from Producer or any other person. CPS shall not be required to distribute or cause any distribution of any Program; CPS shall have discharged fully its obligations hereunder by paying to Producer the sums herein provided in accordance with the terms hereof.

(d) As between CPS and Producer, CPS shall have the sole and exclusive right to produce and distribute, or to cause the production and distribution of, any program or series based upon, derived, or adapted from, any Program or the Series, by any means, uses or media. Producer shall not produce, cause or permit the production of any other program similar to any Program for distribution by means of Non-Standard Television, Standard Television or for Ancillary Uses in the Territory for a period of FIVE (5) years from the First Exhibition.

(e) As used throughout this Agreement the following terms shall have the following meanings:

(i) "Non-Standard Television" shall mean any and all forms of television exhibition and display, whether now existing or developed in the future, other than exhibitions by Standard Television; Non-Standard Television shall include, without limitation, exhibition by pay cable, "over-the-air pay" or Subscription Television ("STV") (including any and all forms of regular and occasional scrambled broadcast for taping) cable, master antenna, low power television, closed circuit, hotel, and other institutional service, multi-point distribution service, direct broadcast satellite service except for theatrical exhibition to paying audiences, all on a subscription, pay-per-view, license, rental, sale or any other basis.

(ii) "Standard Television" shall mean television distributed by a UHF or VHF television broadcast station, the video and audio portions of which are intelligibly receivable without charge by means of standard home roof-top or television set built-in antennas.

(iii) "Ancillary Uses" shall mean any and all means of distribution of any Program other than Non-Standard Television and Standard Television; Ancillary Uses include, without limitation, videotape in all gauges, theatrical motion picture exhibition, publications, merchandising, commercial tie-ups, interactive multimedia, sound recordings and Consumer Video Devices.

(iv) "Consumer Video Devices" shall mean distribution and/or exploitation of any Program by any form of video device, now existing or hereafter devised, including video discs and video cassettes for exhibition by means of a playback device which causes a visual image of any Program on the screen of a television receiver or any comparable device, whether now existing or hereinafter developed, located in consumer homes, including, without limitation, distribution for sale or rent, on a retail, subscription, club, mail order or other direct consumer basis.

(v) "Exhibition Day" shall mean any 24-hour period during which any Program is exhibited by means of Non-Standard Television one or more times at the location and on the program service in question.

(vi) "First Exhibition" shall mean the first exhibition authorized by CPS of any Program.

(v) "Initial Exhibition Period" shall mean for any Program the period terminating ONE (1) year after the First Exhibition of such Program.

Clause 3. PROMOTION AND CONFIDENTIALITY:

Producer shall not cause, authorize, license or permit any distribution, promotion, publicity or advertisement of any Program, or any portion thereof, in any form, by any means, uses or media, other than by CPS as provided hereunder, at any time during the Copyright Term provided that Producer may advertise and promote a Program in trade periodicals; provided, further, that no such advertising or promotion of any Program shall disclose the financial terms of this Agreement or CPS's proposed schedule for exhibition.

Clause 4. PAYMENT:

(a) Subject to the full performance by Producer of its material obligations hereunder, CPS shall pay to Producer, as full compensation for Producer's performance of all its obligations hereunder and all the rights granted to CPS hereunder with respect to the First Program, an aggregate amount equal to the amount of the approved Budget (the "License Fee") payable by checks delivered to Producer at Producer's Address (as hereinafter defined), as follows:

(i) 10% NOT LATER THAN TEN (10) days after the execution and delivery of this Agreement;

(ii) 15% NOT LATER THAN TEN (10) days after the receipt by CPS of notice of the commencement of pre-production;

(iii) 35% NOT LATER THAN TEN (10) days after the later of (A) delivery to CPS of the Script and Schedule; (B) the delivery to CPS of the certificates of insurance required pursuant to this Agreement for the Program; or (C) the approval by CPS of the Budget.

(iv) 20% NOT LATER THAN TEN (10) days after approval by CPS of the rough cut;

(v) 10% NOT LATER THAN TEN (10) days after the approval by CPS of the fine cut; and

(vi) 10% NOT LATER THAN TEN (10) days after the later occurring of (A) delivery to CPS of the acceptable Videotape and CPS's approval thereof; (B) delivery to CPS of an executed and notarized copy of the Assignment in the form of Exhibit I; (C) delivery to CPS of the Music Cue Sheet; (D) delivery to CPS of any Residual Summary (as hereinafter defined); or (E) delivery to CPS of any music synchronization license, music performance license (or any Memorandum of Best Efforts) or stock videotape footage licenses.

Clause 5. OPTION:

(a) Producer hereby irrevocably grants to CPS ONE (1) exclusive option (the "Option") to require Producer to produce and deliver ONE (1) additional Program for the Series, as set forth in this Section.

(b) If CPS does not exercise the Option, all obligations and liabilities between the parties hereto with respect to the First Program shall remain in full force and effect.

(c) If CPS exercises the Option, all terms and provisions of this Agreement applicable to the First Program (with the exception of the License Fee, the Schedule, the Budget and the Delivery Date) shall be applicable to the Production, delivery and distribution of the Optional Program.

(d) CPS may exercise the Option during the period commencing on the date hereof and ending on JUNE 1, 19____.

(e) Within FIFTEEN (15) BUSINESS days after CPS's exercise of the Option, Producer shall deliver to CPS, for CPS's approval, a Schedule specifying dates for each stage of the production and the Delivery Date of the Optional Program, which shall be as soon as practicable and as approved by CPS.

(f) The license fee payable to Producer for Producer's performance of all of its obligations and all the rights granted to CPS with respect to the Optional Program (the "Optional Program License Fee") shall be the amount of the approved Budget.

(g) The Optional Program License Fee shall be payable by checks delivered to Producer at Producer's address, as follows:

(i) 10% WITHIN TEN (10) days of CPS's notice to Producer of CPS's exercise of the Option;

(ii) 15% WITHIN TEN (10) days after the approval by CPS of the Budget;

(iii) 35% WITHIN TEN (10) days after the later occurring of (A) receipt of CPS of the Script and Schedule; or (B) the delivery to CPS of the certificates of insurance required for such Optional Program pursuant to this Agreement;

(iv) 20% WITHIN TEN (10) days after the approval by CPS of the rough cut of such Optional Program;

(v) 10% WITHIN TEN (10) days after approval by CPS of the fine cut of such Optional Program; and

(vi) 10% WITHIN TEN (10) days after the later occurring of (A) CPS's approval of the Videotape of such Optional Program; (B) delivery to CPS of the Assignment; (C) Producer's full compliance with clause 5(a)(v) above; (D) delivery to CPS of the Music Cue Sheet for such Optional Program; or (E) delivery to CPS of any Residual Summary for such Optional Program, and of any music synchronization, music performance licenses (or Memorandum of Best Efforts) or stock footage licenses for such Optional Program).

Clause 6. EXPENSES:

(a) Subject to Subclause 6(c), below, Producer shall pay all costs and expenses required to be paid in connection with the production of each Program and CPS's distribution of such Program hereunder, during the Initial Exhibition Period for each Program, including, without limitation, all residuals or reuse fees (and any pension, health and welfare contributions applicable thereto) prescribed by any applicable union or guild collective bargaining agreement (collectively, "Residuals"); all personnel engaged or employed in connection with such Program; all underlying rights; music synchronization rights, still photo, videotape footage rights and all other material included in such Program.

(b) Subject to Subclause 6(c), below, Producer shall pay all persons and/or entities providing services in connection with each Program and the Series at least the minimum scale compensation prescribed by any union or guild collective bargaining agreement applicable to such Program and also shall make any required contributions to any such union or guild's pension, health and welfare funds. Prior to delivery of each Videotape, Producer shall deliver to CPS a list of all persons providing services in connection with the Program thereof for which any Residuals could accrue pursuant to CPS's exercise of its rights hereunder and for payment of which CPS is obligated hereunder, and setting forth all information necessary for CPS's calculation of payment of any such Residuals (the "Residual Summary"). Notwithstanding any other provision of this Agreement, CPS shall have no obligation or liability to pay any Residuals for any person in any Program unless CPS shall have received such Residual Summary including such person's information for such Program.

(c) Producer shall be solely responsible for obtaining the right to use and to distribute any Program (and all constituent elements thereto) during the entire Copyright Term, provided, that CPS acknowledges that in accordance with industry practice, Producer may not be able to obtain stock footage and music synchronization license rights for the entire Copyright Term. In such event, Producer shall notify CPS (concurrently with the delivery of any Program to CPS) of any restrictions and limitations on any rights obtained by Producer for any footage or music synchronization license, such that CPS shall have sufficient notice to obtain any such additional rights and pay any additional license fees required for the distribution of any program. Except as set forth in the preceding sentence, CPS shall pay all residuals applicable to the distribution of any Program after the Initial Exhibition Period, but shall not be obligated to obtain any such additional rights after such Initial Exhibition Period, which rights Producer shall have obtained for each Program, subject to the aforesaid payments.

Clause 7. COPYRIGHT:

CPS shall be the sole and exclusive owner of each Program. Producer shall include after the credits in each Program a copyright notice, clearly visible for at least THREE (3) seconds, in the following form: "(c) [year of first exhibition] Cable Program Service, Inc. All Rights Reserved." Producer shall execute and deliver to CPS for each Program an assignment of rights substantially in the form appended hereto as Exhibit I, upon delivery of the Videotape thereof. Producer shall execute such assignment or such other assignments and instruments as CPS may from time to time deem reasonably necessary or desirable to evidence, maintain, protect, enforce or defend its right or title in or to any such materials. For such purpose only, Producer hereby irrevocably appoints CPS its true and lawful attorney-in-fact to execute, verify, acknowledge and deliver any and all such assignments and instruments which Producer shall fail or refuse to execute, verify, acknowledge or deliver.

Clause 8. PUBLICITY:

(a) Not later than TEN (10) days after completing videotaping of each Program, or at such earlier time as CPS reasonably request, Producer shall make available at no additional expense to CPS portions of such Program (selected by CPS) for use in CPS's sole discretion in preparing on-air promotional spots for such Program. At CPS's request, Producer shall cooperate with CPS in the preparation of such on-air promotional spots.

(b) Producer shall make available to CPS within FIVE (5) days after CPS's request therefor and in no event later than SIXTY (60) days prior to CPS's proposed First Exhibition of any Program (as notified by CPS to Producer), for CPS's use, and at no additional cost, TWENTY-FOUR (24) color transparencies, TWENTY-FOUR (24) black and white stills, ONE press kit and such other publicity and promotional materials and photographs of persons appearing in such Program as are available or as are made available to Producer.

Clause 9. EARLY TERMINATION; NONCONFORMING DELIVERY:

(a) If Producer is prevented or delayed in the production or delivery of any Program or in complying with any other of its obligations hereunder because of accidents, riots, strikes, epidemics, acts of God, or any other legitimate conditions beyond the affected party's control (each a "force majeure event"), CPS and Producer shall attempt in good faith during the NINETY (90) days following the commencement of such force majeure event to agree upon a mutually acceptable substitute date for delivery of such Program. If by the end of such 90-DAY period CPS and Producer fail to agree upon such substitute date, either party may terminate this Agreement with respect to any Programs affected by such force majeure event. Upon any such termination, Producer shall repay to CPS any amounts paid to Producer pursuant to this Agreement which have not been expended or contractually committed by Producer on the actual production of any Program affected by such termination by the date of such termination. Producer shall account to CPS in writing within TEN (10) days of such termination for any amounts so expended. In such event, Producer shall promptly deliver all elements of any Program affected by such termination produced by such date and all appropriate licenses of rights in such elements to CPS, and CPS (or its licensee or other transferee) shall have the right, but not the obligation, to complete any such Program. CPS's takeover and production of any such Program shall be subject to the provisions of all agreements entered into by Producer in connection with such Program prior to the date of such takeover (other than any provision inconsistent with CPS's takeover rights hereunder). Upon CPS's completion of any such Program, CPS (or its licensees or other transferees) shall have the exclusive right, subject to the aforesaid agreements, to distribute, exhibit and otherwise exploit any such Program (and any and all rights thereto) in any and all media throughout the world.

(b) If Producer fails to deliver the Videotape for any Program to CPS on or before the Delivery Date applicable to such Program (for any reason other than a force majeure event or delays caused by CPS) CPS, in addition to any other remedies it may have in law or in equity, may elect at its sole option either to: (i) reduce the License Fee for such Program by $1000 per day for each day that delivery of such Videotape is delayed (up to a maximum aggregate reduction of FIVE PERCENT (5%) of such License Fee) (such reduction constituting liquidated damages for such late delivery and not a penalty); or (ii) exercise the right of termination set forth in Subclause 9(a), above.

(c) If CPS rejects any Videotape for any Program for reasons of non-conformity with the technical acceptance criteria set forth herein and Producer fails to correct such non-conformity as soon as possible but in no event later than FORTY-EIGHT (48) HOURS (or ONE (1) week, if the exigencies of CPS's scheduling, in CPS's sole discretion, so permit) after notice to Producer of such non-conformity, CPS, in addition to any other remedies it may have in law or equity, may elect, at its sole option, either to: (i) terminate this Agreement with respect to any undelivered Program, whereupon Producer shall repay to CPS all amounts paid to Producer pursuant to this Agreement; or (ii) exercise the right of termination set forth in Subclause 9(a) above.

Clause 10. INSURANCE:

(a) Producer shall (at its own cost and expense) procure and maintain, at all times during the production of each Program the following insurance policies for each Program (each of which shall name CPS as a named insured and shall be issued by an insurance company reasonably acceptable to CPS):

(i) workers' compensation insurance adequate to comply with all statutory requirements covering all persons employed by Producer in connection with such Program, including if applicable, foreign workers' compensation insurance (which policy shall include an employer liability endorsement and a repatriation expense rider);

(ii) public liability insurance (including coverage for owned and hired vehicle liability and hired aircraft liability) having a combined single limit of at least $1,000,000 per occurrence and $2,000,000 in the aggregate, for bodily injuries to any number of persons arising out of the same accident and for property damage;

(iii) insurance (with a limit not less than the Program production budget) covering for such Program (A) the theft, destruction or loss of the Videotape; (B) the theft, destruction or loss of props, sets, wardrobe having a minimum limit of the aggregate budgeted amount for such items; (C) the theft, destruction or loss of all miscellaneous equipment having a minimum amount equal to the replacement value of all equipment owned, rented, leased or loaned; (D) additional expense having a minimum limit reasonably satisfactory to cover all out–of–pocket expenses resulting from such loss; (E) third party property damage having a minimum limit of $250,000; and (F) faulty stock, camera and processing insurance, having a minimum limit reasonably satisfactory to cover all out-of-pocket expenses resulting from such loss;

(iv) cast insurance for such Program with a limit not less than such Program's production budget;

(v) standard producer's liability (errors and omissions) insurance, covering such Program and the title thereof throughout the Initial Exhibition Period, with a customary deductible and with minimum limits of at least $1,000,000 for any claim arising out of a single occurrence and $3,000.000 in the aggregate. Any such producer's liability insurance policy shall not contain, without CPS's prior written consent, any special or non-customary exclusions and shall be cancelable only upon THIRTY (30) days prior written notice to CPS. In the event of such cancellation, and prior to the effective date thereof, Producer shall deliver replacement insurance to CPS issued by an insurance company acceptable to CPS.

(b) Producer shall deliver to CPS valid insurance certificates (in form and substance reasonably satisfactory to CPS) evidencing the insurance coverage required hereby for each Program.

Clause 11. CREDITS:

(a) Producer shall not agree to accord any credits in connection with the advertising or promotion of any Program and the Series without CPS's prior written consent. Producer shall deliver to CPS NINETY (90) days prior to each Delivery Dates, a complete statement ("Producer's Statement") setting forth the credits to be accorded to all persons, firms and corporations in connection with the Program thereof. If no Producer's Statement is received by CPS, CPS shall have the right to rely on the credits as set forth in any Program, and such Program credits shall be deemed to constitute the Producer's Statement for such Program hereunder.

(b) Each Videotape delivered to the Laboratory shall contain only one opening credit which states "CABLE PROGRAM SERVICE, INC. PRESENTS" and a final closing credit which states "THIS HAS BEEN A CABLE PROGRAM SERVICE, INC. PRESENTATION".

(c) No Program shall contain any commercial announcements or promotional or commercial credits. The closing credits for each Program shall not include any logos (other than Producer's non-animated logo), graphics, photographs, addresses, telephone numbers or voice-over mentions. No Program shall contain any visual or audio promotional credits for the sale or distribution of any Consumer Video Devices of such Program or the Series.

Clause 12. PRODUCER'S REPRESENTATIONS, WARRANTIES AND COVENANTS: Producer hereby warrants, represents and covenants to CPS as follows:

(a) With respect solely to material or elements provided by Producer and expressly excluding materials provided by CPS, no Program nor any element thereof shall violate the right of privacy or publicity of, or defame, or violate any copyright, trademark or service mark or other right (including, without limitation, any literary, dramatic, or musical right) of any person, firm or corporation or violate any other applicable law.

(b) (i) Producer has the right to enter into this Agreement, to grant the rights herein granted and to perform fully all of its obligations and agreements hereunder. Producer shall employ or engage writers who shall be the sole authors of each Script and of all the materials contained therein. All such material shall be wholly original with such writers, and not copied in whole or in part from any other work, or is duly licensed or is in the public domain. Producer will enter into appropriate written agreements with third parties providing work in connection with each Program, which agreements shall provide that such work is a work made for hire. Producer has acquired all rights necessary to Producer's grant of rights to CPS hereunder and Producer is the sole owner of all such rights, (and will at CPS's request deliver to CPS copies of all such documents as evidence of Producer's acquisition of such rights) including, without limitation, all copyrights, music synchronization rights, still photo, videotape footage licenses or other appropriate licenses of all elements of each Program or such constituent elements are owned by Producer or are in the public domain.

(ii) Producer shall furnish to CPS, prior to delivery of each Videotape, a Music Cue Sheet, setting forth with respect to each Composition contained in the Program thereof such Composition's running time, composer, publisher and performing rights society.

(c) With respect to each Composition contained in each Program, the non-dramatic musical performing rights necessary for exhibition of the Program hereto are: (i) controlled by American Society of Composers, Authors and Publishers ("ASCAP"), Broadcast Music Inc. ("BMI") or SESAC, (ii) in the public domain or (iii) owned by or licensed to producer. CPS may replace any musical composition in any Program if at any time during the term for exercise of any rights granted to CPS hereunder a performance license from any such performing rights society for such Composition cannot be obtained or maintained as may be necessary for CPS's distribution of such Program hereunder.

(d) The Residual Summary for each Program is complete and accurate for all persons and performers supplying services in connection with such Program, and contains all information necessary to accurately calculate any Residuals that may be due and owing by CPS as a result of CPS's exercise of its rights hereunder with respect to such Program.

(e) The Producer's Statement for each program is complete and accurate and omits no party or entity entitled to any credit for providing services on such Program, nor is any credit provided therein inaccurate, improper or insufficient.

(f) Producer shall cause to be conducted a title search of the title of each Program, confirming that pursuant to such search the title of the Program is available for use for such Program by means of Non-Standard Television, Standard Television and Ancillary Uses in the Territory.

(g) None of the rights herein granted to CPS has been transferred to any third party and said rights are free of any liens, claims and encumbrances whatsoever in favor of any other party, and said rights and the full right to exercise the same, have not been in any way limited, diminished, or impaired. There are no claims, litigation or other proceedings pending or threatened which would adversely affect CPS's rights hereunder.

(h) Producer will announce, or cause to be announced, at each place where videotaping will occur, that such videotaping is occurring and will notify any audience there present that they may be seen on any Program.

(i) Each Videotape shall be delivered by Producer to CPS in accordance with Exhibit II hereto [Technical Specifications].

Clause 13. CPS'S WARRANTIES: CPS hereby represents and warrants to Producer that it has the right to enter into this Agreement and perform all of its obligations hereunder.

Clause 14. INDEMNIFICATION:

(a) Producer assumes liability for, and hereby agrees to indemnify, defend, protect, save and hold harmless CPS from and against any and all claims, actions, suits, costs, liabilities, judgments, obligations, losses, penalties, expenses or damages (including, without limitation, reasonable legal fees and expenses) of whatsoever kind and nature imposed on, incurred by or asserted against CPS, arising out of any breach or alleged breach by Producer of any representation, warranty, covenant or obligation made by Producer pursuant to the Agreement.

(b) CPS assumes liability for, and hereby agrees to indemnify, defend, protect, save and hold harmless Producer from and against any and all claims, actions, suits, costs, liabilities, judgments, obligations, losses, penalties, expenses or damages (including, without limitation, reasonable legal fees and expenses) of whatsoever kind and nature imposed on, incurred by or asserted against Producer, arising out of any breach or alleged breach by CPS of any representation, warranty covenant or obligation made by CPS pursuant to the Agreement.

(c) To seek or receive indemnification hereunder:

(i) the party seeking indemnification must have promptly notified the other of any claim or litigation of which it is aware and to which the indemnification relates; and

(ii) the party seeking indemnification must have afforded the other the opportunity to approve any compromise, settlement, litigation or other resolution or disposition of such claim or litigation provided, that if the indemnifying party does not approve any such compromise, settlement or other resolution it shall, upon the request of the party seeking indemnification, take over at its own cost and expense the control of such litigation.

Clause 15. INDEPENDENT CONTRACTORS:

Producer and CPS are independent contractors with respect to each other. Nothing herein shall create any association, partnership, joint venture or agency relationship between them. All persons employed by Producer in connection with Producer's performance hereunder shall be Producer's employees, and Producer shall be fully responsible for them, including, without limitation, responsibility for all compensation, withholding taxes, worker's compensation insurance and other required payments in connection with such employees, except as otherwise specifically and explicitly provided herein.

Clause 16. CONFIDENTIALITY:

Neither Producer nor CPS shall disclose to any third party (other than its respective employees, in their capacity as such), any information with respect to the financial terms of this Agreement except: (a) to the extent necessary to comply with law or the valid order of a court of competent jurisdiction, in which event the party making such disclosure shall seek confidential treatment of such information; (b) as part of its normal reporting or review procedure to its parent company, its auditors and its attorneys (and said parent company, auditors and attorneys agree to be bound by the provisions of this Clause) and (c) in order to enforce its rights pursuant to this Agreement. Any party disclosing such information hereunder shall give the other party hereto written notice of the nature and scope of such disclosure, and the justification therefore pursuant to this Clause as promptly as possible and in any event reasonably prior to any such disclosure's being made.

Clause 17.   REMEDIES: If CPS breaches any provision of the Agreement, the damage, if any, caused Producer thereby will not be irreparable or otherwise sufficient to entitle Producer to injunctive or other equitable relief. Producer's rights and remedies in any such event shall be strictly limited to the right, if any, to recover damages in an action at law, and Producer shall not be entitled by reason of any such breach to rescind this Agreement, or to restrain CPS's exercise of any of the rights granted to CPS hereunder, or to enjoin or restrain the distribution or exhibition of any version of the Program hereunder, or any advertising, publicity or promotion in connection therewith. All remedies, rights, undertakings, obligations and agreements contained in the Agreement shall be cumulative and none thereof shall be in limitation of any other remedy, right, undertaking, obligation or agreement of either party.

Clause 18.   SEVERABILITY: Nothing contained in this Agreement shall be construed so as to require the commission of any act contrary to law, and wherever there is any conflict between any provision of this Agreement and any statute, law, ordinance, order or regulation contrary to which the parties hereto have no legal right to contract, such statute, law, ordinance, order or regulation shall prevail; provided, that in such event (a) the provision of this Agreement so affected shall be limited only to the extent necessary to permit compliance with the minimum legal requirement, (b) no other provisions of this Agreement shall be affected thereby, and (c) all such other provisions shall continue in full force and effect.

Clause 19.   MISCELLANEOUS

(a) Notices. All notices and other communications between the parties hereto shall be in writing and shall be deemed received when delivered in person, by telex or telegram, or FIVE (5) days after deposited in the United States mails, postage prepaid, certified or registered mail addressed to the other party at the address set forth below (or at such other address as such other party may supply by written notice):

(b) Further Documents. Each party hereto shall execute any and all further documents or instruments which either party hereto may deem reasonably necessary and proper to carry out the purpose of this Agreement.

(c) Prior Agreements, Waivers and Amendments. This Agreement contains the full and complete understanding between the parties hereto, supersedes all prior agreements and understandings, whether written or oral pertaining thereto and cannot be modified except by a written instrument signed by each party hereto. No waiver of any term or condition of this Agreement shall be construed as a waiver of any other term or condition; nor shall any waiver of any default under this Agreement be construed as a waiver of any other default.

(d) Headings, Titles. The descriptive headings of the several sections and paragraphs of this Agreement are inserted for convenience only and do not constitute a part of this Agreement.

(e) Governing Law. This Agreement shall be governed by, and construed in accordance with, the laws of the State of (NAME) applicable to contracts entered into and to be fully performed therein.

(f) Assignments. Producer shall not assign any of its rights or obligations hereunder without the prior written consent of CPS, and any purported assignment without such prior written consent shall be null and void and of no force and effect.

(g) Survival. All representations and warranties contained herein or made by Producer in connection herewith shall survive any independent investigation made by CPS and the execution, delivery, suspension and termination of this Agreement or any provision hereof.

IN WITNESS WHEREOF, each of the parties hereto has duly executed and delivered this Agreement as of the date first written above.

PRODUCER
By: _____

CABLE PROGRAM SERVICE
By: _____

EXHIBIT I

ASSIGNMENT

KNOW ALL PERSONS BY THESE PRESENTS:

In consideration of Ten Dollars, receipt of which is hereby acknowledged, paid by CPS and for other good and valuable consideration, the undersigned does hereby grant and assign to CPS, its successors and assigns, the copyright and all right, title and interest, without reservation, throughout the universe in and to the television program forming a part of the television series tentatively entitled "(TITLE)" and identified more specifically as episode (NAME) of such series (the "Program") and in the script upon which the Program is based. Such rights include without limitation, all of the undersigned's right, title and interest which may affix under any copyright law now or hereinafter in force and effect in the United States of America or in any other country or countries, to be held and enjoyed by CPS, its successors and assigns, fully, entirely and absolutely.

This Assignment is executed in accordance with and is subject to the terms and conditions of the license agreement dated as of FEBRUARY 15, 1986, between the undersigned and CPS relating to the grant and assignment to CPS of the above-mentioned rights in the Program.

IN WITNESS WHEREOF, the undersigned has caused these presents to be signed by its duly authorized officer on the _____day of _____, _____.

PRODUCTIONS, INC.

By: _____

STATE OF (NAME) ss.: COUNTY OF (NAME)

On the (NUMBER) day of (MONTH), (YEAR) before me personally came (NAME), to me known, who, being by me duly sworn, did depose and say that he/she resides at (ADDRESS); that he/she is the (TITLE) of Productions, Inc., the corporation described in and which executed the foregoing instrument; and that he/she signed his/her name thereto by order of the board of directors of said corporation.

_____

Notary Public

Form 9

Option Agreement for Acquisition of Literary Property

Dear [(PURCHASER) or (OWNER)]:

This letter, when countersigned by [(YOU) or (NAME OF PURCHASER)], will confirm the agreement between [(NAME OF PURCHASER)] ("Purchaser") and (NAME OF OWNER) ("Owner") for the acquisition of [DESCRIBE PROPERTY BEING ACQUIRED, E.G. THE LITERARY WORK ENTITLED "(TITLE OF WORK)" OR THE MOTION PICTURE, TELEVISION AND ALLIED RIGHTS IN AND TO THAT CERTAIN ORIGINAL STORY ABOUT (TITLE OF WORK)] (hereinafter called "the Literary Property"). [ADD, AS AND IF APPROPRIATE, written by (NAME OF AUTHOR) ("Author"), published by (NAME OF PUBLISHER) on or about (DATE OF PUBLICATION), in the United States and registered for copyright in the name of (NAME OF COPYRIGHT REGISTRANT) in the United States Copyright Office, registration number (COPYRIGHT REGISTRATION NUMBER).] As used herein, the reference to "Purchaser" includes Purchaser's assignees.

1. OPTION: In consideration of the sum of (AMOUNT, E.G., FIVE THOUSAND) Dollars (E.G., $5,000.00), receipt of which Owner hereby acknowledges, Owner hereby grants to purchaser a (LENGTH OF OPTION, E.G., EIGHTEEN (18) MONTH) exclusive and irrevocable option to (SPECIFY RIGHTS BEING ACQUIRED, E.G.,) [acquire any and all motion picture, allied and ancillary rights in and to the Literary Property except (SPECIFY ANY RESERVED RIGHTS) in order to develop and produce an initial theatrical motion picture based on the Literary Property ("the Picture") and exploit the Picture and all rights acquired herein (or) [obtain and enter into a written agreement with a BONA FIDE third party motion picture company or motion picture production company (collectively the "Motion Picture Company") to develop and produce a motion picture based upon the Literary Property (the "Picture") and to acquire the Literary Property (for the amounts set forth herein) (the "Motion Picture Agreement").] The initial option period shall commence on the date of Owner's execution hereof and may be extended for an additional, consecutive (LENGTH OF ADDITIONAL OPTION PERIOD, E.G., EIGHTEEN (18)) month period by the giving of written notice and the payment to Owner of an additional (AMOUNT, E.G., FIVE THOUSAND) Dollars (E.G., $5,000) at any time prior to the expiration of the initial option period. [(ADD, IF APPLICABLE): Purchaser agrees to immediately notify Owner of any such Motion Picture Agreement and the terms thereof, and to supply Owner with a copy thereof.] [ADD, AS APPLICABLE: If Purchaser exercises its option, [(none) (all) (the first)] of the foregoing payments with respect to the option and any extension thereof will apply and be credited against the first sums payable to Owner as total consideration ("purchase price")].

2. <u>ACQUISITION AND COMPENSATION</u>: If Purchaser timely exercises its option and pays the option price, during the option period, including any extensions, the following terms (OR purchase price) shall apply:

(a) Owner shall grant to Purchaser the rights to produce an initial motion picture [including remakes and sequels] [television long form and series rights] [and] [7,500 word promotional publishing rights and ancillary rights thereto], [subject to Owner's reserved rights and holdback noted in Clause 4 below].

(b) Purchaser [or its assignee] shall pay Owner [or cause the Motion Picture Company to pay Owner] the sum of ($100,000) less the (AMOUNT PAID FOR OPTION) sum theretofore paid in connection with the initial option period] for [(specify, E.G.,) all motion picture, allied and ancillary rights] in and to the Literary Property acquired hereunder, [payable upon exercise of the option granted herein but in any event not later than commencement of principal photography of the Picture].

(c) For any sequel produced based on the Literary Property, in whole or in part, Purchaser will pay or cause Owner to be paid (E.G., ONE-HALF) of the original compensation payable under Subclauses 2(b) and 2(e); and for any remake produced based on the Literary Property, in whole or in part, Purchaser will pay or cause Owner to be paid (E.G., ONE-THIRD) of the original compensation payable under Subclauses 2(b) and 2(e); all the foregoing to be paid to Owner upon commencement of principal photography of any such sequel and/or remake.

(d) For any television series produced, based on the Literary Property, Purchaser will pay or cause to be paid to Owner the following royalties per initial production upon completion of production of each program: up to (E.G., 30) minutes-(E.G., $1,500); over (E.G., 30) but not more than (E.G., 60) minutes-(E.G., $1,750); over (E.G., 60) minutes but not more than (E.G, 90) minutes-(E.G., $2,000); over (E.G., 90) minutes-(E.G., $2,250); and in addition to the foregoing, as a buy out of all royalty obligations, (E.G., ONE HUNDRED) percent (E.G., 100%) in equal installments over (E.G., FIVE) (E.G., 5) reruns, payable within (E.G., THIRTY) (30) days after each such rerun, or subject to the WGA minimum, whichever is greater.

(e) Purchaser shall pay Owner a percentage participation of (E.G., FIVE) percent (E.G., 5%) of one hundred percent (100%) of the net profits (including all allied rights and exploitation) of each motion picture and television program or series based in whole or in part on the Literary Property. The percentage participation shall be defined in the same way as the net profit participation granted to Purchaser [, provided, however, that Owner's percentage shall not be subject to any reductions or preconditions whatsoever, such as but not limited to reductions because of other writers or participants or preconditions to receiving net profits dependent upon writing credits, full performance of services, non-breach of contract and the like. Accountings, statements and audit rights shall be on the same basis as accorded Purchaser, but in any event not less than semi-annual accountings.]

3. <u>REPRESENTATIONS AND WARRANTIES</u>: Owner hereby represents and warrants that: [Owner has the sole, exclusive and unencumbered ownership of all rights of every kind and character throughout the world in and to the Literary Property [, except (LIST ANY EXCEPTIONS)] OR [(a) the Literary Property was written solely by and is original with Owner; (b) neither the Literary Property nor any element thereof infringes upon any other literary property; (c) the production or exploitation of any motion picture or other production based on the Literary Property will not violate the rights to privacy of any person or constitute a defamation against any person, nor will production or exploitation of any motion picture or other production based thereon in any other way violate the rights of any person; (d) Owner owns all rights in the Literary Property as specified hereinabove free and clear of any liens, encumbrances, claims or litigation, whether pending or threatened; (e) Owner has full right and power to make and perform this agreement; and (f) the Literary Property has not previously been exploited as a motion picture, television production, play or otherwise than in book form, and no rights have been granted to any third party to do so. Owner hereby indemnifies Purchaser against any loss or damage (including reasonable attorneys' fees) incurred by reason of any breach or claim of breach of the foregoing representations and warranties. The term "person" as used herein shall mean any person, firm, corporation or other entity.]

4. <u>RIGHTS ACQUIRED/RESERVED</u>: The foregoing option covers [(SPECIFY, E.G.,) the sole, exclusive, perpetual and worldwide motion picture, television and allied and incidental rights in the Literary Property (and any and all screenplays or other adaptations thereof) whether heretofore or hereafter written by Owner or any other person, including theatrical, television (whether filmed, taped or otherwise recorded, and including series rights), cassette and other compact devices, sequel, remake and advertising rights (including 7,500-word synopsis publication rights); all rights to exploit, distribute and exhibit any motion picture or other production produced hereunder in all media now known or hereafter devised; all rights to make any and all changes to and adaptations of the Literary Property; merchandising, sound track, music publishing and exploitation rights; the right to use Author's name in and in connection with the exploitation of the rights granted hereunder; and all other rights customarily obtained in connection with formal literary purchase agreements, as referred to in Clause 9 below.] Purchaser hereby acknowledges that owner reserves [(SPECIFY, E.G.,) nonseries live television, radio, publication and legitimate stage rights], subject to Purchaser's customary limited advertising and promotion rights. Owner will not exercise or dispose of or permit the exercise or disposition of such [(SPECIFY, E.G.,) reserved radio or stage rights for a period of (E.G., SEVEN) (E.G., 7) years after release of the first motion picture based upon the

Literary Property (herein the "Picture"), or (E.G., SEVEN) (E.G., 7) years from
the date on which Purchaser exercises its option, whichever first occurs; nor will
Owner exercise or dispose of or permit the exercise or disposition of Owner's
reserved live television rights for a period of (E.G., FIVE) (E.G., 5) years after
release of the Picture or (E.G. FIVE) (E.G., 5) years after the date on which
Purchaser exercises its option, whichever first occurs.] [At any time that Owner
is entitled to exercise or dispose of any such reserved rights, Purchaser shall have
the right to acquire such rights upon such BONA FIDE terms and conditions
as Owner is offered and is prepared to accept from a third party within (E.G.,
THIRTY (30)) days after Owner notifies purchaser in writing of such terms and
conditions.]

5. EXECUTION OF ADDITIONAL DOCUMENTS: Owner agrees to execute
at Purchaser's request any and all additional documents or instruments, including
a short form option agreement (Exhibit A) and a short form assignment for
purposes of recording in the Copyright Office (Exhibit B), and to do any and
all things necessary or desirable to effectuate the purposes of this agreement.
If such short form assignment is undated, Purchaser is authorized to date such
short form assignment and to file the same in the Copyright Office immediately
upon exercise of the option herein granted. If Owner fails to do anything
necessary or desirable to effectuate the purposes of this agreement, including,
but not limited to, renewing copyrights and instituting and maintaining actions
for infringement of any rights herein granted to Purchaser under copyright or
otherwise, Owner hereby irrevocably appoints Purchaser as Owner's attorney-in-
fact with the right, but not the obligation, to do any such things and renew
copyrights and institute and maintain actions in Owner's name and behalf, but
for Purchaser's benefit, which appointment shall be coupled with an interest and
shall be irrevocable.

6. CREDIT: [Credits shall be provided in accordance with the provisions of the
applicable Writers Guild of America Theatrical and Television Basic Agreement.]
[Subject to the provisions of the applicable Writers Guild of America Theatrical
and Television Basic Agreement,] Purchaser agrees to accord Owner credit on
the positive prints of the Picture substantially as follows:

(a) If the Picture has the same title as the title of the Literary Property, such
credit shall read: "Based on the book by (NAME OF AUTHOR)".

(b) If the Picture does not have the same title as the Literary Property, such
credit shall read: "Based on the book (NAME OF BOOK) by (NAME OF
AUTHOR)". [(AS AN ALTERNATIVE, A SOURCE MATERIAL CREDIT
MAY PROVIDE:) Owner shall be accorded a source material credit in the form
of "Based upon (E.G., THE ORIGINAL STORY) by (NAME OF AUTHOR)."]
[Such credit shall also be provided in paid advertising, subject to any distributor's
and customary exclusions for award, congratulatory and similar ads.] Subject to

the foregoing, the presentation of such credits shall be determined by Purchaser. Any casual or inadvertent failure by Purchaser, or any failure by any third party, to comply with the provisions of this clause shall not be deemed to be a breach of this agreement. In the event of a failure or omission of Purchaser's obligations under this clause, it is expressly agreed that Owner's sole remedy shall be to seek damages in a court of competent jurisdiction, and that in no event shall Owner be entitled to obtain any injunctive or other equitable relief or undertake any legal efforts to restrict Purchaser's right to exploit the Property.

7. ASSIGNMENT: Purchaser shall not have the right to assign this agreement or any part hereof except to a BONA FIDE third party motion picture company or motion picture production company upon the terms and conditions set forth in this agreement, and any such assignment and transfer shall be made specifically subject to the terms and conditions and payments of this agreement, regardless of whether or not Purchaser becomes or remains involved in the production of the Literary Property as writer, producer or otherwise.

8. NOTICES: All checks and notices from Purchaser to Owner shall be sent to Owner (by (MODE OF DELIVERY) (SPECIFY TYPE OF MAIL, E.G., CERTIFIED MAIL return receipt requested)) at the following address (ADDRESS OF OWNER) with a courtesy copy to (NAME AND ADDRESS).

All notices from Owner to Purchaser shall be sent to Purchaser (by (MODE OF DELIVERY) (SPECIFY TYPE OF MAIL, E.G., FACSIMILE OR REGISTERED MAIL)) at the following address (ADDRESS OF PURCHASER) with a courtesy copy to (NAME AND ADDRESS).

[All notices shall be deemed given [(upon receipt by the party to whom they are addressed) OR (upon deposit in the ordinary course of the U.S. mail by the method specified above)].]

9. MORE FORMAL AGREEMENT: Until a more formal agreement is executed incorporating all of the foregoing and additional detailed representations, warranties and other provisions customarily included in such formal literary purchase agreements, this agreement shall be binding upon and inure to the benefit of the parties hereto and their successors, representatives, assigns and licensees.

ADDITIONAL CLAUSES

10. [TECHNICAL] [STORY] CONSULTANT: If Purchaser exercises the option as provided hereinabove, and production of an initial motion picture or television program or series based on the Property is commenced, Purchaser agrees that Owner shall be employed and paid as a [technical] [story] consultant for such motion picture or television program at a guaranteed weekly compensation during production, of (E.G., $1,000 PER WEEK) for a guaranteed period equal to the

period of principal photography of such motion picture or production of such program, but in no event less than an ((E.G., TEN) (E.G., 10)) week period, which sum shall in any event be fully paid no later than the end of said guaranteed period. [Said sum shall be in addition to all other sums paid to Owner hereunder.] Owner shall receive a credit as seen in the motion picture for such services, the size and placement to be at Purchaser's sole discretion.

11. OPTION REVERSION AND TURNAROUND RIGHT:

(a) If the Purchaser does not timely exercise the option and thereafter timely pay the purchase price, the option shall automatically terminate and all rights, title and interests in the Literary Property shall immediately and automatically revert to Owner without any obligation or payment to Purchaser. Owner shall retain all sums thereto paid. Purchaser further agrees to immediately execute and deliver to Owner any and all assignments and documentation required by Owner to implement this Clause, and if Purchaser should fail or be unable to do so, Purchaser hereby grants Owner a power coupled with an interest to execute and deliver such documents as Purchaser's attorney-in-fact.

(b) If the option is timely exercised and the purchase price paid, but purchaser does not [(SPECIFY GROUNDS FOR TURNAROUND, E.G.,) commence principal photography on a motion picture based on the Literary Property within (E.G., FIVE) (E.G., 5) years from acquisition of the Literary Property,] Owner shall have a turnaround right to reacquire and set up the Literary Property elsewhere [(SPECIFY OWNER'S REQUIREMENT TO OBTAIN TURN-AROUND, E.G.,) upon obtaining such other commitment to reimburse the Purchaser or Motion Picture Company for its actual direct out-of-pocket development costs in connection with the Literary Property, such as fees to scriptwriters, (but excluding payments to Owner and any payments to Purchaser not directly related to scriptwriting services)].

[(c) In addition to the above, if Purchaser decides not to exercise the option as provided hereinabove, at any time prior to the expiration of the Option Period, or decides not to extend such option for (SPECIFY ADDITIONAL OPTION LENGTH, E.G., AN ADDITIONAL YEAR), Purchaser agrees to notify Owner of such decision as soon as reasonably possible, but in no event later than the applicable option or extension deadline. When such notice is given, the option granted hereunder to Purchaser shall automatically revert to Owner.]

12. RIGHT TO ENGAGE IN PREPRODUCTION: During said option period or extension thereof, Purchaser shall have the right (at its own expense) to engage in preproduction with respect to a motion picture or other production intended to be based on the Literary Property.

13. FORCE MAJEURE: "Force Majeure" means any fire, flood, earthquake, or public disaster; strike, labor dispute or unrest; embargo, riot, war, insurrection

or civil unrest; any act of God, any act of legally constituted authority; or any other cause beyond Purchaser's control which would excuse Purchaser's performance as a matter of law. If by reason of force majeure, Purchaser's performance hereunder is delayed, hampered or prevented, then the option period provided herein (and any performance by Purchaser) shall be extended for the amount of time of such delay or prevention [up to a maximum of E.G., SIX MONTHS].

Please signify your agreement to the foregoing by signing where indicated below and returning this letter.

AGREED TO AND ACCEPTED:

Very truly yours,

_____
(Purchaser)

_____
(Owner)

Date: _____

Form 10

Agreement to Acquire Literary Material

This Agreement is made on (DATE) by and between
_____ (hereinafter referred to as "Owner") and
_____ (hereinafter referred to as "Purchaser") with re-
spect to Owner's literary work entitled: [E.G., (TITLE), [Written by, (AUTHOR),
which work has been filed in the United States Copyright Office under Copyright
Registration Number _____;] This [work including all
adaptations and/or versions, the titles, characters, plots, themes and storyline]
This is collectively referred to hereinafter as the "Property".

The parties agree as follows:

1. RIGHTS GRANTED: Owner hereby sells, grants, conveys and assigns to
Purchaser, its successors, licensees and assigns exclusively and forever, all
motion picture rights (including all silent, sound, dialogue and musical motion
picture rights), all television motion picture and other television rights, together
with limited radio broadcasting rights and 7,500 word publication rights for
advertisement, publicity and exploitation purposes, [any and all] [certain] allied
and ancillary rights, throughout the universe, in and to the Property and in and
to the copyright thereof and all renewals and extensions of copyright. Included
among the rights granted to Purchaser hereunder (without in any way limiting
the grant of rights hereinabove made) are the following sole and exclusive rights
throughout the universe:

(a) To make, produce, adapt and copyright one or more motion picture
adaptations or versions, whether fixed on film, tape, disc, wire, audio-visual
cartridge, cassette or through any other technical process whether now known
or hereafter devised, based in whole or in part on the Property, of every size,
gauge, color or type, including, but not limited to, musical motion pictures and
remakes of and sequels to any motion picture produced hereunder and motion
pictures in series or serial form, and for such purposes to record and reproduce
and license others to record and reproduce, in synchronization with such motion
pictures, spoken words taken from or based upon the text or theme of the Property
and any and all kinds of music, musical accompaniments and/or lyrics to be
performed or sung by the performers in any such motion picture and any and
all other kinds of sound and sound effects.

(b) To exhibit, perform, rent, lease and generally deal in and with any motion
picture produced hereunder:

(i) by all means or technical processes whatsoever, whether now known or
hereafter devised including, by way of example only, film, tape, disc, wire,
audio-visual cartridge, cassette or television (including commercially

sponsored, sustaining and subscription or pay-per-view television, or any derivative thereof); and

(ii) in any place whatsoever, including homes, theatres and elsewhere, and whether or not a fee is charged, directly or indirectly, for viewing any such motion picture.

(c) To broadcast, transmit or reproduce the Property or any adaptation or version thereof (including without limitations to, any motion picture produced hereunder and/or any script or other material based on or utilizing the Property or any of the characters, themes or plots thereof), by means of television or any process analogous thereto whether now known or hereafter devised (including commercially sponsored, sustaining and subscription or pay-per-view television), through the use of motion pictures produced on films or by means of magnetic tape, wire, disc, audio-visual cartridge or any other device now known or hereafter devised and including such television productions presented in series or serial form, and the exclusive right generally to exercise for television purposes all the rights granted to Purchaser hereunder for motion picture purposes.

(d) Without limiting any other rights granted Purchaser, to broadcast and/or transmit by television or radio or any process analogous thereto whether now known or hereafter devised, all or any part of the Property or any adaptation or version thereof, including any motion picture or other version or versions thereof, and announcements pertaining to said motion picture or other version or versions, for the purpose of advertising, publicizing or exploiting such motion picture or other version or versions, which broadcasts or transmissions may be accomplished through the use of living actors performing simultaneously with such broadcast or transmission or by any other method or means including the use of motion pictures (including trailers) reproduced on film or by means of magnetic tape or wire or through the use of other recordings or transcriptions.

(e) To publish and copyright or cause to be published and copyrighted in the name of Purchaser or its nominee in any and all languages throughout the world, in any form or media, synopses, novelizations, serializations, dramatizations, abridged and/or revised versions of the Property, not exceeding 7,500 words each, adapted from the Property or from any motion picture and/or other version of the Property for the purpose of advertising, publicizing and/or exploiting any such motion picture and/or other version.

(f) For the foregoing purposes to use all or any part of the Property and any of the characters, plots, themes and/or ideas contained therein, and the title of the Property and any title or subtitle of any component of the Property, and to use said titles or subtitles for any motion picture or other version or adaptation whether or not the same is based on or adapted from the Property and/or as the title of any musical composition contained in any such motion picture or other version or adaptation.

(g) To use and exploit commercial or merchandise tie-ups and recordings of any sort and nature arising out of or connected with the Property and/or its motion picture or other versions and/or the title or titles thereof and/or the characters thereof and/or their names or characteristics.

All rights, licenses, privileges and property herein granted Purchaser shall be cumulative and Purchaser may exercise or use any or all said rights, licenses, privileges or property simultaneously with or in connection with or separately and apart from the exercise of any other of said rights, licenses, privileges and property. [If Owner hereafter makes or publishes or permits to be made or published any revision, adaptation, sequel, translation or dramatization or other versions of the Property, then Purchaser shall have and Owner hereby grants to Purchaser without payment therefor all of the same rights therein as are herein granted Purchaser.] The terms "Picture" and "Pictures" as used herein shall be deemed to mean or include any present or future kind of motion picture production based upon the Property, with or without sound recorded and reproduced synchronously therewith, whether the same is produced on film or by any other method or means now or hereafter used for the production, exhibition and/or transmission of any kind of motion picture productions.

2. RIGHTS RESERVED: The following rights are reserved to Owner for Owner's use and disposition, subject, however, to the provisions of this agreement:

(a) Publication Rights: The right to publish and distribute printed versions of the Property owned or controlled by Owner in book form, whether hardcover or softcover, and in magazines or other periodicals, whether in installments or otherwise, subject to Purchaser's rights as provided for in Clause 1, *supra*.

(b) Stage Rights: The right to perform the Property or adaptations thereof on the spoken stage with actors appearing in person in the immediate presence of the audience, provided no broadcast, telecast, recording, photography or other reproduction of such performance is made. Owner agrees not to exercise, or permit any other person to exercise, said stage rights earlier than [E.G., FIVE (5)] years after the first general release or telecast, if earlier, of the first Picture produced hereunder, or [E.G., SEVEN (7)] years after the date of exercise of the purchaser's option to acquire the property, whichever is earlier.

(c) Radio Rights: The right to broadcast the Property by sound (as distinguished from visually) by radio, subject however to Purchaser's right at all times to: (i) exercise its radio rights provided in Clause 1, *supra* for advertising and exploitation purposes by living actors or otherwise, by the use of excerpts from or condensations of the Property or any Picture produced hereunder; and (ii) in any event to broadcast any Picture produced hereunder by radio. Owner agrees not to exercise, or permit any other person to exercise, Owner's radio rights earlier than [E.G., FIVE (5)] years after the first general release or initial telecast, if earlier, of the first Picture produced hereunder or [E.G., SEVEN (7)] years after the date of exercise of purchaser's option to acquire the property, whichever is earlier.

(d) <u>Author-written Sequel</u>: A literary property (story, novel, drama or otherwise), whether written before or after the Property and whether written by Owner or by a successor in interest of Owner, using one or more of the characters appearing in the Property, participating in different events from those found in the Property, and whose plot is substantially different from that of the Property. Owner shall have the right to exercise publication rights; i.e., in book or magazine form, at any time. Owner agrees not to exercise, or permit any other person to exercise any other rights (including but not limited to motion picture or allied rights) of any kind in or to any author-written sequel earlier than [E.G., FIVE (5)] years after the first general release of the first Picture produced hereunder, or [E.G., SEVEN (7)] years after the date of exercise of purchaser's option to acquire the property, whichever is earlier, provided such restriction on Owner's exercise of said author-written sequel rights shall be extended to any period during which there is in effect, in any particular country or territory, a network television broadcasting agreement for a television motion picture, (i) based upon the Property, or (ii) based upon any Picture produced in the exercise of rights assigned herein, or (iii) using a character or characters of the Property, plus one (1) year, which shall also be a restricted period in such country or territory, whether or not such period occurs wholly or partly during or entirely after the (E.G., 5/7) year period first referred to in this clause. [Any disposition of motion picture or allied rights in an author-written sequel made to any person or company other than Purchaser shall be made subject to the following limitations and restrictions:

(i) Inasmuch as the characters of the Property are included in the exclusive grant of motion picture rights to Purchaser, no sequel rights or television series rights may be granted to such other person or company, but such characters from the Property which are contained in the author-written sequel may be used in a motion picture and remakes thereof whose plot is based substantially on the plot of the respective author-written sequel.]

It is expressly agreed that Owner's reserved rights under this subclause relate only to material written or authorized by Owner and not to any revision, adaptation, sequel, translation or dramatization written or authorized by Purchaser, even though the same may contain characters or other elements contained in the Property.

3. <u>RIGHT TO MAKE CHANGES</u>: Owner agrees that Purchaser shall have the unlimited right to vary, change, alter, modify, add to and/or delete from the Property, and to rearrange and/or transpose the Property and change the sequence thereof and the characters and descriptions of the characters contained in the Property, and to use a portion or portions of the Property or the characters, plots,

or theme thereof in conjunction with any other literary, dramatic or other material of any kind. Owner hereby waives the benefits of any provision of law known as the "droit moral" or moral rights or any similar law in any country of the world and agrees not to permit or prosecute any action or lawsuit on the ground that any Picture or other version of the Property produced or exhibited by Purchaser, its assignees or licensees, in any way constitutes an infringement of any of the Owner's "droit moral" or moral rights or is in any way a defamation or mutilation of the Property or any part thereof or contains unauthorized variations, alterations, modifications, changes or translations.

4. <u>DURATION AND EXTENT OF RIGHTS GRANTED</u>: Purchaser shall enjoy, solely and exclusively, all the rights, licenses, privileges and property granted hereunder throughout the world, in perpetuity, as long as any rights in the Property are recognized in law or equity, except insofar as such period of perpetuity may be shortened due to any now existing or future copyright by Owner of the Property and/or any adaptations thereof, in which case Purchaser shall enjoy its sole and exclusive rights, licenses, privileges and property hereunder to the fullest extent permissible under and for the full duration of such copyright or copyrights, whether common law or statutory, and any and all renewals and/or extensions thereof, and shall thereafter enjoy all such rights, licenses, privileges and property nonexclusively in perpetuity throughout the world. The rights granted herein are in addition to and shall not be construed in derogation of any rights which Purchaser may have as a member of the public or pursuant to any other agreement. All rights, licenses, privileges and property granted herein to Purchaser are irrevocable and not subject to rescission, restraint or injunction under any circumstances.

5. <u>CONSIDERATION</u>: As consideration for all rights granted and assigned to Purchaser and for owner's representations and warranties, Purchaser agrees to pay to Owner, and Owner agrees to accept:

(a) For a theatrical motion picture, (E.G., $200,000) [in addition to] [less] any sums paid in connection with the option periods, payable upon exercise of the option to acquire the Property or the commencement of principal photography of a Picture based on the Property, whichever occurs first.

(b) For a television motion picture, (E.G., $80,000) [in addition to] [less] any sums paid in connection with the option periods, payable upon exercise of the option to acquire the Property or the commencement of principal photography of a Picture based on the Property, whichever occurs first.

(c) For any mini-series, (E.G., $20,000) per hour, prorated for part hours [up to a maximum of (E.G. $100,000)].

(d) For any sequel or remake of a theatrical or television motion picture based on the Property, ONE-HALF and ONE-THIRD, respectively, of the amount paid for the initial motion picture, payable UPON COMMENCEMENT OF PRINCI-PAL PHOTOGRAPHY OF THE SUBSEQUENT PRODUCTION.

(e) For any U.S. network primetime television series produced, based on the Property, Purchaser will pay the following royalties per initial production upon completion of production of each program: up to 30 minutes (E.G., $1,250); over 30, but not more than 60, minutes (E.G., $1,750); over 60 minutes (E.G., $2,250); and in addition to the foregoing, as a buy-out of all royalty obligations, (ONE HUNDRED) percent (100%) of the applicable initial royalty amount, in equal installments over (FIVE) (5) reruns, payable within (THIRTY) (30) days after each such rerun.

[(f) As and for contingent compensation (E.G., FIVE) percent (E.G., 5%) of one hundred percent of the net profits (including allied and ancillary rights) of each motion picture and television program or series based on the Property, in whole or in part, with profits defined according to the same definition obtained by Purchaser [; provided, however, that Owner's percentage shall not be subject to any reductions or preconditions whatsoever].]

6. REPRESENTATIONS AND WARRANTIES:

(a) Sole Proprietor: Owner represents and warrants to Purchaser that Owner is the sole and exclusive proprietor, throughout the universe, of [that certain original literary material written by Owner entitled "_____"].

(b) Facts: Owner represents and warrants to Purchaser as follows:

(i) (*Specify as appropriate the nature and status of the ownership of the property, e.g., "(i) Owner is the sole author and creator of the Property.*")

(ii) The Property was first published in (YEAR) by (NAME OF PUB-LISHER) under the title (NAME), and was registered for copyright in the name of (COPYRIGHT REGISTRANT), under copyright registration number (NUMBER), in the Office of the United States Register of Copyrights, Washington, D.C.

(iii) No motion picture or dramatic version of the Property, or any part thereof, has been manufactured, produced, presented or authorized; no radio or television development, presentation, or program based on the Property, or any part thereof, has been manufactured, produced, presented, broadcast or authorized; and no written or oral agreements or commitments whatsoever with respect to the Property, or with respect to any rights therein, have been made or entered into by or on behalf of Owner (except with respect to the publication of the Property as set forth above).

(iv) [Except as otherwise specified herein,] none of the rights granted and assigned to Purchaser have been granted and/or assigned to any person, firm or corporation other than Purchaser.

(c) <u>No Infringement or Violation of Third Party Rights</u>: Owner represents and warrants to Purchaser that Owner has not adapted the Property from any other literary, dramatic or other material of any kind, nature or description, nor, except for material which is in the public domain, has Owner copied or used in the Property the plot, scenes, sequence or story of any other literary, dramatic or other material; that the Property does not infringe upon any common law or statutory rights in any other literary, dramatic or other material; that no material contained in the Property is libelous or violative of the right of privacy of any person; that the full utilization of any and all rights in and to the Property granted by Owner pursuant to this Agreement will not violate the rights of any person, firm or corporation; and that the Property is not in the public domain in any country in the world where copyright protection is available.

(d) <u>No Impairment of Rights</u>: [Except as otherwise specified herein,] Owner represents and warrants to Purchaser that Owner is the exclusive proprietor, throughout the universe, of all rights in and to the Property granted herein to Purchaser; that Owner has not assigned, licensed or in any manner encumbered, diminished or impaired any such rights; that Owner has not committed or omitted to perform any act by which such rights could or will be encumbered, diminished or impaired; and that there is no outstanding claim or litigation pending against or involving the title, ownership and/or copyright in the Property, or in any part thereof, or in any rights granted herein to Purchaser. Owner further represents and warrants that no attempt shall be made hereafter to encumber, diminish or impair any of the rights granted herein and that all appropriate protection of such rights will continue to be maintained by Owner.

7. <u>INDEMNIFICATION</u>: (a) Owner agrees to indemnify Purchaser against all judgments, liability, damages, penalties, losses and expense (including reasonable attorneys' fees) which may be suffered or assumed by or obtained against Purchaser by reason of any breach or failure of any warranty or agreement herein made by Owner.

(b) Purchaser shall not be liable to Owner for damages of any kind in connection with any Picture it may produce, distribute or exhibit, or for damages for any breach of this agreement (except failure to pay the money consideration herein specified) occurring or accruing before Purchaser has had reasonable notice and opportunity to adjust or correct such matters.

[(c) All rights, licenses and privileges herein granted to Purchaser are irrevocable and not subject to rescission, restraint or injunction under any circumstances.]

8. <u>PROTECTION OF RIGHTS GRANTED</u>: Owner hereby grants to Purchaser the free and unrestricted right, but at Purchaser's own cost and expense, to institute in the name and on behalf of Owner, or Owner and Purchaser jointly, any and all suits and proceedings at law or in equity, to enjoin and restrain any

infringements of the rights herein granted, and hereby assigns and sets over to Purchaser any and all causes of action relative to or based upon any such infringement, as well as any and all recoveries obtained thereon. Owner will not compromise, settle or in any manner interfere with such litigation if brought; and Purchaser agrees to indemnify and hold Owner harmless from any costs, expenses, or damages which Owner may suffer as a [direct] result of any such suit or proceeding.

9. <u>COPYRIGHT</u>: Regarding the copyright in and to the Property, Owner agrees that:

(a) Owner will prevent the Property and any arrangements, revisions, translations, novelizations, dramatizations or new versions thereof whether published or unpublished and whether copyrighted or uncopyrighted, from vesting in the public domain, and will take or cause to be taken any and all steps and proceedings required for copyright or similar protection in any and all countries in which the same may be published or offered for sale, insofar as such countries now or hereafter provide for copyright or similar protection. Any contract or agreement entered into by Owner authorizing or permitting the publication of the Property or any arrangements, revisions, translations, novelizations, dramatizations or new versions thereof in any country will contain appropriate provisions requiring such publisher to comply with all the provisions of this clause.

(b) Without limiting the generality of the foregoing, if the Property or any arrangement, revision, translation, novelization, dramatization or new version thereof is published in [the United States or in] any [other] country in which registration is [permitted or] required for copyright or similar protection, Owner will register or cause the same to be registered for copyright or similar protection in accordance with the laws and regulations of such country, and Owner further agrees to affix or cause to be affixed to each copy of the Property or any arrangement, revision, translation, novelization, dramatization or new version thereof which is published or offered for sale such notice or notices as may be required for copyright or similar protection in any country in which such publication or sale occurs.

(c) At least (E.G., SIX (6) MONTHS) prior to the expiration of any copyright required by this provision for the protection of the Property, Owner will renew (or cause to be renewed) such copyright, as permitted by applicable law, and any and all rights granted Purchaser hereunder shall be deemed granted to Purchaser throughout the full period of such renewed copyright, without the payment of any additional consideration, it being agreed that the consideration payable to Owner under this agreement shall be deemed to include full consideration for the grant of such rights to Purchaser throughout the period of such renewed copyright.

(d) If the Property, or any arrangement, revision, translation, novelization, dramatization or new version thereof, shall ever enter the public domain, then nothing contained in this agreement shall impair any rights or privileges that the Purchaser might be entitled to as a member of the public; thus, the Purchaser may exercise any and all such rights and privileges as though this agreement were not in existence. The rights granted herein by Owner to Purchaser, and the representations, warranties, undertakings and agreements made hereunder by Owner shall endure in perpetuity and shall be in addition to any rights, licenses, privileges or property of Purchaser referred to in this Subclause (d).

10. <u>CREDIT OBLIGATIONS</u>: Purchaser shall have the right to publish, advertise, announce and use in any manner or medium, the name, biography and photographs or other likenesses of Owner in connection with any exercise by Purchaser of its rights hereunder, provided such use shall not constitute an endorsement of any product or service.

During the term of the Writer's Guild of America Minimum Basic Agreement ("WGA Agreement"), as it may be amended, the credit provisions of the WGA Agreement shall govern the determination of credits, if any, which the Purchaser shall accord the [OWNER] [AUTHOR] hereunder in connection with photoplays. [If the Purchaser ceases to be a party to said WGA Agreement the provisions of the WGA Agreement shall no longer govern the determination of such credits, and when the WGA Agreement or any amendment, is not effective as between the Purchaser and Writer's Guild of America such credits shall be determined in accordance with EXHIBIT _____ attached hereto.]

[Subject to the foregoing, [OWNER] [AUTHOR] shall be accorded the following credit on a single card on screen and in paid ads controlled by Purchaser and in which any other writer is accorded credit, and in size of type (as to height, width, thickness and boldness) equal to the largest size of type in which any other writer is accorded credit:

(a) If the title of the Picture is the same as the title of the Property (E.G., FOR A NOVEL, ["Based on (E.G., THE NOVEL) by (NAME OF AUTHOR)"]); or

(b) If the title of the Picture differs from the title of the Property, (E.G., FOR A NOVEL, ["Based on (name of novel) by (NAME OF AUTHOR)"]).]

Additionally, if Purchaser shall exploit any other rights in and to the Property, then Purchaser agrees to give appropriate source material credit to the Property, to the extent that such source material credits are customarily given in connection with the exploitation of such rights.

No casual or inadvertent failure to comply with any of the provisions of this clause shall be deemed a breach of this agreement by the Purchaser. Owner hereby expressly acknowledges that in the event of a failure or omission constituting a breach of the provisions of this paragraph, the damage (if any) caused Owner thereby is not irreparable or sufficient to entitle Owner to injunctive or other equitable relief. Consequently, Owner's rights and remedies in the event of such breach shall be limited to the right to recover damages in an action at law. [Purchaser agrees to provide in its contracts with distributors of the Picture that such distributors shall honor Purchaser's contractual credit commitments and agrees to inform such distributors of the credit provisions herein.]

11. RIGHT OF FIRST NEGOTIATION: The Term "Right of First Negotiation" means that if, after the expiration of an applicable time limitation, Owner desires to dispose of or exercise a particular right reserved to Owner herein ("Reserved Right"), whether directly or indirectly, then Owner shall notify Purchaser in writing and immediately negotiate with Purchaser regarding such Reserved Right. If, after the expiration of (E.G., THIRTY DAYS) following the receipt of such notice, no agreement has been reached, then Owner may negotiate with third parties regarding such Reserved Right subject to Clause 12, *infra.*

12. RIGHT OF LAST REFUSAL: The term "Right of Last Refusal" means that if Purchaser and Owner fail to reach an agreement pursuant to Purchaser's right of first negotiation, and Owner makes and/or receives any bona fide offer to license, lease and/or purchase the particular Reserved Right or any interest therein ("Third Party Offer"), [and if the proposed purchase price and other material terms of a Third Party Offer are no more favorable to Owner than the terms which were acceptable to Purchaser during the first negotiation period], Owner shall notify Purchaser, by registered mail or telegram, if Owner proposes to accept such Third Party Offer, the name of the offeror, the proposed purchase price, and other terms of such Third Party Offer. During the period of (E.G., THIRTY (30) DAYS) after Purchaser's receipt of such notice, Purchaser shall have the exclusive option to license, lease and/or purchase, as the case may be, the particular Reserved Right or interest referred to in such Third Party Offer, at the same purchase price and upon the same [financial] terms and conditions as set forth in such notice. If Purchaser elects to exercise the right to purchase such Reserved Right, Purchaser shall notify Owner of the exercise thereof by registered mail or telegram within such (E.G., THIRTY (30) DAY) period, failing which Owner shall be free to accept such Third Party Offer; provided that if any such proposed license, lease and/or sale is not consummated with a third party within (E.G., THIRTY (30) DAYS) following the expiration of the aforesaid (E.G., THIRTY (30) DAY) period, Purchaser's Right of last refusal shall revive and shall apply to each and every further offer or offers at any time received by Owner relating to the particular Reserved Right or any interest therein; provided, further, that Purchaser's option shall continue in full force and effect, upon all of the terms and conditions of this Paragraph, so long as Owner retains any rights, title or interests in or to the particular Reserved Right. Purchaser's Right of Last Refusal shall inure to the benefit of Purchaser, its successors and assigns, and shall bind Owner and Owner's heirs, successors and assigns.

13. <u>NO OBLIGATION TO PRODUCE</u>: Nothing herein shall be construed to obligate Purchaser to produce, distribute, release, perform or exhibit any motion picture, television, theatrical or other production based upon, adapted from or suggested by the Property, in whole or in part, or otherwise to exercise, exploit or make any use of any rights, licenses, privileges or property granted herein to Purchaser.

14. <u>ASSIGNMENT</u>: Purchaser may assign and transfer this agreement or all or any part of its rights hereunder to any person, firm or corporation without limitation, and this Agreement shall be binding upon and inure to the benefit of the parties hereto and their successors, representatives and assigns forever; [provided however, Purchaser shall not be relieved of Purchaser's obligations hereunder unless such assignment and transfer is to a major studio or "mini-major" studio which assumes Purchaser's obligations hereunder.]

15. <u>NO PUBLICITY</u>: Owner will not, without Purchaser's prior written consent in each instance, issue or authorize the issuance or publication of any news story or publicity relating to (i) this Agreement, (ii) the subject matter or terms hereof, or to any use by Purchaser, its successors, licensees and assigns, and (iii) any of the rights granted Purchaser hereunder. This provision shall not be deemed to preclude Owner's incidental, non-derogatory mention in interviews of any Picture based on the Property.

16. <u>AGENT COMMISSIONS</u>: Purchaser shall not be liable for any compensation or fee to any agent of Owner in connection with this agreement.

17. <u>ADDITIONAL DOCUMENTATION</u>: Owner agrees to execute and procure any other and further instruments necessary to transfer, convey, assign and copyright all rights in the Property granted herein by Owner to Purchaser in any country throughout the world. If it shall be necessary under the laws of any country that copyright registration be acquired in the name of Owner, Purchaser is hereby authorized by Owner to apply for said copyright registration thereof; and, in such event, Owner shall and does hereby assign and transfer the same unto Purchaser, subject to the rights in the Property reserved hereunder by Owner. Owner further agrees, upon written request, to duly execute, acknowledge, procure and deliver to Purchaser such short form assignments as may be requested by Purchaser for the purpose of copyright recordation in any country, or otherwise. If Owner shall fail to so execute and deliver, or cause to be executed and delivered, the assignments or other instruments herein referred to, [within E.G., FIVE) business days after Purchaser's request therefor,] Purchaser is hereby irrevocably granted the power coupled with an interest to execute such assignments and instruments in the name of Owner and as Owner's attorney-in-fact. [Purchaser agrees to provide Owner with a copy of any document executed by Purchaser pursuant to the foregoing power of attorney.]

18. <u>NOTICES</u>: All notices to Purchaser under this agreement shall be sent by United States registered mail, postage prepaid, or by telegram addressed to Purchaser at (ADDRESS) with a courtesy copy to (NAME AND ADDRESS OF PURCHASER'S ATTORNEY), and all notices to Owner under this agreement shall be sent by United States registered mail, postage prepaid, or by telegram addressed to at (ADDRESS) owner with a courtesy copy to (NAME AND ADDRESS OF OWNER'S ATTORNEY). The deposit of such notice in the United States mail or the delivery of the telegram message to the telegraph office shall constitute service thereof, and the date of such deposit shall be deemed to be the date of service of such notice.

19. <u>RELATIONSHIP</u>: This agreement between the parties does not constitute a joint venture or partnership of any kind.

20. <u>CUMULATIVE RIGHTS AND REMEDIES</u>: All rights, remedies, licenses, undertakings, obligations, covenants, privileges and other property granted herein shall be cumulative, and Purchaser may exercise or use any of them separately or in conjunction with any one or more of the others.

21. <u>WAIVER</u>: A waiver by either party of any term or condition of this agreement in any instance shall not be deemed or construed to be a waiver of such term or condition for the future, or any subsequent breach thereof.

22. <u>SEVERABILITY</u>: If any provision of this agreement as applied to either party or any circumstances shall be adjudged by a court to be void and unenforceable, such shall in no way affect any other provision of this Agreement, the application of such provision in any other circumstance, or the validity or enforceability of this Agreement.

23. <u>GOVERNING LAW</u>: This Agreement shall be construed in accordance with the laws of the State of (NAME OF STATE) applicable to agreements which are executed and fully performed within said State.

24. <u>HEADINGS</u>: Headings are inserted for reference and convenience only and in no way define, limit or describe the scope of this agreement or intent of any provision.

25. <u>ENTIRE UNDERSTANDING</u>: This agreement (and any exhibits attached hereto) contains the entire understanding of the parties relating to the subject matter, and this Agreement cannot be changed except by written agreement executed by the party to be bound.

IN WITNESS WHEREOF, the parties hereto have signed this Agreement as of the day and year first above written.

_____
("*Owner*")

_____

("*Purchaser*")

By _____

Its _____

Form 11

Director Employment Agreement

(Employment Agreement)

Agreement dated *(date of agreement)* between *(name of director)* ("Director") and *(name of production company)* ("Production Company").

ALTERNATIVE CLAUSE

(Loan-out Agreement)

Agreement dated *(date of agreement)* between *(name of loan-out company)* (a *(name of state)* corporation) ("Lender") and *(name of production company)* (a *(name of state)* corporation) ("Production company.").

(Employment Agreement)

1. <u>EMPLOYMENT</u>: Production Company agrees to employ Director to perform and Director agrees to perform, upon the terms and conditions herein specified, directing services in connection with the Theatrical Motion Picture currently entitled (name of picture) ("Picture").

ALTERNATIVE CLAUSE

(Loan-out Agreement)

1. <u>ENGAGEMENT</u>: Production Company agrees to borrow from Lender and Lender agrees to lend to Production Company, upon the terms and conditions herein specified, the directing services of *(name of director)* ("Director") in connection with the Theatrical Motion Picture currently entitled *(name of picture)* ("Picture"). Lender hereby represents and warrants that it is a corporation organized and existing under and by virtue of the laws of the State of *(state of incorporation of loanout company)*, and that Lender has entered into a written contract with Director which is now in full force and effect and pursuant to which Lender has the full right and authority to lend to Production Company the services of Director upon the terms and conditions herein specified.

2. <u>TERM</u>: The Term hereof shall commence on *(date of commencement of services)* and shall continue until the completion of all of Director's required services on the Picture.

3. <u>SERVICES</u>:

(a) Director shall supervise the preparation of any rewrites of the current screenplay of the Picture, be available to meet the individual producer at the Production Company's office in *(e.g., Los Angeles, California)* and other locations for a reasonable number of meetings concerning the Picture, be available and undertake a location search, assist the individual producer and the production manager selected for the Picture in the preparation of the budget for the Picture and perform such other services as are customarily performed by directors during the period prior to the start of principal photography of a motion picture.

(b) <u>Photography</u>: Director's exclusive services for the Picture shall commence (*specify, e.g., eight weeks*) (*e.g., 8*) weeks prior to the start of principal photography and shall be rendered exclusively thereafter until completion of all photography. The start date of principal photography shall be [as Production Company designates] [mutually approved by Production Company and (Director)(Lender)]. The scheduled start date of principal photography is (specify date).

(c) <u>Post-Production</u>: Director's post-production services shall be rendered on [an exclusive] [a non-exclusive but first-call] basis, if Production Company so requires, [in order to work during the post-production period with the editor] until completion of the final corrected answer print. [Director's other undertakings shall not interfere with Director's post-production services hereunder [or with the post-production time schedule set forth in Exhibits attached hereto and incorporated by this reference herein].] [In connection with post-production:]

[(1) <u>Cooperation with Editor</u>: [Director] [Lender] hereby warrants and agrees that [Director] will do nothing to hinder or delay the assemblage of film by the editor during the photography of the Picture so that the assembled sequences will be completed immediately following the completion of principal photography.]

[(2) <u>Post-Production Schedule</u>: Attached hereto marked Exhibit "S" and by this reference incorporated herein is a schedule for the post-production work on the Picture which has been agreed to by [Director] [Lender] and Production Company. [Director] [Lender] hereby agree(s) that this schedule shall be followed by Director.]

[(3) <u>Final Cutting Authority</u>: (*specify name*) is designated as the Production Company Executive with final cutting authority over the Picture.] [The foregoing shall be subject to applicable guild and union requirements, if any.]

(d) <u>Dailies</u>: Production Company shall have the right to view the dailies during the production of the Picture, the rough cut and all subsequent cuts of the Picture.

(e) <u>Television Cover Shots</u>: Director shall furnish Production Company with protective cover shots necessary for the release of the Picture on television, based on network continuity standards in existence at the time of commencement of principal photography.

(f) <u>Additional Post-Production Services</u>: If after the completion of principal photography, Production Company requires retakes, changes, dubbing, transparencies, added scenes, further photography, trailers, sound track, process shots or other language versions (herein collectively called "retakes, etc.") for the Picture, Director shall report to Production Company for such retakes, etc., at such place or places and on such consecutive or non-consecutive days as Production Company may designate. [Provided Director is not then rendering services (pursuant to a contractual commitment) for another party], [subject to Director's [professional] availability,] [Lender] [Director] shall cooperate to make such services available to Production Company at the earliest possible date.

4. COMPENSATION: As full and complete consideration for Director's [material] services and [Lender's and]/ [Director's] undertakings hereunder and for all rights granted to Production Company hereunder, and subject to [Lender's and]/Director's full compliance with the terms and conditions of this Agreement, Production Company agrees to pay [Director] [Lender] as follows:

(a) Fixed Compensation:

(1) The total sum of [*total amount of fixed compensation, e.g., $500,000*] payable:

(A) $ _____ (*specify amount to be paid, e.g., $50,000*) upon approval of the Budgeted Negative Cost for production of the Picture.

(B) $ _____ (*specify amount, e.g., $100,000*) weekly, pro rated commencing _____ weeks (*specify number of weeks, e.g., 10 weeks*) prior to the start of principal photography of the Picture.

(C) $ _____ (*specify total amount, e.g., $250,000*) payable in equal weekly installments over the scheduled period of principal photography.

(D) $ _____ (*specify amount, e.g., $50,000*) upon delivery of the director's cut.

(E) $ _____ (*specify amount, e.g., $50,000*) upon the completion of the final answer print of the Picture.

(2) Flat Fee Basis: Production Company and [Director] [Lender] hereby mutually acknowledge that the Fixed Compensation as herein above specified is a "flat fee" and [Director] [Lender] shall not be entitled to any additional and/or so-called "overage" compensation for any services rendered by Director during the development, pre-production, production or post-production phases, or for additional post-production services rendered by Director. Without limiting the generality of the foregoing, no additional compensation shall be payable to [Director] [Lender] under Clause 4(a)(i)(C) above if the actual principal photography period for the Picture exceeds the scheduled principal photography period, nor for any services rendered pursuant to Clause 3(f).

[(b) Deferred Compensation: In addition to the Fixed Compensation payable under Clause 4(a), [subject to the production and release of the Picture] [and subject to the performance of all material obligations of Director hereunder,]

Director shall be entitled to receive the sum of (*total amount of deferred compensation* e.g., *$250,000*) which shall be deferred and paid pro rata with all similar deferments of compensation payable [*specify when, e.g., at the point just preceding the payment of percentage participations in the Net Profits of the Picture.*]

(c) <u>Contingent Compensation</u>: In addition to the Fixed Compensation payable under Clause 4(a), [and any Deferred Compensation payable under Clause 4(b),] subject to the production and release of the Picture and subject to the performance of [Lender's and]/[Director's] [material] obligations hereunder [Lender]/ [Director] shall be entitled to receive as Contingent Compensation an amount equal to (*specify percentage e.g., five percent (5%)*) of the Net Profits of the Picture, if any.

(d) <u>Net Profits Definition</u>: "Net Profits" shall be computed, determined and paid in accordance with Exhibit "_____" attached hereto and by this reference incorporated herein.

(e) <u>Conditions Related to Compensation</u>: Notwithstanding anything to the contrary contained in any of the above compensation provisions:

(1) <u>Performance</u>: No compensation shall accrue or become payable to [Lender]/ [Director] during Director's inability, failure or refusal to perform the services contracted for herein according to the terms and conditions of this Agreement.

(2) <u>Pay or Play</u>: Production Company shall not be obligated to utilize Director's services on the Picture, nor shall Production Company be obligated to produce, release, distribute, advertise, exploit or otherwise make use of the Picture; provided, however, that the full amount of the Fixed Compensation herein above specified shall be paid to [Director] [Lender], should Production Company [without legal justification or excuse (as provided elsewhere in this Agreement or by operation of law),] elect not to utilize Director's services.

(f) <u>Vesting</u>: The Fixed Compensation and Contingent Compensation herein-above specified shall be deemed fully vested if, notwithstanding the termination of Director's services due to Producer Disability or Director's Incapacity or [Lender/] Director Default, Director shall be entitled to receive "Directed by" credit pursuant to the Director's Guild of America Basic Agreement of 1987, as same may be amended from time to time ("Basic Agreement"). If the services of Director are terminated by Production Company due to Production Company Disability or Director's Incapacity or [Lender/] Director Default, as defined below, and Director is not entitled to receive credit pursuant to the Basic Agreement, then the Fixed Compensation shall vest and accrue in the same manner as set forth herein and the Contingent Compensation shall accrue and vest in the same ratio that the number of linear feet in the completed Picture as released, which was directed by Director, bears to the total number of linear feet in the completed Picture as released. Notwithstanding the foregoing, if principal photography has not commenced on the scheduled start date as set forth in Clause 3(b) hereof, then the total Fixed Compensation shall vest and accrue on the aforesaid scheduled start date, or if principal photography has commenced on the aforesaid scheduled start date and production of the Picture is thereafter terminated prior to completion of principal photography and/or delivery of the final answer print to Production Company, then that portion of the Fixed Compensation not theretofore accrued shall fully vest and accrue on the date of such termination. If Production Company terminates this Agreement by reason of a [Lender/] Director Default, notwithstanding any vesting of Fixed Compensation and/or Contingent Compensation as set forth above, such vesting shall be subject to any and all the rights accorded to Production Company at law and in equity.

(g) <u>Mitigation</u>: If Production Company elects to exercise its pay or play right as set forth above and/or fails to produce the Picture, [Lender and/or] Director shall [have no obligation] [shall be obligated] to mitigate damages.

5. CREDITS:

(a) <u>Credit</u>: Subject to the production and release of the Picture and provided Director performs his material obligations hereunder, then Production Company shall accord Director credit [in connection with the Picture in accordance with the requirements of the Directors Guild of America, Inc. Basic Agreement of 1987] [before] [immediately after (*e.g., below the main title*)] [which shall be (*specify percentage, e.g., 50%*) of the size of the title] [on a separate card].

(b) <u>Artwork Title Exception</u>: If both a regular (or repeat) title and an artwork title are used, the position and percentage requirements above, as they relate to the title of the Picture, shall relate to the regular (or repeat) title. If only an artwork title is used, the percentage requirements above, as they relate to the title, shall be [not less than] (*e.g., ten percent (10%)*) of the average size of the letters used in the artwork title.

(c) <u>Credit Limitation</u>: Production Company agrees that no other individual and/or entity (other than members of the cast receiving "starring" billing before or after the title of the Picture or the company distributing and/or financing the Picture) shall receive credit [larger than] [the same size as] that used to display the credit accorded to Director [and no other individual or entity shall receive a credit that is larger].

(d) <u>Inadvertent Non-Compliance</u>: No casual or inadvertent failure to comply with the provisions of this Clause shall be deemed to be a breach of this Agreement by Production Company. [Director] [Lender] hereby recognizes and confirms that in the event of a failure or omission by Production Company constituting a breach of Production Company's obligations under this Clause, the damages, if any, caused [Lender and] Director by Production Company are not irreparable or sufficient to entitle [Lender and] Director to injunctive or other equitable relief. Consequently, [Lender's and] Director's rights and remedies hereunder shall be limited to the right, if any, to obtain damages at law and [Lender and]/Director shall have no right in such event to rescind this Agreement or any of the rights assigned to Production Company hereunder or to enjoin or restrain the distribution or exhibition of the Picture. [Production Company agrees to advise its assignees and licensees of the credit requirements herein. If Production Company shall learn of such failure of a third party to give such credit, Production Company shall notify such party of such failure and Production Company may, but shall not be obligated to, take action to cause such party to prospectively cure such failure.]

6. <u>TRANSPORTATION AND EXPENSES</u>: If Director's services are required at Production Company's request to be rendered on location more than (*e.g., fifty (50)*) miles from the [County] [City] of (*name of county or city*), Production Company shall furnish Director first-class round trip transportation for (*e.g., one (1)*) (if available and if used) and Production Company shall reimburse Director for Director's living expenses in the amount of (*specify amount, e.g., $2,000*) per week. [If [Lender] [Director] can demonstrate to Production Company's satisfaction that said living expense allowance is insufficient for any particular location, Production Company shall, at such time, give good faith consideration to an increase.] [For any period week which is less than one (1) week, said reimbursement shall be upon the pro rata basis that one (1) day is equal to one-seventh (1/7) of one (1) week.] [Director] [Lender] shall furnish Production Company with itemized detailed accountings of such living expenses, including vouchers, bills, receipts and statements satisfactory to meet the requirements and regulations of the Internal Revenue Service.

7. <u>PERFORMANCE STANDARDS</u>: Except as specifically provided to the contrary herein, during the Term of this Agreement, Director shall render Director's directing services exclusively to Production Company and, to such extent as Production Company may require, in otherwise assisting in the production of the Picture. Said services shall be rendered either alone or in collaboration with another or other artists in such manner as Production Company may direct, pursuant to the instructions, controls and schedules established by [Production Company] [Production Company's authorized representatives], and at the times, places and in the manner required by [Production Company] [them]. [Such manners, instructions, directions, and controls shall be exercised by Production Company in accordance with standards of reasonableness and also with what is customary practice in the Motion Picture industry.] [Such services shall be rendered in an artistic, conscientious, efficient and punctual manner, to the best of Director's ability and with full regard to the careful, efficient, economical and expeditious production of the Picture within the budget and shooting schedule established by Production Company immediately prior to the commencement of

principal photography [, it being further understood that the production of motion pictures by Production Company involves matters of discretion to be exercised by Production Company with respect to art and taste, and Director's services and the manner of rendition thereof is to be governed entirely by Production Company].]

8. UNIQUE SERVICES: Except as specifically provided to the contrary herein-above, Director's services shall be rendered exclusively to Production Company until expiration of the Term of this Agreement, it being mutually understood that said services are extraordinary, unique and not replaceable, and that there is no adequate remedy at law for breach of this contract by [Lender and/or] [Director] and that Production Company, in the event of such breach by [Lender and/or] [Director] shall be entitled to equitable relief by way of injunction or otherwise to prevent default by [Lender and/or] [Director].

9. RESULTS AND PROCEEDS OF SERVICES: Production Company shall be entitled to and shall solely and exclusively own, in addition to Director's services hereunder, all results and proceeds thereof (including but not limited to all rights, throughout the universe, in perpetuity, of copyright, trademark, patent, produc-tion, manufacture, recordation, reproduction, transcription, performance, broad-cast and exhibition of any art or method now known or hereafter devised, including radio broadcasting, theatrical and nontheatrical exhibition, and exhibi-tion by the medium of television or otherwise), whether such results and proceeds consist of literary, dramatic, musical, motion picture, mechanical or any other forms of works, themes, ideas, compositions, creations or production, together with the rights generally known in the field of literary and musical endeavor as the "moral rights of authors" in and/or to any musical and/or literary proceeds of Director's services, including but not limited to the right to add to, subtract from, arrange, revise, adapt, rearrange, make variations of the property, [and to translate the same into any and all languages, change the sequence, change the characters and the descriptions thereof contained in the property, change the title of the same, [record and photocopy the same with or without sound (including spoken words, dialogue and music synchronously recorded),] use this title or any of its components in connection with works or motion pictures wholly or partially independent of said property, and to use all or any part of the property in new versions, adaptations and sequels in any and all languages, and to obtain copyright therein throughout the universe, and [Lender and] [Director] do(es) assign and transfer to Production Company all the foregoing without reservation, condition, or limitation, and no right of any kind, nature, or description is reserved by [Lender and] [Director]. Furthermore, [Lender and] Director hereby irrevocably assign(s), license(s), and grant(s) to Production Company, exclusively, throughout the universe, and in perpetuity, the rights, if any, of [Lender and] Director to authorize, prohibit, and/or control the renting, lending, fixation, reproduction and/or other exploitation of any motion picture produced based upon the Picture

(or any rights therein) by any media and means now known or hereafter devised as may be conferred upon [Lender and] Director under applicable laws, regulations, or directives including, without limitation, any so-called "Rental Lending Rights" pursuant to any European Economic Community ("EEC") directors and/or enabling or implementing legislation, laws, or regulations enacted by the member nations of the EEC. If Production Company shall desire separate assignments or other documents to implement the foregoing, [Lender and/or] Director shall execute the same upon Production Company's [written] request, and if [Lender and/or] Director fail(s) or refuse(s) to [have the Director] execute and deliver any such separate assignments or other documents, Production Company shall have and is granted the right and authority to execute the same in [Lender's and/or] Director's name and as [Lender's and/or] Director's attorney-in-fact. [Production Company shall supply [Lender and] Director with a copy of any document so executed.]

Wherever in this Agreement the terms "motion picture" or "motion picture production" or terms of similar tenor are used, such terms shall be conclusively deemed and construed to include the present and future developments of the motion picture, television, video tape, videodisc, computer, electronics and telephone industries, including talking motion pictures, videotape, television productions, any and all kinds of electronic and other interactive uses of the Picture and the components thereof, including, but not limited to, CD-ROM, CD-I, interactive multi-media devices, computer discs, and any new variations thereon, and all forms of motion pictures, television, laserdisc, video tape, CD-ROM, CD-I, interactive multimedia devices and similar uses, whether now known or unknown and their accompanying devices which reproduce words, music and/or other sounds in synchronization with, accompaniment of, or supplementary to photography.

10. WARRANTIES RELATED TO CREATED MATERIAL: [Lender and] Director hereby warrant(s) and agree(s) that all material, works, writings, idea, "gags" or dialogue written, composed, prepared, submitted or interpolated by Director in connection with the Picture or its preparation or production, shall be wholly original with Director and shall not be copied in whole or in part from any other work, except that submitted to Director by Production Company as a basis for such material. [Lender and] Director further warrant(s) that neither the said material nor any part thereof will [to the best of [Lender's and] Director's knowledge] violate the rights of privacy or constitute a libel or slander against any person, firm, or corporation, and that the material will not infringe upon the copyright, literary, dramatic or photoplay rights of any person. [Lender and] Director further warrant(s) and agree(s) to indemnify and to hold Production Company and its successors, licensees, and assigns harmless against all liability or loss (including without limitation, reasonable attorneys' fees and costs) which

they or any of them may suffer by reason of the breach of any of the terms or warranties of this Clause.

11. <u>VESTING OF PRODUCTION COMPANY'S RIGHTS</u>: All rights granted or agreed to be granted to Production Company hereunder shall vest in Production Company immediately and shall remain so vested whether this Agreement expires in normal course or is terminated for any [good] cause or reason.

12. <u>NAME AND LIKENESS</u>: Production Company shall always have the right to use and display Director's name and likeness for advertising, publicizing, and exploiting the Picture. However, such advertising may not include the direct endorsement of any product (other than the Picture) without [Lender's] [Director's] consent. Exhibition, advertising, publicizing or exploiting the Picture by any media, even though a part of or in connection with a product or a commercially sponsored program, shall not be deemed an endorsement of any nature.

13. <u>PUBLICITY RESTRICTIONS</u>: [Lender or] [Director] shall not [individually or jointly,] or by means of press agents or publicity or advertising agencies or others, employed or paid by [Lender and/or] [Director] or otherwise, circulate, publish or otherwise disseminate any news stories or articles, books or other publicity, containing [Lender's and/or] [Director's] name relating to Director's employment by Production Company, the subject matter of this contract, the Picture or the services to be rendered by Director or others in connection with the Picture unless first approved by Production Company [in writing] [Lender and/or] Director shall not transfer [or attempt to transfer] any right, privilege, title, or interest in or to any of the things above specified, nor shall [Lender and/or] Director authorize or willingly permit infringement upon the exclusive rights granted to Production Company, and [Lender and] Director authorize(s) Production Company [, at Production Company's expense,] in [Lender's and/or] Director's name or otherwise, to institute any proper legal proceedings to prevent any infringement. [This provision shall not be deemed to preclude Director's incidental, non-derogatory mention in interviews of any Picture based on the Property.]

14. <u>FORCE MAJEURE</u>:

(a) <u>Suspension</u>: If, by reason of fire, earthquake, labor dispute or strike, act of God or public enemy, any municipal ordinance, any state or federal law, governmental order or regulation, or other cause beyond Production Company's control [which would excuse Production Company's performance as a matter of law], Production Company is prevented from or hampered in the production of the Picture, or if, by reason of the closing of substantially all theatres in the United States, [which would excuse Production Company's performance as a matter of law] Production Company's production of the Picture is postponed or suspended, or if, by reason of any of the aforesaid contingencies or any other cause or occurrence not within Production Company's control, including but not limited to the death, illness or incapacity of any principal member of the cast of the Picture, the preparation or production of the Picture is interrupted or delayed [and/or, if Production Company's normal business operations are interrupted or otherwise interfered with by virtue of any disruptive events which are beyond Production Company's control] ("Production Company Disability"), then Production Company may postpone the commencement of or suspend the rendition of services by Director and the running of time hereunder for such time as the Production Company Disability shall continue; and no compensation shall accrue or become payable to [Lender] [Director] hereunder during the period of such suspension. [Such suspension shall end upon the cessation of the cause thereof.] or [Such suspension shall end not later than (*e.g., four weeks*) following the cessation of Production Company Disability or upon the recommencement of principal photography of the Picture after the cessation of Production Company Disability, whichever occurs first.]

(b) Termination:

(1) Production Company Termination Right: If a Production Company Disability continues for a period in excess of (*e.g., eight (8) weeks*), Production Company shall have the right to terminate this Agreement upon written notice to [Lender] [Director].

(2) [Lender's] [Director's] Termination Right: If a Production Company Disability results in compensation being suspended hereunder for a period in excess of (*e.g., eight (8) weeks*), [Lender] [Director] shall have the right to terminate this Agreement upon written notice to Production Company.

(3) Production Company Re-Establishment Right: Despite [Lender's] [Director's] election to terminate this Agreement, within (*e.g., five (5) days*) after Production Company's actual receipt of such written notice from [Lender] [Director], Production Company shall have the right to elect to re-establish the operation of this Agreement.

15. DIRECTOR'S INCAPACITY:

(a) Effect of Director's Incapacity: If, by reason of mental or physical disability, Director is incapacitated from performing or complying with any of the terms or conditions hereof ("Director's Incapacity") for a consecutive period in excess of (*e.g., seven (7) days*) or aggregate period in excess of (*e.g., ten (10) days*), then Production Company shall have the right to terminate this Agreement upon written notice to [Lender] [Director].

(b) Right of Examination: If any claim of mental or physical disability is made by Director or on Director's behalf, Production Company shall have the right to have Director examined by such physicians as Production Company may designate. Director's physician may be present at such examination but shall not interfere therewith. [Any tests performed on Director shall be related to and customary for the treatment, diagnosis or examination to be performed in connection with Director's claim.]

16. [LENDER'S] [DIRECTOR'S] DEFAULT: If [Lender and/] or [Director] fail(s) or refuse(s) to perform or comply with any of the [material] terms or conditions hereof (other than by reason of Director's Incapacity) ["Lender's/ Director's Default"] ["Director's Default"] then Production Company may terminate this Agreement upon written notice to [Lender] [Director]. [[Lender/] Director Default shall not include any failure or refusal of Director to perform or comply with the material terms of this Agreement due to a breach or action by Production Company which makes impossible the performance of services by Director.] [Prior to termination of this Agreement by Production Company based upon [Lender/] Director Default, Production Company shall notify [Lender and] Director specifying the nature of the [Lender/] Director Default and [Lender and] Director shall have a period of (*e.g., 72 hours*) to cure the [Lender/] Director Default. If the [Lender/] Director Default is not cured within said (*e.g., 72 hour*) period, Production Company may terminate this Agreement forthwith.]

17. EFFECT OF TERMINATION: Termination of this Agreement, whether by lapse of time, mutual consent, operation of law, exercise of a right of termination or otherwise shall:

(a) Terminate Production Company's obligation to pay [Lender] [Director] any further compensation. Nevertheless, if the termination is not for Lender's/ Director's Default, Production Company shall pay [Lender] [Director] any compensation due and unpaid prior to the termination, and;

(b) Production Company shall not be deemed to have waived any other rights it may have or alter Production Company's rights or any of [Lender's] [Director's] agreements or warranties relating to the rendition of Director's services prior to termination.

18. PRODUCTION COMPANY RIGHT TO SUSPEND: In the event of Director's Incapacity or [Lender's/] Director's Default, Production Company may postpone [upon written notice] the commencement of or suspend the rendition of services by Director and the running of time hereunder so long as any Director's Disability or [Lender's/] Director's Default shall continue; and no compensation shall accrue or become payable to [Lender] [Director] during the period of such suspension.

(a) [Lender's] [Director's] Right to Cure: Any Director's Incapacity or [Lender's/] Director's Default shall be deemed to continue until Production Company's receipt of written notice from [Lender] [Director] specifying that Director is ready, willing and able to perform the services required hereunder;

provided that any such notice from [Lender] [Director] to Production Company shall not preclude Production Company from exercising any rights or remedies Production Company may have hereunder or at law or in equity by reason of director's Incapacity or [Lender's/] Director's Default.

(b) <u>Alternative Services Restricted</u>: During any period of suspension hereunder, Director shall not render services for any person, firm or corporation other than Production Company. [However, Director shall have the right to render services to third parties during any period of suspension based upon a Production Company Disability, subject, however, to Production Company's right to require Director to resume the rendition of services hereunder upon (*e.g., 24 hours*) prior notice.]

(c) <u>Production Company Right to Extend</u>: If Production Company elects to suspend the rendition of services by Director as herein specified, then Production Company shall have the right (exercisable at any time) [upon written notice] to extend the period of services of Director hereunder for a period equal to the period of such suspension.

(d) <u>Additional Services</u>: If Production Company shall have paid compensation to [Lender] [Director] during any period of Director's Incapacity or [Lender's/] Director's Default, then Production Company shall have the right (exercisable at any time) [upon written notice] to require [Lender] [Director] to render services hereunder without compensation for a period equal to the period for which Production Company shall have paid compensation to [Lender] [Director] during such Director's Incapacity or [Lender's/] Director's Default.

19. <u>FURTHER WARRANTIES</u>: [Lender/and] [Director] hereby warrant(s) that [Director is not] [neither Lender nor Director is] under any obligation or disability, created by law or otherwise, which would in any manner or to any extent prevent or restrict [Lender and] Director from entering into and fully performing this Agreement; [Lender and] Director warrant that [Lender and] Director (has) (have) not entered into any agreement or commitment that would prevent [their] [Director's] fulfilling [its] [Director's] commitments with Production Company hereunder and that [Lender and] [Director] will not enter into any such agreement or commitment without Production Company's specific approval; and [Director hereby accepts the obligations hereunder and agrees to] [Lender agrees that Director shall] devote Director's entire time and attention and best talents and abilities exclusively to Production Company as specified herein, and to observe and to be governed by the rules of conduct established by Production Company for the conduct of its employees.

(a) <u>Indemnity</u>: [Lender and] [Director] shall at all times indemnify Production Company, its successors, assignees and licensees, from and against any and all costs, expenses, losses, damages, judgments and attorneys' fees arising out of or connected with or resulting from any claims, demands or causes of action by any person or entity which is inconsistent with any of [Lender's and/or] Director's representations, warranties or agreements hereunder. [Lender] [Director] will reimburse Production Company on demand for any payment made by Production Company at any time after the date hereof in respect of any liability, loss, damage, cost or expense to which the foregoing indemnity relates.

20. REMEDIES: All remedies accorded herein or otherwise available to either Production Company or [Lender] [Director] shall be cumulative, and no one such remedy shall be exclusive of any other. Without waiving any rights or remedies under this Agreement or otherwise, Production Company may from time to time recover, by action, any damages arising out of any breach of this Agreement by [Lender and/or] [Director], and may institute and maintain subsequent actions for additional damages which may arise from the same or other breaches. The commencement or maintenance of any such action or actions by Production Company shall not constitute an election on Production Company's part to terminate this Agreement nor constitute or result in termination of [Lender's and/or] [Director's] services hereunder unless Production Company shall expressly so elect by written notice to [Lender and/or] [Director]. The pursuit by either Production Company or [Lender] [Director] of any remedy under this Agreement or otherwise shall not be deemed to waive any other or different remedy which may be available under this Agreement or otherwise, either at law or in equity.

Notwithstanding the foregoing, [Lender and] Director hereby recognize(s) and confirm(s) that in the event of failure or omission by Production Company constituting a breach of Production Company's obligations under this Agreement, the damage, if any, caused [Lender and] Director by Production company is not irreparable or sufficient to entitle [Lender and/or] Director to injunctive or other equitable relief. Consequently, [Lender and] Director shall have no right in such event to rescind this Agreement or any of the rights assigned to Production Company hereunder or to enjoin or restrain the distribution or exhibition of the Picture.

21. GUILDS AND UNIONS:

(a) Membership: During the periods when Director is required to render services hereunder, as Production Company may lawfully require [Director so to do, Director, at] [, Lender shall cause Director, at Lender's or] Director's sole cost and expense (and at Production Company's request [shall] [to] remain or become and remain a member in good standing of the then properly designated labor organization or organizations (as defined and determined under the then applicable law) representing persons performing services of the type and character required to be performed by Director hereunder.

(b) Superseding Effect of Guild Agreements: Nothing contained in this Agreement shall be construed so as to require the violation of the Directors Basic

Agreement of 1987, as amended from time to time, or any other written agreement between Production Company and Directors' Guild of America, Inc., which may from time to time be in effect and by its terms controlling with respect to this Agreement; and wherever there is any conflict between any provision of this Agreement and any such agreement, the latter shall prevail, but in such event the provisions of this Agreement shall be curtailed and limited only to the extent necessary to permit compliance with such agreement with Directors' Guild of America, Inc.

[22. PENSION, HEALTH AND WELFARE AND EMPLOYER TAXES: Production Company agrees upon the receipt of appropriate invoices to reimburse Lender in an amount equal to any contributions to pension plans, health and welfare funds required to be paid by Lender to any appropriate Guild or union having jurisdiction over the type of services to be performed by Director hereunder, it being expressly agreed that any amounts to be paid hereunder shall be based upon payments made by Lender in accordance with the applicable provisions of said respective Guild or union basic agreements, and which in any event shall not exceed the amount of the contribution Production Company would have been required to make had Director been employed by Production Company. Production Company shall have no obligation to reimburse Lender for employer taxes of any kind or nature.]

[23. MOTION PICTURE RELIEF FUND OF AMERICA, INC.: [Lender] [Director] hereby authorizes Production Company in Director's behalf to pay to the Motion Picture Relief Fund of America, Inc. one percent (1%) of all compensation accruing to [Lender] [Director] hereunder.]

24. [[GARNISHMENT] [ATTACHMENT]: If Production Company shall be required, because of the service of any [garnishment] [attachment] or by the terms of any contract or assignment executed by [Lender and/or] [Director], to pay all or any portion of the compensation hereunder to any other person, firm or corporation, the withholding of payment of such compensation or any portion thereof, in accordance with the requirements of any such [garnishment] [attachment], contract or assignment shall not be construed as a breach by Production Company of this Agreement.]

25. INSURANCE: Production Company may secure life, health, accident, cast, or other insurance covering Director, the cost of which shall be included in the direct cost budget of the Picture. Such insurance shall be for Production Company's sole benefit and Production Company shall be the beneficiary thereof, and [Lender and] Director shall have no interest in the proceeds thereof. Director shall assist in procuring such insurance by submitting to required examinations and tests and by preparing, signing, and delivering such applications and other documents as may be reasonably required. [Lender and] Director shall, to the

best of [Lender's and] Director's ability, observe all terms and conditions of such insurance of which Production Company notifies [Lender or] Director as necessary for continuing such insurance in effect.

If [Production Company is unable to obtain pre-production or cast insurance covering Director at prevailing standard rates and without any exclusions, restrictions, conditions, or exceptions of any kind, Director shall have the right to pay any premium in excess of the prevailing standard rate in order for Production Company to obtain such insurance. If [Lender] [Director] fails, refuses, to pay such excess premium, or if] Production Company having obtained such insurance, [Lender or] Director fails to observe all terms and conditions necessary to maintain such insurance in effect, Production Company shall have the right to terminate this Agreement without any obligation to [Lender or] Director and by giving [Lender] Director written notice of termination.

26. <u>EMPLOYMENT OF OTHERS</u>: [Lender and] Director agree(s) not to employ any person to serve in any capacity, nor contract for the purchase or renting of any article or material, nor make any agreement committing Production Company to pay any sum of money for any reason whatsoever in connection with the Picture or services to be rendered by Director hereunder or otherwise, without written approval first being had and obtained from Production Company.

[27. <u>WORKERS' COMPENSATION COVERAGE</u>: Lender warrants and represents that Lender maintains workers' compensation coverage for Director at Lender's expense.]

ALTERNATIVE CLAUSE

[27. <u>WORKERS' COMPENSATION</u>: For the purposes of any and all applicable Workers' Compensation statutes, an employment relationship exists between Director and Production Company such that Production Company is Director's special employer (as the term "Special Employer") is understood for purposes of Workers' Compensation statutes). The rights and remedies, if any, of Director and Director's heirs, executors, administrators, successors and assigns, against Production Company and/or its officers, directors, agents, employees, successors, assigns or licensees, by reason of injury, illness, disability or death arising out of or occurring in the course of Director's rendition of services hereunder shall be governed by and limited to those provided under such Workers' Compensation statutes, and neither Production Company, nor its officers, directors, agents, employees, successors, assigns or licensees shall have any other obligation or liability by any reason of any such injury, illness, disability or death. If the applicability of any Workers' Compensation statutes to the engagement of Director's services hereunder is dependent upon, or affected by, an election on the part of Director, such election is hereby made by Director in favor of such application.]

28. <u>RIGHT TO LEND TO OTHERS</u>: Production Company shall have the right to lend Director's services hereunder to (a) any of Production Company's subsidiary or affiliated companies, or (b) any other producer of Motion Pictures provided such producer shall have granted to Production Company the right to distribute the Picture [and further provided that [Lender] [Director] has consented to such lending, which consent shall not be unreasonably withheld]. [If [Lender] [Director] fails to respond to Production Company's request for approval of such lending within (*e.g., three business*) days of Production Company's request therefore, then such request shall automatically be deemed approved.] [No such lending of Director's services shall relieve Production Company of its obligations hereunder.]

29. <u>ASSIGNMENT</u>: This Agreement, at the election of Production Company, shall inure to the benefit of Production Company's administrators, successors, assigns, licensees, grantees, and associated, affiliated and subsidiary companies, and [Lender and] Director agree(s) that Production Company and any subsequent assignee may freely assign this Agreement and grant its rights hereunder, in whole or in part, to any person, firm or corporation [, provided that such person, firm or corporation assumes and agrees in writing to keep and perform all of the executory obligations of Production Company hereunder]. [Unless such assignment is to a major or mini-major studio as such term is commonly understood in the motion picture industry, Production Company shall remain secondarily liable hereunder.]

30. <u>ENTIRE AGREEMENT</u>: This Agreement shall replace and supersede all previous arrangements, understandings, representations, or agreements, either oral or written, with respect to the subject matter hereof and expresses the entire agreement between Production Company and [Lender] [Director] with reference to the terms and conditions for the rendition of Director's services for Production Company in connection with the Picture.

31. <u>NOTICES</u>:

    (a) <u>[Lender's and] Director's Address</u>: All notices from Production Company to [Lender and/or] [Director], in connection with this Agreement, may be given in writing by addressing the same to [Lender and/or] Director in care of (*name and address of recipient of notice*) and by depositing same, so addressed, postage prepaid, in the mail, by facsimile transmission (with a confirmation copy mailed by regular U.S. mail), or at Production Company's option, Production Company may deliver such notice to [Lender and/or] [Director] personally, either orally or in writing. A courtesy copy shall be sent to (*name and address of attorney*). If such notice shall be sent by mail, or by facsimile transmission, as above provided, the date of mailing or facsimile transmission, as applicable, shall be deemed to be the date of service of such notice.

(b) <u>Writing Requirement</u>: Any notice given in respect to any right of termination, suspension, or extension under this Agreement shall be confirmed in writing. If any notice is delivered to [Lender and/or] [Director] personally, a copy of such notice shall be sent to [Lender and/or] [Director], as applicable, at the above address.

(c) <u>Production Company</u>: All notices from [Lender] [Director] to Production Company hereunder shall be given in writing addressed to Production Company as follows: (*name and address of production company*), and by depositing the same, so addressed, postage prepaid, in the mail. A courtesy copy shall be sent to (*name and address of attorney*). Unless otherwise expressly provided, the date of mailing shall be deemed to be the date of service of such notice.

32. <u>EMPLOYMENT ELIGIBILITY</u>: All of Production Company's obligations herein are expressly conditioned upon Director's completion, to Production Company's satisfaction, of the I-9 form (Employee Eligibility Verification Form), and upon [Lender's] [Director's] submission to Production Company of original documents satisfactory to demonstrate to Production Company Director's employment eligibility.

33. <u>GOVERNING LAW</u>: This Agreement shall be construed in accordance with the laws of the State of (*name of state*) applicable to agreements which are executed and fully performed within said State.

34. <u>CAPTIONS</u>: The captions used in connection with the clauses and subclauses of this Agreement are inserted only for the purpose of reference. Such captions shall not be deemed to govern, limit, modify, or in any other manner affect the scope, meaning, or intent of the provisions of this Agreement or any part thereof; nor shall such captions otherwise be given any legal effect.

35. <u>SERVICE OF PROCESS</u>: In any action or proceeding commenced in any court in the state of (*name of state*) for the purpose of enforcing this Agreement or any right granted herein, or any order or decree predicated thereon, any summons, order to show cause, writ, judgment, decree, or other process, issued by such court, may be delivered to [Lender and/or] Director personally without the state of (*name of state*), and when so delivered, [Lender and/or] Director [, as applicable,] shall be subject to the jurisdiction of such court as though the same had been served within the state of (*name of state*), but outside the county in which such action or proceeding is pending.

36. <u>ILLEGALITY</u>: Nothing contained herein shall require the commission of any act or the payment of any compensation which is contrary to an express provision of law or contrary to the policy of express law or any guild or union rules or regulations; and if there shall exist any conflict between any provision contained herein and any such law or policy, or any guild or union rules or

regulations, the latter shall prevail; and the provision or provisions herein affected shall be curtailed, limited or eliminated to the extent (but only to the extent) necessary to remove such conflict; and as so modified this Agreement shall continue in full force and effect.

Other provisions that may be used in the Director Employment (*or Engagement*) Agreement are:

OPTIONAL CLAUSES

37. <u>REMAKE RIGHTS AND SEQUEL MOTION PICTURE RIGHTS</u>: The Remake Rights and the Sequel Motion Picture Rights with respect to the Picture shall be vested in Production Company. Nevertheless, if this Agreement has not been terminated due to [Lender's] Director's Default, and if Director has substantially directed the Picture the following shall apply:

(a) <u>Right of First Negotiation—Theatrical Remakes and Studio Sequel Theatrical Motion Pictures</u>: If (i) [Lender has caused Director to render] [Director has rendered] all services required by Production Company in connection with the Picture; and (ii) if Production Company elects to produce a Theatrical Remake of the Picture or a Studio Sequel Theatrical Motion Picture based upon the Picture within the (*e.g., five year*) period following the Initial Release Date of the Picture; and (iii) if Director has received a "Directed By" credit in connection with each previous Theatrical Remake of the Picture and/or Studio Sequel Theatrical Motion Picture based on the Picture, if any; and (iv) if the Agreement pursuant to which Director renders services in connection with each such remake and/or sequel has not been terminated due to [Lender's] Director's Default; then Production Company shall notify [Lender] [Director] and [Lender] [Director] shall have a period of (*e.g., thirty days*) following such notice within which to negotiate in good faith with Production Company the terms and conditions upon which [Lender] [Director] would furnish the services of Director as the director of such remake or sequel. If no agreement is reached within such (*e.g., thirty day*) period, [Lender's] [Director's] rights of first negotiation as set forth herein shall automatically terminate, and Production Company shall be free to negotiate with any third party with respect to such third party's directing services for such remake or sequel.

(b) <u>Right of First Negotiation — Television Remakes and Studio Sequel Television Motion Pictures</u>: If (i) [Lender has caused Director to render] [Director has rendered] all services required by Production Company in connection with the Picture; and (ii) if Production Company elects to produce a Television Remake of the Picture or a Studio Sequel Television Motion Picture based upon the Picture within the (*e.g., five year*) period following the Initial Release Date of the Picture; and (iii) if Director has received a "Directed By" credit in connection with each previous Television Remake of the Picture and/or Studio

Sequel Television Motion Picture based on the Picture, if any; and (iv) if the Agreement pursuant to which Director renders services in connection with each such remake and/or sequel has not been terminated due to [Lender's] Director's Default; then Production Company shall notify [Lender] [Director] and [Lender] [Director] shall have a period of (*e.g., thirty days*) following such notice within which to negotiate in good faith with Production Company with respect to the terms and conditions upon which [Lender] [Director] would furnish the services of Director as the director of such remake or sequel. If no agreement is reached within such (*e.g., thirty day*) period, [Lender's] [Director's] rights of first negotiation as set forth herein shall automatically terminate, and Production Company shall be free to negotiate with any third party with respect to such third party's directing services for any such remake or sequel.

38. APPROVALS AND SELECTIONS: Provided that [Director is] [Lender and Director are] not in default on their [material] obligations hereunder, and have performed all services required of them by Production Company, and further provided that Production Company elects to proceed to production of the Picture, then:

(a) [Approvals and] Consultation: [Subject to applicable Guild and Union requirements,] Director and Production Company shall fully consult with respect to [and shall have mutual approval of] (*e.g., the principal members of the cast, budgeted negative cost, pre-production schedule, production schedules, post-production schedules, final approved screenplay, locations for shooting sites (both interior and exterior), the laboratory, the main and end titles of the Picture, the site of post-production and final mix of the Picture*). Production Company shall have final approval of all other production elements in connection with the production of the Picture, both "above the line" and "below the line" personnel and elements (except as otherwise set forth herein), and all commitments and contracts relative to any of the foregoing. In addition, Production Company shall have the right, in its sole discretion, to select and designate the location auditor.

(b) *Selections*: [Subject to the applicable Guild and Union requirements,] Director shall have the right to [select and designate] [propose, subject to Production Company approval,] the following key personnel for the Picture: *e.g.*,

(1) Director of Photography;

(2) First Assistant Director;

(3) Production Manager and Unit Manager, if any;

(4) Production Designer;

(5) Costume Designer;

(6) Sound Engineer;

(7) Sound Editors;

(8) Lighting Designer, if any;

(9) Casting Director;

(10) Special Effects Chief;

(11) Music Composer and/or Conductor;

(12) Film Editors;

(13) Music Editors; and

(14) Cameraman,

provided that:

(A) The costs involved for engaging a particular individual for a particular position shall not exceed said individual's then going rate in the Motion Picture industry;

(B) The costs involved for engaging such particular individual for a particular position shall not exceed the amount allocated for the position in the budget;

(C) The particular individual is ready, willing and able to perform services as and when required by Production Company; and

(D) The particular individual's prior work experience with the Production Company, if any, was completed to the satisfaction of Production Company.

(c) Changes Subsequent to [Consultation] [Approval]: Once the pre-production, production, and post-production schedules have been set, these schedules may only be changed by Production Company after full consultation with Director [and subject to Director's approval, which approval shall not be unreasonably withheld]. [Once Director has approved the screenplay, there shall be no material changes made in the final approved screenplay without Director's consent and approval which shall not be unreasonably withheld.]

[(d) Creative Control: Subject to Subclause (e) below, and subject to Production Company's final business decision in the event of a disagreement between Director and Production Company, Director shall have final creative control of the Picture.]

(e) Failure to Approve and Select: If, after Production Company has elected to proceed to production of the Picture, Director and Production Company do not agree on [any of the above elements regarding which Director and Production Company have mutual approval pursuant to Subclause (a) above, or if Director fails or is otherwise unable to select the key personnel to be engaged for the Picture, pursuant to the provisions of Subclause (b) above, (including, the substitute personnel for any previously [approved or] selected individuals who become unavailable) by a date occurring (*e.g., eight weeks*) prior to the commencement of principal photography, then, Production Company may designate such personnel and/or element in its sole discretion].

39. ADVERTISING CAMPAIGN AND DISTRIBUTION PATTERN CONSUL-TATION: Production Company agrees that Director shall have the right to consult with respect to the formulation of the initial advertising campaign and the initial distribution pattern for the theatrical exhibition of the Picture in the United States, including, without limitation, opening in key cities, such as New York, Los Angeles, and Chicago, and that Director shall have the right to consult with respect to the engagement of any third party publicity companies which may render services in connection with the Picture, provided, that Director is available for such consultation at such times and places as Production Company requires and at no expense to Production Company. If the unavailability of Director would in any way hinder or delay Production Company from proceeding with said advertising campaign, and/or the initial distribution of the Picture, and/or the selection of any third party publicity companies to be engaged for the Picture, then Director shall be deemed to have waived such right of consultation. [The availability of Director for such consultation by telephone shall not constitute "unavailability" under this clause.] It is specifically understood and agreed that Production Company has final approval of the initial advertising campaign and the initial distribution pattern.

40. [16MM PRINT] [VHS CASSETTE]: Provided that [Lender and] Director is/are not in default of the Director's obligations hereunder, and have performed all services required by Production Company, and further provided that Production Company produces the Picture, Production Company hereby agrees that it shall furnish Director with one [16mm print] [(*e.g., one VHS cassette*)] of the Picture for Director's home use and entertainment only at such time as and if such [16mm print] [VHS cassette] of the Picture becomes available. In connection therewith, [Lender] [Director] agrees that [Lender and] Director shall execute Production Company's standard form of [print] [video cassette] loan agreement.

41. CUTTING AND EDITING: If Director substantially directs the Picture through the completion of principal photography, Director shall have the "final cut" of the Picture [for purposes of (initial) Theatrical Distribution] *or* [Director shall have one cut and a preview in accordance with the provisions of the DGA Agreement, which shall be deemed to include any and all cuts and previews required under the DGA Agreement,] upon and subject to the following conditions:

(a) The Picture shall have a running time (exclusive of main and end titles) of not less than (*specify number, e.g., 90*) minutes and not more than (*specify number, e.g., 120*) minutes; or including main and end titles not more than (*specify number, e.g., 125*) minutes;

(b) The Picture shall not contain any stock or reused film or sound recordings;

(c) The Picture, as completed, shall be submitted to the Code and Rating Administration of the Motion Picture Association of America ("M.P.A.A.") for a rating and shall qualify for a M.P.A.A. rating not more restrictive than "(*specify rating, e.g.,* "G", "PG-13", "NC-17", *or* "R")";

(d) If requested by Production Company, Director shall photograph and record all necessary "cover shots" for free television exhibition, airline, military and other non-theatrical exhibition and to satisfy "local tastes" in certain foreign markets, at any time not later than [*e.g., three (3) business days*] after the last dailies have been received by Production Company unless otherwise agreed;

(e) Director shall make all cuts and changes as may be deemed necessary by Production Company to meet minimum censorship requirements of any legally constituted censorship board or to eliminate claims or threatened or potential claims for libel, invasion of the right of privacy and other similar legal matters;

(f) Director shall complete [the Director's "final cut"] [the Director's cut] of the Picture within (*e.g., four months*) after the completion of principal photography of the Picture [in accordance with the schedule set forth in Exhibit "S"], as that period may be extended for technical requirements or other events beyond Director's control;

(g) Director may designate any cut as Director's final cut prior to the initial release date of the Picture [, in accordance with the approved post-production schedule as set forth in Exhibit "S"]; provided that Director may not change such designation once made;

(h) [Subject to Director's availability,] Director shall have the right to supervise the cutting and editing required for free television exhibition of the Picture over network television;

(i) Director shall have the right to supervise the dubbing of the (*name of foreign country*) version of the Picture subject to Director's availability. Director shall not be entitled to any additional compensation for such services, but if Director is required to travel in connection therewith, the provisions of Clause 6 [relating to transportation and expenses] shall apply thereto but same shall only apply to Director and not his family nor to Director's companion and/or secretary.

(j) If Director is not available to perform any portion or all of the foregoing cutting and editing in the time contemplated by this Agreement, Production Company shall have the right to perform such cutting and editing after [*e.g., ten business days'*] prior written notice, unless shorter notice is reasonable under the circumstances.

(k) The foregoing cutting and editing rights, as well as all other creative controls of Director, apply solely to Director personally and not to [Lender or] any other corporate entity or other party, and Director shall not delegate or subcontract any of the same.

By signing in the spaces provided below, [Lender] [Director] and Production Company accept and agree to all of the terms and conditions of this Agreement.

(Name of Production Company)

By _____

Its _____

("Production Company")

_____

("Director")

ALTERNATE

_____

(Name of Loan-out Company)

By _____

Its _____

("Lender")

INDUCEMENT

I, (name of director), agree to perform all obligations to be performed by Lender and me hereunder, and make all representations and warranties herein made by Lender, in order to effectuate the terms and conditions of the foregoing Agreement, and I agree to look solely to Lender for payment of any compensation due me. In the event of any breach or threatened breach by Lender, I agree to render all services required of me hereunder directly to Production Company. I hereby accept and acknowledge each and all provisions of the foregoing agreement to the same extent as if I had signed the agreement directly.

_____

(Name of Director)   Date

Form 12

Motion Picture Producer Agreement

(*Loan-out Agreement:*)

Agreement dated as of (*date of agreement*) between (*name of loan-out company*), a (*state of incorporation*) corporation ("Lender"), and (*name of production company*) ("Production Company"), regarding the services of (*name of producer*) ("Producer").

(*Employment Agreement:*)

Agreement dated as of (*date of agreement*) between (*name of individual producer*) ("Producer") and (*name of production company*) ("Production Company").

1. ENGAGEMENT/[EMPLOYMENT]: [Production Company agrees to borrow from Lender and Lender agrees to lend to Production Company upon the terms and conditions herein specified, the services of (*Producer*) as individual producer and to cause Producer] [Producer agrees] to perform all of the services hereinafter described and such other services as are customarily provided by producers in the Motion Picture industry in connection with the development and production of a theatrical motion picture ("Picture") [based upon (*describe source material, e.g., the unpublished screenplay entitled "(name of work)" written by (name of author)*) ("Basic Property").] [The Basic Property, together with all material written based upon the Basic Property, including the final draft screenplay, are referred to as the "Literary Work".] [Lender hereby represents and warrants that it is a corporation organized and existing under and by virtue of the laws of the State of (*state of incorporation of loan-out company*), and that Lender has entered into a written contract with Producer which is now in full force and effect.

2. ACQUISITION OF BASIC PROPERTY:

(a) Options on Basic Property: [Lender] [Producer] has [acquired] [an option to acquire] motion picture and allied rights in and to (*specify, e.g., the Literary work pursuant to that certain Option Agreement dated (date of agreement) between [Lender] [Producer] and (name of seller of literary work)*) ("Option Agreement").

(b) Quitclaim from [Lender] [Producer] to Production Company: [Lender] [Producer] is simultaneously herewith quitclaiming all [its] [*Producer's*] rights in and to (*specify, e.g., the Literary Work and Option Agreement.*)

(c) Chain of Title: [Lender] [Producer] agrees to execute and deliver to Production Company such further documents as Production Company may [reasonably] require in order to perfect the chain of title with respect to the Literary Work, and/or which Production Company deems necessary to effectuate the intent hereof. Production Company's obligations hereunder are conditioned upon the approval by Production Company of the chain of title affecting all the rights in and to the Literary Work (including all screenplay material which has heretofore been written based thereon) and the obtaining by Production Company of all releases and assignments deemed necessary by Production Company in connection with obtaining such rights in form and substance satisfactory to Production Company. [Unless within thirty (30) days following its receipt of the chain of title, Production Company gives notice to [Producer] [Lender] specifying any defects in the chain of title, Production Company shall be deemed to have accepted the chain of title.] [Producer] [Lender] shall have thirty (30) days from receipt of such notice within which to cure any defect in the chain of title. If [Producer] [Lender] fails to provide such cure, [then (*specify consequence of failure to cure; e.g., Production Company shall have the right to terminate this Agreement, and neither party shall have any further obligations to the other hereunder*).] If Production Company does not approve the chain of title and/or Production Company does not so obtain such releases and assignments, this Agreement shall immediately terminate and Production Company and [Lender] [Lender and Producer] shall have no further obligations to each other hereunder; provided, however, that all material developed or contributed by Producer prior to the date of such termination shall remain the sole and exclusive property of Production Company pursuant to Subclause 14(d) hereof and [Lender] [Producer] shall be entitled to receive all sums due and payable to [Lender] [Producer] prior to the date of such termination, if any, pursuant to Clauses 3(c) and 9(a) hereof.

3. DEVELOPMENT AND PRE-PRODUCTION PHASE:

(a) <u>Supervision</u>: [Lender] [Producer], in conjunction with the individual designated to be the director of the Picture ("Director") shall supervise the development and writing, as well as all the revisions and changes [as required by Production Company] in connection with the screenplay, and all pre-production activities [required by Production Company] including the selection of proposed casting and the preparation of the proposed budget to be based on the screenplay determined by Production Company, Director and [Lender] [Producer] to be the final screenplay for the Picture. Producer's services shall be rendered to Production Company pursuant to the terms and conditions of Clause 14 hereof. [All such services shall be rendered on a non-exclusive but first priority basis and the rendition of services by Producer for third parties shall not interfere with Producer's obligations to Production Company hereunder.]

(b) <u>Non-Reimbursed Expenses</u>: During the period of development and pre-production, Production Company shall have no obligation to reimburse [Lender] [Producer] for or make any advances on account of [Lender's] [Producer's] overhead, accounting, legal, living or traveling expenses, or any other charges or expenses of [Lender's] [Producer's] personnel, except as specifically approved by Production Company, in writing, prior to the incurring of such charge or expense, for reasonable and actual expenses incurred by Producer in connection with scouting trips, location surveys, and the like.

(c) <u>Development Fee</u>: Production Company shall pay Producer for all of the aforementioned development and pre-production services to be performed by [Lender] [Producer] [and for the services of Producer provided by Lender] $ (*amount of development fee, e.g., $30,000*), [which shall accrue and be payable weekly over a period of (*e.g., 10 weeks*) at the rate of (*e.g., $3,000 per week*)] [which shall be payable upon execution of this Agreement by Lender and acknowledgment by Producer receipt of which is hereby acknowledged] [which shall be payable one-half upon full execution of this Agreement and one-half upon delivery and acceptance by Production Company of the final draft screenplay of the Picture].

(d) <u>Application of Development Fee</u>: If Production Company proceeds with production of the Picture, the payment specified in Clause 3(c) above shall [not] be applied as a reduction of the Production Fee set forth in Clause 9(a) below.

4. ELECTION TO PROCEED, ABANDONMENT, TURNAROUND:

(a) <u>Election to Proceed</u>: Production Company shall have a period of (*e.g., 30 days*) ("Election Period") to elect to proceed to production or to abandon the Picture after completion of all of the following: (i) delivery of the screenplay determined by [Lender] [Producer] and Production Company as the final draft screenplay; (ii) delivery of the proposed budget approved by [Lender] [Producer]; (iii) delivery of chain of title; and (iv) designation and approval by [Lender] [Producer] of the principal cast and Director. Notice of such election shall be given to [Lender] [Producer] in writing. Failure to give any notice during the election period shall constitute an election not to proceed effective on the (*e.g., thirtieth (30th)*) day of the Election Period. During such Election Period, [Lender shall furnish the services of Producer to] [Producer shall] assist with the preparation of the budget, final shooting script, production schedule, casting and other pre-production matters as required by Production Company.

(b) <u>Turnaround</u>:

(i) <u>Right to Acquire</u>: If during the Election Period Production Company elects not to continue with development of the Picture and/or elects not to proceed to production of the Picture, [Lender] [Producer] shall have the exclusive right for a period of (*e.g., 18*) months after written notice of such election ("Turnaround Period") to acquire all of the right, title and interest of Production Company in and to the Literary Work, by [*e.g.,* reimbursing Production Company for all expenses and charges ("Buy-Out Price") incurred by Production Company in connection with the Picture including all monies paid to [Lender] [Producer] ("Advances"), [plus, *e.g.,* an Administrative Overhead Charge of (*e.g., specify percentage*) of the Advances (collectively "Investment")], plus interest on the Investment computed weekly from the week in which an item of Investment was incurred until repaid to Production Company as herein provided at an annual percentage rate of (*specify amount or method of computation*)]. If during the

Turnaround Period, [Lender] [Producer] shall enter into an agreement for the development or production of the Picture or [Lender or] Producer or any party with whom [Lender or] Producer is negotiating shall do or authorize any writing to be done in connection with the Picture or [Lender or] Producer or any party with whom [Lender or] Producer is negotiating shall commence or authorize the commencement of photography of the Picture, [Lender] [Producer] will upon the occurrence of such event [*e.g.*, pay Production Company the Buy-Out Price and furnish to Production Company an indemnity agreement, in a form satisfactory to Production Company, signed by a party having financial responsibility satisfactory to Production Company, covering all obligations and liabilities in connection with the Picture,] whereupon Production Company will quitclaim its right, title and interest in the Picture to [Lender] [Producer], and Production Company will warrant only that Production Company has not theretofore transferred, hypothecated or otherwise disposed of any of its right, title and interest in the Picture.

[(ii) No Further Rights: If [Lender] [Producer] does not exercise such right within the Turnaround Period, [Lender and/or] Producer shall have no further rights hereunder and/or in the Literary Work and Production Company shall have no obligation whatsoever to involve [Lender and/or] Producer in the Picture and [Lender and/or] Producer shall execute and deliver such instruments as Production Company may reasonably require in order to effectuate the purposes and intents hereof.]

(iii) Changed Elements and Terms: If, prior to Lender paying Production Company the Buy-Out Price within the Turnaround Period, [Lender and/or] Producer introduce(s) any new or alter(s) any existing elements ("Changed Elements") and/or introduce(s) any changed terms and conditions including the financial terms regarding [Lender's and/or] Producer's involvement in connection with the Picture ("Changed Terms"), [Lender] [Producer] shall submit to Production Company in writing such Changed Elements and Changed Terms and Production Company shall have a period of (*e.g.*, *ten (10) business*) days after receipt thereof to reject such submission or to elect to proceed with the development and/or production of the Picture predicated upon the use, presence or involvement of such Changed Elements and Changed Terms, it being agreed that the election of Production Company to proceed shall not require the acceptance of any Changed Elements and Changed Terms which cannot be honored on a financial basis nor the acceptance of financial terms more favorable to [Lender and/or] Producer than the financial terms established herein. If Production Company rejects such submission, [Lender] [Producer] may acquire the right, title and interest of Production Company as herein provided; but the aforesaid first refusal procedure shall be repeated during the Turnaround Period each time [Lender and/or] Producer introduces Changed Elements and/or Changed Terms until [Lender] [Producer] has paid (*e.g.*, *the Buy-Out Price*).

[(iv) <u>Optioned Underlying Properties</u>: Until Production Company has been paid (*e.g., an amount equal to the Buy-Out Price*), if, during or following the Turnaround Period, Production Company fails to extend or exercise the Property Option, if any, regarding the Basic Property, and thereby loses its rights, if any, to the Basic Property, Production Company shall have a security interest and copyright mortgage in any rights which [Lender and/or] Producer may thereafter acquire in the Basic Property, whether directly or indirectly, and [Lender and/or] Producer shall hold such right as trustee for the benefit of Production Company [to the extent of Production Company's unrecouped investment in the Basic Property]. [Lender and] Producer agree(s) to execute such further documents as Production Company may reasonably require to perfect, protect, evidence, renew and/or continue such security interest and copyright mortgage and/or to effectuate the purposes and intents of this clause, including without limitation the execution of a Security Agreement and Financing Statement and copyright mortgage.]

5. <u>PRODUCTION PHASE</u>: If Production Company elects to proceed to production of the Picture and approves the final shooting script, principal cast, Director, and budget, then:

(a) <u>Services Furnished</u>: [Lender shall furnish the services of Producer] [Producer shall act] as individual producer and Producer shall proceed with production of the Picture [, subject to Production Company's approval rights,] and complete the Picture in conformity with the shooting script [approved by Production Company] and the budget and production schedule approved, in writing, by [Lender] [Producer] and Production Company].

(b) <u>Exclusivity</u>: Producer's services shall be exclusive during the period commencing (*e.g., eight weeks*) prior to the commencement, and continuing until completion, of principal photography. At all other times, until completion of the final corrected answer print of the Picture, the services of Producer shall be on a non-exclusive but first priority basis. During such time when services of Producer are on a non-exclusive basis, Producer shall refrain from rendering services elsewhere which would interfere in any way with the services of Producer in connection with the Picture or interfere with the completion of the Picture [in accordance with the post-production schedule set forth in Exhibit "—"]. Producer shall not render services elsewhere which would conflict with post-production services to be rendered by Producer for the Picture.

(c) <u>Running Time</u>: The Picture will have a running time of not less than (*specify number, e.g., 90*) minutes, nor more than (*specify number, e.g., 120*) minutes.

(d) <u>Schedules</u>: Principal photography of the Picture shall commence at the place and on a date designated by Production Company, which shall occur within (*e.g., 90 days*) after Production Company's election to proceed to production, subject to postponement because of delays covered by weather conditions, location unavailability, scheduling problems, force majeure, Director unavailability and/or cast unavailability. [Lender] [Producer] will cause delivery of the Picture to be completed within (*e.g., nineteen weeks*) after completion of principal photography [pursuant to the post-production schedule set forth in Exhibit "S"].

(e) Rating: The Picture, as completed, shall have been submitted to the Code and Rating Administration of the Motion Picture Association of America for a rating, and [unless Production Company approves an "(*specify G, PG, PG-13, R or NC-17*)" rating,] a rating of "(*specify G, PG, PG-13, R or NC-17*)" or "(*specify G, PG, PG-13, R or NC-17*)" shall be obtained before the Picture shall be deemed completed.

[(f) I.A.T.S.E.: The picture must qualify for and bear the I.A.T.S.E. Seal and must comply with Production Company's usual first class production quality and exhibition requirements.]

(g) *Approvals*: Production Company, after consultation with Producer, shall have final approval of the budget, production schedule, post-production schedule, release title, and all other artistic and production elements in connection with the production of the Picture, both "above-the-line" and "below-the-line" personnel and elements, and all commitments and contracts relative to any of the foregoing. [Notwithstanding the foregoing sentence, Producer shall have mutual approval with Production Company and the Director of the key creative personnel (excluding the production manager and location auditor).] [The foregoing shall be subject to applicable guild and union requirements.] If, after Production Company has elected to proceed to production of the Picture pursuant to Clause 4(a), [Lender] [Producer] and Production Company are unable to agree on any element regarding which [Lender] [Producer], Director and Production Company have mutual approval within (*e.g., eight (8) weeks*) prior to the commencement of principal photography of the Picture (including substitutes for any elements previously mutually approved but thereafter unavailable), then, Production Company, after consultation with Producer, shall have the right to designate such element, in its sole discretion. Regarding each decision on which Producer has a right of consultation pursuant to this clause, if Producer is unavailable to exercise such right of consultation, at such times and locations as required by Production Company, such right of consultation shall be deemed to have been waived by Producer. [Producer shall not be deemed unavailable for consultation if Producer is available by telephone.]

(h) Dailies: Production Company, shall have the right to view the dailies during the production of the Picture.

(i) Credit Compliance: [Lender agrees to] [Producer shall] comply with all contractual and union and guild obligations and Production Company requirements of which [Lender] [Producer] is notified in writing with respect to the screen credits for the Picture.

[(j) Television Cover Shots: [Lender agrees to cause Producer to] [Producer shall] furnish to Production Company protective shots necessary for release of the

Picture on television based on network continuity standards in existence at the time of principal photography of the Picture.]

6. RIGHT OF SUBSTITUTION:

(a) Events Occasioning Right of Substitution: Despite any contrary provisions of this Agreement, Production Company may substitute any other person's services for those being provided by the [Lender including those of Producer] [Producer] upon the occurrence of any of the following:

(i) Overbudget: At any time during the production of the Picture, the estimated final Negative Cost thereof exceeds the Budgeted Negative Cost for the Picture by (e.g., 10%) or more; or

(ii) Over-Schedule: At any time during the production of the Picture the principal photography thereof is (e.g., ten) days or more behind the shooting schedule upon which the budget is based; or

(iii) Non-Performance: At any time during the production of the Picture [Lender or] Producer materially defaults in the performance of any obligations under this Agreement.

[(iv) Effect of Election: The exercise of such substitution rights shall not constitute a release of [Lender's] [Producer's] obligations as to the Picture nor limit any other rights or remedies to which Production Company may be entitled.]

(b) Notice of Exercise: Upon the occurrence of any of the aforementioned events, Production Company shall have the right of substitution upon written notice to [Lender] [Producer] of its election to do so. Production Company shall not exercise its substitution rights with respect to the contingencies set forth in subclauses (a)(i) and (ii) above until after (e.g., 10%) of the shooting schedule upon which the Budgeted Negative Cost is based has elapsed, but in no event earlier than after the expiration of the first (e.g., one) week(s) of principal photography.

(c) Events Upon Exercise: If Production Company elects to exercise its substitution rights as hereinabove provided, then:

(i) Assignment of Contracts: [Lender] [Producer] shall assign to Production Company all contracts relating to the Picture to which [Lender] [Producer] is a party.

(ii) Completion of Picture: Production Company shall have the right to proceed with the production and completion of the Picture in such manner as Production Company may deem advisable without interference.

(iii) Expenditures: All expenditures made by Production Company in connection with the production of the Picture shall be included in the Negative Cost of the Picture as a Direct Charge.

(d) Proration of Compensation: If Production Company elects to exercise its substitution rights for any reason other than [Lender and/or] Producer default, and services of [Lender and/or] Producer are no longer required by Production Company (except for such services as are connected with [Lender's] [Producer's] transfer of the production of the Picture to Production Company, Production Company shall pay to [Lender] [Producer] the Fixed Compensation as set forth in Subclause 9(a). If however, Production Company continues to utilize [Lender's] [Producer's] services after exercise of Production Company's substitution rights, [or if Producer's services have been utilized through at least completion of pre-production,] Production Company shall pay to [Lender] [Producer], in addition to the Fixed Compensation, the following percentage of the Contingent Compensation payable to [Lender] [Producer] as set forth in subclause 9(b), and in accordance with the following schedule: (i) (*specify, e.g., Twenty-five percent (25%)*) thereof if [Lender] [Producer] has completed pre-production of the Picture prior to Production Company's exercise of substitution rights; plus,

(ii) (*specify, e.g., Fifty percent (50%)*) thereof prorated in the ratio that the number of weeks of principal photography completed prior to Production Company's exercise of substitution rights bears to the total number of weeks in the scheduled period of principal photography; plus,

(iii) (*specify, e.g., Twelve and one-half percent (12-1/2%)*) thereof if scoring of the Picture has been completed prior to Production Company's exercise of its substitution rights; plus,

(iv) (*specify, e.g., Twelve and one-half percent (12-1/2%)*) if the final corrected answer print is completed prior to Production Company's exercise of its substitution rights.

(e) <u>Substitution on Default</u>: If Production Company exercises its substitution rights based upon an event of [Lender's or] Producer's default, no additional compensation, either Fixed, Deferred, or Contingent, shall be paid to [Lender] [Producer], and all of Production Company's obligations with respect thereto shall terminate.

(f) <u>Effect on Contingent Compensation</u>: [Lender's] [Producer's] share of Contingent Compensation shall be subject to the right of Production Company to deduct therefrom any and all expenses incurred due to the event which gave rise to Production Company's exercise of its substitution rights, plus any and all expenses incurred in connection with the substitution.

(g) <u>Further Rights or Remedies</u>: Nothing in this clause shall be construed to limit or impair any other rights or remedies Production Company may have under this Agreement or at law or in equity by reason of any default by [Lender or] Producer in the performance of [Lender's or] Producer's obligations hereunder.

7. EXPENSES—PRODUCTION AND POST-PRODUCTION PHASES:

(a) <u>Non-Reimbursed Expenses</u>: During the production and post-production phases of the Picture, Production Company shall have no obligation to reimburse

[Lender] [Producer] for or make any advances on account of [Lender's] [Producer's] overhead, accounting, legal, office or secretarial expenses, or living or traveling expenses of any of [Lender's] [Producer's] personnel except as specifically approved by Production Company, or as provided for below.

(b) Office & Secretary: Production Company agrees to furnish [Lender] [Producer] with an office and one (1) secretary [for Producer] during the production and post-production phases of the Picture, provided Production Company elects to proceed with production of the Picture pursuant to Subclause 4(a). [The cost of furnishing said office and secretary shall be charged to the Picture.]

(c) Transportation and Expenses: When Producer's services are required by Production Company on location more than (*e.g., fifty miles from*) [at an overnight location outside of (*name of city or county*)], or from Producer's then principal place of residence), Production Company shall:

(i) Transportation: Furnish Producer with first class round trip transportation [to and from any said location] (if used and if available) [and, one (1) time only, with (*e.g., three*) additional first class round trip transportation (if available and if used) for the use of (*e.g., Producer's wife and children*), and.

(ii) Expenses: Reimburse Producer for Producer's living expenses of (*specify amount, e.g., $2,250*) per week or (*specify amount, e.g., $3,000*) per week if the services are required in a major urban area such as (*specify location, e.g., New York or London*) and (*specify amount, e.g., $1,500*) if such services are required at any other location. [If [Lender] [Producer] demonstrates to Production Company's satisfaction that the foregoing living expense allowance is insufficient for any particular location, Production Company shall, at such time, give good faith consideration to an increase.] [For any period less than one (1) week, said reimbursement shall be upon the pro rata basis that one (1) day is equal to one-seventh (1/7) of one (1) week. Producer agrees to furnish Production Company with itemized accountings for all such expenditures which shall comply with the Internal Revenue Service's regulations, including substantiating vouchers, invoices, and receipts relating to such expenses.]

8. POST-PRODUCTION PHASE:

(a) Cutting Rights: Provided [Lender and] Producer are not in default and have performed all services required of them [and provided further that the Director has no approval rights in connection with the final cut of the Picture and the Director has no right to more than (*e.g., two cuts and/or e.g., two previews*) of the Picture], Producer shall be entitled to (*e.g., one cut and e.g., one preview*) of the Picture. [Such cut and preview shall immediately follow the Director's last cut and preview; [provided, however, that if Producer's cut and preview would delay or otherwise hinder delivery of the Picture to Production Company pursuant to the post-production schedule approved by Production Company in conformity with Production Company's release requirements (including require-ments created by bidding exigencies), Producer's right to (*e.g., one* cut *and e.g., one preview*) shall be forfeited.]] Following delivery of the [Director's [last] cut and] Producer's cut [(if Producer's right to such cut has not been forfeited pursuant to the terms hereof)], Production Company shall have (*specify, e.g., complete and unconditional authority*) to the final cut and the final edit of the Picture.

(b) <u>Post-Production Schedule</u>: [Lender] [Producer] hereby agrees that the post-production period referred to in Subclause 5(d) shall be adhered to, otherwise Production Company shall have the right to proceed with the post-production work on the Picture as it desires. [Such other provisions of Clause 5 as are applicable to the Post-Production Phase shall be deemed incorporated in this clause.]

(c) <u>Right of Consultation</u>: Provided [Lender and] Producer are not in material default hereunder and have performed all services required by them hereunder, Producer shall have a right of consultation [in conjunction with the Director] with respect to the advertising and sales campaigns and the distribution patterns used for the Theatrical Distribution of the Picture in the United States; provided, however, that Production Company shall have the right to make the final decision, in its sole discretion, on all such matters. [If Producer is unavailable to exercise Producer's right of consultation pursuant to this subclause at such times and locations as required by Production Company, such right shall be deemed to have been waived by Producer.] [Producer shall not be deemed to be unavailable for consultation if Producer is available by telephone.]

9. <u>COMPENSATION</u>:

(a) <u>Fixed Compensation</u>: Conditioned upon the performance of [Lender's] [Producer's] obligations [and those of Producer] and Production Company proceeding with production of the Picture, pursuant to Subclause 4(a), Production Company shall pay [Lender] [Producer] as a Production Fee [for the services of Producer] and for all rights granted hereunder (*specify amount, e.g., $500,000*) [but less the Development Fee payable pursuant to Subclause 3(c) hereof]. The Production Fee shall be paid to [Lender] [Producer] as follows:

(i) (*E.g., seventy-five percent*) in equal weekly installments over the (*specify period, e.g., seven (7)*) week pre-production period during which Producer's services are exclusive to Production Company and continuing through the scheduled period of principal photography;

(ii) (*E.g., twelve and one-half percent*) upon completion of scoring of the Picture;

(iii) (*E.g., twelve and one-half percent*) upon completion and delivery of the final corrected answer print and all items required by Production Company for complete delivery of the Picture.

(b) <u>Contingent Compensation</u>: In addition to the Fixed Compensation, [Lender] [Producer] shall be entitled, subject to the production and release of the Picture, and subject to the performance of all obligations of [Lender and] Producer, to receive as Contingent Compensation an amount equal to (*e.g., twelve and one-half percent*) of 100% of (*e.g., Gross Receipts After Breakeven*) [reducible by the following Third Party percentage participations in the following order of priority:

(i) <u>Percentage Participation of (*name of participant*)</u>: (*e.g., Fifty percent*) of sums payable to (*name of participant*) as a percentage participation in Net Profits;

(ii) <u>Other Third Party Percentage Participations (*e.g., One Sixth*)</u>: Thereafter, (*e.g., one-sixth*) of all sums payable to Third Parties (other than (*name of participant*)) as percentage participations in Net Profits ("Third Party Net Participations") and in Gross Participations after Initial Breakeven Point ("Third Party Gross Participations") until the aggregate of such Third Party Net Participations and Third Party Gross Participations deducted pursuant to this subclause equals (*e.g., fifteen percent*) of 100% of Net Profits;

(iii) <u>Remaining Third Party Percentage Participations — [(*e.g., Fifty Percent*)]</u>: Thereafter, (*e.g., fifty percent*) of all remaining Third Party Net Participations and Third Party Gross Participations. [Lender] [Producer] hereby acknowledges that it is the intent of [Production Company and (Lender) (Producer)] that all remaining sums payable as Third Party Net Participations and Third Party Gross Participations that are not applied to reduce [Lender's] [Producer's] Contingent Compensation pursuant to Subclause (ii) hereinabove shall be used to reduce the Contingent Compensation payable to (*name of participant*) in connection with the Picture pursuant to the Agreement dated as of (*date of agreement*) between (*name of participant*) and Production Company and in no event shall the revenues of the Picture to which Production Company is entitled be reduced by such remaining Third Party Net Participations and Third Party Gross Participations.]

[(c) <u>Conversion Factor</u>: For purposes of extrapolating the effect of Third Party Gross Participations on [Lender's] [Producer's] Contingent Compensation prior to actual computation thereof, Third Party Gross Participations shall be converted to a percentage participation of Net Profits by dividing the Third Party Participation by [Production Company's standard conversion factor of (*e.g.,.55,*). To determine the actual reduction of [Lender's] [Producer's] Contingent Compensation by reason of the percentage participations in Net Profits payable to (*name of participant*) and other Third Party Net Participations and/or Third Party Gross Participations, the actual dollar amounts computed to be payable to such third Parties shall be utilized with the dollar amount of Third Party Net Participations used before the dollar amount of any Third Party Gross Participations.]

[(d) <u>Participation Terminology</u>: For purposes of this clause, "Gross Receipts", "Breakeven", "Net Profits" and "Gross Receipts After Breakeven" shall be defined and computed in accordance with Exhibit "_____" attached hereto. For purposes of Exhibit "_____", "Participant's Percentage Participation" shall mean the Contingent Compensation payable to [Lender] [Producer] hereunder.]

10. COPYRIGHT: Production Company shall own the Picture and Basic Property. The Picture shall be registered for copyright in Production Company's name both in the United States and elsewhere. [All music publishing rights and the proceeds of the original music in the Picture shall be owned and controlled by an affiliated music publisher of Production Company, all soundtrack album and commercial recording rights and the proceeds thereof shall be owned and controlled by an affiliated recording company of Producer, and all merchandising and publishing rights in connection with the Picture and the proceeds thereof shall be owned and controlled by Production Company.]

11. NOTICES:

(a) [Lender's] [Producer's] *Address*: All notices from Production Company to [Lender] [Producer] in connection with this Agreement may be given in writing by addressing the same to [Lender] [Producer] in care of (*name and address of recipient of notice*) and by depositing same, so addressed, postage prepaid, in the mail, or, at Production Company's option, Production Company may deliver such notice to [Producer] [Lender] personally, either orally or in writing. Production Company shall send a courtesy copy to (*name and address of attorney*). If such notice shall be sent by mail, as above provided, the date of mailing shall be deemed to be the date of service of such notice. A courtesy copy shall be sent to (name and address of attorney).

(b) Writing Requirement: Any notice given regarding any right of termination, suspension, or extension under this Agreement shall be confirmed in writing. If any notice is delivered to [Producer] [Lender] personally, a copy of such notice shall be sent to [Producer] [Lender] at the above address.

(c) Production Company's Address: All notices from [Lender] [Producer] to Production Company hereunder shall be given in writing, addressed to Production Company as follows: (*name and address of production company*) and by depositing same, so addressed, postage prepaid, in the mail. A courtesy copy shall be sent to (*name and address of attorney*). Unless otherwise expressly provided, the date of mailing shall be deemed to be the date of service of such notice.

12. CREDITS:

(a) Provided that [Lender and] Producer complete(s) all services required hereunder and the Picture is produced and released by Production Company, then Producer shall be accorded credit as hereinafter set forth on the screen and in paid advertising issued by Production Company and under Production Company's control, except advertising of eight (8) column inches or less; group and list advertisements; teasers; publicity; special advertising; billboards of three (3) sheets or more; television trailers, film clips or other advertising on the screen, radio or television ("Excluded Ads"). The credit to be accorded Producer and the conditions relating thereto shall be as follows:

(i) <u>Presentation Credit</u>: Producer shall be accorded a presentation credit in the form of: "(*name*) Production" as follows:

A. <u>On the Screen</u>: On the screen such credit shall be displayed above or before the title of the Picture on a separate card in a size of type not less than (*e.g.*, *fifty percent (50%)* of the size of type used to display the title of the Picture [, but not less than the size of type used to accord the "Film by" credit to the Director].

B. <u>In Paid Advertising</u>: In paid advertising such credit shall be displayed above or before the title of the Picture in a size of type not less than (*e.g.*, *thirty-five percent (35%)*) of the size of type used to display the title of the Picture, [but not less than the size of type used to accord the "Film By" credit to the Director]. [Such credit shall be displayed in any Excluded Ad in which the "Film By" credit accorded the Director also appears except special ads relating to awards, citations, congratulations, nominations or personal appearances of the Director.]

(ii) <u>Producer Credit</u>: Producer shall be accorded producer credit in the form of: "Produced by (*name*)," as follows:

A. <u>On the Screen</u>: On the screen such credit shall be displayed [immediately before the "directed by" credit] on a separate card and in a size of type not less than (*e.g.*, *seventy five percent (75%)*) of the size of type used to display the title of the Picture [but not less than the size of type used to accord the "Directed By" credit to the Director].

B. <u>In Paid Advertising</u>: In paid advertising such credit shall be displayed [above or before the title of the Picture] in a size of type not less than (*e.g.*, *thirty-five percent (35%)*) of the size of type used to display the title of the Picture [, but not less than the size of type used to accord "Directed By" credit to the Director]. [Such credit shall be accorded in any Excluded Ad in which the "Directed By" credit accorded the Director also appears, except special ads relating to awards, citations, congratulations, nominations or personal appearances of the Director.]

(iii) If both a regular (or repeat) title and an artwork title are used in an advertisement, the position and percentage requirements in (ii) above, as they relate to the title of the Picture, shall relate to the regular (or repeat) title. If only an artwork title is used in an advertisement, the percentage requirement in (ii) above, as it relates to the title, shall be [not less than] (*e.g.*, *thirty-five percent (35%)*) of the average size of the letters used in the artwork title.

(b) No casual or inadvertent failure to comply with the provisions of this clause shall be deemed to be a breach of this Agreement by Production Company.

[Lender] [Producer] agree(s) that, in the event of a failure or omission by Production Company constituting a breach of Production Company's obligations under this clause, the damages, if any, caused [Lender] [Producer] by Production Company are not irreparable or sufficient to entitle [Lender] [Producer] to injunctive or other equitable relief. Consequently, [Lender's] [Producer's] rights and remedies hereunder shall be limited to the right, if any, to obtain damages at law and [Lender] [Producer] shall have no right in such event to rescind this Agreement or any of the rights assigned to Production Company hereunder or to enjoin or restrain the distribution or exhibition of the Picture. [Production Company agrees upon receipt of notice from [Lender] [Producer] of Production Company's failure to comply with the provisions of this clause to take such steps as are reasonably practicable to cure such failure with respect to future prints and advertisements on a prospective basis.]

13. REMAKE AND SEQUEL RIGHTS: Subject to the rights, if any, reserved by the original owner of the Basic Property, the remake and sequel rights (including television series rights) with respect to the Picture shall be vested in Production Company.

14. [PRODUCER] SERVICES: Producer's services [which Lender shall furnish to Production Company] shall be rendered as follows:

(a) Availability: [Lender shall cause Producer to] [Producer shall] render services to Production Company to such extent as Production Company may require in the production of the Picture. Producer shall render services to Production Company on a non-exclusive basis during the development [and pre-production phase] of the Picture. The availability of Producer's services to Production Company in connection with the [pre-production,] production and post-production phases shall be governed by Clause 5(b).

(b) Performance Standards: Producer's services shall be rendered [either alone or in collaboration with another or other producers] in such manner as Production Company may direct, under the instructions and in strict accordance with the controls and schedules established by [Production Company] [Production Company's authorized representatives] and at the times, places and in the manner required by [Production Company] [them], which manners, instructions, directions, and controls shall be exercised by Production Company in accordance with standards of reasonableness and also with what is customary practice in the Motion Picture industry. Such services shall be rendered in an artistic, conscientious, efficient and punctual manner to the best of Producer's ability and with full regard to the careful, efficient, economical and expeditious production of the Picture within the budget and shooting schedule established by Production Company immediately prior to the commencement of principal photography [it being understood that such production involves matters of art and taste to be exercised by Production Company, and Producer's services and the manner of rendition thereof are to be governed entirely by Production Company].

(c) <u>Unique Services</u>: It is hereby agreed and understood that Producer's services to be furnished hereunder are special, extraordinary, unique, and not replaceable, and that there is no adequate remedy at law for breach of this contract by [Lender or] [Producer]. Production Company, in the event of such breach by [Lender or] Producer, shall be entitled to [seek] injunctive and other equitable relief to prevent default by [Lender or] Producer. In addition to such equitable relief, Production Company shall be entitled to such other remedies as may be available at law, including damages.

(d) <u>Results and Proceeds</u>: Production Company shall be entitled to and shall solely and exclusively own [and Lender] [Producer] hereby transfers and assigns to Production Company in addition to Producer's services, all the results, product and proceeds thereof (including but not limited to all rights of whatever kind and character, throughout the universe in perpetuity, in any and all languages, of copyright, trademark, patent, production, manufacture, recordation, reproduction, transcription, performance, broadcast and exhibition by any art, method or device now known or hereafter devised, including, without limitation, radio broadcasting, theatrical and non-theatrical exhibition and exhibition, by the medium of television or otherwise), whether such results, products and proceeds consist of literary, dramatic, musical, motion picture, mechanical or any other form or works, themes, ideas, compositions, creation or products. Production Company's acquisition hereunder shall also include all the rights generally known in the field of literary and musical endeavor as the "moral rights of authors" or so-called "droit morale" in and/or to any musical and/or literary proceeds of Producer's services. Production Company shall also have the right [but not the obligation] to add to, subtract from, change, arrange, revise, adapt, rearrange, make variations of said property, and to translate the same into any and all languages, change the sequence, change the characters and the descriptions thereof, change the title of the same, [record and photograph the same with or without sound (including spoken words, dialogue and music synchronously recorded)], use said title or any of its components in connection with works of motion pictures wholly or partially independent thereof [to vend, copy and publish the same as Production Company may desire,] and to use all or any part thereof in new versions, adaptations and sequels in any and all languages, and to obtain copyright therein throughout the world; and [Lender] [Producer] does hereby assign and transfer to Production Company all of the foregoing without reservation, condition or limitations and no right of any kind, nature or description is reserved by [Lender] [Producer]. If Production Company shall desire to secure separate assignments of or for any of the foregoing, [Lender] [Producer] shall [have Producer] execute the same upon Production Company's request therefor.

(i) As part of the foregoing, [Lender and] Producer hereby irrevocably assign[s], license[s], and grant[s] to Production Company, exclusively, throughout the universe, and in perpetuity, the rights, if any, of Producer to authorize, prohibit, and/or control the renting, lending, fixation, reproduction and/or other exploitation of any motion picture produced based upon the Picture (or any rights therein) by any media and means now known or hereafter devised as may be conferred upon Producer under applicable laws, regulations, or directives, including, without limitation, any so-called "Rental Lending Rights" pursuant to any European Economic Community ("EEC") directives and/or enabling or implementing legislation, laws, or regulations enacted by the member nations of the EEC.

(ii) All of the rights granted or agreed to be granted hereunder shall vest in Production Company immediately and shall remain vested whether this Agreement expires in normal course or is terminated for any cause or reason. All of the rights granted herein, including, without limitation, all material created, composed, submitted, added or interpolated by Producer hereunder shall automatically become Production Company's property, and Production Company, for this purpose, shall be deemed author thereof with Producer acting entirely as Production Company's employee. [Lender and] Producer do[es] hereby assign and transfer to Production Company all of the rights herein granted without reservation, condition or limitation, and no right of any kind, nature or description is reserved by [Lender and] Producer. Notwithstanding the foregoing, if any of the rights herein granted are hereafter subject to termination under Section 203 of the Copyright Act, or any similar provisions of said act or subsequent revision thereof, then [Lender and] Producer agree not to make any further grant without giving Production Company the first opportunity to acquire such rights pursuant to a customary right of first negotiation/first refusal.

(iii) [Lender,] Producer and Production Company agree wherever in this Agreement the terms "motion picture" or "motion picture production" or terms of similar tenor are used, such terms shall be conclusively deemed and construed to include the present and future developments of the motion picture, television, video tape, videodisc, computer, electronics and telephone industries, including talking motion pictures, videotape, television productions, any and all kinds of electronic and other interactive uses of the Picture and the components thereof, including, but not limited to, CD-ROM, CD-I, interactive multi-media devices, computer discs, and any new variations thereon, and all forms of motion pictures, television, laserdisc, video tape, CD-ROM, CD-I, interactive multimedia devices and similar uses, whether now known or unknown and their accompanying devices which reproduce words, music and/or other sounds in synchronization with, accompaniment of, or supplementary to photography.

(e) <u>Rights Vesting</u>: [Except as specifically provided otherwise herein,] All rights granted to Production Company hereunder shall vest in Production Company immediately and shall remain vested [whether] [only if] this Agreement expires in normal course or is terminated for any [good] cause or reason.

(f) <u>Use of Name and Likeness</u>: Production Company may use and display Producer's name and likeness for advertising, publicizing and exploiting the Picture. However, such advertising may not include the direct [or indirect] endorsement of any product [or service or commodity] (other than the Picture) without [Lender's] [Producer's] [written] consent. Exhibition, advertising, publicizing or exploiting the Picture by any media, even though a part of or in connection with a product or a commercially sponsored program, shall not be deemed endorsement of any nature.

(g) <u>Force Majeure</u>:

(i) <u>Suspension</u>: If, by reason of fire, earthquake, labor dispute or strike, act of God or public enemy, any municipal ordinance, any state or federal law, governmental order or regulation, or other cause beyond Production Company's control [which would excuse Production Company's performance as a matter of law], Production Company is prevented from or hampered in the production of the Picture, or if, by reason of the closing of substantially all the theatres in the United States for any of the aforesaid or other causes, [which would excuse Production Company's performance as a matter of law] Production Company's production of the Picture is postponed or suspended, or if, by reason of any of the aforesaid contingencies or any other cause or occurrence not within Production Company's control, including but not limited to the death, illness or incapacity of any principal member of the cast of the Picture [or the Director], the preparation, commencement, production or completion of the Picture is hampered, interrupted or interfered with, [and/or, if Production Company's normal business operations are hampered or otherwise interfered with by virtue of any disruptive events which are beyond Production Company's control] ("Production Company Disability"), then Production Company may postpone the commencement of or suspend the rendition of services by Producer and the running of time hereunder for as long as the Production Company Disability shall continue; and no compensation shall accrue or become payable to [Lender] [Producer] hereunder during the period of suspension. [Such suspension shall end upon the cessation of the cause thereof,] *or* [Such suspension shall end not later than (*e.g., four weeks*)] following the cessation of the Production Company Disability or upon the recommencement of principal photography after the cessation of the Production Company Disability, whichever occurs first.

(ii) <u>Termination</u>:

A. <u>Production Company Termination Right</u>: If a Production Company Disability continues for a period exceeding (*e.g., eight weeks*), Production Company may terminate this Agreement upon written notice thereof to [Lender] [Producer].

B. <u>[Lender's] [Producer's] Termination Right</u>: If a Production Company Disability results in the suspension of the payment of compensation hereunder for a period exceeding (*e.g., eight weeks*) [Lender] [Producer] may terminate this Agreement upon written notice to Production Company.

C. <u>Production Company Re-Establishment Right</u>: Despite [Lender's] [Producer's] election to terminate this Agreement, within (*e.g., five days*) after Production Company's actual receipt of such written notice from [Lender] [Producer], Production Company may elect to re-establish the operation of this Agreement.

(h) <u>Producer's Incapacity</u>:

(i) <u>Effect of Producer's Incapacity</u>: If, by reason of mental or physical disability, Producer shall be incapacitated from performing or complying with any of the terms or conditions hereof ("Producer's Incapacity") for a consecutive period exceeding (*e.g., seven*) days or aggregate period exceeding (*e.g., ten*) days, when Producer's services hereunder are exclusive, or for a consecutive period exceeding (*e.g., ten (10)*) days or aggregate period exceeding (*e.g., fourteen (14)*) days when Producer's services hereunder are nonexclusive, then Production Company may terminate this Agreement upon written notice to [Lender] [Producer].

(ii) <u>Right of Examination</u>: If any claim of mental or physical disability is made by Producer or on Producer's behalf, Production Company may have Producer examined by such physicians as Production Company may designate. Producer's physician may be present at such examination, but shall not interfere therewith. [Any tests performed on Producer shall be related to and customary for the treatment, diagnosis or examination to be performed in connection with Producer's claim.]

(i) <u>[Lender/]Producer Default</u>: If [Lender or] Producer fails or refuses to perform or comply with any of the [material] terms or conditions hereof other than by reason of Producer's Incapacity ("[Lender/]Producer Default"), then Production Company may terminate this Agreement upon written notice thereof to [Lender] [Producer]. [Lender/]Producer Default shall not include any failure or refusal of Producer to perform or comply with the material terms of this Agreement due to a breach or action by Production Company (or a third party not an employee of [Lender/]Producer) which makes the performance by Producer of Producer's services impossible.] [Prior to termination of this Agreement by Production Company based upon [Lender/]Producer Default, Production Company shall notify [Lender and] Producer specifying the nature of the [Lender/]Producer Default and [Lender and] Producer shall have (*e.g., 72 hours*) after the giving of such notice within which to cure the [Lender/]Producer Default. If the [Lender/] Producer Default is not cured within the (*e.g., 72 hour*) period, Production Company may terminate this Agreement forthwith.]

(j) <u>Effect of Termination</u>: Termination of this Agreement, whether by lapse of time, mutual consent, operation of law, exercise of a right of termination or otherwise, shall:

(i) Terminate Production Company's obligation to pay [Lender] [Producer] any further compensation. Nevertheless, if the termination is not for [Lender/] Producer Default, Production Company shall pay [Lender] [Producer] any compensation accrued and unpaid prior to the termination;

(ii) Production Company shall not be deemed to have waived any other rights it may have; and

(iii) Termination shall not alter Production Company's rights or any of [Lender's] [Producer's] agreements or warranties in connection with the rendition of Producer's services prior to termination.

(k) <u>Production Company's Right to Suspend</u>: In the event of Producer's Incapacity or [Lender/] Producer Default, Production Company may postpone the commencement of or suspend the rendition of services by Producer and the running of time hereunder as long as any such Producer Incapacity or [Lender/] Producer Default shall continue; and no compensation shall accrue or become payable to [Lender] [Producer] during such suspension.

(i) <u>[Lender's][Producer's] Right to Cure</u>: Any Producer's Incapacity or [Lender/] Producer Default shall be deemed to continue until Production Company's receipt of written notice from [Lender][Producer] specifying that Producer is ready, willing and able to perform the services required hereunder; provided that any such notice from [Lender][Producer] to Production Company shall not preclude Production Company from exercising any rights or remedies Production Company may have hereunder or at law or in equity by reason of Producer's Incapacity or [Lender/] Producer Default.

(ii) <u>Alternative Services Restricted</u>: During any period of suspension, Producer shall not render services for any person, firm or corporation other than Production Company. [However, Producer may render services to third parties during any period of suspension based upon a Production Company Disability, subject, however, to Production Company's right to require Producer to resume services upon (<i>e.g., 24 hours</i>) prior notice.]

(iii) <u>Production Company Right to Extend</u>: If Production Company elects to suspend the rendition of services by Producer as herein specified, then Production Company may (at any time) extend the period of services required of Producer hereunder for a period equal to the period of such suspension.

(iv) <u>Additional Services</u>: If Production Company shall have paid compensation to [Lender] [Producer] during any period of Producer's Incapacity or [Lender/] Producer Default, then Production Company may (at any time) require [Lender to furnish] Producer's services hereunder without compensation for a period equal to the period for which Production Company shall have paid compensation to [Lender] [Producer] during such Producer's Incapacity or [Lender/] Producer Default.

(l) <u>Conditions Related to Compensation</u>: Notwithstanding anything to the contrary contained herein:

(i) <u>Performance</u>: No compensation shall accrue or become payable to [Lender] [Producer] during any Producer's Incapacity or [Lender/] Producer Default.

(ii) <u>Flat Fee Basis</u>: It is hereby mutually agreed that the Fixed Compensation as specified in Clause 9(a) is a "flat fee" and [Lender] [Producer] shall not be entitled to any additional and/or so-called overage compensation for any services rendered by Producer during the development, pre-production, production or post-production phases or for any additional post-production services. [Without limiting the generality of the foregoing, no additional compensation shall be payable to [Lender] [Producer] pursuant to this Agreement if either the actual pre-production and/or the actual principal photography period of the Picture shall exceed the scheduled pre-production and/or the scheduled period of principal photography, and/or the scheduled period of post-production.]

(iii) <u>Pay or Play</u>: Production Company shall not be obligated to use Producer's services in connection with the Picture, nor shall Production Company be obligated to produce, release, distribute, advertise, exploit or otherwise make use of the Picture; provided, however, [that if [Lender and] Producer [are/is] not in [material] default and [have/has] performed all required services hereunder,] the full amount of the Fixed Compensation hereinabove specified shall be paid to [Lender] [Producer] should Production Company, [for any reason] [without legal justification or excuse] (as provided elsewhere herein or by operation of law), elect not to utilize Producer's services after having elected to proceed with the production of the Picture pursuant to Subclause 4(a). In such case, Production Company shall have no further obligation to [Lender] [Producer] hereunder.

(m) <u>[Lender and] [Producer] Warranties</u>: [Lender and] [Producer] hereby warrant(s) that [neither Lender nor] Producer [are/is] [not] under any obligation or disability, created by law or otherwise, which would in any manner or to any extent prevent or restrict [Lender and] Producer from entering into and fully performing this Agreement. [Lender and] [Producer] warrant(s) that [Lender and] [Producer] [have] [has] not entered into any agreement or commitment that would prevent [their] [Producer's] fulfilling [their] [Producer's] commitments with Production Company hereunder and that [Lender and] [Producer] will not enter into any such agreement or commitment without Production Company's specific approval [; and [Lender and] [Producer] hereby agree(s) that Producer shall devote Producer's entire time and attention and best talents and ability exclusively to Production Company as specified herein, and observe and be governed by the rules of conduct established by Production Company for the conduct of its employees].

(n) <u>Warranties Related to Created Material</u>: [Lender and] [Producer] hereby warrant(s) and agree(s) that all material, works, writing, ideas, "gags" or dialogue written, composed, prepared, submitted or interpolated by Producer in connection with the Picture or its preparation or production, shall be wholly original with Producer and shall not be copied in whole or in part from any other work, except that submitted to Producer by Production Company as a basis for such material. [Lender and] [Producer] further warrant(s) that neither the material nor any part thereof will violate the rights of privacy or constitute a libel or slander against any person, firm, or corporation, and that the material will not infringe upon the copyright, literary, dramatic or photoplay rights of any person. [Lender and] [Producer] further warrant(s) and agree(s) to hold Production Company and its successors, licensees, and assigns harmless against all claims, liability, damages, costs, expenses (including attorneys' fees) or loss which they or any of them may suffer by reason of the breach of any of the terms or warranties of this clause.

(o) Guild Membership: During the periods when Producer is required to render services hereunder, as Production Company may lawfully require [Producer so to do, Producer, at] (or) [, Lender shall require Producer, at Lender's or Producer's sole cost and expense (and at Production Company's request)] [shall] [to] remain, or become and remain, a member in good standing of the then properly designated labor organization or organizations (as defined and determined under the then applicable law) representing persons performing services of the type and character required to be performed by Producer hereunder.

(p) Insurance: Production Company may secure life, health, accident, cast or other insurance covering Producer [, the cost of which shall be included as a Direct Charge of the Picture]. Such insurance shall be for Production Company's sole benefit and Production Company shall be the beneficiary thereof, and [Lender and] Producer shall have no interest in the proceeds thereof. [Lender and] Producer shall assist in procuring such insurance by submitting to required examinations and tests and by preparing, signing, and delivering such applications and other documents as may be reasonably required. [Lender and] Producer shall, to the best of [Lender's and] Producer's ability, observe all terms and conditions of such insurance of which Production Company notifies [Lender and] Producer as necessary for continuing such insurance in effect. If Production Company is unable to obtain pre-production or cast insurance covering Producer at prevailing standard rates and without any exclusions, restrictions, conditions, or exceptions of any kind [Producer shall have the right to pay any premium in excess of the prevailing standard rates in order for Production Company to obtain such insurance. If [Lender] [Producer] fails, refuses, or is unable for any reason whatsoever to pay such excess premiums], or if Producer having obtained such insurance, [Lender or] Producer fails to observe all terms and conditions necessary to maintain such insurance in effect, Production Company shall have the right to terminate this Agreement without any obligation to [Lender or] Producer by giving [Lender] [Producer] written notice of termination. [[Lender and] [Producer] shall be named as [an] additional insured [s] under any general liability and errors and omissions insurance policies obtained by Production Company for the picture, subject to the terms, conditions, deductibles and any other limitations of any such policy obtained by Production Company.]

(q) Employment of Personnel: [Lender and] Producer agree(s) not to employ any person to serve in any capacity, nor to contract for the purchase or renting of any article or material, nor make any agreement committing Production Company to pay any sum of money for any reason whatsoever in connection with the Picture or services to be rendered by Producer [or provided by Lender] hereunder, or otherwise, without the prior written consent of Production Company.

15. <u>REMEDIES</u>: All remedies accorded herein or otherwise available to either Production Company or [Lender] [Producer] shall be cumulative, and no one such remedy shall be exclusive of any other. Without waiving any rights or remedies under this Agreement or otherwise, Production Company [or [Lender] [Producer]] may from time to time recover, by action, any damages arising out of any breach of this Agreement by [Lender and/or] Producer, [or Production Company, as applicable] and may institute and maintain subsequent actions for additional damages which may arise from the same or other breaches. The commencement or maintenance of any such action or actions by Production Company [or [Lender or] [Producer]] shall not constitute or result in the termination of [Lender's or] Producer's services hereunder unless Production Company [or [Lender or] [Producer]] shall expressly so elect by written notice to [Lender or] [Producer] [or Production Company]. The pursuit by either Production Company [or [Lender or] [Producer]] of any remedy under this Agreement or otherwise shall not be deemed to waive any other or different remedy which may be available under this Agreement or otherwise, either at law or in equity.

16. <u>ADDITIONAL DOCUMENTS</u>: [Lender] [Producer] agrees to execute and deliver to Production Company such further documents as Production Company may require in order to effectuate the purposes and intents of this Agreement, including without limitation, perfecting the chain of title of the Literary Work, transfer rights to Production Company and creation and perfection of any security interests. [Lender and] [Producer] irrevocably grant(s) Production Company the power coupled with an interest to execute such instruments in [Lender's and] Producer's name(s) and as [Producer's] [Lender's] attorney-in-fact. [Production Company shall provide [Lender] [Producer] with copies of any documents executed by Production Company under this Clause.]

17. <u>[GARNISHMENT]/ [ATTACHMENT]</u>: If Production Company is required, because of the service of any [garnishment] [attachment], writ of execution, or lien, or by the terms of any contract or assignment executed by [Lender or] [Producer], to pay all or any portion of the compensation due [Lender or] [Producer] hereunder to any other person, firm or corporation, or to withhold the same from [Lender or] [Producer], Production Company's compliance with any such [garnishment] [attachment], writ of execution, lien, contract or assignment shall not be deemed a breach of its obligations hereunder.

18. <u>GOVERNMENTAL LIMITATION</u>: If the compensation provided by this Agreement shall exceed the amount permitted by any present or future law or

governmental order or regulation, such stated compensation shall be reduced, while such limitation is in effect, to the amount which is so permitted, and the payment of such reduced compensation shall be deemed to constitute full performance by Production Company of its obligations respecting the payment of compensation hereunder. [Notwithstanding anything to the contrary set forth above, if at such time as the limitation is no longer in effect, there is compensation remaining unpaid for Producer's services hereunder, Production Company shall cooperate with Producer in connection with processing any applications relative to the payment of such unpaid compensation, and Production Company shall pay such compensation to Producer at such time as Production Company is legally permitted to do so.]

19. <u>PUBLICITY RESTRICTIONS</u>: [Lender and] Producer shall not [, individually or jointly,] by means of press agents or publicity or advertising agencies or others, employed or paid by [Lender or] Producer or otherwise, circulate, publish or otherwise disseminate any news stories or articles, books or other publicity containing [Lender's or] Producer's name relating [directly or indirectly] to Producer's [employment] [engagement] by Production Company, the subject matter of this contract, the Picture, or the services to be rendered by Producer or others in connection with the Picture unless the same are first approved by Production Company. [Lender and] [Producer] shall not transfer or attempt to transfer any right, privilege, title or interest in or to any of the things above specified, nor shall [Lender or] [Producer] authorize or willingly permit any infringement upon the exclusive rights granted to Production Company; and [Lender] [Producer] authorize(s) Production Company, [at Production Company's expense,] in [Lender's] [Producer's] name(s) or otherwise, to institute any proper legal proceedings to prevent any infringement.

20. <u>MOTION PICTURE RELIEF FUND OF AMERICA, INC.</u>: [Lender] [Producer] hereby authorizes Production Company on [Lender's and] Producer's behalf to pay the Motion Picture Relief Fund of America, Inc., one percent (1%) of all compensation accruing to [Lender] [Producer] hereunder.

21. <u>RIGHT TO LEND TO OTHERS</u>: Production Company shall have the right to lend Producer's services hereunder to, (a) any of its subsidiary or affiliated companies, or (b) any other producer of motion pictures provided such producer shall have granted to Production Company the right to distribute the Picture [and further, provided that Producer has consented to such lending, which consent shall not be unreasonably withheld]. [No such lending of Producer's services shall relieve Production Company of its obligations hereunder.]

22. <u>ASSIGNMENT</u>: This Agreement, at the election of Production Company, shall inure to the benefit of Production Company's administrators, successors, assigns, licensees, grantees, and associated, affiliated and subsidiary companies,

and [Lender] [Producer] agrees that Production Company and any subsequent assignee may freely assign this Agreement and grant its rights hereunder, in whole or in part, to any person, firm or corporation [, provided that such person, firm or corporation assumes and agrees in writing to keep and perform all of the executory obligations of Production Company hereunder] *or* [provided that notwithstanding such assignment production company shall remain secondarily responsible for all obligations to producer hereunder].

23. ENTIRE AGREEMENT: This Agreement shall replace and supersede all previous arrangements, understandings, representations, or agreements, either oral or written, regarding the subject matter hereof and, together with any exhibits attached hereto and incorporated herein, expresses the entire agreement between Production Company and [Lender] [Producer] with reference to the terms and conditions for the rendition of Producer's services for Production Company in connection with the Picture.

24. VIDEOCASSETTE: Production Company agrees that if Producer completes all required services in connection with the Picture, then Production Company shall lend to Producer, at Production Company's expense, a ½ " VHS videocassette of the Picture, if available, for use solely in Producer's personal home showings pursuant to and subject to the terms and conditions of Production Company's then current print loan practices and its standard videocassette loan-out agreement form. Prior to the loan of such videocassette, Producer shall execute and deliver to Production Company a copy of Production Company's standard videocassette loan-out agreement form.

25. GOVERNING LAW: This Agreement shall be construed in accordance with the laws of the State of (*name of state*) applicable to agreements which are executed and fully performed within said State.

26. CAPTIONS: The captions used in connection with clauses and subclauses of this Agreement are inserted only for the purpose of reference. Such captions shall not be deemed to govern, limit, modify, or in any other manner affect the scope, meaning, or intent of the provisions of this Agreement or any part thereof; nor shall such captions otherwise be given any legal effect.

27. SERVICE OF PROCESS: In any action or proceeding commenced in any court in the State of (*name of state*) for the purpose of enforcing this Agreement or any right granted herein or arising herefrom, or any order or decree predicated thereon, any summons, order to show cause, writ, judgment, decree, or other process, issued by such court, may be delivered to [Lender and/or] Producer personally without the State of (*name of state*); and when so delivered, [Lender and/or] Producer shall be subject to the jurisdiction of such court as though the same had been served within the State of (*name of state*), but outside the county in which such action or proceeding is pending.

28. <u>ILLEGALITY</u>: Nothing contained herein shall require the commission of any act or the payment of any compensation which is contrary to an express provision of law or the policy of express law. If there shall exist any conflict between any provision contained herein and any such law or policy, the latter shall prevail; and the provision or provisions herein affected shall be curtailed, limited or eliminated to the extent (but only to the extent) necessary to remove such conflict, and as so modified, this Agreement shall continue in full force and effect.

29. <u>IF PRODUCER IS MORE THAN ONE PERSON</u>: If this Agreement is entered into with more than one (1) Producer, the term "Producer" shall refer to each and all of them. Further, such Producers represent, warrant and agree that they, and each of them, prior to the date hereof, agreed to collaborate as a team for the services to be rendered or the material to be delivered hereunder, and that they agreed that all compensation specified herein is the combined total for the team. If a separate address for each Producer is provided herein, Production Company shall be deemed to have met its obligations with respect to any payment hereunder by delivering to each Producer at each Producer's respective address, a pro rata amount of any such payment based upon the number of Producers in the team, unless written notice signed by all Producers is delivered to Production Company setting forth a different allocation. All such Producers shall be deemed to have jointly and severally made and entered into all of the representations, warranties, covenants and agreements contained herein and shall be jointly and severally obligated and bound thereby. All of Production Company's rights hereunder relate to and are exercisable against and with respect to each and all of the Producers. Each Producer's representations, warranties and obligations hereunder are made with respect to each and all of them. Upon any Producer's incapacity or default, Production Company may, at its sole option elect to (a) treat such incapacity or default as the incapacity or default of all persons comprising Producer under this Agreement, in which case Production Company may then exercise any and all remedies which Production Company may have for default or incapacity of Producer as set forth herein; or Production Company may (b) treat such incapacity or default as affecting only the person or persons actually so incapacitated or actually in default, and Production Company may require any other persons comprising Producer to continue performance hereunder, in which case Production Company shall continue to compensate the Producer or Producers continuing to render services hereunder for a proportionate amount of the payments otherwise due Producer or Producers [(*e.g., one-half* (½) thereof if two Producers are employed hereunder).]

30. <u>EMPLOYMENT ELIGIBILITY</u>: All of Production Company's obligations herein are expressly conditioned upon Producer's completion, to Production Company's satisfaction, of the I-9 form (Employee Eligibility Verification Form), and upon [Lender's] [Producer's] submission to Production Company of original

documents satisfactory to demonstrate to Production Company Producer's employment eligibility.

31. <u>WORKERS' COMPENSATION</u>: For the purposes of any and all applicable Workers' Compensation statutes, an employment relationship exists between Producer and Production Company such that Production Company is Producer's special employer (as the term "Special Employer") is understood for purposes of Workers' Compensation statutes). The rights and remedies, if any, of Producer and Producer's heirs, executors, administrators, successors and assigns, against Production Company and/or its officers, directors, agents, employees, successors, assigns or licensees, by reason of injury, illness, disability or death arising out of or occurring in the course of Producer's rendition of services hereunder shall be governed by and limited to those provided under such Workers' Compensation statutes, and neither Production Company, nor its officers, directors, agents, employees, successors, assigns or licensees shall have any other obligation or liability by any reason of any such injury, illness, disability or death. If the applicability of any Workers' Compensation statutes to the engagement of Producer's services hereunder is dependent upon, or affected by, an election on the part of Producer, such election is hereby made by Producer in favor of such application.

By signing in the spaces provided below [Lender] [Producer] and Production Company accept and agree to all the terms and conditions of this Agreement.

_____
(*Lender*)

By: _____

_____

or

_____
(*Producer*)

_____
(*Production Company*)

By: _____

_____

[If for a loan-out situation; add Inducement Letter]

INDUCEMENT

I, (*name of individual producer*), agree to perform all obligations to be performed by Lender and me hereunder, and make all representations and warranties herein made by Lender, in order to effectuate the terms and conditions of the foregoing

Agreement, and I agree to look solely to Lender for payment of any compensation due me. I hereby accept and acknowledge each and all provisions of the foregoing agreement and agree to be bound by them to the same extent as if I had signed the agreement directly.

_____

(Producer)

Form 13

Player Agreement-Deal Memorandum

Performer: (NAME AND ADDRESS)

Picture/Role: "(NAME OF PICTURE & ROLE)"

Compensation: ($ (SPECIFY AMOUNT) per week for (SPECIFY NUMBER) weeks) or ($ (STATE TOTAL AMOUNT))

Overage Rate of Compensation: $ (STATE AMOUNT) per week

Contingent Compensation:

As additional consideration for furnishing the services and rights granted hereunder and provided that Performer has fully and faithfully performed all [material] services required of Performer, Production Company shall pay Performer an amount equal to (SPECIFY NUMBER E.G., TEN PERCENT (E.G., 10%)) of 100% of the net profits of the Picture. As used herein, the term "net profits" shall be defined, and the payments hereunder shall be computed and made, in the same manner as provided to Production Company.

Guaranteed Period: (SPECIFY NUMBER) (_____) weeks plus (SPECIFY NUMBER) (_____) free weeks

Start Date: (SPECIFY DATE)

Expenses: (SPECIFY AMOUNT) per week living expense allowance shall be paid to Performer, plus first-class round-trip transportation for (SPECIFY NUMBER) (_____) persons from and to (SPECIFY PLACE), which Performer represents is Performer's permanent residence. [A car will be furnished to Performer while on location in (SPECIFY PLACE).]

Credit:

(a) On the screen: In size of type (E.G., NO LESS THAN 40%) of the size of type used to announce the [nonartwork] title of the Picture [, on a separate card] [, above the title of the Picture];

(b) In paid advertising: In size of type (E.G., NOT LESS THAN 35%] of the size of type used to announce the [nonartwork] title of the Picture [, in first position of all members of the cast] [, above the title of the Picture] [, and no other member of the cast shall receive credit in size of type larger than Performer's credit].

Notices: Notices hereunder shall be in writing. Any notice hereunder shall be given by personal delivery or by mailing (in a postpaid, certified or registered envelope), or telegraphing the same to the appropriate party at the addresses first written above, or transmitting by facsimile, and the date of such personal delivery, mailing, or telegraphing or facsimile transmission shall be the date of the giving of such notice. A courtesy copy of any notices to Performer shall be provided

to (E.G., SPECIFY NAME AND ADDRESS OF AGENT AND/OR ATTOR-
NEY). [If Performer shall be entitled to any contingent compensation, any
accounting statements and payments to which Performer shall be entitled with
respect thereto shall be mailed to Performer at Performer's address first written
above.]

Other Terms: (Any other deal points should be specified; if there are none, then
delete this provision or indicate "not applicable").

Other terms and conditions will be in accordance with customary terms and
conditions of agreements of this nature in the Motion Picture industry.

_____
  ("Production Company")
AGREED:

_____
  ("Performer")

Form 14

Artist Loan-out Agreement

Name and Address of Borrower/Production Company

Re: (*NAME OF PROPERTY OR TITLE OF PICTURE*)

Reference is made to the Agreement dated (DATE OF LENDING AGREE-MENT) ("Lending Agreement"), being executed concurrently herewith, between (NAME OF LOAN-OUT COMPANY) ("Lender") and (NAME OF PRODUC-TION COMPANY) ("Borrower"), covering the loan of the services of the undersigned (NAME OF INDIVIDUAL ARTIST) ("Artist").

1. CONCURRENT EMPLOYMENT AGREEMENT: Artist has heretofore entered into an agreement ("Employment Agreement") with Lender covering the rendition of Artist's services for Lender for a period not less than the period Lender provides Artist's services under the Lending Agreement and that Lender has the right to enter into the Lending Agreement and to furnish the Artist's services and to grant the rights granted pursuant to the terms and conditions therein specified.

2. RATIFICATION OF LENDING AGREEMENT: Artist is familiar with the terms and conditions of the Lending Agreement and consents to the signing thereof; Artist shall perform and comply with all of the terms and conditions of the Lending Agreement requiring performance or compliance by Artist even if the Employment Agreement should hereafter be terminated, suspended or become ineffective; Artist shall render to Borrower all of the services provided to be rendered by Artist under the Lending Agreement; all notices served upon Lender in accordance with the Lending Agreement shall be deemed notices to Artist of the contents thereof with the same effect as if served upon Artist personally. Artist hereby expressly agrees that all of the results and product of all services to be performed by Artist pursuant to the Lending Agreement are results and product specially ordered by Borrower for use as a part of a Motion Picture and shall be considered a work made for hire (as such term is defined under U.S. copyright law) for Borrower and that Borrower shall be the author and copyright owner of such results and product.

3. NO RESTRICTIONS: Artist is under no obligation or disability, by law or otherwise, which would interfere with Artist's full performance and compliance with all of the terms and conditions of the Lending Agreement which require performance or compliance by Artist.

4. REMUNERATION SOLE RESPONSIBILITY OF LENDER: Except as may otherwise be provided in the Lending Agreement, Artist shall look solely to Lender for all compensation and other remuneration for any and all rights and

services which Artist and/or Lender may grant and render to Borrower under the Lending Agreement.

5.   BREACH: Artist's services are unique and extraordinary and the breach of this Inducement Agreement and/or of any of the terms of the Lending Agreement which require performance or compliance by Artist will cause irreparable damage to Borrower. Therefore, in the event of breach or threatened breach by Artist of this Inducement Agreement and/or by Artist or Lender of the Lending Agreement, Borrower shall be entitled to legal or equitable relief by way of injunction or otherwise, against Artist or against Lender or against both, at the discretion of Borrower, to restrain, enjoin and/or prevent such breach by Artist, Lender, or both. All the foregoing shall be to the same extent and with the same force and effect as if Artist was a direct party to the Lending Agreement in the first instance, and as if in the Lending Agreement, Artist had personally agreed to render the services therein provided to be rendered by Artist and to perform and observe each and all the terms and conditions of the Lending Agreement requiring performance or compliance on the part of Artist, Lender, or both.

6.   SUBSTITUTION FOR LENDER: If Lender should be dissolved or should otherwise cease to exist or for any reason whatsoever should fail, neglect, refuse or be unable to perform and observe each and all of the terms or conditions of the Lending Agreement requiring performance or compliance by Lender, Artist shall, at the election of Borrower, be deemed substituted as a direct party to said Lending Agreement in the place and stead of Lender.

7.   GOVERNING LAW: This Inducement Agreement shall be governed and construed by the laws of the State of (NAME OF STATE).

Very truly yours,

_____

(Name of Artist)
Artist

Form 15

Performer Employment Agreement

LOANOUT AGREEMENT:

Agreement dated [as of] (DATE OF AGREEMENT) between (NAME OF LOANOUT COMPANY), a (STATE OF INCORPORATION) corporation ("Lender"), and (NAME OF PRODUCTION COMPANY), a (STATE OF INCORPORATION) corporation ("Production Company"), furnishing the services of _____ (NAME OF PERFORMER) ("Performer").

EMPLOYMENT AGREEMENT:

Agreement dated [as of] _____ between _____("Performer") and _____. ("Production Company").

Clause 1. SERVICES:

(a) [Production Company agrees to borrow from Lender and Lender agrees to lend to Production Company upon the terms and conditions herein specified, the services of Performer] [Performer agrees to perform and Production Company agrees to employ Performer to perform upon the terms and conditions herein specified, services] in connection with the portrayal of the role of (CHARACTER TO BE PLAYED) in the production of the motion picture currently entitled (NAME OF PICTURE) ("Picture").

(b) The consecutive period of the services of Performer hereunder shall commence on a date to be hereafter designated by Production Company, which date shall be [on or about (DATE)] [not earlier than (DATE) nor later than (DATE)] and shall be preceded by the period of Performer's services in connection with rehearsal and other pre-production services as set forth in Clause 2(a) below. The consecutive period of Performer's exclusive services as an [actor] [actress] shall continue thereafter from such date of commencement and continue throughout the period during which Production Company may require Performer's consecutive services for the principal photography of Performer's role in the Picture.

Clause 2. COMPENSATION AND GUARANTY:

(a) As compensation in full for the period hereinafter designated and for the rights granted and/or agreed to be granted to Production Company pursuant to this Agreement, (provided [Lender] [Performer] is not in default and has performed all [material] services required hereunder), Production Company shall pay to [Lender] [Performer] the sum of (SPECIFY AMOUNT) for Performer's services required during the "Guaranteed Period of Services." The Guaranteed Period of Services shall consist of required pre-production services and the scheduled period of (E.G., SEVEN) weeks of principal photography. [Said

Guaranteed Period of Services shall also include (E.G., TWO) free weeks immediately following said scheduled period of principal photography.] The compensation payable for the Guaranteed Period of Services is sometimes herein referred to as the "Guaranteed Compensation." The Guaranteed Compensation shall be payable to [Lender] [Performer] as follows: (SPECIFY, E.G., IN WEEKLY INSTALLMENTS OVER THE SCHEDULED PERIOD OF PRINCI-PAL PHOTOGRAPHY COMMENCING WITH THE START OF PRINCIPAL PHOTOGRAPHY, OR (SPECIFY PAYMENT AMOUNTS AND DATES)).

(b) At any time after the expiration of the Guaranteed Period of Services, Production Company shall be entitled to an additional (E.G., SEVEN) "free days" of Performer's services (which need not be consecutive) for dubbing, looping, and wild lines. Production Company will [endeavor to] schedule such additional services so that Performer will be able to render such additional services on consecutive days. For all other services of Performer rendered after the expiration of the Guaranteed Period of Services, [Lender] [Performer] shall receive compensation payable at the rate set forth in Clause 4.

(c) Unless otherwise expressly provided herein, Performer's services shall be rendered exclusively for Production Company during the Guaranteed Period of Services and Performer shall not undertake any obligation that would interfere with the full and timely performance of such services.

(d) For any period of Performer's services under this Agreement which is less than one (1) week, the compensation provided for in Clause 2(a) shall be computed and paid upon the pro rata basis that one (1) day is equal to one-fifth (1/5) of one (1) week in the case of any "studio work week" and on the basis that one (1) day is equal to one-sixth (1/6) of one (1) week in the case of any "location work week." No additional compensation other than as required by law shall be paid for any services required of the Performer hereunder on any Saturday, Sunday, or holidays [or in the making of promotional films (promoting the Picture) not exceeding (E.G., TWELVE (12)) minutes each in length or the use therein of clips from the Picture]. [Performer's services for such promotional films shall be subject to Performer's approval.] [It is acknowledged that Performer's services performed in (SPECIFY PLACE) shall be considered being performed during a studio work week.]

(e) Production Company shall not be obligated to pay [Lender] [Performer] any compensation hereunder for any period of failure, refusal or inability on Performer's part to render services for Production Company hereunder or to comply with any terms or conditions of this Agreement. A suspension of compensation shall not reduce the Guaranteed Compensation payable to [Lender] [Performer] hereunder unless this Agreement, pursuant to provisions elsewhere herein contained, is terminated prior to the expiration of the Guaranteed Period of Services.

(f) Production Company shall not be obligated to utilize Performer's services in or in connection with the Picture hereunder, Production Company's sole obligation, subject to the terms and conditions of this Agreement, being to pay [Lender] [Performer] the Guaranteed Compensation.

(g) Notwithstanding anything to the contrary contained in this Agreement, if this Agreement has not been terminated because of a [Lender/Performer] default or disability and if Performer appears readily recognizable in the Picture to the general public as released, [Lender] [Performer] shall be paid the Guaranteed Compensation set forth in Clause 2(a) and the Contingent Compensation set forth in Clause 3 hereof.

Clause 3. CONTINGENT COMPENSATION:

Subject to [Lender's] [Performer's] performance and compliance with the material terms and conditions of this Agreement and if Performer appears recognizably in the Picture [and to the general public as released], Production Company shall pay to [Lender] [Performer] in addition to the Guaranteed Compensation set forth in Clause 2(a) the following Contingent Compensation:

[SPECIFY AMOUNT, E.G.: (a) An amount equal to (E.G., FIVE PERCENT (5%)) of one hundred percent (100%) of the Gross Proceeds of the Picture which are in excess of (E.G., $30,000,000) of Gross Proceeds up to (E.G., $35,000,000) of Gross Proceeds plus,

(b) (E.G., FIVE PERCENT (5%)) of one hundred percent (100%) of the Gross Proceeds of the Picture which are in excess of (E.G., $30,000,000) of Gross Proceeds up to (E.G., $35,000,000) of Gross Proceeds which shall accrue but not be payable until a Participation Statement indicates that Gross Proceeds of the Picture equal (E.G., $35,000,000), at which time such accrued (E.G., FIVE PERCENT (5%)) participation shall be paid; and

(c) An amount equal to (E.G., TEN PERCENT (10%)) of one hundred percent (100%) of Gross Proceeds of the Picture in excess of (E.G., $35,000,000) of the Gross Proceeds.

(d) PARTICIPATION TERMINOLOGY: For purposes of this Clause 3, the terms "Gross Receipts," "Gross Proceeds," "Conversion/Transmission Costs," "Taxes," "Checking Costs," "Collection Costs," "Trade Association Fees," "Guild Payments" shall be defined and computed in accordance with Exhibit "A" attached hereto and by this reference incorporated herein.]

OR

[(E.G., TEN percent (10%) of one hundred percent of the Net Profits of the Picture, defined, computed, accounted for and paid in accordance with Production Company's standard definition of Net Profits attached hereto as Exhibit "A" and by this reference incorporated herein.]

Clause 4. CARRYOVER:

(a) If, at the expiration of the Guaranteed Period of Services, Production Company has failed to complete the use of Performer's services in the Picture, and if such failure has not been caused by Performer's mental or physical incapacity or failure or refusal of Performer to render services upon the terms and conditions hereof, then, if Production Company desires, it may require Performer to continue to render Performer's services exclusively hereunder so long as Production Company may require Performer's services or for the additional consecutive period of time necessary to complete the Picture, whichever shall be the shorter period; and, if Production Company requires Performer so to do, Production Company shall pay [Lender] [Performer], during such additional period, compensation on a weekly pro rata basis determined by dividing (SPECIFY AMOUNT) by the number of weeks set forth in the scheduled period of principal photography of the Picture referred to in Clause 2(a). Payments made to [Lender] [Performer] pursuant to this Clause 4(a) shall not be applied against the Contingent Compensation payable to [Lender] [Performer] in accordance with Clause 3 above.

(b) If any such failure to complete the Picture within the guaranteed Period of Services is caused by Performer's mental or physical incapacity or failure or refusal to render services for Production Company upon the terms and conditions hereof, then Performer shall render services hereunder (as and when required by Production Company) without compensation other than the Guaranteed Compensation for a consecutive or non-consecutive period or periods equal to the aggregate period of such incapacity, failure, or refusal to render services for Production Company upon the terms and conditions hereof.

(c) If, after Performer has rendered services hereunder, for a consecutive or non-consecutive period or periods equal to the aggregate period of such incapacity, failure or refusal, Production Company requires additional services hereunder, Production Company shall pay [Lender] [Performer] for such additional services compensation at the rate set forth in Clause 4(a) or pro rata for any period of less than a week on the basis set forth in Clause 2(d). [Lender] [Performer] shall cooperate in every way possible in order to make such services provided in this clause available to Production Company at such times as Production Company requires; and if Performer is unable to report to Production Company at such times as Production Company requires, [Lender] [Performer] shall make such services available to Production Company at the earliest reasonable possible date thereafter [but in any event, Performer shall not be required to provide services under this clause beyond [E.G., ONE YEAR] after the commencement of principal photography of the Picture].

Clause 5. RETAKES, ETC.:

(a) If, after the end of the Guaranteed Period of Services or after the completion of principal photography of the Picture, whichever shall be later, Production

Company requires Performer's services for retakes, changes, transparencies, added scenes, trailers, sound tracks, process shots, and/or other language versions (herein collectively called "retakes, etc.") for the Picture, Performer shall report to Production Company for such retakes, etc., at such place or places and on such day or days as Production Company may designate, provided Performer's services are not unavailable to Production Company due to other contractual commitments [of Lender to have] [Performer] [to] render services as an [actor] [actress].

(b) If the additional services above referred to are required of Performer during the Guaranteed Period of Services, Production Company shall not be obligated to pay any compensation for such services other than the Guaranteed Compensation.

(c) If such additional services are required after the expiration of the Guaranteed Period of Services, Production Company shall compensate [Lender] [Performer] therefor at the rate provided in Clause 4(a) for the day or days upon which Performer is engaged in rendering such additional services[, except the first (SPECIFY NUMBER) days (which need not be consecutive) of Performer's services in connection with dubbing, looping and wild lines, shall be rendered without additional compensation]. However, Production Company shall endeavor to schedule such additional services so that Performer shall be able to render such additional services on consecutive days. [Lender] [Performer] will cooperate in every way possible to make said additional services available to Production Company upon the day or days Production Company shall first request the same; and, if [Lender] [Performer] shall be unable to so arrange Performer's other engagements to return upon the day or days so requested by Production Company, [Lender] [Performer] will endeavor to make Performer's services available to Production Company at the earliest possible date thereafter.

Clause 6. TESTS, FITTINGS, REHEARSALS, ETC.:

During the pre-production period of the Picture, prior to the commencement of the consecutive period of services of Performer hereunder, when Performer is not rendering services for others, and at all times during the consecutive period of services of Performer hereunder, Performer shall report (if and when requested by Production Company) to such place or places as Production Company designates for publicity interviews, publicity photograph sittings, still pictures, tests, fittings, rehearsals, auditions and story, song and production conferences. [Subject to Performer's availability,] after the expiration of the consecutive period of services of Performer hereunder, Performer shall, if requested by Production Company to do so, render similar services; however, no compensation shall be payable for any such services rendered prior to the beginning or after the expiration of such period. [The identity of the person with whom the publicity interviews are to be scheduled shall be subject to the prior approval of [Lender] [Performer], which approval shall not be unreasonably withheld.]

Clause 7. PRE-RECORDINGS:

If Production Company requires Performer's services in connection with pre-recordings for the Picture prior to the commencement of the consecutive period of services of Performer hereunder, [Lender shall provide Performer] [Performer shall], subject to Performer's availability, [to] render services for Production Company in connection therewith at such time or times as Production Company may request; and the rendition of such services shall not be deemed a commence-ment of the Guaranteed Period of Services. However, Production Company shall compensate [Lender] [Performer] for each day of such services at the rate provided in Clause 4(a) and such compensation shall be deemed to be a part of the Guaranteed Compensation payable to [Lender] [Performer] under this Agreement, and each day of such services shall be counted as one (1) day of the Guaranteed Period of Services.

Clause 8. NATURE OF SERVICES:

(a) [Lender shall provide Performer to] [Performer shall] render all services as Production Company may require in connection with the portrayal of Performer's role in the Picture. Said services shall be rendered in such manner as Production Company may direct, at the times and places required by Production Company and in a conscientious and artistic manner, to the best of Performer's ability, with due regard to the efficient production of motion pictures[; it being understood that such production is a matter of art and taste to be exercised by Production Company and that Performer's services and the manner of rendition thereof are to be governed entirely by Production Company].

(b) In connection with the exploitation of the Picture, Production Company shall also have the right to record, produce, reproduce, amplify, enlarge, broadcast, use, perform, and distribute reproductions of Performer's voice and all other sounds of any kind or nature, whether such sounds shall have been created by Performer or by others. Production Company shall have the right to substitute the voice of another or others for Performer's voice, (i) when necessary to expeditiously meet the requirements of foreign exhibition; (ii) when necessary to expeditiously meet censorship requirements both foreign and domestic; (iii) when Performer is not available, [provided, however, that Performer shall have the right to dub Performer's own voice in the English language provided Performer is available as, when and where required by Production Company on (E.G., FOURTEEN (14)) days prior notice and for which services no additional compensation shall be payable]; and (iv) when Performer is unable to meet certain requirements of the role, such as singing or other similar or comparable services requiring special talents or abilities other than those possessed by Performer. Production Company shall also have the right to use a "double" for Performer's acts, poses, plays and appearances to such extent as Production Company may desire[; provided, however, that Production Company obtains Performer's approval of the individual who is to be used as Performer's double, which approval shall not be unreasonably withheld].

Clause 9. INJUNCTIVE RELIEF; EXCLUSIVE SERVICES:

(a) Performer's services to be furnished hereunder are of a special, unique, unusual, extraordinary, and intellectual character and of great and peculiar value to Production Company and Production Company could not, in an action at law, be reasonably or adequately compensated in damages for the loss thereof. [Lender and] [Performer] hereby [grant] [grants] to Production Company the exclusive right and property in and to Performer's services rendered hereunder and the product thereof.

(b) During any period in which Production Company shall be entitled to Performer's services exclusively hereunder, [Lender shall not provide Performer to] [Performer shall not] render services for any person, firm, or corporation other than Production Company.

Clause 10. RESULTS AND PRODUCT:

(a) In addition to Performer's services rendered hereunder, Production Company shall solely and exclusively own all results, product, and proceeds thereof (including, but not limited to, all rights of whatever kind and character throughout the world, in perpetuity in any and all languages of production, manufacture, recordation, reproduction, performance, and exhibition in any manner and by any art, device, or method, now known or hereafter devised, including without limitation radio broadcasting, theatrical and non-theatrical exhibition and exhibition by the medium of television or otherwise, on videotape and video disc, and of copyright, trademark and patent) whether such results, product and proceeds consist of literary, dramatic, musical, motion picture, mechanical or any other form of works, themes, ideas, compositions, creations or products. Production Company's acquisition hereunder shall also include all rights generally known in the field of literary and musical endeavor as the "moral rights of authors" in and/or to any musical and/or literary proceeds of Performer's services. Production Company shall also have the right, in respect to such product, to add to, subtract from, change, arrange, revise, adapt, rearrange, translate into any and all languages, change the sequence, change the characters and the descriptions thereof, change the title of the same, record and photograph the same with or without sound (including spoken words, dialogue and music synchronously recorded), use said title or any of its components in connection with works or motion pictures wholly or partially independent thereof, [to vend, copy and publish the same as Production Company may desire;] and [Lender and] [Performer] hereby [assign] [assigns] to Production Company all of the foregoing without reservation, conditions or limitations and no right of any kind, nature or description is reserved by [Lender] [Performer]. If Production Company shall desire to secure separate assignments of or for any of the foregoing, [Lender]

[Performer] shall execute the same upon Production Company's request. If [Lender] [Performer] shall [unreasonably] fail or refuse to execute and deliver any such separate assignments [or other documents], Production Company shall have and is hereby granted the right, and authority to execute the same in [Lender's and] [Performer's] name as [Lender's] [Performer's] attorney-in-fact. Production Company acknowledges that the aforesaid results, product and proceeds of Performer's services hereunder are acquired in connection with the Picture and that such results, product and proceeds shall not be utilized as an integral or substantial portion of another motion picture.

(b) Production Company shall always have the [sole and exclusive] right [, but only in connection with the Picture or in connection with the character portrayed by Performer in the Picture,] to use and display Performer's name, voice, and likeness for advertising, publicizing and exploiting the Picture, including without limitation souvenir programs, commercial tie-ups, paperback editions of the literary property directly relating to and on which the Picture is based, or any sound recordings. However, such advertising, publicizing and exploiting may not include the direct endorsement of any product [or service or commodity] (other than the Picture) without [Lender's and] [Performer's] consent. The use of Performer's name, voice or likeness in connection with any commercial tie-ups, or on any products such as a paperback edition of the literary property on which the Picture is based, or on any packaging of a multimedia product (whether CD-ROM, CD-I or otherwise) based on the Picture, or on any sound recording, or the cover thereof, containing the score or songs used in the Picture shall not be deemed an endorsement of any product other than the Picture. The exhibition of the Picture by any media, even though a part of or in connection with a commercially sponsored program, shall not be deemed an endorsement of any nature.

(c) [Lender and] Performer hereby irrevocably assign[s], license[s], and grant[s] to Production Company, exclusively, throughout the universe, and in perpetuity, the rights, if any, of Performer to authorize, prohibit, and/or control the renting, lending, fixation, reproduction and/or other exploitation of any motion picture produced based upon the Picture (or any rights therein) by any media and means now known or hereafter devised as may be conferred upon by Performer under applicable laws, regulations, or directives including without limitation, any so-called "Rental Lending Rights" pursuant to any European Economic Community ("EEC") directives and/or enabling or implementing legislation, laws, or regulations enacted by the member nations of the EEC.

(d) All of the rights granted or agreed to be granted hereunder shall vest in Production Company immediately and shall remain vested whether this Agreement expires in normal course or is terminated for any cause or reason. All of the rights granted herein, including, without limitation, all material created, composed, submitted, added or interpolated by Performer hereunder shall automatically become Production Company's property, and Production Company, for this purpose, shall be deemed author thereof with Performer acting entirely as Production Company's employee. [Lender and] Performer do[es] hereby assign and transfer to Production Company all of the rights herein granted without reservation, condition or limitation, and no right of any kind, nature or description is reserved by [Lender and] Performer. Notwithstanding the foregoing, if any of the rights herein granted are hereafter subject to termination under Section 203 of the Copyright Act, or any similar provisions of this Act or subsequent revision thereof, then [Lender and] Performer agree not to make any further grant without giving Production Company the first opportunity to acquire such rights pursuant to a customary right of first negotiation/first refusal.

(e) [Lender,] Performer and Production Company agree wherever in this Agreement the terms "motion picture" or "motion picture production" or terms of similar tenor are used, such terms shall be conclusively deemed and construed to include the present and future developments of the motion picture, television, video tape, videodisc, computer, electronics and telephone industries, including talking motion pictures, videotape, television productions, any and all kinds of electronic and other interactive uses of the Picture and the components thereof, including, but not limited to, CD-ROM, CD-I, interactive multi-media devices, computer discs, and any new variations thereon, and all forms of motion pictures, television, laserdisc, videotape, CD-ROM, CD-I, interactive multimedia devices and similar uses, whether now known or unknown and their accompanying devices which reproduce words, music and/or other sounds in synchronization with, accompaniment of, or supplementary to photography.

Clause 11. MERCHANDISING:

In addition to the rights hereinbefore granted to Production Company in this Agreement, Production Company shall have and is hereby granted the further exclusive right and license, but only in connection with the Picture or in connection with the character portrayed by Performer in the Picture, to use and simulate and to license others to use and simulate Performer's name, likeness and voice in and in connection with any merchandising and/or publishing endeavors whatsoever in which Production Company or its licensees may be or become engaged and commercial tie-ups[; provided, however, Production Company shall first obtain [Lender's and] [Performer's] prior written consent [not to be unreasonably withheld] in connection with each such merchandising item and/or commercial tie-up]. The rights and licenses granted to Production Company in this clause shall extend throughout the universe.

Clause 12. TRANSPORTATION AND EXPENSES:

(a) When Performer's services are required by Production Company to be rendered [during the consecutive period of Performer's services hereunder] at a place more than (E.G., FIFTY (50)) miles [outside of (NAME OF CITY OR

COUNTY)] OR [from Performer's principal place of residence] which Performer represents is (NAME OF CITY AND STATE), Production Company shall furnish Performer with (SPECIFY NUMBER, E.G., TWO) round trip airplane transportation, of a first class nature if used and if available), from (E.G., PERFORMER'S RESIDENCE) to any said location for the Performer [and, on a one time only basis, (SPECIFY NUMBER) additional round trip airplane transportation of a first class nature (if used and if available) to and from (E.G., PERFORMER'S PRINCIPAL RESIDENCE)].

(b) When Performer's services are required by Production Company to be rendered hereunder at a place more than (E.G., FIFTY (50)) miles [outside of (NAME OF CITY OR COUNTY)] OR [from Performer's principal place of residence], Production Company shall reimburse Performer for Performer's living expenses in the amount of (SPECIFY AMOUNT, E.G., $2,250 PER WEEK IN A MAJOR URBAN AREA SUCH AS NEW YORK OR LONDON, $1,750 PER WEEK IN OTHER METROPOLITAN AREAS, AND $1,250 PER WEEK ELSEWHERE). [If Performer can demonstrate to Production Company's satisfaction that the living expense allowance set forth above is insufficient for any particular location, Production Company shall, at such time, give good faith consideration to an increase.] [For any period which is less than one (1) week, said reimbursement shall be upon the pro rata basis that one (1) day is equal to one-seventh (1/7) of one (1) week.] [Performer agrees to furnish Production Company with itemized accountings for all such expenditures, which shall comply with the Internal Revenue Service regulations, including substantiating vouchers, invoices, and receipts relating to such expenses.]

Clause 13. WARDROBE:

(a) [Lender] [Performer] will furnish, at [its] Performer's expense, all wardrobe owned or possessed by Performer which is used or worn by Performer in the portrayal of Performer's role hereunder, except costumes for roles or parts known as costume parts which are not possessed by [Lender] [Performer].

(b) Any costumes, apparel or other articles paid for or furnished by Production Company [shall be returned to Production Company promptly upon its demand therefor] [may be retained by [Lender] [Performer] upon completion of Performer's services in the Picture].

Clause 14. PUBLICITY RESTRICTIONS:

[Lender and] [Performer] shall not [, individually or jointly], by means of press agents or publicity or advertising agencies or others, employed or paid by [Lender or] [Performer] or otherwise, circulate, publish, or otherwise disseminate any news stories or articles, books, or other publicity containing [Lender's or] [Performer's] name relating [directly or indirectly] to Performer's [employment] [engagement], the subject matter of this Agreement, the Picture or the services to be rendered by Performer or others for the Picture unless the same are first approved by Production Company. [Notwithstanding the foregoing sentence, Performer may, or Performer's publicity representatives may, however, disseminate publicity which contains Performer's name and identifies the Picture or Performer's services in connection therewith so long as such publicity (a) is not an advertisement for the Picture, (b) is not derogatory and (c) does not disclose confidential information.] [Lender] [Performer] shall not transfer or attempt to transfer any right, privilege, title, or interest in or to any of the things above specified, nor shall [Lender] [Performer] authorize or willingly permit any person, firm or corporation in any way to infringe upon such rights hereby granted to Production Company, and [Lender] [Performer] authorizes Production Company, at Production Company's expense, in [Lender's] [Performer's] name or otherwise, to institute any proper legal proceedings to prevent any infringement.

Clause 15. CAPACITY TO CONTRACT:

[Lender] [Performer] hereby warrants and represents that [Lender and] [Performer] [is] [are] not under any obligation or disability, created by law or otherwise, which would in any manner or to any extent prevent or restrict [Lender and] [Performer] from entering into and fully performing this Agreement. [Lender and] [Performer] warrant(s) and represent(s) that [Lender and] [Performer] [have] [has] not tethered into any agreement or commitment that would prevent [their] [Performer's] fulfilling [its] [Performer's] commitments with Production Company hereunder and that [Lender and] [Performer] will not enter into any such agreement or commitment without Production Company's specific written approval [; and [Lender and] [Performer] hereby agree(s) that Performer shall devote Performer's entire time and attention and best talents and ability exclusively to Production Company as specified herein, and to observe and to be governed by the rules of conduct established by Production Company for the conduct of its employees].

Clause 16. CREDITS:

If the Performer appears recognizably in the Picture to the general public as released, and this Agreement has not been terminated as a result of Performer's refusal or willful failure to perform Performer's [material] services, then Performer shall be accorded credit [on a separate card] in (NUMBER) position of the entire cast of the Picture [(([(ABOVE) OR (BELOW)] the title) OR (in the main titles [if any are used to identify cast members])] on all positive prints of the Picture and in the billing portion of all paid advertising issued by Production Company herewith, except: group, list, teaser, trailer, special advertising, billboards of three (3) sheets or more, and advertisements of eight (8) column inches or less (herein "excluded ads"). With respect to such credit the following conditions shall apply:

(a) On screen, Performer's name shall be displayed in a size of type not less than (SPECIFY PERCENTAGE, E.G., FORTY PERCENT (40%)) of the size of type used to display the title of the Picture [but in no event less than the size of type used for (E.G., ANY OTHER PERFORMER IN THE PICTURE)].

(b) In paid advertisements (other than excluded ads) issued by Production Company or under its control, Performer's name shall be displayed in a size of type not less than (SPECIFY PERCENTAGE, E.G., THIRTY-FIVE PERCENT (35%)) of the size of type used to display the title of the Picture, [but in no event less than the size of type used for (E.G., ANY OTHER PERFORMER IN THE PICTURE)], provided, however, that

(1) If both an "artwork" title and a regular title are used in any such advertisement, the position and percentage requirements shall relate to the regular title, and

(2) If only an "artwork" title is used in any such advertisement, then the size of type used for Performer's name shall be equal to (SPECIFY PERCENT-AGE, E.G., THIRTY-FIVE PERCENT (35%)) of the average height and width of the letters used in the "artwork" title.

[(c) If the likeness of any other member of the cast of the Picture shall appear in any paid advertisement other than excluded ads, then Performer's likeness shall appear in such advertisement. If the name and/or likeness of any other member of the cast of the Picture shall appear in any of the excluded ads, then Performer's name and/or likeness, as the case may be, shall appear therein but the foregoing shall not apply to special advertisements devoted to other members of the cast, provided Performer's name or likeness appears in an equal number of excluded ads in the same or in similar publications released at approximately the same time; provided, however, that said equal treatment shall not apply to special advertisements relating to awards, citations, congratulations, nominations, or personal appearances of other members of the cast.]

(d) No casual or inadvertent failure to comply with the provisions of this clause shall be deemed a breach of this Agreement by Production Company. [Lender and] [Performer] hereby recognizes and confirms that in the event of failure or omission by Production Company constituting a breach of its obligations under this clause, the damages, if any, caused [Lender and] [Performer] by Production Company are not irreparable or sufficient to entitle [Lender and/or] [Performer] to injunctive or other equitable relief. Consequently, [Lender's and] [Performer's] rights and remedies hereunder shall be limited to the right, if any, to obtain damages at law and [Lender and] [Performer] shall have no right in such event to rescind this Agreement or any rights granted to Production Company hereunder or to enjoin or restrain the distribution or exhibition of the Picture. [Production Company agrees, upon receipt of written notice from Performer of Production Company's failure to comply with this provision, to take such steps as are reasonably practicable to cure such failure in future prints and advertisements.]

Clause 17. [GARNISHMENT]/[ATTACHMENT]:

If by reason of any [garnishment] [attachment] or levy, or by the terms of any contract or assignment executed by [Lender] [Performer], Production Company shall be required to pay any of [Lender's] [Performer's] compensation hereunder to any person, firm, or corporation, or to withhold the same from [Lender] [Performer], Production Company's compliance with any such [garnishment] [attachment], levy, contract, or assignment shall not be deemed a breach of its obligations hereunder.

Clause 18. FORCE MAJEURE:

(a) Suspension: If, by reason of fire, earthquake, labor dispute or strike, act of God or public enemy, any municipal ordinance, any state or federal law, governmental order or regulation, or other cause beyond Production Company's control [which would excuse Production Company's performance as a matter of law], Production Company is prevented from or hampered in the production of the Picture, or if, by reason of the closing of substantially all the theatres in the United States for any of the aforesaid or any other causes, [which would excuse Production Company's performance as a matter of law,] Production Company's production of the Picture is postponed or suspended, or if, by reason of any of the aforesaid contingencies or any other cause or occurrence outside Production Company's control, including without limitation death, illness or incapacity of any other principal member of the cast of the Picture or the director, the preparation, commencement, production or completion of the Picture is hampered, interrupted or interfered with [and/or, if Production Company's normal business operations are hampered or otherwise interfered with by virtue of any disruptive events which are beyond Production Company's control] ("Production Company Disability"), then Production Company may postpone the commencement of or suspend the rendition of services by Performer and the running of time hereunder for such time as the Production Company Disability shall continue [(but any such suspension based upon the death, illness or incapacity of a principal member of the cast shall not exceed (E.G., FOUR) consecutive weeks)] and no compensation shall accrue or become payable to [Lender] [Performer] hereunder during the period of such suspension. [Production Company shall not suspend Performer for a Production Company Disability unless Production Company also suspends all other principal members of the cast.] [If Production Company terminates the suspension with respect to all other principal cast members, it shall terminate the suspension with respect to Performer.] [Production Company shall not suspend Performer more than once with respect to the exact event which causes the Production Company Disability.] [Such suspension shall end no later than (E.G., FOUR WEEKS) following the cessation of the Production Company Disability or upon recommencement of principal photography of the Picture after the cessation of the Production Company Disability, whichever shall occur first.]

(b) Termination:

(1) Production Company Termination Right: If a Production Company Disability continues [for a period exceeding (E.G., FOUR (4)) weeks due to the incapacity or unavailability of the director or of any other principal member of the cast or if a Production Company Disability continues] for a period exceeding (E.G., EIGHT (8)) weeks [due to any other contingency], Production Company may terminate this Agreement upon written notice to Performer.

(2) Performer's Termination Right: If a Production Company Disability results in the payment of compensation being suspended hereunder for a period exceeding (E.G., EIGHT (8)) weeks, [Lender] [Performer] may terminate this Agreement upon written notice to Production Company.

(3) Production Company Re-Establishment Right: Despite [Lender's] [Performer's] election to terminate this Agreement, within (E.G., FIVE (5)) days after Production Company's actual receipt of such written notice from [Lender] [Performer], Production Company may elect to re-establish the operation of this Agreement.

Clause 19. PERFORMER'S INCAPACITY:

(a) Effect of Performer's Incapacity: If (i) Performer shall suffer any facial or other physical injury, impairment, or disfigurement materially detracting from Performer's appearance or [materially impairing Performer's] ability to perform performer's role hereunder, or (ii) by reason of mental or physical disability, Performer shall be incapacitated from performing or complying with any terms or conditions hereof ("Performer's Incapacity") for a consecutive period exceeding (E.G., SEVEN (7)) days or an aggregate period exceeding (E.G., TEN (10)) days, then Production Company may terminate this Agreement upon written notice to [Lender] [Performer].

(b) Right of Examination: If any claim of mental or physical disability is made by Performer or on Performer's behalf, Production Company may have Performer examined by such physicians as Production Company designates. Performer's physician may be present at such examination, but shall not interfere therewith. [Any tests performed on Performer shall be related to and be customary for the treatment, diagnosis or examination to be performed in connection with Performer's claim.]

Clause 20. [LENDER/] PERFORMER DEFAULT:

If [Lender or] Performer fails or refuses to perform or comply with any [material] terms or conditions hereof other than by reason of Performer's Incapacity ("[Lender/] Performer Default"), then Production Company shall have the right to terminate this Agreement upon written notice thereof to [Lender] [Performer]. [[Lender/] Performer Default shall not include any failure or refusal of Performer to perform or comply with the material terms and conditions of this Agreement by reason of a breach or action by Production Company which makes the performance by Performer of Performer's services impossible.] [Prior to termination of this Agreement by Production Company based upon [Lender/] Performer Default, Production Company shall notify [Lender and] Performer, specifying the nature of the [Lender/] Performer Default, and [Lender and] Performer shall have (E.G., 24 HOURS) after the giving of such notice to cure the Default. If the [Lender/] Performer Default is not cured within the (E.G., 24 HOUR) period, Production Company may terminate this Agreement forthwith.]

Clause 21. EFFECT OF TERMINATION:

Termination of this Agreement, whether by lapse of time, mutual consent, operation of law, exercise of a right of termination or otherwise shall:

(a) Terminate Production Company's obligation to pay [Lender] [Performer] any further compensation. Nevertheless, if the termination is not for [Lender/] Performer Default, Production Company shall pay [Lender] [Performer] [in accordance with Clause 2(a) hereof] [any compensation due and unpaid prior to the termination], and

(b) [Neither Production Company nor [Lender and] [Performer] shall be deemed] [Production Company shall not be deemed] to have waived any other rights [they] [it] may have or alter Production Company's rights or any of [Lender's and] [Performer's] agreements or warranties in connection with the rendition of Performer's services prior to termination.

Clause 22. PRODUCTION COMPANY RIGHT TO SUSPEND:

In the event of Performer's Incapacity or [Lender/] Performer Default, Production Company may postpone the commencement of or suspend the rendition of services by Performer and the running of time hereunder so long as any such Performer's Incapacity or [Lender/] Performer Default shall continue; and no compensation shall accrue or become payable to [Lender] [Performer] during the period of such suspension.

(a) [Lender's] [Performer's] Right to Cure: Any Performer's Incapacity or [Lender/] Performer Default shall be deemed to continue until Production Company's receipt of written notice from [Lender] [Performer] specifying that Performer is ready, willing and able to perform the services required hereunder; provided that any such notice from [Lender] [Performer] to Production Company shall not preclude Production Company from exercising any rights or remedies it may have hereunder or at law or in equity by reason of Performer's Incapacity or [Lender/] Performer Default.

(b) Alternative Services Restricted: During any period of suspension hereunder, Performer shall not render services for any person, firm or corporation other than Production Company [; provided, however, that Performer may render services to third parties during any period of suspension based upon a Production Company Disability, subject, however, to Production Company's right to require Performer to resume the rendition of services hereunder upon (E.G., 24 HOURS) prior notice]. [If the period of suspension is not terminated within (E.G., 3 MONTHS), this Agreement shall thereafter be terminated as provided hereinabove.]

(c) Production Company Right to Extend: If Production Company elects to suspend the rendition of services by Performer as herein specified, then Production Company may (at any time) extend the period of services required of Performer hereunder for a period equal to the period of suspension.

(d) Additional Services: If Production Company has paid compensation to [Lender] [Performer] during any period of Performer's Incapacity or [Lender/] Performer Default, then Production Company may (at any time) require [Lender to furnish] Performer's services hereunder without compensation for a period equal to the period for which Production Company shall have paid compensation to [Lender] [Performer] during such Performer's Incapacity or [Lender/] Performer Default.

Clause 23. REMEDIES CUMULATIVE:

All remedies accorded herein or otherwise available to [either] Production Company [or [Lender] [Performer]] shall be cumulative, and no one such remedy shall be exclusive of any other. Without waiving any rights or remedies under this Agreement or otherwise, Production Company [or [Lender] [Performer]] may, from time to time, recover, by action, any damages arising out of any breach of this Agreement by [Lender and/or] Performer [or Production Company, as applicable,] and may institute and maintain subsequent actions for additional damages which may arise from the same or other breaches. The commencement or maintenance of any such action or actions by [Production Company] OR [a party] shall not constitute or result in the termination of Production Company's use of Performer's services hereunder unless [Production Company] OR [such party] shall expressly so elect by written notice to [Lender] [Performer] OR [the other party]. The pursuit by [Production Company] OR [a party] of any remedy under this Agreement or otherwise shall not be deemed to waive any other or different remedy which may be available under this Agreement or otherwise, either at law or in equity, unless specifically limited herein.

Clause 24. INSURANCE:

Production Company may secure life, health, accident, cast or other insurance covering Performer at Production Company's sole expense and for Production Company's sole benefit with Production Company being the beneficiary thereof, and [Lender and] Performer shall not have any interest in the proceeds thereof. [Lender and] Performer shall assist Production Company in procuring such insurance by submitting to required examinations and tests and by preparing signing, and delivering such applications and other documents as may be reasonably required. [Lender and] Performer shall, to the best of [Lender's and] Performer's ability, observe all terms and conditions of such insurance of which Production Company notifies [Lender and] Performer as being necessary for continuing such insurance in effect. [If Production Company is unable to obtain pre-production or cast insurance covering Performer at prevailing standard rates and without any exclusions, restrictions, conditions, or exceptions of any kind, [Lender] [Performer] shall have the right to pay any premium in excess of the prevailing standard rates in order for Production Company to obtain such insurance.] If [Lender] [Performer] fails, refuses, or is unable for any reason whatsoever to pay such excess premium,] or if, having obtained such insurance, [Lender or] [Performer] fails to observe all terms and conditions necessary to maintain such insurance in effect, Production Company shall have the right to terminate this Agreement without any obligation to [Lender and] [Performer] by giving [Lender and] [Performer] written notice of termination.

Clause 25. GUILD MEMBERSHIP:

During the rendition of Performer's services hereunder, at such time or times and during such period or periods as it may be lawful for Production Company to require Performer so to do, [Lender] [Performer], at [Lender's] [Performer's] sole cost and expense, and at Production Company's request, shall [cause Performer to] remain or become and remain a member in good standing of the then properly designated labor organization or organizations (as defined and determined under the then applicable law) representing persons performing services of the kind to be performed by Performer hereunder.

Clause [26. MOTION PICTURE RELIEF FUND OF AMERICA, INC.:

[Lender] [Performer] hereby authorizes Production Company on [Lender's and] Performer's behalf to pay Motion Picture Relief Fund of America, Inc. one percent (1%) of all compensation accruing to [Lender] [Performer] hereunder, which amount [shall] [shall not] be deducted from [Lender's] [Performer's] basic compensation herein.]

Clause [27. GOVERNMENTAL LIMITATION:

If the compensation provided by this Agreement exceeds the amount permitted by any present or future law or governmental order or regulation, such stated compensation shall be reduced, while such limitation is in effect, to the amount which is so permitted, and the payment of such reduced compensation shall constitute full performance by Production Company of its obligation to [Lender] [Performer] respecting the payment of compensation hereunder. [Notwithstanding the foregoing, if at such time as the limitation is no longer in effect, there is compensation remaining unpaid for Performer's services hereunder, Production

Company shall cooperate with Performer in connection with processing any applications relative to the payment of such unpaid compensation, and Production Company shall pay such compensation to Performer at such time as Production Company is legally permitted to do so.]]

Clause 28. EMPLOYMENT OF OTHERS:

[Lender and] Performer agree(s) not to employ any person to serve in any capacity, nor to contract for the purchase or renting of any article or material, nor make any agreement committing Production Company to pay any sum of money for any reason whatsoever in connection with the Picture or services to be rendered by Performer [or provided by Lender] hereunder or otherwise, without the prior written consent of Production Company.

Clause 29. LENDING:

Production Company shall have the right to lend Performer's services hereunder to (a) any of its subsidiary or affiliated companies or (b) any other producer of motion pictures, provided such producer shall have granted to Production Company the right to distribute the Picture [and further provided that Performer has consented to such lending, which consent shall not be unreasonably withheld]. Such lending of Performer's services shall not relieve Production Company of its obligations hereunder.

Clause 30. ASSIGNMENT:

This Agreement, at Production Company's election, shall inure to the benefit of its successors, assigns, licensees, grantees, and associated, affiliated and subsidiary companies, and [Lender] [Performer] agrees that Production Company and any subsequent assignee may freely assign this Agreement and grant the rights obtained hereunder, in whole or in part, to any person, firm or corporation. [If Production Company shall assign this Agreement to a so-called "major" motion picture producer or distributor, provided such assignee shall assume Production Company's obligations hereunder in writing, Production Company shall be forever relieved and discharged of all of its obligations to Performer hereunder. For purposes of this Agreement, a "major" motion picture producer or distributor shall be deemed to include (SPECIFY NAMES). If Production Company shall assign this Agreement to a third party other than a so-called major, Production Company shall remain secondarily liable for the obligations not performed by the assignee.]

Clause 31. ENTIRE AGREEMENT:

This Agreement shall replace and supersede all previous arrangements, understandings, representations, or agreements, either oral or written, regarding the subject matter hereof and expresses the entire agreement between [Lender] [Performer] and Production Company with reference to the terms and conditions for the rendition of Performer's services for Production Company in connection with the Picture.

Clause 32. EMPLOYMENT ELIGIBILITY:

All of Production Company's obligations herein are expressly conditioned upon Performer's completion, to Production Company's satisfaction, of the I-9 form (Employee Eligibility Verification Form), and upon [Lender's] [Performer's] submission to Production Company of original documents satisfactory to demonstrate to Production Company Performer's employment eligibility.

Clause 33. NOTICES:

(a) [Lender's] [Performer's] Address: All notices from Production Company to [Lender] [Performer] in connection with this Agreement may be given in writing by addressing the same to [Lender] [Performer] in care of (NAME AND ADDRESS OF RECIPIENT OF NOTICE) and by depositing same, so addressed, postage prepaid, in the mail, or, at Production Company's option, Production Company may deliver such notice to [Lender] [Performer] personally, either orally or in writing, or by telegraph, cable or facsimile transmission. Production Company shall send a courtesy copy to (NAME AND ADDRESS OF ATTORNEY). [All such notices shall be deemed given when deposited, postage prepaid, in the U.S. Mail, when delivered to a telegraph or cable company, toll prepaid, when transmitted by facsimile, or when personally delivered.] [Three (3) days after the date of mailing, one day after the date of telegraphing, cabling or facsimile transmission, and the date of personal delivery shall be the date of the giving of such notice.]

(b) Writing Requirement: Any notice given in respect to any right of termination, suspension, or extension under this Agreement shall be confirmed in writing. [If any notice is delivered to [Performer] [Lender] personally, a copy of such notice shall be sent to [Performer] [Lender] at the above address.]

(c) Production Company's Address: All notices from [Lender] [Performer] to Production Company hereunder shall be given in writing, addressed to Production Company as follows: (NAME AND ADDRESS OF PRODUCTION COMPANY) and by depositing same, so addressed, postage prepaid, in the mail, or, at [Lender's] [Performer's] option, [Lender] [Performer] may deliver such notice to Production Company personally. A courtesy copy shall be sent to (NAME AND ADDRESS OF ATTORNEY). Unless otherwise expressly provided, the date of mailing shall be deemed to be the date of service of such notice.

(d) Agency Payment. [Lender] [Performer] hereby authorizes Production Company to make all payments for Performer's services to be paid in care of (SPECIFY NAME AND ADDRESS OF AGENT). All payments made in accordance with the preceding sentence shall be deemed as if paid directly to [Lender] [Performer].

Clause 34. GOVERNING LAW:

This Agreement shall be construed in accordance with the laws of the State of (NAME OF STATE) applicable to agreements which are executed and fully performed within said State.

Clause 35. CAPTIONS:

The captions used in this Agreement with the clauses and subclauses are inserted only for the purpose of reference. Such captions shall not be deemed to govern, limit, modify, or otherwise affect the scope, meaning, or intent of the provisions of this Agreement or any part thereof; nor shall such captions otherwise be given any legal effect.

Clause 36. SERVICE OF PROCESS:

In any action or proceeding commenced in any court in the State of (NAME OF STATE) for the purpose of enforcing this Agreement or any right granted herein or growing out hereof, or any order or decree predicated hereon, any summons, order to show cause, writ, judgment, decree, or other process, issued by such court, may be delivered to [Lender and/or] [Performer] personally without the State of (NAME OF STATE); and upon such delivery [Lender and/or] [Performer] shall be subject to the jurisdiction of such court, and amenable to the process so delivered as though the same had been served within the State of (NAME OF STATE), but outside the county in which such action or proceeding is pending.

Clause 37. ILLEGALITY:

Nothing contained in this Agreement shall require the commission of any act, or payment of any monies, which is contrary to an express provision of law or contrary to public policy, or to any provision of applicable guild or collective bargaining agreements. If there shall exist any conflict between any provisions contained herein and any such law, policy or agreement, the latter shall prevail; and the provision or provisions herein affected shall be curtailed, limited or eliminated to the extent (but only to the extent) necessary to remove such conflict; and as so modified this Agreement shall continue in full force and effect.

OPTIONAL PROVISIONS

Clause 38. RECORD ALBUM:

Production Company shall have the right, for itself and its assigns, to utilize Performer's voice and performances on the sound track of the Picture in connection with the manufacture, distribution, sale or other use of commercial phonograph records, including discs, pre-recorded tapes, cartridges and other devices for the reproduction of sound ("Soundtrack Recording"). On condition that [Lender and] Performer fully complete(s) all [material] services which

Production Company may require of [Lender and/or Performer] hereunder, and if the sound track of the Picture is so utilized, Production Company agrees to pay, or to cause the record company involved ("Record Company") to pay to [Lender] [Performer] a royalty which shall be a percentage of the suggested retail selling price (exclusive of all excise, sales and other taxes) of Soundtrack Recordings on ninety percent (90%) [(or on one hundred percent (100%) if Production Company is so accounted to by the Record Company)] of all copies of Soundtrack Recordings sold for which payment has been received less all returns, rebates, credits, cancellations and exchanges. The royalty percentage for Soundtrack Recordings sold in the form of discs in the United States is (E.G., FIVE PERCENT (5%)). The royalty percentage for Soundtrack Recordings sold in the form of discs outside the United States is (E.G., TWO AND ONE-HALF PERCENT (2-1/2%)). As to the sale of Soundtrack Recordings through any direct mail order operation or through record clubs or similar sales plans or schemes, the royalty is computed at (E.G., ONE-HALF (½)) of the royalty percentage otherwise applicable. As to the sale of Soundtrack Recordings in the form of pre-recorded tapes, cartridges, cassettes, or other recorded devices (other than discs), the royalty is computed at (E.G., ONE-HALF (½)) of the royalty percentage otherwise applicable. As to Soundtrack Recordings sold through any direct mail order operation at a price (excluding postage and handling charges) of (E.G., ONE DOLLAR ($1.00)) or less or sold for promotional, sale, incentive, or educational purposes, the applicable royalty percentage shall be computed on the basis of the actual sales price therefor. The proportion of the applicable royalty percentage payable to Performer shall be as the number of bands performed by Performer bears to the total number of bands on the Soundtrack Recording. As to each band embodying Performer's voice and performance with the performance of another artist or artists entitled to a royalty, the applicable royalty percentage shall be further prorated based upon the proportion that the number one bears to the total number of royalty artists whose performances are contained on such band. The Record Company may recoup from such royalties its standard recording costs customarily recognized as recording costs in the recording industry. No royalty is payable on Soundtrack Recordings distributed or sold (a) as premiums, or (b) as samplers, cutouts, scrap, or at close out prices, or (c) on a no charge or nominal charge basis to radio or television stations or networks or transportation facilities or (d) as record club or mail order "free," "bonus," or "dividend" records. If Production Company utilizes Performer's voice in Soundtrack Recordings, Performer shall not perform any selection performed by Performer in such Soundtrack Recordings for any other person, firm, or corporation for the purpose of making phonograph records during the period of (E.G., FIVE (5)) years following the Initial Release Date of the Picture.

Clause 39. APPROVALS [AND CONSULTATIONS]:

If Performer is not in [material] default and has performed all required services hereunder, Performer shall have the following approval [and consultation] rights:

(a) Make-Up Person/Stand-In: Production Company agrees to consult in advance with Performer regarding the selection of Performer's make-up person, and Performer's stand-in for the Picture, Production Company shall consult with Performer regarding said personnel prior to their employment. However, with respect thereto, the employment of any particular person in accordance with Performer's request is subject to the availability of said person, Production Company's determination as to such person's qualifications to perform the services required, and such person's ability to obtain a valid work permit at the place of principal photography of the Picture. [Said personnel who are employed in such capacities to render such services shall receive the applicable minimum compensation payable therefor.]

OR

(a) Make-Up Person: Subject to applicable Guild, union, and government requirements, Performer shall have the right to approve the individual to be engaged to render services as Performer's make-up person for the Picture, provided that: (i) The costs involved for engaging a particular individual are not in excess of the amount allocated for the position in the budget; (ii) the costs involved for engaging a particular individual are not in excess of the individual's then going rate in the motion picture industry; (iii) the particular individual is ready, willing and able to perform services as and when required by Production Company; (iv) the particular individual's prior employment experience, if any, with Production Company has been completed to the satisfaction of Production Company; and (v) the particular individual agrees to be available to render services for other members of the cast of the Picture at no additional cost, provided that Performer shall at all times have "first call" on the services of such individual.

(b) Publicity Representatives: Performer has requested that Production Company engage (SPECIFY NAME) as outside publicity representatives for the Picture. Subject to Clause 14 hereof, Production Company will endeavor to engage (SPECIFY NAME) to render services as outside publicity representatives for the Picture, provided that: (i) the costs involved for engaging same are not in excess of the amount allotted for the position in the budget; (ii) the costs involved for engaging (SPECIFY NAME) are not in excess of their then going rate in the motion picture industry; (iii) they are ready, willing and able to perform services as and when required by Production Company; and (iv) their prior employment experience, if any, with Production Company has been completed to the satisfaction of Production Company.

(c) Failure to Approve and Select: If, after Production Company has elected to proceed to production of the Picture, Performer and Production Company are unable to agree upon any of the above elements with respect to which Performer and Production Company have mutual approval (including substitute personnel for any previously approved or selected individuals who become unavailable) by a date occurring [E.G., EIGHT WEEKS] prior to the scheduled date for commencement of principal photography, then Production Company shall have the right to designate such personnel and/or elements in its sole discretion.

Clause 40. STILL PHOTOGRAPHS, NON-PHOTOGRAPHIC LIKENESSES:

(a) Performer shall have approval [, not to be unreasonably withheld,] of the still photographs in which Performer appears [and of non-photographic likenesses of Performer that may be used in connection with the advertising and exploitation of the Picture]; provided that Performer shall be required to approve at least [E.G., FIFTY PERCENT (50%)] of the total number of still photographs submitted by Production Company to Performer for approval [(which still photographs shall be submitted to Performer in groups of reasonable size and may be in the form of so-called "Contact Sheets") and a reasonable number of non-photographic likenesses]. [Except as otherwise provided in this clause, Production Company agrees that it shall not use the negatives rejected by Performer for any purpose whatsoever. Performer's failure to notify Production Company of disapproval within [E.G., FIVE DAYS] after submission or such reasonably shorter period of time (but not less than [E.G., SEVENTY-TWO HOURS]) shall be deemed to constitute approval. If Performer fails and/or refuses to approve [E.G., FIFTY PERCENT (50%)] of the still photographs submitted or a reasonable number of non-photographic likeness, Production Company shall, in its sole discretion, designate the balance of [E.G., FIFTY PERCENT (50%)] of still photographs [and select a reasonable number of non-photographic likenesses]. [Notwithstanding the foregoing, a non-photographic likeness shall be deemed approved if it is made from an approved still photograph.] Performer agrees to exercise such right of approval of non-photographic likenesses in a reasonable manner, taking into account Production Company's publicity requirements. Once Performer approves a still photograph or a non-photographic likeness, it shall be deemed approved for all permissible purposes hereunder in connection with exploitation of the Picture.

(b) If any other player or players rendering services in connection with the Picture have approval rights with respect to still photographs, Performer and such other player or players must approve at least [E.G., FIFTY PERCENT (50%)] of the total number of still photographs submitted in which said player or players appear with Performer, and failing such mutual approval, then Production Company can select from among those still photographs submitted as Production Company in its sole discretion may determine.

(c) Performer's approval rights with respect to still photographs and non-photographic likenesses of Performer as set forth in this clause shall be applicable to souvenir programs, paperback editions of the literary property on which the Picture is based, [or any Soundtrack Recording made from the soundtrack] or any other items used to exploit, advertise or publicize the Picture which display still photographs and non-photographic likenesses of Performer.

Clause 41. DRESSING ROOM/MOTOR HOME:

Production Company shall provide Performer with a first class dressing room when Performer is rendering services hereunder at the studio of Production Company [for Performer's exclusive use]. When Performer's services are rendered at a location away from Production Company's studio or if Performer's dressing room at such studio facility is not located immediately contiguous to the set or stage where Performer is rendering services, Production Company shall provide Performer with a first class dressing room trailer, which shall be fully furnished and equipped with a private telephone (if available) and with cooking facilities (if available) [for Performer's exclusive use].

Clause 42. CAR AND DRIVER:

Production Company agrees that Performer shall be provided with a car and driver to transport Performer [to and from airports and Performer's location residence and] between Performer's location residence and the location site whenever Performer's services are required by Production Company at the location site. [The car and driver may be part of the production pool of cars and drivers that are used by Production Company in connection with the Picture.] [Performer may select a driver of Performer's choice.] Production Company also agrees that it will furnish Performer with a separate car without driver for Performer's own personal use[, or if Performer determines, in Performer's sole discretion to utilize Performer's own personal car, then Production Company shall furnish Performer with garage space for Performer's personal car].

Clause 43. SECRETARY:

Production Company agrees that it shall reimburse Performer for the salary paid to Performer's personal secretary, in an amount not to exceed (E.G., $500.00) per week (plus such additional sums per week as may be necessary for the payment of reasonable and normal fringe benefits for such secretary) during the period of Performer's services in principal photography. Production Company agrees that it shall also provide such secretary with [first class] round trip air transportation (if available and if used) from (NAME OF CITY OR COUNTY) or such other place of commencement of such secretary's journey, whichever is fewer miles, to and from such location on not more than (E.G., ONE OCCASION) and shall provide each personal secretary with reasonable hotel accommodations and reimbursement for actual reasonable living expenses not to exceed (E.G., FIFTY DOLLARS) per day.

By signing in the spaces provided below, [Lender] [Performer] and Production Company accept and agree to all the terms and conditions of this Agreement.

(NAME OF PRODUCTION COMPANY) ("Production Company")

By   _____

Its   _____

(NAME OF LOAN-OUT COMPANY) ("Lender")

By   _____

Its   _____

OR

_____

(NAME OF PERFORMER)

_____

("Performer")

INDUCEMENT

I, (NAME OF PERFORMER), agree to perform all obligations to be performed by Lender and me hereunder, and make all representations and warranties herein made by Lender, in order to effectuate the terms and conditions of the foregoing Agreement, and I agree to look solely to Lender for payment of any compensation due me. I hereby accept and acknowledge each and all provisions of the foregoing agreement and agree to be bound by them to the same extent as if I had signed the agreement directly.

_____

(PERFORMER)

Form 16

Nudity Rider

Dear:

Reference is made to the Agreement dated _____, 19_____; (the "Agreement") between [(NAME OF COMPANY) ("Loan-out Company") providing the services of] you ("Performer") and (NAME OF PRODUCTION COMPANY), a (CALIFORNIA) corporation ("Production Company") with respect to Performer's acting services in connection with the theatrical motion picture currently entitled (NAME OF PICTURE) (the "Picture").

1. NUDITY/SEX ACTS: It is understood between the parties that, with respect to the services to be rendered by Performer, for the consideration set forth in the Agreement, such services shall require Performer to appear nude and/or semi-nude, and/or perform designated sexual act(s), as the case may be, in the Picture. The general description of the extent of such nudity and the type of physical contact required in such designated sex act(s) is as follows:

[DESCRIBE SEXUAL ACTIVITY AS FULLY AS POSSIBLE, E.G., FULL FRONTAL NUDITY OR SIMULATED SEXUAL INTERCOURSE]

2. PERFORMER'S CONSENT: Performer agrees and consents to render the services set forth above and hereby affirms that Performer agrees to appear nude and/or semi-nude and to perform such designated sex act(s). [In addition, [Lender] [Performer] consents to the use by Production Company of any and all still photography in which Performer appears nude and/or semi-nude or which depicts Performer in a sex act, in connection with the exploitation of the Picture in any and all media.]

3. OWNERSHIP OF PERFORMANCE: Pursuant to the terms and conditions of the Agreement, Production Company owns all results and proceeds of Performer's services rendered pursuant to the Agreement and has the exclusive right to use, license and exploit the Picture and Performer's performance therein, throughout the world in perpetuity in any and all media whether now known or hereafter devised.

All terms and provisions of the Agreement remain in full force and effect without modification or change and the Agreement is hereby affirmed.

Please acknowledge your agreement to the foregoing by signing in the place provided for below.

Very truly yours,

(NAME OF PRODUCTION COMPANY)

By _____

Its _____

AGREED AND ACCEPTED:

_____

"Performer"

OR

(NAME OF LOAN-OUT COMPANY)

By _____

Its _____

The following may be used if the performer uses a loan-out company:

INDUCEMENT

The undersigned, as a material inducement to Production Company to enter into this Agreement, by signing below agrees to be bound by all of the provisions of the above Agreement.

_____

(PERFORMER)

Form 17

Performer Series Engagement

LENDING AGREEMENT

AGREEMENT made and entered into as of this (DAY) of (MONTH, YEAR), by and between (NAME OF PRODUCTION COMPANY) (hereinafter called "Company") and (NAME OF PERFORMER'S LOAN-OUT COMPANY) (hereinafter called "Contractor") for the services of NAME OF PERFORMER) (hereinafter called the "Performer").

The following constitutes our agreement for Contractor to lend to Company the services of Performer to perform acting services in connection with the (one-half hour television) series (which is intended for initial broadcast on (NAME OF NETWORK OR NOTE CABLE OR SYNDICATION) currently entitled (NAME OF SERIES) (hereinafter referred to as the "Series").

Clause 1.

TERM: Contractor hereby lends to Company the services of Performer on a pay-or-play basis, to portray the role of (NAME OF CHARACTER PORTRAYED OR MULTIPLE CHARACTERS IF APPROPRIATE) in connection with the production of the Series for the (*e.g.*, 1993/1994 year). Performer acknowledges that he will be performing the role(s) and rendering services in connection with the Series. For convenience, each episode of the Series is herein referred to as a "Program." The first term and each subsequent term during which Company may require the services of Performer pursuant to the exercise of an option hereunder shall be referred to herein as a "contract year" and each contract year may be referred to for convenience in the order of sequence as the "first contract year," "second contract year," etc.

The first contract year shall commence on approximately (*e.g.*, July 15, 1993) and continue for a term of one (1) year, or until June 30th of the calendar year next following the calendar year in which the first contract year commenced, whichever shall have last occurred, subject to extension as provided herein.

Contractor hereby grants to Company four successive options to extend the term of this agreement for an additional year, each option commencing on the day after the expiration of the prior contract year. Company shall exercise the option by serving written notice of its election to exercise each such option no later than the expiration of the prior contract year, as such term may be extended pursuant to the terms hereof.

If Performer shall not have been engaged in or if Contractor shall not have been paid for at least twenty-six (26) Programs hereunder during any contract year in which Performer is guaranteed at least twenty-six (26) Programs or if Performer shall not have been engaged in or Contractor paid for at least thirteen

(13) Programs hereunder during any contract year for which Performer is guaranteed thirteen (13) or fewer Programs, then for a period commencing six months from Performer's latest engagement in such contract year and continuing until Company's option for the next following contract year is exercised or expires, Performer shall be free to accept other commitments, subject to Company's right of preemption as specified in Section 24(b) of the SAG Agreement as provided in Exhibit A of the applicable AFTRA National Code of Fair Practice for (NETWORK) Television Broadcasting (hereinafter called the "AFTRA Code"). The foregoing shall be inoperative in the event that the compensation specified herein exceeds the minimum amounts specified in the applicable subsection of Section 24(b) of the SAG Agreement as provided in Exhibit A of the AFTRA Code.

If, upon the expiration of any contract year, Company shall not have completed production of all Programs intended for telecast during the then current telecast season, then Company shall have the right, at Company's election, to extend such contract year for such additional period as may be required to enable Company to complete production of such Programs.

If all the Programs to be made hereunder during any one contract year shall have been completed, Company may, at Company's option (exercised by designating to Contractor a date on which Performer is to report) commence in such contract year any Programs provided to be made in any later contract year, provided Company shall have exercised or concurrently therewith exercises Company's option for said additional contract year, with the same effect as if made in such later contract year.

Contractor agrees to keep Company's casting office advised of Performer's whereabouts at all times that Performer's services may be required hereunder in connection with the production of any of the Programs herein provided for, so that Performer may be reached by Company at all reasonable times.

Clause 2.

SERVICES: In the first contract year, Contractor agrees to lend to Company the services of Performer in portraying the role specified in Clause 1 hereinabove in the Series as an employee-for-hire as, when, where and in the manner specified and required by Company. Company guarantees Performer employment on a pay-or-play basis in not fewer than ten (10) Programs in the first contract year. Company shall have the right in Company's sole discretion to employ the services of Performer in up to all of the Programs produced.

Each Program produced hereunder which is greater than thirty (30) minutes in length shall be considered to be two (2) Programs for a sixty (60) minute Program; three (3) Programs for a ninety (90) minute Program, etc.

Performer's services for each contract year shall commence on a date (herein referred to as a "starting date") to be designated by Company and shall continue from and after the starting date designated by Company for such period as Company may require or desire Performer's services hereunder. Each such period shall hereinafter be referred to individually as a "production term." Performer agrees to report to the place designated by Company for commencement of Performer's services on such starting date and Performer will be ready, willing and able to commence the rendition of services at the time and place so designated. Performer shall render Performer's services solely and exclusively for Company during each production term at the times and places designated by Company for the performance of Performer's services hereunder and in the manner specified and required by Company. Performer will promptly and faithfully comply with all directions, requests, rules and regulations made by Company in connection with the services to be performed by Performer hereunder, and Performer will perform such services to the full limit of Performer's capabilities. Company's judgment shall be final and controlling on all matters respecting the rendition of Performer's services, including matters involving artistic taste and judgment.

Without limiting the generality of the foregoing and in furtherance of Company's rights pursuant to Clause 9 hereunder, Contractor agrees that Company shall have the right to make still photographs of Performer, posed with or without any such product or products, in which Performer appears, in or out of costume, either alone or with other members of the cast. Additionally, Contractor agrees, if required by Company, that Performer shall render Performer's services in connection with the making of trailers or transcriptions which may be used for the purpose of advertising and exploiting one (1) or more of the Programs made hereunder or a sponsor of the Programs or the sponsor's product, and in connection therewith, Performer will read lines as required by Company and in which certain products of such sponsor are mentioned. Such transcriptions may be used on the radio or otherwise.

Clause 3.

COMPENSATION: As compensation for Performer's services to be rendered hereunder in connection with the series for the first contract year and for the undertakings hereby made, upon condition that Contractor and Performer fully keep and perform all of the covenants, conditions and obligations on Contractor's and Performer's parts to be kept or performed hereunder and subject to Company's right of suspension, extension and/or termination as hereinafter set forth in the event of Performer's incapacity, default or the occurrence of an event of force majeure, Company agrees to pay Contractor for each Program for which Performer's services are completed hereunder during the first contract year, the sum of (AMOUNT OF PER PROGRAM COMPENSATION) which fee shall be inclusive of all services rendered by Performer hereunder. The fee payable to Contractor hereunder shall increase by (PERCENTAGE OF ANNUAL INCREASES) in each successive contract year of this agreement.

The compensation for each Program set forth above contemplates each Program to be thirty (30) minutes in length. In the event that any program is longer than sixty (60) minutes in length, the per-program compensation for that Program shall increase on a pro-rata basis, but in no event shall be less than minimum scale compensation for programs of such length pursuant to the AFTRA Code.

Upon condition that Contractor and Performer shall fully keep and perform all of the covenants, conditions and obligations on Contractor's and Performer's parts to be kept or performed during the term of this agreement, as the same may be extended, and Performer appears recognizably in any such Program as exhibited, Company agrees to pay to Contractor the minimum amounts required pursuant to the AFTRA Code when and if rerun, supplemental market, theatrical and foreign television (all television outside of the United States and Canada) exhibition rights are exercised by Company, to the extent that Contractor is not prepaid hereunder for the exercise of such right. Contractor shall not be entitled to any compensation for Programs in which Performer appears in the main title, but does not otherwise appear in the Program. If Company shall utilize any portion of any Program (or scenes photographed simultaneously with a separate camera behind the scenes) incorporating Performer's recognizable performance as a trailer to promote the Series for which the Program is intended or to promote any other Program of the Series, the Contractor shall be paid the minimum additional compensation prescribed by the applicable AFTRA Code, except that no such additional compensation shall be payable if Contractor's compensation hereunder is two thousand ($2,000) dollars or more per week. Contractor consents to Company's use of excerpts from the Programs without additional compensation pursuant to Paragraph 73(d)(1)(d) of the AFTRA Code, if applicable.

Company shall be entitled, to the extent permitted under the applicable AFTRA Code, to credit any compensation paid to Performer which is in excess of the applicable guild minimum against any other compensation otherwise due to Performer in connection with his services hereunder, including, but not limited to, rehearsal and extra rehearsal hours and days, overtime (including sixth and seventh day payments), meal penalties, rest period penalties, wardrobe and wardrobe maintenance fees, hazardous performance fees, cosmetic alteration fees, travel payments and promotional announcements. Performer further agrees that Company shall be entitled, to the extent permitted under the applicable AFTRA Code: (i) to credit any compensation paid to Performer which is in excess of two hundred (200%) percent of the applicable guild minimum, against compensation otherwise due to Performer for all domestic re-runs of each Program produced hereunder; and (ii) to credit any compensation paid to Performer which is in excess of the applicable guild minimum against compensation otherwise due to Performer for doubling, whether on or off camera. All of the aforementioned payments and all other Series payments, including without limitation domestic and foreign theatrical and supplemental market payments and residuals will be at the applicable guild minimum.

For the compensation set forth in this Clause 3, Company is entitled to average the workdays of Performer's services for each Program and to intermingle Performer's services in such Programs. For the compensation set forth herein, Company shall be entitled to the maximum wartime and overall production periods provided by the then current AFTRA Code within which to utilize the services of Performer in the production of each Program or each group of Programs. Notwithstanding the foregoing, where no maximum is set forth or where Company is permitted to bargain freely with regard to such time period, then for no additional compensation Company shall be entitled to as much time as may be needed by Company to complete each Program or group of Programs (up to the full period of each contract year). Where a maximum is set forth and Company is not permitted to bargain freely with regard to such time period, then if Performer's employment hereunder continues for an overall period in excess of the maximum period permitted by the AFTRA Code, or if within such overall period performer shall actually render Performer's services for a number of days in excess of the maximum number permitted by the AFTRA Code, Company shall pay Contractor additional compensation for each such additional day for which Performer is required to render services at Company's request at the rate required by the AFTRA Code.

For the purpose of fixing the time of payment of compensation, compensation accruing in any calendar week shall be due and payable during the following week on such day as may from time to time be established as payday by Company's rules and regulations. Company may deduct and withhold from Contractor's compensation all amounts to be deducted and withheld pursuant to any present or future statute, law, ordinance, regulation, order, writ, judgment or decree requiring the withholding of compensation.

It is acknowledged that from time to time, as a result of production exigencies or as a result of production extending into a holiday period, Company may deem it desirable to take a hiatus in a production term. Accordingly, if Company shall deem the same desirable, Contractor hereby agrees, subject to obtaining a waiver from the American Federation of Radio and Television Artists (hereinafter called "AFTRA"), if necessary, to permit Company to lay off production, and thereby to extend the particular production term accordingly without being obligated to pay Contractor any additional compensation for such extension.

Clause 4.

PENSION: Company shall pay directly to the AFTRA Health and Retirement Funds Contributions on Contractor's behalf based on the compensation paid by Company to Contractor with respect to Performer's services hereunder; provided, however, Company shall not be obligated to pay any such contributions which exceed the amount of such contributions which Company would have been obligated to make had Performer been Company's employee.

Clause 5.

EXCLUSIVE EMPLOYMENT: Contractor will notify all advertising agencies for whom Performer has made commercials of Performer's election not to grant exhibition renewal rights for such commercials (and Contractor agrees that upon Contractor's failure to so notify promptly such advertising agencies, Company may give such notice in Performer's name and on Performer's behalf as Performer's attorney-in-fact.

Contractor further warrants and represents that set forth below are the only commercials (a) in connection with which Performer has rendered services during the year immediately preceding the date hereof, and/or (b) wherein the right to continue telecast currently exists. Contractor acknowledges that such warranty and representation is a material inducement to Company to enter into this agreement.

Product and Advertising Agency	When Made	First Telecast	When Telecast Rights Expire

Commencing as of the date hereof and continuing thereafter until the completion of first-run telecasting of the Series (including repeat telecasting which are included in the first-run license of the Series) or sixteen (16) weeks after the expiration of the last contract year for which an option is exercised hereunder, whichever first occurs (hereinafter the "Exclusivity Period"), Performer shall be totally exclusive to Company in television and radio and shall not render any services of any nature whatsoever in television and radio to Contractor, to any third party or on Performer's own behalf except that during said Exclusivity Period other than during any production term, Performer may make not more than three (3) television guest appearances during each thirteen (13) week period of the term hereof; provided that Performer will not appear in a continuing, recurring or host role in such appearances and such appearances shall not be on a program which advertises any product, commodity or services competitive or antithetical to any product, commodity or service of any major sponsor of the Series, or which is intended (at the time Performer renders such services) to be initially telecast or broadcast nationally at the same time as the Series, at the same time as any other program sponsored by a major sponsor of the Series or during the premiere week of the Series. For the purposes of this agreement, a "major sponsor" shall be defined as a sponsor that orders an average of at least one (1) minute per Program per each thirteen week cycle of Programs. During the Exclusivity Period, Performer will not render any services (whether on-camera or off-camera, excluding non-identifiable (voice-overs) to Contractor, to any third party or on Performer's own behalf nor will Performer appear in or permit his likeness to be used in any advertisement, commercial, endorsement or testimonial of any nature whatsoever in any field or medium whatsoever, except as Company may designate pursuant to Clause 2 hereof. Once Performer's episodic compensation hereunder reaches or exceeds the applicable Guild "money-break," Performer may not appear in any commercial without Company's prior written approval in each instance, and subject to Performer's existing commercial commitments and renewals or extensions of the term(s) thereof, Company shall be entitled to major sponsor protection, including on-camera and off-camera (excluding non-identifiable voice-overs) commercial exclusivity. In addition, Performer will not render services in any capacity for Contractor, on Performer's own behalf or for any other person, firm or corporation during any production term, except as provided herein.

It is expressly agreed that the rendition of Performer's services in any field of entertainment or otherwise shall at all times be expressly subject and subordinate to all of the terms and conditions of this agreement and Contractor's obligations hereunder. Company shall be entitled to the maximum exclusivity to Performer's services permitted under the AFTRA Code.

Without limiting the generality of the foregoing, Company and Performer agree that Performer will not render services at any time during the term hereof or thereafter in the portrayal of any role which could be confused with, or which tends to burlesque, satirize or hold up to ridicule, the role or roles to be portrayed by Performer hereunder, whether in motion pictures or on television, radio, the stage, personal appearances or otherwise, and that during the term hereof, Performer will not render services in the portrayal of any role which is similar or unsympathetic to the role or roles to be portrayed by Performer hereunder. Contractor further agrees that Performer will not at any time during the term hereof or thereafter make any reference to the Series or to the characters portrayed therein (including the character portrayed by Performer) in any manner or medium whatsoever, including, but not limited to, radio, television, personal appearances or writings, or make any personal appearance on Performer's own account or for others under the name of Performer's role hereunder, or under any other name, title phrase or expression associated with the Series, and Performer will not, in connection with any such personal appearances, refer to or publicize Performer or allow Performer to be publicized as the name of Performer's role hereunder, or any other name, title phrase, or expression associated with the Series, except as specifically set forth herein.

Contractor agrees that the names and characters of the role or roles to be portrayed by Performer and the title of the Series belong exclusively to Company and Company's successors and assigns and that neither Contractor nor Performer has any right, title or interest therein or thereto and no right to make any use thereof without Company's authority or that of Company's successor or assigns and that Company reserves for Company and to Company's successors and assigns all commercial tie-ups and other rights of use of said title and names.

The exclusivity rights granted by Contractor to Company under this agreement shall also include, subject to the provisions of the applicable Guild agreement, any such additional exclusivity rights as may be required by the applicable television network.

Clause 6.

PROMOTIONAL SERVICES: Contractor and Performer agree that Performer will, upon Company's request, from time to time, render Performer's services and participate in the preparation and presentation of non-commercial announcements (including, without limitation, billboards, openings, closings, lead-ins, lead-outs, bridging lines, signatures and trailers) in connection with any one or more of the Programs, whether or not any of the foregoing is integrated in any of the Programs. No additional compensation shall be payable to Contractor for any of the foregoing. Contractor agrees that Performer will, upon Company's request, from time to time, render services and participate in the preparation and presentation of Series commercials, for which Company agrees that Contractor shall be paid at the minimum rate set forth in the provisions of the AFTRA Code for filmed commercials.

Upon Company's request, during each contract year Performer shall make a reasonable number of non-performing personal appearances before non-paying audiences to promote the Series (which appearances shall include appearances before sales or similar non-public business meetings of a sponsor and/or licensee of the Series). Without limiting the foregoing, Performer also agrees to: (a) participate in publicity-related events and activities for the life of the Series, during the term hereof (including without limitation, broadcast interviews on [LIST POPULAR NETWORK AND SYNDICATED INTERVIEW SHOWS (E.G., GOOD MORNING AMERICA)]); (b) attend the annual NAPE convention if Company requests; (c) make reasonable efforts to support Company's marketing effort when the Series is launched in syndication provided Artist has been a regular Series performer during the life of the Series; and (d) grant a reasonable number of print interviews (whether on the telephone or in person). Such appearances shall be made as, where and when designated by Company, for which Performer shall not be entitled to any additional compensation, except insofar as provided in Clause 2 hereof.

Without limiting Company's rights pursuant to this Clause 6, during the period preceding the initial season telecast of the Series, Contractor further agrees, if requested by Company, that Performer shall make radio and television appearances designated by Company to publicize the Programs and Performer's services in connection therewith.

Clause 7.

ADDITIONAL SERVICES: Performer will render such additional services as may be required by Company for or in connection with added scenes, changes, transparencies, process or trick shots, trailer, foreign versions or additional sound records for or any retakes of any portion of the Programs without the payment of additional compensation to Contractor except as otherwise required under the AFTRA Code. Contractor agrees that Performer will render such services as, when and where designated by Company, subject to Performer's availability during periods other than production terms.

Contractor agrees, if and when requested by Company, that Performer shall report within one (1) week prior to the starting date of the production term to any place Company may designate for wardrobe fittings, publicity interviews, publicity photography sittings, preliminary discussions of roles, making tests, auditions and stills in connection with such Programs without the payment of additional compensation to Contractor. Contractor agrees that Performer will render such services as, when and where designated by Company, subject to Performer's availability.

Clause 8.

GRANT OF RIGHTS: Contractor expressly grants to Company the right to photograph and otherwise reproduce any or all of Performer's acts, poses, plays and appearances of any and all kinds made or done by Performer in, or in connection with, the Programs and the Series and to record Performer's voice and sound effects produced by Performer and to reproduce and transmit the same either separately or in conjunction with such acts, plays, poses and appearances as Company may desire, without any restrictions or limitations of any nature. Contractor further gives and grants perpetually to Company, solely and exclusively, all rights of any kind or character whatsoever (whether or not such rights are now known) in and to such reproductions and recordations and each and all of them, Performer's services and performances pursuant to this agreement and the results and proceeds thereof. All services rendered by Performer hereunder shall be considered "works made for hire." The rights herein granted to Company shall include, without limitation, the complete, unencumbered, exclusive and perpetual rights, throughout the world, to exhibit, record, reproduce, broadcast, transmit, publish, sell, distribute, perform and use for any purpose, in any manner and by any means, whether or not now known, invented, used or contemplated (specifically including, but not limited to, motion pictures, radio, television, televised motion pictures, printing and/or whole or partial recordation of any of the foregoing, or any other similar or dissimilar means and/or manner) all or any part of the matters and things referred to in this clause. Company shall have the right, during the term hereof and thereafter, to make and to use and to permit others to make and use facsimiles of Performer portraying Performer's role herein and all of Performer's acts, poses, plays, vocal expressions, physical appearances and likenesses relating thereto in animated motion pictures without any restrictions or limitations of any nature. Also granted herein is the perpetual and unlimited right to use and to permit others to use Performer's name, voice, actual or simulated likeness, photograph, sobriquet, biography, personal characteristics, signature and other personal identification (herein collectively referred to as the Performer's "likeness") in connection with advertising and exploiting Performer's services hereunder, the Series or any Program, or any of the rights granted to Company hereunder by radio, television, publication and all other similar or dissimilar mediums, whether or not now known. Company shall have the right to "double" or "dub" Performer's act, poses, plays, and appearances and, as well, Performer's voice and other sound effects to be produced by Performer to such extent as may be desired by Company; such doubling or dubbing of Performer's voice to be in English and/or in any other language or languages designated or desired by Company. Company shall have the right to use and permit others to use Performer's likeness in such commercial advertising and/or publicity as Company or they shall desire in any medium in connection with the full utilization and exploitation of any and all rights granted hereunder and in connection with the stations and networks over which the Series or any Program produced hereunder may be telecast. It is understood that Company shall have the right, but not the obligation, to exhibit at any time, whether prior to, concurrently or following the exhibition thereof on television, one or more Programs in all media in perpetuity throughout the universe.

Clause 9.

NAME AND LIKENESS: Contractor hereby grants to Company the following rights: (a) the exclusive, irrevocable and perpetual right throughout the universe to use and license and to grant others the right to use and license Performer's likeness for all merchandising, endorsements, commercial or manufacturing tie-ups and other commercial exploitations of any nature whatsoever in connection with the Series, and Program and/or the character(s) portrayed by Performer hereunder; and (b) the irrevocable right throughout the universe, exclusively during the Exclusivity Period and non-exclusivity for a period of one (1) year following the Exclusivity Period, to use and license and to grant others the right to use and license Performer's likeness for all merchandising, endorsements, commercial or manufacturing tie-ups and other commercial exploitation of any nature whatsoever whether or not related to the Series, and Program and any character(s) portrayed Performer hereunder. All rights granted pursuant to this clause are hereafter referred to collectively as the "merchandising rights." Notwithstanding the foregoing, Company shall not have the right to use and authorize others to use Performer's likeness under this Clause 9 as a direct endorsement of any product or service without first obtaining Contractor's or Performer's written approval for each such use. For purposes of this agreement, the term "merchandising" shall include without limitation the use of Performer's likeness on or in publications of every kind and nature, animated television series and serials, animated motion pictures and other animations, cartoons, comic strips, clothing, toys, novelties, games and household goods, as well as in connection with or on materials which package or enclose any such items. In no event shall a list of cast credits be considered a merchandising use.

Neither the termination, suspension nor expiration of this agreement for any reason prior to the expiration of any license or agreement whereby Company authorizes others to use Performer's likeness as aforesaid shall affect the validity of any such license or agreement or Company's right to enter into further licenses or agreements, and all such licenses or agreements shall remain in full force and effect pursuant to their respective terms.

Contractor hereby warrants and represents that neither Contractor nor Performer has heretofore entered into any merchandising agreement, or any commercial or manufacturing tie-up agreement, or any other agreement or commitment pertaining to the subject matter of this Clause 9, whereby Performer's likeness may be used during the Exclusivity Period or the one (1) year period thereafter, and Contractor further agrees that neither Contractor nor Performer will, following the date hereof and prior to expiration of the Exclusivity Period, enter into any such agreement or commitment except as required by Company hereunder.

Upon condition that Contractor and Performer shall fully keep and perform all of the covenants, conditions and obligations to be kept or performed hereunder, Contractor shall be entitled to a portion of the net proceeds derived from the exercise of merchandising rights in connection with which Performer's likeness is used. Contractor's share of such monies shall be determined and shall be paid to Contractor as more particularly outlined below.

All receipts which Company may receive in the exercise of such merchandising rights are hereinafter referred to as the "gross receipts" of the merchandising rights. With respect to the gross receipts from the exercise of the merchandising rights derived by Company or Company's subsidiaries, Company shall deduct and retain fifty percent (50%) thereof as and for Company's services in exercising and servicing such accounts. Company shall further deduct and retain all direct costs of licensing, which may include, among other things, agents' commissions, trademark and copyright fees, legal enforcement fees and costs of direct mail advertising.

All gross receipts which Company may receive in the exercise of the merchandising rights after deducting Company's servicing fees and all direct costs of licensing in connection therewith are hereafter referred to as the "net proceeds" of the merchandising rights. The net proceeds from the merchandising rights in which Contractor shall be entitled to participate shall be divided as follows:

(i) Five percent (5%) thereof shall be paid to Contractor as and for Contractor's absolute property.

(ii) The balance thereof shall be retained by Company as and for Company's absolute property.

Provided, however, notwithstanding anything to the contrary contained in the foregoing, that if in connection with any item or thing from the exercise of the merchandising rights the likeness of one or more of the other continuing members of the cast of the Series is used in addition to Performer's own, then Contractor's share of the net proceeds from such item or thing shall be reduced on a pro rata basis to not less than two and one-half percent (2-1/2%) of said net proceeds taking into account the number of such other continuing members of the cast whose likenesses are used in connection therewith.

The net proceeds from the merchandising rights in which Contractor shall be entitled to participate shall be those involving the use of Performer's likeness. Contractor shall not be entitled to any share of the net proceeds from the exploitation of the merchandising rights which include only the name of the character portrayed by Performer or a fictional likeness of the character played by Performer (i.e., one in which Performer's likeness is not involved). Notwithstanding anything to the contrary herein, Contractor and Performer will also not be entitled to participate in the net proceeds, if any, derived by Company from either the publication and exploitation of music and/or recordings written for and/or performed in the Series or any Programs whether or not any such exploitation involves the use of Performer's likeness, or from the publication or exploitation of any literary materials derived from or related to the Series or any Program, in which literary materials the Performer's likeness is not the primary subject matter. It is also recognized that Company may exploit the merchandising rights where no revenue is derived.

Contractor shall continue to participate in the net proceeds from the exercise of merchandising rights involving the use of Performer's likeness in accordance with the terms of this clause, notwithstanding the expiration or termination of this agreement.

Distribution of net proceeds shall be made at such times and in such manner as are in accordance with Company's then usual and customary accounting and business practice. Contractor shall have no direct right or claim in or to the actual gross or net proceeds derived from the exercise of said merchandising rights. However, Contractor shall be entitled to be paid sums equivalent to Contractor's percentage participation as set forth above.

Clause 10.

REMEDIES: The remedies herein provided shall be deemed cumulative and the exercise of one shall not preclude the exercise of any other remedy for the same event of disability, force majeure or default; nor shall the specification of remedies herein exclude any rights or remedies at law, or in equity, which may be available, including any rights to damages or injunctive relief.

Contractor specifically agrees that Company may recover by appropriate action, or may withhold from any compensation payable to Contractor hereunder, the amount of the actual damage caused the Company by any failure, refusal or neglect of Performer or Contractor to keep and perform Performer's agreements and warranties herein contained.

Clause 11.

WARDROBE: Contractor agrees to furnish all modern wardrobe and wearing apparel reasonably required for Performer's portrayal of said role; provided, however, should so-called "character" or "period" costumes be required, Company shall supply the same. Any costume furnished by Company shall remain Company's sole property. During the time that Performer is rendering acting services in connection with the Series, but not during hiatus periods, Company shall provide Performer with a dressing facility for Performer's exclusive use.

Clause 12.

TRAVELING EXPENSES: In the event that Performer's services are required in any place other than the City of Los Angeles or its environs, Company agrees to pay Contractor for Performer's first-class (if available) transportation to and from any such other place and reasonable living expenses while Performer is away from the City of Los Angeles as aforesaid. Company shall, however, have no obligation to furnish or reimburse Contractor for the cost of Performer's return transportation to Los Angeles if Performer renders services for any other person, firm or corporation in the entertainment industry prior to returning to Los Angeles.

Clause 13.

CANCELLATION: In the event the Series is canceled by the sponsor or the network, Contractor shall be released from any and all options for Performer's services in the series except where Company exercises its right pursuant to Section 24(c) of the SAG Agreement as provided in exhibit A of the AFTRA Code.

(a) If Company exercises such option for Performer's services pursuant to Section 24(c) of the SAG Agreement as provided in Exhibit A of the AFTRA Code prior to the expiration of the current contract year, then the following contract year will commence on the expiration of the current contract year. If

Company exercises such option after the expiration of the current contract year, then the commencement date for such following contract year shall be within sixty (60) days after exercise of such option, on a date to be designated by Company.

(b) During such additional option periods specified in Section 24(c) of the SAG Agreement as provided in Exhibit A of the AFTRA Code, Performer will comply with all of the provisions of Clause 5 of this agreement with respect to the rendition of Performer's services for others or on Performer's own behalf.

Clause 14.

PAY OR PLAY: Company does not agree to (and Contractor agrees that Company shall have no obligation to) produce, complete, release, distribute, advertise or exploit the Series or any Program or to engage Performer in connection therewith; and Contractor and Performer release Company from any liability for any loss or damage Contractor and Performer may suffer by reason of Company's failure to produce, complete, release, distribute, advertise or exploit any of such Programs or to engage Performer in connection therewith; but nothing in this clause shall be deemed to relieve Company of its obligation to pay Contractor the minimum compensation prescribed for the first contract year or for any contract year for which Company has exercised an option, unless Company's obligation in connection therewith is canceled pursuant to any of the provisions of this agreement.

Clause 15.

GUILD MEMBERSHIP: Contractor warrants and represents to Company and agrees that during the entire term of this agreement (to the extent that and during such period or periods as it may be lawful for Company to require Contractor to do so) Performer will remain, or become and remain, a member in good standing of the properly designated labor organization or organizations (as defined and determined under the applicable law) representing persons performing services of the type and character that are required to be performed by Peformer hereunder.

Clause 16.

MORALS: Contractor agrees that Performer has acted and will act with due regard to public conventions and morals and has not done and will not do anything which will degrade Performer in society or bring Performer into public disrepute, contempt, scorn or ridicule or that will shock, offend or insult the community, public morals or decency, or prejudice Company. In the event of any breach of the terms of this clause, Company may terminate this agreement by written notice to Contractor and thereupon be released of all further obligations hereunder; and Company may (whether or not the term of this agreement has expired or been terminated) refrain from complying with any of the credit provisions hereof. Such right of termination may be exercised by Company no later than whichever of the following dates last occurs: (a) the date which is ninety (90) days from and after the date Company is informed of the occurrence of any act constituting such breach; or (b) seven (7) days after the last date on which any sponsor, network, licensee or distributor of any of the programs produced, or to be produced hereunder, may require Company to exercise the right of termination referred to in this Clause.

Clause 17.

WARRANTIES: Contractor warrants that Contractor is free to execute this agreement and that Contractor has made no agreements or commitments which will prevent or interfere with the performance of Contractor's obligations hereunder.

Contractor is a party to an employment agreement with Performer which grants to Contractor the exclusive right to Performer's services. Contractor hereby further warrants as follows:

(a)   Contractor is a corporation duly organized under the laws of the State of California.

(b)   Contractor presently and exclusively employs and is solely entitled to the services of performer which are or will be required to be performed hereunder and that Contractor controls all rights in the results and proceeds of such services which are or may be loaned to Company hereunder.

(c)   The rights granted to Contractor in Contractor's agreement with Performer are at least as extensive as those contained in this agreement and that the term of said Contractor's agreement shall continue for at least as long as the maximum period contemplated hereunder.

(d)   Contractor has the full right, power and authority to enter into this agreement.

(e)   Contractor will not amend, modify or terminate Contractor's agreement with performer at any time hereafter in such a way as to affect the rights granted to Company hereunder without obtaining Company's prior written consent.

(f)   If Company exercises Company's option to require Contractor to lend the services of Performer to Company in connection with the Series as contemplated in Clause 1 hereof, the minimum guaranteed compensation payable to Performer by Contractor shall be in excess of such amount that would preserve to Contractor and/or Company all of their rights and remedies (including, without limitation, the right to injunctive relief) against Performer under this agreement pursuant to all applicable federal, state and local laws, statutes, regulations and ordinances.

Clause 18.

UNIQUE SERVICES: It is agreed that the services to be rendered by Performer under the terms hereof and the rights and privileges granted to Company by Contractor under the terms hereof are of a special, unique, unusual, extraordinary and intellectual character involving skill of the highest order which gives them a peculiar value, the loss of which cannot be reasonably or adequately compensated by damages in an action at law, and that breach by Contractor or Performer of any of the provisions contained in this agreement will cause Company irreparable injury and damage. Contractor and Performer hereby expressly agree that Company shall be entitled to injunctive relief and other equitable relief to prevent and/or cure any breach or threatened breach of this agreement by Contractor or Performer.

Clause 19.

HAZARDOUS ACTIVITIES: Contractor agrees that Performer will not, prior to the expiration of all of Company's rights to the further use of Performer's services hereunder, engage in hazardous activities or knowingly be subjected to unusual risks. Without limiting the foregoing Performer will not travel in an airplane or any other vehicle which travels in the air other than as a passenger on a recognized airline, but on Company's request by Performer shall travel on recognized airlines whenever required by Company in connection with the production of the Programs. In the event of a breach of the terms of this clause, Company may terminate this agreement.

Clause 20.

POWER OF ATTORNEY: Contractor authorizes Company to institute, in Contractor's name, in Performer's name or otherwise, any legal proceedings to restrain any person, firm or corporation from utilizing, exploiting and/or distributing Performer's likeness and or results or proceeds of Performer's services hereunder for advertising or any other purposes prohibited by the terms hereof.

Clause 21.

EXPIRATION OF AGREEMENT: Neither the expiration of this agreement nor any other termination of this agreement shall diminish, impair or otherwise affect the ownership by Company of the results and proceeds of Performer's services hereunder, any of the rights or privileges of Company hereunder or any warranty or undertaking on the part of Contractor or Performer in connection with such results and proceeds.

Clause 22.

INSURANCE: In the event that Company desires at any time or from time to time to apply in Company's name or otherwise, but at Company's own expense, for health, life, accident or other insurance covering Performer, Contractor agrees that Company may do so and may take out such insurance of any sum which Company may deem necessary to protect Company's interests hereunder. Contractor shall have no right, title or interest in or to such insurance, but Performer agrees nevertheless to assist Company in procuring the same by submitting from time to time at Company's discretion to the usual and customary medical, physical and other examinations and by signing such applications, statements and other instruments in writing as may be reasonably required by any insurer. Performer's failure or inability to qualify for such insurance at customary rates without any exclusions or limitation on the part of the insurer shall be deemed to constitute an event of default hereunder. Contractor hereby warrants and represents that Performer is in sound physical and mental condition and is capable of performing Performer's services in accordance with the requirements of this agreement.

Clause 23.

ASSIGNMENT: Contractor hereby gives and grants to Company the right to assign this agreement without limitation to any person, firm or corporation and this agreement shall inure to the benefit of Company's successors and assigns and the successors and assigns of any such assigns. Company may assign or license any one or more of all the Programs and all or any part of Company's rights with respect to such Programs and the advertising and exploitation thereof and all or any part of the property granted to Company under this agreement or all or any part of Company's rights with respect thereto to any person, firm or corporation and this agreement shall inure to the benefit of all such assignees or their respective successors and assigns, but no such assignment shall relieve Company of its obligations hereunder.

Clause 24.

NOTICES: All notices which Company is required or may desire to serve upon Contractor under or in connection with this agreement shall be given by addressing the same to Contractor in care of [ADDRESS OF CONTRACTOR] or such other address of which Contractor from time to time gives Company written notice, and by depositing the same so addressed, postage prepaid, in the United States mail, by delivering the same, toll prepaid, to a telegraph or cable company, by delivering the same personally to Contractor or Performer or to any agent so named by Contractor or Performer or by delivering the same to Contractor or Performer by telecopier.

All notices which Contractor is or may desire to give to Company under or in connection with this agreement shall be given by addressing the same to

Company at [ADDRESS OF COMPANY], or such other address of which Company from time to time may give Contractor written notice, and by depositing the same so addressed postage prepaid, in the United States mail, by delivering the same, toll prepaid, to a telegraph or cable company or by delivering the same to Company by telecopier.

Any notice mailed, telegraphed, cabled or telecopied as aforesaid shall be deemed to have been given on the date of mailing or telecopying or date of delivery to the telegraph or cable company.

Clause 25.

CONFLICTING LAW: Nothing contained in this agreement shall be construed so as to require the commission of any act contrary to law and wherever there is any conflict between any provisions of this agreement and any material statute, law, ordinance, order or regulation contrary to which Contractor and Company have no legal right to contract, the latter shall prevail; but in such event, any provision of this agreement so affected shall be curtailed and limited only to the extent necessary to remove such conflict; and as so modified, this agreement shall continue in full force and effect.

Nothing in this agreement shall require Company to pay any compensation which violates any present or future law or any governmental or executive order or regulation, and if there shall exist any conflict between the payment of any compensation as provided for hereunder and any such present or future law or any governmental or executive order or regulation, the latter shall prevail; and a reduction in or a failure to increase any such compensation pursuant to any such present or future law or governmental or executive order or regulation shall be deemed to constitute full performance by Company during such period.

Clause 26.

IMMIGRATION ACT: In accordance with the Immigration Reform Act of 1986 and the regulations adopted thereunder, obligations of Company under this agreement are subject to and conditioned upon Performer verifying and delivering to Company, within three (3) business days of Performer's first date of employment, the Form I-9 prescribed by the Immigration and Naturalization Service and to present to the employee of Company designated therefor the original documentation required under the regulations to establish (i) the identity of Performer and (ii) that Performer is lawfully authorized to work in the United States. If Performer is unable to provide the documents required within the aforesaid period, Performer must (a) present to such designated employee within three (3) business days a receipt for the application for the documents prescribed and (b) the original documents required within twenty-one (21) days of Performer's first date of employment. If Performer fails to verify and deliver the Form I-9 and present the required original documents within the stated time period,

Company shall have the right, by notice to such effect given to Performer, to terminate this agreement and thereupon Performer's employment hereunder shall cease and terminate and neither party shall have any right, duty or obligation to the other under this agreement except as shall have accrued prior to the effective date of termination.

Contractor agrees to take all steps which may be required on Performer's part to secure any necessary permission to enter or remain and work in any country designated by Company for the rendition of Performer's services hereunder. Performer shall promptly at the request of Company make application for passports, visas, work permits, membership in labor organizations or other matters which the Company may designate in connection with the services required of Performer hereunder. Company agrees to furnish the required application fees involved in connection with the application for or securing of any of the foregoing; provided that Company shall not be required to pay the Performer's initiation fee or membership dues in connection with any labor organization in the United States or the country in which Performer resides. If Performer is unable to obtain such passports, visas, work permits, membership in any labor organization or any other license or permit which may be necessary to enable Performer to render such services in the country or countries in which the Company requires the rendition thereof, Company shall have the right to terminate this agreement and be relieved of all liability hereunder except compensation, if any, accrued at the date of termination.

Clause 27.

APPLICABLE UNION AGREEMENTS: In the event any provision hereof shall be in violation of the AFTRA Code or any written agreement between Company or Company's distributor and AFTRA, Contractor agrees to join with Company in seeking a waiver from AFTRA to effectuate the terms hereof. Nothing contained in this agreement shall be construed to require the violation of the AFTRA Code or any other written agreement between Company or Company's distributor and AFTRA which may from time to time be in effect and by its terms controlling with respect to this agreement; and wherever there is any conflict between the provisions of this agreement and such AFTRA Code, and if AFTRA shall fail to grant a waiver, the latter shall prevail, but in such event the provisions of this agreement shall be curtailed or limited only to the extent necessary to permit compliance with the AFTRA Code. Except where the terms herein contained shall be more favorable to Contractor, Company shall be entitled to receive the maximum benefits of all of the terms and conditions provided for in the AFTRA Code. In the event that Company elects to produce the Series in a manner where the SAG Agreement would apply, then said SAG Agreement shall govern this agreement in lieu of the AFTRA Code and Company shall be entitled to the maximum rights permitted under the SAG Agreement. In this event, all references herein to the AFTRA Code shall be deemed to refer to the applicable provisions of the SAG Agreement and the SAG minimums where applicable shall be substituted for the AFTRA minimums.

Clause 28.

CREDIT OBLIGATION: On the condition that Contractor and Performer shall keep and perform all of the covenants and agreements to be kept or performed pursuant to this agreement, Company agrees to accord Performer in each public exhibition of each such Program credit in either the opening or closing credits, as Company shall elect in its sole discretion, or not less than a shared card. The size, nature and other characteristics of said credit shall be within Company's sole discretion. If a Program for which Performer is entitled to be accorded credit is combined with one or more other productions to make a single program or is substantially cut or expanded, or exhibited in a medium other than free television, Company may make such changes in Performer's credit (including the size, style and placement thereof) as Company deems justified by the circumstances.

The provisions of this clause shall not apply to group, list, teaser, trailer or other advertising, publicity or exploitation on the air, or to other advertising and publicity not relating primarily to one of the Programs.

No casual or inadvertent failure on Company's part to accord Performer the credit specified herein shall be deemed a breach of this agreement. A breach of any of the provisions of this agreement by any third party shall not constitute a default hereunder. The rights and remedies of Contractor and Performer in the event of a breach of this clause by Company shall be limited to Contractor's rights, if any, to recover damages at law, and in no event shall Contractor or Performer be entitled by reason of any such breach to terminate this agreement or to enjoin or restrain the distribution or exhibition of any programs made hereunder.

Clause 29.

COMMUNICATIONS ACT: Contractor and Performer understand that pursuant to the provisions of the Federal Communications Act, as amended, it is a criminal offense, unless disclosure thereof is made to Company or to the network prior to broadcast, to:

(a) Give or agree to give any member of the production staff, anyone associated in any manner with the Series, or any representative of the network any portion of Contractor's compensation or anything else of value for arranging Performer's employment hereunder.

(b) Accept or agree to accept anything of value, other than Contractor's regular compensation, for services on the Series to promote any product, service or venture on the air or use any prepared material containing such a promotion where Contractor knows the writer received consideration for it.

In addition, Contractor and Performer acknowledge that Contractor and Performer are aware that is Company's policy not to permit the acceptance of payments of any such consideration and that any such acceptance of payment would be a breach of this agreement and cause for Performer's immediate dismissal. In accordance therewith, but not as a limitation thereon, Contractor and Performer hereby expressly represent that Contractor and Performer have not done so and agree not to either accept, pay or agree to accept or pay any such consideration.

Clause 30.

EMPLOYMENT RELATIONSHIP: Contractor hereby agrees and acknowledges that:

(a) Notwithstanding that Contractor is furnishing Performer's services to Company hereunder (as distinguished from the employment of Performer by Company), for the purposes of any applicable Workers' Compensation statute, an employment relationship exists between Company and Performer, Company being Performer's special employer hereunder and Contractor being Performer's general employer (as the terms "special employer" and "general employer" are understood for purposes of the Workers' Compensation statutes).

(b) As between Contractor and Company, Company shall have the exclusive right to direct and control the performance of Performer's services hereunder, including without limitation, the manner and means by which Performer will perform such services.

(c) For purposes of any applicable Workers' Compensation statute, Company is the special employer of each other person (hereinafter "other special employee") whose services are furnished to Company by any corporation or other entity under an agreement pursuant to which Company has the right to direct and control the performance of such other special employee's services.

(d) For purposes of determining the rights and remedies, if any, of Contractor, Performer or Performer's heirs, executors, administrators, successors and assigns, by reason of any injury or illness which falls within the purview of a Workers' Compensation statute and which is sustained by Performer during the period of Performer's services hereunder and/or disability or death by Performer as a result of such an injury or illness, the following shall apply:

(i) the rights and remedies, if any, of Performer or Performer's heirs, executors, administrators, successors and assigns against Company and Company's agents and employees (including, without limitation, any other special employee) by reason of such injury, illness, disability or death shall be governed by and limited to those provided under such Workers' Compensation statute.

(ii) neither Company, nor Company's agents or employees shall have any obligation or liability to Contractor by reason of any such injury, illness, disability or death.

(iii) neither Contractor nor Performer nor any of Performer's heirs, executors, administrators, successors or assigns, shall assert any claim or bring any action by reason of such injury, illness disability or death against any corporation or other entity which furnishes to Company the services of any other special employee.

(iv) Contractor shall indemnify, defend (with counsel acceptable to Company) and hold Company and Company's agents and employees harmless from any loss, cost, liability or expense arising from any claim asserted or action brought by Performer or any other party by reason of any such injury, illness, disability or death other than any claim or action permitted under such Workers' Compensation statute.

(e) If the applicability of any Workers' Compensation statute to the engagement of Performer's services hereunder is dependent upon (or may be affected by) an election on the part of Contractor, Performer or the Company, such election is hereby made.

Clause 31.

NO PUBLICITY WITHOUT WRITTEN CONSENT: Any publicity, paid advertisements, press notices or other information (other than incidental, nonderogatory mention) with respect to this agreement, the Series, the Programs and any of the terms contained herein shall be under the sole control of Company. Therefore, Performer and Contractor shall not consent to and/or authorize any person or entity to release such information without the express prior written approval of Company.

Company shall have the right to open all non-personal mail directed to Performer and to answer such mail, and Company may include in such replies photographs of Performers and facsimiles of Performer's signature and/or signatures purporting to be Performer's signature.

Clause 32.

INDEMNIFICATION: Contractor and Performer agree to indemnify and otherwise hold Company free and harmless from and against any and all claims, demands and expenses (including reasonable attorneys' fees) arising out of or resulting from any breach by either or both of them of the terms, covenants and conditions contained in this agreement.

Clause 33.

DISABILITY OF PERFORMER: An event of "disability" shall be deemed to exist hereunder if Performer becomes incapacitated or prevented from fully performing hereunder or prevented from fully complying with Performer's obligations hereunder by reason of Performer's illness, mental or physical, or any facial, physical or other impairment of Performer's likeness or voice. Any occurrence of a disability as a result of a Performer's use of alcohol, drugs or controlled substances shall be deemed an event of default pursuant to Clause 34 below. If Company alleges that Performer is incapacitated by illness or other disability or by a default of the kind described in the preceding sentence, then Company may, at Company's expense require Performer to submit to a medical examination to be conducted by such physician(s) as may be designated by Company. Performer may, at Performer's own expense, cause Performer's own physician to be present at such examination.

Clause 34.

DEFAULT: An event of "default" shall be deemed to exist hereunder if Performer at any time breaches any provision of this agreement, or if Performer at any time fails, refuses or neglects (other than by reason of disability) or intends to fail, refuse or neglect to report or render services to the full limit of Performer's ability as, when and where required hereunder or to comply fully with Performer's obligations hereunder as required by Company.

Clause 35.

FORCE MAJEURE: An event of "force majeure" shall be deemed to exist hereunder, if, with respect to any Programs in the Series, Company's production operations and/or any normal broadcasting operations are materially impaired, hampered, interrupted, prevented, suspended, postponed or discontinued by reason of any declared or undeclared war, act of public enemy, riot, epidemic, fire, casualty, accident, labor controversy, governmental order or regulation, judicial order or decree, act of God, failure of the producer, director or any other key production personnel or any main character in the cast to perform for any reason, in obtaining facilities, materials and personnel which makes production in accordance with customary or established schedules and practices impracticable, or any other occurrence beyond Company's control.

Clause 36.

RIGHT TO SUSPENSION: If any even of disability, default or force majeure occurs at any time during the term of this agreement, then notwithstanding anything contrary contained in this agreement, Performer's employment pursuant hereto shall be automatically suspended. Unless expressly provided to the contrary in any collective bargaining agreement to which Company is a signatory, no compensation shall accrue or be payable to Performer hereunder during any such period of suspension, except suspension for disability or force majeure shall not prohibit Performer from receiving compensation for Programs in the Series for which Performer has rendered all services required of Performer herein. Any suspension hereunder shall continue until the cause thereof has ceased to exist or until the expiration of the maximum period which Company is permitted to suspend Performer's services pursuant to an applicable collective bargaining agreement to which Company is a signatory, whichever first occurs. With respect to disability or default such suspension shall continue until Performer shall have reported to Producer ready, willing and able to perform his obligations hereunder. Performer shall resume rendering services hereunder on the earliest date that Company shall have prepared for the resumption of Performer's services and shall have notified Performer to appear. During any period of suspension for disability or default, Performer may not render services for any other party or on Performer's own behalf. If suspension is imposed for reasons of force majeure, Performer may render services for others or on his own behalf subject to the terms hereof regarding exclusivity and provided that Performer will be able to immediately resume services hereunder upon receipt of notice from Company. Company shall have the right, at its election, by notice given to Performer at any time during the term of this agreement, to extend this agreement (including, without limitation, the latest date for the exercise of any option or any other right hereunder) by a period of time equal to or less then the aggregate period(s) of suspension hereunder.

Clause 37.

<u>TERMINATION</u>: If any default occurs hereunder, Company shall have the right, at Company's election, to terminate this agreement either during the continuance of such default or within a reasonable time thereafter. In the event of Performer's disability hereunder, Company shall have the right, at Company's election, to terminate this agreement at any time after the continuance of such disability for more than seven (7) consecutive days or an aggregate of fourteen (14) days or more during the period of Performer's employment during any year of the term hereof. If any event of force majeure occurs hereunder, Company shall have the right, at its election, to terminate this agreement at any time after the continuance of such force majeure for a period or aggregate of periods in excess of four (4) weeks during the period of Performer's employment in any year of the term hereof.

If any event of force majeure occurs hereunder, Performer shall have the right, at Performer's election, to terminate this agreement at any time after the continuance of a suspension resulting from an event of force majeure for a period in excess of five (5) consecutive weeks during the period of Performer's employment in any year of the term hereof, provided, however, that any such termination by Performer shall not become effective and this agreement shall continue in full force and effect if Company, within one (1) week of receipt of notice of such termination, lifts the suspension caused by such event of force majeure, and in such event Company shall not thereafter have the right to suspend Performer due to a continuance of the same event of force majeure. Unless expressly provided to the contrary in any collective bargaining agreement to which Company is a signatory, in the event of any termination of this agreement, Company shall be relieved of any and all further obligations to Performer hereunder except that termination shall not relieve Company of its obligations hereunder to Performer with respect to completed Programs of the Series for which Performer has rendered all required services prior to termination.

Clause 38.

ADDITIONAL DOCUMENTS: Contractor and Performer agree to execute and deliver to Company any and all documents which Company shall deem desirable or necessary to effectuate the purposes of this agreement. In the event that Contractor and/or Performer fail or refuse to so execute or deliver, or cause to be executed and delivered, any assignment or other instrument herein provided for, then Contractor and Performer hereby nominate, constitute and appoint Company, and Company shall therefore be deemed to be, Contractor's and/or Performer's true and lawful attorney-in-fact, irrevocably, to execute and deliver all of such documents, instruments and assignments in Contractor's and/or Performer's name and on Contractor's and/or Performer's behalf.

Clause 39.

APPLICABLE LAW: This agreement shall be construed and enforced in accordance with the law of the State of California applicable to contracts negotiated, executed and fully performed within the State of California as to all matters governed by the law of the State of California and shall be construed and enforced in accordance with the federal law of the United States as to all other matters.

As further consideration for Company's execution of this agreement and for good and valuable consideration, Contractor and Performer hereby agree that all actions or proceedings arising directly or indirectly from this agreement shall be litigated only in courts having situs within the State of California and Contractor and Performer hereby consent to the jurisdiction of any local, state or federal court within the State of California. In any action or proceeding commenced in any court in the State of California for the purpose of enforcing this agreement or any right granted herein or growing out hereof, or any order or decree predicated hereon, any summons, order to show cause, writ, judgment, decree, or other process may be delivered to Performer personally without the State of California and when so delivered Contractor and Performer shall be subject to the jurisdiction of such court and amenable to the process so delivered as though the same had been served within the State of California, but outside the county in which such action or proceeding is pending.

Clause 40.

ENTIRE AGREEMENT: This agreement includes the entire understanding between Contractor and Company, and all prior agreements have been merged herein. No representation or warranties have been made other than those expressly provided for herein. This agreement may not be altered, modified or changed in any way except by an instrument in writing signed by the parties.

Clause 41.

WAIVER: No waiver by any party hereto of any breach of any covenants or provisions of this agreement shall be deemed to be a waiver of any preceding or succeeding breach of the same or any other covenant or provision.

Clause 42.

NO PARTNERSHIP BETWEEN PARTIES: Nothing contained in this agreement shall constitute a partnership between or a joint venture by the parties hereto, or constitute either party the agent, of the other or place either party in the position of fiduciary. Neither party shall hold itself out contrary to the terms of this clause as respecting the production or distribution of any Program hereunder and neither party shall become liable by reason of any representation, act or omission of the other contrary to the provisions hereof. This agreement is not for the benefit of any third party and shall not be deemed to give any right or remedy to any such party whether referred to herein or not.

The parties acknowledge their agreement to the terms and conditions hereof by signing below.

CONTRACTOR　　　　　　　　　COMPANY

By: _____　　By: _____

INDUCEMENT LETTER

To induce Company to enter into this agreement with Contractor, Performer acknowledges and agrees:

1. Performer is familiar with all of the terms and provisions of the foregoing agreement.

2. Contractor has the right to enter into the foregoing agreement with reference to Performer's services.

3. Performer will perform all of his services agreed to be supplied by Contractor, in the manner and upon the terms and conditions specified in the foregoing agreement.

4. Performer shall comply with all of the foregoing terms and conditions of the agreement and shall perform all of the services required of Performer thereunder, notwithstanding the existence of any dispute between Performer and Contractor, or the amendment, modification, termination or expiration, by operation of law

or otherwise, of, or the breach by Contractor of, the foregoing agreement or any agreement between Contractor and Performer, or the non-performance by Contractor under any such agreement.

5. Performer shall look solely to Contractor for the payment of any and all compensation or other payments which are required to be made to Performer or on Performer's behalf, or as a reimbursement to Performer, as a result of the rendition by Performer of services pursuant to the foregoing agreement.

6. Performer will indemnify Company for and hold it harmless from and against any and all taxes which Company may have to pay and any and all liabilities (including, but not limited to, judgments, penalties, fines, interests, damages, costs and expenses, including reasonable attorneys' fees) which may be obtained against, imposed upon or suffered by Company or which Company may incur by reason of its failure to deduct and withhold from the compensation payable under the foregoing agreement any amounts required or permitted to be deducted and withheld from the compensation of any employee under the provisions of the Federal and California Income Tax Acts, the Federal Social Security Act, the California Unemployment Insurance Act and any amendments thereof and any other statutes heretofore or hereafter enacted requiring the withholding of any amount from the compensation of any employee.

7. In the event of any breach of terms of the foregoing agreement by Contractor, Company may proceed directly against Performer and may obtain relief at law or in equity with respect to Performer, as though such breach were committed by Performer.

8. All notices served upon Contractor in connection with the agreement shall operate as notice to Performer of the contents thereof.

_____
ARTIST

Form 18

Network Series Production and License Agreement

AGREEMENT made as of (*date*) between NETWORK and (*company*) *Productions, Inc.* ("*Packager*")

Re: *Working Title*

1. SERIES ORDER:

(a) Subject to the provisions of this Agreement, Network hereby orders and Packager hereby agrees to produce and deliver to Network a series of *thirty (30)* minute videotape programs (the "Series") based on and conforming with Packager's written presentation attached hereto. Delivery of the first Series program in accordance with paragraph 5 hereof shall be made in sufficient time for initial broadcast on (*date*) or on such later date as Network shall upon due written notice to Packager designate.

(b) Network hereby orders *eleven (11)* original programs and *two (2)* repeat programs for the first broadcast cycle.

2. SERIES TERM:

(a) The Series term shall commence on the date hereof and shall continue, subject to the right of suspension, termination, and extension hereinafter provided, until the expiration of *five (5)* years from the broadcast date of the first Series program or until the end of the last broadcast cycle for which Network orders new programs hereunder ("Series Term"), whichever first occurs. Said *five (5)* years shall be comprised of *sixteen (16)* broadcast cycles, the first *twelve (12)* of which shall be *thirteen (13)* consecutive weeks in length each and the last *four (4)* of which shall be *twenty-six (26)* consecutive weeks in length, each subject to extension for preemptions as hereinafter provided. The first broadcast cycle is firm, subject to the provisions of this Agreement. Network shall have separate, exclusive, irrevocable, dependent options for the second and succeeding broadcast cycles. Each such option shall be exercisable not later than *twenty-eight (28)* days prior to the end of the then current broadcast cycle.

(b) If the Series Term runs to the end of the *sixteenth (16th)* cycle, Network shall have the right of "first negotiation/first refusal" regarding additional broadcast rights in the Series.

(c) As used in this Agreement, the following terms shall have the meanings set forth below:

(i) **"First Negotiation"** means that Packager shall negotiate in good faith solely with Network during an exclusive negotiation period which shall begin no later than *one hundred and eighty (180)* days and ending no later than *one hundred and fifty (150)* days prior to the expiration of the Series Term; if no agreement is reached during such exclusive negotiation period, Packager shall furnish Network in its last written offer the terms and conditions least favorable to Packager that Packager is willing to accept; and

(ii) **"First Refusal"** means that Packager shall not enter into any agreement with another party on terms less favorable to Packager than Packager's last written offer to Network without first offering in writing (which shall include financial terms) to enter into an agreement with Network on the same terms which Packager and the other party are both willing to accept. Network shall have *ten* (*10*) days after receipt of such written offer in which to accept, however, the offer may not include any provision relating to the place of performance, particular sponsor, or contravening Network's legal responsibilities or requiring any non-financial term which cannot generally be met by companies in the television broadcasting business. If Network fails to accept those terms, Packager may enter into an agreement with the other party. If Packager does not contract with the other party on such terms, the right of first refusal shall continue until Packager accepts an offer which Network refused to accept or for *one* (*1*) year after Network's last broadcast of any Series program ordered pursuant to this Agreement, whichever first occurs.

3. SERIES ORDER PATTERN:

(a) The Series order pattern shall be as follows:

FIRST TWELVE CYCLES	ORDER PATTERN PER CYCLE
1, 2, 5, 6, 9 and 10	eleven (11) originals and two (2) repeats.
3, 7 and 11	ten (10) originals and three (3) repeats.
4, 8 and 12	nine (9) originals and four (4) repeats.

LAST FOUR CYCLES	ORDER PATTERN PER CYCLE
13 and 15	twenty-two (22) originals and four (4) repeats.
14 and 16	twenty (20) originals and six (6) repeats.

(b) In all cycles, repeats will be selected by Network.

(c) Network may extend each broadcast cycle for up to *two* (*2*) weeks due to preemptions.

4. SERIES LICENSE FEES, ADVANCES AND RECOUPMENT:

(a) Payment of any and all license fees is contingent on Network's having previously received an executed copy of Network's Standard Indemnity Letter, and the certificate of Errors and Omissions Insurance described in Clause 16 hereinbelow. The license fees payable by Network to Packager hereunder are:

CYCLE	ORIGINALS
1–4	$ (*amount*) each
5–8	$ (*amount*) each

CYCLE	ORIGINALS
9–12	$ (*amount*) each
13–14	$ (*amount*) each
15–16	$ (*amount*) each

Repeats: Packager's substantiated out-of-pocket repeat costs, plus $ (*amount*), it being understood that the objective of the parties is that such out-of-pocket repeat costs shall not exceed $ (*amount*) per repeat; Packager shall use its best efforts to keep such out-of-pocket repeat costs to a minimum.

(b) License fees for Series programs produced and delivered for broadcasting prior to (*date*) are firm. License fees for Series programs produced and delivered for broadcasting on or after (*date*) are subject to industry-wide union or governmental increases effective on or after (*date*), it being understood that the provisions of this sentence do not apply to any increased or new costs (whether by reason of new collective bargaining or other agreement(s)).

(c) Promptly after the execution of this agreement, Network shall make a non-recoupable pre-production advance to Packager in the full amount of $ (*amount*) it being understood that said advance shall be used by Packager solely for Packager's out-of-pocket production costs.

(d) License fees for originals hereunder shall be paid as follows:

(i) Prior to the commencement of (but not earlier than *four* (4) weeks prior to the commencement of) each cycle for which Network orders programs hereunder, Network shall advance Packager the applicable license fee for one original program in said cycle, and Network shall recoup each such advance by deducting and retaining one-fourth thereof from the applicable license fee payable for each of (A) the last *four* original programs in said cycle, if said cycle is a *thirteen* (13) week cycle or, (B) the *tenth, eleventh, twelfth and thirteenth* original programs in said cycle, if said cycle is a *twenty-six* (26) week cycle;

(ii) Subject to the recoupment provisions set forth in Subclause 4(d)(I) above, license fees for original programs shall be payable 80% thereof upon the commencement of production and 20% thereof upon delivery of the program for which payment is intended.

(e) Subject to the provisions of Subclause 4(a) above, license fees for repeats hereunder shall be paid as follows:

(i) Not later than *ten* (10) days after the telecast of a repeat, Network shall pay Packager $ (*amount*) plus Packager's substantiated out-of-pocket repeat costs for such repeat, provided Packager has furnished to Network, prior to the telecast of such repeat, a reasonably detailed statement, acceptable to Network, of Packager's substantiated out-of-pocket repeat costs for such repeat ("An Acceptable Repeat Statement"), it being understood that Network shall have the right to audit Packager's books and records with respect thereto; or

(ii) If Packager has not furnished Network, prior to the telecast of a repeat, An Acceptable Repeat Statement for such repeat, then, not later than *ten* (*10*) days after the telecast of such repeat, Network shall pay Packager $ (*amount*) plus $ (*amount*) said $ (*amount*) representing an estimate of Packager's substantiated out-of-pocket repeat costs for such repeat, it being understood that an appropriate adjustment shall be made promptly after Packager furnishes to Network An Acceptable Repeat Statement for such repeat and it being further understood that Network shall have the right to audit Packager's books and records with respect thereto.

5. PRODUCTION AND DELIVERY:

(a) The Series programs shall be produced in *New York City*. Network shall deduct from the license fees payable hereunder its charges for below-the-line facilities and personnel used by Packager in the production and delivery of the Series programs. Such charges shall be computed in accordance with Network's then applicable Rate Card.

(b) Delivery of each Series program and all elements thereof shall be in accordance with Network's Standard Tape Program Delivery Requirements attached hereto as Schedule "A" and incorporated herein. Timely delivery of each Series program is of the essence of this Agreement. In the event of Packager's late delivery of any Series program, notwithstanding any other remedies available to Network, Packager shall reimburse Network for any and all resultant costs necessary to facilitate the broadcast of such program as scheduled.

6. BROADCAST TERRITORY: The broadcast territory shall be the United States, its territories and possessions including Puerto Rico (the "Broadcast Territory").

7. OVERLAP PROTECTION; PRE-RELEASE: Network shall be entitled to blackout protection in any territory in which Network has owned and operated or affiliated stations (or acquires the same) within the United States having television broadcasting facilities, over-the-air transmission or cable re-transmission. Packager shall not permit the pre-release of any program for broadcast in Canada prior to its scheduled initial Network broadcast.

8. EXCLUSIVITY: Throughout the Series Term, each Series program and all elements thereof shall be exclusive to Network in the Broadcast Territory in all media, including without limitation, free, pay, subscription, cable, CATV, closed circuit, videocassette and all theatrical and non-theatrical showings (excluding music, publishing, and merchandising) until the expiration of the Series Term except that material which is acquired by Packager from third parties (as distinguished from material produced by Packager for use on the programs hereunder) shall be non-exclusive.

9. APPROVALS:

(a) Network shall have its standard full prior approval rights with respect to all key creative elements in the Series, including but not limited to, line producers, director, head writer (if any), writers, concept, format, program titles, openings and closings, script outlines, scripts (to the extent they vary from approved outlines or contain new or additional matter), cast, and other elements referred to in the attached presentation, music elements and music and guest stars.

(b) The title of the Program shall be subject to the approval of Network.

(c) Each Series program shall be subject to the policies of Network's Broadcast Standards and Compliance and Practices Departments. Packager shall execute the Packager's Disclosure Letter when such instrument is sent to Packager by Network's Compliance and Practices Department.

(d) Designated representatives, including members of the Press and Publicity Departments of Network, may be present during all stages of production including screening of dailies. A rough cut of each Series program shall be made available for viewing by Network.

10. TALENT EXCLUSIVITY:

(a) All continuing cast performers in the Series shall be exclusive to Network in television, to the maximum extent permitted by the applicable union/guild agreements.

(b) It is of the essence of this Agreement that all continuing cast performers in the Series approved by Network shall be furnished by Packager throughout the Series Term and that Packager shall secure exclusive options extending throughout the Series Term for all such continuing cast performers. The name, likeness, voice, and biography of each continuing cast performer in the Series shall be available to Network for publicity purposes.

11. INCIDENTAL RIGHTS & REQUIREMENTS:

(a) Subject to applicable union/guild requirements and provided Network bears all extra costs incurred, Network shall have all the usual and customary incidental rights, including, but not limited to, the following:

(i) to use all program elements for trailers and publicity;

(ii) to use all of the programs for audience tests, sponsor screenings, reference, file, and audition purposes; to make copies for any permitted uses; to make the usual "delayed broadcasts"; and

(iii) to edit all the programs for timing and broadcast standard purposes.

(b) Network agrees not to change or alter any credits, trademark or copyright notices appearing in any of the Series programs.

12. <u>RELATIONSHIP</u>: Packager is an independent contractor. Network shall not share in Packager's program profits nor bear any production risks or losses. Packager shall not share in Network's revenue from the broadcast of the Series. Network shall have the right to sell the programs for sponsorship on behalf of any product or service.

13. <u>REMEDIES AND "PAY OR PLAY"</u>:

(a) Willful failure by Packager to perform hereunder shall cause Network irreparable loss of a unique, intellectual property warranting equitable relief to prevent such loss. While Packager is entitled to damages at law if Network breaches, neither party shall be entitled to consequential damages, such as loss of sponsor or distribution revenues, because of a breach by the other.

(b) Network shall have no obligation to broadcast any program or programs delivered hereunder. Network's only financial obligation shall be payment to Packager of the applicable Series license fee and other sums herein provided.

14. <u>COMPLIANCE</u>:

(a) Packager shall comply with all applicable labor union agreements in connection with the production or use of each Series program.

(b) Packager recognizes Network's policy of equal employment opportunity and that Network applies such policy to all aspects of its operations and Packager agrees that in all aspects of its production activity there will likewise be no discrimination because of race, creed, religion, sex or national origin.

15. <u>REPRESENTATIONS, WARRANTIES AND REMEDIES</u>:

(a) Packager represents and warrants that:

(i) Packager has the right to enter into and fully perform this Agreement and grant the rights granted by Packager under this Agreement;

(ii) Packager has not done and shall not do any act or enter into any agreement which would violate any of the rights granted to Network or interfere with the performance of Packager's obligations under this Agreement;

(iii) On delivery, each program shall be free and clear of any encumbrance, including any lien or tax which is not subordinate and subject to all rights granted to Network by this Agreement;

(iv) The exercise by Network in accordance with the terms of this Agreement of the rights granted to it shall not violate or infringe any rights of any person, firm or corporation; and

(v) On delivery of each program, all performing rights to music in the program are controlled by Packager, ASCAP, BMI, or SESAC, or are in the public domain, and Packager has obtained all recording and synchronization rights to such music.

(b) Packager shall indemnify and hold harmless Network and its parent and subsidiary companies, the stations broadcasting the Program, each Program sponsor and its advertising agency, and the respective officers, directors, agents and employees of each from and against liability, actions, claims, demands, losses or damages (including reasonable attorney's fees) caused by or arising out of the broadcast or other use authorized by Packager of the Program and the material and performances contained in them.

(c) To the extent the Program material at issue in any claim was in fact furnished by Network to Packager in violation of any third party's property rights, Network shall indemnify Packager. Network's review and approval of any elements, material or Program furnished by Packager shall not constitute a waiver of Packager's indemnity.

(d) The indemnitor may, and if any indemnitee requests in writing, the indemnitor shall assume the defense of any claim, demand or action and shall, upon request by the indemnitee give prompt notice of any claim, demand or action covered by this indemnity. If the indemnitee settles any such claim, demand or action without the prior written consent of the indemnitor, the indemnitor shall be released from this indemnity in that instance.

16. INSURANCE: Packager shall carry television producer's errors and omissions insurance with coverage of not less than *One Million/Three Million* (*$1,000,000/$3,000,000*) dollars for the Series, issued by a carrier approved by Network. The coverage of the foregoing insurance shall extend to all claims arising out of the broadcast of each program hereunder regardless of when such claims may be asserted. Packager shall provide Network with a certificate of such insurance prior to the commencement of production of the Series. Said policy must be primary and not excess of or contributory to any other insurance provided for the benefit of or by Network. Packager shall direct its insurer(s) to forward copies of any and all notices involving said policy to Network.

17. FORCE MAJEURE:

(a) If Packager is prevented from timely delivering or Network is prevented from timely broadcasting any Series program ordered hereunder by any event beyond respectively, Packager's or Network's control, including but not limited to, acts of God, war, or labor difficulties ("Force Majeure"), Network shall have the following rights:

(i) The right to reduce accordingly its order of new programs (but only in the case of Packager's inability to produce Series because of Force Majeure) and/or repeat broadcasts for the current broadcast cycle; or, accept late delivery and extend accordingly the broadcast cycle and the Series Term to accommodate Network's later broadcast of any of the Series programs ordered from Packager; or, apply any Series not timely delivered against the minimum program order for any subsequent broadcast cycle; and

(ii) If delivery or broadcast of *four* (*4*) consecutive programs or *six* (*6*) programs in the aggregate is so prevented or delayed in any *thirteen* (*13*) week broadcast cycle, the right to cancel its order of any *one* (*1*) or more programs whose production has not been completed.

(b) Network's option deadline dates shall be extended accordingly in the event of a Force Majeure affecting Packager or Network. The exercise by Network of any of its rights under this paragraph shall not disqualify Network from exercising any or all of its remaining options to order programs hereunder and the exercise of any such rights shall be subject to the limitations imposed (if any) by the applicable union and/or guild agreements and any definition of Force Majeure contained therein.

18. <u>ASSIGNMENT</u>:

(a) This agreement may be assigned by Network only to an entity controlling, controlled by, or under common control with Network, or acquiring a substantial portion of Network's assets, provided however, that such assignment shall not relieve Network of its liability.

(b) Without Network's prior written consent, Packager shall not assign this Agreement prior to Packager's full performance nor shall Packager delegate to another the performance of any of its obligations. Packager does not require Network's consent to assign the proceeds which may become payable under this Agreement as security for monies advanced to finance production of any Series program provided, however, that no secured transaction shall require Packager to assign, pledge, mortgage, hypothecate, or otherwise encumber in any manner any Series program, except subject to Network's rights under this Agreement.

19. <u>NOTICES</u>: Except as otherwise expressly specified, any required notice shall be given in writing by personal delivery, or by mail or telegram sent to the other party at the address set forth above or designated by such party. Notice shall be deemed given on the date of mailing if by certified mail, or upon delivery to a telegraph office if by telegram, charges prepaid or to be billed. No notice shall be deemed given if there is a strike of any means employed. Copies of all notices from Network to Packager shall be sent as a courtesy to (*name and address of Packager's attorney*)

20. <u>APPLICABLE LAW</u>: All controversies or questions with respect to this Agreement shall be determined in accordance with *New York* law applicable to contracts made and to be performed wholly in *New York*.

21. <u>WAIVER</u>: Waiver of any term, condition, or breach of this Agreement shall not be deemed to be a waiver of that breach or any other term or condition in the future.

22. <u>MISCELLANEOUS</u>: This Agreement supersedes all prior agreements between the parties hereto, and both parties acknowledge and agree that neither party has relied on any representations or promises in connection herewith not contained in this Agreement. This Agreement cannot be canceled, modified or waived, in part or in full, except by an instrument in writing signed by all of the parties to this Agreement. The headings of the paragraphs hereof are for convenience only and shall not be deemed to limit or in any way affect the intent of this Agreement or any portion hereof. Should any paragraph or provision of this Agreement be held to be void, invalid, or inoperative, such decision shall not affect any other paragraph or provision hereof, and the remainder of this Agreement shall be effective as though such void, invalid or inoperative paragraph or provision had not been contained herein.

NETWORK   PACKAGER

By: _____   By: _____

Form 19

PRODUCER TERM AGREEMENT

This Agreement consists of the Deal Terms, Schedule I - "Standard Terms and Conditions", Inducement Letter, Exhibit "A" (Net Proceeds - Theatrical), and Exhibit "A-1" (Gross Proceeds Theatrical) attached hereto (collectively the "Agreement Documents").

A. PARTIES: _____, a _____ corporation (ID# _____) ("Lender") and _____("Studio").

B. PRODUCER: _____ (SS# _____) ("Producer") (citizen of _____, with a principal place of residence in _____).

C. DATE: As of _____.

DEAL TERMS

1. CONTINGENCIES: Studio's obligations hereunder are subject to fulfillment of the following conditions precedent:

    a. Signature and delivery of the Agreement Documents to Studio; and

    b. Full compliance by Producer with the IRCA requirements of Paragraph B.17 of the Standard Terms and Conditions.

2. FIRST LOOK/SERVICES: During the "Term" (defined below) Lender and Producer shall submit properties to Studio on an exclusive "first look" basis and Studio may submit properties to Lender and Producer (but shall be under no obligation to do so) for the development and potential production of theatrical motion pictures in accordance with the terms of this Agreement. In connection with any such properties approved for development and potential production, Studio agrees to borrow, and Lender agrees to lend, the services of Producer ("Producing Services"). Subject to the foregoing and to each and all of the other terms and conditions of this Agreement, Lender and Producer may render services for third parties during the Term.

3. TERM: The "Term" shall collectively refer to the "Initial Term" (defined below) and the "Option Term" (defined below).

    a. Initial Term: The "Initial Term" of this Agreement shall be two (2) years commencing on the date hereof.

    b. Option Term: Studio shall have the option, exercisable by written notice given not later than thirty (30) days prior to the expiration of the Initial Term, to extend the Term for a period of one (1) year commencing on the date immediately following the expiration date of the Initial Term ("Option Term").

c.   Exclusivity: Producer's services shall be on an exclusive "first look" basis to Studio with respect to all producing services in the motion picture business throughout the Term ("First Look Submission Obligation").

d.   Outside Projects: The Term and Option Term shall be deemed automatically suspended and extended by Studio, and transportation, expenses and overhead payments hereunder shall be deemed suspended, without notice by Studio during any period in which Producer renders exclusive services for third parties (hereafter "Outside Projects"). Producer's First Look Submission Obligation shall continue during any periods of suspension hereunder and services for third parties shall not materially interfere with Producer's services for Studio hereunder. Studio's right to so suspend the Term shall be at Studio's sole discretion and although Studio has the right, it shall not have the obligation. The Term shall likewise be extended by a time period equal to such period(s) of suspension; provided, however, that Studio may waive such suspension and/or extension.

   (1)   Reimbursement: If the Term is suspended as aforesaid due to an Outside Project, Lender and Producer shall cause the third party for whom services are being rendered to reimburse Studio as set forth in Paragraph 7 below.

   (2)   Pre-emption Right: If Producer receives an offer to render services in connection with an Outside Project during the Term which is permissible pursuant to this subparagraph d. and Producer desires to render such services, Producer shall give Studio not less than thirty (30) days nor more than ninety (90) days written notice prior to the proposed start date for such services. Such notice shall state the title, producer, distributor, nature of services and proposed start and completion date for such services. Producer shall keep Studio advised of the commencement, progress and anticipated completion date of any services for the Outside Project(s). Producer shall not be permitted to render services for an Outside Project during Producer's exclusive services hereunder.

e.   Services After Term: Upon the expiration or earlier termination of the Term, Producer shall continue to render all services required hereunder in accordance with the applicable schedule therefor on all "Projects" and "Pictures" (as such terms are defined herein) for which services have not then been completed.

4.   COMPENSATION:

a.　Compensation/Project Fees:

(1)　Fixed Compensation: Studio shall pay Lender the following compensation in connection with each Picture produced hereunder with respect to which Producer renders Producing Services:

(a)　First Picture: $_____.

(b)　Second Picture: $_____.

(c)　Third and Subsequent Pictures: $_____.

(2)　Participation: For each Picture:

(a)　Gross Proceeds: A sum equal to _____% of 100% of Gross Proceeds, if any, commencing at _____; thereafter

(b)　Net Proceeds: A sum equal to _____% of 100% of Net Proceeds, reducible by all third party participations to a "Soft Floor" of _____% of 100% of Net Proceeds and further reducible to a "Hard Floor" of _____% of 100% of Net Proceeds, subject to Studio's "Hard Floor" of _____% of 100% of Net Proceeds.

(3)　Definitions: For purposes of computing any amounts payable to Lender pursuant to subparagraph (2) above, the following definitions shall apply:

(a)　Net Proceeds: Net Proceeds shall be defined, computed, accounted for and paid in accordance with Exhibit "A" attached hereto and by this reference made a part hereof.

(b)　Gross Proceeds: Gross Proceeds shall be defined, computed, accounted for and paid in accordance with Exhibit "A-1" attached hereto and by this reference made a part hereof.

5.　CREDIT: Individual producer and/or production credit shall be accorded to Producer with respect to each Picture. Such credit shall be subject to Studio's standard exclusions. All other aspects of such credit shall be subject to Studio's discretion.

6.　NOTICES AND PAYMENTS:

a. To Lender and Producer: c/o _____

b. Notices to Studio: _____

7.　SPECIAL PROVISIONS:

a.　Mutual Approval/Consultation: Other than with respect to Added Producers, Producer shall have a right to mutual approval (with Studio retaining the tie-breaker in the event of a disagreement) of third party individual producers in connection with each Picture. In addition,

Producer shall have a right of consultation with respect to the Key Production Crew (i.e., the unit production manager, casting director (unless in-house), cameraman, art director and composer) and the initial theatrical domestic campaign (i.e., the U.S. advertising and publicity campaign, including "artwork") for each Picture.

b. Overhead: Studio shall provide Lender $_____ per year for each year of the Term, payable in arrears in equal monthly installments. Said sum shall be deemed all inclusive and shall cover all expenses and costs in connection herewith, including offices, staffing and related expenses.

c. Miscellaneous:

(1) E & O Insurance: Producer shall be covered as an additional insured under Studio's Errors & Omissions and General Liability insurance policies in connection with any "Project" or "Picture" (as those terms are defined in Schedule I), subject to the limitations, restrictions and terms of said policies. The provisions of this subparagraph shall not be construed so as to limit or otherwise affect any obligation, representation or agreement by Lender or Producer hereunder.

(2) Transportation and Expenses: Producer shall be provided with the following transportation and expenses when required by Studio to render services at a location which is more than fifty (50) miles from Producer's principal residence in connection with a Picture in production.

(a) Transportation: One (1) round-trip fare, first-class, if available, and if used, on a one-time only basis, plus, if Producer is required to remain on location for a period in excess of fourteen (14) consecutive days, Studio shall provide Producer with one (1) additional round-trip fare, first-class, if available, and if used, on a one-time-only basis.

(b) Expense Allowance: $_____ per week in major cities such as New York and London; $_____ per week in other metropolitan areas; and $_____ per week elsewhere. The applicable expense allowance shall be prorated at $\frac{1}{7}$ thereof per day.

(3) Videocassette: One (1) videocassette of each Picture, which shall be provided at such time, if ever, as such Picture is offered for sale to the general public in the United States on videocassette, subject to Lender's and Producer's execution of Studio's standard agreement limiting Lender's and Producer's use of such videocassette to private home use only.

8.   DEFINITION OF TERMS: Terms of art used in these Deal Terms which are not defined herein shall have the meaning set forth in the other Agreement Documents. Terms of art not defined in the Agreement Documents shall be defined as commonly understood in the entertainment industry.

9.   ENTIRE AGREEMENT:

The Agreement Documents constitute the entire agreement between the parties hereto and supersede all prior agreements, representations and warranties, if any, made with respect to the subject matter hereof. This Agreement may be amended only by written agreement executed by all of the parties. To the extent any terms or conditions of the Standard Terms and Conditions are inconsistent with the Deal Terms, the Deal Terms shall govern.

[LENDER]   [STUDIO]
By _____   By _____
        Authorized Signatory   Authorized Signatory

Schedule I

STANDARD TERMS AND CONDITIONS

Standard Terms and Conditions of the Agreement dated as of
_____ between _____ ("Studio")
and _____ ("Lender"), furnishing the services of
_____ ("Producer" or "Employee"). The document to
which this Schedule I is attached is referred to as the "Deal Terms".

A.

STANDARD TERM PRODUCER PROVISIONS

1.   <u>SERVICES</u>: Lender shall cause Producer to render and Producer shall render, all services set forth below and comply with Studio's instructions at all times in all matters. Neither Lender nor Producer may engage the services and/or facilities of any third party without Studio's prior written consent:

   a. <u>Submission of Properties</u>:

     (1) <u>First Look Submissions by Producer</u>: During the Term, Producer shall submit to Studio in writing or orally (provided Producer shall submit upon request a written version of any oral submission) on a "first-look" basis all ideas, concepts or other properties, original or otherwise, whether in book, script, treatment, outline or any other form with respect to which Producer wishes to render Producing Services (each such property shall be referred to herein as a "Submitted Property"); provided, however, that if any Submitted Property is not owned or controlled by Producer or Lender, the motion picture, television, allied and ancillary rights in such Submitted Property must be available to be acquired by Studio on reasonable and customary terms. As used herein, the term "first look" shall mean that each Submitted Property shall be offered solely and exclusively to Studio before same is offered to any other person or entity. Producer shall make a reasonable number of submissions hereunder during the Term.

     (2) <u>Studio Review Period</u>: Studio shall have a period of thirty (30) days after Producer's submission of a Submitted Property within which to give Producer written notice of Studio's election to proceed with the development of a proposed motion picture based upon such Submitted Property upon the terms and conditions hereinafter set forth; provided, however, that such thirty (30) day period may be extended due to an event caused by Producer for

circumstances beyond Studio's control which necessitate a longer period. If there are underlying rights in connection with such Submitted Property and Studio deems it necessary to acquire such rights, all obligations of Studio to Producer hereunder shall be subject to:

(i) Chain-of-Title: Studio's approval of the chain-of-title for the Submitted Property; and

(ii) Acquisition of Rights: The successful acquisition of such rights by Studio upon terms and conditions satisfactory to Studio (including, without limitation, the signature and delivery of all agreements and documents Studio considers necessary, proper or expedient to convey to Studio the rights contemplated therein or to option such rights).

(3) Notification by Studio: If Studio fails to timely notify Producer, or if Studio gives Producer written notice that it elects not to proceed with the development of a Submitted Property, or if the conditions of subdivisions (i) and (ii) above are not met, Studio shall have no further rights under this Agreement in or to such Submitted Property. Producer may thereafter retain or submit such Submitted Property for development alone or in association with any other party, subject to Studio's Pre-emption Right, and the terms and conditions for Outside Projects, as set forth in the Deal Terms, and the "Changed Elements" provision set forth in (4) immediately below.

(4) Changed Elements: If Producer submits to a third party any Submitted Property rejected by Studio and such Submitted Property is comprised of any elements which are new (including, but not limited to, a "spec" script based upon a Submitted Property previously rejected by Studio) or existing elements which are different from the elements originally submitted hereunder (including, but not limited to, script, cast, budget, terms of Producer's employment and services rendered by Producer, etc.) or such Submitted Property is submitted on any material terms and conditions which are more favorable to such third party than the terms and conditions upon which the Submitted Property was last offered to Studio (each of which changes shall be referred to as a "Changed Element"), then Producer shall be obligated in each instance to advise Studio thereof, in writing or orally, and shall offer the Submitted Property to Studio with such different elements and/or on such more favorable terms and conditions. In such event, Studio shall have the right (but not the obligation) to proceed with the development of a motion picture based upon

the Submitted Property (with such different elements and upon such more favorable terms and conditions), which right shall be exercisable by Studio by written notice to Producer within thirty (30) days following Studio's receipt of such notice; provided, however, that with respect to a "spec" script based upon an Submitted Property previously rejected by Studio, if Studio is interested in acquiring such script the parties shall negotiate in good faith the terms and conditions of such acquisition; and provided, further, that if the parties are unable to reach an agreement within ten (10) business days following submission to Studio of such "spec" script, the Producer may retain or submit such script for development alone or in association with any other party, subject to Changed Elements. Producer agrees that any election by Studio to proceed which is predicated upon Changed Elements shall not obligate Studio to meet or accept any Changed Element which cannot be met or accepted easily by one person as another (e.g. the required employment of a certain actor who is not readily available for employment by Studio on terms and conditions customary in the motion picture industry).

(5) Submissions by Studio: During the Term, Studio may elect to submit to Producer any properties on which Studio desires Producer to render Producing Services (each such property shall be referred to herein as a "Studio Proposed Property"). With respect to each Studio Proposed Property, Producer shall have ten (10) business days in which to advise Studio of Producer's approval or disapproval. Submission of a Studio Proposed Property to Producer shall not in and of itself be deemed approval by Studio of the development and/or production thereof and each Studio Proposed Property shall be subject to the approval procedure set forth in Paragraph A.1.a.(2) above, except that the time period in which Studio may approve or disapprove a Studio Proposed Property shall commence on the date on which Producer notifies Studio of Producer's approval of such Property.

(6) Definition of "Projects"/"Picture": Each Submitted Property and Studio Proposed Property with respect to which Studio elects to proceed with development shall be referred to herein as a "Project". Each Submitted Property and Studio Proposed Property with respect to which Studio elects to proceed to production shall be referred to herein as a "Picture".

b.   Terms Applicable to Producing Services: Producer shall render all services set forth below and comply with Studio's instructions at all times in all matters. Producer may not engage the services and/or facilities of any third party without Studio's prior written consent.

(1) <u>Development Services</u>: Development Services shall be rendered during the period commencing on the date Studio elects to proceed with the development of a Submitted Property or Studio Proposed Property and continuing until eight (8) weeks prior to commencement of principal photography of the Picture or abandonment of the Picture pursuant to Paragraph A.1.e.(2) below (whichever first occurs) ("Development Period"). Such services shall consist of all development services to the extent required by Studio and customarily rendered by individual producers in the motion picture industry including but not limited to supervision of the screenplay writer(s) and consulting services on budgeting, proposed casting and crew selection. Such services shall be rendered on a nonexclusive basis, and shall be subject to exclusive and nonexclusive services for third parties provided they are prior contractual commitments of Producer.

(2) <u>Production Services</u>: If Studio elects or is deemed to have elected to proceed to production pursuant to Paragraph A.1.e.(1) below, then during the period commencing eight (8) weeks prior to commencement of principal photography and continuing until completion of principal photography ("Production Period") and during the period commencing upon the completion of principal photography and continuing until the date of completion and delivery of the final answer print of the Picture and all items required by Studio for the distribution and exhibition of the Picture ("Post-Production Period"), Producer shall render all preproduction, production and post-production services requested by Studio and customarily rendered by individual producers in the motion picture industry. Such services shall be exclusive during the Production Period and said services shall be rendered in accordance with the following:

(a) <u>Compliance with Approved Production Elements</u>: The Picture shall be produced in compliance with the budget, production schedule and screenplay therefor approved by Studio. There shall be no deviation from any such element without Studio's prior written consent.

(b) <u>Timely Delivery</u>: The Picture shall be delivered on or before the date specified in the Studio approved post-production schedule, time being of the essence, subject to extensions for force majeure.

(c)   <u>MPAA Rating</u>: The MPAA rating of the Picture shall be no more restrictive than PG.

(d)   <u>T.V. Cover Shots</u>: Producer shall cause to be prepared all such "cover shots" as Studio may request for exhibition of each Picture on U.S. prime-time television, airlines, etc., without hampering the continuity of the Picture.

(e)   <u>Running Time</u>: The Picture shall have a running time of not less than ninety-five (95) minutes nor more than one hundred-ten (110) minutes.

(f)   <u>Compliance with Laws</u>: The Picture will be produced in accordance with all applicable collective bargaining agreements and governmental requirements.

(g)   <u>Studio Facilities</u>: Subject to its availability, Producer shall use only Studio's post-production and sound facilities on its studio premises in Los Angeles to perform the post-production activities required for the Picture.

c.   <u>Election to Proceed to Production/Abandonment</u>:

   (1)   <u>Election to Proceed to Production</u>: Studio may, in its sole discretion, notify Producer at any time that it has elected to proceed to production of a Project. If Studio approves a final screenplay, budget, production schedule and commits to the director and principal cast members for a Project then Studio shall be deemed to have elected to proceed to production of the Project. A Project for which Studio has or is deemed to have elected to proceed to production hereunder shall hereinafter be referred to as a "Picture".

   (2)   <u>Abandonment</u>:

      (a)   <u>Right of Abandonment</u>: Studio shall have the right, in its sole discretion, to abandon a Project or Picture at any time.

      (b)   <u>Inactivity Deemed Abandonment</u>: If for any consecutive nine (9) month period (as such period may be extended by an "Extrinsic Event" [defined below]) there is no active development in connection with a Project (e.g., all writing and reading periods relating to the writing services of the last engaged screenplay writer have expired, no negotiations are ongoing with respect to a writer, cast member, director or financier, and no budgeting or location survey activity is ongoing) then Lender may give Studio written request to resume active development of the Project and, if Studio fails to resume such active development within forty-five (45) days after receipt of such request, the Project shall be deemed abandoned.

(c)   Effect of Abandonment: In the event of abandonment pursuant to subparagraphs (a) and (b) above Studio shall have no obligation to involve Lender or Producer in any later development or production of the Picture at any time thereafter and, Studio's only obligation to Lender shall be the payment of any previously vested and accrued but unpaid Fixed Compensation for services pursuant to Paragraph 4. of the Deal Terms.

d.   Pay or Play: Studio shall have the right to terminate Producer's Producing Services hereunder with respect to a Project or Picture at any time without legal justification or excuse ("Pay-or-Play Termination") whereupon Studio shall have no further obligations to Lender or Producer with respect to such Project or Picture in such capacity. If prior to a Pay-or-Play Termination hereunder, Studio has elected to proceed to production pursuant to Paragraph A.1.e.(1) above or at anytime thereafter elects to proceed to production of Picture, based upon a screenplay supervised by Producer hereunder (with no intervening rewrite, revision or new screenplay not supervised by Producer), Studio shall also pay to Lender any unpaid Fixed Compensation and Participation otherwise payable hereunder to the extent vested on the date of such Pay or Play Termination pursuant to Paragraph A.2.b.(2) below. Notwithstanding the foregoing, if Producer renders services in the entertainment industry during what would have been the Production Period for such Picture had there been no Pay-or-Play Termination, all monies earned by Producer or Lender for such services shall be applied against and reduce the monies payable to Lender pursuant to this Paragraph.

e.   Start Date: The Start Date for each Picture produced hereunder shall be the date of commencement of principal photography of such Picture and shall be automatically extended without notice for a period equal to the duration of any Default, Disability and/or Extrinsic Event (as such terms are defined below and regardless of whether Producer's services are suspended therefor) or due to any location requirements, director and/or cast unavailability, weather conditions, and/or other similar contingencies.

f.   Other Producers: Studio shall have the right to engage other person(s) as individual producers, executive producers or associate producers in connection with the Projects and Pictures hereunder and, subject to the terms of Paragraph A.3. hereof, Studio shall have the right to accord credit to such person(s) in connection with the Picture and advertising and publicity thereof in such form and manner as Studio may determine.

2.   CONSIDERATION: All compensation set forth in Paragraph 4. of the Deal Terms is conditioned upon Lender's and Producer's complete performance of their respective obligations hereunder. Such compensation shall be deemed full consideration for all such performance and for all rights granted Studio hereunder.

   a.   Fixed Compensation: Fixed Compensation for Producing Services shall only become payable if Studio elects or is deemed to have elected to proceed to production of a Project. The payment schedule therefor shall be as follows:

   (1)   Twenty percent (20%) in equal weekly installments commencing eight weeks prior to the date principal photography commences;

   (2)   Sixty percent (60%) in equal weekly installments over the scheduled period of principal photography;

   (3)   Ten percent (10%) upon delivery of the first director's cut; and

   (4)   Ten percent (10%) upon delivery of the final answer print and all items required by Studio for full delivery of the Picture.

   b.   Contingent Compensation: If the Deal Terms provide that the Contingent Compensation payable to Lender is "reducible," such Contingent Compensation shall be reduced by all third-party net proceeds participations on a percentage-point-by-percentage-point basis and thereafter by the dollar amount of all third-party gross participations. If the Deal Terms provide for a "Soft Floor" in connection with the reduction of Lender's Contingent Compensation, such term shall mean that the dollar amount of all third-party participations not utilized in reducing Lender's Contingent Compensation prior to reaching the Soft Floor shall be deducted "off the top"; a "Hard Floor" shall mean that no further deductions shall be made of Lender's Contingent Compensation once the Hard Floor has been reached; provided, however, that notwithstanding the foregoing, if the aggregate Contingent Compensation granted in connection with the Picture (including Lender's Contingent Compensation hereunder) exceed a sum equal to sixty percent (60%) of the Net Proceeds, Lender's Contingent Compensation hereunder shall be calculated as set forth in the Deal Terms.

   (1)   Over-Budget Adjustment: With respect to the Contingent Compensation payable to Lender for Producing Services, if the actual cost of production of the "Photoplay" (as such term is defined in Exhibit "A"), exclusive of the administrative fee, exceeds an amount equal to one hundred seven and one-half percent (107-1/2%) of the approved budget (exclusive of the administrative fee

and contingency, if any), then an amount equal to such excess shall be added to cost of production of the Picture for purposes of determining recoupment of cost of production, Net Proceeds or Gross Proceeds under Exhibit "A" or "A-1"; provided, however, that the administrative fee and interest shall not be charged more than once, and in computing such additional costs of production, the following shall be disregarded: costs caused by an "Extrinsic Event" (defined below), costs due to industry-wide union and guild increases (not contemplated by said budget), costs due to third-party breaches of contract, costs for which Studio will receive insurance reimbursement and costs incurred at Studio's written direction or approval not originally in the budget.

(2) <u>Vesting Schedule</u>: Producer's Participation for Producing Services hereunder shall accrue and vest according to the schedule for payment of the Fixed Compensation pursuant to Paragraph A.2.a. above.

(3) <u>Overhead Costs</u>: All costs incurred or paid by Studio under this Agreement not otherwise specifically allocated to a Project shall be included in the "cost of production" of the First Picture produced hereunder. However, if more than one Project is produced hereunder, such sums shall be apportioned equally as part of the "cost of production" of each such Picture.

3. <u>CREDIT</u>: Credit to be accorded Producer shall be as set forth in Paragraph 5. of the Deal Terms and is contingent on no Default occurring and Producer rendering all material services required hereunder. All other aspects of the credit to be accorded Producer shall be determined by Studio in its sole discretion and shall be subject to the following:

a. <u>Paid Advertising</u>: Studio's obligation hereunder, if any, to accord credit in paid advertising shall be limited to advertising issued by or under the direct control of Studio and shall not include so called "excluded advertising" as follows: (1) group, list or institutional advertising; (2) teaser or special advertising; (3) outdoor advertising; (4) promotional material for exhibitors; (5) publicity, advertising or exploitation relating to the story or literary or dramatic material on which said Picture is based, its title, the authors or writers, the music, the composers or conductor, the director, any members of the cast, or similar matters; (6) any advertising or publicity written in narrative form; (7) a listing in the nature of a cast of characters; (8) trailer or other advertising on the screen; (9) radio or television advertising or exploitation; (10) newspaper or magazine advertising of eight (8) column inches or less; (11) window or lobby displays or advertising; (12) advertising relating to subsidiary or ancillary rights in the Picture (including, without limitation, novelizations, screenplay and other publications, products or merchandising, soundtrack recordings, video-cassettes, videodiscs and other home video devices and the covers, packages, containers or jackets therefor); (13) advertising in which no credit is accorded other than credit to one (1) or two (2) stars of the Picture and/or Studio and/or any other company financing or distributing the Picture; (14) advertising, publicity and exploitation relating to byproducts or commercial tie-ups; (15) other advertising not relating primarily to the Picture; and (16) award, nomination and congratulatory-type ads.

b.   <u>Title</u>: If both artwork and nonartwork titles are used, position and size references to title herein shall apply to the nonartwork title only.

c.   <u>Failure to Comply</u>: Any casual or inadvertent failure to comply with the provisions of this Paragraph A.3. shall not constitute a breach of this Agreement nor entitle Lender or Producer to any relief at law or in equity.

4.   <u>RIGHTS</u>: The results and proceeds of Producer's services hereunder shall be created within the scope of Producer's employment agreement with Lender and shall be a "work made for hire" for Studio as specially commissioned for use as a part of a motion picture in accordance with Sections 101 and 201 of the U.S. Copyright Act. Without limiting the foregoing, Studio shall have the exclusive right to register the copyright in any embodiment of said results and proceeds in Studio's name as owner and author thereof. As between Lender, Producer and Studio, the Picture, all films, tapes, recordings, prints and copies thereof, and all rights therein, shall be the sole property of Studio and may be distributed, exhibited, broadcast and otherwise used and/or exploited, in whole or in part, in perpetuity, in any manner and through any media, whether presently in existence or subsequently devised, as Studio may elect. Neither Lender nor Producer shall not be entitled to any additional compensation in connection with such distribution, exhibition, broadcast, other use and/or exploitation unless such is expressly provided for in this Agreement, or required by law or any applicable collective bargaining agreement to which Studio is a signatory, and then at the minimum amount so required. With respect to any writing services rendered hereunder, Lender and Producer waive the so-called "moral rights", if any, of any author, if any, and Studio shall have the right to add to, subtract from, re-arrange, edit and change the title of Producer's work hereunder. The parties acknowledge that no writing services are required hereunder.

Notwithstanding, if Producer elects to render writing services on a
Project, then Studio and Lender shall enter into a Writer Agreement
on terms to be negotiated in good faith.

5.   SPECIAL TERMS:

    a.   <u>Consultation/Approval Rights</u>: Lender's and Producer's rights of
consultation and/or approval shall be subject to Producer being
available without additional expense to Studio, at the time(s) and
place(s) designated by Studio for such consultation. Such consultation
and/or approval shall not materially delay or otherwise interfere with
Studio's production plans for the Picture. With respect to Lender's
and Producer's consultation rights, Studio's determination with respect
to all such matters shall be final and binding upon Lender and
Producer. With respect to Lender's and Producer's approval rights,
Producer's and Lender's approval of the employment of any of the
individuals in connection with the Picture shall be subject to said
individuals timely being (i) ready, willing, able and available to render
services at the times and places reasonably designated by Studio; (ii)
able to obtain the necessary work visas and satisfy all government
requirements to render services as designated by Studio; (iii) able to
satisfy all applicable union and guild requirements for persons rendering services in the capacities for which they are engaged to; and (iv)
able to render services at their customary rates but in no event in an
amount greater than the budgeted amount for their services as provided
in the final approved budget of the Picture. In the event that any dispute
between Studio and Lender with respect to any of the elements subject
to Lender's approval cannot be resolved, Studio's decision with respect
thereto shall be binding and final upon Lender and Producer.

    b.   <u>Team of Producers</u>: If Lender or Producer consists of more than one
entity or individual furnishing or rendering producing services, the
Agreement and the term "Lender" or "Producer" shall be deemed to
refer to such entities or individuals jointly and/or severally, at Studio's
election. In the event one such entity or individual is unable or
unwilling to perform the obligations required hereunder, Studio may
exercise its rights hereunder either against the nonperforming entity-
(ies) or individual(s) or against all such entity(ies) or individual(s)
hereunder, as it may elect. If Studio elects to terminate this Agreement
as to only the nonperforming entity(ies) or individual(s) Studio's rights
as to the other entity(ies) or individual(s) hereunder shall continue.
All entities constituting Lender and all producers constituting Producer
acknowledge that as a contracting entity they are a producing team
and that their work hereunder constitutes a "joint work" within the

meaning of the United States Copyright Act. All compensation payable to all lenders will be divided equally unless specifically provided otherwise in the Deal Terms.

c. Videocassette: The videocassette copy of the Picture granted Lender in the Deal Terms shall be provided Lender at such time, if ever, as the applicable Picture is offered for sale to the general public in the United States on videocassette and shall be subject to Lender's and Producer's execution of Studio's standard agreement limiting Lender's and Producer's use of such videocassette to private home use only.

d. Insurance:

(1) Right to Insure: At Studio's expense, Studio may secure life, accident, cast or other insurance covering Producer, who shall furnish such information, fill out and sign such forms, and undergo such examinations as reasonably may be required. The proceeds and ownership of such insurance shall be solely Studio's, and neither Lender nor Producer shall have any right, title or interest therein.

(2) Right to Terminate: If Studio is unable to obtain Studio's customary cast insurance covering Producer during the production of the Picture at ordinary rates and with not more than normal deductions and without exclusions or restrictions, then Studio shall have the right to terminate under Paragraph B.4.e.(b)(2) below (with the same effect as a termination for Disability) by giving Lender written notice of termination within ten (10) days after Studio acquires knowledge that Producer has failed to pass a physical examination for such insurance, or otherwise has failed to qualify therefor, but in no event later than one week prior to the start of principal photography (unless the exam occurs within such one-week period). However, provided that Producer is available for the necessary physical examination for such insurance at least two weeks prior to the commencement of principal photography, Studio shall have no right to terminate Producer's services under this subparagraph c. at any time on or after commencement of principal photography hereunder. If such exclusions and/or restrictions can be lifted by the payment of an additional premium, Studio agrees to so notify Producer within said ten days or one week, as the case may be, and if Producer actually makes timely payment of such additional premium, then Studio agrees not to terminate as aforesaid.

(3) Medical Examination: Studio may have medical examinations or tests of Producer made by such physician(s) or other person(s)

as Studio may designate. Producer may have his own physician
or other person present at any examination or test required under
this subparagraph c.(3) at Producer's or Lender's expense.

B.

STANDARD PERSONAL SERVICES PROVISIONS – LOANOUT

1. <u>WARRANTIES</u>:

    a. <u>Employment Agreement</u>: Lender and Employee warrant that during the term of this Agreement there is a valid employment agreement between Lender and Employee under which Employee is engaged to render services exclusively to Lender, and Lender has the right to lend Employee's services as provided herein.

    b. <u>Free to Enter into Agreement</u>: Lender and Employee warrant they are each free to enter into this Agreement and will not do or permit any act which will interfere with or derogate from the full performance of Employee's services or Studio's exercise of the rights herein granted.

    c. <u>Employee's Material</u>: Lender and Employee each warrant that with respect to any material supplied by Employee hereunder, such material:

        (1)   Shall be Employee's original creation (except for material in the public domain and/or material furnished by or included at Studio's direction);

        (2)   Does not and will not defame, infringe upon, or violate the rights of any kind, including the right of privacy, of any person or entity; and

        (3)   Is not the subject of any litigation or claim that might give rise to litigation.

    d. <u>Application of Guild Warranties and Representations</u>: The warranties of Employee pursuant to this Paragraph B.1. are subject to any limitations pertaining thereto under any applicable collective bargaining agreement.

2. <u>INDEMNITY</u>:

    a. <u>By Lender/Employee</u>: Lender and Employee shall each defend, indemnify and hold Studio, its licensees and assigns, and the directors, officers, employees and agents of the foregoing, harmless from all claims, liabilities, damages and costs (including reasonable legal fees and court costs) arising from any breach or alleged breach by Lender or Employee of any warranty or agreement made by either Lender or Employee hereunder or from any use of the rights granted and/or materials supplied by Employee hereunder. Studio shall have the right of approval, not to be unreasonably withheld, of any attorneys or other counsel retained by Lender or Employee in connection with the performance of their obligations pursuant to this Paragraph B.2.a.

b. **By Studio:** Studio shall defend, indemnify and hold Lender and Employee harmless from all claims, liabilities, damages and costs (including reasonable legal fees and court costs) arising from the use of any material supplied Employee by Studio or incorporated at Studio's direction.

c. **Cooperation Between the Parties:** The indemnified party shall cooperate fully with the indemnifying party and shall perform such other acts and deeds as may be reasonably necessary and prudent and requested by the indemnifying party in the performance of the indemnified party's obligations to defend and/or indemnify hereunder.

3. **REMEDIES:**

a. **Against Lender/Employee:** Lender's and Employee's services and the rights herein granted are unique in character and value such that the loss thereof could not be reasonably compensable in damages in an action at law. Accordingly, if Lender or Employee breach this Agreement, Studio shall be entitled to seek any available equitable relief, including but not limited to injunctive relief.

b. **Against Studio:** The sole right of Lender and Employee as to any breach or alleged breach hereunder by Studio shall be the recovery of money damages, if any, and the rights herein granted by Lender and Employee shall not terminate by reason of such breach. In no event may Lender or Employee terminate this Agreement or obtain injunctive or other equitable relief with respect to any breach of Studio's obligations hereunder.

c. **Non-Waiver/Cumulative:** The waiver by any party of any breach hereof shall not be deemed a waiver of any prior or subsequent breach hereof. All remedies of any party shall be cumulative and the pursuit of one remedy shall not be deemed a waiver of any other remedy.

4. **SUSPENSION AND TERMINATION:**

a. **Suspension:**

(1) **Studio's Right of Suspension:** Studio may suspend Employee's services, the running of time and the payment of any compensation hereunder (and thereby postpone any subsequent dates herein specified) during any of the following events:

(a) **Default:** Any failure (whether or not excusable at law) by Lender and/or Employee (other than by reason of Disability) to perform their respective obligations hereunder, or a statement by Lender or Employee or Lender's representative or Employee's representative that Lender and/or Employee will so fail, or Lender's or Employee's failure to confirm to Studio full performance hereunder by notice to Studio given within twenty four (24) hours after receipt by Employee of Studio's notice that Studio requests such confirmation ("Default");

(b) <u>Disability</u>: The inability of Employee to perform Employee's services because of Employee's physical, mental or emotional disability, illness, injury or death ("Disability"); and

(c) <u>Extrinsic Event</u>: Any event which interrupts or materially interferes with Studio's development, production or scheduled release of motion pictures generally or of the Picture with respect to which Employee is engaged hereunder ("Extrinsic Event") including, without limitation, a strike or lockout (whether or not such lockout is beyond Studio's control), or fire, earthquake or other action of the elements, war or civil disturbance or other event beyond Studio's control. Notwithstanding the foregoing:

   (i) <u>Strike by Employee's Guild</u>: Any strike called by the collective bargaining organization (the "Guild") of which Employee is required to be a member pursuant to this Agreement shall not be deemed an "Extrinsic Event," and, accordingly, if Employee respects a strike called by the Guild, a Default shall be deemed to have occurred hereunder; and

   (ii) <u>Strike by Other Guild</u>: If Employee respects a strike or picket line by any party other than the Guild, a Default shall be deemed to have occurred hereunder.

(2) <u>Form of Notice of Suspension</u>: Studio may suspend Employee's services by oral notice to Employee or to Lender's or Employee's agent or by written notice to Lender, but, subject to Studio's right to terminate, such notice shall be given no later than a reasonable time following the end of the event upon which the suspension was based. Studio shall confirm oral suspension by written notice to Lender as soon thereafter as practical, but Studio's failure to do so shall not affect such suspension. Each suspension shall continue until ended by Studio by written notice to Lender. No such suspension shall affect any of Studio's other rights hereunder.

b. <u>Termination</u>:

(1) <u>Employee's Right to Terminate</u>: If a suspension based on an Extrinsic Event continues for more than eight (8) consecutive weeks (or such other period as provided in the collective bargaining agreement of the applicable Guild), Lender may, by written notice to Studio, terminate Employee's services hereunder; provided, however, that if within five (5) business days after Studio's receipt of Lender's notice, Studio terminates the suspension by written notice to Lender, then Lender's termination shall be void, Employee's services and the running of time hereunder shall resume, and Studio shall have no further right to suspend or terminate by reason of the Extrinsic Event upon which such suspension was based.

(2) <u>Studio's Right to Terminate</u>: Studio shall have the right, by written notice to Lender, to terminate Employee's services upon or at any time after any Default, if any Disability continues for three (3) consecutive weeks or a total of five (5) weeks (provided, if Employee is a director or a player, Studio may terminate Employee's services upon or at any time after any Disability) or if any Extrinsic Event continues for five (5) consecutive weeks.

(3) <u>Effect of Termination</u>: If Employee's services are terminated pursuant to this Paragraph B.4.b., Studio shall be released from all further obligations under this Agreement; provided however, that if this Agreement is terminated based upon Disability or an Extrinsic Event, Lender shall be entitled to receive the unpaid portion of the Guaranteed Compensation, Deferred Compensation and Participation granted in Paragraph 3. of the Deal Terms pursuant and subject to the terms and conditions by which such compensation is granted and only to the extent such compensation is vested prior to the commencement of such Disability or Extrinsic Event pursuant to Paragraph A.2. above. No termination of Employee's services hereunder shall affect Studio's rights in or to the Picture, the results and proceeds of Employee's services theretofore rendered hereunder, the use of Employee's name or likeness as granted elsewhere herein or Studio's rights at law and in equity.

5. <u>PERSONALITY AND PUBLICITY RIGHTS</u>: Lender and Employee grant Studio the right to use Employee's name, likeness, voice, and professional biography in credits, advertising, publicity and exploitational material concerning Employee's services and the results and proceeds hereunder, including material containing the name of

commercial products so long as no endorsement or testimonial of such commercial products is attributed to Employee. Neither Lender nor Employee shall issue any publicity nor make any statement concerning Studio, the Picture or Employee's services hereunder without Studio's prior written consent; provided, however, that incidental nonderogatory references to Studio, the Picture or Employee's services in connection therewith shall be permitted.

6. CREDIT NONCOMPLIANCE: No casual or inadvertent failure by Studio, or by any third party, to comply with Studio's credit obligations to Employee hereunder will constitute a breach of this Agreement, but Studio shall exercise reasonable efforts to prospectively cure any such failure. The rights and remedies of the Lender and Employee in the event of a breach of said obligations by Studio shall be limited to an action at law to recover money damages, if any, and in no event shall Lender or Employee be entitled to terminate this Agreement or to enjoin or restrain the distribution or exhibition of the Picture.

7. GUILD MEMBERSHIP: During Employee's engagement, Employee, at Employee's sole cost and expense, shall be a member in good standing of the then properly designated labor organization(s) with which Studio has entered into a collective bargaining agreement or organizations (as defined and determined under the then applicable law) representing persons performing services of the type and character required to be performed by Employee hereunder and having jurisdiction in the premises.

8. WORKERS' COMPENSATION: With respect to any injury, illness, disability or death (herein "Event") which may be suffered by Employee during the period of Employee's engagement hereunder, which Event (including disability or death consequent thereto whether during or following such period of Employee's engagement hereunder) is compensable under any applicable Workers' Compensation statute and the body of law pertaining thereto (herein "Applicable Law"), Lender, Employee and Studio agree as follows:

    a. General/Special Employers: Lender is Employee's general employer and Studio, having the exclusive right to direct and control Employee's performance of services hereunder, shall be Employee's special employer.

    b. Election Under Applicable Law: If the applicability of Applicable Law is dependent upon or is effected by an election by Lender or Employee, or both, Lender and Employee so elect, jointly and severally, to be bound by Applicable Law.

    c.   <u>Rights of Claimants</u>: The rights and remedies of Lender, Employee and all persons (e.g., heirs, executors, administrators, successors, assigns) whose rights are derived through Employee (Lender, Employee and such persons are collectively herein "Claimants") who may have the right to claim compensation or damages for an Event shall be governed by the following:

      (1)   <u>Limitation to Available Rights and Remedies</u>: Such rights and remedies shall be those and only those provided in the Applicable Law;

      (2)   <u>No Obligation Upon Occurrence of Event</u>: Neither Studio nor Studio's agents or employees, general or special, shall have any obligation to Lender by reason of the occurrence of an Event;

      (3)   <u>No Claims Involving Special Employees</u>: None of the Claimants shall assert any claim or cause of action arising out of an Event against any person, or against any entity which furnishes to Studio a person who has the status of a special employee of Studio;

      (4)   <u>Indemnification by Lender</u>: Lender shall indemnify Studio, Studio's agents and employees, general and special, from any loss, cost, liability or expense, including reasonable attorney's fees, arising out of the assertion of a claim or cause of action in breach of the provisions of this Paragraph 8.

9.   <u>NO OBLIGATION TO USE</u>: Studio is not obligated to use Employee's services hereunder or to include any of the results and proceeds thereof in the Picture or to produce, exhibit, advertise or distribute the Picture; but nothing contained in this paragraph shall relieve Studio of its obligations which may become due for Employee's services hereunder and the results and proceeds thereof to the extent provided elsewhere in this Agreement.

10.   <u>CONFORMITY</u>: Nothing in this Agreement shall be construed so as to require any illegal act. Any conflict between any provision hereof and any law or requirement with the force of law or any collective bargaining agreement ("Guild Agreement") to which Studio is a signatory shall be restricted to the extent necessary to bring it within the applicable requirements. Any invalid provision(s) hereof shall be severed, and of no effect, and the remaining provisions shall continue in full force and effect, as if the invalid provision(s) had never been contained herein.

11.   <u>EMPLOYER'S CONTRIBUTIONS</u>: Studio shall pay to the Pension Plan and Health & Welfare Fund established under any applicable Guild Agreement the employer contributions required by said Guild

Agreement with respect to the engagement of Employee's services hereunder, but not exceeding those which Studio would have been obligated to pay had Employee rendered services hereunder as Studio's direct employee.

12.   NOTICES AND PAYMENTS: Any notice by Studio to Lender may be given orally unless required hereunder to be in writing. Any notice by Lender to Studio shall be given in writing. Either Lender or Studio may hereafter designate a substitute address by written notice to the other.

   a.   To Lender: A written notice to Lender shall be delivered to Lender or to Lender's agent, by mail or transmitted through cable, telegraph, or facsimile (provided there is confirmation of receipt of such transmission) at the address for Lender as set forth in the Deal Terms. The date of mailing or transmission of any such notice to Lender shall be deemed the date of service thereof.

   b.   To Studio: A notice to Studio shall be mailed or transmitted by cable, telegraph, or facsimile (provided there is confirmation of receipt of such transmission) to Studio at the address for Studio as set forth in the Deal Terms. The date of mailing or transmission of any such notice to Studio shall be deemed the date of service thereof.

   c.   Payments: All payments to Lender hereunder shall be made by delivery to Lender or to Lender's agent or by mailing same to Lender at the address for Lender as set forth in the Deal Terms. The date of mailing of any payment to Lender hereunder shall be deemed the date of such payment.

13.   FURTHER INSTRUMENTS: Lender and Employee shall execute such documents and do such other acts and deeds as may be reasonably required by Studio or its assignees or licensees to further evidence or effectuate its rights hereunder. If Lender and/or Employee fail to do so, Studio may execute such documents as Lender's and/or Employee's attorney-in-fact, which appointment shall be irrevocable and coupled with an interest.

14.   ASSIGNMENT: Studio shall have the right to freely assign this Agreement and/or any of Studio's rights hereunder to any person, firm or corporation. Studio shall remain secondarily liable to Lender and Employee unless such assignment is to a "major" or "mini-major" motion picture studio or distributor or similarly financially responsible third party which assumes Studio's obligations hereunder in writing, or to any entity with which Studio is merged or consolidated or by which Studio is acquired, and such assignee

accepts Studio's obligations hereunder in writing. Neither Lender nor Employee shall have the right to assign this Agreement except as provided in Paragraph A16. of Exhibit "A."

15.   NO WAIVER: No waiver by either party hereto of any failure by the other party to keep or perform any covenant or condition of this Agreement shall be deemed a waiver of any preceding, succeeding or continuing breach of the same, or any other covenant or condition.

16.   GOVERNING LAW: This Agreement shall be construed in accordance with the laws of the State of California applicable to agreements which are executed and fully performed within the State of California. Any legal proceeding of any nature brought by any party hereto shall be submitted for trial without jury before any court of competent jurisdiction within the State of California. The parties hereto expressly waive trial by jury in any legal proceeding, consent and submit to the jurisdiction of any such court and agree to accept service of process outside the State of California in any matter to be submitted to any such court pursuant hereto.

17.   IMMIGRATION REFORM AND CONTROL ACT OF 1986 ("IRCA"): The engagement of Employee's services hereunder is subject to Employee timely providing Studio with the requisite documents required by IRCA and completing, signing and delivering to Studio the required form I-9 pursuant to IRCA's Section 274 a.2.

INDUCEMENT LETTER

Date: As of _____

Studio

Gentlemen:

As an inducement to you to enter into the contract executed concurrently herewith, between _____ (herein called "Lender") and you, with respect to my producing services, I represent, warrant and agree as follows:

1.   That Lender is now, and will be at all times during the term of said lent contract and at all other times when my services may be rendered or required thereunder, authorized to furnish my services to you as therein provided; and if for any reason my employment contract with Lender should expire or be terminated, I will keep and perform all of the terms and conditions thereof, as though I were a party to said lent contract and had executed it in place of Lender;

2.   That I will keep and perform all of the terms and conditions of said lent contract and will perform my services for you in accordance with the terms and conditions thereof;

3.   That you shall be entitled to apply for equitable relief, by injunction or otherwise, to prevent a breach of said lent contract or of my agreements hereunder;

4.   That I will look solely to Lender for all compensation for my services under said lent contract, and you shall have no obligation to compensate me for any services to be performed by me or for any rights granted to you thereunder;

5.   That I hereby confirm and join in all representations, warranties and agreements (including the obligation to indemnify Studio) of Lender and the grant to you of all rights under said lent contract, including but not limited to all rights granted in and to the results and proceeds of my services and the right to use my name and likeness as set forth therein, whether or not my employment by Lender should expire or be terminated. Without limiting the generality of the foregoing, I certify that all literary or dramatic material written by me relating to said photoplay is or will be written by me as an employee of Lender pursuant to my employment contract and in the performance of my duties thereunder and in the regular course of my employment. I further certify that all such literary or dramatic material shall constitute a work for hire for you pursuant to the lent contract. Accordingly you shall for copyright purposes be deemed the author of said literary or dramatic material, with the right to make such changes therein and such uses as you may desire;

6.   That all notices served on Lender in accordance with the provisions of said lent contract shall be deemed to be notices to me of the contents thereof;

7.   That I shall indemnify and hold you harmless from and against all liabilities, penalties, losses or expenses, including reasonable attorney's fees, imposed upon, sustained or incurred by you by reason of your failure to deduct or withhold from the compensation payable to Lender under said lent contract any amounts required to be deducted or withheld by you under the provisions of any now or hereafter existing law, regulation or collective bargaining agreement; and

8.   That, for purposes of any applicable Workers' Compensation statute, an employment relationship exists between you and me, you being my special employer under said lent contract and, accordingly, in the event that I sustain any injury or illness which falls within the purview of a Workers' Compensation statute, my rights and remedies, and/or

the rights and remedies of my heirs, executors, administrators, successors and assigns, against you and/or your agents and/or employees (including, without limitation, any "other special employee" referred to in said lent contract) and/or any corporation or other entity which furnishes to you the services of any such "other special employee" by reason of such injury or illness, and/or any disability or death suffered by me as a result of such injury or illness, shall be governed by and limited to those provided by such Workers' Compensation statute.

9.   That my social security number is _____.

Very truly yours,

_____

[PRODUCER]

Form 20

Film Writer Agreement

(Employment Agreement)

Agreement dated *(date of agreement)* between *(name of writer)* ("Writer"), and *(name of production company)* ("Production Company").

ALTERNATIVE CLAUSE

(Loan-out Agreement)

Agreement dated *(date of agreement)* between *(name of loan out company)*, (a *(name of state)* corporation) ("Lender"), and *(name of production company)* (a *(name of state)* corporation) ("Production company"), regarding the services of *(name of writer)* ("Writer").

1. <u>EMPLOYMENT</u>: Production Company agrees to employ Writer to perform and Writer agrees to perform, upon the terms and conditions herein specified, writing services for the proposed Theatrical Motion Picture currently entitled "*(name of picture)*" ("Picture"), based upon [*e.g., (name of story, screenplay, etc.)*] *or* [material supplied to Writers by Production Company] (Assigned Material). [Writer shall perform such writing services in collaboration with *(name of second writer)* pursuant to the Employment Agreement dated *(date of agreement)* between *(name of second writer)* and Production company (the "*(name of second writer)* Agreement"). Writer and *(name of second writer)* are hereinafter collectively referred to as the "Team".]

ALTERNATIVE CLAUSE

1. <u>WRITER/ENGAGEMENT</u>: Production Company agrees to borrow from Lender and Lender agrees to lend to Production Company the writing services of ("*Writer*") for the proposed Theatrical Motion Picture currently entitled "*(name of picture)*" ("Picture"), based upon [*e.g., (name of story, screenplay, etc.)*] *or* [material supplied to Writer by Production Company] ("Assigned Material"). Lender represents and warrants that it is a *(state of incorporation)* corporation, that Lender has entered into a written contract with Writer which is now in full force and effect, and that pursuant to such contract Lender has the right and authority to lend to Production Company the services of Writer upon the terms and conditions herein specified.

2. <u>WRITER SERVICES</u> (FLAT DEAL): Writer shall write *(specify the writing products to be delivered by the Writer, e.g., an original first draft screenplay, with two sets of revisions (hereinafter collectively "the Product" and individually the "Product Form"))*.

ALTERNATIVE CLAUSE

2. <u>THE PRODUCT AGREEMENT WITH OPTIONS</u>: The completed results of writer's services hereunder shall be deemed collectively the "Product" and individually the "Product Form," and shall be created as follows:

() Treatment/Outline ("Treatment")

() [*e.g., First*] Revision(s)/Draft(s) of Treatment

() Option for [*e.g., Final*] Revision(s)/Draft(s) of Treatment

() First Draft Screenplay

() Option for first Screenplay with [*e.g., two*] Revision(s)/Draft(s) thereof

() [*e.g., First and Final*] Revision(s)/Draft(s) of Screenplay

() Option for [*e.g., Second*] Revision(s)/Draft(s) of Screenplay

() Rewrite of Screenplay

() Polish of Screenplay

() Other [*e.g., Television revisions*]

---

3. <u>COMMENCEMENT OF SERVICES</u>: [Lender shall cause Writer to] [Writer shall] commence services in writing the (*specify task or initial task*) on [(*specify date*) *or* on a date to be specified by production company, but in any event not later than (*specify date*)]. [*If more than one (1) Product Form is required, add:* [Lender shall cause Writer to] [Writer shall] commence writing each subsequent Product Form on a date to be designated by Production Company, which date may be earlier, but shall not be later than the first business day after expiration of the then current Reading Period or Option Period, as the case may be, described in Clause 4.]

4. <u>TIME REQUIREMENTS (FLAT DEAL)</u>:

Writer's services shall be rendered pursuant to the following time requirements:

(a) <u>Delivery Periods</u>: [Lender shall cause Writer to] [Writer shall] deliver each Product Form within the period ("Delivery Period") which [commences on the date Writer is obligated to commence writing each designated Product Form and which ends upon expiration of the applicable time period listed] [is specified] in Clause 4(c).

(b) <u>Reading Periods</u>: Each time Writer delivers any Product Form, if Writer's engagement herein requires additional writing services, Production Company shall have a period ("Reading Period"), which [commences on the first business day following the delivery of such Product Form and which continues for the length of time listed] [is specified] in Clause 4(c) opposite the description of the Product Form delivered within which to read each Product Form.

(c) Length of Periods: Delivery and Reading Periods shall be the following lengths:

PRODUCT FORM	DELIVERY PERIOD	READING PERIOD
First Draft Treatment	[e.g. four weeks or (date)]	[e.g. two weeks or (date)]
Treatment-First Revision/ Second Draft Treatment	[e.g. two weeks or (date)]	[e.g. two weeks or (date)]
Treatment-Second Revision/ Third Draft Treatment	[e.g. one week or (date)]	[e.g. two weeks or (date)]
First Draft Screenplay	[e.g. twelve weeks or (date)]	[e.g. four weeks or (date)]
First Draft Screenplay First Revision/ Second Draft Screenplay	[e.g. six weeks or (date)]	[e.g. two weeks or (date)]
First Draft Screenplay Second Revision/ Third Draft Screenplay	[e.g. four weeks or (date)]	[e.g. two weeks or (date)]
Rewrite of Screenplay	[e.g. four weeks or (date)]	[e.g. two weeks or (date)]
Polish of Screenplay	[e.g. two weeks or (date)]	[e.g. two weeks or (date)]
Other	[e.g. two weeks or (date)]	[e.g. two weeks or (date)]

ALTERNATIVE CLAUSE

4. TIME REQUIREMENTS (Agreement with Options): Writer's services shall be rendered pursuant to the following time requirements:

(a) Delivery Periods: [Lender shall cause Writer to] [Writer shall] deliver each Product Form within the period ("Delivery Period") which [commences on the date Writer is obligated to commence writing each designated Product Form and which ends upon expiration of the applicable time period listed] [is specified] in Clause 4.(e).

(b) Reading Periods: Each time Writer delivers any Product Form, if Writer's engagement herein requires additional writing services, Production Company shall have a period ("Reading Period"), which [commences on the first business day following the delivery of such Product Form and which continues for the length of time listed] [is specified] in Clause 4(e) opposite the description of the Product Form delivered within which to read such Product Form and advise [Lender to cause Writer] [Writer] to commence writing the next Product Form.

(c) Postponement of Services: If Production Company does not exercise within the applicable Reading Period its right to require [Lender to cause Writer] [Writer] to commence writing [*the next Product Form,* or *e.g., the first or second set of revisions*] or, if Production Company exercises the option set forth in Clause 4(d) for [Lender to cause Writer] [Writer] to commence writing [*e.g., the first and second set of revisions*]. Production Company may nonetheless require [Lender to cause Writer] [Writer] to render such services at any time within the [*e.g., two (2) year*] period commencing upon delivery of the immediately preceding Product Form; provided however, if Writer's services are to be rendered during the first year of said [*e.g., two (2) year*] period, Production Company shall furnish [Lender] [Writer] with [*e.g., thirty (30)*] days' prior written notice of the date designated for the commencement of such services, or, if Writer's services are to be rendered during the second year of said [*e.g., two (2) year*] period, such services shall be subject to [Lender's/Writer's] prior contractual commitments to [render] [provide Writer's] services as a writer in the Theatrical and Television Motion Picture industry, and the applicable Delivery Period for any such previously postponed Product Form shall be extended for such period of time as may be required by reason of [Lender's/ Writer's] prior contractual commitments.] *or* [provided, however, that such services shall be non-exclusive and shall be subject to the contractual commitments of the [Lender/Writer] to render writing services in the Theatrical and Television Motion Picture industry, and that the applicable Delivery Period for any such additional Product Form shall be extended for such period of time as may be required by reason of such other contractual commitments.] [Nevertheless, payment for any such additional Product Form shall be made within [*e.g., five (5) business*] days after the expiration of the Reading Period applicable to such additional Product Form as designated in Clause 4(e).]

(d) Option Periods: Each Option, if any, under Clause 4(e), shall be exercised in writing within the period ("Option Period") which commences on the first business day following the delivery of the Product Form immediately preceding that for which an Option may be exercised, or upon the expiration of the Delivery Period applicable to such Product Form, whichever is later, and which continues for the length of time listed in Clause 4(e) opposite the description of the Product Form delivered. However, if Production Company has the right to request revisions in the Product Form as delivered, but fails to do so before expiration of the Reading Period, the Option Period shall commence on expiration of the Reading Period.

(e) Length of Periods: Delivery, Reading and Option Periods shall be the following lengths:

PRODUCT FORM	DELIVERY PERIOD	READING PERIOD	OPTION PERIOD
First Draft Treatment	[*e.g., four weeks or (date)*]	[*e.g., two weeks or (date)*]	[*e.g., four weeks or (date)*]
Treatment-First Revision/Second Draft Treatment	[*e.g., two weeks or (date)*]	[*e.g., two weeks or (date)*]	[*e.g., two weeks or (date)*]
Treatment-Second Revision/Third Draft Treatment	[*e.g., one week or (date)*]	[*e.g., two weeks or (date)*]	[*e.g., two weeks or (date)*]
First Draft Screenplay	[*e.g., twelve weeks or (date)*]	[*e.g., four weeks or (date)*]	[*e.g., four weeks or (date)*]
First Draft Screenplay First Revision/Second Draft Screenplay	[*e.g., six weeks or (date)*]	[*e.g., two weeks or (date)*]	[*e.g., two weeks or (date)*]
First Draft Screenplay Second Revision/Third Draft Screenplay	[*e.g., four weeks or (date)*]	[*e.g., two weeks or (date)*]	[*e.g., two weeks or (date)*]
Rewrite of Screenplay	[*e.g., four weeks or (date)*]	[*e.g., two weeks or (date)*]	[*e.g., two weeks or (date)*]
Polish of Screenplay	[*e.g., two weeks or (date)*]	[*e.g., two weeks or (date)*]	[*e.g., two weeks or (date)*]
Other	[*e.g., two weeks or (date)*]	[*e.g., two weeks or (date)*]	[*e.g., two weeks or (date)*]

5. [DELIVERY] [TIME OF ESSENCE]:

(a) Effective Delivery: [To allow time for duplication of any Product Form, delivery shall be deemed to occur [*e.g., two (2) business*] days after the Product Form is actually received in the office of [*e.g., the Production Company Executive responsible for Creative Affairs*]. Delivery of Product Form to any person other than [*e.g., said Executive*] shall not constitute delivery of such Product Form as required by this Agreement.] *or* [Delivery of each Product Form shall be deemed to occur upon receipt of such Product Form in Production Company's office at the address specified in Clause 26, *infra*.]

(b) Time of the Essence: [Lender shall cause Writer to] [Writer shall] write and deliver each Product Form [for which Writer is engaged] as soon as reasonably possible after commencement of Writer's services thereon, but not later than the date upon which the applicable Delivery Period expires. Time of delivery is of the essence.

[(c) Revisions: For each Product Form which is in the nature of a Revision, the Writer's services shall include the writing and delivery of such changes as may be required by Production Company within a reasonable time prior to the expiration of the Delivery Period applicable to such Product Form. Delivery shall not be effective until said Product Form incorporating such changes has been delivered to Production Company.]

[(d) Successive Portions: Prior to the completion of any Product Form, Writer shall [if Production Company so requests] deliver to Production Company in a written form the successive portions of such Product Form as soon as such portions shall have been written by Writer [, so that Production Company at all times during the progress of the Writer's writing hereunder will be fully advised of the method and manner of Writer's creation, writing and development of any such Product Form].]

6. COMPENSATION [FLAT DEAL]: On condition that [Lender and] Writer shall fully and completely keep and perform all of [Lender's and] Writer's [material] obligations and agreement, hereunder, and as full consideration for all services [provided by Lender to] [rendered by Writer for] Production Company, and for all rights granted and/or agreed to be granted by [Lender] [Writer] to Production Company, Production Company agrees to pay [Lender] [Writer] and [Lender] [Writer] agrees to accept compensation as follows: [e.g., *($200,000,)* payable *($25,000)* upon commencement of services, *($25,000)* upon delivery of first draft screenplay, *($25,000)* for each of two sets of revisions, and *($100,000,)* upon commencement of principal photography, which shall be subject to reduction to *($50,000)* if screen credit is shared]. [Compensation shall not be due or payable to [Lender] [Writer] for any period or periods during which [Writer] shall fail, refuse or neglect, or shall be unable for any reason to render [Writer's] services as required or desired by Production Company under the terms of this Agreement.] It is agreed that [Lender] [Writer] shall not be entitled to any additional compensation if [Lender] [Writer] shall be required to render [Writer's] services hereunder for a period exceeding the stipulated periods designated in Clause 4 hereof in order to complete all of the literary material required of Writer hereunder. [No additional compensation shall accrue or be payable to [Lender] [Writer] if any of Writer's services are rendered at night, on Sundays or holidays, or after the expiration of any particular number of hours of service in any period.]

ALTERNATIVE CLAUSE

6. COMPENSATION (AGREEMENT WITH OPTIONS):

(a) Fixed Compensation: Production Company shall pay [Lender] [Writer] as set forth below for Writer's services and all rights granted by [Lender][Writer]:

(i) For Treatment: [e.g., ($18,000) (low budget, i.e., less than ($2,500,000)/ ($30,000) (high budget, i.e., over ($2,500,000)

[e.g., (A) ($4,500/$7,500) on commencement of services or on written acknowledgment by [Lender] [Writer] of the deal memorandum covering this Agreement, whichever is later.

(B) ($13,500/$22,500) on delivery of material.]

[e.g., (ii) For Treatment-First Revision/Second Draft Treatment: ($10,000/ $15,000), payable:

(A) ($2,500/$3,750) on commencement of services.

(B) ($7,500/$11,250) on delivery of material.]

[e.g., (iii) For Treatment-Second Revision/Third Draft Treatment: ($5,000/ $7,500), payable:

(A) ($1,250/$1,875) on commencement of services.

(B) ($3,750/$5,625) on delivery of material.]

[e.g., (iv) For First Draft Screenplay: ($16,000/$30,000), payable:

(A) ($4,000/$7,500) on commencement of services.

(B) ($12,000/$22,500) on delivery of material.]

[e.g., (v) For First Draft Screenplay-First Revision/Second Draft Screenplay: ($9,000/$17,000), payable:

(A) ($2,250/$4,250) on commencement of services.

(B) ($6,750/$12,750) on delivery of material.]

[e.g., (vi) For First Draft Screenplay-Second Revision/Third Draft Screenplay: ($9,000/ $16,870), payable:

(A) ($2,250/$4,250) on commencement of services.

(B) ($6,750/$12,750) on delivery of material.]

[e.g., (vii) For Rewrite of Screenplay: ($14,000/$20,000), payable:

(A) ($3,500/$5,000) on commencement of services.

(B) ($10,500/$15,000) on delivery of material.]

[e.g., (viii) For Polish of Screenplay ($7,000/$10,000), payable:

(A) ($1,750/$2,500) on commencement of services.

(B) ($5,250/$7,500) on delivery of material.]

[*e.g.*, (ix) Other: Television revisions: (*$5,000/$10,000*), payable:

  (A) (*$1,250/$2,500*) on commencement of services.

  (B) (*$3,750/$7,500*) on delivery of material.]

(b) <u>Payment</u>: If Production Company does not require [Lender to furnish Writer's] [Writer to render] services for any Product Form regarding which Production Company has the right to require additional services, all compensation which would have been paid to [Lender] [Writer] upon delivery of such Product Form shall be payable to [Lender] [Writer] upon the expiration of the Delivery Period applicable to such Product Form. Production Company shall have no obligation to pay [Lender] [Writer] any compensation with respect to any Product Form for which Production Company has failed to exercise its Option under Clause 4. If Production Company postpones the exercise of any of its rights in Clause 4(c) hereof, compensation for the delivery of any Product Form affected by such postponement shall be made within [*e.g., five (5) business*] days after the expiration of the Reading Period applicable to such Product Form as designated in Clause 4(e).

(c) <u>Bonus Compensation</u>: Subject to the production and release of the Picture, and subject to the performance of all obligations of [Lender and Writer] [Writer] hereunder, in addition to the Fixed Compensation set forth above, [Lender] [Writer] shall be entitled to be paid the following:]

[(i) *Sole Screenplay Credit*: If Writer receives sole screenplay credit pursuant to [*e.g.*, final Writer's Guild of America ("WGA") credit determination] with respect to the Picture, [Lender] [Writer] shall be entitled to receive as Bonus Compensation the sum of [*e.g., ($100,000) over* the compensation provided by Clause 6(a)], less the aggregate of all sums paid to [Lender] [Writer] pursuant to Clause 6(a) above, payable within [*e.g., (ten (10))*] days after the final credit determination for the Picture.]

[(ii) *Shared Screenplay Credit*: If Writer receives shared screenplay credit pursuant to [*e.g.*, final WGA credit determination] with respect to the Picture, [Lender] [Writer] shall be entitled to receive as Bonus Compensation [the sum of (*specify amount, e.g., the initial amount of the bonus for each writer in such case may be $50,000 over the compensation provided by Clause 6(a) supra*) less] or [an amount equal to [*e.g., one-half* (½)] of the difference between [*specify amount, e.g., the initial amount of the bonus for each writer in such case may be $100,000*]) less the aggregate of all sums paid to [Lender][Writer] pursuant to Clause 6(a) above, payable within [*e.g., ten (10)*] days after the final credit determination for the Picture, in lieu of the Bonus Compensation set forth in Clause 6(c)(i) above.]

[(iii) *Time of Payment*: If no other writer is engaged to render services as a writer for the Picture prior to the commencement of principal photography, [and if Production Company believes that Writer shall be accorded sole screenplay credit pursuant to [*e.g.*, final WGA credit determination] for the Picture,] then [Lender][Writer] shall be entitled to be paid ([one-half (½) of the Bonus Compensation set forth in Clause 6(c)(i) above] *or* [the Bonus Compensation set forth in Clause 6(c)(ii) above with respect to shared screenplay credit]) within [*e.g.*, *ten (10)*] days of the commencement of principal photography. ([If Writer does, in fact, receive sole screenplay credit pursuant to [e.g., final WGA credit determination] for the Picture, [Lender] [Writer] shall be entitled to be paid the balance of such Bonus Compensation within [*e.g.*, *ten (10)*] days after final credit determination for the Picture.]) *or* [If [Lender] [Writer] is paid the Bonus Compensation set forth in Clause 6(c)(ii), and if Writer receives sole screenplay credit pursuant to [*e.g.*, final WGA credit determination] for the Picture, [Lender] [Writer] shall be entitled to be paid the difference between the amount so paid to [Lender] [Writer] and the amount Lender is otherwise entitled to be paid pursuant to the provisions of Clause 6(c)(i) above within [*e.g.*, *ten (10)*] days] after the final credit determination for release date of the Picture.]

[(iv) *Repayment*: If [*e.g.*, *one-half (½)*] of the Bonus Compensation set forth in Clause 6(c) above is paid to [Lender] [Writer] as set forth hereinabove, and if Writer receives neither sole screenplay credit nor shared screenplay credit pursuant to [e.g., final WGA credit determination] for the Picture, the [Lender] [Writer] shall repay to Production Company such sum so paid to [Lender] [Writer] within [*e.g.*, *five (5) days*] of such final credit determination.]

[(d) Deferred Compensation: Subject to the production and release of the Picture and subject to the performance of all [material] obligations of [Lender and Writer] [Writer] hereunder, in addition to the Fixed Compensation and Bonus Compensation set forth above, [Lender] [Writer] shall be entitled to be paid the following:]

[(i) *Sole Screenplay Credit*: If Writer receives sole screenplay credit pursuant to [e.g., final WGA credit determination] for the Picture, [Lender] [Writer] shall be entitled to receive as Deferred Compensation the sum of [*e.g.*, *this may be 25% or 50% of the total compensation under Clause 6(a) which may be adjusted upward to offset the deferral aspect*] which shall be deferred and paid pro rata with all similar deferments of compensation at the point just preceding the point at which Net Profit participations in the Picture become payable.]

[(ii) *Shared Screenplay Credit*: If Writer receives shared screenplay credit pursuant to [*e.g.*, final WGA credit determination] for the Picture, [Lender] [Writer] shall be entitled to receive as Deferred Compensation the sum of (*specify amount*) [this will usually be one-half of the amount specified in subclause 6(d)(i)] which shall be deferred and payable pro rata with all similar deferments of compensation at the point just preceding the point at which Net Profit participations in the Picture become payable.]

[(e) <u>Contingent Compensation</u>: Subject to the production and release of the Picture and subject to the performance of all [material obligations of [Lender and Writer] [Writer] hereunder in addition to the Fixed Compensation, Bonus Compensation and Deferred Compensation set forth above, [Lender] [Writer] shall be entitled to be paid the following:]

[(i) *Sole Screenplay Credit*: If Writer receives sole screenplay credit pursuant to [e.g., final WGA credit determination] for the Picture, [Lender] [Writer] shall be entitled to receive as Contingent Compensation an amount equal to [*e.g., five percent 5%*)] of one hundred percent (100%) of the Net Profits of the Picture.]

[(ii) *Shared Screenplay Credit*: If Writer receives shared screenplay credit pursuant to [e.g., final WGA credit determination for the Picture, [Lender] [Writer] shall be entitled to receive as Contingent Compensation an amount equal to [*e.g., two and one-half percent* (2-1/2 %)] of one hundred percent (100%) of the Net Profits of the Picture.]

[(f) <u>Exhibit "A"</u>: For purposes of this Agreement, "Net Profits" shall be computed, determined and paid in accordance with Exhibit "A," attached hereto and incorporated herein by this reference.]

[(g) <u>Additional payments to [Lender] [Writer] for Sequel, Remake and Television Use of the Work; Right of First Negotiation</u>: Subject to the provisions of Clauses 6(h) and 6(i) below, and subject to the production and release of the Picture and the performance of all [material] obligations of [Lender and Writer] [Writer] hereunder:]

[(i) *Studio Sequel Theatrical Motion Pictures*: If Writer receives sole (or shared) screenplay credit or is accorded separation of rights pursuant to [*e.g.*, applicable WGA determination] with respect to the Picture, then for each Studio Sequel Theatrical Motion Picture based on the Picture produced and released by Production Company, [Lender] [Writer] shall be entitled to be paid an amount equal to [*e.g., fifty percent (50%)*] of one hundred percent (100%) of the sum paid to [Lender] [Writer] as Fixed Compensation pursuant to Clause 6(a) above, and a percentage participation in the Net Profits of such Studio Sequel Theatrical Motion Picture in an amount equal to [*e.g., fifty percent (50%)*] of one hundred percent (100%) of the rate of percentage participation in Net Profits of the Picture payable to [Lender] [Writer] as Contingent Compensation pursuant to subclauses 6(e)(i) or 6(e)(ii) above, if any. Net profits shall be computed, determined and paid in accordance with Exhibit "A."]

[(ii) *Theatrical Remakes*: If Writer receives sole (or shared) screenplay credit or is accorded separation of rights pursuant to [*e.g.*, applicable WGA determination] for the Picture, then for each Theatrical Remake of the Picture produced and released by Production Company, [Lender] [Writer] shall be entitled to be paid an amount equal to [*e.g., thirty-three and one-third percent* (33-1/3%)] of one hundred percent (100%) of the sum paid to [Lender] [Writer] as Fixed Compensation pursuant to Clause 6(a), above, and a percentage participation in the Net Profits of such Theatrical Remake in an amount equal to [*e.g., thirty-three and one-third percent* (33-1/3%)] of the rate of percentage participation in Net Profits of the Picture payable to [Lender] [Writer] as Contingent Compensation pursuant to subclauses 6(e)(i) or 6(e)(ii) above, if any. Net Profits shall be computed, determined and paid in accordance with Exhibit "A."]

[(iii) <u>Right of First Negotiation--Studio Sequel Theatrical Motion Pictures and Theatrical Remakes</u>: If Writer is accorded sole (or shared) screenplay credit or is entitled to sole separation of rights with respect to the Picture, and if Production Company elects to produce a Studio Sequel Theatrical Motion Picture based upon the Picture or a Theatrical Remake of the Picture within the period of [*e.g., five (5) years*] after the initial release date of the Picture, and if this Agreement has not been terminated due to [Lender/Writer] Default, Production Company shall so notify [Lender] [Writer] and [Lender] [Writer] shall have a period of [*e.g., thirty (30)*] days following such notice to negotiate with Production Company the terms and conditions upon which [Lender will furnish the services of Writer to] [Writer will] render writing services in connection therewith. [Lender's] [Writer's] rights under this subparagraph shall continue so long as,

(A) Writer is actively engaged as a writer of Theatrical Motion Pictures.

(B) [Lender] [Writer] has furnished Writer's services as a writer for each previous Studio Sequel Theatrical Motion Picture based on the Picture and Theatrical Remake of the Picture, and

(C) The Agreement pursuant to which Writer has rendered such services has not been terminated due to Lender/Writer Default.]

If [Lender furnishes] [Writer provides] Writer's services under this Subclause (iii), the compensation received by [Lender] [Writer] shall be in lieu of any payments to [Lender] [Writer] under Subclauses 6(g)(i) and (ii), above.

[(iv) <u>Studio Sequel Television Motion Pictures and Television Remakes</u>:

(A) *Pilot and Series*: [If Writer is accorded sole (or shared) screenplay credit or separation of rights pursuant to applicable WGA determination with respect to the Picture, then for] *or* [for] each Studio Sequel Television Motion Picture based upon the Picture and/or Television Remake of the Picture which is produced and licensed for exhibition by Production Company and which is a Pilot or an episode of an episodic or anthology [prime time network] television series (collectively "TV Program"), [Lender] [Writer] shall be entitled to receive the following royalties:

(1) [*e.g., $1,250*] for each TV Program of not more than thirty (30) minutes in length.

(2) [*e.g., $1,500*] for each TV Program in excess of thirty (30) minutes but not more than sixty (60) minutes in length.

(3) [*e.g., $1,750*] for each TV Program in excess of sixty (60) minutes in length.

(4) If any TV Program is rerun, [Lender] [Writer] shall be paid [*e.g., twenty percent (20%)*] of the applicable sum initially paid [Lender] [Writer] pursuant to Subclauses (1), (2) or (3) above for the second run, third run, fourth run, fifth run, and sixth run respectively. No further rerun payments shall be due or payable for any rerun after the sixth run.

(5) The applicable amount under Subclauses (1), (2) or (3) above shall be one-half the amount specified if Writer receives shared screenplay credit.

(B) *Movies of the Week and Mini-Series*: [If Writer is accorded sole (or shared) screenplay credit or separation of rights pursuant to applicable WGA determination for the Picture, then for] or [for] each Studio Sequel Television Motion Picture or Television Remake of the Picture which is produced and licensed for exhibition by Production Company and which is a so-called "Movie of the Week" or so-called "Mini-Series", [Lender] [Writer] shall be entitled to receive the following royalties which sum shall constitute full payment for all re-run use and/or other exploitation thereof:

(1) [*e.g., $15,000*] for the first two (2) hours of running time of each such Movie of the Week and/or each such Mini-Series.

(2) [*e.g., $7,500*] for every hour of running time, if any, exceeding the first two (2) hours of running time of such Movie of the Week and/or such Mini-Series [up to a maximum of (*specify amount, e.g., $60,000*.]

[(v) <u>Right of First Negotiation — Studio Sequel Television Motion Pictures and Television Remakes</u>: If Writer is accorded sole (or shared) screenplay credit or is entitled to sole separation of rights with respect to the Picture, and if Production Company elects to produce a Studio Sequel Television Motion Picture based upon the Picture or a Television Remake of the Picture within the period of [*e.g., seven (7)*] years after the initial release date of the Picture, and if this Agreement has not been terminated for Lender/Writer Default [, and subject to the approval of the buyer of such Studio Sequel Television Motion Picture of Television Remake], Production Company shall so notify [Lender][Writer] and [Lender] [Writer] shall have [*e.g., thirty (30)*] days following such notice to negotiate with Production Company the terms and conditions upon which [Lender will furnish the services of Writer to] [Writer will] render writing services in connection therewith. [Lender's] [Writer's] rights under this subparagraph shall continue so long as,

(A) Writer is actively engaged as a Writer of Television Motion Pictures,

(B) [Lender] [Writer] has furnished Writer's services as a Writer for each previous Studio Sequel Television Motion Picture based upon the Picture and Television Remake of the Picture, if any, and

(C) The Agreement pursuant to which Writer has rendered such services has not been terminated due to Lender/Writer Default. If [Lender furnishes] [Writer provides] Writer's services under this Subclause (v), the compensation received by [Lender] [Writer] shall be in lieu of any payments to [Lender] [Writer] under Subclause 6(g)(iv), above.

[(vi) Definitions: The following terms as utilized in connection with this Agreement, shall be defined as set forth below:

(A) "Television Remake": A remake primarily intended to be initially distributed for free-television exhibition.

(B) "Television Studio Sequel Motion Picture": A studio sequel motion picture primarily intended to be initially distributed for free-television exhibition.

(C) "Theatrical Remake": A remake primarily intended to be initially distributed for theatrical exhibition.

(D) "Theatrical Studio Sequel Motion Picture": A studio sequel motion picture primarily intended to be initially distributed for theatrical exhibition.

[(h) Payment to [Lender][Writer] Reducible: Any sum payable to [Lender][Writer] pursuant to Subclauses 6(g)(i), 6(g)(iv) above shall be reducible by all sums payable to any other writer or writers who are also entitled to separation of rights pursuant to applicable WGA determination with respect to the Picture but to not less than one-half (½) of the respective payment or payments provided by said clauses.]

[(i) WGA Agreement: All sums payable to [Lender] [Writer] pursuant to this Agreement shall be in lieu of, and not in addition to, any similar payment to which [Lender] [Writer] may be entitled pursuant to the current Writers Guild of America Theatrical and Television Agreement ("WGA Agreement").]

7. CONDITIONS AFFECTING OR RELATED TO COMPENSATION:

(a) Method of Payment: All compensation which shall become due to [Lender][Writer] hereunder shall be sent to [Lender] [Writer] at the address provided in Clause 26. Such address may be changed to such other address as [Lender] [Writer] may hereafter notify Production Company in accordance with Clause 26.

(b) Performance: Production Company's obligation to pay compensation or otherwise perform hereunder shall be conditioned upon full performance by [Lender and Writer] [Writer] of all [Lender's and Writer's] [Writer's] [material] obligations under the Agreement. No compensation shall accrue or become payable to [Lender] [Writer] during Writer's inability, failure or refusal to perform, according to the terms and conditions of this Agreement, the services contracted for herein, nor shall compensation accrue or become payable during any period of Force Majeure, Suspension or upon Termination except as otherwise herein provided.

(c) Governmental Limitation: No withholding, deduction, reduction or limitation of compensation by Production Company which is required or authorized by law ("Governmental Limitation") shall be a breach of this Agreement by Production Company or relieve [Lender and Writer] [Writer] from [Lender's and Writer's] [Writer's] obligations hereunder. Payment of compensation as permitted pursuant to the Governmental Limitation shall continue while such Governmental Limitation is in effect and shall be deemed to constitute full performance by Production Company of its obligation to pay compensation hereunder.

(d) Garnishment/Attachment: If Production Company is required, because of the service of any [garnishment] [attachment], writ of execution or lien, or by the terms of any contract or assignment executed by [Lender] [Writer] to withhold, or to pay all or any portion of the compensation due [Lender] [Writer] hereunder to any other person, firm or corporation, the withholding or payment of such compensation or portion thereof, pursuant to the requirements of any such [attachment] [garnishment], writ of execution, lien, contract or assignment shall not be construed as a breach by Production Company of this Agreement.

(e) Overpayment/Offset: If Production Company makes any overpayment to [Lender] [Writer] hereunder for any reason or if [Lender and/or] Writer is indebted to Production Company for any reason, [Lender or] Writer shall pay Production Company such overpayment or indebtedness on demand, or at the election of Production Company, Production Company may deduct and retain for its own account an amount equal to all or any part of such overpayment or indebtedness from any sums that may be due or become due or payable by Production Company to [Lender or] Writer or for the account of [Lender or] Writer and such deduction or retention shall not be deemed a breach of this Agreement.

(f) Pay or Play: Production Company shall not be obligated to use Writer's services for the Picture, nor shall Production Company be obligated to produce, release, distribute, advertise, exploit or otherwise make use of the results and proceeds of Writer's services if such services are used. Production Company may elect to terminate Writer's services at any time without legal justification or excuse [as provided in this Agreement or at law] provided that the Fixed Compensation provided in Clause 6(a), which shall have been earned and accrued prior to such termination shall be paid to [Lender] [Writer]. Upon such termination, all other rights of [Lender and] Writer herein shall be deemed void *ab initio* except such rights as may have accrued to Writer in accordance with the terms of Clauses 21 [relating to Guilds and Unions] and 22 [relating to Credits].

8. PERFORMANCE STANDARDS: Writer's services hereunder shall be rendered promptly [either alone or in collaboration with another or other writers] in a diligent, conscientious, artistic and efficient manner to Writer's best ability [, either alone or in collaboration with others]. Writer shall devote all of Writer's time and shall render Writer's services exclusively to Production Company in performing the writing services contemplated hereunder, and shall not render [writing] services for any other party during the period of Writer's engagement. Writer's services shall be rendered in such manner as Production Company may direct pursuant to the instructions, suggestions and ideas of and under the control of and at the times and places [reasonably] required by Production Company's authorized representatives. [Lender shall cause Writer] [Writer shall], as and when requested by Production Company, [to] consult with Production Company's duly authorized representatives and shall be available for conferences with such representatives for such purposes at such times and places during Writer's engagement as may be [reasonably] required by such representatives.

9. RESULTS AND PROCEEDS OF SERVICES:

(a) Ownership: Production Company shall solely and exclusively own, and [Lender] [Writer] hereby transfers and assigns to Production Company, the Product, each Product Form and all of the results and proceeds thereof, in whatever stage of completion as may exist from time to time (including but not limited to all rights of whatever kind and character, throughout the universe, in perpetuity, in any and all languages, of copyright, trademark, patent, production, manufacture, recordation, reproduction, transcription, performance, broadcast and exhibition by any art, method or device, now known or hereafter devised, including without limitation, radio broadcasting, theatrical and non-theatrical exhibition, and television exhibition or otherwise) whether such results and proceeds consist of literary, dramatic, musical, motion picture, mechanical or any other form or works, themes, ideas, compositions, creations or products. Production Company's acquisition hereunder shall also include all rights generally known in the field of literary and musical endeavor as the "moral rights of authors" in and/or to the Product, each Product Form, and any musical and literary proceeds of Writer's services. Production Company shall have the right but not the obligation, with respect to the Product, each Product Form, the results and proceeds thereof, to add to, subtract from, change, arrange, revise, adapt, rearrange, make variations, and to translate the same into any and all languages, change the sequence, change the characters and the descriptions thereof contained therein, change the title of the same, record and photograph the same with or without sound (including spoken words, dialogue and music synchronously recorded), use said title or any of its components in connection with works or motion pictures wholly or partially independent thereof, to sell, copy and publish the same as Production Company may desire and to use all or any part thereof in new versions, adaptations and sequels in any and all languages and to obtain copyright therein throughout the world. [Lender/] Writer hereby expressly waives any and all rights which Writer may have, either in law, in equity, or otherwise, which Writer may have or claim to have as a result of any alleged infringements of Writer's so-called "moral rights of authors." [Lender] [Writer] acknowledges that the results and proceeds of Writer's services are works specially ordered by Production Company for use as part of a motion picture and the results and proceeds of Writer's services shall be considered to be works made for hire for Production Company, and, therefore, Production Company shall be the author and copyright owner of the results and proceeds of Writer's services.

(b) Assignment and Vesting of Rights: All rights granted or agreed to be granted to Production Company hereunder shall vest in Production Company immediately and shall remain vested whether this Agreement expires in normal course or is terminated for any cause or reason, or whether Writer executes the Certificate of Authorship required, *infra*. All material created, composed, submitted, added or interpolated by Writer hereunder shall automatically become Production Company's property, and Production Company, for this purpose, shall be deemed author thereof with Writer acting entirely as Production Company's employee. [Lender/Writer] does hereby assign and transfer to Production Company all of the foregoing without reservation, condition or limitation, and no right of any kind, nature or description is reserved by [Lender or] Writer. [The said assignment and transfer to Production Company by [Lender and] Writer are subject to the limitations contained in the current Writer's Guild of America Theatrical and Television Film Basic Agreement ("WGA Agreement").]

(c) Execution of Other Documents:

(i) Certificate of Authorship: [Lender] [Writer] further agrees, if Production Company requests [Lender] [Writer] to do so, [to cause Writer] to execute and deliver to Production Company, in connection with [the Product] [all material written by writer hereunder], a Certificate of Authorship in substantially the following form:

I hereby certify that I wrote the manuscript hereto attached, entitled "(*name of work*)" based upon "(*name of source*)", as an employee of (*name of production company*) which furnished my services pursuant to an [Employment] Agreement between (*name of writer*) and Production Company dated (*date*), in performance of my duties thereunder and in the regular course of my employment, and that Production Company is the author thereof and entitled to the copyright therein and thereto [and all renewals thereof], with the right to make such changes therein and such uses thereof as it may [from time to time] determine as such author.

IN WITNESS WHEREOF, I have hereto set my hand this (*date*).

If Production Company desires to secure separate assignments or Certificates of Authorship of or for any of the foregoing, [Lender] [Writer] agrees to execute [or to cause Writer to execute] such certificate upon Production Company's request therefor. [Lender and] Writer irrevocably grant(s) Production Company the power coupled with an interest to execute such separate assignments or Certificates of Authorship in [Lender's/] Writer's name and as [Lender's/] Writer's attorney-in-fact.

(ii) [Lender] [Writer] recognizes that the provisions in Subclause 9(c)(iii) dealing with any other documents to be signed by [Lender] [Writer] are not to be construed in derogation of Production Company's rights arising from the employer-employee relationship but are included because in certain jurisdictions and in special circumstances the rights in and to material which flow from the employer-employee relationship may not be sufficient in and of themselves to vest ownership in Production Company.

(iii) If Production Company desires to secure further documents covering, quitclaiming or assigning all or any of the results and proceeds of Writer's services; or all or any rights in and to the same, then [Lender/] Writer agrees to [execute] [to have Writer execute] and deliver to Production Company any such documents at any time and from time to time upon Production Company's request, and in such form as may be prescribed by Production Company; without limiting the generality of the foregoing [Lender/] Writer agrees to [execute] [to have Writer execute] and deliver to Production Company [upon] [within five (5) business days after [Lender's/Writer's] receipt of] Production Company's [written] request therefor an assignment of all rights in the form attached hereto marked Exhibit _____ and made a part hereof by reference, it being agreed that all the representations, warranties and agreements made and to be made by [Lender/] Writer under this Exhibit shall be deemed made by [Lender/] Writer as part of this agreement. If [Lender/] Writer shall fail or refuse to execute and deliver the certificate above described and/or any such documents, [Lender/] Writer hereby irrevocably grants Production Company the power coupled with an interest to execute this certificate and/or documents in [Lender's/] Writer's name and as [Lender's/] Writer's attorney-in-fact. [Lender's/] Writer's failure to execute this certificate and/or documents shall not affect or limit any of Production Company's rights in and to the results and proceeds of Writer's services. [Production Company agrees to provide [Lender/Writer] with a copy of any document signed by Production Company pursuant to the power of attorney granted herein.]

[(d) Publication Rights: Notwithstanding Subclauses (a), (b) and (c) above, if [Lender/] [Writer] is entitled to separation of rights with respect to the Picture pursuant to applicable WGA determination, and subject to the rights of any other

writer or writers entitled to separation of rights under the WGA Agreement, the
following shall apply:]

[(i) The time restrictions contained in Article 16A 3a (1) of the WGA
Agreement shall not apply.]

[(ii) The right to publish or cause to be published, [in printed form] items such
as comic strips, illustrated books, coloring books, picture books, comic books
and Movie-Novels shall be included within the rights granted to Production
Company and shall not be included within the [print] publication rights retained
by [Lender] [Writer].]

[(iii) Subject to the provisions of Article 16A 3a (3) of the WGA Agreement,
[Lender] [Writer] shall enter into an agreement ("Publication Agreement") with
a publisher ("Publisher") for the publication of a paperback novelization
("Novelization") of the Product Form upon which the Picture was based,
subject to the following:]

[(A) [Lender] [Writer] shall cause the Novelization to be written and shall
cause publisher to coordinate the publication thereof with the initial release
date of the Picture.]

[(B) Production Company shall have the publisher's right of approval and
[Lender] [Writer] shall consult with Production Company regarding all
aspects of the Novelization, including, but not limited to, the identity of the
writer of the Novelization (if other than Writer) and the terms of the
Publication Agreement.]

[(C) At Production Company's election, the title of the Novelization shall
be the same as the title of the Picture as of the date of the printing of the
Novelization.]

[(D) [Lender] [Writer] shall submit the final manuscript of the Novelization
to Production Company reasonably in advance of the date scheduled for
publication of the Novelization to enable Production Company to determine
in good faith whether such manuscript is, in fact, a novelization of the final
Product Form upon which the Picture is based. If Production Company
determines that the manuscript is not a novelization of such Product Form,
[Lender] [Writer] shall again submit the manuscript, so revised, to Production
Company for Production Company's approval prior to submitting it to
Publisher.]

[(E) Production Company shall furnish (to the extent available) and Publisher
shall be required to utilize in a manner to be approved by Production
Company, artwork, stills and logos from the Picture, and, in consideration
thereof, shall cause Publisher to pay directly to Production Company an
amount equal to (*e.g. twenty-five percent (25%)*) of one hundred percent
(100%) of all advances and royalties payable to [Lender] [Writer] in
connection with the Novelization.]

[(F) If [Lender] [Writer] has not entered into the Publication Agreement by (*e.g., thirty (30)*) days prior to the date scheduled for commencement of principal photography of the Picture, Production Company shall have the right to enter into the Publishing Agreement, and, in such case, [Lender] [Writer] shall be entitled to receive an amount equal to (*e.g., fifty percent (50%)*) of one hundred percent (100%) of all advances and royalties payable to Production Company by Publisher in connection with the Novelization. Any such payments shall be in lieu of and not in addition to any similar payment to which [Lender] [Writer] may be entitled pursuant to the WGA Agreement.]

[(G) Any advances or royalties payable to or for any other parties who are also entitled to separation of rights pursuant to applicable WGA determination for the Picture shall be borne by [Lender] [Writer] and shall be payable out of that percentage of advances and royalties payable to [Lender] [Writer] hereunder.]

[(iv) Notwithstanding anything to the contrary contained herein, Production Company shall have the right to publish and copyright, or cause to be published and copyrighted, screenplays, teleplays and scripts adapted from or based upon the Product and the novelization of screenplays, teleplays and scripts adapted from or based upon the Product or any Product Form created hereunder.]

[(v) Nothing contained in Subclause (d) shall be interpreted to mean that Production Company has waived any rights (except for those waived pursuant to Subclause (i) above) with respect to Publication Rights in the Product provided under Article 16A of the WGA Agreement.]

10. [LENDER'S AND] WRITER'S WARRANTIES:

(a) <u>Indemnification and Warranties</u>: [Lender and] Writer agrees(s) and warrant(s) that, except as provided in the next sentence hereof, all material composed and/or submitted by Writer for or to Production Company shall be wholly original with Writer and shall not infringe upon or violate the right of privacy of, nor constitute a libel or slander against, nor violate any common law rights or any other rights of any person, firm or corporation. The same agreements and warranties are made by [Lender and] Writer regarding any and all material, incidents, treatments, characters and action which Writer may add to or interpolate in any material assigned by Production Company to Writer for preparation, but are not made regarding violations or infringements contained in the material so assigned by Production Company to Writer. These agreements and warranties on [Lender's and] Writer's part are subject to the limitations contained in the WGA Agreement.

(b) <u>Further Warranties</u>: [Lender and] Writer hereby warrant(s) that [Lender and] Writer (is) (are) under no obligation or disability, created by law or otherwise, which would in any manner or to any extent prevent or restrict [Lender and] Writer from entering into and fully performing this Agreement, and [Lender and]

Writer hereby accept(s) the obligations hereunder. [Lender and] [Writer] warrant(s) that [Lender and] [Writer](has) (have) not entered into any agreement or commitment that would prevent [their] [Writer's] fulfilling [its] [Writer's] commitments with Production Company hereunder and that [Lender and] [Writer] will not enter into any such agreement or commitment without Production Company's specific approval. [[Lender and] [Writer] hereby agrees that Writer shall devote Writer's entire time and attention and best talents and ability exclusively to Production Company as specified herein, and observe and be governed by the rules of conduct established by Production Company for the conduct of its employees.]

(c) <u>Indemnification</u>: [Lender and] Writer agree(s) to indemnify Production Company, its successors, assigns, licensees, officers, directors and employees, and hold them harmless from and against any and all claims, liability, losses, damages, costs, expenses (including but not limited to attorneys' fees), judgments and penalties arising out of, [Lender's and] Writer's breach of any warranty made by [Lender and] Writer under this Agreement.

11. <u>NAME AND LIKENESS</u>: Production Company shall always have the [sole and exclusive] right to use and display Writer's name and likeness in connection with advertising, publicizing and exploiting the Picture or the Product. However, such advertising may not include the direct endorsement of any product (other than the Picture) without Writer's consent. Exhibition, advertising, publicizing or exploiting the Picture by any media, even though a part of or in connection with a product or a commercially-sponsored program, shall not be deemed an endorsement of any nature.

12. <u>PUBLICITY RESTRICTIONS</u>: [Lender or] Writer shall not, [individually or jointly,] or by any means of press agents or publicity or advertising agencies or others, employed or paid by [Lender or] Writer or otherwise, circulate, publish or otherwise disseminate any news stories or articles, books or other publicity, containing [Lender's or] Writer's name relating directly or indirectly to Writer's [engagement] [employment] by Production Company, the subject matter of this Agreement, the Picture, or the services to be rendered by Writer or others for the Picture [,unless first approved by (Production Company); provided, however, that Lender and Writer may issue personal publicity in which the Picture is mentioned incidentally, so long as such references to the Picture are not derogatory.] [Lender and] Writer shall not transfer or attempt to transfer any right, privilege, title or interest in or to any of the aforestated things, nor shall [Lender or] Writer willingly permit any infringement upon the exclusive rights granted to Production Company. [[Lender and] Writer authorize(s) Production Company, at Production Company's expense, in [Lender's or] Writer's name or otherwise, to institute any proper legal proceedings to prevent such infringement.]

13. REMEDIES:

(a) <u>Remedies Cumulative</u>: All remedies of Production Company [or [Lender] [Writer]] shall be cumulative, and no one such remedy shall be exclusive of any other. Without waiving any rights or remedies under this Agreement or otherwise, Production Company [or [Lender] [Writer]] may from time to time recover, by action, any damages arising out of any breach of this Agreement by [Lender and/or] Writer [or Production Company, as applicable] and may institute and maintain subsequent actions for additional damages which may arise from the same or other breaches. The commencement or maintenance of any such action or actions by Production Company shall not constitute or result in the termination of [Lender's] [Writer's] engagement hereunder unless Production Company shall expressly so elect by written notice to [Lender] [Writer]. The pursuit by Production Company [or [Lender] [Writer]] of any remedy under this Agreement or otherwise shall not be deemed to waive any other or different remedy which may be available under this Agreement or otherwise.

(b) <u>Services Unique</u>: [Lender and] Writer acknowledge(s) that Writer's services to be furnished hereunder and the rights herein granted are of a special, unique, unusual, extraordinary and intellectual character which gives them a peculiar value, the loss of which cannot be reasonably or adequately compensated in damages in an action at law, and that [Lender's or] Writer's Default will cause Production Company irreparable injury and damage. [Lender and] Writer agree(s) that Production Company shall be entitled to injunctive and other equitable relief to prevent default by [Lender or] Writer. In addition to such equitable relief, Production Company shall be entitled to such other remedies as may be available at law, including damages.

14. FORCE MAJEURE:

(a) <u>Suspension</u>: If, (i) by reason of fire, earthquake, labor dispute or strike, act of God or public enemy, any municipal ordinance, any state or federal law, governmental order or regulation, or other cause beyond Production Company's control [which would excuse Production Company's performance as a matter of law], Production Company is prevented from or hampered in the development and/or production of the Picture, or if, (ii) by reason of the closing of substantially all the theatres in the United States for any of the aforesaid or other causes [which would excuse Production Company's performance as a matter of law], Production Company's development and/or production of the Picture is postponed or suspended, or if, (iii) by reason of any of the aforesaid contingencies or any other cause or occurrence not within Production Company's control, including but not limited to the death, illness or incapacity of any principal member of the cast of the Picture or the director or individual producer, the preparation, development, commencement, production or completion of the Picture is hampered, interrupted or interfered with, and/or if, (iv) Production Company's normal business operations are hampered or otherwise interfered with by virtue of any disruptive events which are beyond Production Company's control ("Production Company Disability"), then Production Company may postpone the commencement of or suspend the rendition of Writer's services and the running of time hereunder for such time as the Production Company Disability continues; and no compensation shall accrue or become payable to [Lender] [Writer] hereunder during such suspension. [Such suspension shall end upon the cessation of the cause thereof.] *or* [Such suspension shall end no later than (*e.g., four (4) weeks*) following cessation of Production Company Disability or upon the recommencement of principal photography after the cessation of Production Company Disability, whichever shall first occur.] [The maximum suspension of this Agreement due to a Production Company Disability shall be (*e.g., six (6) months*).]

(b) *Termination*:

(i) *Production Company Termination Right*: If a Production Company Disability continues for a period of [*e.g., eight (8) weeks*], Production Company may terminate this Agreement upon written notice to [Lender] [Writer].

(ii) *[Lender's] [Writer's] Termination Right*: If a Production Company Disability results in the payment of compensation being suspended hereunder for a period exceeding [*e.g., eight (8) weeks*], [Lender] [Writer] may terminate this Agreement upon written notice to Production Company.

(iii) *Production Company Re-Establishment Right*: Despite [Lender's] [Writer's] election to terminate this Agreement, within [*e.g., five (5) business days*] after Production Company's actual receipt of such written notice from [Lender] [Writer], Production Company may elect to re-establish the operation of this Agreement by written notice to [Lender] [Writer] and recommencement of the provision of Writer's services and the payment of any compensation due [Lender] [Writer].

15. WRITER'S INCAPACITY: If, by reason of mental or physical disability, Writer shall be incapacitated from performing or complying with any (of the terms or conditions hereof ("Writer's Incapacity") for a consecutive period exceeding (*e.g., seven (7) days*) or an aggregate period exceeding (*e.g., ten (10) days*)) during the performance of Writer's services, then:

(a) Suspension: Production Company may suspend the rendition of services by Writer and the running of time hereunder so long as Writer's Incapacity shall continue.

(b) Termination: Production Company may terminate this Agreement and all of Production Company's obligations and liabilities hereunder upon written notice to [Lender] [Writer].

(c) Right of Examination: If any claim of mental or physical disability is made by Writer or on Writer's behalf, the Production Company may have Writer examined by such physicians as Production Company may designate. Writer's physician may be present at such examination, and shall not interfere therewith. [Any tests performed on Writer shall be related to and be customary for the treatment, diagnosis or examination to be performed in connection with Writer's claim.]

16. [LENDER/] [WRITER] DEFAULT: If Writer fails or refuses to write, complete and deliver to Production Company the Product Form provided for herein within the respective periods specified or if [Lender and/or] Writer otherwise fails or refuses to perform or comply with any of the [material] terms or conditions hereof (other than by reason of Writer's Incapacity) ("Lender/Writer Default"), then:

(a) Suspension: Production Company may suspend the rendition of services by Writer and the running of time hereunder so long as the [Lender/] Writer Default shall continue.

(b) Termination: Production Company may terminate this Agreement and all of Production Company's obligations and liabilities hereunder upon written notice to [Lender] [Writer].

[(c) [Lender/] Writer Default shall not include any failure or refusal of Writer to perform or comply with the material terms of this Agreement by reason of a breach or action by Production Company which makes the performance of services by Writer impossible.]

[(d) Prior to termination of this Agreement by Production Company based upon [Lender/] Writer Default, Production Company shall notify [Lender and] Writer specifying the nature of the [Lender/] Writer Default and [Lender/] Writer shall have a period of [*e.g., 72 hours*] after the giving of such notice to cure the [Lender/] Writer Default. If the [Lender/] Writer Default is not cured within said [*e.g., 72 hours*] period, Production Company may terminate this Agreement forthwith.]

17. EFFECT OF TERMINATION: Termination of this Agreement, whether by lapse of time, mutual consent, operation of law, exercise of right of termination or otherwise shall:

(a) Compensation: Terminate Production Company's obligation to pay [Lender] [Writer] any further compensation. Nevertheless, if the termination is not for [Lender/] Writer Default, Production Company shall pay [Lender] [Writer] any compensation due and unpaid prior to termination;

(b) Refund/Delivery: If termination occurs pursuant to Clauses 14, 15, or 16, prior to Writer's delivery to Production Company of the Product Form on which Writer is then currently working, then [Lender or] Writer (or upon Writer's death, Writer's estate) shall, as Production Company requests, either forthwith refund to Production Company the compensation which may have been paid to [Lender]

[Writer] as of that time for such Product Form, or immediately deliver to Production Company all of the Product then completed or in progress, in whatever stage of completion it may be. [[Lender's and] Writer's representations and warranties set forth herein shall survive any termination of this Agreement.]

18. <u>EFFECT OF SUSPENSION</u>: No compensation shall accrue or become payable to [Lender] [Writer] during any suspension. During any period of suspension hereunder, [Lender shall not permit Writer to] [Writer shall not] render services for [Lender,] Writer or any party other than Production Company. [However, Writer shall have the right to render services to third parties during any period of suspension based upon a Production Company Disability subject, however, to Production Company's right to require Writer to resume the rendition of services hereunder upon (*e.g.*, *24 hours*) prior notice.] Production Company shall have the right (exercisable at any time) to extend the period of services of Writer hereunder for a period equal to the period of such suspension. If Production Company shall have paid compensation to [Lender] [Writer] during any period of Writer's Incapacity or [Lender/] Writer Default, then Production Company shall have the right (exercisable at any time) to require Writer to render services hereunder without compensation for a period equal to the period [Lender] [Writer] received compensation during such Writer's Incapacity or [Lender/] Writer Default.

19. <u>[LENDER'S] [WRITER'S] RIGHT TO CURE</u>: Any Writer's Incapacity or [Lender/] Writer Default shall be deemed to continue until Production Company's receipt of written notice from [Lender or] Writer specifying that Writer is ready, willing and able to perform the services required hereunder; provided that any such notice from [Lender or] Writer to Production Company shall not preclude Production Company from exercising any rights or remedies Production Company may have hereunder or at law or in equity by reason of Writer's Incapacity or [Lender/] Writer Default.

20. <u>TEAM OF WRITERS</u>: The provisions of this Clause 20 shall apply if more than one individual is engaged as Writer pursuant to this Agreement ("Team of Writers"). The obligations of the Team of Writers under this Agreement shall be joint and several, and all references in this Agreement to Writer shall be deemed to refer to the Team of Writers jointly and severally. Should any right of termination arise as a result of the Incapacity or Default of any one of the Team of Writers, the remedies of the Production Company may be exercised either as to such Writer or as to the Team of Writers [or as to Lender], at Production Company's election. Should Production Company elect to exercise its remedies only as to the Writer affected, the engagement of the other Writer or Writers shall continue [and [Lender] [such remaining Writer] shall receive only a pro-rated share of the compensation provided for herein.]

———

ALTERNATIVE CLAUSE

20. <u>IF WRITER IS MORE THAN ONE PERSON</u>: If this Agreement is entered into with more than one (1) Writer, the term "Writer" shall refer to each and all of them. Further, such Writers represent, warrant and agree that they, and each of them, prior to the date hereof, agreed to collaborate as a team for the services to be rendered or the material to be delivered hereunder, and that they agreed that all compensation specified herein is the combined total for the team. If a separate address for each Writer is provided herein, Production Company shall be deemed to have met its obligations with respect to any payment hereunder by delivering to each Writer at each Writer's respective address, a pro rata amount of any such payment based upon the number of Writers in the team. All such Writers shall be deemed to have jointly and severally made and entered into all of the representations, warranties, covenants and agreements contained herein and shall be jointly and severally obligated and bound thereby. All the Production Company's rights hereunder relate to and are exercisable against and with respect to each and all the Writers. Each Writer's representations, warranties and obligations hereunder are made with respect to each and all of them. Upon any Writer's incapacity or default, Production Company may, at its sole option elect to (a) treat such incapacity or default as the incapacity or default of all persons comprising Writer under this Agreement, in which case Production Company may then exercise any and all remedies which Production Company may have for default or incapacity of Writer as set forth herein; or Production Company may (b) treat such incapacity or default as affecting only the person or persons actually so incapacitated or actually in default, and Production Company may require any other persons comprising Writer to continue performance hereunder, in which case Production Company shall continue to compensate the Writer or Writers continuing to render services for a proportionate amount of the payments otherwise due Writer or Writers (*e.g.*, *one-half* (½) thereof if two Writers are employed hereunder).

———

[21. <u>GUILDS AND UNIONS</u>:

(a) <u>Membership</u>: During Writer's engagement hereunder, as Production Company may lawfully require, Writer at [Lender's] [Writer's] sole cost and expense (and at Production Company's request) shall remain or become and remain a member in good standing of the then properly designated labor organization or organizations (as defined and determined under the then applicable law) representing persons performing services of the type and character required to be performed by Writer hereunder.

(b) <u>Superseding Effect of Guild Arrangements</u>: Nothing contained in this Agreement shall be construed so as to require the violation of the applicable WGA Agreement, which by its terms is controlling with respect to this Agreement; and whenever there is any conflict between any provision of this Agreement and any such WGA Agreement, the latter shall prevail. In such event the provisions of this Agreement shall be curtailed and limited only to the extent necessary to permit compliance with such WGA Agreement.]

22. <u>CREDITS</u>:

(a) <u>Billing</u>: Provided that [Lender and] Writer fully perform[s] all of [Lender's and] Writer's obligations hereunder and the Picture is completed and distributed, Production Company agrees that credits for authorship by Writer shall be determined and accorded pursuant to the provisions of the WGA Agreement in effect at the time of such determination. [If Production Company is not a party to the WGA Agreement at the time for determination of such credits, then [such determination shall be made and] the credits shall be accorded in the same manner as provided for in said WGA Agreement, subject to Production Company's right to determine the contribution of each writer to the literary material for the Picture]. [The provisions of Exhibit "X" attached hereto and incorporated by this reference shall govern such credit].

(b) <u>Inadvertent Non-Compliance</u>: [Subject to the foregoing provisions, Production Company shall determine, in Production Company's discretion, the manner of presenting such credits.] No casual or inadvertent failure to comply with the provisions of this clause [, nor any failure of any other person, firm or corporation to comply with its agreements with Production Company relating to such credits,] shall constitute a breach by Production Company of Production Company's obligations under this Clause. [Lender and] Writer hereby agree that if through inadvertence Production Company breaches any of its obligations pursuant to this clause, the damages (if any) caused [Lender and/or] Writer by Production Company are not irreparable or sufficient to entitle [Lender and/or] Writer to injunctive or other equitable relief. Consequently, [Lender's and/or] Writer's rights and remedies in such event, shall be limited to [Lender's and/or] Writer's rights, if any, to recover damages in an action at law, and [Lender and/or] Writer shall not be entitled to rescind this agreement or any of the rights granted to Production Company hereunder, or to enjoin or restrain the distribution or exhibition of the Picture or any other rights granted to Production Company. [Production Company agrees upon receipt of notice from [Lender] [Writer] of Production Company's failure to comply with the provisions of this Clause, to take such steps as are reasonably practicable to cure such failure on future prints and advertisements.]

[(c) If contingent or other compensation of any kind is payable hereunder conditioned upon Writer's entitlement to a particular credit, the following shall be applicable: (1) If Writer receives such credit as the result of a unanimous agreement among the participating writers pursuant to the applicable provisions of the WGA Agreement, such credit shall not govern for the purpose of determining whether such contingent or other compensation based on credit shall be payable; but the determination as to whether such contingent or other compensation based on credit shall be payable shall be determined by Production Company solely on the basis of Writer's contribution to the final screenplay; (2) If Writer receives such credit in the notice of tentative credits which tentative credits become final within the time specified in the WGA Agreement, or a WGA determination through its arbitration committee, then, in either such event, such contingent or other compensation based on credit shall be payable hereunder.]

23. <u>INSURANCE</u>: Production Company may secure life, health, accident, cast or other insurance covering Writer, the cost of which shall be included as a direct charge of the Picture. Such insurance shall be for Production Company's sole benefit and Production Company shall be the beneficiary thereof, and [Lender and] Writer shall have no interest in the proceeds thereof. [Lender and] Writer shall assist in procuring such insurance by submitting to required examinations and tests and by preparing, signing and delivering such applications and other documents as may be reasonably required. [Lender and] Writer shall, to the best of [Lender's and] Writer's ability, observe all terms and conditions of such insurance of which Production Company notifies [Lender or] Writer as necessary for continuing such insurance in effect. [If Production Company is unable to obtain pre-production or cast insurance covering Writer at prevailing standard rates and without any exclusions, restrictions, conditions or exceptions of any kind, [Lender] [Writer] shall have the right to pay any premium in excess of prevailing standard rates in order for Production Company to obtain such insurance.] If [[Lender] [Writer] fails, refuses, or is unable for any reason whatsoever to pay such excess premium,] or if Production Company has obtained such insurance but [Lender or] Writer fails to observe all terms and conditions necessary to maintain such insurance in effect, Production Company may terminate this Agreement without any obligation to [Lender or] Writer by giving [Lender] [Writer] written notice of termination. [If Production Company obtains Errors and Omissions Insurance with respect to the Picture, [Lender and] Writer shall be included as [an] additional insured(s), to the extent that such coverage is reasonably available for [Lender and] Writer.]

24. <u>EMPLOYMENT OF OTHERS</u>: [Lender and] Writer agree(s) not to employ any person to serve in any capacity, nor contract for the purchase or renting of any article or material, nor make any agreement committing Production Company to pay any sum of money for any reason whatsoever in connection with the Picture or services to be rendered by Writer [or provided by Lender] hereunder, or otherwise, without written approval first being had and obtained from Production Company.

25. ASSIGNMENT AND LENDING:

(a) Assignability: This Agreement is non-assignable by [Lender and/or] [Writer]. Production Company and any subsequent assignee may freely assign this Agreement and grant its rights hereunder, in whole or in part to any person, firm, or corporation [provided that such assignee is a major or "mini-major" studio as that term is commonly understood in the motion picture industry] [provided that such party assumes and agrees in writing to keep and perform all the executory obligations of Production Company hereunder] [and Production Company remains secondarily responsible for the performance of all such obligations].

(b) Right to Lend to Others: [Lender] [Writer] understands and acknowledges that the actual production entity of a motion picture to be made from the Product may be a party other than Production Company. In such event, [and provided that Writer has consented to such lending, which consent shall not be unreasonably withheld] Writer's services shall be rendered hereunder for the actual production entity but without releasing Production Company from its obligations hereunder.

26. NOTICES:

(a) [Lender's] [Writer's] Address: All notices from Production Company to [Lender and/or] [Writer] in connection with this Agreement may be given in writing by addressing the same to [Lender and/or] [Writer] at (name of address of person to receive notice) and by depositing the same, so addressed, postage prepaid, in the mail, or at Production Company's option, Production Company may deliver such notice to [Lender] [Writer] personally, either orally or in writing. A courtesy copy shall be given to (name and address of attorney). If such notice is sent by mail, as above provided, the date of mailing shall be deemed to be the date of service of such notice.

(b) Writing Requirement: Any oral notice given in respect to any right of termination, suspension or extension under this Agreement shall be confirmed in writing. If any notice is delivered to [Lender and/or] [Writer] personally, a copy of such notice shall be sent to [Lender and/or] [Writer] at the above address.

(c) Producer's Address: All notices from [Lender and/or] [Writer] to Production Company hereunder shall be given in writing addressed to Production Company as follows: (name of responsible production company executive and production company's address) and by depositing the same, so addressed, postage prepaid, in the mail. A courtesy copy shall be given to (name and address of attorney). Unless otherwise expressly provided, the date of mailing shall be deemed to be the date of service of such notice.

27. TRANSPORTATION AND EXPENSES: When Writer's services are required by Production Company to be rendered hereunder at a place more than

[*e.g., fifty (50)*] miles outside of (*name of place*), Production Company shall [:] [furnish Writer transportation to and from such places and meals and [*e.g., first class*] lodging accommodations while Writer is on location to render Writer's services.]

OR

(a) furnish Writer with [(or reimburse Lender for)] [*e.g., first class*] round trip [air] transportation from (*name of place*) to such location (if used and if available) and, one (1) time only, with (*number*) additional [*e.g., first class*] round trip air transportation (if available and if used) for the use of Writer's (*name or relationship*), and

(b) reimburse [Lender] [Writer] for Writer's living expenses in the amount of (*specify amount, e.g., $2,000*) per week if the services are required in a major urban area, such as New York or London, (*specify amount, e.g., $1,500*) if the services are required in any other metropolitan city, and (*specify amount, e.g., $1,000*) if the services are required anywhere else. For any period less than one (1) week, said reimbursement shall be upon the pro rata basis that one (1) day is equal to one-seventh (1/7) of one (1) week.

[(c) Production Company shall give good faith consideration to increasing the applicable allowance if at the time Writer is at such location Writer demonstrates that such allowance is insufficient to meet Writer's reasonable expenses. However, in the event of any dispute, Production Company's [reasonable] decision shall prevail.]

28. <u>GOVERNING LAW</u>: This agreement shall be construed in accordance with the laws of the State of (*name of state*) applicable to agreements which are executed and fully performed within said State.

29. <u>CAPTIONS</u>: The captions used in connection with the clauses and subclauses of this Agreement are inserted only for the purpose of reference. Such captions shall not be deemed to govern, limit, modify, or in any other manner affect the scope, meaning or intent of the provisions of this Agreement or any part thereof; nor shall such captions otherwise be given any legal effect.

30. <u>SERVICE OF PROCESS</u>: In any action or proceeding commenced in any court in the State of (*name of state*) for the purpose of enforcing this Agreement or any right granted herein or growing out hereof, or any order or decree predicated thereon, any summons, order to show cause, writ, judgment, decree, or other process, issued by such court, may be delivered to [Lender or] Writer personally without the State of (*name of state*); and when so delivered, [Lender and] Writer shall be subject to the jurisdiction of such court as though the same had been served within the State of (*name of state*), but outside the county in which such action or proceeding is pending.

31. <u>ILLEGALITY</u>: Nothing contained herein shall require the commission of any act or the payment of any compensation which is contrary to an express provision of law or contrary to the policy of express law [, or to any provision of applicable guild or collective bargaining agreements]. If there shall exist any conflict between any provision contained herein and any such law or policy, the latter shall prevail; and the provision or provisions herein affected shall be curtailed, limited or eliminated to the extent (but only to the extent) necessary to remove such conflict; and as so modified the remaining provisions of this Agreement shall continue in full force and effect.

[32. <u>MOTION PICTURE RELIEF FUND</u>: [Lender] [Writer] authorizes Production Company to deduct from each payment of compensation hereunder one percent (1%) of the gross amount thereof and to pay the amount so deducted to the Motion Picture Relief Fund of America, Inc.]

[33. <u>PENSION, HEALTH & WELFARE & EMPLOYER TAXES</u>: Production Company agrees upon the receipt of appropriate invoices to reimburse Lender in an amount equal to any contributions to Pension plans, Health and Welfare funds required to be paid by Lender to any appropriate Guild or union having jurisdiction over the type of services to be performed by Writer hereunder, it being expressly agreed that any amounts to be paid hereunder shall be based upon payments made by Lender pursuant to the applicable provisions of the respective Guild or union basic agreements, which in any event shall not exceed the amount of the contribution Production Company would have been required to make had Writer been employed by Production Company. Production Company shall have no obligation to reimburse Lender for employer taxes of any kind or nature.]

34. <u>EMPLOYMENT ELIGIBILITY</u>: All of Production Company's obligations herein are expressly conditioned upon Writer's completion, to Production Company's satisfaction, of the I-9 form (Employee Eligibility Verification Form), and upon Writer's submission to Production Company of original documents satisfactory to demonstrate to Production Company Writer's employment eligibility.

35. <u>ENTIRE AGREEMENT</u>: This Agreement contains the entire agreement of the parties and all previous agreements, warranties and representations, if any, are merged herein.

Film Writer Agreement

By signing in the spaces provided below, [Lender] [Writer] and Production Company accept and agree to all the terms and conditions of this agreement.

_____

("Lender")

By: _____

Its: _____

[OR]

_____

("Writer")

_____

("Production Company")

By: _____

Its: _____

[If a loan-out corporation is used, add the following:]

INDUCEMENT

By countersigning this Agreement, Writer confirms all grants made by Lender and agrees to perform the services herein provided for in accordance with the terms hereof, and Writer will look solely to Lender for any and all compensation hereunder.

_____

(*Name of Writer*)

Form 21

Definitions of Net Profits

Exhibit "A" of the document entitled _____("Main Agreement") and forming a part of the _____Agreement ("Agreement") dated as of _____between TWENTIETH CENTURY FOX FILM CORPORATION (referred to as "_____" in the Main Agreement and as "Fox" herein) and _____ (referred to as "_____" in the Main Agreement and as "Participant" herein), in connection with the Motion Picture entitled "_____".

INDEX

EXHIBIT "A"

I. DEFINED TERMS

A. "Identification": All words appearing within the text of this Exhibit with initial letters capitalized (except the first word of a sentence and proper nouns) and all words appearing within underlined paragraph captions with initial letters capitalized and within quotation marks and the words "including" "in perpetuity" are specifically defined terms, the definitions for which are set forth within the text of this Exhibit or in the Glossary attached hereto as Schedule "1". Words which appear within parentheses with initial letters capitalized and within quotation marks are specifically defined terms defined by the text immediately preceding the parentheses.

B. "Fox": Fox means Twentieth Century Fox Film Corporation, a Delaware corporation, or its successor in interest.

C. "Distributor": Distributor means Fox and Subsidiaries and Affiliates engaged in the distribution of a Motion Picture for exhibition by other Parties. The term Distributor shall not include the following: theatres, television broadcast stations, electronic transmission systems (including cable, direct broadcast satellite, microwave and master antenna), program delivery services and radio stations (and other exhibitors of Motion Pictures to viewers by any means now known or hereafter devised), or laboratories producing and/or distributing Motion Picture Copies, or merchandisers, manufacturers, sellers, wholesale dealers or retail dealers of Cassettes or of any other products, or book or music publishers, or Parties producing or distributing Sound Records, or Pay-TV/Cassette Marketers, or any Parties similar to any of the foregoing excluded Parties (whether or not any of the foregoing excluded Parties are Subsidiaries or Affiliates), or Subdistributors.

II. "PICTURE":

Picture means the Theatrical Motion Picture covered by the Agreement in all versions thereof, including subtitled, dubbed and narrated versions. If the Agreement covers more than 1 Theatrical Motion Picture, Picture refers to each Theatrical Motion Picture individually, or the particular Theatrical Motion Picture involved as the context requires.

III. "PARTICIPANT'S PERCENTAGE PARTICIPATION":

Participant's Percentage Participation refers to the percentage of Net Profits to which Participant is entitled under the Agreement and which shall be computed, accounted for and paid as provided in this Exhibit.

IV. "NET PROFITS":

Net Profits means the amount of Gross Receipts remaining, if any, after first deducting from Gross Receipts, on a continuing and cumulative basis, the aggregate of the following items in the order of priority set forth below based upon financial data determined, recorded and computed as of the end of the particular Statement Period for which a periodic Participation Statement is being rendered:

A. "Fox Distribution Fees": Fox Distribution Fees as set forth in Section V., Paragraphs C.1. through C.5. shall be applied to all Gross Film Rentals and Theatrical Outright Sale Receipts.

B. "Distribution Expenses": See Section V., Paragraph D.

C. "DEFERMENTS" AND "PERCENTAGE PARTICIPATIONS": Before or At "Initial Breakeven Point": Any amounts not included within Negative Cost payable prior to or at the initial Breakeven Point to any Party, including Participant, for rights, services, materials, or facilities granted or used in connection with the Picture, whether as a fixed sum, the payment of which vests upon the expiration of a period of time and/or the attainment of a specified level of receipts or profits of the Picture ("Deferment") or as a percentage of the receipts of the Picture which remain after giving effect to specified exclusions and deductions ("Percentage Participation"), if any, all as set forth in the agreement providing for such payment, whether or not such Deferment or Percentage Participation is defined or computed in the same manner as set forth in this Exhibit.

D. "Interest" On "Negative Cost": The aggregate of the sums ("Interest") computed as a percentage of Negative Cost commencing as of the week in which an amount chargeable to Negative Cost is incurred and continuing until the end of the Statement Period with respect to which such amount chargeable to Negative Cost is recouped from Gross Receipts as provided in Section IV. at an annual percentage rate 1/2% above the prime lending rate charged by Security Pacific Bank from time to time in effect, plus a charge of 20% on said annual percentage rate ("Interest Rate").

E. "Negative Cost": See Section V., Paragraph E.

F. "Agreed Overbudget Deduction": Fox and Participant contemplate that the Picture can be produced at the Budgeted Negative Cost. However, as the Negative Cost may exceed the Budgeted Negative Cost and thereby increase the risk borne by Fox by reason of additional investment in the Picture, Fox and Participant specifically agree that the Agreed Overbudget Deduction shall be deductible in the computation of Net Profits. "Agreed Overbudget Deduction" means an amount equal to the sum by which the Negative Cost (after adjustment of the Negative Cost for foreign currency exchange fluctuations using the same rate of foreign currency exchange for expenditures in a foreign currency as used in determining the Budgeted Negative Cost regardless of the actual rate of foreign currency exchange and after excluding Direct Charges already included within Negative Cost which arise by reason of events of Force Majeure, scenes not originally contemplated in the Final Approved Screenplay being required by Fox which have not been agreed to by Participant in writing, and industry wide union and guild wage and fringe benefit increases not contemplated in the Budgeted Negative Cost) exceeds the aggregate of Budgeted Negative Cost plus a contingency allowance of 10% of the initial $1,500,000 of the Budgeted Negative Cost and 5% of the Budgeted Negative Cost in excess of $1,500,000. Such contingency allowance shall be reduced by an amount equal to any contingency allowance established within the Budgeted Negative Cost.

G. "Deferments" After "Initial Breakeven Point": Any amounts not included within Negative Cost payable after the Initial Breakeven Point to any Party, including Participant, as a Deferment whether or not such Deferment is defined or computed in the same manner as set forth in this Exhibit.

H. "Percentage Participations" After "Initial Breakeven Point": Any amounts not included within Negative Cost payable after the Initial Breakeven Point to any Party, including Participant, as a Percentage Participation (other than percentage participations in Net Profits), which amounts have not otherwise been applied in reduction of Participant's Percentage Participation pursuant to an express provision of the Agreement whether or not such Percentage Participation is defined or computed in the same manner as set forth in this Exhibit.

V. FINANCIAL TERMINOLOGY: As used in this Exhibit and the Agreement, the following terms have the following meanings:

A. "Gross Receipts": The aggregate of Gross Film Rentals, Theatrical Outright Sale Receipts, Government Subsides, Net Recoveries, Music Publishing Receipts, Music Recording Receipts, Merchandising and Literary Publishing Receipts, and Net Trailer and Advertising Accessory Income.

1. "Gross Film Rentals": The aggregate of the following:

(a) "Theatre Rentals": All monies actually received and earned by Distribution from the Theatrical Distribution of the Picture other than Theatrical Distribution Outright Sales of the Picture.

(b) "Four Wall Engagement Receipts": The box office receipts received and earned by Distributor from Four Wall Engagements less all expenses incurred or paid by Distributor in connection with the operation of the theatres used and any payments made and/or shares of box office receipts paid to or allowed to such theatres ("Four Wall Expenses"), whether or not such theatres are owned, operated, managed or controlled by Distributor, but not including advertising and publicity expenses which shall be deductible as a Distribution Expense. If the aggregate of the Four Wall Expenses, other than the aforesaid advertising and publicity expenses deductible as a Distribution Expense exceeds box office receipts from Four Wall Engagements, such excess shall be deductible as a Distribution Expense. Participant acknowledges there is no obligation to exhibit the Picture by means of Four Wall Engagements.

(c) "Free Television Rentals": The aggregate of the following:

(i) "Cash Sales": All monies actually received and earned by Distributor from the Free Television Distribution of the Picture other than Net Advertising Revenues.

(ii) "Barter Sales": All Net Advertising Revenues if Distributor sells commercial time for the advertising of products and/or services of sponsors or advertisers in connection with the Free Television Exhibition of the Picture ("Barter Sales"). "Net Advertising Revenues" means the gross income actually received and earned by Distributor from Barter Sales after Deduction of advertising agency commission and expenses, any credits and so-called "make goods" in connection with such program audience guarantee policy as may be applicable, and all commissions, fees and expense reimbursements payable to or retained by any sales agent Distributor may engage.

(iii) "Copyright Royalties": All royalties, fees or other revenues actually received and earned by Distributor pursuant to any statute or governmental regulation or by operation of Law based upon or in connection with any secondary transmission of the Television Exhibition of the Picture or the recording of the signal embodying the Television Exhibition of the Picture. Fox shall determine the amount allocable to the Picture consistent with empirical data reasonably available to Fox in the ordinary course of business.

(d) "Supplemental Television Rentals": The aggregate of the following:

(i) "Pay Television Receipts": All monies actually received and earned by Distributor from the Pay Television Distribution of the Picture. No monies other than the license fees directly derived by Distributor from and related to the licensing of the Picture by Distributor for Pay Television Distribution and/or Pay Television Exhibition shall be included in Gross Film Rentals by reason of or in connection with the Pay Television Distribution and/or Pay Television Exhibition of the Picture.

(ii) "Home Video Receipts": Product royalty amounts equal to the following, as and when actually received and earned by Distributor from the Home Video Distribution of the Picture:

(A) Sales: 20% of "Net Wholesale Price". Net Wholesale Price shall mean 100% of the monies derived by the Party (whether an Affiliate, Subsidiary or other Party) engaged in Home Video Distribution directly to wholesale dealers which sell Cassettes to retail outlets ("Home Video Distributor"), less amounts (however denominated) remitted as sales, use, excise, value added and similar taxes (collectively, "Sales Taxes") and returns and bad debts.

(B) <u>Rentals</u>: 20% of "Net Rental Income." Net Rental Income shall mean 100% of the monies derived by the Home Video Distributor from the Home Video Distribution of the Picture to the extent such monies are received from wholesale dealers which account to the Home Video Distributor based on rentals of Cassettes, less Sales Taxes, return and bad debts.

(C) <u>Direct Marketing Sales</u>: 15% of "Net Direct Marketing Income". Net Direct Marketing Income shall mean 100% of the monies received by the Party directly engaged in Home Video Distribution of the Picture by means of direct marketing to consumers for Home Video Exhibition (e.g., through direct mail, mail order, telephone order, club member-ships, continuity series offerings or single title offerings), less Sales Taxes, returns, credits and bad debts.

No monies other than the product royalty based solely on the amounts described in this Section V., Paragraphs A.1(d)(ii)(A), (B) and (C) derived from the sale or rental of Cassettes shall be included in Gross Film Rentals by reason of or in connection with the Home Video Distribution and/or Home Video Exhibition of the Picture.

(e) <u>"Non-Theatrical Rentals"</u>: All monies actually received and earned by Distributor from Non-Theatrical Distribution of the Picture.

2. <u>"Theatrical Outright Sale Receipts"</u>: All monies actually received and earned by Distributor from Theatrical Distribution Outright Sales of the Picture.

3. <u>"Government Subsidies"</u>: All monies actually received by Distributor by reason of Motion Picture subsidies being granted solely with respect to the Picture by a governmental agency. Motion Picture subsidies granted for use in connection with subsequent production activity and tax credits in the nature of investment tax credits or other governmental incentive credits, allowances or payments shall not be included.

4. <u>"Net Recoveries"</u>:

(a) <u>Unauthorized Exhibition/Copyright Infringement</u>: All monies actually received by Distributor by reason of the settlement of any dispute or on account of any judgment or decree in any litigation relative to any claims for unauthorized exhibition, distribution or other use of the Picture and/or for infringement, plagiarism or other interference by any Party with the copyright of the Picture remaining after first deducting all costs and expenses incurred in connection with obtaining such monies, including reasonable attorneys' fees. Costs and expenses in excess of monies received shall be deductible as Copyright Infringement Costs.

(b) <u>Breach of Contract</u>: All monies actually received by Distributor by reason of the settlement of any dispute or on account of any judgment or decree in any litigation relating to any claims for breach of contract in connection with the distribution and/or exhibition of the Picture remaining after first deducting all costs and expenses incurred in connection with obtaining such monies, including reasonable attorneys' fees. Costs and expenses in excess of monies received shall be deductible as Collection Costs.

5. "Music Publishing Receipts": As to music and/or lyrics originally composed specifically for and synchronized in the Picture ("Picture Music") and with respect to which Fox acquired the right to exploit Music Publishing Rights, the following shall apply:

(a) Administering Publisher: If a Subsidiary ("Music Subsidiary") is the sole publisher or an administering co-publisher of Picture Music, then Music Publishing Receipts shall be 50% of all monies actually received in the United States by the Music Subsidiary ("Music Income") which remain after first deducting (i) a Music Subsidiary administration fee of 15% of Music Income and (ii) all costs and expenses of the Music Subsidiary in connection therewith, including all royalties and shares of Music Income payable to any Party, including Participant (other than by reason of inclusion of Music Publishing Receipts in Gross Receipts), if any, all charges of any agent, trustee or administrator involved in the collection of monies or administering the Music Publishing Rights, and (iii) any co-publisher's share of such monies.

(b) Non-Administering Co-Publisher: If a Music Subsidiary is a non-administering co-publisher of Picture Music, then Music Publishing Receipts shall be 50% of all monies actually received in the United States by the Music Subsidiary from the administering co-publisher net of any administering co-publisher's share of such monies which remain after first deducting all costs and expenses of the Music Subsidiary in connection therewith, including all royalties and shares of such monies payable to any Party, including Participant (other than by reason of inclusion of Music Publishing Receipts in Gross Receipts), if any.

(c) Third Party Music Publisher: If a Music Subsidiary is neither the sole publisher nor a co-publisher of Picture Music, then Music Publishing Receipts shall be all monies actually received in the United States by Fox from the publisher of the Picture Music, which remain after first deducting a Fox administration fee of 15% of all such monies actually received, and all royalties and shares of such monies payable to any Party in connection therewith, including Participant (other than by reason of inclusion of Music Publishing Receipts in Gross Receipts), if any.

6. "Music Recording Receipts": As to Sound Records manufactured for sale to the public, which embody music and/or dialogue as taken from the actual soundtrack of the Picture or a re-recording of all or a portion of the soundtrack

of the Picture performed by the same artist who originally performed that portion of the actual soundtrack, which re-recording is licensed by Fox in lieu of the actual soundtrack ("Soundtrack Recordings"), and with respect to which Fox acquired the right to exploit Soundtrack Recording Rights, the following shall apply:

(a) <u>Releasing</u>: If a Subsidiary ("Recording Subsidiary") engages in the business of releasing a Soundtrack Recording, then Music Recording Receipts shall be a record royalty which shall be a percentage ("Royalty Percentage") of the suggested retail list price from time-to-time in effect (exclusive of all excise, sales, or other taxes) of the applicable Soundtrack Recordings, after first deducting standard packaging charges, on 100% of all copies of such Soundtrack Recordings sold for which payment has been received in the United States by Recording Subsidiary, less all returns, rebates, credits, exchanges and cancellations of any kind. The Royalty Percentage for Soundtrack Recordings sold in the form of LP recordings (e.g., vinyl discs, audio cassettes, compact discs) in the United States through normal retail distribution channels is 10%, and the Royalty Percentage for Soundtrack Recordings sold in the form of non-LP recordings (including singles and EP discs) in the United States through normal retail distribution channels is 5%. The applicable Royalty Percentage shall be reduced by all record royalties and participations payable to any other Parties in connection with the applicable Soundtrack Recordings; provided, however, that the Royalty Percentage shall not be reduced by more than 50%. The Royalty Percentage shall be subject to standard reduction with respect to sales of Soundtrack Recordings in the United States other than through normal retail distribution channels (including sales of budget records and mid-price records, and sales of Soundtrack Recordings through Armed Forces PXs, record clubs and direct mail order). The Royalty Percentage for sales outside the United States shall be 75% of the otherwise applicable Royalty Percentage for similar sales in the United States (and with respect to sales outside the United States, the Royalty Percentage shall be calculated, at Recording Subsidiary's election, either upon the suggested retail list price of such Soundtrack Recording in the Territory of manufacture or the Territory of sale or such other royalty base as Recording Subsidiary employs with respect to the majority of its similar type releases in such Territory). Record royalties with respect to sales of Soundtrack Recordings outside the United States shall be computed in the national currency of the Territory of sale or the Territory of manufacture, as Recording Subsidiary elects, and shall be paid at the same rate of exchange as Recording Subsidiary is paid. Recording Subsidiary will recoup from the record royalties derived from the exploitation of the Soundtrack Recordings a pro rata share of the recording costs, reuse fees, re-recording fees, union and guild payments, re-mixing and remastering costs customary in the phonograph recording industry. Such proration shall be based upon a fraction, the numerator of which is the applicable Royalty Percentage and the denominator of which is the aggregate of all record royalties payable with respect to the applicable Soundtrack Recording including the applicable Royalty Percentage hereunder. No record royalty shall be included in Music Recording Receipts with respect to Soundtrack Recordings distributed or sold: (i) as premiums, or (ii) as samplers, cutouts, scrap, or at close out prices, or (iii) on a no charge or nominal charge basis to radio or television stations, networks, program services or transportation facilities, or (iv) as record club or mail order "free", "bonus" or "dividend" Sound Records, or as "free goods". As to Sound Records not consisting entirely of a Soundtrack Recording, the record royalties to be included in Music Recording Receipts shall be pro-rated by multiplying the applicable Royalty Percentage by a fraction, the numerator of which is the number of selections of such Sound Record which consist of a Soundtrack Recording and the denominator of which is the total number of selections on such Sound Record.

(b) Licensing: If Fox licenses the right to release Soundtrack Recordings to a third Party other than a Recording Subsidiary, then Music Recording Receipts shall be all monies actually received in the United States by or on behalf of Fox from such third Party which remain after first deducting a Fox administration fee of 15% of all such monies, and all royalties and shares of such monies payable by or on behalf of Fox to any Party in connection therewith, including Participant (other than by reason of inclusion of Music Publishing Receipts in Gross Receipts), if any.

7. "Merchandising and Literary Publishing Receipts": As to Merchandising Rights and Literary Publishing Rights with respect to the Picture which Fox acquired the right to exploit, the following shall apply:

(a) Licensing: If Fox or Subsidiary, or any agent or licensee of Fox or Subsidiary ("Fox Merchandising Agent") licenses to a third Party Merchandising Rights or Literary Publishing Rights with respect to the Picture ("Merchandise License"), then Merchandising and Literary Publishing Receipts shall be all monies actually received in the United States by Fox or Subsidiary or Fox Merchandising Agent pursuant to the Merchandise License remaining after first deducting (i) a Fox administration fee of 40% of all such monies if Fox or Subsidiary solicited the Merchandise License or 15% of all such monies if Fox Merchandising Agent solicited the Merchandise License and (ii) all royalties and shares of such monies payable to any Party in connection therewith, including royalty payments to Participant, if any, and (iii) all commissions and fees payable to or retained by any Fox Merchandising Agent, if any, and (iv) all costs of proprietary protection in the form of trademarks, patents and copyrights, and (v) all costs, expenses and charges paid, advanced or incurred by Fox, Subsidiary and

Fox Merchandising Agent in connection with or relative to the derivation of monies from the exercise of Merchandising Rights and Literary Publishing Rights with respect to the Picture.

(b) <u>Manufacturing and Distributing</u>: If Fox or Subsidiary directly engages in the business of exploiting Merchandising Rights or Literary Publishing Rights with respect to the Picture, then Merchandising and Literary Receipts shall be an amount equal to 5% of the Net Merchandising Sales of Fox or Subsidiary. "Net Merchandising Sales" means the gross sales price actually received by Fox or Subsidiary for all sales in connection with the exercise of Merchandising Rights and Literary Publishing Rights with respect to the Picture, less Sales Taxes, quantity and trade discounts, returns, credits and bad debts.

8. <u>"Net Trailer and Advertising Accessory Income"</u>: All monies received and earned by Distributor from the license or distribution of trailers and advertising accessories (including display matter, lithographs and stills), if and when used in connection with the Theatrical Distribution and Theatrical Exhibition of the Picture, remaining after first deducting the aggregate of all costs and expenses incurred by Distributor in connection with the preparation, manufacture, license and distribution thereof. Costs and expenses in excess of monies received and earned shall be deductible as Advertising Costs.

B. <u>Exclusions from "Gross Receipts"</u>: In no event shall the following be included in Gross Receipts:

1. <u>Box Office Receipts/Exhibitor Receipts</u>: The monies derived (including ticket sales, subscription fees, and advertising income) by any theatre or other exhibitor from exhibition of the Picture, whether or not such theatre or other exhibitor is owned, operated, managed or controlled by Distributor or Subdistributor except as set forth in Section V., Paragraph A.1(b) with respect to Four Wall Engagements.

2. <u>Advances/Guarantees</u>: Advance payments and security deposits, until earned or forfeited. Non-returnable guarantees are deemed advanced payments and excluded from Gross Receipts until earned.

3. <u>Rebates/Refunds/Adjustments/Allowances/Settlements</u>: All rebates, refunds, adjustments, allowances or settlements given to licensees of the Picture by Distributor or Subdistributors as to license fees, advertising allowances, operating expenses and/or otherwise. To the extent any such amounts represent a return of amounts previously included in Gross Receipts, an appropriate adjustment in Gross Receipts and Fox Distribution Fees shall be made.

4. <u>"Subdistributor Receipts"</u>: Monies derived by a Subdistributor from the distribution of the Picture are specifically excluded from Gross Receipts, except that solely for purposes of computing Net Profits, all monies actually received

and earned by a Subdistributor from Theatrical Distribution shall be included within Theatre Rentals.

5. <u>Charitable Contributions</u>: Gross Film Rentals from the exhibition of the Picture contributed or paid to charitable organizations.

6. <u>Collected Taxes</u>: Any amounts collected by Distributor or Subdistributor or licensee of the Picture as taxes or for payment as taxes, such as admission, sales, use and value-added taxes.

7. <u>Salvage</u>: All monies received by Distributor or Subdistributor from the scrapping or disposal of Motion Picture Copies or salvage of other materials.

8. <u>Physical Properties</u>: All monies received by Fox from the sale, rental or other disposition of materials and supplies, including props, sets, costumes and equipment purchased, designed, created or constructed for use in connection with production and/or distribution of the Picture. As between Fox and Participant, Fox shall be the owner of such materials and supplies.

9. <u>Stock Footage/Featurettes/Still Photographs</u>: All monies received by Distributor from the exploitation or use of stock footage, film, tape, sound and other materials retained for library purposes, featurettes and still photographs which relate to or are derived from the Picture.

10. <u>Ancillary Rights</u>: Subject to the specific provisions set forth elsewhere in the Agreement and this Exhibit, all monies received by Distributor by reason of the exploitation of any subsidiary rights with respect to the Picture including Soundtrack Recording Rights, Music Publishing Rights, Merchandising Rights, Literary Publishing Rights, Commercial Tie-In Rights, Live Television Rights, Radio Rights, Legitimate Stage Rights, Remake Rights, Sequel Motion Picture Rights and Additional Motion Picture Rights.

C. "<u>Fox Distribution Fees</u>": The following establishes the percentage rates Fox shall apply as Fox Distribution Fees and retain for its own account. The determination as to what items and personnel are furnished for the Fox Distribution Fees shall be made in all respects in the same manner as Fox customarily determines such matters. The application of the Fox Distribution Fees shall in no way diminish the charges included as Distribution Expenses pursuant to Section V., Paragraph D.

1. "<u>Domestic Territory</u>": 30% of Gross Film Rentals derived from the Domestic Territory.

2. "<u>British Territory</u>" and "<u>Continental Europe</u>": 37 1/2% of Gross Film Rentals derived from the British Territory and Continental Europe.

3. "<u>International Territory</u>": 40% of Gross Film Rentals derived from the International Territory.

4. "<u>Theatrical Distribution Outright Sales</u>": 15% of Theatrical Outright Sale Receipts.

5. <u>Subdistribution</u>: The foregoing notwithstanding, as to Theatre Rentals actually received and earned by a Subdistributor, the Fox Distribution Fee shall be the greater of the following:

(a) The applicable Fox Distribution Fee set forth above as applied to the Theatre Rentals of the Subdistributor, or

(b) The distribution fee percentage payable to or deductible by the Subdistributor plus 10% as applied to the Theatre Rentals of the Subdistributor.

D. "<u>Distribution Expenses</u>": The aggregate of:

1. "<u>Distribution Costs</u>": All costs, expenses and charges (collectively "costs") paid, advanced or incurred by Distributor by reason of, in connection with, or relative to the derivation of Gross Receipts with respect to the Picture including:

(a) "Conversion/Transmission Costs": All costs of conversion of monies, including cable expenses and any discounts taken for the conversion thereof directly or indirectly into United States Dollars and all costs of transmission of such monies to the United States.

(b) "Taxes": All taxes, imposts, duties, tariffs and governmental fees of any nature, however denominated or characterized, imposed by any taxing authority in any Territory, directly or indirectly, on any receipts (irrespective of character or origin) of the Picture or in connection with the Picture, Motion Picture Copies, trailers, and other material relating to the Picture, or the lease, license, distribution, exhibition or other disposition thereof, or the collection, conversion or remittance of monies, including personal property, turnover, sales, use, transaction, film hire, excise, stamp, censorship, added value, remittance, release, income and franchise taxes irrespective of whether such amounts relate to the Picture or a group of Motion Pictures in which the Picture may be included as reasonably allocated by Fox. Where local law limits Participant's right to receive any payment to an amount less than as provided in the Agreement, Distributor shall be entitled to deduct, from the amount allowed to be paid to Participant pursuant to such local Law, the total amount of all taxes payable with respect to any monies which would otherwise have been payable to Participant pursuant to the Agreement except for such limitation. Any amount withheld by reason of such limitation shall constitute Restricted Proceeds. All monies required to be paid on account of import fees, export fees, duties, imposts, customs, and costs to acquire permits in connection with shipment, delivery, license, exhibition or other use of the Picture and Motion Picture Copies; all payments and expenses with respect to contesting, compromising or settling (whether by litigation or otherwise) of any Taxes, together with any interest and penalties with respect thereto shall be treated as Taxes. If any monies are required to be paid to a local institution, group, individual or fund, such payments shall be treated as Taxes. In no event shall Participant be entitled, directly or indirectly, to claim, share or participate in any credits, deductions, or other benefits of any kind or nature with respect to any Taxes, nor shall the deductible amount of any Taxes (however determined) be decreased (nor Gross Receipts increased) because of the manner in which Taxes and tax credits are treated by Distributor in filing its net income, corporate franchise, excess profits or other similar tax returns. Participant shall not be required to pay or participate in Distributor's own United States Federal and State income taxes and franchise taxes (however denominated) based on Distributor's actual net earnings or any income tax (however denominated) payable by Distributor to any Territory, based on the actual net earnings of Distributor in such Territory, it being agreed that any Taxes (however denominated) required to be withheld by any Territory in order to permit the remittance of monies from any such Territory shall not be deemed to be a tax based on the actual net earnings of Distributor.

(c) "Checking Costs": All costs incurred to check attendance and receipts at theatres and to audit subscriber counts and exhibitions by television exhibitors, program delivery services and the like in order to determine the accuracy of box office reports and accounting statements and to investigate unauthorized exhibition or distribution of the Picture and to determine full utilization of the rights granted, whether such costs are direct expenses or an allocable portion of the aggregate general checking and auditing expenses incurred by Distributor in connection with the distribution of Motion Pictures.

(d) "Collection Costs": All costs incurred in connection with the collection of monies includable within Gross Receipts, including reasonable fees of attorneys and auditors, and loss, damage or liability suffered or incurred by Distributor in the collection of such monies, whether by litigation or otherwise.

(e) "Trade Association Fees": An allocable portion of dues, assessments and contributions of Distributor to the Motion Picture Association of America, Alliance of Motion Picture and Television Producers, Motion Picture Export Association of America, Academy of Motion Picture Arts and Sciences, and any similarly constituted or substitute organizations throughout the world.

(f) "Guild Payments": All costs incurred with respect to payments required, including employer fringe benefits and taxes payable with respect thereto, under applicable Collective Bargaining Agreements by reason of or as a condition to any exhibition of the Picture, or any part thereof, or any use or reuse thereof for any purpose or in any media whatsoever. If Participant or any principal stockholder of Participant is entitled, either directly or by way of participation in any fund, to any Guild Payments ("Participant's Residuals"), the amount of Participant's Residuals shall be a deductible

Distribution Expense, and shall not be treated as an advance against Participant's Percentage Participation; and any Participant's Percentage Participation paid to Participant shall not constitute and advance against Participant's Residuals.

(g) "Advertising Costs": The aggregate of the costs enumerated in the following Paragraphs D.1.(g)(i) and (ii):

(i) "General Advertising Costs": All costs incurred, which are related to or allocable to (as Fox may determine) the advertising, publicizing and promoting of the Picture in any way, including the following:

(A) Publications: Costs of purchasing advertising space in newspapers, magazines, periodicals, trade papers and other printed publications.

(B) Radio and Television: Costs of purchasing advertising time on radio and television; costs of physical materials used in the production and broadcasting of commercials by radio and television; costs of preparation, production and shipping of commercials; costs of placement, integration and monitoring of commercials.

(C) Direct Mail: Costs of preparing and mailing printed advertising and promotional material.

(D) Display: Costs of purchasing advertising space on billboards and other locations, and of preparation, production and distribution of display materials.

(E) Advertising Agency/Consultant Fees: Fees of advertising and/or publicity agencies and/or consultants engaged in connection with the advertising and/or promotion of the Picture.

(F) Promotional Activities: Salaries, fees and living, travel and business expenses of publicists, press representatives, consultants and field and exploitation persons, allocated on the basis of time spent on the Picture, whether paid to Distributor employees or other persons; salaries, fees and living, travel and business expenses relating to tours and personal appearances of personalities connected with the Picture, whether paid to Distributor employees or other persons; costs of previews, screenings and premieres (including overtime salaries of Distributor employees when involved with previews, screening and premieres); living, travel and business expenses of any of Distributor's employees (excluding straight time regular salaries but including overtime salaries) involved with the advertising and promotion of the Picture when travel (including sales conventions, instruction sessions and the like) is directly attributable to or occasioned by the Picture.

(G) Entertainment: Costs of entertaining press, exhibitors and personalities.

(H) Commercial Tie-Ins: Costs of creation, procurement, preparation, placement and supervision of promotional tie-ins with commercial products, including the purchase of advertising space and time.

(I) Research, Surveys and Tests: Costs of formulation, performance and evaluation of research, surveys, studies and tests of advertising concepts, advertising campaigns, media effectiveness, box office statistics, market demographics and the like on a qualitative and quantitative basis.

(J) Promotional Materials: Costs of creation (including re-use fees and rights payments), preparation, production, fabrication and distribution of press books, press kits, screening invitations, tickets, programs, featurettes, teaser trailers, trailers, film clips, video press kits, "making of" programs, music videos, special photography, biographies, synopses, billing sheets, lobby displays, stills, publicity releases, posters, advertising accessories and Sound Records.

(K) Printing Materials: Costs of creation, preparation, production and fabrication of artwork, engravings, cuts, plates, color separations and mechanicals, including the physical materials required therefor.

(ii) "Advertising Overhead": An amount equal to 10% of the aggregate of all costs deductible under Paragraph D.1.(g)(i) above (including Advertising Costs incurred by a Subdistributor pursuant to Paragraph D.2. below) to cover salaries and indirect operating costs of Distributor's advertising and publicity personnel. Advertising overhead shall accrue and be deducted concurrently with the respective amounts of Advertising Costs to which it applies. The determination as to what items and personnel are furnished for the Advertising Overhead shall be made in all respects in the same manner as Fox customarily determines such matters. The application of Advertising Overhead shall in no way diminish the charges deductible pursuant to Paragraph D.1.(g)(i) above, which charges are subject to Advertising Overhead as provided in this Paragraph D.1.(g)(ii).

(iii) "Media Advertising for Theatrical Exhibition": That portion of the General Advertising Costs incurred to advertise, publicize and promote the Picture by means of national, regional or local publications (other than trade papers), radio and television, direct mail, display advertising, promotional activities, entertainment, and commercial tie-ins, in connection with the Theatrical Exhibition of the Picture, whether engaged in by Distributor directly or where Distributor pays, shares in, or is charged with all or a portion of the costs thereof (whether effected by credits against or deductions from Theatre Rentals). Any costs of Media Advertising for Theatrical Exhibition contributed by exhibitors from exhibitor's share of box office receipts shall not be included hereunder and shall not be deductible as a Distribution Cost. Allowances to exhibitors or allowable deductions from Distributor's share of box office receipts for Media Advertising for Theatrical Exhibition shall not be deemed a reduction of box office receipts or Gross Film Rentals for the purpose of computation of Fox Distribution Fees.

(h) "Foreign Version Costs": All costs, if not included within Negative Cost, incurred to make and deliver foreign language versions of the Picture, whether dubbed and/or subtitled in one or more languages including translation, narration, looping re-titling, superimposing, re-cutting, spotting, re-recording, re-mixing, re-dubbing and re-editing of the Picture and trailers; and transportation, packing and handling of Motion Picture Copies and parts thereof with respect to the preparation of foreign language versions of the Picture.

(i) "Re-Editing Costs": All costs (including charges established pursuant to the then current published Fox Studio Rental Rates and Price Schedule for facilities, equipment and personnel of Fox furnished and utilized in connection with the matters set forth in this Paragraph D.1.(i) and related imputed fringe charges at the percentage rates established pursuant to the then current published Fox Studio Rental Rates and Price Schedule as applied to all direct salaries of all personnel utilized in connection with the matters set forth in this Paragraph D.1.(i)), if not included in Negative Cost, incurred to re-cut, re-edit, re-record, re-score, re-mix and re-dub the Picture, including changes, eliminations or additions with respect to the Picture for Television Exhibition, Home Video Exhibition and Non-Theatrical Exhibition; and conforming (voluntarily or involuntarily) the Picture to requirements of censorship, classification and rating by governmental or local organizations or other Parties, including exhibitors and religious and ethnic groups, and to national and/or political regulations or prejudices of any Territory.

(j) "Physical Material Costs": All costs of Motion Picture Copies, including laboratory (including charges established pursuant to the then current published Film Price List of Deluxe Laboratories or other affiliated entity of Distributor), labor, service, materials and facilities costs in connection therewith.

(k) "Shipping/Delivery/Transmission Costs": All costs of inspection, repair and renovation of Motion Picture Copies, reels and containers, all costs of packing, storing, shipping and delivery of Motion Picture Copies, reels and containers, all costs of inspecting and checking projection, sound, exhibition and transmission equipment and facilities of exhibitors and all costs of transmission of Motion Pictures by any electronic or other means now known or hereafter devised.

(l) "Royalties": All costs, if not included within Negative Cost, of all licenses required to permit exhibition, distribution or other use of the Picture, trailers and Motion Picture Copies thereof, including fees for use of any patented equipment or processes; synchronization, recording and performing royalties and fees with respect to performance of lyrics and music and Literary Material; any re-use fees and costs, if not included within Negative Cost, advanced by Distributor; any costs, not included in Negative Costs, incurred to acquire, use and publish Picture Music advanced by Distributor.

(m) "Insurance Costs": All costs, if not included in Negative Cost, for insurance coverage of any and all risks of loss with respect to the Picture and any components thereof, including errors and omissions insurance and loss or damage to Motion Picture Copies and physical material insurance. Distributor may elect to self insure as to any items or risk and charge as an Insurance Cost an amount equal to the insurance premium Distributor would otherwise have paid for such insurance. Distributor shall, in its sole discretion, determining whether or not to obtain or maintain any insurance or to self insure any items of risk.

(n) "Copyrighting Costs": All costs, if not included in Negative Cost, to obtain copyright and the extension and renewal thereof, and other similar protections throughout the world, wherever and whenever incurred within Distributor's sole discretion.

(o) "Copyright Infringement Costs": All costs, if not included in Negative Cost, incurred to protect the copyright ownership in the Picture and to prevent any infringement of copyright or violation of rights in and to the Picture or any elements thereof (whether by litigation or otherwise) and reasonable attorneys' fees in connection therewith.

(p) "Claims and Litigation Costs": All costs, if not included in Negative Costs, incurred by reason of claims asserted by third Parties which arise out of the production, distribution, exhibition and/or exploitation of the Picture (including claims of infringement, unfair competition, violation of any right of privacy, right of publicity, defamation or breach of contract) including reasonable attorneys's fees, litigation expenses, investigation expenses, and reasonable reserves established by Distributor in its good faith business judgment as reasonably necessary to protect against the probability of ultimate expense, loss, damage or liability as to claims Distributor determines in its sole business judgment to be of sufficient merit as to warrant such reserves. Distributor shall have the right, in its sole discretion, to settle and pay any such claim. After settlement or final judicial determination of any such claim, any reserve taken shall be adjusted to reflect the actual costs paid by Distributor. Nothing herein contained shall be construed as a waiver of any of Participant's warranties contained in the Agreement, or a waiver of any right or remedy which may exist in favor of Fox, including the right to require Participant to reimburse Fox on demand for any liability, cost, damage or expense arising out of, or resulting from, any breach by Participant of any warranty, undertaking or obligation by Participant, or any right on the part of Fox to recoup or recover any such cost or expense out of Participant's Percentage Participation.

(q) "Industry Assessments": An allocable portion of industry assessments, including industry campaigns endorsed and supported by all or substantially all the major Parties in the Motion Picture industry; contributions to legal fees and related overhead of counsel retained to monitor and investigate infringement of copyright in Motion Pictures distributed by Distributor; assessments for awards, settlements, contributions, judgments, legal fees and other costs incurred in connection with prosecuting and defending actions of any kind under antitrust Laws, communication Laws and other Laws regarding the distribution, exhibition and/or exploitation of the Picture (including law suits and arbitrations) in which Distributor is involved.

(r) "Quota Losses": Expenditures in a Territory which result from the acquisition of Motion Picture product produced in such Territory as a prerequisite to the eligibility of the Picture for distribution in such Territory.

(s) "Miscellaneous Distribution Costs": Other costs customarily incurred by Distributor in connection with the distribution of Motion Pictures, including telephone, telegraph, cable, postage, messenger and copying costs.

2. "Subdistributor Distribution Costs": All costs, expenses and charges paid, advanced or incurred by a Subdistributor of the kind described in Section V., Paragraph D.1., with respect to Subdistributor Receipts which are accountable as Gross Receipts, including the application of Advertising Overhead.

E. "Negative Cost": The sum of "Direct Charges" and "Fox Administrative Overhead Charge".

1. "Direct Charges": The aggregate of all costs, charges and expenses which are paid, incurred or accrued in connection with the acquisition of all underlying literary rights and musical rights with respect to the Picture (including costs of copyright and title searches, clearances and registrations, and royalty and license fees) and in connection with the preparation, production, completion and delivery of the completed Picture, including the costs of materials, equipment, physical properties, personnel and services utilized in connection with the Picture, both above-the-line and below-the-line (including charges for insurance and production auditor, charges established pursuant to the then current published Fox Studio Rental Rates and Price Schedule for facilities, equipment and personnel of Fox furnished and utilized in connection with the Picture and related imputed employer fringe charges at the percentage rates established pursuant to the then current published Fox Studio Rental Rates and Price Schedule as applied to all direct salaries of all personnel utilized in connection with the Picture, both above-the-line and below-the-line), actual costs of financing and of completion bond charges and recoupments and

laboratory charges (including charges established pursuant to the then current published Film Price List of Deluxe Laboratories or other affiliated entity of Fox). If the individual producer, executive producer and/or director for the Picture is engaged by Fox to render services in connection with the development of Motion Picture projects in addition to the Picture, the actual amount of fees paid or allocated for services rendered in connection with the Picture plus an allocable share (as reasonably determined by Fox) of the general development expenses (including charges for office space and refurbishing, office equipment and supplies, telephone, travel, business expenses, research, and support and development personnel) incurred in connection with all services of such individual producer, executive producer and/or director performed for Fox shall be included as Direct Charges. However, unless otherwise expressly provided in the Agreement, no direct costs of Motion Picture projects involving such individual producer, executive producer and/or director abandoned by Fox shall be included as Direct Charges. Fox may elect to self insure any items of risk in connection with the preparation, production, completion and delivery of the Picture and charge as a Direct Charge an amount equal to the insurance premium Fox would otherwise have paid for such insurance. Fox shall, in its sole discretion, determine whether or not to obtain or maintain any insurance or to self insure any item of risk. The amount of losses recovered from insurance proceeds shall be used to reduce Direct Charges.

2. "Fox Administrative Overhead Charge": An amount equal to 15% of Direct Charges irrespective of where or by whom the Picture is produced anywhere in the world. The Fox Administration Overhead Charge shall accrue and be included in Negative Cost concurrently with the incurring of the respective items of Direct Charges to which it applies. The determination as to what items and personnel are furnished for the Fox Administrative Overhead Charge shall be made in all respects in the same manner as Fox customarily determines such matters. The application of the Fox Administration Overhead Charge shall in no way diminish the charges established pursuant to the Fox Studio Rental Rates and Price Schedule, which charges are included as Direct Charges pursuant to Paragraph E.1. above and subject to the Fox Administrative Overhead Charge as provided in this Paragraph E.2.

F. "Initial Breakeven Point": The Initial Breakeven Point shall be deemed to be that amount of Gross Receipts at which a Participation Statement first reflects that the aggregate amount of Gross Receipts is sufficient to recoup the aggregate amount of all the items deductible from Gross Receipts in realizing Net Profits pursuant to Section IV, based upon financial data determined, recorded and computed as of the end of the Statement Period for which said Participation Statement is rendered, except that the deductible amount of Fox Distribution Fees shall be the aggregate of Fox Distribution Fees applied with respect to only that amount of Gross Receipts necessary to recoup the aggregate of the items set forth in Section IV., Paragraphs A. through F. in the order of priority set forth in Section IV. The ratio that the aggregate amount of Fox Distribution Fees computed on a continuing and cumulative basis pursuant to Section IV., Paragraph C. bears to the aggregate amount of Gross Film Rentals and Theatrical Outright Sale Receipts computed on a continuing and cumulative basis shall be used to calculate the applicable percentage rate of Fox Distribution Fee for purposes of determining the amount of Fox Distribution Fees deductible in determining the Initial Breakeven Point. The Statement Period as to which a Participation Statement reflects achievement of the Initial Breakeven Point is referred to as the "Initial Breakeven Statement Period."

VI. GENERAL ACCOUNTING PROVISIONS:

A. Records: Fox shall maintain books of account which pertain to the production and distribution of the Picture at such place or places as may from time to time be customary with Fox pursuant to its ordinary business practices.

B. Accounting Practices: All financial matters, including the determination of items constituting Direct Charges, Gross Receipts and Distribution Expenses shall be determined, accounted for and calculated in all respects pursuant to participation accounting practices customarily used by Fox for Theatrical Motion Pictures produced and/or distributed by Fox. All computations hereunder, including Direct Charges, Interest, Gross Receipts and Distribution Expenses, shall be on a continuing and cumulative basis based upon financial data determined, recorded and computed as of the end of the particular Statement Period for which a periodic Participation Statement is being rendered. Fox may establish reasonable reserves for anticipated Direct Charges, Deferments, Percentage Participations and/or Distribution Expenses.

C. Foreign Currencies:

1. Foreign Remittances: Monies received by Distributor in a Restricted Currency are not includable in Gross Receipts. Monies paid to and received by Distributor in a currency of a Territory outside the United States which is not a Restricted Currency shall be deemed to have been converted into the United States Dollars at the monthly average of the daily U.S. working day rate of foreign currency exchange as reported in the Wall Street Journal and shall be deemed to have been remitted to Fox in the United States as of the end of the Statement Period during which such monies were received by Distributor. Monies paid to and received by Distributor in United States Dollars in a Territory outside the United States which are freely remittable to the United States shall be deemed to have been remitted to Fox in the United States as of the end of the Statement Period during which such monies were received by Distributor.

2. "Restricted Proceeds": Such monies which are not includable in Gross Receipts by reason of being in a Restricted Currency.

(a) Notification: At the request of Participant, the amount of Restricted Proceeds, if any, shall be reported on the next regularly scheduled Participation Statement in the currency units of the Restricted Currency.

(b) Partial Remittance: If only a portion of the total amount of a Restricted Currency which has accumulated in a Territory outside the United States with respect to the Picture and other Theatrical Motion Pictures distributed by Distributor in such Territory is remitted and actually received in the United States by Fox ("Remittance"), there shall be allocated to Gross Receipts a portion of the Remittance determined by multiplying the Remittance by a fraction, the numerator of which is the Restricted Proceeds in such Territory and the denominator of which is the then current total amount of Restricted Currency which has accumulated in such Territory with respect to the Picture and other Theatrical Motion Pictures distributed by Distributor in such Territory. The foregoing notwithstanding, if the Remittance is designated by the governmental authorities of such Territory (i) as funds derived during a specific period, then the aforementioned fraction shall be determined with respect to the specific period so designated, or (ii) as funds derived from a specific Motion Picture or Motion Pictures, then the Remittance shall be deemed to be a Remittance only as to the specific Motion Picture or Motion Pictures so designated.

(c) Deposit of "Restricted Proceeds": As and when the Participant's Percentage Participation becomes payable to Participant, Participant may notify Fox in writing that Participant elects to require settlement of Participant's share of the Restricted Proceeds remaining in any Territory outside the United States (not yet converted into United States Dollars and therefore not includable in Gross Receipts) in the currency of such Territory, by designating a bank or other representative in such Territory, to whom payment may be made for Participant's account. Subject to applicable Laws, such payment shall be made to such bank or representative at Participant's expense. Such payment shall fully satisfy Fox's obligations to Participant as to such Restricted Proceeds and Participant's share thereof. Any taxes or expenses incurred in connection with the making of such payment shall be deducted from the amount so paid, or otherwise charged to or paid by the Participant, in advance, if so required.

D. Statements:

1. "Negative Cost Statement": Concurrently with the rendition of the first Participation Statement, Fox shall furnish Participant an itemized summary of the Negative Cost of the Picture without prejudice to Fox's right to render subsequent Negative Cost Statements for the purpose of revision and correction.

2. "Participation Statement": Fox shall render to Participant periodic Participation Statements showing, in summary form, Gross Receipts and permitted deductions therefrom, accompanied with payment of the amount, if any, shown thereon to be due Participant by check drawn to the order of Participant in United States Dollars except as otherwise provided in Section VI., Paragraph C.2.(c). A Participation Statement shall be rendered for the period not greater than 6 months in length from the end of the month in which the Initial Release Date of the Picture occurred and then for periods not greater than 3 months in length for a minimum of 8 quarters and then for periods not greater than 6 months in length for the next 2–year period, and thereafter for periods not greater than 12 months in length. The period covered by a Participation Statement as hereinabove provided is referred to as a "Statement Period". Each Participation Statement shall be furnished no later than 90 days after the close of the Statement Period for which the Participation Statement is rendered, but such reporting time shall be increased to no later than 120 days as to Participation Statements covering Statement Periods which commence after the expiration of 5 years from the Initial Release Date of the Picture. Any Participation Statement may be changed from time to time to effectuate periodic adjustments determined by Fox's Accounting Department or its certified public accountants or to correct any errors or omissions. After the expiration of 3 years from the Initial Release Date of the Picture, no Participation Statement need be rendered for any Statement Period with respect to which no amounts would be shown to be due Participant.

3. Mailing: Negative Cost Statements and Participation Statements to be furnished to Participant shall be mailed to Participant at Participant's then current address for Notices under the Agreement.

E. Withholdings: There shall be deducted from any payments to or for the account of Participant hereunder, the amount of any tax or other withholding which, pursuant to applicable Laws, is required to be made by Fox, based upon, measured by, or resulting from payments to or for the account of Participant. Such deduction shall be in accordance with the good faith interpretation by Fox of such Laws. Fox shall not be liable to Participant for the amount of such deductions because of the payment of said amount to the Party involved. Participant shall make and prosecute any and all claims which it may have as to such tax deductions and/or withholdings directly with the Party involved.

F. Overpayment/Offset: If Fox makes any overpayment to Participant hereunder for any reason or if Participant is indebted to Fox for any reason, Participant shall pay Fox such overpayment or indebtedness on demand, or at the election of Fox, Fox may deduct and retain for its own account an amount equal to any such overpayment or indebtedness from any sums that may become due or payable by Fox or any affiliated entity of Fox to Participant or for the account of Participant.

G. <u>Audit</u>: If Participant requests by written notice pursuant to the Notices provision of the Agreement, Fox shall permit, at the sole cost and expense of Participant, a first class and reputable firm of certified public accountants designated by Participant in such written notice, the designation of which shall be subject to the reasonable approval of Fox ("Participation Auditor"), to examine the Fox books of account which relate to the Picture, in order to verify the accuracy of the transactions or items of information as first reflected in any Negative Cost Statement (the mailing date of which occurred during the 24-month period prior to the date of the commencement of the field work examination by the Participation Auditor) and of any Participation Statement (the mailing date of which occurred during the 24-month period prior to the date of the commencement of the field work examination by the Participation Auditor). The Participation Auditor may make copies of, or make excerpts from only such part of the Fox books of account which relate to matters and time frame subject to examination as herein provided. Such examination shall be only at such place where said Fox books of account are maintained and during reasonable business hours in such manner as not to interfere with Fox's normal business activities and not more frequently than once during any consecutive 12-month period. Such examination shall continue for no longer than 90 calendar days and for such additional times as is reasonably necessary for the Participation Auditor to complete the examination of those Fox books of account as relate to matters and time frame subject to examination as herein provided. The records supporting the transactions or items of information reflected in the particular Negative Cost Statement or Participation Statement shall not be examined more than once. A true copy of all reports made by the Participation Auditor pursuant to the foregoing provisions shall be delivered to Fox at such time as written objection is delivered to Fox as to transactions or items of information. Such right to examine is limited to the Picture and under no circumstances shall Participant or the Participation Auditor have the right to examine records relating to Fox's business generally or with respect to any other Motion Picture for purposes of comparison or otherwise, provided, however, that where any original income or expense document with third Parties relate to the Picture and to other Motion Pictures, Participant Auditor shall have the right to examine the entire document without deletion therefrom subject to the signature by Participant and the Participation Auditor of a Confidentiality Agreement in Fox's usual form if Fox elects to require a Confidentiality Agreement.

H. <u>Incontestability</u>: All transactions and items of information reflected within any Negative Cost Statement or Participation Statement including any and all information contained in the Fox books of account and Distributor records and all supporting documentation therein ("Picture Records") which in any way pertain to such transactions and items of information shall be deemed correct and shall be conclusive and binding upon Participant and Participant shall forever be barred from objecting for any reason or maintaining or instituting any action or proceeding which relates to any transactions or questions the accuracy of any item of information reflected therein, including any and all information contained in the Picture Records which pertain in any way to such transactions and items of information, unless a written objection specifying in detail the transactions or items of information to which Participant objects and the nature and reasons for such objection is delivered to Fox within 33–months from the date of mailing of the Negative Cost Statement or Participation Statement in which the transaction or item of information is first reflected irrespective of when or if an audit of such Negative Cost Statement or Participation Statement, as the case may be, was initiated or completed. Transactions or items of information not specified in such written objection may not be raised subsequent to the expiration of said 33–month period. If Participant's objections are not resolved amicably, Participant's objections shall be deemed to have been waived unless Participant maintains or institutes an action or proceeding with respect thereto within 6 months after the expiration of said 33–month period. The inclusion in any Negative Cost Statement or Participation Statement of transactions or items of information which have appeared in a previous Negative Cost Statement or Participation Statement shall not make any such transactions or items of information including any and all information contained in the Picture Records which in any way pertain to such transactions or items of information subject to objection again nor recommence the running of the 33–month period as to such transactions or items of information, including any and all information contained in the Picture Records which in any way pertain to such transactions or items of information. The right to examine and/or object and/or to maintain or institute any action or proceeding shall not be extended by reason of requesting an opportunity to audit. Participant agrees that Participant's sole right to receive accountings in connection with the Picture, to examine Picture Records, and/or to object as to transactions or items of information and/or any other matter with respect to Participant's Participation and/or to maintain or institute any action or proceeding shall be only as provided in this Exhibit, and Participant hereby waives the benefits of any applicable Law under which Participant otherwise may be entitled to an accounting, rights of examination and/or rights of objection and/or rights to maintain or institute any action or proceeding and agrees that the accountings to Participant in connection with the Picture as provided in this Exhibit shall not be deemed a book account or an open account between Fox and Participant and shall not be viewed in any way so as to deny the applicability of the incontestability provisions set forth in this Exhibit. The applicable Picture Records need not be retained and may be destroyed after the expiration of said 33-month period following the date of mailing of the Negative Cost Statement or applicable Participation Statement, as the case may be, unless Participant has duly objected prior thereto and instituted an action as herein provided.

VII. GENERAL TERMS AND CONDITIONS:

A. No Representations: Fox has not made any express or implied representation, warranty, guarantee or agreement that the Picture will be produced, or if produced, that the Picture will be released or distributed or the quality of the Picture will equal or exceed any minimum standard of quality, or if produced and released, that the Picture will earn any minimum amount of Gross Receipts or Net Profits or any minimum amount of monies will be expended in connection therewith or Participant's Percentage Participation will equal or exceed any minimum amount or the Picture will be distributed or exploited in any particular manner.

B. Distribution and Exploitation of the Picture: As between Participant and Fox, Fox shall have the complete, exclusive and unqualified control of the distribution, marketing, advertising, publicizing, exhibition, exploitation and other disposition of the Picture directly or by any Subsidiary, Affiliate, or other Party in all media throughout the world in perpetuity, in accordance with such sales methods, plans, patterns, programs, policies, terms and conditions as Fox in its sole business judgment may determine proper or expedient. The enumeration of the following rights of distribution and exploitation shall in no way limit the generality or effect of the foregoing:

1. Refrain from Distribution, Exhibition or Exploitation: Fox may refrain from the release, distribution, re-issue or exhibition of the Picture at any time, in any location or Territory, in any media, or in any form as Fox in its sole business judgment may determine. Participant acknowledges that there is no obligation to exploit the Soundtrack Recording Rights or Music Publishing Rights or Merchandising Rights or Literary Publishing Rights, it being agreed that Fox may elect to exercise any one or more of said rights or to refrain from exercising any or all of said rights as Fox in its sole business judgment may determine.

2. "Outright Sales": Fox may make Outright Sales of the Picture as Fox in its sole business judgment may determine, whether or not Fox maintains its own distributing organization in the Territory involved. Only net monies actually received and earned by Fox with respect to Outright Sales of the Picture shall be included within Gross Film Rentals.

3. Contracts and Settlements: Fox may, in the exercise of its sole business judgment, make, alter or cancel contracts with exhibitors, Subdistributors and other licensees and adjust and settle disputes, make allowances and adjustments and given credits with respect thereto.

4. Collections: Fox shall, in the exercise of its sole business judgment, determine the extent to audit, check or verify the computation of any payments or to press for the collection of any monies which, if collected, would constitute Gross Receipts. There shall be no responsibility or liability to Participant for failure to audit, check, or verify or to collect any monies payable.

5. <u>Advertising</u>: Fox shall not be obligated to expend any minimum or maximum amount with respect to the advertising and publicizing of the Picture, and Fox, in the exercise of its sole business judgment, shall determine the amount of the advertising and publicizing budget and the extent of the advertising and publicizing campaign.

6. <u>Expenses</u>: Fox may incur any expenses which Fox, in the exercise of its sole business judgment, deems appropriate with respect to the Picture or the exercise of any of Fox's rights hereunder including the number of Motion Picture Copies of the Picture ordered.

C. <u>Sale of "Picture"</u>: Fox shall have the unlimited right at any time to sell, transfer or assign all of its right, title and interest in the Picture and the negative and copyright thereof to any Party. Any such sale, transfer or assignment shall be subject to Participant's rights hereunder, and Fox shall not be relieved of its obligations hereunder. However, if such sale, transfer or assignment be to any Subsidiary or Affiliate or other Party which shall succeed to all or substantially all of Fox's assets or to all or substantially all of Fox's Theatrical Distribution organization and if such Subsidiary, Affiliate or other Party shall assume in writing and agree to perform all of the obligations of Fox hereunder, then upon assumption by such Subsidiary, Affiliate or other Party of all of Fox's obligations hereunder, such sale, transfer or assignment shall be deemed a novation and Fox shall be forever released and discharged from any further liability or obligation to Participant for the payment of any monies which may thereafter become payable hereunder, and Participant shall look solely to such Subsidiary, Affiliate or other Party for any such payment. No monies received by Fox from any such sale, transfer or assignment shall be included in Gross Receipts and the terms of such sale, transfer or assignment and the monies paid to Fox thereunder shall be of no relevance to Participant. Nothing herein contained shall be deemed to limit or prevent Fox from assigning or hypothecating all or a portion of its share of monies derived hereunder.

D. <u>Assignment by "Participant"</u>:

1. <u>Assignment</u>: Subject to all applicable Laws and to the rights of Fox hereunder, Participant may assign the rights to Participant's Percentage Participation hereunder at any time after the Initial Release Date of the Picture, provided both a Notice of Irrevocable Assignment and a Distributor's Acceptance in Fox's usual form shall be executed by Participant and by the assignee and delivered to Fox. Any such assignment shall, at all times, be subject to all Laws and to all rights of Fox hereunder. Fox shall not be obligated to pay in accordance with any partial assignment if the formula or basis of computation creates any doubt of interpretation whereby Fox takes any risk whatsoever and/or if all the assignees fail to execute and deliver an agreement in Fox's usual form appointing a single person as a disbursing agent, to whom Fox may make all such payments thereafter regardless of any further assignment(s).

Fox's payment in accordance with any such assignment or designation shall be deemed to be equivalent of payment to Participant hereunder and shall release and discharge Fox from any further liability or obligation to Participant for the payment of monies hereunder. Participant's rights to inspect and audit the Fox books of account shall not be assignable without Fox's prior written consent.

2. <u>First Refusal</u>: If Participant shall propose to sell or assign the rights to Participant's Percentage Participation hereunder, Fox shall have the right of first refusal to acquire Participant's Percentage Participation, exercisable within 10 business days after receipt of written notice from Participant which specifies the Party to whom the proposed sale or assignment is to be made and the consideration and other terms and conditions upon which Participant proposes to make such sale or assignment. If Fox fails to exercise said right of first refusal, then Participant may make such proposed sale or assignment, but only to the Party and for the consideration and upon the terms and conditions specified in the notice to Fox. If Participant fails to make such proposed sale or assignment, Participant shall not thereafter make a sale or assignment to any other Party for a consideration or upon terms and conditions more favorable to such other Party than those specified in the notice to Fox without again giving Fox the opportunity to exercise its right of first refusal in accordance with the foregoing procedure.

E. <u>Creditor-Debtor Relationship</u>: Participant expressly acknowledges the relationship between Participant and Fox to be that of creditor and debtor with respect to all matters including the production, distribution, exploitation and any other disposition of the Picture, any elements thereof or rights therein and the computation and payment of any monies due Participant hereunder. Furthermore, Participant expressly acknowledges there is no fiduciary relationship between Fox and Participant and waives any right to make any claim to the contrary. Nothing contained in the Agreement, including this Exhibit, shall be construed to create an agency, trust, fiduciary obligation or specific fund as to Gross Receipts or Net Profits of the Picture or Participant's share thereof or of any other monies, or as to any other matter with respect to the Picture, or to prevent or preclude Fox from commingling Gross Receipts or Net Profits or any monies due Participant with any other monies or to give Participant a lien on the Picture or an assignment of the proceeds thereof. Fox's obligation to pay Participant hereunder shall not bear interest nor entitle Participant to gains which may accrue to such funds prior to payment to Participant.

F. <u>Litigation</u>: Participant waives any right which Participant may have at law or equity to revoke, terminate, diminish or enjoin any rights granted or acquired by Fox hereunder by reason of any claim which Participant may assert for non-payment of any monies claimed due and payable hereunder, it being agreed that

Participant shall be limited to an action at law for recovery of any such monies claimed.

G. <u>No Joint Venture or Partnership</u>: Nothing contained in the Agreement, including this Exhibit, shall be construed so as to create a joint venture or partnership between Participant and Fox or any other relationship other than creditor and debtor, or a third Party beneficiary relationship as to any third Party. Except as otherwise specifically set forth herein, neither Participant nor Fox shall be authorized or empowered to make any representation or commitment or to perform any act which shall be binding on the other unless expressly authorized or empowered in writing.

H. <u>Captions</u>: Captions of paragraphs hereof are inserted for reference and convenience only and in no way define, limit or describe the scope or intent of any provision hereof other than as provided in Section I. with respect to the identification of defined terms in the caption by the use of quotation marks.

GLOSSARY

Schedule "1" of Exhibit "A" forming a part of the _____Agreement dated as of _____between TWENTIETH CENTURY FOX FILM CORPORATION and_____.

The following words have the following meanings:

A. "Additional Motion Picture": A Motion Picture based upon some portion of the plot or story line from Literary Material, which portion was not used in a prior Motion Picture, and which is not a Studio Sequel Motion Picture or a Remake.

B. "Additional Motion Picture Rights": The right to make one or more Additional Motion Pictures and the right to exploit any or all rights therein and thereto.

C. "Affiliate": A joint venture, partnership or other entity, other than a corporate entity, as to which Fox or a Subsidiary is the sole Party with respect to, or shares in, the actual management, operation, and expenses thereof; or a corporate entity in which Fox or a Subsidiary has a controlling interest represented by stock ownership in excess of 20%, but not more than 50%, of the total issued and outstanding voting stock of such corporate entity.

D. "Author Sequel Motion Picture": A Motion Picture based upon an Author-Written Sequel.

E. "Author-Written Sequel": New Literary Material written by the author of pre-existing Literary Material in which

(1) One or more of the principal characters of the new Literary Material is taken from the pre-existing Literary Material of such author; and

(2) Said principal character(s) is shown as participating in new and different events and situations from the events and situations in which said principal character(s) participated in the pre-existing Literary Material of such author.

F. "Books-On-Sound-Records": Sound Records containing the single voice non-dramatic reading of Literary Material.

G. "Books-On-Sound-Records Rights": The right to license, manufacture, distribute and sell Books-On-Sound-Records.

H. "British Territory": The United Kingdom of Great Britain and Northern Ireland, Republic of Ireland, Isle of Man, the Channel Islands, Malta and Gibraltar, and military installations, aircraft and/or ships flying the British flag, and aircraft and/or ships owned or operated by any entity whose principal administrative office is located within any of the aforementioned Territories but excluding territorial areas and possessions.

I. "Budgeted Negative Cost": The total Negative Cost of a Motion Picture established in the budget upon which the principal photography of such Motion Picture commences or upon which principal photography of such Motion Picture is intended to commence.

J. "Canada": Canada and military installations, aircraft and/or ships flying the Canadian flag, and aircraft and/or ships owned or operated by any entity whose principal administrative office is located within any of the aforementioned Territories but excluding territorial areas and possessions.

K. "Canadian Network": At least 40 terrestrial over-the-air television broadcast stations all of which are affiliated with Canadian Broadcasting Corporation which stations broadcast Motion Pictures for Free Television Exhibition in the English language or at least 19 terrestrial over-the-air television stations all of which are affiliated with CTV Television Network Ltd. which stations broadcast Motion Pictures for Free Television Exhibition with audio in the English language.

L. "Cassettes": Motion Picture Copies in the form of a cassette, cartridge, videogram, video disc, tape or other similar device now known or hereafter devised and designed to be used in conjunction with a reproduction apparatus which causes a Motion Picture to be visible on the screen of a television receiver, television monitor or comparable device now known or hereafter devised.

M. "Commercial Tie-In Rights": The right to license the use of characters, designs, visual representations, names, likenesses and/or characteristics of artists, physical properties or other materials appearing or used in or in connection with a Motion Picture or all or any part of the Literary Material in connection with (1) the advertising, publicizing, promoting and/or packaging of (but not embodying on or in) merchandise, products or services and/or (2) premiums and/or promotions.

N. "Continental Europe": France, Belgium, Netherlands, Luxembourg, Federal Republic of Germany, Lichtenstein, Monaco, Austria, Switzerland, Spain, Portugal, Italy, Denmark, Norway, Sweden, Finland, Iceland, Greece, the Vatican, Andorra and San Marino, and military installations, aircraft and/or ships flying the flags thereof, and aircraft and/or ships owned or operated by any entity whose principal administrative office is located within any of the aforementioned Territories but excluding territorial areas and possessions.

O. "Distributor": Fox and Subsidiaries and Affiliates engaged in the distribution of a Motion Picture for exhibition by other Parties. The term Distributor shall not include the following: theatres, television broadcast stations, electronic transmission systems (including cable, direct broadcast satellite, microwave and master antenna), program delivery services and radio stations (and other exhibitors of Motion Pictures to viewers by any means now known or hereafter devised), or laboratories producing and/or distributing Motion Picture Copies, or merchandisers, manufacturers, sellers, wholesale dealers or retail dealers of Cassettes or of any other products, or book or music publishers, or Parties producing or distributing Sound Records, or Pay-TV/Cassette Marketers, or any Parties similar to any of the foregoing excluded Parties (whether or not any of the foregoing excluded Parties are Subsidiaries or Affiliates), or Subdistributors.

P. "Domestic Territory": The United States and Canada.

Q. "Episode": Each individual Television Motion Picture which is part of a Television Series.

R. "Final Approved Screenplay" or "Final Approved Teleplay": The version of the Literary Material with respect to which the Budgeted Negative Cost of a Motion Picture is computed.

S. "Force Majeure": The interruption of or material interference with the preparation, commencement, production, completion, or distribution of a particular Motion Picture or of a substantial number of Motion Pictures produced and/or distributed or proposed to be produced and/or distributed by Fox by any cause or occurrence beyond the control of Fox or Participants as the case may be, including fire, flood, epidemic, earthquake, explosion, accident, riot, war (declared or undeclared), blockade, embargo, act of public enemy, civil disturbance, labor dispute, strike, lockout, inability to secure sufficient labor, power, essential commodities, necessary equipment or adequate transportation or transmission facilities, failure or non-availability of any means for electronic transmission or reception of Motion Pictures, any applicable Law, any act of God, or the incapacity or unavailability or default (including refusal to perform) of the director of the Picture other than Participant (unless such default or refusal was caused by or in any way related to or connected with any action or inaction by Participant) or a principal member of the cast of the Picture other than Participant (unless such default or refusal was caused by or in any way related to or connected with any action or inaction by Participant).

T. "Foreign Territory": All Territories other than the United States.

U. "Four Wall Engagement": The Theatrical Exhibition of a Motion Picture pursuant to an arrangement whereby Distributor pays a rental fee for the right to exhibit the Motion Picture in a theatre and pursuant to which Distributor directly controls the collection and disbursement of box office receipts.

V. "Free Movie-For-Television": A Movie-For-Television primarily intended to be initially distributed for Free Television Exhibition.

W. "Free Television Distribution": The lease or license of a Motion Picture to one or more Parties with the right to engage in the Free Television Exhibition of the Motion Picture and/or to grant licenses to other Parties to engage in the Free Television Exhibition and/or Free Television Distribution of the Motion Picture.

X. "Free Television Exhibition": Television Exhibition, other than Pay Television Exhibition, without any fee being charged to the viewer for the privilege of unimpaired reception of such exhibition. For purposes of this definition, any government imposed fees or taxes applicable to the use of television receivers generally or a regular periodic access, carriage or equipment fee (but not any optional premium subscription charge or fee paid with respect to Pay Television Exhibition) paid by a subscriber to a cable television transmission service or other transmission service or agency for the privilege of unimpaired reception shall not be deemed a fee charged to the viewer.

Y. "Free Television Mini-Series": A Television Mini-Series primarily intended to be initially distributed for Free Television Exhibition.

Z. "Free Television Motion Picture": A Television Motion Picture primarily intended to be initially distributed for Free Television Exhibition.

AA. "Free Television Series": A Television Series primarily intended to be initially distributed for Free Television Exhibition.

AB. "Home Video Distribution": The lease or license of a Motion Picture to one or more Parties with the right to engage in the manufacture, distribution, rental and/or sale of Cassettes of the Motion Picture to one or more Parties for Home Video Exhibition of the Motion Picture and/or to engage in the further lease or license of the Motion Picture to other Parties with the right to engage in the manufacture, distribution, rental and/or sale of Cassettes of the Motion Picture for Home Video Exhibition of the Motion Picture.

AC. "Home Video Exhibition": The non-public exhibition of a Motion Picture by means of a Cassette in a private residence for viewing at the place of origin of such exhibition.

AD. "Home Video Motion Picture": A Motion Picture primarily intended to be initially distributed by means of Cassettes for Home Video Exhibition.

AE. "Including": Whenever examples are used with the word including (or any derivation thereof), such examples are intended to be illustrative only and shall not limit the generality of the words accompanying the word including (or any derivation thereof).

AF. "Initial Release Date": The date on which Theatrical Exhibition of a Motion Picture commences on a regularly scheduled basis in at least one major metropolitan area in the United States, other than previews, premieres, charitable screenings, test market screenings, screenings for Academy Award consideration, Theatrical Exhibition for Academy Award qualification, and other similar special exhibitions of a Motion Picture.

AG. "In perpetuity": The most extensive period of time permitted, including renewal and extension periods, if any, by any applicable Law.

AH. "International Territory": All Territories other than the Domestic Territory, British Territory and Continental Europe.

AI. "Law": Any present or future statute or ordinance, whether municipal, county, state, national or territorial; any executive, administrative or judicial regulation, order, judgment or decree; any treaty or international convention; any rule or principle of common law or equity, or any requirement with force of law.

AJ. "Legitimate Stage Rights": The right to present Literary Material upon the spoken stage with living performers appearing and speaking in the immediate presence of the viewing audience. The right to present Literary Material upon the spoken stage with living performers appearing and speaking, whether or not in the immediate presence of a viewing audience, for the primary purpose of photographing and recording such presentation for use in or in connection with a Motion Picture or for the promotion or publicity of a Motion Picture is an exercise of rights with respect to Motion Pictures and not an exercise of Legitimate Stage Rights.

AK. "Literary Material": Written matter, whether published or unpublished, in any form, including a novel, treatment, outline, screenplay, teleplay, story, manuscript, play or otherwise, which may be included in or upon which a Motion Picture may be based.

AL. "Literary Publishing Rights": The right to publish and distribute for sale to the public hardcover or soft-cover printed publications (including novelizations, screenplays and teleplays) of all or any part of the Literary Material or other material (other than music and/or lyrics) used in connection with a Motion Picture, including artwork, logos or photographic stills (but solely to the extent that the right to make such use of such other material has been separately obtained from the owner thereof), other than the publications included within Merchandising Rights.

AM. "Live Television Rights": Television Exhibition of the performance of living performers at the same time such performance actually takes place rather than the Television Exhibition of such performance by use of a Motion Picture Copy. However, Live Television Rights shall also encompass the limited right to reproduce a live Free Television Exhibition using a Motion Picture Copy and to exhibit such reproduction by means of Free Television Exhibition during the period of 30 days after the original live Free Television Exhibition, but only for the limited purpose of supplemental coverage and/or delayed broadcast in those few localities within the Territory where such original live Free Television Exhibition occurred but which were not reached by such original live Free Television Exhibition.

AN. "Merchandising Rights": The right to license, manufacture, distribute, and sell articles of merchandise and/or products (including toys, board and video games, novelties, trinkets, souvenirs, wearing apparel, fabric, foods, beverages and cosmetics) and the right to license, distribute, and sell services, which embody on or in such merchandise, products or services, characters, designs, visual representations, names, likenesses and/or characteristics of artists, physical properties or other materials appearing or used in or in connection with a Motion Picture or all or any part of the Literary Material and the right to publish, distribute, and sell souvenir programs, picture books, comic books, post cards, movie novels, photo novels, illustration books, and activity books or booklets which embody on or in the foregoing any or all of the characters, designs, visual representations, names, likenesses and/or characteristics of artists, physical properties or other materials appearing or used in or in connection with a Motion Picture or all or any part of the Literary Material.

BD. "Pilot": A Television Motion Picture produced as a prototype for the purpose of interesting an exhibitor, sponsor or distributing entity in ordering a Television Series based upon such Television Motion Picture.

BE. "Radio Rights": The right to transmit sound alone by means of radio devices.

BF. "Remake": A Motion Picture which is based upon a prior Motion Picture and in which one or more of the principal characters is shown as participating in substantially the same events and situations as in such prior Motion Picture. The term Remake does not include:

(1) an Additional Motion Picture;

(2) an Author Sequel Motion Picture;

(3) a Studio Sequel Motion Picture; or

(4) foreign, shortened, expanded or other modified versions of such prior Motion Picture.

BG. "Remake Rights": The right to make one or more Remakes and the right to exploit any or all rights therein and thereto.

BH. "Restricted Currency": A currency which is or becomes subject to moratorium, embargo, banking or exchange restrictions, or restrictions against remittances, or which in the business judgment of Fox is commercially impracticable to remit.

BI. "Sequel": A Studio Sequel Motion Picture or Author Sequel Motion Picture.

BJ. "Sequel Motion Picture Rights": The right to make one or more Author Sequel Motion Pictures and/or Studio Sequel Motion Pictures and the right to exploit any or all rights therein and thereto.

BK. "Sound Records": Sound only recordings and reproductions of every kind and character including all present and future developments of the sound recording and Motion Picture industries whether produced by means of any electrical, electronic, mechanical or other process or device now known or hereafter devised, and any accompanying process or device whereby sound only may be recorded for later transmission or playback but not simultaneously or in synchronization or timed relation with Motion Pictures.

BL. "Soundtrack Recording Rights": The right to license, manufacture, distribute and sell Sound Records made from the soundtrack of a Motion Picture or from a re-recording of the soundtrack of the Motion Picture.

BM. "Studio Sequel Motion Picture": A Motion Picture in which

(1) One or more of the principal characters of such Motion Picture is taken from the Literary Material upon which a prior Motion Picture is based and/or from the prior Motion Picture; and

(2) Said principal character(s) is/are shown as participating in new and different events and situations from the events and situations in which said principal character(s) participated (whether or not as principal characters) in said Literary Material or in said prior Motion Picture or any Remake thereof or in any earlier Studio Sequel Motion Picture or any Remake thereof or in any Additional Motion Picture; and

(3) The events and situations differ from that of said Literary Material or of said prior Motion Picture or any Remake thereof or of any earlier Studio Sequel Motion Picture or any Remake thereof or of any Additional Motion Picture.

The term Studio Sequel Motion Picture does not include any Additional Motion Picture, any Remake of said prior Motion Picture, any Remake of any Studio Sequel Motion Picture, or any Remake of any Remake.

BN. "Subdistributor": A Party licensed by Distributor to distribute or license a Motion Picture for exhibition in any one or more Territories, other than a Subsidiary, Affiliate, exhibitor, a licensee of an Outright Sale transaction, or a licensee which is a program delivery service for Television Exhibition (such as a network system for over-the-air television broadcast stations and/or for cable systems and/or for direct broadcast satellite service and/or for hotels and/or for hospitals).

BO. "Subsidiary": A corporate entity in which Fox or a Subsidiary has a controlling interest represented by stock ownership in excess of 50% of the total issued and outstanding voting stock of such Party.

BP. "Television Distribution": The lease or license of a Motion Picture to one or more Parties with the right to engage in the Television Exhibition of the Motion Picture and/or to grant licenses to other Parties to engage in the Television Exhibition and/or Television Distribution of the Motion Picture.

BQ. "Television Exhibition": The exhibition of a Motion Picture using any form of Motion Picture Copy for transmission by any means now known or hereafter devised (including over-the-air, cable, wire, fiber, master antennae, satellite, microwave, closed circuit, laser, multi-point distribution services or direct broadcast systems) which transmission is received, directly or indirectly by retransmission or otherwise, impaired or unimpaired, for viewing the Motion Picture on the screen of a television receiver or comparable device now known or hereafter devised (including high definition television), other than Home Video Exhibition or Theatrical Exhibition.

BR. "Television Mini-Series": A closed end Television Series consisting of a limited number of Episodes (in excess of one Episode), each of which is in excess of 60 minutes of running time.

BS. "Television Motion Picture": A Motion Picture primarily intended to be initially distributed for Television Exhibition.

BT. "Television Series": Related Episodes intended to be distributed as a group in episodic format (in which a continuing cast of characters performs roles in different factual situations in each Episode in accordance with an established story line) or anthology format (in which there is no continuing cast of characters performing roles and no continuing established story line) or a combination of an episodic and an anthology format.

BU. "Territory": Any specific geographic area constituting a nation, country, state, governmental entity or any subdivision thereof located anywhere in the universe.

BV. "Theatrical Distribution": The lease or license of a Motion Picture to one or more Parties with the right to engage in Theatrical Exhibition of the Motion Picture and/or to grant licenses to other Parties to engage in the Theatrical Exhibition and/or Theatrical Distribution of the Motion Picture.

BW. "Theatrical Distribution Outright Sale": An Outright Sale of a Motion Picture solely for Theatrical Distribution for a period in excess of 2 years. Theatrical Distribution Outright Sale does not include the license to an exhibitor, whether or not such license includes the right to license the Motion Picture to other Parties for Theatrical Exhibition.

BX. "Theatrical Exhibition": The exhibition of a Motion Picture using any form of Motion Picture Copy by any process now known or hereafter devised in walk-in or drive-in theatres open to the general public on a regularly scheduled basis where a fee is charged for admission to view the Motion Picture.

BY. "Theatrical Motion Picture": A Motion Picture primarily intended to be initially distributed for Theatrical Exhibition.

BZ. "Theatrical Re-Issue": A re-release of a Motion Picture for Theatrical Exhibition on a percentage basis or Four Wall Engagement basis in first-run theatres.

CA. "United States": The continental United States of America, including the District of Columbia, and the States of Alaska and Hawaii, and military installations, aircraft and/or ships flying the United States flag, and aircraft and/or ships owned or operated by any entity whose principal administrative office is located within any of the aforementioned Territories but excluding territorial areas, possessions and commonwealths.

CB. "U.S. Network": At least 50 terrestrial over-the-air television broadcast stations which broadcast Motion Pictures for Free Television Exhibition and all of which are affiliated with either ABC or CBS or NBC.

Form 22

Real-Life Story Rights Option Agreement

THIS AGREEMENT is made this (*date*) between *John Doe* ("Owner") and *Productions, Inc.* ("Purchaser") concerning the rights in Owner's life story. Owner agrees that he is willing to permit Purchaser, and any of Purchaser's successors, licensees or assigns, on the terms and conditions herein contained to exploit Owner's story rights, and any of the material furnished by Owner or others to Purchaser, or in the public domain, involving Owner's story (*describe*) (hereinafter the "Material"). Each such means of exploitation based on the Material is hereinafter referred to as a "Product".

The following terms and conditions shall constitute the understanding and agreement between Owner and Purchaser concerning the foregoing:

1. <u>OPTION</u>: In consideration of the mutual promises contained herein, and the payment to Owner of $ (*amount*) which sum is applicable against the purchase price if Purchaser exercises its option herein, Owner hereby grants Purchaser the exclusive, irrevocable right and option (hereinafter the "Option") to purchase the motion picture, television and all allied, ancillary and subsidiary rights as such rights are understood in the television industry (hereinafter the "Rights") in and to the Material subject to the terms and conditions of a Purchase Agreement (hereinafter the "Purchase Agreement"), a copy of which is attached hereto as Exhibit "A" and made a part hereof.

2. <u>OPTION TERM</u>: The initial period of time during which the Option may be exercised shall be twelve (12) months, commencing on the date of execution hereof. Purchaser shall have the right to extend the initial period of time for an additional twelve (12) months by sending notice to Owner prior to the expiration of the initial period, along with an additional payment of $ (*amount*) which sum shall be applicable against the purchase price. If Purchaser so extends the Option period as aforesaid, Purchaser will have the right to further extend the Option for an additional six months by sending notice to Owner plus making an additional payment of $ (*amount*) prior to the expiration of the preceding Option Period, which sum shall be applicable against the purchase price.

Purchaser may exercise the option at any time during the Option term as it may be extended, by giving written notice to Owner and by currently paying the compensation set forth in Clause 2(a) or 2(b), of the Purchase Agreement, whichever is applicable.

3. <u>EXECUTION AND DELIVERY OF AGREEMENT</u>: Concurrently with the execution of this Option Agreement, Owner is executing and depositing with Purchaser the Purchase Agreement and a Short Form Assignment of Option Rights (attached hereto as Exhibit "B" and executed for the purpose of copyright

registration). If Purchaser exercises the Option, upon such exercise the Purchase Agreement shall be deemed dated as of the date of such exercise, and the Purchase Agreement shall be a valid and binding agreement between the parties hereto without further execution or delivery. If Purchaser shall fail to exercise the Option, the Purchase Agreement shall be of no force and effect and Purchaser shall return the documents to Owner.

4. <u>DISCLOSURE AND CONSULTATION:</u> Prior to the time that the option is exercised, and thereafter if the Option is exercised, Owner shall, at Purchaser's request, disclose to Purchaser and Purchaser's representatives, freely completely and candidly, all information in Owner's possession or under Owner's control including, without limitation, copies of any newspaper or magazine clippings, photographs, transcripts, notes, recordings, or other physical materials relating to Owner's story and all Owner's thoughts, observations, recollections, reactions and experiences surrounding, arising out of, and concerning all those events, circumstances, and activities, relating to Owner's story.

If Purchaser specifically requires Owner to travel or to incur telephone expenses in connection with such disclosure or consultation, then Purchaser shall reimburse Owner for reasonable out of pocket travel and living expenses for services performed by Owner away from Owner's home and for long distance telephone calls incurred at Purchaser's request.

5. <u>GRANT OF RIGHTS:</u> Owner hereby grants to Purchaser the perpetual, exclusive and irrevocable rights to depict Owner, whether wholly or partially factual or fictional, and to use Owner's name(s), likeness, voice, and biography in connection with the Material and any Production (as that term is defined in Clause 1(a) of the Purchase Agreement appended hereto) and the advertising and exploitation thereof or any rights thereto, in any and all media except as may be specifically limited in this agreement and the Purchase agreement, provided, however, that unless and until the Option is exercised, the rights herein granted to Purchaser shall be exercised only in connection with customary development and preproduction activities in the television industry including, but not limited to, preparation and submission of treatments and scripts. Owner acknowledges that if Purchaser exercises the Option, Purchaser shall have the rights, in addition to the other rights granted in the Purchase Agreement, in connection with any such Product to use any information, documents, news reports, clippings, photographs, recordings and other materials dealing with, depicting or concerning Owner and the Materials whether furnished by Owner, others, or in the public domain. Purchaser shall have the right to include or cause to be included in any such Product such actual or fictional events, scenes, situations, dialogue and other materials as Purchaser may consider desirable or necessary in Purchaser's sole and absolute discretion.

Notwithstanding anything contained in this Clause 5 to the contrary, it is Purchaser's intention to portray Owner's story as factually as possible with the understanding that Purchaser has the right to deviate from the facts to enhance the dramatic value of the Material.

6. <u>WAIVER:</u> Owner hereby waives and relinquishes any rights or remedies at law, in equity or otherwise, and further releases Purchaser and Purchaser's employees, agents, successors, licensees, and assigns from, and covenants not to sue Purchaser, or any of them, with respect to any claim, cause of action, liability or damage of any nature whatsoever arising out of or in connection with the exercise of any of the rights herein granted to Purchaser or granted pursuant to the Purchase Agreement. Such liabilities include, without limitation, defamation, libel, slander or invasion of any right of privacy or publicity in any jurisdiction. The aforesaid waivers are hereby made by Owner, both on Owner's own behalf and on the behalf of Owner's heirs.

7. <u>REPRESENTATIONS AND WARRANTIES:</u>

(a)   Owner represents and warrants that Owner has not heretofore granted, and Owner hereby agrees that hereafter Owner shall not grant, during the Option Term, or thereafter if the Option is exercised, to any party, nor shall Owner exercise or authorize, or permit to be exercised, any right to use or exploit any of the rights granted or to be granted to Purchaser herein or in the Purchase Agreement; and that Owner has not entered into, and shall not enter into during the aforesaid periods, any agreements or activities which will hinder, compete, conflict, or interfere with the exercise of, or diminish, any of the rights granted to Purchaser. Owner has no knowledge of any claim or potential claim by any party which might in any way affect Purchaser's right to use and exploit the rights granted herein.

(b)   Owner represents and warrants that none of the information to be provided by Owner or on Owner's behalf is, or will be a violation of the rights of any third party, including, without limitation, a defamation, libel, slander or violation of any right of privacy or publicity.

(c)   Owner represents and warrants that Owner has the right, authority and legal capacity to grant the rights granted to Purchaser hereunder and in the Purchase Agreement.

(d)   Owner shall defend, indemnify and hold Purchaser, and Purchaser's employees, agents, successors, licensees and assigns, harmless from and against any and all claims, damages, liabilities, losses or expenses (including reasonable attorney's fees and costs) which Purchaser or any such party may suffer or incur arising out of or in connection with the breach by Owner of any of the representations and warranties set forth herein or in the Purchase Agreement.

(e)   Purchaser shall defend, indemnify and hold Owner harmless from and against any and all claims, damages, liabilities, losses or expenses (including reasonable attorney's fees and costs) which Owner may suffer or incur arising out of any fictional material added to the Material by Purchaser.

8. <u>ADDITIONAL RELEASES</u>: Owner agrees to use Owner's best efforts to procure for Purchaser for no additional cost, those releases Purchaser deems necessary from individuals who are a part of Owner's life story or depicted in any information or materials Owner may supply to Purchaser herein.

9. <u>NO OBLIGATION TO EXPLOIT</u>: The terms of this Option Agreement and the Purchase Agreement shall not obligate Purchaser to exercise any of Purchaser's rights hereunder or under the Purchase Agreement or to continue such exploitation if commenced.

10. <u>ADDITIONAL ASSURANCES AND DOCUMENTS</u>: This Option Agreement is irrevocable, and this Option Agreement and the Purchase Agreement apply equally to any and all Products and is not only for Purchaser's benefit, but also for the benefit of any other party to whom Purchaser may sell, assign, and/or license any or all of the rights, privileges, powers and/or immunities granted herein or in the Purchase Agreement. Owner will prevent the use by others of Owner's name, likeness, voice, character and/or life story in a manner inconsistent with the grant of rights to Purchaser hereunder. Purchaser may prosecute, and Owner irrevocably grants to Purchaser full power and authority to do so, in Owner's name and to take any and all steps as Purchaser, in Purchaser's sole discretion may elect, to restrain and prevent others from so depicting, presenting and/or otherwise using Owner's name, likeness, voice, character and/or life story. Owner further agrees to execute, acknowledge and deliver to Purchaser or procure the execution, acknowledgment and delivery to Purchaser of any and all further assignments and other instruments, in form approved by counsel for Purchaser, necessary or expedient to carry out and effectuate the purposes and intent of the parties as herein expressed and, if Purchaser shall exercise the Option hereunder, to convey to Purchaser all rights granted to Purchaser in the Purchase Agreement. If Owner shall fail, refuse or neglect to so execute and deliver or cause to be so executed and delivered any such assignment or other instrument, Purchaser shall be deemed to be, and Owner irrevocably appoints Purchaser, the true and lawful attorney-in-fact of Owner, to execute and deliver any and all such assignments and other instruments in the name of Owner.

11. <u>PUBLIC INFORMATION</u>: Under no circumstances shall Purchaser, or Purchaser's successors, licensees or assigns, be in a less favorable situation than Purchaser would have been had Purchaser not secured from Owner the rights described herein or in the Purchase Agreement.

12. <u>REMEDIES</u>: If Purchaser shall fail to make any of the payments to Owner provided for in the Purchase Agreement or if Purchaser breaches any other covenant or condition hereof or of the Purchase Agreement, Owner acknowledges and agrees that Owner's sole remedy shall be an action at law to recover such payments and/or monetary damages. In no event shall any of the rights granted or to be granted and/or the releases made herein or in the Purchase Agreement revert to Owner, nor shall Owner have a right of rescission or right to injunctive or other equitable relief.

13. <u>ASSIGNMENT</u>: Purchaser may assign, license, transfer or otherwise dispose of this Option Agreement and the Purchase Agreement, and any of the rights, licenses, privileges or property conveyed, in whole or in part with the prior consent of Owner, which consent shall be not be unreasonably withheld or delayed. Notwithstanding any such sale, assignment, license transfer or disposal, Purchaser shall remain primarily liable to Owner for the payments described in Clause 2 of the Purchase Agreement.

14. <u>FORCE MAJEURE</u>: If engagement in any preproduction activities in connection with any version of the Material to be produced hereunder, including the writing of any treatments or teleplays, shall be prevented or interrupted due to epidemic, fire, action of the elements, strikes, labor disputes, governmental order, court order, act of God, public enemy, wars, riots, or civil commotion, the Option period shall be extended for the number of days such event of force majeure existed.

15. <u>GOVERNING LAW</u>: This Option Agreement and the Purchase Agreement shall in all respects be governed and controlled by the laws of the *State of New York.*

16. <u>NOTICES</u>: All notices and statements which either party shall be required or shall desire to give to the other party shall be given in one of the following ways:

    (a)   By courier or other personal delivery;

    (b)   By deposit, addressed as specified below, registered or certified mail, postage prepaid, in the United States mail, or;

    (c)   By telefax to compatible equipment.

If so delivered, mailed, or telefaxed, each such notice, statement or other document shall be conclusively deemed to have been given when personally delivered, or telefaxed or on the first business day following the date of mailing, as the case may be. The addresses of the parties shall be those of which the other party actually receives written notice and, until further notice are: (*address*)

With copies to parties' attorneys at: (*addresses*)

17. <u>ENTIRE AGREEMENT:</u> This Option Agreement and Exhibits and Schedules attached hereto, constitute the entire agreement between the parties and cannot be modified except by written instrument executed and delivered to Purchaser and Owner. Neither Purchaser nor Owner has made any representations, promises or warranties not set forth herein. In witness whereof the parties have caused this Option agreement to be duly executed and delivered the day and year first above written.

_____
Purchaser

_____
Owner

Form 23

Real-Life Story Rights Purchase Agreement

THIS AGREEMENT is made and entered into by and between Owner and Purchaser on this *(date)*. This Agreement is composed of the following terms and conditions:

1. <u>GRANT OF RIGHTS:</u> Owner does hereby exclusively sell, grant, convey, transfer, set over and assign to Purchaser, Purchaser's successors, licensees and assigns all rights in and to the Material, including, but not limited to the following:

(a) <u>Production and Distribution:</u> The sole and exclusive right to make television programs and motion picture versions or adaptations of the Material or any part thereof, and to produce one or more television productions of any type based upon or adapted in whole or in part from the Material, or any part thereof, or any such versions or adaptations (all of such programs, motion pictures, versions or adaptations thereof being hereinafter referred to as "productions"), and to produce, remake, distribute, exhibit, broadcast, perform, sell, license for exhibition, exploit, dispose of and generally deal in any manner with one or more productions.

(b) <u>Adaptation and Fictionalization:</u> The sole and exclusive rights to translate into all languages, and to freely adapt, revise rearrange, add to and subtract from the Material, or any part thereof, and the title, theme, plot, sequences, incidents, and characterizations thereof, to make sequels to and new versions or adaptations of the Material or any part thereof; to make serials of the Material or any part thereof; to use any part or parts of the Material or the theme thereof or any incidents, characters, character names, scenes, and sequences therein contained in conjunction with any other material or materials; and to separately or cumulatively do any or all of the foregoing, to such extent as Purchaser in Purchaser's sole discretion may deem expedient or desirable in the exercise of any of the rights, licenses or privileges herein conveyed. Purchaser has the right to fictionalize, simulate, portray or impersonate Owner's name, likeness and biography in the productions, and to make use of incidents which have occurred in relation to the Material, factually or fictionally, and Purchaser may employ any actor to portray Owner, in Purchaser's sole discretion. Notwithstanding anything contained in this Clause 1(b) to the contrary, it is Purchaser's intention to portray Owner's story as factually as possible with the understanding that Purchaser has the right to deviate from the facts to enhance the dramatic value of the Material.

(c) <u>Copyright:</u> The sole and exclusive right to secure copyright registration (or equivalent protection in countries where no copyright law exists) of such productions, and any other versions or adaptations of Material, and any soundtracks or recordings in connection therewith, in all countries of the world under any now existing or hereafter created laws, regulations or rules, in the name of Purchaser or any other person, firm or corporation. Purchaser shall be deemed to have acquired and is hereby granted and assigned all rights in the Material under any copyright which may have been herein granted, sold, assigned and set over to Purchaser. If requested by Purchaser, Owner agrees to execute, acknowledge and deliver, or cause to be executed, acknowledged and delivered to Purchaser, any instruments that may be required by Purchaser or that may be necessary, proper or expedient in the opinion of Purchaser to establish and vest in Purchaser such rights under such copyright.

(d) <u>Publicity and Advertising:</u> Purchaser shall have the customary right for advertising and publicity purposes to broadcast, prepare, publish and copyright publications in newspapers, magazines and periodicals of all types, of any synopses, excerpts, summaries, and stories (all of which shall collectively be referred to as "synopses" herein and may not exceed *2,500 words)* of the Material or any part thereof, and the right to use said synopses in posters, lobby displays, pressbooks, trade publications, newspapers, magazines and other periodicals, and all other media of advertising and publicity whatsoever (and to copyright said synopses in Purchaser's name in all countries and languages of the world).

The foregoing rights, licenses, privileges and properties shall be enjoyed by Purchaser throughout the world, and the enumeration thereof shall not be deemed to restrict or limit in any way the generality of the grant made in this clause.

Nothing herein contained shall be interpreted or construed to obligate Purchaser to produce any production of the Material, or exercise any of the other rights, licenses or privileges herein conveyed.

2. <u>COMPENSATION:</u> As full consideration for all rights, licenses, privileges and property herein conveyed, and all warranties, representations, and covenants herein made by Owner, Purchaser agrees to pay Owner the following sums, as applicable:

(a) If Purchaser shall produce or cause to be produced a program or mini-series intended for initial exhibition over commercial television the purchase price shall be *thirty thousand (30,000)* dollars, payable upon exercise of the option. The Option payments will be applicable against and deducted from the Purchase Price.

(b) If Purchaser shall produce or cause to be produced a motion picture intended for initial release in theaters, Purchaser shall pay Owner an additional sum of *ten thousand (10,000)* dollars, payable on first theatrical exhibition.

(c) If Purchaser shall produce or cause to be produced a remake of any production hereunder, Purchaser shall pay Owner *50%* of the applicable Purchase Price, payable on commencement of principal photography of the remake.

(d) If Purchaser shall produce or cause to be produced any sequel to any production hereunder, Purchaser shall pay Owner *33 1/3%* of the applicable

Purchase Price, payable on commencement or principal photography of the sequel.

3. <u>OWNER'S RIGHT OF REVERSION:</u> Notwithstanding anything to the contrary herein, if Purchaser shall fail to commence principal photography within *seven (7)* years of the date of exercise of the option herein, then all rights granted by Owner hereunder shall automatically revert to Owner for Owner's use, benefit and disposition. Purchaser shall execute any documents required by Owner to evidence a reversion of rights back to Owner.

4. <u>OWNER'S PUBLICATION RIGHTS:</u> If Owner at any time enters into a publishing agreement relating in any way to Owner's story or to the Materials, and Owner receives revenues pursuant thereto prior to the procurement of a firm development or production commitment from a network, sponsor or other financing entity, Purchaser shall receive no consideration therefrom. Upon obtaining a firm development or production commitment from a network, sponsor or other financing entity, however, Purchaser shall receive *10%* of all gross royalties, advances and other consideration paid or to be paid to Owner therefrom commencing with the date upon which such commitment is made (of which Purchaser shall give Owner notice). Purchaser's percentage shall be increased by *5%* to an aggregate *15%* of all gross royalties, advances and other consideration paid or to be paid to Owner therefrom commencing with the date of the initial telecast, or theatrical release of the first production produced pursuant hereto, if any, and continuing in perpetuity.

Owner shall cause the publisher to pay Purchaser's share directly to Purchaser as a third party beneficiary at the same time it pays Owner's share, and Purchaser shall have the same rights as Owner to receive statements from the publisher as well as the same rights to audit and object to statements. Such a provision shall be inserted into the agreement with the publisher, as well as a provision stating that such provision may not be modified or stricken without Purchaser's written consent. If such percentage is not paid directly to Purchaser as above-described, then Owner shall pay it within one week of Owner's receipt in each instance.

The parties hereby agree to all the terms and conditions set forth above by signing below.

_____

Owner

_____

Purchaser

MUSIC AGREEMENTS

Form 24

ASCAP General License Agreement--Restaurants, Taverns, Nightclubs, and Similar Establishments

827

GENERAL LICENSE AGREEMENT—RESTAURANTS, TAVERNS, NIGHTCLUBS, AND SIMILAR ESTABLISHMENTS

Agreement between AMERICAN SOCIETY OF COMPOSERS, AUTHORS AND PUBLISHERS ("SOCIETY"), located at

and

("LICENSEE"), located at   as follows:

1. Grant and Term of License

(a) SOCIETY grants and LICENSEE accepts for a term of one year, commencing and continuing thereafter for additional terms of one year each unless terminated by either party as hereinafter provided, a license to perform publicly at

("the premises"), and not elsewhere, non-dramatic renditions of the separate musical compositions now or hereafter during the term hereof in the repertory of SOCIETY, and of which SOCIETY shall have the right to license such performing rights.

(b) This license authorizes performances by means of "jukebox(es)" as defined in the Rate Schedule attached to and made a part of this Agreement.

(c) This Agreement shall enure to the benefit of and shall be binding upon the parties hereto and their respective successors and assigns, but no assignment shall relieve the parties hereto of their respective obligations hereunder as to performances rendered, acts done and obligations incurred prior to the effective date of the assignment.

(d) Either party may, on or before thirty days prior to the end of the initial term or any renewal term, give notice of termination to the other. If such notice is given the Agreement shall terminate on the last day of such initial or renewal term.

2. Limitations on License

(a) This license is not assignable or transferable by operation of law or otherwise, except as provided in subparagraph "1(c)" hereof, and is limited to the LICENSEE and to the premises.

(b) This license does not authorize the broadcasting, telecasting or transmission by wire or otherwise, of renditions of musical compositions in SOCIETY's repertory to persons outside of the premises, other than by means of a music-on-hold telephone system operated by LICENSEE at the premises.

(c) This license is limited to non-dramatic performances, and does not authorize any dramatic performances. For purposes of this Agreement, a dramatic performance shall include, but not be limited to, the following:

    (i) performance of a "dramatico-musical work" (as hereinafter defined) in its entirety;

    (ii) performance of one or more musical compositions from a "dramatico-musical work" (as hereinafter defined) accompanied by dialogue, pantomime, dance, stage action, or visual representation of the work from which the music is taken;

    (iii) performance of one or more musical compositions as part of a story or plot, whether accompanied or unaccompanied by dialogue, pantomime, dance, stage action, or visual representation;

    (iv) performance of a concert version of a "dramatico-musical work" (as hereinafter defined).

The term "dramatico-musical work" as used in this Agreement shall include, but not be limited to, a musical comedy, opera, play with music, revue, or ballet.

3. License Fees and Payments

(a) In consideration of the license granted herein, LICENSEE agrees to pay SOCIETY the applicable license fee set forth in the Rate Schedule annexed hereto and made a part hereof, based on "LICENSEE's Operating Policy." The term "LICENSEE's Operating Policy" shall mean all of the factors which determine the license fee applicable to the premises under the Rate Schedule.

(b) LICENSEE warrants that the Statement of LICENSEE's Operating Policy attached to and made a part of this Agreement is true and correct as of the date hereof.

(c) The current applicable license fee for the premises is   annually, based on the factors set forth in the Statement of LICENSEE's Operating Policy.

(d) LICENSEE agrees to pay SOCIETY the license fee due hereunder in installments of one-third the applicable annual fee in advance on or before January 1, May 1 and September 1 of each year provided, however, that if LICENSEE does not otherwise owe SOCIETY any fees under this or any prior license agreement, and if LICENSEE pays the full annual fee on or before January 31st of any year, the applicable license fee for that year shall be reduced by 20%.

(e) LICENSEE agrees to pay SOCIETY a $25 service charge for each unpaid check, draft or other form of monetary instrument submitted by LICENSEE to SOCIETY.

(f) In the event LICENSEE shall be delinquent in payment of license fees due hereunder by 30 days or more, LICENSEE agrees to pay a finance charge on the license fees due of 1½% per month, or the maximum rate permitted by the law of the state in which the premises licensed hereunder are located, whichever is less, from the date such license fees became due.

(g) In the event that LICENSEE's payment of fees under this Agreement causes SOCIETY to incur a liability to pay a gross receipts, sales, use, business use, or other tax which is based on the amount of SOCIETY's receipts from LICENSEE, the number of licensees of SOCIETY, or any similar measure of SOCIETY's activities, and (i) SOCIETY has taken reasonable steps to be exempted or excused from paying such tax; and (ii) SOCIETY is permitted by law to pass through such tax to its licensees, LICENSEE agrees to pay to SOCIETY the full amount of such tax.

4. Changes in LICENSEE's Operating Policy

(a) LICENSEE agrees to give SOCIETY thirty days prior written notice of any change in LICENSEE's Operating Policy. For purposes of this Agreement, a change in LICENSEE's Operating Policy shall be one in effect for at least thirty days.

(b) Upon any change in LICENSEE's Operating Policy resulting in an increase in the license fee, based on the annexed Rate Schedule, LICENSEE agrees to pay SOCIETY the increased license fee, effective as of the initial date of such change, whether or not written notice of such change has been given pursuant to subparagraph "4(a)" hereof.

(c) Upon any change in LICENSEE's Operating Policy resulting in a reduction in the license fee, based on the annexed Rate Schedule, LICENSEE shall be entitled to the reduction, effective as of the initial date of such change, and to a *pro rata* credit for any unearned license fees paid in advance, provided LICENSEE has given SOCIETY thirty days prior written notice of such change. If LICENSEE fails to give SOCIETY thirty days prior written notice, any reduction and credit shall be effective thirty days after LICENSEE gives SOCIETY written notice of the change.

(d) Within thirty days of any change in LICENSEE's Operating Policy, LICENSEE shall furnish to SOCIETY a current Statement of LICENSEE's Operating Policy and shall certify that it is true and correct.

(e) If LICENSEE discontinues the performance of music at the premises, LICENSEE or SOCIETY may terminate this Agreement upon thirty days notice, the termination to be effective at the end of the thirty day period. In the event of such termination, SOCIETY shall refund to LICENSEE a *pro rata* share of any unearned license fees paid in advance. For purposes of this Agreement, a discontinuance of music shall be one in effect for no less than thirty days.

5. Breach or Default

Upon any breach or default by LICENSEE of any term or condition herein contained, SOCIETY may terminate this license by giving LICENSEE thirty days notice to cure the breach or default, and in the event that it has not been cured within the thirty day period, this license shall terminate on the expiration of that period without further notice from SOCIETY to LICENSEE.

6. Interference in SOCIETY's Operations

In the event of:

(a) any major interference with the operations of SOCIETY in the state, territory, dependency, possession or political subdivision in which LICENSEE is located, by reason of any law of such state, territory, dependency, possession or political subdivision; or

(b) any substantial increase in the cost to SOCIETY of operating in such state, territory, dependency, possession or political subdivision, by reason of any law of such state, territory, dependency, possession or political subdivision, which is applicable to the licensing of performing rights,

SOCIETY shall have the right to terminate this Agreement forthwith by written notice and shall refund to LICENSEE any unearned license fees paid in advance.

7. Notices

All notices required or permitted to be given by either party to the other hereunder shall be duly and properly given if:

(a) mailed to the other party by registered or certified United States Mail; or

(b) sent by electronic transmission (i.e., Mailgram, facsimile or similar transmission); or

(c) sent by generally recognized same-day or overnight delivery service,

addressed to the party at the address stated above. Each party agrees to inform the other of any change of address.

IN WITNESS WHEREOF, this Agreement has been duly executed by SOCIETY and LICENSEE

this   day of   , 19

AMERICAN SOCIETY OF COMPOSERS,
AUTHORS AND PUBLISHERS

By _____   By _____

_____   _____
            Title   Title

(Fill in capacity in which signed:
(a) If corporation, state corporate office held;
(b) If partnership, write word "partner" under signature of signing partner;
(c) If individual owner, write "individual owner" under signature.)

STATEMENT OF OPERATING POLICY

ROOM NO. _____

Indicate only applicable factors:

I. Seating Capacity _____

		No. Days/Nights Per Week	Days/Nights Used (Circle)
II. Live Entertainment			
A. Single instrumentalist	☐	_____	Su M Tu W Th F Sa
B. Two or more instrumentalists	☐	_____	Su M Tu W Th F Sa

		No. Days/Nights Per Week	Days/Nights Used (Circle)
III. Mechanical music not otherwise licensed			
A. Audio-only			
1. Compact discs		_____	Su M Tu W Th F Sa
2. Jukebox	☐	_____	Su M Tu W Th F Sa
3. Karaoke	☐	_____	Su M Tu W Th F Sa
4. Radio-over-speakers	☐	_____	Su M Tu W Th F Sa
5. Records	☐	_____	Su M Tu W Th F Sa
6. Tapes	☐	_____	Su M Tu W Th F Sa
7. Other_____	☐	_____	Su M Tu W Th F Sa

		No. Days/Nights Per Week	Days/Nights Used (Circle)
B. Audio-Visual			
1. Karaoke with video	☐	_____	Su M Tu W Th F Sa
2. Large-screen television	☐	_____	Su M Tu W Th F Sa
Approximate screen size:_____ inches diagonally			
3. Laser disc	☐	_____	Su M Tu W Th F Sa
4. Multiple televisions	☐	_____	Su M Tu W Th F Sa
5. Video cassette recorder	☐	_____	Su M Tu W Th F Sa
6. Video jukebox	☐	_____	Su M Tu W Th F Sa
7. Other (describe)_____	☐	_____	Su M Tu W Th F Sa

IV. Mechanical music furnished by licensed background music supplier ☐

Name and address of supplier: _____
_____
_____

		No. Days/Nights Per Week	Days/Nights Used (Circle)
V. Variables			
A. Act(s)	☐	_____	Su M Tu W Th F Sa
B. Dancing and/or disc jockey	☐	_____	Su M Tu W Th F Sa
C. Show	☐	_____	Su M Tu W Th F Sa
D. Vocalist(s)	☐	_____	Su M Tu W Th F Sa

		No. Days/Nights Per Week	Days/Nights Used (Circle)
VI. Charges made: $_____			
A. Admission	☐	_____	Su M Tu W Th F Sa
B. Cover	☐	_____	Su M Tu W Th F Sa
C. Entertainment	☐	_____	Su M Tu W Th F Sa
D. Minimum	☐	_____	Su M Tu W Th F Sa
E. Similar charge (describe) _____		_____	Su M Tu W Th F Sa

		No. Days/Nights Per Week	Days/Nights Used (Circle)
VII. Alternate or relief music provided by instrumentalist(s) ☐		_____	Su M Tu W Th F Sa

VIII. Jukebox (see definition in Rate Schedule): Yes ☐ No ☐
A. Number of jukeboxes:_____

IX. Music-on-hold: Yes ☐ No ☐

X. Number of rooms with musical entertainment _____
(If music is performed in more than one room, fill out and attach a separate Statement of Operating Policy for each room)

XI. If seasonal operation, indicate seasonal period: Opening date _____ Closing date _____

Rate based on above policy $ _____

(If more than one room,
total rate for premises $ _____)

10M 4/95 (C)

ASCAP General License Agreement

STATEMENT OF OPERATING POLICY

OWNER _____

PREMISES _____

FULL ADDRESS _____

_____ ZIP CODE _____

TELEPHONE NO. _____ ROOM NO. _____

Indicate only applicable factors:

I. Seating Capacity _____

		No. Days/Nights Per Week	Days/Nights Used (Circle)
II. Live Entertainment			
A. Single instrumentalist	☐	_____	Su M Tu W Th F Sa
B. Two or more instrumentalists	☐	_____	Su M Tu W Th F Sa
III. Mechanical music not otherwise licensed		No. Days/Nights Per Week	Days/Nights Used (Circle)
A. Audio-only			
1. Compact discs		_____	Su M Tu W Th F Sa
2. Jukebox	☐	_____	Su M Tu W Th F Sa
3. Karaoke	☐	_____	Su M Tu W Th F Sa
4. Radio-over-speakers	☐	_____	Su M Tu W Th F Sa
5. Records	☐	_____	Su M Tu W Th F Sa
6. Tapes	☐	_____	Su M Tu W Th F Sa
7. Other_____	☐	_____	Su M Tu W Th F Sa
B. Audio-Visual		No. Days/Nights Per Week	Days/Nights Used (Circle)
1. Karaoke with video	☐	_____	Su M Tu W Th F Sa
2. Large-screen television	☐	_____	Su M Tu W Th F Sa
Approximate screen size:_____inches diagonally			
3. Laser disc	☐	_____	Su M Tu W Th F Sa
4. Multiple televisions	☐	_____	Su M Tu W Th F Sa
5. Video cassette recorder	☐	_____	Su M Tu W Th F Sa
6. Video jukebox	☐	_____	Su M Tu W Th F Sa
7. Other (describe)_____	☐	_____	Su M Tu W Th F Sa

IV. Mechanical music furnished by licensed background music supplier ☐

Name and address of supplier: _____

_____

_____

		No. Days/Nights Per Week	Days/Nights Used (Circle)
V. Variables			
A. Act(s)	☐	_____	Su M Tu W Th F Sa
B. Dancing and/or disc jockey	☐	_____	Su M Tu W Th F Sa
C. Show	☐	_____	Su M Tu W Th F Sa
D. Vocalist(s)	☐	_____	Su M Tu W Th F Sa
VI. Charges made: $_____		No. Days/Nights Per Week	Days/Nights Used (Circle)
A. Admission	☐	_____	Su M Tu W Th F Sa
B. Cover	☐	_____	Su M Tu W Th F Sa
C. Entertainment	☐	_____	Su M Tu W Th F Sa
D. Minimum	☐	_____	Su M Tu W Th F Sa
E. Similar charge (describe) _____		_____	Su M Tu W Th F Sa

VII. Alternate or relief music provided by instrumentalist(s) ☐   No. Days/Nights Per Week   Days/Nights Used (Circle)

_____   Su M Tu W Th F Sa

VIII. Jukebox (see definition in Rate Schedule): Yes ☐ No ☐

A. Number of jukeboxes_____

IX. Music-on-hold: Yes ☐ No ☐

X. Number of rooms with musical entertainment _____

(If music is performed in more than one room, fill out and attach a separate Statement of Operating Policy for each room)

XI. If seasonal operation, indicate seasonal period: Opening date _____ Closing date _____

Rate based on above policy $ _____

(If more than one room,
total rate for premises $ _____)

Entertainment Law Document Supplement

RATE SCHEDULE
LICENSE FEES FOR CALENDAR YEAR 1997

This Rate Schedule applies to Bars, Grills, Taverns, Restaurants, Lounges, Supper Clubs, Night Clubs, Ballrooms, Dance Clubs, Discos, Piano Bars, Cabarets, Roadhouses and similar establishments.

Seating Capacity (A)	No. Days/ Nights Per Week	LIVE MUSIC—SINGLE INSTRUMENTALIST Base Rate	NO. OF VARIABLES (B) (1)	(2)	(3)	Mech Music Audio-Only (C) Add	Mech Music with A/V (D) Add	LIVE MUSIC—TWO OR MORE INSTRUMENTALISTS Base Rate	NO. OF VARIABLES (E) (1)	(2)	(3)	Mech Music Audio-Only (C) Add	Mech Music with A/V (D) Add	NO LIVE MUSIC Mech Music Audio-Only (C) Base Rate	NO. OF VARIABLES (F) (1)	(2)	Mech Music With A/V (D) Base Rate	NO. OF VARIABLES (F) (1)	(2)
75 & under	1	$231	$305	$406	$544	$89	$135	$305	$406	$544	$725	$89	$135	$209	$305	$406	$311	$458	$609
	2-3	318	419	557	746	115	173	456	610	812	1079	115	173	231	419	557	346	626	833
	4-7	391	520	696	939	139	210	610	812	1079	1446	139	210	253	520	696	380	782	1046
76-150	1	305	406	544	724	127	191	406	544	724	964	127	191	298	406	544	446	609	819
	2-3	456	610	812	1079	165	248	610	812	1079	1446	165	248	332	610	812	497	915	1216
	4-7	610	812	1079	1446	203	303	812	1079	1446	1929	203	303	366	812	1079	549	1216	1618
151-225	1	406	544	724	966	165	248	544	724	964	1295	165	248	389	544	724	583	819	1088
	2-3	610	812	1079	1446	216	325	823	1088	1461	1940	216	325	433	812	1079	690	1216	1618
	4-7	812	1079	1446	1929	267	402	1088	1461	1940	2588	267	402	476	1079	1446	715	1618	2169
226-300	1	504	674	899	1203	203	303	684	913	1217	1622	203	303	481	674	899	721	1009	1347
	2-3	784	1014	1356	1814	267	402	1029	1370	1827	2434	267	402	534	1014	1356	800	1523	2035
	4-7	1014	1356	1814	2412	332	497	1370	1827	2434	3248	332	497	587	1356	1799	861	2035	2700
301-375	1	610	812	1079	1446	240	360	823	1103	1471	1955	240	360	570	812	1079	854	1216	1618
	2-3	913	1217	1622	2165	318	477	1245	1652	2206	2928	318	477	632	1217	1622	947	1827	2434
	4-7	1217	1622	2165	2878	391	587	1652	2194	2928	3907	391	587	684	1622	2165	1043	2434	3248
376-450	1	713	952	1267	1689	279	418	964	1281	1712	2283	279	418	862	952	1267	995	1430	1901
	2-3	1065	1432	1892	2524	371	556	1446	1929	2574	3422	371	556	734	1419	1892	1162	2128	2837
	4-7	1419	1904	2524	3362	456	684	1929	2574	3422	4568	456	684	807	1904	2524	1213	2855	3706
451-525	1	713	952	1267	1689	279	418	1103	1471	1965	2612	318	477	756	1079	1461	1134	1618	2192
	2-3	1065	1432	1892	2524	371	556	1659	2206	2944	3932	419	628	839	1622	2194	1258	2434	3290
	4-7	1419	1904	2524	3362	456	684	2206	2944	3920	5226	520	782	923	2157	2917	1384	3236	4376
526-600	1	713	952	1267	1689	279	418	1245	1659	2206	2944	354	531	844	1203	1652	1287	1803	2477
	2-3	1065	1432	1892	2524	371	556	1866	2486	3310	4415	469	704	930	1814	2473	1409	2720	3708
	4-7	1419	1904	2524	3362	456	684	2486	3310	4415	5895	582	874	1032	2412	3290	1540	3819	4949
601-675	1	713	952	1267	1689	279	418	1383	1838	2460	3272	391	587	935	1332	1836	1404	1998	2796
	2-3	1065	1432	1892	2524	371	556	2079	2765	3690	4909	520	782	1040	2004	2765	1567	3007	4190
	4-7	1419	1904	2524	3362	456	684	2765	3690	4909	6542	645	968	1143	2685	3666	1717	3999	5518
676-750	1	713	952	1267	1689	279	418	1519	2026	2702	3603	433	650	1027	1461	2026	1541	2192	3042
	2-3	1065	1432	1892	2524	371	556	2283	3041	4059	5404	573	860	1140	2194	3041	1711	3290	4581
	4-7	1419	1904	2524	3362	456	684	3041	4059	5404	7203	713	1068	1254	2917	4059	1882	4376	6089
751 & over	1	713	952	1267	1689	279	418	1519	2026	2702	3603	469	704	1121	1585	2219	1680	2378	3329
	2-3	1065	1432	1892	2524	371	556	2283	3041	4059	5404	621	933	1245	2382	3336	1857	3574	5006
	4-7	1419	1904	2524	3362	456	684	3041	4059	5404	7203	778	1162	1369	3171	4440	2053	4757	6661

(A) "Seating Capacity" for ballrooms, dance clubs, discos and similar operations means the total allowable occupancy of the premises under local fire or similar regulations, and shall not be limited to the total number of available seats, provided that if no such local fire or similar regulations are in effect, then "seating capacity" means 10 people per 100 square feet or portion thereof of the room(s) in which music is performed.

(B) VARIABLES (Applicable to single instrumentalist):
  – Show or act(s) or vocalist(s).
  – Admission, minimum, cover, entertainment or similar charge.
  – Alternate or relief music (live) by a single instrumentalist. Music provided solely at the time of the show or act(s) shall not be deemed to be alternate or relief music.

(C) "Mechanical Music Audio-Only" means performances other than by live musicians, e.g., records, tapes, compact discs, karaoke, or similar media or by a radio-over-loudspeaker system licensable under the United States Copyright Law, but shall not include music presented by means of a music-on-hold telephone system or a jukebox (as hereinafter defined).

(D) "Mechanical Music Audio-Visual" means performances such as, for example, by means of a television with screen measuring greater than 36 inches diagonally, multiple televisions regardless of screen size, laser discs, video tapes, karaoke with video, or video jukeboxes. If performances are presented by both audio-only and audio-visual mechanical means, add only the applicable additional fee specified for "mechanical music audio-visual."

(E) VARIABLES (Applicable to two or more instrumentalists):
  – Show or act(s).
  – Admission, minimum, cover, entertainment or similar charge.
  – Alternate or relief music (live) by any instrumentalist(s). Music provided solely at the time of the show or act(s) shall not be deemed to be alternate or relief music.

(F) VARIABLES (Applicable when there is no live music, to audio-only and audio-visual mechanical music):
  – Admission, minimum, cover, entertainment or similar charge.
  – Dancing (patrons or performers), show or act(s) (including disc jockey, video jockey or master of ceremonies).

FEE FOR PERFORMANCES BY MEANS OF JUKEBOX(ES)

For purposes of this Agreement, a "jukebox" is a machine or device that is (i) employed solely for the non-dramatic performance of musical works by means of phonorecords, compact discs or similar medium and which is activated by insertion of coins, currency, tokens, or other monetary units or their equivalent; (ii) is located in an establishment making no direct or indirect charge for admission; (iii) is accompanied by a list of the titles of all musical works available for performance on the jukebox, which list is affixed to the jukebox or posted in the establishment in a prominent position where it can be readily examined by the public; (iv) affords a choice of works available for performance and permits the choice to be made by the patrons of the establishment in which it is located; and (v) for which neither a compulsory license nor a license from the Jukebox License Office nor a license from SOCIETY other than this license is in effect. For purposes of this Agreement, the term "jukebox" does not include devices commonly known as "video jukeboxes," or any other audio-visual devices.

For performances given by means of jukebox(es), the annual license fee shall be $227 per jukebox.

FEE FOR PERFORMANCES BY MEANS OF MUSIC-ON-HOLD TELEPHONE SYSTEM

For performances given by means of a music-on-hold telephone system at the premises, the annual license fee shall be $169.

COMPUTATION OF FEE FOR MIXED POLICIES

1. Compute fee for the higher policy for the number of days/nights that the higher policy is in effect. The higher policy is the policy which generates the highest fee for any one day/night. If the higher policy is in effect for four or more days/nights per week, stop here: Your fee is the fee for the higher policy. If the higher policy is in effect for fewer than four days/nights per week, continue with steps 2 through 6 below to complete the computation of the fee for your mixed policy.

2. Note total number of days/nights entertainment is provided.

3. Compute fee for the lower policy using the total number of days/nights entertainment is provided under both the higher and lower policies.

4. Compute fee for the lower policy using the number of days/nights the higher policy is in effect.

5. Subtract fee computed in step 4 from fee computed in step 3.

6. Add fee computed in step 1 to fee computed in step 5 for total fee.

SEASONAL FEES

For seasonal licensees, the fees for periods up to four months of operation are 1/2 the annual license fee; for each additional month the fee is 1/12 the annual license fee. The seasonal license fee will in no case be more than the annual license fee.

FEE FOR OCCASIONAL PERFORMANCES

For policies in effect for any three or fewer days/nights per month, the fee is the applicable annual fee for the highest of such policies as if such highest policy were in effect for one day/night per week. For policies in effect for any six or fewer days/nights per calendar year, the fee is 1/3 the applicable annual fee for the highest of such policies as if such highest policy were in effect for one day/night per week.

ANNUAL LICENSE FEE FOR CALENDAR YEARS 1998 AND THEREAFTER

The annual license fee for each calendar year commencing 1998 shall be the license fee for the preceding calendar year, adjusted in accordance with the increase in the Consumer Price Index, All Urban Consumers – (CPI-U) between the preceding October and the next preceding October.

Form 25

BMI Music Performance Agreement--Restaurants, Nightclubs, Cocktail Lounges, Taverns, Disco's, and Other Establishments

BMI Music Performance Agreement

BMI Music Performance Agreement

Restaurants, Nightclubs, Bars, Cocktail Lounges, Taverns, Disco's, and Other Establishments

```
┌──┬──┬──┬──┬──┬──┐ ┌──┐
│  │  │  │  │  │  │─│08│
└──┴──┴──┴──┴──┴──┘ └──┘
      ACCOUNT #
```

LI-94/04-08

AGREEMENT, made at New York, N.Y. on _(Date Will Be Entered By BMI Upon Execution)_ _____ between BROADCAST MUSIC, INC. (hereinafter BMI), a State of New York corporation with its principal offices at 320 West 57th Street, New York, N.Y. 10019 and the entity described below and referred to thereafter as LICENSEE:

ENTER LEGAL NAME ▶	_Name of Corporation, Partnership, or Individual Owner_
ENTER TRADE NAME ▶	_(Doing business under the name of)_
CHECK APPROPRIATE BOX AND COMPLETE ▶	☐ Corporation ☐ Partnership (Enter names of partners) ☐ Individual Owner _(indicate residence address below under Mailing Address)_
	(State of Incorporation)

PREMISES ADDRESS	MAILING ADDRESS
	(Street Address)
(State) _(Zip)_	_(City)_ _(State)_ _(Zip)_
(Premises Name)	_(Telephone No.)_ _(Contact Name)_
(Title)	_(Title)_

1. DEFINITIONS

(a) **Live music:** music performed by musicians, singers or other entertainers actually present and performing at the licensed premises.

(b) **Live music and entertainment costs:** expenditures of every kind (whether money or any other consideration) made by or for LICENSEE for live music. The services of LICENSEE and/or non-compensated musicians or entertainers shall be included in "entertainment costs" at the prevailing rate for such services in the community. Also included in "entertainment costs" are expenditures for room and board where LICENSEE is obligated to provide them as part of the consideration for such entertainment services.

(c) **Recorded music:** the performance of music by mechanical or electronic devices for background, foreground, or as part of audio-visual presentations, etc., which include, but are not limited to, records, tapes, CD's, broadcasts, satellite signals and/or cablecasts.

(d) **Dancing:** patrons, performers or employees dancing to recorded music anywhere on the licensed premises.

(e) **Discontinuance:** to permanently stop the use of all music, both live and recorded.

2. BMI GRANT

(a) BMI hereby grants to LICENSEE a non-exclusive license to perform publicly at the licensed premises all of the musical works the rights to grant public performance licenses of which BMI controls during the term. This license does not include: (i) dramatic rights, the right to perform dramatico-musical works in whole or in substantial part, the right to present individual works in a dramatic setting or the right to use the music licensed hereunder in any other context which may constitute an exercise of the "grand rights" therein; (ii) the right to broadcast, telecast, cablecast, or otherwise transmit the performances licensed hereunder to persons outside of the premises; or (iii) performances of music by means of a coin-operated phonorecord player (jukebox) as defined in the Copyright Law (17 U.S.C. § 116).

(b) BMI reserves the right at its discretion to withdraw from the license granted hereunder any musical work as to which any legal action has been instituted or a claim made that BMI does not have the right to license the performing rights in such work or that such work infringes another composition.

3. TERM OF AGREEMENT

The initial term of this annual agreement shall begin on the first day of _____ _Month/Year_ and end on the last day of _____ _Month/Year_ and continue for additional periods of one (1) year each, unless cancelled by either party at the end of any period, upon 30 days advance written notice. Each one (1) year period is a "contract year."

4. FEES

(a) LICENSEE agrees to pay to BMI for each contract year an estimated fee as an advance of the actual fee. The estimated fee shall then be adjusted in accordance with Paragraph 5. The first estimated annual fee due shall be payable upon the signing of the agreement by LICENSEE. The resulting actual fee shall be determined as follows:

PLEASE COMPLETE ALL SHADED AREAS

1

(i) **LIVE MUSIC AND ENTERTAINMENT ONLY** -- LICENSEE shall pay the applicable fee as indicated. See page 4, License Fee Schedule, Category 1.

(ii) **RECORDED AND LIVE MUSIC** -- LICENSEE shall pay the applicable fee as indicated. See page 4, License Fee Schedule, Category 1 and 2.

(iii) **RECORDED MUSIC ONLY** -- LICENSEE shall pay the applicable fee as indicated. See page 4, License Fee Schedule, Category 3.

(b) For each subsequent contract year the estimated license fee is due and payable no later than 20 days after each anniversary date of this agreement. Beginning with the second contract year and at the option of LICENSEE upon written request, payment of the estimated fee may be made in quarterly installments, provided that they are made no later than twenty (20) days after the start of each quarterly period. If any quarterly payment is not received on time, this option terminates, and the balance of the then-current year's estimate will immediately be due and payable. All subsequent estimates will then be due and payable annually. The estimated fee for each contract year after the first contract year is the actual annual fee payable by LICENSEE for the previous contract year, pursuant to this paragraph.

5. REPORTING

(a) After the first contract year at the same time that the estimated annual fee is paid, LICENSEE will furnish BMI (on BMI forms) a report certified either by an officer, owner, operator or by the auditor of LICENSEE, including the following information for such contract year: if live music was performed, the total live music and entertainment costs; if recorded music was performed, the maximum occupancy of the entire licensed premises; whether or not there is dancing at the premises; and whether or not licensable audiovisual performances of recorded music were given. These reports will continue to be made during any period of discontinuance.

(b) If after processing the annual report, the actual fee due BMI is less than the estimated fee already paid for such contract year, BMI will credit the difference to the account of LICENSEE and, if such difference occurs during the last year of the term, BMI will return same promptly.

(c) If after processing the annual report, the actual fee due BMI is greater than the estimated fee already paid for such contract year, LICENSEE will pay the difference between the actual and estimated license fee within thirty (30) days of receipt of BMI's adjusted statement.

(d) If LICENSEE fails to timely submit to BMI the annual report required by Paragraph 5 or 6, LICENSEE hereby appoints and authorizes BMI, at BMI's option, to assess a reasonable estimated license fee for such contract year. BMI shall give written notice to LICENSEE of the fee calculated. LICENSEE shall have ninety (90) days after such written notice by BMI to submit the report. If BMI does not receive from LICENSEE the report within those 90 days, BMI and LICENSEE agree that BMI's estimated fee shall then be established as the actual fee for the year unreported by LICENSEE. BMI and LICENSEE further agree that such established actual fee shall also become the estimated fee for the following contract year. LICENSEE agrees to waive its right to file its report for any contract year in which BMI's estimated fee becomes the actual fee.

6. DISCONTINUANCE OF MUSIC

In the event that LICENSEE discontinues the use of all music or if LICENSEE ceases to operate the premises during the term and so notifies BMI in writing, within thirty (30) days after receipt of such notice a pro rata adjustment for recorded music shall be made by BMI for that contract year, provided that LICENSEE submits a report as required by Paragraph 5 for all music used up to the date of discontinuance. In no event shall any fee be less than the lowest applicable Category 1, Category 2 and Category 3 fee in that contract year. LICENSEE will not be obligated to make future payments to BMI for the discontinued music (provided all previously due license fees have been paid) unless LICENSEE resumes the use of music. If LICENSEE discontinues the use of either live or recorded music, but not both, this agreement shall continue to be applicable to the music which continues to be used. LICENSEE will send written notice of any resumption of music to BMI within thirty (30) days thereof and at the same time provide BMI with the information required in Paragraph 5. If discontinuance and resumption occur in the same contract year, license fees shall be payable as if discontinuance never occurred and LICENSEE's estimated fee immediately prior to discontinuance shall be reinstated.

7. REVIEW OF STATEMENTS AND/OR ACCOUNTINGS

BMI will have the right, by its authorized representatives, at any time during customary business hours, and upon thirty (30) days advance written notice, to examine those portions of LICENSEE's books and records of account to such extent as may be necessary to verify any and all statements and/or accountings made hereunder or under any prior agreement with BMI. BMI shall consider all data and information coming to its attention as the result of any such examination of LICENSEE's books and records as confidential.

8. INDEMNITY BY BMI

BMI agrees to indemnify, save harmless and defend LICENSEE, its officers and employees, from and against any and all claims, demands or suits that may be made or brought against them or any of them with respect to the performance of any material licensed under this agreement. This indemnity shall be limited to works which are licensed by BMI at the time of LICENSEE's performances. BMI will, upon reasonable written request, advise LICENSEE whether particular musical works are available for performance as part of BMI's repertoire. LICENSEE shall provide the title and the writer/composer of each musical composition requested to be identified. LICENSEE agrees to give BMI immediate notice of any such claim, demand or suit, to deliver to BMI any papers pertaining thereto, and to cooperate with BMI with respect thereto, and BMI shall have full charge of the defense of any such claim, demand or suit.

2

9. CANCELLATION OF ENTIRE CATEGORY
BMI shall have the right to cancel this agreement along with the simultaneous cancellation of the agreements of all other licensees of the same class and category as LICENSEE, as of the end of any month during the term, upon sixty (60) days advance written notice.

10. OFFER OF COMPARABLE AGREEMENT
In the event that BMI, at any time during the term hereof, shall for the same class and category as that of LICENSEE, issue licenses granting rights similar to those in this agreement on a more favorable basis, BMI shall, for the balance of the term, offer LICENSEE a comparable agreement.

11. BREACH OR DEFAULT/WAIVER
Upon any breach or default of the terms and conditions of this agreement, BMI has the right to cancel this agreement, but any such cancellation shall only become effective if the breach or default continues thirty (30) days after the date of BMI's written notice to LICENSEE. The right to cancel is in addition to any and all other remedies which BMI may have. No waiver by BMI of full performance of this agreement by LICENSEE in any one or more instances will be a waiver of the right to require full and complete performance of this agreement thereafter or of the right to cancel this agreement in accordance with the terms of this paragraph.

12. ARBITRATION
All disputes of any kind, nature or description arising in connection with the terms and conditions of this agreement shall be submitted to the American Arbitration Association in the City, County and State of New York, for arbitration under its then prevailing arbitration rules. The arbitrator(s) to be selected as follows: Each of the parties shall, by written notice to the other, have the right to appoint one arbitrator. If, within ten (10) days following the giving of such notice by one party the other shall not, by written notice, appoint another arbitrator, the first arbitrator shall be the sole arbitrator. If two arbitrators are so appointed, they shall appoint a third arbitrator. If ten (10) days elapse after the appointment of the second arbitrator and the two arbitrators are unable to agree upon a third arbitrator, then either party may, in writing, request the American Arbitration Association to appoint the third arbitrator. The award made in the arbitration shall be binding and conclusive on the parties and judgment may be, but need not be, entered in any court having jurisdiction. Such award shall include the fixing of the costs, expenses and attorneys' fees of arbitration, which shall be borne by the unsuccessful party.

13. NOTICES
Any notice under this agreement will be in writing and deemed given upon mailing when sent by ordinary first-class U.S. mail to the party intended, at its mailing address above stated, or any other address which either party may designate. Any such notice sent to BMI shall be to the attention of the General Licensing Department. Any such notice sent to LICENSEE shall be to the attention of the person signing this agreement on behalf of LICENSEE or such other person as LICENSEE may advise BMI in writing.

14. MISCELLANEOUS
This agreement is the entire understanding between the parties, will not be binding until signed by both parties, and cannot be waived or added to or modified orally, and no waiver, addition or modification will be valid unless in writing and signed by the parties. This agreement is executed by the duly authorized representative of BMI and LICENSEE. The rights of LICENSEE are not assignable. This agreement, its validity, construction and effect, will be governed by the laws of the State of New York. The fact that any provisions are found by a court of competent jurisdiction to be void or unenforceable will not affect the validity or enforceability of any other provisions. All headings in this agreement are for the purpose of convenience and shall not be considered to be part of this agreement.

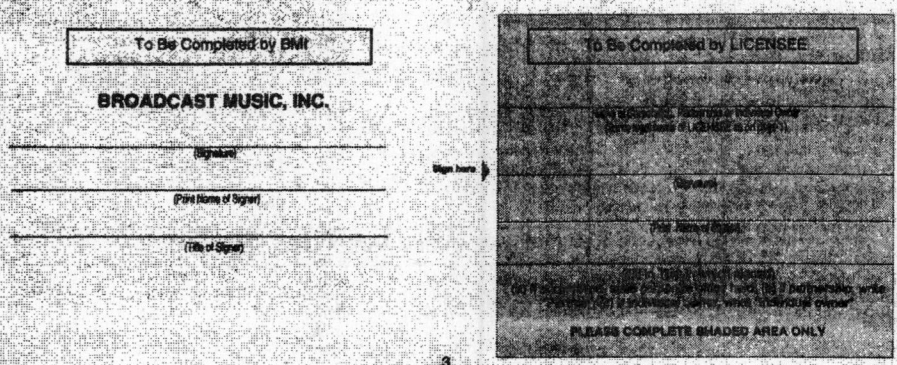

3

LICENSE FEE SCHEDULE

AVERAGE WEEKLY -OR- ANNUAL ENTERTAINMENT COSTS (LIVE MUSIC FEE CATEGORY 1)	ANNUAL LIVE MUSIC FEE	MAXIMUM OCCUPANCY OF ALL ROOMS, FLOORS AND AREAS OF LICENSED PREMISES (PER LOCAL FIRE OR BUILDING AUTHORITY)	ANNUAL RECORDED MUSIC (When Live Music is Used) CATEGORY 2 NO DANCING	DANCING			ANNUAL RECORDED MUSIC (When No Live Music is Used) CATEGORY 3 NO DANCING	DANCING		
$99 or less (Less than $5,000)	$175									
100-149 (5,000-7,999)	220	1-75	$105	$141.75	$190	$256.50	$195	$263.25	$315	$425.25
150-199 (8,000-9,999)	260	76-150	160	216	260	351	235	317.25	455	614.25
200-299 (10,000-14,999)	330	151-225	210	283.50	325	438.75	300	405	595	803.25
300-499 (15,000-24,999)	440	226-300	280	378	400	540	360	486	725	982.25
500-699 (25,000-34,999)	535	301-375	310	418.50	470	634.50	430	580.50	875	1,181.25
700-899 (35,000-49,999)	610	376-450	370	499.50	520	702	480	648	1,015	1,370.25
900-1,199 (50,000-64,999)	690	451-525	420	567	620	837	540	729	1,155	1,559.25
1,200-1,499 (65,000-79,999)	765	526-600	475	641.25	660	891	600	810	1,310	1,768.50
1,500-1,899 (80,000-99,999)	910	601-675	525	708.75	750	1,012.50	665	897.75	1,435	1,937.25
1,900-2,099 (100,000-119,999)	1,095	676-750	580	783	805	1,086.75	725	978.75	1,575	2,126.25
2,100-2,699 (120,000-139,999)	1,275	751 & OVER	630	850.50	900	1,215	800	1,080	1,715	2,315.25
2,700-3,099 (140,000-159,999)	1,530									
3,100 or more (160,000 or more)	1,530 + 8/10 of 1% (.008) of each dollar of expense over 160,000									

MUSIC POLICY STATEMENT

LIVE MUSIC

1. Is live music used? ☐ yes ☐ no

2. If yes, calculate Weekly Entertainment Costs as indicated below:

(Avg. no. of musicians per night) x (Avg. payment per musician) x (No. of nights with live music per week) = (Avg. Weekly Entertainment Costs)

OR

3. Indicate prior year's Annual Entertainment Costs (if available) $

4. Using the table above (Category 1) Indicate Estimated Annual Live Music Fee (if not applicable, write N/A). $

RECORDED MUSIC

5. Is recorded music used? ☐ yes ☐ no

6. Is there dancing to recorded music? ☐ yes ☐ no

7. Indicate maximum occupancy of all rooms, floors and areas of entire licensed premises (per local fire or building authority)

8. Is a jukebox used? ☐ yes ☐ no
If yes, ☐ Coin-operated ☐ Free-play ☐ Or Both

9. Jukebox Supplier's Name:

Phone:

10. Jukebox License Office (JLO) Certificate #:

11. Using the table above (Category 2 or 3) Indicate Estimated Annual Recorded Music Fee (if not applicable, write N/A). $

TOTAL ESTIMATED LIVE AND RECORDED ANNUAL FEE (Add line 4 and line 11) → $

4

Form 26

BMI Single Station Radio Blanket License Agreement

839

BMI

BROADCAST MUSIC, INC.

SINGLE STATION RADIO BLANKET LICENSE AGREEMENT

SHORT METHOD OPTION OR LONG METHOD OPTION

AGREEMENT made at New York, New York, on this _____ day of _____ 19___, between BROADCAST MUSIC, INC., a corporation organized under the laws of the State of New York (hereinafter BMI) with principal offices at 320 West 57th Street, New York, N.Y. 10019 and _____

_____

(Legal Name of LICENSEE)

PLEASE CHECK APPROPRIATE BOX AND COMPLETE

☐ A corporation organized under the laws of the State of _____

☐ A partnership consisting of _____

☐ An individual residing at _____

(hereinafter called LICENSEE) with offices presently located at _____

_____

(Street Address)

City _____ State _____ Zip _____ Telephone No. (_____) _____
Area Code

and operating the radio broadcasting station presently located at _____

_____

(Street Address)

City _____ State _____ Zip _____ Telephone No. (_____) _____
Area Code

and presently designated by the call letters _____
☐ AM
☐ FM and assigned frequency _____

(Check Appropriate Box)

1. Term.

The Term of this License Agreement commences as of January 1, 1992 and ends on December 31, 1996, unless earlier terminated as hereinafter provided.

2. Definitions.

A. **"Radio broadcasting"** shall mean aural broadcasting in all of its forms.

B. **"Local program"** shall mean any radio program, including a "cooperative program," broadcast by a station other than a "network program". For the purposes of this License Agreement, sports, special events and other programs furnished by networks not licensed by BMI, as well as any program originating from a station which holds a BMI Single Station Radio Blanket License Agreement, shall be deemed to be "local programs".

C. **"Cooperative program"** shall mean any program furnished by a network to the station under an agreement permitting the station to broadcast such program on a sustaining basis or on a commercial basis under the sponsorship of a local, regional or national advertiser contracting directly with the station or its representative for the incorporation of the commercial credits of such advertiser into such program, as broadcast by the station.

D. **"Network program"** shall mean any radio program simultaneously broadcast by any means by any network licensed as a network by BMI. "Network program" shall include "rebroadcasts," "delayed broadcasts" and "repeat broadcasts" of a network program as those terms are now understood in the broadcasting industry, even though non-simultaneous. Payments made to the originating network by an affiliated station in connection with such program may not be deducted. LICENSEE shall report all billings to and/or cash received from the furnishing network. "Billing(s)" as used in this License Agreement shall exclude the non-cash portion of transactions such as trade and barter sales with respect to a station reporting on a Billing Basis as referred to in Paragraph 2.F.(1).

PLEASE COMPLETE SHADED AREAS ONLY

(1) Any program furnished by a network which is not licensed as a network by BMI shall be deemed to be a local program. With respect to any such program:

(a) LICENSEE shall report all billings to and/or cash received from the furnishing network; and

(b) LICENSEE may deduct amounts paid to the furnishing network for: (i) the use of interconnecting facilities necessary to broadcast the program from outside the station's studios (not more than the amount actually paid to a utility company for such), and (ii) broadcast rights (not more than the amount actually paid to or for the original holder of the broadcast rights for the program).

(2) Any program which originates from a station which holds a BMI Single Station Radio Blanket License Agreement shall be deemed to be a local program. With respect to any such program:

(a) The originating station shall report all billings to and/or cash received from, or on behalf of, (1) the sponsors of any such program, and (2) affiliated stations. The following deductions shall be allowed against such revenue:

(i) The actual payments made to an outside vendor (e.g., a utility or satellite company) for the use of transmission facilities necessary to broadcast the program from outside the station's studios;

(ii) The actual payments made for broadcast rights, but not more than the amount actually paid to or for the original holder of them; and

(iii) The actual payments made by the originating station to its affiliates in connection with such program.

(b) The affiliated station shall include all billings to and/or cash received from the originating station in connection with such program, or from or on behalf of sponsors of cooperative announcements. If payments are made to the originating station by the affiliated station in connection with such program, the affiliated station may deduct such payments.

E. "Simulcast program" shall mean any program broadcast by two or more stations which are owned by LICENSEE, and are broadcast either simultaneously or on a "delayed broadcast" or "repeat broadcast" basis. Simulcast programs shall also include such programs for which LICENSEE acts as a "Local Manager."

F. "Gross Revenue" shall mean:

(1) When reporting on a "Billing Basis" (see Paragraph 5.B.), all billings (standard accrual method) charged to or on behalf of sponsors and donors, but excluding non-cash billings applicable to transactions such as trade and barter sales, for the use of the broadcasting facilities of the station from:

(a) local programs (including programs furnished by a network not licensed as a network by BMI and programs originating from another station which holds a BMI Single Station License Agreement);

(b) network programs;

(c) cooperative programs;

(d) simulcast programs;

(e) contributions and donations; and

(f) the cash portion of billings attributed to Time Brokers or providers of "program services" in "barter" arrangements by such parties that have no direct or indirect managerial ownership or connection with LICENSEE.

(2) When reporting on a "Cash Receipts Basis" (see Paragraph 5.B.), all cash payments made by or on behalf of sponsors and donors for the use of the radio broadcasting facilities of the station in the areas indicated in Paragraph 2.F.(1)(a) through (f) above.

(3) Gross Revenue shall also include all billings on behalf of (if reporting on a Billing Basis) and payments made directly to (if reporting on a Cash Receipts Basis), or as authorized by, LICENSEE, its employees, representatives, agents or any other person acting on LICENSEE's behalf, and all billings on behalf of and payments made to any company, firm or corporation under the same or substantially the same ownership, management or control as LICENSEE. Such billings and payments shall not include billings on behalf of and payments made to third parties, such as networks or program suppliers, that are not under the same ownership, management or control as the LICENSEE, or non-cash payments such as payments in goods or services commonly referred to as trade or barter. Subject to Paragraph 2.D., above, if LICENSEE is owned or controlled by a network, Gross Revenue shall not include billings by or cash payments to the network.

(4) In the event LICENSEE acts as a Local Manager for another station's facilities, Gross Revenues shall also include all billings charged to, or cash payments made by, sponsors or donors for the use of the managed station's facilities in the areas indicated in Paragraph 2.F.(1)(a) through (f), above, subject to the terms of any LMA-92-A Agreement entered into by LICENSEE pursuant to Paragraph 8, below.

2

(5) In the event that LICENSEE owns or controls one or more stations which are licensed by BMI under separate Blanket or Per Program license agreements, and LICENSEE's Gross Revenues are derived from any source, either in whole or in part, as the result of offerings of the stations' broadcast facilities in combination, LICENSEE shall make an allocation on a reasonable basis of the *combined* Gross Revenues and applicable deductions when filing Annual Statements and/or Annual Financial Reports required under the terms of the BMI Single Station Radio Blanket and Per Program License Agreements.

G. **"Net Revenue"** shall mean:

(1) When reporting on a Billing Basis, Gross Revenue

reduced by,

    (i) bad debts written off (increased by any bad debt recoveries) or rebates paid;

    (ii) rate card discounts (cash, quantity and/or frequency actually allowed); and

    (iii) advertising agency commissions actually incurred (not to exceed 15% of commissionable sales).

(2) When reporting on a Cash Receipts Basis, Gross Revenue *reduced by* advertising agency commissions actually incurred (not to exceed 15% of commissionable sales). The deduction for advertising agency commissions shall not be permitted if LICENSEE reports its net cash received from such agency sales as Gross Revenue.

H. **"Adjusted Net Revenue"** shall mean Net Revenue less any sums received for the broadcasting of local political programs.

I. **"Amount Subject to BMI Fee"** shall mean Adjusted Net Revenue (Short Method Option—See Paragraph 4.A.) or, at the option of LICENSEE, Adjusted Net Revenue less the total of the following itemized deductions to the extent they exceed 15% of Adjusted Net Revenue (Long Method Option—See Paragraph 4.B.):

(1) Net Talent Fees Allowed. All compensation in excess of the Total Yearly Amount set forth below actually paid by the station directly to "on-air" personnel acting as: (a) master of ceremonies or disk jockey on musical programs; (b) vocalist or instrumentalist engaged for a special program; (c) featured newscaster or news commentator; (d) featured sportscaster; (e) master of ceremonies on an entertainment program; or (f) announcer. If such person(s) has a 40% or more ownership interest in the station, this deduction shall not be allowed. If such person(s) holds a managerial capacity at the station and spends less than 100% of his or her time performing any of the duties enumerated in this Paragraph 2.I.(1), the total compensation amount shall be reduced in proportion to the amount of time spent on said duties.

Station's Annual Adjusted Net Revenue	Total Yearly Amount
Less than $50,000	$ 6,200
$ 50,000 to $149,999	18,600
$150,000 to $299,999	27,900
$300,000 to $499,999	41,900
$500,000 to $749,999	46,500
$750,000 to $999,999	53,700
$1,000,000 and over	62,000

The names, description of on-air duties and compensation must be indicated separately on the Annual Statement supplied by BMI. If the Annual Statement covers less than a full calendar year, Adjusted Net Revenue must be annualized, and the corresponding Total Yearly Amount must be prorated over the reporting period.

(2) News Service and Audio News Service. LICENSEE may deduct the actual payment made by it to an independent supplier of news service (e.g., AP, UPI), whether for hard or electronic copy or audio service. These costs must be for general news services and must be paid to an independent supplier of news service.

(3) The actual cost incurred by the station for a specific local commercial program for: (a) payments to the telephone company or similar transmission facility for remote pick-up necessary to broadcast such program from outside the station's studios; and (b) rights for broadcasting a sports or other special event but not to exceed the amount actually paid to or for the original holder of the broadcast rights for the program.

J. **"Time Broker"** shall mean any entity that has no direct or indirect managerial ownership or connection with LICENSEE that purchases and resells any portion of the station's air time or the station's radio broadcasting facilities.

K. "Local Manager" shall mean any entity not under common ownership or control of LICENSEE which is authorized to resell 10% or more of the station's air time and (1) simulcasts or sells announcements on the station in combination with a radio station owned or operated by the entity, which station has entered into a BMI Single Station Radio License Agreement; or (2) has assumed, contractually or otherwise, responsibility for the management of the station. An entity which would otherwise qualify as a Local Manager but which is authorized to resell less than 10% of the station's air time shall be deemed to be a Time Broker.

L. "Local Management Agreement" shall mean any agreement under which any other entity becomes a Local Manager in regard to the station licensed under this License Agreement.

3. BMI Grant.

A. BMI hereby grants to LICENSEE, for the Term hereof, a non-exclusive license to perform, by radio broadcasting on LICENSEE's local programs by the station, non-dramatic performances of all musical works, the right to grant public performance rights of which BMI may, during the Term hereof, own or control.

B. The rights granted hereby shall not include the right to perform more than thirty (30) minutes of a full-length dramatic or dramatico-musical work (or a substantial part of a short dramatic or dramatico-musical work) such as an opera, operetta, musical show or ballet, but this exclusion shall not apply to such performances from (1) a score originally written for and performed as part of a radio program, or (2) the original cast, soundtrack or similar album of a dramatic or dramatico-musical work other than an opera.

C. The performances licensed hereunder may originate at any place, whether or not such place is licensed to publicly perform the musical works licensed hereunder, and regardless of the manner, means or methods of such origination. Nothing in this License Agreement shall be deemed to grant a license to anyone authorizing any public performance in such other place of any such composition.

D. Nothing herein shall be construed as authorizing LICENSEE to grant to any cable system (including MMDS or similar wireless services) the right to retransmit to the public or publicly perform by any means, method or process whatsoever, any of the musical compositions licensed hereunder.

E. BMI will, upon specific reasonable written request made by LICENSEE, indicate whether a number of specific musical compositions listed by LICENSEE are licensed by BMI. LICENSEE shall provide: (1) title; (2) writer/composer; (3) publisher; and (4) recording artist of each musical composition requested to be identified. In the event LICENSEE does not provide BMI with all of the information requested herein, BMI will attempt to identify whether such musical compositions are licensed by BMI, but will be under no obligation to make such identifications.

4. Fee Computation Options; Minimum Fee; Taxes.

A. *SHORT METHOD OPTION:*
The fee under the Short Method Option will
be calculated as follows:

Gross Revenue*

Less:

    (1) Bad debts written off or rebates paid
    (2) Rate card discounts and
    (3) Advertising agency commissions

Equals:
Net Revenue*

Less:
Net Revenue from Political Broadcasting

Equals:
Adjusted Net Revenue* (Amount
Subject to BMI Fee*)
Apply the applicable rate for the
calendar year indicated:

Year	If Net Revenue is $150,000 or greater	If Net Revenue is less than $150,000
1992	1.475%	1.328%
1993	1.510%	1.359%
1994	1.535%	1.382%
1995	1.585%	1.427%
1996	1.605%	1.445%

Equals:
License Fee

B. *LONG METHOD OPTION:*
The fee under the Long Method Option will be
calculated as follows:

Gross Revenue*

Less:

    (1) Bad debts written off or rebates paid
    (2) Rate card discounts and
    (3) Advertising agency commissions

Equals:
Net Revenue*

Less:
Net Revenue from Political Broadcasting

Equals:
Adjusted Net Revenue*
*Less amount by which sum of the following
exceeds 15% of Adjusted Net Revenue:*

    (1) Net Talent Fees Allowed
    (2) News Services
    (3) Remote Lines
    (4) Broadcast Rights

Equals:
Amount Subject to BMI Fee*
Apply the applicable rate for the
calendar year indicated:

Year	If Net Revenue is $150,000 or greater	If Net Revenue is less than $150,000
1992	1.475%	1.328%
1993	1.510%	1.359%
1994	1.535%	1.382%
1995	1.585%	1.427%
1996	1.605%	1.445%

Equals:
License Fee

*DEFINED IN PARAGRAPH 2.

C. In either case LICENSEE shall pay a minimum fee per calendar year for each year this License
Agreement is in effect in the amount of $412 for 1992, and for each subsequent year an amount equal to the
minimum fee for the prior year adjusted to reflect any percentage increase in the Consumer Price Index (National,
All Items) between October of the preceding year and October of the next preceding year.

D. In the event that the payment of any license fee to BMI by LICENSEE pursuant to this License
Agreement causes BMI to become liable to pay any state or local tax which is based upon the license fees received
by BMI from licensees, the LICENSEE agrees to pay to BMI the full amount of such tax together with
LICENSEE's fee payment(s) as invoiced by BMI; provided, however, that (1) BMI shall make reasonable efforts
to be exempted or excused from paying such tax, and (2) BMI is permitted by law to pass through such tax to
LICENSEE.

5. Annual Statements; LICENSEE Breach.

A. Commencing on or before April 1, 1993, and on or before April 1 of each year thereafter, LICENSEE
shall render Annual Statements to BMI, on forms supplied by BMI, covering the period of the preceding calendar
year with respect to billings and/or cash receipts for the use of the facilities of the station for the broadcasting of
local programs. If LICENSEE reports via the Long Method Option, it must show all deductions in order to arrive
at Amount Subject to BMI Fee as herein provided. In the event that LICENSEE shall fail to make payment or
render any report or Annual Statement under this License Agreement, when and as due, BMI may, in addition to
any and all other remedies which it has at law or in equity, terminate this License Agreement upon thirty (30)
days' notice in writing, and this License Agreement shall thereupon so terminate at the end of such period unless
said default shall previously have been cured. The right to cancel shall be in addition to any and all other remedies

5

which BMI may have. No waiver by BMI of full performance of this License Agreement by LICENSEE in any one or more instances shall be deemed a waiver of the right to require full and complete performance of this License Agreement thereafter or of the right to cancel this License Agreement in accordance with the terms of this Paragraph 5.

Reporting Basis

B. (1) LICENSEE must report for the Term of this License Agreement on a Billing Basis unless:

(a) LICENSEE has filed its 1991 and 1992 Annual Statements on a Cash Receipts Basis, or

(b) LICENSEE is a new owner of the station, which was previously licensed by BMI, and both the prior licensee maintained and LICENSEE maintains the books and records of account of the station on a Cash Receipts Basis.

(2) If LICENSEE reported on a Cash Receipts Basis for calendar year 1992, LICENSEE may report for the Term of this License Agreement on a Billing Basis, but only after paying any fees owed BMI for receipts accrued in calendar year 1992 but not reported to BMI, and after receiving written permission from BMI. However, nothing herein shall be interpreted to permit LICENSEE to change the basis of reporting retroactively.

(3) All billings made prior to the termination of this License Agreement with respect to local radio broadcasts made during the Term hereof shall be accounted for by LICENSEE as and when such billings are made by LICENSEE.

C. If any Annual Statement is not received by BMI within sixty (60) days after the due date, LICENSEE will be required to use the Short Method Option for such statement.

Joint Annual Statement

D. If LICENSEE owns an AM and FM station in the same market, LICENSEE will be governed as follows:

(1) If LICENSEE filed a joint Annual Statement for its first contract year of this License Agreement for said AM/FM stations, LICENSEE must continue to file Annual Statements on a combined basis for the duration of this License Agreement. If one of the stations is sold after the initial joint Annual Statement has been filed by LICENSEE, no other station may be substituted in place of the station sold. Under no circumstances may a joint Annual Statement be filed with BMI where the AM/FM stations are in separate markets.

(2) If LICENSEE filed separate Annual Statements for its first contract year of this License Agreement for the AM/FM stations, LICENSEE must continue to file separate Annual Statements for said AM/FM stations for the duration of this License Agreement.

Estimated Fees

E. For each month during the Term hereof LICENSEE shall, on or before the first day of the following month, pay to BMI a sum equal to one twelfth of the annual fee payable hereunder for the preceding calendar year (if less than a calendar year, said sum shall be annualized), adjusted to reflect the percentage increase in the Consumer Price Index (National, All Items) between October of the preceding year and October of the next preceding year; provided, however, that if, as and when any Annual Statement required to be supplied to BMI by LICENSEE pursuant to this Paragraph 5 is not received when due, all subsequent monthly payments due hereunder shall be increased by an amount equal to 24% thereof, and such increase shall remain in effect up to and including the month in which any such overdue statement is finally received by BMI. Notwithstanding any of the foregoing, in any calendar year of the Term hereof, as of the month when BMI receives the Annual Statement required to be supplied by Paragraph 5.A. hereof applicable to any immediately prior year, any adjustment required by a discrepancy between prior billings and monthly payments actually due in accordance with this Paragraph 5.E. shall, at BMI's option, be prorated over the remaining monthly payments due during that calendar year.

Adjustments

F. (1) For calendar year 1992, if the annual license fee exceeds the amount previously billed for that year, LICENSEE shall pay any such additional amount to BMI within thirty (30) days of invoicing by BMI.

(2) If the annual license fee for any calendar year of the Term subsequent to 1992 exceeds the monthly installments applicable to such year's fee, LICENSEE shall pay any such additional amount to BMI at the time the Annual Statement is due.

(3) If the amount paid by LICENSEE for any calendar year exceeds the annual license fee due for said year, LICENSEE will be entitled to a credit of the overage paid; provided, however, that if the overage paid is greater than three times the monthly payments required by Paragraph 5.E. for said calendar year, BMI shall, within thirty (30) days of receipt of written request from LICENSEE, refund the excess payment; and provided

6

further that LICENSEE shall be entitled to a refund only if the overage (which exceeds three times LICENSEE's monthly payments) by LICENSEE, results in a net balance due LICENSEE. In this event, the amount of the refund shall not exceed the amount of the net balance due the LICENSEE. Any fees subject to a good faith dispute as a result of a BMI audit shall not be considered in determining whether there is a net balance due LICENSEE for purposes of this subparagraph.

Late Payment Charge

G.   BMI may impose a late payment charge of 1½% per month from the date the payment was due on any monthly or annual payment that is received by BMI more than one month after the date payment was due.

Audits

H.   (1)   BMI shall have the right by its duly authorized representatives, during customary business hours, on notice in writing of not less than ten (10) business days, to examine the books and records of account of LICENSEE only to such extent as may be necessary to verify any Annual Statements required by this License Agreement. All data and information coming to BMI's attention as a result of any such examination of LICENSEE's books and records shall be held completely and entirely confidential and shall not be used by BMI other than in connection with its administration of this License Agreement.

(2)   The period for which BMI may audit pursuant to Paragraph 5.H.(1) hereof shall be limited to four (4) calendar years preceding the year in which the audit is made; provided, that if an audit is postponed at the request of LICENSEE, and BMI grants such postponement, BMI shall have the right to audit for the period commencing with the fourth calendar year preceding the year in which notification of intention to audit was first given by BMI to LICENSEE. Notwithstanding the above, BMI shall not audit LICENSEE's books and records for years prior to calendar year 1991, unless: (a) no Annual Statement was filed by LICENSEE for such earlier calendar year(s); or (b) the audit for calendar year 1991 or subsequent calendar year(s) pursuant to this License Agreement reveals a deficiency of 20% or more in license fees payable to BMI by LICENSEE. The four year limitation on BMI's right to audit shall not apply if LICENSEE fails or refuses after written notice from BMI to produce the books and records necessary to verify any report or statement required hereunder; however, in such instance BMI shall not audit for any reported calendar years prior to 1989.

(3)   In the event that any BMI audit reveals that additional license fees are owed to BMI, LICENSEE shall pay interest on such additional license fees of 1½% per month from the date(s) such fees should have been paid pursuant to this License Agreement if the underpayment is 7% or more of the annual license fee previously reported, and at least $1,000. LICENSEE shall pay interest on such additional license fees of 1½% per month beginning thirty (30) days after the date BMI invoices such additional license fees to LICENSEE if the underpayment is less than 7% or less than $1,000.

(4)   If LICENSEE disputes all or part of BMI's claim for such additional license fees arising from an audit, LICENSEE shall, within thirty (30) days from the date BMI invoices additional fees, (a) notify BMI in writing, of the basis for such dispute and (b) pay to BMI any license fees not in dispute together with the applicable interest on additional license fees not in dispute in accordance with subparagraph (3) above. If there is a good faith dispute between LICENSEE and BMI with respect to all or part of the additional license fees which BMI has invoiced pursuant to this Paragraph, upon resolution of the disputed amount, subparagraph (3) shall govern payment of the interest due; provided, however, that no interest will be charged LICENSEE for the disputed license fees for the period beginning on the date of LICENSEE's written notice to BMI of the dispute and ending sixty (60) days after BMI responds to LICENSEE's notice of the dispute.

(5)   Interest calculated in accordance with this Paragraph and concerning additional license fees which LICENSEE disputes in accordance with subparagraph (4) above shall be adjusted pro-rata to the amount arrived at by LICENSEE and BMI in resolution of the dispute with respect to additional license fees due.

I.   The period for which LICENSEE may amend any Annual Statement submitted pursuant to this License Agreement shall be limited to four (4) calendar years (but in no event prior to calendar year 1991) following the year for which such statement was required to be filed pursuant to Paragraph 5.A.; provided, however, that if BMI audits for years prior to 1991, LICENSEE may amend its Annual Statement for such year(s). LICENSEE shall have the right to amend any portion of a previously submitted Annual Statement and the right to correct computational or reporting errors. Once LICENSEE submits an Annual Statement to BMI pursuant to this License Agreement, LICENSEE may amend said Annual Statement only one time. If LICENSEE amends an Annual Statement pursuant to this provision, the time for BMI to audit said Annual Statement will be four (4) years after the filing of said amended Annual Statement by LICENSEE.

BMI Single Station Radio Blanket License Agreement

6. Per Program Option.

The BMI Single Station Radio Per Program License Agreement for the Term ending December 31, 1996 is being offered to LICENSEE simultaneously with this License Agreement. In accepting this License Agreement LICENSEE acknowledges that it has been offered the option of entering into either this License Agreement or the BMI Single Station Radio Per Program License Agreement with BMI. LICENSEE may, as of the first day of any month, upon not less than thirty (30) days written notice to BMI elect to enter into the BMI Single Station Radio Per Program License Agreement, provided LICENSEE is current in all payments (excluding payments subject to a good faith dispute as a result of a BMI audit), reports and Annual Statements required by the BMI Single Station Radio Blanket License Agreement as of the effective date of LICENSEE's election.

7. Indemnification.

BMI agrees to indemnify, save and hold harmless and to defend LICENSEE, its advertisers and their advertising agencies, and its and their officers, employees and artists, from and against all claims, demands and suits that may be made or brought against them or any of them with respect to the performance under this License Agreement of any material licensed hereunder; provided that this indemnity shall not apply to broadcasts of any musical work performed by LICENSEE after written request from BMI to LICENSEE that LICENSEE refrain from performance thereof. LICENSEE agrees to give BMI immediate notice of any such claim, demand or suit, and agrees immediately to deliver to BMI all papers pertaining thereto. BMI shall have full charge of the defense of any such claim, demand or suit, and LICENSEE shall cooperate fully with BMI therein.

8. Local Management Agreement.

A. In the event LICENSEE enters into a Local Management Agreement as defined in Paragraph 2.L. hereof, within thirty (30) days of such agreement (1) LICENSEE shall provide BMI with a copy of such agreement and (2) LICENSEE and Local Manager shall provide BMI with two (2) fully executed copies of BMI's LMA-92-A Agreement, a sample copy of which is annexed hereto and made part hereof. The fully executed LMA-92-A Agreement makes Local Manager a party to this License Agreement, and this License Agreement shall be deemed amended by said LMA-92-A Agreement.

B. In the event LICENSEE becomes a Local Manager by entering into a Local Management Agreement with another station, LICENSEE shall notify BMI within thirty (30) days of entering into the agreement.

C. In the event that LICENSEE and/or Local Manager do not provide to BMI, on a timely basis, the documentation required by Paragraph 8.A., this License Agreement may be terminated by BMI on ten (10) days' written notice.

D. In the event that the Local Management Agreement provided to BMI terminates prior to its stated termination date, LICENSEE and Local Manager shall immediately notify BMI of such termination.

9. Assignment.

This License Agreement shall be non-assignable except to the person, firm or corporation acquiring the Federal Communications Commission license of the station, and upon assignment to such station and upon acceptance in form approved by BMI of the application of LICENSEE hereunder, LICENSEE shall be relieved of future liability under this License Agreement as long as all Annual Statements have been filed by LICENSEE and all fees due BMI under this License Agreement have been paid to BMI.

10. Arbitration.

All disputes of any kind, nature or description arising in connection with the terms and conditions of this License Agreement shall be submitted to the American Arbitration Association in the City and State of New York for arbitration under its then prevailing rules, the arbitrator(s) to be selected as follows: Each of the parties hereto shall by written notice to the other have the right to appoint one arbitrator. If, within ten (10) days following the giving of such notice by one party, the other shall not, by written notice, appoint another arbitrator, the first arbitrator shall be the sole arbitrator. If two arbitrators are so appointed, they shall appoint a third arbitrator. If ten (10) days elapse after the appointment of the second arbitrator and the two arbitrators are unable to agree upon the third arbitrator, then either party may, in writing, request the American Arbitration Association to appoint the third arbitrator. The award made in the arbitration shall be binding and conclusive on the parties and judgment may be, but need not be, entered in any court having jurisdiction. Such award shall include the fixing of the costs, expenses and reasonable attorneys' fees of arbitration, which shall be borne by the unsuccessful party.

MISCELLANEOUS

11. LICENSEE, upon written request from BMI made not less than one (1) week's notice specifying the period to be covered, agrees to furnish to BMI (upon forms to be supplied by BMI) a report of LICENSEE's performances of all musical works, indicating the compositions performed by title, writer/composer and artist, or by such other convenient method as may be designated by BMI, but such report need not be furnished for more than one (1) week of each year of the Term.

12. In the event that the Federal Communications Commission revokes or fails to renew the broadcasting license of LICENSEE, or in the event that the governmental rules and regulations applicable to the station are suspended or amended so as to forbid the broadcasting of commercial programs by LICENSEE, LICENSEE may notify BMI thereof, and BMI, within ten (10) days of the receipt of such notice shall, by written notice to LICENSEE, at BMI's option, either terminate or suspend this License Agreement and all payments and services hereunder for the period that such condition continues. In the event that BMI elects to suspend this License Agreement, such suspension shall not continue for longer than six (6) months, and this License Agreement shall automatically terminate at the end of six (6) months' suspension. In the event that the condition giving rise to the suspension shall continue for less than six (6) months, BMI at its option, and on written notice to LICENSEE, may reinstate this License Agreement at any time within thirty (30) days after the cessation of such condition.

13. In the event that any law now or hereafter enacted of the state, or political subdivision thereof, in which the station and/or LICENSEE is located shall result in major interference with BMI's operations or in the refusal of a substantial number of radio stations therein to enter into license agreements with BMI or to make payments to BMI, BMI shall have the right at any time to terminate this License Agreement on no less than sixty (60) days' written notice to LICENSEE.

14. Any notice required or permitted to be given under this License Agreement shall be in writing and shall be deemed duly given when sent by ordinary first-class U.S. mail to the party for whom it is intended, at its address hereinabove stated, or any other address which either party hereto may from time to time designate for such purpose, and when such notice is so mailed, it shall be deemed given upon the mailing thereof. Any such notice sent to BMI shall be to the attention of the Licensing-Telecommunications Department. Any such notice sent to LICENSEE shall be to the attention of the person signing this License Agreement on behalf of LICENSEE or such other person as LICENSEE may advise BMI in writing.

15. On written notice to LICENSEE, BMI may, effective with such notice, withdraw from the license granted hereunder any musical work as to which any legal action has been instituted or a claim made that BMI does not have the right to license the performing rights in such work or that such work infringes another composition.

16. This License Agreement shall enure to the benefit of and shall be binding upon the parties and their respective successors and assigns, but no assignment shall relieve the parties of their respective obligations under this License Agreement.

17. This License Agreement constitutes the entire understanding between the parties, shall not be binding until signed by both parties and cannot be waived or added to or modified orally, and no waiver, addition or modification shall be valid unless in writing and signed by the parties. This License Agreement, its validity, construction and effect shall be governed by the laws of the State of New York. The fact that any provisions herein are found to be void or unenforceable by a court of competent jurisdiction shall in no way affect the validity or enforceability of any other provisions. All headings in this License Agreement are for the purpose of convenience and shall not be considered to be part of this License Agreement.

BROADCAST MUSIC, INC.

_____
LICENSEE (Legal Name)

By _____   By _____
          (Signature)   (Signature)

_____   _____
     (Print Name of Signer)   (Print Name of Signer)

_____   _____
       (Title of Signer)   (Title of Signer)

PLEASE COMPLETE SHADED AREA ONLY

LMA-92-A

LMA AGREEMENT

Whereas, radio station _____ ("STATION") has entered into a Local Management Agreement with _____ ("LOCAL MANAGER") for the period _____ through _____ ; and

Whereas, STATION and LOCAL MANAGER wish to add LOCAL MANAGER as a party to the Single Station Radio License Agreement in effect between STATION and BMI ("the License Agreement") with all of the rights and obligations of LICENSEE as set forth in the License Agreement for the period of the Local Management Agreement beginning January 1, 1992 and ending at the time referred to above;

It is hereby agreed as follows:

1. For all periods that STATION simulcasts or is sold in combination with another radio station owned or operated by LOCAL MANAGER ("MANAGER's STATION") that has a BMI Single Station Radio License Agreement, all Gross Revenue (as defined in the License Agreement) of STATION shall be reported as follows:

a. All LOCAL MANAGER Gross Revenue relating to STATION will be included in LOCAL MANAGER's license fee reports for MANAGER's STATION. If such Gross Revenue constitutes all Gross Revenue for STATION, no license fee or license fee reports will be required of STATION.

b. The balance of STATION's Gross Revenue will be included in STATION's license fee reports.

c. Amounts payable by LOCAL MANAGER to STATION pursuant to the Local Management Agreement shall not be reportable by STATION or deductible by MANAGER's STATION.

d. In the event that STATION and MANAGER's STATION have different forms of BMI License Agreement, all LOCAL MANAGER's Gross Revenue relating to programs of STATION which are simulcast or sold in combination with MANAGER's STATION shall be apportioned between STATION and MANAGER's STATION in the same ratio as the Adjusted Net Revenue of STATION and MANAGER's STATION bear to each other for the most recent year prior to the Local Management Agreement reported by STATION and MANAGER's STATION to BMI (annualized for any period less than a year). Any such Gross Revenue apportioned to, and reported for, STATION pursuant to this paragraph shall not be reportable by LOCAL MANAGER on its license fee reports for MANAGER's STATION.

2. If STATION fully simulcasts programs broadcast by MANAGER's STATION and has no separate programs, STATION and LOCAL MANAGER agree to maintain the same form of BMI license (blanket or per program) for STATION as LOCAL MANAGER has for MANAGER's STATION. In the event that LOCAL MANAGER has a different form of license for MANAGER's STATION at the time this agreement is executed, it is agreed that such other form of license shall be substituted in place of the License Agreement, and the appropriate documentation shall be executed.

In the event that STATION and MANAGER's STATION have the per program form of license at the time this agreement is executed, and LOCAL MANAGER subsequently changes or is converted to the blanket form of license, such change or conversion shall be deemed to apply as well to STATION.

3. For all periods that STATION has a per program license agreement, MANAGER's STATION shall submit the reports required by Paragraph 4 of the per program license for all programs provided by MANAGER's STATION which are broadcast by STATION, and STATION shall submit such reports for all other programs broadcast by STATION. If STATION fully simulcasts programs broadcast by MANAGER's STATION and has no separate programs, and if all Gross Revenue relating to STATION is included in LOCAL MANAGER's license fee reports for MANAGER's STATION in accordance with Paragraph 1.a. above, STATION shall not be required to submit separate reports pursuant to Paragraph 4 of the per program license.

10

4. If STATION has a Local Management Agreement with a LOCAL MANAGER that does not own or operate another local radio station that has a BMI Single Station Radio License Agreement, then all Gross Revenue relating to STATION shall be reported as follows:

     a. All LOCAL MANAGER Gross Revenue relating to STATION will be included in LOCAL MANAGER's license fee reports to BMI. If such revenue constitutes all Gross Revenue for STATION, no license fee or license fee reports will be required of STATION.

     b. The balance of STATION's Gross Revenue will be included in STATION's license fee reports.

     c. Amounts payable by LOCAL MANAGER to STATION pursuant to the Local Management Agreement shall not be reportable by STATION, or deductible by LOCAL MANAGER.

     d. If STATION's License Agreement is a per program license agreement, then LOCAL MANAGER will be responsible for submitting Monthly Music Reports required by Paragraph 4 of the License Agreement for the programming covered by the Local Management Agreement.

     5. STATION and LOCAL MANAGER jointly designate the following single address for billing and other regular correspondence, and the following single address for any notices in accordance with the license agreement (Paragraph 14 of the blanket license or Paragraph 24 of the per program license):

Billing Address: _____   Notice Address: _____

_____   _____

_____   _____

     6. In the event that the Local Management Agreement between STATION and LOCAL MANAGER terminates, STATION and LOCAL MANAGER shall notify BMI of the termination within 20 days, and submit all required statements, reports and payments through the date of said termination. In the event that both STATION and LOCAL MANAGER fail to notify BMI of the termination of the Local Management Agreement between STATION and LOCAL MANAGER, then both STATION and LOCAL MANAGER shall remain obligated under this agreement for all statements, reports and payments.

_____   _____
LICENSEE (Legal Name)   LOCAL MANAGER (Legal Name)

BY: _____   _____
        (Signature)   (Call Letters, if applicable)

                      BY: _____
_____
    (Print Name of Signer)   (Signature)

_____   _____
    (Title of Signer)   (Print Name of Signer)

                      _____
                      (Title of Signer)

Accepted and agreed:
BROADCAST MUSIC, INC.

BY: _____

_____
       (Title)

Date: _____

[Reserved]

Form 27 through 30

[Reserved]

Form 31

ASCAP Experimental License Agreement for Computer Online Services, Electronic Bulletin Boards, Internet Sites, and Similar Operations

> **ASCAP EXPERIMENTAL LICENSE AGREEMENT FOR COMPUTER ONLINE SERVICES, ELECTRONIC BULLETIN BOARDS, INTERNET SITES, AND SIMILAR OPERATIONS**

1.   Parties: This is an agreement between the American Society of Composers, Authors and Publishers ("We," "Us" or "ASCAP"), located at One Lincoln Plaza, New York, New York 10023 and

("You" or "Licensee"), located at

2.   Experimental Agreement: This is an experimental agreement which applies for its term only and is entered into without prejudice to any position you or we may take for any period subsequent to its termination.

3.   Computer Service Defined: Your "Computer Service" is a computer online service, electronic bulletin board, Internet site or similar operation,

known as	
with the Internet Protocol (IP) address of	
the Universal Resource Locator (URL) of	
the primary telephone dial-up (modem) number of	
or which may otherwise be accessed by the public as follows:	

4.   Computer Service Users Defined: "Computer Service Users" are all persons, firms or corporations who access your Computer Service.

5.   Repertory Defined: Our "Repertory" consists of all copyrighted musical compositions written or published by our members or by the members of affiliated foreign performing rights societies, including compositions written or published during the term of this agreement, and of which we have the right to license non-dramatic public performances.

6.   Grant of License: We grant you a license to publicly perform, or cause to be publicly performed, by means of transmissions on your Computer Service, non-dramatic renditions of the separate musical compositions in our Repertory.

7.   Term of License: The license granted by this agreement commences on   , 19   (the "Effective Date"), and ends on December 31 of the same calendar year, and continues after that for additional terms of one year each unless you or we terminate it by giving the other party notice at least thirty days prior to the end of a calender year.

8.   **Limitations on License:**

   (a)   This license extends only to you and your Computer Service and is limited to performances presented by means of transmissions on your Computer Service, and by no other means, to Computer Service Users.

   (b)   This license may not be assigned without our written consent.

   (c)   This license is limited to the United States, its territories and possessions, and the Commonwealth of Puerto Rico.

   (d)   Nothing in this agreement grants you, or authorizes you to grant to any Computer Service User, or to anyone else, any right to reproduce, copy or distribute by any means, method or process whatsoever, any of the musical compositions licensed by this agreement, including, but not limited to, transferring or copying any such musical composition to a computer hard drive, or otherwise downloading the composition onto any other storage medium.

   (e)   Nothing in this agreement grants, or authorizes you to grant, to any Computer Service User, or to anyone else, any right to perform by any means, method or process whatsoever, any of the musical compositions licensed under this agreement.

   (f)   This license is limited to non-dramatic performances, and does not authorize any dramatic performances. For purposes of this agreement, a dramatic performance shall include, but not be limited to, the following:

      (i)   performance of a "dramatico-musical work" in its entirety;

      (ii)   performance of one or more musical compositions from a "dramatico-musical work" accompanied by dialogue, pantomime, dance, stage action, or visual representation of the work from which the music is taken;

      (iii) performance of one or more musical compositions as part of a story or plot, whether accompanied or unaccompanied by dialogue, pantomime, dance, stage action, or visual representation; and

      (iv)   performance of a concert version of a "dramatico-musical work."

   The term "dramatico-musical work" includes, but is not limited to, a musical comedy, opera, play with music, revue, or ballet.

9.   **License Fees:** For each year during the term of this agreement you agree to pay us the license fee applicable to your "Amount Subject to Fee" as defined in the Rate Schedule applicable for that year.

10.   **Rate Schedules:** There are four alternative Rate Schedules attached to and made a part of this agreement. Rate Schedule "A" contains rates based on your Computer Service's gross revenue; Rate Schedule "B" contains rates based on your Computer Service's total music revenue; Rate Schedule "C" contains rates based on your Computer Service's total ASCAP music revenue; and Rate Schedule "D," which only applies to non-profit corporations, contains rates based on the total budget for your Computer Service. Each Rate Schedule includes a specific definition of "Amount Subject to Fee" applicable to that Rate Schedule and a Statement of Account for providing required reports. Rate Schedules "B" or "C" may only be used if (a) you maintain your books and records in a manner which enables you to furnish the required information, (b) your Annual License Fee Report is submitted when due, and (c) you are current in payment of license fees. In all other instances, the rates contained in Rate Schedule "A" apply.

2

11. **Reports and Payments:** You agree to furnish license fee reports and payments to us as follows:

   (a) Annual License Fee Reports. You will submit an Annual License Fee Report for each year of this agreement, by the first day of April of the following year, by fully completing the Statement of Account form on the applicable Rate Schedule.

   (b) Initial License Fee Report. Within thirty days after you and we execute this agreement, you will submit an Initial License Fee Report based on a good faith estimate of your Computer Service's "Amount Subject to Fee" for the first full year of operation from the Effective Date of this agreement.

   (c) Quarterly License Fee Payments. You will submit license fee payments quarterly on or before the first day of January, April, July and October of each year. The payments due by April 1, July 1 and October 1 of each year, and by January 1 of the following year, are each equal to one-fourth of the license fee for the preceding calendar year (annualized for any reported period less than a year).

   (d) Late Report Payments. If we do not receive your Annual License Fee Report when due, you will submit quarterly license fee payments that are 24% higher than the quarterly payments due for the preceding year, and payments will continue at that increased rate until we receive the late report.

   (e) Annual Adjustment. With each annual report you will submit payment of any license fees due over and above all amounts that you paid for that year. If the fee is less than the amount that you paid, we will apply the excess to the next quarterly payment due under this agreement. If the excess is greater than one quarterly payment, we will refund it to you at your written request.

   (f) Late Payment Charge. You will pay a finance charge of 1-1/2% per month, from the date due, on any required payment that is not made within thirty days of its due date.

12. **Report Verification:**

   (a) We have the right to examine your books and records in order to verify any required report. We may exercise this right by giving you thirty days notice of our intention to conduct an examination. We will consider all data and information derived from our examination as completely confidential. You agree to furnish all pertinent books and records, including electronic records, to our authorized representatives, during customary business hours.

   (b) If our examination shows that you underpaid license fees, you agree to pay a finance charge of 1-1/2% per month on the license fees due from the date we bill you for that amount or, if the underpayment is 5% or more, from the date or dates that the license fees should have been paid.

   (c) You may dispute all or part of our claim for additional fees. You may do so by advising us in writing within thirty days from the date we bill the additional fees to you of the basis for your dispute, and by paying the undisputed portion of our claim with the applicable finance charges. If there is a good faith dispute between us concerning all or part of our claim, we will defer finance charges on the disputed amount until sixty days after we have responded to you, and will pro-rate finance charges based on our resolution of the dispute.

3

13. Breach or Default: If you fail to perform any of the terms or conditions required of you by this agreement, we may terminate your license by giving you thirty days notice to cure your breach or default. If you do not do so within that thirty day period, your license will automatically terminate at the end of that period without any further notice from us.

14. Interference With ASCAP's Operations: We have the right to terminate this license effective immediately, if there is any major interference with, or substantial increase in the cost of, our operation as a result of any law in the state, territory, dependency, possession or political subdivision in which you or your Computer Service is located which is applicable to the licensing of performing rights.

15. Indemnification: We will indemnify you from any claim made against you with respect to the non-dramatic performance under this agreement of any composition(s) in our Repertory, and will have full charge of the defense against the claim. You agree to notify us immediately of any such claim, furnish us with all the papers pertaining to it, and cooperate fully with us in its defense. If you wish, you may engage your own counsel, at your expense, who may participate in the defense. Our liability under this paragraph is strictly limited to the amount of license fees that you actually paid us under this agreement for the calendar year(s) in which the performance(s) which are the subject of the claim occurred.

16. Notices: We or you may give any notice required by this agreement by (a) sending the notice to the other party's last known address by United States Mail or by generally recognized same-day or overnight delivery service, or (b) transmitting the notice electronically to the other party's last known facsimile number or e-mail (or similar electronic transmission) address. We each agree to inform the other in writing of any change of address.

IN WITNESS WHEREOF, this Agreement has been duly executed by ASCAP and Licensee this ████ day of ████████████, 19████.

AMERICAN SOCIETY OF COMPOSERS,
AUTHORS AND PUBLISHERS

By _____

_____
Title

Licensee Name

By _____
Signature

_____
Print Your Name

_____
Title
(Fill in capacity in which signed: (a) If corporation, state corporate office held; (b) If partnership, write word "partner" under printed name of signing partner; (c) If individual owner, write "individual owner" under printed name.)

4

```
RATE SCHEDULE "A" – STATEMENT OF ACCOUNT
        COMPUTER SERVICE REVENUE REPORT
  ASCAP EXPERIMENTAL LICENSE AGREEMENT FOR
COMPUTER ONLINE SERVICES, ELECTRONIC BULLETIN BOARDS,
      INTERNET SITES AND SIMILAR OPERATIONS
```

PART I.   ACCOUNT INFORMATION   REPORT PERIOD: ▨▨▨▨ THRU ▨▨▨▨

LICENSEE:

ADDRESS:

COMPUTER SERVICE NAME:

FACSIMILE NUMBER: ▨▨▨▨   PHONE NUMBER: ▨▨▨▨

PART II.   DEFINITIONS

NOTE: Definitions of Licensee's "Computer Service" and "Computer Service Users" are contained in paragraphs 3 and 4 of the license agreement. All "Revenue" definitions include all specified payments whether made directly to Licensee, any entity under the same or substantially the same ownership, management or control as Licensee, or to any other person, firm or corporation as directed or authorized by Licensee or any of Licensee's agents or employees.

1. "COMPUTER SERVICE USER REVENUE" means all payments made by or on behalf of Computer Service Users for the Computer Service including, but not limited to, subscriber fees and connect time charges.

2. "SPONSOR REVENUE" means all payments made by or on behalf of sponsors, advertisers, program suppliers, content providers, or others for the use of the facilities of the Computer Service including, but not limited to, payments made for "hotlinks."

3. "ADJUSTMENTS TO SPONSOR REVENUE" means: (a) advertising agency commissions not to exceed 15% actually allowed to an advertising agency that has no direct or indirect ownership or managerial connection with Licensee or the Computer Service; and (b) bad debts actually written off and discounts allowed or rebates paid.

4. "NET SPONSOR REVENUE" means all Sponsor Revenue less Adjustments to Sponsor Revenue.

5. "PROMOTIONAL REVENUE" is the reasonable value of the facilities of the Computer Service for promotion of any product(s) or service(s), other than the Computer Service, offered by Licensee or any entity under the same or substantially the same ownership, management or control as Licensee.

6. "AMOUNT SUBJECT TO FEE" is the total of Computer Service User Revenue, Net Sponsor Revenue and Promotional Revenue.

PART III. AMOUNT SUBJECT TO FEE COMPUTATION

1.   Computer Service User Revenue .... $_____
2.   Net Sponsor Revenue (from Part IV, line 9)...................... $_____
3.   Promotional Revenue.. $_____
4.   Amount Subject to Fee (add lines 1, 2 and 3)................... $_____

PART IV. NET SPONSOR REVENUE CALCULATION

5.   Sponsor Revenue... $_____
6.   Advertising Commissions......................$_____
7.   Bad Debts...................................$_____
8.   Total Adjustments to Sponsor Revenue (add lines 6 and 7).......... $_____
9.   Net Sponsor Revenue (line 5 minus line 8)......................... $_____

PART V. LICENSE FEE

10. The annual license fee under this Rate Schedule "A" is the applicable fee based on Amount Subject to Fee (from Part III, line 4), as shown in the Table below (pro-rated for partial year)..................... $_____

Amount Subject to Fee	Annual License Fee
Less than $ 31,000.00	$ 500.00
$ 31,000 to $ 39,999.99	$ 575.00
$ 40,000 to $ 49,999.99	$ 725.00
$ 50,000 to $ 59,999.99	$ 890.00
$ 60,000 to $ 69,999.99	$ 1,050.00
$ 70,000 to $ 79,999.99	$ 1,210.00
$ 80,000 to $ 89,999.99	$ 1,370.00
$ 90,000 to $ 99,999.99	$ 1,535.00
$ 100,000 to $ 119,999.99	$ 1,777.00
$ 120,000 to $ 139,999.99	$ 2,100.00
$ 140,000 to $ 159,999.99	$ 2,423.00
$ 160,000 to $ 179,999.99	$ 2,745.00
$ 180,000 to $ 199,999.99	$ 3,068.00
$ 200,000 to $ 224,999.99	$ 3,432.00
$ 225,000 or More	$3,432.00 plus 1.615% of the Amount Subject to Fee in excess of $225,000

PART VI. CERTIFICATION

We certify that all books and records necessary to verify this report are now and will continue to be available for your examination in accordance with the terms of the license agreement.

_____   _____
Signature   Date

_____
Print Name and Title

A - 2

ASCAP Experimental License Agreement

> *RATE SCHEDULE "B" – STATEMENT OF ACCOUNT*
> *MUSIC REVENUE REPORT*
> *ASCAP EXPERIMENTAL LICENSE AGREEMENT FOR*
> *COMPUTER ONLINE SERVICES, ELECTRONIC BULLETIN BOARDS,*
> *INTERNET SITES AND SIMILAR OPERATIONS*

PART I.   ACCOUNT INFORMATION   REPORT PERIOD: ▨▨▨ THRU ▨▨▨

LICENSEE:

ADDRESS:

COMPUTER SERVICE NAME:

FACSIMILE NUMBER: ▨▨▨   **PHONE NUMBER:** ▨▨▨

PART II.   DEFINITIONS

NOTE: Definitions of Licensee's "Computer Service" and "Computer Service Users" are contained in paragraphs 3 and 4 of the license agreement. All "Revenue" definitions include all specified payments whether made directly to Licensee, any entity under the same or substantially the same ownership, management or control as Licensee, or to any other person, firm or corporation as directed or authorized by Licensee or any of Licensee's agents or employees.

1.   "COMPUTER SERVICE USES" means the total number of "hits" or "accesses" of the Computer Service by Computer Service Users.

2.   "MUSIC SERVICE(S)" means any area(s) offered by Licensee, or otherwise available to Computer Service Users as part of the Computer Service, which contain(s) music.

3.   "MUSIC SERVICE USERS" means all Computer Service Users who access any Music Service(s).

4.   "MUSIC SERVICE USES" means the total number of "hits" or "accesses" of the Music Service(s) by Music Service Users.

5.   "COMPUTER SERVICE USER REVENUE" means all payments made by or on behalf of Computer Service Users for the Computer Service including, but not limited to, subscriber fees and connect time charges.

6.   "MUSIC SERVICE CONNECTION REVENUE" means all payments made by or on behalf of Music Service Users for access to the Music Service(s).

7.   "NON-MUSIC COMPUTER SERVICE USER REVENUE" means all Computer Service User Revenue that is not Music Service Connection Revenue.

8. "SPONSOR REVENUE" means all payments made by or on behalf of sponsors, advertisers, program suppliers, content providers, or others for the use of the facilities of the Computer Service including, but not limited to, payments made for "hotlinks."

9. "TARGETED SPONSOR REVENUE" means all Sponsor Revenue that is targeted for specific area(s) offered by Licensee, or otherwise available to Computer Service Users as part of the Computer Service, and that are only available to Computer Service Users who access those area(s).

10. "TARGETED MUSIC SERVICE SPONSOR REVENUE" means all Targeted Sponsor Revenue for the Music Service(s).

11. "NON-TARGETED SPONSOR REVENUE" means all Sponsor Revenue that is not Targeted Sponsor Revenue.

12. "PROMOTIONAL REVENUE" is the reasonable value of the facilities of the Computer Service for promotion of any product(s) or service(s), other than the Computer Service, offered by Licensee or any entity under the same or substantially the same ownership, management or control as Licensee.

13. "TARGETED PROMOTIONAL REVENUE" means all Promotional Revenue that is targeted for specific area(s) offered by Licensee, or otherwise available to Computer Service Users as part of the Computer Service, and that are only available to Computer Service Users who access those area(s).

14. "TARGETED MUSIC SERVICE PROMOTIONAL REVENUE" means all Targeted Promotional Revenue for the Music Service(s).

15. "NON-TARGETED PROMOTIONAL REVENUE" means all Promotional Revenue that is not Targeted Promotional Revenue.

16. "ATTRIBUTABLE REVENUE" is that portion of the total of (a) Non-Music Computer Service User Revenue, (b) Non-Targeted Sponsor Revenue, and (c) Non-Targeted Promotional Revenue which bears the same ratio to that total as the total number of Music Service Uses bears to the total number of Computer Service Uses.

17. "MUSIC REVENUE/AMOUNT SUBJECT TO FEE" is the total of Music Service Connection Revenue, Targeted Music Service Sponsor Revenue, Targeted Music Service Promotional Revenue and Attributable Revenue.

PART III. AMOUNT SUBJECT TO FEE COMPUTATION

1. Music Service Connection Revenue .... $_____
2. Targeted Music Service Sponsor Revenue .... $_____
3. Targeted Music Service Promotional Revenue .... $_____
4. Attributable Revenue (from Part IV, line 13) .... $_____
5. Amount Subject to Fee (add lines 1, 2, 3 and 4) .... $_____

PART IV. ATTRIBUTABLE REVENUE CALCULATION

6. Non-Music Computer Service User Revenue............................... $_____
7. Non-Targeted Sponsor Revenue.. $_____
8. Non-Targeted Promotional Revenue...................................... $_____
9. Total (add lines 6, 7 and 8).. $_____
10. Total Music Service Uses.................................... _____
11. Total Computer Service Uses................................ _____
12. Ratio (divide line 10 by line 11)(to 3 decimals)................... _____
13. Attributable Revenue (multiply line 9 by line 12).................. $_____

B - 2
—

RATE SCHEDULE "C" – STATEMENT OF ACCOUNT
ASCAP MUSIC REVENUE REPORT
ASCAP EXPERIMENTAL LICENSE AGREEMENT FOR
COMPUTER ONLINE SERVICES, ELECTRONIC BULLETIN BOARDS,
INTERNET SITES AND SIMILAR OPERATIONS

PART I.   ACCOUNT INFORMATION   REPORT PERIOD: ▓▓▓▓▓ THRU ▓▓▓▓▓

LICENSEE:
▓▓

ADDRESS:
▓▓

COMPUTER SERVICE NAME:
▓▓

FACSIMILE NUMBER: ▓▓▓▓▓▓▓▓▓   PHONE NUMBER: ▓▓▓▓▓▓▓▓▓

PART II.   DEFINITIONS

NOTE: Definitions of Licensee's "Computer Service" and "Computer Service Users" are contained in paragraphs 3 and 4 of the license agreement. All "Revenue" definitions include all specified payments whether made directly to Licensee, any entity under the same or substantially the same ownership, management or control as Licensee, or to any other person, firm or corporation as directed or authorized by Licensee or any of Licensee's agents or employees.

1.   "COMPUTER SERVICE USES" means the total number of "hits" or "accesses" of the Computer Service by Computer Service Users.

2.   "MUSIC SERVICE(S)" means any area(s) offered by Licensee, or otherwise available to Computer Service Users as part of Licensee's Computer Service, which contain(s) music.

3.   "MUSIC SERVICE USERS" means all Computer Service Users who access any Music Service(s).

4.   "MUSIC SERVICE USES" means the total number of "hits" or "accesses" of the Music Service(s) by Music Service Users.

5.   "MUSIC USES" means the total number of "hits," "accesses," "downloads," "plays" or other transmissions on the Computer Service of musical works.

6.   "ASCAP MUSIC USES" means the total number of "hits," "accesses," "downloads," "plays" or other transmissions on the Computer Service of works in the ASCAP repertory.

7.   "ASCAP MUSIC USE CONNECTION REVENUE" means all payments made by or on behalf of Music Service Users for ASCAP Music Uses.

8.   "COMPUTER SERVICE USER REVENUE" means all payments made by or on behalf of Computer Service Users for Licensee's Computer Service including, but not limited to, subscriber fees and connect time charges.

9.   "MUSIC SERVICE CONNECTION REVENUE" means all payments made by or on behalf of Music Service Users for access to the Music Service(s).

10.   "NON-MUSIC COMPUTER SERVICE USER REVENUE" means all Computer Service User Revenue that is not Music Service Connection Revenue.

11. "SPONSOR REVENUE" means all payments made by or on behalf of sponsors, advertisers, program suppliers, content providers, or others for the use of the facilities of the Computer Service including, but not limited to, payments made for "hotlinks."

12. "TARGETED SPONSOR REVENUE" means all Sponsor Revenue that is targeted for specific area(s) offered by Licensee, or otherwise available to Computer Service Users as part of Licensee's Computer Service, and that are only available to Computer Service Users who access those area(s).

13. "TARGETED MUSIC SERVICE SPONSOR REVENUE" means all Targeted Sponsor Revenue for the Music Service(s).

14. "NON-TARGETED SPONSOR REVENUE" means all Sponsor Revenue that is not Targeted Sponsor Revenue.

15. "PROMOTIONAL REVENUE" is the reasonable value of the facilities of the Computer Service for promotion of any product(s) or service(s), other than the Computer Service, offered by Licensee or any entity under the same or substantially the same ownership, management or control as Licensee.

16. "TARGETED PROMOTIONAL REVENUE" means all Promotional Revenue that is targeted for specific area(s) offered by Licensee, or otherwise available to Computer Service Users as part of the Computer Service, and that are only available to Computer Service Users who access those area(s).

17. "TARGETED MUSIC SERVICE PROMOTIONAL REVENUE" means all Targeted Promotional Revenue for the Music Service(s).

18. "NON-TARGETED PROMOTIONAL REVENUE" means all Promotional Revenue that is not Targeted Promotional Revenue.

19. "ATTRIBUTABLE REVENUE" is that portion of the total of (a) Non-Music Computer Service User Revenue, (b) Targeted Music Service Sponsor Revenue, (c) Non-Targeted Sponsor Revenue, (d) Targeted Music Service Promotional Revenue, and (e) Non-Targeted Promotional Revenue which bears the same ratio to that total as the total number of Music Service Uses bears to the total number of all Computer Service Uses.

20. "ATTRIBUTABLE ASCAP MUSIC REVENUE" is that portion of Attributable Revenue that bears the same ratio to that amount as the total number of ASCAP Music Uses bears to the total of all Music Uses.

21. "ASCAP MUSIC REVENUE/AMOUNT SUBJECT TO FEE" is the total of ASCAP Music Use Connection Revenue and Attributable ASCAP Music Revenue.

PART III. AMOUNT SUBJECT TO FEE COMPUTATION

1. ASCAP Music Use Connection Revenue .... $_____
2. Attributable ASCAP Music Revenue (from Part V, line 18)................. $_____
3. Amount Subject to Fee (add lines 1 and 2)...................................... $_____

PART IV. ATTRIBUTABLE REVENUE CALCULATION

4.   Non-Music Computer Service User Revenue...................................... $_____
5.   Targeted Music Service Sponsor Revenue.. $_____
6.   Non-Targeted Sponsor Revenue.. $_____
7.   Targeted Music Service Promotional Revenue................................... $_____
8.   Non-Targeted Promotional Revenue.. $_____
9.   Total (add lines 4, 5, 6, 7, and 8)... $_____
10. Total Music Service Uses... _____
11. Total Computer Service Uses.. _____
12. Ratio (divide line 10 by line 11)(to 3 decimals)............... _____
13. Attributable Revenue (multiply line 9 by line 12) .... $_____

C - 2

> **RATE SCHEDULE "D" – STATEMENT OF ACCOUNT**
> **COMPUTER SERVICE BUDGET REPORT**
> **ASCAP EXPERIMENTAL LICENSE AGREEMENT FOR**
> **COMPUTER ONLINE SERVICES, ELECTRONIC BULLETIN BOARDS,**
> **INTERNET SITES AND SIMILAR OPERATIONS**

NOTE: This Rate Schedule "D" applies only if: (a) the Computer Service is owned or operated by a not-for-profit entity recognized under Title 26, United States Code, § 501(c)(3); and (b) "Computer Service Budget," as defined below, is greater than the Amount Subject to Fee which would otherwise apply under Rate Schedules "A," "B" and "C."

PART I.   ACCOUNT INFORMATION   REPORT PERIOD: ░░░░░░ THRU ░░░░░░

LICENSEE:

ADDRESS:

COMPUTER SERVICE NAME:

FACSIMILE NUMBER: ░░░░░░░░   PHONE NUMBER: ░░░░░░░░

NOTE: If you identify and track "Computer Service Uses" and "Music Service Uses," each as defined below, you may complete either Parts III and IV or Parts V and VI.   Otherwise, you must complete Parts III and IV, and omit Parts V and VI.

PART II.   DEFINITIONS

NOTE: Definitions of Licensee's "Computer Service" and "Computer Service Users" are contained in paragraphs 3 and 4 of the license agreement.

1.   "COMPUTER SERVICE BUDGET" means the total operating budget of the Computer Service.

2.   "COMPUTER SERVICE USES" means the total number of "hits" or "accesses" of the Computer Service by Computer Service Users.

3.   "MUSIC SERVICE(S)" means any area(s) offered by Licensee, or otherwise available to Computer Service Users as part of Licensee's Computer Service, which contain(s) music.

4.   "MUSIC SERVICE USES" means the total number of "hits" or "accesses" of any Music Service(s) by Computer Service Users.

5.   "AMOUNT SUBJECT TO FEE" under Part III below is your Computer Service Budget, and "Amount Subject to Fee" under Part V below is that portion of your Computer Service Budget which bears the same ratio to that amount as the total number of Music Service Uses bears to all Computer Service Uses.

PART III. AMOUNT SUBJECT TO FEE

1. Computer Service Budget/Amount Subject to Fee.. $____________________

PART IV. LICENSE FEE

2. The annual license fee is the applicable fee based on Amount Subject to Fee (from Part III, line 1), as shown in Table I below (pro-rated for partial year).. $____________________

TABLE I

Amount Subject to Fee	Annual License Fee
Less than $ 31,000	$ 500.00
$ 31,000 to $ 39,999.99	$ 575.00
$ 40,000 to $ 49,999.99	$ 725.00
$ 50,000 to $ 59,999.99	$ 890.00
$ 60,000 to $ 69,999.99	$ 1,050.00
$ 70,000 to $ 79,999.99	$ 1,210.00
$ 80,000 to $ 89,999.99	$ 1,370.00
$ 90,000 to $ 99,999.99	$ 1,535.00
$ 100,000 to $ 119,999.99	$ 1,777.00
$ 120,000 to $ 139,999.99	$ 2,100.00
$ 140,000 to $ 159,999.99	$ 2,423.00
$ 160,000 to $ 179,999.99	$ 2,745.00
$ 180,000 to $ 199,999.99	$ 3,068.00
$ 200,000 to $ 224,999.99	$ 3,432.00
$ 225,000 or More	$3,432.00 plus 1.615% of the Amount Subject to Fee in excess of $225,000

D - 2

ASCAP Experimental License Agreement

PART V. LICENSE FEE

14. The annual license fee under this Rate Schedule "B" is the applicable fee based on Amount Subject to Fee (from Part III, line 5), as shown in the Table below (pro-rated for partial year) .... $_____

Amount Subject to Fee	Annual License Fee
Less than $ 20,650	$ 500.00
$ 20,700 to $ 25,999.99	$ 585.00
$ 26,000 to $ 31,999.99	$ 702.00
$ 32,000 to $ 39,999.99	$ 872.00
$ 40,000 to $ 49,999.99	$ 1,089.00
$ 50,000 to $ 62,999.99	$ 1,367.00
$ 63,000 to $ 78,999.99	$ 1,718.00
$ 79,000 to $ 99,999.99	$ 2,166.00
$ 100,000 to $ 125,999.99	$ 2,735.00
$ 126,000 to $ 159,999.99	$ 3,461.00
$ 160,000 to $ 199,999.99	$ 4,356.00
$ 200,000 to $ 249,999.99	$ 5,245.00
$ 250,000 to $ 299,999.99	$ 6,655.00
$ 300,000 or more	$ 6,655.00 plus 2.17% of the Amount Subject to Fee in excess of $300,000

PART VI. CERTIFICATION

        We attach to this report a written statement of the method used to identify and track Computer Service Uses, Music Service Uses, and that portion of the revenue of the Computer Service that is derived from, or in connection with, or is attributable to, performances of music on the Computer Service. We certify that all books and records necessary to verify this report are now and will continue to be available for your examination in accordance with the terms of the license agreement.

Signature   **Date**

Print Name and Title

B - 3

PART V.   ATTRIBUTABLE ASCAP MUSIC REVENUE CALCULATION

14.   Attributable Revenue (from Part IV, line 13)...................................... $_____
15.   Total ASCAP Music Uses.................................   _____
16.   Total Music Uses...   _____
17.   Ratio (divide line 15 by line 16)(to 3 decimals)....................................   _____
18.   Attributable ASCAP Music Revenue (multiply line 14 by line 17)..................... $_____

PART VI. LICENSE FEE

19.   The annual license fee under this Rate Schedule "C" is the applicable fee based on Amount Subject to Fee (from Part III, line 3), as shown in the Table below (pro-rated for partial year)..................... $_____

Amount Subject to Fee	Annual License Fee
Less than $ 11,200	$ 500.00
$ 11,200 to $ 14,999.99	$ 630.00
$ 15,000 to $ 19,999.99	$ 780.00
$ 20,000 to $ 26,999.99	$ 1,070.00
$ 27,000 to $ 35,999.99	$ 1,405.00
$ 36,000 to $ 47,999.99	$ 1,765.00
$ 48,000 to $ 63,999.99	$ 2,498.00
$ 64,000 to $ 84,999.99	$ 3,293.00
$ 85,000 to $112,999.99	$ 4,415.00
$113,000 to $149,999.99	$ 5,855.00
$150,000 to $199,999.99	$ 7,805.00
$200,000 to $264,999.99	$ 10,372.00
$ 265,000 to $ 349,999.99	$13,714.00
$350,000 or More	$13,714.00 plus 4.46% of the Amount Subject to Fee in excess of $350,000

PART VII. CERTIFICATION

We attach to this report a written statement of the method used to identify and track Computer Service Uses, Music Service Uses, Music Uses, ASCAP Music Uses, and that portion of the revenue of the Computer Service that is derived from, or in connection with, or is attributable to, performances on the Computer Service of music in the ASCAP Repertory. We certify that all books and records necessary to verify this report are now and will continue to be available for your examination in accordance with the terms of the license agreement.

_____   _____
Signature   Date

_____
Print Name and Title

C - 3

PART V.   AMOUNT SUBJECT TO FEE COMPUTATION

1. Computer Service Budget... $_____
2. Total Music Service Uses... _____
3. Total Computer Service Uses... _____
4. Ratio (divide line 2 by line 3) (to 3 decimals)............................... _____
5. Amount Subject to Fee (multiply line 1 by line 4) .... $_____

PART VI.   LICENSE FEE

6. The annual license fee is the applicable fee based on Amount Subject to Fee (from Part V, line 5), as shown in Table II below (pro-rated for partial year)... $_____

TABLE II

Amount Subject to Fee	Annual License Fee
Less than $ 20,650	$ 500.00
$ 20,650 to $ 25,999.99	$ 565.00
$ 26,000 to $ 31,999.99	$ 702.00
$ 32,000 to $ 39,999.99	$ 873.00
$ 40,000 to $ 49,999.99	$ 1,089.00
$ 50,000 to $ 62,999.99	$ 1,367.00
$ 63,000 to $ 78,999.99	$ 1,718.00
$ 79,000 to $ 99,999.99	$ 2,166.00
$ 100,000 to $ 125,999.99	$ 2,735.00
$ 126,000 to $ 159,999.99	$ 3,461.00
$ 160,000 to $ 199,999.99	$ 4,356.00
$ 200,000 to $ 249,999.99	$ 5,445.00
$ 250,000 to $ 299,999.99	$ 6,655.00
$ 300,000 or More	$6,655.00 plus 2.42% of the Amount Subject to Fee in excess of $300,000

PART VII.   CERTIFICATION

If our annual license fee is based on the Amount Subject to Fee from Part V, line 5, we attach to this report a written statement of the method used to identify and track Computer Service Uses and Music Service Uses. In all instances, we certify that all books and records necessary to verify this report are now and will continue to be available for your examination in accordance with the terms of the license agreement.

_____   _____
Signature   Date

_____
Print Name and Title

D-3

Form 32

A.F.M. EXCLUSIVE AGENT-MUSICIAN AGREEMENT
(Not for Use in California)

_____   _____

Legal Name of Musician   Name of Agent

_____

Professional Name of Musician or Agent

_____

Name of Musician's A.F.M. Booking Orchestra or Group   Agent Number

_____

Musician's A.F.M. Locals

   This Agreement Begins on _____, 19 ____, and Ends on _____,
19____.

1. <u>SCOPE OF AGREEMENT</u>: Musician hereby employs Agent and Agent
hereby accepts employment as Musician's exclusive booking agent, manager and
representative throughout the world with respect to musician's services, appearances and endeavors as a musician. As used in this agreement "Musician" refers
to the undersigned musician and to musicians performing with any orchestra or
group which Musician leads or conducts and whom Musician shall make subject
to the terms of this agreement; "A.F.M." refers to the American Federation of
Musicians of the United States and Canada.

2. <u>DUTIES OF AGENT</u>:

   (a) Agent agrees to use reasonable efforts in the performance of the following
duties: assist Musician in obtaining, obtain offers of, and negotiate, engagements
for Musician; advise, aid, counsel and guide musician with respect to Musician's
professional career; promote and publicize Musician's name and talents; carry
on business correspondence in Musician's behalf relating to Musician's professional career; cooperate with duly constituted and authorized representatives of
Musician in the performance of such duties.

   (b) Agent will maintain office, staff and facilities reasonably adequate for the
rendition of such services.

   (c) Agent will not accept any engagements for Musician without Musician's
prior approval which shall not be unreasonably withheld.

   (d) Agent shall fully comply with all applicable laws, rules and regulations
of governmental authorities and secure such licenses as may be required for the
rendition of services hereunder.

3. RIGHTS OF AGENT:

(a) Agent may render similar services to others and may engage in other businesses and ventures, subject, however, to the limitations imposed by 8 below.

(b) Musician will promptly refer to Agent all communications, written or oral, received by or on behalf of Musician relating to the services and appearances by Musician.

(c) Without Agent's written consent, Musician will not engage any other person, firm or corporation to perform the services to be performed by Agent hereunder (except that Musician may employ a personal manager) nor will Musician perform or appear professionally or offer so to do except through Agent.

(d) Agent may publicize the fact that Agent is the exclusive booking agent and representative for Musician.

(e) Agent shall have the right to use or to permit others to use Musician's name and likeness in advertising or publicity relating to Musician's services and appearances but without cost or expense to Musician unless Musician shall otherwise specifically agree in writing.

(f) In the event of Musician's breach of this agreement, Agent's sole right and remedy for such breach shall be the receipt from Musician of the commissions specified in this agreement, but only if, as, and when, Musician receives moneys or other consideration on which such commissions are payable hereunder.

4. COMPENSATION OF AGENT:

(a) In consideration of the services to be rendered by Agent hereunder, Musician agrees to pay to Agent commissions equal to the percentages, set forth below, of the gross moneys received by Musician, directly or indirectly, for each engagement on which commissions are payable hereunder:

(1) Fifteen per cent (15%) if the duration of the engagement is two (2) or more consecutive days per week.

(2) Twenty per cent (20%) for Single Miscellaneous Engagements of one (1) day duration each for a different employer in a different location.

(3) In no event, however, shall the payment of any such commissions result in the retention by Musician for any engagement of net moneys or other consideration in an amount less than the applicable minimum scale of the A.F.M. or of any local thereof having jurisdiction over such engagement.

(4) In no event shall the payment of any such commissions result in the receipt by Agent for any engagement of commissions, fees or other consideration, directly, or indirectly, from any person or persons, including the Musician, which in aggregate exceed the commissions provided for in this agreement. Any commission, fee, or other consideration received by Agent

from any source other than Musician, directly or indirectly, on account of, as a result of, or in connection with supplying the services of Musician shall be reported to Musician and the amount thereof shall be deducted from the commissions payable by the Musician hereunder.

(b) Commissions shall become due and payable to Agent immediately following the receipt thereof by Musician or by anyone else in Musician's behalf.

(c) No commissions shall be payable on any engagement if Musician is not paid for such engagement irrespective of the reasons for such non-payment to Musician, including but not limited to non-payment by reason of the fault of Musician. This shall not preclude the awarding of damages by the International Executive Board to a booking agent to compensate him for actual expenses incurred as the direct result of the cancellation of an engagement when such cancellation was the fault of the member.

(d) Agent's commissions shall be payable on all moneys or other considerations received by Musician pursuant to contracts for engagements negotiated or entered into during the term of this agreement; if specifically agreed to by Musician by initialing the margin hereof, to contracts for engagements in existence at the commencement of the term hereof (excluding, however, any engagements as to which Musician is under prior obligation to pay commissions to another agent); and to any modifications, extensions and renewals thereof or substitutions therefor or substitutions therefor regardless of when Musician shall receive such moneys or other considerations.

(e) As used in this paragraph and elsewhere in this agreement the term "gross earnings" shall mean the gross amounts received by Musician for each engagement less costs and expenses incurred in collecting amounts due for any engagement, including costs of arbitration, litigation and attorney's fees.

(f) If specifically agreed to by Musician by initialing the margin hereof, the following shall apply:

(1) Musician shall advance to Agent against Agent's final commissions an amount not exceeding the following percentages of the gross amounts received for each engagement 15% on engagements of three (3) days or less; 10% on all other engagements.

(2) If Musician shall so request and shall simultaneously furnish Agent with the data relating to deductions, the Agent within 45 days following the end of each 12 months period during the term of this agreement and within 45 days following the termination of this Agreement, shall account to and furnish Musician with a detailed statement itemizing the gross amounts received for all engagements during the period to which such accounting relates, the moneys or other considerations upon which Agent's commissions are based, and the amount of Agent's commissions resulting from such

computations. Upon request, a copy of such statement shall be furnished promptly to the Office of the President of the A.F.M.

(3) Any balances owed by or to the parties shall be paid as follows: by the Agent at the time of rendering such statement; by the Musician within 30 days after receipt of such statement.

5. DURATION AND TERMINATION OF AGREEMENT:

(a) The term of this agreement shall be as stated in the opening heading hereof, subject to termination as provided in 5(b), 6 and 10 below.

(b) In addition to termination pursuant to other provisions of this agreement, this agreement may be terminated by either party, by notice as provided below, if Musician

(1) is unemployed for four (4) consecutive weeks at any time during the term hereof; or

(2) does not obtain employment for at least twenty (20) cumulative weeks of engagements to be performed during each of the first and second six (6) months periods during the term hereof; or

(3) does not obtain employment for at least forty (40) cumulative weeks of engagements to be performed during each subsequent year of the term hereof.

(c) Notice of such termination shall be given by certified mail addressed to the addressee at his last known address and a copy thereof shall be sent to the A.F.M. Such termination shall be effective as of the date of mailing of such notice if and when approved by the A.F.M. Such notice shall be mailed no later than two (2) weeks following the occurrence of any event described in (i) above: two (2) weeks following a period in excess of thirteen (13) of the cumulative weeks of unemployment specified in (ii) above; and two (2) weeks following a period in excess of twenty-six (26) of the cumulative weeks of unemployment specified in (iii) above. Failure to give notice as aforesaid shall constitute a waiver of the right to terminate based upon the happening of such prior events.

(d) Musician's disability resulting in failure to perform engagements and Musician's unreasonable refusal to accept and perform engagements shall not by themselves either deprive Agent of its right to or give Musician the right to terminate (as provided in (b) above).

(e) As used in this agreement, a "week" shall commence on Sunday and terminate on Saturday. A "week of engagements" shall mean any one of the following:

(1) a week during which Musician is to perform on at least four (4) days; or

(2) a week during which Musician's gross earnings equals or exceeds the lowest such gross earnings obtained by Musician for performances rendered during any one of the immediately preceding six (6) weeks; or

(3) a week during which Musician is to perform engagements on commercial television or radio or in concert for compensation equal at least to three (3) times the minimum scales of the A.F.M. or of any local thereof having jurisdiction applicable to such engagements.

6. AGENT'S MAINTENANCE OF A.F.M. BOOKING AGENT AGREEMENT: Agent represents that Agent is presently a party to an A.F.M. Booking Agent Agreement which is in full force and effect. If such A.F.M. Booking Agent Agreement shall terminate, the rights of the parties hereunder shall be governed by the terms and conditions of said Booking Agent Agreement relating to the effect of termination of such agreements which are incorporated herein by reference.

7. NO OTHER AGREEMENTS: This is the only and the complete agreement between the parties relating to all or any part of the subject matter covered by this agreement. There is no other agreement, arrangement or participation between the parties, nor do the parties stand in any relationship to each other which is not created by this agreement, whereby the terms and conditions of this agreement are avoided or evaded, directly or indirectly, such as, by way of example but not limitation, contracts, arrangements, relationships or participations relating to publicity services, business management, personal management, music publishing, or instruction.

8. INCORPORATION OF A.F.M. BYLAWS, ETC.: There are incorporated into and made part of this agreement, as though fully set forth herein, the present and future provisions of the Bylaws, Rules, Regulations and Resolutions of the A.F.M. and those of its locals which do not conflict therewith. The parties acknowledge their responsibility to be fully acquainted, now and for the duration of this agreement, with the contents thereof.

9. SUBMISSION AND DETERMINATION OF DISPUTES: Every claim, dispute, controversy or difference arising out of, dealing with, relating to, or affecting the interpretation or application of this agreement, or the violation or breach, or the threatened violation or breach thereof shall be submitted, heard and determined by the International Executive Board of the A.F.M., in accordance with the rules of such Board (regardless of the termination or purported termination of this agreement or of the Agent's A.F.M. Booking Agent Agreement), and such determination shall be conclusive, final and binding on the parties.

10. NO ASSIGNMENT OF THIS AGREEMENT: This agreement shall be personal to the parties and shall not be transferable or assignable by operation

of law or otherwise without the prior consent of the Musician and of the A.F.M. The obligations imposed by this agreement shall be binding upon the parties. The Musician may terminate this agreement at any time within ninety (90) days after the transfer of a controlling interest in the Agent.

11. NEGOTIATION FOR RENEWAL: Neither party shall enter into negotiations for or agree to the renewal or extension of this agreement prior to the beginning of the final year of the term hereof.

12. APPROVAL BY A.F.M.: This agreement shall not become effective unless, within (30) days following its execution, an executed copy thereof is filed with and is thereafter approved in writing by the A.F.M.

IN WITNESS WHEREOF, the parties hereto have executed this agreement the _____ day of _____, 19_____.

_____   _____
        Agent   Musician

By _____   _____
    Title or Capacity

                                    _____
                                    City State Zip Code

Agent Representing No More Than Two Clients

If specifically agreed to by the parties by signing below:

(a) Agent warrants and represents that Agent presently serves, and Agent agrees that during the term hereof Agent will restrict its activities to serving, as booking agent, or manager, or representative, no more than one other musical soloist, orchestra, band or performing group. If such warranty and representation is untrue, this agreement is null and void. If such agreement is broken, this agreement shall automatically terminate.

(b) In consideration thereof, the parties agree that the provisions of 4(a) (i) and (ii) and 4(f) above shall be inapplicable and that the compensation of Agent shall be as set forth in Schedule 1 attached. In no event, however, shall the payment of any commission result in the retention by Musician for any engagement of net moneys or other consideration in an amount less than the applicable minimum scale of the A.F.M. or of any local thereof.

_____   _____
Agent   Musician

By _____
    Title or Capacity

Form 33
Copyright Application Form PA

Copyright Application Form PA

FORM PA
For a Work of the Performing Arts
UNITED STATES COPYRIGHT OFFICE

REGISTRATION NUMBER

_____

PA   PAU

EFFECTIVE DATE OF REGISTRATION

_____

Month   Day   Year

DO NOT WRITE ABOVE THIS LINE. IF YOU NEED MORE SPACE, USE A SEPARATE CONTINUATION SHEET.

1

TITLE OF THIS WORK ▼

PREVIOUS OR ALTERNATIVE TITLES ▼

NATURE OF THIS WORK ▼ See instructions

---

2 a

NAME OF AUTHOR ▼

DATES OF BIRTH AND DEATH
Year Born ▼   Year Died ▼

Was this contribution to the work a "work made for hire"?
☐ Yes
☐ No

AUTHOR'S NATIONALITY OR DOMICILE
Name of Country
OR { Citizen of ▶
Domiciled in ▶

WAS THIS AUTHOR'S CONTRIBUTION TO THE WORK
Anonymous? ☐ Yes ☐ No
Pseudonymous? ☐ Yes ☐ No

If the answer to either of these questions is "Yes," see detailed instructions.

NATURE OF AUTHORSHIP Briefly describe nature of material created by this author in which copyright is claimed. ▼

NOTE
Under the law, the "author" of a "work made for hire" is generally the employer, not the employee (see instructions). For any part of the work that was "made for hire" check "Yes" in the space provided, give the employer (or other person for whom the work was prepared) as "Author" of that part, and leave the space for dates of birth and death blank.

b

NAME OF AUTHOR ▼

DATES OF BIRTH AND DEATH
Year Born ▼   Year Died ▼

Was this contribution to the work a "work made for hire"?
☐ Yes
☐ No

AUTHOR'S NATIONALITY OR DOMICILE
Name of Country
OR { Citizen of ▶
Domiciled in ▶

WAS THIS AUTHOR'S CONTRIBUTION TO THE WORK
Anonymous? ☐ Yes ☐ No
Pseudonymous? ☐ Yes ☐ No

If the answer to either of these questions is "Yes," see detailed instructions.

NATURE OF AUTHORSHIP Briefly describe nature of material created by this author in which copyright is claimed. ▼

c

NAME OF AUTHOR ▼

DATES OF BIRTH AND DEATH
Year Born ▼   Year Died ▼

Was this contribution to the work a "work made for hire"?
☐ Yes
☐ No

AUTHOR'S NATIONALITY OR DOMICILE
Name of Country
OR { Citizen of ▶
Domiciled in ▶

WAS THIS AUTHOR'S CONTRIBUTION TO THE WORK
Anonymous? ☐ Yes ☐ No
Pseudonymous? ☐ Yes ☐ No

If the answer to either of these questions is "Yes," see detailed instructions.

NATURE OF AUTHORSHIP Briefly describe nature of material created by this author in which copyright is claimed. ▼

---

3 a

YEAR IN WHICH CREATION OF THIS WORK WAS COMPLETED
This information must be given
◀ Year in all cases.

b DATE AND NATION OF FIRST PUBLICATION OF THIS PARTICULAR WORK
Complete this information
ONLY if this work
has been published.
Month ▶   Day ▶   Year ▶   ◀ Nation

4

COPYRIGHT CLAIMANT(S) Name and address must be given even if the claimant is the same as the author given in space 2 ▼

See instructions before completing this space.

TRANSFER If the claimant(s) named here in space 4 is (are) different from the author(s) named in space 2, give a brief statement of how the claimant(s) obtained ownership of the copyright. ▼

APPLICATION RECEIVED

ONE DEPOSIT RECEIVED

TWO DEPOSITS RECEIVED

FUNDS RECEIVED

DO NOT WRITE HERE
OFFICE USE ONLY

MORE ON BACK ▶
• Complete all applicable spaces (numbers 5-9) on the reverse side of this page.
• See detailed instructions.
• Sign the form at line 8.

DO NOT WRITE HERE

Page 1 of ____ pages

EXAMINED BY	FORM PA
CHECKED BY	
☐ CORRESPONDENCE Yes	FOR COPYRIGHT OFFICE USE ONLY

DO NOT WRITE ABOVE THIS LINE. IF YOU NEED MORE SPACE, USE A SEPARATE CONTINUATION SHEET.

PREVIOUS REGISTRATION Has registration for this work, or for an earlier version of this work, already been made in the Copyright Office?
☐ Yes ☐ No If your answer is "Yes," why is another registration being sought? (Check appropriate box) ▼
a. ☐ This is the first published edition of a work previously registered in unpublished form.
b. ☐ This is the first application submitted by this author as copyright claimant.
c. ☐ This is a changed version of the work, as shown by space 6 on this application.
If your answer is "Yes," give: **Previous Registration Number** ▼   **Year of Registration** ▼

5

DERIVATIVE WORK OR COMPILATION Complete both space 6a and 6b for a derivative work; complete only 6b for a compilation.
a. Preexisting Material Identify any preexisting work or works that this work is based on or incorporates. ▼

b. Material Added to This Work Give a brief, general statement of the material that has been added to this work and in which copyright is claimed. ▼

6

See instructions before completing this space.

DEPOSIT ACCOUNT If the registration fee is to be charged to a Deposit Account established in the Copyright Office, give name and number of Account.
Name ▼   Account Number ▼

7

CORRESPONDENCE Give name and address to which correspondence about this application should be sent. Name/Address/Apt/City/State/ZIP ▼

Area Code and Telephone Number ▶

Be sure to give your daytime phone number

CERTIFICATION* I, the undersigned, hereby certify that I am the
Check only one ▼
☐ author
☐ other copyright claimant
☐ owner of exclusive right(s)
☐ authorized agent of _____
Name of author or other copyright claimant, or owner of exclusive right(s) ▲

8

of the work identified in this application and that the statements made
by me in this application are correct to the best of my knowledge.

Typed or printed name and date ▼ If this application gives a date of publication in space 3, do not sign and submit it before that date.
Date ▶

Handwritten signature (X) ▼

MAIL CERTIFICATE TO
Name ▼
Number/Street/Apt ▼
City/State/ZIP ▼

Certificate will be mailed in window envelope

9

*17 U.S.C. § 506(e): Any person who knowingly makes a false representation of a material fact in the application for copyright registration provided for by section 409, or in any written statement filed in connection with the application, shall be fined not more than $2,500.

May 1995—300,000   ♻ PRINTED ON RECYCLED PAPER   ☆U.S. GOVERNMENT PRINTING OFFICE: 1995-387-237/46

■Filling Out Application Form PA

Detach and read these instructions before completing this form.
Make sure all applicable spaces have been filled in before you return this form.

BASIC INFORMATION

When to Use This Form: Use Form PA for registration of published or unpublished works of the performing arts. This class includes works prepared for the purpose of being "performed" directly before an audience or indirectly "by means of any device or process." Works of the performing arts include: (1) musical works, including any accompanying words, (2) dramatic works, including any accompanying music; (3) pantomimes and choreographic works, and (4) motion pictures and other audiovisual works.

Deposit to Accompany Application: An application for copyright registration must be accompanied by a deposit consisting of copies or phonorecords representing the entire work for which registration is made. The following are the general deposit requirements as set forth in the statute:

Unpublished Work: Deposit one complete copy (or phonorecord)

Published Work: Deposit two complete copies (or one phonorecord) of the best edition.

Work First Published Outside the United States: Deposit one complete copy (or phonorecord) of the first foreign edition.

Contribution to a Collective Work: Deposit one complete copy (or phonorecord) of the best edition of the collective work

Motion Pictures: Deposit: both of the following: (1) a separate written description of the contents of the motion picture; and (2) for a published work, one complete copy of the best edition of the motion picture; or, for an unpublished work, one complete copy of the motion picture or identifying material. Identifying material may be either an audiorecording of the entire soundtrack or one frame enlargement or similar visual print from each 10 minute segment.

The Copyright Notice: For works first published on or after March 1, 1989, the law provides that a copyright notice in a specified form "may be placed on all publicly distributed copies from which the work can be visually perceived." Use of the copyright notice is the responsibility of the copyright owner and does not require advance permission from the Copyright Office. The required form of the notice for copies generally consists of three elements: (1) the symbol "©", or the word "Copyright," or the abbreviation "Copr."; (2) the year of first publication; and (3) the name of the owner of copyright. For example: "© 1990 Jane Cole." The notice is to be affixed to the copies "in such manner and location as to give reasonable notice of the claim of copyright." Works first published prior to March 1, 1989, must carry the notice or risk loss of copyright protection.

For information about requirements for works published before March 1, 1989, or other copyright information, write: Information Section, LM-401, Copyright Office, Library of Congress, Washington, D.C. 20559-6000.

LINE-BY-LINE INSTRUCTIONS

Please type or print using black ink.

1 SPACE 1: Title

Title of This Work: Every work submitted for copyright registration must be given a title to identify that particular work. If the copies or phonorecords of the work bear a title (or an identifying phrase that could serve as a title), transcribe that wording *completely and exactly* on the application. Indexing of the registration and future identification of the work will depend on the information you give here. If the work you are registering is an entire "collective work" (such as a collection of plays or songs), give the overall title of the collection. If you are registering one or more individual contributions to a collective work, give the title of each contribution, followed by the title of the collection. For an unpublished collection, you may give the titles of the individual works after the collection title.

Previous or Alternative Titles: Complete this space if there are any additional titles for the work under which someone searching for the registration might be likely to look, or under which a document pertaining to the work might be recorded.

Nature of This Work: Briefly describe the general nature or character of the work being registered for copyright. Examples: "Music"; "Song Lyrics"; "Words and Music"; "Drama"; "Musical Play"; "Choreography"; "Pantomime"; "Motion Picture"; "Audiovisual Work."

2 SPACE 2: Author(s)

General Instructions: After reading these instructions, decide who are the "authors" of this work for copyright purposes. Then, unless the work is a "collective work," give the requested information about every "author" who contributed any appreciable amount of copyrightable matter to this version of the work. If you need further space, request additional Continuation Sheets. In the case of a collective work, such as a songbook or a collection of plays, give the information about the author of the collective work as a whole.

Name of Author: The fullest form of the author's name should be given. Unless the work was "made for hire," the individual who actually created the work is its "author." In the case of a work made for hire, the statute provides that "the employer or other person for whom the work was prepared is considered the author."

What is a "Work Made for Hire"? A "work made for hire" is defined as: (1) "a work prepared by an employee within the scope of his or her employment"; or (2) "a work specially ordered or commissioned for use as a contribution to a collective work, as a part of a motion picture or other audiovisual work, as a translation, as a supplementary work, as a compilation, as an instructional text, as a test, as answer material for a test, or as an atlas, if the parties expressly agree in a written instrument signed by them that the work shall be considered a work made for hire." If you have checked "Yes" to indicate that the work was "made for hire," you must give the full legal name of the employer (or other person for whom the work was prepared). You may also include the name of the employee along with the name of the employer (for example: "Elster Music Co., employer for hire of John Ferguson").

"Anonymous" or "Pseudonymous" Work: An author's contribution to a work is "anonymous" if that author is not identified on the copies or phonorecords of the work. An author's contribution to a work is "pseudonymous" if that author is identified on the copies or phonorecords under a fictitious name. If the work is "anonymous" you may: (1) leave the line blank; or (2) state "anonymous" on the line; or (3) reveal the author's identity. If the work is "pseudonymous" you may: (1) leave the line blank; or (2) give the pseudonym and identify it as such (example: "Huntley Haverstock, pseudonym"); or (3) reveal the author's name, making clear which is the real name and which is the pseudonym (for example: "Judith Barton, whose pseudonym is Madeline Elster"). However, the citizenship or domicile of the author must be given in all cases.

Dates of Birth and Death: If the author is dead, the statute requires that the year of death be included in the application unless the work is anonymous or pseudonymous. The author's birth date is optional, but is useful as a form of identification. Leave this space blank if the author's contribution was a "work made for hire."

Author's Nationality or Domicile: Give the country of which the author is a citizen, or the country in which the author is domiciled. Nationality or domicile must be given in all cases.

Nature of Authorship: Give a brief general statement of the nature of this particular author's contribution to the work. Examples: "Words"; "Coauthor of Music"; "Words and Music"; "Arrangement"; "Coauthor of Book and Lyrics"; "Dramatization"; "Screen Play"; "Compilation and English Translation"; "Editorial Revisions."

3 SPACE 3: Creation and Publication

General Instructions: Do not confuse "creation" with "publication." Every application for copyright registration must state "the year in which creation of the work was completed." Give the date and nation of first publication only if the work has been published

Creation: Under the statute, a work is "created" when it is fixed in a copy or phonorecord for the first time. Where a work has been prepared over a period of time, the part of the work existing in fixed form on a particular date constitutes the created work on that date. The date you give here should be the year in which the author completed the particular version for which registration is now being sought, even if other versions exist or if further changes or additions are planned.

Publication: The statute defines "publication" as "the distribution of copies or phonorecords of a work to the public by sale or other transfer of ownership, or by rental, lease, or lending"; a work is also "published" if there has been an "offering to distribute copies or phonorecords to a group of persons for purposes of further distribution, public performance, or public display." Give the full date (month, day, year) when, and the country where, publication first occurred. If first publication took place simultaneously in the United States and other countries, it is sufficient to state "U.S.A."

4 SPACE 4: Claimant(s)

Name(s) and Address(es) of Copyright Claimant(s): Give the name(s) and address(es) of the copyright claimant(s) in this work even if the claimant is the same as the author. Copyright in a work belongs initially to the author of the work (including, in the case of a work made for hire, the employer or other person for whom the work was prepared). The copyright claimant is either the author of the work or a person or organization to whom the copyright initially belonging to the author has been transferred.

Transfer: The statute provides that, if the copyright claimant is not the author, the application for registration must contain "a brief statement of how the claimant obtained ownership of the copyright." If any copyright claimant named in space 4 is not an author named in space 2, give a brief statement explaining how the claimant(s) obtained ownership of the copyright. Examples: "By written contract"; "Transfer of all rights by author"; "Assignment"; "By will." Do not attach transfer documents or other attachments or riders.

5 SPACE 5: Previous Registration

General Instructions: The questions in space 5 are intended to show whether an earlier registration has been made for this work and, if so, whether there is any basis for a new registration. As a general rule, only one basic copyright registration can be made for the same version of a particular work.

Same Version: If this version is substantially the same as the work covered by a previous registration, a second registration is not generally possible unless: (1) the work has been registered in unpublished form and a second registration is now being sought to cover this first published edition; or (2) someone other than the author is identified as copyright claimant in the earlier registration, and the author is now seeking registration in his or her own name. If either of these two exceptions apply, check the appropriate box and give the earlier registration number and date. Otherwise, do not submit Form PA, instead, write the Copyright Office for information about supplementary registration or recordation of transfers of copyright ownership.

Changed Version: If the work has been changed, and you are now seeking registration to cover the additions or revisions, check the last box in space 5, give the earlier registration number and date, and complete both parts of space 6 in accordance with the instructions below.

Previous Registration Number and Date: If more than one previous registration has been made for the work, give the number and date of the latest registration.

6 SPACE 6: Derivative Work or Compilation

General Instructions: Complete space 6 if this work is a "changed version," "compilation," or "derivative work," and if it incorporates one or more earlier works that have already been published or registered for copyright or that have fallen into the public domain. A "compilation" is defined as "a work formed by the collection and assembling of preexisting materials or of data that are selected, coordinated, or arranged in such a way that the resulting work as a whole constitutes an original work of authorship." A "derivative work" is "a work based on one or more preexisting works." Examples of derivative works include musical arrangements, dramatizations, translations, abridgments, condensations, motion picture versions, or "any other form in which a work may be recast, transformed, or adapted." Derivative works also include works "consisting of editorial revisions, annotations, or other modifications" if these changes, as a whole, represent an original work of authorship.

Preexisting Material (space 6a): Complete this space and space 6b for derivative works. In this space identify the preexisting work that has been recast, transformed, or adapted. For example, the preexisting material might be: "French version of Hugo's 'Le Roi s'amuse'." Do not complete this space for compilations.

Material Added to This Work (space 6b): Give a brief, general statement of the additional new material covered by the copyright claim for which registration is sought. In the case of a derivative work, identify this new material. Examples: "Arrangement for piano and orchestra"; "Dramatization for television"; "New film version"; "Revisions throughout; Act III completely new." If the work is a compilation, give a brief, general statement describing both the material that has been compiled and the compilation itself. Example: "Compilation of 19th Century Military Songs."

7,8,9 SPACE 7, 8, 9: Fee, Correspondence, Certification, Return Address

Deposit Account: If you maintain a Deposit Account in the Copyright Office, identify it in space 7. Otherwise leave the space blank and send the fee of $20 with your application and deposit.

Correspondence (space 7): This space should contain the name, address, area code, and telephone number of the person to be consulted if correspondence about this application becomes necessary.

Certification (space 9): The application cannot be accepted unless it bears the date and the handwritten signature of the author or other copyright claimant, or of the owner of exclusive right(s), or of the duly authorized agent of the author, claimant, or owner of exclusive right(s).

Address for Return of Certificate (space 9): The address box must be completed legibly since the certificate will be returned in a window envelope.

MORE INFORMATION

How to Register a Recorded Work:
If the musical or dramatic work that you are registering has been recorded (as a tape, disk, or cassette), you may choose either copyright application Form PA (Performing Arts) or Form SR (Sound Recordings), depending on the purpose of the registration.

Form PA should be used to register the underlying musical composition or dramatic work. Form SR has been developed specifically to register: a "sound recording" as defined by the Copyright Act—a work resulting from the "fixation of a series of sounds," separate and distinct from the underlying musical or dramatic work. Form SR should be used when the copyright claim is limited to the sound recording itself. (In one instance, Form SR may also be used to file for a copyright registration for both kinds of works—see (4) below.) Therefore:

(1) File Form PA if you are seeking to register the musical or dramatic work, not the "sound recording," even though what you deposit for copyright purposes may be in the form of a phonorecord.

(2) File Form PA if you are seeking to register the audio portion of an audiovisual work, such as a motion picture soundtrack; these are considered integral parts of the audiovisual work.

(3) File Form SR if you are seeking to register the "sound recording" itself, that is, the work that results from the fixation of a series of musical, spoken, or other sounds, but not the underlying musical or dramatic work.

(4) File Form SR if you are the copyright claimant for both the underlying musical or dramatic work and the sound recording, and you prefer to register both on the same form.

(5) File both forms PA and SR if the copyright claimant for the underlying work and sound recording differ, or you prefer to have separate registration for them.

"Copies" and "Phonorecords":
To register for copyright, you are required to deposit "copies" or "phonorecords." These are defined as follows:

Musical compositions may be embodied (fixed) in "copies," objects from which a work can be read or visually perceived, directly or with the aid of a machine or device, such as manuscripts, books, sheet music, film, and videotape. They may also be fixed in "phonorecords," objects embodying fixations of sounds, such as tapes and phonograph disks, commonly known as phonograph records. For example, a song (the work to be registered) can be reproduced in sheet music ("copies") or phonograph records ("phonorecords"), or both.

Form 34

ASCAP Membership Agreement

879

**MEMBERSHIP
AGREEMENT**

A S C A P

AGREEMENT BETWEEN

_____

AND
AMERICAN SOCIETY OF COMPOSERS, AUTHORS & PUBLISHERS

ONE LINCOLN PLAZA NEW YORK, NY 10023
PHONE (212) 621-6000

ASCAP Membership Agreement

ASCAP
MEMBERSHIP
AGREEMENT

Agreement made between the Undersigned (for brevity called "*Owner*") and the AMERICAN SOCIETY OF COMPOSERS, AUTHORS AND PUBLISHERS (for brevity called "*Society*"), in consideration of the premises and of the mutual covenants hereinafter contained, as follows:

1. The *Owner* grants to the *Society* for the term hereof, the right to license non-dramatic public performances (as hereinafter defined), of each musical work:

Of which the *Owner* is a copyright proprietor; or

Which the *Owner*, alone, or jointly, or in collaboration with others, wrote, composed, published, acquired or owned; or

In which the *Owner* now has any right, title, interest or control whatsoever, in whole or in part; or

Which hereafter, during the term hereof, may be written, composed, acquired, owned, published or copyrighted by the *Owner*, alone, jointly or in collaboration with others; or

In which the *Owner* may hereafter, during the term hereof, have any right, title, interest or control, whatsoever, in whole or in part.

The right to license the public performance of every such musical work shall be deemed granted to the *Society* by this instrument for the term hereof, immediately upon the work being written, composed, acquired, owned, published or copyrighted.

The rights hereby granted shall include:

(a) All the rights and remedies for enforcing the copyright or copyrights of such musical works, whether such copyrights are in the name of the *Owner* and/or others, as well as the right to sue under such copyrights in the name of the *Society* and/or in the name of the *Owner* and/or others, to the end and that the *Society* may effectively protect and be assured of all the rights hereby granted.

(b) The non-exclusive right of public performance of the separate numbers, songs, fragments or arrangements, melodies or selections forming part or parts of musical plays and dramatico-musical compositions, the *Owner* reserving and excepting from this grant the right of performance of musical plays and dramatico-musical compositions in their entirety, or any part of such plays or dramatico-musical compositions on the legitimate stage.

(c) The non-exclusive right of public performance by means of radio broadcasting, telephony, "wired w reless," a l forms of synchronism with motion pictures, and/or any method of transmitting sound other than television broadcasting.

(d) The non-exclusive right of public performance by television broadcasting; provided, however, that:

(i) This grant does not extend to or include the right to license the public performance by television broadcasting or otherwise of any rendition or performance of (a) any opera, operetta, musical comedy, play or like production, as such, in whole or in part, or (b) any composition from any opera, operetta, musical comedy, play or like production (whether or not such opera, operetta, musical comedy, play or like production was presented on the stage or in motion picture form) in a manner which recreates the performance of such composition with substantially such distinctive scenery or costums as was used in the presentation of such opera, operetta, musical comedy, play or like production (whether or not such opera, operetta, musical comedy, play or like production was presented on the stage or in motion picture form): provided, how-

ever, that the rights hereby granted shall be deemed to include a grant of the right to license non-dramatic performances of compositions by television broadcasting of a motion picture containing such composition if the rights in such motion picture other than those granted hereby have been obtained from the parties in interest.

(ii) Nothing herein contained shall be deemed to grant the right to license the public performance by television broadcasting of dramatic performances. Any performance of a separate musical composition which is not a dramatic performance, as defined herein, shall be deemed to be a non-dramatic performance. For the purposes of this agreement, a dramatic performance shall mean a performance of a musical composition on a television program in which there is a definite p ot depicted by action and where the performance of the musical composition is woven into and carries forward the plot and its accompanying action. The use of dialogue to establish a mere program format or the use of any non-dramatic dev ce merely to introduce a performance of a composition shall not be deemed to make such performances dramatic.

(iii) The definition of the terms "dramatic" and "non-dramatic" performances contained herein are purely for the purposes of this agreement and for the term thereof and shall not be binding upon or prejudicial to any pos tion taken by either of us subsequent to the term hereof or for any purpose other than this agreement.

(e) The *Owner* may at any time and from time to time, in good fa th, restrict the radio or television broadcasting of compositions from musical comedies, operas, operettas and motion pictures, or any other composition being excessively broadcast, only for the purpose of preventing harmful effect upon such musical comedies, operas, operettas, motion pictures or compositions, in respect of other interest or dor the copyrights thereof; provided, however, that the right to grant limited icenses will be given, upon application, as to restricted compositions, if and when the *Owner* is unable to show reasonable hazards to his or its major nterests likely to result from such radio or television broadcasting; and provided further that such right to restrict any such composition sha l no be exercised for the purpose of permitting the fixing or regulating of fees for the recording or transcribing of such composition, and provided further that in no case shall any charges, "free plugs," or other consideration be required in respect of any permission granted to perform a restricted composition; and provided further that in no event shall any composition, after the initial radio or television broadcast thereof, be restricted for the purpose of confining further radio or television broadcasts thereof to a particular artist, station, network or program. The *Owner* may also at anytime and from time to time, in good faith, restrict the radio or television broadcasting of any composition, as to which any suit has been brought or threatened on a claim that such composition infringes a composition not contained in the repertory of *Society* or on a claim by a non-member of *Society* that *Society* does not have the right to license the public performance of such composition by radio or television broadcasting.

2. The term of this Agreement shall be for a period commencing on the date hereof and continuing indefinitely thereafter unless terminated by either party in accordance with the Articles of Association.

3. The *Society* agrees, during the term hereof, in good faith to use its best endeavors to promote and carry out the objects for which it was organized, and to hold and apply all royalties, profits, benefits and advantages arising from the exploitation of the rights assigned to it by its several members, including the *Owner*, to the uses and purposes as

provided in its Articles of Association (which are hereby incorporated by reference), as now in force or as hereafter amended.

4. The *Owner* hereby irrevocably, during the term hereof, authorizes, empowers and vests in the *Society* the right to enforce and protect such rights of public performance under any and all copyrights, whether standing in the name of the *Owner* and/or others, in any and all works copyrighted by the *Owner*, and/or by others; to prevent the infringement thereof, to litigate, collect and receipt for damages arising from infringement, and in its sole judgment to join the *Owner* and/or others in whose names the copyright may stand, as parties plaintiff or defendants in suits or proceedings; to bring suit in the name of the *Owner* and/or in the name of the *Society*, or others in whose name the copyright may stand, or otherwise, and to release, compromise or refer to arbitration any actions, in the same manner and to the same extent and to all intents and purposes as the *Owner* might or could do, had this instrument not been made.

5. The *Owner* hereby makes, constitutes and appoints the *Society*, or its successor, the *Owner*'s true and lawful attorney, irrevocably during the term hereof, and in the name of the *Society* or its successor, or in the name of the *Owner*, or otherwise, to do all acts, take all proceedings, execute, acknowledge and deliver any and all instruments, papers, documents process and pleadings that may be necessary, proper or expedient to restrain infringements and recover damages in respect to or for the infringement or other violation of the rights of public performance in such works, and to discontinue, compromise or refer to arbitration any such proceedings or actions, or to make any other disposition of the differences in relation to the premises.

6. The *Owner* agrees from time to time, to execute, acknowledge and deliver to the *Society*, such assurances, powers of attorney or other authorizations or instruments as the *Society* may deem necessary or expedient to enable it to exercise, enjoy and enforce, in its own name or otherwise, all rights and remedies aforesaid.

7 It is mutually agreed that during the term hereof the Board of Directors of the *Society* shall be composed of an equal number of writers and publishers respectively, and that the royalties distributed by the Board of Directors shall be divided into two (2) equal sums and one (1) each of such sums credited respectively to and for division amongst (a) the writer members, and (b) the publisher members, in accordance with the system of apportionment and distribution of royalties as determined by the Board of Directors in accordance with the Articles of Association as they may be amended from time to time.

8. The *Owner* agrees that the apportionment and distribution of royalties by the *Society* as determined from time to time by the Board of Directors of the *Society*, in case of appeal by him, shall be final, conclusive and binding upon him.

The *Society* shall have the right to transfer the right of review of any apportionment and distribution of royalties from the Board of Directors to any other agency or instrumentality that in its discretion and good judgment it deems best adapted to assuring to the *Society*'s membership; a just, fair, equitable and accurate apportionment and distribution of royalties.

The *Society* shall have the right to adopt from time to time such systems, means, methods and formulae for the establishment of a member's apportionment and distribution of royalties as will assure a fair, just and equitable distribution of royalties among the membership.

9. **"Public Performance" Defined.** The term *"public performance"* shall be construed to mean vocal, instrumental and/or mechanical renditions and "representations in any manner or by any method whatsoever, including transmissions by radio and television broadcasting stations, transmission by telephony and/or "wired wireless"; and/or reproductions of performances and renditions by means of devices for reproducing sound recorded in synchronism or timed relation with the taking of motion pictures.

10. **"Musical Works" Defined.** The phrase *"musical works"* shall be construed to mean musical compositions and dramatico-musical compositions the words and music thereof, and the respective arrangements thereof, and the selections therefrom.

11. The powers, rights, authorities and privileges by this instrument vested in the *Society*, are deemed to include the World; provided, however, that such grant of rights for foreign countries shall be subject to any agreements now in effect, a list of which are noted on the reverse side hereof.

12. The grant made herein by the owner is modified by and subject to the provisions of (a) the Amended Final Judgment (Civil Action No. 13-95) dated March 14, 1950 in *U.S.A. v. ASCAP* as further amended by Order dated January 7, 1960, (b) the Final Judgment (Civil Action No. 42-245) in *U.S.A. v. ASCAP*, dated March 14, 1950, and (c) the provisions of the Articles of association and resolutions of the Board of Directors adopted pursuant to such judgments and order.

SIGNED, SEALED AND DELIVERED, on this _____ day of _____ 19____

Owner {
_____
_____

Society {
AMERICAN SOCIETY OF COMPOSERS, AUTHORS AND PUBLISHERS,
By_____
President and Chairman of the Board

ASCAP Membership Agreement

ASCAP
MEMBERSHIP
AGREEMENT

FOREIGN AGREEMENTS AT THIS DATE IN EFFECT
(See paragraph 11 of within agreement)

COUNTRY	WITH (Name of Firm)	EXPIRES	REMARKS

Form 35

BMI Writer Agreement

BMI Writer Agreement

BMI • 320 West 57th Street, New York, NY 10019-3790 • 212-586-2000 • FAX 212-245-8986

Date

Dear

The following shall constitute the agreement between us:

1. As used in this agreement:

(a) The word "Period" shall mean the term from   to
and continuing thereafter for additional terms of two years each unless terminated by either party at the end of said initial term
or any additional term, upon notice by registered or certified mail not more than six (6) months or less than three (3) months prior
to the end of any such term.

(b) The words "Work" or "Works" shall mean:

(I) All musical compositions (including the musical segments and individual compositions written for a dramatic or
dramatico-musical work) composed by you alone or with one or more co-writers during the Period; and

(ii) All musical compositions (including the musical segments and individual compositions written for a dramatic or
dramatico-musical work) composed by you alone or with one or more co-writers prior to the Period, except those in which there
is an outstanding grant of the right of public performance to a person other than a publisher affiliated with BMI.

2. You agree that:

(a) Within ten (10) days after the execution of this agreement you will furnish to us a completed clearance form available
in blank from us with respect to each Work heretofore composed by you which has been published in printed copies or recorded
commercially or synchronized commercially with film or tape or which is being currently performed or which you consider as likely
to be performed.

(b) In each instance that a Work for which a clearance form has not been submitted to us pursuant to sub-paragraph 2(a)
is published in printed copies or recorded commercially or in synchronization with film or tape or is considered by you as likely
to be performed, whether such Work is composed prior to the execution of this agreement or hereafter during the Period, you will
promptly furnish to us a completed clearance form with respect to each such Work.

(c) If requested by us in writing, you will promptly furnish to us a legible lead sheet or other written or printed copy
of a Work.

3. The submission of each clearance form pursuant to paragraph 2 shall constitute a warranty and representation by you that
all of the information contained thereon is true and correct and that no performing rights in such Work have been granted to or
reserved by others except as specifically set forth therein in connection with Works heretofore written or co-written by you.

4. Except as otherwise provided herein, you hereby grant to us for the Period:

(a) All the rights that you own or acquire publicly to perform, and to license others to perform, anywhere in the world,
any part or all of the Works.

(b) The non-exclusive right to record, and to license others to record, any part or all of any of the Works on electrical
transcriptions, wire, tape, film or otherwise, but only for the purpose of performing such Work publicly by means of radio and
television or for archive or audition purposes. This right does not include recording for the purpose of sale to the public or for
the purpose of synchronization (i) with motion pictures intended primarily for theatrical exhibition or (ii) with programs distributed
by means of syndication to broadcasting stations, cable systems or other similar distribution outlets.

(c) The non-exclusive right to adapt or arrange any part or all of any of the Works for performance purposes, and to
license others to do so.

5. Notwithstanding the provisions of sub-paragraph 4(a):

(a) The rights granted to us by sub-paragraph 4(a) shall not include the right to perform or license the performance of
more than one song or aria from a dramatic or dramatico-musical work which is an opera, operetta or musical show or more than

five (5) minutes from a dramatic or dramatico-musical work which is a ballet, if such performance is accompanied by the dramatic action, costumes or scenery of that dramatic or dramatico-musical work.

(b) You, together with all the publishers and your co-writers, if any, shall have the right jointly, by written notice to us, to exclude from the grant made by sub-paragraph 4(a) performances of Works comprising more than thirty (30) minutes of a dramatic or dramatico-musical work, but this right shall not apply to such performances from (i) a score originally written for or performed as part of a theatrical or television film, (ii) a score originally written for or performed as part of a radio or television program, or (iii) the original cast, sound track or similar album of a dramatic or dramatico-musical work.

(c) You, the publishers and/or your co-writers, if any, retain the right to issue non-exclusive licenses for performances of a Work or Works in the United States, its territories and possessions (other than to another performing rights licensing organization), provided that within ten (10) days of the issuance of such license we are given written notice thereof and a copy of the license is supplied to us.

6. (a) As full consideration for all rights granted to us hereunder and as security therefor, we agree to pay to you, with respect to each of the Works in which we obtain and retain performing rights during the Period:

(i) For radio and television performances of a Work in the United States, its territories and possessions, amounts calculated pursuant to our then current standard practices upon the basis of the then current performance rates generally paid by us to our affiliated writers for similar performances of similar compositions. The number of performances for which you shall be entitled to payment shall be estimated by us in accordance with our then current system of computing the number of such performances.

You acknowledge that we license performances of the Works of our affiliates by means other than on radio and television, but that unless and until such time as methods are adopted for tabulation of such performances, payment will be based solely on performances in those media and locations then currently surveyed. In the event that during the Period we shall establish a system of separate payment for performances by means other than radio and television, we shall pay you upon the basis of the then current performance rates generally paid by us to our other affiliated writers for similar performances of similar compositions.

(ii) In the case of a Work composed by you with one or more co-writers, the sum payable to you hereunder shall be a pro rata share, determined on the basis of the number of co-writers, unless you shall have transmitted to us a copy of an agreement between you and your co-writers providing for a different division of payment.

(iii) Monies received by us from any performing rights licensing organization outside of the United States, its territories and possessions, which are designated by such performing rights licensing organization as the author's share of foreign performance royalties earned by your Works after the deduction of our then current handling charge applicable to our affiliated writers and in accordance with our then current standard practices of payment for such performances.

(b) Notwithstanding the provisions of sub-paragraph 6(a), we shall have no obligation to make payment hereunder with respect to (i) any performance of a Work which occurs prior to the date on which we have received from you all of the information and material with respect to such Work which is referred to in paragraphs 2 and 3, or (ii) any performance of a Work as to which a direct license as described in sub-paragraph 5(c) has been granted by you, your co-writers, if any, or the publishers, or (iii) any performance for which no license fee shall be collected by us, or (iv) any performance of a Work which you claim was either omitted from or miscalculated on a royalty statement and for which we shall not have received written notice from you of such claimed omission or miscalculation within nine (9) months of the date of such statement.

7. In accordance with our then current standard practices, we will furnish periodic statements to you during each year of the Period showing the monies due pursuant to sub-paragraph 6(a). Each such statement shall be accompanied by payment of the sum thereby shown to be due you, subject to all proper deductions, if any, for taxes, advances or amounts due BMI from you.

8. (a) Nothing in this agreement requires us to continue to license the Works subsequent to the termination of this agreement. In the event that we continue to license your interest in any Work, however, we shall continue to make payments to you for such Work for so long as you do not make or purport to make directly or indirectly any grant of performing rights in such Work to any other licensing organization. The amounts of such payments shall be calculated pursuant to our then current standard practices upon the basis of the then current performance rates generally paid by us to our affiliated writers for similar performances of similar compositions. You agree to notify us by registered or certified mail of any grant or purported grant by you directly or indirectly of performing rights to any other performing rights organization within ten (10) days from the making of such grant or purported grant and if you fail so to inform us thereof and we make payments to you for any period after the making of any such grant or purported grant, you agree to repay to us all amounts so paid by us promptly with or without demand by us. In addition, if we inquire of you by registered or certified mail, addressed to your last known address, whether you have made any such grant or purported grant and you fail to confirm to us by registered or certified mail within thirty (30) days of the mailing of such inquiry that you have not made any such grant or purported grant, we may, from and after such date, discontinue making any payments to you.

(b) Our obligation to continue payment to you after the termination of this agreement for performances outside of the United States, its territories and possessions, of Works which BMI continues to license after such termination shall be dependent upon our receipt in the United States of payments designated by foreign performing rights organizations as the author's share of foreign performance royalties earned by your Works. Payment of such foreign royalties shall be subject to deduction of our then current handling charge applicable to our affiliated writers and shall be in accordance with our then current standard practices of payment for such performances.

(c) In the event that we have reason to believe that you will receive, are entitled to receive, or are receiving payment from a performing rights licensing organization other than BMI for or based on United States performances of one or more of your Works during a period when such Works were licensed by us pursuant to this agreement, we shall have the right to withhold payment for such performances from you until receipt of evidence satisfactory to us that you were not or will not be so paid by such other organization. In the event that you were or will be so paid or do not supply such evidence within eighteen (18) months from the date of our request therefor, we shall be under no obligation to make any payment to you for performances of such Works during such period.

9. In the event that this agreement shall terminate at a time when, after crediting all earnings reflected by statements rendered to you prior to the effective date of such termination, there remains an unearned balance of advances paid to you by us, such termination shall not be effective until the close of the calendar quarterly period during which (a) you shall repay such unearned balance of advances, or (b) you shall notify us by registered or certified mail that you have received a statement rendered by us at our normal accounting time showing that such unearned balance of advances has been fully recouped by us.

10. You warrant and represent that you have the right to enter into this agreement; that you are not bound by any prior commitments which conflict with your commitments hereunder; that each of the Works, composed by you alone or with one or more co-writers, is original; and that exercise of the rights granted by you herein will not constitute an infringement of copyright or violation of any other right of, or unfair competition with, any person, firm or corporation. You agree to indemnify and hold harmless us, our licensees, the advertisers of our licensees and their respective agents, servants and employees from and against any and all loss or damage resulting from any claim of whatever nature arising from or in connection with the exercise of any of the rights granted by you in this agreement. Upon notification to us or any of the other parties herein indemnified of a claim with respect to any of the Works, we shall have the right to exclude such Work from this agreement and/or to withhold payment of all sums which become due pursuant to this agreement or any modification thereof until receipt of satisfactory written evidence that such claim has been withdrawn, settled or adjudicated.

11. (a) We shall have the right, upon written notice to you, to exclude from this agreement, at any time, any Work which in our opinion is similar to a previously existing composition and might constitute a copyright infringement, or has a title or music or lyric similar to that of a previously existing composition and might lead to a claim of unfair competition.

(b) In the case of Works which in our opinion are based on compositions in the public domain, we shall have the right, upon written notice to you, either (i) to exclude any such Work from this agreement, or (ii) to classify any such Work as entitled to receive only a fraction of the full credit that would otherwise be given for performances thereof.

(c) In the event that any Work is excluded from this agreement pursuant to paragraph 10 or sub-paragraph 11(a) or (b), all rights in such Work shall automatically revert to you ten (10) days after the date of our notice to you of such exclusion. In the event that a Work is classified for less than full credit under sub-paragraph 11(b)(ii), you shall have the right, by giving notice to us, within ten (10) days after the date of our notice advising you of the credit allocated to the Work, to terminate our rights therein, and all rights in such Work shall thereupon revert to you.

12. In each instance that you write, or are employed or commissioned by a motion picture producer to write, during the Period, all or part of the score of a motion picture intended primarily for exhibition in theaters, or by the producer of a musical show or revue for the legitimate stage to write, during the Period, all or part of the musical compositions contained therein, we agree, on request, to advise the producer of the film that such part of the score as is written by you may be performed as part of the exhibition of said film in theaters in the United States, its territories and possessions, without compensation to us, or to the producer of the musical show or revue that your compositions embodied therein may be performed on the stage with living artists as part of such musical show or revue, without compensation to us. In the event that we notify you that we have established a system for the collection of royalties for performance of the scores of motion picture films in theaters in the United States, its territories and possessions, we shall no longer be obligated to take such action with respect to motion picture scores.

13. You make, constitute and appoint us, or our nominee, your true and lawful attorney, irrevocably during the Period, in our name or that of our nominee, or in your name, or otherwise, in our sole judgment, to do all acts, take all proceedings, execute, acknowledge and deliver any and all instruments, papers, documents, process or pleadings that, in our sole judgment, may be necessary, proper or expedient to restrain infringement of and/or to enforce and protect the rights granted by you hereunder, and to recover damages in respect to or for the infringement or other violation of said rights, and in our sole judgment to join you and/or others in whose names the copyrights to any of the Works may stand; to discontinue, compromise or refer to arbitration, any such actions or proceedings or to make any other disposition of the disputes in relation to the Works, provided that any action or proceeding commenced by us pursuant to the provisions of this paragraph shall be at our sole expense and for our sole benefit. Notwithstanding the foregoing, nothing in this paragraph 13 requires us to take any proceeding or other action against any person, firm, partnership or other entity or any writer or publisher, whether or not affiliated with us, who you claim may be infringing your Works or otherwise violating the rights granted by you hereunder. In addition, you understand and agree that the licensing by us of any musical compositions which you claim may be infringing your Works or otherwise violating the rights granted by you hereunder, shall not constitute an infringement of your Works on our part.

14. BMI shall have the right, in its sole discretion, to terminate this agreement on at least thirty (30) days' notice by registered or certified mail if you, your agents, employees or representatives, directly or indirectly, solicit or accept payment from writers for composing music for lyrics to music or for writing lyrics to music or for reviewing, publishing, promoting, recording or rendering other services connected with the exploitation of any composition, or permit use of your name or your affiliation with us in connection with any of the foregoing. In the event of such termination no payments shall be due to you pursuant to paragraph 8.

15. No monies due or to become due to you shall be assignable, whether by way of assignment, sale or power granted to an attorney-in-fact, without our prior written consent. If any assignment of such monies is made by you without such prior written consent, no rights of any kind against us will be acquired by the assignee, purchaser or attorney-in-fact.

16. In the event that during the Period (a) mail addressed to you at the last address furnished by you pursuant to paragraph 20 shall be returned by the post office, or (b) monies shall not have been earned by you pursuant to paragraph 6 for a period of two consecutive years or more, or (c) you shall die, BMI shall have the right to terminate this agreement on at least thirty (30) days' notice by registered or certified mail addressed to the last address furnished by you pursuant to paragraph 20 and, in the case of your death, to the representative of your estate, if known to BMI. In the event of such termination no payments shall be due to you pursuant to paragraph 8.

17. You acknowledge that the rights obtained by you pursuant to this agreement constitute rights to payment of money and that during the Period we shall hold title to the performing rights granted to us hereunder. In the event that during the Period you shall file a petition in bankruptcy, such a petition shall be filed against you, you shall make an assignment for the benefit of creditors, you shall consent to the appointment of a receiver or trustee for all or part of your property, or you shall institute or shall have instituted against you any other insolvency proceeding under the United States bankruptcy laws or any other applicable law, we shall retain title to the performing rights in all Works the rights to which are granted to us hereunder and shall subrogate your trustee in bankruptcy or receiver and any subsequent purchasers from them to your right to payment of money for said Works in accordance with the terms and conditions of this agreement.

18. (a) You hereby authorize us to negotiate for and collect royalties or monies to which you may become entitled as a writer pursuant to the Audio Home Recording Act of 1992 and/or any amendments thereto or substitutions therefor and, to the extent possible, collect for and distribute to you royalties arising from or as compensation for home recording in countries outside the United States, its territories and possessions. This authorization with respect to royalties and monies under the Audio Home Recording Act of 1992 may be revoked by you at the end of any calendar year on prior written notice by you to us by registered or certified mail. Such revocation shall be effective beginning with the calendar year subsequent to the time of notice and shall in no way affect the Period of this agreement with respect to any of the other rights granted to BMI by you hereunder.

(b) We agree to distribute to you royalties and monies collected by us pursuant to the authorization granted in sub-paragraph 18(a), pursuant to our then prevailing practices, including deduction of our expenses therefor.

19. All disputes of any kind, nature or description arising in connection with the terms and conditions of this agreement shall be submitted to the American Arbitration Association in New York, New York, for arbitration under its then prevailing rules, the arbitrator(s) to be selected as follows: Each of us shall, by written notice to the other, have the right to appoint one arbitrator. If, within ten (10) days following the giving of such notice by one of us, the other shall not, by written notice, appoint another arbitrator, the first arbitrator shall be the sole arbitrator. If two arbitrators are so appointed, they shall appoint a third arbitrator. If ten (10) days elapse after the appointment of the second arbitrator and the two arbitrators are unable to agree upon the third arbitrator, then either of us may, in writing, request the American Arbitration Association to appoint the third arbitrator. The award made in the arbitration shall be binding and conclusive on both of us and shall include the fixing of the costs, expenses and reasonable attorneys' fees of arbitration, which shall be borne by the unsuccessful party. Judgment may be entered in New York State Supreme Court or any other court having jurisdiction.

20. You agree to notify our Department of Writer/Publisher Administration promptly in writing of any change in your address. Any notice sent to you pursuant to the terms of this agreement shall be valid if addressed to you at the last address so furnished by you.

21. This agreement constitutes the entire agreement between you and us, cannot be changed except in a writing signed by you and us and shall be governed and construed pursuant to the laws of the State of New York.

22. In the event that any part or parts of this agreement are found to be void by a court of competent jurisdiction, the remaining part or parts shall nevertheless be binding with the same force and effect as if the void part or parts were deleted from this agreement.

Very truly yours,

BROADCAST MUSIC, INC.

ACCEPTED AND AGREED TO:

By...

....   Vice President

4/94

Form 36

BMI Publisher Agreement

889

BMI AGREEMENT made on .... between BROADCAST MUSIC, INC. ("BMI"), a

New York corporation, whose address is 320 West 57th Street, New York, N.Y. 10019-3790 and ....

....

a .... doing business as ....

.... ("Publisher"), whose address is ....

....

WITNESSETH:

FIRST: The term of this agreement shall be the period from ....

to ...., and continuing thereafter for additional periods of five (5) years each unless terminated by either party at the end of such initial period or any additional period, upon notice by registered or certified mail not more than six (6) months or less than three (3) months prior to the end of any such period.

SECOND: As used in this agreement, the word "Work" or "Works" shall mean:

A. All musical compositions (including the musical segments and individual compositions written for a dramatic or dramatico-musical work) whether published or unpublished, now owned or copyrighted by Publisher or in which Publisher owns or controls performing rights, and

B. All musical compositions (including the musical segments and individual compositions written for a dramatic or dramatico-musical work) whether published or unpublished, in which hereafter during the term Publisher acquires ownership of copyright or ownership or control of the performing rights, from and after the date of the acquisition by Publisher of such ownership or control.

THIRD: Except as otherwise provided herein, Publisher hereby sells, assigns and transfers to BMI, its successors or assigns, for the term of this agreement:

A. All the rights which Publisher owns or acquires publicly to perform, and to license others to perform, anywhere in the world, any part or all the Works.

B. The non-exclusive right to record, and to license others to record, any part or all of any of the Works on electrical transcriptions, wire, tape, film or otherwise, but only for the purpose of performing such Work publicly by means of radio and television or for archive or audition purposes. This right does not include recording for the purpose of sale to the public or for the purpose of synchronization (1) with motion pictures intended primarily for theatrical exhibition or (2) with programs distributed by means of syndication to broadcasting stations, cable systems or other similar distribution outlets.

C. The non-exclusive right to adapt or arrange any part or all of any of the Works for performance purposes, and to license others to do so.

FOURTH: Notwithstanding the provisions of subparagraph A of paragraph THIRD hereof:

A. The rights granted to BMI by said subparagraph A shall not include the right to perform or license the performance of more than one song or aria from a dramatic or dramatico-musical work which is an opera, operetta or musical show or more than five (5) minutes from a dramatic or dramatico-musical work which is a ballet, if such performance is accompanied by the dramatic action, costumes or scenery of that dramatic or dramatico-musical work.

B. Publisher, together with all the writers and co-publishers, if any, shall have the right jointly, by written notice to BMI, to exclude from the grant made by subparagraph A of paragraph THIRD hereof performances of Works comprising more than thirty (30) minutes of a dramatic or dramatico-musical work, but this right shall not apply to such performances from (1) a score originally written for or performed as part of a theatrical or television film, (2) a score originally written for or performed as part of a radio or television program, or (3) the original cast, sound track or similar album of a dramatic or dramatico-musical work.

C. Publisher, the writers and/or co-publishers, if any, retain the right to issue non-exclusive licenses for performances of a Work or Works in the United States, its territories and possessions (other than to another performing rights licensing organization), provided that within ten (10) days of the issuance of such license BMI is given written notice thereof and a copy of the license is supplied to BMI.

FIFTH:

A. As full consideration for all rights granted to BMI hereunder and as security therefor, BMI agrees to make the following payments to Publisher with respect to each of the Works in which BMI has performing rights:

(1) For radio and television performances of Works in the United States, its territories and possessions, BMI will pay amounts calculated pursuant to BMI's then standard practices upon the basis of the then current performance rates generally paid by BMI to its affiliated publishers for similar performances of similar compositions. The number of performances for which Publisher shall be entitled to payment shall be estimated by BMI in accordance with its then current system of computing the number of such performances.

Publisher acknowledges that BMI licenses performances of the Works of its affiliates by means other than on radio and television, but that unless and until such time as methods are adopted for tabulation of and payment for such performances, payment will be based solely on performances in those media and locations then currently surveyed. In the event that during the term of this agreement BMI shall establish a system of separate payment for performances by means other than radio and television, BMI shall pay Publisher upon the basis of the then current performance rates generally paid by BMI to its other affiliated publishers for similar performances of similar compositions.

(2) For performances of Works outside of the United States, its territories and possessions, BMI will pay to Publisher monies received by BMI in the United States from any performing rights licensing organization which are designated by such organization as the publisher's share of foreign performance royalties earned by any of the Works after the deduction of BMI's then current handling charge applicable to its affiliated publishers and in accordance with BMI's then standard practices of payment for such performances.

(3) In the case of Works which, or rights in which, are owned by Publisher jointly with one or more other publishers, the sum payable to Publisher under this subparagraph A shall be a pro rata share determined on the basis of the number of publishers, unless BMI shall have received from Publisher a copy of an agreement or other document signed by all of the publishers providing for a different division of payment.

B. Notwithstanding the provisions of subparagraph A of this paragraph FIFTH, BMI shall have no obligation to make payment hereunder with respect to (1) any performance of a Work which occurs prior to the date on which BMI shall have received from

Publisher of all the material with respect to such Work referred to in subparagraph A of paragraph TENTH hereof, and in the case of foreign performances, the information referred to in subparagraph B of paragraph FOURTEENTH hereof, or (2) any performance of a Work as to which a direct license as described in subparagraph C of paragraph FOURTH hereof has been granted by Publisher, its co-publishers or the writers, or (3) any performance for which no license fees shall be collected by BMI, or (4) any performance of a Work which Publisher claims was either omitted from or miscalculated on a royalty statement and for which BMI shall not have received written notice from Publisher of such claimed omission or miscalculation within nine (9) months of the date of such statement.

SIXTH: In accordance with BMI's then current standard practices, BMI will furnish periodic statements to Publisher during each year of the term showing the monies due pursuant to subparagraph A of paragraph FIFTH hereof. Each such statement shall be accompanied by payment of the sum thereby shown to be due to Publisher, subject to all proper deductions, if any, for taxes, advances or amounts due to BMI from Publisher.

SEVENTH:

A.   Nothing in this agreement requires BMI to continue to license the Works subsequent to the termination of this agreement. In the event that BMI continues to license Publisher's interest in any Work, however, BMI shall continue to make payments to Publisher for such Work for so long as Publisher does not make or purport to make directly or indirectly any grant of performing rights in such Work to any other licensing organization. The amounts of such payments shall be calculated pursuant to BMI's then current standard practices upon the basis of the then current performance rates generally paid by BMI to its affiliated publishers for similar performances of similar compositions. Publisher agrees to notify BMI by registered or certified mail of any grant or purported grant by Publisher directly or indirectly of performing rights to any other performing rights organization within ten (10) days from the making of such grant or purported grant and if Publisher fails so to inform BMI thereof and BMI makes payments to Publisher for any period after the making of any such grant or purported grant, Publisher agrees to repay to BMI all amounts so paid by BMI promptly with or without demand by BMI. In addition, if BMI inquires of Publisher by registered or certified mail, addressed to Publisher's last known address, whether Publisher has made any such grant or purported grant and Publisher fails to confirm to BMI by registered or certified mail within thirty (30) days of the mailing of such inquiry that Publisher has not made any such grant or purported grant, BMI may, from and after such date, discontinue making any payments to Publisher.

B.   BMI's obligation to continue payment to Publisher after the termination of this agreement for performances outside of the United States, its territories and possessions, of Works which BMI continues to license after such termination shall be dependent upon BMI's receipt in the United States of payments designated by foreign performing rights licensing organizations as the publisher's share of foreign performance royalties earned by the Works. Payment of such foreign royalties shall be subject to deduction of BMI's then current handling charge applicable to its affiliated publishers and shall be in accordance with BMI's then standard practices of payment for such performances.

C.   In the event that BMI has reason to believe that Publisher will receive, or is entitled to receive, or is receiving payment from a performing rights licensing organization other than BMI for or based on United States performances of one or more of the Works during a period when such Works were licensed by BMI pursuant to this agreement, BMI shall have the right to withhold payment for such performances from Publisher until receipt of evidence satisfactory to BMI that Publisher was not or will not be so paid by such other organization. In the event that Publisher was or will be so paid or does not supply such evidence within eighteen (18) months from the date of BMI's request therefor, BMI shall be under no obligation to make any payment to Publisher for performances of such Works during such period.

EIGHTH: In the event that this agreement shall terminate at a time when, after crediting all earnings reflected by statements rendered to Publisher prior to the effective date of such termination, there remains an unearned balance of advances paid to Publisher by BMI, such termination shall not be effective until the close of the calendar quarterly period during which (A) Publisher shall repay such unearned balance of advances, or (B) Publisher shall notify BMI by registered or certified mail that Publisher has received a statement rendered by BMI at its normal accounting time showing that such unearned balance of advances has been fully recouped by BMI.

NINTH:

A.   BMI shall have the right, upon written notice to Publisher, to exclude from this agreement, at any time, any Work which in BMI's opinion is similar to a previously existing composition and might constitute a copyright infringement, or has a title or music or lyric similar to that of a previously existing composition and might lead to a claim of unfair competition.

B.   In the case of Works which in the opinion of BMI are based on compositions in the public domain, BMI shall have the right, at any time, upon written notice to Publisher, either (1) to exclude any such Work from this agreement, or (2) to classify any such Work as entitled to receive only a stated fraction of the full credit that would otherwise be given for performances thereof.

C.   In the event that any Work is excluded from this agreement pursuant to subparagraph A or B of this paragraph NINTH, or pursuant to subparagraph C of paragraph TWELFTH hereof, all rights of BMI in such Work shall automatically revert to Publisher ten (10) days after the date of the notice of such exclusion given by BMI to Publisher. In the event that a Work is classified for less than full credit under subparagraph B(2) of this paragraph NINTH, Publisher shall have the right, by giving notice to BMI within ten (10) days after the date of BMI's notice to Publisher of the credit allocated to such Work, to terminate all rights in such Work granted to BMI herein and all such rights of BMI in such Work shall thereupon revert to Publisher.

TENTH:

A.   With respect to each of the Works which has been or shall be published or recorded commercially or synchronized with motion picture or television film or tape or which Publisher considers likely to be performed, Publisher agrees to furnish to BMI:

(1) A completed clearance form available in blank from BMI, unless a cue sheet with respect to such Work is furnished pursuant to subparagraph A(3) of this paragraph TENTH.

(2) If such Work is based on a composition in the public domain, a legible lead sheet or other written or printed copy of such Work setting forth the lyrics, if any, and music correctly metered; provided that with respect to all other Works, such copy need be furnished only if requested by BMI pursuant to subsection (b) of subparagraph D(2) of this paragraph TENTH.

(3) If such Work has been or shall be synchronized with or otherwise used in connection with motion picture or television film or tape, a cue sheet showing the title, writers, publisher and nature and duration of the use of the Work in such film or tape.

B.   Publisher shall submit the material described in subparagraph A of this paragraph TENTH with respect to Works heretofore published, recorded or synchronized within ten (10) days after the execution of this agreement and with respect to any of the Works hereafter so published, recorded, synchronized or likely to be performed prior to the date of publication or release of the recording, film or tape or anticipated performance.

C.   The submission of each clearance form or cue sheet shall constitute a warranty and representation by Publisher that all of the information contained thereon is true and correct and that no performing rights in any of the Works listed thereon have been granted to or reserved by others except as specifically set forth therein.

D.   Publisher agrees:

(1) To secure and maintain copyright protection of the Works pursuant to the Copyright Law of the United States and pursuant to the laws of such other nations of the world where such protection is afforded; and to give BMI, upon request, prompt written notice of the date and number of copyright registration and/or renewal of each Work registered in the United States Copyright Office.

(2) At BMI's request:

(a) To register each unpublished and published Work in the United States Copyright Office pursuant to the Copyright Law of the United States.

(b) To obtain and deliver to BMI copies of: unpublished and published Works; copyright registration and/or renewal certificates issued by the United States Copyright Office; any agreements, assignments, instruments or documents of any kind by which Publisher obtained the right to publicly perform and/or the right to publish, co-publish or sub-publish any of the Works.

E. Publisher agrees to give BMI prompt notice by registered or certified mail in each instance when, pursuant to the Copyright Law of the United States, (1) the rights granted to BMI by Publisher in any Work shall revert to the writer or the writer's representative, or (2) copyright protection of any Work shall terminate.

ELEVENTH: Publisher warrants and represents that:

A. Publisher has the right to enter into this agreement; Publisher is not bound by any prior commitments which conflict with its undertakings herein; the rights granted by Publisher to BMI herein are the sole and exclusive property of Publisher and are free from all adverse encumbrances and claims; and exercise of such rights will not constitute infringement of copyright or violation of any right of, or unfair competition with, any person, firm, corporation or association.

B. Except with respect to Works in which the possession of performing rights by another person, firm, corporation or association is specifically set forth on a clearance form or cue sheet submitted to BMI pursuant to subparagraph A of paragraph TENTH hereof, Publisher has performing rights in each of the Works by virtue of written grants thereof to Publisher signed by the authors and composers or other owners of such Work.

TWELFTH:

A. Publisher agrees to defend, indemnify, save and hold BMI, its licensees, the advertisers of its licensees and their respective agents, servants and employees, free and harmless from and against any and all demands, loss, damage, suits, judgments, recoveries and costs, including counsel fees, resulting from any claim of whatever nature arising from or in connection with the exercise of any of the rights granted by Publisher in this agreement; provided, however, that the obligations of Publisher under this paragraph TWELFTH shall not apply to any matter added to, or changes made in, any Work by BMI or its licensees.

B. Upon the receipt by BMI or any of the other parties herein indemnified of any notice, demand, process, papers, writ or pleading, by which any such claim, demand, suit or proceeding is made or commenced against them, or any of them, which Publisher shall be obliged to defend hereunder, BMI shall, as soon as may be practicable, give Publisher notice thereof and deliver to Publisher such papers or true copies thereof, and BMI shall have the right to participate and direct such defense on behalf of BMI and/or its licensees by counsel of its own choice, at its own expense. Publisher agrees to cooperate with BMI in all such matters.

C. In the event of such notification of claim or service of process on any of the parties herein indemnified, BMI shall have the right, from the date thereof, to exclude the Work with respect to which a claim is made from this agreement and/or to withhold payment of all sums which may become due pursuant to this agreement or any modification thereof until receipt of satisfactory written evidence that such claim has been withdrawn, settled or adjudicated.

THIRTEENTH: Publisher makes, constitutes and appoints BMI, or its nominee, Publisher's true and lawful attorney, irrevocably during the term hereof, in the name of BMI or that of its nominee, or in Publisher's name, or otherwise, in BMI's sole judgment, to do all acts, take all proceedings, and execute, acknowledge and deliver any and all instruments, papers, documents, process or pleadings that, in BMI's sole judgment, may be necessary, proper or expedient to restrain infringement of and/or to enforce and protect the rights granted by Publisher hereunder, and to recover damages in respect of or for the infringement or other violation of said rights, and in BMI's sole judgment to join Publisher and/or others in whose names the copyrights to any of the Works may stand, and to discontinue, compromise or refer to arbitration, any such actions or proceedings or to make any other disposition of the disputes in relation to the Works; provided that any action or proceeding commenced by BMI pursuant to the provisions of this paragraph THIRTEENTH shall be at its sole expense and for its sole benefit. Notwithstanding the foregoing, nothing in this paragraph THIRTEENTH requires BMI to take any proceeding or other action against any person, firm, partnership or other entity or any writer or publisher, whether or not affiliated with BMI, who Publisher claims may be infringing Publisher's Works or otherwise violating the rights granted by Publisher hereunder. In addition, Publisher understands and agrees that the licensing by BMI of any musical compositions which Publisher claims may be infringing Publisher's Works or otherwise violating the rights granted by Publisher hereunder, shall not constitute an infringement of Publisher's Works on BMI's part.

FOURTEENTH:

A. It is acknowledged that BMI has heretofore entered into, and may during the term of this agreement enter into, contracts with performing rights licensing organizations for the licensing of public performing rights controlled by BMI in territories outside of the United States, its territories and possessions (herein called "Foreign Territories"). Upon Publisher's written request, BMI agrees to permit Publisher to grant performing rights in any or all of the Works for any Foreign Territory for which, at the time such request is received, BMI has not entered into any such contract with a performing rights licensing organization; provided, however, that any such grant of performing rights by Publisher shall terminate at such time when BMI shall have entered into a contract with a performing rights licensing organization covering such Foreign Territory and shall have notified Publisher thereof. Nothing herein contained, however, shall be deemed to restrict Publisher from assigning to its foreign publisher or representative the right to collect a part or all of the publishers' performance royalties earned by any or all of the Works in any Foreign Territory as part of an agreement for the publication, exploitation or representation of such Works in such territory, whether or not BMI has entered into such a contract with a performing rights licensing organization covering such territory.

B. Publisher agrees to notify BMI promptly in writing in each instance when publication, exploitation or other rights in any or all of the Works are granted for any Foreign Territory. Such notice shall set forth the title of the Work, the Foreign Territory or Territories involved, the period of such grant, the name of the person, firm, corporation or association entitled to collect performance royalties earned in the Foreign Territory and the amount of such share. Within ten (10) days after the execution of this agreement Publisher agrees to submit to BMI, in writing, a list of all Works as to which Publisher has, prior to the effective date of this agreement, granted to any person, firm, corporation or association performing rights and/or the right to collect publisher performance royalties earned in any Foreign Territory.

FIFTEENTH: BMI shall have the right, in its sole discretion, to terminate this agreement if:

A. Publisher, its agents, employees, representatives or affiliated companies, directly or indirectly during the term of this agreement:

(1) Solicits or accepts payment from or on behalf of authors for composing music for lyrics, or from or on behalf of composers for writing lyrics to music.

(2) Solicits or accepts music and/or lyrics from composers or authors in consideration of any payments to be made by or on behalf of such composers or authors for reviewing, arranging, promotion, publication, recording or any other services connected with the exploitation of any composition.

(3) Permits Publisher's name, or the fact of its affiliation with BMI, to be used by any other person, firm, corporation or association engaged in any of the practices described in subparagraphs A(1) and A(2) of this paragraph FIFTEENTH.

(4) Submits to BMI, as one of the Works to come within this agreement, any musical composition with respect to which any payments described in subparagraphs A(1) and A(2) of this paragraph FIFTEENTH have been made by or on behalf of a composer or author to any person, firm, corporation or association.

B. Publisher, its agents, employees or representatives directly or indirectly during the term of this agreement makes any effort to ascertain from, or offers any inducement or consideration to, anyone, including but not limited to any radio or television licensee of BMI or to the agents, employees or representatives of BMI or of any such licensee, for information regarding the time or times when any such BMI licensee is to report its performances to BMI, or to attempt in any way to manipulate performances or affect the representative character or accuracy of BMI's system of sampling or logging performances.

C. Publisher fails to notify BMI's Department of Writer/Publisher Administration promptly in writing of any change of firm name, ownership or address of Publisher.

In the event BMI exercises its right to terminate this agreement pursuant to the provisions of subparagraphs A, B or C of this paragraph FIFTEENTH, BMI shall give Publisher at least thirty (30) days' notice by registered or certified mail of such termination. In the event of such termination, no payments shall be due to Publisher pursuant to paragraph SEVENTH hereof.

SIXTEENTH: In the event that during the term of this agreement (1) monies shall not have been earned by Publisher pursuant to paragraph FIFTH hereof for a period of two consecutive years or more, or (2) the proprietor, if Publisher is a sole proprietorship, shall die, BMI shall have the right to terminate this agreement on at least thirty (30) days' notice by registered or certified mail addressed to the last address furnished by Publisher in writing to BMI's Department of Writer/Publisher Administration and, in the case of the death of a sole proprietor, to the representative of said proprietor's estate, if known to BMI. In the event of such termination, no payments shall be due Publisher pursuant to paragraph SEVENTH hereof.

SEVENTEENTH: Publisher acknowledges that the rights obtained by it pursuant to this agreement constitute rights to payment of money and that during the term BMI shall hold title to the performing rights granted to BMI hereunder. In the event that during the term Publisher shall file a petition in bankruptcy, such a petition shall be filed against Publisher, Publisher shall make an assignment for the benefit of creditors, Publisher shall consent to the appointment of a receiver or trustee for all or part of its property, Publisher shall file a petition for corporate reorganization or arrangement under the United States bankruptcy laws, or Publisher shall institute or shall have instituted against it any other insolvency proceeding under the United States bankruptcy laws or any other applicable law, or, in the event Publisher is a partnership, all of the general partners of said partnership shall be adjudged bankrupts, BMI shall retain title to the performing rights in all Works the rights to which are granted to BMI hereunder and shall subrogate Publisher's trustee in bankruptcy or receiver and any subsequent purchasers from them to Publisher's right to payment of money for said Works in accordance with the terms and conditions of this agreement.

EIGHTEENTH: All disputes of any kind, nature or description arising in connection with the terms and conditions of this agreement shall be submitted to the American Arbitration Association in New York, New York, for arbitration under its then prevailing rules, the arbitrator(s) to be selected as follows:

Each of the parties shall, by written notice to the other, have the right to appoint one arbitrator. If, within ten (10) days following the giving of such notice by one party, the other shall not, by written notice, appoint another arbitrator, the first arbitrator shall be the sole arbitrator. If two arbitrators are so appointed, they shall appoint a third arbitrator. If ten (10) days elapse after the appointment of the second arbitrator and the two arbitrators are unable to agree upon the third arbitrator, then either party may, in writing, request the American Arbitration Association to appoint the third arbitrator. The award made in the arbitration shall be binding and conclusive on the parties and shall include the fixing of the costs, expenses and reasonable attorneys' fees of arbitration, which shall be borne by the unsuccessful party. Judgment may be entered in New York State Supreme Court or any other court having jurisdiction.

NINETEENTH: Publisher agrees that it shall not, without the written consent of BMI, assign any of its rights hereunder. No rights of any kind against BMI will be acquired by the assignee if any such purported assignment is made by Publisher without such written consent.

TWENTIETH: Any notice sent to Publisher pursuant to the terms of this agreement shall be valid if addressed to Publisher at the last address furnished in writing by Publisher to BMI's Department of Writer/Publisher Administration.

TWENTY-FIRST: This agreement constitutes the entire agreement between BMI and Publisher, cannot be changed except in a writing signed by BMI and Publisher and shall be governed and construed pursuant to the laws of the State of New York.

TWENTY-SECOND: In the event that any part or parts of this agreement are found to be void by a court of competent jurisdiction, the remaining part or parts shall nevertheless be binding with the same force and effect as if the void part or parts were deleted from this agreement.

IN WITNESS WHEREOF, the parties hereto have caused this agreement to be duly executed as of the day and year first above written.

BROADCAST MUSIC, INC.

By...
Vice President

....

By...

(Title of Signer)...

Form 37

EXCLUSIVE SONGWRITING AND CO-PUBLISHING AGREEMENT

This agreement ("Agreement") is made and entered into this _____ day of _____, 1997, by and between _____ ("Publisher"), at _____, and _____ (such songwriters shall be collectively referred to hereunder as "Writers," whereas the publishing companies of such songwriters shall be collectively referred to hereunder as "Co-Publishers"), all c/o _____.

1. (a) The initial contract period ("Initial Period") of this Agreement shall commence upon the date hereof and shall terminate ten (10) business days after receipt by Publisher of written notice confirming delivery to and acceptance by the applicable record company of the third studio album hereunder which, when released, would satisfy the "Minimum Release Requirement" (hereafter defined) for the "Renewal Period" (hereafter defined), as well as the receipt by Publisher of written confirmation from such record company of a specifically scheduled date of release for such album, provided, however, that all musical compositions embodied on such third studio album, as well as all musical compositions created after release of the second studio album, shall not be subject to this Agreement if Publisher does not exercise its option for the Renewal Period (subject to the last sentence of subparagraph 1[b] below).

(b) Publisher shall have one (1) option to renew this Agreement for one (1) additional contract period ("Renewal Period"). The Renewal Period shall be deemed to have commenced upon termination of the Initial Period if Publisher shall have given Writers written notice of its exercise of its option for the Renewal Period no later than the end of the Initial Period, and shall terminate upon satisfaction of the Minimum Release Requirement for the Renewal Period.

(c) For all purposes of 1(a)-(b) above, copies of the third studio album must be presented to Publisher before Publisher need exercise its option for the Renewal Period. (The Initial Period and Renewal Period, to the extent Publisher has exercised its option for such period, shall be collectively referred to as the "Term" hereunder.)

2. (a) Writers and Co-Publishers hereby grant, convey and assign to Publisher fifty percent (50%) of the copyright ownership and any and all other rights, titles and interests, throughout the universe (the "Territory"), of every kind, nature and description, existing under any present or future law, other governmental regulation or judicial decision, that are attributable to Writers's fractional creative shares of all musical compositions partially or wholly written or composed by Writers, whether alone or in collaboration with other songwriters: (i) prior to the Term hereof ("Back Catalog"), and Writers and Co-Publishers warrant that all such compositions are listed on Schedule "A," attached hereto (with the

exception of musical compositions described in 2[e] below), along with accurate identification of other Songwriters and music publishers, and the percentages attributable to each; (ii) during the term of this Agreement ("Term Compositions"); as well as any such rights as are attributable to any ownership share derived from the creative contribution of any songwriters other than Writers in the creation of any musical compositions, whether or not co-written by Writers ("Other Songwriters"), that are embodied on any recording whatsoever featuring the performances of one or more of Writers (or any group of which one or more of Writers are then members), and which ownership share has been acquired by Writers, Co-Publishers or any company owned or controlled by Writers or Co-Publishers, in whole or in part, directly or indirectly, prior to or during the term hereof ("Acquired Share"), regardless of when such Acquired Share was created, provided, however, that: (A) with respect to any so-called "catalog" or other such purchase Writers or Co-Publishers wish to make which requires an advance or other payment, Publisher shall have only the right to match such offer in accordance with the terms of Paragraph 25 hereunder; (B) in the event Publisher pays such advance and makes such purchase ("Special Acquired Share") such catalog shall be co-published between Co-Publishers and Publisher (and also, if applicable, with the music publishing designee of the third party selling, assigning, conveying or otherwise transferring such rights ["Third Party"]) in accordance with the terms hereof, and, to the extent such advance or purchase price is not recoupable from the Third Party or any other person or entity, fifty percent (50%) of such advance or purchase price shall be recoupable solely from the royalties and other sums (except other advances) payable to Co-Publishers generated by such Special Acquired Share; and (C) any Special Acquired Share shall otherwise be subject to all terms and provisions hereof respecting any Acquired Share, provided, however, that notwithstanding Subparagraph 22(c) hereunder, Publisher acknowledges that neither Writers nor Co-Publishers make any warranty or other representation concerning the originality of any Acquired Share or Special Acquired Share.

(b) Any musical composition written or composed by Writers, in whole or in part, alone or in collaboration with other Songwriters, which is first commercially exploited (*e.g.*, released, exhibited or broadcast, by means of any form of analog or digital audio or audio-visual product, whether a CD, theatrical motion picture, television program, interactive media device or otherwise) within thirty (30) days following the expiration of the term of this Agreement shall retroactively be deemed created during the Term for purposes of Subparagraphs 2(a)-(c) above, unless: (i) Writers can establish that such musical composition was created after expiration of the Term hereof; or (ii) Publisher has not exercised its option for the Renewal Period hereunder, and such commercial exploitation occurs after the Initial Period, and such exploitation is by means of an audio-only or audio-visual product featuring the performance of one or more of Writers (or any group of which one or more of Writers is a member) and released by the record company to which one or more of the performing Writers is then signed an exclusive recording artist.

(c) Writers shall provide Publisher with the names of all other Songwriters and music publishers for each Composition, as well as the creative and ownership percentages of all such parties, and Writers further agree to render reasonable assistance to Publisher in obtaining the signatures of such collaborators and other music publishers for any documents deemed necessary by Publisher to verify such information.

(d) Respecting Term Compositions, the assignment of ownership and other rights to Publisher hereunder derived from Writers's creative share shall be deemed to occur immediately upon creation of such Composition. Therefore, neither Writers nor Co-Publishers shall have any right, power or authority to assign any portion of such ownership or other rights to any party without Publisher's express written consent.

(e) Musical compositions Writers have previously written or composed, in whole or in part, alone or in collaboration with other songwriters, and for which no ownership or administration rights can be assigned to Publisher hereunder, because such Compositions are the subject of previously existing agreements with persons or business entities unrelated to Writers or Co-Publishers (also identified on Schedule "B") which would prevent such an assignment to Publisher, are listed on Schedule "B," attached hereto ("Schedule 'B' Compositions"), and Writers warrants the accuracy of such list. Writers shall submit any written agreements for inspection by Publisher. If, at any time during the Term hereof, any ownership or administration rights in any such Schedule "B" Compositions are re-assigned to or revert to Writers, Co-publishers or any entity owned or controlled, in whole or in part, directly or indirectly, by Writers or Co-Publishers, whether by operation of law or otherwise, all such reverted or reassigned rights shall be immediately deemed assigned to Publisher hereunder, and such Composition shall then become part of Back Catalog.

3. Notwithstanding the co-ownership of the Compositions or any Acquired Share, the grant, conveyance and assignment to Publisher from Writers and Co-Publishers in Paragraph 2 shall vest exclusively in Publisher the sole and exclusive right, throughout the Territory, on behalf of Writers, Publisher and Co-Publishers:

(a) to register the copyright for the Compositions and any Acquired Share in the name of Publisher and Co-Publishers (and Publisher hereby expressly assumes the obligation for such registration as to any Compositions or Acquired Share that have been commercially exploited), or for any Compositions or Acquired Shares that have previously been registered for copyright, to record an assignment to Publisher of the appropriate percentage of such copyright in accordance with the terms of this Agreement, but fully subject to the re-assignment of all rights hereunder to Writers and Co-Publishers when required by the terms of Paragraph 22 hereunder;

(b) subject to any restrictions expressed in this Agreement, to administer, use and exploit all interests in the Compositions and any Acquired Share generally described in Paragraph 2 in any manner, mode or medium, of every kind, nature or description, whether such manner, mode or medium is now known and developed, or is developed at any time in the future,

(c) to receive and collect one hundred percent (100%) of all music publishing income derived from the ownership and administration rights granted to Publisher hereunder, and generated from any use, exploitation or other exercise of rights respecting the Compositions or any Acquired Share in the Territory, with the sole exception of the "songwriters' share" payable to Writers or Other Songwriters for public performance income from any performing rights society (as such share is now commonly computed and understood in the music publishing industry);

(d) to make or authorize any and all revisions, arrangements, adaptations, translations, dramatizations or other musical or non-musical works derived in whole or in part from the Compositions; and

(e) to enter into and execute, on behalf of Publisher, Writers and Co-Publishers, any and all agreements or other legal documents respecting the Compositions in Publisher's sole discretion, upon terms determined solely in Publisher's reasonable business judgment.

4. With respect to the use of any Compositions Writers desire to create for television programs or theatrical motion pictures, Publisher acknowledges that producers of such entertainment properties may require assignment of a portion of music publishing income and administration rights in such situations. In such event, Publisher shall negotiate with such parties in good faith, in Publisher's sole discretion and business judgment, respecting the use of any Compositions in such entertainment properties, provided, however, that mutual consultation and agreement between and among Writers, Co-Publishers and Publisher shall be required, on a case-by-case basis, regarding the issue of whether any co-publishing ownership or income rights requested by such party shall be assigned from Publisher's and Co-Publishers' share jointly, as well as the issue of whether Writers shall be permitted to enter into a direct agreement with any such party respecting creation of any musical work.

5. During the Initial Period no less than two (2) "Qualifying Albums" (as such term is defined below) shall be released, and during the Renewal Period (if Publisher exercises its option for such contract period), one (1) Qualifying Album shall be released (the foregoing requirement for each contract period of the Term shall be referred to as the "Minimum Release Requirement"). The term "Qualifying Album" shall be defined as a "phonorecord" (as such term is defined under

U.S. Copyright Law) produced, performed and recorded in a recording studio, released and distributed for sale to the public in the United States by a major record company, comprised of no fewer than nine (9) master recordings featuring the performances of Writers, or any group of which any of Writers are regular performing and recording members ("Writers' Group"), embodying musical compositions not previously released for sale to the public on phonorecords featuring the performance of Writers or Writers' Group. No release of an album embodying musical compositions which are essentially versions in a different language of musical compositions previously released in English featuring the performances of Writers shall be deemed a Qualifying Album. For all purposes of this Agreement, a "major record company" shall be defined as a record company which shall effect distribution of recorded products in the Territory embodying Compositions hereunder by or through one of the six (6) major distribution groups now in existence (*e.g.*, EMD [EMI Record Distribution], MCA, SONY, BMG, WEA or POLYGRAM), or any subsequent distribution group of relatively equal size and financial stature to such distribution groups.

6. Subject to the provisions of Paragraphs 7 and 8 below, Publisher shall pay to Writers and Co-Publishers jointly the following advances during the Term:

(a) _____ dollars ($ _____) upon execution of this Agreement;

(b) _____ dollars ($ _____) upon release for sale to the public in the United States of the first Qualifying Album during the Initial Period;

(c) upon release for sale to the public in the United States of the second Qualifying Album during the Initial Period in compliance with the Minimum Release Requirement, an advance equal to seventy-five percent (75%) of the royalties credited to the group for the first Qualifying Album hereunder, with a minimum advance of _____ dollars ($ _____) and a maximum advance of _____ dollars ($_____), provided, however, that if the cumulative accounts of Writers and Co-Publishers are unrecouped at such time, such advance shall be reduced by the amount of the unrecouped balance, but shall be no less than _____ dollars ($_____); and

(d) if Publisher has exercised its option for the Renewal Period, then within ten (10) days after release of third Qualifying Album in compliance with the Minimum Release Requirement, an advance equal to seventy-five percent (75%) of the royalties credited to the group for the second Qualifying Album hereunder, with a minimum advance of _____ dollars ($_____) and a maximum advance of _____ dollars ($ _____), provided, however, that if the cumulative accounts of Writers and Co-Publishers are unrecouped at such time, such advance shall be reduced by the amount of the unrecouped balance, but shall be no less than _____ dollars ($_____).

7. Notwithstanding anything to the contrary expressed or implied in Paragraph 6 or anywhere else in this Agreement, to the extent that the mechanical royalties

payable to Publisher for top-line, U.S. sales of the First Qualifying Album hereunder are equal to less than ten (10) times one hundred percent (100%) of the current statutory rate (10 X 100% X $.0695 = .695/copy), or that royalties payable to Publisher for top-line, U.S. sales of the second or third Qualifying Album hereunder are equal to less than ten (10) times one hundred percent (100%) of statutory rate used by the releasing record company in its formula to determine mechanical royalties payable for the applicable album (with respect to each album hereunder, the "Minimum Per-Album Rate") (customary "controlled composition" reductions in Writers' recording artist agreement, such as for "free goods," "mid-price," "budget line," "close-out," "scrap," etc., shall not affect such determination), the otherwise payable advances described in Paragraph 6 shall be reduced pro-rata accordingly.

8.   (a) After the computations and reductions, if any, required in Paragraphs 6 and 7, and notwithstanding Publisher's acknowledgment and acceptance of the "controlled composition" terms of Writers' current recording artist agreement later in this Agreement, no advance payable pursuant to Paragraphs 6 and 7 shall be paid until receipt by Publisher of written confirmation from the record company releasing the applicable album of specific amounts, if any, that have either been recouped to date, or are then recoupable, from mechanical royalties or any other sums otherwise collectible by Publisher hereunder. To the extent, if any, at the time such advance would otherwise be payable, that any amounts either have been recouped or are claimed to be recoupable by [name of record company] or any other record company from mechanical royalties or other amounts otherwise collectible by Publisher hereunder, and which amounts were incurred on account of any album hereunder or any musical compositions embodied on such albums (including, but not limited to, recoupment for extraneous advances or overbudget recording, packaging, artwork or video costs), Publisher shall deduct from such advance otherwise due hereunder the amount of any such sums either claimed to be recoupable or actually recouped, provided, however, that to the extent any amounts claimed to be recoupable by any such company are subsequently recouped by such company from other sources of income not otherwise payable to Publisher (*e.g.*, recording artist royalties), or to the extent such record company confirms in writing that they no longer deem such amounts recoupable, Publisher shall pay the corresponding amount of any such reduction jointly to Writers and Co-Publishers.

(b) Writers and Co-Publishers warrant and represent that, as of the date of execution of this Agreement, no amounts whatsoever are recoupable by [name of record company] (or any other person or business entity) from mechanical royalties or other amounts otherwise collectible by Publisher hereunder for exploitation of the first Qualifying Album, and nothing in this Paragraph 8 shall be interpreted or construed to negate, dilute or diminish in any manner such warranty, promise and representation.

9. Publisher and Writers shall mutually select the Compositions for which demonstration recordings shall be produced, although Writers shall not be required to perform for such demos, provided, however, that Writers' consent shall be required prior to the recording of any demonstration recording featuring the performance of any individual who is not one of Writers. If Publisher and Writers have both approved a Composition for recording, Publisher shall approve a budget for such recording, and Publisher shall only pay for documented, out-of-pocket costs. If the cost of any demo exceeds the budget approved by Publisher for a given Composition, for any reason attributable solely to Writers, Co-Publishers or any person or business entity retained by Writers or Co-Publishers, Writers and Co-Publishers shall pay such excess costs, unless Publisher pays such costs on behalf of Writers and Co-Publishers, in which event such excess costs shall be one hundred percent (100%) recoupable hereunder. To the extent not constituting a breach of Writers' then current exclusive recording artist agreement, the copyright in the each demonstration recording shall be co-owned by Publisher and Co-Publishers, but neither Publisher, Writers nor Co-Publishers shall have the right to use or license the use of such demonstration recordings, other than for normal activities promoting the applicable Composition, without mutual written consent.

10. Except as otherwise specifically set forth in this Agreement, or otherwise subsequently agreed upon by Writers, Co-Publishers and Publisher, all advances and other chargeable costs described in this Agreement shall be fully recoupable from all income due Writers and Co-Publishers hereunder pursuant to Paragraph 11 from any use, exploitation or other exercise of rights respecting the Compositions, but not from any form of advances.

11. (a) For any use, exploitation or other exercise of rights respecting the Compositions, Publisher shall pay to Writers and Co-Publishers (or credit to Writers' and Co-Publishers' accounts if unrecouped), the following percentages of "gross music publishing income" (as hereafter defined) received by Publisher for the exploitation of the Compositions:

(i) to Writers, fifty percent (50%), and to Co-Publishers, twenty-five percent (25%), of mechanical royalties;

(ii) to Writers, fifty percent (50%), and to Co-Publishers, twenty percent (20%), of all synchronization license fees procured substantially through the efforts of Publisher;

(iii) to Co-Publishers, fifty percent (50%) of the so-called "publisher's share" of public performance royalties; and

(iv) to Writers, fifty percent (50%), and to Co-Publishers, twenty-five percent (25%) of any and all other income sources.

(b) With respect to any Acquired Share, Publisher shall pay Co-Publishers (or credit to Co-Publishers' accounts, if then unrecouped) fifty percent (50%)

of "net music publishing income" (as such term is defined in Subparagraph 12(g) below).

12. All payments (or credits) in Paragraph 11 are subject to the following:

(a) Neither Writers nor Co-Publishers shall be entitled to any portion of any advance payments, guarantee payments, or minimum royalty payments which Publisher may receive in connection with any subpublishing, collection, licensing or other agreement that covers the Compositions, unless such agreement pertains only to one or more of the Compositions, or only to the catalog of Writers.

(b) If Publisher or its affiliates shall ever directly engage in the business of printing, publishing and selling in the United States and Canada printed versions of the Compositions (other than primarily through one exclusive print licensee), then:

(i) for purposes of this Agreement, gross music publishing income for all copies of printed editions actually sold, paid for, and not returned, and for which such income has been received by Publisher, or credited to Publisher against a prior advance, shall be deemed to be twenty percent (20%) of the suggested retail list price ("SRLP") for piano/vocal sheet music, twelve and one-half percent (12-1/2%) of the SRLP for folios other than "personality folios," "fake books" or "educational editions," seventeen and one-half percent (17-1/2%) of the SRLP for personality folios, ten percent (10%) of the SRLP for fake books and educational editions, and ten percent (10%) of the SRLP for all forms of printed editions not encompassed by one of the foregoing descriptions (all of the royalties described in this subparagraph shall be reduced pro-rata to the extent other musical compositions are included in such product which are not covered hereunder);

(ii) the foregoing "deemed" gross music publishing income for each Composition shall be reduced pro-rata to the extent the applicable Composition was less than one hundred percent (100%) created by Writers; and

(iii) with respect to print music sales described in this Subparagraph 12(b), Publisher may maintain a reasonable reserve for anticipated returns, which reserve shall in no event shall exceed twenty-five percent (25%) of such copies distributed, and the reserve established in a particular semi-annual accounting period shall be liquidated within two (2) semi-annual accounting periods thereafter.

(c) The term "gross music publishing income" shall be defined as all music publishing income attributable to either Writers' creative share of each Composition or any Acquired Share and received by Publisher or credited to Publisher. Throughout this Agreement, the term "received by Publisher" shall include only the actual receipts of Publisher, its affiliates or its subsidiaries.

The term "credited to Publisher" shall include only sums credited to the account of Publisher (or any entity owned by Publisher) with an accounting statement in reduction of a prior advance to Publisher (but only to the extent Writers and Co-Publishers did not participate in such advance).

(d) with the exception of costs for demonstration recordings, fifty percent (50%) of the following direct expenses incurred by Publisher shall be recoupable from the amounts otherwise payable to Co-Publishers pursuant to Paragraph 11: audits, reasonable purchases of recorded products (for administrative and promotional purposes only), record promotion, publicity, copyright registration, transcribing for lead sheets, and litigation with third parties (except to the extent such expenses have been recovered or reimbursed from a cash settlement, recovery or award from such litigation). With respect to the costs of demonstration recordings, fifty percent (50%) shall be recoupable from amounts otherwise payable to Writers pursuant to Paragraph 11, and twenty-five percent (25%) shall be recoupable from amounts otherwise payable to Co-Publishers pursuant to Paragraph 11. Nothing in the foregoing shall be interpreted or construed to limit Publisher's right, with respect to any discretionary expenditure requested by Writers or Co-Publishers (e.g., promotion and publicity, travel expenses), to either decline such request or to require Writers and Co-Publishers to agree that one hundred percent (100%) of such amount shall be recoupable hereunder as a condition of Publisher making such payment.

(e) Payments to persons either creating new foreign lyrics or translations of Writers' lyrics (who shall not be paid amounts in excess of those required by societies with jurisdiction over such services) shall be recoupable as follows: (i) flat-fee payments shall be fifty percent (50%) recoupable from Co-Publishers; and (ii) royalty payments shall be deducted from Writers' otherwise payable royalties for such versions.

(f) Respecting any Acquired Share, sums payable to Other Songwriters, as well as any income participation percentage payable to a music publishing company deriving its rights from such Other Songwriters, as well as any direct expenses of Publisher respecting such Acquired Share, including, but not limited to, demo costs and litigation expenses, shall be deducted "off-the-top" from gross music publishing income (except to the extent any such direct expenses have been recouped from some other party), with the remaining balance of income deemed "net music publishing income" from which Co-Publishers shall be paid in accordance with Subparagraph 11(b).

(g) Income derived from any settlement or damages obtained by or awarded to Publisher, Writers or Co-Publishers in any infringement or other legal action against a third party respecting the Compositions shall be payable directly to Publisher, and shall be included in gross music publishing income after the deduction of all actual, direct, out-of-pocket legal fees and costs incurred by

Publisher in obtaining such sums, provided, however, that any recovery by Writers or Co-Publishers, on the one hand, or by Publisher, on the other hand, specifically allocated to any causes of action not mutually possessed by the other (*e.g.*, general right of publicity or privacy, defamation, interference with prospective advantage, etc.) shall be payable directly to the applicable party, and shall not be included in gross music publishing income, provided further, however, that Publisher must approve any settlement agreement purporting to dispose of any claim or cause of action jointly possessed by Publisher.

13. It shall be Writers' sole responsibility to monitor and collect Writers' shares of performing rights payments from Writers' respective performing rights societies or other collection agent. Writers warrant that they and their respective music publishing companies are members of [name of performing rights society], and such society is hereby authorized to pay Publisher or its collection agents one hundred percent (100%) of the "publisher's share" of royalties collected and computed by such society derived from the Compositions.

14.   (a) Publisher shall send accounting statements to Writers and Co-Publishers on or before the last day of February each year respecting gross music publishing income received by Publisher or credited to Publisher during the semi-annual period ending the preceding December 31st, and on or before August 31st each year respecting gross music publishing income received by Publisher or credited to Publisher during the semi-annual period ending the preceding June 30th, accompanied by payment of any amounts due both Writers and Co-Publishers after deduction of any unrecouped advances or other chargeable costs hereunder paid prior to the end of the applicable accounting period.

(b) All advances, reimbursements and accounting statements shall be sent to and made payable to Writers and Co-Publishers as follows: (i) the execution advance shall be sent and made payable to _____, and the tax identification number of such party is _____; (ii) all accounting statements, future advances and future royalties shall be sent and made payable to _____; and (iii) all royalties earned hereunder shall be credited against all unrecouped amounts in the joint account of Writers and Co-Publishers until recouped, regardless of the songwriting or copublishing share hereunder from which such royalties were generated, but with respect to any accounting period ending with no unrecouped balances, royalties earned hereunder shall be separately payable to [names of songwriters] in direct relation to the actual songwriting shares of such parties for the Compositions generating such sums, with all such checks being sent as follows: _____.

(c) Writers and Co-Publishers acknowledge that any future instruction or direction to alter any payee, method of payment or address for payment that is described in Subparagraph 14(b) shall be accepted by Publisher only if contained in a letter of direction signed by all individuals comprising Writers, unless only the Writer requesting such change would be affected by such instruction. Notwithstanding the foregoing, Publisher's manner of "cross-collateralizing" all royalties hereunder against the unrecouped balances in all accounts, regardless of the songwriter to whom the royalties would otherwise be paid if all accounts were recouped, shall not be changed without Publisher's written consent.

15. Writers and Co-Publishers shall have the joint right, at their sole cost and expense, only once per year and once per accounting statement, at Publisher's place of business, during Publisher's normal business hours, after no less than ten (10) business days written notice, to audit Publisher's books and records regarding sums due Writers and Co-Publishers pursuant to any accounting statement received not more than two (2) years prior to the date of the audit, provided, however, that any independent auditor must sign a letter of confidentiality containing terms customary in the industry respecting such audit. With the exception of specific written objections given to Publisher by Writers within two (2) years after the date a particular statement was received by Writers and/or Co-Publishers, each such statement shall be binding upon Writers and Co-Publishers and not subject to objection for any reason. Furthermore, neither Writers nor Co-Publishers may commence any legal action pertaining to royalties earned or due during a particular accounting period, unless such action is filed within three (3) years after the date the accounting statement for such period was received by Writers and/or Co-Publishers. Only for purposes of the foregoing limitations on audits, objections and legal actions respecting accounting statements and accompanying payments, unless Writers notify Publisher within ninety (90) days after the due date of a particular statement and payment that such statement and payment was either late or not received, statements and payments for both Writers and Co-Publishers shall be deemed received ten (10) days after the date due. Failure by Writers or Co-Publishers to submit such notice, however, shall not affect Publisher's obligation hereunder to render such accounting statement and payment thereafter.

16. Writers hereby grant to Publisher the right, which shall be exclusive during the term and non-exclusive thereafter, to use and authorize the use of any legal or professional name used by Writers or any Writers' Group, now or in the future, in connection with the use or exploitation of the Compositions or the institutional advertising of Publisher. The foregoing shall not be construed, however, to prevent or restrict such usage by any record company or other company releasing recorded products featuring the performance by one or both of Writers of a Composition or other musical composition.

17. Writers and Co-Publishers expressly waive any so-called "moral rights" in and to the Compositions which may now or hereafter exist under any law, other governmental regulation or judicial decision throughout the Territory, but only to the extent permissible under any such present or future legal authority.

18. Writers shall not, during the Term of this Agreement, write or compose any musical compositions, directly or indirectly, in whole or in part, alone or in collaboration with others, in which rights derived from Writers' creative contributions will be owned or administered by any party other than Publisher without Publisher's express written consent (the foregoing shall not, however, be interpreted or construed to restrict the rights of Writers' performing rights society to collect public performance income on behalf of Writers). All provisions affecting Writers and Co-Publishers hereunder shall be binding on any other company or business entity owned by, controlled by, or affiliated with, Writers or Co-Publishers, in whole or in part, directly or indirectly.

19.   (a) Publisher acknowledges that Writers are currently signed to one or more agreements with _____ Records ("Record Company") covering, among other things, the licensing and use of musical compositions performed and written, in whole or in part, by Writers ("Record Company Compositions") for both sound-alone recordings and audio-visual devices (the "Record Company Agreements"), and, subject to the provisions of Subparagraph 8(a) above, Publisher agrees to be bound by any provisions of such agreements that exist on the date hereof relating to Compositions hereunder. Writers hereby warrant, however, that the Record Company Agreements do not contain any provision: (i) assigning any ownership or income participation rights in or to the Record Company Compositions to Record Company or any other party; or (ii) allowing Record Company to recoup or offset any advances or other amounts whatsoever from mechanical royalties that would otherwise be collectible by Publisher hereunder, with the sole exception of so-called "overbudget" recording costs or indemnity provisions relating to claims that one or more of the Compositions infringe the copyright of other musical compositions.

   (b) If Writers or Co-Publishers shall desire to either revise, amend, replace, substitute for or otherwise modify the Record Company Agreements, or if the Record Company Agreements terminate and Writers or Co-Publishers desire to enter into any other exclusive recording artist agreement affecting or respecting licensing of Compositions hereunder, the restrictions of Paragraph 20 shall apply to any such modifications or new agreement.

20. Except as already provided for pursuant to the Record Company Agreements, without the express written approval of Publisher, neither Writers, Co-Publishers, nor any person or business entity acting on Writers' or Co-Publishers' behalf, or deriving rights from or through Writers or Co-Publishers, may receive any advance, loan or other payment from Record Company, a performing rights society, another record company or other third party, or may agree that any such party may incur any expense or make any payment on behalf of Writers or Co-Publishers, which is or may be recoupable from (or otherwise subject to offset against) monies which would otherwise be collectible by Publisher hereunder.

If Writers or Co-Publishers shall violate the terms of this Paragraph 20, then in addition to any other rights and remedies available to Publisher, Publisher shall be entitled: (a) to send a letter of direction in Writers' and Co-Publishers' name advising such party of Publisher's rights and the prohibition against such terms in this Agreement, and instructing such party that, after recoupment of whatever sums have been charged against or recouped from such mechanical royalties, such party must provide Publisher with an accounting statement reflecting the mechanical royalties that would otherwise have been payable; and (b) to reimburse itself from any and all royalties otherwise due Writers and Co-Publishers hereunder, for any amount charged or recouped by such party against or from such mechanical royalties, provided, however, that to the extent Publisher is later paid any portion of such amounts by such party, Writers and Co-Publishers shall then be repaid any such sums previously deducted.

21. Publisher shall have the sole and exclusive right to take (or refrain from taking) such action as Publisher deems necessary, on behalf of Publisher, Writers and Co-Publishers, to protect all legal rights and interests in the Compositions, including, but not limited to, the right to institute or defend against any legal action, claim, demand or other proceeding affecting the Compositions, as well as to resolve such matters in Publisher's sole discretion, but after consultation with Writers and Co-Publishers. Publisher shall notify Writers and Co-Publishers of any such pending matter, and Writers and Co-Publishers shall have the right to participate in any such matter with Writers' own counsel, provided, however, that the cost of such counsel shall be borne solely by Writers, Co-Publishers or all such parties, as applicable, and that Publisher shall have final approval of, and shall control the prosecution and/or defense, of any such action. Writers and Co-Publishers shall also have the right, at Writers' sole cost and expense, to prosecute or defend matters for which Publisher has declined to initiate prosecution or defense within thirty (30) days after written request from Writers or Co-Publishers respecting such matter, provided, however, that without Publisher's written approval, such matters may only be prosecuted or defended in the name of Writers and Co-Publishers, and only with respect to the copyright ownership and income participation share of Writers and Co-Publishers hereunder.

22. Notwithstanding anything to the contrary expressed or implied in this Agreement, twenty (20) years after expiration of the Term, if the accounts of Writers and Co-Publishers hereunder are recouped at such time (if not, then twenty-five [25] years after expiration of the term), but only after receipt of written notice by Publisher signed by all living members of Writers, all rights, titles and interests assigned to Publisher hereunder, including, but not limited to, all copyrights throughout the Territory, shall be deemed automatically reassigned to Writers and Co-Publishers in the shares specified in such written

notice, although Publisher shall nonetheless execute any appropriate document reasonably requested by Writers at such time to evidence said reassignment.

23. Writers and Co-Publishers hereby warrant, promise and represent that:

(a) they have full right, power and authority to enter into this Agreement;

(b) they have full legal right to assign, convey, grant and transfer to Publisher all rights hereunder, free and clear of any and all claims, demands or rights of any other parties whatsoever;

(c) the Compositions are and will be each new and original, and no Compositions are or will be an imitation or copy of any other musical composition, or do or will violate or infringe upon any common law, statutory or other rights of any party;

(d) any use by Publisher of the name "[group name of recording artist]" or any subsequent professional or trade name of Writers or any Writers' Group as permitted hereunder, or in a manner consistent with reasonably common practice among music publishers relating to their exclusive song-writers/artists, will not violate or infringe upon any common law, statutory or other rights of any party;

(e) neither Writers nor Co-Publishers shall attempt to make any license, assignment, grant, conveyance or other transfer of rights in violation of this Agreement;

(f) no advance, loan or other payment has been received by Writers or Co-Publishers (or by any other party on their behalf), and no payment has been made or expense incurred, which would violate the terms of Paragraph 20; and

(g) all relevant provisions of the Record Company Agreements and any other agreement affecting or potentially affecting the Compositions hereunder have been submitted to Publisher for inspection prior to execution hereof.

24. (a) Publisher, on the one hand, and Writers and Co-Publishers, on the other hand, indemnify, save, and holds harmless each other, their respective parent, affiliated and subsidiary companies, and their licensees and other successors in interest, as indemnitees, from any and all damages, liabilities, costs, losses or expenses arising out of or connected with any claim, demand, action or proceeding by a third party which is inconsistent with any of the warranties, promises, covenants or representations made by the indemnitor in this Agreement, and which is either: (i) fully adjudicated adverse to the indemnitor by a court, arbitrator or other forum of competent jurisdiction; or (ii) settled with the indemnitor's consent, which consent shall not be unreasonably withheld. If within ten (10) business days after the indemnitor's receipt of notice from the indemnitee of a settlement offer deemed acceptable by the indemnitee, the indemnitor shall

not have given written consent to such offer, then the indemnitee, in addition to any other legal remedies, may require that the indemnitor maintain all further action in regard to the claim at the indemnitor's sole cost and expense, with counsel selected jointly by Publisher, Writer and Co-Publisher, provided, however, that the indemnitor shall retain approval rights over any settlement or, other disposition of such matter which involves any payment by the indemnitor or any dilution or other negative effect respecting rights otherwise possessed by indemnitor hereunder.

(b) Pending the determination of any matter described in 24(a), Publisher shall have the right to withhold payment of any monies otherwise payable to Writers and Co-Publishers hereunder in an amount reasonably related to the claim asserted and estimated reasonable attorneys' fees and costs related thereto, provided, however, that: (i) such sums shall be released to Writers and Co-Publishers if no legal action is instituted against Publisher within one (1) year after Publisher was notified of such claim; and (ii) in lieu of such withholding, Writers or Co-Publishers may post an indemnity or surety bond, in a form satisfactory to Publisher, which shall cover the amount of the claim and estimated legal fees and costs.

25. Except as expressly limited by Paragraph 22, Publisher's rights and duties under this Agreement shall exist for the maximum term of copyright in each Composition throughout the Territory, including any extensions and renewals thereof, allowed under any present or future law, other governmental regulation or judicial decision. Furthermore, Publisher may assign, grant, license, delegate or otherwise transfer any or all of such rights or duties to any person or business entity, in Publisher's sole discretion, upon terms determined solely in Publisher's reasonable business judgment, provided, however, that any assignment of this entire Agreement shall require that the assignee assume all obligations and duties of Publisher hereunder, and shall be made only to a company owned by, controlled by, or affiliated with Publisher, in whole or in part, or which owns or controls Publisher, in whole or in part, or which acquires all or substantially all of Publisher's catalog.

26. Writers and Co-Publishers shall deliver to Publisher copies of any agreements respecting or affecting any Compositions on the date hereof, including, but not limited to, all relevant provisions of the Record Company Agreements and any licenses of any musical compositions comprising Back Catalog, and the identity and general description of all such agreements is listed on Schedule "C," attached hereto. Writers and Co-Publishers shall also execute and deliver to Publisher any and all documents, including, but not limited to, the Assignment of Copyright attached hereto as Exhibit "A," the letters of direction to Co-Publishers' respective performing rights societies, and the general letter of direction, which Publisher may reasonably request to evidence, establish

and protect the rights granted hereunder, and to carry out and effectuate the intent and purposes of this Agreement. If Writers or Co-Publishers shall fail, within fifteen (15) business days after receipt of a written request by Publisher, to execute any such document reasonably requested, Writers and Co-Publishers constitute and appoint Publisher as Writers' and Co-Publishers' attorney-in-fact, with full powers of substitution and delegation, to execute such document on behalf of Writers and/or Co-Publishers (as applicable). Such power-of-attorney is coupled with an interest and therefore irrevocable.

27. Publisher shall neither be deemed in default hereunder nor to have committed a material breach of this Agreement unless Writers or Co-Publishers shall notify Publisher of such alleged default or breach in writing, and unless Publisher shall thereafter fail to remedy such default or breach within thirty (30) days after receipt of such notice. The foregoing "cure-of-breach" provision shall also apply to any curable breaches of Writers or Co-Publishers, provided, however, that such cure-of-breach period shall not delay Publisher's right, in accordance with the terms of this Agreement, to extend any contract period hereunder or withhold any advance or other payment otherwise due. Notwithstanding the foregoing, with respect to any claim by Writers or Co-Publishers that additional monies are payable pursuant to this Agreement, whether or not such claim is based upon an audit of Publisher's books and records, Publisher shall not be deemed in material breach of this Agreement justifying termination, rescission, reformation or any other equitable remedy, unless either: (a) within ten (10) business days after Publisher's receipt of written notice of such claim, together with a copy of any audit report upon which such claim is based, if any, Publisher neither pays the sums requested in such claim nor contests such claim by written notice to Writers or Co-Publishers; or (b) such claim is reduced to a final, non-appealable judgment in favor of Writers or Co-Publishers granting the applicable equitable remedy.

28. Writers and Co-Publishers understand and acknowledge that, although Co-Publishers shall be a co-owner of the copyright in the Compositions, as between Publisher and Co-Publishers, the only rights retained by Co-Publishers hereunder are strictly limited to those specified in this Agreement, including, but not limited to, the reassignment of rights provided for in Paragraph 22 above.

29. All promises, warranties, representations, indemnities, potential liabilities and other legal and contractual duties and obligations of Writers and Co-Publishers, as well as Publisher's rights of recoupment, shall be deemed granted and made by Writers and Co-Publishers jointly and severally, and no individual entity or person comprising Co-Publishers or Writers hereunder shall be released or otherwise absolved from any such liabilities, duties or obligations without the written consent of Publisher.

30. All official or legal notices, statements and payments which either party shall be required or shall desire to give the other must be in writing, addressed to the receiving party as specified hereunder, or to such other address as the receiving party may designate in writing from time to time, and shall be sent certified or registered U.S. mail, return receipt requested, provided, however, that accounting statements and payments shall be sent by regular, first-class U.S. mail. Subject to the provisions of Paragraph 15 regarding accounting statements, if mailed in accordance with the foregoing, each such notice, statement or other document shall be conclusively deemed to have been received either on the date of actual delivery or receipt, the date when any attempted delivery was refused at the receiving party's address (which refusal shall be evidenced in writing by the person attempting such delivery), five (5) business days after mailing by the required means, or the date it can be established that the then current attorney or personal manager of the Writer or Writers to which such notice is directed have received such notice (provided that such party shall not be deemed "then-current" unless such party has acted on behalf of such Writer or Writers within three months prior to the date of such notice), whichever is earlier. All notices to Publisher shall be sent to _____, with courtesy copies sent concurrently to _____. Courtesy copies of all legal notices to Writers shall be sent to _____, provided, however, that no failure to send such copy shall be deemed a breach of this Agreement, nor shall any such failure affect the validity of such legal notice.

31. This Agreement sets forth the entire understanding of the parties hereto relating to the subject matter hereof. No modification, amendment, waiver, termination or discharge of its terms shall be effective, and no form of waiver shall be deemed a continuing waiver, unless contained in a separate written document executed by all parties hereto.

·32. This Agreement shall be construed, interpreted and enforced under the laws of the State of New York applicable to agreements to be wholly performed therein, as well as any applicable provisions of the Copyright Law of the United States.

IN WITNESS WHEREOF, the parties hereto have executed this Agreement on the date first written above.

_____   _____

_____   _____

ASSIGNMENT OF COPYRIGHT

For good and valuable consideration, the undersigned _____ (collectively "Assignors"), hereby assign, convey, grant and transfer exclusively to _____ ("Assignee"), its successors and assigns, fifty percent (50%) of all right, title and interest, including copyright, of every kind, nature and description throughout the universe (whether such rights exist now or in the future under any law, other governmental regulation or judicial decision) in and to the musical compositions listed on Schedule "A," attached hereto (the "Compositions"), for the maximum term (including any renewals or extensions thereof) available now or in the future throughout the universe under any law, other governmental regulation or judicial decision, but subject to the provisions of the Agreement dated _____, 1997, by and between Assignors and Assignee.

Notwithstanding such joint ownership, Assignors hereby assign, convey, grant and transfer exclusively to Assignee, its successors and assigns: the sole and exclusive right to administer, exploit and authorize exploitation of the Compositions; the sole and exclusive right to collect all sums received from any exploitation of the Compositions; any past, present and future legal causes of action respecting infringement of the Compositions; and all works based upon or derived from the Compositions.

This Assignment is subject to all terms and conditions of the Agreement dated the _____ day of _____, 1997, by and between Assignee, on the one hand, and Assignors, on the other hand.

Executed by Assignors as of the _____ day of _____, 1997.

_____

SCHEDULE "A"
(Back Catalog pursuant to Paragraph 2)

<u>Song Title</u>	<u>Songwriters %</u>	<u>Publishers %</u>

*   *   *

SCHEDULE "B"
(musical compositions not initially assigned hereunder)
(third party agreements affecting such compositions)

<u>Song Title</u>	<u>Nature of Agreement</u>	<u>Publisher</u>

*   *   *

SCHEDULE "C"
(third party agreements affecting compositions)

Form 38

MUSIC PUBLISHING ADMINISTRATION AGREEMENT

This agreement ("Agreement") is made and entered into this 1st of January, 1997, by and between _____ ("Administrator"), at _____ and _____ ("Owner"), _____.

The parties hereby agree as follows:

1. The term of this Agreement shall be deemed to have commenced on January 1, 1997, and shall extend until terminated by either party on at least sixty (60) days written notice, with such termination to be effective only at the end of a semi-annual accounting period (*i.e.*, June 30 or December 31) (the "Term"), provided, however, Administrator shall have the right to continue to collect, for a period not to exceed two (2) semi-annual accounting periods after expiration of the Term, all sums earned hereunder but not collected during the Term ("Collection Period").

2. Owner hereby grants, conveys and assigns exclusively to Administrator, throughout the world (the "Territory"), all so-called "administration rights" (as such term is commonly understood in the music publishing industry and further described hereunder) to one hundred percent (100%) of Owner's copyright Ownership and all of Owner's other rights, titles and interests throughout the Territory, of every kind, nature and description, existing under any present or future law, other governmental regulation or judicial decision, in and to all musical compositions owned in whole or in part by Owner (the "Compositions"), including, but not limited to, those Compositions listed on Schedule "A," attached hereto.

3. (a) Subject to the restrictions, limitations and reservations expressed in Subparagraphs 3(b)-(d) below, the rights granted, conveyed and assigned by Owner to Administrator in Paragraph 2 shall include, but shall not be limited to, the sole and exclusive right, throughout the Territory, on behalf of Owner:

    (i) for any Compositions that have not previously been registered for copyright, to register the copyright for the Compositions in the name of Owner and any other appropriate parties, and Administrator expressly assumes the obligation to register such copyrights with respect to all Compositions that are, or have been, commercially exploited;

    (ii) for any Compositions that have not previously been registered with the appropriate performing rights societies, to register such Compositions in the name of Owner and any other appropriate parties with such societies, and Administrator expressly assumes the obligation to register such Compositions that are, or have been, commercially exploited;

(iii) to administer, use and license the use of the Compositions in any manner, mode or medium, of every kind, nature or description, whether such manner, mode or medium is now known, or is developed at any time in the future;

(iv) to receive and collect one hundred percent (100%) of all gross music publishing income (as hereafter defined) payable to or received by Owner, Administrator or their respective collection agents during the Term, regardless of when earned, subject to the rights of Warner/Chappell Music ("Warner/Chappell") under the Administration Agreement dated October 19, 1990, between Owner and Warner/Chappell (the "Warner/Chappell Agreement");

(v) to make or authorize any and all revisions, arrangements, adaptations, translations, dramatizations or other musical or non-musical works derived in whole or in part from the Compositions, provided, however, that, notwithstanding anything to the contrary expressed or implied in this Agreement, all translations, arrangements and adaptations of the Compositions shall be made at the sole cost and expense of Administrator (except to the extent that the rules of a local society require a portion of the royalties generated by a translation or adaptation to be paid to the local translator or adaptor, in which event the amount of such royalties shall be deducted before the calculation of "net music publishing income" payable to Owner), although any such materials shall be the sole and exclusive property of Owner (but shall remain subject hereto during the Term).

(vi) to enter into and execute, on behalf of Owner, any and all licenses, agreements or other legal documents respecting exploitation of the Compositions in Administrator's sole discretion, upon terms determined solely in Administrator's reasonable business judgment, including, but not limited to, the right to amend the Warner/Chappell Agreement with respect to any provisions having effect after December 31, 1994, and, notwithstanding anything to the contrary expressed or implied in this Agreement, Administrator shall have the specific right, power and authority hereunder to issue non-exclusive licenses for the use of any of the Compositions for periods of time in excess of the Term hereof;

(vii) to change the registration of the Compositions with mechanical, performing and other rights societies and collection agents worldwide to reflect Administrator as exclusive administrator.

(b) Notwithstanding anything to the contrary expressed or implied in Subparagraph 3(a) above or anywhere else in this Agreement, the copyright in each of the Compositions, as well as the copyright to any derivative works based upon or derived from the Compositions, as well as Ownership of all proprietary rights to the titles of the Compositions, shall be reserved to Owner throughout the Territory.

4. (a) From gross music publishing income received by Administrator or credited to Administrator in the Territory and generated by the rights granted by Owner hereunder, Administrator shall, in the following order: (i) deduct an administration fee of _____ percent (____%); (ii) compute and pay to the applicable songwriter, co-publisher or other party designated by Owner, amounts due pursuant to Owner's agreement with such party or parties (or, if so instructed by Owner, credit such amounts to such party or parties and pay such amounts to Owner); (iii) deduct the direct expenses of Administrator incurred respecting the Compositions, if any; and (iv) pay the balance, representing "net music publishing income," to Owner.

(b) Sums payable to persons either creating new foreign lyrics or translations of the existing lyrics of any Composition (who shall not be paid amounts in excess of those permissible under local society regulations and standards), as well as the sums payable to any co-publisher on account of such lyrics, shall be deducted "off-the-top" from gross music publishing income prior to computing either the administration fee of Administrator or the amounts due Owner.

5. Notwithstanding anything to the contrary expressed or implied anywhere in this Agreement:

(a) Owner shall not be entitled to any portion of any advance payments, guarantee payments, or minimum royalty payments which Administrator may receive in connection with any collection, licensing or other agreement, unless such agreement covers only Compositions hereunder or specifically allocates to one (1) or more Compositions hereunder an identifiable portion of such payment, in which event such sums shall be deemed gross music publishing income hereunder; and

(b) no sums shall be payable to Owner for any use of the Compositions for which sums are not received by or credited to Administrator.

6. If Administrator or its affiliates shall ever directly engage in the business of printing, publishing and selling printed versions of the Compositions (other than through a print licensee):

(a) for purposes of this Agreement, gross music publishing income generated by such operations for all copies of printed editions actually sold, paid for, and not returned, and for which such income has been received by Administrator or credited to Administrator, shall be deemed to be twenty percent (20%) of the suggested retail list price ("SRLP") for piano/vocal sheet music, twelve and one-half percent (12-1/2%) of the SRLP for folios other than "personality folios," "fake books" or "educational editions," seventeen and one-half percent (17-1/2%) for personality folios, and ten percent (10%) of the SRLP for fake books and educational editions (prorated in either event in the case of mixed folios); and

(b) the foregoing "deemed" gross music publishing income shall be reduced pro-rata to the extent the applicable Composition is less than one hundred percent (100%) owned by Owner and one hundred percent (100%) subject to this Agreement

7. Throughout this Agreement, the following terms shall be defined as indicated:

(a) "gross music publishing income" — subject to Paragraph 6, all music publishing income generated throughout the Territory and received by Administrator or credited to Administrator from exploitation of the Compositions, and which is derived from the rights granted hereunder;

(b) "received by Administrator" — actual receipts of Administrator in the U.S. from any use, exploitation or other exercise of rights respecting the Compositions in the Territory, after any and all deductions or charges imposed by third parties not owned or controlled by Administrator, its affiliates, or its subsidiaries;

(c) "credited to Administrator" — sums credited to the account of Administrator for any use, exploitation or other exercise of rights respecting the Compositions, anywhere in the Territory, in reduction of a prior advance to Administrator (but only to the extent Owner did not participate in such advance).

(d) "net music publishing income" — that gross music publishing income remaining after deduction and payment (or credit) of the amounts described pursuant to Subparagraphs 4(a)(i)-(iii).

8. Owner hereby authorizes ASCAP, BMI, SESAC and any other domestic or foreign performing rights societies or collection agents to pay Administrator one hundred percent (100%) of the "publisher's share" of royalties derived from Owner's copyright Ownership share of the Compositions and collected and computed by such societies.

9. (a) Administrator shall submit accounting statements to Owner on or before the last day of February each year respecting gross music publishing income received by Administrator or credited to Administrator during the semi-annual period ending the preceding December 31st, and on or before August 31st each year respecting gross music publishing income received by Administrator or credited to Administrator during the semi-annual period ending the preceding June 30th, accompanied by payment of any amounts due.

(b) All advances, accounting statements and royalties shall be sent and made payable to _____, at _____, and the social security or other federal tax identification number of such party is _____.

10. Owner shall have the right, at its sole cost and expense, at the place of business of Administrator, during the normal business hours of Administrator, after no less than fifteen (15) days written notice, to audit the books and records of Administrator regarding sums due Owner hereunder.

11. All grants, conveyances, assignments, other transfers, warranties, covenants, promises, representations, duties, obligations and rights made, assumed or possessed by Owner hereunder are deemed made, assumed and possessed by Owner on behalf of itself and all songwriters and other parties having assigned, or in the future assigning, rights to Owner.

12. Administrator shall have the right, only upon consultation with and approval of Owner, to take (or refrain from taking) such action as Administrator deems necessary, on behalf of Owner, to protect all legal rights and interests in the Compositions, including, but not limited to, the right, only upon consultation with and approval of Owner, to institute or defend any legal action, claim, demand or other proceeding affecting the Compositions, and to resolve such matters with the approval of Owner. Administrator shall have the obligation to notify Owner of any such pending matter or potential legal dispute promptly. Any recovery in such matter shall be deemed gross music publishing income hereunder only after reimbursement to Owner and Administrator of all legal fees and costs incurred in such matter. Nothing in this paragraph, however, shall be interpreted or construed: (a) to prevent or limit in any manner Owner's independent right to institute or defend any such action, claim, demand or other proceeding affecting any of the Compositions, either alone or in conjunction with Administrator; or (b) to prevent or limit in any manner the right of Administrator to defend its own legal interests with respect to any claim, demand, legal action or other legal proceeding instituted against Administrator, or in which Administrator has been named as defendant, as well as to settle any such claim only with respect to Administrator (not Owner).

13. Owner hereby warrants, promises and represents that: Owner has full right, power and authority to enter into this Agreement and to assign, convey, grant and transfer to Administrator all rights hereunder. Owner hereby indemnifies, saves and holds harmless Administrator, its parent, affiliated and subsidiary companies, and its licensees and other successors in interest, from any damages suffered on account of any claim, demand, action or proceeding by a third party which is inconsistent with the foregoing warranty, promise, covenant and representation, and which: (a) is fully adjudicated adverse to Administrator by a court, arbitrator or other forum of competent jurisdiction; or (b) is settled with

Owner's consent. Notwithstanding the foregoing, it shall be the duty of Administrator to promptly notify Owner of any such adverse claim, demand, action or proceeding, and the duty of Owner to assume control of the defense in any such matter.

14. Except as expressly limited hereunder, Administrator may assign, grant, license, delegate or otherwise transfer any or all of its rights or duties hereunder to any person or business entity, in Administrator's sole discretion, upon terms determined solely in Administrator's reasonable business judgment, provided, however, that any assignment of this entire Agreement shall require that the assignee assume all applicable obligations and duties of Administrator hereunder.

15. Neither party shall be deemed in default hereunder or to have committed a material breach of this Agreement, unless the party claiming such breach or default shall have notified the other party of such alleged default or breach in writing, and unless the party allegedly in breach or default shall thereafter fail to remedy such breach or default within thirty (30) days after receipt of such notice.

16. All official or legal notices, statements and payments which either party shall be required or shall desire to give the other must be in writing, addressed to the receiving party as specified hereunder, or to such other address as the receiving party may designate in writing from time to time, and shall be sent certified or registered U.S. mail, return receipt requested, provided, however, that accounting statements and payments shall be sent by regular, first-class U.S. mail. If mailed in accordance with the foregoing, each such notice, statement or other document shall be conclusively deemed to have been received on either the date of actual delivery or receipt, or the date when any attempted delivery was refused at the receiving party's address (which refusal shall be evidenced in writing by the person attempting such delivery), whichever is earlier. All notices to Administrator shall be sent to _____, with courtesy copies sent concurrently to _____. All legal notices directed to Owner shall be sent to _____, with a courtesy copy to _____.

17. This Agreement sets forth the entire understanding of the parties hereto relating to the subject matter hereof. No modification, amendment, waiver, termination or discharge of its terms shall be effective unless contained in a separate written document executed by all parties hereto.

18. This Agreement shall be construed, interpreted and enforced under the laws of the State of New York applicable to agreements to be wholly performed therein, as well as any applicable provisions of the Copyright Law of the United States.

OWNER   ADMINISTRATOR

By: _____   By: _____
    An Authorized Signatory   An Authorized Signatory

January 1, 1997

American Society of Composers,
    Authors & Publishers
One Lincoln Plaza
New York, NY 10023

Gentlemen:

You are hereby authorized and directed to pay to our administrator, _____ ("Administrator"), at _____, and we hereby assign to Administrator, all monies payable to the undersigned from and after January 1, 1997, regardless of when earned, as the so-called "publisher's share" of performance royalties respecting the ownership share of _____, in all musical compositions, and copies of all statements respecting such publisher's share shall be sent solely to Administrator.

The foregoing authorization and direction shall remain in full force and effect until modified or terminated by both the undersigned and Administrator.

Very truly yours,

[name of Owner]

By: _____
        An Authorized Signatory

Music Publishing Administration Agreement

January 1, 1997

Broadcast Music, Inc.
8730 Sunset Boulevard, 3rd Floor West
Los Angeles, CA 90069-9109

To Whom it May Concern:

This is to advise BMI that we have entered into an agreement with another BMI publisher for the administration of our catalog, and that BMI's records should be marked to reflect the agreement as follows:

1. Name of BMI publisher acting as our administrator:

_____

2. Effective date of agreement — immediately, including all royalties now payable or which hereafter become payable, regardless of when performances took place.

3. Checks for all our BMI royalties, both domestic and foreign, should be made payable to the administrator and should be sent together with statements and all other correspondence to the administrator at its address on BMI's records.

We understand that BMI cannot mark its records at this time so as to indicate the termination date of the administration agreement and that, therefore, the above information will continue to be reflected on BMI's records until such time as we or the administrator notifies BMI that the administration agreement is about to terminate.

Very truly yours,

_____

[Name of Owner]

By: _____
An Authorized Signatory

Dated: As of January 1, 1997

To Whom it May Concern:

Please be advised that effective January 1, 1997, the undersigned, _____, entered into an exclusive administration agreement with _____ ("Administrator"), granting to Administrator 100% of the administration rights to all musical compositions owned or controlled, in whole or in part, by _____ (the "Compositions"). With respect to such Compositions, you are hereby authorized and directed to pay Administrator, _____, all income of any nature, payable from and after January 1, 1997, regardless of when earned, otherwise payable to _____. With respect to mechanical royalties, such payments should be sent to Administrator, c/o The Harry Fox Agency, 205 E. 42nd Street, 18th Floor, New York, New York 10017.

Please mark your records accordingly.

We would appreciate your acknowledging receipt of this notification by signing the enclosed copy and returning it to Administrator at the address noted in the preceding paragraph.

The foregoing authorization and direction shall remain in full force and effect until modified or terminated by both the undersigned and Administrator.

Very truly yours,   Acknowledged by:

_____   _____

An Authorized Signatory

Form 39

Exclusive Recording Artist Agreement

AN AGREEMENT made this (DATE) between XYZ CORP. (hereinafter referred to as "XYZ") and (NAME OF ARTIST(S)' LOAN OUT COMPANY) (hereinafter referred to as "you").

1. <u>REPRESENTATIONS, WARRANTIES AND COVENANTS:</u>

1.01. During the term of this agreement, you will furnish to XYZ the exclusive recording services of (NAME OF ARTIST OR GROUP) (hereinafter collectively and individually referred to as "Artist") in the Territory.

1.02. You are authorized, empowered and able to enter into and fully perform your obligations under this agreement. Neither this agreement nor the fulfillment hereof by any party infringes upon the rights of any Person. There is in existence between you and Artist a valid and enforceable written agreement (the "Artist Agreement") pursuant to which Artist is required to perform exclusively for you during the term of this agreement and which otherwise contains appropriate provisions to allow you to comply with your obligations hereunder. You will not modify or amend the Artist Agreement nor waive your rights thereunder in any manner that might impair the rights granted to XYZ hereunder. You shall take all steps necessary and desirable to keep the Artist Agreement in full force and effect during the term hereof. Simultaneously with the execution of this agreement, you shall deliver to XYZ an agreement between XYZ and Artist in the form annexed hereto as Exhibit "A"; you hereby give your consent and approval to the contents thereof and Exhibit A is hereby made a part hereof. You will require full and complete performance by the Artist of said agreement. If Artist breaches said agreement, you will immediately notify XYZ in writing of the details of such breach. If you do not enforce any of your rights under said agreement, XYZ may, without limitation of XYZ's rights or remedies, enforce such rights in your name and/or the name of XYZ. You have no knowledge of any claim or purported claim which would interfere with XYZ's rights hereunder or create any liability on the part of XYZ.

[OPTIONAL CLAUSE 1.03. THIS OPTIONAL CLAUSE APPEARS ONLY IN EXCLUSIVE RECORDING ARTIST AGREEMENTS THAT APPLY OR ARE GOVERNED BY CALIFORNIA LAW]

[FIRST ALTERNATIVE CLAUSE 1.03. THE FIRST ALTERNATIVE TO THE OPTIONAL CLAUSE IS A TYPICAL MINIMUM GUARANTEED COMPENSATION PROVISION FOUND IN EXCLUSIVE ARTIST RECORDING AGREEMENTS THAT APPLY OR ARE GOVERNED BY CALIFORNIA LAW AND THAT ARE ENTERED INTO AFTER JANUARY 1, 1994]

1.03. MINIMUM COMPENSATION: You warrant and represent that the Artist Agreement provides that, as of the end of each of the first seven Contract

Years of the Artist Agreement (or, if later, the first seven Contract Years of this agreement), [each [Key Member] member of] Artist will have received Compensation (as defined below) of not less than the following amounts:

First Contract Year: Nine Thousand Dollars ($9,000.00);

Second Contract Year: Twelve Thousand Dollars ($12,000.00);

Third Contract Year: Fifteen Thousand Dollars ($15,000.00);

Fourth Contract Year: Fifteen Thousand Dollars ($15,000.00);

Fifth Contract Year: Fifteen Thousand Dollars ($15,000.00);

Sixth Contract Year: Fifteen Thousand Dollars ($15,000.00); and

Seventh (and any applicable succeeding) Contract Year: Fifteen Thousand Dollars ($15,000.00).

Compensation paid in any Contract Year in excess of the minimums specified above shall apply to reduce the Compensation otherwise required above to be paid in any subsequent Contract Year. You warrant and represent that the term of the Artist Agreement commenced on (INSERT DATE THAT THE ARTIST AGREEMENT COMMENCED), and that you have paid all minimum Compensation required above for that portion of the term of the Artist Agreement prior to the commencement of the term hereof. You warrant and represent that the Artist Agreement provides that in the event the Compensation paid to [any [Key Member] member of] Artist is below the amount described above as of THIRTY (30) days prior to the end of the applicable Contract Year, [such member of] Artist will give you and XYZ written notice containing specific reference to this paragraph 1.03 and specifying such deficiency. Such notice may be given no earlier than THIRTY (30) days nor later than FIFTEEN (15) days prior to the expiration of the Contract Year concerned. Promptly after its receipt of such notice, during the term of this agreement, XYZ will pay the actual amount of any such deficiency, which payment shall be a pre-payment of any monies due you hereunder (other than Mechanical Royalties). Any failure by XYZ to make such payment will not constitute a material breach of this agreement. As used in this paragraph 1.03: (a) Contract Year means the annual period beginning on the first day of the term of the Artist Agreement or this agreement, as applicable, and each subsequent annual period during the continuance of the term; [and] (b) Compensation means all monies paid by you or XYZ to [the member of] Artist (including, but not limited to, Advances and Record royalties, but not including Mechanical Royalties) [; and (c) Key Member means (name of member) and any other member of Artist who is (1) a lead vocalist on Artist's most recent Album of the Recording Commitment, (2) a lead instrumentalist for a substantial portion of the material on Artist's most recent Album of the Recording Commitment, or (3) a producer of a substantial portion of the material on Artist's most recent Album of the Recording Commitment]. [You hereby warrant and represent that all Compensation paid to Artist under the Artist Agreement has been and will be divided in such a way so as to ensure payment of the minimum Compensation as required in this paragraph 1.03.]

1.04. There now exist no prior unreleased recorded performances by Artist other than those listed on the attached Schedule A. You warrant and represent that you own all rights in and to the Masters listed on Schedule A and that no recordings from those Masters will be released during the term hereof.

1.05. The Masters hereunder and performances embodied thereon shall be produced in accordance with the rules and regulations of the American Federation of Musicians, the American Federation of Television and Radio Artists and all other unions having jurisdiction. Artist is or will become and remain, to the extent necessary to enable the performance of this agreement, a member in good standing of all labor unions or guilds, membership in which may be required for the performance of Artist's services hereunder.

1.06. You have the sole and exclusive right to the services of Artist as required herein. Artist will not perform for (and neither you nor Artist will license or consent to or permit the use by any Person other than XYZ of Artist's name or likeness for) or in connection with the recording or exploitation of any Phonograph Record embodying any Composition recorded by Artist under this agreement prior to the later of the date (E.G., FIVE (5)) years subsequent to the date of delivery to XYZ hereunder of the last Master embodying that Composition or the date (E.G., TWO (2)) years subsequent to the expiration or termination of the term of this agreement, or any subsequent agreement between you and any Person relating to Artist's recording services for XYZ, provided the term of such subsequent agreement commences no later than (E.G., THREE (3)) months after the term hereof terminates. Your agreement with the individual Producer of a Master hereunder shall restrict said producer from producing the Composition on another Master for any Person other than XYZ for at least (E.G., TWO (2)) years from the date of Delivery to XYZ of such Master.

1.07. None of the Masters hereunder, nor the performances embodied thereon, nor any other Materials, as hereinafter defined, nor any authorized use thereof by XYZ or its grantees, licensees or assigns, will violate or infringe upon the rights of any third party. "Materials" as used herein means: all Controlled Compositions; each name or sobriquet used by you or Artist, individually or as a group; and all other musical, dramatic, artistic and literary materials, ideas and other intellectual properties furnished or selected by you, the Artist or any individual producer and contained in or used in connection with any Recordings made hereunder or the packaging, sale, distribution, advertising, publicizing or other exploitation thereof.

1.08. Without limiting the foregoing, XYZ shall not be required to make any payments of any nature for, or in connection with, the acquisition, exercise or exploitation of rights by XYZ pursuant to this agreement, except as specifically provided in this agreement. You shall be solely responsible for and shall pay all sums due Artist, and the individual producers of Masters hereunder, and all other Persons entitled to receive royalties or other payments in connection with the sale of Phonograph Records derived from Masters hereunder. You shall not be responsible for AFM, AFTRA, or other similar "per-record" payments or normal costs of manufacture and distribution of Records. Each person who will render any services in connection with the recording of the Masters will grant to you and XYZ the rights referred to in this agreement and will have the rights to so render such services and grant such rights. None of the persons whose performances are embodied in the Masters or whose services are used in the recording of such Masters shall be bound by any agreement with any other Person that would prevent or restrict such performances or services (or to the extent otherwise bound, you will obtain all necessary clearances with respect thereto).

1.09.   (a) Neither you nor Artist shall authorize or knowingly permit the Artist's performances to be recorded for any purpose without an express written agreement prohibiting the use of such recording on Phonograph Records in violation of the restrictions herein, and you and Artist shall take reasonable measures to prevent the manufacture, distribution and sale at any time by any Person other than XYZ of such Phonograph Records. Neither you, Artist, nor any Person deriving any rights from you or Artist, shall use or authorize or permit any Person other than XYZ to use your or Artist's name (including any professional name or sobriquet), likeness (including picture, portrait or caricature) or biography in connection with the manufacture and/or exploitation of Masters or Phonograph Records.

(b) Artist will perform under a professional name, to be chosen by you and agreed to by XYZ. You will be the sole owner of such professional name and no other Person has or will have the right to use such name in connection with Phonograph Records during the term. Artist shall not use a different name in connection with Phonograph Records unless you and XYZ mutually agree in writing. You agree that XYZ may cause a search to be instituted to determine whether there have been any third party uses for Phonograph Record purposes of such name. XYZ may cause a federal application to USA federal registration of the name to be made in favor of Artist for Phonograph Record and/or entertainment purposes. You agree that any amounts up to but not exceeding (E.G., SIX HUNDRED DOLLARS ($600)) expended by XYZ pursuant to this clause will be deemed Advances hereunder. If the trademark search indicates that such name should not be so used, XYZ and you shall mutually agree upon a substitute name for Artist. Nothing contained herein shall release you from your indemnification of XYZ in respect of XYZ's use of such name.

1.10. Neither you, nor Artist, nor any Person deriving any rights from you, shall at any time, do or authorize any Person to do, anything inconsistent with, or which in XYZ's reasonable business judgment is likely to diminish, impair or interfere with any of XYZ's rights hereunder or the full and prompt performances of your obligations hereunder. [Neither Artist nor you shall endorse blank tapes.]

1.11. Neither you nor Artist is under any disability, restriction or prohibition respecting Compositions that Artist records for XYZ.

[1.12. You agree to and do hereby indemnify, save and hold XYZ and its licensees harmless of and from any and all liability, loss, damage, cost or expense (including legal expenses and reasonable attorney fees) arising out of or connected with any breach or alleged breach of this agreement or any claim which is inconsistent with any of the warranties or representations made by you in this agreement, and you agree to reimburse XYZ on demand for any payment made or incurred by XYZ with respect to the foregoing provided the claim concerned has been settled or has resulted in a final judgment against XYZ or its licensees. Pending the determination of any claim in respect of which XYZ is entitled to be indemnified, XYZ shall not withhold monies which would otherwise be payable to you hereunder in an amount exceeding your potential liability to XYZ pursuant to this clause. If XYZ pays more than $7,500 in settlement of any claim not reduced to judgment, you will not be obligated to reimburse XYZ for the excess unless you have consented to the settlement. If you do not consent to any settlement proposed by XYZ for an account exceeding $7,500, you will nevertheless be required to reimburse XYZ for the full amount unless you make bonding arrangements, satisfactory to XYZ in its sole discretion, to assure XYZ of reimbursement for all damages, liabilities, costs and expenses (including legal expenses and counsel fees) which XYZ or its licensees may incur as a result of that claim. XYZ will release any withheld monies if (i) no action is commenced on such claim and (ii) no settlement discussions have taken place and no further demand has been made on the claim for any period of one (1) full year. XYZ will notify you of any action commenced on such a claim. You may participate in the defense of any such claim through counsel of your selection at your own expense, but XYZ will have the right at all times, in its sole discretion, to retain or resume control of the defense of such claim.]

2. <u>TERM</u>:

2.01. The term of this agreement will commence on the date hereof and continue, unless extended as provided herein, for a first Contract Period (sometimes referred to as the "initial Contract Period") ending (E.G., SEVEN (7)) months after the date of the delivery to XYZ of all Masters required in fulfillment of your Recording Commitment for such Period but in no event earlier than (E.G., TWELVE (12)) months after the date of the commencement of such period.

2.02. Additionally, you hereby grant XYZ three (3) separate options to extend the term of this agreement for additional Contract Periods ("Option Periods") on the same terms and conditions applicable to the initial Contract Period except as otherwise provided herein. XYZ may exercise each of those options by sending you a notice at any time before the expiration of the Contract Period which is then in effect. If XYZ exercises such an option, the Option Period concerned will begin immediately after the end of the current Contract Period. The term of each option period will end (E.G., SEVEN (7)) months after the date of delivery to XYZ of all Masters required in fulfillment of your Recording Commitment for such Period but not earlier than (E.G., EIGHTEEN (18)) months after the date of commencement of the first and second Option Periods and (E.G., TWELVE (12)) months after the date of commencement of the third Option Period.

3. DELIVERY OBLIGATIONS:

3.01. During each Contract Period you will deliver to XYZ commercially satisfactory Masters. Such Masters shall embody the featured vocal performances of Artist of contemporary selections which have not been recorded at a "live" or "in concert" performance, and which have not been previously recorded by Artist, whether hereunder or otherwise. (Any Masters accepted hereunder by XYZ that were partially or completely recorded prior to the term of this agreement shall be deemed to have been recorded during the initial Contract Period.) Neither Multiple Record LPs nor Joint Recordings shall be recorded as part of your Recording Commitment hereunder without your and XYZ's prior written consent (your delivery of a Multiple Record LP or Joint Recording shall be deemed your consent). Without limiting the foregoing, XYZ shall have the right to reject any Master which XYZ reasonably deems offensive to reasonable standards of public taste or which infringes on the rights of others.

3.02. During each Contract Period, you will cause the Artist to perform for the recording of Masters and you will deliver to XYZ those Masters (the "Recording Commitment") necessary to satisfy the following schedule:

CONTRACT PERIOD	RECORDING COMMITMENT
Initial Contract Period	2 LPs
First Option Period	2 LPs
Second Option Period	2 LPs
Third Option Period	1 LP

3.03. During each Contract Period, you will deliver the first LP in fulfillment of your Recording Commitment for each Period within the first (E.G., FOUR (4)) months of the commencement of each Period (except for the first LP in the initial Contract Period, which shall be delivered within (E.G., THREE (3)) months after the execution hereof) and you will deliver the second LP in fulfillment of your Recording Commitment, if applicable, not earlier than (E.G., SIX (6)) months or later than (E.G., NINE (9)) months after the date of the delivery of the first LP in such Period.

3.04. You shall not deviate from the delivery schedule specified in clause 3.03 without XYZ's written consent; timely delivery as provided therein shall be deemed a material obligation hereunder. You further agree not to commence the recording of any LP hereunder until (E.G., SIX (6)) months after the date of delivery to XYZ of the immediately preceding LP in fulfillment of your Recording Commitment hereunder. Each LP will consist entirely of Masters made in the course of that LP recording project.

3.05. You shall deliver to XYZ each Master hereunder in the form of a two-track stereo tape master (and, if requested by XYZ, a monaural tape master) as well as reference discs which are representative of such tape masters. You shall deliver at the same time any multi-track master tapes recorded in connection with the recording project including, without limitation, any (E.G., TWO (2)) track master tapes. The two-track stereo tape master (and the monaural tape master, if applicable) shall be fully edited, mixed, equalized and leadered for the production of parts from which satisfactory Phonograph Records can be manufactured. All such tapes (together with the information specified in clause 3.06 below) shall be delivered to XYZ's Vice President of Administration at the address specified at the beginning hereof; within (E.G., TWO (2)) weeks thereafter, you shall send a written notice specifying that you have so delivered and the date of such delivery to XYZ's Vice President of Legal Affairs. The two-track stereo tapes for the Masters comprising each Record to be delivered hereunder shall be assembled on one (1) master tape reel or, if necessary, on two (2) master tape reels.

3.06. As used in this agreement, delivery shall mean the receipt of the tape masters as provided in clauses 3.01 and 3.05 as well as the submission by you in a written form of all necessary information, consents, licenses and permissions such that XYZ may manufacture, distribute and release the Phonograph Records concerned including, without limitation, all label copy, publishing and songwriting information (including applicable music performance rights organizations), LP credits, the timings of each Composition contained on a Record, ancillary materials prepared by or for you which are required hereunder, first use mechanical licenses, sideperson permissions and any information required to be delivered to unions, guilds or other third parties. Deliveries will also include a reference disc approved by XYZ from which metal parts can be prepared. XYZ's election to make a payment to you which was to have been made upon delivery of Masters or to release a Record derived from such Master shall not be deemed to be its acknowledgment that such "delivery" was properly made, and XYZ shall not be deemed to have waived either its right to require such complete and proper performance thereafter or its remedies for your failure to perform in accordance therewith.

4. RECORDING PROCEDURE:

4.01. You shall schedule and conduct recording sessions only after first obtaining XYZ's written approval of the individual producer, the places of recording, the Compositions to be recorded and the Authorized Budget (as the term "Authorized Budget" is hereinafter defined). You shall request such approvals at least (E.G., FOURTEEN (14)) days prior to the proposed first date of recording, and XYZ shall not unreasonably withhold any such approval. If XYZ disapproves any of the foregoing, you shall promptly submit alternative proposals, but in all instances allowing XYZ a reasonable period of review prior to the proposed first date of recording. XYZ shall approve any first-class recording studio if its use would not be inconsistent with any of XYZ's union agreements or cause labor difficulties for other reasons, and if XYZ anticipates that its use would not require expenditures inconsistent with the Authorized Budget. The scheduling and booking of all studio time will be done by XYZ.

4.02. You shall engage artists, producers, musicians, recording studios or other personnel for the recording sessions hereunder, but only after having submitted a written estimate of all Recording Costs (as the term "Recording Costs" is hereinafter defined) to be incurred in connection therewith and having obtained a written authorization therefor signed by one of XYZ's officers. Such estimate shall provide for payment to you or Artist only of union scale for your and Artist's services and shall not contain a charge for arrangements or orchestrations supplied by you or Artist. The written authorization to conduct such session or sessions shall indicate the maximum amount which you may expend for the session or sessions authorized (the "Authorized Budget"). The granting of authorizations and the approval of Authorized Budgets shall be entirely within XYZ's discretion provided that in connection with the first and second LP hereunder, the Authorized Budget shall be mutually approved by you and XYZ. XYZ agrees to approve an Authorized Budget for any particular LP which does not exceed (E.G., SEVENTY PERCENT (70%)) of the applicable Recording Fund for such LP pursuant to clause 6.02 hereof (as same may be reduced pursuant to the provisions of this agreement) and is otherwise in conformity with the requirements hereof. XYZ shall have the right to have a representative attend all recording sessions conducted pursuant to this agreement. Without limiting XYZ's other rights or remedies in such event, if it reasonably appears to XYZ that the Recording Costs for any Masters will exceed the Authorized Budget therefor, XYZ shall have the right to require you to discontinue recording unless you can establish to XYZ's reasonable satisfaction that you can and will pay or reimburse XYZ for any Recording Costs in excess of the Authorized Budget.

4.03. XYZ agrees to advance Recording Costs for the production of each particular LP of the Recording Commitment in an amount not in excess of the Authorized Budget therefor. You will deliver copies of substantiating invoices, receipts, Form B's, vouchers and similar satisfactory documentary evidence of such costs, and if you fail to do so, XYZ's obligation to pay further Recording Costs will be suspended until delivery thereof. You agree to deliver, or cause the individual producer of the Masters to deliver, Form B's and W-4's to XYZ within (E.G., SEVENTY-TWO (72)) hours after each session hereunder so that XYZ may timely make all required union payments, and you agree to deliver all other invoices, receipts, vouchers and documents within (E.G., ONE (1)) week after your receipt thereof. If XYZ incurs late-payment penalties by reason of your failure to make timely delivery of any such materials, you will reimburse XYZ for same upon demand and, without limiting its other rights and remedies, XYZ may deduct an amount equal to all such penalties from monies otherwise payable to you under this agreement. XYZ shall be responsible for late-payment penalties caused solely by XYZ's acts or omissions. If XYZ, in its sole discretion, shall pay any Recording Costs for any Masters hereunder in excess of the Recording Fund in respect thereof, you shall repay any such excess upon demand and, without limiting its other rights and remedies, XYZ may deduct same from any monies payable to you pursuant to this agreement. You further agree, represent and warrant that all Masters delivered by you to XYZ hereunder will be free and clear of any claims by any person AND agree to indemnify XYZ from any claims by any person (i) with regard to Recording Costs of any Masters hereunder in excess of the Recording Fund and/or (ii) inconsistent with the foregoing warranties and representations.

4.04. Without limiting the foregoing, your obligations will include furnishing the services of the individual producers of Masters hereunder, and you shall be solely responsible for engaging and paying them.

4.05. With respect to all LPs in fulfillment of your Recording Commitment hereunder, you hereby request and irrevocably authorize XYZ to pay all mutually approved Producers, engaged by you and to whom you become obligated to pay royalties, a royalty (the "Producing Royalty") on Net Sales of Phonograph Records derived from Master Recordings produced by the Producer concerned hereunder. XYZ shall have the right to approve in writing, in advance of any commitment being made by you, all compensation due any such Producer. If the Recording Costs combined with the Producer's advance for a particular LP do not exceed (E.G., SEVENTY PERCENT (70%)) percent of the Minimum Recording Fund (or Approved Budget, if the LP is recorded in the initial Contract Period) for that LP and if the Producing Royalty does not exceed a basic rate of (E.G., THREE PERCENT (3%)), pursuant to clause 7.01(A)(i) below, with proportionate deductions for other sales, such Producer's advance and Producing Royalty shall be deemed approved. The Producing Royalty shall be recoupable only from royalties payable or becoming payable to or on behalf of you, pursuant to this agreement. The Producing Royalty shall be paid at the same times and subject to the same conditions that royalties are paid to you hereunder. In each instance the Producing Royalty will not, without your and XYZ's written consent, exceed a basic rate of (E.G., THREE PERCENT (3%)), as computed under clause 7.01(A)(i) below, with proportionate reductions on all sales for which reduced royalties are payable hereunder; and may be payable from the first Record sold, in each instance, after recoupment of the Recording Costs attributable to the Record concerned. The recoupment of such Recording Costs shall be computed at your net royalty rate as reduced to reflect the deduction of the Producing Royalty. You shall notify XYZ so that it can comply with this (clause) promptly after you engage the Producer concerned, but in no event later than the release of any record so produced and shall supply XYZ with all necessary information in order to so pay such Producer (XYZ shall have no liability to pay such Producer absent such timely notice). To the extent that you supply XYZ with all of the information that it needs to pay the applicable Producing Royalty and to the extent such Producing Royalty payments are in conformance with the terms and conditions hereof, XYZ agrees to make all applicable Producing Royalty payments on your behalf in accordance with the terms and conditions hereof with respect to all LPs in fulfillment of your Recording Commitment. XYZ's compliance with this authorization will constitute an accommodation to you alone, and nothing herein shall constitute the Producer, or any payee on behalf of the Producer, a beneficiary of or party to this instrument or any other agreement between you and XYZ. All Producing Royalty payments hereunder will constitute payment to you and XYZ will have no liability by reason of any payment. You will indemnify and hold XYZ harmless against any claims asserted against XYZ or any damages, losses or expenses incurred by XYZ by reason of any such Producing Royalty payment or otherwise in connection therewith.

5. RECOUPABLE COSTS:

5.01. XYZ will pay all union scale payments required to be made to Artist in connection with Masters made hereunder, all costs of instrumental, vocal and other personnel specifically approved by XYZ for the recording of such Masters, and all other amounts required to be paid by XYZ pursuant to any applicable law or any collective bargaining agreement between XYZ and any union representing persons who render services in connection with such Masters.

5.02. All amounts described in clause 5.01 above plus all other amounts representing direct expenses paid by XYZ, or incurred in connection with the recording of Masters hereunder (including, without limitation, travel, rehearsal, and equipment rental and cartage expenses, advances to individual producers, transportation costs, hotel and living expenses approved by XYZ, and all studio and engineering charges, in connection with XYZ's facilities and personnel or otherwise) are herein sometimes called "Recording Costs" and shall constitute Advances. All packaging costs in excess of XYZ's then standard design, engraving or manufacturing costs with respect to a standard single disc package shall be recoupable from all monies payable to you hereunder, provided XYZ advises you in advance of such excess packaging costs and you do not object to such Packaging in writing within _____ (NUMBER) (_____) days after XYZ so advises you. All costs incurred by XYZ in connection with the production of Videos made for use in promoting sales of Records made under this agreement will constitute Advances. Notwithstanding the foregoing, fifty percent (50%) of such costs incurred in connection with the production of Videos shall be recoupable only from monies otherwise payable to you due to the exploitation of Videos hereunder. With respect to the preparation of a lacquer, copper or equivalent master from a fully mixed, edited and equalized master tape, an amount equal to the normal engineering charges which would reasonably be incurred in connection with the production of such master on a real time basis at (NAME) Studios (or other first class studios designated by XYZ) will be excluded in the calculation of Recording Costs, but all costs in excess of those normal engineering charges will be included in that calculation. Payments to the AFM Special Payments Fund and the Music Performance Trust Fund based upon record sales as well as analogous AFTRA or other union payments (so-called "per-record royalties"), shall not constitute Advances and shall be paid by XYZ. Nothing contained in this agreement shall be deemed to make you or Artist XYZ's agent or authorize you or Artist to incur any costs on XYZ's behalf under this agreement.

5.03. The portion of the Recording Costs applicable to any Joint Recording which are chargeable under this clause against your royalties will be computed by multiplying the aggregate amount of those Recording Costs by the same fraction used in determining the royalties payable to you in respect of that Joint Recording.

6. ADDITIONAL ADVANCES:

6.01. All monies paid to or on behalf of you or Artist pursuant hereto or at your request or to which you consent during the term of this agreement, other than royalties paid pursuant to this agreement, shall constitute Advances unless expressly agreed to the contrary in writing by XYZ.

6.02.

(a) In connection with each LP delivered in the initial Contract Period, XYZ will pay you an advance for the LP concerned of (AMOUNT IN DOLLARS) ($_____).

(b) In connection with each LP delivered in fulfillment of your Recording Commitment in the first, second, and third Option Periods, XYZ will pay you an Advance in the amount by which the applicable sum indicated below ("Recording Fund") exceeds the Recording Costs for the LP concerned:

(1) First LP recorded during the first Option Period: (AMOUNT IN DOLLARS) ($ _____).

(2) Second LP recorded during the first Option Period: (AMOUNT IN DOLLARS) ($_____).

(3) LPs recorded during the second and third Option Periods: (AMOUNT IN DOLLARS) ($_____).

(c) This subclause 6.02(c) shall apply in respect of each timely delivered LP recorded in fulfillment of your Recording Commitment for the Option Periods hereof and no other LPs. Subject to subclause 6.02(d) below and provided you have timely fulfilled all of your material obligations under this agreement, the Recording Fund for each LP specified in the preceding sentence shall be the amount as determined pursuant to this subclause 6.02(c) rather than the applicable sum as set forth in subclause 6.02(b) above, if the sum as computed pursuant to this subclause 6.02(c) is greater than the applicable sum set forth in subclause 6.02(b) for the LP concerned:

(1) An amount equal to (E.G., 66 PERCENT (66%)) of the average royalties earned by Artist on USNRC Net Sales of the last two LPs of Artist's Recording Commitment (after provisions for reserves for returns and credits of (E.G., FIFTY PERCENT (50%)) computed according to XYZ's month's end accounting statement for Artist's royalty account hereunder as of the earlier of the date of the commencement of recording of the LP concerned or the date (E.G., TWELVE (12)) months after the initial United States release date of each such LP.

(d) Notwithstanding anything to the contrary contained in subclause 6.02(c), the Recording Funds for LPs recorded in fulfillment of your Recording Commitment for the Option Periods hereof shall not exceed:

(1) First LP recorded in the first Option Period: (AMOUNT IN DOLLARS) ($).

(2) Second LP recorded in the first Option Period: (AMOUNT IN DOLLARS) ($).

(3) LPs recorded in the second and third Option Periods: (AMOUNT IN DOLLARS) ($).

(e) Each Advance, where applicable, shall be paid according to the following schedule:

(1) With respect to the first LP:

(A) (AMOUNT IN DOLLARS) ($) promptly after execution hereof.

(B) The balance upon delivery of the LP.

(2) With respect to the second LP:

(A) (AMOUNT IN DOLLARS) ($) promptly after commencement of recording of the LP.

(B) The balance promptly after delivery of the LP.

(3) With respect to each subsequent LP:

(A) (NUMBER) percent (%) of the Minimum Recording Fund applicable to that LP as set forth in subclause 6.02(a) above after commencement of recording of the LP concerned, but in no event shall such payment reduce the remainder of the Minimum Recording Fund for said LP to an amount less than (NUMBER) percent (%) of the actual Recording Costs for the last LP delivered by you.

(B) The balance promptly after delivery of the LP concerned.

6.03. If the Recording Costs paid or reimbursed by XYZ for any Recording in fulfillment of your Recording Commitment exceed the Recording Fund (or Authorized Budget initially established by XYZ with respect to LPs recorded in the initial Contract Period), payable with respect to such Recording, you shall be solely responsible for such excess, it being agreed that if XYZ elects to pay such excess, such payments shall be a direct debt from you to XYZ which, in addition to any other available remedies, XYZ may recover from any sums payable to you and/or Artist hereunder.

7. ROYALTIES:

7.01. In consideration of (i) the copyright ownership provided below; (ii) XYZ's rights to use Artist's name and likeness as provided herein; and (iii) the other agreements, representations and warranties contained herein, XYZ agrees to pay you in connection with the Net Sale of Phonograph Records consisting entirely of Masters hereunder and sold by XYZ or its licensees, a royalty computed at the applicable percentage indicated below, of the applicable Royalty Base Price with respect to the Record concerned, it being agreed that such royalties will be computed and paid in accordance with clause 8 below and the other provisions set forth herein:

(A) On Records sold for distribution through normal retail channels in the United States ("USNRC Net Sales"):

(i) On LPs:

(a) On Masters made during the initial Contract Period: (NUMBER, E.G., 14%).

(b) The royalty rate pursuant to clause 7.01(A)(i)(a) shall apply to the first (NUMBER, E.G., 250,000) units of USNRC Net Sales of LPs comprised of such Masters. The royalty rate will be:

(1) 14 1/2% rather than 14% on the next (NUMBER, E.G., 250,000) units of any such LP (*i.e.*, USNRC Net Sales between (NUMBER, E.G., 250,000) units and (NUMBER, E.G., 500,000) units); and

(2) 15% on USNRC Net Sales of any such LP in excess of (E.G., 500,001) units.

(c) On Masters made during the first Option Period: (NUMBER) %

(d) The royalty rate pursuant to clause 7.01(A)(i)(c) shall apply to the first (NUMBER) units of USNRC Net Sales of LPs comprised of such Masters. The royalty rate will be:

(1) (NO.)% rather than (NO.)% on the next (NUMBER) units of any such LP (*i.e.*, USNRC Net Sales between (NUMBER) units and (NUMBER) units); ·

(2) (NO.)% on the next (NUMBER) units of any such LP (*i.e.*, USNRC Net Sales between (NUMBER) units and (NUMBER) units); and

(3) (NO.)% on USNRC Net Sales of any such LP in excess of (NUMBER) units.

(e) On Masters made during the second and third Option Periods: (NO.)%.

(f) The royalty rate pursuant to clause 7.01(a)(i)(e) shall apply to the first (NUMBER) units of UNSRC Net Sales of LPs comprised of such Masters. The royalty rate will be:

(1) (NO.)% rather than (NO.)% on the next units of any such LP (*i.e.*, USNRC Net Sales between units and (NUMBER) units); and

(2) (NO.)% on the next (NUMBER) units of any such LP (*i.e.*, USNRC Net Sales between (NUMBER) units and (NUMBER) units); and

(3) (NO.)% on USNRC Net Sales of any such LP in excess of (NUMBER) units.

(ii) On Singles: (E.G., 10%)

(B)   (i) Except as provided in clause 7.01(b)(ii) below, on Records sold for distribution through normal retail channels outside the United States, the royalty rate shall be one-half (½) of the applicable royalty rate provided in clauses 7.01(A)(i)(a), 7.01(A)(i)(c), 7.01(A)(i)(e), or 7.01(A)(ii), as the case may be.

(ii) On Records sold for distribution through normal retail channels in the Territory of Canada, the royalty rate shall be (E.G., EIGHTY-FIVE PERCENT (85%)) of the royalty rate provided in clauses 7.01(A)(i)(a), 7.01(A)(i)(c), 7.01(A)(i)(e), or 7.01(A)(ii), as the case may be. On Records sold for distribution through normal retail channels in the Territories of France, Japan and Holland, the royalty rate shall be two-thirds (2/3) of the royalty rate provided in clauses 7.01(A)(i)(a), 7.01(A)(i)(c), 7.01(A)(i)(e), or 7.01(A)(ii), as the case may be. On LPs sold for distribution through normal retail channels in the Territory of the United Kingdom, the royalty rate shall be (E.G., ELEVEN PER-CENT (11%)). On LPs sold for distribution through normal retail channels in the Territories of West Germany and Australia, the royalty rate shall be (E.G., TEN PERCENT (10%)). The royalty rate on single Records sold for distribution in the Territories of the United Kingdom, West Germany and Australia shall be determined by reducing the LP royalty rate in the applicable territory in the same proportion that the United States single royalty rate is reduced as compared to the LP royalty rate on the applicable LP.

7.02.   (a) With respect to Mid-line Records, the royalty rate shall be two-thirds (2/3) of the otherwise applicable basic rate. With respect to Records sold to the Armed Forces Post Exchanges or to the United States or a state or local government, the royalty rate shall be three-quarters (3/4) of the otherwise applicable basic rate. With respect to long play singles, the royalty rate shall be three-quarters (3/4) of the otherwise applicable single Record Rate. With respect to Budget Records, premium records, EPs, or with respect to Records other than LPs not specifically referred to herein, the royalty rate shall be one-half (½) of the otherwise applicable basic rate (without regard to escalations of such basic rate). With respect to any Multiple Record LP, if any, the royalty rate shall be the full otherwise applicable royalty rate if, at the beginning of the royalty accounting period when such Record is initially released, the Suggested Retail List Price of such LP is at least twice the Suggested Retail List Price for XYZ's "top-line" single disc LPs marketed by XYZ or its principal licensee in the territory where the Multiple Record LP is sold. If a different Suggested Retail List Price applies to such Multiple Record LP, the royalty rate prescribed in the preceding sentence will be reduced in proportion to the variance in the Suggested Retail List Price (but will not be less than one-half (½) of the applicable royalty rate prescribed in clause 7.01 for such LP). With respect to Net Sales of Records sold in the form of compact discs or other new audio Record configurations, XYZ shall pay you, with respect to each such Record, a royalty equal to the same dollars and cents (or other currency) royalty amount as is payable hereunder with respect to a top-line single LP not in the form of a compact disc or such new configuration. Notwithstanding the foregoing, said royalty shall be in effect for (E.G., TWO (2)) years from the date hereof. At any time after such date, at your written request, XYZ shall review the sale of its Records.

(b) If during the year previous to the date of such request, XYZ's sales of Records in the form of compact discs comprise at least (NUMBER) percent (NO.%) of total sales of all of XYZ's Records in all other configurations during such period, then, at that time, XYZ and you shall negotiate in good faith regarding the royalty payable with respect to such compact disc sales commencing with the next full accounting period. The royalty payable with respect to such compact discs shall never exceed the applicable royalty rate set forth in clause 7 hereunder.

7.03. With respect to the following Records and/or exploitation of Masters, the royalty hereunder shall be a sum equal to (E.G., FIFTY PERCENT (50%)) of XYZ's net receipts with respect to such exploitation: (i) Records derived from Masters sold through record clubs or similar sales plans; (ii) licenses of Masters for methods of distribution such as "key outlet marketing" (distribution through retail fulfillment centers in conjunction with special advertisements on radio or television), direct mail, or mail order, or by any combination of the methods set forth above or other methods; and (iii) licenses of Masters on a flat fee or cent rate. Notwithstanding anything to the contrary herein, with respect to Records sold through record clubs pursuant to subsection (i) above, XYZ will pay you as provided herein on up to (E.G., FIFTY PERCENT (50%)) of Records distributed as "free" or bonus Records provided that the record club concerned pays XYZ on such Records.

7.04.   (a) If XYZ licenses Videos (i.e., sight and sound records designed to reproduce the audio performances of recording artists together with a visual image) or makes commercial use of such Videos embodying Artist's performances (other than as provided below), the royalty payable by XYZ to you shall be one-half (½) of XYZ's net receipts derived therefrom after deducting (i) any and all direct costs and/or third party payments in connection with the creation, manufacture, exploitation or use of the Videos from Artist's share of net receipts; and (ii) an additional fee in lieu of any overhead or distribution fee of (E.G., TWENTY-FIVE PERCENT (25%)) of the gross receipts in connection therewith (XYZ shall not be entitled to the deduction described in this clause 7.04(a)(ii) if the use concerned is covered by the first sentence of clause 7.04(b) below). If any item of direct costs is attributable to receipts from such uses of Masters made under this agreement and other master recordings, the amount of the expense item which will be deductible in computing the net receipts under this paragraph will be determined by apportionment. It is specifically agreed that XYZ shall have the right to license Videos to third parties (e.g., club services) without any payment to you as long as XYZ does not receive any such payment. To the extent XYZ receives any payment for such promotional uses, XYZ will credit your account with one-half (½) of the net receipts as provided in this clause 7.04.

(b) With respect to so-called home video devices embodying Artist's performances (e.g., video cassettes or discs intended primarily for home use), if XYZ licenses a third party to manufacture and distribute such devices, clause 7.04(a) shall apply (if such third party is an affiliated company as XYZ HOME VIDEO, XYZ shall negotiate with such company at arm's length). If XYZ RECORDS manufactures and distributes such devices, you will be entitled to a royalty computed as provided in this clause, but the following rates shall apply instead of the rates specified in clause 7.01 above: (A) On units sold for distribution in the United States: (E.G., 15%) of the applicable Royalty Base Price; and (B) On units sold for distribution outside the United States: (E.G., 10%) of the applicable Royalty Base Price. Said royalties shall be inclusive of any third party payments required in connection with the sale of such devices including, without limitation, artist and producer royalties and copyright payments.

7.05. The terms "net receipts," "net sums," or "net amount received" and similar terms in this clause shall mean amounts received by XYZ in connection with the subject matter thereof which are solely attributable to the Masters hereunder, less any costs or expenses which XYZ is required to pay or credit to third parties with whom XYZ deals at arm's length (such as, without limitation, production costs, mechanical royalties, AF of M and other union or guild payments).

7.06. As to Records not consisting entirely of Masters, the royalty rates otherwise payable to you hereunder shall be prorated on the basis of the number of Masters which are embodied on such records compared to the total number of masters (including the Masters) contained on each such Record. As to Joint Recordings, the royalty rate due shall be the royalty rate provided for herein divided by the number of artists with respect to whom XYZ is obligated to pay a royalty (including Artist).

7.07. No royalties shall be due or payable in respect of (i) Records furnished on a no-charge basis or sold for less than (E.G., FIFTY PERCENT (50%)) of XYZ's or the XYZ DISTRIBUTOR'S (or their respective licensees') posted wholesale list price to disc jockeys, publishers, employees of XYZ or the XYZ DISTRIBUTOR (or their respective licensees'), motion picture companies, radio and television stations and other customary recipients of free, discounted or promotional Records; (ii) Records sold by XYZ or the XYZ DISTRIBUTOR at close-out prices or for scrap, or at less than XYZ's or its Distributor's (or their respective licensees') inventory cost; (iii) Records (or fractions thereof) given away or shipped on a so-called "no charge" or "freebie" basis or sold for (E.G., FIFTY PERCENT (50%)) or less of XYZ's or XYZ DISTRIBUTOR'S (or their respective licensees') posted wholesale list price, to distributors, subdistributors, dealers and others whether or not such Records are intended for sale to third parties; (iv) Records sold by XYZ or the XYZ DISTRIBUTOR (or their respective licensees) directly to consumers for a price of (E.G., $3.00) or less per single disc LP or the tape equivalent (whether sold singly or in Multiple Record LP packages); and (v) when XYZ, an XYZ DISTRIBUTOR or their respective licensees sells Records at a discount from XYZ's, and XYZ DISTRIB-UTOR'S or their respective licensees', as applicable, posted wholesale list price (but for more than (E.G., FIFTY PERCENT (50%)) of such price), the number of Records determined by applying such discount to the total number of Records shipped. For convenience, those Records sold at a discount in lieu of Records furnished on a so-called "no charge" basis (definitionally determined herein as the percentage amount of such discount multiplied by the number of Records sold at such discount) and Records furnished on such a so-called "no charge" basis are collectively sometimes referred to herein as "Free Goods". References in this agreement to "Records for which no royalties are payable hereunder," or words of similar connotation, shall include, without limitation, all Free Goods. Free Goods embodying LPs hereunder are sometimes referred to herein as "LP Free Goods", and Free Goods embodying single Records hereunder are some-times referred to herein as "Single Free Goods." XYZ and you acknowledge and agree that, with respect to each LP and Mini-LP hereunder, XYZ shall ship LP Free Goods in accordance with the current policy of the current XYZ DISTRIBU-TOR, which policy is that (E.G., FIFTEEN PERCENT (15%)) of the aggregate units of each LP sold by XYZ hereunder or shipped by XYZ or the XYZ DISTRIBUTOR hereunder shall be LP Free Goods. XYZ and you acknowledge and agree that, with respect to each single Record hereunder, XYZ shall ship single Free Goods in accordance with the current policy of the current XYZ DISTRIBUTOR, which policy is that (E.G., TWENTY-THREE PERCENT (23%)) of the aggregate units of such single Record sold by XYZ or the XYZ DISTRIBUTOR or shipped by XYZ or the XYZ DISTRIBUTOR hereunder shall be Single Free Goods. XYZ agrees that, with respect to each LP and Mini-LP hereunder, XYZ and the XYZ DISTRIBUTOR shall not ship Special LP Free Goods (hereinafter defined) in excess of (E.G., TEN PERCENT (10%)) of all Records embodying such LP and/or Mini-LP sold by XYZ or the XYZ DISTRIB-UTOR hereunder or shipped by XYZ or the XYZ DISTRIBUTOR hereunder. XYZ agrees that, with respect to each single Record hereunder, XYZ and the XYZ DISTRIBUTOR shall not ship Special Single Free Goods (hereinafter defined) in excess of (E.G., TEN PERCENT (10%)) of the aggregate units of such single Record sold by XYZ or the XYZ DISTRIBUTOR or shipped by XYZ or the XYZ DISTRIBUTOR hereunder. In the event XYZ or the XYZ DISTRIBUTOR shall ship Free Goods in excess of the limitations provided for herein, XYZ and the XYZ DISTRIBUTOR shall not be deemed in breach hereof and XYZ's only obligation to you in such event shall be to pay you royalties as provided herein in respect of such excess Free Goods. From time to time, XYZ and the XYZ DISTRIBUTOR may conduct special programs with respect to the marketing and merchandising of Records of various artists which may include Artist hereunder, or special "impact" programs concerning the marketing and merchandising of recordings hereunder, and all of said special programs may involve the distribution of additional Free Goods; all such additional Free Goods shipped pursuant to any such special program are herein referred to as "Special Free Goods," all additional LP Free Goods shipped pursuant to any such special program are herein referred to as "Special LP Free Goods," and all additional Single Free Goods shipped pursuant to any such special program are herein referred to as "Special Single Free Goods." If XYZ distributes LPs hereunder as "free" or "no-charge" for resale in the United States which are tied to the sale of LPs of other artists for the purpose of selling such other artists' LPs rather than your own, then XYZ shall pay you the applicable royalty on such free LPs so distributed. By way of clarification, this is specifically not intended to restrict XYZ or XYZ's licensees from distributing your LPs through any club operation or any other similar program wherein a customer may select among a variety of LPs, some of which are free and some of which are paid for.

7.08. The royalty payable to you hereunder includes all royalties due Artist, the individual producers and any other Persons on account of the sale of Records hereunder (other than AF of M or other similar per-record royalties and mechanical royalties).

8. ROYALTY ACCOUNTINGS:

8.01. XYZ will compute your royalties as of each (JUNE 30) and (DECEMBER 30) for the prior six (6) months, in respect of each such six (6) month period in which there are sales or returns of Records on which royalties are payable to you. On or before the next September 30th with respect to the period ending June 30th, and on or before March 31st with respect to the period ending December 31st, XYZ will send you a statement covering those royalties and will remit to you the net amount of such royalties, if any, after deducting any and all unrecouped Advances and chargeable costs under this agreement and such amount, if any, which XYZ may be required to withhold pursuant to the CALIFORNIA REVENUE AND TAXATION CODE, the U.S. Tax Regulations or any other applicable statute, regulation, treaty or law. After the term hereof, no royalty statements shall be required for periods during which no additional royalties accrue. In computing the number of Records sold, only Records for which XYZ has been paid or credited shall be deemed sold, and XYZ shall have the right to deduct returns and credits of any nature and to withhold reasonable reserves (which shall be liquidated within four (4) full accounting periods after the period in which such reserves were initially established) therefor from payments otherwise due you. If XYZ makes any overpayment to you (e.g., by reason of an accounting error or by paying royalties on Records returned later), you shall reimburse XYZ for it but only to the extent XYZ does not deduct such sums from monies due you hereunder. XYZ may at any time elect to utilize a different method of computing royalties so long as such method does not decrease the net monies received by or credited to you hereunder. Notwithstanding the foregoing, returns will be apportioned between Records sold and "free goods" in the same ratio in which XYZ's customer's account is credited.

8.02. Royalties for Records sold for distribution outside the United States ("foreign sales") shall be computed in the same national currency as XYZ is accounted to by its licensees with respect to the sale concerned and shall be paid at the same rate of exchange as XYZ is paid, and shall be proportionately subject to any taxes applicable to royalties remitted by or received from foreign sources; provided, however, that royalties on Records sold outside the United States shall not be due and payable by XYZ until payment therefor has been received by XYZ (less cost of conversion) in the United States in United States dollars. For purposes of accounting to you, XYZ will treat any foreign sale as a sale made during the same six (6) month period in which XYZ receives its licensee's accounting and payment for that sale. If XYZ does not receive payment in the United States in United States dollars, and shall be required to accept payment in foreign currency or in a foreign country, XYZ shall deposit to your credit (at your request and expense) in such currency in a depository selected by you in the country in which XYZ is required to accept payment, your share of royalties due and payable with respect to such sales, and shall notify you of such deposit upon your written request. Deposit as aforesaid shall fulfill XYZ's obligations as to Phonograph Record sales to which such royalty payments are applicable. If any law, government ruling or other restriction affects the amount of the payments which XYZ's licensees can remit to XYZ, XYZ may deduct from your royalties an amount proportionate to the reduction in such licensee's remittances and appropriately credit your account when and if such reduction is rectified.

8.03. All royalty statements rendered by XYZ shall be conclusively binding upon you and not subject to any objection by you for any reason unless specific objection in writing, stating the basis thereof, is given to XYZ within (NUMBER) (NO.) years from the date such statement is rendered. Each statement shall be deemed rendered when due unless you notify XYZ to the contrary within (E.G., SIXTY (60)) days after the applicable due date specified in clause 8.01 above. Failure to make specific objection within the (E.G., TWO (2)) years time period shall be deemed approval of such statement. You will not have the right to sue XYZ in connection with any royalty accounting, or to sue XYZ for royalties on Records sold during the period a royalty accounting covers, unless you commence the suit within that two years after the date rendered.

8.04. You may, at your own expense, directly audit XYZ's books and records relating to this agreement that report the sales of Phonograph Records or other exploitation of Masters for which royalties are payable hereunder. You may make such audit only for the purpose of verifying the accuracy of statements sent to you hereunder and only as provided herein. You shall have the right to audit said books by notice to XYZ at least (E.G., THIRTY (30)) days prior to the date you intend to commence your audit. Said audit shall be conducted by a reputable independent certified public accountant experienced in recording industry audits, shall be conducted in such a manner so as not to disrupt XYZ's other functions and shall be completed promptly. You may make such an examination for a particular statement only once and only within (E.G., TWO (2)) years after the date any such statement is due as provided in clause 8.01 above. Any such audit shall be conducted only during XYZ's usual business hours and at the place where it keeps the books and records to be examined. Your auditor shall review his tentative findings with a member of XYZ's finance staff designated and made available by XYZ before rendering a report to you so as to remedy any factual errors and clarify any issues that may have resulted from misunderstanding.

9.   XYZ's ADDITIONAL RIGHTS:

9.01. You warrant, represent and agree that throughout the Territory, XYZ is the sole, exclusive and perpetual owner of all Masters delivered hereunder or recorded by Artist during the term of this agreement, which ownership entitles XYZ, among other things, to all right, title and interest in the copyright in and to the Masters (but excluding the copyrights of the musical compositions contained therein). Each Master made under this agreement or during its term, from the inception of its recording, will be considered a "work made for hire" for XYZ; if any such Master is determined not to be such a "work," it will be deemed transferred to XYZ by this agreement, together with all rights and title in and to it. All Masters made under this agreement or during its term (including duplicates, work tapes, etc.), the performances contained thereon and the Recordings derived therefrom shall, from the inception of their creation, be the sole property of XYZ, in perpetuity, free from any claims by you, Artist or any other Person and XYZ shall have the right to use and control same subject to the terms herein. XYZ (or XYZ's designees) shall have the exclusive right to copyright all such Masters in its name as the author and owner of them and to secure any and all renewals and extensions of such copyright throughout the Territory. You will execute and deliver to XYZ such instruments of transfer and other documents regarding the rights of XYZ or its designees in the Masters subject to this agreement as XYZ may reasonably request to carry out the purposes of this agreement, and XYZ may sign such documents in your name or the name of Artist (and you hereby appoint XYZ your agent and attorney-in-fact for such purposes) and make appropriate disposition of them consistent with this agreement.

9.02. Without limiting the generality of the foregoing, XYZ and any Person authorized by XYZ shall have the unlimited and exclusive rights to manufacture Records by any method(s) now or hereafter known embodying any portion(s) or all of the performances embodied on Masters hereunder; to publicly perform such Records and to permit the public performance thereof in any medium; to import, export, sell, transfer, lease, rent, deal in or otherwise dispose of such Masters and Records derived therefrom throughout the Territory under any trademarks, trade names or labels designated by XYZ; to edit or adapt the Masters to conform to technological or commercial requirements in various formats now or hereafter known or developed, or to eliminate material which might subject XYZ to any legal action; to use the Masters for background music, synchronization in motion pictures and television soundtracks and other similar purposes, including, without limitation, use on transportation facilities, without any payment other than as provided herein; or XYZ and its subsidiaries, affiliates and licensees may, at their election, delay or refrain from doing any one or more of the foregoing.

9.03. XYZ and any licensee of XYZ each shall have the perpetual right, without liability to any Person, and may grant to others the right, to reproduce, print, publish or disseminate in any medium your name, the names, portraits, pictures and likenesses of the Artist and individual producer and all other persons performing services in connection with Masters made under this agreement (including, without limitation, all professional, group and other assumed or fictitious names used by them), and biographical material concerning them for purposes of advertising, promotion and trade in connection with you or Artist, the making and exploitation of Records hereunder and general goodwill advertising. During the term hereof, XYZ or its licensees may, in the Territory, bill, advertise and describe Artist as an Exclusive XYZ Artist or by a similar designation. XYZ's rights as described in this clause shall be exclusive during the term of this agreement and non-exclusive thereafter. Artist shall be available from time to time to appear for photography, poster and cover art and the like, under the reasonable direction of XYZ or its nominees, and to appear for interviews with representatives of the communications media and XYZ's publicity personnel. [You and Artist shall not be entitled to any compensation for such services, except as may be required by applicable union agreements; provided, however, that if you or Artist is required to travel outside of a fifty mile radius of your or Artist's then place of residence, XYZ shall reimburse you or Artist (as the case may be) for the reasonable travel and living expenses incurred by you or Artist in connection with the rendition of services rendered at XYZ's direction as provided herein pursuant to a budget approved in advance by XYZ in writing.]

10.   MARKETING AND MISCELLANEOUS RESTRICTIONS:

10.01. Within (E.G., TEN (10)) days following the execution hereof, you may supply XYZ with an approved biography and (E.G., SIX (6)) approved pictures of Artist to be used by XYZ pursuant to clause 9.03 above. Such submission shall be made to XYZ's Vice President of Artist Development; concurrently therewith, you shall also notify XYZ of such fact. If XYZ disapproves of the biography or pictures supplied by you, XYZ will make available to you for your approval biographical material and pictures concerning Artist to be so used by XYZ. Your approval will not be unreasonably withheld, and will be deemed given unless your notice of disapproval (including the reason) has been received by XYZ within (E.G., FIVE (5)) business days after the material has been made available to you. In the event that you timely disapprove of any biographical material or pictures, you will, within (E.G., SEVEN (7)) days of the date of your disapproval notice, supply to XYZ approved biographical material or pictures. If the biographical material or pictures supplied by you, pursuant to the preceding sentence, are not satisfactory to XYZ or in the event that you do not supply the biographical material or pictures to XYZ pursuant to this clause, XYZ shall thereafter have the right to select and use such biographical material and pictures as it shall determine, in its sole discretion, and you shall have no approval rights in respect thereof. You may from time to time supply XYZ with more recent approved pictures than in XYZ's possession at that time. If you do so, the procedures set forth in this paragraph shall apply. No inadvertent failure by XYZ to comply with this clause will constitute a breach of this agreement.

10.02. During the term of this agreement, with respect to Records manufactured for sale in the United States, XYZ will not without your consent:

(a) initially release any LP in fulfillment of your Recording Commitment under any Record label other than XYZ in the United States and Canada, or other label then used by XYZ for performances by XYZ's best selling artists then under exclusive term contract to XYZ;

(b) couple during any one year period more than (NUMBER) (NO.) Masters made hereunder on any disc Record with Recordings not embodying Artist's performances hereunder, except promotional Records and programs for use on public transportation carriers and facilities;

(c) use Masters made under this agreement on premium Records to promote the sale of any product or service other than Phonograph Records;

(d) release any LP consisting of Masters made hereunder as a Budget Record or Mid-line Record within (E.G., TWELVE (12)) months after such LP's initial release, unless XYZ pays you the otherwise applicable royalty rate (i.e., without reduction of the rate provided in clause 7.02 above with respect to LPs sold prior to such date). Nothing contained in this subclause 10.02(d) shall be deemed to limit XYZ's rights to initially release an LP made hereunder as a Mid-line Record or Budget Record as part of a "new or developing artist" type of program to stimulate the sales of Artist's LP.

(e) sell Phonograph Records derived from any Master made hereunder as "cut-outs", within (E.G., SIX (6)) months after the initial United States release of the Master concerned.

10.03. If XYZ determines during the term of this agreement to edit or remix any Masters made under this agreement for release on LPs in the United States, it will accord you a period of (E.G., SEVEN (7)) days in which to do that work, unless that delay would interfere with a scheduled release, in which case XYZ will accord you as many days as is possible without so interfering with the scheduled release. Any costs incurred in connection therewith shall be deemed additional recording costs in connection with the project concerned. The preceding sentence will not apply to editing or remixing for the purpose of equalizing the running time of tracks on LPs in non-disc configurations. An inadvertent failure by XYZ to comply with the preceding clause shall not be deemed a breach of this agreement.

10.04. In connection with the release of the first three (3) LPs hereunder, XYZ and you shall produce an aggregate of three (3) Videos. In connection with such Videos, as well as any other Videos which XYZ and you mutually decide to produce during the term hereof (which neither XYZ nor you are under any obligation whatsoever to do), the following shall be applicable:

(a) The selection(s) to be embodied in each Video shall be mutually designated by you and XYZ.

(b) Each Video shall be shot on a date or dates and at a location or locations to be mutually designated by you and XYZ and subject to Artist's reasonable availability.

(c) The producer and director of each Video, and the concept or script for each Video, shall be approved by both you and XYZ. XYZ shall engage the producer, director and other production personnel for each Video, and shall be responsible for and shall pay the production costs of each Video in an amount not in excess of a budget to be established in advance by you and XYZ (the "Production Budget"). You shall be responsible for and shall pay the production costs for each Video which are in excess of the Production Budget. In the event that XYZ shall pay any production costs for which you are responsible pursuant to the foregoing (which XYZ is in no way obligated to do), you shall promptly reimburse XYZ for such excess upon demand and, without limiting XYZ's other rights and remedies. XYZ may deduct an amount equal to such excess from any monies otherwise payable to you hereunder. Artist's compensation for performing in such Videos (as opposed to your compensation with respect to the exploitation of such Videos which is provided elsewhere herein) shall be limited to any minimum amounts required to be paid for such performance pursuant to any collective bargaining agreements pertaining thereto; provided, however, that Artist hereby waives any right to receive such compensation to the extent such right may be waived.

(d) XYZ shall be the sole owner of all worldwide rights in and to each Video (including the worldwide copyrights therein and thereto).

(e) You shall issue (or shall cause the music publishing companies having the right to do so to issue) (i) worldwide, perpetual synchronization licenses, and (ii) perpetual licenses for public performance in the United States (to the extent that ASCAP and BMI are unable to issue same), to XYZ at no cost for the use of all Controlled Compositions in any such Videos effective as of the commencement of production of the applicable Video (and your execution of this agreement shall constitute the issuance of such licenses by any music publishing company which is owned or controlled by you, Artist or by any Person owned or controlled by you or Artist). If you shall fail to cause any such music publishing company to issue any such license to XYZ, and if XYZ shall be required to pay any fee to such music publishing company in order to obtain any such license, then XYZ shall have the right to deduct the amount of such license fee from any and all sums otherwise payable to you hereunder.

(f) XYZ shall have the right to use and allow others to use each Video for advertising and promotional purposes with no payment to you or Artist except as otherwise provided herein. As used herein, "advertising and promotional purposes" shall mean all uses for which XYZ receives no monetary consideration from licensees in excess of any incidental fee, a reasonable amount as reimbursement for its administrative costs, and the actual costs incurred by XYZ for tape stock, duplication of the Videos and shipping. Compensation derived from such promotional uses and due you hereunder shall be credited to your account as provided in clause 7.04 above.

(g) XYZ shall also have the right to use and allow others to use the Videos for commercial purposes. As used in this subclause 10.04(g), "commercial purposes" shall mean any use for which XYZ receives monetary consideration in excess of any incidental fee, a reasonable amount as reimbursement for its administrative costs, and the actual costs incurred by XYZ for tape stock, duplication of the Videos and shipping. Compensation derived from such commercial exploitation and due you hereunder shall be credited to your account as provided in clause 7.04 above.

(h) Each Video shall be deemed a Material as provided herein and XYZ shall have the rights otherwise applicable hereto with respect to Masters made hereunder including, without limitation, the right to use and publish, and to permit others to use and publish, your and Artist's name and likeness in each Video and for advertising and purposes of trade in connection therewith.

10.05. Notwithstanding anything to the contrary contained herein, any member of Artist shall have the right, during the term hereof, to perform as a background vocalist or background instrumentalist for the purpose of making audio Phonograph Records for others subject to the following:

(a) You have then fulfilled all your obligations hereunder, and the engagement does not interfere with the continuing prompt performance of your obligations to XYZ nor with any professional engagements to which you or Artist is committed and which are intended to aid in the promotion of Records hereunder;

(b) The member of Artist will not render a solo or "step-out performance" and the musical style of the recording will not be substantially similar to the characteristic musical style of Recordings made by Artist for XYZ;

(c) The member of Artist will not record any material embodied on a Master theretofore or thereafter delivered by you hereunder, and neither you nor Artist shall be restricted from recording the same material for XYZ (which you shall not do without XYZ's written consent);

(d) The name of the member performing (but not the group name of Artist) may be used in a courtesy credit to XYZ Records on the LP liners used for such Records, in the same position as the credits accorded to other sidepersons and in type identical in size, prominence and all other respects. Except as provided in this subclause (d), neither the Artist's name, the name of the performing member, nor likeness nor biographical material may be used in any manner in connection with such Recordings. Without limiting the foregoing, the name of the performing member and/or his likeness shall not be used on the front cover of LPs, on sleeves or labels used for single records, or in advertising, publicity or other forms of exploitation, without XYZ's express written consent which XYZ may withhold in its absolute discretion.

(e) No more than one (1) member of Artist shall perform as a sideperson on any LP, EP or Recording.

10.06. In preparation for the initial release in the United States during the term of this agreement of each LP in fulfillment of your Recording Commitment, XYZ shall consult with you or Artist regarding the proposed album artwork. No inadvertent failure by XYZ to comply with the terms of this clause shall be a breach of this agreement. XYZ's decision on all packaging elements shall be final. This clause shall apply only to LPs timely delivered.

10.07. (a) XYZ will release each LP recorded in fulfillment of your Recording Commitment in the United States within (E.G., FOUR (4)) months after delivery of the LP concerned. If XYZ fails to do so, you may notify XYZ within (E.G., FIFTEEN (15)) days after the end of the four (4) months period concerned, that you intend to terminate the term of this agreement unless XYZ releases the LP within (E.G., SIXTY (60)) days after XYZ's receipt of your notice (the "cure period"). If XYZ fails to release the LP before the end of the cure period, you may terminate the term of this agreement by giving XYZ notice within (E.G., THIRTY (30)) days after the end of the cure period.

On receipt by XYZ of your termination notice, the term of this agreement will end and all parties will be deemed to have fulfilled all of their obligations under it except those obligations which survive the end of the term (e.g., warranties, re-recording restrictions and obligations to pay royalties). Your only remedy for failure by XYZ to release an LP will be termination in accordance with this clause. If you fail to give XYZ either of those notices within the period specified, your right to terminate will lapse.

(b) (1) XYZ will release each LP recorded in fulfillment of your Recording Commitment in the Territories of Canada, the United Kingdom, and West Germany (the "Release Territories") within (E.G., FOUR (4)) months after the release of the applicable LP in the United States.

(2) If XYZ fails to comply with subclause 10.07(b)(1) in any Release Territory, you may notify XYZ within (E.G., SIXTY (60)) days after the end of the four-month period concerned that you intend to invoke this subclause 10.07(b)(2) if XYZ does not release that LP in that (E.G., THIRTY (30)) days after XYZ's receipt of your notice ("Cure Period"). If XYZ fails to do so, you will have the right ("Termination Option") to terminate XYZ's rights to manufacture and distribute Records derived from the Recordings comprised in that LP in that Release Territory. If XYZ fails to so release (E.G., TWO (2)) consecutive LPs within such cure periods, you will have the right ("Termination Option") to terminate XYZ's right to manufacture and distribute the second such unreleased LP and all subsequent LPs in the Territory. You may exercise either Termination Option by giving XYZ notice within (E.G., THIRTY (30)) days after the end of the Cure Period. Your only remedy for failure by XYZ to release an LP will be termination of XYZ's territorial rights in the Recordings in it, in accordance with this clause. If you fail to give XYZ either of those notices within the period specified, your rights under this subclause will lapse. If you exercise a Termination Option, XYZ will prepare and transmit to you for execution a license agreement authorizing you to exploit those Recordings in the Release Territory concerned, subject to the following conditions:

(i) You will be required to obtain and deliver to XYZ, in advance: (A) all consents by other Persons which XYZ may require (including but not limited to consents by recording artists); and (B) all agreements by other Persons which XYZ may require to look to you, and not to XYZ, for the fulfillment of any obligations arising in connection with the manufacture or distribution of Records under the license (including such agreements by unions and funds established under union agreements). You will also become a first party to the Phonograph Record Manufacturers' Special Payments Fund Agreement dated November 1979, entered into by XYZ with the American

Federation of Musicians of the United States and Canada, or the successor agreement then in effect. The license will not become effective until you have complied with all the provisions of this subsection (i).

(ii) You will make all payments required in connection with the manufacture, sale or distribution in that Release Territory of Phonograph Records made from those Master Recordings after the effective date of the license, including, without limitation, all royalties and other payments to performing artists, producers, owners of copyrights in musical compositions, the Music Performance Trust Fund and Special Payments Funds, and any other unions and union funds. You will comply with the applicable rules and regulations of the American Federation of Musicians and any other union having jurisdiction and any other applicable laws, rules and regulations covering any use of the Recordings by you or any Person deriving rights from you, in the manufacture and sale of Phonograph Records or otherwise.

(iii) No warranty or representation, express or implied, will be made by XYZ in connection with the Recordings, the license, or otherwise. You will indemnify and hold harmless XYZ and its licensees against all claims, damages, liabilities, costs, and expenses, including reasonable counsel fees, arising out of any use of the Recordings or exercise of such rights by you or any Person deriving rights from you.

(iv) XYZ will instruct its licensees in that Release Territory not to manufacture Records derived from those Master Recordings for sale there, except as permitted under subclause 10.07(b)(2)(vii) below. If you notify XYZ of such manufacture, XYZ will instruct the licensee concerned to discontinue it, but neither XYZ nor the XYZ Licensee shall have any liability by reason of such manufacture occurring before XYZ's receipt of such notice, and XYZ shall have no liability by reason of such manufacture at any time.

(v) Each Record made under the license will bear a sound recording copyright notice identical to the notice used by XYZ for its initial United States release of the Recording concerned, or such other notice as XYZ shall require. Otherwise, those Records will not be identified directly or indirectly with XYZ.

(vi) All gross proceeds in any form whatever derived by you from the exploitation of those Master Recordings will be paid to XYZ promptly following your receipt of the proceeds concerned; (E.G., FIFTY PERCENT (50%)) of all such monies received by XYZ will be credited to your royalty account. XYZ will have the right to examine your books and records for the purpose of verifying the accuracy of the accountings rendered by you to XYZ under this subclause. All agreements entered into by you with others regarding the exploitation of such rights will require them to pay such sums directly to XYZ and furnish XYZ with duplicate copies of all accountings rendered by them to you, and will provide for such examination of their books and records by XYZ. XYZ will remit to you any overpayments made to it by reason of the preceding sentence.

(vii) XYZ and its licensees will have the continuing right at all times to manufacture and sell recompilation LPs (defined below) which may contain those Master Recordings in that Release Territory. (A "recompilation LP" is an LP containing Master Recordings previously released in different LP combinations, such as a "Greatest Hits" or "Best of" LP.)

(viii) Notwithstanding the foregoing, if any LP other than the first LP delivered hereunder fails to achieve at least a Top 20 position on the Billboard Pop Album chart within (E.G., FOUR (4)) months after release in the United States, that LP will not be subject to any provisions of this subclause 10.07(b).

(c) The running of each of the periods referred to in Subclauses 10.07(a) and 10.07(b) will be suspended (and the expiration date of each of those periods will be postponed) for the period of any suspension of the running of the term of this agreement. If any such period would otherwise expire on a date between October 15 and the next January 16, its running will be suspended for the duration of the period between October 15 and January 16 and its expiration date will be postponed by the same amount of time. If any LP is delivered to XYZ later than the time prescribed in clause 3, this clause will not apply to that LP.

11. LICENSES FOR MUSICAL COMPOSITIONS:

11.01.   (a)(1) You hereby grant to XYZ an irrevocable license under copyright to reproduce such Controlled Compositions on Phonograph Records and distribute them in the United States and Canada.

(2) For that license, XYZ will pay Mechanical Royalties, on the basis of Net Sales, at the following rates:

(i) ON RECORDS MANUFACTURED FOR DISTRIBUTION IN THE UNITED STATES: The rate equal to seventy-five percent (75%) of the minimum compulsory license rate applicable to the use of musical compositions on Phonograph Records under the United States copyright law at the time of the commencement of the recording of the Master concerned but in no event later than the last date for timely delivery of such Master. (That minimum statutory rate is currently

6.60 cents per Composition, effective January 1, 1994.) Notwithstanding the foregoing, in the event any LP delivered in fulfillment of your Recording Commitment achieves USNRC Net Sales in excess of one million (1,000,000) units, the mechanical royalty payable on all Controlled Compositions in respect of each LP sold after such sales level is achieved shall be at the minimum statutory rate, as determined above.

(ii) ON RECORDS MANUFACTURED FOR DISTRIBUTION IN CANADA:

(A) The rate equal to (E.G., FOUR PERCENT (4%)) of the minimum compulsory license rate applicable to the use of musical works on phonorecords under the copyright law of Canada at the time of the commencement of recording of the Master pursuant to clause 3 hereof but in no event later than the last date for timely delivery of such Master pursuant to clause 3.

(B) The rate applicable under this clause (ii) will not be less than two cents ($0.02) per Composition and not more than the rate which would be applicable to the Records concerned under subclause 11.01(a)(2)(i) above if they were manufactured for distribution in the United States.

(b) The total Mechanical Royalty for all Compositions (including Controlled Compositions) with respect to (i) each single disc LP (or the equivalent thereof) shall be not more than ten (10) times the minimum statutory rate referred to in subclause 11.01(a)(2)(i); (ii) twice that amount on each single Record released hereunder; (iii) five (5) times that amount of any Mini-LP; and (iv) with respect to Multiple Record LPs (if any), the maximum aggregate Mechanical Royalty shall not be more than the maximum Mechanical Royalty applicable to a single disc LP or the equivalent Record (as set forth above) multiplied by a fraction, the numerator of which is the Suggested Retail List Price of such Multiple Record LP at the commencement of the accounting period when such LP is initially released, and the denominator of which is the applicable Suggested Retail List Price of "top-line" single disc LPs at the time of initial release of such Multiple Record LP. With respect to the exploitation or sale of Records as described in clauses 7.02 (other than with respect to EPs, singles and Multiple Record LPs), 7.03 (other than with respect to club sales through third parties such as the RCA RECORD CLUB where a separate license is negotiated between such club and the copyright proprietor and paid by such club) and 7.06, the Mechanical Royalty maximums shall be three-fourths (3/4) of the amounts prescribed in the previous sentence. Any amounts in excess of the applicable maximums pursuant to this subclause 11.01(b) shall be treated as described in subclause 11.01(f) below.

(c) Mechanical Royalties shall not be payable with respect to Records otherwise not royalty bearing hereunder, with respect to non-musical material or with respect to Compositions of one minute or less in duration. No Mechanical Royalties shall be payable in respect of Controlled Compositions which are in the public domain or are arrangements of Compositions in the public domain except that if such arrangement is credited by ASCAP or BMI, then the Mechanical Royalty otherwise payable hereunder will be apportioned in the same ratio used by ASCAP or BMI in determining the credits for public performance of the work, provided you furnish XYZ with satisfactory evidence of that ratio.

(d) XYZ will compute Mechanical Royalties on Controlled Compositions as of the end of each calendar quarter-annual period in which there are sales or returns of Records on which Mechanical Royalties are payable to you. On the next May 15th, August 15th, November 15th, or February 15th, XYZ will send a statement covering those royalties and will pay any net royalties which are due. Mechanical Royalty reserves maintained by XYZ against anticipated returns and credits will not be held for an unreasonable period of time. If XYZ makes any overpayment of Mechanical Royalties on Controlled Compositions (e.g., but, without limitation, by reason of an accounting error or by paying Mechanical Royalties on Records returned) such excess shall be treated as described in subclause 11.01(f) below. Your right to audit XYZ's books and records as the same relate to Mechanical Royalties for Controlled Compositions shall be subject to the terms and conditions set forth in clause 8.

(e) Any assignment made of the ownership of copyright in, or the rights to license or administer the use of, any Controlled Composition shall be made subject to the provisions of this clause 11.

(f) You agree to indemnify and hold XYZ harmless from the payment of Mechanical Royalties in excess of the applicable amounts in the provisions of this clause 11. If XYZ pays any such excess, such payments shall be a direct debt from you to XYZ, which, in addition to any other remedies available, XYZ may recover from royalties or any other payments hereunder.

12. FAILURE OF PERFORMANCE:

12.01. XYZ reserves the right by written notice to you to suspend the operation of this agreement and its obligations hereunder for the duration of any contingencies by reason of which XYZ is materially hampered in its recording, manufacture, distribution or sale of Records, or its normal business operations become commercially impracticable: for example, labor disagreements; fire; catastrophe; shortage of materials; or any cause beyond XYZ's control. A number of days equal to the total of all such days of suspension may be added to the Contract Period in which such contingency occurs and the dates for the exercise by XYZ of its options as set forth in clause 1, the dates of commencement of subsequent Contract Periods and the term of this agreement shall be deemed extended accordingly. Any such suspension of the term of this agreement shall not exceed (E.G., SIX (6)) consecutive months, unless the contingencies causing such extension affect at least one other record company in addition to XYZ. Notwithstanding the above, XYZ shall continue to account to you and pay royalties unless such force majeure circumstance affects XYZ's ability to do so.

12.02. If, in respect of any Contract Period, XYZ, except for reasons set forth in clause 12.01 above, refuses to allow you to fulfill your Recording Commitment for such Period and if, not later than (E.G., SIXTY (60)) days after that refusal takes place, you notify XYZ of your desire to fulfill such Recording Commitment, then XYZ may permit you to fulfill said Recording Commitment by notice to you to such effect within (E.G., THIRTY (30)) days of XYZ's receipt of your notice. Should XYZ fail to give such notice, you shall have the option to terminate the term of this agreement by notice given to XYZ within thirty-five (35) days after the expiration of the (E.G., THIRTY (30)) day period referred to above; on receipt by XYZ of such notice the term of this agreement shall terminate and all parties will be deemed to have fulfilled all their obligations hereunder, except those obligations which survive the end of the term (e.g., warranties, re-recording restrictions and obligation to pay royalties), at which time XYZ shall pay to you, in full settlement of its obligation in connection therewith, an Advance in the amount equal to:

(a) The aggregate of the Minimum Recording Funds fixed in clause 6.02 for each LP, then remaining unrecorded, of the Recording Commitment for the Contract Period in respect of which such termination occurs;

LESS:

(b) The average amount of the Recording Costs for the last two (2) LPs recorded hereunder in fulfillment of your Recording Commitment (or, if only one LP has been recorded, the amount of the Recording Costs for that LP), multiplied by the number of such unrecorded LPs referred to in subclause 12.02(a).

Notwithstanding the foregoing, with respect to the first two (2) LPs hereunder, the Advance shall be NINETY THOUSAND dollars ($90,000) rather than the amount determined pursuant to subclauses 12.02(a) and (b). If you fail to give XYZ either notice within the period specified therefor, XYZ shall be under no obligation to you for failing to permit you to fulfill such Recording Commitment.

13.   XYZ's ADDITIONAL REMEDIES:

13.01. Without limiting any other rights and remedies of XYZ hereunder, if you fail to deliver any Masters hereunder within the time prescribed in clause 3, XYZ will have the following options, each exercisable by notice to you:

(a) to suspend XYZ's obligations to make payments to you under this agreement until you have cured the default (other than any obligation under clause 1.03);

(b) to terminate the term of this agreement at any time, whether or not you have commenced curing the default before such termination occurs; and

(c) to require you to repay to XYZ the amount not then recouped of any Advance previously paid to you by XYZ and not specifically attributable under clause 6 to an LP which has actually been fully delivered.

If XYZ terminates the term of this agreement under Subclause 13.01(c) above, all parties will be deemed to have fulfilled all of their obligations under this agreement, except those obligations which survive the end of the term of this agreement (such as indemnification obligations, XYZ's obligation to account and pay royalties to you, re-recording restrictions, and your obligations under subclause 13.01(b)). No exercise of an option under this clause will limit XYZ's rights to recover damages by reason of your default, its rights to exercise any other option under this clause, or any of its other rights.

13.02. If Artist's voice should be or become materially and permanently impaired or if Artist should otherwise become physically disabled to perform recording and/or personal appearances and/or if Artist should cease to pursue a career as an entertainer, XYZ may elect to terminate this agreement, by notice to you at any time during the period in which such contingency arose or continues, and thereby be relieved of any liability for the executory provisions of this agreement.

13.03. You acknowledge, recognize and agree that Artist's services hereunder are of a special, unique, unusual, extraordinary and intellectual character which gives them a peculiar value, the loss of which cannot be reasonably or adequately compensated for by damages in an action at law. Inasmuch as a breach of such services will cause XYZ irreparable damages, XYZ shall be entitled to injunctive and other equitable relief, in addition to whatever legal remedies are available, to prevent or cure any such breach or threatened breach. Nothing herein shall prevent you from opposing such relief on grounds which do not negate your acknowledgment expressed in the first sentence hereof.

13.04. In the event of your dissolution or the liquidation of your assets, or the filing by or against you of a petition for liquidation or reorganization under Title 11 of the United States Code as now or hereafter in effect or under any similar statute relating to insolvency, bankruptcy, liquidation or reorganization, or in the event of the appointment of a trustee, receiver or custodian for you or for any of your property, or if you shall make an assignment for the benefit or creditors or commit any act for, or in, bankruptcy or become insolvent, or in the event you shall fail to fulfill any of your obligations under this agreement for any other reason, then at any time after the occurrence of any such event, in addition to any other remedies which may be available, XYZ shall have the option by notice to you to either terminate this agreement or to require Artist to render Artist's personal services directly to XYZ for the remaining balance of the term of this agreement, including any extension thereof, for the purpose of making Phonograph Records, upon all the same terms and conditions as are herein contained. In such event the Artist shall be deemed substituted for you as a party to this agreement as of the date of XYZ's option exercise, and, in respect of Masters of the Artist's performances recorded subsequently, the royalties and any Advances payable hereunder shall be reduced to two-thirds (2/3) of the amounts prescribed in this agreement.

13.05. The rights and remedies of the parties as specified in this agreement are not to the exclusion of each other or of any other rights or remedies of the parties; either party may decline to exercise one or more of its rights and remedies as it may deem appropriate without jeopardizing any other of its rights or remedies; and all of each party's rights and remedies shall survive the expiration of the term of this agreement. Notwithstanding anything in this agreement, XYZ may at any time exercise any right which it now has or at any time hereafter may be entitled to as a member of the public as though this agreement were not in existence.

14.   DEFINITIONS:

14.01. "Record" or "Phonograph Record" means all forms of reproductions, now or hereafter known, manufactured or distributed primarily for home use, school use, juke box use or use in means of transportation, including records of sound alone and audiovisual Recordings.

14.02. "Master," "Master Recording" or "Recording" means any recording of sound, whether or not coupled with a visual image, by any method and on any substance or material, whether now or hereafter known, which is intended for use in the recording, production and/or manufacture of Phonograph Records.

14.03. "Performance" means singing, speaking, conducting or playing an instrument, alone or with others.

14.04. The words "Single Record" or "Single" means a Record containing not more than three (3) Sides.

14.05. "Long Play Single" means a 12-inch 33-1/3 rpm disc Phonograph Record embodying not more than three (3) Sides.

14.06. "Mini LP" or "EP" means a Record containing not less than four (4) or more than seven (7) Sides and not less than twenty (20) minutes of playing time.

14.07. The term "Multiple Record LP" means an LP containing two or more 12-inch 33-1/3 rpm records packaged as a single unit or equivalent. For purposes of the Recording Commitment hereunder and for computing the applicable Recording Fund or Advance, a Multiple Record LP accepted by XYZ shall be deemed only one (1) LP.

14.08. "Person" means any individual, corporation, partnership, association or other organized group of persons or legal successors or representatives of the foregoing.

14.09. "Side" means a Recording of sufficient playing time to constitute one side of a 45 rpm record, but not less than three (3) minutes of continuous sound embodying performances by Artist.

14.10.(a) "Suggested Retail List Price" means (i) with respect to Records sold for distribution in the United States, XYZ's suggested retail list price in the United States during the applicable accounting period for the computation of royalties to be made hereunder, it being understood that a separate calculation of the suggested retail list price shall be made for each price configuration of Phonograph Records manufactured and sold by XYZ; and (ii) with respect to Records sold hereunder for distribution outside the United States, XYZ's or its licensees' suggested or applicable retail price in the country of manufacture or sale, as XYZ is paid, or, in the absence in a particular country of such suggested retail list price, the price as may be established by XYZ or its licensee(s) in conformity with the general practice of the recording industry in such country, provided that XYZ shall not be obligated to utilize the price adopted by the local mechanical copyright collection agency for the collection of Mechanical Royalties.

(b) XYZ may at some time change the method by which it computes royalties in the United States from a retail basis to some other basis (the "New Basis"), such as, without limitation, a wholesale basis. The New Basis will replace the then-current Royalty Base Price and the royalty rates shall be adjusted to the appropriate royalty which would be applied to the New Basis so that the dollars-and-cents royalty amounts payable with respect to the top-line product through normal retail channels would be the same as that which was payable immediately prior to such New Basis; for sales other than top-line product, for which there is a New Basis, the adjusted royalty rate shall be reduced in the ratio of the royalty rate for such sales to the royalty rates for sales of top-line product. If there are other adjustments made by XYZ that would otherwise make the New Basis more favorable (a particular example of which might be the distribution of small quantities of free goods than theretofore distributed), then the benefits of such other adjustments will be taken into consideration in adjusting the royalty rate.

(c) Notwithstanding anything to the contrary contained herein, the Suggested Retail List Price for premium Records shall be XYZ's actual sales price of such Records.

(d) Notwithstanding anything to the contrary herein, the Suggested Retail List Price with respect to so-called home video devices manufactured and distributed by XYZ RECORDS shall be XYZ's published wholesale price as of the commencement of the accounting period concerned.

14.11. "Container Charge" shall mean ten percent (10%) of the Suggested Retail List Price for a single-fold disc Record in a standard sleeve with no inserts or for any other Record other than as hereinafter provided (provided that if the sleeve of such LP is other than plain white stock paper, the Container Charge shall mean twelve and one-half percent (12½%) of the Suggested Retail List Price); fifteen percent (15%) of the Suggested Retail List Price for an LP in a double-fold or gatefold jacket, or non-standard jacket or with inserts; and twenty percent (20%) of such Price for Records in non-disc form, audiovisual Records, or compact discs. The placement of a sticker on an otherwise standard jacket will not in and of itself render the jacket or sleeve non-standard for the purposes of this clause. There will be no container charge on single Records shipped in XYZ's plain stock sleeve.

14.12. "Royalty Base Price" means the Suggested Retail List Price less all excise, sales and similar taxes included therein and less the applicable Container Charge.

14.13. "LP" or "Album" means a sufficient number of Masters embodying Artist's performances to comprise one (1) or more 12-inch, 33 1/3, long-playing Phonograph Record album, or the equivalent, of not less than thirty-eight (38) minutes of playing time.

14.14. The words "term of this agreement" or "period of this agreement" or "term hereof" or "so long as this agreement remains in force" or words of similar connotation shall include the initial period of this agreement and the period of all renewals, extensions and substitutions or replacements of this agreement.

14.15. "United States" mean the United States of America, its territories, possessions and military exchanges.

14.16. "Contract Period" means the initial period, or any option period, of the term hereof (as such periods may be suspended or extended as provided herein).

14.17. "Composition" means a single musical composition, irrespective of length, including all spoken words and bridging passages and including a medley.

14.18. "Controlled Composition" means a Composition wholly or partly written, owned or controlled by you, the Artist, an individual producer or any Person in which you, the Artist or an individual producer has a direct or indirect interest.

14.19. (a) "Budget Record" means a Record bearing a Suggested Retail List Price that is no more than sixty-seven (67%) of the Suggested Retail List Price in the country concerned of top-line single disc LPs.

(b) "Mid-line Record" means a Record bearing a Suggested Retail List Price that is between eighty percent (80%) and sixty-seven percent (67%) of the Suggested Retail List Price in the country concerned of top-line single disc LPs.

14.20. "Net Sales" means sales of Records paid for or credited and not returned, less returns and credits, after deduction of reasonable reserves against anticipated returns and credits.

14.21. "Advance" means a prepayment of royalties and shall be chargeable against and recoupable from any royalties other than mechanical royalties otherwise payable hereunder, but not otherwise returnable.

14.22. "Territory" shall mean the Universe.

14.23. "Sales Through Normal Retail Channels" means sales other than as described in clauses 7.02, 7.03, 7.04, 7.06, and 7.07.

14.24. "Mechanical Royalties" means royalties payable to any Person for the right to reproduce and distribute copyrighted musical compositions on Phonograph Records.

14.25. "Joint Recordings" means Masters embodying the Artist's performance and any performance by another artist with respect to whom XYZ is obligated to pay royalties.

15. NOTICES AND PAYMENTS:

15.01. All notices required to be given to XYZ shall be sent to XYZ at its address first mentioned herein, and all royalties, royalty statements and payments and any and all notices to you shall be sent to you at your address first mentioned herein, or such other address as each party respectively may hereafter designate by notice in writing to the other. All notices sent under this agreement shall be in writing and, except for royalty statements, shall be sent by personal delivery, registered or certified mail (return receipt requested) or telegraph (prepaid) and the day of mailing (or transmission in the case of telegraphs) of any such notice shall be deemed the date of the giving thereof (except notices of change of address, the date of which shall be the date of receipt by the receiving party). All notices to XYZ shall be served upon XYZ to the attention of the VICE PRESIDENT, LEGAL AFFAIRS.

16. MISCELLANEOUS:

16.01. Unless otherwise provided, all matters to be determined by mutual agreement, or as to which any approval or consent is required, such agreement, approval or consent will not be unreasonably withheld.

16.02. Your agreement, approval or consent, whenever required, shall be deemed to have been given unless you notify XYZ otherwise within five (5) business days following the date of XYZ's written request to you for it.

16.03. The invalidity or unenforceability of any provision shall not affect the validity or enforceability of any other provision. This agreement contains the entire understanding of the parties relating to its subject matter. No change of this agreement will be binding unless signed by the party to be charged. A waiver by either party of any provision of this agreement in any instance shall not be deemed to waive it for the future. All remedies, rights, undertakings and obligations contained in this agreement shall be cumulative and none of them shall limit any other remedy, right, undertaking or obligation.

16.04. XYZ shall have the right at any time during the term hereof to obtain insurance on the life of you or any member of Artist, at XYZ's sole expense and cost, with XYZ being the sole beneficiary thereof. You agree that you and Artist will fully cooperate with XYZ in connection with the obtaining of such a policy, including, without limitation, your and/or any member of Artist submitting to any required physical examination and completing any documents necessary or desirable in respect thereof. Neither you, Artist, nor your estate(s) shall have any right to claim the benefit of any such policy obtained by XYZ.

16.05. XYZ may assign its rights under this agreement in whole or in part to any subsidiary, affiliated or controlling corporation, to any person owning or acquiring a substantial portion of the stock or assets of XYZ, or to any partnership or other venture in which XYZ participates, and such rights may be assigned by any assignee. No such assignment shall relieve XYZ of any of its obligations. XYZ may also assign its rights to any of its licensees if advisable in XYZ's sole discretion to implement the license granted. You may assign your rights under this agreement to a corporation a majority of whose capital stock is owned and controlled by the Artist. No such assignment shall affect XYZ's rights hereunder nor relieve you or Artist of any obligations under this agreement.

16.06. You shall not be entitled to recover damages or to terminate the term of this agreement by reason of any breach by XYZ of its material obligations hereunder, unless XYZ has failed to remedy such breach within a reasonable time following receipt of your notice therefor.

16.07. XYZ shall assist you and endeavor to obtain appropriate immigration clearances, including a "green card" for (NAME OF MEMBER). XYZ shall pay costs involved in such endeavor (but in no event more than (E.G., SIX THOUSAND DOLLARS ($6,000)), which payment shall be an Advance.

16.08. You recognize that the sale of Records is speculative and agree that the judgment of XYZ with respect to matters affecting the sale, distribution and exploitation of such Records shall be binding upon you. Nothing contained in this agreement shall obligate XYZ to make, sell, license or distribute Records manufactured from the Sides recorded hereunder except as specified herein.

16.09. This agreement has been entered into in the STATE OF CALIFORNIA and the validity, interpretation and legal effect of this agreement shall be governed by the laws of the STATE OF CALIFORNIA applicable to contracts entered into and performed entirely within such STATE. The CALIFORNIA courts (state and federal) only will have jurisdiction of any controversies regarding this agreement and the parties hereto consent to the jurisdiction of said courts. Any process in any action, suit or proceeding arising out of or relating to this agreement may, among other methods, be served upon you by delivering it or mailing it in accordance with clause 15 above. Any such process may, among other methods, be served upon Artist or any other Person who approves, ratifies or assents to this agreement to induce XYZ to enter into it, by delivering the process or mailing it to the Artist or the other Person concerned in the manner prescribed in clause 15. Any such delivery or mail service shall be deemed to have the same force and effect as personal service in CALIFORNIA.

16.10. In entering into this agreement and in providing services pursuant hereto, you and the Artist have and shall have the status of independent contractors and nothing herein contained shall contemplate or constitute you or Artist as XYZ's agents or employees.

16.11. The headings of the clauses herein are intended for convenience only, and shall not be of any effect in construing the contents of this agreement.

16.12. This agreement shall not become effective until executed by all parties hereto.

16.13. Any and all riders, exhibits or schedules annexed hereto together with this basic document shall constitute this agreement.

17. GROUP ARTIST

17.01. The Artist's obligations under this agreement are joint and several. All references to "Artist" include all members of the group collectively and each member individually, unless otherwise specified herein.

17.02. "Artist" shall refer to the members of the group as presently comprised and such other individual(s) who at any given time during the term hereof shall then comprise the group. The substitution of, addition to, or subtraction from any of the present members of Artist shall be done only upon the prior written approval of you and XYZ, provided that any substituted individual will be deemed a party to this agreement and shall agree in writing to be bound by all of the terms and conditions of this agreement. You shall promptly deliver to XYZ any documents as XYZ may require executed by such substituted member as XYZ, in its judgment, may deem necessary or advisable to effectuate the institution of such substituted member.

17.03. If any member of Artist ceases to perform as a member of the group ("leaving member"), you shall promptly give XYZ written notice of such occurrence (the "Leaving Member Notice"). If the group disbands, each member of the group shall be deemed a leaving member.

(a) If XYZ should so request within sixty (60) days after XYZ's receipt of the Leaving Member Notice, you shall promptly deliver to XYZ a "demo tape," at XYZ's expense, embodying the performances of such leaving member and/or of such remaining members of the group. At XYZ's election, such leaving member and/or such remaining members shall hold a live audition.

(b) None of the individuals herein named as Artist ("Present Members") or any who may hereafter become substituted therefor ("Substitute Members") shall, during the term hereof record for anyone other than XYZ, individually or as part of any other group. Each of the Present Members and Substitute Members agree that, without limiting any of XYZ's other rights and/or remedies, if there is a leaving member during the term hereof:

(i) XYZ shall have the right to terminate the term of this agreement with respect to the remaining members of Artist by notice given to you at any time before the expiration of ninety (90) days after XYZ's receipt of the Leaving Member Notice (or, if later, the date of the delivery to XYZ of the demo tape or the occurrence of the live audition, if applicable). In the event of such termination, all of the members of Artist shall be deemed leaving members as of the date of XYZ's notice to you (subclause (c) below shall then apply to any or all of such members).

(ii) If XYZ does not terminate the term of this agreement with respect to the remaining members, the royalties otherwise payable pursuant to clause 7.01 above and each of the Advances otherwise payable pursuant to the terms of this agreement with respect to such remaining members shall be those payable as if the first LP delivered thereafter were the first LP delivered in the initial Contract Period, the second LP delivered thereafter were the second LP delivered in the initial Contract Period, and so forth, except as follows: (1) in each contract period, the minimum Recording Commitment shall be one (1) LP, and XYZ shall have the option, exercisable any time before the end of the applicable period, to request you to record the second LP; and (2) the Advance payable in the initial Contract Period shall be (E.G., FIFTY THOUSAND DOLLARS ($50,000)) if the leaving member was (NAME) and (E.G., TWENTY-FIVE THOUSAND DOLLARS ($25,000)) if the leaving member was (NAME).

(c) You and the Artist hereby grant to XYZ an irrevocable option to engage the exclusive services of any leaving member as a recording artist. Said option, with respect to such individual, may be exercised by XYZ by giving you notice at any time before the expiration of ninety (90) days after XYZ's receipt of the Leaving Member Notice (or, if later, the date of the delivery to XYZ of the demo tape or the occurrence of the live audition, if applicable). In the event of XYZ's exercise of such option, you and such leaving member shall be deemed to have entered into an agreement with XYZ with respect to such individual's exclusive recording services upon all the terms and conditions of this agreement except that: (i) the Minimum Recording Obligation in the initial Contract Period shall be for sufficient Masters to constitute four (4) Sides and the right to overcall such number of Masters as shall constitute up to two (2) LPs, with five (5) additional number of options granted to XYZ to extend the term of such agreement for consecutive option periods for one (1) LP each, which options shall be exercised within nine (9) months after delivery to XYZ of the Minimum Recording Obligation; (ii) the Advance payable for each of the first two LPs delivered shall be (E.G., FIFTY THOUSAND DOLLARS ($50,000)) if the leaving member is (NAME) and (TWENTY-FIVE THOUSAND DOLLARS ($25,000)) if the leaving member is (NAME); thereafter the Advances payable will be those payable as if the next LP were the first LP delivered in the initial Contract Period hereunder, and so forth; (iii) the royalties otherwise payable pursuant to clause 7.01 above shall be those payable as if the first LP delivered thereafter were the first LP delivered in the initial Contract Period, the second LP delivered thereafter were the second LP delivered in the initial Contract Period, and so forth; (iv) XYZ shall be entitled to combine such leaving member's account with the Artist account hereunder; and (v) Recordings by such individual shall not be applied in diminution of your Minimum Recording Obligation as set forth in this agreement.

(d) A leaving member shall not, without XYZ's consent, use the professional name of the group in any commercial artistic endeavor; said professional name shall remain the property of the group who continue to perform their obligations hereunder and whose engagements are not terminated.

By _____

AGREED AND ACCEPTED:

By _____(AN AUTHORIZED SIGNATORY)

Federal I.D. No.: _____

Form 40

Tour Merchandising License Agreement

License Agreement dated as of the (number) day of (month), (year) by and between (name of corporation), a California corporation, (address) (hereinafter referred to as "Licensor") and (name of corporation), a California corporation, (address) (hereinafter referred to as "Licensee").

RECITALS

WHEREAS, Licensor has the sole and exclusive right to use and to license others to use the name and likeness of (name of artist) (hereinafter referred to as "Artist") for the purposes of merchandising in connection with live concert engagements of Artist; and

WHEREAS, Artist is a popular performer in the entertainment industry appearing from time-to-time in live concert engagements; and

WHEREAS, Licensee provides services in the area of merchandising at live concert engagements; and

WHEREAS, Licensor and Licensee desire to do business on the terms and conditions set forth hereinafter;

NOW, THEREFORE, in consideration of the mutual promises and undertakings herein contained, and for other good and valuable considerations, Licensor and Licensee agree as follows:

1. DEFINITIONS:

A. "Territory" shall mean the United States of America and Canada, their territories and possessions, including but not limited to Puerto Rico.

B. "Term" shall mean the period commencing on (date) and ending on (date).

C. "Tour" shall man each and every live concert engagement of Artist in the Territory during the Term. The tentative tour itinerary is attached hereto as Exhibit "A" and made a part hereof.

ALTERNATIVE SUBCLAUSES

B. "Tour" shall mean each and every live concert engagement of artist in the Territory occurring on or after (date) and ending on or about (date) in accordance with the tentative Tour itinerary attached hereto as Exhibit "A" and made a part hereof. Notwithstanding the foregoing, the Tour shall be extended to include any live concert engagement(s) of Artist in the Territory occurring after (date) provided that:

(i) the personnel, staging, presentation and other elements of such live concert engagement do not vary materially from live concert engagements on the Tour prior to such date; and

(ii) such live concert engagement occurs no later than two (2) weeks following any prior live concert engagement of Artist on the Tour.

C. "Term" shall mean the period commencing as of the date hereof and expiring at the end of the Tour.

D. "Licensed Subject Matter" shall mean the name, symbols, emblems, designs, depictions, characterizations, likenesses and visual representations of Artist and/or the Tour and the trademarks, logos, copyrights, and all other authorized material owned or controlled by Artist and/or Licensor all of which are approved by Artist with respect to Products as said term is defined below.

E. "Products" shall mean merchandise items approved by Licensor and Licensee embodying any of the Licensed Subject Matter or which otherwise relate to Artist and/or Artist's performances(s), whether recorded or live. Products may include without limitation, T-shirts, jerseys, sweatshirts, programs, posters, pictures, buttons and lights. It is hereby agreed by Licensor and Licensee that with respect to the Tour the tentatively approved Products are set forth in Exhibit "B" attached hereto and made a part thereof.

F. "Concert Hall" shall mean each and every concert hall, arena, stadium or theatre in which Artist shall perform on the Tour.

G. "Actual Cost" or "Licensee's Cost" of the Products shall mean all costs actually incurred by Licensee in its design (including Artwork as defined hereinbelow), manufacturing and shipping of the Products and registering of trademarks and/or copyrights therefor, all as evidenced by invoices and bills paid by Licensee. For purposes hereof, no overhead and/or interest shall be included in the calculation of the Actual Cost of the Products.

2.   <u>GRANT OF LICENSE</u>: Licensor hereby grants to Licensee, and Licensee hereby accepts from Licensor, subject to the terms hereof, the sole and exclusive right and license:

(i) to manufacture Products or have Products manufactured on its behalf during the Term; and

(ii) to distribute and sell Products in and around (and only in and around) the immediate vicinity of each and every Concert Hall.

3.   <u>LICENSEE'S OBLIGATIONS</u>:

A. Licensee agrees that all use of the Licensed Subject Matter shall be only upon merchandise items manufactured by or for Licensee in accordance with quality and artistic standards approved by Licensor prior to the commencement of manufacture of Products. Licensee agrees to furnish Licensor, free of cost, for its approval as to quality and style, one (1) sample of each of the merchandise items covered by this Agreement before the Licensed Subject Matter is embodied thereon. No Products shall be manufactured or sold by Licensee without such prior approval by Licensor.

B. In the event that the quality standards hereinabove referred to are not met, or in the event that said quality standards are not maintained throughout the period of manufacture of any Products hereunder, then upon written notice from Licensor, Licensee will immediately discontinue the manufacture and distribution of such Products that do not meet the said quality standards.

C. It is agreed that Licensee shall submit for Licensor's prior approval a schedule of Licensee's recommended retail prices for each of the Products, and that Licensor shall be deemed to have granted approval with respect thereto if it does not notify Licensee to the contrary within ten (10) business days (i.e., excluding weekends and holidays) after Licensor's receipt thereof.

D. Licensee agrees to execute and deliver to Licensor at Licensor's cost any and all documents which may be necessary to record Licensee as a registered user of the Licensed Subject Matter; it being understood and agreed that Licensee's right to use the Licensed Subject Matter shall exist only when and so long as this Agreement remains in effect. Licensee agrees that upon or immediately after the expiration or termination of this Agreement for any reason, it shall prepare, execute and deliver to Licensor, in such form as Licensor shall reasonably request, any and all documents which may be necessary to cancel the recordation of Licensee as a registered user of the Licensed Subject Matter, but if Licensor should prefer first to complete the recordation of Licensee as a registered user before canceling the same, also to provide any and all documents which may be necessary or desirable to achieve this purpose.

E. Licensee shall manufacture or have manufactured on its behalf only so many Products as Licensee reasonably calculates are required for sale in connection with the license granted to Licensee hereunder.

F. Licensee shall have the right to determine the manner of distribution and sale of the Products with respect to each Concert Hall. Said distribution and sale of the Products shall not in any way interfere with Artist's performances during the Tour.

G. Licensee shall negotiate with each Concert Hall with respect to the payment each Concert Hall (including vendors) shall receive and with respect to the obligations each Concert Hall shall undertake in connection with the sale of the Products.

H. Licensee shall inventory the Products prior to the commencement of the Tour and thereafter shall transport and/or arrange transportation of such Products from city to city in which the Tour is held, check in all Products at each Concert

Hall, obtain the signature of an authorized agent or employee of each such Concert Hall on the exact count of all Products in and out of said Concert Hall, supervise all sales and conduct sales where necessary, check out all remaining Products following the close of each performance of Artist, and account and pay all sums due hereunder to Licensor as set forth herein. Notwithstanding the foregoing, Licensor, at its own expense, shall have the right at all reasonable times to conduct a physical inventory of Products where they are maintained and the right to have a representative present during the check-in and check-out of all Products at each Concert Hall, at Licensor's election.

I. Licensee shall supply Licensor with an inventory showing the number and type of all Products on hand with respect to each Concert Hall engagement, and the costs of the Concert Hall and any vendors for such engagement. Licensee shall also supply Licensor with detailed reports of all Products manufactured within thirty (30) days after their manufacture.

J. Licensee shall pay all costs and expenses in connection with the merchandising of the Products including production, manufacturing, packaging, shipping, distribution, sales personnel and concessionaires (except when a Concert Hall requires its own concessionaires). Licensee shall use its best efforts to provide its own personnel to transport and sell the Products.

K. In the event that Licensor, subject to Clause 4E, grants a Tour sponsor the right to distribute items of merchandise in and around Concert Halls, Licensee shall not be obligated in any way nor shall Licensee incur any cost or expense nor be liable for same with respect to the production, manufacture, packing, shipping, transportation, distribution, use, sale and/or exhibition of any such items of merchandise.

L. Licensee agrees that during the Term hereof it will diligently and continuously maintain a reasonable supply of Products to satisfy the reasonably anticipated demands of sales of the Products and shall furthermore diligently and continuously distribute and offer said Products for sale subject to the following:

(i) In the event that any Concert Hall (including vendors) requires as payment in connection with the sale of Products a commission of more than forty percent (40%) of the gross receipts of all such sales, excluding sales tax, Licensee shall have the right, in Licensee's sole discretion, to refrain from selling Products at such Concert Hall, and Licensee shall notify Licensor of its decision to so refrain within a reasonable time prior to said Concert Hall engagement.

(ii) With respect to Concert Hall engagement(s) in Canada, Licensee shall have the right to sub-license the rights granted hereunder to a third party approved by Licensor (which such approval shall not be unreasonably withheld), it being acknowledged by Licensor that the importation to Canada of such Products manufactured outside Canada results in tariffs, levies and taxes which would cause Licensee to operate at a loss and frustrate the intent of this Agreement.

If Licensee cannot sub-license the aforementioned rights to a third party approved by Licensor, Licensee shall have the right, upon giving notice to Licensor no later than ten (10) business days prior to any such Canadian Concert Hall engagement(s), to refrain from selling Products thereat. Licensee shall be responsible and liable for any and all acts, negligent or intentional, of its Canadian sub-licensee(s), and Licensee hereby indemnifies and holds Licensor and Artist harmless from any such act(s) of said sub-licensee(s).

(iii) Licensee shall have the right to refrain from selling Products at those Concert Hall engagement(s) at which Licensee is unable for any reason to render the services described herein due to the fault of Licensor, said Concert Hall(s) or an act constituting force majeure as described in Clause 14. Upon the Licensee's determination that it shall be unable to render the services described herein due to any of the foregoing reasons, Licensee shall provide notice to Licensor thereof as soon as is reasonably possible.

(iv) If Licensee does not sell Products at any Concert Hall engagement(s) for any reason other than the fault of Licensor or Artist or their employees, agents or assigns, Licensor shall have the right, but not the obligation, to sell Products thereat and retain all gross receipts therefrom with respect to such sales and, in such event, Licensee hereby agrees to use its best efforts to sell a reasonable amount of Products to Licensor at Licensee's Actual Cost therefor plus fifteen percent (15%) and shipping costs, and any payment made to Licensee in connection therewith shall be deemed excluded from royalty bearing gross receipts as described herein. Licensee shall use its best efforts to deliver said Products to Licensor within seventy-two (72) hours of Licensee's receipt from Licensor of the payment by Licensor of fifty percent (50%) of the Licensee's Actual Cost of said Products plus the full cost of shipping said Products to Licensor. The balance of Licensee's Actual Cost of the Products plus the fifteen percent (15%) shall be paid upon delivery to Licensor of the Products.

M. Licensee agrees to sell Licensor a reasonable number of Products for Licensor's personal use at a price equal to Licensee's Actual Costs therefor plus fifteen percent (15%) plus shipping. Said Products shall be delivered to Licensor upon the receipt by Licensee of payment in full. Said payment shall be deemed excluded from royalty bearing gross receipts as described herein.

N. Licensee agrees that all of its sublicensees hereunder shall be subject to Licensor's prior written approval, such approval not to be unreasonably withheld.

4. LICENSOR'S OBLIGATIONS:

A. Licensor agrees throughout the term hereof to give prompt written notice to Licensee of any and all modifications, changes, deletions and additions with respect to the Tour itinerary.

B. Licensor shall promptly furnish Licensee with sufficient information about the Tour to enable Licensee to adequately plan its sales and merchandising program. Said information shall include, but not be limited to, the approximate length of Artist's performance and intermissions and, if applicable, the scheduling of any acts playing prior to or after Artist's performance (as well as notification of any changes of any of the foregoing information) with respect to each Concert Hall engagement.

C. Licensor acknowledges Licensee's reliance upon the Tour itinerary, as revised from time to time, and upon the information provided therein in ordering inventory of Products, transporting stock, employing manpower, and incurring other related business expenses. If Licensor determines that Artist will be unable to perform at any Concert Hall engagement during the Tour for any reason, Licensor shall immediately so notify Licensee.

D. Licensor shall use its reasonable efforts to ensure that any opening (or closing) act for Artist shall be limited to selling no more than two (2) tour merchandising items and that said items shall not be a concert book, whether featuring Artist or otherwise.

E. Licensor shall not have the right to grant to any Tour sponsor of Artist nor any other person or entity the right to distribute any items of merchandise, whether for free or otherwise, in and around Concert Halls without the express prior written approval of Licensee, which such approval may be withheld in Licensee's sole discretion.

F. It is the essence of this Agreement and Licensor does hereby guarantee that the aggregate paid attendance for all Concert Hall engagements of Artist on the Tour at which Artist is the sole headline performer and at which Licensee renders its services subject to the terms hereof shall be no less than (number) thousand persons (the "Guaranteed Attendance").

ALTERNATIVE SUBCLAUSE

F. It is the essence of this Agreement and Licensor does hereby warrant and represent that (i) Artist shall perform on the Tour at no fewer than (number) separate and different Concert Hall engagements, and (ii) the aggregate Adjusted Seating Capacity of the Concert Halls for said engagements shall be no fewer than (written number) thousand (number) seats (the "Guaranteed Adjusted Seating Capacity"). For the purposes of example only, two performances by Artist at the Concert Hall shall constitute two separate and different Concert Hall engagements. For purposes of this Agreement, the term "Adjusted Seating Capacity" shall mean the actual authorized seating capacity of each Concert Hall less the number of seats that are not placed on sale to the public for Concert Hall engagements of Artist.

5. MATERIAL AND ARTWORK:

A. Licensor agrees upon the execution hereof to furnish Licensee (at Licensor's sole expense) with camera ready photographs, transparencies and/or other artwork and other material which Licensee requires for the manufacture a Tour book and/or poster, if any. Licensee shall pay for the initial retouching in connection therewith and Licensor shall pay for any subsequent retouching. Any such retouching shall be subject to the approval of the Licensor.

B. Licensee agrees to submit for Licensor's prior approval the artwork, packaging design, advertising material and all other proposed materials to be used in connection with the Products including the artwork for the Licensed Subject Matter appearing on the Products (hereinafter collectively referred to as the "Artwork") and Licensor shall be deemed to have granted approval with respect thereto if it does not notify Licensee to the contrary (stating specific objections) within ten (10) business days after Licensor's receipt thereof. Any Artwork submitted by Licensor to Licensee shall be deemed approved unless expressly stated otherwise in writing or unless such Artwork is materially altered in any way by Licensee.

C. Licensor and Licensee shall each pay one-half (½) of any and all costs of "C" prints incurred by Licensee and any sum paid by Licensee on behalf of Licensor in connection therewith may be deducted from any royalties paid to Licensor hereunder.

D. Except as expressly provided in Subclauses 5A and 5C above, Licensee agrees to pay any and all costs in connection with the creation of the Artwork and all right title and interest in and to the elements (such as screens, color separations, etc.) comprising same shall be owned by Licensee; provided, however, that Licensor shall retain all right, title and interest in and to the Licensed Subject Matter and any elements thereof supplied by Licensor. Licensor shall have the right, but not the obligation, following the expiration of the Term, to purchase all right, title and interest in and to any and all of the elements comprising the Artwork upon payment to Licensee of a sum to be mutually agreed by the parties and not to exceed one-half (½) of Licensee's Actual Cost for the Artwork so purchased by Licensor. In connection therewith, Licensee shall, upon the request of Licensor, provide Licensor with copies of all invoices and bills paid by Licensee in connection with the cost of creation, design and production of the Artwork. After the end of the Term, Licensee shall have no rights whatsoever to use or exploit the Artwork for any reason. If at the end of the Term Licensor does not exercise its above right to purchase the Artwork, the following shall apply:

(i) Any and all elements of the Artwork (including screens) shall be delivered to a mutually designated third party and held by said party for a ninety (90) day period. If Licensor does not purchase the Artwork as aforesaid during said ninety

(90) day period, then the Artwork shall be destroyed (with a certificate of destruction to be supplied to both Licensor and Licensee);

(ii) After the Term, and notwithstanding the foregoing, Licensor shall have the right to use or exploit any of the elements of said Artwork supplied by Licensor hereunder.

E. Licensor agrees that, subject to the terms hereof, the Artwork may be used, copied, reproduced and/or exploited by Licensee in any manner in connection with the manufacture of the Products.

F. Licensee agrees to comply with Licensor's reasonable instructions regarding the form, placement and other details of the Licensed Subject Matter with respect to the Products, including, without limitation, placement of the required copyright, trademark and/or service mark notices on the Products. In connection therewith, Licensee shall, at Licensee's cost therefore, use its best efforts to comply with all legal requirements. Notwithstanding the foregoing, the filing of applicable copyright, trademark and/or service mark registration forms shall be the responsibility of Licensor at Licensor's sole expense. Licensee shall cause the following notice to appear on all Products embodying Licensed Subject Matter and on any advertising and promotional materials and containers: "© 1990 (Name of Licensor or Other Designated Party). All Rights Reserved."

G. Licensee recognizes the value of the publicity and good will associated with the Licensed Subject Matter, and in such connection, acknowledges that such good will exclusively belongs to Licensor and its grantors and that the Licensed Subject Matter has acquired a secondary meaning in the mind of the purchasing public.

H. Licensor reserves all rights pertaining to the Licensed Subject Matter except as specifically granted to Licensee hereunder.

6. ROYALTIES, ADVANCE AND GUARANTEE:

A. In consideration of the rights and license herein granted, Licensee hereby agrees to pay to Licensor: a royalty computed on the gross receipts received by Licensee from sales of Products pursuant to the terms hereof less all sales taxes, value added taxes and any equivalent taxes, without deduction of any other kind ("Gross Receipts") in the amount of (written number) percent (number %).

ALTERNATIVE SUBCLAUSE

A royalty computed on the gross receipts received by Licensee from sales of Products pursuant to the terms hereof less all sales taxes, value added taxes and any equivalent taxes, without deduction of any kind ("Gross Receipts") in the following amounts:

(i) (written number) Percent (number %) of all Gross Receipts up to (written number) dollars ($ number);

(ii) (written number) Percent (number %) of all Gross Receipts in excess of (written number) dollars ($ number).

B. Notwithstanding the foregoing, if the commission paid by Licensee to a Concert Hall (the "Concert Hall Commission") with respect to the sale of Products at such Concert Hall is:

(i) (written number) percent (number %) or more, then the royalty paid to Licensor solely with respect to Products sold at such Concert Hall shall be reduced (written number) Percent (number %);

(ii) (written number) percent (number %) or less, then the royalty paid to Licensor solely with respect to Products sold at such Concert Hall shall be increased (written number) percent (number %).

C. Notwithstanding the foregoing, with respect to all monies received by or credited to Licensee from the sale of Products by sub-licensees approved by Licensor hereunder, Licensee agrees to pay to Licensor a royalty in the amount of (written number) percent (number %) of the difference between said monies and Licensee's direct manufacturing, distribution and shipping costs in connection with such Products.

D. The royalties payable to Licensor hereunder shall be based upon the currency in which the gross receipts are received by Licensee. Any gross receipts received by Licensee in a foreign currency, including but not limited to Canadian currency, shall first be converted into United States currency at the applicable currency exchange rate in existence on the date of conversion for purposes of calculating Licensee's gross receipts.

E. Licensee agrees to pay to Licensor an advance (the "Advance") in the amount of (written number) Dollars ($ number). (Written number) dollars ($ number) of said Advance shall be paid upon the date of execution of this Agreement by Licensee and the balance of said Advance shall be paid on the date of the first Concert Hall engagement. Said Advance shall be recoupable by Licensee from any and all royalties payable to Licensor hereunder.

ADDITIONAL CLAUSE E(i)

[(i) If, at the end of the Term, the Advance shall not be fully recouped by Licensee, Licensor agrees to reimburse Licensee the unrecouped balance of said Advance within ten (10) business days after the end of the Term.]

ADDITIONAL CLAUSE E(ii)

[(ii) Notwithstanding the foregoing, Licensor shall have the option in its sole discretion exercised by notice to Licensee within (number) days prior to the end of the Term to extend the Term until such time as either: (i) the unrecouped balance is in fact recouped by Licensee or (ii) the Licensor pays to Licensee the unrecouped balance then remaining, at which time the Term shall expire, but in no event shall the Term be extended more than one (1) year and, if at the end of the said year there remains an unrecouped balance, Licensor shall immediately pay in full to Licensee said unrecouped balance.]

ADDITIONAL CLAUSE E(iii)

[(iii) Upon expiration of the Term, if the aggregate paid attendance for all Concert Hall engagements of Artist on the Tour at which Artist is the sole headline performer and at which Licensee renders its services subject to the Terms hereof shall be less than the Guaranteed Attendance, then Licensor hereby agrees to refund to Licensee a pro rata portion of the Advance or the unrecouped balance of said Advance, whichever is less. Said pro rata portion of the Advance shall be calculated by multiplying the Advance by a fraction, the numerator of which is the difference between the aggregate paid attendance as described above and the Guaranteed Attendance and the denominator of which is the Guaranteed Attendance. Said refund shall be paid to Licensor within ten (10) business days after written request therefore by Licensor.]

7. ACCOUNTING:

A. Licensee shall render to Licensor, nightly at the close of each Concert Hall engagement, an informal accounting in writing of gross receipts derived from the sale of Products in connection with such engagement and all other pertinent and relevant data necessary to compute royalties payable to Licensor. Licensor's authorized representative may be present with Licensee when such accounting occurs, but may not interfere with Licensee's operations.

B. Licensee shall pay or, if applicable, shall credit Licensor all royalties due, if any, in connection with the sale of Products for each Concert Hall engagement no later than ten (10) business days after the date on which Licensee receives payment of gross receipts in connection with such sale.

C. Licensee shall furnish to Licensor a complete and final accounting of gross receipts derived from the sale of Products within a reasonable period of time (not to exceed thirty (30) days) after the expiration of the Term with detailed concession reports for each Concert Hall, a statement of all Gross Receipts derived from the sale of the Products indicating the number and description of each item of the Products sold and the gross sales prices of each such item less applicable taxes, and the calculation of Licensor's royalty. Said final accounting shall be accompanied by the payment of the balance, if any, of any and all royalties payable to Licensor pursuant to the terms hereof.

D. Licensee shall keep accurate books of account governing all transactions relating to the Products and Licensor, or its duly authorized representative, shall have the right at any time, but in no event later than two (2) years after the date that the final accounting is rendered to Licensor, at its sole expense, to audit the books and records of Licensee with respect to the sale of the Products, upon reasonable notice to Licensee; provided, however, that said audit is conducted at a time and place determined solely by Licensee so as not to unreasonably interfere with Licensee's business. If an audit conducted by Licensor in accordance with the above accurately reveals that Licensee has made an underpayment to Licensor of Licensor's royalty, Licensee shall pay Licensor the amount of said underpayment and, in addition thereto, interest at the rate of ten percent (10%) per annum commencing upon the date the error causing such underpayment occurred. [Notwithstanding the foregoing, if as a result of said audit it is found that Licensee has underpaid Licensor in an amount greater than (written number) percent (number %) of the total payment including the Advance and royalties paid to Licensor, then Licensee agrees to reimburse Licensor the reasonable costs of Licensor's audit.]

E. All accountings and statements rendered by Licensee shall be binding upon Licensor and shall not be subject to objection for any reason unless specific objection is made by Licensor by written notice to Licensee stating the basis thereof within two (2) years after the date that the final accounting is rendered to Licensor. [Licensor shall not have the right to maintain any action, claim or proceeding against Licensee in any forum or tribunal with respect to any accounting or statement due hereunder unless such action, claim or proceeding is commenced against Licensee in a court of competent jurisdiction within (number) years after the date such accounting or statement is rendered.]

8.   WARRANTIES AND REPRESENTATIONS:

A. Licensor hereby warrants and represents to Licensee that Licensor has the exclusive right and authority to grant to Licensee the rights granted herein.

B. Each party hereto warrants and represents that it is under no disability, restriction or prohibition, whether contractual or otherwise, with respect to its rights to execute this Agreement, to grant the rights herein granted and to perform its obligations hereunder.

C. Licensor warrants and represents that none of the Artwork furnished or to be furnished by Licensor or its agents for use by Licensee pursuant to the terms hereof, nor the exploitation or use thereof in accordance with the terms hereof, will violate or infringe upon any common law or statutory law or rights of any party, including without limitation contractual rights, trademarks, copyrights, and rights of publicity and privacy.

D. It is the essence of this Agreement and Licensor warrants and represents that Licensor has not granted and shall not grant any right, title or interest to any other person or entity effective during the Term hereof which would conflict with or be in limitation of any of the rights granted herein. Without limiting the foregoing, Licensor shall not enter into any other agreement effective during the Term hereof with any other party with respect to the manufacture, distribution, sale or advertisement in the Territory of merchandising items including, without limitation, Products, relating to the Tour or which are intended for distribution, sale or advertisement at Concert Hall engagements of Artist.

E. Licensee acknowledges that no rights in the Licensed Subject Matter are granted to Licensee except as otherwise expressly provided by this Agreement and except as so provided, Licensor reserves all rights therein.

F. Licensee will not enter into any agreement relating to the Licensed Subject Matter for commercial tie-ups or combination sales of any kind, nor will Licensee give away Products as premiums or otherwise without Licensor's prior written consent.

G. Licensee will not make or authorize any use, direct or indirect, of the Licensed Subject Matter in any areas outside the Territory and it will not knowingly sell Products covered by this Agreement to persons who intend or are likely to re-sell them in any manner other than as set forth herein.

H. Licensee will not attack the title of Licensor in and to the Licensed Subject Matter or any copyright or trademark pertaining thereto, nor will it attack the validity of the license granted hereunder.

I. Licensee will not harm, misuse or bring into disrepute the Licensed Subject Matter.

J. Licensee will not create any expenses chargeable to Licensor without the prior written approval of Licensor.

9. INDEMNIFICATION: The parties hereto shall indemnify, defend, protect, save and hold each other harmless from and against any and all actions, claims, suits, losses, judgments, penalties, liabilities, damages, costs and expenses (including without limitation reasonable attorney's fees and court costs) of whatever kind and nature imposed on, incurred by or asserted, brought or made against either party arising out of the other party's breach of any of its representations, warranties, or obligations made pursuant to this Agreement or through the negligence or intentional acts of its officers, directors, employees, or representatives. The parties hereto shall give each other prompt written notice of any such action, claim or suit and the party so noticed shall have the opportunity, at its option, to participate in the defense thereof through counsel of its own choice at such party's sole cost and expense.

10. INSURANCE: Prior to the sale of any Products, Licensee shall, at its own expense, obtain and maintain during the Term hereof a Products Liability Insurance Policy from a recognized insurance company qualified to do business in the State of (e.g. California). Said policy shall name Licensor and Artist as additional insureds against any claims, suits, losses, or damages arising out of the use of the Products and any alleged defects in the Products. Said policy shall be in an amount of not less than One Million Dollars ($1,000,000). Licensor and Artist shall be provided with a certificate of insurance evidencing the existence of said policy and the coverage of Licensor "and Artist. Said policy shall provide that Licensor and Artist shall be given notice by said insurance company at least ten (10) days prior to the cancellation or expiration of the policy.

11. SELL-OFF:

A. After expiration or termination of this Agreement, Licensee may, on a non-exclusive basis and in the ordinary course of its business, other than at Concert Halls, dispose of all remaining Products then on hand for a period of three (3) months (hereinafter referred to as the "Sell-Off Period") including but not limited to selling Products to retail outlets. Prior to selling any Products during the Sell-Off Period, Licensee shall give Licensor a full and complete written inventory of the remaining Products. Licensor shall have the right within ten (10) business days after receipt of such inventory to buy all or any portion of the remaining Products at Licensee's cost therefor plus Fifteen Percent (15%) and Licensor shall pay all shipping costs in connection with Products so purchased. Licensor's payment to Licensee for Products shall not be deemed gross receipts for which a royalty is paid to Licensor.

B. With respect to sales of Products made by Licensee during the Sell-Off Period, Licensee shall pay Licensor a percentage royalty equal to Fifty Percent (50%) multiplied by the difference, if any, between the gross receipts (less all applicable taxes) received from the sale of such Products and Licensee's Actual Cost therefor. During the Sell-Off Period Licensee shall not engage in "distress" or "close-out" sales.

C. If the Products to be sold by Licensee pursuant to this Paragraph are to be sold at or below Licensee's Actual Cost therefor, Licensor shall be given the right of first refusal by written notice to purchase said Products at such offered price and Licensor must exercise said right within ten (10) business days after its receipt of said notice. Within fifteen (15) business days after the expiration of the Sell-Off Period, all Products then remaining in Licensee's inventory shall be either:

   (i)   Sold to Licensor at a price to be agreed by the parties hereto; or

   (ii) if they can't agree as to the price or if Licensor elects not to purchase said remaining Products, destroyed by Licensee with a certificate of destruction supplied to Licensor.

D. With respect to sales of Products made by Licensee during the Sell-Off Period, Licensee shall pay Licensor a percentage royalty equal to fifty percent (50%) multiplied by the difference, if any, between the gross receipts (less all applicable taxes) received from the sale of such Products and Licensee's Actual Cost therefor. During the Sell-Off Period, Licensee shall not engage in "distress" or "close-out" sales.

12. INFRINGEMENT:

A. Licensor, at its sole expense, shall register and maintain or cause to be registered and maintained appropriate copyright(s), trademark(s), and/or service-marks(s) for the Licensed Subject Matter throughout the Territory.

B. Licensor and Licensee shall use their best efforts to protect Licensor's and Licensee's rights in and to the Licensed Subject Matter and the Products, including without limitation using their best efforts to discover, prevent and prohibit the illegal sale of Products, facsimiles of Products and/or items of merchandise similar to Products by unlicensed third parties. Each party hereto shall promptly notify the other of an infringement or other unauthorized exploitation of the Licensed Subject Matter or Products by any third party. Licensor and Licensee shall have the right, but not the obligation, to take whatever steps at their own expense they deem necessary to prevent any further such infringement or unauthorized exploitation, including but not limited to the commencement of any legal and/or equitable action provided, however, that such action shall be their own name. In the event that Licensee initiates any action or proceeding in connection with the foregoing and Licensor elects to join with Licensee in pursuing such action or proceeding, then Licensor agrees to contribute and pay fifty percent (50%) of any and all costs and expenses including but not limited to legal and court costs and fees incurred in connection therewith. If Licensor has agreed to pay Licensee the fifty percent (50%) contribution described above and if Licensee recovers on account of any such action or proceeding to which Licensor has so contributed, Licensor shall be entitled to receive a sum equal to fifty percent (50%) of the proceeds of such recovery, after deduction of any and all reasonable costs and expenses incurred by Licensee and/or Licensor in prosecuting such action.

13. TERMINATION:

A. If either party hereto breaches any of the material terms and conditions of this Agreement, the party claiming such breach shall have the right, if it so elects, to serve upon the party alleged to be in breach of the Agreement a written notice of its intention to terminate this Agreement and the party alleged to be in breach shall thereupon have a period of ten (10) business days within which to remedy said breach. If the party alleged to be in breach fails to so remedy said breach, then upon the expiration of said ten (10) business day period this Agreement shall automatically terminate.

B. Termination of this Agreement pursuant to the provisions of this clause shall be without prejudice to any other rights which either party may otherwise have against the other.

C. If either party hereto becomes insolvent or files a petition in bankruptcy, or if a petition in bankruptcy is filed against either party, or either party makes an assignment for the benefit of creditors or makes any arrangement pursuant to any bankruptcy law or a receiver is appointed, this Agreement may be automatically terminated by the other party at its election.

D. If at any time during the Term hereof by reason of any act of God, fire, earthquake, flood, explosion, strike, labor disturbance, civil commotion, act of government, its agencies or officers, any order, regulation, ruling or action of any labor union or association of artists, musicians, composers or employees affecting Licensor, Artist or Licensee, its subsidiaries or affiliates or the industry in which it is or they are engaged or any shortage of or failure or delays in the delivery of materials, supplies, labor or equipment or any other cause or causes beyond the control of Artist, Licensor, and/or licensee, the performance of Licensor's or Licensee's obligations hereunder is delayed, hampered, interrupted or interfered with or otherwise becomes impossible or impracticable, and if such condition exists for ninety (90) consecutive days or for a total of ninety (90) days in any six (6) month period during the Term, then either party may upon notice to the other terminate this agreement [if applicable, add] and the Advance, or a portion thereof, shall be returned to Licensee in accordance with Clause 6E within ten (10) days after said notice of termination.

E. Licensee shall have the right to suspend the running of the term of this agreement and of its obligations hereunder upon written notice to licensor if for any reason whatsoever artist's voice or artist's ability to perform as a vocalist shall become impaired or if artist shall refuse, neglect or be unable to comply with any of its obligations in connection with the tour. Such suspension shall be for the duration of any such event or contingency, and, unless licensee notifies licensor to the contrary in writing, the term hereof shall be automatically extended by such number of days as equal to total number of days of any such suspension. During any such suspension, artist shall not render services as a performer in live concert engagements.

14. ASSIGNMENT: Neither licensor nor licensee shall assign this agreement without the prior written consent of the other party except that licensee shall have the right to assign this agreement to any wholly owned subsidiary, or to any person, firm or corporation owning or acquiring a substantial portion of licensee's stock or assets, provided said subsidiary, person, firm or corporation is a bona fide concert merchandiser for musical artists of artist's stature.

15. NOTICES: All notices and statements provided for herein shall be in writing and, together with all payments provided for herein, shall be sent by United States

mail, postage prepaid, or sent by telex or telegraph with all charges prepaid to the address set forth above or such other address as may be designated in writing from time-to-time. A copy of all notices to licensee shall be sent to (name and address) A copy of all notices to licensor shall be sent to (name and address). Properly addressed notices delivered or sent as provided herein shall be deemed given when post-marked if delivered by mail, or on the date thereof if sent by telex or telegraph.

16.   <u>MISCELLANEOUS</u>:

A. This agreement sets forth the entire understanding of the parties hereto relating to the subject matter hereof. No modification, amendment, waiver, termination or discharge of this agreement or any of the terms or provisions hereof shall be binding upon either of the parties unless confirmed by a written instrument signed by the parties. No waiver by either party of any term or provision of this agreement or of any default hereunder shall affect such party's rights thereafter to enforce such term or provision or to exercise any right or remedy in the event of any other default, whether or not similar.

B. If any provision of this Agreement shall be held void, voidable, invalid or inoperative, no other provision of this Agreement shall be affected as a result thereof, and, accordingly, the remaining provisions of this Agreement shall remain in full force and effect as though such void, voidable, invalid or inoperative provision had not been contained herein. Notwithstanding the foregoing, in the event any provision held void, voidable, invalid or inoperative shall impair Licensor's right to receive royalties hereinunder or impair Licensee's right to manufacture, distribute and sell Products in accordance with the Terms hereof, then this agreement shall be deemed to terminate.

C. Nothing herein contained shall constitute a partnership or a joint venture between the parties. Neither party hereto shall have the right to obligate or bind the other in any manner whatsoever nor hold itself out contrary to the terms of this paragraph, and neither party shall become liable for any representation, act or omission of the other contrary to the provisions hereof.

D. In the event of any action, suit or proceeding arising from or based upon this Agreement brought by either party hereto against the other, the prevailing party shall be entitled to recover from the other its reasonable attorneys' fees in connection therewith in addition to the costs of such action, suit or proceeding.

E. Except as otherwise provided in this Agreement all rights and remedies herein or otherwise shall be cumulative and none of them shall be in limitation of any other right or remedy.

F. This Agreement has been entered into in the State of (e.g., California), and its validity, construction, interpretation and legal effect shall be governed by the laws of the State of (e.g., California) applicable to contracts entered into and performed entirely within the State of (e.g., California). The parties hereto agree that any lawsuit or proceeding initiated by one party against the other in connection with this Agreement shall be brought in (name of place).

IN WITNESS THEREOF, the parties hereto have signed this agreement on the date first set forth above.

("Licensor")

_____
(signature)

By _____, its _____

("Licensee")

_____
(signature)

By _____, its _____

Exhibit A (Tentative Tour Itinerary)

Exhibit B (Tentatively Approved Products)

BOOK PUBLISHING AGREEMENTS

Form 41

Author-Agent Contract

1. <u>SUBMITTING MANUSCRIPTS AND PROPOSALS</u>. All submissions should be accompanied by self-addressed stamped envelopes. Agency prefers to see manuscript material rather than synopses. Agency also needs to have some background about Author's professional experience, particularly that which is relevant to Author's book, as well as a list of previously published works. Agency is usually fairly prompt in responding to submissions — from between ONE to THREE weeks on average. Agency does require, however, that all authors fully advise us as to whom any particular project, in any form, has been previously submitted to publishers and what their response was. Author must also advise us upon submission if a project has been sent to another agent. Some literary agencies charge fees to read or review manuscripts or book proposals in addition to any commissions on sold works. ABC LITERARY AGENCY does not.

2. <u>COMMISSIONS</u>. Our commission is 15% of all proceeds of a work we represent, except for foreign (non-U.S.) rights retained from the initial sale, which are subject to a 20% commission. All proceeds means all royalties, expense or production funds or reimbursements, and other payments with respect to the work or its derivative works, such as subsidiary rights retained in the initial sale. All commissions accrue to the Agent upon the initial sale of primary rights in the work. Agent is entitled to receive proceeds directly from the publisher or other purchaser and to deduct his commission share of each payment received along with expenses due. Commissions received are not returnable for any reason. Author's balances are remitted within 10 to 15 days after our receipt.

3. <u>EXPENSES</u>. The Author is responsible for the Agent's costs of out-of-house photocopying or for buying books or galleys for manuscript or proposal submissions, long-distance telephone calls, messengers, and long-distance courier services such as Federal Express. Any other expenses must be approved by the Author. The ABC LITERARY AGENCY will do our best to minimize all expenses.

4. <u>ARTICLES</u>. For Authors we currently represent we may, when requested by the Author, handle articles for publication in national periodicals, subject to our standard 15% or 20% commission (if we require a co-agent for a sale abroad). We do not otherwise obtain a commission from an author's journalism, except for sales of serial or syndication rights of books we represent.

5. <u>CO-AGENTS</u>. We may retain co-agents at our sole expense and our sole discretion. Co-agents are commonly used in the industry to assist the agent in sales of certain subsidiary rights, such as foreign publication rights.

6. <u>EXCLUSIVITY OF AGENCY</u>. Agency is the author's sole and exclusive agent for sales, licenses, or other forms of disposition (sales) of that project and

any project that may be derived from it (such as rights retained for the author from the initial sale). Exclusivity means, of course, that an Author may not submit a project his agent has already worked on, or agreed to represent, to any other agent, nor may the Author make an independent deal with a publisher or other exploiter of rights with respect to the project. Potential buyers approaching the Author directly always should be referred to the Author's agent.

7. IRREVOCABILITY OF THE AGENT'S INTEREST. Agent will provide substantial editorial help to Author, as well as invest time and energy in promoting the Author and the Author's work. Therefore, after we undertake to represent a particular project, our Agency's interest in proceeds of that project and its derivative works are irrevocable. This means that we would be entitled to be designated as Agent on all contracts, receive all proceeds, and deduct our full commissions, regardless of who makes the sale, or when, unless we otherwise agree. In practice, we will release any unsold project, as submitted, either on our own initiative or upon Author's request, if, in our opinion, we have had sufficient opportunity to market the work and no longer anticipate success. In such event, we would be entitled to retain all copies of materials marked up with, or incorporating, our own manuscript editing or our own ideas or other intellectual property, and Author would not be entitled to use such property, though he would be free to do as he pleased with material exclusively his own.

8. TERMINATION OF AGENCY. Either we or the Author are free to terminate the agency relationship upon notice to the other at any time. Author should understand, however, that terminating an agent affects only future works and not the agent's interest in proceeds of works (including derivative works) he undertook to represent prior to termination.

9. LEGAL ADVICE. Agency wishes to advise Author that we do not engage in the practice of law and may not furnish legal services to Author. Accordingly, we suggest that it is in your best interest to engage an attorney of your choice in situations where you want legal advice.

If the above meets with your approval, please sign below.

Dated:

_____
Author

ABC Literary Agency, Inc.

By _____

Form 42

Author-Publisher Hardcover Trade Book Contract

AGREEMENT, entered into this (DAY) of (MONTH), 1991 between (NAME AND ADDRESS OF PUBLISHING COMPANY), (hereinafter called "Publisher"), and (NAME AND ADDRESS OF AUTHOR) (hereinafter called "Author"). In consideration of the premises and promises hereinafter set forth, Publisher and Author agree together as follows with respect to the work tentatively entitled (TITLE AND DESCRIPTION OF BOOK) (hereinafter called "the Work").

1. <u>RIGHTS GRANTED:</u> Author grants and assigns to Publisher the following rights and privileges in, to and in connection with the Work during the full terms of copyright and all renewals and extensions thereof, under the present or future laws of any country covered by this Agreement:

(e.g., The sole and exclusive right to publish and sell the Work or cause the same to be published and sold in book form in the English language in the United States of America, its dependencies, in the Republic of the Philippines, and in the Dominion of Canada. In addition, publisher shall have the non-exclusive rights to sell the Work in the English language in book form in all other parts of the world, excluding the British Commonwealth and Empire (excluding Canada) as constituted at the date of this Agreement.)

2. <u>ADVANCES:</u> Subject to the provisions hereof, Publisher agrees to pay to Author as an advance against royalties to be earned at the rates hereinafter set forth and on account of all monies accruing to Author under this Agreement, the sum of ($ AMOUNT) payable ($ AMOUNT) upon signature of this Agreement; ($ AMOUNT) upon delivery and acceptance of one-half (½) the completed manuscript; and ($ AMOUNT) upon delivery and acceptance of the completed manuscript.

3. <u>ROYALTIES:</u> Publisher shall pay to Author royalties as follows, based upon net retail sales less a reserve for returns of _____%.

(a) Except as provided hereinafter, a royalty upon the regular trade edition sold in the United States of America of TEN percent (10%) of the retail price on the first 5,000 copies sold in regular course; TWELVE AND ONE HALF PERCENT (12 ½%) on the next 5,000 copies sold; and FIFTEEN PERCENT (15%) on all copies sold thereafter, except that on reprintings of 2,500 copies or fewer made during the twelve (12) months immediately after the date of first publication the royalties shall be ten percent (10%) on copies sold unless there shall be two (2) or more reprintings of at least 2,500 copies made within the first six (6) months after the first date of publication, which printings will then earn royalties at the regular stipulated rate. After twelve (12) months from the date of first publication, one-half (½) of the regular stipulated rate on all copies sold from a reprinting of 2,500 copies or less, providing that the regular sales in the six (6) months period immediately preceding such reprinting do not exceed five hundred (500) copies; if such sales do exceed five hundred (500) copies, ten percent (10%) on such reprintings. These reduced royalties are provided because of the increased cost of manufacture of small reprintings and to enable Publisher to keep the work in print and in circulation as fully and as long as possible.

(b) A royalty of twelve and one-half percent (12 ½%) of the amount received by Publisher on all sales in Canada of copies of any hardcover edition published by Publisher.

(c) Two-thirds (2/3) of any amount received by Publisher for the sale of the right to publish a hardcover edition of the Work on a royalty basis or for an outright sum in Canada.

(d) A royalty of ten percent (10%) of the amount received by Publisher on sales of copies or unbound sheets of any hardcover edition of the Work published by Publisher, sold outside the continental limits of the United States of America and Canada, and on sales at a discount of sixty percent (60%) or more from the retail price to reading circles, to recognized book clubs, and to organizations outside the regular book-selling channels.

(e) A royalty of ten percent (10%) of the retail price of each copy sold within the continental limits of the United States of America of any hardcover edition issued by Publisher at a retail price of not more than two-thirds (2/3) of the original retail price.

(f) Fifty percent (50%) of any license fee or royalty charge for the right granted another publisher to issue and distribute a reprint edition or visual reproduction (microfilm) of the Work.

(g) Fifty percent (50%) of the gross amount paid by a book club as royalty for the right to publish the Work in whole or in part for distribution to its members. If, by the terms of such license for the right to publish an edition by a book club, Publisher is required to provide the book club with more than one complete set of plates and binder's dies, the cost of such extra sets of plates and binder's dies shall be borne equally by Author and Publisher.

(h) Fifty percent (50%) of the amount actually received by Publisher for permissions to publish extracts from the Work.

(i) Ten percent (10%) of the amount received by Publisher for the cloth-bound edition and five percent (5%) for a lower-price edition on sales of copies of overstock at a discount between fifty percent (50%) and sixty percent (60%) or more, or for the use of the plates by any governmental agency. No royalties shall be payable on copies furnished gratis to Author for review, advertising, sample, publicity, promotion, or like purposes, or on copies destroyed by fire or water, or on copies sold at or below the cost of manufacture.

(j) Where the discount to jobbers or to wholesale distributors or booksellers (except as provided for in Subclauses 3(d) and 3(i) hereof) on copies of any edition published by Publisher is forty-eight percent (48%) or more, Publisher shall pay Author the prevailing rate of royalty less one-half (½) difference between a forty-four percent (44%) discount and the discount granted [it being understood that the amount paid to Author shall not be less than one-half (½) the stipulated royalty].

(k) On hardcover copies sold through mail order coupon advertising or direct-by-mail circulation: FIVE PERCENT (5%) of the net amount received by Publisher.

(l) On rack-size paperback copies sold in the United States, its territories and possessions: EIGHT PERCENT (8%) of the retail cover price on the first 150,000 copies sold; TEN PERCENT (10%) of the retail cover price on all copies sold thereafter.

(m) On trade paperback copies sold in the United States, its territories and possessions: SIX PERCENT (6%) of the retail cover price on the first 20,000 copies sold and SEVEN AND ONE-HALF PERCENT (7 ½%) of the retail cover price on all copies sold above 20,000 copies.

(n) On paperback copies sold in foreign countries: FOUR PERCENT (4%) of the United States retail cover price on all such copies sold.

(o) On paperback copies sold to a bona-fide book club or sold to be distributed as a premium: FIVE PERCENT (5%) of the net amount received by Publisher.

(p) On paperback copies sold in bulk to organizations other than book clubs, on a non-returnable basis, for the specific purpose of achieving distribution in special markets: One-half (½) of the prevailing royalty rate set forth in Subclause 3(a) above. Publisher shall have the right to imprint the colophon of the organization on such copies for the purpose of identification, and such special printings shall still be considered Publisher's editions.

(q) If, in the opinion of Publisher, the paperback edition shall have ceased to have a remunerative sale, Publisher shall be at liberty to dispose of all or part of the existing stock and will pay Proprietor a royalty of FIVE PERCENT (5%) of the net amount received from the sale thereof. No royalties shall be paid on any such copies sold at or below cost, but, all copies sold at Ten (10) Cents or less shall be considered as remainders and shall not be subject to royalty.

(r) On paperback copies sold through mail orders: One-half (½) of the prevailing paperback royalty on all copies sold.

(s) Publisher shall have the further right to break up into hardcover and/or paperback editions any of the material in the Work, and to use the material separately at any time. Publisher shall have the right to publish the material in any number of volumes it seems suitable at any time. If there is a Continuity

Program of the Work either through the mail or in chain and supermarkets, the royalty payable shall be Five percent (5%) of the net amount received by Publisher on all such copies sold.

No royalties shall be payable on copies of either the hardcover or paperback edition damaged or destroyed or on copies furnished gratis for review, publicity or like purposes.

Author's right to payments shall be subject to Publisher's prior right to deduct any and all advance payments made by Publisher to Author. However, Publisher shall account to Author for any reserve against returns within (SIX MONTHS) following the end of the period within which book stores or other purchasers may obtain credit for returned books.

4. SUBSIDIARY RIGHTS:

(a) Publisher is further granted the exclusive right, in the territories set forth in Clause 1, to sell or license (including among others, the licensing of Publisher's own divisions) the use of the Work, for publication in whole or part, in any form, upon such terms as it deems advisable. The net proceeds of such sales or licenses shall be divided as follows, and Author's share, less the amount of any advances then unearned, shall be paid at the time of the next accounting:

	AUTHOR'S SHARE	PUBLISHER'S SHARE
Reprint licenses including mass market paperback or trade paperback:	50	50
First Serial (use of serializations, condensations, excerpts, digests, etc., in newspapers, magazines or other periodicals before publication of the Work in book form in the relevant territory)	90	10
Second Serial (use of serializations, condensations, excerpts, digests, etc., in newspapers, magazines, or other periodicals or books AFTER publication of the Work in book form in the relevant territory)	50	50
Book Club	50	50
Storage, Retrieval, Microfilm, Microfiche, Other forms of non-dramatic electronic reproduction, including non-dramatic readings of the entire book or portions thereof	50	50

British Hardcover and/or Paperback (which may include the right of such licensee to sub-license ancillary rights in that market)	80	20
Translation	75	25
Other Book Publication (including, but not limited to, hardcover, large format paperback, large print editions, mail order, calendar)	50	50
Commercial and Merchandising (derivative products such as the use of a title or character for greeting cards, clothing)	50	50
Performance (television, radio, dramatic, motion picture rights and allied merchandising rights derived therefrom)	90	10
Electronic Publishing (such as computer software, audio and video cassettes)	50	50

Alternative Electronic Rights Provision

Electronic Publishing (the right to record and transmit the verbatim text of the Work or parts of the Work by any means, electronic or otherwise, the result of which serves as a substitute for sales of the work in book form)	50	50

If Publisher exercises any of the foregoing rights itself in lieu of sublicensing same, the royalty rates, where not otherwise specified above, shall be subject to agreement between the parties.

(b) If Author controls any of the foregoing rights which Publisher has the capacity to exercise itself, Author agrees to give Publisher the right of first refusal for the separate acquisition of such rights before licensing such rights elsewhere.

(c) Publication of the work in Braille, or photocopying, recording and microfilming the work for the physically handicapped: Publisher is hereby authorized to license such publication without fee and with no royalty to Author. Should any compensation be received, however, it shall be divided equally between Author and Publisher.

ADDITIONAL "PASS-THROUGH" CLAUSE

After the advance has been recouped by Publisher, Publisher agrees to pay Author, Author's share of net licensing revenue received by Publisher over $1,000 within THIRTY (30) DAYS of receipt by Publisher.

ELECTRONIC RIGHTS PROVISIONS ALTERNATIVE ELECTRONIC RIGHTS CLAUSE (I)

The Publisher shall also have the following rights with respect to which the Publisher alone may make arrangements both on its own behalf and on behalf of the author in the exclusive market granted herein, and the division of the net receipts from the sale or other disposition of these rights shall be as follows:

(a) publication or utilization of the text of the work, or any portion thereof, in any form by any electronic, computerized, or any other means now known or hereafter invented by which the text may be stored, preserved, entered, displayed, transmitted, communicated, disclosed: fifty percent (50%) to the author and fifty percent (50%) to the publisher.

(b) in the event the rights noted above in subclause (a) are conveyed, it is understood that the exact text may be communicated, transmitted or performed or through sound recordings in connection with the electronic or computerized versions of the text.

ALTERNATIVE ELECTRONIC RIGHTS CLAUSE (II)

The Publisher shall also have all electronic rights to the work. "Electronic rights" shall mean the sole and exclusive right to use or adapt, and to authorize others to use or adapt, the Literary Work or any portion thereof, for one or more "electronic versions." As used herein, the term "electronic versions" shall mean any and all methods of copying, recording, storage, retrieval or transmission of all or any portion of the Literary Work, alone or in combination with other works, including in any multimedia work or electronic book, by any electronic, electromagnetic or other means now known or hereafter devised, including, without limitation, by analog or digital signal, whether in sequential or non-sequential order, on any and all physical media now known or hereafter devised including, without limitation, magnetic tape, floppy disks, interactive CD, CD-ROM, laser disk, optical disk, integrated circuit card or chip and any other human or machine-readable medium, whether or not permanently affixed in such media, and the broadcast or transmission thereof by any means now known or hereafter devised, but excluding audio recording rights, video recording rights and all uses encompassed in the definitions of motion picture rights and television rights (provided that the exercise of any of the foregoing rights, if reserved herein by the Author or licensed to any third party, shall not preclude the exercise of electronic rights).

*   *   *

ALTERNATE ELECTRONIC RIGHTS CLAUSE (VI)

A. Publisher shall have the right to exercise, and with author's prior written consent (not to be unreasonably withheld), license the exercise of, the Electronic Rights (as defined herein).

B. "Electronic Rights" shall include, and be limited to, the right to nondramatic reproduction of the verbatim text of the Book in its entirety in an electronic form the result of which serves as a substitute for sales of the Book in book form, with the same content, form, organization, text and other material contained in the Book in its printed form, in the same order and without embellishment or abridgement or other additions, deletions or changes of any kind unless the Author's written consent thereto shall have first been obtained.

C. The following shall also be subject to the Author's prior written approval in connection with the exploitation of Electronic Rights; any product which constitutes an exploitation of the Electronic Rights; any commercial tie-in; any direct or indirect endorsement of any product, service, business and/or organization; and any advertising done in conjunction with such product.

D. Without limiting anything contained herein, it is expressly understood and agreed that in connection with the exploitation of the Electronic Rights, the Book may not be coupled with any other work without the Author's prior written approval.

E. The Publisher acknowledges that if the Author consents to the use of any additional new material to be written and used for a product which constitutes an exploitation of the Electronic Rights, the Author shall have first option to write any such material on terms to be agreed upon or on terms no less favorable than the Publisher or its licensee would pay to a third party to write such material.

*   *   *

ALTERNATIVE ELECTRONIC RIGHTS CLAUSE (VIII)

Author conveys to the Publisher electronic rights, that is the right to use, and to authorize others to use, the verbatim text of the work or any portion thereof and to add to such text images, photographs, or narration for the purpose of illustrating the text material (this shall not, however, be construed as granting the Publisher any rights to license the dramatic rights), as a basis for electronic or digital copying, recording or transmission, including without limitation copying, recording or transmission by magnetic, laser or electronic means, whether on disc or other computer software, and the broadcast and transmission thereof. The Publisher shall consult with the Author prior to exercising or disposing of any such rights; the Author shall have the absolute right to approve any editing or revision of the text of the work; the Publisher shall not use or authorize the use of dramatized images with the work; and the Publisher shall not exercise or dispose of any electronic rights in such a way as to adversely affect the motion picture, television, radio and allied rights, which are reserved to the Author. Notwithstanding the foregoing, the Author reserves the specific right to produce, market, publish and distribute a traditional audio recording of the text of the work and/or a traditional video recording based upon the work (it being understood that all other electronic rights, including but not limited to computer-oriented audio and video technology rights (E.G. CD-ROM and CD-I) are among the electronic rights granted exclusively to the Publisher hereunder.

5.   Publisher shall forward to Author, or his agent, royalty statements to be computed as of June 30th and December 31st of each year of this Agreement within one hundred twenty (120) days following such respective dates, and shall make the payments indicated to be due thereby together therewith. If no payments are due in any accounting period, Publisher shall not be obligated to render statements.

Whenever Author has received an overpayment, other than any unearned advance as may herein be specifically provided, it is agreed that Publisher may deduct the amount of such overpayment from any further earnings accruing to Author on account of the Work. In all cases royalties paid on copies subsequently returned shall be treated as overpayment.

Upon written request, Author may examine or cause to be examined through certified public accountants the books of account of Publisher in so far as they relate to the sale or licensing of the Work.

ALTERNATIVE AUDIT RIGHTS CLAUSE

Author may, at its own expense, audit the books and records of Publisher relating to the publication of the Work pursuant to this agreement at the place where Publisher maintains such books and records in order to verify statements rendered to Author. Any such audit shall be conducted only by a reputable public accountant during reasonable business hours in such manner as not to interfere with Publisher's normal business activities. An audit with respect to any statement shall not commence later than twelve (12) months from the date of dispatch to Author of such statement nor shall any audit continue for longer than five (5) consecutive business days nor shall audits be made more frequently than twice annually, nor shall the records supporting any such statements be audited more than once. All statements rendered hereunder shall be binding upon Author and not subject to objection for any reason unless such objection is made in writing stating the basis thereof and delivered to Publisher within twelve (12) months from delivery of such statement, or if an audit is commenced prior thereto, within thirty (30) days from the completion of the relative audit.

6.   DELIVERY: Author agrees to deliver to Publisher on or before (DATE) in duplicate, and in final revised form and content satisfactory to Publisher, an English-language manuscript of approximately (NUMBER) words. Unless postponed by mutual agreement, failure to make delivery of the manuscript of the work on or before the date shall be deemed just cause for Publisher, at its option, to terminate this Agreement by giving written notice, whereupon Author agrees to repay forthwith all monies which may have been advanced hereunder and shall further pay other damages as Publisher may sustain by reason of such breach. The foregoing does not exclude any other remedies at law or equity that the publisher may have. It is understood and agreed that no duty shall devolve upon Publisher under this Agreement until such time as the manuscript has been completed to the satisfaction of Publisher. It is understood that in the ordinary course of preparing the manuscript for the printer Publisher is authorized to exercise editorial privilege and to make the manuscript conform to its house style in spelling, punctuation and usage.

Publisher shall have the right, in its sole discretion and at its sole cost and expense, to submit the Work, or any parts thereof, to its legal counsel for review. Publisher shall have ninety (90) days after Publisher's receipt of the Work in Manuscript Form to notify Author in writing whether Publisher shall submit the Work to its legal counsel for review. If Publisher so notifies Author, then, notwithstanding anything herein contained, the Work shall not be deemed to be satisfactory to Publisher hereunder unless and until any and all changes which may be required by Publisher's legal counsel have been made. Additionally, payment of the advance or any part thereof or any other sums to Author hereunder, including any payment upon or following delivery of the Work, shall not be deemed to be evidence either that the Work is satisfactory to Publisher, that Author has fulfilled his obligations hereunder, or that Publisher has waived any of its rights hereunder. It is specifically agreed and understood by the parties that nothing contained in this subparagraph shall in any way alter or vary any of Publisher's rights hereunder including but not limited to Publisher's rights pursuant to Author's representations and warranties set forth in Clause _____ and the indemnification provisions of Clause _____.

7.   PERMISSIONS:

(a) If permission from others is required for publication of any material contained in the Work or for the exercise of any other right conferred by this Agreement, Author agrees to obtain such permissions at Author's own expense, and to deliver such permissions, in form acceptable to Publisher, on the due date for the final manuscript. Permissions shall cover the territorial market and uses as licensed herein, as specified in Clause 1 hereunder.

(b) Copies of the signed agreements between Author and each of the contributors shall be attached to this Agreement and shall become a part thereof.

8. <u>REJECTION OF MANUSCRIPT</u>: If, in the opinion of Publisher, the manuscript is unacceptable or unsatisfactory to Publisher, Publisher may reject it by written notice within sixty (60) days of delivery, in which event any sums previously advanced under this agreement pursuant to Clause 2 shall be repaid by Author, this Agreement shall be deemed terminated, and there shall be no further obligation upon Publisher to publish the Work or to make any further payment hereunder.

ALTERNATIVE CLAUSE (I)

8. <u>TIME FOR ACCEPTANCE</u>: Publisher will convey to Author its comments concerning the acceptability of the Work or any portion thereof delivered in accordance with Clause 6 above or the need for revisions within ninety (90) days of its receipt of the completed Work or any portion thereof. If Publisher concludes that the Work or any portion thereof is unacceptable but could be revised to Publisher's satisfaction in a timely fashion, Publisher and Author shall agree on an appropriate period of time for the revision process. Should Publisher conclude that the Work or any portion thereof as first submitted cannot be revised to its satisfaction within a timely period or should Publisher find the revised Work or any portion thereof unacceptable for any reason, Publisher may reject it. Upon rejection of one-half the manuscript as described in Clause 1 above, Author may retain ONE THOUSAND DOLLARS ($1,000). Upon rejection of the completed manuscript as described in clause above, Author may retain TWO THOUSAND DOLLARS ($2,000) and all other monies paid to Author by Publisher shall be returned to Publisher and Publisher shall not be obligated to make any further payment. Thereafter Author may grant the rights to the Work to another publisher subject to Author's obligation to repay Publisher the retained sum out of first monies received from such other publisher for the Work, and, except for such repayment obligation, this Agreement shall be deemed terminated.

ALTERNATIVE CLAUSE (II)

8. <u>TIME FOR ACCEPTANCE</u>: If supervening events or circumstances have, in the sole judgment of Publisher, materially adversely changed the economic expectations of Publisher in respect to the Work on the giving of timely notice, all Publisher's rights shall terminate and revert to Author and in any such event, Author shall be entitled to retain all payments previously made to him.

ALTERNATIVE CLAUSE (III)

8. <u>TIME FOR ACCEPTANCE</u>: If the Work is unsatisfactory or unacceptable to Publisher, Author shall be at liberty to submit the manuscript to others, and if the manuscript is accepted elsewhere, Author shall thereupon return, or cause to be returned, to Publisher all monies which may have been advanced to Author.

ALTERNATIVE CLAUSE (IV)

8.   TIME FOR ACCEPTANCE: Author will direct any third party publishing the manuscript to assign and pay directly to Publisher all monies due to Author until the advance is repaid and advise any such third party that Publisher's release of its rights under this Agreement is conditional upon Author and the third party complying with the preceding.

ALTERNATIVE CLAUSE (V)

8.   TIME FOR ACCEPTANCE: Publisher shall not be obligated to accept the Work unless the Work, in Manuscript Form, is delivered at the time specified in Clause [] above and is, in Publisher's sole editorial judgment, satisfactory in form and content. Timely and satisfactory delivery of the Work is of the essence of this Agreement. If the Work is not satisfactory to Publisher or if the Work is not delivered on time Publisher may, without waiving any of its other rights or remedies, serve notice of Publisher's intention to terminate this Agreement. Upon the giving of this notice of termination, all Publisher's obligations hereunder shall automatically be suspended and Author shall then have the right to offer the manuscript of the Work to other bona fide publishers, it being understood that Publisher's exclusive rights granted shall continue in full force and effect until such time that Author or such other publishers have actually repaid to Publisher all sums paid to Author under this Agreement, including but not limited to any advances set forth in Clause [] hereof from the first (and all) proceeds of any agreements with such other publishers or from alternate arrangements for such repayment satisfactory to Publisher. Should Author breach the provisions of the previous sentence Author shall be obligated to pay all of Publisher's costs of recovering such sums including Publisher's legal fees and expenses. Publisher shall have the right, upon written notice to Author, to revoke its notice of termination at any time prior to the entering into of an agreement by Author with another publisher with respect to the Work.

9.   EDITORIAL CHANGES: Publisher is authorized, in its sole discretion, to make any editorial changes, deletions, abridgment and condensation whatsoever in the text of the Work, and is further authorized to title, sub-title and change the title and the chapters of the Work, and such authorization shall extend to each reprinting of same in any form.

Publisher reserves the right to omit any part of the Work submitted by Author, and to request substitutions or additional material prior to publication; and Author agrees to make such revisions, substitutions and alterations in the Work as Publisher may reasonably request. Final decision as to title and retail price shall be within Publisher's sole discretion.

Author agrees to read, revise, correct and return promptly galleys of the Work within ten (10) days of receipt. If Author fails to return such proofs within such agreed upon period of time, Publisher shall have the right to publish the Work in the condition it was deemed satisfactory and acceptable to Publisher, subject to the provisions of Clause 6 concerning the customary preparation for the printer. Author agrees to have charged against it any sums accruing to it under the terms of this Agreement, the cost of alterations in type or in plates, required by Author, other than those due to printer's errors, in excess of ten (10%) of the cost of setting type. If Publisher elects to charge these costs against sums accruing to Author hereunder and such sums do not cover the cost within one (1) year from the date of first publication, Author shall at that time on notice from Publisher pay in cash the balance of the costs outstanding. Publisher will forward a statement of charges at Author's request any time after thirty (30) days of the receipt of the printer's bills, and the corrected proofs will be presented on request for Author's inspection.

ALTERNATIVE CLAUSE

9. EDITORIAL CHANGES:

   (a) No changes in the manuscript or the provisional title shall be made without the consent of Author. However, Publisher shall not be obligated to publish a work which in its opinion violates the copyright of any third party or the right of privacy of any person or contains libelous or obscene matter.

10. COPYRIGHT: Publisher is authorized, upon first publication of the Work, to secure copyright to it in the name of (NAME OF AUTHOR) to credit (NAME OF AUTHOR) as Author and to use his name, picture, likeness for advertising purposes or purposes of trade in connection with the Work as finally published hereunder, as well as the name, picture, likeness, for advertising purposes or purposes of trade in connection with the Work as finally published of any and all of the contributors contributing materials to the Work, and to arrange for sale of the Work in Canada simultaneously with first sale in the United States. Author agrees to make timely application for renewals and extensions of the copyright. With respect or any portions of the Work which are or have been published prior to publication of the Work by Publisher, Publisher shall see to it that any such publication bears a proper copyright notice as specified by the United States Copyright Law and the Universal Copyright Convention. If, in connection with any such publication, Author shall promptly deliver to Publisher an assignment of such copyright in form for recordation in the Copyright office. If such publication is outside the United States, Author shall promptly deliver to Publisher three (3) copies of the Work or part thereof so published and inform Publisher of the date of such publication.

11. PUBLICATION DATE: Publisher agrees to publish and commence distribution of the hardcover edition within twelve months after approval and acceptance of Author's final manuscript. Unless otherwise agreed, the paperback

edition will be published not earlier than twelve months after hardcover publication and not later than TWELVE MONTHS after hardcover publication.

ADDITIONAL CLAUSE

11. MANNER OF PUBLICATION: Publisher shall have the right: (1) to publish the Work in such style as it deems best suited to the sale of the Work; (2) to fix or alter the prices at which the Work shall be sold; (3) to determine the method and means of advertising, publicizing, and selling the Work, the number and destination of free copies, and all other publishing details, including the number of copies to be printed, form, style, size, type, paper to be used and like details.

ALTERNATIVE CLAUSE

11. CONTROL OVER ASPECTS OF PRODUCTION BY WRITER: The title under which the book is to be published shall be designated by Author. The dust jacket of the trade edition shall include a biography and photograph of Author which shall be subject to her approval. Author shall have approval of the artwork of the dust jacket for the United States trade edition of the book and of the artwork to be used on the cover of the first paperback edition of the Work to be published. Publisher shall consult in advance with Author concerning the format and style of the trade edition, and its graphic material. The sequence in which the stores are to appear in the Work shall be designated by Author.

12. DEMAND FOR PUBLICATION: If Publisher shall fail to publish and distribute either the hardcover or paperback edition of the Work by the date, Author may, at any time after the date, serve a written demand on Publisher, by Registered Mail, return receipt requested, requiring Publisher to commence manufacture and publication within six (6) months from the date of such written demand, and if Publisher shall fail to comply with such written demand, this Agreement shall be terminated forthwith on expiration of the six (6) months. In such instance, however, such payments as shall have been made to Author as advances shall constitute full payment to Author for all his rights, efforts and all materials supplied under this Agreement and no other damages, claims, actions or proceedings, either legal or equitable, founded on such breach, default or failure to publish by Publisher may be claimed, instituted or maintained by Author against Publisher. However, Publisher shall not be obligated to publish a work which in its opinion violates the common law or statutory copyright or the work of privacy of any person or contains libelous or obscene matter.

13. AUTHOR COPIES: On publication, Publisher shall give Author TEN (10) COPIES of the hardcover and paperback editions of the published Work, and should Author desire any more copies for personal use they shall be supplied

at FORTY PERCENT (40%) OF THE RETAIL PRICE IF AVAILABLE FOR SUCH USE. COPIES THUS SUPPLIED SHALL NOT BE RESOLD.

14. OUT-OF-PRINT:

(a) If, in the sole discretion and determination of Publisher, further publication and sale of either the hardcover or paperback edition of the Work will no longer be a profitable venture, Publisher may discontinue publishing, distributing and selling same.

ALTERNATIVE CLAUSE

14. OUT-OF-PRINT: If the work becomes out of print in the United States and Publisher fails to bring out a new edition within six months of Publisher's receipt of written request from Author to do so, or if within the six-month period a reprint edition has not been arranged for, then this Agreement shall terminate and all rights under this Agreement shall revert to Author without further notice.

15. WARRANTIES: Author warrants and represents that the Work is original and has not before been published; that he is the sole Author of the Work and has full power, free of any prior contract, lien or rights of any nature in anyone which might interfere therewith, to enter into this Agreement and to grant the rights hereby conveyed to Publisher; that the Work contains no matter which is libelous, obscene, or otherwise unlawful, infringes no right of privacy, proprietary right or copyright (whether statutory or common law); that he has not heretofore and will not hereafter during the term of this agreement enter into any agreement or understanding with any person, firm or corporation other than Publisher for the rights granted hereunder. If Author shall breach this warranty, Publisher shall be entitled to injunctive relief in addition to all other remedies which may be available to it. Author further agrees that he will hold Publisher, its distributors, employees, licensees, agents and any retailer harmless against any suit, claim, demand, proceeding, prosecution, recovery or penalty and any expense, including attorneys' and litigation expenses arising out of same, by reason of any claim or violation of any of the foregoing warranties or representations.

In defending any such claim, demand, action or proceeding, Publisher shall have the right to select counsel and the right to withhold amounts otherwise payable to Author under this or any other agreement and to apply such amounts (as required) in satisfaction of the foregoing indemnities. If monies are withheld under this clause, they shall be set aside in an interest bearing account, and any balance after payment of legal fees, expenses, settlement costs and/or judgments shall be paid to Author along with the interest on such amount. The foregoing warranties and indemnities shall be effective without regard to what Publisher may suggest or advise or fail to suggest or advise with respect to the manuscript as submitted and shall apply to the final manuscript as it appears in corrected printer's proofs and shall survive the termination of this Agreement.

ALTERNATIVE CLAUSE

15. INSURANCE:

(a) Notwithstanding anything to the contrary in the Agreement, Publisher agrees to add Author as an insured to the Media Special Perils Program, Policy No._____, which Publisher currently carries with _____ Insurance Company. A copy of the policy is attached and forms a part of this Agreement.

As an insured, Author will be covered subject to the terms of the policy against claims arising from the Work for libel, invasion of the right of privacy, plagiarism, infringement of copyright, trademark infringement and unfair competition. (See the policy for a more detailed list of claims covered.) Coverage will be solely for the publication of the Work by Publisher, or by its licensee, and will be subject to the limits of liability and the deductible provisions set forth in the policy.

The policy's limits of liability are [$5 MILLION] for all occurrences in any policy year for all books published by Publisher or under license from Publisher.

Author and Publisher, have the same coverage under the policy for the Work. The coverage includes legal expenses as well as judgments. However, if Author elects to have separate counsel for any reason, the cost of such counsel must be borne by Author and the counsel must cooperate with the counsel engaged under the policy.

Publisher will pay the premium for the coverage described herein.

The deductible for each individual loss or claim is [$50,000.] It will be handled as follows: Publisher will pay the first [$1500] of all costs and expenses (including legal fees and disbursements) incurred in connection with any claims asserted which, if true, would constitute a breach by author of author's representation and warranties in the agreement. Publisher and Author agree to bear any such additional costs or expenses above [$1500] constituting the balance of the deductible in the policy on a 50/50 basis. If there are costs and expenses in excess of the deductible which for any reason are not paid by the insurance corporation, then those amounts will be handled in accordance with the terms of this Agreement, as if this modification had not been made.

16. ASSIGNMENT OF ROYALTIES:

(a) Author agrees to furnish Publisher with a copy of any assignment which Author may make of his rights to royalties under this Agreement, and to specify in writing to whom and where future royalty payments may be made. Such assignments shall not be binding on Publisher unless Author shall receive from Publisher written acknowledgment of receipt of a copy of such assignment. The performance of the terms of this Agreement are personal to Author and may not be assigned.

(b) This Agreement may be assigned by Publisher as part of the sale or transfer of all or substantially all Publisher's business or as part of the merger or consolidation of Publisher with another corporation. This Agreement may be assigned by Publisher to any corporate subsidiary or affiliate, or any company or entity owned or controlled by it.

17. RIGHT OF FIRST REFUSAL: Author grants Publisher the first refusal of his next completed book-length work, on the same terms and conditions as are set forth herein, except that the amount of the advance and the royalties shall be subject to negotiation. Such negotiation shall not commence until four months after the publication of the present Work. If Author and Publisher cannot agree upon advance and royalties within thirty (30) days after the commencement of negotiations, Author shall then be free to negotiate with other publishers, provided that Publisher shall have the option to obtain the right to publish by matching terms which Author shall have obtained elsewhere. Author shall communicate such terms to Publisher in writing, and Publisher shall have ten (10) days after Publisher's receipt of such communication in which to exercise such option.

18. PAYMENT TO AGENT: Publisher is authorized to pay all monies due Author to (NAME AND ADDRESS OF AUTHOR'S AGENT) whose receipt shall be full and valid discharge of Publisher's obligations.

19. BINDING EFFECT: The provisions of this Agreement shall be binding upon and shall inure to the benefit of the parties, their respective successors, legal representatives, and assigns.

20. FORCE MAJEURE: This Agreement and performance thereof by Publisher shall in all respects be subject to delays or inability to perform all or any portion thereof by reasons of strikes, lockouts, market shortages of labor or materials, acts of God, accidents arising out of circumstances and conditions not directly due to negligence of Publisher, or which may affect Publisher's suppliers, or subcontractors; and without limitation by reason of any of the foregoing, by reason of any cause, condition or circumstances beyond the control of Publisher, including but not limited to the intervention of any rules, law or regulation of any Government, or any bureau or department, or any sovereign act, and the term of this Agreement or any obligation of Publisher hereunder shall be extended by the period of such delay.

21. NON-COMPETITION: Author agrees that during the term of this Agreement it will not, without the written permission of Publisher, publish or permit to be published any material, in book or pamphlet form, based on material in the Work.

22. <u>NOTIFICATION</u>: Author agrees to notify Publisher promptly of the disposition of any right which Author has retained for itself.

23. <u>DISPOSAL OF MANUSCRIPT</u>: Except for loss or damage due to its negligence, Publisher shall not be responsible for loss of or damage to any property of Author, and in the absence of written request from Author prior to publication for their return, Publisher, after publication of the Work, may dispose of the original manuscript and proofs.

24. <u>NO WAIVER</u>: A waiver of any breach of this Agreement or of any of the terms or conditions by either party, shall not be deemed a waiver or any repetition of such breach or any ways affect any other terms or conditions hereof; no waiver shall be valid or binding unless it shall be in writing and signed by the party making the waiver.

25. <u>CROSS-COLLATERALIZATION</u>: Any sums due and owing from Author to Publisher, arising out of this or any other agreement, may be deducted from any sum due or to become due from Publisher or Author pursuant to this Agreement or any other agreement between the parties.

26. <u>BANKRUPTCY</u>: If (a) a petition in bankruptcy is filed by Publisher, or (b) a petition in bankruptcy is filed against Publisher and such petition is finally sustained, or (c) a petition for arrangement is filed by Publisher or a petition for reorganization is filed by or against Publisher, and an order is entered directing the liquidation of Publisher as in bankruptcy, or (d) Publisher makes an assignment for the benefit of creditors, or (e) Publisher liquidates its business for any cause whatever, Author may terminate this agreement by written notice and thereupon all rights granted by him hereunder shall revert to him. Upon such termination, Author, at his option, may purchase the plates as provided in Clause 16 and the remaining copies at one-half of the manufacturing cost, exclusive of overhead. If he fails to exercise such option within sixty (60) days after the happening of any one of the events above referred to, the trustee, receiver, or assignee may destroy the plates and sell the copies remaining on hand, subject to the royalty provisions of Clause 10.

ADDITIONAL CLAUSES

27. <u>INFRINGEMENT</u>: If the copyright in the Work is infringed, and if the parties proceed jointly, the expenses and recoveries, if any, shall be shared equally, and if they do not proceed jointly, either party shall have the right to prosecute such action, and such party shall bear the expenses thereof, and any recoveries shall belong to such party [or, any recoveries after the deduction of such expenses shall be divided between them.]

28. <u>ARBITRATION</u>: Any controversy arising under this Agreement shall be submitted to arbitration before the American Arbitration Association in

accordance with its rules, and judgment confirming the arbitrator's award may be entered in any court of competent jurisdiction.

29. LIFE INSURANCE: Publisher shall have the right to obtain life insurance coverage on Author's life of up to FIVE HUNDRED THOUSAND ($500,000.00) DOLLARS, and Author shall cooperate with Publisher to the extent necessary to enable Publisher to obtain such coverage, including submission to a physical examination if required by Publisher's insurance carrier.

30. PUBLISHER'S EDITOR: It is understood and agreed that Author has entered into this agreement in reliance upon the representation that [NAME OF EDITOR] shall work with Author as the editor of this Work. If at any time [EDITOR] leaves the employ of Publisher or ceases to act as editor of this Work without the consent of Author, then Author may terminate this agreement by giving 90 days notice of his intent to terminate. Within that 90-day period, Author shall repay all advances made under this agreement or arrange for a satisfactory method of repayment. Upon receipt of such sums or upon Publisher indicating in writing that it would accept a proposed method of repayment, all rights granted hereunder shall revert to Author.

31. NEW YORK LAW APPLIES: This Agreement shall be interpreted according to the laws of the STATE OF NEW YORK, applicable to agreements made and to be performed therein. This Agreement constitutes the complete understanding of the parties. No modification or waiver of any provision shall be valid unless in writing and signed by both parties.

IN WITNESS WHEREOF, the parties have duly executed this Agreement the day and year first written above.

AUTHOR: PUBLISHERS:

_____   _____

(Name of author)   (Publishing Company)

LIVE THEATRICAL AGREEMENTS

Form 43

Production Contract for Plays (Non-APC)

This contract made and entered into as of the 1st day of March, 1995, between Harold Jones, whose address is 1531 Broadway, New York, NY 10036, hereinafter referred to as Producer, and Samuel Yardley, whose address is 1234 La Cienega Boulevard, Los Angeles, CA 90967, hereinafter sometimes referred to as Bookwriter. The Bookwriter and the Composer, who has not yet been engaged, and the lyricist, who has not yet been engaged, are hereinafter jointly referred to as Author of the proposed Play based on the motion picture "The Blues Crooner."

WITNESSETH:

WHEREAS, Author has been or will be writing the book of a musical play, now entitled "The Blues Crooner," hereinafter referred to as the "Play;" and

WHEREAS, Producer is in the business of producing plays and desires to acquire the sole and exclusive rights to produce the Play in the United States, its territories and possessions, including Puerto Rico and Canada (the "Territory") and to acquire Author's services in connection therewith;

Now, THEREFORE, in consideration of the mutual covenants herein contained and other good and valuable consideration, the parties hereto agree as follows:

1.(a) <u>Grant of Rights to Produce a Play</u>: Subject to the terms of this Contract, Author hereby grants to Producer the sole and exclusive rights to present the Play for one or more First Class Performances. For the purposes of this Contract, the term "First Class Performances" shall mean live stage productions of the Play on the speaking stage, within the Territory, under Producer's own management, in a regular evening bill in a first class theatre in a first class manner, with a first class cast and a first class director.

(b) <u>Author's Services</u>: Author hereby agrees to perform such services as may be reasonably necessary in making revisions to the Play; to assist in the selection of the cast and consult with, assist and advise the Producer, director, scenic, lighting and costume designers and the choreographer and/or dance director, conductor and sound designer, if any, regarding any problem arising out of the production of the Play; to attend rehearsals of the Play as well as out-of-town performances prior to the Official Press Opening of the Play in New York City, provided, however, that Author may be excused from such attendance on showing reasonable cause.

(c) <u>Rights Terminate if Play Not Produced</u>: Although nothing herein shall be deemed to obligate Producer to produce the Play, nevertheless, unless Producer presents the first paid public First Class Performance of the Play within the applicable Option Period described herein for which the prescribed payment has been made, Producer's rights to produce the Play and to the services of Author shall then automatically and without notice terminate.

(d) <u>Continuous Production Rights:</u> If the first paid public First Class Performance of the Play hereunder is presented within one of the Option Periods (including the extensions, if any, set forth herein), the rights granted to present the Play shall continue subject to the reopening provisions herein.

(e) <u>Reservation of Rights:</u> Author shall retain sole and complete title in and to the Play and to all rights and uses of every kind except as otherwise specifically provided herein. Author reserves all rights and uses now in existence or which may hereafter come into existence, except as specifically provided herein. Any rights reserved shall not be deemed competitive with any of Producer's rights and may be exercised by Author at any time except as otherwise specifically provided herein. All contracts for the publication of the music and lyrics of the Play shall provide that the copyright be in the names of the Composer and Lyricist.

(f) <u>Author Defined:</u> "Author" shall mean each bookwriter, composer and lyricist whose literary or musical material is used in the Play. The term "Author" shall include any person who is involved in the initial stages of a collaborative process and who is deserving of billing credit as an Author and whose literary or musical contribution will be an integral part of the Play as presented in subsequent productions by other producers. The term "Author" shall not include any owner of underlying rights, except as otherwise provided herein.

2.(a) <u>Option Periods and Option Payments:</u> In consideration of the foregoing grant of rights and Author's agreement to perform services in connection with the production of the Play, Producer agrees to pay Author the following sums ("Option Payments") for the rights to present the Play, on condition that the first paid public First Class Performance of the Play occurs prior to the expiration of the applicable "Option Period" described as follows: (i) "First Option Period"—$ 6,000 for one year from the Date of this Agreement, payable upon the execution of this Contract; (ii) "Second Option Period"—$ 3,000 for a second one-year period payable on or before the last day of the First Option Period; (iii) "Third Option Period"—$ 300 per month for a maximum of 12 consecutive months. Payment for each successive month shall be made before the termination of the preceding option period.

(b) <u>Option Payments Non-Returnable:</u> Each of the foregoing Option Payments made by Producer shall be nonreturnable but shall be deductible, to the extent permitted by the terms herein, from the Advance Payments and Royalties otherwise payable to Author.

(c) <u>Extension of Option Until Delivery of Completed Play:</u> If the Play is not completed at the time of execution of the Agreement, the option period and all other time periods shall be measured from the date of delivery of a completed Play. Producer shall maintain the sole and exclusive rights and option to present the Play while Producer awaits delivery of the Completed Play. A "Completed Play" shall mean the Play consisting of a book of at least 80 single-spaced pages plus a score consisting of music and lyrics for at least 12 songs. Producer may terminate this contract upon written notice to Author if the Completed Play is not delivered within six months after the Effective Date of this Contract. Time is of the essence as to such delivery date.

(d) Extension of Option for Try-Out Performances: If, during one of the Option Periods, Producer presents Second Class Performances or Developmental Productions of the Play, the expiration of the Option Periods and due dates for subsequent Option Payments shall be extended for a period equal to the number of days on which performances of the Play were so presented (up to a maximum of 8 weeks) plus an additional 60 days.

3.(a) Calculation and Due Dates of Advance Payments: Producer shall pay Author the following "Advance Payments," at the stated times, (i) on the first day of rehearsal at which Producer requires the attendance of all cast members of the Principal Company, but in no event later than five business days before the initial First Class Performance of the Play, Producer shall pay Author 2% of the amounts constituting Capitalization (as defined herein) at such date; (ii) thereafter, at such times as additional amounts, if any are contributed towards Capitalization, Producer shall pay Author, within 10 business days after Producer's receipt thereof, a sum equal to 2% of such additional contributions; (iii) the sums otherwise payable by Producer pursuant to the foregoing calculation in this Clause shall be reduced by an amount equal to 2% of such sums. The net amounts paid to Author shall constitute the Advance Payments.

(b) Maximum Advance: In any event, the total Advance Payments payable by Producer pursuant to Clause 3.(a) shall not exceed $60,000.

4.(a) Definitions: The following terms shall have the indicated meanings:

(i) "Out-of-Town Performances"— First Class Performances of the Play outside of New York City before presentation of Preview or Regular Performances in New York City.

(ii) "Preview Performances"— First Class Performances of the Play in New York City before the Official Press Opening in New York City.

(iii) "Regular Performances"— First Class Performances of the Play in New York City commencing with the first performance of the Play following the Official Press Opening of the Play in New York City.

(iv) "Touring Performances"— First Class Performances of the Play outside of New York City, presented by a Company simultaneously with or subsequent to Out-of-Town, Preview or Regular Performances.

(v) "Fixed-Fee Performances"— All performances of the Play (other than Preview and Regular Performances) produced by a grant of rights from Producer, in return for which Producer receives compensation based in whole or in part on a fixed guaranteed fee.

(vi) "Performance Week"— The six - or seven-day period, beginning on either Monday or, if there is no performance on Monday, then on Tuesday and continuing through Sunday, during which one or more performances of the Play are presented.

(vii) "Full Performance Week"— Any Performance Week during which at least eight performances of the Play are presented.

(viii) "New York City"— The theatrical district of the Borough of Manhattan of the city of New York.

(ix) "LORT Productions"— Productions of the Play presented on the main stage of a theatre that is a member of the League of Regional Theatres or any comparable resident theatre.

(x) "Production Costs" shall mean the estimated costs of producing the Principal Company (including any contingency reserves), as described in the offering documents used in connection with the financing of such Company, including costs that may be paid, if permitted by the terms of such documents, by an overcall, but not including weekly operating expenses.

(xi) "Capitalization" shall mean:

(A) the aggregate of the following sums actually received by Producer (after all necessary bank clearances) for the purpose of paying Production Costs:

(I) all amounts contributed as Equity Capital. For the purposes of this Contract, "Equity Capital" shall mean the amounts contributed by investors in order to pay Production Costs and obtain an ownership interest in the venture producing the Principal Company, including all amounts received by Producer pursuant to an overcall but only to the extent such sums exceed 10% of the total Equity Capital contributions received by Producer from all investors immediately prior to the date on which the demand for such overcall is issued and only to the extent such sums are used by Producer to pay Production Costs; and

(II) should Producer find it necessary to obtain loans to pay Production Costs, then the amount of such loan proceeds shall also be included to the extent such proceeds are in excess of 20% of the estimated Production Costs (or if the documents used in connection with the financing of the Principal Company set forth an amount representing minimum estimated Production Costs, then such amount); however, if Producer receives no Equity Capital pursuant to an overcall, then the amount of such loan proceeds shall be included to the extent such proceeds are in excess of 30% of such estimated Production Costs;

(B) but not including the foregoing, to the extent allocated to pay the following items of Production Costs:

(I) all security bonds, deposits and other guarantees to be provided to any union or other collective bargaining organization, theatre or other entity;

(II) all Option Payments to Author;

(III) advertising, promotional and press-related costs in excess of 10% of the minimum estimated Production Costs; and

(IV) all sums herein which are included as Production Costs and paid to a third party who presented the Play in the Territory as a Developmental Production or as other non-First Class Performances.

All sums received by Producer to pay the operating costs of paid public performances of the Play (rather than Production Costs) shall be excluded in determining the amount of Capitalization, regardless of the source of any such sums or the manner in which such sums may be contributed.

(xii) "Gross Weekly Box Office Receipts" shall be computed upon all sums received by Producer from all ticket sales to the Play allocable to performances given in such week, less the following deductions:

(A) federal or other admission taxes;

(B) customary commissions and fees, as may be prevailing from time to time, paid to or retained by third parties in connection with theatre parties, benefits, American Express or other similar credit card plans, telephone sales, automated ticket distribution or remote box offices, e.g., Ticketron and Ticket World (but not ticket brokers), and commissions or fees for group sales;

(C) those sums equivalent to the former 5% New York City Amusement Tax, the proceeds of which are now paid to the pension and/or welfare funds of various theatrical unions;

(D) subscription fees;

(E) receipts from Actors' Fund Benefit performances, provided the customary payments are made by the Actors' Fund to The Dramatists Guild Fund, Inc.;

(F) receipts from two performances of the Play in each calendar year to the extent such receipts are contributed for theatre-related eleemosynary purposes; and

(G) if applicable, library discounts, value added taxes and entertainment taxes, if any.

Producer may also deduct from Gross Weekly Box Office Receipts allocable to any Performance Week any sums included as Gross Weekly Box Office Receipts in a prior Performance Week which were included in Author's Royalty calculation but which sums subsequently were refunded or uncollectible due to dishonored checks, invalidated credit card receipts or for any other reason.

If the Play is presented simultaneously by more than one Company, Gross Weekly Box Office Receipts received by each such Company shall be computed and paid separately.

(xiii) The terms "Recouped" or "Recoupment" shall mean the recovery of all costs incurred in presenting such Company after payment or accrual of all operating expenses for such Company. Each Company will be separately treated for this computation.

The profits or losses attributable to one Company shall not affect the calculation of Recoupment for any other Company. Recoupment shall be determined by the accountant engaged by Producer, and the determination made by such accountant shall be final and binding among the parties. Upon such determination by the accountant, Producer shall send Author written notice that Recoupment has occurred.

The costs incurred in presenting a Play shall include the following "Production Expenses:" fees of designers, directors, general and company managers; cost of sets, curtains, drapes and costumes; cost or payments on account of properties, furnishings, lighting and electrical equipment; premiums for bonds and insurance; unrecouped option and advance payments to persons other than the Author; rehearsal charges; transportation charges; reasonable legal and accounting expenses; advance advertising; publicity and press expenses; and other expenses and losses actually incurred in connection with the production and presentation of the Play up to and including the Official Press Opening of such Company.

In calculating Recoupment, the amounts of bonds, deposits or other returnable items shall not be included as costs to be recovered. Recoupment of the amounts incurred for any Company shall be deemed final so that once Recoupment has been attained subsequent expenses incurred by such Company will not change the fact that the Company has Recouped.

5.(a) Royalties: Except for fixed-fee performances, Bookwriter, Composer and Lyricist will jointly be entitled to nine points in a royalty pool, which will be shared equally by the bookwriter, composer, lyricist, that is, three points for each. The royalty pool will be composed of 32 ½% of the net receipts until recoupment of total production costs, at which time it will be increased to 35% of such net receipts. Net receipts shall mean all gross weekly box office receipts less all customary and reasonable expenses except those variable expenses payable to royalty participants as part of this formula. The total points in the royalty pool will not exceed twenty-two. Each royalty participant will receive a guaranteed payment of $600 per point.

(b) <u>Fixed-Fee Performance Royalties:</u> For the purposes of this Clause, the term "Producer" shall mean Producer's grantee in those cases where Fixed-Fee Performances are produced by such grantee. Author's Royalty for Fixed-Fee Performances of the Play shall be calculated as 6% of any fixed fee paid to Producer by such local promoter or sponsor for such Performances plus 6% of Producer's share of box office receipts and any profits of such Performances (including box office receipts and profits paid as a salary, fee, royalty or other type of compensation for Producer's services) paid to Producer by such local promoter or sponsor.

6.(a) <u>Deductions from Advances:</u> Option Payments made for all but the First Option Period shall be deducted from the Advance Payments otherwise payable to Author.

(b) <u>Deductions from Royalties:</u> After recoupment, 50% of the Royalties earned from all companies will be used to pay all option and advance payments to Author, but, in any case, Author will not be paid less than $3,000 for any full performance week.

7. <u>Royalty Due Dates And Statements:</u> (a) The Producer agrees to hold the Author's share of any receipts or weekly profits in trust for the benefit of the Author, and such funds will be deemed trust funds whether the money is physically segregated or not. Author may, at his option, pursue his remedies at law or in equity in lieu of the arbitration procedure in the event of the breach of the trust created by this contract. Producer shall send to the Agent of each party comprising the Author within seven (7) days after the end of each performance week the monies due the Author for Royalties for such week together with the daily box office statements signed by the treasurer of the theatre in which the performances are given, and also signed by the Producer or his duly authorized representative. For Plays presented more than 500 miles from New York City, the statements and payments due shall be sent within fourteen (14) days after the end of each performance week and in Canada within twenty-one (21) days after the end of each week unless the payments are delayed or blocked by the action of government authorities where the Play is being presented.

(b) All checks will be sent to the Author or his Agent if so requested by the Author, and the checks will be drawn to the Author or to the Agent. Royalties accruing from each Company shall be computed and paid separately if the Play is being presented simultaneously by more than one Company.

8.(a) <u>General Terms of Contract:</u> Producer, recognizing that the Play is the artistic creation of Author and that as such Author is entitled to protect the type and nature of the production of Author's creation, hereby agrees:

(i) Under his own management to rehearse, present and continue to present the Play, with a cast, director, scenic, lighting, costume and, where appropriate, sound designer, conductor, choreographer and/or dance director mutually agreeable to Producer and to Author, and to announce the name of Author as sole Author of the book, music and lyrics of the Play upon all programs and in all advertising matter in accordance with the terms herein. Any change in the cast or any replacement of a director, conductor, choreographer and/or dance director, scenic, lighting, costume and, where appropriate, sound designer, shall likewise be subject to the approval of Author, provided, however, that Author must exercise his right of approval or disapproval within 24 hours after receiving notice from Producer of any proposed change or replacement.

(ii) To rehearse, produce, present and continue to present the Play, including road companies thereof, with no additions, omissions or alterations in the Play or title without the consent of both Producer and the author of the affected portion of the Play (i.e., Bookwriter, Composer or Lyricist), with any change in the title requiring approval of a majority of Bookwriter, Composer and Lyricist. Any change of any kind whatsoever in the manuscript, title, stage business or performance of the Play which is acceptable to Author shall be the property of the Bookwriter, Composer or Lyricist, as the case may be. Neither Bookwriter, Composer nor Lyricist shall be obligated to make payment to any person suggesting or making any such changes unless he has entered into a bona fide written agreement to do so. Similarly, Producer shall not be required to make payment to any person solicited by Bookwriter, Composer or Lyricist to suggest or make changes unless Producer has entered into a bona fide written agreement to do so.

(b) <u>Right to Attend Rehearsals:</u> Author shall have the right to attend all rehearsals and performances of the Play prior to the Official Press Opening in New York City. Author shall use all best efforts to be available one month ahead of scheduled rehearsal dates to perform the services required by the terms of this Contract.

(c) <u>Author's Approval Rights:</u> Where the approval or consent of Author is required, the Bookwriter, Composer and Lyricist of the Play shall vote as three separate units (regardless of the number of persons constituting each such unit), with each unit having one vote and with a majority of such votes controlling.

If, after the Play has been presented for at least three weeks in New York City, Producer, because of some emergency, requests the approval of Author to make changes or replacements and Producer is unable to obtain any response from Bookwriter, Composer or Lyricist, within 72 hours after requesting same, then the right to vote of such person failing to timely respond shall not be counted and the votes of the others shall control.

(d) Expenses: Producer shall reimburse Author for reasonable hotel and travel expenses as Author may incur in making trips to attend rehearsals and up to 12 weeks of Out-of-Town Performances and Preview Performances and the Official Press Opening in New York City, and at any other time when the presence of Author is required by Producer. Author's hotel and travel accommodations shall be of a class equal to the greater of the class charged to the Company by Producer or Director.

(e) Designs: Pursuant to the rules and regulations of the United Scenic Artists Local 829, Author undertakes and agrees that Author will not sell, lease, license or authorize the use of any of the original designs of scenery, lighting or costumes created by the designers, without the written consent of the owner of such designs.

(f) Artwork: To the extent that the Producer owns the artwork or logo for the production, the Producer will grant permission to the Author to use such artwork and logo in connection with exploitation of the Play, but not for the purpose of creating commercial use products. The use by the Author will be subject to all payments which must be made to other parties for such use, and Author will indemnify the Producer for any liability which may arise due to such use.

(g) Production Script: Prior to the last performance of the Play under this Contract or prior to one month after the Official Press Opening in New York City, whichever is earlier, Producer shall deliver to Author or Author's representative, as Author's property, a neat and legible script of the Play, as currently presented.

(h) Promotion of Play: Author hereby grants to Producer and Producer's licensees and permitted assigns, the right to use the names of Bookwriter, Composer and Lyricist and each of their biographies, photographs, likenesses or recorded voice, and the title of and excerpts from the Play for advertising, press and promotional purposes by any means or medium, subject to approval of Author. If the Bookwriter, Composer or Lyricist does not advise Producer within 72 hours of receipt of the materials of desired changes, the materials are approved as submitted. Producer shall include Author's biography in all programs used by Producer in which any other biography appears.

(i) Author's Billing Credit: Author shall receive billing credit whenever Producer and/or Director is accorded billing credit. However, with respect to ABC listings and "teaser" advertisements, radio and television advertisements and marquees, billing credit may be accorded to any one or more of Producer, Author or Director without according billing credit to the other(s), if such person(s) has achieved a level of prominence greater than those not receiving billing credit and such that the use of the name(s) of the person(s) excluded would not enhance the commercial value of the Play.

Author's billing shall be on one or more separate lines beneath the title of the Play, in a type size no less than 40% of the type size used for the title of the Play (other than logo titles), provided, however, if the title of the Play appears more than once in any one advertisement, the placement and size of Author's billing shall be in relation to the title where used in closest proximity to the billing accorded to others involved in the Play. In no event shall Author's billing be smaller than the type size used for the billing accorded to Director and/or Producer. Wherever credits are accorded in connection with the Play in a so-called "billing box" pursuant to which the Author is entitled to credit, the size of both the Author's and Producer's credit shall be determined by the size of the title of the Play in such "billing box" and will appear only in the billing box.

(j) Radio and TV Publicity: Producer shall have the right to authorize one or more radio and/or television excerpts of or based on the Play, not exceeding 15 minutes each, for the purpose of exploiting and publicizing the theatre industry, performances of the Play, any person performing in the Play and for use on awards programs, without any additional approval by or payment to Author, provided Producer receives no compensation therefrom other than reimbursement of out-of-pocket expenses; however, Author shall have approval of any change in the book, music or lyrics made in an excerpt produced under the control of Producer.

(k) Producer's Billing Credit: If Producer has presented the Play for its Official Press Opening, Author will use best efforts to require that Producer receive conspicuously placed billing credit if all or any portion of the Play is published, the credit shall appear on a page preceding the first page of the text of the Play; if a motion picture or television production is produced based on the Play, the credit shall appear on the screen separately with no other credit and, in the case of any Revival, Stock, Amateur or Ancillary Performances, as those terms are defined herein, the credit shall appear on the first page of credits in all programs used therefore.

Such credit shall contain the name(s) of Producer and co-producers, if any, and shall state that the Play was originally produced by them. The order, title and relative size and spacing of the names of Producer (and co-producers, if any) shall be identical to the billing contained in the program for the Play at the time of the Official Press Opening.

No casual or inadvertent failure to comply with the provisions of this Clause shall be deemed a breach of this Contract unless such failure can, but shall not, be rectified as soon as practicable.

(l) House Seats: Producer shall hold two (2) pairs of adjoining house seats for Author or his designee, for all performances of the Play in New York City, Los Angeles and London in the first ten (10) rows in the center section of the orchestra. Additionally, Author shall have the right to purchase four (4) additional pairs of seats in good orchestra locations for Opening Night. Such house seats shall be held forty-eight (48) hours prior to the scheduled performance and shall be paid for at the regularly established box office prices. Author acknowledges and agrees that the theatre tickets made available hereunder cannot, except in accordance with the regulations promulgated by the office of the Attorney General of the state of New York, be resold at a premium or otherwise, and that complete and accurate records will be maintained by him, which may be inspected at reasonable times by a duly designated representative of Producer and/or the Attorney General of the state of New York, with respect to the disposition of all tickets made available hereunder.

(m) <u>Cast Albums</u>: Producer and Author will jointly control the rights to make Cast Albums. The term "Cast Albums" shall mean all audio recordings of the Play (or any portion thereof) performed by the cast of any production that is presented by or under lease or license from Producer. Author and Producer shall calculate and share, in perpetuity, the proceeds (other than amounts advanced by record companies for the creation of the album or for investment in the Play) received from the worldwide exploitation of such Cast Albums and Author shall receive 60% and Producer 40% of such proceeds not included in calculating recoupment.

(n) <u>Musical Scores</u>: Producer shall in the first instance furnish all necessary orchestral scores, conductor's scores, orchestra parts and vocal parts ("Scores") at Producer's own expense. Producer shall be the sole and exclusive owner of the physical Scores (as distinguished from the copyrights therein) and Producer may, subject to Author's copyrights in such Scores, sell, license, assign, rent or otherwise dispose of such Scores and retain any sums received therefrom, which sums shall not be counted in the calculation of Recoupment.

Notwithstanding the foregoing, if Author elects to own the Scores and gives Producer written notice thereof, the following provisions shall apply:

(i) The Scores shall belong jointly to the Lyricist and Composer of the Play immediately upon delivery thereof to Producer and may be used by the Lyricist and Composer at any time after the close of the First Class Performances in the Territory;

(ii) The Composer and Lyricist alone shall have the right to contract for the publication of the music and lyrics of the Play or any part thereof, without prejudice to the right of Producer to arrange for separate payment to Producer by the music publisher. The Composer and Lyricist alone may permit the reproduction of the music and lyrics or any part thereof by discs or any other means or devices;

(iii) Producer may deduct from the Royalties otherwise payable to each of the Composer and Lyricist $600 in the aggregate in each Performance

Week in which such deduction would not reduce the Royalties payable to Author to less than $4,000 for Out-of-Town and Preview Performances or less than $3,000 for all other performances hereunder, until a sum equal to 50% of the Producer's actual expenditure for the Scores shall have been recovered by Producer;

(iv) The Composer and Lyricist may at their option pay outright to the Producer at any time a sum equal to 50% of Producer's expenditures for such Scores or such remaining balance thereof as may then be unpaid;

(v) For purposes of this Contract, "Additional Collaborator" may mean any replacement author and/or any person who assists the original authors or who assists a replacement author as defined herein in the creation of literary or musical material that is used in the Play, but shall not include any Director and/or Choreographer.

(o) <u>Deleted Music and Lyrics</u>: All rights in and to any music and lyrics which shall be deleted from the Play prior to the Official Press Opening in New York City shall revert to the Composer and Lyricist, respectively, for their use, free from any claim by the Producer provided, however, that the Composer and Lyricist shall not have any right to use or authorize the use of any such lyrics which (i) refer to any character in the Play by the same name as the character in the Play if the name is sufficiently distinctive to identify with the Play or (ii) depict or portray an important situation which is contained in the Play or (iii) contain any distinctive dialogue or distinctive phrases from the Play or (iv) have as their title the name of any character in, or the title of the Play if such name is sufficiently distinctive to identify with the Play. If any such compositions are included in any agreement for an Audio-Visual Production of the Play, the Composer and Lyricist shall not be entitled to any larger additional compensation by reason thereof and the Producer's share of the income therefrom shall not be diminished.

9.(a) <u>Second Class Performance Rights</u>: Author hereby grants Producer the sole and exclusive right to produce one or more Second Class Performances of the Play in the Territory during the time that Producer continues to have rights to present the Play. The term "Second Class Performances" shall mean all performances of the Play other than Stock, Amateur and Ancillary Performances (as those terms are defined herein), Off-Broadway Performances (as defined herein), and First Class Performances and Developmental (i.e., "workshop") Productions. Author's Royalties for Second Class Performances shall be calculated and paid in the manner set forth in this contract.

(b) <u>Off-Broadway Rights</u>: If the Producer has vested in the territory, then the Producer will be entitled to the sole and exclusive rights to produce one or more Off-Broadway performances of the Play during the period that he continues to have rights to produce the Play. This right is conditioned on the Producer not simultaneously presenting any other performances of the Play in New York City. The Royalties payable for such Off-Broadway performances shall be calculated and paid in the manner set forth in this agreement.

(c) <u>British Isles, Australia and New Zealand Rights:</u> If Producer has vested in the territory, Author grants to Producer the sole and exclusive rights to produce one or more productions of the Play for a consecutive run, (including tryout performances) in a first class manner, in a first class theatre, on the speaking stage in one or more of the following "Additional Territories:" (i) The United Kingdom of Great Britain (i.e., England, Northern Ireland, Scotland and Wales) and in Ireland (collectively the "British Isles"); (ii) Australia and (iii) New Zealand.

In order to produce the Play pursuant to a lease or license to a third party in Australia or New Zealand, Producer shall give Author written notice of the terms of any third party offer for the production of the Play in such Additional Territory. Producer may accept the offer unless Author shall, within six business days after receipt of Producer's notice, give Producer written notice that the offer is unacceptable, stating Author's reasons therefor, together with a definite offer from a third party, on terms at least as favorable to Producer as those contained in the offer which Producer is willing to accept. If within the prescribed period of time Author submits such an offer, Producer may accept such offer. If within the prescribed period of time Author fails to submit such an offer, then Producer may accept the original offer.

(d) <u>Payments for Rights in Additional Territories:</u>

(i) Producer's rights to present the Play in such Additional Territory shall automatically terminate unless Producer presents the first paid public performance of the Play in an Additional Territory within six months after the close of First Class Performances in New York City, unless such rights are extended as provided herein;

(ii) Producer shall be entitled to three consecutive six-month extensions of such rights upon payment of $750 for the first extension, $1,500 for the second extension and $2,000 for the third extension, which payment must be made prior to the expiration of the rights period then in effect, provided, however, that for the third extension, Producer must give Author, simultaneously with the payment of $2,000, written notice of the intended date of the first paid public performance together with copies of either a commitment for the licensing of the Additional Territory equivalent of a first class theatre, with occupancy to occur before the end of the third extension period or contracts for the engagement of the principal members of the cast or the director, pursuant to which such person(s) agrees to render services before the end of the third extension period.

(e) <u>Royalty Payments for Additional Territories:</u> Author's Royalties for performances of the Play in the British Isles, shall be calculated and paid in accordance with the Royalty Pool herein set forth. Author's Royalties for performances in Australia and New Zealand shall be 6% of the Gross Weekly Box Office Receipts.

Sums payable to Author in connection with performances of the Play in any Additional Territory shall be paid after deduction of all withholding and other taxes due thereon pursuant to the laws of the applicable Additional Territory, all conversion and remittance costs applicable to such payments and all payments required to be made to any author's society or similar organizations. Producer shall not be liable for losses incurred due to fluctuations in the exchange rate.

(f) Rights to Assign to Additional Territory Producer: Subject to Author's written consent and subject to the terms of this Agreement, Producer may produce the Play alone or in association with or under lease or license to an Additional Territory producer or manager. In such case, Producer's obligations to make the payments herein provided shall remain unimpaired.

(g) Author's Attendance in Additional Territories: Author shall have the right to be present for up to three weeks in order to attend rehearsals, tryouts and the opening of the first production of the Play in any Additional Territory. Producer shall reimburse Author for hotel and travel expenses during such period and at any other time when the presence of Author is required by Producer.

10.(a) Reopenings in Territories: Provided Producer has Vested in the Territory, Producer may, within four months after the last performance of the Play in the Territory, notify Author in writing of Producer's intention to reopen the Play in the Territory and may reopen the Play within 12 months following such last performance; provided, however, that if the Play is not reopened within four months from such last performance, Producer must, in order to retain his rights to reopen the Play, pay Author the following nonreturnable advances against the Royalties payable: $400 per month for up to four months, commencing with the fourth month following the last performance, and $1,000 per month for up to an additional four months.

If Producer closes the Play in the Territory prior to having Vested, Producer may reopen the Play provided he gives the Author written notice, within 30 days after such closing, of Producer's intention to reopen the Play, pays Author $600 per month (as nonreturnable advances against the Royalties payable), commencing one month following the closing until the Play has reopened, and commences rehearsals for such production no later than four months after the closing. All the provisions of this Clause shall apply to each reopening in the Territory, whether First Class, Second Class or Off-Broadway.

(b) Reopenings in Additional Territories: All of the terms and conditions above set forth with respect to reopenings in the Territory shall be applicable in each instance to reopenings in the additional Territories. The times set forth and the amounts therein set forth shall be identical in the case of reopenings in the respective additional territories.

(c) <u>Closing:</u> Producer shall give written notice to the Author immediately upon the determination to close a run of the Play anywhere in the world.

11.(a) <u>Subsidiary Rights:</u> "Subsidiary Rights" shall mean the following rights in the Play:

(i) "Media Productions"—motion picture, television, video cassette and video disc productions; soundtrack albums, tapes and discs, radio for all of the foregoing; and all other kinds of visual and audio-visual productions in connection with the Play, whether now existing or developed in the future;

(ii) "Commercial Use Products"—toys; games; figures; dolls; novelties or any other physical property representing a character in the Play or using the name, character or the title of the Play or otherwise connected with the Play or its title and souvenir books and programs;

(iii) "Stock Performances"—all performances of the Play presented in the English language pursuant to one of the Actors' Equity Association agreements as that term is commonly used in the business;

(iv) "Amateur Performances"—performances of the Play in the English language using only non-union actors;

(v) "Ancillary Performances"—all performances of the Play presented in the English language as condensed and tabloid versions, so-called concert tour versions and opera versions based on the Play as well as foreign language performances of all kinds in the Territory or each Additional Territory, as the case may be;

(vi) "Revival Performances"—

(A) In the city of New York—A First Class, Second Class and Off-Broadway Performance of the Play in the city of New York and all performances at Lincoln Center (regardless of how classified), presented after the expiration of Producer's rights to present the Play in the Territory; and

(B) Outside the city of New York—all First and Second Class Performances of the Play in the Territory, presented after the expiration of Producer's rights to present the Play in the Territory presented outside the city of New York, provided that, with respect to each contract entered into for such production, the Play is presented in at least three cities throughout the Territory. Notwithstanding the foregoing, if any of such cities is the city of New York, the three-city minimum shall automatically be waived;

(C) In the Additional Territories—all performances of the Play in any of the Additional Territories (which are the Additional Territory equivalents of First or Second Class Performances in the Territory) presented after the expiration of Producer's rights to present the Play in such Additional Territory;

(D) Remakes, Prequels, Sequels and Spin-Offs—Revival Performances shall also include performances of all "remakes," "prequels" (i.e., stories which occur at an earlier point in time than the story in the Play), "sequels" and "spin-offs" of the Play produced in the manner described above.

(b) <u>Definition of Vested:</u> "Vested" shall mean presentation of the Play in the Territory, for either (i) 10 paid public First Class Preview Performances plus the Official Press Opening of the Play in New York City, or (ii) 5 paid public First Class Preview Performances plus the Official Press Opening in New York City plus 5 Regular Performances, or (iii) for 64 consecutive paid public Out-of-Town Performances, whether or not the Play has its Official Press Opening in New York City, provided that breaks may be made in performances outside of New York City because of the necessities of travel so long as the 64 performances shall have been given within 80 days of the first performance, or (iv) for 64 consecutive Out-of-Town Performances in arenas or auditoriums if, because of the nature of the Play or the size or complexity of its contemplated production, the performance of the Play in a traditional first class theatre would not be feasible or desirable.

Rights shall have vested for a production in the British Isles if the Play is first produced in London for 21 consecutive performances or if first produced outside of London, for 64 performances within 80 days after the first performance, whether presented partly inside or outside of London.

(c) <u>Subsidiary Rights Participation:</u> Although Producer is acquiring rights in the Play and Author's services solely in connection with the production of the Play, Author recognizes that by a successful production Producer makes a contribution to the value of other rights in the Play. Therefore, although the relationship between the parties is limited to play production as herein provided, and Author alone owns and controls the Play with respect to all other uses, nevertheless, if Producer has Vested in the Territory and Producer is not in breach of any provision of this Contract, Author hereby agrees that:

(i) <u>No Outright Sale:</u> Author will not authorize or permit any outright sale of the right to use said Play for any of the Subsidiary Rights purposes during the period therein specified without Producer's prior consent. In no event shall there be any outright sale of any such rights prior to the first paid public First Class Performance of the Play;

(ii) <u>Best Efforts:</u> Author will use best efforts to exploit the Play for Subsidiary Rights purposes.

(iii) <u>"Producer's Alternatives":</u>

(A) Producer may choose Alternative I or II of the 3 Producer's Alternatives hereinafter set forth in this Clause. The choice of Alternative III must be specified by Author and Producer upon the signing of this Contract. The choice of Alternative I or II must be made by giving Author written notice of such choice on or before 12 o'clock midnight on the first day of rehearsal at which Producer requires all cast members of the Principal Company. If Producer fails to give such timely notice, Author may choose which Producer's Alternative will apply upon giving Producer written notice of such choice on or before 12 o'clock midnight on the next business day following said rehearsal date. If both Producer and Author fail to choose a Producer's Alternative in a timely manner, Producer's Alternative III will apply.

(B) Participation in Territory: With respect to the exploitation of Subsidiary Rights in the Territory, Author shall promptly pay to Producer, based on the applicable Producer's Alternative, the designated percentage of Author's compensation directly or indirectly earned (after deduction of agents' commissions, if any), from the disposition of the specified Subsidiary Rights anywhere in the Territory, pursuant to each contract entered into on or after the effective date of this Contract but prior to the expiration of the periods described in the applicable Producer's Alternative (regardless of when such compensation is paid); provided, however, that with respect to Media Productions, Producer's participation shall be in

Author's compensation earned from exploitations anywhere in the world:

Under Producer's Alternative	If any of the following Subsidiary Rights are disposed of	Author will pay Producer, based on the following percentages of Author's compensation directly or indirectly earned (after deduction of agents' commissions, if any) from such dispositions pursuant to each contract entered into on or after the Effective Date of this Contract but prior to the expiration of the specified periods of time after the last performance of the Play hereunder (regardless when such compensation is paid):
I	Media Productions	50% perpetuity
	Stock and Ancillary	50% for the first 5 years then
	Performances	25% for the next 5 years
	Amateur Performances	25% for 5 years
	Revival Performances	20% for 40 years
	Commercial Use	
	Products	See Clause 11.(e)
II	Media Productions	50% in perpetuity
	Stock and Ancillary	
	Performances	30% for 36 years
	Amateur Performances	0%
	Revival Performances	20% for 40 years
	Commercial Use	
	Products	See Clause 11.(e)
III	Media Productions	30% in perpetuity
	Stock, Amateur and	30% for the first 20 years then
	Ancillary Performances	25% for the next 10 years and 20% for the next 10 years (total of 40 years)
	Revival Performances	20% for 40 years
	Commercial Use	
	Products	See Clause 11.(e)

(iv) <u>Revival Participation</u>: In paying Producer's financial participation in Revival Performances, Author shall secure the payment of one-half of such sum (i.e., 10%) from the producer of the Revival Performances.

(v) <u>Foreign Participation:</u> Author shall have the exclusive right to negotiate and contract for all Performances of the Play and for other Subsidiary Rights purposes described in this Clause outside the Territory and outside the Additional Territories, and Author shall promptly pay Producer 30% of the compensation earned by Author (after deduction of agents' commissions, if any), regardless of when paid, in connection with each such contract (other than contracts for Media Productions in which Producer will have previously acquired a worldwide interest) entered into on or after the effective date of this Contract but prior to 6 years from the date on which Producer vested in the Territory. With respect to contracts for Foreign Local Television Productions, Author shall pay Producer 40% of such compensation earned by Author (after deduction of agents' commissions, if any) for such contracts entered into on or after the effective date of this Contract but prior to 12 years from the date on which Producer vested in the Territory.

(vi) <u>Participation in Audio-Visual Sequels:</u> If the producer of the Audio-Visual Production makes one or more Audio-Visual Production remakes, prequels, sequels or spin-offs upon the payment of additional compensation, then, if and when such additional compensation is paid, Producer's share of such compensation shall be one-half of the Media Productions percentage set forth in the applicable Producer's Alternative.

(d) <u>Author's Share of Subsidiary Rights:</u> No one not an Author may participate in the Author's share of Subsidiary Rights income for each collaborator, adaptor, and owner of underlying rights whose material is used in the Play and in the Author's share of subsidiary rights income for Additional Collaborators.

(e) <u>Commercial Use Products:</u> Producer shall have the sole and exclusive rights for the Territory and for each Additional Territory in which Producer presents or licenses the rights to present the Play to create, manufacture and sell (or have created, manufactured and sold) Commercial Use Products, during the time that Producer retains any rights to present the Play except that if a contract exists with a third party for the creation, manufacture or sale of Commercial Use Products, then such contract will continue in full force until the end of its term, but in no event for more than 6 years from the date of such contract, or the last extension thereof. In connection with each contract entered into for the exploitation of Commercial Use Products, Producer shall pay Author the following amounts, regardless of when paid: (i) for sales of such products on the premises of Theatres in which Producer presents the Play, a sum equal to 10% of the gross retail sales (after deduction of taxes) not to exceed 50% of the Producer's license fee; (ii) with respect to sales of such products in other locations, a sum equal to 40% of Producer's net receipts from such sales (i.e., the gross amounts paid to Producer less all customary third-party costs actually incurred in the creation, manufacture and sale of such Commercial Use Products).

After Producer's rights to exploit Commercial Use Products expire, Author may exploit or enter into contracts for the exploitation of Commercial Use Products in any location in which Producer's rights have expired, subject to any contracts which may continue in effect as herein described. If Producer has vested in such location, Author will pay Producer the following amounts (after deduction of agents' commissions, if any) regardless of when paid, in connection with each such contract entered into before the expiration of 42 years after the last performance of the Play in the Territory or such Additional Territory, as the case may be: (i) for sales of such products on the premises of theatres in which Author's Play is presented, a sum equal to 15% of the gross retail sales (after deduction of taxes) not to exceed 50% of the Author's license fee; (ii) for sales of such products in other locations, a sum equal to 40% of Author's net receipts from such sales (i.e., the gross amounts paid to Author less all customary third-party costs actually incurred in the creation, manufacture and sale of such Commercial Use Products).

If Producer has vested in the Territory, Producer shall also have such rights and financial interest worldwide where the rights to exploit Commercial Use Products are disposed of together with dispositions by Author of rights to exploit any or all Media Productions.

The sums paid to or retained by Producer in connection with the exploitation of Commercial Use Products, shall not be included in the calculation of Recoupment.

(f) Consultation with Producer on Subsidiary Rights: If Producer shall be entitled to share in Author's Subsidiary Rights income, Author will not grant any Subsidiary Rights during the periods in which Producer is entitled to so share, without giving Producer the reasonable opportunity to consult with Author in connection with the exploitation of all such rights.

(g) Limitations on Dispositions by Author: Author represents that Author has not authorized or permitted, and shall not authorize or permit, unless Producer first consents in writing, the exploitation (or publicity regarding future exploitations) of any of the rights hereinbelow described, prior to the dates specified below:

Rights	Specified Date
(i) Worldwide Media Productions (other than radio) and Foreign Local Television Productions	the Effective Date of this Contrant
(ii) Separately with respect to the Territory and each Additional Territory: First and Second Class; Stock; Amateur; Ancillary; Off-Broadway and Revival Performances (and their equivalents outside the Territory; and radio;	the date on which all of Producer's rights to produce the Play have ended in the Territory, or the date on which Producer has in writing stated that he will not reopen the Play.
(iii) Commercial Use Products, separately with respect to the Territory and each Additional Territory:	the date on which all of Producer's rights to produce the play have ended in the Territory, subject to any contracts which may continue in effect as above set forth.
(iv) Worldwide music publishing and mechanical reproduction rights including, without limitation, cast album rights (note that songs may be released for radio use at any time).	the date of the Official Press Opening of the Play in New York City.

If Author disposes of any rights in the Territory before the date of this Contract and if Producer vests in the Territory, Producer will receive a sum equal to one-half (½) the amount Producer would have been entitled to receive had Producer vested in the Territory prior to the disposition of such rights. Except to the extent that such sums have been previously paid by Author, such sums shall be paid to Producer from Author's share of the first monies received by Author after the effective date of this Contract from all Subsidiary Rights uses.

12. WARRANTIES AND REPRESENTATIONS: Author warrants, represents and covenants with respect to his contribution that the Play is not in the public domain, that he is the sole and exclusive Author, owner and the copyright proprietor of the Play and of all rights of every kind or nature therein, and that Author has the right and authority to enter into this Contract and to grant the rights granted herein. The use of the Play will not infringe the copyright of any other person or violate any other rights.

13.(a) Conduct of Defense: If a third party claims an infringement or interference with rights because of the production of the Play, then Producer and Author shall jointly conduct the defense of any such action, unless either of them chooses to engage separate counsel. In no event shall Author be responsible for any material in the Play supplied by Producer. If any suit is brought against

Author or Producer alone, such person shall promptly inform the other of such suit.

(b) <u>Expenses of Defense:</u> If Producer and Author conduct a joint defense of such third-party action, they will equally share the expenses thereof; however, if Producer or Author engage separate counsel, they shall each bear their own expenses. If Author writes the Play at the request of Producer from material supplied by Producer and an action is brought on the grounds of plagiarism, then Producer shall defend the action at Producer's own expense and pay all damages that may be found as a result of the plagiarism and pay any judgment rendered against Author on account thereof. If the act or omission upon which any claim is based is caused by either Author or Producer alone, then no part of the expenses shall be paid by the party not at fault, who shall be entitled to all legal remedies.

14.(a) <u>Failure to Produce Play/Improper Assignment:</u> All rights granted to Producer under this Contract shall terminate automatically and without notice if Producer fails to produce the Play within the time and in the manner provided herein or fails to vest prior to the expiration of Producer's production rights hereunder, or fails to make any Option or Advance Payment when it becomes due or if Producer assigns the rights except as herein permitted.

(b) <u>Termination:</u> If the rights of Producer to present the Play shall cease and terminate, Producer shall immediately stop dealing with the Play in any manner and shall forthwith return to the Author all literary materials relating to the Play which are in Producer's possession or control, except that Producer may retain one copy of such materials, but not for commercial use or sale. If termination occurs due to Producer's failure to make any Advance Payment to Author, Author shall retain all Option and Advance Payments made to date.

15. <u>ARBITRATION:</u> Any claim, dispute, or controversy arising between Producer and Author under or in connection with or out of this Contract, or the breach thereof, shall be submitted to arbitration. Judgment upon the award rendered may be entered in the highest court of the forum, whether state or federal, having jurisdiction. The arbitrators shall be selected from the panel of the American Arbitration Association and the arbitration shall be held in accordance with the rules of said Association.

16.(a) <u>Assignability of Rights:</u> Except as provided below, neither this Contract nor the rights granted herein to Producer shall be licensed or assigned by Producer without his first having obtained the consent in writing of the Author. Notwithstanding the foregoing, Producer may, without Author's consent, license or assign this Contract or any of the rights contained herein to a Limited Liability Company, a corporation, partnership or other entity of which any person comprising Producer is a controlling party or controlling shareholder or has a controlling interest, provided that any licensee or assignee shall assume all of the obligations of this Contract and that Producer shall remain personally liable for the fulfillment thereof in the same manner as though no such license or assignment had been made.

(b) Inspection of Contracts: Author and Producer shall each have the right to inspect contracts entered into by the other if such contracts would affect the inspecting party's financial interest hereunder.

(c) Notices: All notices given pursuant to this Contract shall be in writing and delivered either in person, by wire communication or by registered or certified mail, return receipt requested, to the party being notified, at the address first above written (or such other address as may be designated by written notice). Unless specified to the contrary herein, notices shall be deemed given on the day received (at any time prior to 5 p.m. on such day) at the address specified for delivery of such notices.

(d) Equal Employment Opportunity: Author and Producer agree, that in connection with the presentation of the Play, they will promote equal employment opportunities consistent with the artistic integrity of the Play.

(e) Counting of Business Days: Whenever this Contract provides for the measurement of time by the passage of "business days," Saturdays, Sundays and legal holidays in the Territory, and if applicable in any Additional Territory, shall not be counted. If such measurement is made in "days," then only such legal holidays shall not be counted.

(f) Changes in Writing: This Contract may not be amended and no amendment will be effective unless the amendment is reduced to writing, signed by the parties hereto. Any attempted oral amendment of this Contract shall be null and void and of no legal effect.

(g) Binding Nature of Contract: This Contract shall be binding upon and inure to the benefit of the respective parties hereto and their respective successors in interest and permitted assigns.

(h) Severability: Should any part, term or provision of this Contract be decided by the courts to be in conflict with any law of the state where made or of the United States, the validity of the remaining parts, terms or provisions shall not be affected thereby.

(i) Applicable Law: This Contract shall be governed by and construed in accordance with the substantive laws of the state of New York without reference to rules regarding the conflict of laws.

(j) Counterparts: This Contract may be executed in several counterparts and all counterparts so executed by all the parties hereto and affixed to this Contract shall constitute a valid and binding agreement, even though all of the parties have not signed the same counterpart.

(k) <u>Headings and Captions:</u> The headings and captions in this Contract are inserted for convenience only and shall not be used to define, limit, extend or describe the scope or intent of any provision herein.

(l) <u>Pronouns:</u> Whenever the context may require, any pronoun used herein shall include the corresponding masculine, feminine or neuter forms.

In witness whereof, the parties hereto have executed this Agreement as of the day and year first above written.

_____   _____
Harold Jones   Samuel Yardley
Producer   Bookwriter

Form 44

Director Agreement for SSDC First Class Performance (Broadway) with Rider

---

This Agreement must be signed in quintuplicate. The Producer must file one copy with SSDC upon execution. The Director, Choreographer, Director/ Choreographer must file one copy upon execution. Each party retains one copy. One copy is for the agent or attorney of employee. Attach Riders to each copy as needed.

The following constitutes our Agreement:

1.   This Agreement is entered into on the 1st day of January, 1995. Pursuant to all the terms and conditions herein set forth The First Production Company, Inc., (Producer) agrees to engage the services of Harold (Director, Choreographer, Director/Choreographer) and he/she agrees to accept such engagement with respect to the production of "Going Crazy" (the Play), rehearsal to begin on or about (date) and the opening shall be on or about (date).

2.   This Agreement is subject to and incorporates all terms and conditions of the Collective Agreement between the Society of State Directors and Choreographers, Inc. (SSDC), and the League of American Theatres and Producers, Inc. (League), effective September 1, 1990. (Society-American League Agreement) or its successor Agreement, and binds the undersigned Producer to its terms for the duration of said Agreement or its successor Agreement.

3. COMPENSATION

FEE: In consideration of full and timely performance by Director, Choreographer, Director/Choreographer hereunder, Producer agrees to compensate Director, Choreographer, Director/Choreographer as follows:

FEE AND PAYMENT SCHEDULE (fee total includes nonreturnable advance against royalties):

Fee	$25,000.00	Payment Schedule:	$12,500.00	upon signing this Agreement
Advance	$25,000.00		$12,500.00	on start of 1st wk of rehearsal
Fee Total	$50,000.00		$12,500.00	on start of 2nd wk of rehearsal
			$12,500.00	on start of 3rd wk of rehearsal

ROYALTY: Producer agrees to pay Director, Choreographer, Director/ Choreographer weekly either a sum equal to _____% of all gross weekly box office receipts or a royalty pool payment as provided in the Minimum Basic Agreement, with the specific agreement of Director, Choreographer, Director/ Choreographer as expressed in Rider attached hereto. All such payments shall be sent to SSDC pursuant to the Minimum Basic Agreement.

The Producer is authorized to make checks payable to (name).

All payments drawn to the Director, Choreographer, Director/Choreographer shall be sent in care of SSDC accompanied by appropriate box office statements and/or royalty pool reports.

4.   Director, Choreographer, Director/Choreographer requests and Producer agrees to deduct two and one-half (2 ½ %) percent working assessments from all monies earned by Director, Choreographer, Director/Choreographer under this Agreement and to remit same to SSDC, with a maximum payment of annual assessment on royalties of $5,000 from each company of the Play.

5.   PENSION AND WELFARE: The Producer shall make pension and welfare contributions to the Society/League Pension Fund and the Society/League Welfare Fund as specified in the SSDC-American League Agreement.

6.   GRIEVANCE OR DISPUTE: Any grievance or dispute arising out of this Agreement shall be settled pursuant to the procedures contained in the SSDC-American League Agreement.

7.   RIDERS: (Additional Riders to be attached to each copy of this Agreement.)

_____

_____

Accepted: Producer __must__ sign contract first.

DIRECTOR, CHOREOGRAPHER,   PRODUCER
DIRECTOR/CHOREOGRAPHER

(Signature)_____   (Signature)_____
(Please Type Name)Harold Harold___   (Please Type Name) The First
                                             Production Company, Inc.___
Date 1st, January 1995_____   Date 1st, January 1995_____
Address c/o John Jones_____   Address 100 Park Avenue_____
500 Park Avenue_____   New York, NY Zip 10016___
New York, NY Zip 10022___
Phone_____   Phone_____
Social Security No._____   Employer Federal I.D. No._____
Member of SSDC: Yes_____ No_____   Member of American League:
                                             Yes_____No_____

RIDER TO AGREEMENT dated JUNE 1, 1995 by and between the Producer and the Director hereinafter named concerning the Play hereinafter specified.

PLAY:	*GOING CRAZY*
AUTHOR:	*ROBERT ROBERT*
PRODUCER:	*THE FIRST PRODUCTION*
	COMPANY, INC.
	100 PARK AVENUE
	NEW YORK, NY 10016
DIRECTOR:	*HAROLD HAROLD*
	c/o John Jones
	100 Park Ave.
	New York, NY 10022
REHEARSAL DATE:	*AUGUST 1, 1995*

WITNESSETH:

The parties mutually agree as follows:

1. <u>EMPLOYMENT</u>:

(a) The Producer hereby engages the services of the Director as the sole and exclusive director to direct and stage the Producer's production of the above Play. The Director hereby accepts such employment and agrees to perform to the best of his talents and abilities all of the services customarily performed by the director of a Broadway legitimate stage production, including but not limited to advising with respect to casting, script revisions, sets, costumes, props and similar matters; consulting with the various designers; and attending, conducting and directing all auditions, rehearsals, tryouts (out-of-town or otherwise), previews and invitational performances, if any, prior to the official New York City opening.

(b) After the New York City opening, the Director agrees at the request of the Producer to use his best efforts to render services in refining and polishing the production and rendering customary services in connection with re-rehearsals, rehearsals of cast replacements and maintenance of the quality of the production without additional compensation (except for travel and living expenses when the Director's presence is required by the Producer away from New York City and its environs). Failure by the Director to do so shall not be a breach of this agreement. If the original company moves from Broadway, requiring rehearsal of a new cast amounting to more than the usual "brush ups", it will be considered a production of an additional company.

(c) For the purpose of computing fees, advances and royalties hereunder, all performances of the Play presented by the Producer as a tour or out-of-town tryout prior to the official New York City opening shall be deemed part of the original New York City company, and not additional companies.

2. REHEARSALS AND EXCLUSIVITY: The Play will go into rehearsal on the Rehearsal Date indicated in the Agreement, or within TWO weeks thereafter, the exact date to be selected by the Producer upon at least 30 days prior written notice to the Director. If rehearsals are prevented or interrupted by reason of force majeure, as hereinafter defined, the Producer shall have the right to change the Rehearsal Date or continue rehearsals as soon as practicable after such force majeure ceases to prevent rehearsals. The Director's services will become exclusive to the Producer commencing ONE week prior to rehearsals and continuing until the official New York City opening, provided that said exclusivity shall not be required to exceed TWELVE weeks.

3. DEFINITIONS:

(a) "Royalty Participants" shall mean the Author, the Director and the Producer (with respect to the Producer's management fee).

(b) "Company Participants" shall mean the general and limited partners of the production company (or managing or investor members of the Limited Liability Company) formed by the Producer to present the Play hereunder, and their designees.

(c) "Royalty Participants' Share" shall aggregate 37½% of the Weekly Operating Profits (defined below) of each Company, computed separately for each week, which shall increase prospectively to 40% of the Weekly Operating Profits of each Company, computed separately, commencing with the week following "125% of Recoupment", which is increased prospectively to 42½% of the weekly operating profits of each Company, computed separately, commencing with the week following "150% of Recoupment", as defined below, of such Company.

(d) "Company Participants' Share" shall aggregate 62½% of the Weekly Operating Profits of each Company, computed separately for each week, which shall decrease prospectively to 60% of the Weekly Operating Profits of each Company, computed separately, commencing with the week following 125% of Recoupment, which shall decrease prospectively to 57.5% of the weekly operating profits of each Company, computed separately, commencing with the week following 150% of Recoupment of such Company.

(e) "Gross weekly box office receipts" shall mean all receipts for the sale of tickets, less:

(i) any governmental admission taxes or other similar admission taxes or value added taxes;

(ii) commissions or fees paid or discounts allowed in connection with theatre parties, group sales and benefits, and British library discounts;

(iii) actual fees for box office computer service charge and automated ticket distribution or remote box offices (but not ticket brokers), which shall not exceed 20 cents per ticket for box office computer service charge and 30 cents per ticket for Ticketron sales;

(iv) actual fees paid to credit card companies for credit card sales;

(v) telemarketing fees actually paid;

(vi) TKTS returns for tickets to the extent that payment for the tickets was included in Gross Weekly Box Office Receipts;

(vii) sums paid to pension and welfare funds of theatrical unions, which shall not exceed 4.5% of Gross Weekly Box Office Receipts before other deductions hereunder (except TKTS returns) plus additional sums paid to said funds for which the Producer is assessed with respect to the Producer's performance hereunder; and

(viii) actual League of American Theatres' fees paid, which shall not exceed $50 per performance (to the extent permitted by SSDC), and receipts from Actors' Equity Fund Benefit performances to the extent paid to said Fund.

With respect to road tour or other performances, and provided that a profit pool is not being used, in weeks when the Producer is compensated on the basis of a Company Share, fixed fee or guarantee plus a percentage, Gross Weekly Box Office Receipts shall mean any gross receipts derived by the Producer (in its capacity as producer) from such engagement plus any sums paid by the promoter or theatre directly to a star, provided that the Author's royalty and Producer's management fee are computed in the same manner.

(f) "Weekly Operating Profits" shall mean Gross Weekly Box Office Receipts for each week less the "Running Expenses" and "Other Expenses", as defined in the "Limited Partnership Agreement," (or Limited Liability Company Operating Agreement) as defined below, for said week in connection with the Play. In computing Weekly Operating Profits:

(i) The Royalty Participants' Share and the Company Participants' Share shall not be deducted as Running Expenses, but all payments to theatres for rent and/or expenses (including but not limited to compensation to a theatre computed as a fixed fee, percentage of Gross Box Office receipts, Weekly Operating Profits, Net Profits, Adjusted Net Profits, or any combination thereof) shall be deducted as Running Expenses.

(ii) Weekly Operating Profits shall be computed separately for each week for each Company presenting the Play (whether or not a separate production entity is formed for each such Company) and shall not be cross-collateralized against Weekly Operating Profits for any other week or any other Company for the purpose of computing the Director's royalties, except that expenses paid in any week that are not customarily treated as expenses for a single week shall be amortized over the number of weeks to which they pertain or such other number of weeks as is customary. No items charged as "Production Expenses" (as defined in the Limited Partnership Agreement or the Limited Liability Company Operating Agreement) shall be charged against Weekly Operating Profits, or vice versa.

(g) "Production Contract" shall mean an Option Agreement dated JANUARY 15, 1995 between the Owner of the rights and Producer above named, a copy of which has been furnished to the Director. The Director's rights hereunder, to the extent they are determined with respect to the Production Contract, shall also be determined with respect to any extensions, modifications or substitutions of or for the Production Contract applicable to all of the investors of the initial Broadway production of the Play.

(h) "Limited Partnership Agreement" (or Limited Liability Company Operating Agreement) shall mean the limited partnership agreement of "Going Crazy Limited Partnership," (or "Going Crazy Limited Liability Company") (hereafter the "Limited Partnership") (or Limited Liability Company Operating Agreement) (or "Limited Liability Company"), a copy of which shall be furnished to the Director. The Director agrees to be bound by the terms of the Limited Partnership Agreement (or Limited Liability Company Operating Agreement), insofar as the Director is concerned, with respect to all matters concerning the definition and payment of Net Profits, the statements relating thereto, and the extent of the rights of the Limited Partnership (or Limited Liability Company), except that the Director shall not be deemed a limited partner (or Investor Member) of the Limited Partnership (or Limited Liability Company) by virtue of the foregoing.

(i) "Recoupment" shall mean the time that the Gross Weekly Box Office Receipts from the Play plus all other income of the Producer with respect to the exploitation of rights in the Play held by it hereunder, from all sources, equal the Production Expenses of the Play (excluding bonds, deposits and other recoverable items) plus the Running Expenses and Other Expenses (to the extent not included in Production Expenses), as those terms are defined in the Limited Partnership Agreement (or Limited Liability Company Operating Agreement). Recoupment shall be computed separately for each Company presenting the Play. Whether or not a separate production entity is formed for each such Company the Royalty Pool will be in the amount of 37½% of the net receipts. For the purpose of determining the Director's increase in royalty upon recoupment and multiple recoupment, actual repayment to the investors shall not be necessary.

(j) "Net Profits" shall be defined as in the Limited Partnership Agreement (or the Limited Liability Company Operating Agreement). Notwithstanding the foregoing, Net Profits shall be defined on a most favored basis vis-a-vis the definition of Net Profits of the Author and Producer.

(k) "Force Majeure" shall be defined as strike, boycott, job action or other labor disturbance; fire, storm, accident or other casualty or act of God or nature;

civil or armed hostilities; public commotion, disturbance or demonstration; government regulation, law, order, mandate or injunction; or any other similar or dissimilar cause beyond the Producer's control.

(l) "SSDC Agreement" shall mean the Collective Agreement between the Society of Stage Directors and Choreographers, Inc. and the League of American Theatres and Producers, Inc. dated SEPTEMBER 1, 1990 and any successor agreement in effect prior to the Rehearsal Date, or which becomes effective retroactively on the Rehearsal Date.

4. COMPENSATION:

In consideration of the full compliance by the Director with his obligations hereunder and for the rights herein granted by him, the Producer agrees to pay and the Director agrees to accept the following compensation:

(a) With respect to the original Company of the Play presented by the Producer, a non-returnable, non-recoupable fee of $25,000, payable 25% upon the execution hereof and the balance in THREE equal weekly payments starting on the first day of rehearsals, provided that the foregoing payments shall be payable upon the sooner abandonment of the production pursuant to Clause 11 below.

(b) With respect to the original Company of the Play presented by the Producer, a non-returnable advance of $25,000 against royalties hereunder, payable 25% upon the execution hereof and the balance in THREE equal weekly payments starting on the first day of rehearsals; provided that the foregoing payments shall be payable upon the sooner abandonment of the production pursuant to Clause 11 below.

(c) With respect to the original Company of the Play presented by the Producer, a royalty equal to THREE (3%) percent of the gross weekly box office receipts from performances of the Play, which shall increase prospectively to FOUR (4%) percent of the gross weekly box office receipts commencing with the week following Recoupment of such Company. Notwithstanding the foregoing, in lieu of the aforesaid royalty, the Director agrees to accept and the Producer agrees to pay a "Formula Royalty" for all performances presented by the Producer hereunder equal to 3/15 of the Royalty Participants' Share of each Company, computed separately for each Company for each week. If a Formula Royalty is used, the Producer cannot change to a gross royalty payment without the written approval of the Director.

(d) FIVE (5%) percent of 100% of the Net Profits, as defined above, of each separate producing entity organized by the Producer within the period of the Producer's production and reopening rights to produce the Play and turn to account rights therein pursuant to the Production Contract, computed without deduction of any other participation in the Net Profits of the producing entity. Statements of production costs and net profits and payments, if any, shall be furnished at least monthly during the period that any First-Class Company hereunder is running, and thereafter not less frequently than annually. The Producer shall keep books and records relating to said production costs and net profits and the Director or his representative shall have the reasonable right to audit same.

(e) Reasonable living expenses for each day that the Producer requires the Director's services outside of New York City and its environs, plus transportation for the Director from New York City to and from such other place. All air transportation to be furnished by the Producer shall be first class. If the Director is outside the city of New York at the request of the Producer, he will be furnished with an automobile, hotel, and a per diem of $125 for each night that he is away from the city. He will be furnished with a telephone credit card for use in connection with the show and will be reimbursed for all reasonable and proper expenses incurred with the show. The foregoing obligations of the Producer shall not apply if such expenses are paid, provided or reimbursed to the Director by a third party.

(f) Notwithstanding the provisions of Subclauses 4(c), 6(b), 6(c) and 6(d), the royalty payable to the Director in any week in which the profit pool is used shall not be less than $750 per point.

5. ADDITIONAL ROYALTY PROVISIONS:

(a) The Author's royalty shall be TEN FIFTEENTHS (10/15THS) of the Royalty Participants' Share of each Company, computed separately for each Company for each week.

(b) The Producer's management fee shall be TWO FIFTEENTHS (2/15THS) of the Royalty Participants' Share of each Company, computed separately for each Company for each week.

(c) No Royalty Participants shall receive a royalty computed as a percentage of gross box office receipts, except as provided for in clause 4 and except that designers may receive a fixed fee or gross royalty which shall be included as expenses in computing Weekly Operating Profits.

(d) The Director's definition of Weekly Operating Profits shall be defined on a basis at least as favorable to the Director as for any other Royalty Participant therein.

6. ADDITIONAL COMPANIES:

(a) Provided that the Director shall have complied with his obligations with respect to the Producer's original Company of the Play to its official New York City opening, the Director shall have the right, if he so elects, to direct each additional First-Class (including First-Class bus-and-truck) Company of the Play pursuant to the Production Contract, in the United States, Canada and the British

Isles, wholly or partly under the Producer's management, authority, ownership or control or under assignment, lease or license of rights from the Producer or the original stage production Company. The Director shall receive at least 45 days but not more than 90 days written notice of the commencement of rehearsals, and unless he notifies the Producer in writing within TEN days after receipt of the aforementioned notice of rehearsals that he elects to direct such additional Company, he shall be deemed to have elected not to direct such additional Company, and the Producer may employ another director for that purpose. Any declination by the Director shall not affect his right to direct any additional Company of the Play.

(b) For each additional Company which the Director elects to direct, and provided that the Director complies with his obligations hereunder, he shall receive a fee of $25,000 plus an advance of $25,000 against a royalty defined in accordance with Subclause 4(c) above (the "Full Royalty"). The foregoing fee and advance shall be payable 25% upon the Director's giving of notice that he will direct the additional Company and the balance in three equal weekly payments starting on the first day of rehearsals. The Director shall be required to render the same services for the additional Company as are applicable to an original Company, including conducting all rehearsals of the additional Company. When the Director's services are required away from New York City and its environs, the Director shall receive the travel and living expenses described in Subclause 4(e) above.

(c) For each additional Company produced by the Producer which the Director elects not to direct, he shall receive a fee of $10,000 and an advance of $10,000 against a royalty equal to the Full Royalty, from which royalty shall be deducted any royalties or amounts in lieu thereof paid to the director of the additional Company, provided that the Director's royalty rate for the additional Company shall not be less than ONE-HALF of the Full Royalty. The foregoing fee and advance shall be payable in FOUR equal weekly payments starting on the first day of rehearsals.

(d) For each additional Company licensed by the Producer which the Director elects not to direct, he shall receive no fee or advance, and he shall receive a royalty equal to the Full Royalty, from which royalty shall be deducted any royalties or amounts in lieu thereof paid to the director of the additional Company, provided that the Director's royalty rate for the additional company shall not be less than ONE-HALF of the Full Royalty.

7. <u>APPROVALS:</u> The Director shall have the right to approve the cast, scenic, costume, lighting and sound designers and their designs, and the stage manager of each company he directs and, if he is available, replacements thereof, which approvals the Director shall not unreasonably withhold. No biography or photograph of MR. HAROLD shall be printed and distributed by the Producer

without the Director's prior approval, unless the Director fails to notify the Producer of his disapproval within 72 hours after the Producer requests approval.

8.   BILLING:

(a) With respect to each Company of the Play which the Director directs, he shall receive billing in last position in the form "Directed by HAROLD HAROLD" whenever and wherever the Author is billed as author of the Play (including the Author's possessory credit) in all programs, souvenir books, houseboards, billboards, paid advertisements and publicity, and in all marquees in New York City and in marquees elsewhere where possible, under the control of the production company organized by the Producer to present the original Company of the Play, in size no less than the Author's billing but in any event not less than 50% of the size of the majority of the letters in the title. No names shall be equal to the Director in size or prominence of type or color except that of the author and stars. No names except stars billed above the title shall be larger or more prominent than that of the Director.

(b) Notwithstanding the foregoing, billing need not be given in ABC ads unless anyone other than the Author is given credit therein (except that in any event, if the Author is given credit, billing shall be given to the Director in Monday, Wednesday and Friday NEW YORK TIMES ABC ads and ABC ads that appear in PLAYBILL), and billing to the Director shall not be required by virtue of the appearance of names other than the Director in critics' quotes. If a "billing box" or other billing area is used, or if an "artwork title" (as opposed to a "regular title" or "billing title") is used, the size and location of billing to the Director shall be determined solely by the size and location of the "regular title", "billing title", billing box or other billing area, provided that all other persons receiving credit are billed on the same basis.

(c) Provided that the Director has directed the original Company of the Play to its official opening as aforesaid, he shall receive billing credit with respect to each Company produced by the Producer which he elects not to direct, wherever and whenever the director of said Company is billed, in a size, prominence and color equal to that of the director of said Company, except that the form shall be:

"Original Production Directed by HAROLD HAROLD" "Restaged by ____" and said billing shall appear before the name of the director of such Company. In any event, the Director shall receive said billing in all programs, houseboards and window cards.

(d) No inadvertent failure by the Producer to give the above billing credit shall be deemed a breach unless not corrected prospectively, promptly after written notice from the Director. With respect to companies produced under license or other grant of rights from the Producer, the Producer shall by contract require its licensees or assignees to give the foregoing billing to the Director, but failure of such persons to give proper billing shall not be deemed a breach of this agreement by the Producer.

9.   HOUSE SEATS: For each performance of the Play directed by the Director the Producer shall cause FOUR adjoining house seats (except one pair for benefit, subscription and theatre party performances) in the first 12 rows of the center section of the orchestra, and FIVE additional pairs in good orchestra locations for the Producer's official openings directed by the Director pursuant to this agreement, to be held available at the box office for the Director or the Director's designee to purchase at the regular box office price. Such tickets shall be so held until FIFTY hours prior to the respective performance. However, should the Play, the Author, the Director or any of the cast or designers be nominated for a Tony Award, there will be no house seats available to the Director during the Tony voting period, provided the same applies to all other house seat recipients in connection with the Play. The Director shall keep, and furnish on request to the Producer, such house seat records as may be required by the New York state Attorney General.

10.   RIGHTS:

In consideration of the payments to the Director pursuant to Subclause 4(d) above, all direction, stage business, script changes and other ideas, suggestions and material of the same or different nature heretofore or hereafter contributed by the Director to the Play or its production, whether or not required hereunder, including all worldwide copyrights and renewal and extended copyrights therein under present or future laws, shall belong perpetually to the Producer and the Author (as their respective interests may appear) and their assigns, to whom the Director hereby assigns the same, with the unrestricted right to use, change, adapt or refrain from using same free from any claim by the Director, except for payments, if any, required pursuant to Clauses 4, 5 and 6 above.

11.   ABANDONMENT, POSTPONEMENT:

(a) In the event that the Producer abandons the Producer's original Company of the Play prior to its official New York City opening, or postpones the Rehearsal Date for more than two weeks (unless the postponement is for reasons of force majeure), its sole obligation shall be to pay the unpaid remainder of the fee and advance payment described in Clauses 4(a) and (b), and this agreement shall terminate and each party shall be released from all other obligations hereunder, except that the provisions of Clauses 10 and 12 shall survive such termination and remain in effect.

(b) Notwithstanding the foregoing, if a new commencement date is set by the Producer, the Director shall be given not less than 30 and not more than 90 days notice of such date and, only if within TEN (10) business days after the Director's receipt of such notice the Director so notifies the Producer in writing, the Director shall have the right to direct the Play according to all the terms of this Agreement. If the Director agrees to direct the reinstated Company, any fee or advance payment paid with respect to the terminated or suspended Company of the Play shall be deemed applied to the reinstated Company. Declination shall not affect the Director's right to receive such option with respect to any further change or postponement.

12. <u>ARBITRATION</u>: Any and all disputes arising out of, under or in connection with this agreement, including without limitation the making, validity, interpretation, performance, termination and breach hereof, shall be settled by ONE arbitrator in New York City pursuant to the rules of the American Arbitration Association. Any award rendered shall be final and conclusive upon the parties and judgment thereon may be entered in the highest state or federal court in New York having jurisdiction.

13. <u>TELEVISION</u>: The Producer agrees not to film, televise, tape, transmit or otherwise reproduce audio-visually the complete or partial performance of any Company of the Play directed by the Director or authorize others to do the same without first agreeing with him for additional compensation, provided however that excerpts of not more than FIFTEEN minutes may be broadcast on television for the purpose of publicizing stage productions or for award presentations, without payment to the Director, provided the Producer receives no compensation therefor other than reimbursement for out-of-pocket expenses. Provided that the Director has directed the original Company of the Play to its official opening as aforesaid, if the Producer's production of the Play is then taped or filmed, the Director will be given an option of first refusal to direct such television or motion picture production upon terms to be negotiated by the parties in good faith, and such rights are in addition to any rights given to the Director under the SSDC Agreement.

14. <u>PAYMENTS, STATEMENTS AND NOTICES</u>:

(a) All fees and royalties hereunder for the Director shall be made payable to the order of HAROLD HAROLD and sent to JOHN JONES, 100 PARK AVENUE, NEW YORK, NEW YORK 10022, and the Director agrees to accept the receipt by said agent as full evidence and satisfaction of such payments and delivery of statements. Royalties shall be payable within SEVEN days after the end of each playing week (FOURTEEN days with respect to foreign performances) and shall be accompanied by customary box office statements. Payments to the Director of royalties for performances outside the United States shall be subject to delays, restrictions and withholdings under applicable foreign laws and regulations, but the Director may elect to receive payment in foreign currency to the extent permitted by law.

(b) All notices hereunder shall be in writing and sent by registered or certified mail, return receipt requested, prepaid telegram or personal delivery with receipt obtained, or by telefax, to the parties at their respective addresses above set forth. Copies of notices to the Producer shall be sent to his attorney, DONALD C. FARBER, 99 PARK AVENUE, 25TH FLOOR, NEW YORK, NEW YORK 10016.

15. GOVERNING LAW; AGREEMENT BINDING; WRITING REQUIRED; NO WAIVER: All matters concerning this agreement and its validity, performance or breach shall be governed by the laws of the state of New York. This agreement shall be binding upon and enure to the benefit of the parties and their respective heirs, executors, administrators, successors and assigns. No agreement changing, amending, extending, superseding, rescinding, terminating or discharging this agreement or any provisions hereof shall be valid unless in writing and signed by the party to be charged. No waiver of any provisions hereunder shall be binding unless in writing and signed by the party to be charged; no waiver of any breach hereof shall be construed to be a continuing waiver or consent to any subsequent breach hereof.

16. SSDC: This agreement shall be subject to the terms of the Collective Agreement between the Society of Stage Directors and Choreographers, Inc. and the League of American Theatres and Producers, Inc. dated SEPTEMBER 1, 1990, and any successor agreement in effect prior to the Rehearsal Date, or which becomes effective retroactively to the Rehearsal Date, provided however that anything in this agreement which is more favorable to the Director shall prevail. Notwithstanding the foregoing, the Director agrees to cooperate with the Producer if necessary to obtain SSDC approval of the provisions of Clauses 4, 5 and 6 above.

17. DIRECTOR'S ASSISTANT: The Producer shall provide and pay for an assistant of Director's choice at compensation, per diem, transportation and term of employment to be mutually agreed to by the Producer and Director.

18. PENSION AND WELFARE: The Producer shall make all applicable union pension and welfare payments for LLOYD RICHARDS.

19. VISAS: If MR. HAROLD'S services hereunder are required at any time outside of the United States, the Producer, at its expense, shall file for any required labor permits or visas.

20. CHANGES: Notwithstanding the provisions of Clause 10 above, no changes in the staging, performance or presentation of the Play or any portion thereof, of any company under the Producer's control directed by the Director, shall be made without the Director's approval, provided that he is available within 72 hours to exercise his right of approval, except that the foregoing shall not be deemed to give the Director approval over the script.

THE GOING CRAZY LIMITED   The First Production Company, Inc.
PARTNERSHIP
(or Limited Liability Company)

By: _____   By: _____
Harold Harold   **James James**

In consideration of the execution of this contract by Director, the undersigned hereby agrees to be liable with the Producer for the full performance of each and every covenant and provision of this contract on Producer's part to be performed including, but not limited to, the payment of all monies due the Director hereunder.

_____

James James

Form 45

Actors' Equity Association Standard Minimum Production Contract

COPY **Actors' Equity Association**
STANDARD **MINIMUM PRODUCTION CONTRACT**

TO BE ISSUED TO ACTORS PERFORMING AS CHORUS
MUST BE SIGNED BY ACTOR AND PRODUCER BEFORE ACTOR'S FIRST REHEARSAL

Agreement made this _____ day of _____ 19_____,

between the undersigned Producer(s) and _____, hereinafter "Actor".

1. The Producer engages the Actor to render services as Chorus _____
                              (Specify: dancer/singer, singer/dancer, understudy, named part, specialty, swing, etc.)

in the play now called " _____,"

and the Actor hereby accepts such employment upon the following terms:

2. **FIRST PAID PERFORMANCE.** The day of the first paid public performance shall be the _____ day of _____, 19_____, or not later than 14 days thereafter. Employment hereunder shall begin on the date of the Actor's first rehearsal, which may not commence earlier than the number of weeks prior to the first paid public performance as set forth herein, and as per Rule 58 of the Agreement and Rules Governing Employment under the Production Contract (hereinafter "Rules").

3. **ORGANIZATION POINT.** It is agreed that the point of organization of the company shall be (please select and circle one of the following):

    NEW YORK CITY, CHICAGO, LOS ANGELES, SAN FRANCISCO. (If no choice is made, the organization point shall be New York City).

4. **COMPENSATION.** The Producer shall pay the Actor the sum of _____ dollars

($_____) for each week of employment during the rehearsal period and shall pay the sum of _____

_____ dollars ($_____) for each week of employment commencing with the first paid public performance. In addition, the Actor shall receive $_____ for out-of-town expenses in accordance with the Rules. No reduction of this compensation shall be binding on the Actor without the written consent of Actors' Equity Association (hereinafter "Equity"). All weekly compensation due shall be paid no later than the day before the last banking day of the week.

5. The Producer recognizes Equity as the exclusive bargaining representative of the Actor for the purpose of collective bargaining and the administration of matters within the scope of this agreement. Both the Producer and the Actor agree that each and every provision, including the Arbitration Rules, contained in the Basic Agreement between Equity and the League of American Theatres and Producers and contained in the Rules, is and becomes a part of this agreement, as though set forth herein at length; that they have read said Rules and admit actual notice and knowledge of same; that each and every term of said Rules is of the essence of the contractual relationship between them; that said Rules set forth the minimum conditions under which the Actor may work for the Producer; and that said Rules may not be waived or modified without the written consent of Equity.

6. **SECURITY.** It is the essence of this contract and a condition precedent to the engagement of the Actor that the Producer shall file and shall at all times maintain with Equity security satisfactory to it as required by the Security Agreement and the Rules.

7. **CHECK-OFF AUTHORIZATION.** The Actor hereby assigns to Equity from any compensation to be earned in connection with this contract, such amounts for dues, initiation fees, and assessments certified by Equity as due and authorizes and directs the deduction of such amounts from Actor's compensation and the remission of the same to Equity. This assignment, authorization and direction covers all compensation earned as a result of employment under this contract (regardless of how characterized or when paid) including but not limited to compensation earned pursuant to Rule 70, provided that with respect to such compensation, Equity has first required that payment thereof be made by the Producer to the Actor. This assignment, authorization and direction shall remain in effect and be irrevocable, and shall be continued automatically, unless Actor revokes it by giving written notice to the Producer and Equity by registered mail not more than 30 days and not less than 15 days prior to the expiration of each successive one year period or of each successive Collective Bargaining Agreement, whichever occurs sooner. Such revocation shall become effective the first day of the calendar month following its receipt. This clause shall be operative unless stricken by the Actor in which case the Actor is liable for direct payment of dues to the Association. If the Actor strikes this clause and elects to pay dues directly to the Association and is in default of payment of any legally required dues, the Actor is subject to discharge from employment for dues delinquency.

8. **INDIVIDUAL SIGNATURE REQUIRED.** The Producer agrees that execution of this contract binds not only the producing company, but also the individual signatory to this contract as well as any person under whose authority this contract is executed.

Producer's Name (MUST SIGN FIRST)	Actor
Name of the Producing Organization	Address
City and State	City, State, Zip
Unemployment Insurance Registration #	Social Security # (MUST BE FILLED IN)

COPY   8/95

ACTOR'S COPY

Form 46
Actors' Equity Association Standard Minimum Production Contract

Actors' Equity Association
Standard Minimum Production Contract

TO BE ISSUED ONLY TO ACTORS PERFORMING AS PRINCIPALS

EACH COPY MUST BE SIGNED BY ACTOR AND PRODUCER BEFORE ACTOR'S FIRST REHEARSAL

Agreement made this _____ _____ day of _____ 19_____,

between the undersigned Producer or Producers and _____ Actor.

1. AGREEMENT OF EMPLOYMENT. The Producer engages the Actor to render services in the part (or understudy) of _____

_____

in the play now called "_____
and the Actor hereby accepts such employment upon the following terms:

2. FIRST PAID PUBLIC PERFORMANCE. The date of the first paid public performance shall be the _____ day of _____, 19____, or not later than fourteen (14) days thereafter. Employment hereunder shall begin on the date of beginning of rehearsals, which date shall not be earlier than six (6) weeks [seven (7) weeks in the case of musicals] prior to the first paid public performance herein agreed upon.

3. ORGANIZATION POINT. It is agreed between the Actor and the Producer that the organization point of the Company shall be one of the following: (Please Circle One) NEW YORK CITY, CHICAGO, SAN FRANCISCO, LOS ANGELES. If no choice is made, the Organization point shall be New York City.

4. COMPENSATION.

(A) The Producer agrees to pay the Actor each week on the day before the last banking day of the week the sum of _____
_____ Dollars ($_____) for employment at the Organization Point.

(B) The Producer agrees to pay the Actor each week on the day before the last banking day of the week the sum of _____
_____ Dollars ($_____) for employment outside the Organization Point.

In addition, the Actor will receive $_____ for out-of-town expenses in accordance with the Agreement and Rules Governing Employment under the Production Contract.

(C) No reduction of this compensation shall be binding on the Actor without the written consent of Equity.

5. EQUITY RULES
(A) The Producer recognizes Actors' Equity Association ("EQUITY") as the exclusive bargaining representative for the Actor for the purpose of collective bargaining and the administration of matters within the scope of this Agreement.

(B) Both the Producer and the Actor agree that each and every provision including the Arbitration Rule contained in the Basic Agreement between Equity and the League of New York Theatres and Producers, Inc. and the Agreement and Rules Governing Employment under the Production Contract is and becomes a part of this Agreement, as though set forth herein at length; that they have read said Rules and admit actual notice and knowledge of same; that each and every term of said Rules is of the essence of the contractual relationship between them and that said Rules set forth the minimum conditions under which the Actor may work for the Producer; and that said Rules may not be waived or modified without the written consent of Equity. Nothing herein shall be construed contrary to the Basic Agreement.

6. SECURITY. It is the essence of this contract and a condition precedent to the engagement of the Actor that the Producer shall file and shall at all times maintain with Actors' Equity Association security satisfactory to Equity as required by its existing Security Agreement and Rules.

7. AUTHORIZATION. Actor hereby assigns to Equity from any compensation to be earned in connection with this Contract, such amounts for: dues, initiation fees, and assessments certified by Equity as due and authorizes and directs the deduction of such amounts from Actor's compensation and the remission of the same to Equity. This assignment, authorization, and direction covers all compensation earned as a result of employment under this Contract (regardless of how characterized or when paid) including but not limited to compensation earned pursuant to Rule 70 of the Basic Agreement, provided that with respect to such Rule 70 compensation, Equity has first required that payment thereof be made by the Producer to the Actor. This assignment, authorization and direction shall remain in effect and be irrevocable, and shall be continued automatically, unless Actor revokes it by giving written notice to the Producer and Equity by registered mail not more than 30 days and not less than 15 days prior to the expiration of each successive one year period or if each successive Collective Bargaining Agreement, whichever occurs sooner. Such revocation shall become effective the first day of the calendar month following its receipt.

8. INDIVIDUAL SIGNATURE REQUIRED. The Producer agrees that execution of this Contract binds not only the producing company, but the individual signator to this Contract as well as any person under whose authority this Contract is executed.

(PRODUCER MUST SIGN FIRST)

_____   _____
Actor   Producer (must sign first)

_____   _____
Address   Employer's Registration Number for Unemployment Insurance

_____   _____
Social Security Number   Name of Company Registered for Unemployment Insurance and Social Security

_____
Agent (if any)

OBLIGATION FOR ACTORS' FUND: SEE RULE 5.

COPY

MISCELLANEOUS AGREEMENTS

Form 47

PHILIPS MEDIA LICENSE AGREEMENT *

AGREEMENT dated as of _____, 1995 (the "Agreement") between _____ a corporation with its principal place of business at _____ ("Provider") and Philips Media, Inc., a Delaware corporation, with its principal place of business at 10960 Wilshire Boulevard, Seventh Floor, Los Angeles, California 90024 ("PMI").

WHEREAS, Provider owns or controls certain rights to intellectual property having commercial value; and

WHEREAS, PMI is in the business and developing and marketing multimedia software; and

WHEREAS, PMI desires to obtain and Provider desires to grant certain of Provider's rights in connection with PMI's contemplated development of certain multimedia software based in part on Provider's intellectual property;

NOW, THEREFORE, the parties hereto agree as follows:

1. Definitions:

The following terms used in this Agreement shall have the meanings hereinafter set forth.

(a) "Multimedia Program" - The term "Multimedia Program" means a software program whether in fixed medium configuration or non-fixed medium configuration, regardless of platform, format or the like, for interactive presentation of video, audio, graphics, animation, text and/or data.

(b) "Program" - The term "Program" means any Multimedia Program (or Programs) (including foreign language, edited, derivative, new, spinoff and sequel versions thereof) contemplated to be created and exploited by PMI utilizing the Source Materials (as hereinafter defined) pursuant to PMI's license under this Agreement and tentatively titled "_____."

(c) "Disc" - The term "Disc" means the Program in the event it is physically embodied in or on any fixed medium configuration and/or tangible storage medium (by way of example and not limitation: compact disc, floppy disc, or magnetic tape).

(d) "Delivery Items" - The term "Delivery Items" means the items specified in Exhibit "A".

(e) "Distributor" - The term "Distributor" means PMI and solely insofar as concerns Provider and (without thereby creating any third party beneficiary rights) any subdistributor, licensee or sublicensee of PMI.

* Reprinted with permission of Philips Media.

   (f) "Effective Date" - The term "Effective Date" means the date of full and complete execution of this Agreement by the parties hereto.

   (g) "Rights Period" - The term "Rights Period" means the period of time during which Distributor may exploit all of Distributor's rights in the Program, which period commences upon the first commercial release of the Program hereof and shall endure in perpetuity.

[Use when Rights Period is less than perpetuity:

   (h) "Sell-Off Period" - The term "Sell-Off Period" shall mean the twelve (12) month period of time during which PMI (or any Distributor) may sell or rent (but not manufacture) units of the Program after the expiration or termination of the Rights Period.]

   (i) "Source Materials" - The term "Source Materials" means:

      (A) Generally, the sources or subject matter upon which the Program is to be based and which are licensed herein, more specifically identified in subparagraph 1(i)(B) below.

      (B) In particular, the Source Materials shall be .

   (j) "Territory" - The term "Territory" means the entire universe.

2.   Grant of Rights:

   (a) Provider hereby irrevocably grants, licenses and assigns to PMI the exclusive right, title and interest, throughout the Territory during the Rights Period, in all electronic multimedia and allied and analogous rights in and to the Source Materials and in any and all adaptations and versions thereof owned or controlled by Provider, and all its elements, including without limitation, the title, characters and characterizations, under copyright, trademark or otherwise, to create, develop, adapt, produce, convert, port, advertise, promote, market, distribute, bundle, exhibit, broadcast, display, sell, lease, rent, perform, merchandise and exploit the Program and the Discs (including any foreign and/or dual language versions, edited versions, sequel and/or spinoff versions and other derivative or new versions of the Program and Discs) and, in connection therewith, the Source Materials, as PMI in PMI's sole discretion may determine, for release in all media now known or hereafter developed, including but not limited to all configurations in all languages for all multimedia technology/ systems, whether fixed medium configurations (including, but not limited to, compact disc, floppy disc and cartridge) or non-fixed medium configurations (including, but not limited to, on-line, Infobahn, video-on-demand, interactive television) whether such configurations and/or technology systems are now known or hereafter developed, under whatever title(s) PMI may designate and the right, license and authority to sub-license any of the aforementioned rights. Without limiting the generality of the foregoing, PMI shall enjoy and be entitled fully to exploit all of Provider's rights in all music, lyrics, characters and images contained in, or synchronized with, or credited or composed for, the Program or the Discs including, without limitation, all soundtrack and music publishing rights and all merchandising, television and motion picture rights in or to the Program or Discs.

(b)Exclusivity: Blocking Rights.During the Rights Period, Provider may not grant any rights to any person or entity to exploit the Source Materials in any Multimedia Program.

(c) Trademark and Associated Rights. Provider further licenses to PMI the right to use Provider's trademarks, trade names, trade dress, logos and other similar proprietary rights in connection with the Program and with PMI's marketing, distribution, promotion, packaging, advertising, sale, and/or rental of the Program [subject to the limitations set forth in Exhibit "_____"].

(d)Publicity Rights. Provider hereby grants to PMI for and during the Rights Period and throughout the Territory for the purpose of advertising, publicizing, and/or promoting the Program, the right to use and otherwise exploit the names, photographs, likenesses, voices and other sound effects of Provider and all persons appearing in the Source Materials or providing creative services in connection with the production of the Source Materials.

(e) Advertising and Promotional Rights. PMI shall have the right to perform, display, and/or exhibit excerpts of the Source Materials or the Program (or the Program in its entirety if for non-revenue generating purposes) in all media now known or hereafter developed, including, but not limited to, radio, television, cable, videodisc, videocassette, audio disc, satellite telephony, whether by living actors, electrical transcriptions, film, tape, disc, cassette or otherwise in any language in the Territory for the purpose of advertising, publicizing and/or promoting the Program or the system on which the Program may be exhibited.

(f) Assignment. PMI shall have the right to assign or convey all or any part of PMI's rights and obligations under this Agreement and to license others to exploit all or any part of the foregoing rights granted to PMI, as PMI in FMI's sole discretion may determine. Provider shall not have the right to assign Provider's rights or obligations under this Agreement, except the right to assign payment of royalties conditioned upon receipt of written notice of irrevocable authority in a form satisfactory to PMI, and executed by Provider. PMI's payment in accordance with such assignment shall be deemed to be the equivalent of payment to Provider hereunder. Subject to the foregoing, this Agreement shall be binding upon and inure to the benefit of the parties hereto and their respective legal successors and assigns.

3.   Delivery: At such time(s) as PMI may request, Provider shall deliver the Delivery Items to PMI at Provider's expense to a location designated by PMI. Provider shall likewise deliver the same materials with respect to all future

versions and editions of the Source Materials to PMI as they become available. Provider shall assist PMI in the research and acquisition of additional images, photographs, drawings and the like. Any original images photographs and/or drawings delivered to PMI by Provider shall be returned to Provider when PMI has finished using same.

4. Defaults and Termination:

(a) Each of the following events shall constitute an "event of default" for the purposes hereof:

(i) If Provider materially breaches or defaults under any provision of this Agreement; and/or

(ii) If the Program, any of the rights licensed by Provider hereunder or any of the Source Materials relating thereto is attached or levied upon by a creditor or claimant of Provider or of any entity related to Provider, and such attachment or levy is not released within five (5) days; and/or

(iii) If any representation or warranty made by Provider in this Agreement is false or misleading.

(b) If any event of default shall occur, PMI may (but shall not be obligated to):

(i) Terminate any or all of PMI's obligations hereunder; and/or

(ii) Offset against any sums which may be or become due Provider and/or any related entity, under this Agreement or any other agreement; and/or

(iii) Exercise any other available right or remedy.

(c) All costs incurred by PMI in proceeding under this paragraph 4 (including, without limitation, reasonable attorneys' fees) shall be added to any sums due PMI by Provider. All of PMI's rights and remedies are cumulative and the exercise of one shall not limit or affect PMI's right concurrently or subsequently to exercise any other right or remedy.

(d) If PMI breaches this Agreement, Provider's rights and remedies shall be limited to Provider's rights, if any, to recover damages in an action at law, and Provider shall not be entitled to terminate, revoke, or rescind this Agreement or any of the rights granted to PMI, or to enjoin or restrain PMI or PMI's licensees from exercising any of the rights granted to PMI.

(e) With respect to any breach by PMI, Provider may not exercise any remedy other than suspension of Provider's performance unless PMI fails to fully cure the breach within thirty (30) days after Provider gives written notice thereof.

(f) Neither party shall be liable to the other for any incidental damages, consequential damages or lost profits resulting from a breach or default, and any right to recover lost profits or consequential damages is hereby expressly waived by both PMI and Provider.

5. <u>Credits</u>: PMI shall cause Provider to be accorded an appropriate credit in the Program as the licensor of the Source Materials. The precise form of such credit, the size and placement thereof and all other matters relating to credit shall be determined by PMI in PMI's discretion. Upon Provider's request, PMI will consult with Provider regarding credits accorded in connection with the Program and will give good faith consideration to Provider's reasonable requests. No casual or inadvertent failure by PMI or any failure by any third party to accord credit in compliance with the credit provisions hereunder shall constitute a breach of this Agreement.

6. <u>Copyright Ownership, Protection and Enforcement</u>:

(a) All rights not granted hereunder are reserved by Provider.

(b) PMI shall own the exclusive right, title and interest under copyright, trademark or otherwise in and to the Program included but not limited to the tools, utilities, design processes, software systems, source and object codes, program logic, interactive program structures, retrieval software systems, user interface designs and other procedures and methods of operation which are utilized in connection with the Program, including, without limitation, the copyrights therein throughout the universe and shall be exclusively entitled to produce, reproduce, display, perform, distribute and otherwise exploit the Program throughout the universe in perpetuity in all media now known or hereafter developed.

(c) Copyright registration of the Program and notices on each unit of the Program shall be in the name of PMI unless such registration and/or notices are customarily done in the name of the individual distributor or licensee in the applicable territory.

(d) Distributor shall have full and complete authority either in the name of Provider or otherwise as Distributor deems appropriate, to take such steps as Distributor (or Distributor's licensees) deems appropriate by action at law, or otherwise, to prevent unauthorized replication, manufacture and/or distribution of the Program and Discs in the Territory or any infringement upon the rights of PMI or Provider in the Program and Discs; and Distributor or Distributor's nominee may, as Provider's attorney-in-fact (coupled with an interest) execute, acknowledge, verify and deliver all pleadings and/or instruments pertaining thereto in the name of and on behalf of Provider as Distributor deems appropriate. Distributor may (but shall not be obligated to) take such steps as Distributor shall deem appropriate, by action at law, or otherwise, to recover monies due with respect to the exploitation, distribution or exhibition of the Program and Discs. Any and all recoveries from any such action shall be applied first to recover all expenses incurred in such action and Provider shall be entitled to Provider's percentage royalty of the balance (after paying to the licensee for such territory such amount as Distributor is contractually obligated to pay such licensee).

7. Sales Policies:

(a) Distributor may exploit and distribute the Program and Discs and exercise any and all rights herein granted, in accordance with such sales or rental methods, policies, practices and terms as Distributor may determine in Distributor's sole discretion. Without limitation, Distributor may adjust and increase or decrease any allowances to any published prices; allow reasonable "free goods" whether on a regular or special promotion basis; permit reasonable returns for any reason; license the distribution of the Program and Discs for a particular country (other than distribution through regular retail channels in the United States, Canada, Great Britain, France, Germany, Spain, Italy, Japan or Australia) on a flat sum basis; license the distribution of the Program and Discs upon a percentage of receipts, royalty, or flat amount per unit; bundle, sell or license the Program and Discs together with other programs or separately, as Distributor shall deem desirable; and refrain from distribution in any place at any time, as Distributor, in Distributor's sole discretion, may elect. No royalty will be payable with respect to Program and Discs sold by Distributor to Distributor's employees. Distributor shall be obligated to deal with related persons and entities on a good faith arms' length basis.

(b) Distributor has not made any express or implied representation, warranty, or agreement as to the amount of royalties or receipts which shall be derived from the distribution of the Program and Discs, nor has Distributor made any express or implied representation, warranty, or agreement that there will be any royalties or other sums payable to Provider, or that the Program will be favorably received by retailers or the public. PMI makes no express or implied representation, warranty, or agreement as to whether a Program will be developed, produced, and/or marketed and reserves the right not to create the Program and/or to create the Program at a later time, as PMI in PMI's sole discretion may determine. Neither party shall incur any liability hereunder based upon any claim that either party has failed to realize revenues or to effectuate sales which should have been realized.

(c) Provider acknowledges that PMI may develop and/or distribute other products in competition with the Program and shall be under no duty to avoid competing products, or to expend the same promotional efforts for and on behalf of the Program as PMI expends for other products, irrespective of the similarity of potential market. Whenever a licensee pays for the right to manufacture and distribute a number of products, including the Program, under an agreement which does not specify what portion of the license payments apply to each of the respective products in the group, Distributor may, in good faith, allocate to the Program for the purpose hereof, such portion of such total license payment as Distributor may in good faith consider proper. PMI has no obligation to actually produce or release the Program or to actually use any of the Source Materials in connection therewith.

8. <u>Advance; Royalties:</u>

(a) Upon execution of this Agreement, PMI shall pay Provider the sum of _____ as an advance against royalties (the "Advance"). No royalties shall be paid to Provider until such time, if ever, as PMI has recouped the Advance out of amounts otherwise payable to Provider as royalties.

(b) In full consideration of all rights granted to PMI hereunder by Provider, and provided Provider is not in material breach or default of this Agreement, and provided PMI actually uses the Source Materials in whole or in part in the Program, PMI agrees to pay Provider the following royalties in connection with the marketing and distribution of Program and Discs:

(i) PMI shall pay to Provider a royalty of _____ Percent (%) of PMI's Net Receipts (as hereinafter defined) derived and actually received by PMI from exploitation of the Program in the United States until Recoupment (as hereinafter defined) ("U.S. Royalty"). Following recoupment, on a prospective basis only, the U.S. Royalty shall be increased to _____ Percent (_____ %) of Net Receipts.

(ii) The royalty payable to Provider for exploitation of the Program outside the United States shall be equal to the Net Receipts in the applicable country of the Territory outside the United States multiplied by one-half (½) of the applicable U.S. Royalty provided in subparagraph 8(b)(i) above.

(iii) Notwithstanding any of the foregoing, in the event of Scrap, Budget, or Mid-Priced sales of Programs hereunder, the applicable percentage royalty rate as defined in Paragraph 8 hereof shall be modified as follows:

	Reduction in Paragraph 8 Rate
Scrap Sales	100%
Budget Sales	50%
Mid-Price Sales	25%

Scrap or Budget sales will only be made in order to liquidate existing inventory or in the event that continuing sales of the Program are less than one hundred (100) units per month.

For purposes of the foregoing table, "Scrap Sales" shall mean Discs furnished free to users or sold as scrap or "cut-outs" at prices equal to or less than 33-1/3% of the original Wholesale Price which was set as of the initial commercial release of the Program and/or Discs, and on Discs furnished on a so-called "no charge" basis to distributors, subdistributors, dealers or others; "Budget Sales" shall mean the sale or license of Discs at prices equal to or less than 50% (but more than 33-1/3%) of the original Wholesale Price which was set as of the initial commercial release of the Program and/or Discs; and "Mid-Price Sales" shall mean the sale or license of Discs at prices equal or less than 66-2/3% (but more than 50%) of the original Wholesale Price which was set as of the initial commercial release of the Program and/or Discs.

(iv) Provider hereby agrees that Provider shall be solely responsible for all accountings and payments out of Provider's share of royalties hereunder to any and all third-party royalty participants however denominated with whom Provider has contracted and who are entitled to compensation based on exploitation of the Program or Source Materials out of Provider's share of royalties hereunder.

(c) As used herein, and subject to cross-collateralization by PMI, Net Receipts shall mean the gross receipts actually received by PMI from all sales and licenses of the Program less the following amounts:

(i) Taxes on sale or license, including but not limited to sales, use, excise or other taxes;

(ii) Sales commissions payable;

(iii) Amounts reimbursed to customers for expenses actually incurred, including but not limited to insurance, shipping and similar charges;

(iv) Promotional amounts actually credited, including but not limited to credits, cash discounts, freight discounts, rebates or promotional allowances to customers, copies supplied for promotional purposes to the press, trade, sales representatives, employees, or potential customers;

(v) Amounts for returns, replacement of defectives, including but not limited to credits, refunds or allowances; and

(vi) Currency exchange fees incurred by PMI with respect to receipts other than in United States Dollars.

(d) (i) The term "Wholesale Price" as used herein shall mean the published price to dealer (net of "free goods") for the Program sold or otherwise distributed.

(ii) The term "Recoupment" as used herein shall mean the point at which PMI has recouped one hundred thirty percent (130%) of PMI's development and production costs including all packaging, mastering and product testing costs) incurred in connection with the Program hereunder out of thirty two percent (32%) of PMI's Net Receipts, less all amounts payable as pre-Recoupment royalties to Provider and/or any third parties in connection with the Program.

9. Royalty Statements: Within sixty (60) days after the end of each calendar quarter, subject to delay on account of events or circumstances beyond PMI's control, PMI shall send Provider statements showing, in summary form, (i) the net number of units of the Program reported to PMI during the period as having been sold or rented (whether or not actually sold or rented during that accounting period), and (ii) the royalties, if any, due with respect to such units of the Program

for the accounting period covered by such statement. All statements may be submitted on a billings or collections basis as PMI may from time to time elect, and if such statements are changed from one basis to another, such statements may thereafter be amended to reflect adjustments by reason thereof. In the event the statements are submitted on a billings basis, PMI may either establish reasonable reserves (as established by Distributor) for unpaid units, or charges against sales and bad debts as they are recognized. Should PMI make any overpayment for any reason, PMI shall have the right to deduct and retain an amount equal to any such overpayment from any sums that may thereafter become due or payable to Provider or for Provider's account, and/or may demand repayment from Provider, in which event Provider agrees to repay the same when such demand is made. Any amounts payable to Provider pursuant to any such statement shall be payable simultaneously with the rendering of such statement, subject to any provision in this Agreement relieving PMI from such obligation; provided, however, that all amounts payable to Provider hereunder shall be subject to all laws and regulations now or hereafter in existence requiring or permitting the deduction or withholding of payment for taxes or other amounts payable by, or assessable against, Provider. Provider shall make and prosecute any and all claims which Provider may have with respect to the same directly with the governmental agency having jurisdiction in the premises. Notwithstanding any sub-license or distribution arrangement, Provider will look solely to PMI to perform all obligations undertaken by PMI or PMI's designee pursuant to this Agreement, including the payment of all royalties. At PMI's election, however, PMI may cause a third party to perform PMI's obligation to account to Provider as provided in paragraphs 8, 9, 10 and 11 hereof.

10. _Accounting Records and Audit Rights Relating to Distribution of Program:_ PMI shall keep reasonably adequate books of account relating to the distribution of the Program. With twenty (20) days written notice to PMI, Provider may, at Provider's own expense audit the applicable records at the place where PMI maintains the same to verify royalty statements hereunder. Any such audit shall be conducted only by a certified public accountant during business hours and in such manner as not to interfere with PMI's normal business activities. A copy of all reports made by Provider's accountant pursuant to any such audit shall be delivered to PMI at the same time such reports are delivered to Provider. No audit with respect of any royalty statements shall commence later than twelve (12) months from the date of the royalty statement on which the audited matter is initially reflected; nor shall any audit continue for longer than such time reasonably necessary to complete it; nor shall audits be made hereunder more frequently than once in any year; nor shall the records supporting any royalty statement be audited more than once. Provider shall be forever barred from maintaining or instituting any action or proceeding in any way relating to any transactions had by Distributor in connection with the Program and the accounting

embraced in any statement or account delivered hereunder, and such statements and accounts shall be final and binding on Provider, unless written objection thereto is given to PMI within said twelve (12) month period and such action or proceeding is commenced within twenty-four (24) months after the date of the subject statement. The right to examine books of account and other documents herein granted to Provider may only be exercised by Provider with respect to the Program, and Provider shall have no right to inspect or examine the books of account or any other documents with respect to any other products distributed by PMI.

11. Foreign Currency: Foreign receipts shall be converted to United States Dollars at the same rate at which such funds were actually converted into and received by PMI in the United States in U.S. dollars. Provider's pro rata portion of foreign currency conversion and transmission charges will be deducted from the royalty otherwise payable.

12. Supplemental Documents; Power of Attorney: Provider will execute, acknowledge and deliver such instruments as PMI may request to evidence, maintain, effectuate, or defend any and all of the rights granted to PMI under this Agreement, including, without limitation, an Instrument of Transfer evidencing PMI's rights. If Provider shall fail to execute, acknowledge or deliver to PMI any such instrument, PMI is irrevocably appointed Provider's attorney-in-fact, with full right and authority to execute, acknowledge and deliver the same in the name and on behalf of Provider. Provider agrees that such authority and agency is a power coupled with a pecuniary interest and shall survive the dissolution or other cessation of existence of Provider.

13. Representations and Warranties:

   (a) PMI and Provider each represent and warrant that it is duly organized, validly existing and in good standing under the laws of its state of incorporation and is qualified to do business in any state or country where such qualification is necessary; that it has sole right, power, and authority to enter into and perform this Agreement, and to grant all of the rights granted and agreed to be granted pursuant hereto; that it has taken all necessary action to authorize the execution and performance of this Agreement; and that the same does not and will not violate or require any consent under any provision of its charter documents, or of any agreement or instrument to which it is a party or by which a material part of its assets are bound, nor will such execution or performance violate any judgment or decree by which it is bound.

   (b) Provider further represents and warrants as follows:

      (i) That Provider has not sold, transferred or conveyed and will not sell, transfer or convey to any person, firm, corporation or other entity, any of the rights licensed and granted to PMI hereunder or any right or interest which is inconsistent with the rights granted to PMI or that Provider has reserved such rights, that no Multimedia Program based on the Source Materials has been made or produced and no right or license to do so remains outstanding;

(ii) That Provider owns all necessary rights, including, without limitation, all such rights in all applicable copyrights, trademarks, trade names, titles and similar rights, in and to the Source Materials furnished by Provider to grant PMI the rights granted to PMI under this Agreement, without payment of any additional sums therefor by Provider or PMI;

(iii) That there are and shall be no claims, demands, liens, encumbrances or rights of any kind or nature in or to the Program or Source Materials or any part thereof, or the copyright thereto resulting from any act or omission by Provider, which can or will impair or interfere with the rights of PMI under this Agreement nor will Provider take any action which would interfere with PMI's enjoyment of the rights granted hereunder and that nothing contained in the Source Materials nor any use thereof by PMI permitted hereunder will violate any right of any third party; and

(iv) That neither the Source Materials, nor the Source Materials' use in any form, adaptation, or version allowed under this Agreement, nor the exercise of any of the rights herein granted or conveyed, will in any way infringe upon any copyright, literary, dramatic, photoplay or common laws right(s) of any person, firm or corporation whatsoever, or constitute a libel or defamation of, or invasion of any rights (including, without limitation the right of privacy or publicity) of any party.

14.   Indemnity: Each party shall indemnify, defend and hold harmless the other party, its successors, assigns, parents, subsidiaries, affiliates, licensees, officers, employees, agents and representatives, from and against any and all loss, damage, liability, expense, claim or action (including reasonable attorneys' fees) arising in connection with any breach by either party of its warranties, representations or agreements made hereunder whether a final determination as to such breach is rendered by a fact-finder (including by way of example, a judge or arbitrator) or by the parties hereto as part of a settlement. If any claim or action shall be asserted or brought alleging facts which, if true, would constitute a breach by the indemnitor hereunder, or involving any matter connected with the Program caused by or under the control of the indemnitor, the indemnitor shall, at indemnitor's expense, cause counsel reasonably satisfactory to the indemnitee to defend such claim or action. The indemnitee shall have the right at indemnitee's election to withhold payment of any monies otherwise payable to the indemnitor in an amount reasonably related to the claim and potential liability, provided that the indemnitee shall not withhold such monies, if and to the extent that the indemnitor provides a surety bond issued by a company and in a form

satisfactory to the indemnitee. Any amount withheld shall be released if a proceeding with respect to the subject claim is not commenced within eighteen (18) months following the commencement of the applicable withholding. The foregoing does not limit the indemnitee's right to recommence withholding at any time if a proceeding is subsequently commenced. No settlement of any such action shall be made by the indemnitor without the indemnitee's express approval, not to be unreasonably withheld. The foregoing indemnification shall not diminish rights set forth elsewhere in this Agreement relative to a default or breach.

15. Notices:

   (a) All notices hereunder shall be given in writing and sent to the other party at the addresses specified below:

TO PROVIDER: **TO PMI:**
_____   Philips Media, Inc.
_____   10960 Wilshire Boulevard, 7th floor
_____   Los Angeles, CA 90024
Attn: _____   Attn: Vice President, Business Affairs

   (b) Notices shall be sent postage prepaid by certified mail, return receipt requested. Accounting statements shall be in writing and shall be sent by first class mail only, postage prepaid to the address to which notices are to be sent. All notices given as aforesaid shall be deemed received on the third business day following deposit in the United States mails; in the case of a telex or facsimile transmission on the date of transmission of the notice. Any notice given in any other manner shall be effective only when actually received.

16. Sell-Off Period: Upon expiration of the Rights Period, PMI shall have the right for the duration of the Sell-Off Period to sell and rent (but not manufacture or reproduce) units of the Program on all of the terms and conditions set forth in the Agreement, including payment of royalties. Upon expiration of the Sell-Off Period, Provider shall either purchase all the inventories of the Program then owned by PMI (and PMI's affiliated sublicensees or distributors) at the actual cost of manufacture within thirty (30) days after the end of the Sell-Off Period, or Provider shall be deemed to have authorized the sale of all such units, with PMI's royalty obligation being reduced in the same proportion that the sales price of such units bears to the regular price to dealers of such units.

17. Arbitration: With respect to any dispute or disagreement between the parties arising out of or in connection with this Agreement, the parties shall make a good faith effort to resolve that dispute by discussions between them. If they are unable to resolve that dispute or disagreement within forty-five (45) calendar days after one party has given the other notice of such dispute or disagreement, then the dispute or disagreement shall, upon written demand of either party, be

settled by binding arbitration pursuant to the Rules of the American Arbitration Association. Arbitration shall take place in Los Angeles County, California and both parties consent to the in personam jurisdiction of the federal and state courts of such County. An award of arbitration may be entered as a judgment in any court having jurisdiction in the matter, or application may be made to such a court for acceptance of the award and for an order of enforcement as the case may require. Unless otherwise ordered by the arbitrator, each party shall bear its own costs and expenses of the arbitration and one-half (½) of the arbitrator's fees and costs.

18. Miscellaneous: Nothing contained herein shall constitute a partnership between or joint venture by the parties or constitute either party the agent of the other. Neither party shall hold itself out contrary to the terms hereof and neither party shall become liable by any representation, act or omission of the other contrary to the provisions hereof. This Agreement is not entered into for the benefit of any third party and shall not be deemed to give any right or remedy to any such party whether or not referred to herein. No waiver by either party hereto of any breach of this Agreement shall be deemed to be a waiver of any preceding or succeeding breach of the same or any other provision hereof. The exercise of any right granted to either party hereunder shall not operate as a waiver. No remedy or election hereunder shall be deemed exclusive but shall, wherever possible, be cumulative with all other remedies at law or in equity. This Agreement shall be construed and interpreted pursuant to the laws of the State of California applicable to agreements entered into and fully performed in California. If any provision hereof is deemed to be unenforceable as written the provision shall be modified so as to make the provision in its general interest enforceable and as so modified shall form part of this Agreement. Nothing contained herein shall be construed so as to require the commission of any act contrary to law, and wherever there is any conflict between any provision of this Agreement and any material statute, law or ordinance the latter shall prevail, but in such event the provision of this Agreement affected shall be curtailed and limited only to the extent necessary to bring the provision within the legal requirements. This Agreement is the product of negotiation at arms' length between parties' knowledge concerning its subject matter who have had the opportunity to consult with counsel concerning this Agreement and each of its terms prior to the execution thereof. It is therefore agreed that this Agreement shall be considered jointly drafted by the parties hereto and that any rule of law that would require interpretation of any term in this Agreement against the party responsible for its inclusion herein, including, without limitation, California Civil Code Section 1654, or its equivalent, shall have no effect on the interpretation of this Agreement. This Agreement and the schedules, exhibits and attachments hereto constitute the entire Agreement and supersedes and cancels all prior negotiations, undertakings and agreements, both oral and written, between the

parties with respect to the subject matter hereof and shall be binding only when executed by both parties hereto. The parties acknowledge that no officer, employee or representative of either party has any authority to make any representation or promise not contained in this Agreement and neither party has executed this Agreement in reliance on any representation or promise not contained herein. No waiver, modification or cancellation of any term or condition of this Agreement shall be effective unless executed in writing by an authorized representative of the party charged therewith. If this Agreement is executed in counterparts, such counterparts shall constitute one and the same instrument.

IN WITNESS WHEREOF, the parties hereto have executed this Agreement as of the day and year first above written.

ACCEPTED AND AGREED TO:

By: _____

Name:_____

Title:_____

Date:_____

PHILIPS MEDIA, INC.

By: _____

Its: _____

Effective Date:_____

EXHIBIT "A"

DELIVERY ITEMS

Form 48

PHILIPS MEDIA PRODUCTION AGREEMENT *

AGREEMENT dated _____, 1995 (the "Agreement") between _____, a _____ corporation, with its principal place of business at _____ ("Provider") and Philips Media, Inc., a Delaware corporation, with its principal place of business at 10960 Wilshire Boulevard, Seventh Floor, Los Angeles, California 90024 ("PMI").

The parties hereto agree as follows:

1. Definitions:

The following terms used in this Agreement shall have the meanings hereinafter set forth.

(a) "Multimedia Program" - The term "Multimedia Program" means a software program whether in fixed medium configuration or non-fixed medium configuration, regardless of platform, format or the like, for interactive presentation of video, audio, graphics, animation, text and/or data.

(b) "Program" - The term "Program" means any Multimedia Program (or Programs) (including foreign language, edited, derivative, new, spinoff and sequel versions thereof) contemplated to be created and exploited by PMI utilizing the Source Materials (as hereinafter defined) pursuant to PMI's license under this Agreement and tentatively titled "_____." It is understood and agreed that the Program will be delivered by Provider in the form of _____.

(c) "Disc" - The term "Disc" means the Program as it is physically embodied in any fixed interactive software medium configuration by way of example and not limitation: compact disc, floppy disc, or magnetic tape).

(d) "PMI's Production Advance Commitment" - The term "PMI's Production Advance Commitment" means the maximum aggregate amount of Production Cost Advances which PMI has agreed or may agree to make.

(e) "Completion Date" - The term "Completion Date" means the date provided in the Production and Delivery Schedule (as hereinafter defined) for the delivery of the Master Materials (as hereinafter defined).

(f) "Distributor" - The term "Distributor" means PMI and solely insofar as concerns Provider and Distributor (and without thereby creating any third party beneficiary rights) any distributor, subdistributor, licensee or sublicensee of PMI.

(g) "Effective Date" - The term "Effective Date" means the date of full and complete execution of this Agreement by the parties hereto.

---

* Reprinted with permission of Philips Media.

(h) "<u>Master Materials</u>" - The term "Master Materials" means (i) the source and object code for the Program; (ii) all audio and visual data in a format specified by PMI (including, without limitation, the Master Materials and the digitized master tapes of the Program); and (iii) all supporting documentation and items required by PMI to properly master the tape disc image as specified in Exhibit "B" which is attached hereto and made a part hereof. The Master Materials shall also include all rights documentation required by PMI, including, without limitation, the following: (i) All rights and releases for pre-recorded video or stock film; (ii) All rights and permission regarding the use of images scanned or otherwise digitized in the creation of graphics; (iii) Releases from all graphic artists; (iv) Talent release forms -voice and picture; (v) Synchronization rights (if any); (vi) Master music cue sheets (necessary for international distribution); (vii) All rights and releases for Source Materials and any third party characters, trademarks, trade names and/or service marks used in the Program; and (viii) A concise summary of any limitations (whether to time, place, format or otherwise) in connection with the foregoing rights and releases.

(i) "<u>Production and Delivery Schedule</u>" - The term "Production and Delivery Schedule" means the time schedule for completing various steps in developing and producing the Program which schedule has been or will be prepared by Provider and approved in writing by PMI. The Production and Delivery Schedule shall be prepared in form substantially as set forth in Exhibit "A" which is attached hereto and made a part hereof.

(j) "<u>Production Budget</u>" - The term "Production Budget" means the budget of costs for developing and producing the Program, which has been or will be prepared by Provider and approved in writing by PMI. The Production Budget shall be attached hereto and made a part hereof as Exhibit "C."

(k) "<u>Production Costs</u>" - The term "Production Costs" means the actual direct cost of developing and producing the Program and, unless otherwise expressly approved by PMI in writing, (i) shall not include any overhead or general or administrative charges or costs not specifically and directly incurred by Provider in connection with development or production of the Program, (ii) shall not include charges for salaries, payroll taxes or burden or fringe benefits of Provider's executive or managerial personnel who provide supervisorial services to Provider's development and production activities, (iii) shall not include interest, taxes, attorneys' fees, (iv) shall not include charges for rental of Provider's facilities, tools or equipment, but (v) shall include all costs and charges incurred by Provider which directly relate to the Program being produced and which are payable to unaffiliated third parties.

(l) "<u>Production Cost Advances</u>" - The term "Production Cost Advances" means the advances of Production Costs made by PMI from time to time with respect to development and production of the Program.

(m) "Production Milestone" - The term "Production Milestone" means the satisfaction of the delivery preconditions pursuant to paragraph 4 hereinbelow for each Production Cost Advance hereunder.

(n) "Production Term" - The term "Production Term" means the period commencing upon the Effective Date hereof and continuing until the delivery to and acceptance by PMI of the "gold" master disc of the Program and all the Master Materials for the Program produced hereunder; provided, however, that the Production Term may be terminated by PMI under the terms and conditions hereunder.

(o) "Program Participants" - The term "Program Participants" means those key persons providing creative or production services to the production of the Program, such as producer, director, writer, composer, art director, and any featured artist, actor, actress, narrator, programmer, graphic designer and interactive designer.

(p) "Project" - The term "Project" means the development and production effort relative to the Program.

(q) "Reference Rate" - The term "Reference Rate" means the daily rate of interest announced by Citibank, N.A. (main New York office) as its "prime" or "reference" interest rate for unsecured loans of less than one (1) year maturity.

(r) "Rights Period" - The term "Rights Period" means the period of time during which Distributor may exploit all of its rights in the Program, which period commences upon the Effective Date hereof and shall endure in perpetuity.

(s) "Source Materials" - The term "Source Materials" means:

(i) Generally, the sources or subject matter upon which the Program is to be based, more specifically identified in paragraph 1(s)(ii) below.

(ii) In particular, the Source Materials shall be _____

_____

_____.

(t) "Territory" - The term "Territory" means the entire universe.

2.   (Intentionally deleted.) [Add G.O.R. paragraph if producer is bringing third party rights to the table]

3.   Production Terms and Conditions:

(a) Production Budget and Delivery Schedule: Within ten (10) days from the Effective Date hereof, Provider will submit a Production and Delivery Schedule (in accordance with the form set forth in Exhibit "A") setting forth all required Production Milestones, the dates by which such Production Milestones must be satisfactorily completed and delivered to PMI, and the payments of PMI's Production Cost Advances associated with the completion and delivery of the

Production Milestones required hereunder and a Production Budget (which shall be attached hereto and made a part hereof as Exhibit "C"). If PMI requests Provider to modify the Production Budget and/or Production and Delivery Schedule, Provider shall promptly consult with PMI in order to modify the same to PMI's satisfaction. Upon PMI's prior written approval, the Production and Delivery Schedule shall become the "Approved Schedule" and the Production Budget shall become the "Approved Budget."

(b) <u>Production Funding and Payment Schedule:</u>

(i) PMI's Production Advance Commitment for the Program shall be such sum as PMI may approve in writing following Provider's submission and PMI's acceptance of the Production Budget. Provider shall contribute all of the remaining Production Costs, if any, contained in the Approved Budget and Provider shall produce the Program in accordance therewith. Subject to the provisions of paragraph 4(c) hereinbelow, the total dollar amount of Production Costs for the Program shall not exceed the Approved Budget and any Production Costs in excess of the Approved Budget shall be borne solely by Provider.

(ii) PMI's Production Cost Advance Commitment pursuant to paragraph 3(b)(i) hereinabove shall be paid to Provider in installments in accordance with the Approved Schedule upon the completion and satisfaction of the associated Production Milestones approved in writing by PMI.

(c) <u>Production Cost Advances:</u> Prior to receipt by Provider of each Production Cost Advance hereunder, Provider shall submit to PMI a complete and itemized written statement of all expenditures in accordance with the Production Budget format incurred or made by Provider constituting the Production Costs of the Program incurred to the date of each Production Milestone in accordance with the Production Budget format. Such statement shall certify that all costs so incurred by Provider have been paid in full and such certificate shall be certified as true and accurate by an officer of the Provider. If the Production Budget includes an allowance for supplies or other consumables or for use of facilities, the cost thereof shall be deemed incurred ratably over the Production Term hereunder.

(d) <u>Program Specifications:</u> The Program shall (i) be fully scored, edited and composed with visuals, text, music, images, graphics, sound and other audio or visual features fully synchronized, (ii) generally, when performed or played, correspond to the approved script, approved interactive design and approved storyboards, and (iii) meet the technical requirements of the specifications supplied by PMI and shall be of a first-class quality technically satisfactory for formatting on any platform(s) designated by PMI.

(e) <u>Approval of Production Elements:</u> Provider shall develop and submit to PMI for approval, in accordance with the Production and Delivery Schedule, all deliverables, including but not limited to the final script (including, without limitation, written text, music, narration, sound effects) storyboards, the user interface, the interactive design, the source and object code, the retrieval software system, artwork and graphic design and all packaging material ("Production Elements") each of which shall conform to the approved outline. PMI shall have a right of approval over each Production Element hereunder and the completed Program (including, without limitation, the completed "gold" master disc of the Program). If PMI disapproves any of the Production Elements by determining that any of the Production Elements are not in conformance with PMI's standards of delivery, then Provider shall make such changes as are necessary to make such Production Elements conform to PMI's standards of delivery. In the event Provider is unwilling to make revisions as requested by PMI, PMI shall have the option, at PMI's sole election, to abandon the development or production of the Program, or to take over the production of the Program, at PMI's sole cost and expense and Provider shall thereupon be excused from any obligation to advance any further Production Costs hereunder. Any Program so completed by PMI shall nevertheless be marketed by PMI pursuant to the terms of this Agreement with no royalty due Provider. Provider shall be responsible for all testing and debugging (including, without limitation, all costs associated therewith) of all Production Elements, including but not limited to the completed final "gold" master disc; provided, however, that PMI shall be responsible for one (1) round of testing of the completed final "gold" master disc.

(f) Technical Assistance: PMI shall provide Reasonable Technical Assistance required by Provider. "Reasonable Technical Assistance" as used herein means (i) providing Provider with interpretation of the so-called "Green Book," "Red Book," "White Book," and "Yellow Book" specifications and (ii) making available for use by Provider any unique authoring tools and/or utilities, if any, developed by or licensed to PMI; provided, however, that such use by Provider shall not violate any license between PMI and a third party.

(g) Abandonment; Postponement; Discontinuance:

(i) Notwithstanding anything to the contrary contained elsewhere in the Agreement but subject only to the provisions of subparagraph (ii) below, PMI shall have the right (in PMI's sole and absolute discretion) to abandon and/or postpone the development and/or production of the Program at any time, for any reason ("Abandonment"). PMI shall have no obligation to make, produce, distribute or exploit the Program, or, if commenced, to continue the production, distribution or exploitation of the Program. PMI shall have no obligation to use the services of Provider hereunder, and if PMI elects (in PMI's sole and absolute discretion) to discontinue the services of Provider, PMI may continue the development and/or production of the Program without Provider's further participation.

(ii) In the event of any Abandonment of the Program and/or the services of Provider as provided in subparagraph (a) above, PMI will be obligated to pay Provider only for such Milestone(s) or portion(s) thereof which are completed and delivered by Provider and approved by PMI as of the date of abandonment, postponement or discontinuance. With respect to any royalties otherwise payable to Provider pursuant to Paragraph 17 below, in the event that Provider's services are discontinued hereunder for reasons other than default or breach of this Agreement, and if PMI actually produces and distributes the Program using assets created by Provider hereunder, then Provider's royalties for the Program under Paragraph 17 hereof shall vest in the same proportion that the aggregate payments made to Provider with respect to the development and/or production of the Program prior to the date of such discontinuance bear to the total development and production budget for the Program. (For example, if the aggregate of the milestone payments made to Provider amounts to Fifty Percent (50%) to the total budget for the development and production of the Program, then provider will receive Fifty Percent (50%) of the royalties otherwise payable to Provider pursuant to Paragraph 17 below).

(iii) Neither party shall be liable to the other for any incidental damages, consequential damages or lost profits resulting from any abandonment, postponement or discontinuance of the Program as provided hereunder, and any right to recover such incidental or consequential damages or lost profits is hereby expressly waived by both PMI and Provider.

(iv) Upon any abandonment, postponement, or discontinuance hereunder, PMI may require Provider to return any assets created by Provider hereunder to PMI, and if PMI so requires, Provider will immediately comply.

(h) Equipment: Any equipment furnished by PMI to Provider in connection with the Production of the Program shall at all times remain the sole and exclusive property of PMI and shall be returned to PMI upon PMI's demand.

4. Progress Reports; Delivery; Completion of the Program:

(a) (i) Provider shall on a monthly basis provide PMI with progress reports on the production effort hereunder, advise PMI of the cumulative costs incurred to that date and advise PMI of any anticipated requests for modifications to the Approved Budget.

(ii) Within ninety (90) days following delivery of the Master Materials for the Program, Provider shall submit to PMI a full, complete, detailed and itemized written statement of all expenditures incurred or made by Provider constituting the Production Costs of the Program hereunder in accordance with the Production Budget Format. Such statement shall be certified as true and accurate by an officer of Provider. PMI shall in no event have any responsibility of any sort for any other costs that may thereafter be alleged to constitute Production Costs hereunder. The final Production Costs shown on such statement, along with the costs incurred by PMI and so certified, shall be used by the parties in determining the Production Costs to be recouped in calculating royalties payable hereunder to Provider.

(b) Provider shall, on or before the Completion Date, deliver to PMI each of the Master Materials. Delivery to PMI shall not be deemed made unless and until each of the Master Materials have been delivered to PMI. Provider shall, at all times, maintain duplicate or safety "back-up" copies of all Master Materials produced from time to time at a venue sufficiently separate from Provider's primary place of business. After proper delivery hereunder Provider shall continue to store a duplicate of all Master Materials so delivered until advised by PMI that duplicates of such Master Materials have been made by or for PMI's benefit.

(c) Provider hereby agrees to the completion of production and delivery of the Program (hereinafter "Completion of the Program") on or before the Completion Date (subject to "Force Majeure" as specified in paragraph 8 below) in accordance with the Approved Budget and the Approved Schedule hereunder, time being of the essence. Provider may perform Provider's obligations with respect to the Approved Budget, at Provider's option, either (i) by assuming all costs in excess of the Approved Budget required to meet the costs of Completion of the Program, or (ii) by abandoning production of the Program and refunding to PMI within five (5) days of such abandonment all Production Cost Advances previously advanced, less the value of materials delivered by Provider to PMI in connection with the Program (such value to be based on Production Costs which PMI reasonably anticipates that PMI will save by using such materials in completing the Program), together with interest thereon at the Reference Rate from the date of such advance to the date of repayment of such advance, and (iii) turning over to PMI, if PMI so desires, all items necessary to complete production of the Program.

5. Accounting Records Relating to Production of Program:

(a) Provider shall keep or cause to be kept at Provider's principal place of business full and proper books of accounts, records, and contracts, together with vouchers and receipts representing production charges for the Project, which books shall be kept in accordance with generally accepted monthly accounting principles.

(b) PMI shall have the right, during reasonable business hours, until the expiration of twenty-four (24) months from delivery of the Master Materials hereunder, at PMI's expense, to examine and take excerpts from the accounts, vouchers, receipts, records and contracts maintained by Provider for the purpose of inquiring into any records or transactions relating to credits or charges, at the place where Provider maintains such books and records. In addition, all such accounts, records, contracts, vouchers and receipts shall be kept by Provider for a time period of not less than three (3) years, and PMI and all appropriate tax authorities, with PMI's consent, shall have access to such documents during such time period.

6. Confidentiality of Information: PMI and Provider shall treat all proprietary data and other information received by one from the other relating to laser optical hardware systems, software for such systems and procedures for developing such systems and software (collectively "Information") as confidential and proprietary to such other party. Moreover, neither party shall duplicate or use any Information received from the other hereunder for any purpose other than for the Project. In addition, neither party shall disclose any Information to any party that is not specifically authorized by the other party to receive it and who has not agreed to the same obligations specified in this paragraph 6. Each party, respectively, further agrees that it will disclose the Information only on a need-to-know basis to persons known to it to be under the same obligations as set forth herein with respect to that Information. After Provider has delivered the Master Materials to PMI, Provider shall return to PMI all tangible Information provided to Provider by PMI in connection with the Project, and PMI shall return to Provider all tangible Information provided to PMI by Provider in connection with the Project.

7. Insurance:

(a) Provider shall, before the commencement of development of any Program and until delivery to PMI of the Master Materials hereunder, insure the Program against fire, theft, vandalism or other malicious mischief and other insurable risks generally covered by an extended coverage casualty policy. The cost of such insurance shall be paid by Provider, subject to reimbursement to the extent of the sum included in respect thereof in the Approved Budget.

(b) Provider shall obtain and maintain all required worker's compensation insurance, meeting the laws of the various states or countries in which Provider may have employees furnishing services with regard to the Project, for the benefit of all employees directly engaged by Provider, as well as public liability and property damage insurance relative to the acts or omissions of such employees and the condition of the premises and facilities maintained by Provider. None of the premium costs (or deductibles) of such insurance policies shall be included in the Production Costs of the Program. Provider shall indemnify, defend and hold PMI harmless from and against any and all damages, claims, actions, obligations, liabilities and expenses which may be asserted by or on behalf of any person engaged directly by Provider in connection with the Project by reason of injury or death arising out of and in the course of his/her employment, or by or on behalf of any person by reason of accident, injury, death, or property damage resulting from any negligence or fault of Provider or which is in any way connected with the preproduction or production of the Program.

(c) Provider shall obtain producer's errors and omission insurance against third party claims, including claims for damages for infringement of copyrights or other literary property rights, libel, slander, or any other forms of defamation, invasion of rights of privacy, unauthorized use of names, plagiarism, and similar matters. Said insurance shall be in the amount specified by PMI up to Five Million Dollars ($5,000,000.00) for any claim arising out of a single occurrence and Five Million Dollars ($5,000,000.00) for all claims in the aggregate, and shall have no exclusions and no deductible greater than Ten Thousand Dollars ($10,000.00). Provider shall provide PMI an insurance certificate within 15 days of PMI's election to proceed with production of the Program that demonstrates the necessary coverage as required above and confirms PMI as an additional insured. The premium cost of such insurance shall be charged as a Production Cost of the Program. Provider shall comply with the requirements of such insurance regarding the giving of notices and cooperating with the carrier in the defense of claims under the policy, and Provider shall maintain such insurance policy for the period ending at least five (5) years after the delivery of the Master Materials.

(d) All insurance obtained by Provider or PMI hereunder shall be for the benefit of PMI and Provider as their respective interests may appear. All policies, endorsements, and certificates relating to any insurance obtained pursuant to this Paragraph 7, shall provide for losses to be adjusted with and (with the exception of Worker's Compensation) be payable to PMI.

8. Force Majeure: Provider shall not be deemed in default hereunder and shall not be liable to PMI if and to the extent Provider is unable to commence or complete production of the Program at the times herein required by reason of fire, earthquake, flood, hurricanes, tornados (but not including any other weather conditions), epidemic, accident, explosion, casualty, strike, lockout, labor controversy, riot, civil disturbance, act of public enemy, embargo, war, act of God, any municipal, county, state or national ordinance or law, any executive or judicial order enacted or in effect, any failure of any electrical equipment of any laboratory or production facility or any failure beyond Provider's control to obtain material or power, or any other essential thing required to produce the Program or similar causes beyond Provider's control and without fault of Provider. The Completion Date may, at Provider's option, be postponed for a period equal to the period the production of the Program is prevented or delayed by reason of the occurrence of any event referred to in the foregoing sentence. If completion of production of the Program is prevented or delayed for a period of ninety (90) days or more by reason of any events referred to hereinabove, PMI may, at PMI's option, at any time thereafter, terminate any or all of PMI's obligations hereunder with respect to furnishing or causing to be furnished Production Cost Advances.

9. Defaults and Termination:

(a) Each of the following events shall constitute an "event of default" for the purposes hereof:

(i) If Provider (or any affiliated person or entity) materially breaches or defaults under any provision of this Agreement; and/or

(ii) If the Program or any of the Master Materials relating thereto is attached or levied upon by a creditor or claimant of Provider or an affiliated person or entity of Provider, and such attachment or levy is not released within five (5) days after such levy; and/or

(iii) If any representation or warranty made by Provider in this Agreement is false or misleading; and/or

(iv) If Provider fails or refuses to implement any change to any deliverable (including, without limitation, the Production Elements) that is necessary to obtain PMI's approval under Paragraph 3(e) when Provider is instructed by PMI to so implement.

(b) If any event of default shall occur, PMI may (but shall not be obligated to):

(i) Suspend, or require any other party to suspend, any or all of its obligations with respect to the furnishing of Production Cost Advances; and/or

(ii) Take over production of the Program; and/or

(iii) Terminate any or all of PMI's obligations hereunder including, but not limited to, the furnishing of Production Cost Advances; and/or

(iv) Offset against any sums which may be or become due Provider and/or any affiliated person or entity, under this Agreement or any other agreement; and/or

(v) Exercise any other available right or remedy; and/or

(vi) Enter upon any premises where the physical elements of the Program may be and take possession thereof; demand and receive possession from anyone who has possession thereof; remove, keep, and store the Program, Master Materials or any portion thereof, or put a custodian in charge thereof; and take such other measures as PMI may deem appropriate for the protection thereof including, but not limited to, the right to complete the Program and to cause it to be delivered for distribution.

(c) All costs incurred by PMI in proceeding under this Paragraph 9 (including, without limitation, reasonable attorneys' fees) shall be added to any sums due PMI by Provider.

(d) All of PMI's rights and remedies are cumulative and the exercise of one shall not limit of affect PMI's right concurrently or subsequently to exercise any other right or remedy.

(e) If PMI breaches this Agreement, Provider's rights and remedies shall be limited to Provider's rights, if any, to recover damages in an action at law, and Provider shall not be entitled to terminate, revoke, or rescind this Agreement or any of the rights granted to PMI, or to enjoin or restrain PMI or PMI's licensees from exercising any of the rights granted to PMI.

(f) If this Agreement is terminated, or production of the Program is abandoned for Provider's default, or if PMI takes over production because of Provider's default, PMI shall be released and discharged from any liability whatsoever to Provider hereunder with respect to such Program, including but not limited to the payment of royalties as set forth in Paragraph 17 in the event PMI releases and distributes the Program.

[If Provider will not agree to losing royalties in the event of their default, add:

, and if PMI actually produces and distributes the Program using assets created by Provider hereunder, then Provider's royalties for the Program as set forth in Paragraph 17 hereof shall vest in the same proportion that PMI uses assets created by Provider hereunder bear to the total assets actually used in the completed Program.

(g) With respect to any breach by PMI, Provider may not exercise any remedy other than suspension of Provider's performance unless PMI fails to fully cure the breach within thirty (30) days after Provider gives written notice thereof.

(h) Neither party shall be liable to the other for any incidental damages, consequential damages or lost profits resulting from a breach or default, and any right to recover incidental damages, lost profits or consequential damages is hereby expressly waived by both PMI and Provider.

10. <u>Right of Termination:</u> If PMI exercises a right of termination of this Agreement pursuant to paragraph 9 hereinabove before the completion of the Production Term, then all funds advanced by PMI to Provider in connection with the production of the Program (*i.e.*, any sums paid to Provider prior to the date they are due under the milestone schedule, but not any funds paid when due hereunder) shall be immediately repayable by Provider to PMI, except as otherwise provided hereunder.

11. <u>Exclusive Rights in Physical Materials:</u> As between Distributor and Provider and subject to this Agreement, Distributor shall have full rights to use, possess and enjoy all pre-mastering and Master Materials utilized in creating the Program.

12. <u>Publicity Rights:</u> Provider hereby grants to PMI for and during the Rights Period and throughout the Territory for the purpose of advertising, publicizing, and/or promoting the Program, the right to use and otherwise exploit the names, photographs, likenesses, voices and other sound effects of Provider and all

persons appearing in the Source Materials or providing creative services in connection with the production of the Source Materials.

13.. <u>Advertising and Promotional Rights:</u> Distributor shall have the right to perform, display, and/or exhibit excerpts of the Source Materials or the Program (or the Program in its entirety if for non-revenue generating purposes) in all media now known or hereafter developed, including, but not limited to, radio, television, cable, videodisc, videocassette, audio disc, satellite telephony, whether by living actors, electrical transcriptions, film, tape, disc, cassette or otherwise in any language in the Territory for the purpose of advertising, publicizing and/or promoting the Program or the system on which the Program may be exhibited.

14. <u>Credits:</u> On each Disc or unit of the Program, PMI's "bumper" (*i.e.*, animated logo presentation sequence) and the following credits shall appear in the main titles or opening credits and the packaging of each Disc or unit of the Program: "Produced by _____ in Association with Philips Media, Inc." and "Distributed by Philips Media, Inc." The packaging of each Disc or unit of the Program may contain additional or substitute distribution credits as determined by PMI. The precise form of the credit, the size and placement thereof and all other matters relating to credit shall be determined by PMI in PMI's discretion Upon Provider's request, PMI will consult with Provider regarding credits accorded in connection with the Program and will give good faith consideration to Provider's reasonable requests. No casual or inadvertent failure by PMI or any failure by any third party to accord credit in compliance with the credit provisions hereunder shall constitute a breach of this Agreement.

15. <u>Grant of Rights; Copyright Ownership, Protection and Enforcement:</u>

(a) Provider acknowledges that as between PMI and Provider, PMI shall own all right, title and interest in and to: (i) the Program, and the Discs, including the copyright therein throughout the universe; and (ii) all tools, utilities, design processes, software systems, source and object codes, program logic, interactive program structures, retrieval software systems, user interface designs and other procedures and methods of operation which are utilized in connection with the Program, including, without limitation, the copyrights therein throughout the world. Provider hereby grants to PMI a non-exclusive, perpetual license throughout the Territory to any and all components, routines, sub-routines, mathematical techniques, programs, modules and effects currently owned by Provider and used in the development and production of the Development Delivery Items described herein.

(b) PMI and Provider agree that the results and proceeds of Provider's services and Provider's employees' and independent contractors' services in connection with the Program (including, without limitation, any copyrights) under this Agreement shall be a "work-made-for-hire" for PMI. Provider further agrees that all the results and proceeds of Provider's services and Provider's employees' and independent contractors' services, whether solely or in collaboration with others, whether or not same is made at the request or suggestion of PMI, or during or outside regular hours of work, shall at all times be and remain the sole and exclusive property of PMI, and PMI shall own all rights in such results and proceeds, exploitable by PMI in any and all media whether now known or hereafter developed throughout the Territory in perpetuity. In the event that it is ever determined pursuant to the U.S. Copyright Act or otherwise that such results and proceeds are not a "work-made-for-hire" by Provider for PMI, Provider hereby irrevocably grants and assigns exclusively to PMI without any reservations of any kind any and all rights whatsoever in and to all results and proceeds of Provider's services hereunder (including without limitation, the Program, Discs, Source Materials, Master Materials and all delivery items hereunder) including the copyright therein throughout the universe in perpetuity exploitable by PMI through any and all means whether now known or hereafter developed. Provider shall cause all of Provider's employee's and independent contractors who render services in connection with the Program to execute written "work-made-for-hire" agreements in a form satisfactory to PMI and shall deliver copies of such agreements to PMI together with the Master Materials. Provider waives and relinquishes any claim of "droit moral" or moral rights that Provider may have in connection with Provider's services hereunder or, if it is ever deemed that such rights may not be waived or relinquished, said rights are hereby granted and assigned exclusively and irrevocably to PMI.

(c) PMI shall cause the due and timely registration of copyright throughout the Territory of the Program. As between PMI and Provider, copyright registration of the Program and notices on each unit of Disc or Program shall be in PMI's name unless such registration and/or notices are customarily done in the name of the individual distributor or licensee in such territory. Distributor and PMI agree to take all reasonable action to instruct third party licensees, subdistributors and others authorized to exploit the Program to comply with all copyright notice and registration requirements and further agree to refrain from taking any action and from authorizing others to take action, which would cause or allow the Program to become part of the public domain in the United States or in any other country of the world adhering to either or both the Berne Convention or the Universal Copyright Convention, provided that PMI shall have no liability arising from any inadvertent failure to take such action.

(d) Distributor shall have full and complete authority, either in the name of PMI and Provider or otherwise as Distributor deems appropriate, to take such steps (including but not limited to the placement on the Program and/or the packaging thereof a warning that piracy of the Program is prohibited under local law) as Distributor (or Distributor's licensee) deems appropriate by action at law, or otherwise, to prevent unauthorized replication, manufacture and/or distribution of the Program in the Territory or any infringement upon the rights of PMI or Provider in the Program; and Distributor or Distributor's nominee may, as PMI's and Provider's attorney-in-fact, execute, acknowledge, verify and deliver all pleadings and/or instruments pertaining thereto in the name of and on behalf of PMI and Provider as Distributor deems appropriate. Distributor may (but shall not be obligated to) take such steps as Distributor shall deem appropriate, by action at law, or otherwise, to recover monies due with respect to the distribution or exhibition of the Discs or Program. Any and all recoveries from any such action shall be applied first to recover all expenses incurred in such action and the balance (after paying to the licensee for such territory such amount as Distributor is contractually obligated to pay such licensee) shall be divided equally between PMI and Provider.

16. Sales Policies:

(a) Distributor may exploit and distribute the Discs or Program and exercise any and all rights herein granted, in accordance with such sales or rental methods, policies, practices and terms as it may determine in its sole discretion. Distributor may adjust and increase or decrease any allowances to any published prices; allow reasonable "free goods" whether on a regular or special promotion basis; permit reasonable returns for any reason; license the distribution of the Discs or Program for a particular country (other than the United States, Canada, Great Britain, France, Germany, Spain, Italy, Japan or Australia) on a flat sum basis; license the distribution of the Discs or Program upon a percentage of receipts, royalty, or flat amount per unit; bundle, sell or license the Discs or Program together with other discs or separately, as it shall deem desirable; and refrain from distribution in any place at any time, as Distributor, in Distributor discretion, may elect. Distributor shall be obligated to deal with related persons and entities on a good faith, arm's-length basis.

(b) Distributor has not made any express or implied representation, warranty, or agreement as to the amount of royalties or receipts which shall be derived from the distribution of the Discs or Program, nor has Distributor made any express or implied representation, warranty or agreement that there will be any royalties or other sums payable to Provider, or that the Discs or Program will be favorably received by retailers or the public. Neither party shall incur any liability hereunder based upon any claim that either party has failed to realize revenues or to effectuate sales which should have been realized.

(c) Provider acknowledges that PMI may distribute other programs or discs in competition with the Discs or Program and shall be under no duty to avoid competing products, or to expend the same promotional efforts for and on behalf of the Discs or Program as Distributor's expends for other discs or programs, irrespective of the similarity of potential market. Whenever a licensee pays for the right to manufacture and distribute a number of discs, including the Discs or Program, under an agreement which does not specify what portion of the license payments apply to each of the respective discs in the group, Distributor may, in good faith, allocate to the Discs or Program for the purpose hereof, such portion of such total license payment as Distributor may in good faith consider proper. PMI has no obligation to actually produce or release the Program or to actually use any of the Source Materials in connection therewith.

17. Royalties:

(a) In full consideration of all services rendered and expenses incurred by Provider hereunder and all rights granted to PMI by Provider hereunder, and conditioned upon Provider's full performance of Provider's material obligations, and provided Provider is not in material breach or default of this Agreement, PMI agrees to pay Provider the following royalties in connection with the marketing and distribution of Discs or Program:

(i) PMI shall pay to Provider a royalty of _____ Percent (%) of PMI's Net Receipts (as hereinafter defined) derived and actually received by PMI from exploitation of the Program in the United States until Recoupment (as hereinafter defined) ("U.S. Royalty"). Following recoupment, on a prospective basis only, the U.S. Royalty shall be increased to _____ Percent (%) of Net Receipts.

(ii) The foreign royalty payable to Provider for exploitation of the Program outside the United States shall be equal to the Net Receipts derived and actually received by PMI from exploitation in the applicable country of the Territory outside the United States multiplied by one-half (½) of the applicable U.S. Royalty provided in sub-paragraph 17(a)(i) above.

(iii) PMI shall have the right hereunder to sell each Disc "bundled" with the sale of Philips or other hardware manufacturer's players. If PMI negotiates an agreement to "bundle" the Discs or Program with players, Provider and PMI shall be entitled to a royalty equal to one-third (1/3) of the otherwise applicable royalty.

(iv) (intentionally deleted).

(v) Provider hereby agrees that Provider shall be solely responsible for all accountings and payments to any and all third party royalty participants with whom Provider has contracted and who are entitled to compensation based on exploitation of the Program out of Provider's share of royalties hereunder.

(vi) Notwithstanding any of the foregoing, in the event of Scrap, Budget, or Mid-Priced sales of Discs hereunder, the applicable percentage royalty rate as defined in Paragraph 17(a) hereof shall be modified as follows:

	Reduction in Paragraph 17(a) Rate
Scrap Sales	100%
Budget Sales	50%
Mid-Price Sales	25%

Scrap or Budget sales will only be made in order to liquidate existing inventory or in the event that continuing sales of the Discs are less than 100 units per month.

For purposes of the foregoing table, "Scrap Sales" shall mean Discs furnished free to users or sold as scrap or "cut-outs" at prices equal to or less than 33.3% of the Wholesale Price (as hereinafter defined), and on Discs furnished on a so-called "no charge" basis to distributors, subdistributors, dealers or others; "Budget Sales" shall mean the sale or license of Discs at prices equal to or less than 50% (but more than 33.3%) of the Wholesale Price; and "Mid-Price Sales" shall mean the sale or license of Discs at prices equal or less than 66.6% (but more than 50%) of the Wholesale Price.

(b) As used herein, Net Receipts shall mean the gross receipts actually received by PMI from all sales and licenses of the Program less the following amounts:

(i) Taxes on sale or license, including but not limited to sales, use, excise or other taxes;

(ii) Sales commissions payable;

(iii) Amounts reimbursed to customers for expenses actually incurred, including but not limited to insurance, shipping and similar charges;

(iv) Promotional amounts, including but not limited to credits, cash discounts, freight discounts, rebates or promotional allowances to customers, copies supplied for promotional purposes to the press, trade, sales representatives, employees, or potential customers;

(v) Amounts for scrap or replacement of defectives;

(vi) Amounts for returns, such as credits, refunds or allowances; and

(vii) Currency exchange fees incurred by PMI with respect to receipts other than in United States Dollars.

(c) The term "Wholesale Price" as used herein shall mean the published price to dealer (net of "free goods") for the Program sold or otherwise distributed.

(d) The term "Recoupment" as used herein shall mean the point at which PMI has recouped one hundred thirty percent (130%) of PMI's development and production costs including all packaging, mastering and product testing costs) incurred in connection with the Program hereunder out of the following revenues:

(A) Thirty Percent (30%) of the U.S. Net Receipts with respect to each unit of the Program sold by PMI and/or PMI's designee, paid for and not returned in the United States, plus

(B) Eighty Percent (80%) of the Net Receipts with respect to each unit of the Program sold by PMI and/or PMI's designee, paid for and not returned outside of the United States; less

(C) All amounts payable as pre-Recoupment royalties to Provider and/or any third parties in connection with the Program.

18.   Royalty Statements: Within sixty (60) days after the end of each calendar quarter, subject to delay on account of events or circumstances beyond PMI's control, PMI shall send Provider statements showing, in summary form, (i) the net number of the units of the Program reported to PMI during the period as having been sold (whether or not actually sold during that accounting period), and (ii) the royalties, if any, due with respect to such units of the Program for the accounting period covered by such statement. All statements may be submitted on a billings or collections basis as PMI may from time to time elect, and if such statements are changed from one basis to another, such statements may thereafter be amended to reflect adjustments by reason thereof. In the event the statements are submitted on a billings basis, PMI may either establish reasonable reserves (as established by Distributor) for unpaid units, or charges against sales and bad debts as they are recognized. Should PMI make any overpayment for any reason, PMI shall have the right to deduct and retain an amount equal to any such overpayment from any sums that may thereafter become due or payable to Provider or for Provider's account, and/or may demand repayment from Provider, in which event Provider agrees to repay the same when such demand is made. No royalties shall be payable on employee sales. Any amounts payable to Provider pursuant to any such statement shall be payable simultaneously with the rendering of such statement, subject to any provision in this Agreement relieving PMI from such obligation; provided, however, that all amounts payable to Provider hereunder shall be subject to all laws and regulations now or hereafter in existence requiring or permitting the deduction or withholding of payment for taxes or other amounts payable by, or assessable against, Provider. Provider shall make and prosecute any and all claims which it may have with respect to the same directly with the governmental agency having jurisdiction in the premises. Notwithstanding any sub-license or distribution arrangement, Provider will look solely to PMI to perform all obligations undertaken by PMI or its designee pursuant to this Agreement, including the payment of all royalties. At PMI's election, however, PMI may cause a third party to perform its obligation to account to Provider as provided in paragraphs 18, 19 and 20 hereof.

19.   Accounting Records and Audit Rights Relating to Distribution of Discs or Program: PMI shall keep reasonably adequate books of account relating to the distribution of the Discs or Program. With twenty (20) days written notice to PMI, Provider may, at Provider's own expense, audit the applicable records at

the place where PMI maintains the same in order to verify royalty statements hereunder. Any such audit shall be conducted only by a certified public accountant during business hours and in such manner as not to interfere with PMI's normal business activities. A copy of all reports made by Provider's accountant pursuant to any such audit shall be delivered to PMI at the same time such reports are delivered to Provider. No audit with respect of any royalty statements shall commence later than twelve (12) months from the date of the royalty statement on which the audited matter is initially reflected; nor shall any audit continue for longer than such time reasonably necessary to complete it; nor shall audits be made hereunder more frequently than once in any year; nor shall the records supporting any royalty statement be audited more than once. Provider shall be forever barred from maintaining or instituting any action or proceeding in any way relating to any transactions had by Distributor in connection with the Discs or Program and the accounting embraced in any statement or account delivered hereunder, and such statements and accounts shall be final and binding on Provider, unless written objection thereto is given to PMI within said twelve (12) month period and such action or proceeding is commenced within twenty-four (24) months after the date of the subject statement. The right to examine books of account and other documents herein granted to Provider may only be exercised by Provider with respect to the Discs or Program, and Provider shall have no right to inspect or examine the books of account or any other documents with respect to any other discs distributed by PMI.

20.   Foreign Currency: Foreign receipts shall be converted to United States Dollars at the same rate at which such funds were actually converted into and received by PMI in the United States in U.S. dollars. Provider's pro rata portion of foreign currency conversion and transmission charges will be deducted from the royalty otherwise payable.

21.   Supplemental Documents; Power of Attorney: Provider will execute, acknowledge and deliver such instruments as PMI may request to evidence, maintain, effectuate, or defend any and all of the rights granted to PMI under this Agreement. If Provider shall fail to execute, acknowledge or deliver to PMI any such instrument, PMI is irrevocably appointed Provider's attorney-in-fact, with full right and authority to execute, acknowledge and deliver the same in the name and on behalf of Provider. Provider agrees that such authority and agency is a power coupled with a pecuniary interest and shall survive the dissolution or other cessation of existence of Provider.

22.   Representations and Warranties: (a) PMI and Provider each represent and warrant that it is duly organized, validly existing and in good standing under the laws of its state of incorporation and is qualified to do business in any state or country where such qualification is necessary; that it has full right, power,

and authority to enter into and perform this Agreement, and to grant all of the rights granted and agreed to be granted pursuant hereto; that it has taken all necessary action to authorize the execution and performance of this Agreement; and that the same does not and will not violate or require any consent under any provision of its charter documents, or of any agreement or instrument to which it is a party or by which a material part of its assets are bound, nor will such execution or performance violate any judgment or decree by which it is bound.

(b) Provider further represents and warrants to PMI as follows:

(i) That Provider has not sold, assigned, transferred or conveyed and will not sell, assign, transfer or convey to any person, firm, corporation or other entity, any right, title or interest in or to the Source Materials, the Program, the Discs or any part thereof, any of the rights licensed and granted to PMI hereunder or any right or interest which is inconsistent with the rights granted to PMI or that Provider has reserved such rights;

(ii) That Provider shall, on or before the Completion Date have paid or made adequate provision for payment of all known bills and other sums payable or due as a result of the production of the Program including, without limitation, all contributions made to any collective bargaining unit, or health or welfare fund administered by any such entity, except to the extent that Provider is contesting such obligation in good faith and no lien or security interest has attached or will attach to the Program or the Discs as a consequence of non-payment, nor will PMI be deemed to have assumed any legal responsibility for payment of such sums by PMI's exercise of the rights granted hereunder;

(iii) That Provider owns all necessary rights, including, without limitation, all such rights in all applicable copyrights, trademarks, trade names, titles and similar rights, in and to any assets furnished by Provider so that Provider is able to grant PMI all of the rights granted under this Agreement, without payment of any additional sums therefor by Provider or PMI;

(iv) That there are and shall be no claims, demands, liens, encumbrances or rights of any kind in the materials furnished by Provider, including, but not limited to the Program, the Discs or any part thereof, or the copyright therein resulting from any act or omission caused by Provider, which can or will impair or interfere with the rights of PMI and that nothing contained in the Source Materials furnished by Provider nor any use thereof by PMI permitted hereunder will violate any right of any third party;

(v) That Provider owns all necessary rights in all music and lyrics used in the Program and furnished by Provider, including, without limitation, not less than a good and valid synchronization license in customary form issued by the copyright proprietor of such music and/or lyrics, or his/her agent or trustee, in each case together with the nonexclusive, irrevocable right to publicly perform such music and lyrics in the advertising, display or promotion of the Program or the Discs and the right to make and sell copies of the Program or the Discs in the United States without payment of any additional sums by Provider or Distributor and the right to perform publicly such music and lyrics outside the United States, subject only to clearance by applicable performing rights societies in accordance with their customary practices and payment of their customary fees and the right to produce and sell copies of the Program or the Discs without payment of any additional sums by Provider or Distributor;

(vi) That Provider owns all necessary rights in (or licenses to) all previously trademarked characters, logos, captions or slogans that are furnished by Provider, used in or appearing on the Program and/or the Discs or its packaging, without payment of any additional sums therefor by Provider or PMI; and

(vii) That neither the Master Materials or the Program, nor the Master Materials' or Program's use in any form, adaptation, or version allowed under this Agreement, nor the exercise of any of the rights herein granted or conveyed, will in any way infringe upon any copyright, literary, dramatic, photoplay or common law right(s) of any person, firm or corporation whatsoever, or constitute a libel or defamation of, or invasion of any rights (including, without limitation the right of privacy or publicity) of any party.

23. Indemnity: Each party shall indemnify, defend and hold harmless the other party from and against any and all loss, cost, damage, liability, expense, claim, demand, suit or action (including reasonable attorneys' fees) (collectively "Claims") arising in connection with any breach by either party of its warranties, representations or agreements made hereunder whether a final determination as to such breach is rendered by a fact-finder (including by way of example, a judge or arbitrator) or by the parties hereto as part of a settlement. If any claim, suit, action or demand shall be asserted, made or brought against the indemnitee alleging facts which, if true, would constitute a breach by the indemnitor hereunder, or involving any matter connected with the Program caused by or under the control of the indemnitor, the indemnitor shall, at its expense, cause counsel reasonably satisfactory to the indemnitee to defend such claim or action. If PMI is the indemnitee, PMI shall have the right at its election to withhold payment of any monies otherwise payable to Provider in an amount reasonably related to the claim and potential liability, provided that PMI shall not withhold such monies, if and to the extent that Provider provides PMI with a surety bond issued by a company and in a form satisfactory to PMI. Any amount withheld shall be released if a proceeding with respect to the subject claim is not commenced within eighteen (18) months following the commencement of the applicable withholding. The foregoing does not limit PMI's right to recommence

withholding at any time if a proceeding is subsequently commenced. No settlement of any such action shall be made by the indemnitor without the indemnitee's express approval. The foregoing indemnification shall not diminish rights set forth elsewhere in this Agreement relative to a default or breach.

24. <u>Notices:</u>

(a) All notices and accounting statements delivered hereunder shall be given in writing and sent to the other party at the addresses specified below:

TO PROVIDER:	TO PMI:
_____	Philips Media, Inc.
_____	10960 Wilshire Boulevard, 7th floor
_____	Los Angeles, CA 90024
Attn: _____	Attn: Vice President, Business Affairs

(b) Any notice to be served hereunder shall be deemed to have been served in the case of delivery on the day of delivery; in the case of service by certified mail within ten (10) working days from the day it was posted; and in the case of a telex or facsimile transmission on the date of transmission of the notice. Any notice given in any other manner shall be effective only when actually received.

25. <u>Assignment:</u> Neither party hereto shall assign or otherwise transfer all or any of its rights hereunder without the consent of the other party, except that PMI shall have the right to assign or otherwise transfer all or any of PMI's rights hereunder to any parent, affiliate, subsidiary or successor to substantially all of its capital stock or business assets, or company into which PMI merges, all without the consent of Provider. Provider shall not have the right to and shall not sell, assign, transfer or hypothecate (collectively "assign") all or any part of Provider's right to receive royalties, at any time, while Provider is indebted to PMI or while any advances hereunder including, without limitation, Production Cost Advances, have not as of yet been recouped by PMI pursuant to the terms of this Agreement. In all events, any assignment shall be subject to all of PMI's rights hereunder. No assignment shall relieve Provider of any obligation to PMI pursuant to this Agreement. PMI's obligation to pay royalties to an assignee in accordance with any such assignment shall be further conditioned upon receipt of written notice of irrevocable authority in form satisfactory to PMI and executed by Provider. PMI's payment in accordance with any such assignment shall be deemed to be the equivalent of payment to Provider hereunder. Subject to the foregoing, this Agreement shall be binding upon and inure to the benefit of the parties hereto and their respective legal successors and assigns.

26. <u>Arbitration:</u> With respect to any dispute or disagreement between the parties arising out of or in connection with this Agreement, the parties shall make a good faith effort to resolve that dispute by discussions between them. If they

are unable to resolve that dispute or disagreement within forty-five (45) calendar days after one party has given the other notice of such dispute or disagreement, then the dispute or disagreement may, upon written demand of either party, be settled by binding arbitration pursuant to the Rules of the Southern California Chapter of the American Arbitration Association. Arbitration shall take place in Los Angeles County, California and both parties consent to the *in personam* jurisdiction of the federal and state courts of such County. An award of arbitration may be entered as a judgment in any court having jurisdiction in the matter, or application may be made to such a court for acceptance of the award and for an order of enforcement as the case may require. Each party shall bear its own costs and expenses of the arbitration and one-half (½) of the arbitrator's fees and costs, subject to such a different award as the arbitrator may make.

27. <u>Miscellaneous</u>: Nothing contained herein shall constitute a partnership between or joint venture by the parties or constitute either party the agent of the other. Neither party shall hold itself out contrary to the terms hereof and neither party shall become liable by any representation, act or omission of the other contrary to the provisions hereof. This Agreement is not entered into for the benefit of any third party and shall not be deemed to give any right or remedy to any such party whether or not referred to herein. No waiver by either party hereto of any breach of this Agreement shall be deemed to be a waiver of any preceding or succeeding breach of the same or any other provision hereof. The exercise of any right granted to either party hereunder shall not operate as a waiver. No remedy or election hereunder shall be deemed exclusive but shall, wherever possible, be cumulative with all other remedies at law or in equity. This Agreement shall be construed and interpreted pursuant to the laws of the State of California applicable to agreements entered into and fully performed in California. If any provision hereof is deemed to be unenforceable as written the provision shall be modified so as to make the provision in its general interest enforceable and as so modified shall form part of this Agreement. Nothing contained herein shall be construed so as to require the commission of any act contrary to law, and wherever there is any conflict between any provision of this Agreement and any material statute, law or ordinance the latter shall prevail, but in such event the provision of this Agreement affected shall be curtailed and limited only to the extent necessary to bring the provision within the legal requirements. This Agreement is the product of negotiation at arm's length between parties knowledgeable concerning its subject matter who have had the opportunity to consult with counsel concerning this Agreement and each of its terms prior to the execution thereof. It is therefore agreed that this Agreement shall be considered jointly drafted by the parties hereto and that any rule of law that would require interpretation of any term in this Agreement against the party responsible for its inclusion herein, including, without limitation, California Civil Code Section 1654, or its equivalent, shall have no effect on the interpretation

of this Agreement. This Agreement and the schedules, exhibits and attachments hereto constitute the entire Agreement and supersedes and cancels all prior negotiations, undertakings and agreements, both oral and written, between the parties with respect to the subject matter hereof and shall be binding only when executed by both parties hereto. The parties acknowledge that no officer, employee or representative of either party has any authority to make any representation or promise not contained in this Agreement and neither party has executed this Agreement in reliance on any representation or promise not contained herein. No waiver, modification or cancellation of any term or condition of this Agreement shall be effective unless executed in writing by an authorized representative of the party charged therewith. If this Agreement is executed in counterparts, such counterparts shall constitute one and the same instrument.

IN WITNESS WHEREOF, the parties hereto have executed this Agreement by their respective officers, thereunto duly authorized, as of the day and year first above written.

_____
("Provider")
By:_____
Its:_____
PHILIPS MEDIA, INC.
("PMI")
By:_____
Its:_____

EXHIBIT "A"

PRODUCTION AND DELIVERY SCHEDULE

1. _____ Dollars ($ ____) of PMI's Production Cost Advance Commitment, upon Provider's delivery to and written approval by PMI of the Approved Budget and Approved Schedule for the Program hereunder.

2. _____ Dollars ($ ____) of PMI's Production Cost Advance Commitment, upon Provider's delivery to and written approval by PMI of the written production script and interactive design specifications for the Program;

3. _____ Dollars ($ ____) of PMI's Production Cost Advance Commitment, upon Provider's delivery to and design review and written approval by PMI of an implementation of proposed production procedures, techniques and methods for a representative example of program display for the Program ("Production Testing Results Phase"). During the Production Testing Results Phase, PMI shall make a final determination with respect to (a) the Completion Date, which shall be no later than _____, 199_ and (b) the

production procedures and methods to be implemented in the production of the Program. (During the Production Testing Results Phase, the Completion Date and production procedures and methods shall be specified on _____.)

4. _____ Dollars ($ _____) of PMI's Production Cost Advance Commitment, upon Provider's delivery to and design review and written approval by PMI of the final art work and graphic design for the Program;

5. _____ Dollars ($ _____) of PMI's Production Cost Advance Commitment, upon Provider's delivery to and written approval by PMI of the final audio test including, without limitation, all final music, narration and sound effects of the Program;

6. _____ Dollars ($ _____) of PMI's Production Cost Advance Commitment, upon Provider's delivery to and written approval by PMI of the Alpha tape of the Program;

7. _____ Dollars ($ _____) of PMI's Production Cost Advance Commitment, upon Provider's delivery to and written approval by PMI of the Beta tape of the Program, all assets necessary for the packaging of the Program and all items set forth in paragraph 4 of the Master Materials set forth in Exhibit "B"; and

8. The remaining _____ Dollars ($ _____) of PMI's Production Cost Advance Commitment, upon Provider's delivery to and written approval by PMI of the remaining Master Materials identified on Exhibit "B" hereto including, but not limited to, the master tapes in system machine code (O/S9 68000 executable object code) for the Program hereunder which shall be technically satisfactory for formatting.

EXHIBIT "B"

MASTER MATERIALS

1. Presentation Asset Inventory:

   Listing of all media used in Program.

2. Analog Audio:

   All final, mixed audio in the following format:

   1/4" center striped time code, 30 ips (unless otherwise specified); and

   In addition, all M and E's (music and effects tracks are also required).

3. Analog Video/Visual Data:

   All visual data (including slides, flat art, photographs, video and film); and

   All final input videotape including master tapes on 1" tape, Betacam and Umatic.

All graphics files used in the production of the Program.

4. <u>Rights & Permission Documentation:</u>

All rights and releases for pre-recorded video or stock film;

All rights and permission regarding the use of images scanned or otherwise digitized in the creation of graphics. Releases from all graphic artists that stipulate PMI as the owner thereof;

Talent release forms - voice and picture;

Synchronization rights (if any); and

Master music cue sheets (necessary for international distribution).

5. <u>Support Documentation:</u>

The master Program Specification Document including all storyboards and flowcharts, Hypercard stacks; and

All scripts, cue sheets and production edit decision lists.

The following items shall be delivered in complete computer program text source code in machine-readable text files in either Apple Macintosh format (on 800K floppy), DOS format (on 5 ¼" or 3" floppy) or Sun Unix tape format (on 1/4" tape, tape cartridge on ½" tape reel):

6. <u>Video Presentation Assets:</u>

All digitized images, including animated, computer generated or captured as captured or created (originals);

All final edited versions of the originals (e.g., resizings, croppings, touch-ups);

All encoded versions of the images into formats as they are used in the title, i.e., CLUT7, DYUV, etc., versions;

All script files used to control the editing and encoding of the originals; and

Specifications of the process by which the originals are edited and encoded into the final versions, i.e., what authoring system, utilities, etc.

7. <u>Audio Presentation Assets:</u>

All digitized sounds as captured (originals);

All final edited versions of the originals (e.g., cuts, fades, etc.);

All encoded versions of the images into formats as they are used in the title, e.g., ADPCM level A stereo versions;

All script files used to control the editing and encoding of the originals; and

Specification of the process by which the originals are edited and encoded into final versions, i.e., what authoring system, utilities, etc.

8. <u>Text Presentation Assets:</u>

All ASCII text data; and

All fonts (in format) used in the Program

9. <u>Real-Time Records and Files:</u>

All real-time records and real-time files used in the Program;

All script files used to control the generation of the real-time records and real-time files;

and

Specification of the process by which the presentation assets are converted into real-time records and real-time files, i.e., what tool or utility processed the scripts and presentation assets.

10. <u>Program Source Code:</u>

Commented source code which implements the control code for the Program;

All script files used to control the building of the executable image; and

Specification of the process by which the source code is converted into an executable image, i.e., what development system and libraries are used.

11. <u>External Applications:</u>

Specification of any external applications used by the Program (e.g., retrieval engine).

12. <u>Disc Image:</u>

Digital version of the actual Disc image;

All script files used to control the building of the Disc image; and

Specification of the process by which the Disc elements (items 6-11 hereinabove) are converted into a Disc image, i.e., what disc building system is used.

13. <u>Master Tape:</u>

Magnetic digital tape which is used to physically create the Disc;

All script files used to control the generation of the master tape; and

Specification of the process by which the Disc image is converted into a master tape, i.e., what utility software and pressing plant is utilized.

EXHIBIT "C"

PRODUCTION BUDGET FORMAT

Form 49

Retainer Agreement

(LAW FIRM STATIONARY)

_____, 1997

_____

_____

_____

Re: _____

Dear _____:

Thank you for selecting (NAME OF LAW FIRM) to represent you in the above-referenced matter. This letter shall set forth our understanding with respect to fees, costs and disbursements for which you will be responsible.

As we have discussed, (NAME OF LAW FIRM) charges for attorney time on a varying hourly basis with the fees for the individual attorneys ranging from _____ Dollars ($ _____) to _____ Dollars ($ _____) per hour. These rates are subject to periodic revision and you will be notified in writing of any increase. In addition, you will be billed for any and all costs and fees advanced including, without limitation, all travel, photocopying and filing fees.

You will receive a monthly statement listing all charges and describing the services provided. All accounts are due and payable in full upon receipt of the monthly statement therefor, and our filing system requires the payment of a finance charge on account balances not paid within sixty (60) days of the date of the statement.

The finance charge will be applicable to both disbursements advanced by us on your behalf and fees for services rendered. No finance charge will be imposed upon an amount billed for disbursements or fees if we receive payment within sixty (60) days of the date shown on the statement. Any portion not paid within sixty (60) days will thereafter be subject to the monthly finance charge which will be imposed retroactive to the date of the statement on which the charge first appeared. All finance charges will be calculated and posted to your account concurrently with the preparation of your monthly statement.

The monthly finance charge is determined by looking at the current balance of your account at the beginning of each month before a new monthly billing cycle. The unpaid balance is then multiplied by the finance charge periodic rate of .833% per month (10% annual percentage rate). This finance charge is then added to your current balance to arrive at the new billing figure.

All payments received shall be first applied to disbursements, next to fees, and lastly to finance charges. Within each of these three categories, payments shall be applied to the oldest balance first.

All attorney time is logged by the various attorneys on individual time sheets and compiled monthly on a computer printout. These time sheets and printouts will be available for your review and discussion should you have a question concerning any monthly statement and fail to receive a satisfactory explanation from the attorney or attorneys involved.

If you understand and agree to the terms and conditions described herein, please indicate your consent by signing and returning the enclosed copy together with your retainer check in the amount of _____ Dollars ($_____). This retainer will be maintained in our client trust account and applied to your account monthly as the charges accrue. Should there be a balance remaining upon the resolution of this matter, said balance will be promptly refunded along with the closing statement.

Thank you again for selecting (NAME OF LAW FIRM). We will of course always do our utmost to provide you with efficient service and strive to achieve the best results possible in this and any other matter you might refer to us for handling. As always, please feel free to contact me at any time if you have any questions or comments.

Very truly yours,
(NAME OF LAW FIRM)

_____

AGREED TO AND ACCEPTED: _____

DATE: _____

Form 50

Partnership Agreement

This Agreement is made and entered into as of (DATE), by and between (among) [INSERT NAMES] (hereinafter individually referred to as "Partner" and collectively as "Partners"):

W I T N E S S E T H:

WHEREAS, the Partners hereto desire to form a General Partnership, subject to the terms and conditions hereinafter set forth;

ALTERNATIVE CLAUSE

WHEREAS, the Partners hereto have heretofore been and are conducting business as a partnership under the name of (GROUP NAME), pursuant to an oral agreement entered into by the Partners on or about (DATE), under which each of the Partners has been sharing in the profits and losses in the percentage described herein; and

WHEREAS, the Partners desire to continue conducting their business as a Partnership and to commit their agreement to writing;

NOW, THEREFORE, in consideration of the mutual covenants hereinafter contained, it is hereby agreed as follows:

Clause 1.

FORMATION: The Partners hereby constitute themselves as a General Partnership (the "Partnership") under the laws of the State of (NAME OF STATE).

Clause 2.

NAME OF PARTNERSHIP: The Partnership shall operate and conduct business under the name of (GROUP NAME).

Clause 3.

TERM: The Partnership shall commence on (DATE) and shall continue thereafter until dissolved in any manner provided herein.

Clause 4.

PLACE OF BUSINESS: The principal office and place of business of the Partnership shall be located at (ADDRESS) or such other place as the Partners may from time to time designate.

Clause 5.

PURPOSE: The purpose of the Partnership is for the Partners to engage in the entertainment, amusement, music, recording and publishing industries (the "entertainment field") as the musical group (the "Group") known as (GROUP NAME) (the "Group Name") including, without limitation, recording commercial phonorecords, performing personal appearances, exploiting and merchandising the names (both legal and professional), likeness, sobriquet and biographical materials ("Merchandising Rights") of each Partner, either individually or collectively as members of the Group, and the Group Name and all other present and future activities of the Partners and the Partnership in the entertainment field during the term of this Agreement. Except as otherwise expressly provided herein, the Partners shall render their services in the entertainment field on an exclusive basis to the Partnership. However, it is specifically understood and agreed that the copyrighting and exploiting of original musical compositions heretofore or hereafter composed by any Partner individually or jointly with any other Partner or Partners or any other person shall not be within the scope of this Agreement, and the Partnership shall have no right or claim to the ownership or control of such musical compositions or to any monies received by any Partner which are attributable to the publishing and/or writing of such musical compositions.

Clause 6.

DUTIES: Each partner agrees to devote his entire time and attention to the affairs of the partnership and to fully perform any and all activities unanimously agreed upon by the partners.

Clause 7.

CONTRIBUTIONS:

    (a) Initial Contributions:

        (i) Contributions of Services and Merchandising Rights. As a contribution to the Partnership, each Partner is contributing his exclusive services in the entertainment field including, without limitation, service as a recording artist with respect to phonorecords which may be recorded and exploited by the Partnership hereunder, services as a musical performer in all media and on the live stage, and his rights to Merchandising Rights.

        (ii) Capital Contributions. The Partnership's initial capital shall consist of the amounts in cash and/or in property shown in Exhibit "A" attached hereto and incorporated herein by reference. Exhibit "A" sets forth the capital contributions to be made by the respective Partners, the nature of their respective contributions, and, for contributions consisting of property, the amounts that the Partners agree are the market value of their respective properties. Each Partner shall pay in full or convey his contribution to the Partnership within sixty (60) days after the date of this agreement.

ALTERNATIVE CLAUSE

Clause 7.

CONTRIBUTIONS:

   (a) Instruments, Equipment, Etc.: All of the instruments, musical, sound and video equipment owned by each Partner and used in connection with the activities of the Partnership shall continue to belong to such Partner according to such Partner's present ownership therein, but during the term of the Partnership, during which such Partner shall remain a Partner, the Partnership shall be entitled to the full use thereof, free of expense, except for insurance and repairs. All other instruments, musical and/or video equipment hereafter acquired in connection with the Partnership activities shall be paid for from the Partnership monies and shall be deemed additional capital of the Partnership.

   (b) Additional Capital: Whenever it is determined by the unanimous approval of the Partners that the capital of the Partnership is likely to become insufficient for the conduct of the Partnership business, the Partners shall make additional capital contributions in the proportions in which such Partners are then entitled to share in the profits of the Partnership.

   (c) Failure to Make Capital Contributions: If any Partner fails to make any contribution to the Partnership's capital at the time and in the amount required by this agreement, any other Partner may, at its sole discretion, loan money to said defaulting Partner on such terms as may be agreed upon by the parties or, in the alternative, may withdraw its own capital contribution and instead lend money to the Partnership pursuant to Clause 8 below.

   (d) Withdrawals of Capital: No Partner may withdraw capital from the Partnership without the unanimous agreement of the Partners.

Clause 8.

LOANS TO PARTNERSHIP: Any loans to the Partnership (whether from the Partners or from unrelated third parties) shall be payable by the Partnership on such terms as the parties shall mutually agree, may bear reasonable interest and shall constitute an obligation of the Partnership which shall be prior to the return of capital or any distribution provided herein.

Clause 9.

DIVISION OF PROFITS AND LOSSES: The Partnership's profits and losses shall be shared by the Partners in the same proportion as their capital accounts bear to each other.

FIRST ALTERNATIVE CLAUSE

The Partners shall share equally in all of the profits, losses, rights and obligations of the Partnership. Should any Partner at any time bear or satisfy a disproportionate share of financial obligations of the Partnership, such Partner shall be entitled to reimbursement from the other Partners proportionately out of the sums otherwise distributable to them as Partners.

SECOND ALTERNATIVE CLAUSE

The Partners shall share in all net profits and bear all losses of the Partnership in the following percentages: (DESCRIBE).

Clause 10.

DISTRIBUTION OF PROFITS:

(a) Net profits shall be distributed in cash to the Partners from time to time but only as expressly authorized by the unanimous consent of the Partners. The aggregate amounts distributed to the Partners from the Partnership's profits shall not, however, exceed the amount of cash available for distribution, taking into account the Partnership's reasonable working capital needs as determined by the unanimous vote of the Partners.

(b) For the purpose of this agreement, "net profits" as used herein shall mean all income, commissions, royalties, bonuses, payments (other than repayment of loans), dividends, stock bonuses, interests or monies of any kind or nature paid to the Partnership or to any Partner (except as provided in Clause 5 above) as a result of the Partnership's or any Partner's activities in the entertainment field after deducting the sum total of all reasonable salaries, management and agency fees, rent, promotional costs, travel costs, office expenditures, telephone costs, accounting and legal fees, entertainment costs and any and all legitimate Partnership expenses incurred by the Partnership while conducting Partnership business.

(c) The Partners shall be entitled to draw from time to time against the net profits of the Partnership so credited to their respective accounts in such amounts which may be agreed upon by the unanimous consent of the Partners. Any profits distributed in accordance with the foregoing shall be less any sum which any Partner may have previously drawn on account thereof, and if it is determined that any Partner shall have drawn out more than his share of the profits, such Partner shall immediately repay the excess to the Partnership. [OPTIONAL LANGUAGE: No Partner may withdraw capital from the Partnership without the unanimous agreement of the Partners.]

(d) No Partner shall receive any salary, bonus or goods or other assets of the Partnership in excess of that received by any other Partner, except upon the unanimous vote of all the Partners (or as may be provided for elsewhere in this agreement).

Clause 11.

MANAGEMENT: Each Partner shall have one vote on all matters to be decided by the Partnership and shall have the right to participate equally in the control, management and direction of the business of the Partnership. A two-thirds (2/3) affirmative vote of the Partners shall be required to adopt any Partnership decision, except that a unanimous vote of the Partners shall be required in the following matters:

(a) Making any amendment to this agreement, except an amendment by operation of law, in the event of a death of a Partner. Said Partner's right to vote on any Partnership matter shall terminate with his death.

(b) Making any expenditure on behalf of the Partnership in excess of (AMOUNT).

(c) Borrowing money in the Partnership's name or making, executing, delivering or guaranteeing any commercial paper, compromise or release of debts owing to the Partnership.

(d) Selling, leasing, assigning, transferring, pledging, compromising, licensing or otherwise encumbering any Partnership claim, debts or Partnership property.

(e) Entering into, making, executing and/or delivering any contracts or agreements to hire or agree to hire any person or persons to manage the Partnership (and, if so voted, such designation and delegation shall be irrevocable during the engagement of such manager except by an unanimous vote of the Partners).

(f) Determining that a Partner is under permanent disability, that a Partner shall be expelled from the Partnership or that a Partner shall be added to the Partnership as described more fully herein.

(g) The engagement by any Partner in any activity and/or enterprise in the entertainment field other than in connection with the Partnership (except as expressly provided herein).

(h) Dispose of the good will of the Partnership business.

(i) Engage in any act which will make it impossible to carry on the ordinary business of the Partnership.

(j) Pledge or transfer in any matter any interest in the Partnership except to another Partner.

Clause 12.

MEETINGS OF PARTNERS: Upon reasonable notice, a majority of the Partners may, from time to time, elect to call a meeting of the Partners at any reasonable time at the Partnership's principal place of business. In such event, any and all expenses incurred by the Partners in attending such meeting shall be borne solely by each said Partner unless a majority of the Partners agree otherwise.

Clause 13.

NEW PARTNERS: A new Partner may be admitted to the Partnership but only with the unanimous written consent of the Partners. A new Partner shall be admitted only if he executes an agreement with the Partnership under the terms of which such Partner agrees to be bound by all of the provisions hereof, as amended, as if a signatory hereto. Unless expressly agreed upon by the unanimous vote of the Partners, such new Partner shall have no interest whatsoever in the Group Name apart from the limited right to be known as a member of the Group. Such new Partner's capital contribution, if any, and share of the Partnership's net profits and losses shall be agreed upon in the written consent of all of the Partners approving the admission of the new Partner.

Clause 14.

PARTNER'S DEATH, DISABILITY, OR VOLUNTARY WITHDRAWAL:

(a) A Partner may become disassociated from the Partnership by reason of his death, his disability or his resignation. For the purposes hereof, the term "disability" shall include, without limitation, the inability of a Partner to render the services described herein for a continuous period of six (6) months. If a Partner retires from the Partnership, he shall give thirty (30) days prior written notice of such resignation to each of the other Partners. A Partner (or, in the event of disassociation by death, his executor or personal representative) who is disassociated shall be entitled to receive an amount equal to his proportionate share of the new worth of the Partnership as of the date of his disassociation, but he shall not be entitled to any of the earnings of the Partnership received thereafter (nor shall he have any interest in the Group name, nor shall he be subject to any of the liabilities of the Partnership incurred thereafter; provided, however, such Partner shall be entitled to receive a pro rata or other agreed share of any royalties earned from the exploitation of any phonorecord recorded hereunder and embodying his performances as and when such royalties are actually received by the Partnership, less his pro rata or other agreed share of any expenses. It is hereby agreed by the Partners that for the purposes of determining the new worth of a disassociating Partner, the Group Name shall be valued at all times at One Dollar ($1.00).

(b) The net worth of the Partnership shall be determined as of the date of disassociation by an accountant selected by the remaining Partners other than the Partnership's regular accountant, and other than the personal accountant of any Partner, which accountant shall be familiar with the music industry. The accountant shall make said determination in accordance with generally accepted accounting practices and principles, taking into consideration, among other factors, the fair market value of the assets of the Partnership (other than the Group Name), its liabilities (including the disassociated Partner's entitlement to future record royalties as provided in Subclause (a) hereinabove), its past profits and losses. In the event of voluntary resignation, the determination of said accountant shall be final. However, if the disassociated Partner or his legal representative should disagree with the accountant's determination in the event of disassociation for any other reason, the disassociated Partner or such representative may within thirty (30) days after receipt of the accountant's determination submit the issue of the fair market value of the Partnership to arbitration in (STATE), under the applicable rules of the American Arbitration Association. Unless the remaining Partner(s) elect to pay the disassociated Partner's share of the value of the Partnership sooner, said share (including interest on the unpaid balance at the rate of (NUMBER) percent (#%) per annum accruing from said date of final determination) shall be payable in (NUMBER) equal monthly installments commencing one month following the date of the final determination of said net worth; provided however, that if said share is in excess of $(AMOUNT) but less than $(AMOUNT), the remaining Partner(s) may elect to pay same in (NUMBER) equal monthly installments.

Clause 15.

DISSOLUTION:

(a) This Agreement shall terminate, and the Partnership shall be dissolved, upon the first to occur of the following events:

(i) The written agreement of all of the Partners to dissolve the Partnership; or

(ii) By operation of law, except as otherwise provided herein. The addition of a new Partner (as provided in Clause 13 hereof) or the disassociation of a Partner (as provided in Clause 14 hereof) shall not terminate the Agreement, and it shall remain in full force and effect among the remaining Partners.

(b) Upon termination of the Partnership, the Partnership's receivables shall be collected and its assets liquidated forthwith (except as provided in Subclauses (d) and (e) below). The proceeds from the liquidation of the Partnership assets and collection of the Partnership receivables shall be applied in the following order:

(i) First, to the expense of liquidation and debts of the Partnership other than debts owing to any of the Partners;

(ii) Next, to the debts owing to any of the Partners, including debts arising from loans made to or for the benefit of the Partnership, except that if the amount of such proceeds is insufficient to pay such debts in full, payment shall be made on a pro rata basis;

(iii) Next, in payment to each Partner of any financial capital investment made by him in the Partnership belonging to him, except that if the amount of such proceeds is insufficient to pay such financial capital investment in full, payment shall be made on a pro rata basis;

(iv) Next, in payment to each Partner on a pro rata basis of any of such proceeds remaining.

(c) The Partners shall execute all such instruments for facilitating the collection of the Partnership receivables and liquidation of the Partnership assets, and for the mutual indemnity or release of the Partners as may be appropriate.

(d) Any property, including, but not limited to, the Group Name and all rights and interest in contracts, agreements, options, choses in action and Merchandising Rights, owned or controlled by the Partnership at the time of dissolution from which income is being derived shall not be sold, but shall be retained and distributed in the manner hereinafter set forth. After the payments provided for in Clause 9(b)(i), (ii) and (iii) have been made in full, any such property owned by the Partnership and the continuing earnings received as a result of the exploitation thereof shall be valued by an accountant selected by the Partners who is experienced in the music industry. Said property shall then be distributed as nearly as possible, in equal shares among the Partners.

(e) Notwithstanding the foregoing, upon dissolution the Group Name shall be the joint property of each of the Partners but shall not be used in any manner by any Partner alone or with other Partner(s) without the written consent of all of the Partners.

Clause 16.

ACCOUNTING:

(a) Fiscal Year: The fiscal year of the Partnership shall be determined by the Partners after consultation with the Partnership's accountants.

(b) Accounting Method: The Partnership books shall be kept on a cash basis.

(c) Capital Accounts: An individual capital account shall be maintained for each Partner and his capital contribution shall be credited to that account.

(d) Determination of Profit and Loss: The Partnership shall render yearly accountings to each Partner on the first day of (YEAR) and every year during the term of the Partnership.

Clause 17.

BOOKS AND RECORDS: Proper and complete books of account of the Partnership business shall be kept at the Partnership's principal place of business and shall be open to inspection by the Partners or their accredited representatives at any reasonable time during normal business hours.

Clause 18.

PARTNERSHIP BANK ACCOUNTS: One or more Partnership bank accounts may be opened and maintained by the Partners with such bank or banks as the Partners may determine and any checks or withdrawals from or against any bank account or accounts shall be upon the signature of any, (NUMBER) (#) of the Partners or any other person as the Partners may unanimously select; provided, however, that such checks or withdrawals shall be subject to the approval process set out in Clause 7 hereinabove.

Clause 19.

ASSIGNMENT OF PARTNERS' INTEREST: No Partner, or executor or administrator of a deceased Partner, shall sell, assign or transfer all or any portion of his financial or other interest in the Partnership or right to receive a share of Partnership assets, profits or other distributions without the prior written consent of all of the other Partners and any such purported sale, assignment or transfer in contravention of the foregoing shall be null and void. The Partners acknowledge that a part of the capital contribution of each Partner is the unique personal services required to be rendered on the exclusive account of the Partnership by each Partner, for which no presently adequate substitute exists; and that the other Partners are the sole and exclusive judges of the adequacy of any future substitution.

Clause 20.

MISCELLANEOUS:

(a) Notices: All accountings and notices required to be given hereunder, and notices of any action by the Partnership which has the effect of altering any Partner's share of profits or losses shall be given in writing, by personal delivery or by mail or by telegram at the respective addresses of the Partners set forth above, or at such other addresses as may be designated in writing by registered mail by any Partner. Notice given by mail or by telegram shall be deemed given on the date of mailing thereof or on the date of delivery of such telegram to a telegraph office, charges prepaid.

(b) Liability: The liability of the Partnership or the Partners arising out of any activities of the Partnership shall to the extent possible be covered by appropriate policies of insurance. In the event that any liability shall not be adequately covered by insurance, the amount of liability not so insured against shall first be satisfied out of the assets of the Partnership.

(c) Indemnity: Each Partner hereby indemnifies the other Partner(s) and holds such other Partner(s) harmless against and from all claims, demands, actions and rights of action which shall or may arise by virtue of anything done or admitted to be done by him (through or by agents, employees or other representatives) outside the scope of or in breach of the terms of this Agreement. Each Partner shall promptly notify the other Partner(s) if such Partner knows the existence of a claim, demand, action or right of action.

(d) <u>Successors and Assigns:</u> Subject to the restrictions on assignments set forth in this Agreement, the provisions of this Agreement shall be binding upon and inure to the benefit of the heirs, executors, administrators, successors and assigns of the Partnership.

(e) <u>Severability:</u> If any term, provision, covenant or condition of this Agreement is held to be illegal or invalid for any reason whatsoever, such illegality or invalidity shall not affect the validity of the remainder of this Agreement.

(f) <u>Gender:</u> Wherever required in this Agreement, the singular shall include the plural, and the masculine gender shall include the feminine and the neuter.

Clause 21.

<u>CONSTRUCTION</u>: This Agreement shall be governed by and construed in accordance with the laws of the State of (NAME) applicable to contracts entered into and fully to be performed in (NAME). In the event of any action, arbitration, suit or proceeding arising from or under this Agreement, the prevailing party shall be entitled to recover reasonable attorneys' fees and costs of said action, suit, arbitration or proceeding. This is the entire understanding of the parties relating to the subject matter hereof and supersedes all prior and collateral agreements, understandings, and negotiations of the parties. Each party acknowledges that no representation, inducements, promises, understandings or agreements, oral or written, with reference to the subject matter hereof have been made other than as expressly set forth herein. Each Partner acknowledges that he has consulted with legal counsel of his choice with respect to the contents of this Agreement prior to execution hereof, and has been advised by such counsel with respect to the meaning and consequences hereof. This Agreement cannot be changed, rescinded or terminated except by a writing signed by each of the Partners. The titles of the clauses of this Agreement are for convenience only, and shall not in any way affect the interpretation of any clauses of this Agreement or of the Agreement itself.

IN WITNESS WHEREOF, the parties have executed this Agreement as of the day and year first above written.

"PARTNERS"

_____

_____

_____

_____

Form 51

Certificate of Doing Business as Partners Under Assumed Name (N.Y.)

_____ and _____ do hereby certify pursuant to Section 130 of the General Business Law of the State of New York that they conduct and transact business in this state in the County of _____, at _____ Street, _____, New York, as a partnership under the name or designation of _____ and that the full names of all the persons, including the names of all partners, who conduct business under such name or designation, with their respective residence addresses, are as follows:

_____, residing at _____ Street, _____, New York.

_____, residing at _____ Street, _____, New York.

AND WE DO FURTHER CERTIFY that all of the persons are over eighteen years of age.

AND FURTHER that we are successors in interest to _____, who have previously used the above name in the carrying on or transacting of business at _____, New York.

IN WITNESS WHEREOF, we have executed this certificate this _____ day of _____ 19 ____.

STATE OF NEW YORK

County of _____

On the _____ day of _____ 19____ before me personally appeared _____, and _____ to me known to be the individuals described in and who executed the foregoing instrument and acknowledged that they executed the same.

_____
Notary Public

State of_____
County of_____
    on the day_____

_____

_____

_____
Notary Public

Form 52

Copyright Assignment

ASSIGNMENT

In consideration of the sum of One Dollar ($1.00) and other good and valuable consideration, receipt of which is hereby acknowledged, the undersigned, (NAME OF OWNER) ("Assignor") does hereby sell, transfer, assign and convey to (NAME OF PURCHASER) or its designee ("Assignee") an undivided (E.G., FIFTY) percent (50%) interest in Assignor's share of the copyright and all other rights, title and interest in and to the musical compositions listed on Schedule "A" attached hereto and by this reference made a part hereof, including, but not limited to, the copyright and all renewals and extensions thereof for the United States of America and all countries of the world and any and all claims or causes of action whether asserted or not relating thereto.

By _____

Notary _____

Form 53

ARTIST-INFOMERCIAL AGREEMENT

JONES PRODUCTS LLC
1734 EAST 10TH STREET
CHICAGO, ILLINOIS 60609

[Date]

Smith Productions, Inc. f/s/o Ms. Television Personality
c/o Jerome Salespitch
Salespitch & Associates, Inc.
351 Ventura Boulevard, Suite 1500
Sherman Oaks, California 91403

Re: Television Personality/"The Widget" Infomercial

Gentlepersons:

This letter, when executed by Smith Productions ("Smith") and by Jones Products, LLC ("Jones"), will constitute a valid and binding agreement between Smith and Jones with respect to Smith furnishing the services of Television Personality (hereinafter referred to as "Artist") to Jones to advertise and promote Jones's fitness product tentatively titled "The Widget" and (subject to her approval) related upsell products (collectively "Products"), via a 30-minute commercial ("Infomercial"), 30-120 second commercials (Short Form Infomercials) (Infomercials and Short Form Infomercials shall collectively be known as Commercials"), home shopping channels, personal appearances, and all other forms of advertising, including, but not limited to, print, credit card, retail, stand placements, trade shows, fairs and direct mail (all collectively known as "Advertising").

A. NATURE OF SERVICES

1. We hereby engage Artist and Smith agrees to provide Artist's services to Jones as follows:

a. During the Test Term (as defined below) to render services in or about August, 1995, at two (2) twelve (12) hour sessions in the Los Angeles metropolitan area for the purpose of performing as an on camera host in the Commercials to promote the Products. Jones shall also have the right to have Artist render one additional twelve (12) hour session for re-shoots, looping and revising the Commercials. Jones shall further have the right to have Artist sit for one photo session. Jones shall have the right to use the Commercials in all media including, but not limited to, free-tv, pay-tv, cable, closed circuit, and in-store television. Commercials may be on film, tape, disc and any other method of recording now or hereafter invented.

b. During any Option Term (as defined below), to render services as set forth in A1 and, as requested by Jones, to render services of up to six (6) days for personal appearances to promote the Products on a home shopping channel.

All services will be rendered in accordance with Jones's reasonable instructions and under Jones's control or the control of an agent designated by Jones. The materials to be produced hereunder and the rendition of Artist's services will be at such times and locations as Jones may determine, subject to reasonable prior notice to Smith and Artist's prior bona fide professional commitments. Jones acknowledges Artist's professional commitment to host a program on the Family Channel (the "Family Channel Program") and further acknowledges that from time to time there may be unforseen scheduling conflicts between Artist's services hereunder and Artist's services with the Family Channel Program. The parties will use their reasonable efforts to avoid such conflicts and nothing herein shall be construed as a breach of the agreement if an unforseen conflict arises, with respect to Artist's services on the Family Channel Program, after notice by Jones to Smith.

B. TERM AND AREA OF USE

1. The initial term of this agreement ("Test Term") will commence on the date of the first broadcast of the Infomercial or December 1, 1995, whichever is sooner, and continue for a period of ninety (90) days.

2. Jones shall also have three (3) successive options to extend the term of this agreement for additional periods of one (1) year each (hereinafter referred to, respectively, as the "First Option Term," "Second Option Term," and "Third Option Term"). Said options shall be exercised, in writing, no less than ten (10) days prior to the end of the Test Term and thirty (30) days prior to the end of any preceding Option Term. At the time of exercising any option Jones shall pay Smith for additional services as it relates to "The Widget" product, as an advance against any royalty (as defined below) due Smith hereunder the sum of one hundred thousand dollars ($100,000) which Jones shall pay to Smith in equal quarterly installments. If an option is exercised, Jones shall have the right to require Artist to render all of the same services with respect to the applicable option period as Jones had with respect to the Test Term as well as the services set forth in A1a and b above. Further, Jones shall have the right to continue to use all materials previously produced hereunder during any extension of the term. The Initial Term, together with any option periods for which the option has been exercised, will hereinafter be referred to, collectively, as the "term."

3. During the Test Term, the materials produced hereunder may be used throughout North America. During any Option Term the materials produced hereunder may be used throughout the universe ("Territory").

C. COMPENSATION

1. Jones agrees to pay to Smith and Smith and Artist agree to accept, in consideration of all services rendered by Artist and the use of the results thereof, and all rights granted by Smith to Jones, the following compensation:

a. With respect to Artist's services as set forth in paragraph A1a, which are performed during the Test Term, Jones shall pay Smith the sum of twenty-five thousand dollars ($25,000) payable one-half upon execution of this agreement and one-half upon completion of Artist's first two days of services during the Test Term. This amount shall be applied against any royalty that may be due Smith hereunder. For Artist's services, under paragraph A1a rendered during any Option Term, in excess of the days of services as set forth in A1a (excluding travel), Jones shall pay Smith the sum of ten thousand dollars ($10,000) per day which amount will not be applicable against any royalty due Smith or Artist.

b. With respect to Artist's services as set forth in paragraph A1a and b, Jones shall pay Smith the sum of two thousand five hundred dollars ($2,500) payable prior to Artist's departure to render services. Any payment under this paragraph shall be applied against any royalty that may be due Smith hereunder.

c. For The Widget sold via the Commercials, Jones shall pay Smith a royalty ("Royalty") equal to one percent (1%) of the gross retail selling price of the Product and other products sold through the Commercials, less any returns, bad checks, chargebacks, credit card declines and cancel, shipping and handling, taxes and credit card fees. For sales of the Product via retail or any other Direct Response Advertising channels of distribution Jones shall pay Smith a royalty equal to one percent (1%) of the gross wholesale price, less any returns, bad checks, chargebacks, credit card declines and cancel, freight, shipping and handling, taxes and credit card fees.

d. For any other Product that Jones desires to use Artist's services, during the Term, to advertise and promote, the parties shall, after approval of the Product by Artist, negotiate in good faith an appropriate Royalty taking into account price, distribution, marketing channels and prior performance of other products.

e. With respect to Artist's services set forth herein, if Artist is required to travel, Jones shall provide two round trip first class airfares, two first class hotel rooms, limousine service to portal and a per diem of three hundred dollars ($300) per day. Artist and/or Smith shall be responsible for all other incidental expenses.

f. Jones shall, during the term of this agreement, account and provide to Smith on a quarterly basis, a statement showing the amount of all sales in the previous quarter, all returns and uncollectibles and a payment, if any, of the Royalties due Smith. Smith shall have access to our books and records as they relate to the sales of the Products and Jones's Royalties. Smith shall have two (2) years from the date of Smith's receipt of each statement within which to audit Jones's books and records and a further year within which to commence mediation and/or arbitration as set forth herein with respect to each statement after which that statement will be deemed closed and not subject to further objection. The cost and expense of any audit shall be borne by Smith unless there is discovered a discrepancy in the amount paid and the amount owed of more than five percent (5%) in which case the cost of the audit shall be borne by Jones.

2. If required, Jones shall make any SAG or AFTRA Pension and Health Fund ("P&H") payments applicable to Artist's services in connection with the production of the Commercials. For the purpose of computing such P&H payments, the amount allocated to Artist's broadcast services shall be twenty-five thousand dollars ($25,000) during the test term and ten thousand dollars ($10,000) during any option term.

3. Payments to be made hereunder will not be subject to any deductions, as Artist is an independent contractor. Artist and Smith agree, however, to indemnify Jones should Artist and/or Smith fail to pay any assessments or taxes due on Artist's compensation hereunder. Smith warrants that Smith will pay Artist the minimum compensation provided in the collective bargaining agreements applicable to Artist's services for the production of the Commercials and that Smith will otherwise comply with all obligations imposed upon an employer of performers under such applicable collective bargaining agreement. Smith will be responsible for all payments to be made to any agent with respect to Artist's services hereunder. Smith acknowledges that for the purposes of retaining Artist's services hereunder, Artist will not be considered an employee of Jones and will not, by way of example and not by way of limitation, be entitled to any benefits from workers compensation, disability benefits, health, medical or life insurance programs, pension, profit-sharing or other employee-benefit plans or programs maintained by Jones.

D. EXCLUSIVITY AND ENDORSEMENTS

1. Smith warrants and represents that it and the Artist have not authorized, will not authorize or permit the use of Artist's performance, name, voice, signature, photograph or other likeness, nor will Artist render services in connection with any direct response advertising project nor act as a spokesperson or participate in any other advertising or promotion activity, for any fitness products or services that are directly competitive or similar with The Widget Product. This exclusivity shall encompass any other Products, in the future, Artist may agree to endorse or advertise for Jones. Nothing herein shall prohibit Artist from appearing as a guest on any television program regardless of sponsorship of said program nor discussing any fitness product in relation to her providing services to the Family Channel Program.

2. Smith warrants, represents and agrees that at no time will Smith or Artist disparage Smith or Artist's association with Jones or the Products.

3. Smith agrees that Jones may utilize the results of Artist's services to endorse the Products and in that connection, Artist will execute the letter attached hereto as Exhibit A.

E.   USE OF NAME AND LIKENESS

1. Subject to and in accordance with the limitations set forth in this Agreement and during the term, Smith hereby grants to Jones the right to use Artist's name, performance, voice, signature, photograph and likeness (subject to Artist's approval as provided below) in connection with the Commercials and Direct Response Advertising produced hereunder.

2. Artist will have approval over the script of the Commercials, any photos of Artist and any advertising copy in which Artist's image is made a part thereof. Such approvals shall not be unreasonably withheld. Approvals must be given within five (5) working days and if no response is received the materials shall then be deemed approved. For any still photographs to be used by Jones, Artist shall be required to approve at least fifty percent (50%) of the total number of still photographs submitted by Jones. If Artist fails to approve fifty percent (50%) of the photographs Jones shall have the right, in its sole discretion to designate the balance of fifty percent (50%) of the still photographs to be used.

3. Smith also hereby grants Jones the right to publicize Artist's association with Jones and the Products.

4. Upon the termination of this agreement, no materials produced hereunder will be disseminated by Jones beyond a run-off period of six (6) months, to allow for the conclusion of any media purchases, following termination of this agreement. Jones shall continue to pay Smith Royalties as set forth above during the run-off period.

F.   MISCELLANEOUS PROVISIONS

1. Services Unique

It is expressly understood and agreed that the services to be performed by Artist and the rights and privileges granted to Jones hereunder are special, unique, extraordinary and impossible of replacement, which gives them a peculiar value, the loss of which cannot be reasonably or adequately compensated in an action at law and that Smith and Artist's failure or refusal to perform their obligations hereunder would cause irreparable harm or damage. Should Smith or Artist fail or refuse to perform such obligations, Jones shall in addition to any monetary damages Jones may be entitled to, including but not limited to a complete refund of all monies paid to Smith and/or Artist, Jones shall also be entitled to ex parte injunctive or other equitable relief against Smith and Artist to prevent the continuance of such failure or refusal or to prevent Artist from performing services or granting rights to others in violation of this agreement.

2. Union Membership

In the event any expenses, including any fine or penalty, as a result of Jones's change of relationship with any union or guild, then such monies will be paid by Jones rather than Smith or Artist.

3. Indemnities

a. Smith and Artist will at all times indemnify and hold Jones and its respective directors, officers, employees, licensees, agents and assigns harmless from and against any and all claims, damages, liabilities, expenses, non-cancellable production costs and/or media expenditures and any other costs and expenses, including counsel fees, arising out of any breach by Smith or Artist of any warranty or agreement made by Smith or Artist herein or in the performance of their respective obligations hereunder.

b. Jones shall indemnify Smith and Artist and hold Smith and Artist harmless, with respect to any claims, damages, liabilities, and costs and expenses, including counsel fees, arising out of materials prepared by us concerning the advertising, distribution, exploitation or usage of Jones's Products. Smith and Artist shall be named as an additional insured on all of Jones's relevant insurance policies, which currently are a product liability policy with limits of two (2) million dollars in the aggregate and an umbrella policy with a five (5) million dollar limit. Both policies shall be in place prior to the first broadcast of the Commercials.

4. Ownership of Materials

You acknowledge that neither Smith nor Artist has or will claim any right, title or interest in or to the Commercials, Direct Response Advertising or other materials produced hereunder, or in or to any of our trademarks, service marks, trade names or copyrights.

5. Professional Behavior

If Artist has committed or commits any act or becomes involved in any situation or occurrence which brings Artist into public disrepute, contempt, scandal or ridicule or which shocks, insults or offends the people of this nation or any class or group thereof or reflects unfavorably upon Jones, or Jones's Products, Jones shall have the right to immediately terminate this agreement. Jones's decision on all matters arising under this paragraph will be conclusive, provided that Jones's decision to terminate hereunder must be exercised, if at all, not later than forty-five (45) days after the facts giving rise to such right under this paragraph are brought to Jones's attention.

6. Force Majeure

If for any reason, such as strikes, boycotts, war, acts of God, labor troubles, riots, delays of commercial carriers, restraints of public authority, or for any other reason, similar or dissimilar, beyond Jones's control, Jones shall be unable to use and/or reuse the materials produced hereunder or Artist is unable to render services as required by Jones during any period of the term hereof, then Jones shall have the right to extend the term hereof for an equivalent period, without any additional compensation to Smith or Artist.

G.   Death

In the event of Artist's death during the term hereof, Jones shall have the right, in its sole discretion, to either terminate this agreement or continue to use the materials in which Artist participated upon payment of the required compensation to you hereunder.

H.   Disability

If Artist should fail to fulfill Artist's obligations hereunder due to any illness, accident or other physical or mental impairment which renders Artist incapable of performing or unqualified to perform services whenever required under this agreement, then Jones may, in its sole discretion, either extend the term by such number of days that Jones fails to provide Artist's services or terminate this agreement.

I.   Breach

Except with respect to the application of Jones's rights under Paragraphs G and H above, Jones or Artist at any time commit a breach of any provision of this agreement or at any time fail or refuse to fulfill your respective obligations hereunder, then Jones may terminate this agreement, provided, however, that written notice of such breach must be served upon Smith, and Smith will thereupon have fifteen (15) days in which to cure such breach, if it is curable. If not or upon Smith's failure to cure within such period, termination will be deemed effective on the date Smith originally receives notice.

J.   Rights Upon Breach

In the event of a breach of this agreement by Smith or Artist, in addition to any other legal remedies Jones may have, Jones shall have the right to resort to injunctive or other equitable relief, and the exercise of such right will not constitute a waiver of any other or additional rights at law or pursuant to the terms of this agreement which Jones may have against Smith or Artist as a result of such breach. .

K.   Full Power

a. Smith represents and warrants that:

(i) Artist is employed by Smith;

(ii) Smith and Artist have the full right and power to enter into and fully perform this agreement in accordance with its terms;

(iii) The execution, delivery, and performance of this agreement will not infringe upon the rights of any third party or violate the provisions of any agreement to which Smith or Artist are a party; and

(iv) Artist has read and executed the letter attached hereto as Exhibit B simultaneously with Smith's execution of this agreement.

L.   Notices

Service of all notices, payments and correspondence under this agreement will be sufficient if given personally, mailed or faxed to Smith at:

Smith Productions, Inc. f/s/o Ms. Television Personality
c/o Jerome Salespitch
Salespitch & Associates, Inc.
351 Ventura Boulevard, Suite 1500
Sherman Oaks, California 91403

And to Jones at

Jones Products, LLC
1734 East 10th Street
Chicago, Illinois 60609

with a copy to:

Hall, Dickler, Lawler, Kent, Friedman & Wood LLP
2029 Century Park East
Los Angeles, California 90067
Attention: Alan Feldstein, Esq.

Any notice mailed or faxed pursuant hereto shall be deemed to have been given on the day it is mailed or telefaxed or, if delivered in person by hand, on the day it is delivered.

M.   Waiver

The failure by Jones to exercise rights granted to Jones hereunder upon the occurrence of any of the contingencies set forth in this agreement will not constitute a waiver of such rights upon the recurrence of such contingency.

N.   Governing Law

This agreement will be construed in accordance with the laws of the State of California pertaining to contracts made and performed entirely therein and Smith agrees and consents that jurisdiction and venue of all matters relating to this agreement will be vested exclusively in the federal, state and local courts within the State of California, County of Los Angeles unless otherwise super-seded by the mediation/arbitration provisions contained in any applicable collective bargaining agreement to which Jones are signatories.

O.   Professional Rendition of Services

Artist will attend and participate in all rehearsals, filming, taping or photography sessions required and will render her services hereunder in accordance with the scripts or other materials which Jones shall furnish to Artist for such purposes. Smith agrees that Artist will render her services in a competent and artistic manner to the best of her ability, and that all her services will be subject to Jones's approval, direction and reasonable control at all times. Artist will promptly comply with whatever reasonable instructions, suggestions and recommendations Jones may give Artist in connection with the rendition of such services.

P.   Severability

In the event any provision of this agreement is determined to be invalid by a court of competent jurisdiction, such determination shall in no way affect the validity or enforceability of any other provision herein.

Q.   Assignment

This agreement, including the right to receive compensation, may not be assigned by Smith or Artist. Jones shall have the right to assign this agreement.

R.   Independent Contractor

Smith will discharge all Jones's obligations imposed by any federal, state or local law, regulation or order now or hereafter in force including, but not limited to, the filing of all returns and reports required and the payment of assessments, taxes, contributions and other sums required of Smith, and Smith will indemnify and hold us harmless against all claims and demands resulting from Smith's failure to comply with the provisions of this paragraph.

S.   Entire Agreement

This agreement constitutes the entire understanding between Smith and Jones with respect to the subject matter of this agreement and supersedes all prior agreements. No waiver modifications or additions to this agreement will be valid unless in writing and signed by the parties hereto.

Please confirm your acceptance of, and agreement to the foregoing by affixing your signature in the place indicated below.

Very truly yours,

Jones Products, LLC

By: _____

Artist-Infomercial Agreement

ACCEPTED AND AGREED:
Smith PRODUCTIONS, INC.

By: _____

Title: _____

Federal I.D. Number: _____

EXHIBIT A

Date:

Jones ELLIS FITNESS, LLC
2945 WEST 31ST STREET
CHICAGO, ILLINOIS 60623

Gentlepersons:

Pursuant to a separate agreement ("Agreement"), you have retained my services in connection with the production of various materials in which I may deliver testimonials for products owned by you ("Products".)

I hereby certify to you that except as I may promptly otherwise advise you in writing, any statements attributed to me are or will be true and an expression of my personal experience and belief. I have used the Products and promise that I shall continue to use said Products for so long as you have the right to use the materials produced pursuant to the Agreement.

Nothing contained in this letter shall constitute an amendment or addition to the Agreement, the terms and conditions of which shall remain in full force and effect.

Very truly yours,

Television Personality

Witness:

EXHIBIT B

Date:

JONES PRODUCTS, LLC
2945 WEST 31ST STREET
CHICAGO, ILLINOIS 60623

Gentlepersons:

Reference is made to an Agreement dated _____, 19_____ between you and SMITH PRODUCTIONS, INC.

In consideration of your entering into the Agreement with SMITH PRODUC-TIONS, INC. and in order to induce your execution thereof, I hereby confirm that I have read said Agreement and that I agree to perform all of the obligations and undertakings required of me thereunder and to abide by all the restrictions contained therein as they are applicable to me, regardless of whether SMITH PRODUCTIONS, INC. continues throughout the term of the Agreement to be my employer in connection with such services.

I acknowledge that payment by you to SMITH PRODUCTIONS, INC., as set forth in said Agreement shall fully discharge your obligations to me.

I warrant and represent that SMITH PRODUCTIONS, INC. is authorized by me to contract for my services as set forth in said Agreement and represent that I am not obligated to any third parties in any manner that would interfere with my ability to perform as required under said Agreement.

Very truly yours,
Television Personality

Form 54

Retail Merchandising License

LICENSE AGREEMENT made _____, 199 ____, by and between (hereinafter referred to as "LICENSOR") and _____, whose address is _____ Attn: _____ (hereinafter referred to as "LICENSEE").

WITNESSETH:

The parties hereto mutually agree as follows:

1. DEFINITIONS: As used in this Agreement, the following terms shall have the following respective meanings:

    (a) Channels of Distribution: Licensee may sell the Licensed Products through the following channels of distribution only:

    (b) Guaranteed Consideration: The sum of $ _____.00 payable as follows:

        $_____.00 payable simultaneously with the execution of this Agreement;

    and

        $_____.00 payable on or before _____.

        $_____.00 payable on or before _____.

        $_____.00 payable on or before _____.

        $_____.00 payable on or before _____.

    (c) Licensed Product(s):

    (d) Licensed Property:

    (e) Marketing Date:

    (f) Royalty Rate:

    (g) Term:

    (h) Territory: United States (fifty states)

2. GRANT OF LICENSE:

    (a) Subject to the restrictions, limitations, reservations and conditions and Licensor's approval rights set forth in this Agreement, Licensor hereby grants to Licensee and Licensee hereby accepts for the Term of this Agreement, a license to utilize the Licensed Property solely on or in connection with the manufacture, distribution and sale of the Licensed Products as specified above for the ultimate retail sale to the public throughout the Territory on a non-exclusive basis.

(b) Without limiting any other approval rights of Licensor as contained herein, no television commercials may be utilized under this Agreement without the specific prior written approval of Licensor.

3. RESERVATION OF RIGHTS; PREMIUMS:

(a) Licensor reserves all rights not expressly conveyed to Licensee hereunder, and Licensor may grant licenses to others to use the Licensed Property, artwork and textual matter in connection with other uses, services and products without limitation.

(b) Notwithstanding anything to the contrary stated herein, Licensor specifically reserves the right, without limitation throughout the world, to itself use, or license any third party(s) of its choice to use the Licensed Property for the manufacture, distribution and sale of products similar or identical to those licensed herein in Paragraph 1(c) above for sale through any catalogue(s) produced or distributed by or on behalf of Licensor or its affiliated companies, or for sale or distribution in any theaters or arenas, or for sale or distribution in any retail stores operated by or on behalf of Licensor, its affiliated companies or franchisees, or for sale or distribution in any theme/amusement parks operated by or on behalf of Licensor and its affiliated companies, including without limitation, the parks. In addition, Licensor reserves the right to allow _____ to manufacture (or have manufactured by a third party) products similar or identical to those licensed herein for distribution or sale in theme and/or amusement parks owned or operated by _____. Further, Licensor reserves the right to use, or license others to use, and/or manufacture products similar or identical to those licensed herein for use as premiums.

(c) Licensee specifically understands and agrees that no rights are granted herein with respect to the logo or trademark, or any other trademark(s), logo(s) or copyrights owned by Licensor other than those specifically set forth above in the Licensed Property, it being understood that all rights in and to said properties are reserved exclusively to Licensor for use and/or licensing as it deems appropriate to third party(s) of its choice.

(d) Licensee agrees that it will not use, or knowingly permit the use of, and will exercise due care that its customers likewise will refrain from the use of, the Licensed Products as a premium, except with the prior written consent of Licensor. Subject to Licensor's prior written approval as aforesaid, Licensee shall pay to Licensor a sum equal to TWELVE PERCENT (12%) of all premium sales. For purposes of this paragraph, the term "premium" shall be defined as including, but not necessarily limited to, combination sales, free or self-liquidating items offered to the public in conjunction with the sale or promotion of a product or service, including traffic building or continuity visits by the consumer/customer, or any similar scheme or device, the prime intent of which is to use the Licensed Products in such a way as to promote, publicize and or sell the products, services or business image of the user of such item.

4. CONSIDERATION:

   (a) The Guaranteed Consideration paid by Licensee as set forth above shall be applied against such royalties as are, or have become, due to Licensor. No part of such Guaranteed Consideration shall be repayable to Licensee. Royalties earned in excess of the Guaranteed Consideration applicable to the Term hereof shall not offset any Guaranteed Consideration required in respect of the succeeding renewal term (if any); likewise, royalties earned in excess of the Guaranteed Consideration applicable to the renewal term (if any) shall not offset any Guaranteed Consideration applicable to any prior term.

   (b) Royalty Payments: Licensee shall pay to Licensor a sum equal to the Royalty Rate as set forth above of all net sales by Licensee of the Licensed Products covered by this Agreement. The term "net sales" herein shall mean the gross invoice price billed customers, less actual quantity discounts and actual returns, but no deductions shall be made for uncollectible accounts and deductions for actual returns may not exceed 5% of total sales. No costs incurred in the manufacture, sale, distribution, advertisement, or exploitation of the Licensed Products shall be deducted from any royalties payable by Licensee.

   (c) Royalties shall be payable concurrently with the periodic statements required in Paragraph 5 hereof, except to the extent offset by Guaranteed Consideration theretofore remitted.

5. PERIODIC STATEMENTS:

   (a) Within thirty (30) days after the initial shipment of the Licensed Products and promptly on the 15th day of every month thereafter, Licensee shall furnish to Licensor complete and accurate statements certified to be accurate by Licensee, or if a corporation, by an officer of Licensee, showing with respect to all Licensed

Products distributed and sold by Licensee during the preceding calendar month the (i) number of units; (ii) country in which manufactured, sold and/or to which shipped; (iii) description (as such term is defined below) of the Licensed Products; (iv) gross sales price; and (v) itemized deductions from gross sales price, and net sales price together with any returns made during the preceding calendar month. Such statements shall be furnished to Licensor whether or not any of the Licensed Products have been sold during calendar months to which such statements refer. Receipt or acceptance by Licensor of any of the statements furnished pursuant to this Agreement or of any sums paid hereunder shall not preclude Licensor from questioning the correctness thereof at any time, and in the event that any inconsistencies or mistakes are discovered in such statements or payments, they shall immediately be rectified and the appropriate payments made by Licensee. Upon demand of Licensor, Licensee shall at its own expense, but not more than once in any twelve (12) month period, furnish to Licensor a detailed statement by an independent certified public accountant showing the (i) number of units; (ii) country in which manufactured, sold and/or to which shipped; (iii) description of the Licensed Products; (iv) gross sales price; and (v) itemized deductions from gross sales price and net sales price of the Licensed Products covered by this Agreement distributed and/or sold by Licensee up to and including the date upon which Licensor has made such demand. For purposes of this Subparagraph, the term "Description" shall mean a detailed description of the Licensed Products including the nature of each of the Licensed Products, any and all names and likenesses, whether live actors or animated characters, tram the Licensed Property utilized on the Licensed Products and/or any related packaging and/or wrapping material, and any other components of the Licensed Property utilized on the Licensed Products and/or any related packaging and/or wrapping material. In the event Licensor is responsible for the payment of any additional third party participations based on Licensee not reporting by character name and likeness as provided above, Licensee shall be responsible for reimbursing Licensor for the full amount of all such third party claims, including without limitation, the participation itself, interest, audit and attorneys' fees. Licensee understands and agrees that it is a material term and condition of this Agreement that Licensee include the Description on all statements. In the event Licensee fails to do so, Licensor shall have the right to terminate this Agreement, in accordance with the provisions of Paragraph 14 herein.

(b)   The statements and payments required hereunder shall be delivered to: _____.

(c)   Any payments which are made to Licensor hereunder after the due date required therefor, shall bear interest at the then current prime rate plus six (6%) percent (or the maximum rate permissible by law, if less than the current prime rate) from the date such payments are due to the date of payment. Licensor's right hereunder to interest on late payments shall not preclude Licensor from exercising any of its other rights or remedies pursuant to this Agreement or otherwise with regard to Licensee's failure to make timely remittances.

(d)   Licensee agrees to provide, at Licensor's request: (i) a grant to Licensor of a first-priority lien and security interest in Licensee's inventory, contract rights and accounts receivable, and all proceeds thereof, with respect to the Licensed Products; and/or (ii) a letter of credit issued in favor of Licensor from a financial institution as approved by Licensor in an amount up to the Guaranteed Consideration; and/or (iii) such other form of security acceptable to Licensor. Licensee agrees to execute all documentation as Licensor may require in connection with perfecting such security interests.

6. BOOKS AND RECORDS:

(a)   Licensee shall keep, maintain and preserve (in Licensee's principal place of business) for at least two (2) years following termination or expiration of the Term of this Agreement or any renewal(s) hereof (if applicable), complete and accurate records of accounts including, without limitation, purchase orders, inventory records, invoices, correspondence, banking and financial and other records pertaining to the various items required to be submitted by Licensee as well as to ensure Licensee's compliance with local laws as required pursuant to Paragraph 13(k) hereof. Such records and accounts shall be available for inspection and audit at any time or times during or after the Term of this Agreement or any renewal(s) hereof (if applicable) during reasonable business hours and upon reasonable notice by Licensor or its nominees. Licensee agrees not to cause or permit any interference with Licensor or nominees of Licensor in the performance of their duties. During such inspections and audits, Licensor shall have the right to take extracts and/or make copies of Licensee's records as it deems necessary.

(b) The exercise by Licensor in whole or in part, at any time of the right to audit records and accounts or of any other right herein granted, or the acceptance by Licensor of any statement or statements or the receipt and/or deposit by Licensor, of any payment tendered by or on behalf of Licensee shall be without prejudice to any rights or remedies of Licensor and such acceptance, receipt and/or deposit shall not preclude or prevent Licensor from thereafter disputing the accuracy of any such statement or payment.

(c) If pursuant to its right hereunder Licensor causes an audit and inspection to be instituted which thereafter discloses a deficiency between the amount found to be due to Licensor and the amount actually received or credited to Licensor, then Licensee shall, upon Licensor's demand, promptly pay the deficiency, together with interest thereon at the then current prime rate from the date such amount became due until the date of payment, and, if the deficiency is more than 3% of all royalties paid by Licensee during the period covered by the audit, then Licensee shall pay the reasonable costs and expenses of such audit and inspection.

(d) PUT IN THIS SUBDIVISION ONLY IF MASS MARKET DISTRIBUTION: Licensee understands and agrees that Licensor shall have access to Licensee's sell-through information, with respect to the Licensed Products, pertaining to _____ stores through _____ computer retail link (the "_____"). Licensor agrees to keep confidential all information obtained by Licensor through the _____ except: (i) to the extent necessary to comply with a law or the valid order of a court of competent jurisdiction, in which event the party making such disclosure shall so notify the other and shall seek confidential treatment of such information; (ii) as part of normal reporting or review procedure to the respective parties' boards of directors, parent company, auditors and attorneys who agree to be bound by the provisions of this subparagraph; (iii) in order to enforce its rights or perform its obligations under this Agreement; or (iv) when discussing the sale of Licensed Products with _____ in an effort to improve business results.

7. INDEMNIFICATIONS:

(a) During the Term, and continuing after the expiration or termination of this Agreement, Licensor shall indemnify Licensee and shall hold it harmless from any loss, liability, damage, cost or expense, arising out of any claims or suits which may be brought or made against Licensee by reason of the breach of Licensor of the warranties or representations as set forth in Paragraph 12 hereof, provided that Licensee shall give prompt written notice, and full cooperation and assistance to Licensor relative to any such claim or suit and provided, further, that Licensor shall have the option to undertake and conduct the defense of any suit so brought. Licensee shall not, however, be entitled to recover for lost profits. Licensee shall cooperate fully in all respects with Licensor in the conduct and defense of said suit and/or proceedings related thereto.

(b)   During the Term, and continuing after the expiration or termination of this Agreement, Licensee shall indemnify Licensor and shall hold it harmless from any loss, liability, damage, cost or expense arising out of any claims or suits which may be brought or made against Licensor by reason of: (i) any breach of Licensee's covenants and undertakings hereunder; (ii) any unauthorized use by Licensee of the Licensed Property; (iii) any use of any trademark, copyright, design, patent, process, method or device, except for those uses of the Licensed Property that are specifically approved by Licensor pursuant to the terms of this Agreement; (iv) Licensee's non-compliance with any applicable federal, state or local laws or with any other applicable regulations; and (v) any alleged defects and/or inherent dangers (whether obvious or hidden) in the Licensed Products or the use thereof.

(c)   With regard to 7(b)(v) above, Licensee agrees to obtain, at its own expense, product liability insurance providing adequate protection for Licensor and Licensee against any such claims or suits in amounts no less than three million dollars ($3,000,000) per occurrence, combined single limits. Simultaneously with the execution of this Agreement, Licensee undertakes to submit to Licensor a fully paid policy or certificate of insurance naming Licensor as an additional insured party and, requiring that the insurer shall not terminate or materially modify such policy or certificate of insurance without written notice to Licensor at least twenty (20) days in advance thereof. Such insurance and the delivery of the policy or certificate are material obligations of Licensee.

8.   ARTWORK; COPYRIGHT AND TRADEMARK NOTICES:

(a)   The Licensed Property shall be displayed or used only in such form and in such manner as has been specifically approved in writing by Licensor in advance and Licensee undertakes to assure usage of the trademark(s) and character(s) solely as approved hereunder. Licensee further agrees and acknowledges that any and all Artwork (defined below) created, utilized, approved and/or authorized for use hereunder by Licensor in connection with the Licensed Products or which otherwise features or includes the Licensed Property shall be owned in its entirety exclusively by Licensor. Artwork as used herein shall include, without limitation, all pictorial, graphic, visual, audio, audio-visual, digital, literary, animated, artistic, dramatic, sculptural, musical or any other type of creations and applications, whether finished or not, including, but not limited to, animation, drawings, designs, sketches, images, illustrations, film, video, electronic, digitized or computerized information, software, object code, source code, on-line elements, music, text, dialogue, stories, visuals, effects, scripts, voiceovers, logos, one-sheets, promotional pieces, packaging, display materials, printed materials, photographs, interstitials, notes, shot logs, character profiles and translations, produced by Licensee or for Licensee, pursuant to this Agreement. Licensor reserves for itself or its designees all rights to use any and all Artwork created, utilized and/or approved hereunder without limitation.

(b) Licensee acknowledges that, as between Licensor and Licensee, the Licensed Property and Artwork and all other depictions, expressions and derivations thereof, and all copyrights, trademarks and other proprietary rights therein are owned exclusively by Licensor and Licensee shall have no interest in or claim thereto, except for the limited right to use the same pursuant to this Agreement and subject to its terms and conditions.

Licensee agrees and acknowledges that any Artwork created by Licensee or for Licensee hereunder is a "work made for hire" for Licensor under the U.S. Copyright Act, and any and all similar provisions of law under other jurisdictions, and that Licensor is the author of such works for all purposes, and that Licensor is the exclusive owner of all the rights comprised in the undivided copyright and all renewals, extensions and reversions therein, in and to such works in perpetuity and throughout the universe. Licensee hereby waives and releases in favor of Licensor all rights (if any) of "droit moral," rental rights and similar rights in and to the Artwork (the "Intangible Rights") and agrees that Licensor shall have the right to revise, condense, abridge, expand, adapt, change, modify, add to, subtract from, re-title, re-draw, re-color, or otherwise modify the Artwork, without the consent of Licensee.

Licensee hereby irrevocably grants, transfers and assigns to Licensor all right, title and interest, including copyrights, trademark rights, patent rights and other proprietary rights, it may have in and to the Artwork, in perpetuity and throughout the universe, and to all proprietary depictions, expressions or derivations of the Licensed Property created by or for Licensee. Licensee acknowledges that Licensor shall have the right to terminate this Agreement in the event Licensee asserts any rights (other than those specifically granted pursuant to this Agreement) in or to the Licensed Property or Artwork.

Licensee hereby warrants that any and all work created by Licensee under this Agreement apart from the materials provided to Licensee by Licensor is and shall be wholly original with or fully cleared by Licensee and shall not copy or otherwise infringe the rights of any third parties, and Licensee hereby indemnities Licensor and will hold Licensor harmless from any such claim of infringement or otherwise involving Licensee's performance hereunder. At the request of Licensor, Licensee shall execute such form(s) of assignment of copyright or other papers as Licensor may reasonably request in order to confirm and vest in Licensor the rights in the properties as provided for herein. In addition, Licensee hereby appoints Licensor as Licensee's Attorney-in-Fact to take such actions and to make, sign, execute, acknowledge and deliver all such documents as may from time to time be necessary to confirm in Licensor, its successors and assigns, all rights granted herein. If any third party makes or has made any contribution to the creation of Artwork authorized for use hereunder, Licensee agrees to obtain from such party a full confirmation and assignment of rights so that the foregoing rights shall vest fully in Licensor, in the form of the contributor's Agreement attached hereto as Exhibit 2 and by this reference made a part hereof, prior to commencing work, ensuring that all rights in the Artwork and Licensed Property arise in and are assigned to Licensor. Promptly upon entering into each such Agreement, Licensee shall give Licensor a copy of such Agreement. Licensee assumes all responsibility for such parties and agrees that Licensee shall bear any and all risks arising out of or relating to the performance of services by them and to the fulfillment of their obligations under the Contributor's Agreement.

Upon expiration or termination of this Agreement for any reason, or upon demand by Licensor at any time, Licensee shall promptly deliver to Licensor all Artwork or Licensed Property, whether finished or not, including drawings, drafts, sketches, illustrations, screens, data, digital files and information, copies or other items, information or things created in the course of preparing the Licensed Property and all materials provided to Licensee by Licensor hereunder, or, at Licensor's option and instruction, shall destroy some or all of the foregoing and shall confirm to Licensor in writing that Licensee has done so. Licensee shall not use such Artwork or Licensed Property, items, information or things, material, for any purpose other than is permitted under this Agreement.

(c)   Licensee shall, within thirty (30) days of receiving an invoice, pay Licensor for artwork executed for Licensee by Licensor (or by third parties under contract to Licensor) for use in the development of the Licensed Products and any related packaging, display and promotional materials at Licensor's prevailing commercial art rates. The foregoing shall include any artwork that, in Licensor's opinion, is necessary to modify artwork initially prepared by Licensee and submitted for approval. Estimates of artwork charges are available upon request.

(d)   Licensee shall cause to be imprinted, irremovably and legibly on each Licensed Products manufactured, distributed or sold under this Agreement, and all advertising, promotional, packaging and wrapping material wherein the Licensed Property appears, the following copyright and/or trademark notice(s):

(e)   In no event shall Licensee use, in respect to the Licensed Products and/or in relation to any advertising, promotional, packaging or wrapping material, any copyright or trademark notices which shall conflict with, be confusing with, or negate, any notices required hereunder by Licensor in respect to the Licensed Property.

(f)   Licensee agrees to deliver to Licensor free of cost six (6) of each of the Licensed Products together with their packaging and wrapping material for trademark registration purposes in compliance with applicable laws, simultaneously upon distribution to the public. Any copyrights or trademarks with respect to the Licensed Products shall be procured by and for the benefit of Licensor and at Licensor's expense. Licensee further agrees to provide Licensor with the date of the first use of the Licensed Products in interstate and intrastate commerce.

(g)   Licensee shall assist Licensor, at Licensor's expense, in the procurement, protection, and maintenance of Licensor's rights to the Licensed Property. Licensor may, in its sole discretion, commence or prosecute and effect the disposition of any claims or suits relative to the imitation, infringement and/or unauthorized use of the Licensed Property either in its own name, or in the name of Licensee, or join Licensee as a party in the prosecution of such claims or suits. Licensee agrees to cooperate fully with Licensor in connection with any such claims or suits and undertakes to furnish full assistance to Licensor in the conduct of all proceedings in regard thereto. Licensee shall promptly notify Licensor in writing of any infringements or imitations or unauthorized uses by others of the Licensed Property, on or in relation to products identical to, similar to or related to the Licensed Products. Licensor shall in its sole discretion have the right to settle or effect compromises in respect thereof. Licensee shall not institute any suit or take any action on account of such infringements, imitations or unauthorized uses.

9. APPROVALS AND QUALITY CONTROLS:

   (a) Licensee agrees to strictly comply and maintain compliance with the quality standards, specifications and rights of approval of Licensor in respect to any and all usage of the Licensed Property on or in relation to the Licensed Products throughout the Term of this Agreement and any renewals or extensions thereof (if applicable). Licensee agrees to furnish to Licensor free of cost for its written approval as to quality and style, samples of each of the Licensed Products, together with their packaging, hangtags, and wrapping material, as follows in the successive stages indicated: (i) rough sketches/layout concepts; (ii) finished artwork or final proofs; (iii) pre-production samples or strike-offs; and (iv) finished products, including packaged samples.

   (b) No Licensed Products and no material utilizing the Licensed Property shall be manufactured, sold, distributed or promoted by Licensee without prior written approval. Licensee may, subject to Licensor's prior written approval, use textual and/or pictorial matter pertaining to the Licensed Property on such promotional, display and advertising material as may, in its reasonable judgment, promote the sale of the Licensed Products. All advertising and promotional material relating to the Licensed Products must be submitted to the Licensor for its written approval at the following stages appropriate to the medium used: (i) rough concepts; (ii) layout, storyboard, script; and (iii) finished materials.

   (c) Approval or disapproval shall lie in Licensor's sole discretion. Any Licensed Products not so approved in writing shall be deemed unlicensed and shall not be manufactured or sold. If any unapproved Licensed Products are being sold, Licensor may, together with other remedies available to it including, but not limited to, immediate termination of this Agreement, require such Licensed Products to be immediately withdrawn from the market and to be destroyed, such destruction to be attested to in a certificate signed by an officer of Licensee.

(d) Any modification of a Licensed Product must be submitted in advance for Licensor's written approval as if it were a new Licensed Product. Approval of a Licensed Product which uses particular artwork does not imply approval of such artwork for use with a different Licensed Product.

(e) Licensed Products must conform in all material respects to the final production samples approved by Licensor. If in Licensor's reasonable judgement, the quality of a Licensed Product originally approved has deteriorated in later production runs, or if a Licensed Product has otherwise been altered, Licensor may, in addition to other remedies available to it, require that such Licensed Product be immediately withdrawn from the market.

(f) Licensee shall permit Licensor, to inspect Licensee's manufacturing operations, testing and payroll records (including those operations and records of any supplier or manufacturer approved pursuant to Paragraph 10(b) hereof) with respect to the Licensed Products.

(g) If any changes or modifications are required to be made to any material submitted to Licensor for its written approval in order to ensure compliance with Licensor's specifications or standards of quality, Licensee agrees promptly to make such changes or modifications.

(h) Subsequent to final approval, no fewer than twenty-four (24) production samples of Licensed Products will be sent to Licensor, to ensure quality control simultaneously upon distribution to the public. In addition, Licensee shall provide Licensor with six (6) catalogs which display all of Licensee's products, not just the Licensed Products. Further, Licensor shall have the right to purchase any and all Licensed Products in any quantity at the maximum discount price Licensee charges its best customer.

(i) To avoid confusion of the public, Licensee agrees not to associate other characters or properties with the Licensed Property on the Licensed Products or in any packaging, promotional or display materials unless Licensee receives Licensor's prior written approval. Furthermore, Licensee agrees not to use the Licensed

Property (or any component thereof) on any business sign, business cards, stationery or forms, nor as part of the name of Licensee's business or any division thereof.

(j) Licensee shall use its best efforts to notify its customers of the requirement that Licensor has the right to approve all promotional, display and advertising material pursuant to this Agreement.

(k) It is understood and agreed that any animation used in electronic media, including but not limited to animation for television commercials and character voices for radio commercials, shall be produced pursuant to a separate agreement between Licensee and _____, subject to customary rates. Any payment made for such animation shall be in addition to and shall not offset the Guaranteed Consideration set forth in Paragraph 1(b) hereof.

(l) Licensor's approval of Licensed Products (including without limitation, the Licensed Products themselves as well as promotional, display, and advertising materials) shall in no way constitute or be construed as an approval by Licensor of Licensee's use of any trademark, copyright and/or other proprietary materials, not owned by Licensor.

10. DISTRIBUTION; SUB-LICENSE MANUFACTURE:

(a) Within the Channels of Distribution set forth in Paragraph 1(a) hereof, Licensee shall sell the Licensed Products either to jobbers, wholesalers, distributors or retailers for sale or resale and distribution directly to the public. Unless explicitly set forth in Paragraph 1(a) hereof, Licensee shall not sell the Licensed Products through any cable home shopping service or through electronic media, including on any on-line network or service. If Licensee sells or distributes the Licensed Products at a special price, directly or indirectly, to itself, including without limitation, any subsidiary of Licensee or to any other person, firm, or corporation affiliated with Licensee or its officers, directors or major stockholders, for ultimate sale to unrelated third parties, Licensee shall pay royalties with respect to such sales or distribution, based upon the price generally charged the trade by Licensee.

(b) Licensee shall not be entitled to sub-license any of its rights under this Agreement. In the event Licensee is not the manufacturer of the Licensed Products, Licensee shall, subject to the prior written approval of Licensor, which approval shall not be unreasonably withheld, be entitled to utilize a third party manufacturer in connection with the manufacture and production of the Licensed Products, provided that such manufacturer shall execute a letter in the form of Exhibit 1 attached hereto and by this reference made a part hereof. In such event, Licensee shall remain primarily obligated under all of the provisions of this Agreement and any default of this Agreement by such manufacturer shall be deemed a default by Licensee hereunder. In no event shall any such third party manufacturer agreement include the right to grant any rights to subcontractors.

11. GOOD WILL: Licensee recognizes the great value of the publicity and good will associated with the Licensed Property and acknowledges: (i) such good will is exclusively that of Licensor; and (ii) that the Licensed Property has acquired a secondary meaning as Licensor's trademarks and/or identifications in the mind of the purchasing public. Licensee further recognizes and acknowledges that a breach by Licensee of any of its covenants, agreements or undertakings hereunder will cause Licensor irreparable damage, which cannot be readily remedied in damages in an action at law, and may, in addition thereto, constitute an infringement of Licensor's copyrights, trademarks and/other proprietary rights in, and to the Licensed Property, thereby entitling Licensor to equitable remedies, and costs.

12. LICENSOR'S WARRANTIES AND REPRESENTATIONS: Licensor represents and warrants to Licensee that:

(a) It has, and will have throughout the Term of this Agreement, the right to license the Licensed Property to Licensee in accordance with the terms and provisions of this Agreement; and

(b) The making of this Agreement by Licensor does not violate any agreements, rights or obligations of any person, firm or corporation.

13. LICENSEE'S WARRANTIES AND REPRESENTATIONS: Licensee represents and warrants to Licensor that, during the Term and thereafter:

(a) It will not attack the title of Licensor (or third parties that have granted rights to Licensor) in and to the Licensed Property or any copyright or trademarks pertaining thereto, nor will it attack the validity of the license granted hereunder;

(b) It will not harm, misuse or bring into disrepute the Licensed Property, but on the contrary, will maintain the value and reputation thereof to the best of its ability;

(c) It will manufacture, sell, promote and distribute the Licensed Products in an ethical manner and in accordance with the terms and intent of this Agreement, and in compliance with all applicable government regulations and industry standards;

(d)   It will not create any expenses chargeable to Licensor without the prior written approval of Licensor in each and every instance. It will not cause or allow any liens or encumbrances to be placed against the Licensed Property;

(e)   It will protect to the best of its ability its right to manufacture, sell, promote, and distribute the Licensed Products hereunder;

(f)   It will at all times comply with all government laws and regulations, including but not limited to product safety, food, health, drug, cosmetic, sanitary or other similar laws, and all voluntary industry standards relating or pertaining to the manufacture, sale, advertising or use of the Licensed Products, and shall maintain its appropriate customary high quality standards during the Term hereof. It shall comply with any regulatory agencies which shall have jurisdiction over the Licensed Products and shall procure and maintain in force any and all permissions, certifications and/or other authorizations from governmental and/or other official authorities that may be required in response thereto. Each Licensed Product and component thereof distributed hereunder shall comply with all applicable laws, regulations and voluntary industry standards. Licensee shall follow reasonable and proper procedures for testing that all Licensed Products comply with such laws, regulations and standards. Licensee shall permit Licensor or its designees to inspect testing records and procedures with respect to the Licensed Products for compliance. Licensed Products that do not comply with all applicable laws, regulations and standards shall automatically be deemed unapproved and immediately taken off the market;

(g)   It shall, upon Licensor's request, provide credit information to Licensor including, but not limited to, fiscal year-end financial statements (profit-and-loss statement and balance sheet) and operating statements;

(h)   It will provide Licensor with the date(s) of first use of the Licensed Products in interstate and intrastate commerce, where appropriate;

(i)   It will, pursuant to Licensor's instructions, duly take any and all necessary steps to secure execution of all necessary documentation for the recordation of itself as user of the Licensed Property in any jurisdiction where this is required or where Licensor reasonably requests that such recordation shall be effected.

Licensee further agrees that it will at its own expense cooperate with Licensor in cancellation of any such recordation at the expiration of this Agreement or upon termination of Licensee's right to use the Licensed Property. Licensee hereby appoints Licensor its Attorney-in-Fact for such purpose;

(j) It will not deliver or sell Licensed products outside the Territory or knowingly sell Licensed Products to a third party for delivery outside the Territory;

(k) It will not use any labor that violates any local labor laws, including all wage and hour laws, laws against discrimination and that it will not use prison, slave or child labor in connection with the manufacture of the Licensed Products;

(1) It shall at all times comply with all manufacturing, sales, distribution, retail and marketing policies and strategies promulgated by Licensor from time-to-time;

(m) If requested by Licensor to do so, it will utilize specific design elements of the Licensed Property provided to Licensee by Licensor on hangtags, labels, and other materials.

14. TERMINATION BY LICENSOR:

(a) Licensor shall have the right to terminate this Agreement without prejudice to any rights which it may have, whether pursuant to the provisions of this Agreement, or otherwise in law, or in equity, or otherwise, upon the occurrence of any one or more of the following events (herein called "defaults"):

(i) Licensee defaults in the performance of any of its obligations provided for in this Agreement; or

(ii) Licensee shall have failed to deliver to Licensor or to maintain in full force and effect the insurance referred to in Paragraph 7(c) hereof; or

(iii) Licensee shall fail to make any payments due hereunder on the date due; or

(iv) Licensee shall fail to deliver any of the statements required herein or to give access to the premises and/or license records pursuant to the provisions hereof to Licensor's authorized representatives for the purposes permitted hereunder; or

(v) Licensee shall fail to comply with any laws, regulations or voluntary industry standards as provided in Paragraph 13(f) hereof or any governmental agency or other body, office or official vested with appropriate authority finds that the

Licensed Products are harmful or defective in any way, manner or form, or are being manufactured, sold or distributed in contravention of applicable laws, regulations or standards, or in a manner likely to cause harm; or

(vi)   Licensee shall be unable to pay its debts when due, or shall make any assignment for the benefit of creditors, or shall file any petition under the bankruptcy or insolvency laws of any jurisdiction, county or place, or shall have or suffer a receiver or trustee to be appointed for its business or property, or be adjudicated a bankrupt or an insolvent; or

(vii)   Licensee does not commence in good faith to manufacture, distribute and sell each Licensed Products and utilize each character set forth in the Licensed Property ("Character") throughout the Territory on or before the Marketing Date and thereafter fails to diligently and continuously manufacture, distribute and sell each of the Licensed Products and utilize each Character throughout the Territory. Such default and Licensor's resultant right of termination (or recapture) shall only apply to the specific Character(s) and/or the specific Licensed Products, which or wherein Licensee fails to meet said Marketing Date requirement; or

(viii) Licensee shall manufacture, sell or distribute, whichever first occurs, any of the Licensed Products(s) without the prior written approval of Licensor as provided in Paragraph 9 hereof; or

(ix)   Licensee undergoes a substantial change of management or control; or

(x)   A manufacturer approved pursuant to Paragraph 10(b) hereof shall sell Licensed Products to parties other than Licensee or engage in conduct, which conduct if engaged in by Licensee would entitle Licensor to terminate this Agreement; or

(xi)   Licensee delivers or sells Licensed Products outside the Territory or knowingly sells Licensed Products to a third party who Licensee knows intends to, or who Licensee reasonably should suspect intends to, sell or deliver such Licensed Products outside the Territory; or

(xii)   Licensee uses any labor that violates any local labor laws and/or it uses prison, slave or child labor in connection with the manufacture of the Licensed Products; or

(xiii)   Licensee has made a material misrepresentation or has omitted to state a material fact necessary to make the statements not misleading; or

(xiv)   Licensee shall breach any other agreement in effect between Licensee on the one hand and Licensor on the other.

(b)   In the event any of these defaults occur, Licensor shall give notice of termination in writing to Licensee by facsimile and certified mail. Licensee shall have ten (10) days from the date of giving notice in which to correct any of these defaults (except subdivisions (vii), (viii), (xi) and (xiii) above, which are not curable), and failing such, this Agreement shall thereupon immediately terminate, and any and all payments then or later due from Licensee hereunder (including Guaranteed Consideration) shall then be promptly due and payable in full and no portion of those prior payments shall be repayable to Licensee.

15.   FINAL STATEMENT UPON TERMINATION OR EXPIRATION: Licensee shall deliver, as soon as practicable, but not later than thirty (30) days following expiration or termination of this Agreement, a statement indicating the number and description of Licensed Products on hand together with a description of all advertising and promotional materials relating thereto. Following expiration or termination of this Agreement, Licensee shall immediately cease any and all manufacturing of the Licensed Product. However, if Licensee has complied with all the terms of this Agreement, including, but not limited to, complete and timely payment of the Guaranteed Consideration and Royalty Payments, then Licensee may continue to distribute and sell its remaining inventory for a period not to exceed sixty (60) days following such termination or expiration (the "Sell-Off Period"), subject to payment of applicable royalties thereto. In no event, however, may Licensee distribute and sell during the Sell-Off Period an amount of Licensed Products that exceeds the average amount of Licensed Products sold during any consecutive sixty (60) day period during the Term. In the event this Agreement is terminated by Licensor for any reason under this Agreement, Licensee shall be deemed to have forfeited its Sell-Off Period. If Licensee has any remaining inventory of the Licensed Products following the Sell-Off Period, Licensee shall, at Licensor's option, make available such inventory to Licensor for purchase at or below cost, deliver up to Licensor for destruction said remaining inventory or furnish to Licensor an affidavit attesting to the destruction of said remaining inventory. Licensor shall have the right to conduct a physical inventory in order to ascertain or verify such inventory and/or statement. In the event that Licensee refuses

to permit Licensor to conduct such physical inventory, Licensee shall forfeit its right to the Sell-Off Period hereunder or any other rights to dispose of such inventory. In addition to the forfeiture, Licensor shall have recourse to all other legal remedies available to it.

16. NOTICES: Except as otherwise specifically provided herein, all notices which either party hereto is required or may desire to give to the other shall be given by addressing the same to the other at the address set forth above, or at such other address as may be designated in writing by any such party in a notice to the other given in the manner prescribed in this paragraph. All such notices shall be sufficiently given when the same shall be deposited so addressed, postage prepaid, in the United States mail and/or when the same shall have been delivered, so addressed, by facsimile or by overnight delivery service and the date of transmission by facsimile, receipt of overnight delivery service or two business days after mailing shall for the purposes of this Agreement be deemed the date of the giving of such notice.

17. NO PARTNERSHIP, ETC.: This Agreement does not constitute and shall not be construed as constitution of a partnership or joint venture between Licensor and Licensee. Neither party shall have any right to obligate or bind the other party in any manner whatsoever, and nothing herein contained shall give, or is intended to give, any rights of any kind to any third persons.

18. NO SUB-LICENSING/NON-ASSIGNABILITY: This Agreement shall bind and inure to the benefit of Licensor, its successors and assigns. This Agreement is personal to Licensee. Licensee shall not sub-license, franchise or delegate to third parties its rights hereunder (except as set forth in Paragraph 10(b) hereof). Neither this Agreement nor any of the rights of Licensee hereunder shall be sold transferred or assigned by Licensee and no rights hereunder shall devolve by operation of law or otherwise upon any receiver, liquidator, trustee or other party.

19. CONSTRUCTION: This Agreement shall be construed in accordance with the laws of the State of California of the United States of America without regard to its conflicts of laws provisions.

20. WAIVER, MODIFICATION, ETC.: No waiver, modification or cancellation of any term or condition of this Agreement shall be effective unless executed in writing by the party charged therewith. No written waiver shall excuse the performance of any acts other than those specifically referred to therein. The fact that the Licensor has not previously insisted upon Licensee expressly complying with any

provision of this Agreement shall not be deemed to be a waiver of Licensor's future right to require compliance in respect thereof and Licensee specifically acknowledges and agrees that the prior forbearance in respect of any act, term or condition shall not prevent Licensor from subsequently requiring full and complete compliance thereafter. If any term or provision of this Agreement is held to be invalid or unenforceable by any court of competent jurisdiction or any other authority vested with jurisdiction, such holding shall not affect the validity or enforceability of any other term or provision hereto and this Agreement shall be interpreted and construed as if such term or provision, to the extent the same shall have been held to be invalid, illegal or unenforceable, had never been contained herein. Headings of paragraphs herein are for convenience only and are without substantive significance.

21. ACCEPTANCE BY LICENSOR: This instrument, when signed by Licensee, shall be deemed an application for license and not a binding agreement unless and until accepted by Licensor by signature of a duly authorized officer and the delivery of such a signed copy to Licensee. The receipt and/or deposit by Licensor of any check or other consideration given by Licensee and/or delivery of any material by Licensor to Licensee shall not be deemed an acceptance by Licensor of this application. The foregoing shall apply to any documents relating to renewals or modifications hereof.

This Agreement shall be of no force or effect unless and until it is signed by all of the parties listed below:

AGREED AND ACCEPTED: AGREED AND ACCEPTED:

LICENSOR: LICENSEE:

By:_____   By:_____

Date:_____   Date:_____

EXHIBIT 1

RE: Approval of Third Party Manufacturer

Gentlemen:

    This letter will serve as notice to you that pursuant to Paragraph 10(b) of the License Agreement dated _____, 199_____, between _____ and _____ ("Licensee"), we have been engaged as the manufacturer for Licensee in connection with the manufacture of the Licensed Products as defined in the aforesaid License Agreement. We hereby acknowledge that we may not manufacture Licensed Products for, or sell or distribute Licensed Products to, anyone other than Licensee. We hereby further acknowledge that we have received a copy and are cognizant of the terms and conditions set forth in said License Agreement and hereby agree to observe those provisions of said License Agreement which are applicable to our function as manufacturer of the Licensed Products. It is expressly understood that we are obligated to comply with all local laws, including without limitation, labor laws, wage and hour laws and anti-discrimination laws and that you or your representatives shall, at anytime, have the right to inspect our facilities and review our records to ensure compliance therewith. It is understood that this engagement is on a royalty free basis and that we may not subcontract any of our work without your prior written approval.

    We understand that our engagement as the manufacturer for Licensee is subject to your written approval. We request, therefore, that you sign in the space below, thereby showing your acceptance of our engagement as aforesaid.

Very truly yours,

_____

manufacturer/company name

By: _____

signature

_____

print name

_____

address

_____

_____

AGREED TO AND ACCEPTED:

By:_____

Date:_____

EXHIBIT 2

CONTRIBUTOR' S AGREEMENT

I, _____ the undersigned ("Contributor"), have been engaged by _____ ("Licensee") to work on or contribute to the creation of Licensed Products, described as _____ by Licensee under an Agreement between Licensee and Licensor dated _____.

I understand and agree that the Licensed Products, and all artwork or other results of my services for Licensee in connection with such Licensed Products ("Work") is a "work made for hire" for Licensor and that all right, title and interest in and to the Work shall vest and remain with Licensor. I reserve no rights therein. Without limiting the foregoing, I hereby assign and transfer to Licensor all other rights whatsoever, in perpetuity throughout the universe which I may have or which may arise in me or in connection with the Work. I hereby waive all moral rights in connection with such Work together with any other rights which are not capable of assignment. I further agree to execute any further documentation relating to such transfer or waiver or relating to such Work at the request of Licensor or Licensee, failing which Licensor is authorized to execute same as my Attorney-in-Fact.

Contributor:

By:_____

Date:_____

Licensor:

By:_____

Date:_____

Form 55

Consent and Release Form

To: (*NAME AND ADDRESS OF PRODUCTION COMPANY*)

I understand that you desire to use all or parts of the events of my life in order to have one or more screenplays written and to produce, distribute, exhibit and exploit one or more motion pictures of any length in any and all' media now known or hereafter devised and sound recordings in any and all media now known or hereafter devised, and to publish one or more publications of any kind, based upon, derived from or suggested by all or parts of the events of my life. I have agreed to grant you certain rights in that connection. This Consent and Release confirms our agreement as follows:

1. <u>CONSIDERATION; GRANT OF RIGHTS:</u> In consideration of the payment to me of *(AMOUNT OF PAYMENT) ($(AMOUNT))* (payable upon your receipt of this Consent and Release signed by me) or (payable on *(SPECIFY DATE))* with full knowledge I hereby grant you, perpetually and irrevocably, the unconditional and exclusive right throughout the world to use, simulate and portray my name, likeness, voice, personality, personal identification and personal experiences, incidents, situations and events which heretofore occurred or hereafter occur (in whole or in part) based upon or taken from my life or otherwise in and in connection with motion pictures, sound recordings, publications and any and all other media of any nature whatsoever, whether now known or hereafter devised. Without limiting the generality of the foregoing, it is understood and agreed that said exclusive right includes theatrical, television, dramatic stage, radio, sound recording, music, publishing, commercial tie-up, merchandising, advertising and publicity rights in all media of every nature whatsoever whether now known or hereafter devised. I reserve no rights with respect to such uses. (All said rights are hereinafter referred to as the "Granted Rights.") It is further understood and agreed that the Granted Rights may be used in any manner and by any means, whether now known or unknown, and either factually or with such fictionalization, portrayal, impersonation, simulation and/or imitation or other modification as you, your successors and assigns, determine in your sole discretion. I further acknowledge that I am to receive no further payment with respect to any matter referred to herein. Any or all of the Granted Rights shall be freely assignable by you.

2. <u>RELEASE:</u> I agree hereby to release and discharge you, your employees, agents, licensees, successors and assigns from any and all claims, demands or causes of action that I may now have or may hereafter have for libel, defamation, invasion of privacy or right of publicity, infringement of copyright or violation of any other right arising out of or relating to any utilization of the Granted Rights or based upon any failure or omission to make use thereof.

3.   NAME-PSEUDONYM: You have informed me and I agree that in exercising the Granted Rights, you, if you so elect, may refrain from using my real name and may use a pseudonym which will be dissimilar to my real name, however, such agreement does not preclude you from the use of my real name should you in your sole discretion elect and that in connection therewith I shall have no claim arising out of the so-called right of privacy and/or right of publicity.

4.   FURTHER DOCUMENTS: I agree to execute such further documents and instruments as you may reasonably request in order to effectuate the terms and intentions of this Consent and Release, and in the event I fail or am unable to execute any such documents or instruments, I hereby appoint you as my irrevocable attorney in fact to execute any such documents or instruments, provided that said documents and instruments shall not be inconsistent with the terms and conditions of this Consent and Release. Your rights under this Clause 4 constitute a power coupled with an interest and are irrevocable.

5.   REMEDIES: No breach of this Consent and Release shall entitle me to terminate or rescind the rights granted to you herein, and I hereby waive the right, in the event of any such breach, to equitable relief or to enjoin, restrain or interfere with the production, distribution, exploitation, exhibition or use of any of the Granted Rights granted, it being my understanding that my sole remedy shall be the right to recover damages with respect to any such breach.

6.   PUBLIC DOMAIN MATERIAL: Nothing in this Consent and Release shall ever be construed to restrict, diminish or impair the rights of either you or me to utilize freely, in any work or media, any story, idea, plot, theme, sequence, scene, episode, incident, name, characterization or dialogue which may be in the public domain from whatever source derived.

7.   ENTIRE UNDERSTANDING: This Consent and Release expresses the entire understanding between you and me, and I agree that no oral understandings have been made with regard thereto. This Consent and Release may be amended only by written instrument signed by you and me. I acknowledge that in granting the Granted Rights I have not been induced to do so by any representations or assurances, whether written or oral, by you or your representatives relative to the manner in which the Granted Rights may be exercised and I agree that you are under no obligation to exercise any of the Granted Rights and agree I have not received any promises or inducements other than as herein set forth. The provisions hereof shall be binding upon me and my heirs, executors, administrators and successors. I acknowledge that you have explained to me that this Consent, Release has been prepared by your attorney and that you have recommended to me that I consult with my attorney in connection with this Consent and Release, and that I have either consulted with an attorney of my own choosing or have voluntarily chosen not to do so. [This Consent and Release

shall be construed in accordance with the laws of the State of CALIFORNIA applicable to agreements which are fully signed and performed within the State of CALIFORNIA and I hereby waive any rights I may have, known or unknown, pursuant to SECTION 1542 OF THE CALIFORNIA CIVIL CODE WHICH PROVIDES: "A GENERAL RELEASE DOES NOT EXTEND TO CLAIMS WHICH THE CREDITOR DOES NOT KNOW OR SUSPECT TO EXIST IN HIS FAVOR AT THE TIME OF EXECUTING THE RELEASE, WHICH IF KNOWN BY HIM MUST HAVE MATERIALLY AFFECTED HIS SETTLE-MENT WITH THE DEBTOR."]

In witness hereof and in full understanding of the foregoing, I have signed this Consent and Release on this (DATE).

_____
(*Signature*)

_____
(*Name, Please Print*)

_____
(Address, Please Print)

AGREED:

(Name of Production Company)

By _____

Its _____

STATUTES

STATUTES

Federal Trademark Statutes:

California Statutes:

Indiana Statutes:

Ind. Code §§

New York Statutes:

FEDERAL COPYRIGHT STATUTES:

17 U.S.C. § 101. Definitions

Except as otherwise provided in this title, as used in this title, the following terms and their variant forms mean the following:

An "anonymous work" is a work on the copies or phonorecords of which no natural person is identified as author.

An "architectural work" is the design of a building as embodied in any tangible medium of expression, including a building, architectural plans, or drawings. The work includes the overall form as well as the arrangement and composition of spaces and elements in the design, but does not include individual standard features.

"Audiovisual works" are works that consist of a series of related images which are intrinsically intended to be shown by the use of machines or devices such as projectors, viewers, or electronic equipment, together with accompanying sounds, if any, regardless of the nature of the material objects, such as films or tapes, in which the works are embodied.

The "Berne Convention" is the Convention for the Protection of Literary and Artistic Works, signed at Berne, Switzerland, on September 9, 1886, and all acts, protocols, and revisions thereto.

A work is a "Berne Convention work" if—

(1) in the case of an unpublished work, one or more of the authors is a national of a nation adhering to the Berne Convention, or in the case of a published work, one or more of the authors is a national of a nation adhering to the Berne Convention on the date of first publication;

(2) the work was first published in a nation adhering to the Berne Convention, or was simultaneously first published in a nation adhering to the Berne Convention and in a foreign nation that does not adhere to the Berne Convention;

(3) in the case of an audiovisual work—

(A) if one or more of the authors is a legal entity, that author has its headquarters in a nation adhering to the Berne Convention; or

(B) if one or more of the authors is an individual, that author is domiciled, or has his or her habitual residence in, a nation adhering to the Berne Convention;

(4) in the case of a pictorial, graphic, or sculptural work that is incorporated in a building or other structure, the building or structure is located in a nation adhering to the Berne Convention; or

(5) in the case of an architectural work embodied in a building, such building is erected in a country adhering to the Berne Convention.

For purposes of paragraph (1), an author who is domiciled in or has his or her habitual residence in, a nation adhering to the Berne Convention is considered to be a national of that nation. For purposes of paragraph (2), a work is considered to have been simultaneously published in two or more nations if its dates of publication are within 30 days of one another.

The "best edition" of a work is the edition, published in the United States at any time before the date of deposit, that the Library of Congress determines to be most suitable for its purposes.

A person's "children" are that person's immediate offspring, whether legitimate or not, and any children legally adopted by that person.

A "collective work" is a work, such as a periodical issue, anthology, or encyclopedia, in which a number of contributions, constituting separate and independent works in themselves, are assembled into a collective whole.

A "compilation" is a work formed by the collection and assembling of preexisting materials or of data that are selected, coordinated, or arranged in such a way that the resulting work as a whole constitutes an original work of authorship. The term "compilation" includes collective works.

A "computer program" is a set of statements or instructions to be used directly or indirectly in a computer in order to bring about a certain result.

"Copies" are material objects, other than phonorecords, in which a work is fixed by any method now known or later developed, and from which the work can be perceived, reproduced, or otherwise communicated, either directly or with the aid of a machine or device. The term "copies" includes the material object, other than a phonorecord, in which the work is first fixed.

'Copyright owner", with respect to any one of the exclusive rights comprised in a copyright, refers to the owner of that particular right.

For purposes of section 411, a work is a "United States work" only if—

(1) in the case of a published work, the work is first published—

(A) in the United States;

(B) simultaneously in the United States and another treaty party or parties, whose law grants a term of copyright protection that is the same as or longer than the term provided in the United States;

(C) simultaneously in the United States and a foreign nation that is not a treaty party; or

(D) in a foreign nation that is not a treaty party, and all of the authors of the work are nationals, domiciliaries, or habitual residents of, or in the case of an audiovisual work legal entities with headquarters in, the United States;

(2) in the case of an unpublished work, all the authors of the work are nationals, domiciliaries, or habitual residents of the United States, or, in the case of an unpublished audiovisual work, all the authors are legal entities with headquarters in, the United States; or

(3) in the case of a pictorial, graphic, or sculptural work incorporated in a building or structure, the building or structure is located in the United States.

A work is "created" when it is fixed in a copy or phonorecord for the first time; where a work is prepared over a period of time, the portion of it that has been fixed at any particular time constitutes the work as of that time, and where the work has been prepared in different versions, each version constitutes a separate work.

A "derivative work" is a work based upon one or more preexisting works, such as a translation, musical arrangement, dramatization, fictionalization, motion picture version, sound recording, art reproduction, abridgment, condensation, or any other form in which a work may be recast, transformed, or adapted. A work consisting of editorial revisions, annotations, elaborations, or other modifications which, as a whole, represent an original work of authorship, is a "derivative work".

A "device," "machine," or "process" is one now known or later developed.

A "digital transmission" is a transmission in whole or in part in a digital or other non-analog format.

To "display" a work means to show a copy of it, either directly or by means of a film, slide, television image, or any other device or process or, in the case of a motion picture or other audiovisual work, to show individual images nonsequentially.

An "establishment" is a store, shop, or any similar place of business open to the general public for the primary purpose of selling goods or services in which the majority of the gross square feet of space that is nonresidential is used for that purpose, and in which nondramatic musical works are performed publicly.

A "food service or drinking establishment" is a restaurant, inn, bar, tavern, or any other similar place of business in which the public or patrons assemble for the primary purpose of being served food or drink, in which the majority of the gross square feet of space that is nonresidential is used for that purpose, and in which nondramatic musical works are performed publicly.

A work is "fixed" in a tangible medium of expression when its embodiment in a copy or phonorecord, by or under the authority of the author, is sufficiently permanent or stable to permit it to be perceived, reproduced, or otherwise communicated for a period of more than transitory duration. A work consisting of sounds, images, or both, that are being transmitted, is "fixed" for purposes of this title if a fixation of the work is being made simultaneously with its transmission.

The "Geneva Phonograms Convention" is the Convention for the Protection of Producers of Phonograms Against Unauthorized Duplication of Their Phonograms, concluded at Geneva, Switzerland, on October 29, 1971.

The "gross square feet of space" of an establishment means the entire interior space of that establishment, and any adjoining outdoor space used to serve patrons, whether on a seasonal basis or otherwise.

The terms "including" and "such as" are illustrative and not limitative.

An "international agreement" is—

    (1) the Universal Copyright Convention;

    (2) the Geneva Phonograms Convention;

    (3) the Berne Convention;

    (4) the WTO Agreement;

(5) [Caution: This paragraph takes effect upon the entry into force of the WIPO Copyright Treaty with respect to the United States, as provided by § 105(b)(1) of Act Oct. 28, 1998, Pub. L. 105-304, which appears as a note to this section.] the WIPO Copyright Treaty;

(6) [Caution: This paragraph takes effect upon the entry into force of the WIPO Performances and Phonograms Treaty with respect to the United States, as provided by § 105(b)(2) of Act Oct. 28, 1998, Pub. L. 105-304, which appears as a note to this section.] the WIPO Performances and Phonograms Treaty; and

(7) any other copyright treaty to which the United States is a party.

A "joint work" is a work prepared by two or more authors with the intention that their contributions be merged into inseparable or interdependent parts of a unitary whole.

"Literary works" are works, other than audiovisual works, expressed in words, numbers, or other verbal or numerical symbols or indicia, regardless of the nature of the material objects, such as books, periodicals, manuscripts, phonorecords, film, tapes, disks, or cards, in which they are embodied.

"Motion pictures" are audiovisual works consisting of a series of related images which, when shown in succession, impart an impression of motion, together with accompanying sounds, if any.

To "perform" a work means to recite, render, play, dance, or act it, either directly or by means of any device or process or, in the case of a motion picture or other audiovisual work, to show its images in any sequence or to make the sounds accompanying it audible.

A "performing rights society" is an association, corporation, or other entity that licenses the public performance of nondramatic musical works on behalf of copyright owners of such works, such as the American Society of Composers, Authors and Publishers (ASCAP), Broadcast Music, Inc. (BMI), and SESAC, Inc.

"Phonorecords" are material objects in which sounds, other than those accompanying a motion picture or other audiovisual work, are fixed by any method now known or later developed, and from which the sounds can be perceived, reproduced, or otherwise communicated, either directly or with the aid of a machine or device. The term "phonorecords" includes the material object in which the sounds are first fixed.

"Pictorial, graphic, and sculptural works" include two-dimensional and three-dimensional works of fine, graphic, and applied art, photographs, prints and art reproductions, maps, globes, charts, diagrams, models, and technical drawings, including architectural plans. Such works shall include works of artistic craftsmanship insofar as their form but not their mechanical or utilitarian aspects are concerned; the design of a useful article, as defined in this section, shall be considered a pictorial, graphic, or sculptural work only if, and only to the extent that, such design incorporates pictorial, graphic, or sculptural features that can be identified separately from, and are capable of existing independently of, the utilitarian aspects of the article.

A "proprietor" is an individual, corporation, partnership, or other entity, as the case may be, that owns an establishment or a food service or drinking establishment, except that no owner or operator of a radio or television station licensed by the Federal Communications Commission, cable system or satellite carrier, cable or satellite carrier service or programmer, provider of online services or network access or the operator of facilities therefor, telecommunications company, or any other such audio or audiovisual service or programmer now known or as may be developed in the future, commercial subscription music service, or owner or operator of any other transmission service, shall under any circumstances be deemed to be a proprietor.

The term "financial gain" includes receipt, or expectation of receipt, of anything of value, including the receipt of other copyrighted works.

A "pseudonymous work" is a work on the copies or phonorecords of which the author is identified under a fictitious name.

'Publication' is the distribution of copies or phonorecords of a work to the public by sale or other transfer of ownership, or by rental, lease, or lending. The offering to distribute copies or phonorecords to a group of persons for purposes of further distribution, public performance, or public display, constitutes publication. A public performance or display of a work does not of itself constitute publication.

To perform or display a work "publicly" means—

(1) to perform or display it at a place open to the public or at any place where a substantial number of persons outside of a normal circle of a family and its social acquaintances is gathered; or

(2) to transmit or otherwise communicate a performance or display of the work to a place specified by clause (1) or to the public, by means of any device or process, whether the members of the public capable of receiving the performance or display receive it in the same place or in separate places and at the same time or at different times.

"Registration", for purposes of sections 205(c)(2), 405, 406, 410(d), 411, 412, and 506(e), means a registration of a claim in the original or the renewed and extended term of copyright.

"Sound recordings" are works that result from the fixation of a series of musical, spoken, or other sounds, but not including the sounds accompanying a motion picture or other audiovisual work, regardless of the nature of the material objects, such as disks, tapes, or other phonorecords, in which they are embodied.

"State" includes the District of Columbia and the Commonwealth of Puerto Rico, and any territories to which this title is made applicable by an Act of Congress.

A "transfer of copyright ownership" is an assignment, mortgage, exclusive license, or any other conveyance, alienation, or hypothecation of a copyright or of any of the exclusive rights comprised in a copyright, whether or not it is limited in time or place of effect, but not including a nonexclusive license.

A "transmission program" is a body of material that, as an aggregate, has been produced for the sole purpose of transmission to the public in sequence and as a unit.

To "transmit" a performance or display is to communicate it by any device or process whereby images or sounds are received beyond the place from which they are sent.

A "treaty party" is a country or intergovernmental organization other than the United States that is a party to an international agreement.

The "United States", when used in a geographical sense, comprises the several States, the District of Columbia and the Commonwealth of Puerto Rico, and the organized territories under the jurisdiction of the United States Government.

A "useful article" is an article having an intrinsic utilitarian function that is not merely to portray the appearance of the article or to convey information. An article that is normally a part of a useful article is considered a "useful article".

The author's "widow" or "widower" is the author's surviving spouse under the law of the author's domicile at the time of his or her death, whether or not the spouse has later remarried.

[Caution: This subdivision takes effect upon the entry into force of the WIPO Copyright Treaty with respect to the United States, as provided by § 105(b)(1) of Act Oct. 28, 1998, Pub. L. 105-304, which appears as a note to this section.] The "WIPO Copyright Treaty" is the WIPO Copyright Treaty concluded at Geneva, Switzerland, on December 20, 1996.

[Caution: This paragraph takes effect upon the entry into force of the WIPO Performances and Phonograms Treaty with respect to the United States, as provided by § 105(b)(2) of Act Oct. 28, 1998, Pub. L. 105-304, which appears as a note to this section.] The "WIPO Performances and Phonograms Treaty" is the WIPO Performances and Phonograms Treaty concluded at Geneva, Switzerland, on December 20, 1996.

A "work of visual art" is—

(1) a painting, drawing, print, or sculpture, existing in a single copy, in a limited edition of 200 copies or fewer that are signed and consecutively numbered by the author, or, in the case of a sculpture, in multiple cast, carved, or fabricated sculptures of 200 or fewer that are consecutively numbered by the author and bear the signature or other identifying mark of the author; or

(2) a still photographic image produced for exhibition purposes only, existing in a single copy that is signed by the author, or in a limited edition of 200 copies or fewer that are signed and consecutively numbered by the author.

A work of visual art does not include—

(A) (i) any poster, map, globe, chart, technical drawing, diagram, model, applied art, motion picture or other audiovisual work, book, magazine, newspaper, periodical, data base, electronic information service, electronic publication, or similar publication;

(ii) any merchandising item or advertising, promotional, descriptive, covering, or packaging material or container;

(iii) any portion or part of any item described in clause (i) or (ii);

(B) any work made for hire; or

(C) any work not subject to copyright protection under this title.

A "work of the United States Government" is a work prepared by an officer or employee of the United States Government as part of that person's official duties.

A "work made for hire" is—

(1) a work prepared by an employee within the scope of his or her employment; or

(2) a work specially ordered or commissioned for use as a contribution to a collective work, as a part of a motion picture or other audiovisual work, as a translation, as a supplementary work, as a compilation, as an instructional text, as a test, as answer material for a test, or as an atlas, if the parties expressly agree in a written instrument signed by them that the work shall be considered a work made for hire. For the purpose of the foregoing sentence, a "supplementary work" is a work prepared for publication as a secondary adjunct to a work by another author for the purpose of introducing, concluding, illustrating, explaining, revising, commenting upon, or assisting in the use of the other work, such as forewords, afterwords, pictorial illustrations, maps, charts, tables, editorial notes, musical arrangements, answer material for tests, bibliographies, appendixes, and indexes, and an "instructional text" is a literary, pictorial, or graphic work prepared for publication and with the purpose of use in systematic instructional activities.

The terms "WTO Agreement" and "WTO member country" have the meanings given those terms in paragraphs (9) and (10), respectively, of section 2 of the Uruguay Round Agreements Act [19 USCS § 3501].

(Amended Dec. 12, 1980, Pub. L. 96-517, § 10(a), 94 Stat. 3028; Oct. 31, 1988, Pub. L. 100-568, § 4(a)(1), 102 Stat. 2854; Dec. 1, 1990, Pub. L. 101-650, Title VI, § 602, Title VII, § 702, 104 Stat. 5128, 5133; June 26, 1992, Pub. L. 102-307, Title I, § 102(b)(2), 106 Stat. 266; Oct. 28, 1992, Pub. L. 102-563, § 3(b), 106 Stat. 4248; Nov. 1, 1995, Pub. L. 104-39, § 5(a), 109 Stat. 348; Nov. 13, 1997, Pub. L. 105-80, § 12(a)(3), 111 Stat. 1534; Dec. 16, 1997, Pub. L. 105-147, § 2(a), 111 Stat. 2678; Oct. 27, 1998, Pub. L. 105-298, Title II, § 205, 112 Stat. 2833; Oct. 28, 1998, Pub. L. 105-304, Title I, § 102(a), 112 Stat. 2861.)

17 U.S.C. § 102.   Subject matter of copyright

(a) Copyright protection subsists, in accordance with this title, in original works of authorship fixed in any tangible medium of expression, now known or later developed, from which they can be perceived, reproduced, or otherwise communicated, either directly or with the aid of a machine or device. Works of authorship include the following categories:

(1)   literary works;

(2)   musical works, including any accompanying words;

(3)   dramatic works, including any accompanying music;

(4)   pantomimes and choreographic works;

(5)   pictorial, graphic, and sculptural works;

(6)   motion pictures and other audiovisual works;

(7)   sound recordings; and

(8)   architectural works.

(b) In no case does copyright protection for an original work of authorship extend to any idea, procedure process, system, method of operation, concept, principle, or discovery, regardless of the form in which it is described, explained, illustrated, or embodied in such work.

17 U.S.C. § 103.   Compilations and derivative works

(a) The subject matter of copyright as specified by section 102 includes compilations and derivative works, but protection for a work employing preexisting material in which copyright subsists does not extend to any part of the work in which such material has been used unlawfully.

(b) The copyright in a compilation or derivative work extends only to the material contributed by the author of such work, as distinguished from the preexisting material employed in the work, and does not imply any exclusive right in the preexisting material. The copyright in such work is independent of, and does not affect or enlarge the scope, duration, ownership, or subsistence of, any copyright protection in the preexisting material.

17 U.S.C. § 104.   National origin

(a) Unpublished works. The works specified by sections 102 and 103, while unpublished, are subject to protection under this title without regard to the nationality or domicile of the author.

(b) Published works. The works specified by sections 102 and 103, when published, are subject to protection under this title if—

(1) on the date of first publication, one or more of the authors is a national or domiciliary of the United States, or is a national, domiciliary, or sovereign authority of a treaty party, or is a stateless person, wherever that person may be domiciled; or

(2) the work is first published in the United States or in a foreign nation that, on the date of first publication, is a treaty party; or

(3) the work is a sound recording that was first fixed in a treaty party; or

(4) the work is a pictorial, graphic, or sculptural work that is incorporated in a building or other structure, or an architectural work that is embodied in a building and the building or structure is located in the United States or a treaty party; or

(5) the work is first published by the United Nations or any of its specialized agencies, or by the Organization of American States; or

(6) the work comes within the scope of a Presidential proclamation. Whenever the President finds that a particular foreign nation extends, to works by authors who are nationals or domiciliaries of the United States or to works that are first published in the United States, copyright protection on substantially the same basis as that on which the foreign nation extends protection to works of its own nationals and domiciliaries and works first published in that nation, the President may by proclamation extend protection under this title to works of which one or more of the authors is, on the date of first publication, a national, domiciliary, or sovereign authority of that nation, or which was first published in that nation. The President may revise, suspend, or revoke any such proclamation or impose any conditions or limitations on protection under a proclamation.

For purposes of paragraph (2), a work that is published in the United States or a treaty party within 30 days after publication in a foreign nation that is not a treaty party shall be considered to be first published in the United States or such treaty party, as the case may be.

(c) Effect of Berne Convention. No right or interest in a work eligible for protection under this title may be claimed by virtue of, or in reliance upon, the provisions of the Berne Convention, or the adherence of the United States thereto. Any rights in a work eligible for protection under this title that derive from this title, other Federal or State statutes, or the common law, shall not be expanded or reduced by virtue of, or in reliance upon, the provisions of the Berne Convention, or the adherence of the United States thereto.

(d) Effect of phonograms treaties [Caution: This subsection takes effect upon the entry into force of the WIPO Performances and Phonograms Treaty with respect to the United States, as provided by § 105(b)(2) of Act Oct. 28, 1998, Pub. L. 105-304, which appears as 17 USCS § 101 note.]. Notwithstanding the provisions of subsection (b), no works other than sound recordings shall be eligible for protection under this title solely by virtue of the adherence of the United States to the Geneva Phonograms Convention or the WIPO Performances and Phonograms Treaty.

(Amended Oct. 31, 1988, Pub. L. 100-568, § 4(a)(2), (3), 102 Stat. 2855; Oct. 28, 1998, Pub. L. 105-304, Title I, § 102(b), 112 Stat. 2862.)

17 U.S.C. § 104A. Copyright in restored works

(a) Automatic protection and term.

(1) Term.

(A) Copyright subsists, in accordance with this section, in restored works, and vests automatically on the date of restoration.

(B) Any work in which copyright is restored under this section shall subsist for the remainder of the term of copyright that the work would have otherwise been granted in the United States if the work never entered the public domain in the United States.

(2) Exception. Any work in which the copyright was ever owned or administered by the Alien Property Custodian and in which the restored copyright would be owned by a government or instrumentality thereof, is not a restored work.

(b) Ownership of restored copyright. A restored work vests initially in the author or initial rightholder of the work as determined by the law of the source country of the work.

(c) Filing of notice of intent to enforce restored copyright against reliance parties. On or after the date of restoration, any person who owns a copyright in a restored work or an exclusive right therein may file with the Copyright Office a notice of intent to enforce that person's copyright or exclusive right or may serve such a notice directly on a reliance party. Acceptance of a notice by the Copyright Office is effective as to any reliance parties but shall not create a presumption of the validity of any of the facts stated therein. Service on a reliance party is effective as to that reliance party and any other reliance parties with actual knowledge of such service and of the contents of that notice.

(d) Remedies for infringement of restored copyrights.

(1) Enforcement of copyright in restored works in the absence of a reliance party. As against any party who is not a reliance party, the remedies provided in chapter 5 of this title [17 USCS §§ 501 et seq.] shall be available on or after the date of restoration of a restored copyright with respect to an act of infringement of the restored copyright that is commenced on or after the date of restoration.

(2) Enforcement of copyright in restored works as against reliance parties. As against a reliance party, except to the extent provided in paragraphs (3) and (4), the remedies provided in chapter 5 of this title [17 USCS §§ 501 et seq.] shall be available, with respect to an act of infringement of a restored copyright, on or after the date of restoration of the restored copyright if the requirements of either of the following subparagraphs are met:

(A) (i) The owner of the restored copyright (or such owner's agent) or the owner of an exclusive right therein (or such owner's agent) files with the Copyright Office, during the 24-month period beginning on the date of restoration, a notice of intent to enforce the restored copyright; and

(ii) (I) the act of infringement commenced after the end of the 12-month period beginning on the date of publication of the notice in the Federal Register;

(II) the act of infringement commenced before the end of the 12-month period described in subclause (I) and continued after the end of that 12-month period, in which case remedies shall be available only for infringement occurring after the end of that 12-month period; or

(III) copies or phonorecords of a work in which copyright has been restored under this section are made after publication of the notice of intent in the Federal Register.

(B) (i) The owner of the restored copyright (or such owner's agent) or the owner of an exclusive right therein (or such owner's agent) serves upon a reliance party a notice of intent to enforce a restored copyright; and

(ii) (I) the act of infringement commenced after the end of the 12-month period beginning on the date the notice of intent is received;

(II) the act of infringement commenced before the end of the 12-month period described in subclause (I) and continued after the end of that 12-month period, in which case remedies shall be available only for the infringement occurring after the end of that 12-month period; or

(III) copies or phonorecords of a work in which copyright has been restored under this section are made after receipt of the notice of intent.

In the event that notice is provided under both subparagraphs (A) and (B), the 12-month period referred to in such subparagraphs shall run from the earlier of publication or service of notice.

(3) Existing derivative works.

(A) In the case of a derivative work that is based upon a restored work and is created—

(i) before the date of the enactment of the Uruguay Round Agreements Act [enacted Dec. 8, 1994], if the source country of the restored work is an eligible country on such date, or

(ii) before the date on which the source country of the restored work becomes an eligible country, if that country is not an eligible country on such date of enactment,

a reliance party may continue to exploit that derivative work for the duration of the restored copyright if the reliance party pays to the owner of the restored copyright reasonable compensation for conduct which would be subject to a remedy for infringement but for the provisions of this paragraph.

(B) In the absence of an agreement between the parties, the amount of such compensation shall be determined by an action in United States district court, and shall reflect any harm to the actual or potential market for or value of the restored work from the reliance party's continued exploitation of the work, as well as compensation for the relative contributions of expression of the author of the restored work and the reliance party to the derivative work.

(4) Commencement of infringement for reliance parties. For purposes of section 412, in the case of reliance parties, infringement shall be deemed to have commenced before registration when acts which would have constituted infringement had the restored work been subject to copyright were commenced before the date of restoration.

(e) Notices of intent to enforce a restored copyright.

(1) Notices of intent filed with the copyright office.

(A) (i) A notice of intent filed with the Copyright Office to enforce a restored copyright shall be signed by the owner of the restored copyright or the owner of an exclusive right therein, who files the notice under subsection (d)(2)(A)(i) (hereafter in this paragraph referred to as the "owner"), or by the owner's agent, shall identify the title of the restored work, and shall include an English translation of the title and any other alternative titles known to the owner by which the restored work may be identified, and an address and telephone number at which the owner may be contacted. If the notice is signed by an agent, the agency relationship must have been constituted in a writing signed by the owner before the filing of the notice. The Copyright Office may specifically require in regulations other information to be included in the notice, but failure to provide such other information shall not invalidate the notice or be a basis for refusal to list the restored work in the Federal Register.

(ii) If a work in which copyright is restored has no formal title, it shall be described in the notice of intent in detail sufficient to identify it.

(iii) Minor errors or omissions may be corrected by further notice at any time after the notice of intent is filed. Notices of corrections for such minor errors or omissions shall be accepted after the period established in subsection (d)(2)(A)(i). Notices shall be published in the Federal Register pursuant to subparagraph (B).

(B) (i) The Register of Copyrights shall publish in the Federal Register, commencing not later than 4 months after the date of restoration for a particular nation and every 4 months thereafter for a period of 2 years, lists identifying restored works and the ownership thereof if a notice of intent to enforce a restored copyright has been filed.

(ii) Not less than 1 list containing all notices of intent to enforce shall be maintained in the Public Information Office of the Copyright Office and shall be available for public inspection and copying during regular business hours pursuant to sections 705 and 708.

(C) The Register of Copyrights is authorized to fix reasonable fees based on the costs of receipt, processing, recording, and publication of notices of intent to enforce a restored copyright and corrections thereto.

(D) (i) Not later than 90 days before the date the Agreement on Trade-Related Aspects of Intellectual Property referred to in section 101(d)(15) of the Uruguay Round Agreements Act [19 USCS § 3511(d)(15)] enters into force with respect to the United States, the Copyright Office shall issue and publish in the Federal Register regulations governing the filing under this subsection of notices of intent to enforce a restored copyright.

(ii) Such regulations shall permit owners of restored copyrights to file simultaneously for registration of the restored copyright.

(2) Notices of intent served on a reliance party.

(A) Notices of intent to enforce a restored copyright may be served on a reliance party at any time after the date of restoration of the restored copyright.

(B) Notices of intent to enforce a restored copyright served on a reliance party shall be signed by the owner or the owner's agent, shall identify the restored work and the work in which the restored work is used, if any, in detail sufficient to identify them, and shall include an English translation of the title, any other alternative titles known to the owner by which the work may be identified, the use or uses to which the owner objects, and an address and telephone number at which the reliance party may contact the owner. If the notice is signed by an agent, the agency relationship must have been constituted in writing and signed by the owner before service of the notice.

(3) Effect of material false statements. Any material false statement knowingly made with respect to any restored copyright identified in any notice of intent shall make void all claims and assertions made with respect to such restored copyright.

(f) Immunity from warranty and related liability.

(1) In general. Any person who warrants, promises, or guarantees that a work does not violate an exclusive right granted in section 106 shall not be liable for legal, equitable, arbitral, or administrative relief if the warranty, promise, or guarantee is breached by virtue of the restoration of copyright under this section, if such warranty, promise, or guarantee is made before January 1, 1995.

(2) Performances. No person shall be required to perform any act if such performance is made infringing by virtue of the restoration of copyright under the provisions of this section, if the obligation to perform was undertaken before January 1, 1995.

(g) Proclamation of copyright restoration. Whenever the President finds that a particular foreign nation extends, to works by authors who are nationals or domiciliaries of the United States, restored copyright protection on substantially the same basis as provided under this section, the President may by proclamation extend restored protection provided under this section to any work—

(1) of which one or more of the authors is, on the date of first publication, a national, domiciliary, or sovereign authority of that nation; or

(2) which was first published in that nation. The President may revise, suspend, or revoke any such proclamation or impose any conditions or limitations on protection under such a proclamation.

(h) Definitions. For purposes of this section and section 109(a):

(1) The term "date of adherence or proclamation" means the earlier of the date on which a foreign nation which, as of the date the WTO Agreement enters into force with respect to the United States, is not a nation adhering to the Berne Convention or a WTO member country, becomes—

(A) a nation adhering to the Berne Convention;

(B) a WTO member country;

(C) [Caution: This subparagraph takes effect upon the entry into force of the WIPO Copyright Treaty with respect to the United States, as provided by § 105(b)(1) of Act Oct. 28, 1998, Pub. L. 105-304, which appears as 17 USCS § 101 note.] a nation adhering to the WIPO Copyright Treaty;

(D) [Caution: This subparagraph takes effect upon the entry into force of the WIPO Performances and Phonograms Treaty with respect to the United States, as provided by § 105(b)(2) of Act Oct. 28, 1998, Pub. L. 105-304, which appears as 17 USCS § 101 note.] a nation adhering to the WIPO Performances and Phonograms Treaty; or

(E) subject to a Presidential proclamation under subsection (g).

(2) The "date of restoration" of a restored copyright is—

(A) January 1, 1996, if the source country of the restored work is a nation adhering to the Berne Convention or a WTO member country on such date, or

(B) the date of adherence or proclamation, in the case of any other source country of the restored work.

(3) The term "eligible country" means a nation, other than the United States, that—

(A) becomes a WTO member country after the date of the enactment of the Uruguay Round Agreements Act [enacted Dec. 8, 1994];

(B) on such date of enactment is, or after such date of enactment becomes, a nation adhering to the Berne Convention;

(C) [Caution: This subparagraph takes effect upon the entry into force of the WIPO Copyright Treaty with respect to the United States, as provided by § 105(b)(1) of Act Oct. 28, 1998, Pub. L. 105-304, which appears as 17 USCS § 101 note.] adheres to the WIPO Copyright Treaty;

(D) [Caution: This subparagraph takes effect upon the entry into force of the WIPO Performances and Phonograms Treaty with respect to the United States, as provided by § 105(b)(2) of Act Oct. 28, 1998, Pub. L. 105-304, which appears as 17 USCS § 101 note.] adheres to the WIPO Performances and Phonograms Treaty; or

(E) after such date of enactment becomes subject to a proclamation under subsection (g).

(4) The term "reliance party" means any person who—

(A) with respect to a particular work, engages in acts, before the source country of that work becomes an eligible country, which would have violated section 106 if the restored work had been subject to copyright protection, and who, after the source country becomes an eligible country, continues to engage in such acts;

(B) before the source country of a particular work becomes an eligible country, makes or acquires 1 or more copies or phonorecords of that work; or

(C) as the result of the sale or other disposition of a derivative work covered under subsection (d)(3), or significant assets of a person described in subparagraph (A) or (B), is a successor, assignee, or licensee of that person.

(5) The term "restored copyright" means copyright in a restored work under this section.

(6) The term "restored work" means an original work of authorship that—

(A) is protected under subsection (a);

(B) is not in the public domain in its source country through expiration of term of protection;

(C) is in the public domain in the United States due to—

(i) noncompliance with formalities imposed at any time by United States copyright law, including failure of renewal, lack of proper notice, or failure to comply with any manufacturing requirements;

(ii) lack of subject matter protection in the case of sound recordings fixed before February 15, 1972; or

(iii) lack of national eligibility; and

(D) has at least one author or rightholder who was, at the time the work was created, a national or domiciliary of an eligible country, and if published, was first published in an eligible country and not published in the United States during the 30-day period following publication in such eligible country.

(7) The term "rightholder" means the person—

(A) who, with respect to a sound recording, first fixes a sound recording with authorization, or

(B) who has acquired rights from the person described in subparagraph (A) by means of any conveyance or by operation of law.

(8) The "source country" of a restored work is—

(A) a nation other than the United States;

(B) in the case of an unpublished work—

(i) the eligible country in which the author or rightholder is a national or domiciliary, or, if a restored work has more than 1 author or rightholder, of which the majority of foreign authors or rightholders are nationals or domiciliaries; or

(ii) if the majority of authors or rightholders are not foreign, the nation other than the United States which has the most significant contacts with the work; and

(C) in the case of a published work—

(i) the eligible country in which the work is first published, or

(ii) if the restored work is published on the same day in 2 or more eligible countries, the eligible country which has the most significant contacts with the work.

(Added Dec. 8, 1993, Pub. L. 103-182, Title III, Subtitle C, § 334(a), 107 Stat. 2115; Amended Dec. 8, 1994, Pub. L. 103-465, Title V, Subtitle A, § 514(a), 108 Stat. 4976; Oct. 11, 1996, Pub. L. 104-295, § 20(e)(2), 110 Stat. 3529; Nov. 13, 1997, Pub. L. 105-80, § 2, 111 Stat. 1530; Oct. 28, 1998, Pub. L. 105-304, Title I, § 102(c), 112 Stat. 2862.)

17 U.S.C. § 106. Exclusive rights

Subject to sections 107 through 120, the owner of copyright under this title has the exclusive rights to do and to authorize any of the following:

(1) to reproduce the copyrighted work in copies or phonorecords;

(2) to prepare derivative works based upon the copyrighted work;

(3) to distribute copies or phonorecords of the copyrighted work to the public by sale or other transfer of ownership, or by rental, lease, or lending;

(4) in the case of literary, musical, dramatic, and choreographic works, pantomimes, and motion pictures and other audiovisual works, to perform the copyrighted work publicly; and

(5) in the case of literary, musical, dramatic, and choreographic works, pantomimes, and pictorial, graphic, or sculptural works, including the

individual images of a motion picture or other audiovisual work, to display the copyrighted work publicly.

(6) in the case of sound recordings, to perform the copyrighted work publicly by means of a digital audio transmission.

17 U.S.C. § 106A. Rights of attribution and integrity

(a) **Rights of Attribution and Integrity.** Subject to section 107 and independent of the exclusive rights provided in section 106, the author of a work of visual art—

(1) shall have the right—

(A) to claim authorship of that work, and

(B) to prevent the use of his or her name as the author of any work of visual art which he or she did not create;

(2) shall have the right to prevent the use of his or her name as the author of the work of visual art in the event of a distortion, mutilation, or other modification of the work which would be prejudicial to his or her honor or reputation; and

(3) subject to the limitations set forth in section 113(d), shall have the right—

(A) to prevent any intentional distortion, mutilation, or other modification of that work which would be prejudicial to his or her honor or reputation, and any intentional distortion, mutilation, or modification of that work is a violation of that right, and

(B) to prevent any destruction of a work of recognized stature, and any intentional or grossly negligent destruction of that work is a violation of that right.

(b) **Scope and Exercise of Rights.** Only the author of a work of visual art has the rights conferred by subsection (a) in that work, whether or not the author is the copyright owner. The authors of a joint work of visual art are co-owners of the rights conferred by subsection (a) in that work.

(c) **Exceptions.**

(1) The modification of a work of visual art which is a result of the passage of time or the inherent nature of the materials is not a distortion, mutilation, or other modification described in subsection (a)(3)(A).

(2) The modification of a work of visual art which is the result of conservation, or of the public presentation, including lighting and placement, of the work is not a destruction, distortion, mutilation, or other modification described in subsection (a)(3) unless the modification is caused by gross negligence.

(3) The rights described in paragraphs (1) and (2) of subsection (a) shall not apply to any reproduction, depiction, portrayal, or other use of a work in, upon, or in any connection with any item described in subparagraph (A) or

(B) of the definition of "work of visual art" in section 101, and any such reproduction, depiction, portrayal, or other use of a work is not a destruction, distortion, mutilation, or other modification described in paragraph (3) of subsection (a).

(d) **Duration of Rights.**

(1) With respect to works of visual art created on or after the effective date set forth in section 610(a) of the Visual Artists Rights Act of 1990, the rights conferred by subsection (a) shall endure for a term consisting of the life of the author.

(2) With respect to works of visual art created before the effective date set forth in section 610(a) of the Visual Artists Rights Act of 1990, but title to which has not, as of such effective date, been transferred from the author, the rights conferred by subsection (a) shall be coextensive with, and shall expire at the same time as, the rights conferred by section 106.

(3) In the case of a joint work prepared by two or more authors, the rights conferred by subsection (a) shall endure for a term consisting of the life of the last surviving author.

(4) All terms of the rights conferred by subsection (a) run to the end of the calendar year in which they would otherwise expire.

(e) **Transfer and Waiver.**

(1) The rights conferred by subsection (a) may not be transferred, but those rights may be waived if the author expressly agrees to such waiver in a written instrument signed by the author. Such instrument shall specifically identify the work, and uses of that work, to which the waiver applies, and the waiver shall apply only to the work and uses so identified. In the case of a joint work prepared by two or more authors, a waiver of rights under this paragraph made by one such author waives such rights for all such authors.

(2) Ownership of the rights conferred by subsection (a) with respect to a work of visual art is distinct from ownership of any copy of that work, or of a copyright or any exclusive right under a copyright in that work. Transfer of ownership of any copy of a work of visual art, or of a copyright or any exclusive right under a copyright, shall not constitute a waiver of the rights conferred by subsection (a). Except as may otherwise be agreed by the author in a written instrument signed by the author, a waiver of the rights conferred by subsection (a) with respect to a work of visual art shall not constitute a transfer of ownership of any copy of that work, or of ownership of a copyright or of any exclusive right under a copyright in that work.

17 U.S.C. § 107. Fair use

Notwithstanding the provisions of sections 106 and 106A, the fair use of a copyrighted work, including such use by reproduction in copies or phonorecords or by any other means specified by that section, for purposes such as criticism, comment, news reporting, teaching (including multiple copies for classroom use), scholarship, or research, is not an infringement of copyright. In determining whether the use made of a work in any particular case is a fair use the factors to be considered shall include—

(1) the purpose and character of the use, including whether such use is of a commercial nature or is for nonprofit educational purposes;

(2) the nature of the copyrighted work;

(3) the amount and substantiality of the portion used in relation to the copyrighted work as a whole; and

(4) the effect of the use upon the potential market for or value of the copyrighted work.

The fact that a work is unpublished shall not itself bar a finding of fair use if such finding is made upon consideration of all the above factors.

17 U.S.C. § 108. Limitations on exclusive rights: Reproduction by libraries and archives

(a) Except as otherwise provided in this title and notwithstanding the provisions of section 106, it is not an infringement of copyright for a library or archives, or any of its employees acting within the scope of their employment, to reproduce no more than one copy or phonorecord of a work, except as provided in subsections (b) and (c), or to distribute such copy or phonorecord, under the conditions specified by this section, if—

(1) the reproduction or distribution is made without any purpose of direct or indirect commercial advantage;

(2) the collections of the library or archives are (i) open to the public, or (ii) available not only to researchers affiliated with the library or archives or with the institution of which it is a part, but also to other persons doing research in a specialized field; and

(3) the reproduction or distribution of the work includes a notice of copyright that appears on the copy or phonorecord that is reproduced under the provisions of this section, or includes a legend stating that the work may be protected by copyright if no such notice can be found on the copy or phonorecord that is reproduced under the provisions of this section.

(b) The rights of reproduction and distribution under this section apply to three copies or phonorecords of an unpublished work duplicated solely for purposes of preservation and security or for deposit for research use in another library or archives of the type described by clause (2) of subsection (a), if—

(1) the copy or phonorecord reproduced is currently in the collections of the library or archives; and

(2) any such copy or phonorecord that is reproduced in digital format is not otherwise distributed in that format and is not made available to the public in that format outside the premises of the library or archives.

(c) The right of reproduction under this section applies to three copies or phonorecords of a published work duplicated solely for the purpose of replacement of a copy or phonorecord that is damaged, deteriorating, lost, or stolen, or if the existing format in which the work is stored has become obsolete, if—

(1) the library or archives has, after a reasonable effort, determined that an unused replacement cannot be obtained at a fair price; and

(2) any such copy or phonorecord that is reproduced in digital format is not made available to the public in that format outside the premises of the library or archives in lawful possession of such copy.

For purposes of this subsection, a format shall be considered obsolete if the machine or device necessary to render perceptible a work stored in that format is no longer manufactured or is no longer reasonably available in the commercial marketplace.

(d) The rights of reproduction and distribution under this section apply to a copy, made from the collection of a library or archives where the user makes his or her request or from that of another library or archives, of no more than one article or other contribution to a copyrighted collection or periodical issue, or to a copy or phonorecord of a small part of any other copyrighted work, if—

(1) the copy or phonorecord becomes the property of the user, and the library or archives has had no notice that the copy or phonorecord would be used for any purpose other than private study, scholarship, or research; and

(2) the library or archives displays prominently, at the place where orders are accepted, and includes on its order form, a warning of copyright in accordance with requirements that the Register of Copyrights in accordance with requirements that the Register of Copyrights shall prescribe by regulation.

(e) The rights of reproduction and distribution under this section apply to the entire work, or to a substantial part of it, made from the collection of a library or archives where the user makes his or her request or from that of another library or archives, if the library or archives has first determined, on the basis of a reasonable investigation, that a copy or phonorecord of the copyrighted work cannot be obtained at a fair price, if—

(1) the copy or phonorecord becomes the property of the user, and the library or archives has had no notice that the copy or phonorecord would be used for any purpose other than private study, scholarship, or research; and

(2) the library or archives displays prominently, at the place where orders are accepted, and includes on its order form, a warning of copyright in

accordance with requirements that the Register of Copyrights shall prescribe by regulation.

(f) Nothing in this section—

— (1) shall be construed to impose liability for copyright infringement upon a library or archives or its employees for the unsupervised use of reproducing equipment located on its premises: Provided, That such equipment displays a notice that the making of a copy may be subject to the copyright law;

(2) excuses a person who uses such reproducing equipment or who requests a copy or phonorecord under subsection (d) from liability for copyright infringement for any such act, or for any later use of such copy or phonorecord, if it exceeds fair use as provided by section 107;

(3) shall be construed to limit the reproduction and distribution by lending of a limited number of copies and excerpts by a library or archives of an audiovisual news program, subject to clauses (1), (2), and (3) of subsection (a); or

(4) in any way affects the right of fair use as provided by section 107, or any contractual obligations assumed at any time by the library or archives when it obtained a copy or phonorecord of a work in its collections.

(g) The rights of reproduction and distribution under this section extend to the isolated and unrelated reproduction or distribution of a single copy or phonorecord of the same material on separate occasions, but do not extend to cases where the library or archives, or its employee—

(1) is aware or has substantial reason to believe that it is engaging in the related or concerted reproduction or distribution of multiple copies or phonorecords of the same material, whether made on one occasion or over a period of time, and whether intended for aggregate use by one or more individuals or for separate use by the individual members of a group; or

(2) engages in the systematic reproduction or distribution of single or multiple copies or phonorecords of material described in subsection (d): Provided, That nothing in this clause prevents a library or archives from participating in interlibrary arrangements that do not have, as their purpose or effect, that the library or archives receiving such copies or phonorecords for distribution does so in such aggregate quantities as to substitute for a subscription to or purchase of such work.

(h) (1) For purposes of this section, during the last 20 years of any term of copyright of a published work, a library or archives, including a nonprofit educational institution that functions as such, may reproduce, distribute, display, or perform in facsimile or digital form a copy or phonorecord of such work, or portions thereof, for purposes of preservation, scholarship, or research, if such library or archives has first determined, on the basis of a reasonable investigation, that none of the conditions set forth in subparagraphs (A), (B), and (C) of paragraph (2) apply.

(2) No reproduction, distribution, display, or performance is authorized under this subsection if—

(A) the work is subject to normal commercial exploitation;

(B) a copy or phonorecord of the work can be obtained at a reasonable price; or

(C) the copyright owner or its agent provides notice pursuant to regulations promulgated by the Register of Copyrights that either of the conditions set forth in subparagraphs (A) and (B) applies.

(3) The exemption provided in this subsection does not apply to any subsequent uses by users other than such library or archives.

(i) The rights of reproduction and distribution under this section do not apply to a musical work, a pictorial, graphic or sculptural work, or a motion picture or other audiovisual work other than an audiovisual work dealing with news, except that no such limitation shall apply with respect to rights granted by subsections (b) and (c), or with respect to pictorial or graphic works published as illustrations, diagrams, or similar adjuncts to works of which copies are reproduced or distributed in accordance with subsections (d) and (e).

(Amended June 26, 1992, Pub. L. 102-307, Title III, § 301, 106 Stat. 272; Nov. 13, 1997, Pub. L. 105-80, § 12(a)(4), 111 Stat. 1534; Oct. 27, 1998, Pub. L. 105-298, Title I, § 104, 112 Stat. 2829; Oct. 28, 1998, Pub. L. 105-304, Title IV, § 404, 112 Stat. 2889.)

17 U.S.C. § 109. Effect of transfer of particular copy or phonorecord

(a) Notwithstanding the provisions of section 106(3), the owner of a particular copy or phonorecord lawfully made under this title, or any person authorized by such owner, is entitled, without the authority of the copyright owner, to sell or otherwise dispose of the possession of that copy or phonorecord. Notwithstanding the preceding sentence, copies or phonorecords of works subject to restored copyright under section 104A that are manufactured before the date of restoration of copyright or, with respect to reliance parties, before publication or service of notice under section 104A(e), may be sold or otherwise disposed of without the authorization of the owner of the restored copyright for purposes of direct or indirect commercial advantage only during the 12-month period beginning on —

(1) the date of the publication in the Federal Register of the notice of intent filed with the Copyright Office under section 104A(d)(2))A), or

(2) the date of the receipt of actual notice served under section 104A(d)(2)(B), whichever occurs first.

(b)(1)(A) Notwithstanding the provisions of subsection (a), unless authorized by the owners of copyright in the sound recording or the owner of copyright in a computer program (including any tape, disk, or other medium embodying such program), and in the case of a sound recording in the musical works embodied therein, neither the owner of a particular phonorecord nor any person in possession of a particular copy of a computer program (including any tape, disk, or other medium embodying such program), may, for the purposes of direct or indirect commercial advantage, dispose of, or authorize the disposal of, the possession of that phonorecord or computer program (including any tape, disk, or other medium embodying such program) by rental, lease, or lending, or by any other act or practice in the nature of rental, lease, or lending. Nothing in the preceding sentence shall apply to the rental, lease, or lending of a phonorecord for nonprofit purposes by a nonprofit library or nonprofit educational institution. The transfer of possession of a lawfully made copy of a computer program by a nonprofit educational institution to another nonprofit educational institution or to faculty, staff, and students does not constitute rental, lease, or lending for direct or indirect commercial purposes under this subsection.

(B) This subsection does not apply to—

(i) a computer program which is embodied in a machine or product and which cannot be copied during the ordinary operation or use of the machine or product; or

(ii) a computer program embodied in or used in conjunction with a limited purpose computer that is designed for playing video games and may be designed for other purposes.

(C) Nothing in this subsection affects any provision of chapter 9 of this title.

(2)(A) Nothing in this subsection shall apply to the lending of a computer program for nonprofit purposes by a nonprofit library, if each copy of a computer program which is lent by such library has affixed to the packaging containing the program a warning of copyright in accordance with requirements that the Register of Copyrights shall prescribe by regulation.

(B) Not later than three years after the date of the enactment of the Computer Software Rental Amendments Act of 1990, and at such times thereafter as the Register of Copyright considers appropriate, the Register of Copyrights, after consultation with representatives of copyright owners and librarians, shall submit to the Congress a report stating whether this paragraph has achieved its intended purpose of maintaining the integrity of the copyright system while providing nonprofit libraries the capability to fulfill their function. Such report shall advise the Congress as to any information or recommendations that the Register of Copyrights considers necessary to carry out the purposes of this subsection.

(3) Nothing in this subsection shall affect any provision of the antitrust laws. For purposes of the preceding sentence, "antitrust laws" has the meaning given that term in the first section of the Clayton Act and includes section 5 of the Federal Trade Commission Act to the extent that section relates to unfair methods of competition.

(4) Any person who distributes a phonorecord or a copy of a computer program (including any tape, disk, or other medium embodying such program) in violation of paragraph (1) is an infringer of copyright under section 501 of this title and is subject to the remedies set forth in sections 502, 503, 504, 505, and 509. Such violation shall not be a criminal offense under section 506 or cause such person to be subject to the criminal penalties set forth in section 2319 of title 18.

(c) Notwithstanding the provisions of section 106(5), the owner of a particular copy lawfully made under this title, or any person authorized by such owner, is entitled, without the authority of the copyright owner, to display that copy publicly, either directly or by the projection of no more than one image at a time, to viewers present at the place where the copy is located.

(d) The privileges prescribed by subsections (a) and (c) do not, unless authorized by the copyright owner, extend to any person who has acquired possession of the copy or phonorecord from the copyright owner, by rental, lease, loan, or otherwise, without acquiring ownership of it.

(e) Notwithstanding the provisions of sections 106(4) and 106(5), in the case of an electronic audiovisual game intended for use in coin-operated equipment, the owner of a particular copy of such a game lawfully made under this title, is entitled, without the authority of the copyright owner of the game, to publicly perform or display that game in coin-operated equipment, except that this subsection shall not apply to any work of authorship embodied in the audiovisual game if the copyright owner of the electronic audiovisual game is not also the copyright owner of the work of authorship.

17 U.S.C. § 110. Limitations on exclusive rights: Exemption of certain performances and displays

Notwithstanding the provisions of section 106, the following are not infringements of copyright:

(1) performance or display of a work by instructors or pupils in the course of face-to-face teaching activities of a nonprofit educational institution, in a classroom or similar place devoted to instruction, unless, in the case of a motion picture or other audiovisual work, the performance, or the display of individual images, is given by means of a copy that was not lawfully made under this title, and that the person responsible for the performance knew or had reason to believe was not lawfully made;

(2) performance of a nondramatic literary or musical work or display of a work, by or in the course of a transmission, if—

(A) the performance or display is a regular part of the systematic instructional activities of a governmental body or a nonprofit educational institution; and

(B) the performance or display is directly related and of material assistance to the teaching content of the transmission; and

(C) the transmission is made primarily for—

(i) reception in classrooms or similar places normally devoted to instruction, or

(ii) reception by persons to whom the transmission is directed because their disabilities or other special circumstances prevent their attendance in classrooms or similar places normally devoted to instruction, or

(iii) reception by officers or employees of governmental bodies as a part of their official duties or employment;

(3) performance of a nondramatic literary or musical work or of a dramatico-musical work of a religious nature, or display of a work, in the course of services at a place of worship or other religious assembly;

(4) performance of a nondramatic literary or musical work otherwise than in a transmission to the public, without any purpose of direct or indirect commercial advantage and without payment of any fee or other compensation for the performance to any of its performers, promoters, or organizers, if—

(A) there is no direct or indirect admission charge; or

(B) the proceeds, after deducting the reasonable costs of producing the performance, are used exclusively for educational, religious, or charitable purposes and not for private financial gain, except where the copyright owner has served notice of objection to the performance under the following conditions;

(i) the notice shall be in writing and signed by the copyright owner or such owner's duly authorized agent; and

(ii) the notice shall be served on the person responsible for the performance at least seven days before the date of the performance, and shall state the reasons for the objection; and

(iii) the notice shall comply, in form, content, and manner of service, with requirements that the Register of Copyrights shall prescribe by regulation;

(5) (A) except as provided in subparagraph (B), communication of a transmission embodying a performance or display of a work by the public reception of the transmission on a single receiving apparatus of a kind commonly used in private homes, unless—

[(i)](A) a direct charge is made to see or hear the transmission; or

[(ii)](B) the transmission thus received is further transmitted to the public;

(B) communication by an establishment of a transmission or retransmission embodying a performance or display of a nondramatic musical work intended to be received by the general public, originated by a radio or television broadcast station licensed as such by the Federal Communications Commission, or, if an audiovisual transmission, by a cable system or satellite carrier, if—

(i) in the case of an establishment other than a food service or drinking establishment, either the establishment in which the communication occurs has less than 2,000 gross square feet of space (excluding space used for customer parking and for no other purpose), or the establishment in which the communication occurs has 2,000 or more gross square feet of space (excluding space used for customer parking and for no other purpose) and—

(I) if the performance is by audio means only, the performance is communicated by means of a total of not more than 6 loudspeakers, of which not more than 4 loudspeakers are located in any 1 room or adjoining outdoor space; or

(II) if the performance or display is by audiovisual means, any visual portion of the performance or display is communicated by means of a total of not more than 4 audiovisual devices, of which not more than 1 audiovisual device is located in any 1 room, and no such audiovisual device has a diagonal screen size greater than 55 inches, and any audio portion of the performance or display is communicated by means of a total of not more than 6 loudspeakers, of which not more than 4 loudspeakers are located in any 1 room or adjoining outdoor space;

(ii) in the case of a food service or drinking establishment, either the establishment in which the communication occurs has less than 3,750 gross square feet of space (excluding space used for customer parking and for no other purpose), or the establishment in which the communication occurs has 3,750 gross square feet of space or more (excluding space used for customer parking and for no other purpose) and—

(I) if the performance is by audio means only, the performance is communicated by means of a total of not more than 6 loudspeakers, of which not more than 4 loudspeakers are located in any 1 room or adjoining outdoor space; or

(II) if the performance or display is by audiovisual means, any visual portion of the performance or display is communicated by means of a total of not more than 4 audiovisual devices, of which not more than one audiovisual device is located in any 1 room, and no such audiovisual device has a diagonal screen size greater than 55 inches, and any audio portion of the performance or display is communicated by means of a total of not more than 6 loudspeakers, of which not more than 4 loudspeakers are located in any 1 room or adjoining outdoor space;

(iii) no direct charge is made to see or hear the transmission or retransmission;

(iv) the transmission or retransmission is not further transmitted beyond the establishment where it is received; and

(v) the transmission or retransmission is licensed by the copyright owner of the work so publicly performed or displayed;

(6) performance of a nondramatic musical work by a governmental body or a nonprofit agricultural or horticultural organization, in the course of an annual agricultural or horticultural fair or exhibition conducted by such body or organization; the exemption provided by this clause shall extend to any liability for copyright infringement that would otherwise be imposed on such body or organization, under doctrines of vicarious liability or related infringement, for a performance by a concessionnaire, business establishment, or other person at such fair or exhibition, but shall not excuse any such person from liability for the performance;

(7) performance of a nondramatic musical work by a vending establishment open to the public at large without any direct or indirect admission charge, where the sole purpose of the performance is to promote the retail sale of copies or phonorecords of the work, or of the audiovisual or other devices utilized in such performance, and the performance is not transmitted beyond the place where the establishment is located and is within the immediate area where the sale is occurring;

(8) performance of a nondramatic literary work, by or in the course of a transmission specifically designed for and primarily directed to blind or other handicapped persons who are unable to read normal printed material as a result of their handicap, or deaf or other handicapped persons who are unable to hear the aural signals accompanying a transmission of visual signals, if the performance is made without any purpose of direct or indirect commercial advantage and its transmission is made through the facilities of: (i) a governmental body; or (ii) a noncommercial educational broadcast station (as defined in section 397 of title 47); or (iii) a radio subcarrier authorization (as defined in 47 CFR 73.293-73.295 and 73.593-73.595); or (iv) a cable system (as defined in section 111(f));

(9) performance on a single occasion of a dramatic literary work published at least ten years before the date of the performance, by or in the course of a transmission specifically designed for and primarily directed to blind or other handicapped persons who are unable to read normal printed material as a result of their handicap, if the performance is made without any purpose of direct or indirect commercial advantage and its transmission is made through the facilities of a radio subcarrier authorization referred to in clause (8)(iii), Provided, That the provisions of this clause shall not be applicable to more than one performance of the same work by the same performers or under the auspices of the same organization; and

(10) notwithstanding paragraph (4), the following is not an infringement of copyright: performance of a nondramatic literary or musical work in the

course of a social function which is organized and promoted by a nonprofit veterans' organization or a nonprofit fraternal organization to which the general public is not invited, but not including the invitees of the organizations, if the proceeds from the performance, after deducting the reasonable costs of producing the performance, are used exclusively for charitable purposes and not for financial gain. For purposes of this section the social functions of any college or university fraternity or sorority shall not be included unless the social function is held solely to raise funds for a specific charitable purpose.

The exemptions provided under paragraph (5) shall not be taken into account in any administrative, judicial, or other governmental proceeding to set or adjust the royalties payable to copyright owners for the public performance or display of their works. Royalties payable to copyright owners for any public performance or display of their works other than such performances or displays as are exempted under paragraph (5) shall not be diminished in any respect as a result of such exemption.

(Amended Oct. 15, 1982, Pub. L. 97-366, § 3, 96 Stat. 1759; Nov. 13, 1997, Pub. L. 105-80, § 12(a)(6), 111 Stat. 1534; Oct. 27, 1998, Pub. L. 105-298, Title II, § 202, 112 Stat. 2830.)

17 U.S.C. § 112. Limitations on exclusive rights: Ephemeral recordings

(a) (1) Notwithstanding the provisions of section 106, and except in the case of a motion picture or other audiovisual work, it is not an infringement of copyright for a transmitting organization entitled to transmit to the public a performance or display of a work, under a license, including a statutory license under section 114(f), or transfer of the copyright or under the limitations on exclusive rights in sound recordings specified by section 114(a), or for a transmitting organization that is a broadcast radio or television station licensed as such by the Federal Communications Commission and that makes a broadcast transmission of a performance of a sound recording in a digital format on a nonsubscription basis, to make no more than one copy or phonorecord of a particular transmission program embodying the performance or display, if—

(A) the copy or phonorecord is retained and used solely by the transmitting organization that made it, and no further copies or phonorecords are reproduced from it; and

(B) the copy or phonorecord is used solely for the transmitting organization's own transmissions within its local service area, or for purposes of archival preservation or security; and

(C) unless preserved exclusively for archival purposes, the copy or phonorecord is destroyed within six months from the date the transmission program was first transmitted to the public.

(2) In a case in which a transmitting organization entitled to make a copy or phonorecord under paragraph (1) in connection with the transmission to the public of a performance or display of a work is prevented from making

such copy or phonorecord by reason of the application by the copyright owner of technical measures that prevent the reproduction of the work, the copyright owner shall make available to the transmitting organization the necessary means for permitting the making of such copy or phonorecord as permitted under that paragraph, if it is technologically feasible and economically reasonable for the copyright owner to do so. If the copyright owner fails to do so in a timely manner in light of the transmitting organization's reasonable business requirements, the transmitting organization shall not be liable for a violation of section 1201(a)(1) of this title for engaging in such activities as are necessary to make such copies or phonorecords as permitted under paragraph (1) of this subsection.

(b) Notwithstanding the provisions of section 106, it is not an infringement of copyright for a governmental body or other nonprofit organization entitled to transmit a performance or display of a work, under section 110(2) or under the limitations on exclusive rights in sound recordings specified by section 114(a), to make no more than thirty copies or phonorecords of a particular transmission program embodying the performance or display, if—

(1) no further copies or phonorecords are reproduced from the copies or phonorecords made under this clause; and

(2) except for one copy or phonorecord that may be preserved exclusively for archival purposes, the copies or phonorecords are destroyed within seven years from the date the transmission program was first transmitted to the public.

(c) Notwithstanding the provisions of section 106, it is not an infringement of copyright for a governmental body or other nonprofit organization to make for distribution no more than one copy or phonorecord, for each transmitting organization specified in clause (2) of this subsection, of a particular transmission program embodying a performance of a nondramatic musical work of a religious nature, or of a sound recording of such a musical work, if—

(1) there is no direct or indirect charge for making or distributing any such copies or phonorecords; and

(2) none of such copies or phonorecords is used for any performance other than a single transmission to the public by a transmitting organization entitled to transmit to the public a performance of the work under a license or transfer of the copyright; and

(3) except for one copy or phonorecord that may be preserved exclusively for archival purposes, the copies or phonorecords are all destroyed within one year from the date the transmission program was first transmitted to the public.

(d) Notwithstanding the provisions of section 106, it is not an infringement of copyright for a governmental body or other nonprofit organization entitled to transmit a performance of a work under section 110(8) to make no more than ten copies or phonorecords embodying the performance, or to permit the use of any such copy or phonorecord by any governmental body or nonprofit organization entitled to transmit a performance of a work under section 110(8), if—

(1) any such copy or phonorecord is retained and used solely by the organization that made it, or by a governmental body or nonprofit organization entitled to transmit a performance of a work under section 110(8), and no further copies or phonorecords are reproduced from it; and

(2) any such copy or phonorecord is used solely for transmissions authorized under section 110(8), or for purposes of archival preservation or security; and

(3) the governmental body or nonprofit organization permitting any use of any such copy or phonorecord by any governmental body or nonprofit organization under this subsection does not make any charge for such use.

(e) Statutory license.

(1) A transmitting organization entitled to transmit to the public a performance of a sound recording under the limitation on exclusive rights specified by section 114(d)(1)(C)(iv) or under a statutory license in accordance with section 114(f) is entitled to a statutory license, under the conditions specified by this subsection, to make no more than 1 phonorecord of the sound recording (unless the terms and conditions of the statutory license allow for more), if the following conditions are satisfied:

(A) The phonorecord is retained and used solely by the transmitting organization that made it, and no further phonorecords are reproduced from it.

(B) The phonorecord is used solely for the transmitting organization's own transmissions originating in the United States under a statutory license in accordance with section 114(f) or the limitation on exclusive rights specified by section 114(d)(1)(C)(iv).

(C) Unless preserved exclusively for purposes of archival preservation, the phonorecord is destroyed within 6 months from the date the sound recording was first transmitted to the public using the phonorecord.

(D) Phonorecords of the sound recording have been distributed to the public under the authority of the copyright owner or the copyright owner authorizes the transmitting entity to transmit the sound recording, and the transmitting entity makes the phonorecord under this subsection from a phonorecord lawfully made and acquired under the authority of the copyright owner.

(3) Notwithstanding any provision of the antitrust laws, any copyright owners of sound recordings and any transmitting organizations entitled to a statutory license under this subsection may negotiate and agree upon

royalty rates and license terms and conditions for making phonorecords of such sound recordings under this section and the proportionate division of fees paid among copyright owners, and may designate common agents to negotiate, agree to, pay, or receive such royalty payments.

(4) No later than 30 days after the date of the enactment of the Digital Millennium Copyright Act [enacted Oct. 28, 1998], the Librarian of Congress shall cause notice to be published in the Federal Register of the initiation of voluntary negotiation proceedings for the purpose of determining reasonable terms and rates of royalty payments for the activities specified by paragraph (2) of this subsection during the period beginning on the date of the enactment of such Act [enacted Oct. 28, 1998] and ending on December 31, 2000, or such other date as the parties may agree. Such rates shall include a minimum fee for each type of service offered by transmitting organizations. Any copyright owners of sound recordings or any transmitting organizations entitled to a statutory license under this subsection may submit to the Librarian of Congress licenses covering such activities with respect to such sound recordings. The parties to each negotiation proceeding shall bear their own costs.

(5) In the absence of license agreements negotiated under paragraph (3), during the 60-day period commencing 6 months after publication of the notice specified in paragraph (4), and upon the filing of a petition in accordance with section 803(a)(1), the Librarian of Congress shall, pursuant to chapter 8 [17 USCS §§ 801 et seq.], convene a copyright arbitration royalty panel to determine and publish in the Federal Register a schedule of reasonable rates and terms which, subject to paragraph (6), shall be binding on all copyright owners of sound recordings and transmitting organizations entitled to a statutory license under this subsection during the period beginning on the date of the enactment of the Digital Millennium Copyright Act [enacted Oct. 28, 1998] and ending on December 31, 2000, or such other date as the parties may agree. Such rates shall include a minimum fee for each type of service offered by transmitting organizations. The copyright arbitration royalty panel shall establish rates that most clearly represent the fees that would have been negotiated in the marketplace between a willing buyer and a willing seller. In determining such rates and terms, the copyright arbitration royalty panel shall base its decision on economic, competitive, and programming information presented by the parties, including—

(A) whether use of the service may substitute for or may promote the sales of phonorecords or otherwise interferes with or enhances the copyright owner's traditional streams of revenue; and

(B) the relative roles of the copyright owner and the transmitting organization in the copyrighted work and the service made available to the public with respect to relative creative contribution, technological contribution, capital investment, cost, and risk.

In establishing such rates and terms, the copyright arbitration royalty panel may consider the rates and terms under voluntary license agreements negotiated as provided in paragraphs (3) and (4). The Librarian of Congress shall also establish requirements by which copyright owners may receive reasonable notice of the use of their sound recordings under this section, and under which records of such use shall be kept and made available by transmitting organizations entitled to obtain a statutory license under this subsection.

(6) License agreements voluntarily negotiated at any time between 1 or more copyright owners of sound recordings and 1 or more transmitting organizations entitled to obtain a statutory license under this subsection shall be given effect in lieu of any determination by a copyright arbitration royalty panel or decision by the Librarian of Congress.

(7) Publication of a notice of the initiation of voluntary negotiation proceedings as specified in paragraph (4) shall be repeated, in accordance with regulations that the Librarian of Congress shall prescribe, in the first week of January 2000, and at 2-year intervals thereafter, except to the extent that different years for the repeating of such proceedings may be determined in accordance with paragraph (4). The procedures specified in paragraph (5) shall be repeated, in accordance with regulations that the Librarian of Congress shall prescribe, upon filing of a petition in accordance with section 803(a)(1), during a 60-day period commencing on July 1, 2000, and at 2-year intervals thereafter, except to the extent that different years for the repeating of such proceedings may be determined in accordance with paragraph (4). The procedures specified in paragraph (5) shall be concluded in accordance with section 802.

(8) (A) Any person who wishes to make a phonorecord of a sound recording under a statutory license in accordance with this subsection may do so without infringing the exclusive right of the copyright owner of the sound recording under section 106(1)—

(i) by complying with such notice requirements as the Librarian of Congress shall prescribe by regulation and by paying royalty fees in accordance with this subsection; or

(ii) if such royalty fees have not been set, by agreeing to pay such royalty fees as shall be determined in accordance with this subsection.

(B) Any royalty payments in arrears shall be made on or before the 20th day of the month next succeeding the month in which the royalty fees are set.

(9) If a transmitting organization entitled to make a phonorecord under this subsection is prevented from making such phonorecord by reason of the application by the copyright owner of technical measures that prevent

the reproduction of the sound recording, the copyright owner shall make available to the transmitting organization the necessary means for permitting the making of such phonorecord as permitted under this subsection, if it is technologically feasible and economically reasonable for the copyright owner to do so. If the copyright owner fails to do so in a timely manner in light of the transmitting organization's reasonable business requirements, the transmitting organization shall not be liable for a violation of section 1201(a)(1) of this title for engaging in such activities as are necessary to make such phonorecords as permitted under this subsection.

(10) Nothing in this subsection annuls, limits, impairs, or otherwise affects in any way the existence or value of any of the exclusive rights of the copyright owners in a sound recording, except as otherwise provided in this subsection, or in a musical work, including the exclusive rights to reproduce and distribute a sound recording or musical work, including by means of a digital phonorecord delivery, under sections 106(1), 106(3), and 115, and the right to perform publicly a sound recording or musical work, including by means of a digital audio transmission, under sections 106(4) and 106(6).

(f) The transmission program embodied in a copy or phonorecord made under this section is not subject to protection as a derivative work under this title except with the express consent of the owners of copyright in the preexisting works employed in the program.

(Amended Oct. 28, 1998, Pub. L. 105-304, Title IV, §§ 402, 405(b), 112 Stat. 2888.)

17 U.S.C. § 113. Scope of exclusive rights in pictorial, graphic, and sculptural works

(a) Subject to the provisions of subsections (b) and (c) of this section, the exclusive right to reproduce a copyrighted pictorial, graphic, or sculptural work in copies under section 106 includes the right to reproduce the work in or on any kind of article, whether useful or otherwise.

(b) This title does not afford, to the owner of copyright in a work that portrays a useful article as such, any greater or lesser rights with respect to the making, distribution, or display of the useful article so portrayed than those afforded to such works under the law, whether title 17 or the common law or statutes of a State, in effect on December 31, 1977, as held applicable and construed by a court in an action brought under this title.

(c) In the case of a work lawfully reproduced in useful articles that have been offered for sale or other distribution to the public, copyright does not include any right to prevent the making, distribution, or display of pictures or photographs of such articles in connection with advertisements or commentaries related to the distribution or display of such articles, or in connection with news reports.

(d)(1) In a case in which—

(A) a work of visual art has been incorporated in or made part of a building in such a way that removing the work from the building will cause the destruction, distortion, mutilation, or other modification of the work as described in section 106A(a)(3), and

(B) the author consented to the installation of the work in the building either before the effective date set forth in section 610(a) of the Visual Artists Rights Act of 1990, or in a written instrument executed on or after such effective date that is signed by the owner of the building and the author and that specifies that installation of the work may subject the work to destruction, distortion, mutilation, or other modification, by reason of its removal,

then the rights conferred by paragraphs (2) and (3) of section 106A(a) shall not apply.

(2) If the owner of a building wishes to remove a work of visual art which is a part of such building and which can be removed from the building without the destruction, distortion, mutilation, or other modification of the work as described in section 106A(a)(3), the author's rights under paragraphs (2) and (3) of section 106A(a) shall apply unless—

(A) the owner has made a diligent, good faith attempt without success to notify the author of the owner's intended action affecting the work of visual art, or

(B) the owner did provide such notice in writing and the person so notified failed, within 90 days after receiving such notice, either to remove the work or to pay for its removal.

For purposes of subparagraph (A), an owner shall be presumed to have made a diligent, good faith attempt to send notice if the owner sent such notice by registered mail to the author at the most recent address of the author that was recorded with the Register of Copyrights pursuant to paragraph (3). If the work is removed at the expense of the author, title to that copy of the work shall be deemed to be in the author.

(3) The Register of Copyrights shall establish a system of records whereby any author of a work of visual art that has been incorporated in or made part of a building, may record his or her identity and address with the Copyright Office. The Register shall also establish procedures under which any such author may update the information so recorded, and procedures under which owners of buildings may record with the Copyright Office evidence of their efforts to comply with this subsection.

17 U.S.C. § 114. Scope of exclusive rights in sound recordings

(a) The exclusive rights of the owner of copyright in a sound recording are limited to the rights specified by clauses (1), (2), (3) and (6) of section 106, and do not include any right of performance under section 106(4).

(b) The exclusive right of the owner of copyright in a sound recording under clause (1) of section 106 is limited to the right to duplicate the sound recording in the form of phonorecords or copies that directly or indirectly recapture the actual sounds fixed in the recording. The exclusive right of the owner of copyright in a sound recording under clause (2) of section 106 is limited to the right to prepare a derivative work in which the actual sounds fixed in the sound recording are rearranged, remixed, or otherwise altered in sequence or quality. The exclusive rights of the owner of copyright in a sound recording under clauses (1) and (2) of section 106 do not extend to the making or duplication of another sound recording that consists entirely of an independent fixation of other sounds, even though such sounds imitate or simulate those in the copyrighted sound recording. The exclusive rights of the owner of copyright in a sound recording under clauses (1), (2), and (3) of section 106 do not apply to sound recordings included in educational television and radio programs (as defined in section 397 of title 47) distributed or transmitted by or through public broadcasting entities (as defined by section 118(g): Provided, That copies or phonorecords of said programs are not commercially distributed by or through public broadcasting entities to the general public.

(c) This section does not limit or impair the exclusive right to perform publicly, by means of a phonorecord, any of the works specified by section 106(4).

(d) Limitations on exclusive right. Notwithstanding the provisions of section 106(6)—

(1) Exempt transmissions and retransmissions. The performance of a sound recording publicly by means of a digital audio transmission, other than as a part of an interactive service, is not an infringement of section 106(6) if the performance is part of—

(A) a nonsubscription broadcast transmission;

(B) a retransmission of a nonsubscription broadcast transmission: Provided, That, in the case of a retrans mission of a radio station"s broadcast transmission—

(i) the radio station's broadcast transmission is not willfully or repeatedly retransmitted more than a radius of 150 miles from the site of the radio broadcast transmitter, however—

(I) the 150 mile limitation under this clause shall not apply when a nonsubscription broadcast transmission by a radio station licensed by the Federal Communications Commission is retrans mitted on a nonsubscription basis by a terrestrial broadcast station, terrestrial translator, or terrestrial repeater licensed by the Federal Communications Commission; and

(II) in the case of a subscription retransmission of a nonsubscription broadcast retrans mission covered by subclause (I), the 150 mile radius shall be measured from the transmitter site of such broadcast retransmitter;

    (ii) the retransmission is of radio station broadcast transmissions that are—

      (I) obtained by the retransmitter over the air;

      (II) not electronically processed by the re transmitter to deliver separate and discrete signals; and

      (III) retransmitted only within the local communities served by the retransmitter;

    (iii) the radio station's broadcast transmission was being retransmitted to cable systems (as defined in section 111(f)) by a satellite carrier on January 1, 1995, and that retransmission was being retransmitted by cable systems as a separate and discrete signal, and the satellite carrier obtains the radio station's broadcast transmission in an analog format: Provided, That the broadcast transmission being retransmitted may embody the programming of no more than one radio station; or

    (iv) the radio station's broadcast transmission is made by a noncommercial educational broadcast station funded on or after January 1, 1995, under section 396(k) of the Communications Act of 1934 (47 U.S.C. 396(k)), consists solely of noncommercial educational and cultural radio programs, and the retransmission, whether or not simultaneous, is a nonsubscription terrestrial broadcast retransmission; or

(C) a transmission that comes within any of the following categories—

    (i) a prior or simultaneous transmission incidental to an exempt transmission, such as a feed received by and then retransmitted by an exempt transmitter: Provided, That such incidental transmissions do not include any subscription transmission directly for reception by members of the public;

    (ii) a transmission within a business establishment, confined to its premises or the immediately surrounding vicinity;

    (iii) a retransmission by any retransmitter, including a multichannel video programming distributor as defined in section 602(12) of the Communications Act of 1934 (47 U.S.C. 522(12)), of a transmission by a transmitter licensed to publicly perform the sound recording as a part of that transmission, if the retransmission is simultaneous with the licensed transmission and authorized by the transmitter; or

    (iv) a transmission to a business establishment for use in the ordinary course of its business: Provided, That the business recipient does not retransmit the transmission outside of its premises or the immediately surrounding vicinity, and that the transmission does not exceed the sound recording performance complement. Nothing in this clause shall limit the scope of the exemption in clause (ii).

(2) Statutory licensing of certain transmissions. The performance of a sound recording publicly by means of a subscription digital audio

transmission not exempt under paragraph (1), an eligible nonsubscription transmission, or a transmission not exempt under paragraph (1) that is made by a preexisting satellite digital audio radio service shall be subject to statutory licensing, in accordance with subsection (f) if—

(A) (i) the transmission is not part of an interactive service;

(ii) except in the case of a transmission to a business establishment, the transmitting entity does not automatically and intentionally cause any device receiving the transmission to switch from one program channel to another; and

(iii) except as provided in section 1002(e), the transmission of the sound recording is accompanied, if technically feasible, by the information encoded in that sound recording, if any, by or under the authority of the copyright owner of that sound recording, that identifies the title of the sound recording, the featured recording artist who performs on the sound recording, and related information, including information concerning the underlying musical work and its writer;

(B) in the case of a subscription transmission not exempt under paragraph (1) that is made by a preexisting subscription service in the same transmission medium used by such service on July 31, 1998, or in the case of a transmission not exempt under paragraph (1) that is made by a preexisting satellite digital audio radio service—

(i) the transmission does not exceed the sound recording performance complement; and

(ii) the transmitting entity does not cause to be published by means of an advance program schedule or prior announcement the titles of the specific sound recordings or phonorecords embodying such sound recordings to be transmitted; and

(C) in the case of an eligible nonsubscription transmission or a subscription transmission not exempt under paragraph (1) that is made by a new subscription service or by a preexisting subscription service other than in the same transmission medium used by such service on July 31, 1998—

(i) the transmission does not exceed the sound recording performance complement, except that this requirement shall not apply in the case of a retransmission of a broadcast transmission if the retransmission is made by a transmitting entity that does not have the right or ability to control the programming of the broadcast station making the broadcast transmission, unless—

(I) the broadcast station makes broadcast transmissions—

(aa) in digital format that regularly exceed the sound recording performance complement; or (bb) in analog format, a substantial portion of which, on a weekly basis, exceed the sound recording performance complement; and

(II) the sound recording copyright owner or its representative has notified the transmitting entity in writing that broadcast transmissions of the copyright owner's sound recordings exceed the sound recording performance complement as provided in this clause;

(ii) the transmitting entity does not cause to be published, or induce or facilitate the publication, by means of an advance program schedule or prior announcement, the titles of the specific sound recordings to be transmitted, the phonorecords embodying such sound recordings, or, other than for illustrative purposes, the names of the featured recording artists, except that this clause does not disqualify a transmitting entity that makes a prior announcement that a particular artist will be featured within an unspecified future time period, and in the case of a retransmission of a broadcast transmission by a transmitting entity that does not have the right or ability to control the programming of the broadcast transmission, the requirement of this clause shall not apply to a prior oral announcement by the broadcast station, or to an advance program schedule published, induced, or facilitated by the broadcast station, if the transmitting entity does not have actual knowledge and has not received written notice from the copyright owner or its representative that the broadcast station publishes or induces or facilitates the publication of such advance program schedule, or if such advance program schedule is a schedule of classical music programming published by the broadcast station in the same manner as published by that broadcast station on or before September 30, 1998;

(iii) the transmission—

(I) is not part of an archived program of less than 5 hours duration;

(II) is not part of an archived program of 5 hours or greater in duration that is made available for a period exceeding 2 weeks;

(III) is not part of a continuous program which is of less than 3 hours duration; or

(IV) is not part of an identifiable program in which performances of sound recordings are rendered in a predetermined order, other than an archived or continuous program, that is transmitted at—

(aa) more than 3 times in any 2-week period that have been publicly announced in advance, in the case of a program of less than 1 hour in duration, or

(bb) more than 4 times in any 2-week period that have been publicly announced in advance, in the case of a program of 1 hour or more in duration,

except that the requirement of this subclause shall not apply in the case of a retransmission of a broadcast transmission by a transmitting entity that does not have the right or ability to control the programming of the broadcast transmission, unless the transmitting entity is given notice in writing by the copyright owner of the sound recording that the broadcast station makes broadcast transmissions that regularly violate such requirement;

(iv) the transmitting entity does not knowingly perform the sound recording, as part of a service that offers transmissions of visual images contemporaneously with transmissions of sound recordings, in a manner that is likely to cause confusion, to cause mistake, or to deceive, as to the affiliation, connection, or association of the copyright owner or featured recording artist with the transmitting entity or a particular product or service advertised by the transmitting entity, or as to the origin, sponsorship, or approval by the copyright owner or featured recording artist of the activities of the transmitting entity other than the performance of the sound recording itself;

(v) the transmitting entity cooperates to prevent, to the extent feasible without imposing substantial costs or burdens, a transmission recipient or any other person or entity from automatically scanning the transmitting entity's transmissions alone or together with transmissions by other transmitting entities in order to select a particular sound recording to be transmitted to the transmission recipient, except that the requirement of this clause shall not apply to a satellite digital audio service that is in operation, or that is licensed by the Federal Communications Commission, on or before July 31, 1998;

(vi) the transmitting entity takes no affirmative steps to cause or induce the making of a phonorecord by the transmission recipient, and if the technology used by the transmitting entity enables the transmitting entity to limit the making by the transmission recipient of phonorecords of the transmission directly in a digital format, the transmitting entity sets such technology to limit such making of phonorecords to the extent permitted by such technology;

(vii) phonorecords of the sound recording have been distributed to the public under the authority of the copyright owner or the copyright owner authorizes the transmitting entity to transmit the sound recording, and the transmitting entity makes the transmission from a phonorecord lawfully made under the authority of the copyright owner, except that the requirement of this clause shall not apply to a retransmission of a broadcast transmission by a transmitting entity that does not have the right or ability to control the programming of the broadcast transmission, unless the transmitting entity is given notice in writing by the copyright owner of the sound recording that the broadcast station makes broadcast transmissions that regularly violate such requirement;

(viii) the transmitting entity accommodates and does not interfere with the transmission of technical measures that are widely used by sound recording copyright owners to identify or protect copyrighted works, and that are technically feasible of being transmitted by the transmitting entity without imposing substantial costs on the transmitting entity or resulting in perceptible aural or visual degradation of the digital signal, except that the requirement of this clause shall not apply to a satellite digital audio service that is in operation, or that is licensed under the authority of the Federal Communications Commission, on or before July 31, 1998, to the extent that such service has designed, developed, or made commitments to procure equipment or technology that is not compatible with such technical measures before such technical measures are widely adopted by sound recording copyright owners; and

(ix) the transmitting entity identifies in textual data the sound recording during, but not before, the time it is performed, including the title of the sound recording, the title of the phonorecord embodying such sound recording, if any, and the featured recording artist, in a manner to permit it to be displayed to the transmission recipient by the device or technology intended for receiving the service provided by the transmitting entity, except that the obligation in this clause shall not take effect until 1 year after the date of the enactment of the Digital Millennium Copyright Act [enacted Oct. 28, 1998] and shall not apply in the case of a retransmission of a broadcast transmission by a transmitting entity that does not have the right or ability to control the programming of the broadcast transmission, or in the case in which devices or technology intended for receiving the service provided by the transmitting entity that have the capability to display such textual data are not common in the marketplace.

(3) Licenses for transmissions by interactive services.

(A) No interactive service shall be granted an exclusive license under section 106(6) for the performance of a sound recording publicly by means of digital audio transmission for a period in excess of 12 months, except that with respect to an exclusive license granted to an interactive service by a licensor that holds the copyright to 1,000 or fewer sound recordings, the period of such license shall not exceed 24 months: Provided, however, That the grantee of such exclusive license shall be ineligible to receive another exclusive license for the performance of that sound recording for a period of 13 months from the expiration of the prior exclusive license.

(B) The limitation set forth in subparagraph (A) of this paragraph shall not apply if—

(i) the licensor has granted and there remain in effect licenses under section 106(6) for the public performance of sound recordings by means of digital audio transmission by at least 5 different interactive services: Provided, however, That each such license must be for a minimum of 10 percent of the copyrighted sound recordings owned by the licensor that have been licensed to interactive services, but in no event less than 50 sound recordings; or

(ii) the exclusive license is granted to perform publicly up to 45 seconds of a sound recording and the sole purpose of the performance is to promote the distribution or performance of that sound recording.

(C) Notwithstanding the grant of an exclusive or nonexclusive license of the right of public performance under section 106(6), an interactive service may not publicly perform a sound recording unless a license has been granted for the public performance of any copyrighted musical work contained in the sound recording: Provided, That such license to publicly perform the copyrighted musical work may be granted either by a performing rights society representing the copyright owner or by the copyright owner.

(D) The performance of a sound recording by means of a retransmission of a digital audio transmission is not an infringement of section 106(6) if—

(i) the retransmission is of a transmission by an interactive service licensed to publicly perform the sound recording to a particular member of the public as part of that transmission; and

(ii) the retransmission is simultaneous with the licensed transmission, authorized by the transmitter, and limited to that particular member of the public intended by the interactive service to be the recipient of the transmission.

(E) For the purposes of this paragraph—

(i) a "licensor" shall include the licensing entity and any other entity under any material degree of common ownership, management, or control that owns copyrights in sound recordings; and

(ii) a "performing rights society" is an association or corporation that licenses the public performance of nondramatic musical works on behalf of the copyright owner, such as the American Society of Composers, Authors and Publishers, Broadcast Music, Inc., and SE-SAC, Inc.

(4) Rights not otherwise limited.

(A) Except as expressly provided in this section, this section does not limit or impair the exclusive right to perform a sound recording publicly by means of a digital audio transmission under section 106(6).

(B) Nothing in this section annuls or limits in any way—

(i) the exclusive right to publicly perform a musical work, including by means of a digital audio transmission, under section 106(4);

(ii) the exclusive rights in a sound recording or the musical work embodied therein under sections 106(1), 106(2) and 106(3); or

(iii) any other rights under any other clause of section 106, or remedies available under this title, as such rights or remedies exist either before or after the date of enactment of the Digital Performance Right in Sound Recordings Act of 1995 [enacted Nov. 1, 1995].

(C) Any limitations in this section on the exclusive right under section 106(6) apply only to the exclusive right under section 106(6) and not to any other exclusive rights under section 106. Nothing in this section shall be construed to annul, limit, impair or otherwise affect in any way the ability of the owner of a copyright in a sound recording to exercise the rights under sections 106(1), 106(2) and 106(3), or to obtain the remedies available under this title pursuant to such rights, as such rights and remedies exist either before or after the date of enactment of the Digital Performance Right in Sound Recordings Act of 1995 [enacted Nov. 1, 1995].

(e) Authority for negotiations.

(1) Notwithstanding any provision of the antitrust laws, in negotiating statutory licenses in accordance with subsection (f), any copyright owners of sound recordings and any entities performing sound recordings affected by this section may negotiate and agree upon the royalty rates and license terms and conditions for the performance of such sound recordings and the proportionate division of fees paid among copyright owners, and may designate common agents on a nonexclusive basis to negotiate, agree to, pay, or receive payments.

(2) For licenses granted under section 106(6), other than statutory licenses, such as for performances by interactive services or performances that exceed the sound recording performance complement—

(A) copyright owners of sound recordings affected by this section may designate common agents to act on their behalf to grant licenses and receive and remit royalty payments: Provided, That each copyright owner shall establish the royalty rates and material license terms and conditions unilaterally, that is, not in agreement, combination, or concert with other copyright owners of sound recordings; and

(B) entities performing sound recordings affected by this section may designate common agents to act on their behalf to obtain licenses and collect and pay royalty fees: Provided, That each entity performing sound recordings shall determine the royalty rates and material license terms and conditions unilaterally, that is, not in agreement, combination, or concert with other entities performing sound recordings.

(f) Licenses for certain nonexempt transmissions.

(1) (A) No later than 30 days after the enactment of the Digital Performance Right in Sound Recordings Act of 1995 [enacted Nov. 1, 1995], the Librarian of Congress shall cause notice to be published in the Federal Register of the initiation of voluntary negotiation proceedings for the purpose of determining reasonable terms and rates of royalty payments for subscription transmissions by preexisting subscription services and transmissions by preexisting satellite digital audio radio services specified by subsection (d)(2) of this section during the period beginning on the effective date of such Act and ending on December 31, 2001, or, if a copyright arbitration royalty panel is convened, ending 30 days after the Librarian issues and publishes in the Federal Register an order adopting the determination of the copyright arbitration royalty panel or an order setting the terms and rates (if the Librarian rejects the panel's determination). Such terms and rates shall distinguish among the different types of digital audio transmission services then in operation. Any copyright owners of sound recordings, preexisting subscription services, or preexisting satellite digital audio radio services may submit to the Librarian of Congress licenses covering such subscription transmissions with respect to such sound recordings. The parties to each negotiation proceeding shall bear their own costs.

(B) In the absence of license agreements negotiated under subparagraph (A), during the 60-day period commencing 6 months after publication of the notice specified in subparagraph (A), and upon the filing of a petition in accordance with section 803(a)(1), the Librarian of Congress shall, pursuant to chapter 8 [17 USCS § 801 et seq.], convene a copyright arbitration royalty panel to determine and publish in the Federal Register a schedule of rates and terms which, subject to paragraph (3), shall be binding on all copyright owners of sound recordings and entities performing sound recordings affected by this paragraph. In establishing rates and terms for preexisting subscription services and preexisting satellite digital audio radio services, in addition to the objectives set forth in section 801(b)(1), the copyright arbitration royalty panel may consider the rates and terms for comparable types of subscription digital audio transmission services and comparable circumstances under voluntary license agreements negotiated as provided in subparagraph (A).

(C) (i) Publication of a notice of the initiation of voluntary negotiation proceedings as specified in subparagraph (A) shall be repeated, in accordance with regulations that the Librarian of Congress shall prescribe—

(I) no later than 30 days after a petition is filed by any copyright owners of sound recordings, any preexisting subscription services, or any preexisting satellite digital audio radio services indicating that a new type of subscription digital audio transmission service on which sound recordings are performed is or is about to become operational; and

(II) in the first week of January 2001, and at 5-year intervals thereafter.

(ii) The procedures specified in subparagraph (B) shall be repeated, in accordance with regulations that the Librarian of Congress shall prescribe, upon filing of a petition in accordance with section 803(a)(1) during a 60-day period commencing—

(I) 6 months after publication of a notice of the initiation of voluntary negotiation proceedings under subparagraph (A) pursuant to a petition under clause (i)(I) of this subparagraph; or

(II) on July 1, 2001, and at 5-year intervals thereafter.

(iii) The procedures specified in subparagraph (B) shall be concluded in accordance with section 802.

(2) (A) No later than 30 days after the date of the enactment of the Digital Millennium Copyright Act [enacted Oct. 28, 1998], the Librarian of Congress shall cause notice to be published in the Federal Register of the initiation of voluntary negotiation proceedings for the purpose of determining reasonable terms and rates of royalty payments for public performances of sound recordings by means of eligible nonsubscription transmissions and transmissions by new subscription services specified by subsection (d)(2) during the period beginning on the date of the enactment of such Act and ending on December 31, 2000, or such other date as the parties may agree. Such rates and terms shall distinguish among the different types of eligible nonsubscription transmission services and new subscription services then in operation and shall include a minimum fee for each such type of service. Any copyright owners of sound recordings or any entities performing sound recordings affected by this paragraph may submit to the Librarian of Congress licenses covering such eligible nonsubscription transmissions and new subscription services with respect to such sound recordings. The parties to each negotiation proceeding shall bear their own costs.

(B) In the absence of license agreements negotiated under subparagraph (A), during the 60-day period commencing 6 months after publication of the notice specified in subparagraph (A), and upon the filing of a petition in accordance with section 803(a)(1), the Librarian of Congress shall, pursuant to chapter 8 [17 USCS §§ 801 et seq.], convene a copyright arbitration royalty panel to determine and publish in the Federal Register a schedule of rates and terms which, subject to paragraph (3), shall be binding on all copyright owners of sound recordings and entities performing sound recordings affected by this paragraph during the period beginning on the date of the enactment of the Digital Millennium

Copyright Act [enacted Oct. 28, 1998] and ending on December 31, 2000, or such other date as the parties may agree. Such rates and terms shall distinguish among the different types of eligible nonsubscription transmission services then in operation and shall include a minimum fee for each such type of service, such differences to be based on criteria including, but not limited to, the quantity and nature of the use of sound recordings and the degree to which use of the service may substitute for or may promote the purchase of phonorecords by consumers. In establishing rates and terms for transmissions by eligible nonsubscription services and new subscription services, the copyright arbitration royalty panel shall establish rates and terms that most clearly represent the rates and terms that would have been negotiated in the marketplace between a willing buyer and a willing seller. In determining such rates and terms, the copyright arbitration royalty panel shall base its decision on economic, competitive and programming information presented by the parties, including—

(i) whether use of the service may substitute for or may promote the sales of phonorecords or otherwise may interfere with or may enhance the sound recording copyright owner's other streams of revenue from its sound recordings; and

(ii) the relative roles of the copyright owner and the transmitting entity in the copyrighted work and the service made available to the public with respect to relative creative contribution, technological contribution, capital investment, cost, and risk.

In establishing such rates and terms, the copyright arbitration royalty panel may consider the rates and terms for comparable types of digital audio transmission services and comparable circumstances under voluntary license agreements negotiated under subparagraph (A).

(C) (i) Publication of a notice of the initiation of voluntary negotiation proceedings as specified in subparagraph (A) shall be repeated in accordance with regulations that the Librarian of Congress shall prescribe—

(I) no later than 30 days after a petition is filed by any copyright owners of sound recordings or any eligible nonsubscription service or new subscription service indicating that a new type of eligible nonsubscription service or new subscription service on which sound recordings are performed is or is about to become operational; and

(II) in the first week of January 2000, and at 2-year intervals thereafter, except to the extent that different years for the repeating of such proceedings may be determined in accordance with subparagraph (A).

(ii) The procedures specified in subparagraph (B) shall be repeated, in accordance with regulations that the Librarian of Congress shall prescribe, upon filing of a petition in accordance with section 803(a)(1) during a 60-day period commencing—

(I) 6 months after publication of a notice of the initiation of voluntary negotiation proceedings under subparagraph (A) pursuant to a petition under clause (i)(I); or

(II) on July 1, 2000, and at 2-year intervals thereafter, except to the extent that different years for the repeating of such proceedings may be determined in accordance with subparagraph (A).

(iii) The procedures specified in subparagraph (B) shall be concluded in accordance with section 802.

(3) License agreements voluntarily negotiated at any time between 1 or more copyright owners of sound recordings and 1 or more entities performing sound recordings shall be given effect in lieu of any determination by a copyright arbitration royalty panel or decision by the Librarian of Congress.

(4) (A) The Librarian of Congress shall also establish requirements by which copyright owners may receive reasonable notice of the use of their sound recordings under this section, and under which records of such use shall be kept and made available by entities performing sound recordings.

(B) Any person who wishes to perform a sound recording publicly by means of a transmission eligible for statutory licensing under this subsection may do so without infringing the exclusive right of the copyright owner of the sound recording—

(i) by complying with such notice requirements as the Librarian of Congress shall prescribe by regulation and by paying royalty fees in accordance with this subsection; or

(ii) if such royalty fees have not been set, by agreeing to pay such royalty fees as shall be determined in accordance with this subsection.

(C) Any royalty payments in arrears shall be made on or before the twentieth day of the month next succeeding the month in which the royalty fees are set.

(g) Proceeds from licensing of transmissions.

(1) Except in the case of a transmission licensed under a statutory license in accordance with subsection (f) of this section—

(A) a featured recording artist who performs on a sound recording that has been licensed for a transmission shall be entitled to receive payments from the copyright owner of the sound recording in accordance with the terms of the artist's contract; and

(B) a nonfeatured recording artist who performs on a sound recording that has been licensed for a transmission shall be entitled to receive payments from the copyright owner of the sound recording in accordance with the terms of the nonfeatured recording artist's applicable contract or other applicable agreement.

(2) The copyright owner of the exclusive right under section 106(6) of this title to publicly perform a sound recording by means of a digital audio transmission shall allocate to recording artists in the following manner its receipts from the statutory licensing of transmission performances of the sound recording in accordance with subsection (f) of this section:

(A) 2 1/2 percent of the receipts shall be deposited in an escrow account managed by an independent administrator jointly appointed by copyright owners of sound recordings and the American Federation of Musicians (or any successor entity) to be distributed to nonfeatured musicians (whether or not members of the American Federation of Musicians) who have performed on sound recordings.

(B) 2 1/2 percent of the receipts shall be deposited in an escrow account managed by an independent administrator jointly appointed by copyright owners of sound recordings and the American Federation of Television and Radio Artists (or any successor entity) to be distributed to nonfeatured vocalists (whether or not members of the American Federation of Television and Radio Artists) who have performed on sound recordings.

(C) 45 percent of the receipts shall be allocated, on a per sound recording basis, to the recording artist or artists featured on such sound recording (or the persons conveying rights in the artists' performance in the sound recordings).

(h) Licensing to affiliates.

(1) If the copyright owner of a sound recording licenses an affiliated entity the right to publicly perform a sound recording by means of a digital audio transmission under section 106(6), the copyright owner shall make the licensed sound recording available under section 106(6) on no less favorable terms and conditions to all bona fide entities that offer similar services, except that, if there are material differences in the scope of the requested license with respect to the type of service, the particular sound recordings licensed, the frequency of use, the number of subscribers served, or the duration, then the copyright owner may establish different terms and conditions for such other services.

(2) The limitation set forth in paragraph (1) of this subsection shall not apply in the case where the copyright owner of a sound recording licenses—

(A) an interactive service; or

(B) an entity to perform publicly up to 45 seconds of the sound recording and the sole purpose of the performance is to promote the distribution or performance of that sound recording.

(i) No effect on royalties for underlying works. License fees payable for the public performance of sound recordings under section 106(6) shall not be taken into account in any administrative, judicial, or other governmental proceeding to set or adjust the royalties payable to copyright owners of musical works for the public performance of their works. It is the intent of Congress that royalties payable to copyright owners of musical works for the public performance of their works shall not be diminished in any respect as a result of the rights granted by section 106(6).

(j) Definitions. As used in this section, the following terms have the following meanings:

(1) An "affiliated entity" is an entity engaging in digital audio transmissions covered by section 106(6), other than an interactive service, in which the licensor has any direct or indirect partnership or any ownership interest amounting to 5 percent or more of the outstanding voting or non-voting stock.

(2) An "archived program" is a predetermined program that is available repeatedly on the demand of the transmission recipient and that is performed in the same order from the beginning, except that an archived program shall not include a recorded event or broadcast transmission that makes no more than an incidental use of sound recordings, as long as such recorded event or broadcast transmission does not contain an entire sound recording or feature a particular sound recording.

(3) A "broadcast" transmission is a transmission made by a terrestrial broadcast station licensed as such by the Federal Communications Commission.

(4) A "continuous program" is a predetermined program that is continuously performed in the same order and that is accessed at a point in the program that is beyond the control of the transmission recipient.

(5) A "digital audio transmission" is a digital transmission as defined in section 101, that embodies the transmission of a sound recording. This term does not include the transmission of any audiovisual work.

(6) An "eligible nonsubscription transmission" is a noninteractive nonsubscription digital audio transmission not exempt under subsection (d)(1) that is made as part of a service that provides audio programming consisting, in whole or in part, of performances of sound recordings, including retransmissions of broadcast transmissions, if the primary purpose of the service is to provide to the public such audio or other entertainment programming, and the primary purpose of the service is not to sell, advertise, or promote particular products or services other than sound recordings, live concerts, or other music-related events.

(7) An "interactive service" is one that enables a member of the public to receive a transmission of a program specially created for the recipient, or on request, a transmission of a particular sound recording, whether or

not as part of a program, which is selected by or on behalf of the recipient. The ability of individuals to request that particular sound recordings be performed for reception by the public at large, or in the case of a subscription service, by all subscribers of the service, does not make a service interactive, if the programming on each channel of the service does not substantially consist of sound recordings that are performed within 1 hour of the request or at a time designated by either the transmitting entity or the individual making such request. If an entity offers both interactive and noninteractive services (either concurrently or at different times), the noninteractive component shall not be treated as part of an interactive service.

(8) A "new subscription service" is a service that performs sound recordings by means of noninteractive subscription digital audio transmissions and that is not a preexisting subscription service or a preexisting satellite digital audio radio service.

(9) A "nonsubscription" transmission is any transmission that is not a subscription transmission.

(10) A "preexisting satellite digital audio radio service" is a subscription satellite digital audio radio service provided pursuant to a satellite digital audio radio service license issued by the Federal Communications Commission on or before July 31, 1998, and any renewal of such license to the extent of the scope of the original license, and may include a limited number of sample channels representative of the subscription service that are made available on a nonsubscription basis in order to promote the subscription service.

(11) A "preexisting subscription service" is a service that performs sound recordings by means of noninteractive audio-only subscription digital audio transmissions, which was in existence and was making such transmissions to the public for a fee on or before July 31, 1998, and may include a limited number of sample channels representative of the subscription service that are made available on a nonsubscription basis in order to promote the subscription service.

(12) A "retransmission" is a further transmission of an initial transmission, and includes any further retransmission of the same transmission. Except as provided in this section, a transmission qualifies as a "retransmission" only if it is simultaneous with the initial transmission. Nothing in this definition shall be construed to exempt a transmission that fails to satisfy a separate element required to qualify for an exemption under section 114(d)(1).

(13) The "sound recording performance complement" is the transmission during any 3-hour period, on a particular channel used by a transmitting entity, of no more than—

(A) 3 different selections of sound recordings from any one phonorecord lawfully distributed for public performance or sale in the United States, if no more than 2 such selections are transmitted consecutively; or

(B) 4 different selections of sound recordings—

(i) by the same featured recording artist; or

(ii) from any set or compilation of phonorecords lawfully distributed together as a unit for public performance or sale in the United States,

if no more than three such selections are transmitted consecutively:

Provided, That the transmission of selections in excess of the numerical limits provided for in clauses (A) and (B) from multiple phonorecords shall nonetheless qualify as a sound recording performance complement if the programming of the multiple phonorecords was not willfully intended to avoid the numerical limitations prescribed in such clauses.

(14) A "subscription" transmission is a transmission that is controlled and limited to particular recipients, and for which consideration is required to be paid or otherwise given by or on behalf of the recipient to receive the transmission or a package of transmissions including the transmission.

(15) A "transmission" is either an initial transmission or a retransmission.

(Amended Nov. 1, 1995, Pub. L. 104-39, § 3, 109 Stat. 336; Nov. 13, 1997, Pub. L. 105-80, § 3, 111 Stat. 1531; Oct. 28, 1998, Pub. L. 105-304, Title IV, § 405(a)(1)-(4), 112 Stat. 2890.)

17 U.S.C. § 115. Scope of exclusive rights in nondramatic musical works: Compulsory license for making and distributing phonorecords

In the case of nondramatic musical works, the exclusive rights provided by clauses (1) and (3) of section 106, to make and to distribute phonorecords of such works, are subject to compulsory licensing under the conditions specified by this section.

(a) Availability and scope of compulsory license.

(1) When phonorecords of a nondramatic musical work have been distributed to the public in the United States under the authority of the copyright owner, any other person, including those who make phonorecords or digital phonorecord deliveries, may, by complying with the provisions of this section, obtain a compulsory license to make and distribute phonorecords of the work. A person may obtain a compulsory license only if his or her primary purpose in making phonorecords is to distribute them to the public for private use, including by means of a digital phonorecord delivery. A person may not obtain a compulsory license for use of the work in the making of phonorecords duplicating a sound recording fixed by another, unless: (i) such sound recording was fixed lawfully; and (ii) the making of the phonorecords was authorized by the owner of copyright in the sound recording or, if the sound recording was fixed before February 15, 1972,

by any person who fixed the sound recording pursuant to an express license from the owner of the copyright in the musical work or pursuant to a valid compulsory license for use of such work in a sound recording.

(2) A compulsory license includes the privilege of making a musical arrangement of the work to the extent necessary to conform it to the style or manner of interpretation of the performance involved, but the arrangement shall not change the basic melody or fundamental character of the work, and shall not be subject to protection as a derivative work under this title, except with the express consent of the copyright owner.

(b) Notice of intention to obtain compulsory license.

(1) Any person who wishes to obtain a compulsory license under this section shall, before or within thirty days after making, and before distributing any phonorecords of the work, serve notice of intention to do so on the copyright owner. If the registration or other public records of the Copyright Office do not identify the copyright owner and include an address at which notice can be served, it shall be sufficient to file the notice of intention in the Copyright Office. The notice shall comply, in form, content, and manner of service, with requirements that the Register of Copyrights shall prescribe by regulation.

(2) Failure to serve or file the notice required by clause (1) forecloses the possibility of a compulsory license and, in the absence of a negotiated license, renders the making and distribution of phonorecords actionable as acts of infringement under section 501 and fully subject to the remedies provided by sections 502 through 506 and 509. *

(c) Royalty payable under compulsory license.

(1) To be entitled to receive royalties under a compulsory license, the copyright owner must be identified in the registration or other public records of the Copyright Office. The owner is entitled to royalties for phonorecords made and distributed after being so identified, but is not entitled to recover for any phonorecords previously made and distributed.

(2) Except as provided by clause (1), the royalty under a compulsory license shall be payable for every phonorecord made and distributed in accordance with the license. For this purpose and other than as provided in paragraph (3), a phonorecord is considered "distributed" if the person exercising the compulsory license has voluntarily and permanently parted with its possession. With respect to each work embodied in the phonorecord, the royalty shall be either two and three-fourths cents, or one-half of one cent per minute of playing time or fraction thereof, whichever amount is larger.

---

* Section 115(c) as amended by the Act of Oct. 4, 1984, Pub. L. 98–450 (98 Stat. 1727). For Section 4 of that Act see the footnote to Section 109 *supra*.

(3)(A) A compulsory license under this section includes the right of the compulsory licensee to distribute or authorize the distribution of a phonorecord of a nondramatic musical work by means of a digital transmission which constitutes a digital phonorecord delivery, regardless of whether the digital transmission is also a public performance of the sound recording under section 106(6) of this title or of any nondramatic musical work embodied therein under section 106(4) of this title. For every digital phonorecord delivery by or under the authority of the compulsory licensee—

(i) on or before December 31, 1997, the royalty payable by the compulsory licensee shall be the royalty prescribed under paragraph (2) and chapter 8 of this title; and

(ii) on or after January 1, 1998, the royalty payable by the compulsory licensee shall be the royalty prescribed under subparagraphs (B) through (F) and chapter 8 of this title.

(B) Notwithstanding any provision of the antitrust laws, any copyright owners of nondramatic musical works and any persons entitled to obtain a compulsory license under subsection (a)(1) may negotiate and agree upon the terms and rates of royalty payments under this paragraph and the proportionate division of fees paid among copyright owners, and may designate common agents to negotiate, agree to, pay or receive such royalty payments. Such authority to negotiate the terms and rates of royalty payments includes, but is not limited to, the authority to negotiate the year during which the royalty rates prescribed under subparagraphs (B) through (F) and chapter 8 of this title shall next be determined.

(C) During the period of June 30, 1996, through December 31, 1996, the Librarian of Congress shall cause notice to be published in the Federal Register of the initiation of voluntary negotiation proceedings for the purpose of determining reasonable terms and rates of royalty payments for the activities specified by subparagraph (A) during the period beginning January 1, 1998, and ending on the effective date of any new terms and rates established pursuant to subparagraph (C), (D) or (F), or such other date (regarding digital phonorecord deliveries) as the parties may agree. Such terms and rates shall distinguish between (i) digital phonorecord deliveries where the reproduction or distribution of a phonorecord is incidental to the transmission which constitutes the digital phonorecord delivery, and (ii) digital phonorecord deliveries in general. Any copyright owners of nondramatic musical works and any persons entitled to obtain a compulsory license under subsection (a)(1) may submit to the Librarian of Congress licenses covering such activities. The parties to each negotiation proceeding shall bear their own costs.

(D) In the absence of license agreements negotiated under subparagraphs (B) and (C), upon the filing of a petition in accordance with section

803(a)(1), the Librarian of Congress shall, pursuant to chapter 8, convene a copyright arbitration royalty panel to determine and publish in the Federal Register a schedule of rates and terms which, subject to subparagraph (E), shall be binding on all copyright owners of nondramatic musical works and persons entitled to obtain a compulsory license under subsection (a)(1) during the period beginning January 1, 1998, and ending on the effective date of any new terms and rates established pursuant to subparagraph (C), (D) or (F), or such other date (regarding digital phonorecord deliveries) as may be determined pursuant to subparagraphs (B) and (C). Such terms and rates shall distinguish between (i) digital phonorecord deliveries where the reproduction or distribution of a phonorecord is incidental to the transmission which constitutes the digital phonorecord delivery, and (ii) digital phonorecord deliveries in general. In addition to the objectives set forth in section 801(b)(1), in establishing such rates and terms, the copyright arbitration royalty panel may consider rates and terms under voluntary license agreements negotiated as provided in subparagraphs (B) and (C). The royalty rates payable for a compulsory license for a digital phonorecord delivery under this section shall be established de novo and no precedential effect shall be given to the amount of the royalty payable by a compulsory licensee for digital phonorecord deliveries on or before December 31, 1997. The Librarian of Congress shall also establish requirements by which copyright owners may receive reasonable notice of the use of their works under this section, and under which records of such use shall be kept and made available by persons making digital phonorecord deliveries.

(E)(i) License agreements voluntarily negotiated at any time between one or more copyright owners of nondramatic musical works and one or more persons entitled to obtain a compulsory license under subsection (a)(1) shall be given effect in lieu of any determination by the Librarian of Congress. Subject to clause (ii), the royalty rates determined pursuant to subparagraph (C), (D) or (F) shall be given effect in lieu of any contrary royalty rates specified in a contract pursuant to which a recording artist who is the author of a nondramatic musical work grants a license under that person's exclusive rights in the musical work under paragraphs (1) and (3) of section 106 or commits another person to grant a license in that musical work under paragraphs (1) and (3) of section 106, to a person desiring to fix in a tangible medium of expression a sound recording embodying the musical work.

(ii) The second sentence of clause (i) shall not apply to—

(I) a contract entered into on or before June 22, 1995, and not modified thereafter for the purpose of reducing the royalty rates determined pursuant to subparagraph (C), (D) or (F) or of increasing the number of musical works within the scope of the contract covered by the reduced rates, except if a contract entered into on or before June 22, 1995, is modified thereafter for the purpose of increasing the number of musical works within the scope of the contract, any contrary royalty rates specified in the contract shall be given effect in lieu of royalty rates determined pursuant to subparagraph (C), (D) or (F) for the number of musical works within the scope of the contract as of June 22, 1995; and

(II) a contract entered into after the date that the sound recording is fixed in a tangible medium of expression substantially in a form intended for commercial release, if at the time the contract is entered into, the recording artist retains the right to grant licenses as to the musical work under paragraphs (1) and (3) of section 106.

(F) The procedures specified in subparagraphs (C) and (D) shall be repeated and concluded, in accordance with regulations that the Librarian of Congress shall prescribe, in each fifth calendar year after 1997, except to the extent that different years for the repeating and concluding of such proceedings may be determined in accordance with subparagraphs (B) and (C).

(G) Except as provided in section 1002(e) of this title, a digital phonorecord delivery licensed under this paragraph shall be accompanied by the information encoded in the sound recording, if any, by or under the authority of the copyright owner of that sound recording, that identifies the title of the sound recording, the featured recording artist who performs on the sound recording, and related information, including information concerning the underlying musical work and its writer.

(H)(i) A digital phonorecord delivery of a sound recording is actionable as an act of infringement under section 501, and is fully subject to the remedies provided by sections 502 through 506 and section 509, unless—

(I) the digital phonorecord delivery has been authorized by the copyright owner of the sound recording; and

(II) the owner of the copyright in the sound recording or the entity making the digital phonorecord delivery has obtained a compulsory license under this section or has otherwise been authorized by the copyright owner of the musical work to distribute or authorize the distribution, by means of a digital phonorecord delivery, of each musical work embodied in the sound recording.

(ii) Any cause of action under this subparagraph shall be in addition to those available to the owner of the copyright in the nondramatic musical work under subsection (c)(6) and section 106(4) and the owner of the copyright in the sound recording under section 106(6).

(I) The liability of the copyright owner of a sound recording for infringement of the copyright in a nondramatic musical work embodied in the sound recording shall be determined in accordance with applicable law, except that the owner of a copyright in a sound recording shall not be liable for a digital phonorecord delivery by a third party if the owner of the copyright in the sound recording does not license the distribution of a phonorecord of the nondramatic musical work.

(J) Nothing in section 1008 shall be construed to prevent the exercise of the rights and remedies allowed by this paragraph, paragraph (6), and chapter 5 in the event of a digital phonorecord delivery, except that no action alleging infringement of copyright may be brought under this title against a manufacturer, importer or distributor of a digital audio recording device, a digital audio recording medium, an analog recording device, or an analog recording medium, or against a consumer, based on the actions described in such section.

(K) Nothing in this section annuls or limits (i) the exclusive right to publicly perform a sound recording or the musical work embodied therein, including by means of a digital transmission, under sections 106(4) and 106(6), (ii) except for compulsory licensing under the conditions specified by this section, the exclusive rights to reproduce and distribute the sound recording and the musical work embodied therein under sections 106(1) and 106(3), including by means of a digital phonorecord delivery, or (iii) any other rights under any other provision of section 106, or remedies available under this title, as such rights or remedies exist either before or after the date of enactment of the Digital Performance Right in Sound Recordings Act of 1995.

(L) The provisions of this section concerning digital phonorecord deliveries shall not apply to any exempt transmissions or retransmissions under section 114(d)(1). The exemptions created in section 114(d)(1) do not expand or reduce the rights of copyright owners under section 106 (1) through (5) with respect to such transmissions and retransmissions.

(4) A compulsory license under this section includes the right of the maker of a phonorecord of a nondramatic musical work under subsection (a)(1) to distribute or authorize distribution of such phonorecord by rental, lease, or lending (or by acts or practices in the nature of rental, lease, or lending). In addition to any royalty payable under clause (2) and chapter 8 of this title, a royalty shall be payable by the compulsory licensee for every act of distribution of a phonorecord by or in the nature of rental, lease, or lending, by or under the authority of the compulsory licensee. With respect to each nondramatic musical work embodied in the phonorecord, the royalty shall be a proportion of the revenue received by the compulsory licensee from every such act of distribution of the phonorecord under this clause

equal to the proportion of the revenue received by the compulsory licensee from distribution of the phonorecord under clause (2) that is payable by a compulsory licensee under that clause and under chapter 8. The Register of Copyrights shall issue regulations to carry out the purpose of this clause.

(5) Royalty payments shall be made on or before the twentieth day of each month and shall include all royalties for the month next preceding. Each monthly payment shall be made under oath and shall comply with requirements that the Register of Copyrights shall prescribe by regulation. The Register shall also prescribe regulations under which detailed cumulative annual statements of account, certified by a certified public accountant, shall be filed for every compulsory license under this section. The regulations covering both the monthly and the annual statements of account shall prescribe the form, content and manner of certification with respect to the number of records made and the number of records distributed.

(6) If the copyright owner does not receive the monthly payment and the monthly and annual statements of account when due, the owner may give written notice to the licensee that, unless the default is remedied within thirty days from the date of the notice, the compulsory license will be automatically terminated. Such termination renders either the making or the distribution, or both, of all phonorecords for which the royalty has not been paid, actionable as acts of infringement under section 501 and fully subject to the remedies provided by sections 502 through 506 and 509.

(d) Definition.—As used in this section, the following term has the following meaning: A "digital phonorecord delivery" is each individual delivery of a phonorecord by digital transmission of a sound recording which results in a specifically identifiable reproduction by or for any transmission recipient of a phonorecord of that sound recording, regardless of whether the digital transmission is also a public performance of the sound recording or any nondramatic musical work embodied therein. A digital phonorecord delivery does not result from a real-time, non-interactive subscription transmission of a sound recording where no reproduction of the sound recording or the musical work embodied therein is made from the inception of the transmission through to its receipt by the transmission recipient in order to make the sound recording audible.

(Amended Oct. 4, 1984, Pub. L. 98-450, § 3, 98 Stat. 1727; Nov. 1, 1995, Pub. L. 104-39, Sec. 4, 109 Stat. 344; Nov. 13, 1997, Pub. L. 105-80, 111 Stat. 1531, 1534-35.)

17 U.S.C. § 117. Limitations on exclusive rights: Computer programs

(a) Making of additional copy or adaptation by owner of copy. Notwithstanding the provisions of section 106, it is not an infringement for the owner of a copy of a computer program to make or authorize the making of another copy or adaptation of that computer program provided:

(1) that such a new copy or adaptation is created as an essential step in the utilization of the computer program in conjunction with a machine and that it is used in no other manner, or

(2) that such new copy or adaptation is for archival purposes only and that all archival copies are destroyed in the event that continued possession of the computer program should cease to be rightful.

(b) Lease, sale, or other transfer of additional copy or adaptation. Any exact copies prepared in accordance with the provisions of this section may be leased, sold, or otherwise transferred, along with the copy from which such copies were prepared, only as part of the lease, sale, or other transfer of all rights in the program. Adaptations so prepared may be transferred only with the authorization of the copyright owner.

(c) Machine maintenance or repair. Notwithstanding the provisions of section 106, it is not an infringement for the owner or lessee of a machine to make or authorize the making of a copy of a computer program if such copy is made solely by virtue of the activation of a machine that lawfully contains an authorized copy of the computer program, for purposes only of maintenance or repair of that machine, if—

(1) such new copy is used in no other manner and is destroyed immediately after the maintenance or repair is completed; and

(2) with respect to any computer program or part thereof that is not necessary for that machine to be activated, such program or part thereof is not accessed or used other than to make such new copy by virtue of the activation of the machine.

(d) Definitions. For purposes of this section—

(1) the "maintenance" of a machine is the servicing of the machine in order to make it work in accordance with its original specifications and any changes to those specifications authorized for that machine; and

(2) the "repair" of a machine is the restoring of the machine to the state of working in accordance with its original specifications and any changes to those specifications authorized for that machine.

(Amended Dec. 12, 1980, Pub. L. 96-517, § 10(b), 94 Stat. 3028; Oct. 28, 1998, Pub. L. 105-304, Title III, § 302, 112 Stat. 2887.)

17 U.S.C. § 120. Scope of exclusive rights in architectural works

(a) **Pictorial Representations Permitted.** The copyright in an architectural work that has been constructed does not include the right to prevent the making, distributing, or public display of pictures, paintings, photographs, or other pictorial representations of the work, if the building in which the work is embodied is located in or ordinarily visible from a public place.

(b) **Alterations to and Destruction of Buildings.** Notwithstanding the provisions of section 106(2), the owners of a building embodying an architectural work may, without the consent of the author or copyright owner of the architectural work, make or authorize the making of alterations to such building, and destroy or authorize the destruction of such building.

17 U.S.C. § 201. Ownership of copyright

(a) **Initial Ownership.** Copyright in a work protected under this title vests initially in the author or authors of the work. The authors of a joint work are co-owners of copyright in the work.

(b) **Works Made for Hire.** In the case of a work made for hire, the employer or other person for whom the work was prepared is considered the author for purposes of this title, and, unless the parties have expressly agreed otherwise in a written instrument signed by them, owns all of the rights comprised in the copyright.

(c) **Contributions to Collective Works.** Copyright in each separate contribution to a collective work is distinct from copyright in the collective work as a whole, and vests initially in the author of the contribution. In the absence of an express transfer of the copyright or of any rights under it, the owner of copyright in the collective work is presumed to have acquired only the privilege of reproducing and distributing the contribution as part of that particular collective work, any revision of that collective work, and any later collective work in the same series.

(d) **Transfer of Ownership.**

(1) The ownership of a copyright may be transferred in whole or in part by any means of conveyance or by operation of law, and may be bequeathed by will or pass as personal property by the applicable laws of intestate succession.

(2) Any of the exclusive rights comprised in a copyright, including any subdivision of any of the rights specified by section 106, may be transferred as provided by clause (1) and owned separately. The owner of any particular exclusive right is entitled, to the extent of that right, to all of the protection and remedies accorded to the copyright owner by this title.

(e) **Involuntary Transfer.** When an individual author's ownership of a copyright, or of any of the exclusive rights under a copyright, has not previously been transferred voluntarily by that individual author, no action by any governmental body or other official or organization purporting to seize, expropriate, transfer, or exercise rights of ownership with respect to the copyright, or any of the exclusive rights under a copyright, shall be given effect under this title except as provided under Title 11.

17 U.S.C. § 202. Ownership of copyright as distinct from ownership of material object

Ownership of a copyright, or of any of the exclusive rights under a copyright, is distinct from ownership of any material object in which the work is embodied.

Transfer of ownership of any material object, including the copy or phonorecord in which the work is first fixed, does not of itself convey any rights in the copyrighted work embodied in the object; nor, in the absence of an agreement, does transfer of ownership of a copyright or of any exclusive rights under a copyright convey property rights in any material object.

17 U.S.C. § 203. Termination of transfers and licenses granted by author

(a) Conditions for termination. In the case of any work other than a work made for hire, the exclusive or nonexclusive grant of a transfer or license of copyright or of any right under a copyright, executed by the author on or after January 1, 1978, otherwise than by will, is subject to termination under the following conditions:

(1) In the case of a grant executed by one author, termination of the grant may be effected by that author or, if the author is dead, by the person or persons who, under clause (2) of this subsection, own and are entitled to exercise a total of more than one-half of that author's termination interest. In the case of a grant executed by two or more authors of a joint work, termination of the grant may be effected by a majority of the authors who executed it; if any of such authors is dead, the termination interest of any such author may be exercised as a unit by the person or persons who, under clause (2) of this subsection, own and are entitled to exercise a total of more than one-half of that author's interest.

(2) Where an author is dead, his or her termination interest is owned, and may be exercised, as follows:

(A) the widow or widower owns the author's entire termination interest unless there are any surviving children or grandchildren of the author, in which case the widow or widower owns one-half of the author's interest;

(B) the author's surviving children, and the surviving children of any dead child of the author, own the author's entire termination interest unless there is a widow or widower, in which case the ownership of one-half of the author's interest is divided among them;

(C) the rights of the author's children and grandchildren are in all cases divided among them and exercised on a per stirpes basis according to the number of such author's children represented; the share of the children of a dead child in a termination interest can be exercised only by the action of a majority of them.

(D) In the event that the author's widow or widower, children, and grandchildren are not living, the author's executor, administrator, personal representative, or trustee shall own the author's entire termination interest.

(3) Termination of the grant may be effected at any time during a period of five years beginning at the end of thirty-five years from the date of execution of the grant; or, if the grant covers the right of publication of the work, the period begins at the end of thirty-five years from the date of publication of the work under the grant or at the end of forty years from the date of execution of the grant, whichever term ends earlier.

(4) The termination shall be effected by serving an advance notice in writing, signed by the number and proportion of owners of termination interests required under clauses (1) and (2) of this subsection, or by their duly authorized agents, upon the grantee or the grantee's successor in title.

(A) The notice shall state the effective date of the termination, which shall fall within the five-year period specified by clause (3) of this subsection, and the notice shall be served not less than two or more than ten years before that date. A copy of the notice shall be recorded in the Copyright Office before the effective date of termination, as a condition to its taking effect.

(B) The notice shall comply, in form, content, and manner of service, with requirements that the Register of Copyrights shall prescribe by regulation.

(5) Termination of the grant may be effected notwithstanding any agreement to the contrary, including an agreement to make a will or to make any future grant.

(b) Effect of termination. Upon the effective date of termination, all rights under this title that were covered by the terminated grants revert to the author, authors, and other persons owning termination interests under clauses (1) and (2) of subsection (a), including those owners who did not join in signing the notice of termination under clause (4) of subsection (a), but with the following limitations:

(1) A derivative work prepared under authority of the grant before its termination may continue to be utilized under the terms of the grant after its termination, but this privilege does not extend to the preparation after the termination of other derivative works based upon the copyrighted work covered by the terminated grant.

(2) The future rights that will revert upon termination of the grant become vested on the date the notice of termination has been served as provided by clause (4) of subsection (a). The rights vest in the author, authors, and other persons named in, and in the proportionate shares provided by, clauses (1) and (2) of subsection (a).

(3) Subject to the provisions of clause (4) of this subsection, a further grant, or agreement to make a further grant, of any right covered by a terminated grant is valid only if it is signed by the same number and proportion of the owners, in whom the right has vested under clause (2)

of this subsection, as are required to terminate the grant under clauses (1) and (2) of subsection (a). Such further grant or agreement is effective with respect to all of the persons in whom the right it covers has vested under clause (2) of this subsection, including those who did not join in signing it. If any person dies after rights under a terminated grant have vested in him or her, that person's legal representatives, legatees, or heirs at law represent him or her for purposes of this clause.

(4) A further grant, or agreement to make a further grant, of any right covered by a terminated grant is valid only if it is made after the effective date of the termination. As an exception, however, an agreement for such a further grant may be made between the persons provided by clause (3) of this subsection and the original grantee or such grantee's successor in title, after the notice of termination has been served as provided by clause (4) of subsection (a).

(5) Termination of a grant under this section affects only those rights covered by the grants that arise under this title, and in no way affects rights arising under any other Federal, State, or foreign laws.

(6) Unless and until termination is effected under this section, the grant, if it does not provide otherwise, continues in effect for the term of copyright provided by this title.

(Amended Oct. 27, 1998, Pub. L. 105-298, Title I, § 103, 112 Stat. 2829.)

17 U.S.C. § 204. Execution of transfers of copyright ownership

(a) A transfer of copyright ownership, other than by operation of law, is not valid unless an instrument of conveyance, or a note or memorandum of the transfer, is in writing and signed by the owner of the rights conveyed or such owner's duly authorized agent.

(b) A certificate of acknowledgment is not required for the validity of a transfer, but is prima facie evidence of the execution of the transfer if—

(1) in the case of a transfer executed in the United States, the certificate is issued by a person authorized to administer oaths within the United States; or

(2) in the case of a transfer executed in a foreign country, the certificates issued by a diplomatic or consular officer of the United States, or by a person authorized to administer oaths whose authority is proved by a certificate of such an officer.

17 U.S.C. § 205. Recordation of transfers and other documents

(a) **Conditions for Recordation.** Any transfer of copyright ownership or other document pertaining to a copyright may be recorded in the Copyright Office if the document filed for recordation bears the actual signature of the person who executed it, or if it is accompanied by a sworn or official certification that it is a true copy of the original, signed document.

(b) **Certificate of Recordation.** The Register of Copyrights shall, upon receipt of a document as provided by subsection (a) and of the fee provided by section 708, record the document and return it with a certificate of recordation.

(c) **Recordation as Constructive Notice.** Recordation of a document in the Copyright Office gives all persons constructive notice of the facts stated in the recorded document, but only if—

(1) the document, or material attached to it, specifically identifies the work to which it pertains so that, after the document is indexed by the Register of Copyrights, it would be revealed by a reasonable search under the title or registration number of the work; and

(2) registration has been made for the work.

(d) **Priority Between Conflicting Transfers.** As between two conflicting transfers, the one executed first prevails if it is recorded, in the manner required to give constructive notice under subsection (c), within one month after its execution in the United States or within two months after its execution outside the United States, or at any time before recordation in such manner of the later transfer. Otherwise the later transfer prevails if recorded first in such manner, and if taken in good faith, for valuable consideration or on the basis of a binding promise to pay royalties, and without notice of the earlier transfer.

(e) **Priority Between Conflicting Transfer of Ownership and Nonexclusive License.** A nonexclusive license, whether recorded or not, prevails over a conflicting transfer of copyright ownership if the license is evidenced by a written instrument signed by the owner of the rights licensed or such owner's duly authorized agent, and if—

(1) the license was taken before execution of the transfer; or

(2) the license was taken in good faith before recordation of the transfer and without notice of it.

17 U.S.C. § 301. Preemption with respect to other laws

(a) On and after January 1, 1978, all legal or equitable rights that are equivalent to any of the exclusive rights within the general scope of copyright as specified by section 106 in works of authorship that are fixed in a tangible medium of expression and come within the subject matter of copyright as specified by sections 102 and 103, whether created before or after that date and whether published or unpublished, are governed exclusively by this title. Thereafter, no person is entitled to any such right or equivalent right in any such work under the common law or statutes of any State.

(b) Nothing in this title annuls or limits any rights or remedies under the common law or statutes of any State with respect to—

(1) subject matter that does not come within the subject matter of copyright as specified by sections 102 and 103, including works of authorship not fixed in any tangible medium of expression; or

(2) any cause of action arising from undertakings commenced before January 1, 1978;

(3) activities violating legal or equitable rights that are not equivalent to any of the exclusive rights within the general scope of copyright as specified by section 106; or

(4) State and local landmarks, historic preservation, zoning, or building codes, relating to architectural works protected under section 102(a)(8).

(c) With respect to sound recordings fixed before February 15, 1972, any rights or remedies under the common law or statutes of any State shall not be annulled or limited by this title until February 15, 2067. The preemptive provisions of subsection (a) shall apply to any such rights and remedies pertaining to any cause of action arising from undertakings commenced on and after February 15, 2067. Notwithstanding the provisions of section 303, no sound recording fixed before February 15, 1972, shall be subject to copyright under this title before, on, or after February 15, 2067.

(d) Nothing in this title annuls or limits any rights or remedies under any other Federal statute.

(e) The scope of Federal preemption under this section is not affected by the adherence of the United States to the Berne Convention or the satisfaction of obligations of the United States thereunder.

(f) (1) On or after the effective date set forth in section 610(a) of the Visual Artists Rights Act of 1990 [17 USCS § 106A note], all legal or equitable rights that are equivalent to any of the rights conferred by section 106A with respect to works of visual art to which the rights conferred by section 106A apply are governed exclusively by section 106A and section 113(d) and the provisions of this title relating to such sections. Thereafter, no person is entitled to any such right or equivalent right in any work of visual art under the common law or statutes of any State.

(2) Nothing in paragraph (1) annuls or limits any rights or remedies under the common law or statutes of any State with respect to—

(A) any cause of action from undertakings commenced before the effective date set forth in section 610(a) of the Visual Artists Rights Act of 1990 [17 USCS § 106A note];

(B) activities violating legal or equitable rights that are not equivalent to any of the rights conferred by section 106A with respect to works of visual art; or

(C) activities violating legal or equitable rights which extend beyond the life of the author.

(Amended Oct. 31, 1988, Pub. L. 100-568, § 6, 102 Stat. 2857; Dec. 1, 1990, Pub. L. 101-650, Title VI, § 605, Title VII, § 705, 104 Stat. 5131, 5134; Oct. 27, 1998, Pub. L. 105-298, Title I, § 102(a), 112 Stat. 2827.)

17 U.S.C. § 302. Duration of copyright: Works created on or after January 1, 1978

(a) In general. Copyright in a work created on or after January 1, 1978, subsists from its creation and, except as provided by the following subsections, endures for a term consisting of the life of the author and 70 years after the author's death.

(b) Joint works. In the case of a joint work prepared by two or more authors who did not work for hire, the copyright endures for a term consisting of the life of the last surviving author and 70 years after such last surviving author's death.

(c) Anonymous works, pseudonymous works, and works made for hire. In the case of an anonymous work, a pseudonymous work, or a work made for hire, the copyright endures for a term of 95 years from the year of its first publication, or a term of 120 years from the year of its creation, whichever expires first. If, before the end of such term, the identity of one or more of the authors of an anonymous or pseudonymous work is revealed in the records of a registration made for that work under subsections (a) or (d) of section 408, or in the records provided by this subsection, the copyright in the work endures for the term specified by subsection (a) or (b), based on the life of the author or authors whose identity has been revealed. Any person having an interest in the copyright in an anonymous or pseudonymous work may at any time record, in records to be maintained by the Copyright Office for that purpose, a statement identifying one or more authors of the work; the statement shall also identify the person filing it, the nature of that person's interest, the source of the information recorded, and the particular work affected, and shall comply in form and content with requirements that the Register of Copyrights shall prescribe by regulation.

(d) Records relating to death of authors. Any person having an interest in a copyright may at any time record in the Copyright Office a statement of the date of death of the author of the copyrighted work, or a statement that the author is still living on a particular date. The statement shall identify the person filing it, the nature of that person's interest, and the source of the information recorded, and shall comply in form and content with requirements that the Register of Copyrights shall prescribe by regulation. The Register shall maintain current records of information relating to the death of authors of copyrighted works, based on such recorded statements and, to the extent the Register considers practicable, on data contained in any of the records of the Copyright Office or in other reference sources.

(e) Presumption as to author's death. After a period of 95 years from the year of first publication of a work, or a period of 120 years from the year of its creation, whichever expires first, any person who obtains from the Copyright Office a certified report that the records provided by subsection (d) disclose nothing to indicate that the author of the work is living, or died less than 70 years before, is entitled to the benefit of a presumption that the author has been dead for at least 70 years. Reliance in good faith upon this presumption shall be a complete defense to any action for infringement under this title.

(Amended Oct. 27, 1998, Pub. L. 105-298, Title I, § 102(b), 112 Stat. 2827.)

17 U.S.C. § 303. Duration of copyright: Works created but not published or copyrighted before January 1, 1978

(a) Copyright in a work created before January 1, 1978, but not theretofore in the public domain or copyrighted, subsists from January 1, 1978, and endures for the term provided by section 302. In no case, however, shall the term of copyright in such a work expire before December 31, 2002; and, if the work is published on or before December 31, 2002, the term of copyright shall not expire before December 31, 2047.

(b) The distribution before January 1, 1978, of a phonorecord shall not for any purpose constitute a publication of the musical work embodied therein.

(Amended Nov. 13, 1997, Pub. L. 105-80, § 11, 111 Stat. 1534; Oct. 27, 1998, Pub. L. 105-298, Title I, § 102(c), 112 Stat. 2827.)

17 U.S.C. § 304.

(a) Copyrights in their first term on January 1, 1978.

(1) (A) Any copyright, the first term of which is subsisting on January 1, 1978, shall endure for 28 years from the date it was originally secured.

(B) In the case of—

(i) any posthumous work or of any periodical, cyclopedic, or other composite work upon which the copyright was originally secured by the proprietor thereof, or

(ii) any work copyrighted by a corporate body (otherwise than as assignee or licensee of the individual author) or by an employer for whom such work is made for hire, the proprietor of such copyright shall be entitled to a renewal and extension of the copyright in such work for the further term of 67 years.

(C) In the case of any other copyrighted work, including a contribution by an individual author to a periodical or to a cyclopedic or other composite work—

(i) the author of such work, if the author is still living,

(ii) the widow, widower, or children of the author, if the author is not living,

(iii) the author's executors, if such author, widow, widower, or children are not living, or

(iv) the author's next of kin, in the absence of a will of the author, shall be entitled to a renewal and extension of the copyright in such work for a further term of 67 years.

(2) (A) At the expiration of the original term of copyright in a work specified in paragraph (1)(B) of this subsection, the copyright shall endure for a renewed and extended further term of 67 years, which—

(i) if an application to register a claim to such further term has been made to the Copyright Office within 1 year before the expiration of the original term of copyright, and the claim is registered, shall vest, upon the beginning of such further term, in the proprietor of the copyright who is entitled to claim the renewal of copyright at the time the application is made; or

(ii) if no such application is made or the claim pursuant to such application is not registered, shall vest, upon the beginning of such further term, in the person or entity that was the proprietor of the copyright as of the last day of the original term of copyright.

(B) At the expiration of the original term of copyright in a work specified in paragraph (1)(C) of this subsection, the copyright shall endure for a renewed and extended further term of 67 years, which—

(i) if an application to register a claim to such further term has been made to the Copyright Office within 1 year before the expiration of the original term of copyright, and the claim is registered, shall vest, upon the beginning of such further term, in any person who is entitled under paragraph (1)(C) to the renewal and extension of the copyright at the time the application is made; or

(ii) if no such application is made or the claim pursuant to such application is not registered, shall vest, upon the beginning of such further term, in any person entitled under paragraph (1)(C), as of the last day of the original term of copyright, to the renewal and extension of the copyright.

(3) (A) An application to register a claim to the renewed and extended term of copyright in a work may be made to the Copyright Office—

(i) within 1 year before the expiration of the original term of copyright by any person entitled under paragraph (1) (B) or (C) to such further term of 67 years; and

(ii) at any time during the renewed and extended term by any person in whom such further term vested, under paragraph (2) (A) or (B), or by any successor or assign of such person, if the application is made in the name of such person.

(B) Such an application is not a condition of the renewal and extension of the copyright in a work for a further term of 67 years.

(4) (A) If an application to register a claim to the renewed and extended term of copyright in a work is not made within 1 year before the expiration of the original term of copyright in a work, or if the claim pursuant to such application is not registered, then a derivative work prepared under authority of a grant of a transfer or license of the copyright that is made before the expiration of the original term of copyright may continue to be used under the terms of the grant during the renewed and extended term of copyright without infringing the copyright, except that such use does not extend to the preparation during such renewed and extended term of other derivative works based upon the copyrighted work covered by such grant.

(B) If an application to register a claim to the renewed and extended term of copyright in a work is made within 1 year before its expiration, and the claim is registered, the certificate of such registration shall constitute prima facie evidence as to the validity of the copyright during its renewed and extended term and of the facts stated in the certificate. The evidentiary weight to be accorded the certificates of a registration of a renewed and extended term of copyright made after the end of that 1-year period shall be within the discretion of the court.*

(b) Copyrights in their renewal term at the time of the effective date of the Sonny Bono Copyright Term Extension Act. Any copyright still in its renewal term at the time that the Sonny Bono Copyright Term Extension Act becomes effective [effective Oct. 27, 1998] shall have a copyright term of 95 years from the date copyright was originally secured.

---

* Before the enactment of the Copyright Renewal Act of 1992 (effective June 26, 1992), § 304(a) read:

(a) Copyrights in their first term on January 1, 1978. Any copyright, the first term of which is subsisting on January 1, 1978, shall endure for twenty-eight years from the date it was originally secured: *Provided,* That in the case of any posthumous work or of any periodical, cyclopedic, or other composite work upon which the copyright was originally secured by the proprietor thereof, or of any work copyrighted by a corporate body (otherwise than as assignee or licensee of the individual author) or by an employer for whom such work is made for hire, the proprietor of such copyright shall be entitled to a renewal and extension of the copyright in such work for the further term of forty-seven years when application for such renewal and extension shall have been made to the Copyright Office and duly registered therein within one year prior to the expiration of the original term of copyright: *And provided further,* That in the case of any other copyrighted work, including a contribution by an individual author to a periodical or to a cyclopedic or other composite work, the author of such work, if still living, or the widow, widower, or children of the author, if the author be not living, or if such author, widow, widower, or children be not living, then the author's executors, or in the absence of a will, his or her next of kin shall be entitled to a renewal and extension of the copyright in such work for a further term of forty-seven years when application for such renewal and extension shall have been made to the Copyright Office and duly registered therein within one year prior to the expiration of the original term of copyright: *And provided further,* That in default of the registration of such application for renewal and extension, the copyright in any work shall terminate at the expiration of twenty-eight years from the date copyright was originally secured.

(c) Termination of transfers and licenses covering extended renewal term. In the case of any copyright subsisting in either its first or renewal term on January 1, 1978, other than a copyright in a work made for hire, the exclusive or nonexclusive grant of a transfer or license of the renewal copyright or any right under it, executed before January 1, 1978, by any of the persons designated by subsection (a)(1)(C) of this section, otherwise than by will, is subject to termination under the following conditions:

(1) In the case of a grant executed by a person or persons other than the author, termination of the grant may be effected by the surviving person or persons who executed it. In the case of a grant executed by one or more of the authors of the work, termination of the grant may be effected, to the extent of a particular author's share in the ownership of the renewal copyright, by the author who executed it or, if such author is dead, by the person or persons who, under clause (2) of this subsection, own and are entitled to exercise a total of more than one-half of that author's termination interest.

(2) Where an author is dead, his or her termination interest is owned, and may be exercised, as follows:

(A) the widow or widower owns the author's entire termination interest unless there are any surviving children or grandchildren of the author, in which case the widow or widower owns one-half of the author's interest;

(B) the author's surviving children, and the surviving children of any dead child of the author, own the author's entire termination interest unless there is a widow or widower, in which case the ownership of one-half of the author's interest is divided among them;

(C) the rights of the author's children and grandchildren are in all cases divided among them and exercised on a per stirpes basis according to the number of such author's children represented; the share of the children of a dead child in a termination interest can be exercised only by the action of a majority of them.

(D) In the event that the author's widow or widower, children, and grandchildren are not living, the author's executor, administrator, personal representative, or trustee shall own the author's entire termination interest.

(3) Termination of the grant may be effected at any time during a period of five years beginning at the end of fifty-six years from the date copyright was originally secured, or beginning on January 1, 1978, whichever is later.

(4) The termination shall be effected by serving an advance notice in writing upon the grantee or the grantee's successor in title. In the case of a grant executed by a person or persons other than the author, the notice shall be signed by all of those entitled to terminate the grant under clause (1) of this subsection, or by their duly authorized agents. In the case of a

grant executed by one or more of the authors of the work, the notice as to any one author's share shall be signed by that author or his or her duly authorized agent or, if that author is dead, by the number and proportion of the owners of his or her termination interest required under clauses (1) and (2) of this subsection, or by their duly authorized agents.

(A) The notice shall state the effective date of the termination, which shall fall within the five-year period specified by clause (3) of this subsection, or, in the case of a termination under subsection (d), within the five-year period specified by subsection (d)(2), and the notice shall be served not less than two or more than ten years before that date. A copy of the notice shall be recorded in the Copyright Office before the effective date of termination, as a condition to its taking effect.

(B) The notice shall comply, in form, content, and manner of service, with requirements that the Register of Copyrights shall prescribe by regulation.

(5) Termination of the grant may be effected notwithstanding any agreement to the contrary, including an agreement to make a will or to make any future grant.

(6) In the case of a grant executed by a person or persons other than the author, all rights under this title that were covered by the terminated grant revert, upon the effective date of termination, to all of those entitled to terminate the grant under clause (1) of this subsection. In the case of a grant executed by one or more of the authors of the work, all of a particular author's rights under this title that were covered by the terminated grant revert, upon the effective date of termination, to that author or, if that author is dead, to the persons owning his or her termination interest under clause (2) of this subsection, including those owners who did not join in signing the notice of termination under clause (4) of this subsection. In all cases the reversion of rights is subject to the following limitations:

(A) A derivative work prepared under authority of the grant before its termination may continue to be utilized under the terms of the grant after its termination, but this privilege does not extend to the preparation after the termination of other derivative works based upon the copyrighted work covered by the terminated grant.

(B) The future rights that will revert upon termination of the grant become vested on the date the notice of termination has been served as provided by clause (4) of this subsection.

(C) Where the author's rights revert to two or more persons under clause (2) of this subsection, they shall vest in those persons in the proportionate shares provided by that clause. In such a case, and subject to the provisions of subclause (D) of this clause, a further grant, or agreement to make a further grant, of a particular author's share with respect to any right covered by a terminated grant is valid only if it is signed by the same number and proportion of the owners, in whom the right has vested under this clause, as are required to terminate the grant under clause (2) of this subsection. Such further grant or agreement is effective with respect to all of the persons in whom the right it covers has vested under this subclause, including those who did not join in signing it. If any person dies after rights under a terminated grant have vested in him or her, that person's legal representatives, legatees, or heirs at law represent him or her for purposes of this subclause.

(D) A further grant, or agreement to make a further grant, of any right covered by a terminated grant is valid only if it is made after the effective date of the termination. As an exception, however, an agreement for such a further grant may be made between the author or any of the persons provided by the first sentence of clause (6) of this subsection, or between the persons provided by subclause (C) of this clause, and the original grantee or such grantee's successor in title, after the notice of termination has been served as provided by clause (4) of this subsection.

(E) Termination of a grant under this subsection affects only those rights covered by the grant that arise under this title, and in no way affects rights arising under any other Federal, State, or foreign laws.

(F) Unless and until termination is effected under this subsection, the grant, if it does not provide otherwise, continues in effect for the remainder of the extended renewal term.

(d) Termination rights provided in subsection (c) which have expired on or before the effective date of the Sonny Bono Copyright Term Extension Act. In the case of any copyright other than a work made for hire, subsisting in its renewal term on the effective date of the Sonny Bono Copyright Term Extension Act [effective October 27, 1998] for which the termination right provided in subsection (c) has expired by such date, where the author or owner of the termination right has not previously exercised such termination right, the exclusive or nonexclusive grant of a transfer or license of the renewal copyright or any right under it, executed before January 1, 1978, by any of the persons designated in subsection (a)(1)(C) of this section, other than by will, is subject to termination under the following conditions:

(1) The conditions specified in subsections (c)(1), (2), (4), (5), and (6) of this section apply to terminations of the last 20 years of copyright term as provided by the amendments made by the Sonny Bono Copyright Term Extension Act.

(2) Termination of the grant may be effected at any time during a period of 5 years beginning at the end of 75 years from the date copyright was originally secured.

(Amended June 26, 1992, Pub. L. 102-307, Title I, § 102(a), (d), 106 Stat. 264, 266; Nov. 13, 1997, Pub. L. 105-80, § 12(a)(9), 111 Stat. 1535; Oct. 27, 1998, Pub. L. 105-298, Title I, §§ 102(d)(1), 103, 112 Stat. 2827, 2829.)

17 U.S.C. § 305. Duration of copyright: Terminal date

All terms of copyright provided by sections 302 through 304 run to the end of the calendar year in which they would otherwise expire.

17 U.S.C. § 410. Registration and issuance of certificate

(a) When, after examination, the Register of Copyrights determines that, in accordance with the provisions of this title, the material deposited constitutes copyrightable subject matter and that the other legal and formal requirements of this title have been met, the Register shall register the claim and issue to the applicant a certificate of registration under the seal of the Copyright Office. The certificate shall contain the information given in the application, together with the number and effective date of the registration.

(b) In any case in which the Register of Copyrights determines that, in accordance with the provisions of this title, the material deposited does not constitute copyrightable subject matter or that the claim is invalid for any other reason, the Register shall refuse registration and shall notify the applicant in writing of the reasons for such refusal.

(c) In any judicial proceedings the certificate of a registration made before or within five years after first publication of the work shall constitute prima facie evidence of the validity of the copyright and of the facts stated in the certificate. The evidentiary weight to be accorded the certificate of a registration made thereafter shall be within the discretion of the court.

(d) The effective date of a copyright registration is the day on which an application, deposit, and fee, which are later determined by the Register of Copyrights or by a court of competent jurisdiction to be acceptable for registration, have all been received in the Copyright Office.

17 U.S.C. § 411. Registration and infringement actions

(a) Except for an action brought for a violation of the rights of the author under section 106A(a), and subject to the provisions of subsection (b), no action for infringement of the copyright in any United States work shall be instituted until registration of the copyright claim has been made in accordance with this title. In any case, however, where the deposit, application, and fee required for registration have been delivered to the Copyright Office in proper form and registration has been refused, the applicant is entitled to institute an action for infringement if notice thereof, with a copy of the complaint, is served on the Register of Copyrights. The Register may, at his or her option, become a party to the action with respect to the issue of registrability of the copyright claim by entering an appearance within sixty days after such service, but the Register's failure to become a party shall not deprive the court of jurisdiction to determine that issue.

(b) In the case of a work consisting of sounds, images, or both, the first fixation of which is made simultaneously with its transmission, the copyright owner may, either before or after such fixation takes place, institute an action for infringement under section 501, fully subject to the remedies provided by sections 502 through 506 and sections 509 and 510, if, in accordance with requirements that the Register of Copyrights shall prescribe by regulation, the copyright owner—

(1) serves notice upon the infringer, not less than 48 hours before such fixation, identifying the work and the specific time and source of its first transmission, and declaring an intention to secure copyright in the work; and

(2) makes registration for the work, if required by subsection (a), within three months after its first transmission.

(Amended Oct. 31, 1988, Pub. L. 100-568, § 9(b)(1), 102 Stat. 2859; Dec. 1, 1990, Pub. L. 101-650, Title VI, § 606(c)(1), 104 Stat. 5131; Nov. 13, 1997, Pub. L. 105-80, § 6, 111 Stat. 1532; Oct. 28, 1998, Pub. L. 105-304, Title I, § 102(d), 112 Stat. 2863.)

17 U.S.C. § 412. Registration as prerequisite to certain remedies for infringement

In any action under this title, other than an action brought for a violation of the rights of the author under section 106A(a) or an action instituted under section 411(b), no award of statutory damages or of attorney's fees, as provided by sections 504 and 505, shall be made for—

(1) any infringement of copyright in an unpublished work commenced before the effective date of its registration; or

(2) any infringement of copyright commenced after first publication of the work and before the effective date of its registration, unless such registration is made within three months after the first publication of the work.

17 U.S.C. § 501. Infringement of copyright

(a) Anyone who violates any of the exclusive rights of the copyright owner as provided by sections 106 through 118 or of the author as provided in section 106A(a), or who imports copies or phonorecords into the United States in violation of section 602, is an infringer of the copyright or right of the author, as the case may be. For purposes of this chapter (other than section 506), any reference to copyright shall be deemed to include the rights conferred by section 106A(a). As used in this subsection the term "anyone" includes any State, any instrumentality of a State, and any officer or employee of a State or instrumentality of a State acting in his or her official capacity. Any State, and any such instrumentality, officer, or employee, shall be subject to the provisions of this title in the same manner and to the same extent as any nongovernmental entity.

(b) The legal or beneficial owner of an exclusive right under a copyright is entitled, subject to the requirements of section 411, to institute an action for any infringement of that particular right committed while he or she is the owner of it. The court may require such owner to serve written notice of the action with a copy of the complaint upon any person shown, by the records of the Copyright Office or otherwise, to have or claim an interest in the copyright, and shall require that such notice be served upon any person whose interest is likely to be affected by a decision in the case. The court may require the joinder, and shall permit the intervention, of any person having or claiming an interest in the copyright.

(c) For any secondary transmission by a cable system that embodies a performance or a display of a work which is actionable as an act of infringement under subsection (c) of section 111, a television broadcast station holding a copyright or other license to transmit or perform the same version of that work shall, for purposes of subsection (b) of this section, be treated as a legal or beneficial owner if such secondary transmission occurs within the local service area of that television station.

(d) For any secondary transmission by a cable system that is actionable as an act of infringement pursuant to section 111(c)(3), the following shall also have standing to sue: (i) the primary transmitter whose transmission has been altered by the cable system; and (ii) any broadcast station within whose local service area the secondary transmission occurs.

(e) With respect to any secondary transmission that is made by a satellite carrier of a primary transmission embodying the performance or display of a work and is actionable as an act of infringement under section 119(a)(5), a network station holding a copyright or other license to transmit or perform the same version of that work shall, for purposes of subsection (b) of this section, be treated as a legal or beneficial owner if such secondary transmission occurs within the local service area of that station.

17 U.S.C. § 502. Injunctions

(a) Any court having jurisdiction of a civil action arising under this title may, subject to the provisions of section 1498 of title 28, grant temporary and final injunctions on such terms as it may deem reasonable to prevent or restrain infringement of a copyright.

(b) Any such injunction may be served anywhere in the United States on the person enjoined; it shall be operative throughout the United States and shall be enforceable, by proceedings in contempt or otherwise, by any United States court having jurisdiction of that person. The clerk of the court granting the injunction shall, when requested by any other court in which enforcement of the injunction is sought, transmit promptly to the other court a certified copy of all the papers in the case on file in such clerk's office.

17 U.S.C. § 503. Impounding and disposition of infringing articles

(a) At any time while an action under this title is pending, the court may order the impounding, on such terms as it may deem reasonable, of all copies or phonorecords claimed to have been made or used in violation of the copyright owner's exclusive rights, and of all plates, molds, matrices, masters, tapes, film negatives, or other articles by means of which such copies or phonorecords may be reproduced.

(b) As part of a final judgment or decree, the court may order the destruction or other reasonable disposition of all copies or phonorecords found to have been made or used in violation of the copyright owner's exclusive rights, and of all plates, molds, matrices, masters, tapes, film negatives, or other articles by means of which such copies or phonorecords may be reproduced.

17 U.S.C. § 504. Remedies for infringement: Damages and profits

(a) In general. Except as otherwise provided by this title, an infringer of copyright is liable for either—

(1) the copyright owner's actual damages and any additional profits of the infringer, as provided by subsection (b); or

(2) statutory damages, as provided by subsection (c).

(b) Actual damages and profits. The copyright owner is entitled to recover the actual damages suffered by him or her as a result of the infringement, and any profits of the infringer that are attributable to the infringement and are not taken into account in computing the actual damages. In establishing the infringer's profits, the copyright owner is required to present proof only of the infringer's gross revenue, and the infringer is required to prove his or her deductible expenses and the elements of profit attributable to factors other than the copyrighted work.

(c) Statutory damages.

(1) Except as provided by clause (2) of this subsection, the copyright owner may elect, at any time before final judgment is rendered, to recover, instead of actual damages and profits, an award of statutory damages for all infringements involved in the action, with respect to any one work, for which any one infringer is liable individually, or for which any two or more infringers are liable jointly and severally, in a sum of not less than $ 500 or more than $ 20,000 as the court considers just. For the purposes of this subsection, all the parts of a compilation or derivative work constitute one work.

(2) In a case where the copyright owner sustains the burden of proving, and the court finds, that infringement was committed willfully, the court in its discretion may increase the award of statutory damages to a sum of not more than $ 100,000. In a case where the infringer sustains the burden of proving, and the court finds, that such infringer was not aware and had no reason to believe that his or her acts constituted an infringement of copyright, the court in its discretion may reduce the award of statutory damages to a sum of not less than $ 200. The court shall remit statutory

damages in any case where an infringer believed and had reasonable grounds for believing that his or her use of the copyrighted work was a fair use under section 107, if the infringer was: (i) an employee or agent of a nonprofit educational institution, library, or archives acting within the scope of his or her employment who, or such institution, library, or archives itself, which infringed by reproducing the work in copies or phonorecords; or (ii) a public broadcasting entity which or a person who, as a regular part of the nonprofit activities of a public broadcasting entity (as defined in subsection (g) of section 118) infringed by performing a published nondramatic literary work or by reproducing a transmission program embodying a performance of such a work.

(d) Additional damages in certain cases. In any case in which the court finds that a defendant proprietor of an establishment who claims as a defense that its activities were exempt under section 110(5) did not have reasonable grounds to believe that its use of a copyrighted work was exempt under such section, the plaintiff shall be entitled to, in addition to any award of damages under this section, an additional award of two times the amount of the license fee that the proprietor of the establishment concerned should have paid the plaintiff for such use during the preceding period of up to 3 years.

(Amended Oct. 31, 1988, Pub. L. 100-568, § 10(b), 102 Stat. 2860; Nov. 13, 1997, Pub. L. 105-80, § 12(a)(13), 111 Stat. 1535; Oct. 27, 1998, Pub. L. 105-298, Title II, § 204, 112 Stat. 2833.)

17 U.S.C. § 505. Costs and attorney's fees

In any civil action under this title, the court in its discretion may allow the recovery of full costs by or against any party other than the United States or an officer thereof. Except as otherwise provided by this title, the court may also award a reasonable attorney's fee to the prevailing party as part of the costs.

17 U.S.C. § 507. Limitations on actions

(a) Criminal proceedings. Except as expressly provided otherwise in this title, no criminal proceeding shall be maintained under the provisions of this title unless it is commenced within 5 years after the cause of action arose.

(b) Civil actions. No civil action shall be maintained under the provisions of this title unless it is commenced within three years after the claim accrued.

(Amended Dec. 16, 1997, Pub. L. 105-147, § 2(c), 111 Stat. 2678; Oct. 28, 1998, Pub. L. 105-304, Title I, § 102(e), 112 Stat. 2863.)

17 U.S.C. § 512. Determination of reasonable license fees for individual proprietors [Caution: This section was added by Pub. L. 105-298. Another § 512 was added by Pub. L. 105-304.]*

In the case of any performing rights society subject to a consent decree which provides for the determination of reasonable license rates or fees to be charged

---

* Effective date of section: This section took effect 90 days after enactment, pursuant to § 207 of Act Oct. 27, 1998, Pub. L. 105-298, which appears as 17 USCS § 101 note.

by the performing rights society, notwithstanding the provisions of that consent decree, an individual proprietor who owns or operates fewer than 7 non-publicly traded establishments in which nondramatic musical works are performed publicly and who claims that any license agreement offered by that performing rights society is unreasonable in its license rate or fee as to that individual proprietor, shall be entitled to determination of a reasonable license rate or fee as follows:

(1) The individual proprietor may commence such proceeding for determination of a reasonable license rate or fee by filing an application in the applicable district court under paragraph (2) that a rate disagreement exists and by serving a copy of the application on the performing rights society. Such proceeding shall commence in the applicable district court within 90 days after the service of such copy, except that such 90-day requirement shall be subject to the administrative requirements of the court.

(2) The proceeding under paragraph (1) shall be held, at the individual proprietor's election, in the judicial district of the district court with jurisdiction over the applicable consent decree or in that place of holding court of a district court that is the seat of the Federal circuit (other than the Court of Appeals for the Federal Circuit) in which the proprietor's establishment is located.

(3) Such proceeding shall be held before the judge of the court with jurisdiction over the consent decree governing the performing rights society. At the discretion of the court, the proceeding shall be held before a special master or magistrate judge appointed by such judge. Should that consent decree provide for the appointment of an advisor or advisors to the court for any purpose, any such advisor shall be the special master so named by the court.

(4) In any such proceeding, the industry rate shall be presumed to have been reasonable at the time it was agreed to or determined by the court. Such presumption shall in no way affect a determination of whether the rate is being correctly applied to the individual proprietor.

(5) Pending the completion of such proceeding, the individual proprietor shall have the right to perform publicly the copyrighted musical compositions in the repertoire of the performing rights society by paying an interim license rate or fee into an interest bearing escrow account with the clerk of the court, subject to retroactive adjustment when a final rate or fee has been determined, in an amount equal to the industry rate, or, in the absence of an industry rate, the amount of the most recent license rate or fee agreed to by the parties.

(6) Any decision rendered in such proceeding by a special master or magistrate judge named under paragraph (3) shall be reviewed by the judge of the court with jurisdiction over the consent decree governing the performing rights society. Such proceeding, including such review, shall be concluded within 6 months after its commencement.

(7) Any such final determination shall be binding only as to the individual proprietor commencing the proceeding, and shall not be applicable to any other proprietor or any other performing rights society, and the performing rights society shall be relieved of any obligation of nondiscrimination among similarly situated music users that may be imposed by the consent decree governing its operations.

(8) An individual proprietor may not bring more than one proceeding provided for in this section for the determination of a reasonable license rate or fee under any license agreement with respect to any one performing rights society.

(9) For purposes of this section, the term 'industry rate' means the license fee a performing rights society has agreed to with, or which has been determined by the court for, a significant segment of the music user industry to which the individual proprietor belongs.

(Added Oct. 27, 1998, Pub. L. 105-298, Title II, § 203(a), 112 Stat. 2831.)

17 U.S.C. § 512. Limitations on liability relating to material online [Caution: This section was added by Pub. L. 105-304. Another § 512 was added by Pub. L. 105-298.] *

(a) Transitory digital network communications. A service provider shall not be liable for monetary relief, or, except as provided in subsection (j), for injunctive or other equitable relief, for infringement of copyright by reason of the provider's transmitting, routing, or providing connections for, material through a system or network controlled or operated by or for the service provider, or by reason of the intermediate and transient storage of that material in the course of such transmitting, routing, or providing connections, if—

(1) the transmission of the material was initiated by or at the direction of a person other than the service provider;

(2) the transmission, routing, provision of connections, or storage is carried out through an automatic technical process without selection of the material by the service provider;

(3) the service provider does not select the recipients of the material except as an automatic response to the request of another person;

(4) no copy of the material made by the service provider in the course of such intermediate or transient storage is maintained on the system or network in a manner ordinarily accessible to anyone other than anticipated recipients, and no such copy is maintained on the system or network in a manner ordinarily accessible to such anticipated recipients for a longer period than is reasonably necessary for the transmission, routing, or provision of connections; and

---

* Effective date of section: This section took effect on October 28, 1998, pursuant to § 203 of Act Oct. 28, 1998, Pub. L. 105-304, which appears as a note to this section.

(5) the material is transmitted through the system or network without modification of its content.

(b) System caching.

(1) Limitation on liability. A service provider shall not be liable for monetary relief, or, except as provided in subsection (j), for injunctive or other equitable relief, for infringement of copyright by reason of the intermediate and temporary storage of material on a system or network controlled or operated by or for the service provider in a case in which—

(A) the material is made available online by a person other than the service provider;

(B) the material is transmitted from the person described in subparagraph (A) through the system or network to a person other than the person described in subparagraph (A) at the direction of that other person; and

(C) the storage is carried out through an automatic technical process for the purpose of making the material available to users of the system or network who, after the material is transmitted as described in subparagraph (B), request access to the material from the person described in subparagraph (A), if the conditions set forth in paragraph (2) are met.

(2) Conditions. The conditions referred to in paragraph (1) are that—

(A) the material described in paragraph (1) is transmitted to the subsequent users described in paragraph (1)(C) without modification to its content from the manner in which the material was transmitted from the person described in paragraph (1)(A);

(B) the service provider described in paragraph (1) complies with rules concerning the refreshing, reloading, or other updating of the material when specified by the person making the material available online in accordance with a generally accepted industry standard data communications protocol for the system or network through which that person makes the material available, except that this subparagraph applies only if those rules are not used by the person described in paragraph (1)(A) to prevent or unreasonably impair the intermediate storage to which this subsection applies;

(C) the service provider does not interfere with the ability of technology associated with the material to return to the person described in paragraph (1)(A) the information that would have been available to that person if the material had been obtained by the subsequent users described in paragraph (1)(C) directly from that person, except that this subparagraph applies only if that technology—

(i) does not significantly interfere with the performance of the provider's system or network or with the intermediate storage of the material;

(ii) is consistent with generally accepted industry standard communications protocols; and

(iii) does not extract information from the provider's system or network other than the information that would have been available to the person described in paragraph (1)(A) if the subsequent users had gained access to the material directly from that person;

(D) if the person described in paragraph (1)(A) has in effect a condition that a person must meet prior to having access to the material, such as a condition based on payment of a fee or provision of a password or other information, the service provider permits access to the stored material in significant part only to users of its system or network that have met those conditions and only in accordance with those conditions; and

(E) if the person described in paragraph (1)(A) makes that material available online without the authorization of the copyright owner of the material, the service provider responds expeditiously to remove, or disable access to, the material that is claimed to be infringing upon notification of claimed infringement as described in subsection (c)(3), except that this subparagraph applies only if—

(i) the material has previously been removed from the originating site or access to it has been disabled, or a court has ordered that the material be removed from the originating site or that access to the material on the originating site be disabled; and

(ii) the party giving the notification includes in the notification a statement confirming that the material has been removed from the originating site or access to it has been disabled or that a court has ordered that the material be removed from the originating site or that access to the material on the originating site be disabled.

(c) Information residing on systems or networks at direction of users.

(1) In general. A service provider shall not be liable for monetary relief, or, except as provided in subsection (j), for injunctive or other equitable relief, for infringement of copyright by reason of the storage at the direction of a user of material that resides on a system or network controlled or operated by or for the service provider, if the service provider—

(A) (i) does not have actual knowledge that the material or an activity using the material on the system or network is infringing;

(ii) in the absence of such actual knowledge, is not aware of facts or circumstances from which infringing activity is apparent; or

(iii) upon obtaining such knowledge or awareness, acts expeditiously to remove, or disable access to, the material;

(B) does not receive a financial benefit directly attributable to the infringing activity, in a case in which the service provider has the right and ability to control such activity; and

(C) upon notification of claimed infringement as described in paragraph (3), responds expeditiously to remove, or disable access to, the material that is claimed to be infringing or to be the subject of infringing activity.

(2) Designated agent. The limitations on liability established in this subsection apply to a service provider only if the service provider has designated an agent to receive notifications of claimed infringement described in paragraph (3), by making available through its service, including on its website in a location accessible to the public, and by providing to the Copyright Office, substantially the following information:

(A) the name, address, phone number, and electronic mail address of the agent.

(B) other contact information which the Register of Copyrights may deem appropriate.

The Register of Copyrights shall maintain a current directory of agents available to the public for inspection, including through the Internet, in both electronic and hard copy formats, and may require payment of a fee by service providers to cover the costs of maintaining the directory.

(3) Elements of notification.

(A) To be effective under this subsection, a notification of claimed infringement must be a written communication provided to the designated agent of a service provider that includes substantially the following:

(i) A physical or electronic signature of a person authorized to act on behalf of the owner of an exclusive right that is allegedly infringed.

(ii) Identification of the copyrighted work claimed to have been infringed, or, if multiple copyrighted works at a single online site are covered by a single notification, a representative list of such works at that site.

(iii) Identification of the material that is claimed to be infringing or to be the subject of infringing activity and that is to be removed or access to which is to be disabled, and information reasonably sufficient to permit the service provider to locate the material.

(iv) Information reasonably sufficient to permit the service provider to contact the complaining party, such as an address, telephone number, and, if available, an electronic mail address at which the complaining party may be contacted.

(v) A statement that the complaining party has a good faith belief that use of the material in the manner complained of is not authorized by the copyright owner, its agent, or the law.

(vi) A statement that the information in the notification is accurate, and under penalty of perjury, that the complaining party is authorized to act on behalf of the owner of an exclusive right that is allegedly infringed.

(B) (i) Subject to clause (ii), a notification from a copyright owner or from a person authorized to act on behalf of the copyright owner that fails to comply substantially with the provisions of subparagraph (A) shall not be considered under paragraph (1)(A) in determining whether a service provider has actual knowledge or is aware of facts or circumstances from which infringing activity is apparent.

(ii) In a case in which the notification that is provided to the service provider's designated agent fails to comply substantially with all the provisions of subparagraph (A) but substantially complies with clauses (ii), (iii), and (iv) of subparagraph (A), clause (i) of this subparagraph applies only if the service provider promptly attempts to contact the person making the notification or takes other reasonable steps to assist in the receipt of notification that substantially complies with all the provisions of subparagraph (A).

(d) Information location tools. A service provider shall not be liable for monetary relief, or, except as provided in subsection (j), for injunctive or other equitable relief, for infringement of copyright by reason of the provider referring or linking users to an online location containing infringing material or infringing activity, by using information location tools, including a directory, index, reference, pointer, or hypertext link, if the service provider—

(1) (A) does not have actual knowledge that the material or activity is infringing;

(B) in the absence of such actual knowledge, is not aware of facts or circumstances from which infringing activity is apparent; or

(C) upon obtaining such knowledge or awareness, acts expeditiously to remove, or disable access to, the material;

(2) does not receive a financial benefit directly attributable to the infringing activity, in a case in which the service provider has the right and ability to control such activity; and

(3) upon notification of claimed infringement as described in subsection (c)(3), responds expeditiously to remove, or disable access to, the material that is claimed to be infringing or to be the subject of infringing activity, except that, for purposes of this paragraph, the information described in subsection (c)(3)(A)(iii) shall be identification of the reference or link, to material or activity claimed to be infringing, that is to be removed or access to which is to be disabled, and information reasonably sufficient to permit the service provider to locate that reference or link.

(e) Limitation on liability of nonprofit educational institutions.

(1) When a public or other nonprofit institution of higher education is a service provider, and when a faculty member or graduate student who

is an employee of such institution is performing a teaching or research function, for the purposes of subsections (a) and (b) such faculty member or graduate student shall be considered to be a person other than the institution, and for the purposes of subsections (c) and (d) such faculty member's or graduate student's knowledge or awareness of his or her infringing activities shall not be attributed to the institution, if—

(A) such faculty member's or graduate student's infringing activities do not involve the provision of online access to instructional materials that are or were required or recommended, within the preceding 3-year period, for a course taught at the institution by such faculty member or graduate student;

(B) the institution has not, within the preceding 3-year period, received more than two notifications described in subsection (c)(3) of claimed infringement by such faculty member or graduate student, and such notifications of claimed infringement were not actionable under subsection (f); and

(C) the institution provides to all users of its system or network informational materials that accurately describe, and promote compliance with, the laws of the United States relating to copyright.

(2) Injunctions. For the purposes of this subsection, the limitations on injunctive relief contained in subsections (j)(2) and (j)(3), but not those in (j)(1), shall apply.

(f) Misrepresentations. Any person who knowingly materially misrepresents under this section—

(1) that material or activity is infringing, or

(2) that material or activity was removed or disabled by mistake or misidentification,

shall be liable for any damages, including costs and attorneys' fees, incurred by the alleged infringer, by any copyright owner or copyright owner's authorized licensee, or by a service provider, who is injured by such misrepresentation, as the result of the service provider relying upon such misrepresentation in removing or disabling access to the material or activity claimed to be infringing, or in replacing the removed material or ceasing to disable access to it.

(g) Replacement of removed or disabled material and limitation on other liability.

(1) No liability for taking down generally. Subject to paragraph (2), a service provider shall not be liable to any person for any claim based on the service provider's good faith disabling of access to, or removal of, material or activity claimed to be infringing or based on facts or circumstances from which infringing activity is apparent, regardless of whether the material or activity is ultimately determined to be infringing.

(2) Exception. Paragraph (1) shall not apply with respect to material residing at the direction of a subscriber of the service provider on a system or network controlled or operated by or for the service provider that is removed, or to which access is disabled by the service provider, pursuant to a notice provided under subsection (c)(1)(C), unless the service provider—

(A) takes reasonable steps promptly to notify the subscriber that it has removed or disabled access to the material;

(B) upon receipt of a counter notification described in paragraph (3), promptly provides the person who provided the notification under subsection (c)(1)(C) with a copy of the counter notification, and informs that person that it will replace the removed material or cease disabling access to it in 10 business days; and

(C) replaces the removed material and ceases disabling access to it not less than 10, nor more than 14, business days following receipt of the counter notice, unless its designated agent first receives notice from the person who submitted the notification under subsection (c)(1)(C) that such person has filed an action seeking a court order to restrain the subscriber from engaging in infringing activity relating to the material on the service provider's system or network.

(3) Contents of counter notification. To be effective under this subsection, a counter notification must be a written communication provided to the service provider's designated agent that includes substantially the following:

(A) A physical or electronic signature of the subscriber.

(B) Identification of the material that has been removed or to which access has been disabled and the location at which the material appeared before it was removed or access to it was disabled.

(C) A statement under penalty of perjury that the subscriber has a good faith belief that the material was removed or disabled as a result of mistake or misidentification of the material to be removed or disabled.

(D) The subscriber's name, address, and telephone number, and a statement that the subscriber consents to the jurisdiction of Federal District Court for the judicial district in which the address is located, or if the subscriber's address is outside of the United States, for any judicial district in which the service provider may be found, and that the subscriber will accept service of process from the person who provided notification under subsection (c)(1)(C) or an agent of such person.

(4) Limitation on other liability. A service provider's compliance with paragraph (2) shall not subject the service provider to liability for copyright infringement with respect to the material identified in the notice provided under subsection (c)(1)(C).

(h) Subpoena to identify infringer.

(1) Request. A copyright owner or a person authorized to act on the owner's behalf may request the clerk of any United States district court to issue a subpoena to a service provider for identification of an alleged infringer in accordance with this subsection.

(2) Contents of request. The request may be made by filing with the clerk—

(A) a copy of a notification described in subsection (c)(3)(A);

(B) a proposed subpoena; and

(C) a sworn declaration to the effect that the purpose for which the subpoena is sought is to obtain the identity of an alleged infringer and that such information will only be used for the purpose of protecting rights under this title.

(3) Contents of subpoena. The subpoena shall authorize and order the service provider receiving the notification and the subpoena to expeditiously disclose to the copyright owner or person authorized by the copyright owner information sufficient to identify the alleged infringer of the material described in the notification to the extent such information is available to the service provider.

(4) Basis for granting subpoena. If the notification filed satisfies the provisions of subsection (c)(3)(A), the proposed subpoena is in proper form, and the accompanying declaration is properly executed, the clerk shall expeditiously issue and sign the proposed subpoena and return it to the requester for delivery to the service provider.

(5) Actions of service provider receiving subpoena. Upon receipt of the issued subpoena, either accompanying or subsequent to the receipt of a notification described in subsection (c)(3)(A), the service provider shall expeditiously disclose to the copyright owner or person authorized by the copyright owner the information required by the subpoena, notwithstanding any other provision of law and regardless of whether the service provider responds to the notification.

(6) Rules applicable to subpoena. Unless otherwise provided by this section or by applicable rules of the court, the procedure for issuance and delivery of the subpoena, and the remedies for noncompliance with the subpoena, shall be governed to the greatest extent practicable by those provisions of the Federal Rules of Civil Procedure governing the issuance, service, and enforcement of a subpoena duces tecum.

(i) Conditions for eligibility.

(1) Accommodation of technology. The limitations on liability established by this section shall apply to a service provider only if the service provider—

(A) has adopted and reasonably implemented, and informs subscribers and account holders of the service provider's system or network of, a policy that provides for the termination in appropriate circumstances of subscribers and account holders of the service provider's system or network who are repeat infringers; and

(B) accommodates and does not interfere with standard technical measures.

(2) Definition. As used in this subsection, the term "standard technical measures" means technical measures that are used by copyright owners to identify or protect copyrighted works and—

(A) have been developed pursuant to a broad consensus of copyright owners and service providers in an open, fair, voluntary, multi-industry standards process;

(B) are available to any person on reasonable and nondiscriminatory terms; and

(C) do not impose substantial costs on service providers or substantial burdens on their systems or networks.

(j) Injunctions. The following rules shall apply in the case of any application for an injunction under section 502 against a service provider that is not subject to monetary remedies under this section:

(1) Scope of relief.

(A) With respect to conduct other than that which qualifies for the limitation on remedies set forth in subsection (a), the court may grant injunctive relief with respect to a service provider only in one or more of the following forms:

(i) An order restraining the service provider from providing access to infringing material or activity residing at a particular online site on the provider's system or network.

(ii) An order restraining the service provider from providing access to a subscriber or account holder of the service provider's system or network who is engaging in infringing activity and is identified in the order, by terminating the accounts of the subscriber or account holder that are specified in the order.

(iii) Such other injunctive relief as the court may consider necessary to prevent or restrain infringement of copyrighted material specified in the order of the court at a particular online location, if such relief is the least burdensome to the service provider among the forms of relief comparably effective for that purpose.

(B) If the service provider qualifies for the limitation on remedies described in subsection (a), the court may only grant injunctive relief in one or both of the following forms:

(i) An order restraining the service provider from providing access to a subscriber or account holder of the service provider's system or network who is using the provider's service to engage in infringing activity and is identified in the order, by terminating the accounts of the subscriber or account holder that are specified in the order.

(ii) An order restraining the service provider from providing access, by taking reasonable steps specified in the order to block access, to a specific, identified, online location outside the United States.

(2) Considerations. The court, in considering the relevant criteria for injunctive relief under applicable law, shall consider—

(A) whether such an injunction, either alone or in combination with other such injunctions issued against the same service provider under this subsection, would significantly burden either the provider or the operation of the provider's system or network;

(B) the magnitude of the harm likely to be suffered by the copyright owner in the digital network environment if steps are not taken to prevent or restrain the infringement;

(C) whether implementation of such an injunction would be technically feasible and effective, and would not interfere with access to noninfringing material at other online locations; and

(D) whether other less burdensome and comparably effective means of preventing or restraining access to the infringing material are available.

(3) Notice and ex parte orders. Injunctive relief under this subsection shall be available only after notice to the service provider and an opportunity for the service provider to appear are provided, except for orders ensuring the preservation of evidence or other orders having no material adverse effect on the operation of the service provider's communications network.

(k) Definitions.

(1) Service provider.

(A) As used in subsection (a), the term "service provider" means an entity offering the transmission, routing, or providing of connections for digital online communications, between or among points specified by a user, of material of the user's choosing, without modification to the content of the material as sent or received.

(B) As used in this section, other than subsection (a), the term "service provider" means a provider of online services or network access, or the operator of facilities therefor, and includes an entity described in subparagraph (A).

(2) Monetary relief. As used in this section, the term "monetary relief" means damages, costs, attorneys' fees, and any other form of monetary payment.

(l) Other defenses not affected. The failure of a service provider's conduct to qualify for limitation of liability under this section shall not bear adversely upon the consideration of a defense by the service provider that the service provider's conduct is not infringing under this title or any other defense.

(m) Protection of privacy. Nothing in this section shall be construed to condition the applicability of subsections (a) through (d) on—

(1) a service provider monitoring its service or affirmatively seeking facts indicating infringing activity, except to the extent consistent with a standard technical measure complying with the provisions of subsection (i); or

(2) a service provider gaining access to, removing, or disabling access to material in cases in which such conduct is prohibited by law.

(n) Construction. Subsections (a), (b), (c), and (d) describe separate and distinct functions for purposes of applying this section. Whether a service provider qualifies for the limitation on liability in any one of those subsections shall be based solely on the criteria in that subsection, and shall not affect a determination of whether that service provider qualifies for the limitations on liability under any other such subsection.

(Added Oct. 28, 1998, Pub. L. 105-304, Title II, § 202(a), 112 Stat. 2877.)

17 U.S.C. § 1001. Definitions

As used in this chapter, the following terms have the following meanings:

(1) A "digital audio copied recording" is a reproduction in a digital recording format of a digital musical recording, whether that reproduction is made directly from another digital musical recording or indirectly from a transmission.

(2) A "digital audio interface device" is any machine or device that is designed specifically to communicate digital audio information and related interface data to a digital audio recording device through a nonprofessional interface.

(3) A "digital audio recording device" is any machine or device of a type commonly distributed to individuals for use by individuals, whether or not included with or as part of some other machine or device, the digital recording function of which is designed or marketed for the primary purpose of, and that is capable of, making a digital audio copied recording for private use, except for—

(A) professional model products, and

(B) dictation machines, answering machines, and other audio recording equipment that is designed and marketed primarily for the creation of sound recordings resulting from the fixation of nonmusical sounds.

(4)(A) A "digital audio recording medium" is any material object in a form commonly distributed for use by individuals, that is primarily marketed or most commonly used by consumers for the purpose of making digital audio copied recordings by use of a digital audio recording device.

(B) Such term does not include any material object—

(i) that embodies a sound recording at the time it is first distributed by the importer or manufacturer; or

(ii) that is primarily marketed and most commonly used by consumers either for the purpose of making copies of motion pictures or other audiovisual works or for the purpose of making copies of nonmusical literary works, including computer programs or data bases.

(5)(A) A "digital musical recording" is a material object—

(i) in which are fixed, in a digital recording format, only sounds, and material, statements, or instructions incidental to those fixed sounds, if any, and

(ii) from which the sounds and material can be perceived, reproduced, or otherwise communicated, either directly or with the aid of a machine or device.

(B) A "digital musical recording" does not include a material object—

(i) in which the fixed sounds consist entirely of spoken word recordings, or

(ii) in which one or more computer programs are fixed, except that a digital musical recording may contain statements or instructions constituting the fixed sounds and incidental material, and statements or instructions to be used directly or indirectly in order to bring about the perception, reproduction, or communication of the fixed sounds and incidental material.

(C) For purposes of this paragraph—

(i) a "spoken word recording" is a sound recording in which are fixed only a series of spoken words, except that the spoken words may be accompanied by incidental musical or other sounds, and

(ii) the term "incidental" means related to and relatively minor by comparison.

(6) "Distribute" means to sell, lease, or assign a product to consumers in the United States, or to sell, lease, or assign a product in the United States for ultimate transfer to consumers in the United States.

(7) An "interested copyright party" is—

(A) the owner of the exclusive right under section 106(1) of this title to reproduce a sound recording of a musical work that has been embodied in a digital musical recording or analog musical recording lawfully made under this title that has been distributed;

(B) the legal or beneficial owner of, or the person that controls, the right to reproduce in a digital musical recording or analog musical recording a musical work that has been embodied in a digital musical recording or analog musical recording lawfully made under this title that has been distributed;

(C) a featured recording artist who performs on a sound recording that has been distributed; or

(D) any association or other organization—

(i) representing persons specified in subparagraph (A), (B), or (C), or

(ii) engaged in licensing rights in musical works to music users on behalf of writers and publishers.

(8) To "manufacture" means to produce or assemble a product in the United States. A "manufacturer" is a person who manufactures.

(9) A "music publisher" is a person that is authorized to license the reproduction of a particular musical work in a sound recording.

(10) A "professional model product" is an audio recording device that is designed, manufactured, marketed, and intended for use by recording professionals in the ordinary course of a lawful business, in accordance with such requirements as the Secretary of Commerce shall establish by regulation.

(11) The term "serial copying" means the duplication in a digital format of a copyrighted musical work or sound recording from a digital reproduction of a digital musical recording. The term "digital reproduction of a digital musical recording" does not include a digital musical recording as distributed, by authority of the copyright owner, for ultimate sale to consumers.

(12) The "transfer price" of a digital audio recording device or a digital audio recording medium—

(A) is, subject to subparagraph (B)—

(i) in the case of an imported product, the actual entered value at United States Customs (exclusive of any freight, insurance, and applicable duty), and

(ii) in the case of a domestic product, the manufacturer's transfer price (FOB the manufacturer, and exclusive of any direct sales taxes or excise taxes incurred in connection with the sale); and

(B) shall, in a case in which the transferor and transferee are related entities or within a single entity, not be less than a reasonable arms-length price under the principles of the regulations adopted pursuant to section 482 of the Internal Revenue Code of 1986, or any successor provision to such section.

(13) A "writer" is the composer or lyricist of a particular musical work.

(Added Oct. 28, 1992, Pub. L. 102-563, § 2, 106 Stat. 4237.)

17 U.S.C. § 1002. Incorporation of copying controls

(a) Prohibition on importation, manufacture, and distribution.— No person shall import, manufacture, or distribute any digital audio recording device or digital audio interface device that does not conform to—

(1) the Serial Copy Management System;

(2) a system that has the same functional characteristics as the Serial Copy Management System and requires that copyright and generation status information be accurately sent, received, and acted upon between devices using the system's method of serial copying regulation and devices using the Serial Copy Management System; or

(3) any other system certified by the Secretary of Commerce as prohibiting unauthorized serial copying.

(b) Development of verification procedure.—The Secretary of Commerce shall establish a procedure to verify, upon the petition of an interested party, that a system meets the standards set forth in subsection (a)(2).

(c) Prohibition on circumvention of the system.— No person shall import, manufacture, or distribute any device, or offer or perform any service, the primary purpose or effect of which is to avoid, bypass, remove, deactivate, or otherwise circumvent any program or circuit which implements, in whole or in part, a system described in subsection (a).

(d) Encoding of information on digital musical recordings.—

(1) Prohibition on encoding inaccurate information.— No person shall encode a digital musical recording of a sound recording with inaccurate information relating to the category code, copyright status, or generation status of the source material for the recording.

(2) Encoding of copyright status not required.— Nothing in this chapter requires any person engaged in the importation or manufacture of digital musical recordings to encode any such digital musical recording with respect to its copyright status.

(e) Information accompanying transmissions in digital format.— Any person who transmits or otherwise communicates to the public any sound recording in digital format is not required under this chapter to transmit or otherwise communicate the information relating to the copyright status of the sound recording. Any such person who does transmit or otherwise communicate such copyright status information shall transmit or communicate such information accurately.

(Added Oct. 28, 1992, Pub. L. 102-563, § 2, 106 Stat. 4240.)

17 U.S.C. § 1003. Obligation to make royalty payments

(a) Prohibition on importation and manufacture.— No person shall import into and distribute, or manufacture and distribute, any digital audio recording device or digital audio recording medium unless such person records the notice specified by this section and subsequently deposits the statements of account and applicable royalty payments for such device or medium specified in section 1004.

(b) Filing of notice.— The importer or manufacturer of any digital audio recording device or digital audio recording medium, within a product category or utilizing a technology with respect to which such manufacturer or importer has not previously filed a notice under this subsection, shall file with the Register of Copyrights a notice with respect to such device or medium, in such form and content as the Register shall prescribe by regulation.

(c) Filing of quarterly and annual statements of account.—

(1) Generally.— Any importer or manufacturer that distributes any digital audio recording device or digital audio recording medium that it manufactured or imported shall file with the Register of Copyrights, in such form and content as the Register shall prescribe by regulation, such quarterly and annual statements of account with respect to such distribution as the Register shall prescribe by regulation.

(2) Certification, verification, and confidentiality.— Each such statement shall be certified as accurate by an authorized officer or principal of the importer or manufacturer. The Register shall issue regulations to provide for the verification and audit of such statements and to protect the confidentiality of the information contained in such statements. Such regulations shall provide for the disclosure, in confidence, of such statements to interested copyright parties.

(3) Royalty payments.— Each such statement shall be accompanied by the royalty payments specified in section 1004.

(Added Oct. 28, 1992, Pub. L. 102-563, § 2, 106 Stat. 4240.)

17 U.S.C. § 1004. Royalty payments

(a) Digital audio recording devices. —

(1) Amount of payment. —The royalty payment due under section 1003 for each digital audio recording device imported into and distributed in the United States, or manufactured and distributed in the United States, shall be 2 percent of the transfer price. Only the first person to manufacture and distribute or import and distribute such device shall be required to pay the royalty with respect to such device.

(2) Calculation for devices distributed with other devices.—With respect to a digital audio recording device first distributed in combination with one or more devices, either as a physically integrated unit or as separate components, the royalty payment shall be calculated as follows:

(A) If the digital audio recording device and such other devices are part of a physically integrated unit, the royalty payment shall be based on the transfer price of the unit, but shall be reduced by any royalty payment made on any digital audio recording device included within the unit that was not first distributed in combination with the unit.

(B) If the digital audio recording device is not part of a physically integrated unit and substantially similar devices have been distributed separately at any time during the preceding 4 calendar quarters, the royalty payment shall be based on the average transfer price of such devices during those 4 quarters.

(C) If the digital audio recording device is not part of a physically integrated unit and substantially similar devices have not been distributed separately at any time during the preceding 4 calendar quarters, the royalty payment shall be based on a constructed price reflecting the proportional value of such device to the combination as a whole.

(3) Limits on royalties.—Notwithstanding paragraph (1) or (2), the amount of the royalty payment for each digital audio recording device shall not be less than $1 nor more than the royalty maximum. The royalty maximum shall be $8 per device, except that in the case of a physically integrated unit containing more than 1 digital audio recording device, the royalty maximum for such unit shall be $12. During the 6th year after the effective date of this chapter, and not more than once each year thereafter, any interested copyright party may petition the Librarian of Congress to increase the royalty maximum and, if more than 20 percent of the royalty payments are at the relevant royalty maximum, the Librarian of Congress shall prospectively increase such royalty maximum with the goal of having no more than 10 percent of such payments at the new royalty maximum; however the amount of any such increase as a percentage of the royalty maximum shall in no event exceed the percentage increase in the Consumer Price Index during the period under review.

(b) Digital audio recording media.—The royalty payment due under section 1003 for each digital audio recording medium imported into and distributed in the United States, or manufactured and distributed in the United States, shall be 3 percent of the transfer price. Only the first person to manufacture and distribute or import and distribute such medium shall be required to pay the royalty with respect to such medium.

(Added Oct. 28, 1992, Pub. L. 102-563, § 2, 106 Stat. 4241; Amended Dec. 17, 1993, Pub. L. 103-198, § 6(b)(1), 107 Stat. 2312.)

17 U.S.C. § 1005. Deposit of royalty payments and deduction of expenses

The Register of Copyrights shall receive all royalty payments deposited under this chapter and, after deducting the reasonable costs incurred by the Copyright Office under this chapter, shall deposit the balance in the Treasury of the United States as offsetting receipts, in such manner as the Secretary of the Treasury directs. All funds held by the Secretary of the Treasury shall be invested in interest-bearing United States securities for later distribution with interest under section 1007. The Register may, in the Register's discretion, 4 years after the close of any calendar year, close out the royalty payments account for that calendar year, and may treat any funds remaining in such account and any subsequent deposits that would otherwise be attributable to that calendar year as attributable to the succeeding calendar year.

(Added Oct. 28, 1992, Pub. L. 102-563, § 2, 106 Stat. 4242; Amended Dec. 17, 1993, Pub. L. 103-198, § 6(b)(2), 107 Stat. 2312.)

17 U.S.C. § 1006. Entitlement to royalty payments

(a) Interested copyright parties.—The royalty payments deposited pursuant to section 1005 shall, in accordance with the procedures specified in section 1007, be distributed to any interested copyright party—

(1) whose musical work or sound recording has been—

(A) embodied in a digital musical recording or an analog musical recording lawfully made under this title that has been distributed, and

(B) distributed in the form of digital musical recordings or analog musical recordings or disseminated to the public in transmissions, during the period to which such payments pertain; and

(2) who has filed a claim under section 1007.

(b) Allocation of royalty payments to groups.—The royalty payments shall be divided into 2 funds as follows:

(1) The Sound Recordings Fund.—66 2/3 percent of the royalty payments shall be allocated to the Sound Recordings Fund. 2 5/8 percent of the royalty payments allocated to the Sound Recordings Fund shall be placed in an escrow account managed by an independent administrator jointly appointed by the interested copyright parties described in section 1001(7)(A) and the American Federation of Musicians (or any successor entity) to be distributed to nonfeatured musicians (whether or not members of the American Federation of Musicians or any successor entity) who have performed on sound recordings distributed in the United States. 1 3/8 percent of the royalty payments allocated to the Sound Recordings Fund shall be placed in an escrow account managed by an independent administrator jointly appointed by the interested copyright parties described in section 1001(7)(A) and the American Federation of Television and Radio Artists (or any successor entity) to be distributed to nonfeatured vocalists (whether or not members of the American Federation of Television and Radio Artists or any successor entity) who have performed on sound recordings distributed in the United States. 40 percent of the remaining royalty payments in the Sound Recordings Fund shall be distributed to the interested copyright parties described in section 1001(7)(C), and 60 percent of such remaining royalty payments shall be distributed to the interested copyright parties described in section 1001(7)(A).

(2) The Musical Works Fund.—

(A) 33 1/3 percent of the royalty payments shall be allocated to the Musical Works Fund for distribution to interested copyright parties described in section 1001(7)(B).

(B)(i) Music publishers shall be entitled to 50 percent of the royalty payments allocated to the Musical Works Fund.

(ii) Writers shall be entitled to the other 50 percent of the royalty payments allocated to the Musical Works Fund.

(c) Allocation of royalty payments within groups.—If all interested copyright parties within a group specified in subsection (b) do not agree on a voluntary proposal for the distribution of the royalty payments within each group, the Librarian of Congress shall convene a copyright arbitration royalty panel which shall, pursuant to the procedures specified under section 1007(c), allocate royalty payments under this section based on the extent to which, during the relevant period—

(1) for the Sound Recordings Fund, each sound recording was distributed in the form of digital musical recordings or analog musical recordings; and

(2) for the Musical Works Fund, each musical work was distributed in the form of digital musical recordings or analog musical recordings or disseminated to the public in transmissions.

(Added Oct. 28, 1992, Pub. L. 102-563, § 2, 106 Stat. 4242; Amended Dec. 17, 1993, Pub. L. 103–198, § 6(b)(3), 107 Stat. 2312; Nov. 13, 1997, Pub. L. 105–80, 111 Stat. 1535.)

17 U.S.C. § 1007. Procedures for distributing royalty payments

(a) Filing of claims and negotiations.—

(1) Filing of claims.—During the first 2 months of each calendar year after calendar year 1992, every interested copyright party seeking to receive royalty payments to which such party is entitled under section 1006 shall file with the Librarian of Congress a claim for payments collected during the preceding year in such form and manner as the Librarian of Congress shall prescribe by regulation.

(2) Negotiations.—Notwithstanding any provision of the antitrust laws, for purposes of this section interested copyright parties within each group specified in section 1006(b) may agree among themselves to the proportionate division of royalty payments, may lump their claims together and file them jointly or as a single claim, or may designate a common agent, including any organization described in section 1001(7)(D), to negotiate or receive payment on their behalf; except that no agreement under this subsection may modify the allocation of royalties specified in section 1006(b).

(b) Distribution of payments in the absence of a dispute.—After the period established for the filing of claims under subsection (a), in each year after 1992, the Librarian of Congress shall determine whether there exists a controversy concerning the distribution of royalty payments under section 1006(c). If the Librarian of Congress determines that no such controversy exists, the Librarian of Congress shall, within 30 days after such determination, authorize the distribution of the royalty payments as set forth in the agreements regarding the distribution of royalty payments entered into pursuant to subsection (a), after deducting its reasonable administrative costs under this section.

(c) Resolution of disputes.—If the Librarian of Congress finds the existence of a controversy, the Librarian shall, pursuant to chapter 8 of this title, convene a copyright arbitration royalty panel to determine the distribution of royalty payments. During the pendency of such a proceeding, the Librarian of Congress shall withhold from distribution an amount sufficient to satisfy all claims with respect to which a controversy exists, but shall, to the extent feasible, authorize the distribution of any amounts that are not in controversy. The Librarian of Congress shall, before authorizing the distribution of such royalty payment, deduct the reasonable administrative costs incurred by the Librarian under this section.

(Added Oct. 28, 1992, Pub. L. 102-563, § 2, 106 Stat. 4244; Amended Dec. 17, 1993, Pub. L. 103-198, § 6(b)(4), 107 Stat. 2312; Nov. 13, 1997, Pub. L. 105–80, 111 Stat. 1535.)

17 U.S.C. § 1008. Prohibition on certain infringement actions

No action may be brought under this title alleging infringement of copyright based on the manufacture, importation, or distribution of a digital audio recording device, a digital audio recording medium, an analog recording device, or an analog recording medium, or based on the noncommercial use by a consumer of such a device or medium for making digital musical recordings or analog musical recordings.

(Added Oct. 28, 1992, Pub. L. 102-563, § 2, 106 Stat. 4244.)

17 U.S.C. § 1009. Civil remedies

(a) Civil actions.— Any interested copyright party injured by a violation of section 1002 or 1003 may bring a civil action in an appropriate United States district court against any person for such violation.

(b) Other civil actions. — Any person injured by a violation of this chapter may bring a civil action in an appropriate United States district court for actual damages incurred as a result of such violation.

(c) Powers of the court. — In an action brought under subsection (a), the court —

(1) may grant temporary and permanent injunctions on such terms as it deems reasonable to prevent or restrain such violation;

(2) in the case of a violation of section 1002, or in the case of an injury resulting from a failure to make royalty payments required by section 1003, shall award damages under subsection (d);

(3) in its discretion may allow the recovery of costs by or against any party other than the United States or an officer thereof; and

(4) in its discretion may award a reasonable attorney's fee to the prevailing party.

(d) Award of damages.—

(1) Damages for section 1002 or 1003 violations. —

(A) Actual damages.—(i) In an action brought under subsection (a), if the court finds that a violation of section 1002 or 1003 has occurred, the court shall award to the complaining party its actual damages if the complaining party elects such damages at any time before final judgment is entered.

(ii) In the case of section 1003, actual damages shall constitute the royalty payments that should have been paid under section 1004 and deposited under section 1005. In such a case, the court, in its discretion, may award an additional amount of not to exceed 50 percent of the actual damages.

(B) Statutory damages for section 1002 violations. —

(i) Device. —A complaining party may recover an award of statutory damages for each violation of section 1002 (a) or (c) in the sum of not more than $2,500 per device involved in such violation or per device on which a service prohibited by section 1002(c) has been performed, as the court considers just.

(ii) Digital musical recording. — A complaining party may recover of section 1002(d) in the sum of not more than $25 per digital musical recording involved in such violation, as the court considers just.

(iii) Transmission. — A complaining party may recover an award of damages for each transmission or communi cation that violates section 1002(e) in the sum of not more than $10,000, as the court considers just.

(2) Repeated violations.— In any case in which the court finds that a person has violated section 1002 or 1003 within 3 years after a final judgment against that person for another such violation was entered, the court may increase the award of damages to not more than double the amounts that would otherwise be awarded under paragraph (1), as the court considers just.

(3) Innocent violations of section 1002.—The court in its discretion may reduce the total award of damages against a person violating section 1002 to a sum of not less than $250 in any case in which the court finds that the violator was not aware and had no reason to believe that its acts constituted a violation of section 1002.

(e) Payment of damages.—Any award of damages under subsection (d) shall be deposited with the Register pursuant to section 1005 for distribution to interested copyright parties as though such funds were royalty payments made pursuant to section 1003.

(f) Impounding of articles.—At any time while an action under subsection (a) is pending, the court may order the impounding, on such terms as it deems reasonable, of any digital audio recording device, digital musical recording, or device specified in section 1002(c) that is in the custody or control of the alleged violator and that the court has reasonable cause to believe does not comply with, or was involved in a violation of, section 1002.

(g) Remedial modification and destruction of articles.—In an action brought under subsection (a), the court may, as part of a final judgment or decree finding a violation of section 1002, order the remedial modification or the destruction of any digital audio recording device, digital musical recording, or device specified in section 1002(c) that—

(1) does not comply with, or was involved in a violation of, section 1002, and

(2) is in the custody or control of the violator or has been impounded under subsection (f).

(Added Oct. 28, 1992, P.L. 102-563, § 2, 106 Stat. 4245.)

17 U.S.C. § 1010. Arbitration of certain disputes

(a) Scope of arbitration.—Before the date of first distribution in the United States of a digital audio recording device or a digital audio interface device, any party manufacturing, importing, or distributing such device, and any interested copyright party may mutually agree to binding arbitration for the purpose of determining whether such device is subject to section 1002, or the basis on which royalty payments for such device are to be made under section 1003.

(b) Initiation of arbitration proceedings.—Parties agreeing to such arbitration shall file a petition with the Librarian of Congress requesting the commencement of an arbitration proceeding. The petition may include the names and qualifications of potential arbitrators. Within 2 weeks after receiving such a petition, the Librarian of Congress shall cause notice to be published in the Federal Register of the initiation of an arbitration proceeding. Such notice shall include the names and qualifications of 3 arbitrators chosen by the Librarian of Congress from a list of available arbitrators obtained from the American Arbitration Association or such similar organization as the Librarian of Congress shall select, and from potential arbitrators listed in the parties' petition. The arbitrators selected under this subsection shall constitute an Arbitration Panel.

(c) Stay of judicial proceedings.—Any civil action brought under section 1009 against a party to arbitration under this section shall, on application of one of the parties to the arbitration, be stayed until completion of the arbitration proceeding.

(d) Arbitration proceeding.—The Arbitration Panel shall conduct an arbitration proceeding with respect to the matter concerned, in accordance with such procedures as it may adopt. The Panel shall act on the basis of a fully documented written record. Any party to the arbitration may submit relevant information and proposals to the Panel. The parties to the proceeding shall bear the entire cost thereof in such manner and proportion as the Panel shall direct.

(e) Report to Librarian of Congress.—Not later than 60 days after publication of the notice under subsection (b) of the initiation of an arbitration proceeding, the Arbitration Panel shall report to the Librarian of Congress its determination concerning whether the device concerned is subject to section 1002, or the basis on which royalty payments for the device are to be made under section 1003. Such report shall be accompanied by the written record, and shall set forth the facts that the Panel found relevant to its determination.

(f) Action by the Librarian of Congress.—Within 60 days after receiving the report of the Arbitration Panel under subsection (e), the Librarian of Congress shall adopt or reject the determination of the Panel. The Librarian of Congress shall adopt the determination of the Panel unless the Librarian of Congress finds that the determination is clearly erroneous. If the Librarian of Congress rejects the determination of the Panel, the Librarian of Congress shall, before the end of that 60-day period, and after full examination of the record created in the arbitration proceeding, issue an order setting forth the Librarian's decision and the reasons therefor. The Librarian of Congress shall cause to be published in the Federal Register the determination of the Panel and the decision of the Librarian of Congress under this subsection with respect to the determination (including any order issued under the preceding sentence).

(g) Judicial review.—Any decision of the Librarian of Congress under subsection (f) with respect to a determination of the Arbitration Panel may be appealed, by a party to the arbitration, to the United States Court of Appeals for the District of Columbia Circuit, within 30 days after the publication of the decision in the Federal Register. The pendency of an appeal under this subsection shall not stay the decision of the Librarian of Congress. The court shall have jurisdiction to modify or vacate a decision of the Librarian of Congress only if it finds, on the basis of the record before the Librarian of Congress, that the Arbitration Panel or the Librarian of Congress acted in an arbitrary manner. If the court modifies the decision of the Librarian of Congress, the court shall have jurisdiction to enter its own decision in accordance with its final judgment. The court may further vacate the decision of the Librarian of Congress and remand the case for arbitration proceedings as provided in this section.

(Added Oct. 28, 1992, Pub. L. 102-563, § 2, 106 Stat. 4246; Amended Dec. 17, 1993, Pub. L. No. 103-198, Sec. 6(b)(5), 107 Stat. 2312.)

17 U.S.C. § 1101. Unauthorized fixation and trafficking in sound recordings and music videos

(a) **Unauthorized Acts.** Anyone who, without the consent of the performer or performers involved—

(1) fixes the sounds or sounds and images of a live musical performance in a copy or phonorecord, or reproduces copies or phonorecords of such a performance from an unauthorized fixation,

(2) transmits or otherwise communicates to the public the sounds or sounds and images of a live musical performance, or

(3) distributes or offers to distribute, sells or offers to sell, rents or offers to rent, or traffics in any copy or phonorecord fixed as described in paragraph (1), regardless of whether the fixations occurred in the United States, shall be subject to the remedies provided in sections 502 through 505, to the same extent as an infringer of copyright.

(b) **Definition.** As used in this section, the term "traffic in" means transport, transfer, or otherwise dispose of, to another, as consideration for anything of value, or make or obtain control of with intent to transport, transfer, or dispose of.

(c) **Applicability.** This section shall apply to any act or acts that occur on or after the date of the enactment of the Uruguay Round Agreements Act.

(d) **State law not preempted.** Nothing in this section may be construed to annul or limit any rights or remedies under the common law or statutes of any State.

17 U.S.C. § 1201. Circumvention of copyright protection systems

(a) Violations regarding circumvention of technological measures.

(1) (A) No person shall circumvent a technological measure that effectively controls access to a work protected under this title. The prohibition contained in the preceding sentence shall take effect at the end of the 2-year period beginning on the date of the enactment of this chapter [enacted Oct. 28, 1998].

(B) The prohibition contained in subparagraph (A) shall not apply to persons who are users of a copyrighted work which is in a particular class of works, if such persons are, or are likely to be in the succeeding 3-year period, adversely affected by virtue of such prohibition in their ability to make noninfringing uses of that particular class of works under this title, as determined under subparagraph (C).

(C) During the 2-year period described in subparagraph (A), and during each succeeding 3-year period, the Librarian of Congress, upon the recommendation of the Register of Copyrights, who shall consult with the Assistant Secretary for Communications and Information of the Department of Commerce and report and comment on his or her views in making such recommendation, shall make the determination in a rulemaking proceeding on the record for purposes of subparagraph (B) of whether persons who are users of a copyrighted work are, or are likely to be in the succeeding 3-year period, adversely affected by the prohibition under subparagraph (A) in their ability to make noninfringing uses under this title of a particular class of copyrighted works. In conducting such rulemaking, the Librarian shall examine—

(i) the availability for use of copyrighted works;

(ii) the availability for use of works for nonprofit archival, preservation, and educational purposes;

(iii) the impact that the prohibition on the circumvention of technological measures applied to copyrighted works has on criticism, comment, news reporting, teaching, scholarship, or research;

(iv) the effect of circumvention of technological measures on the market for or value of copyrighted works; and

(v) such other factors as the Librarian considers appropriate.

(D) The Librarian shall publish any class of copyrighted works for which the Librarian has determined, pursuant to the rulemaking conducted under subparagraph (C), that noninfringing uses by persons who are users of a copyrighted work are, or are likely to be, adversely affected, and the prohibition contained in subparagraph (A) shall not apply to such users with respect to such class of works for the ensuing 3-year period.

(E) Neither the exception under subparagraph (B) from the applicability of the prohibition contained in subparagraph (A), nor any determination made in a rulemaking conducted under subparagraph (C), may be used as a defense in any action to enforce any provision of this title other than this paragraph.

(2) No person shall manufacture, import, offer to the public, provide, or otherwise traffic in any technology, product, service, device, component, or part thereof, that—

(A) is primarily designed or produced for the purpose of circumventing a technological measure that effectively controls access to a work protected under this title;

(B) has only limited commercially significant purpose or use other than to circumvent a technological measure that effectively controls access to a work protected under this title; or

(C) is marketed by that person or another acting in concert with that person with that person's knowledge for use in circumventing a technological measure that effectively controls access to a work protected under this title.

(3) As used in this subsection—

(A) to "circumvent a technological measure" means to descramble a scrambled work, to decrypt an encrypted work, or otherwise to avoid, bypass, remove, deactivate, or impair a technological measure, without the authority of the copyright owner; and

(B) a technological measure "effectively controls access to a work" if the measure, in the ordinary course of its operation, requires the application of information, or a process or a treatment, with the authority of the copyright owner, to gain access to the work.

(b) Additional violations.

(1) No person shall manufacture, import, offer to the public, provide, or otherwise traffic in any technology, product, service, device, component, or part thereof, that—

(A) is primarily designed or produced for the purpose of circumventing protection afforded by a technological measure that effectively protects a right of a copyright owner under this title in a work or a portion thereof;

(B) has only limited commercially significant purpose or use other than to circumvent protection afforded by a technological measure that effectively protects a right of a copyright owner under this title in a work or a portion thereof; or

(C) is marketed by that person or another acting in concert with that person with that person's knowledge for use in circumventing protection afforded by a technological measure that effectively protects a right of a copyright owner under this title in a work or a portion thereof.

(2) As used in this subsection—

(A) to "circumvent protection afforded by a technological measure" means avoiding, bypassing, removing, deactivating, or otherwise impairing a technological measure; and

(B) a technological measure "effectively protects a right of a copyright owner under this title" if the measure, in the ordinary course of its operation, prevents, restricts, or otherwise limits the exercise of a right of a copyright owner under this title.

(c) Other rights, etc., not affected.

(1) Nothing in this section shall affect rights, remedies, limitations, or defenses to copyright infringement, including fair use, under this title.

(2) Nothing in this section shall enlarge or diminish vicarious or contributory liability for copyright infringement in connection with any technology, product, service, device, component, or part thereof.

(3) Nothing in this section shall require that the design of, or design and selection of parts and components for, a consumer electronics, telecommunications, or computing product provide for a response to any particular technological measure, so long as such part or component, or the product in which such part or component is integrated, does not otherwise fall within the prohibitions of subsection (a)(2) or (b)(1).

(4) Nothing in this section shall enlarge or diminish any rights of free speech or the press for activities using consumer electronics, telecommunications, or computing products.

(d) Exemption for nonprofit libraries, archives, and educational institutions.

(1) A nonprofit library, archives, or educational institution which gains access to a commercially exploited copyrighted work solely in order to make a good faith determination of whether to acquire a copy of that work for the sole purpose of engaging in conduct permitted under this title shall not be in violation of subsection (a)(1)(A). A copy of a work to which access has been gained under this paragraph—

(A) may not be retained longer than necessary to make such good faith determination; and

(B) may not be used for any other purpose.

(2) The exemption made available under paragraph (1) shall only apply with respect to a work when an identical copy of that work is not reasonably available in another form.

(3) A nonprofit library, archives, or educational institution that willfully for the purpose of commercial advantage or financial gain violates paragraph (1)—

(A) shall, for the first offense, be subject to the civil remedies under section 1203; and

(B) shall, for repeated or subsequent offenses, in addition to the civil remedies under section 1203, forfeit the exemption provided under paragraph (1).

(4) This subsection may not be used as a defense to a claim under subsection (a)(2) or (b), nor may this subsection permit a nonprofit library, archives, or educational institution to manufacture, import, offer to the public, provide, or otherwise traffic in any technology, product, service, component, or part thereof, which circumvents a technological measure.

(5) In order for a library or archives to qualify for the exemption under this subsection, the collections of that library or archives shall be—

(A) open to the public; or

(B) available not only to researchers affiliated with the library or archives or with the institution of which it is a part, but also to other persons doing research in a specialized field.

(e) Law enforcement, intelligence, and other government activities. This section does not prohibit any lawfully authorized investigative, protective, information security, or intelligence activity of an officer, agent, or employee of the United States, a State, or a political subdivision of a State, or a person acting pursuant to a contract with the United States, a State, or a political subdivision of a State. For purposes of this subsection, the term "information security" means activities carried out in order to identify and address the vulnerabilities of a government computer, computer system, or computer network.

(f) Reverse engineering.

(1) Notwithstanding the provisions of subsection (a)(1)(A), a person who has lawfully obtained the right to use a copy of a computer program may circumvent a technological measure that effectively controls access to a particular portion of that program for the sole purpose of identifying and analyzing those elements of the program that are necessary to achieve interoperability of an independently created computer program with other programs, and that have not previously been readily available to the person engaging in the circumvention, to the extent any such acts of identification and analysis do not constitute infringement under this title.

(2) Notwithstanding the provisions of subsections (a)(2) and (b), a person may develop and employ technological means to circumvent a technological measure, or to circumvent protection afforded by a technological measure, in order to enable the identification and analysis under paragraph (1), or for the purpose of enabling interoperability of an independently created computer program with other programs, if such means are necessary to achieve such interoperability, to the extent that doing so does not constitute infringement under this title.

(3) The information acquired through the acts permitted under paragraph (1), and the means permitted under paragraph (2), may be made available to others if the person referred to in paragraph (1) or (2), as the case may be, provides such information or means solely for the purpose of enabling interoperability of an independently created computer program with other programs, and to the extent that doing so does not constitute infringement under this title or violate applicable law other than this section.

(4) For purposes of this subsection, the term "interoperability" means the ability of computer programs to exchange information, and of such programs mutually to use the information which has been exchanged.

(g) Encryption research.

(1) Definitions. For purposes of this subsection—

(A) the term "encryption research" means activities necessary to identify and analyze flaws and vulnerabilities of encryption technologies applied to copyrighted works, if these activities are conducted to advance the state of knowledge in the field of encryption technology or to assist in the development of encryption products; and

(B) the term "encryption technology" means the scrambling and descrambling of information using mathematical formulas or algorithms.

(2) Permissible acts of encryption research. Notwithstanding the provisions of subsection (a)(1)(A), it is not a violation of that subsection for a person to circumvent a technological measure as applied to a copy, phonorecord, performance, or display of a published work in the course of an act of good faith encryption research if—

(A) the person lawfully obtained the encrypted copy, phonorecord, performance, or display of the published work;

(B) such act is necessary to conduct such encryption research;

(C) the person made a good faith effort to obtain authorization before the circumvention; and

(D) such act does not constitute infringement under this title or a violation of applicable law other than this section, including section 1030 of title 18 and those provisions of title 18 amended by the Computer Fraud and Abuse Act of 1986 [18 USCS § 1030(a)-(c), (e), (f)].

(3) Factors in determining exemption. In determining whether a person qualifies for the exemption under paragraph (2), the factors to be considered shall include—

(A) whether the information derived from the encryption research was disseminated, and if so, whether it was disseminated in a manner reasonably calculated to advance the state of knowledge or development of encryption technology, versus whether it was disseminated in a manner that facilitates infringement under this title or a violation of applicable law other than this section, including a violation of privacy or breach of security;

(B) whether the person is engaged in a legitimate course of study, is employed, or is appropriately trained or experienced, in the field of encryption technology; and

(C) whether the person provides the copyright owner of the work to which the technological measure is applied with notice of the findings and documentation of the research, and the time when such notice is provided.

(4) Use of technological means for research activities. Notwithstanding the provisions of subsection (a)(2), it is not a violation of that subsection for a person to—

(A) develop and employ technological means to circumvent a technological measure for the sole purpose of that person performing the acts of good faith encryption research described in paragraph (2); and

(B) provide the technological means to another person with whom he or she is working collaboratively for the purpose of conducting the acts of good faith encryption research described in paragraph (2) or for the purpose of having that other person verify his or her acts of good faith encryption research described in paragraph (2).

(5) Report to Congress. Not later than 1 year after the date of the enactment of this chapter [enacted Oct. 28, 1998], the Register of Copyrights and the Assistant Secretary for Communications and Information of the Department of Commerce shall jointly report to the Congress on the effect this subsection has had on—

(A) encryption research and the development of encryption technology;

(B) the adequacy and effectiveness of technological measures designed to protect copyrighted works; and

(C) protection of copyright owners against the unauthorized access to their encrypted copyrighted works.

The report shall include legislative recommendations, if any.

(h) Exceptions regarding minors. In applying subsection (a) to a component or part, the court may consider the necessity for its intended and actual incorporation in a technology, product, service, or device, which—

(1) does not itself violate the provisions of this title; and

(2) has the sole purpose to prevent the access of minors to material on the Internet.

(i) Protection of personally identifying information.

(1) Circumvention permitted. Notwithstanding the provisions of subsection (a)(1)(A), it is not a violation of that subsection for a person to circumvent a technological measure that effectively controls access to a work protected under this title, if—

(A) the technological measure, or the work it protects, contains the capability of collecting or disseminating personally identifying information reflecting the online activities of a natural person who seeks to gain access to the work protected;

(B) in the normal course of its operation, the technological measure, or the work it protects, collects or disseminates personally identifying information about the person who seeks to gain access to the work protected, without providing conspicuous notice of such collection or dissemination to such person, and without providing such person with the capability to prevent or restrict such collection or dissemination;

(C) the act of circumvention has the sole effect of identifying and disabling the capability described in subparagraph (A), and has no other effect on the ability of any person to gain access to any work; and

(D) the act of circumvention is carried out solely for the purpose of preventing the collection or dissemination of personally identifying information about a natural person who seeks to gain access to the work protected, and is not in violation of any other law.

(2) Inapplicability to certain technological measures. This subsection does not apply to a technological measure, or a work it protects, that does not collect or disseminate personally identifying information and that is disclosed to a user as not having or using such capability.

(j) Security testing.

(1) Definition. For purposes of this subsection, the term "security testing" means accessing a computer, computer system, or computer network, solely

for the purpose of good faith testing, investigating, or correcting, a security flaw or vulnerability, with the authorization of the owner or operator of such computer, computer system, or computer network.

(2) Permissible acts of security testing. Notwithstanding the provisions of subsection (a)(1)(A), it is not a violation of that subsection for a person to engage in an act of security testing, if such act does not constitute infringement under this title or a violation of applicable law other than this section, including section 1030 of title 18 and those provisions of title 18 amended by the Computer Fraud and Abuse Act of 1986.

(3) Factors in determining exemption. In determining whether a person qualifies for the exemption under paragraph (2), the factors to be considered shall include—

(A) whether the information derived from the security testing was used solely to promote the security of the owner or operator of such computer, computer system or computer network, or shared directly with the developer of such computer, computer system, or computer network; and

(B) whether the information derived from the security testing was used or maintained in a manner that does not facilitate infringement under this title or a violation of applicable law other than this section, including a violation of privacy or breach of security.

(4) Use of technological means for security testing. Notwithstanding the provisions of subsection (a)(2), it is not a violation of that subsection for a person to develop, produce, distribute or employ technological means for the sole purpose of performing the acts of security testing described in subsection (2), provided such technological means does not otherwise violate section (a)(2).

(k) Certain analog devices and certain technological measures.

(1) Certain analog devices.

(A) Effective 18 months after the date of the enactment of this chapter [enacted Oct. 28, 1998], no person shall manufacture, import, offer to the public, provide or otherwise traffic in any—

(i) VHS format analog video cassette recorder unless such recorder conforms to the automatic gain control copy control technology;

(ii) 8mm format analog video cassette camcorder unless such camcorder conforms to the automatic gain control technology;

(iii) Beta format analog video cassette recorder, unless such recorder conforms to the automatic gain control copy control technology, except that this requirement shall not apply until there are 1,000 Beta format analog video cassette recorders sold in the United States in any one calendar year after the date of the enactment of this chapter [enacted Oct. 28, 1998];

(iv) 8mm format analog video cassette recorder that is not an analog video cassette camcorder, unless such recorder conforms to the automatic gain control copy control technology, except that this requirement shall not apply until there are 20,000 such recorders sold in the United States in any one calendar year after the date of the enactment of this chapter [enacted Oct. 28, 1998]; or

(v) analog video cassette recorder that records using an NTSC format video input and that is not otherwise covered under clauses (i) through (iv), unless such device conforms to the automatic gain control copy control technology.

(B) Effective on the date of the enactment of this chapter [enacted Oct. 28, 1998], no person shall manufacture, import, offer to the public, provide or otherwise traffic in—

(i) any VHS format analog video cassette recorder or any 8mm format analog video cassette recorder if the design of the model of such recorder has been modified after such date of enactment so that a model of recorder that previously conformed to the automatic gain control copy control technology no longer conforms to such technology; or

(ii) any VHS format analog video cassette recorder, or any 8mm format analog video cassette recorder that is not an 8mm analog video cassette camcorder, if the design of the model of such recorder has been modified after such date of enactment so that a model of recorder that previously conformed to the four-line colorstripe copy control technology no longer conforms to such technology.

Manufacturers that have not previously manufactured or sold a VHS format analog video cassette recorder, or an 8mm format analog cassette recorder, shall be required to conform to the four-line colorstripe copy control technology in the initial model of any such recorder manufactured after the date of the enactment of this chapter [enacted Oct. 28, 1998], and thereafter to continue conforming to the four-line colorstripe copy control technology. For purposes of this subparagraph, an analog video cassette recorder "conforms to" the four-line colorstripe copy control technology if it records a signal that, when played back by the playback function of that recorder in the normal viewing mode, exhibits, on a reference display device, a display containing distracting visible lines through portions of the viewable picture.

(2) Certain encoding restrictions. No person shall apply the automatic gain control copy control technology or colorstripe copy control technology to prevent or limit consumer copying except such copying—

(A) of a single transmission, or specified group of transmissions, of live events or of audiovisual works for which a member of the public has exercised choice in selecting the transmissions, including the content of the transmissions or the time of receipt of such transmissions, or both, and as to which such member is charged a separate fee for each such transmission or specified group of transmissions;

(B) from a copy of a transmission of a live event or an audiovisual work if such transmission is provided by a channel or service where payment is made by a member of the public for such channel or service in the form of a subscription fee that entitles the member of the public to receive all of the programming contained in such channel or service;

(C) from a physical medium containing one or more prerecorded audiovisual works; or

(D) from a copy of a transmission described in subparagraph (A) or from a copy made from a physical medium described in subparagraph (C).

In the event that a transmission meets both the conditions set forth in subparagraph (A) and those set forth in subparagraph (B), the transmission shall be treated as a transmission described in subparagraph (A).

(3) Inapplicability. This subsection shall not—

(A) require any analog video cassette camcorder to conform to the automatic gain control copy control technology with respect to any video signal received through a camera lens;

(B) apply to the manufacture, importation, offer for sale, provision of, or other trafficking in, any professional analog video cassette recorder; or

(C) apply to the offer for sale or provision of, or other trafficking in, any previously owned analog video cassette recorder, if such recorder was legally manufactured and sold when new and not subsequently modified in violation of paragraph (1)(B).

(4) Definitions. For purposes of this subsection:

(A) An "analog video cassette recorder" means a device that records, or a device that includes a function that records, on electromagnetic tape in an analog format the electronic impulses produced by the video and audio portions of a television program, motion picture, or other form of audiovisual work.

(B) An "analog video cassette camcorder" means an analog video cassette recorder that contains a recording function that operates through a camera lens and through a video input that may be connected with a television or other video playback device.

(C) An analog video cassette recorder "conforms" to the automatic gain control copy control technology if it—

(i) detects one or more of the elements of such technology and does not record the motion picture or transmission protected by such technology; or

(ii) records a signal that, when played back, exhibits a meaningfully distorted or degraded display.

(D) The term "professional analog video cassette recorder" means an analog video cassette recorder that is designed, manufactured, marketed, and intended for use by a person who regularly employs such a device for a lawful business or industrial use, including making, performing, displaying, distributing, or transmitting copies of motion pictures on a commercial scale.

(E) The terms "VHS format", "8mm format", "Beta format", "automatic gain control copy control technology", "colorstripe copy control technology", "four-line version of the colorstripe copy control technology", and "NTSC" have the meanings that are commonly understood in the consumer electronics and motion picture industries as of the date of the enactment of this chapter [enacted Oct. 28, 1998].

(5) Violations. Any violation of paragraph (1) of this subsection shall be treated as a violation of subsection (b)(1) of this section. Any violation of paragraph (2) of this subsection shall be deemed an "act of circumvention" for the purposes of section 1203(c)(3)(A) of this chapter.

(Added Oct. 28, 1998, Pub. L. 105-304, Title I, § 103(a), 112 Stat. 2863.)

17 U.S.C. § 1202. Integrity of copyright management information

(a) False copyright management information. No person shall knowingly and with the intent to induce, enable, facilitate, or conceal infringement—

(1) provide copyright management information that is false, or

(2) distribute or import for distribution copyright management information that is false.

(b) Removal or alteration of copyright management information. No person shall, without the authority of the copyright owner or the law—

(1) intentionally remove or alter any copyright management information,

(2) distribute or import for distribution copyright management information knowing that the copyright management information has been removed or altered without authority of the copyright owner or the law, or

(3) distribute, import for distribution, or publicly perform works, copies of works, or phonorecords, knowing that copyright management information has been removed or altered without authority of the copyright owner or the law, knowing, or, with respect to civil remedies under section 1203, having reasonable grounds to know, that it will induce, enable, facilitate, or conceal an infringement of any right under this title.

(c) Definition. As used in this section, the term "copyright management information" means any of the following information conveyed in connection with copies or phonorecords of a work or performances or displays of a work, including in digital form, except that such term does not include any personally identifying information about a user of a work or of a copy, phonorecord, performance, or display of a work:

(1) The title and other information identifying the work, including the information set forth on a notice of copyright.

(2) The name of, and other identifying information about, the author of a work.

(3) The name of, and other identifying information about, the copyright owner of the work, including the information set forth in a notice of copyright.

(4) With the exception of public performances of works by radio and television broadcast stations, the name of, and other identifying information about, a performer whose performance is fixed in a work other than an audiovisual work.

(5) With the exception of public performances of works by radio and television broadcast stations, in the case of an audiovisual work, the name of, and other identifying information about, a writer, performer, or director who is credited in the audiovisual work.

(6) Terms and conditions for use of the work.

(7) Identifying numbers or symbols referring to such information or links to such information.

(8) Such other information as the Register of Copyrights may prescribe by regulation, except that the Register of Copyrights may not require the provision of any information concerning the user of a copyrighted work.

(d) Law enforcement, intelligence, and other government activities. This section does not prohibit any lawfully authorized investigative, protective, information security, or intelligence activity of an officer, agent, or employee of the United States, a State, or a political subdivision of a State, or a person acting pursuant to a contract with the United States, a State, or a political subdivision of a State. For purposes of this subsection, the term "information security" means activities carried out in order to identify and address the vulnerabilities of a government computer, computer system, or computer network.

(e) Limitations on liability.

(1) Analog transmissions. In the case of an analog transmission, a person who is making transmissions in its capacity as a broadcast station, or as a cable system, or someone who provides programming to such station or system, shall not be liable for a violation of subsection (b) if—

(A) avoiding the activity that constitutes such violation is not technically feasible or would create an undue financial hardship on such person; and

(B) such person did not intend, by engaging in such activity, to induce, enable, facilitate, or conceal infringement of a right under this title.

(2) Digital transmissions.

(A) If a digital transmission standard for the placement of copyright management information for a category of works is set in a voluntary, consensus standard-setting process involving a representative cross-section of broadcast stations or cable systems and copyright owners of a category of works that are intended for public performance by such stations or systems, a person identified in paragraph (1) shall not be liable for a violation of subsection (b) with respect to the particular copyright management information addressed by such standard if—

(i) the placement of such information by someone other than such person is not in accordance with such standard; and

(ii) the activity that constitutes such violation is not intended to induce, enable, facilitate, or conceal infringement of a right under this title.

(B) Until a digital transmission standard has been set pursuant to subparagraph (A) with respect to the placement of copyright management information for a category or works, a person identified in paragraph (1) shall not be liable for a violation of subsection (b) with respect to such copyright management information, if the activity that constitutes such violation is not intended to induce, enable, facilitate, or conceal infringement of a right under this title, and if—

(i) the transmission of such information by such person would result in a perceptible visual or aural degradation of the digital signal; or

(ii) the transmission of such information by such person would conflict with—

(I) an applicable government regulation relating to transmission of information in a digital signal;

(II) an applicable industry-wide standard relating to the transmission of information in a digital signal that was adopted by a voluntary consensus standards body prior to the effective date of this chapter; or

(III) an applicable industry-wide standard relating to the transmission of information in a digital signal that was adopted in a voluntary, consensus standards-setting process open to participation by a representative cross-section of broadcast stations or cable systems and copyright owners of a category of works that are intended for public performance by such stations or systems.

(3) Definitions. As used in this subsection—

(A) the term "broadcast station" has the meaning given that term in section 3 of the Communications Act of 1934 (47 U.S.C. 153); and

(B) the term "cable system" has the meaning given that term in section 602 of the Communications Act of 1934 (47 U.S.C. 522).

(Added Oct. 28, 1998, Pub. L. 105-304, Title I, § 103(a), 112 Stat. 2872.)

17 U.S.C. § 1203. Civil remedies

(a) Civil actions. Any person injured by a violation of section 1201 or 1202 may bring a civil action in an appropriate United States district court for such violation.

(b) Powers of the court. In an action brought under subsection (a), the court—

(1) may grant temporary and permanent injunctions on such terms as it deems reasonable to prevent or restrain a violation, but in no event shall impose a prior restraint on free speech or the press protected under the 1st amendment to the Constitution;

(2) at any time while an action is pending, may order the impounding, on such terms as it deems reasonable, of any device or product that is in the custody or control of the alleged violator and that the court has reasonable cause to believe was involved in a violation;

(3) may award damages under subsection (c);

(4) in its discretion may allow the recovery of costs by or against any party other than the United States or an officer thereof;

(5) in its discretion may award reasonable attorney's fees to the prevailing party; and

(6) may, as part of a final judgment or decree finding a violation, order the remedial modification or the destruction of any device or product involved in the violation that is in the custody or control of the violator or has been impounded under paragraph (2).

(c) Award of damages.

(1) In general. Except as otherwise provided in this title, a person committing a violation of section 1201 or 1202 is liable for either—

(A) the actual damages and any additional profits of the violator, as provided in paragraph (2), or

(B) statutory damages, as provided in paragraph (3).

(2) Actual damages. The court shall award to the complaining party the actual damages suffered by the party as a result of the violation, and any profits of the violator that are attributable to the violation and are not taken into account in computing the actual damages, if the complaining party elects such damages at any time before final judgment is entered.

(3) Statutory damages.

(A) At any time before final judgment is entered, a complaining party may elect to recover an award of statutory damages for each violation of section 1201 in the sum of not less than $ 200 or more than $ 2,500 per act of circumvention, device, product, component, offer, or performance of service, as the court considers just.

(B) At any time before final judgment is entered, a complaining party may elect to recover an award of statutory damages for each violation of section 1202 in the sum of not less than $ 2,500 or more than $ 25,000.

(4) Repeated violations. In any case in which the injured party sustains the burden of proving, and the court finds, that a person has violated section 1201 or 1202 within 3 years after a final judgment was entered against the person for another such violation, the court may increase the award of damages up to triple the amount that would otherwise be awarded, as the court considers just.

(5) Innocent violations.

(A) In general. The court in its discretion may reduce or remit the total award of damages in any case in which the violator sustains the burden of proving, and the court finds, that the violator was not aware and had no reason to believe that its acts constituted a violation.

(B) Nonprofit library, archives, or educational institutions. In the case of a nonprofit library, archives, or educational institution, the court shall remit damages in any case in which the library, archives, or educational institution sustains the burden of proving, and the court finds, that the library, archives, or educational institution was not aware and had no reason to believe that its acts constituted a violation.

(Added Oct. 28, 1998, Pub. L. 105-304, Title I, § 103(a), 112 Stat. 2874.)

17 U.S.C. § 1204. Criminal offenses and penalties

(a) In general. Any person who violates section 1201 or 1202 willfully and for purposes of commercial advantage or private financial gain—

(1) shall be fined not more than $ 500,000 or imprisoned for not more than 5 years, or both, for the first offense; and

(2) shall be fined not more than $ 1,000,000 or imprisoned for not more than 10 years, or both, for any subsequent offense.

(b) Limitation for nonprofit library, archives, or educational institution. Subsection (a) shall not apply to a nonprofit library, archives, or educational institution.

(c) Statute of limitations. No criminal proceeding shall be brought under this section unless such proceeding is commenced within 5 years after the cause of action arose.

(Added Oct. 28, 1998, Pub. L. 105-304, Title I, § 103(a), 112 Stat. 2876.)

17 U.S.C. § 1205. Savings clause

Nothing in this chapter [17 USCS §§ 1201 et seq.] abrogates, diminishes, or weakens the provisions of, nor provides any defense or element of mitigation in a criminal prosecution or civil action under, any Federal or State law that prevents the violation of the privacy of an individual in connection with the individual's use of the Internet.

(Added Oct. 28, 1998, Pub. L. 105-304, Title I, § 103(a), 112 Stat. 2876.)

28 USCS § 4001 Assumption of contractual obligations related to transfers of rights in motion pictures.

(a)   Assumption of obligations.

   (1)   In the case of a transfer of copyright ownership under United States law in a motion picture (as the terms "transfer of copyright ownership" and "motion picture" are defined in section 101 of title 17) that is produced subject to 1 or more collective bargaining agreements negotiated under the laws of the United States, if the transfer is executed on or after the effective date of this chapter [effective Oct. 28, 1998] and is not limited to public performance rights, the transfer instrument shall be deemed to incorporate the assumption agreements applicable to the copyright ownership being transferred that are required by the applicable collective bargaining agreement, and the transferee shall be subject to the obligations under each such assumption agreement to make residual payments and provide related notices, accruing after the effective date of the transfer and applicable to the exploitation of the rights transferred, and any remedies under each such assumption agreement for breach of those obligations, as those obligations and remedies are set forth in the applicable collective bargaining agreement, if

     (A)   the transferee knows or has reason to know at the time of the transfer that such collective bargaining agreement was or will be applicable to the motion picture; or

     (B)   in the event of a court order confirming an arbitration award against the transferor under the collective bargaining agreement, the transferor does not have the financial ability to satisfy the award within 90 days after the order is issued.

   (1)   For purposes of paragraph (1)(A), "knows or has reason to know' means any of the following:

     (A)   Actual knowledge that the collective bargaining agreement was or will be applicable to the motion picture.

     (B)(i)Constructive knowledge that the collective bargaining agreement was or will be applicable to the motion picture, arising from recordation of a document pertaining to copyright in the motion picture under section 205 of title 17 or from publication, at a site available to the public on-line that is operated by the relevant union, of information that identifies the motion picture as subject to a collective bargaining agreement with that union, if the site permits commercially reasonable verification of the date on which the information was available for access.

(ii)   Clause (i) applies only if the transfer referred to in subsection (a)(1) occurs

(I)   after the motion picture is completed, or

(II)   before the motion picture is completed and

(aa)   within 18 months before the filing of an application for copyright registration for the motion picture under section 408 of title 17, or

(bb)   if no such application is filed, within 18 months before the first publication of the motion picture in the United States.

(A)   Awareness of other facts and circumstances pertaining to a particular transfer from which it is apparent that the collective bargaining agreement was or will be applicable to the motion picture.

(a)   Scope of exclusion of transfers of public performance rights. For purposes of this section, the exclusion under subsection (a) of transfers of copyright ownership in a motion picture that are limited to public performance rights includes transfers to a terrestrial broadcast station, cable system, or programmer to the extent that the station, system, or programmer is functioning as an exhibitor of the motion picture, either by exhibiting the motion picture on its own network, system, service, or station, or by initiating the transmission of an exhibition that is carried on another network, system, service, or station. When a terrestrial broadcast station, cable system, or programmer, or other transferee, is also functioning otherwise as a distributor or as a producer of the motion picture, the public performance exclusion does not affect any obligations imposed on the transferee to the extent that it is engaging in such functions.

(b)   Exclusion for grants of security interests. Subsection (a) shall not apply to

(1)   a transfer of copyright ownership consisting solely of a mortgage, hypothecation, or other security interest; or

(2)   a subsequent transfer of the copyright ownership secured by the security interest described in paragraph (1) by or under the authority of the secured party, including a transfer through the exercise of the secured party's rights or remedies as a secured party, or by a subsequent transferee. The exclusion under this subsection shall not affect any rights or remedies under law or contract.

(a)   Deferral pending resolution of bona fide dispute. A transferee on which obligations are imposed under subsection (a) by virtue of paragraph (1) of that subsection may elect to defer performance of such obligations that are subject to a bona fide dispute between a union and a prior transferor until that dispute is resolved, except that such deferral shall not stay accrual of any union claims due under an applicable collective bargaining agreement.

(b)   Scope of obligations determined by private agreement. Nothing in this section shall expand or diminish the rights, obligations, or remedies of any person under the collective bargaining agreements or assumption agreements referred to in this section.

(c)   Failure to notify. If the transferor under subsection (a) fails to notify the transferee under subsection (a) of applicable collective bargaining obligations before the execution of the transfer instrument, and subsection (a) is made applicable to the transferee solely by virtue of subsection (a)(1)(B), the transferor shall be liable to the transferee for any damages suffered by the transferee as a result of the failure to notify.

(d)   Determination of disputes and claims. Any dispute concerning the application of subsections (a) through (f) shall be determined by an action in United States district court, and the court in its discretion may allow the recovery of full costs by or against any party and may also award a reasonable attorney's fee to the prevailing party as part of the costs.

(e)   Study. The Comptroller General, in consultation with the Register of Copyrights, shall conduct a study of the conditions in the motion picture industry that gave rise to this section, and the impact of this section on the motion picture industry. The Comptroller General shall report the findings of the study to the Congress within 2 years after the effective date of this chapter

[effective Oct. 28, 1998]. HISTORY: (Added Oct. 28, 1998, P.L. 105-304, Title IV, §   406(a), 112 Stat. 2903.)

FEDERAL TRADEMARK STATUTES:

15 U.S.C. § 1114 (§ 32 of the Lanham Act). Liability of infringers; remedies

(1) Any person who shall, without the consent of the registrant—

(a) use in commerce any reproduction, counterfeit, copy, or colorable imitation of a registered mark in connection with the sale, offering for sale, distribution, or advertising of any goods or services on or in connection with which such use is likely to cause confusion, or to cause mistake, or to deceive; or

(b) reproduce, counterfeit, copy, or colorably imitate a registered mark and apply such reproduction, counterfeit, copy, or colorable imitation to labels, signs, prints, packages, wrappers, receptacles or advertisements intended to be used in commerce upon or in connection with the sale, offering for sale, distribution, or advertising of goods or services on or in connection with which such use is likely to cause confusion, or to cause mistake, or to deceive,

shall be liable in a civil action by the registrant for the remedies hereinafter provided. Under subsection (b) of this section, the registrant shall not be entitled to recover profits or damages unless the acts have been committed with knowledge that such imitation is intended to be used to cause confusion, or to cause mistake, or to deceive.

As used in this subsection, the term "any person" includes any State, any instrumentality of a State, and any officer or employee of a State or instrumentality of a State acting in his or her official capacity. Any State, and any such instrumentality, officer, or employee, shall be subject to the provisions of this chapter in the same manner and to the same extent as any nongovernmental entity.

15 U.S.C. § 1115 (§ 33 of the Lanham Act). Registration as prima facie evidence

(a) Any registration issued under the Act of March 3, 1881, or the Act of February 20, 1905, or of a mark registered on the principal register provided by this chapter and owned by a party to an action shall be admissible in evidence and shall be prima facie evidence of the validity of the registered mark and of the registration of the mark, of the registrant's ownership of the mark, and of the registrant's exclusive right to use the registered mark in commerce on or in connection with the goods or services specified in the registration subject to any conditions or limitations stated therein, but shall not preclude another person from proving any legal or equitable defense or defect, including those set forth in subsection (b) of this section, which might have been asserted if such mark had not been registered.

15 U.S.C. § 1116 (§ 34 of the Lanham Act). Injunctions

(a) The several courts vested with jurisdiction of civil actions arising under this chapter shall have power to grant injunctions, according to the principles of equity and upon such terms as the court may deem reasonable, to prevent the violation of any right of the registrant of a mark registered in the Patent and Trademark Office or to prevent a violation under section 1125(a) of this title. Any such injunction may include a provision directing the defendant to file with the court and serve on the plaintiff within thirty days after the service on the defendant of such injunction, or such extended period as the court may direct, a report in writing under oath setting forth in detail the manner and form in which the defendant has complied with the injunction. Any such injunction granted upon hearing, after notice to the defendant, by any district court of the United States, may be served on the parties against whom such injunction is granted anywhere in the United States where they may be found, and shall be operative and may be enforced by proceedings to punish for contempt, or otherwise, by the court by which such injunction was granted, or by any other United States district court in whose jurisdiction the defendant may be found.

15 U.S.C. § 1117 (§ 35 of the Lanham Act). Damages, costs and attorney fees

(a) When a violation of any right of the registrant of a mark registered in the Patent and Trademark Office, or a violation under section 1125(a) of this title, shall have been established in any civil action arising under this chapter, the plaintiff shall be entitled, subject to the provisions of sections 1111 and 1114 of this title, and subject to the principles of equity, to recover (1) defendant's profits, (2) any damages sustained by the plaintiff, and (3) the costs of the action. The court shall assess such profits and damages or cause the same to be assessed under its direction. In assessing profits the plaintiff shall be required to prove defendant's sales only; defendant must prove all elements of cost or deduction claimed. In assessing damages the court may enter judgment, according to the circumstances of the case, for any sum above the amount found as actual damages, not exceeding three times such amount. If the court shall find that the amount of the recovery based on profits is either inadequate or excessive the court may in its discretion enter judgment for such sum as the court shall find to be just, according to the circumstances of the case. Such sum in either of the above circumstances shall constitute compensation and not a penalty. The court in exceptional cases may award reasonable attorney fees to the prevailing party.

15 U.S.C. § 1125 (§ 43 of the Lanham Act). False designations of origin, dilution

(a) Civil action

(1) Any person who, on or in connection with any goods or services, or any container for goods, uses in commerce any word, term, name, symbol, or device, or any combination thereof, or any false designation of origin, false or misleading description of fact, or false or misleading representation of fact, which—

(A) is likely to cause confusion, or to cause mistake, or to deceive as to the affiliation, connection, or association of such person with another person, or as to the origin, sponsorship, or approval of his or her goods, services, or commercial activities by another person, or

(B) in commercial advertising or promotion, misrepresents the nature, characteristics, qualities, or geographic origin of his or her or another person's goods, services, or commercial activities, shall be liable in a civil action by any person who believes that he or she is or is likely to be damaged by such act.

(2) As used in this subsection, the term "any person" includes any State, instrumentality of a State or employee of a State or instrumentality of a State acting in his or her official capacity. Any State, and any such instrumentality, officer, or employee, shall be subject to the provisions of this chapter in the same manner and to the same extent as any nongovernmental entity.

* * *

(c) Remedies for dilution of famous marks

(1) The owner of a famous mark shall be entitled, subject to the principles of equity and upon such terms as the court deems reasonable, to an injunction against another person's commercial use in commerce of a mark or trade name, if such use begins after the mark has become famous and causes dilution of the distinctive quality of the mark, and to obtain such other relief as is provided in this subsection. In determining whether a mark is distinctive and famous, a court may consider factors such as, but not limited to—

(A) the degree of inherent or acquired distinctiveness of the mark;

(B) the duration and extent of use of the mark in connection with the goods or services with which the mark is used;

(C) the duration and extent of advertising and publicity of the mark;

(D) the geographical extent of the trading area in which the mark is used;

(E) the channels of trade for the goods or services with which the mark is used;

(F) the degree of recognition of the mark in the trading areas and channels of trade used by the marks' owner and the person against whom the injunction is sought;

(G) the nature and extent of use of the same or similar marks by third parties; and

(H) whether the mark was registered under the Act of March 3, 1881, or the Act of February 20, 1905, or on the principal register.

(2) In an action brought under this subsection, the owner of the famous mark shall be entitled only to injunctive relief unless the person against whom the injunction is sought willfully intended to trade on the owner's reputation or to

cause dilution of the famous mark. If such willful intent is proven, the owner of the famous mark shall also be entitled to the remedies set forth in sections 1117(a) and 1118 of this title, subject to the discretion of the court and the principles of equity.

(3) The ownership by a person of a valid registration under the Act of March 3, 1881, or the Act of February 20, 1905, or on the principal register shall be a complete bar to an action against that person, with respect to that mark, that is brought by another person under the common law or a statute of a State and that seeks to prevent dilution of the distinctiveness of a mark, label, or form of advertisement.

(4) The following shall not be actionable under this section:

(A) Fair use of a famous mark by another person in comparative commercial advertising or promotion to identify the competing goods or services of the owner of the famous mark.

(B) Noncommercial use of a mark.

(C) All forms of news reporting and news commentary.

CALIFORNIA STATUTES:

Cal. Bus. & Prof. Code § 14330. Dilution

(a) Likelihood of injury to business reputation or of dilution of the distinctive quality of a mark registered under this chapter, or a mark valid at common law, or a trade name valid at common law, shall be a ground for injunctive relief notwithstanding the absence of competition between the parties or the absence of confusion as to the source of goods or services.

Cal. Civ. Code § 982. Transfers of ownership; right of reproduction

(a) The owner of any rights in any original works of authorship not fixed in any tangible medium of expression may transfer the ownership therein.

(b) The owner of any invention or design, or of any representation or expression thereof, may transfer his or her proprietary interest in it.

(c) Notwithstanding any other provision in this section, whenever a work of fine art is transferred, whether by sale or on commission or otherwise, by or on behalf of the artist who created it, or that artist's heir, legatee, or personal representative, the right of reproduction thereof is reserved to such artist or such heir, legatee, or personal representative until it passes into the public domain by act or operation of law, unless that right is expressly transferred by a document in writing in which reference is made to the specific right of reproduction, signed by the owner of the rights conveyed or that person's duly authorized agent. If the transfer is pursuant to an employment relationship, the right of reproduction is transferred to the employer, unless it is expressly reserved in writing. If the transfer is pursuant to a legacy or inheritance, the right of reproduction is transferred to the legatee or heir, unless it is expressly reserved by will or codicil. Nothing contained herein, however, shall be construed to prohibit the fair use of such work of fine art.

(d) As used in subdivision (c):

(1) "Fine art" means any work of visual art, including but not limited to, a drawing, painting, sculpture, mosaic, or photograph, a work of calligraphy, a work of graphic art (including an etching, lithograph, offset print, silk screen, or a work of graphic art of like nature), crafts (including crafts in clay, textile, fiber, wood, metal, plastic, and like materials), or mixed media (including a collage, assemblage, or any combination of the foregoing art media).

(2) "Artist" means the creator of a work of fine art.

(3) "Right of reproduction," at the present state of commerce and technology shall be interpreted as including, but shall not be limited to, the following: reproduction of works of fine art as prints suitable for framing; facsimile casts of sculpture; reproductions used for greeting cards; reproductions in general books and magazines not devoted primarily to art, and in newspapers in other than art or news sections, when such reproductions in books, magazines, and

newspapers are used for purposes similar to those of material for which the publishers customarily pay; art films; television, except from stations operated for educational purposes, or on programs for educational purposes from all stations; and reproductions used in any form of advertising, including magazines, calendars, newspapers, posters, billboards, films or television.

(e) The amendments to this section made at the 1975-76 Regular Session shall only apply to transfers made on or after January 1, 1976.

Cal. Civ. Code § 985. Private writings

Letters and other private communications in writing belong to the person to whom they are addressed and delivered; but they cannot be published against the will of the writer, except by authority of law.

Cal. Civ. Code § 986 Artist resale royalties for sale of works of fine art

(a) Whenever a work of fine art is sold and the seller resides in California or the sale takes place in California, the seller or the seller's agent shall pay to the artist of such work of fine art or to such artist's agent 5 percent of the amount of such sale. The right of the artist to receive an amount equal to 5 percent of the amount of such sale may be waived only by a contract in writing providing for an amount in excess of 5 percent of the amount of such sale. An artist may assign the right to collect the royalty payment provided by this section to another individual or entity. However, the assignment shall not have the effect of creating a waiver prohibited by this subdivision.

(1) When a work of fine art is sold at an auction or by a gallery, dealer, broker, museum, or other person acting as the agent for the seller the agent shall withhold 5 percent of the amount of the sale, locate the artist and pay the artist.

(2) If the seller or agent is unable to locate and pay the artist within 90 days, an amount equal to 5 percent of the amount of the sale shall be transferred to the Arts Council.

(3) If a seller or the seller's agent fails to pay an artist the amount equal to 5 percent of the sale of a work of fine art by the artist or fails to transfer such amount to the Arts Council, the artist may bring an action for damages within three years after the date of sale or one year after the discovery of the sale, whichever is longer. The prevailing party in any action brought under this paragraph shall be entitled to reasonable attorney fees, in an amount as determined by the court.

(4) Moneys received by the council pursuant to this section shall be deposited in an account in the Special Deposit Fund in the State Treasury.

(5) The Arts Council shall attempt to locate any artist for whom money is received pursuant to this section. If the council is unable to locate the artist and the artist does not file a written claim for the money received by the council

within seven years of the date of sale of the work of fine art, the right of the artist terminates and such money shall be transferred to the council for use in acquiring fine art pursuant to the Art in Public Buildings program set forth in Chapter 2.1 (commencing with Section 15813) of Part 10b of Division 3 of Title 2, of the Government Code.

(6) Any amounts of money held by any seller or agent for the payment of artists pursuant to this section shall be exempt from enforcement of a money judgment by the creditors of the seller or agent.

(7) Upon the death of an artist, the rights and duties created under this section shall inure to his or her heirs, legatees, or personal representative, until the 20th anniversary of the death of the artist. The provisions of this paragraph shall be applicable only with respect to an artist who dies after January 1, 1983.

(b) Subdivision (a) shall not apply to any of the following:

(1) To the initial sale of a work of fine art where legal title to such work at the time of such initial sale is vested in the artist thereof.

(2) To the resale of a work of fine art for a gross sales price of less than one thousand dollars ($1,000).

(3) Except as provided in paragraph (7) of subdivision (a), to a resale after the death of such artist.

(4) To the resale of the work of fine art for a gross sales price less than the purchase price paid by the seller.

(5) To a transfer of a work of fine art which is exchanged for one or more works of fine art or for a combination of cash, other property, and one or more works of fine art where the fair market value of the property exchanged is less than one thousand dollars ($1,000).

(6) To the resale of a work of fine art by an art dealer to a purchaser within 10 years of the initial sale of the work of fine art by the artist to an art dealer, provided all intervening resales are between art dealers.

(7) To a sale of a work of stained glass artistry where the work has been permanently attached to real property and is sold as part of the sale of the real property to which it is attached.

(c) For purposes of this section, the following terms have the following meanings:

(1) "Artist" means the person who creates a work of fine art and who, at the time of resale, is a citizen of the United States, or a resident of the state who has resided in the state for a minimum of two years.

(2) "Fine art" means an original painting, sculpture, or drawing, or an original work of art in glass.

(3) "Art dealer" means a person who is actively and principally engaged in or conducting the business of selling works of fine art for which business such person validly holds a sales tax permit.

(d) This section shall become operative on January 1, 1977, and shall apply to works of fine art created before and after its operative date.

(e) If any provision of this section or the application thereof to any person or circumstance is held invalid for any reason, such invalidity shall not affect any other provisions or applications of this section which can be effected, without the invalid provision or application, and to this end the provisions of this section are severable.

(f) The amendments to this section enacted during the 1981-82 Regular Session of the Legislature shall apply to transfers of works of fine art, when created before or after January 1, 1983, that occur on or after that date.

Cal. Civ. Code § 987. California Art Preservation Act

(a) The Legislature hereby finds and declares that the physical alteration or destruction of fine art, which is an expression of the artist's personality, is detrimental to the artist's reputation, and artists therefore have an interest in protecting their works of fine art against any alteration or destruction; and that there is also a public interest in preserving the integrity of cultural and artistic creations.

(b) As used in this section:

(1) "Artist" means the individual or individuals who create a work of fine art.

(2) "Fine art" means an original painting, sculpture, or drawing, or an original work of art in glass, of recognized quality, but shall not include work prepared under contract for commercial use by its purchaser.

(3) "Person" means an individual, partnership, corporation, limited liability company, association or other group, however organized.

(4) "Frame" means to prepare, or cause to be prepared, a work of fine art for display in a manner customarily considered to be appropriate for a work of fine art in the particular medium.

(5) "Restore" means to return, or cause to be returned, a deteriorated or damaged work of fine art as nearly as is feasible to its original state or condition, in accordance with prevailing standards.

(6) "Conserve" means to preserve, or cause to be preserved, a work of fine art by retarding or preventing deterioration or damage through appropriate treatment in accordance with prevailing standards in order to maintain the structural integrity to the fullest extent possible in an unchanging state.

(7) "Commercial use" means fine art created under a work-for-hire arrangement for use in advertising, magazines, newspapers, or other print and electronic media.

(c)(1) No person, except an artist who owns and possesses a work of fine art which the artist has created, shall intentionally commit, or authorize the intentional commission of, any physical defacement, mutilation, alteration, or destruction of a work of fine art.

(2) In addition to the prohibitions contained in paragraph (1), no person who frames, conserves, or restores a work of fine art shall commit, or authorize the commission of, any physical defacement, mutilation, alteration, or destruction of a work of fine art by any act constituting gross negligence. For purposes of this section, the term "gross negligence" shall mean the exercise of so slight a degree of care as to justify the belief that there was an indifference to the particular work of fine art.

(d) The artist shall retain at all times the right to claim authorship, or, for a just and valid reason, to disclaim authorship of his or her work of fine art.

(e) To effectuate the rights created by this section, the artist may commence an action to recover or obtain any of the following:

(1) Injunctive relief.

(2) Actual damages.

(3) Punitive damages. In the event that punitive damages are awarded, the court shall, in its discretion, select an organization or organizations engaged in charitable or educational activities involving the fine arts in California to receive any punitive damages.

(4) Reasonable attorneys' and expert witness fees.

(5) Any other relief which the court deems proper.

(f) In determining whether a work of fine art is of recognized quality, the trier of fact shall rely on the opinions of artists, art dealers, collectors of fine art, curators of art museums, and other persons involved with the creation or marketing of fine art.

(g) The rights and duties created under this section:

(1) Shall, with respect to the artist, or if any artist is deceased, his or her heir, beneficiary, devisee, or personal representative, exist until the 50th anniversary of the death of the artist.

(2) Shall exist in addition to any other rights and duties which may now or in the future be applicable.

(3) Except as provided in paragraph (1) of subdivision (h), may not be waived except by an instrument in writing expressly so providing which is signed by the artist.

(h) (1) If a work of fine art cannot be removed from a building without substantial physical defacement, mutilation, alteration, or destruction of the work, the rights and duties created under this section, unless expressly reserved by an instrument in writing signed by the owner of the building, containing a legal description of the property and properly recorded, shall be deemed waived. The instrument, if properly recorded, shall be binding on subsequent owners of the building.

(2) If the owner of a building wishes to remove a work of fine art which is a part of the building but which can be removed from the building without substantial harm to the fine art, and in the course of or after removal, the owner intends to cause or allow the fine art to suffer physical defacement, mutilation, alteration, or destruction, the rights and duties created under this section shall apply unless the owner has diligently attempted without success to notify the artist, or, if the artist is deceased, his or her heir, beneficiary, devisee, or personal representative, in writing of his or her intended action affecting the work of fine art, or unless he or she did provide notice and that person failed within 90 days either to remove the work or to pay for its removal. If the work is removed at the expense of the artist, his or her heir, beneficiary, devisee, or personal representative, title to the fine art shall pass to that person.

(3) If a work of fine art can be removed from a building scheduled for demolition without substantial physical defacement, mutilation, alteration, or destruction of the work, and the owner of the building has notified the owner of the work of fine art of the scheduled demolition or the owner of the building is the owner of the work of fine art, and the owner of the work of fine art elects not to remove the work of fine art, the rights and duties created under this section shall apply, unless the owner of the building has diligently attempted without success to notify the artist, or, if the artist is deceased, his or her heir, beneficiary, devisee, or personal representative, in writing of the intended action affecting the work of fine art, or unless he or she did provide notice and that person failed within 90 days either to remove the work or to pay for its removal. If the work is removed at the expense of the artist, his or her heir, beneficiary, devisee, or personal representative, title to the fine art shall pass to that person.

(4) Nothing in this subdivision shall affect the rights of authorship created in subdivision (d) of this section.

(i) No action may be maintained to enforce any liability under this section unless brought within three years of the act complained of or one year after discovery of the act, whichever is longer.

(j) This section shall become operative on January 1, 1980, and shall apply to claims based on proscribed acts occurring on or after that date to works of fine art whenever created.

(k) If any provision of this section or the application thereof to any person or circumstance is held invalid for any reason, the invalidity shall not affect any other provisions or applications of this section which can be effected without the invalid provision or application, and to this end the provisions of this section are severable.

Cal. Civ. Code § 988. Reservation of ownership rights in work of art

(a) For the purpose of this section:

(1) The term "artist" means the creator of a work of art.

(2) The term "work of art" means any work of visual or graphic art of any media including, but not limited to, a painting, print, drawing, sculpture, craft, photograph, or film.

(b) Whenever an exclusive or nonexclusive conveyance of any right to reproduce, prepare derivative works based on, distribute copies of, publicly perform, or publicly display a work of art is made by or on behalf of the artist who created it or the owner at the time of the conveyance, ownership of the physical work of art shall remain with and be reserved to the artist or owner, as the case may be, unless such right of ownership is expressly transferred by an instrument, note, memorandum, or other writing, signed by the artist, the owner, or their duly authorized agent.

(c) Whenever an exclusive or nonexclusive conveyance of any right to reproduce, prepare derivative works based on, distribute copies of, publicly perform, or publicly display a work of art is made by or on behalf of the artist who created it or the owner at the time of the conveyance, any ambiguity with respect to the nature or extent of the rights conveyed shall be resolved in favor of the reservation of rights by the artist or owner, unless in any given case the federal copyright law provides to the contrary.

Cal. Civ. Code § 989. Preservation of integrity of cultural and artistic creations

(a) The Legislature hereby finds and declares that there is a public interest in preserving the integrity of cultural and artistic creations.

(b) As used in this section:

(1) "Fine art" means an original painting, sculpture, or drawing, or an original work of art in glass, of recognized quality, and of substantial public interest.

(2) "Organization" means a public or private not-for-profit entity or association, in existence at least three years at the time an action is filed pursuant to this section, a major purpose of which is to stage, display, or otherwise present works of art to the public or to promote the interests of the arts or artists.

(3) "Cost of removal" includes reasonable costs, if any, for the repair of damage to the real property caused by the removal of the work of fine art.

(c) An organization acting in the public interest may commence an action for injunctive relief to preserve or restore the integrity of a work of fine art from acts prohibited by subdivision (c) of Section 987.

(d) In determining whether a work of fine art is of recognized quality and of substantial public interest the trier of fact shall rely on the opinions of those described in subdivision (f) of Section 987.

(e)(1) If a work of fine art cannot be removed from real property without substantial physical defacement, mutilation, alteration, or destruction of such work, no action to preserve the integrity of the work of fine art may be brought under this section. However, if an organization offers some evidence giving rise to a reasonable likelihood that a work of art can be removed from the real property without substantial physical defacement, mutilation, alteration, or destruction of the work, and is prepared to pay the cost of removal of the work, it may bring a legal action for a determination of this issue. In that action the organization shall be entitled to injunctive relief to preserve the integrity of the work of fine art, but shall also have the burden of proof. The action shall commence within 30 days after filing. No action may be brought under this paragraph if the organization's interest in preserving the work of art is in conflict with an instrument described in paragraph (1) of subdivision (h) of Section 987.

(2) If the owner of the real property wishes to remove a work of fine art which is part of the real property, but which can be removed from the real property without substantial harm to such fine art, and in the course of or after removal, the owner intends to cause or allow the fine art to suffer physical defacement, mutilation, alteration, or destruction the owner shall do the following:

(A) If the artist or artist's heir, legatee, or personal representative fails to take action to remove the work of fine art after the notice provided by paragraph (2) of subdivision (h) of Section 987, the owner shall provide 30 days' notice of his or her intended action affecting the work of art. The written notice shall be a display advertisement in a newspaper of general circulation in the area where the fine art is located. The notice required by this paragraph may run concurrently with the notice required by subdivision (h) of Section 987.

(i) If within the 30-day period an organization agrees to remove the work of fine art and pay the cost of removal of the work, the payment and removal shall occur within 90 days of the first day of the 30-day notice.

(ii) If the work is removed at the expense of an organization, title to the fine art shall pass to that organization.

(B) If an organization does not agree to remove the work of fine art within the 30-day period or fails to remove and pay the cost of removal of the work of fine art within the 90-day period the owner may take the intended action affecting the work of fine art.

(f) To effectuate the rights created by this section, the court may do the following:

(1) Award reasonable attorney's and expert witness fees to the prevailing party, in an amount as determined by the court.

(2) Require the organization to post a bond in a reasonable amount as determined by the court.

(g) No action may be maintained under this section unless brought within three years of the act complained of or one year after discovery of such act, whichever is longer.

(h) This section shall become operative on January 1, 1983, and shall apply to claims based on acts occurring on or after that date to works of fine art, whenever created.

(i) If any provision of this section or the application thereof to any person or circumstances is held invalid, such invalidity shall not affect other provisions or applications of this section which can be given effect without the invalid provision or application, and to this end the provisions of this section are severable.

Cal. Civ. Code § 990. Unauthorized use of deceased personality's name, voice, signature, photograph or likeness

(a) Any person who uses a deceased personality's name, voice, signature, photograph, or likeness, in any manner, on or in products, merchandise, or goods, or for purposes of advertising or selling, or soliciting purchases of, products, merchandise, goods, or services, without prior consent from the person or persons specified in subdivision (c), shall be liable for any damages sustained by the person or persons injured as a result thereof. In addition, in any action brought under this section, the person who violated the section shall be liable to the injured party or parties in an amount equal to the greater of seven hundred fifty dollars ($750) or the actual damages suffered by the injured party or parties, as a result of the unauthorized use, and any profits from the unauthorized use that are attributable to the use and are not taken into account in computing the actual damages. In establishing these profits, the injured party or parties shall be required to present proof only of the gross revenue attributable to the use and the person who violated the section is required to prove his or her deductible expenses. Punitive damages may also be awarded to the injured party or parties. The prevailing party or parties in any action under this section shall also be entitled to attorneys' fees and costs.

(b) The rights recognized under this section are property rights, freely transferable, in whole or in part, by contract or by means of trust or testamentary documents, whether the transfer occurs before the death of the deceased personality, by the deceased personality or his or her transferees, or, after the death of the deceased personality, by the person or persons in whom the rights vest under this section or the transferees of that person or persons.

(c) The consent required by this section shall be exercisable by the person or persons to whom the right of consent (or portion thereof) has been transferred in accordance with subdivision (b), or if no such transfer has occurred, then by the person or persons to whom the right of consent (or portion thereof) has passed in accordance with subdivision (d).

(d) Subject to subdivisions (b) and (c), after the death of any person, the rights under this section shall belong to the following person or persons and may be exercised, on behalf of and for the benefit of all of those persons, by those persons who, in the aggregate, are entitled to more than a one-half interest in the rights:

(1) The entire interest in those rights belong to the surviving spouse of the deceased personality unless there are any surviving children or grandchildren of the deceased personality, in which case one-half of the entire interest in those rights belong to the surviving spouse.

(2) The entire interest in those rights belong to the surviving children of the deceased personality and to the surviving children of any dead child of the deceased personality unless the deceased personality has a surviving spouse, in which case the ownership of a one-half interest in rights is divided among the surviving children and grandchildren.

(3) If there is no surviving spouse, and no surviving children or grandchildren, then the entire interest in those rights belong to the surviving parent or parents of the deceased personality.

(4) The rights of the deceased personality's children and grandchildren are in all cases divided among them and exercisable in the manner provided in Section 240 of the Probate Code according to the number of the deceased personality's children represented; the share of the children of a dead child of a deceased personality can be exercised only by the action of a majority of them.

(e) If any deceased personality does not transfer his or her rights under this section by contract, or by means of a trust or testamentary document, and there are no surviving persons as described in subdivision (d), then the rights set forth in subdivision (a) shall terminate.

(f)(1) A successor-in-interest to the rights of a deceased personality under this section or a licensee thereof may not recover damages for a use prohibited by this section that occurs before the successor-in-interest or licensee registers a claim of the rights under paragraph (2).

(2) Any person claiming to be a successor-in-interest to the rights of a deceased personality under this section or a licensee thereof may register that claim with the Secretary of State on a form prescribed by the Secretary of State and upon payment of a fee of ten dollars ($10). The form shall be verified and shall include the name and date of death of the deceased personality, the name and address of the claimant, the basis of the claim, and the rights claimed.

(3) Upon receipt and after filing of any document under this section, the Secretary of State may microfilm or reproduce by other techniques any of the filings or documents and destroy the original filing or document. The microfilm

or other reproduction of any document under the provision of this section shall be admissible in any court of law. The microfilm or other reproduction of any document may be destroyed by the Secretary of State 50 years after the death of the personality named therein.

(4) Claims registered under this subdivision shall be public records.

(g) No action shall be brought under this section by reason of any use of a deceased personality's name, voice, signature, photograph, or likeness occurring after the expiration of 50 years from the death of the deceased personality.

(h) As used in this section, "deceased personality" means any natural person whose name, voice, signature, photograph, or likeness has commercial value at the time of his or her death, whether or not during the lifetime of that natural person the person used his or her name, voice, signature, photograph, or likeness on or in products, merchandise or goods, or for purposes of advertising or selling, or solicitation of purchase of, products, merchandise, goods or service. A "deceased personality" shall include, without limitation, any such natural person who has died within 50 years prior to January 1, 1985.

(i) As used in this section, "photograph" means any photograph or photographic reproduction, still or moving, or any video tape or live television transmission, of any person, such that the deceased personality is readily identifiable. A deceased personality shall be deemed to be readily identifiable from a photograph when one who views the photograph with the naked eye can reasonably determine who the person depicted in the photograph is.

(j) For purposes of this section, a use of a name, voice, signature, photograph, or likeness in connection with any news, public affairs, or sports broadcast or account, or any political campaign, shall not constitute a use for which consent is required under subdivision (a).

(k) The use of a name, voice, signature, photograph, or likeness in a commercial medium shall not constitute a use for which consent is required under subdivision (a) solely because the material containing the use is commercially sponsored or contains paid advertising. Rather it shall be a question of fact whether or not the use of the deceased personality's name, voice, signature, photograph, or likeness was so directly connected with the commercial sponsorship or with the paid advertising as to constitute a use for which consent is required under subdivision (a).

(l) Nothing in this section shall apply to the owners or employees of any medium used for advertising, including, but not limited to, newspapers, magazines, radio and television networks and stations, cable television systems, billboards, and transit ads, by whom any advertisement or solicitation in violation of this section is published or disseminated, unless it is established that the owners or employees had knowledge of the unauthorized use of the deceased personality's name, voice, signature, photograph, or likeness as prohibited by this section.

(m) The remedies provided for in this section are cumulative and shall be in addition to any others provided for by law.

(n) This section shall not apply to the use of a deceased personality's name, voice, signature, photograph, or likeness, in any of the following instances:

(1) A play, book, magazine, newspaper, musical composition, film, radio or television program, other than an advertisement or commercial announcement not exempt under paragraph (4).

(2) Material that is of political or newsworthy value.

(3) Single and original works of fine art.

(4) An advertisement or commercial announcement for a use permitted by paragraph (1), (2), or (3).

Cal. Civ. Code § 1670.5. Unconscionable contract

(a) If the court as a matter of law finds the contract or any clause of the contract to have been unconscionable at the time it was made, the court may refuse to enforce the contract, or it may enforce the remainder of the contract without the unconscionable clause, or it may so limit the application of any unconscionable clause as to avoid any unconscionable result.

(b) When it is claimed or appears to the court that the contract or any clause thereof may be unconscionable, the parties shall be afforded a reasonable opportunity to present evidence as to its commercial setting, purpose, and effect to aid the court in making the determination.

Cal. Civ. Code § 3344. Use of another's name, voice, signature, photograph, or likeness

(a) Any person who knowingly uses another's name, voice, signature, photograph, or likeness, in any manner, on or in products, merchandise, or goods, or for purposes of advertising or selling, or soliciting purchases of, products, merchandise, goods or services, without such person's prior consent, or, in the case of a minor, the prior consent of his parent or legal guardian, shall be liable for any damages sustained by the person or persons injured as a result thereof. In addition, in any action brought under this section, the person who violated the section shall be liable to the injured party or parties in an amount equal to the greater of seven hundred fifty dollars ($750) or the actual damages suffered by him or her as a result of the unauthorized use, and any profits from the unauthorized use that are attributable to the use and are not taken into account in computing the actual damages. In establishing such profits, the injured party or parties are required to present proof only of the gross revenue attributable to such use, and the person who violated this section is required to prove his or her deductible expenses. Punitive damages may also be awarded to the injured party or parties. The prevailing party in any action under this section shall also be entitled to attorney's fees and costs.

(b) As used in this section, "photograph" means any photograph or photographic reproduction, still or moving, or any videotape or live television transmission, of any person, such that the person is readily identifiable.

(1) A person shall be deemed to be readily identifiable from a photograph when one who views the photograph with the naked eye can reasonably determine that the person depicted in the photograph is the same person who is complaining of its unauthorized use.

(2) If the photograph includes more than one person so identifiable, then the person or persons complaining of the use shall be represented as individuals rather than solely as members of a definable group represented in the photograph. A definable group includes, but is not limited to, the following examples: a crowd at any sporting event, a crowd in any street or public building, the audience at any theatrical or stage production, a glee club, or a baseball team.

(3) A person or persons shall be considered to be represented as members of a definable group if they are represented in the photograph solely as a result of being present at the time the photograph was taken and have not been singled out as individuals in any manner.

(c) Where a photograph or likeness of an employee of the person using the photograph or likeness appearing in the advertisement or other publication prepared by or in behalf of the user is only incidental, and not essential, to the purpose of the publication in which it appears, there shall arise a rebuttable presumption affecting the burden of producing evidence that the failure to obtain the consent of the employee was not a knowing use of the employee's photograph or likeness.

(d) For purposes of this section, a use of a name, voice, signature, photograph, or likeness in connection with any news, public affairs, or sports broadcast or account, or any political campaign, shall not constitute a use for which consent is required under subdivision (a).

(e) The use of a name, voice, signature, photograph, or likeness in a commercial medium shall not constitute a use for which consent is required under subdivision (a) solely because the material containing such use is commercially sponsored or contains paid advertising. Rather it shall be a question of fact whether or not the use of the person's name, voice, signature, photograph, or likeness was so directly connected with the commercial sponsorship or with the paid advertising as to constitute a use for which consent is required under subdivision (a).

(f) Nothing in this section shall apply to the owners or employees of any medium used for advertising, including, but not limited to, newspapers, magazines, radio and television networks and stations, cable television systems, billboards, and transit ads, by whom any advertisement or solicitation in violation of this section is published or disseminated, unless it is established that such owners or employees had knowledge of the unauthorized use of the person's name, voice, signature, photograph, or likeness as prohibited by this section.

(g) The remedies provided for in this section are cumulative and shall be in addition to any others provided for by law.

Cal. Civ. Code § 3423. Denial of injunction

An injunction may not be granted:

(a) To stay a judicial proceeding pending at the commencement of the action in which the injunction is demanded, unless this restraint is necessary to prevent a multiplicity of proceedings.

(b) To stay proceedings in a court of the United States.

(c) To stay proceedings in another state upon a judgment of a court of that state.

(d) To prevent the execution of a public statute, by officers of the law, for the public benefit.

(e) To prevent the breach of a contract the performance of which would not be specifically enforced, other than a contract in writing for the rendition of personal services from one to another where the promised service is of a special, unique, unusual, extraordinary, or intellectual character, which gives it peculiar value, the loss of which cannot be reasonably or adequately compensated in damages in an action at law, and where the compensation for the personal services is as follows:

(1) As to contracts entered into on or before December 31, 1993, the minimum compensation provided in the contract for the personal services shall be at the rate of six thousand dollars ($6,000) per annum.

(2) As to contracts entered into on or after January 1, 1994, the criteria of subparagraph (A) or (B), as follows, are satisfied:

(A) The compensation is as follows:

(i) The minimum compensation provided in the contract shall be at the rate of nine thousand dollars ($9,000) per annum for the first year of the contract, twelve thousand dollars ($12,000) per annum for the second year of the contract, and fifteen thousand dollars ($15,000) per annum for the third to seventh years, inclusive, of the contract.

(ii) In addition, after the third year of the contract, there shall actually have been paid for the services through and including the contract year during which the injunctive relief is sought, over and above the minimum contractual compensation specified in clause (i), the amount of fifteen thousand dollars ($15,000) per annum during the fourth and fifth years of the contract, and thirty thousand dollars ($30,000) per annum during the sixth and seventh years of the contract. As a condition to petitioning for an injunction, amounts payable under this clause may be paid at any time prior to seeking injunctive relief.

(B) The aggregate compensation actually received for the services provided under a contract that does not meet the criteria of subparagraph (A), is at least 10 times the applicable aggregate minimum amount specified in clauses (i) and (ii) of subparagraph (A) through and including the contract year during which the injunctive relief is sought. As a condition to petitioning for an injunction, amounts payable under this subparagraph may be paid at any time prior to seeking injunctive relief.

(3) Compensation paid in any contract year in excess of the minimums specified in subparagraphs (A) and (B) of paragraph (2) shall apply to reduce the compensation otherwise required to be paid under those provisions in any subsequent contract years.

However, an injunction may be granted to prevent the breach of a contract entered into between any nonprofit cooperative corporation or association and a member or stockholder thereof in respect to any provision regarding the sale or delivery to the corporation or association of the products produced or acquired by the member or stockholder.

(f) To prevent the exercise of a public or private office, in a lawful manner, by the person in possession.

(g) To prevent a legislative act by a municipal corporation.

Cal. Civ. Code § 3504. Definitions

As used in this title:

(a) "Animal" means any amphibian, bird, mammal or reptile. It does not include any fish or insect.

(b) "Motion picture" means any motion picture, regardless of length or content, which is exhibited in a motion picture theater to paying customers, or is exhibited on television to paying customers or under the sponsorship of a paying advertiser. It shall not include motion pictures made for scientific, research, or educational purposes, or motion pictures exhibited as home movies, or amateur films, which are shown free or at cost to friends, neighbors or civic groups.

(c) "Person" means individuals, corporations, associations, partnerships, limited liability companies, trustees, lessees, agents and assignees.

Cal. Civ. Code § 3505. Exhibition of motion picture containing intentional killing or cruelty

(a) The exhibition of any motion picture, if any intentional killing of, or cruelty to, a human being or an animal is shown in the motion picture and such intentional killing of, or cruelty to, a human being or an animal actually occurred in the production of the motion picture for the purpose of such production, is a nuisance, which shall be enjoined, abated, and prevented.

(b) As used in this section, "killing" and "cruelty" mean conduct which both (1) results in the death or the infliction of any physical injury or wound, including, but not limited to, any temporary or permanent physical harm resulting from the administration of any drug or chemical, and (2) is patently offensive to the average person, applying contemporary statewide community standards. It does not include conduct committed against a human being to which the human being has given his or her consent. In determining whether conduct is patently offensive, the trier of fact may consider any or all of the following: (i) the degree or extent of the physical injury inflicted, (ii) the manner in which the injury is inflicted, (iii) the extent to which the injuring or wounding or acts resulting therein are depicted on the screen, (iv) the number of instances of infliction of injury, wound or harm occurring in the making of the motion picture, and (v) whether such conduct is lawful or unlawful under any provision of law other than this title.

(c) For the purposes of this section, it shall not be a requirement that the entire motion picture and all of the conduct resulting therein be taken into account in determining whether a nuisance exists, and to this end, the Legislature finds and declares that any specific conduct which intentionally results in the killing of, or cruelty to, an animal or a human being in the making of a motion picture is unnecessary and is a nuisance, and that if a motion picture cannot be completed in the absence of such conduct, it is, therefore, a nuisance in its entirety.

Cal. Civ. Code § 3506. Commencement of nuisance actions

Whenever there is reasonable cause to believe that a nuisance as defined in this title is kept, maintained or is in existence in any county, the district attorney or the Attorney General, in the name of the people of the State of California, shall, on a proper showing, commence an action in equity to abate and prevent the nuisance and to perpetually enjoin the person conducting or maintaining it, and the owner, lessee or agent of the building, or place, in or upon which the nuisance exists, from maintaining or permitting it. As used herein, a proper showing to commence an action under this title must be based upon evidence independent of the motion picture itself that intentional killing of, or cruelty to, a human being or an animal actually occurred in the production of the motion picture for the purpose of such production.

Cal. Civ. Code § 3507. Injunctions

Whenever an action is initiated under this title to abate an alleged nuisance, an adversary trial on the merits shall be held pursuant to Section 3507.2. If the court finds that the exhibition of the particular motion picture constitutes a nuisance, it shall issue a permanent injunction to abate and prevent the continuance or recurrence of such nuisance. No temporary restraining order or preliminary injunction shall be granted in such an action. An appeal may be taken from an order issuing a permanent injunction, and any injunction issued pursuant to this title by the trial court may be stayed by such court pending the outcome of such appeal. No appeal may be taken from a ruling by the trial court denying an injunction requested under this title.

Cal. Civ. Code § 3507.1. Motion picture admissible as evidence

In actions brought under this title, the motion picture shall be admissible into evidence. The burden of proof that the exhibition of the particular motion picture constitutes a nuisance shall be met by the district attorney or Attorney General only when clear and convincing evidence, independent of the motion picture itself, is provided that the acts alleged actually occurred in the production of the motion picture.

Cal. Civ. Code § 3507.2. Expeditious adjudication

Actions brought under this title shall be brought as promptly as possible. Such actions shall have precedence over all actions, excepting criminal proceedings and election contests. It is also the intent of the Legislature that actions commenced under this title be adjudicated in the most speedy and expeditious manner.

Cal. Civ. Code § 3507.3. Punishment for violations

Any violation or disobedience of an injunction or order expressly provided for by this title is punishable as a contempt of court by a fine of not less than two hundred dollars ($200) nor more than one thousand dollars ($1,000).

Cal. Civ. Code § 3507.4. Joint and several liability of distributors and producers

The distributor who furnished a motion picture to a person who is made a defendant in an action under this title, and the producer of a motion picture which is the subject of this title shall be jointly and severally liable, upon proof and after an opportunity to appear and interpose any appropriate defenses, to such person and the exhibitor for damages, including loss of profits, attorney's fees, and other costs of defending such action. Such distributor and such producer shall actively assist in such defense to the extent that such person possesses information necessary to such defense concerning the production of the motion picture which is not otherwise available to the defendant. The exhibitor shall not be liable upon any portion of any contract made on or after January 1, 1979, which requires the exhibition or advertisement of a motion picture subject to this title on or after the date of the filing of any action under this title, if the motion picture by final decision of a court is determined to be a nuisance under this title.

Cal. Civ. Code § 3508. Application of title

(a) This title shall not apply to any of the following:

(1) The exhibition of any motion picture, such as a newsreel or documentary, involving acts of killing or cruelty which were not intentionally committed for the purpose of producing the motion picture.

(2) Any motion picture made, in whole or in part, prior to January 1, 1979.

(3) Any motion picture all or part of which has been edited or remade so that any previous conduct which constituted a nuisance under this title no longer appears.

(4) The taking of any animal as permitted by any provision of the Fish and Game Code or pursuant thereto in accordance with regulations adopted by the Fish and Game Commission unless the time, place, or manner of such taking violates any provision of law except this title. This title shall apply to any other animal whether or not the time, place, or manner of the taking is prohibited by any laws other than this title, however, this title shall not apply to the taking of any animal authorized by law in any other jurisdiction unless the time, place or manner of such taking is prohibited by law or regulation.

(5) A motion picture which includes scenes of killing or cruelty to animals if the acts constituting the killing or cruelty were authorized by the laws governing such acts in the jurisdiction where the scenes were filmed.

(6) Any motion picture which bears within its contents a statement from the producer of the motion picture that all scenes depicting animals were filmed without the intentional killing of, or cruelty to an animal or that any killing or cruelty to an animal was authorized by the laws of the jurisdiction where the scenes were filmed or that the film is otherwise exempt under this title.

(7) Any motion picture if the exhibitor thereof has a written signed statement, or a copy thereof, from the producer of the motion picture that all scenes depicting animals were filmed without the intentional killing of, or cruelty to an animal or that any killing or cruelty to an animal was authorized by the laws of the jurisdiction where the scenes were filmed or that the film is otherwise exempt under this title.

(b) This title shall not apply in any case in which it would conflict with federal supremacy in the field of television broadcasting.

Cal. Civ. Code § 3508.1. Misstatements by producers

Any producer who willfully misstates or causes to be misstated any fact contained in a statement under paragraph (6) or (7) of Section 3508 is guilty of a misdemeanor.

Civ. Proc. Code § 526. Granting or denial of injunction

(a) An injunction may be granted in the following cases:

(1) When it appears by the complaint that the plaintiff is entitled to the relief demanded, and the relief, or any part thereof, consists in restraining the commission or continuance of the act complained of, either for a limited period or perpetually.

(2) When it appears by the complaint or affidavits that the commission or continuance of some act during the litigation would produce waste, or great or irreparable injury, to a party to the action.

(3) When it appears, during the litigation, that a party to the action is doing, or threatens, or is about to do, or is procuring or suffering to be done, some act in violation of the rights of another party to the action respecting the subject of the action, and tending to render the judgment ineffectual.

(4) When pecuniary compensation would not afford adequate relief.

(5) Where it would be extremely difficult to ascertain the amount of compensation which would afford adequate relief.

(6) Where the restraint is necessary to prevent a multiplicity of judicial proceedings.

(7) Where the obligation arises from a trust.

(b) An injunction cannot be granted in the following cases:

(1) To stay a judicial proceeding pending at the commencement of the action in which the injunction is demanded, unless the restraint is necessary to prevent a multiplicity of proceedings.

(2) To stay proceedings in a court of the United States.

(3) To stay proceedings in another state upon a judgment of a court of that state.

(4) To prevent the execution of a public statute by officers of the law for the public benefit.

(5) To prevent the breach of a contract the performance of which would not be specifically enforced, other than a contract in writing for the rendition of personal services from one to another where the promised service is of a special, unique, unusual, extraordinary, or intellectual character, which gives it peculiar value, the loss of which cannot be reasonably or adequately compensated in damages in an action at law, and where the compensation for the personal services is as follows:

(A) As to contracts entered into on or before December 31, 1993, the minimum compensation provided in the contract for the personal services shall be at the rate of six thousand dollars ($6,000) per annum.

(B) As to contracts entered into on or after January 1, 1994, the criteria of clause (i) or (ii), as follows, are satisfied:

(i) The compensation is as follows:

(I) The minimum compensation provided in the contract shall be at the rate of nine thousand dollars ($9,000) per annum for the first year of the contract, twelve thousand dollars ($12,000) per annum for the second year of the contract, and fifteen thousand dollars ($15,000) per annum for the third to seventh years, inclusive, of the contract.

(II) In addition, after the third year of the contract, there shall actually have been paid for the services through and including the contract year during which the injunctive relief is sought, over and above the minimum contractual compensation specified in subclause (I), the amount of fifteen thousand dollars ($15,000) per annum during the fourth and fifth years of the contract, and thirty thousand dollars ($30,000) per annum during the sixth and seventh years of the contract. As a condition to petitioning for an injunction, amounts payable under this clause may be paid at any time prior to seeking injunctive relief.

(ii) The aggregate compensation actually received for the services provided under a contract that does not meet the criteria of subparagraph (A), is at least 10 times the applicable aggregate minimum amount specified in subclauses (I) and (II) of clause (i) through and including the contract year during which the injunctive relief is sought. As a condition to petitioning for an injunction, amounts payable under this subparagraph may be paid at any time prior to seeking injunctive relief.

(C) Compensation paid in any contract year in excess of the minimums specified in clauses (i) and (ii) of subparagraph (B) shall apply to reduce the compensation otherwise required to be paid under those provisions in any subsequent contract years. However, an injunction may be granted to prevent the breach of a contract entered into between any nonprofit cooperative corporation or association and a member or stockholder thereof, in respect to any provision regarding the sale or delivery to the corporation or association of the products produced or acquired by the member or stockholder.

(6) To prevent the exercise of a public or private office, in a lawful manner, by the person in possession.

(7) To prevent a legislative act by a municipal corporation.

Cal. Fam. Code § 6710. Right of disaffirmance

Except as otherwise provided by statute, a contract of a minor may be disaffirmed by the minor before majority or within a reasonable time afterwards or, in case of the minor's death within that period, by the minor's heirs or personal representative.

Cal. Fam. Code § 6750. Minor's contracts in art, entertainment and professional sports

This chapter applies to the following contracts:

(a) A contract pursuant to which a person is employed or agrees to render artistic or creative services. "Artistic or creative services" includes, but is not limited to, services as an actor, actress, dancer, musician, comedian, singer, or other performer or entertainer, or as a writer, director, producer, production executive, choreographer, composer, conductor, or designer.

(b) A contract pursuant to which a person agrees to purchase, or otherwise secure, sell, lease, license, or otherwise dispose of literary, musical, or dramatic properties, either tangible or intangible, or any rights therein for use in motion pictures, television, the production of phonograph records, the legitimate or living stage, or otherwise in the entertainment field.

(c) A contract pursuant to which a person is employed or agrees to render services as a participant or player in a professional sport, including, but not limited to, services as a professional boxer, professional wrestler, or professional jockey.

Cal. Fam. Code § 6751. Disaffirmance of contracts approved by court

(a) A contract, otherwise valid, of a type described in Section 6750, entered into during minority, cannot be disaffirmed on that ground either during the minority of the person entering into the contract, or at any time thereafter, if the contract has been approved by the superior court in the county in which the minor resides or is employed or, if the minor neither resides in nor is employed in this state, by the superior court of the county in which any party to the contract has its principal office in this state for the transaction of business.

(b) Approval of the court may be given on petition of either party to the contract, after such reasonable notice to the other party to the contract as is fixed by the court, with opportunity to such other party to appear and be heard.

(c) Approval of the court given under this section extends to the whole of the contract and all of its terms and provisions, including, but not limited to, any optional or conditional provisions contained in the contract for extension, prolongation, or termination of the term of the contract.

Cal. Fam. Code § 6752. Court preservation of net earnings of minor

(a) Notwithstanding any other statute, in an order approving a contract of a minor of a type described in Section 6750, the court may require that the portion of the net earnings of the minor, not exceeding one-half thereof, that the court determines is just and proper, be set aside and preserved for the benefit of the minor, either in a trust fund or other savings plan approved by the court.

(b) The court may withhold approval of the contract until the parent or parents or guardian, as the case may be, execute and file with the court written consent to the making of the order described in subdivision (a).

(c) "Net earnings of the minor" for the purposes of this section means the total sum received for the services of the minor pursuant to the contract less all of the following:

(1) All sums required by law to be paid as taxes to any government or governmental agency.

(2) Reasonable sums expended for the support, care, maintenance, education, and training of the minor.

(3) Fees and expenses paid in connection with procuring the contract or maintaining the employment of the minor.

(4) Attorney's fees for services rendered in connection with the contract and other business of the minor.

Cal. Lab. Code § 1700. "Person" defined

As used in this chapter, "person" means any individual, company, society, firm, partnership, association, corporation, limited liability company, manager, or their agents or employees.

Cal. Lab. Code § 1700.1. "Theatrical engagement," "motion picture engagement," and "emergency engagement" defined

As used in this chapter:

(a) "Theatrical engagement" means any engagement or employment of a person as an actor, performer, or entertainer in a circus, vaudeville, theatrical, or other entertainment, exhibition, or performance.

(b) "Motion picture engagement" means any engagement or employment of a person as an actor, actress, director, scenario, or continuity writer, camera man, or in any capacity concerned with the making of motion pictures.

(c) "Emergency engagement" means an engagement which has to be performed within 24 hours from the time when the contract for such engagement is made.

Cal. Lab. Code § 1700.2. "Fee" and "registration fee" defined

(a) As used in this chapter, "fee" means any of the following:

(1) Any money or other valuable consideration paid or promised to be paid for services rendered or to be rendered by any person conducting the business of a talent agency under this chapter.

(2) Any money received by any person in excess of that which has been paid out by him or her for transportation, transfer of baggage, or board and lodging for any applicant for employment.

(3) The difference between the amount of money received by any person who furnished employees, performers, or entertainers for circus, vaudeville, theatrical, or other entertainments, exhibitions, or performances, and the amount paid by him or her to the employee, performer, or entertainer.

(b) As used in this chapter, "registration fee" means any charge made, or attempted to be made, to an artist for any of the following purposes:

(1) Registering or listing an applicant for employment in the entertainment industry.

(2) Letter writing.

(3) Photographs, film strips, video tapes, or other reproductions of the applicant.

(4) Costumes for the applicant.

(5) Any activity of a like nature.

Cal. Lab. Code § 1700.3. "License" and "licensee" defined

As used in this chapter:

(a) "License" means a license issued by the Labor Commissioner to carry on the business of a talent agency under this chapter.

(b) "Licensee" means a talent agency which holds a valid, unrevoked, and unforfeited license under this chapter.

Cal. Lab. Code § 1700.4. "Talent agency" and "artists" defined

(a) "Talent agency" means a person or corporation who engages in the occupation of procuring, offering, promising, or attempting to procure employment or engagements for an artist or artists, except that the activities of procuring, offering, or promising to procure recording contracts for an artist or artists shall not of itself subject a person or corporation to regulation and licensing under this chapter. Talent agencies may, in addition, counsel or direct artists in the development of their professional careers.

(b) "Artists" means actors and actresses rendering services on the legitimate stage and in the production of motion pictures, radio artists, musical artists, musical organizations, directors of legitimate stage, motion picture and radio productions, musical directors, writers, cinematographers, composers, lyricists, arrangers, models, and other artists and persons rendering professional services in motion picture, theatrical, radio, television and other entertainment enterprises.

Cal. Lab. Code § 1700.5. Requirement of talent agency license

No person shall engage in or carry on the occupation of a talent agency without first procuring a license therefor from the Labor Commissioner. The license shall be posted in a conspicuous place in the office of the licensee. The license number shall be referred to in any advertisement for the purpose of the solicitation of talent for the talent agency.

Licenses issued for talent agencies prior to the effective date of this chapter shall not be invalidated thereby, but renewals of those licenses shall be obtained in the manner prescribed by this chapter.

Cal. Lab. Code § 1700.23. Approval of talent agency contracts

Every talent agency shall submit to the Labor Commissioner a form or forms of contract to be utilized by such talent agency in entering into written contracts with artists for the employment of the services of such talent agency by such artists, and secure the approval of the Labor Commissioner thereof. Such approval shall not be withheld as to any proposed form of contract unless such proposed form of contract is unfair, unjust and oppressive to the artist. Each such form of contract, except under the conditions specified in Section 1700.45, shall contain an agreement by the talent agency to refer any controversy between the artist and the talent agency relating to the terms of the contract to the Labor

Commissioner for adjustment. There shall be printed on the face of the contract in prominent type the following: "This talent agency is licensed by the Labor Commissioner of the State of California."

Cal. Lab. Code § 1700.25. Trust funds

(a) A licensee who receives any payment of funds on behalf of an artist shall immediately deposit that amount in a trust fund account maintained by him or her in a bank or other recognized depository. The funds, less the licensee's commission, shall be disbursed to the artist within 30 days after receipt. However, notwithstanding the preceding sentence, the licensee may retain the funds beyond 30 days of receipt in either of the following circumstances:

(1) To the extent necessary to offset an obligation of the artist to the talent agency that is then due and owing.

(2) When the funds are the subject of a controversy pending before the Labor Commissioner under Section 1700.44 concerning a fee alleged to be owed by the artist to the licensee.

(b) A separate record shall be maintained of all funds received on behalf of an artist and the record shall further indicate the disposition of the funds.

(c) If disputed by the artist and the dispute is referred to the Labor Commissioner, the failure of a licensee to disburse funds to an artist within 30 days of receipt shall constitute a "controversy" within the meaning of Section 1700.44.

(d) Any funds specified in subdivision (a) that are the subject of a controversy pending before the Labor Commissioner under Section 1700.44 shall be retained in the trust fund account specified in subdivision (a) and shall not be used by the licensee for any purpose until the controversy is determined by the Labor Commissioner or settled by the parties.

(e) If the Labor Commissioner finds, in proceedings under Section 1700.44, that the licensee's failure to disburse funds to an artist within the time required by subdivision (a) was a willful violation, the Labor Commissioner may, in addition to other relief under Section 1700.44, order the following:

(1) Award reasonable attorney's fees to the prevailing artist.

(2) Award interest to the prevailing artist on the funds wrongfully withheld at the rate of 10 percent per annum during the period of the violation.

(f) Nothing in subdivision (c), (d), or (e) shall be deemed to supersede Section 1700.45 or to affect the enforceability of a contractual arbitration provision meeting the criteria of Section 1700.45.

Cal. Lab. Code § 1700.26. Records of talent agency

Every talent agency shall keep records in a form approved by the Labor Commissioner, in which shall be entered all of the following:

(1) The name and address of each artist employing the talent agency.

(2) The amount of fee received from the artist.

(3) The employments secured by the artist during the term of the contract between the artist and the talent agency, and the amount of compensation received by the artists pursuant thereto.

(4) Any other information which the Labor Commissioner requires.

No talent agency, its agent or employees, shall make any false entry in any records.

Cal. Lab. Code § 1700.27. Inspection of books and records

All books, records, and other papers kept pursuant to this chapter by any talent agency shall be open at all reasonable hours to the inspection of the Labor Commissioner and his agents. Every talent agency shall furnish to the Labor Commissioner upon request a true copy of such books, records, and papers or any portion thereof, and shall make such reports as the Labor Commissioner prescribes.

Cal. Lab. Code § 1700.29. Rules and regulations

The Labor Commissioner may, in accordance with the provisions of Chapter 4 (commencing at Section 11370), Part 1, Division 3, Title 2 of the Government Code, adopt, amend, and repeal such rules and regulations as are reasonably necessary for the purpose of enforcing and administering this chapter and as are not inconsistent with this chapter.

Cal. Lab. Code § 1700.36. Unlawful employment of minors

No talent agency shall accept any application for employment made by or on behalf of any minor, as defined by subdivision (c) of Section 1286, or shall place or assist in placing any such minor in any employment whatever in violation of Part 4 (commencing with Section 1171).

Cal. Lab. Code § 1700.37. Judicially approved contract not disaffirmable by minor

A minor cannot disaffirm a contract, otherwise valid, entered into during minority, either during the actual minority of the minor entering into such contract or at any time thereafter, with a duly licensed talent agency as defined in Section 1700.4 to secure him engagements to render artistic or creative services in motion pictures, television, the production of phonograph records, the legitimate or living stage, or otherwise in the entertainment field including, but without being limited to, services as an actor, actress, dancer, musician, comedian, singer, or other performer or entertainer, or as a writer, director, producer, production executive, choreographer, composer, conductor or designer, the blank form of which has been approved by the Labor Commissioner pursuant to Section 1700.23, where such contract has been approved by the superior court of the county where such minor resides or is employed.

Such approval may be given by the superior court on the petition of either party to the contract after such reasonable notice to the other party thereto as may be fixed by said court, with opportunity to such other party to appear and be heard.

Cal. Lab. Code § 1700.39. Fee-splitting

No talent agency shall divide fees with an employer, an agent or other employee of an employer.

Cal. Lab. Code § 1700.40. Prohibition of registration or referral fees; conflicts of interest

(a) No talent agency shall collect a registration fee. In the event that a talent agency shall collect from an artist a fee or expenses for obtaining employment for the artist, and the artist shall fail to procure the employment, or the artist shall fail to be paid for the employment, the talent agency shall, upon demand therefor, repay to the artist the fee and expenses so collected. Unless repayment thereof is made within 48 hours after demand therefor, the talent agency shall pay to the artist an additional sum equal to the amount of the fee.

(b) No talent agency may refer an artist to any person, firm, or corporation in which the talent agency has a direct or indirect financial interest for other services to be rendered to the artist, including, but not limited to, photography, audition tapes, demonstration reels or similar materials, business management, personal management, coaching, dramatic school, casting or talent brochures, agency-client directories, or other printing.

(c) No talent agency may accept any referral fee or similar compensation from any person, association, or corporation providing services of any type expressly set forth in subdivision (b) to an artist under contract with the talent agency.

Cal. Lab. Code § 1700.41. Reimbursement for traveling expenses

In cases where an artist is sent by a talent agency beyond the limits of the city in which the office of such talent agency is located upon the representation of such talent agency that employment of a particular type will there be available for the artist and the artist does not find such employment available, such talent agency shall reimburse the artist for any actual expenses incurred in going to and returning from the place where the artist has been so sent unless the artist has been otherwise so reimbursed.

Cal. Lab. Code § 1700.44. Disputes referred to Labor Commissioner

(a) In cases of controversy arising under this chapter, the parties involved shall refer the matters in dispute to the Labor Commissioner, who shall hear and determine the same, subject to an appeal within 10 days after determination, to the superior court where the same shall be heard de novo. To stay any award for money, the party aggrieved shall execute a bond approved by the superior court in a sum not exceeding twice the amount of the judgment. In all other cases the bond shall be in a sum of not less than one thousand dollars ($1,000) and approved by the superior court.

The Labor Commissioner may certify without a hearing that there is no controversy within the meaning of this section if he or she has by investigation established that there is no dispute as to the amount of the fee due. Service of the certification shall be made upon all parties concerned by registered or certified mail with return receipt requested and the certification shall become conclusive 10 days after the date of mailing if no objection has been filed with the Labor Commissioner during that period.

(b) Notwithstanding any other provision of law to the contrary, failure of any person to obtain a license from the Labor Commissioner pursuant to this chapter shall not be considered a criminal act under any law of this state.

(c) No action or proceeding shall be brought pursuant to this chapter with respect to any violation which is alleged to have occurred more than one year prior to commencement of the action or proceeding.

(d) It is not unlawful for a person or corporation which is not licensed pursuant to this chapter to act in conjunction with, and at the request of, a licensed talent agency in the negotiation of an employment contract.

Cal. Lab. Code § 1700.45 Arbitration

Notwithstanding Section 1700.44, a provision in a contract providing for the decision by arbitration of any controversy under the contract or as to its existence, validity, construction, performance, nonperformance, breach, operation, continuance, or termination, shall be valid:

(a) If the provision is contained in a contract between a talent agency and a person for whom the talent agency under the contract undertakes to endeavor to secure employment, or

(b) If the provision is inserted in the contract pursuant to any rule, regulation, or contract of a bona fide labor union regulating the relations of its members to a talent agency, and

(c) If the contract provides for reasonable notice to the Labor Commissioner of the time and place of all arbitration hearings, and

(d) If the contract provides that the Labor Commissioner or his or her authorized representative has the right to attend all arbitration hearings.

Except as otherwise provided in this section, any arbitration shall be governed by the provisions of Title 9 (commencing with Section 1280) of Part 3 of the Code of Civil Procedure.

If there is an arbitration provision in a contract, the contract need not provide that the talent agency agrees to refer any controversy between the applicant and the talent agency regarding the terms of the contract to the Labor Commissioner for adjustment, and Section 1700.44 shall not apply to controversies pertaining to the contract.

A provision in a contract providing for the decision by arbitration of any controversy arising under this chapter which does not meet the requirements of this section is not made valid by Section 1281 of the Code of Civil Procedure.

Cal. Lab. Code § 1700.47. Unlawful discrimination

It shall be unlawful for any licensee to refuse to represent any artist on account of that artist's race, color, creed, sex, national origin, religion, or handicap.

Cal. Lab. Code § 2855. Enforcement of contract to render personal service; time limit

(a) Except as otherwise provided in subdivision (b), a contract to render personal service, other than a contract of apprenticeship as provided in Chapter 4 (commencing with Section 3070), may not be enforced against the employee beyond seven years from the commencement of service under it. Any contract, otherwise valid, to perform or render service of a special, unique, unusual, extraordinary, or intellectual character, which gives it peculiar value and the loss of which can not be reasonably or adequately compensated in damages in an action at law, may nevertheless be enforced against the person contracting to render the service, for a term not to exceed seven years from the commencement of service under it. If the employee voluntarily continues to serve under it beyond that time, the contract may be referred to as affording a presumptive measure of the compensation.

(b) Notwithstanding subdivision (a):

(1) Any employee who is a party to a contract to render personal service in the production of phonorecords in which sounds are first fixed, as defined in Section 101 of Title 17 of the United States Code, may not invoke the provisions of subdivision (a) without first giving written notice to the employer in accordance with Section 1020 of the Code of Civil Procedure, specifying that the employee from and after a future date certain specified in the notice will no longer render service under the contract by reason of subdivision (a).

(2) Any party to such a contract shall have the right to recover damages for a breach of the contract occurring during its term in an action commenced during or after its term, but within the applicable period prescribed by law.

(3) In the event a party to such a contract is, or could contractually be, required to render personal service in the production of a specified quantity of the phonorecords and fails to render all of the required service prior to the date specified in the notice provided in paragraph (1), the party damaged by the failure shall have the right to recover damages for each phonorecord as

to which that party has failed to render service in an action which, notwithstanding paragraph (2), shall be commenced within 45 days after the date specified in the notice.

Cal. Lab. Code § 2924. Termination of employment by employer

An employment for a specified term may be terminated at any time by the employer in case of any willful breach of duty by the employee in the course of his employment, or in case of his habitual neglect of his duty or continued incapacity to perform it.

Cal. Lab. Code § 2925. Termination of employment by employee

An employment for a specified term may be terminated by the employee at any time in case of any wilful or permanent breach of the obligations of his employer to him as an employee.

INDIANA STATUTES

Ind. Code § 32-13-1-1. Application of chapter

Sec. 1.(a) This chapter applies to an act or event that occurs within Indiana, regardless of a personality's domicile, residence, or citizenship.

(b) This chapter does not affect rights and privileges recognized under any other law that apply to a news reporting or an entertainment medium.

(c) This chapter does not apply to the following:

(1) The use of a personality's name, voice, signature, photograph, image, likeness, distinctive appearance, gestures, or mannerisms in any of the following:

(A) Literary works, theatrical works, musical compositions, film, radio, or television programs.

(B) Material that has political or newsworthy value.

(C) Original works of fine art.

(D) Promotional material or an advertisement for a news reporting or an entertainment medium that:

(i) uses all or part of a past edition of the medium's own broadcast or publication; and

(ii) does not convey or reasonably suggest that a personality endorses the news reporting or entertainment medium.

(E) An advertisement or commercial announcement for a use described under this subdivision.

(2) The use of a personality's name to truthfully identify the personality as:

(A) the author of a written work; or

(B) a performer of a recorded performance;

under circumstances in which the written work or recorded performance is otherwise rightfully reproduced, exhibited, or broadcast.

(3) The use of a personality's:

(A) name;

(B) voice;

(C) signature;

(D) photograph;

(E) image;

(F) likeness;

(G) distinctive appearance;

(H) gestures; or

(I) mannerisms;

in connection with the broadcast or reporting of an event or a topic of general or public interest.

Ind. Code § 32-13-1-2. 'Commercial purpose" defined

Sec. 2. As used in this chapter, "commercial purpose" means the use of an aspect of a personality's right of publicity as follows:

(1) On or in connection with a product, merchandise, goods, services, or commercial activities.

(2) For advertising or soliciting purchases of products, merchandise, goods, services, or for promoting commercial activities.

(3) For the purpose of fundraising.

"Ind. Code § 32-13-1-3. "Name" defined

Sec. 3. As used in this chapter, "name" means the actual or assumed name of a living or deceased natural person that is intended to identify the person.

Ind. Code § 32-13-1-4. "News reporting or an entertainment medium" defined

Sec. 4. As used in this chapter, "news reporting or an entertainment medium" means a medium that publishes, broadcasts, or disseminates advertising in the normal course of its business, including the following:

(1) Newspapers.

(2) Magazines.

(3) Radio and television networks and stations.

(4) Cable television systems.

Ind. Code § 32-13-1-5. "Person" defined

Sec. 5. As used in this chapter, "person" means a natural person, a partnership, a firm, a corporation, or an unincorporated association.

Ind. Code § 32-13-1-6. "Personality" defined

Sec. 6. As used in this chapter, "personality" means a living or deceased natural person whose:

(1) name;

(2) voice;

(3) signature;

(4) photograph;

(5) image;

(7) distinctive appearance;

(8) gesture; or

(9) mannerism;

has commercial value, whether the person uses or authorizes the use of the person's rights of publicity for a commercial purpose during the person's lifetime.

Ind. Code § 32-13-1-7. "Right of publicity" defined

Sec. 7. As used in this chapter, "right of publicity" means a personality's property interest in the personality's:

(1) name;

(2) voice;

(3) signature;

(4) photograph;

(5) image;

(6) likeness;

(7) distinctive appearance;

(8) gestures; or

(9) mannerisms.

Ind. Code § 32-13-1-8. Duration of right; consent

Sec. 8. A person may not use an aspect of a personality's right of publicity for a commercial purpose during the personality's lifetime or for one hundred (100) years after the date of the personality's death without having obtained previous written consent from a person specified in section 17 of this chapter.

Ind. Code § 32-13-1-9. Jurisdictional acts

Sec. 9. A person who:

(1) engages in conduct within Indiana that is prohibited under section 8 of this chapter;

(2) creates or causes to be created within Indiana goods, merchandise, or other materials prohibited under section 8 of this chapter;

(3) transports or causes to be transported into Indiana goods, merchandise, or other materials created or used in violation of section 8 of this chapter; or

(4) knowingly causes advertising or promotional material created or used in violation of section 8 of this chapter to be published, distributed, exhibited, or disseminated within Indiana;

submits to the jurisdiction of Indiana courts.

Ind. Code § 32-13-1-10. Damages

Sec. 10. A person who violates section 8 of this chapter may be liable for any of the following:

(1) Damages in the amount of:

(A) one thousand dollars ($1,000); or

(B) actual damages, including profits derived from the unauthorized use; whichever is greater.

(2) Treble or punitive damages, as the injured party may elect, if the violation under section 8 of this chapter is knowing, willful, or intentional.

Ind. Code § 32-13-1-11. Proof of profits

Sec. 11. In establishing the profits under section 10(1)(B) of this chapter:

(1) the plaintiff is required to prove the gross revenue attributable to the unauthorized use; and

(2) the defendant is required to prove properly deductible expenses.

Ind. Code § 32-13-1-12. Additional remedies

Sec. 12. In addition to any damages awarded under section 10 of this chapter, the court:

(1) shall award to the prevailing party reasonable attorney's fees, costs, and expenses relating to an action under this chapter; and

(2) may order temporary or permanent injunctive relief, except as provided by section 13 of this chapter.

Ind. Code § 32-13-1-13. Restrictions on injunctive relief

Sec. 13. Injunctive relief is not enforceable against a news reporting or an entertainment medium that has:

(1) contracted with a person for the publication or broadcast of an advertisement; and

(2) incorporated the advertisement in tangible form into material that has been prepared for broadcast or publication.

Ind. Code § 32-13-1-14 Impoundment of materials

Sec. 14. (a) This section does not apply to a news reporting or an entertainment medium.

(b) During any period that an action under this chapter is pending, a court may order the impoundment of:

(1) goods, merchandise, or other materials claimed to have been made or used in violation of section 8 of this chapter; and

(2) plates, molds, matrices, masters, tapes, negatives, or other items from which goods, merchandise, or other materials described under subdivision (1) may be manufactured or reproduced.

(c) The court may order impoundment under subsection (b) upon terms that the court considers reasonable.

Ind. Code § 32-13-1-15. Destruction of offending materials

Sec. 15. (a) This section does not apply to a news reporting or an entertainment medium.

(b) As part of a final judgment or decree, a court may order the destruction or other reasonable disposition of items described in section 14(b) of this chapter.

Ind. Code § 32-13-1-16. Transferability of property rights

Sec. 16. The rights recognized under this chapter are property rights, freely transferable and descendible, in whole or in part, by the following:

(1) Contract.

(2) License.

(3) Gift.

(4) Trust.

(5) Testamentary document.

(6) Operation of the laws of intestate succession applicable to the state administering the estate and property of an intestate deceased personality, regardless of whether the state recognizes the property rights set forth under this chapter.

Ind. Code § 32-13-1-17 Exercise and enforcement of rights and remedies

Sec. 17. (a) The written consent required by section 8 of this chapter and the rights and remedies set forth in this chapter may be exercised and enforced by:

(1) a personality; or

(2) a person to whom the recognized rights have been transferred under section 16 of this chapter.

(b) If the transfer described under subsection (a) has not occurred, a person or personality to whom the rights recognized are transferred under section 18 of this chapter may exercise and enforce the rights and remedies under this chapter.

Ind. Code § 32-13-1-18. Exercise and enforcement of rights and remedies following death of intestate personality

Sec. 18. (a) Subject to sections 16 and 17 of this chapter, after the death of an intestate personality, the rights and remedies of this chapter may be exercised and enforced by a person who possesses a total of not less than one-half (½) interest of the rights.

(b) A person described in subsection (a) shall account to any other person in whom the rights have vested to the extent that the other person's interest may appear.

Ind. Code § 32-13-1-19. Termination of untransferred rights following personality's death

Sec. 19. If:

(1) a deceased personality has not transferred the deceased person's rights under this chapter by:

    (A) contract;

    (B) license;

    (C) gift;

    (D) trust; or

    (E) testamentary document; and

(2) there are no surviving persons as described in section 17 of this chapter; the rights set forth in this chapter terminate.

Ind. Code § 32-13-1-20. Additional rights and remedies

Sec. 20. The rights and remedies provided for in this chapter are supplemental to any other rights and remedies provided by law.

NEW YORK STATUTES

N.Y. Arts & Cult. Aff. § 14.01 Right to reproduce works of fine art

1. Whenever a work of fine art is sold or otherwise transferred by or on behalf of the artist who created it, or his heirs or personal representatives, the reproduction right thereto is reserved to the grantor until it passes into the public domain by act or operation of law unless such right is sooner expressly transferred by an instrument, note or memorandum in writing signed by the owner of the rights conveyed or his duly authorized agent.

2. Whenever an exclusive or non-exclusive conveyance of any reproduction right is made by the holder of such right, or his duly authorized agent, ownership of the physical work of fine art shall be presumed to remain with and be reserved to the grantor unless expressly transferred in writing by an instrument, note or memorandum or by other written means, signed by the grantor or his duly authorized agent.

3. This article shall not apply to the sale, conveyance, donation or other transfer of the physical work of fine art which does not include a conveyance of a reproduction right in such work.

4. Nothing herein contained, however, shall be construed to prohibit the fair use of such work of fine art.

5. Nothing in this section shall operate or be construed to conflict with any rights or liabilities under federal copyright law.

N.Y. Arts & Cult. Aff. § 14.03 Artists authorship rights

1. Except as limited by subdivision three of this section, on and after January first, nineteen hundred eighty-five, no person other than the artist or a person acting with the artist's consent shall knowingly display in a place accessible to the public or publish a work of fine art or limited edition multiple of not more than three hundred copies by that artist or a reproduction thereof in an altered, defaced, mutilated or modified form if the work is displayed, published or reproduced as being the work of the artist, or under circumstances under which it would reasonably be regarded as being the work of the artist, and damage to the artist's reputation is reasonably likely to result therefrom, except that this section shall not apply to sequential imagery such as that in motion pictures.

2. (a) Except as limited by subdivision three of this section, the artist shall retain at all times the right to claim authorship, or, for just and valid reason, to disclaim authorship of such work. The right to claim authorship shall include the right of the artist to have his or her name appear on or in connection with such work as the artist. The right to disclaim authorship shall include the right of the artist to prevent his or her name from appearing on or in connection with such work as the artist. Just and valid reason for disclaiming authorship shall include that the work has been altered, defaced, mutilated or modified

other than by the artist, without the artist's consent, and damage to the artist's reputation is reasonably likely to result or has resulted therefrom.

(b) The rights created by this subdivision shall exist in addition to any other rights and duties which may now or in the future be applicable.

3.   (a) Alteration, defacement, mutilation or modification of such work resulting from the passage of time or the inherent nature of the materials will not by itself create a violation of subdivision one of this section or a right to disclaim authorship under subdivision two of this section; provided such alteration, defacement, mutilation or modification was not the result of gross negligence in maintaining or protecting the work of fine art.

(b) In the case of a reproduction, a change that is an ordinary result of the medium of reproduction does not by itself create a violation of subdivision one of this section or a right to disclaim authorship under subdivision two of this section.

(c) Conservation shall not constitute an alteration, defacement, mutilation or modification within the meaning of this section, unless the conservation work can be shown to be negligent.

(d) This section shall not apply to work prepared under contract for advertising or trade use unless the contract so provides.

(e) The provisions of this section shall apply only to works of fine art or limited edition multiples of not more than three hundred copies knowingly displayed in a place accessible to the public, published or reproduced in this state.

4.   (a) An artist aggrieved under subdivision one or subdivision two of this section shall have a cause of action for legal and injunctive relief.

(b) No action may be maintained to enforce any liability under this section unless brought within three years of the act complained of or one year after the constructive discovery of such act, whichever is longer.

N.Y. Arts & Cult. Aff. § 35.01 Child performers

1. It shall be unlawful, except as otherwise provided in this section, to employ, or to exhibit or cause to be exhibited, or to use, or have custody of, for the purpose of exhibition, use or employment, any child under the age of sixteen years, or for one who has the care, custody or control of such child as a parent, relative, guardian, employer or otherwise, to exhibit, use or to procure or consent to the use or exhibition of such child, or to neglect or to refuse to restrain such child from engaging or acting in a public or private place, except as hereinafter provided, whether or not an admission fee is charged and whether or not such child or any other person is to be compensated for the use of such child therein, in the following activities:

(a) In singing; or dancing; or playing upon a musical instrument; or acting, or in rehearsing for, or performing in a theatrical performance or appearing in a pageant; or as a subject for use, in or for, or in connection with the making of a motion picture film; or

(b) In rehearsing for or performing in a radio or television broadcast or program.

2. The provisions of subdivision one of this section shall not apply to the participation or employment, use or exhibition of any child in a church, academy or school, including a dancing or dramatic school, as part of the regular services or activities thereof respectively; or in the annual graduation exercises of any such academy or school; or in a private home; or in any place where such performance is under the direction, control or supervision of a department of education; or in the performance of radio or television programs in cases where the child or children broadcasting do so from a school, church, academy, museum, library or other religious, civic or educational institution, or for not more than two hours a week from the studios of a regularly licensed broadcasting company, where the performance of the child or children is of a nonprofessional character and occurs during hours when attendance for instruction is not required in accordance with the education law.

3. Notwithstanding the foregoing provisions of subdivision one of this section, such a child may be employed, used or exhibited in any of the exhibitions, rehearsals or performances set forth in subdivision one of this section if a child performer permit has been issued as hereinafter provided.

4. A child performer permit shall be issued by the mayor or other chief executive officer of the city, town or village where the exhibition, rehearsal or performance will take place.

5. An application for a child performer permit shall be made on a form prescribed by the issuing authority and shall contain such matters as the issuing authority may deem to be necessary, including the following:

(a) The true and stage name and the age of the child, and the name and address of his parent or guardian;

(b) The written consent of the parent or guardian;

(c) The nature, time, duration and number of performances, together with the place and nature of the exhibition;

(d) A detailed description of the entire part to be taken and each and every act and thing to be done and performed, except that if the performance is in connection with a radio or television program, the application shall contain a general statement describing the part or parts to be taken by the child and the nature of the radio or television program.

6. The mayor or other chief executive officer of the city, town or village where the exhibition, rehearsal or performance will take place may solicit the assistance of the Society for the Prevention of Cruelty to Children in New York City, and outside New York City, with the Society for the Prevention of Cruelty to Children

or other child protective organization, if there be one and such other state and local agencies as he may determine.

7. No child shall perform except as provided in the permit. No permit shall be issued for the exhibition, rehearsal or performance of a child which is harmful to the welfare, development or proper education of such child. A permit may be revoked by the issuing authority for good cause.

8. Violation of this section shall be a misdemeanor.

N.Y. Arts & Cult. Aff. § 35.03 Judicial approval of certain contracts for services of infants; guardianship of savings

1. A contract made by an infant or made by a parent or guardian of an infant, or a contract proposed to be so made, under which (a) the infant is to perform or render services as an actor, actress, dancer, musician, vocalist or other performing artist, or as a participant or player in professional sports, or (b) a person is employed to render services to the infant in connection with such services of the infant or in connection with contracts therefor, may be approved by the supreme court or the surrogate's court as provided in this section where the infant is a resident of this state or the services of the infant are to be performed or rendered in this state. If the contract is so approved the infant may not, either during his minority or upon reaching his majority, disaffirm the contract on the ground of infancy or assert that the parent or guardian lacked authority to make the contract. A contract modified, amended or assigned after its approval under this section shall be deemed a new contract.

2. (a) Approval of the contract pursuant to this section shall not exempt any person from any other law with respect to licenses, consents or authorizations required for any conduct, employment, use or exhibition of the infant in this state, nor limit in any manner the discretion of the licensing authority or other persons charged with the administration of such requirements, nor dispense with any other requirement of law relating to the infant.

(b) No contract shall be approved which provides for an employment, use or exhibition of the infant, within or without the state, which is prohibited by law and could not be licensed to take place in this state.

(c) No contract shall be approved unless (i) the written acquiescence to such contract of the parent or parents having custody, or other person having custody of the infant, is filed in the proceeding or (ii) the court shall find that the infant is emancipated.

(d) No contract shall be approved if the term during which the infant is to perform or render services or during which a person is employed to render services to the infant, including any extensions thereof by option or otherwise, extends for a period of more than three years from the date of approval of the contract. If the contract contains any other covenant or condition which extends beyond such three years, the same may be approved if found to be reasonable and for such period as the court may determine.

(e) If the court which has approved a contract pursuant to this section shall find that the well-being of the infant is being impaired by the performance thereof, it may, at any time during the term of the contract during which services are to be performed by the infant or rendered by or to the infant or during the term of any other covenant or condition of the contract, either revoke its approval of the contract, or declare such approval revoked unless a modification of the contract which the court finds to be appropriate in the circumstances is agreed upon by the parties and the contract as modified is approved by order of the court. Application for an order pursuant to this paragraph may be made by the infant, or his parent or parents, or guardian, or his limited guardian appointed pursuant to this section, or by the person having the care and custody of the infant, or by a special guardian appointed for the purpose by the court on its own motion. The order granting or denying the application shall be made after hearing, upon notice to the parties to the proceeding in which the contract was approved, given in such manner as the court shall direct. Revocation of the approval of the contract shall not affect any right of action existing at the date of the revocation, except that the court may determine that a refusal to perform on the ground of impairment of the well-being of the infant was justified.

3.   (a) The court may withhold its approval of the contract until the filing of consent by the parent or parents entitled to the earnings of the infant, or of the infant if he is entitled to his own earnings, that a part of the infant's net earnings for services performed or rendered during the term of the contract be set aside and saved for the infant pursuant to the order of the court and under guardianship as provided in this section, until he attains his majority or until further order of the court. Such consent shall not be deemed to constitute an emancipation of the infant.

(b) The court shall fix the amount or proportion of net earnings to be set aside as it deems for the best interests of the infant, and the amount or proportion so fixed may, upon subsequent application, be modified in the discretion of the court, within the limits of the consent given at the time the contract was approved. In fixing such amount or proportion, consideration shall be given to the financial circumstances of the parent or parents entitled to the earnings of the infant and to the needs of their other children, or if the infant is entitled to his own earnings and is married, to the needs of his family. Unless the infant is at the time thereof entitled to his own earnings and has no dependents, the court shall not condition its approval of the contract upon consent to the setting aside of an amount or proportion in excess of one-half of the net earnings.

(c) For the purposes of this subdivision, net earnings shall mean the gross earnings received for services performed or rendered by the infant during the term of the contract, less (i) all sums required by law to be paid as taxes to any government or subdivision thereof with respect to or by reason of such earnings; (ii) reasonable sums to be expended for the support, care, education, training and professional management of the infant; and (iii) reasonable fees and expenses paid or to be paid in connection with the proceeding, the contract and its performance.

4.   (a) A proceeding for the approval of a contract shall be commenced by verified petition of the guardian of the infant's person or property, or of the infant, or of a parent, or of any interested person, or of any relative of the infant on his behalf. If a guardian of the infant's person or property has been appointed or qualified in this state, the petition shall be made to the court by which he was appointed or in which he qualified. If there is no such guardian, the petition shall be made to the supreme court or the surrogate's court in the county in which the infant resides, or if he is not a resident of the state, in any county in which the infant is to be employed under the contract.

(b) The following persons, other than one who is the petitioner or joins in the petition, shall be served with an order or citation to show cause why the petition should not be granted: (i) the infant, if over the age of fourteen years, (ii) his guardian or guardians, if any, whether or not appointed or qualified in this state; (iii) each party to the contract; (iv) the parent or parents of the infant; (v) any person having the care and custody of the infant; (vi) the person with whom the infant resides; and (vii) if it appears that the infant is married, his spouse. Service shall be made in such manner as the court shall direct, at least eight days before the time at which the petition is noticed to be heard, unless the court shall fix a shorter time.

5. The petition shall have annexed a complete copy of the contract or proposed contract and shall set forth:

(a) The full name, residence and date of birth of the infant;

(b) The name and residence of any living parent of the infant, the name and residence of the person who has care and custody of the infant, and the name and residence of the person with whom the infant resides;

(c) Whether the infant has had at any time a guardian appointed by will or deed or by a court of any jurisdiction;

(d) Whether the infant is a resident of the state, or if he is not a resident, that the petition is for approval of a contract for performance or rendering of services by the infant and the place in the state where the services are to be performed or rendered;

(e) A brief statement as to the infant's employment and compensation under the contract or proposed contract;

(f) (i) A statement that the term of the contract during which the infant is to perform or render services or during which a person is employed to render services to the infant can in no event extend for a period of more than three years from the date of approval of the contract, and (ii) an enumeration of any other covenants or conditions contained in the contract which extend beyond such three years or a statement that the contract contains no such other covenants or conditions;

(g) A statement as to who is entitled to the infant's earnings and, if the infant is not so entitled, facts regarding the property and financial circumstances of the parent or parents who are so entitled;

(h) The facts with respect to any previous application for the relief sought in the petition or similar relief with respect to the infant;

(i) A schedule showing the infant's gross earnings, estimated outlays and estimated net earnings as defined in subdivision three of this section;

(j) The interest of the petitioner in the contract or proposed contract or in the infant's performance under it;

(k) Such other facts regarding the infant, his family and property, as show that the contract is reasonable and provident and for the best interests of the infant.

If no guardian of the property of the infant has been appointed or qualified in this state, the petition shall also pray for the appointment of a limited guardian as provided in subdivision seven of this section. The petition may nominate a person to be appointed as such limited guardian, setting forth reasons why the person nominated would be a proper and suitable person to be appointed as limited guardian and setting forth the interest of the person so nominated in the contract or proposed contract or in the infant's performance under it.

6. At any time after the filing of the petition, the court, if it deems it advisable, may appoint a special guardian to represent the interests of the infant.

7. If a guardian of the property of the infant has been appointed or qualified in this state, he shall receive and hold any net earnings directed by the court to be set aside for the infant as provided in subdivision three. In any other case a limited guardian shall be appointed for such purpose. A parent, guardian or other petitioner is not ineligible to be appointed as limited guardian by reason of his interest in any part of the infant's earnings under the contract or proposed contract or by reason of the fact that he is a party to or otherwise interested in the contract or in the infant's performance under the contract, provided such interest is disclosed.

If the contract is approved and if the court shall direct that a portion of the net earnings be set aside as provided in subdivision three of this section, the limited guardian shall qualify in the manner provided with respect to a general guardian of the property of the infant appointed by the court in which the proceeding is had, and with respect to net earnings ordered to be set aside shall be subject to all provisions applicable to a general guardian so appointed.

If a guardian of the property of the infant is appointed or qualifies after the appointment of a limited guardian, the limited guardian may continue to act with respect to earnings under the contract approved by the court until the termination of the contract; upon such termination he shall transfer to the guardian of the infant's property the funds of the infant in his hands.

8. (a) The infant shall attend personally before the court upon the hearing of the petition. Upon such hearing, and upon such proof as it deems necessary and advisable, the court shall make such order as justice and the best interests of the infant require.

(b) The court at such hearing or on an adjournment thereof may, by order:

(i) determine any issue arising from the pleadings or proof and required to be determined for final disposition of the matter, including issues with respect to the age or emancipation of the infant or with respect to entitlement of any person to his earnings;

(ii) disapprove the contract or proposed contract or approve it, or approve it upon such conditions, with respect to modification of the terms thereof or otherwise, as it shall determine;

(iii) appoint a limited guardian as provided in subdivision seven of this section.

(c) If the contract is approved upon condition of consent that a portion of the net earnings of the infant under the contract be set aside, the court shall fix the amount or proportion of net earnings to be set aside and if the court shall find that consent or consents thereto have been filed as provided in subdivision three of this section, shall give directions with respect to computation of and payment of sums to be set aside.

N.Y. Arts & Cult. Aff. § 35.05 Employment of children as models

1. It shall be unlawful to employ, use, exhibit or cause to be exhibited a minor as a model unless:

(a) A child model work permit has been issued as hereinafter provided; and

(b) Such employment, use or exhibition is in accordance with the rules and regulations promulgated by the commissioner of education as hereinafter provided.

2. It shall be unlawful for any parent or guardian of a minor to obtain or consent to the employment or exhibition of such minor as a model unless a permit has been issued in accordance with this section.

3. An application for a permit for the employment or exhibition of a minor as a model shall be made by such minor or by his parent or guardian on a form prescribed by the commissioner of education and shall contain such matters as the commissioner may determine to be necessary, including the following:

(a) The minor's name, address, date of birth, and if the minor is of school age, the name and address of the school the minor attends and, if the application is made by his parent or guardian of a minor over twelve years of age the consent of such minor;

(b) The name and address of the parent or guardian, and the consent of the parent or guardian to the issuance of the permit;

(c) A certificate from a physician showing that the minor is physically fit to be employed or exhibited as a model. In a city of over one million population such certificate shall be issued by a physician designated by the department of health if the minor is of school age.

4. A child model work permit shall be issued upon application to the superintendent of schools in cities and school districts employing a superintendent of schools and elsewhere upon application to the district superintendent of schools. A superintendent of schools or district superintendent of schools may, in accordance with regulations of the commissioner of education, designate in writing one or more public school officials to act as certificating officer in his stead.

5. A child model work permit may be issued by the certificating officer if he finds that the employment or exhibition of the minor as a model will not be harmful to his health and welfare, and that, in the case of a minor of school age, the minor's education will not be neglected.

6. A child model work permit:

(a) Shall be signed by each person employing, using, or exhibiting the minor prior to the commencement of the minor's employment or exhibition and shall permit the employment, use or exhibition of such minor only when signed by such person;

(b) Shall not be valid when attendance for instruction is required in accordance with the education law;

(c) Shall terminate one year after the date of issuance;

(d) May be revoked by the certificating officer at any time for good cause.

7. The commissioner of education may promulgate rules and regulations to carry out the provisions of this section. Such rules and regulations shall be designed to protect the health and welfare of child models and to insure that the conditions under which such child models are employed, used or exhibited will not impair their health or welfare.

8. This section shall not apply to the employment, use, or exhibition of a minor as a model:

(a) In a television broadcast or program for whom a permit has been issued pursuant to section 35.01 of this article;

(b) By a federal, state or municipal government or political subdivision or agency thereof, or by any corporation, unincorporated association, community chest, fund or foundation organized and operated exclusively for religious, charitable or educational purposes, no part of the net earnings of which inures to the benefit of any private shareholder or individual.

9. Violation of this section shall be a misdemeanor.

N.Y. Arts & Cult. Aff. § 37.01 Definitions

As used in sections 37.03 and 37.05 of this article:

1. "Person" means any individual, company, society, association, corporation, manager, contractor, subcontractor, partnership, bureau, agency, service, office or the agent or employee of the foregoing.

2. "Fee" means anything of value, including any money or other valuable consideration charged, collected, received, paid or promised for any service, or act rendered or to be rendered by an employment agency, including but not limited to money received by such agency or its emigrant agent which is more than the amount paid by it for transportation, transfer of baggage, or board and lodging on behalf of any applicant for employment.

3. "Theatrical employment agency" means any person (as defined in subdivision one hereof) who procures or attempts to procure employment or engagements for circus, vaudeville, the variety field, the legitimate theater, motion pictures, radio, television, phonograph recordings, transcriptions, opera, concert, ballet, modeling or other entertainments or exhibitions or performances, but such term does not include the business of managing such entertainments, exhibitions or performances, or the artists or attractions constituting the same, where such business only incidentally involves the seeking of employment therefor.

4. "Theatrical engagement" means any engagement or employment of a person as an actor, performer or entertainer in employment described in subdivision three of this section.

N.Y. Arts & Cult. Aff. § 37.03 Theatrical employment; contracts

Every licensed person who shall procure for or offer to an applicant a theatrical engagement shall have executed in duplicate a contract or deliver to the parties as herein set forth a statement containing the name and address of the applicant; the name and address of the employer of the applicant and of the person acting for such employer in employing such applicant; the time and duration of such engagement; the amount to be paid to such applicant; the character of entertainment to be given or services to be rendered; the number of performances per day or per week that are to be given by said applicant; if a vaudeville engagement, the name of the person by whom the transportation is to be paid, and if by the applicant, either the cost of transportation between the places where said entertainment or services are to be given or rendered, or the average cost of transportation between the places where such services are to be given or rendered; and if a dramatic engagement, the cost of transportation to the place where the services begin, if paid by the applicant; and the gross commission or fees to be paid by said applicant and to whom. Such contracts or statements shall contain no other conditions and provisions except such as are equitable between the parties thereto and do not constitute an unreasonable restriction of business. Forms of such contract and statement in blank shall be first approved by the commissioner and his determination shall be reviewable by certiorari. One of such duplicate contracts or of such statements shall be delivered to the person engaging the applicant and the other shall be retained by the applicant. The licensed person procuring such engagement for such applicant shall keep on file or enter in a book provided for

N.Y. Arts & Cult. Aff. § 37.05 Theatrical employment; financial investigations

A theatrical employment agent shall investigate whether or not any employer (person, firm or corporation) who is offering employment to an applicant for employment, has defaulted in the payment of salaries, fees or other compensation to any performer or group of performers or has left stranded any performing companies or individuals or groups, during the five years preceding the date of the application. An agent shall not procure or undertake to procure employment or engagements on the part of any performer or groups of performers for an employer who has failed to pay salaries, fees or other compensation, or who has left stranded any performer or groups of performers or any performing companies or individuals during the five years preceding the date of the application, unless such employer (person, firm or corporation) shall provide sufficient security for the direct benefit of the performer or performers and in an amount ample to pay the performer or performers their full compensation for the specified employment or engagement designated in the employment or engagement contract. The provisions of this section shall not apply to employment or engagements in modeling.

N.Y. Arts & Cult. Aff. § 37.07 Performing artists; ads for availability of employment

1. It shall be unlawful for any person, firm, corporation, association, or agent or employee thereof, holding itself out to the public by any designation indicating a connection with show business including, but not limited to, talent agent, talent scout, personal manager, artist manager, impresario, casting director, public relations advisor or consultant, promotion advisor or consultant, to

(a) Make, publish, disseminate, circulate or place before the public or cause directly or indirectly to be made, published, disseminated, circulated or placed before the public in this state an advertisement, solicitation, announcement, notice or statement which represents that such person, firm, corporation or association has employment available or is able to secure any employment in the field of show business, including, but not limited to, theatre, motion pictures, radio, television, phonograph records, commercials, opera, concerts, dance, modeling or any other entertainments, exhibitions or performances when an advance fee of any nature is a condition to such employment; or

(b) Accept from a member of the public any fee, retainer, salary, advance payment or other compensation of any nature in return for services or otherwise, other than (i) repayment for advances or expenses actually incurred for or on behalf of such member of the public, or (ii) agreed commissions, royalties or similar compensation based upon payments received by or on behalf of such member of the public as a result of his employment in the field of show business.

2. Whenever there shall be a violation of this section, an application may be made by the attorney general in the name of the people of the state of New York to a court or justice having jurisdiction to issue an injunction, and upon notice to the defendant of not less than five days, to enjoin and restrain the continuance of such violations; and if it shall appear to the satisfaction of the court or justice that the defendant has, in fact, violated this section, an injunction may be issued by such court or justice, enjoining and restraining any further violation, without requiring proof that any person has, in fact, been injured or damaged thereby. In any such proceeding, the court may make allowances to the attorney general as provided in paragraph six of subdivision (a) of section eighty-three hundred three of the civil practice law and rules, and direct restitution. In connection with any such proposed application, the attorney general is authorized to take proof and make a determination of the relevant facts and to issue subpoenas in accordance with the civil practice law and rules.

N.Y. Civ. Rights § 50. Right of privacy

A person, firm or corporation that uses for advertising purposes, or for the purposes of trade, the name, portrait or picture of any living person without having first obtained the written consent of such person, or if a minor of his or her parent or guardian, is guilty of a misdemeanor.

N.Y. Civ. Rights § 51. Action for injunction and for damages

Any person whose name, portrait, picture or voice is used within this state for advertising purposes or for the purposes of trade without the written consent first obtained as above provided [§ 50] may maintain an equitable action in the supreme court of this state against the person, firm or corporation so using his name, portrait, picture or voice, to prevent and restrain the use thereof; and may also sue and recover damages for any injuries sustained by reason of such use and if the defendant shall have knowingly used such person's name, portrait, picture or voice in such manner as is forbidden or declared to be unlawful by section fifty of this article, the jury, in its discretion, may award exemplary damages. But nothing contained in this article shall be so construed as to prevent any person, firm or corporation from selling or otherwise transferring any material containing such name, portrait, picture or voice in whatever medium to any user of such name, portrait, picture or voice, or to any third party for sale or transfer directly or indirectly to such a user, for use in a manner lawful under this article; nothing contained in this article shall be so construed as to prevent any person, firm or corporation, practicing the profession of photography, from exhibiting in or about his or its establishment specimens of the work of such establishment, unless the same is continued by such person, firm or corporation after written notice objecting thereto has been given by the person portrayed; and nothing contained in this article shall be so construed as to prevent any person, firm or corporation from using the name, portrait, picture or voice of any manufacturer or dealer in connection with the goods, wares and merchandise manufactured, produced or dealt in by him which he has sold or disposed of with such name, portrait, picture or voice used in connection therewith; or from using the name, portrait, picture or voice of any author, composer or artist in connection with his literary, musical or artistic productions which he has sold or disposed of with such name, portrait, picture or voice used in connection therewith. Nothing contained in this section shall be construed to prohibit the copyright owner of a sound recording from disposing of, dealing in, licensing or selling that sound recording to any party, if the right to dispose of, deal in, license or sell such sound recording has been conferred by contract or other written document by such living person or the holder of such right. Nothing contained in the foregoing sentence shall be deemed to abrogate or otherwise limit any rights or remedies otherwise conferred by federal law or state law.

N.Y. Gen. Bus. Law § 170. Application to employment agencies

This article shall apply to all employment agencies in the state.

N.Y. Gen. Bus. Law § 171. Definitions

Whenever used in this article:

1. "Commissioner" means the industrial commissioner of the state of New York, except that in the application of this article to the city of New York the term "commissioner" means the commissioner of consumer affairs of such city.

2. a. "Employment agency" means any person (as hereinafter defined) who, for a fee, procures or attempts to procure:

(1) employment or engagements for persons seeking employment or engagements, or

(2) employees for employers seeking the services of employees.

b. "Employment agency" shall include any person engaged in the practice of law who regularly and as part of a pattern of conduct, directly or indirectly, recruits, supplies, or attempts or offers to recruit or supply, an employee who resides outside the continental United States (as defined in section one hundred eighty-four-a of this article) for employment in this state and who receives a fee in connection with the arrangement for the admission into this country of such workers for employment.

c. "Employment agency" shall include any person who, for a fee, renders vocational guidance or counseling services and who directly or indirectly:

(1) procures or attempts to procure or represents that he can procure employment or engagements for persons seeking employment or engagements;

(2) represents that he has access, or has the capacity to gain access, to jobs not otherwise available to those not purchasing his services; or

(3) provides information or service of any kind purporting to promote, lead to or result in employment for the applicant with any employer other than himself.

d. "Employment agency" shall include any nurses' registry and any theatrical employment agency (as hereinafter defined).

e. "Employment agency" shall not include: (1) any employment bureau conducted by a duly incorporated bar association, hospital, association of registered professional nurses, registered medical institution, or by a duly incorporated association or society of professional engineers, or by a duly incorporated association or society of land surveyors, or by a duly incorporated association or society of registered architects; (2) any speakers' bureau as defined in subdivision eleven hereof; (3) any organization operated by or under the exclusive control of a bonafide nonprofit educational, religious, charitable or eleemosynary institution; (4) any person, firm, corporation or organization defined and regulated by sections one hundred ninety-one through one hundred ninety-three of this chapter.

3. "Fee" means anything of value, including any money or other valuable consideration charged, collected, received, paid or promised for any service, or act rendered or to be rendered by an employment agency, including but not limited to money received by such agency or its emigrant agent which is more than the amount paid by it for transportation, transfer of baggage, or board and lodging on behalf of any applicant for employment.

4. "Agency manager" means the person designated by the applicant for a license who is responsible for the direction and operation of the placement activities of the agency at the premises covered by the license.

5. "Placement employee" shall mean any agency manager, director, counselor, interviewer, or any other person employed by an employment agency who spends a substantial part of his time interviewing, counseling or conferring with job applicants or employers for the purpose of placing or procuring job applicants, but shall not include employees of an employment agency who are primarily engaged in clerical occupations.

6. "Nurses' registry" means any employment agency, bureau, office or other place which procures or attempts to procure employment or engagements for

nurses licensed pursuant to article one hundred thirty-nine of the education law as a registered professional nurse or licensed practical nurse.

7. "Person" means any individual, company, society, association, corporation, manager, contractor, subcontractor, partnership, bureau, agency, service, office or the agent or employee of the foregoing.

8. "Theatrical employment agency" means any person (as defined in subdivision seven of this section) who procures or attempts to procure employment or engagements for circus, vaudeville, the variety field, the legitimate theater, motion pictures, radio, television, phonograph recordings, transcriptions, opera, concert, ballet, modeling or other entertainments or exhibitions or performances, but such term does not include the business of managing such entertainments, exhibitions or performances, or the artists or attractions constituting the same, where such business only incidentally involves the seeking of employment therefor.

9. "Theatrical engagement" means any engagement or employment of a person as an actor, performer or entertainer in employment described in subdivision eight of this section.

10. "Emigrant agent" shall mean any person, on behalf of an employment agency who, for a fee, procures or attempts to procure employment for persons outside the state or outside the continental United States seeking such employment, or employees from outside the state or outside the continental United States for employers seeking the services of such employees.

11. "Speakers' bureau" means any person whose principal business is to provide lecture business management and promotional services on behalf of lecturers or speakers and procures on behalf of a lecturer or speaker, speaking engagements to appear in lecture programs established by an individual or institutional sponsor and who charges a fee, directly or indirectly, to such lecturer or speaker.

Whenever used in this article words in the singular shall include the plural.

N.Y. Gen. Bus. Law § 172. License requirement

No person shall open, keep, maintain, own, operate or carry on any employment agency unless such person shall have first procured a license therefor as provided in this article. Such license shall be issued by the commissioner of labor, except that if the employment agency is to be conducted in the city of New York such license shall be issued by the commissioner of consumer affairs of such city. Such license shall be posted in a conspicuous place in said agency.

N.Y. Gen. Bus. Law § 181. Contract and information requirement

It shall be the duty of every employment agency to give to each applicant for employment:

1. A true copy of every contract executed between such agency and such applicant, which shall have printed on it or attached to it a statement setting forth in a clear and concise manner the provisions of sections one hundred eighty-five, and one hundred eighty-six of this article.

2. Information as to the name and address of the person to whom the applicant is to apply for such employment, the kind of service to be performed, the anticipated rate of wages or compensation, the agency's fee for the applicant based on such anticipated wages or compensation, whether such employment is permanent or temporary, the name and address of the person authorizing the hiring of such applicant, and the cost of transportation if the services are required outside of the city, town or village where such agency is located. If the job is a conditionally fee-paid job, the conditions under which the applicant will be required to pay a fee shall be clearly set forth in a separate agreement in ten-point type signed by the job applicant.

3. A receipt for any fee, deposit, consideration, or payment which such agency receives from such applicant, which shall have printed or written on it the name of the applicant, the name and address of the employment agency, the date and amount of such fee, deposit, consideration or payment or portion thereof for which the receipt is given, the purpose for which it was paid, and the signature of the person receiving such payment. If the applicant for employment has been recruited from outside the state for domestic or household employment the receipt shall have printed on it, or attached to it, a copy of section one hundred eighty-four of this article.

4. The original or duplicate-original copy of each such contract and receipt shall be retained by every employment agency for three years following the date on which the contract is executed or the payment is made, and shall be made available for inspection by the commissioner or his duly authorized agent or inspector, upon his request. Notwithstanding the other provisions of such contracts, the monetary consideration to be paid by the applicant shall not exceed the fee ceiling provided in subdivision eight of section one hundred eighty-five.

N.Y. Gen. Bus. Law § 185. Fees

1. Circumstances permitting fee. An employment agency shall not charge or accept a fee or other consideration unless in accordance with the terms of a written contract with a job applicant, except for class "A" and "A-1" employment, and except after such agency has been responsible for referring such job applicant to an employer or such employer to a job applicant and where as a result thereof such job applicant has been employed by such employer. The maximum fees provided for herein for all types of placements or employment may be charged to the job applicant and a similar fee may be charged to the employer provided, however, that with regard to placements in class "B" employment, a fee of up to one and one-half times the fee charged to the job applicant may be charged

to the employer. By agreement with an employment agency, the employer may voluntarily assume payment of the job applicant's fee. The fees charged to employers by any licensed person conducting an employment agency for rendering services in connection with, or for providing employment in classes "A," "A-1" and "B," as hereinafter defined in subdivision four of this section where the applicant is not charged a fee shall be determined by agreement between the employer and the employment agency. No fee shall be charged or accepted for the registration of applicants for employees or employment.

2. Size of fee; payment schedule. The gross fee charged to the job applicant and the gross fee charged to the employer each shall not exceed the amounts enumerated in the schedules set forth in this section, for any single employment or engagement, except as hereinabove provided; and such fees shall be subject to the provisions of section one hundred eighty-six of this article. Except as otherwise provided herein, an employment agency shall not require an applicant while employed in the continental United States, and paid weekly to pay any fee at a rate greater than in ten equal weekly instalments each of which shall be payable at the end of each of the first ten weeks of employment, or if paid less frequently, in five equal installments, each of which shall be payable at the end of the first five pay periods following his employment, or within a period of ten weeks, whichever period is longer. An employer's fee shall be due and payable at the time the applicant begins employment, unless otherwise determined by agreement between the employer and the agency.

3. Deposits, advance fees. Notwithstanding any other provisions of this section, an employment agency may not require a deposit or advance fee from any applicant except an applicant for class "A" or class "A1" employment, and only to the extent of the maximum fees hereinafter provided. Such deposit or advance fee shall be offset against any fee charged or accepted when such employment is obtained. Any excess above the lawful fee shall be returned without demand therefor, immediately after the employment agency has been notified that such employment has been obtained; and all of such deposit or advance fee shall be returned immediately upon demand therefor, if at the time of the demand such employment has not been obtained.

4. Types of employment. For the purpose of placing a ceiling over the fees charged by persons conducting employment agencies, types of employment shall be classified as follows:

Class "A"—domestics, household employees, unskilled or untrained manual workers and laborers, including agricultural workers;

Class "A1"—non-professional trained or skilled industrial workers or mechanics;

Class "B"—commercial, clerical, executive, administrative and professional employment, all employment outside the continental United States, and all other employment not included in classes "A," "A1," "C" and "D";

Class "C"—theatrical engagements;

Class "D"—nursing engagements as defined in article one hundred thirty-nine of the education law.

* * *

8. Fee ceiling: For a placement in class "C" employment, the gross fee shall not exceed, for a single engagement, ten per cent of the compensation payable to the applicant, except that for employment or engagements for orchestras and for employment or engagements in the opera and concert fields such fees shall not exceed twenty percent of the compensation.

N.Y. Gen. Bus. Law § 187. Agency prohibitions

An employment agency shall not engage in any of the following activities or conduct:

(1) Induce or attempt to induce any employee to terminate his employment in order to obtain other employment through such agency, provided, however, that this provision shall not apply to an employee not placed in employment by the employment agency who is offered an executive administrative or professional position where the first year's compensation is $12,000.00 or more or procure or attempt to procure the discharge of any person from his employment.

(2) Publish or cause to be published any false, fraudulent or misleading information, representation, promise, notice or advertisement.

(3) Advertise in newspapers or otherwise, or use letterheads or receipts or other written or printed matter, unless such advertising or other matter contains the name and address of the employment agency and the word "agency."

(4) Direct an applicant to an employer for the purpose of obtaining employment without having first obtained a bona fide order therefor; however, a qualified applicant may be directed to an employer who has previously requested that he regularly be accorded interviews with applicants of certain qualifications if a confirmation of the order is sent to the employer. Likewise an employment agency may attempt to sell the services of an applicant to an employer from whom no job order has been received as long as this fact is told to the applicant before he is directed to the employer. Any applicant who is referred to an employer contrary to the provisions of this subdivision without obtaining employment thereby, shall be reimbursed by the employment agency for all ordinary and necessary travel expenses incurred by the applicant as a result of such referral, within twenty-four hours of making a demand therefor.

(5) Send or cause to be sent any person to any employer where the employment agency knows, or reasonably should have known, that the prospective employment is or would be in violation of state or federal laws governing minimum wages or child labor, or in violation of article sixty-five of the education law

relating to compulsory education or article four of the labor law, or, that a labor dispute is in progress, without notifying the applicant of such fact, and delivering to him a clear written statement that a labor dispute exists at the place of such employment, or make any referral to an employment or occupation prohibited by law.

(6) Send or cause to be sent any person to any place which the employment agency knows or reasonably should have known is maintained for immoral or illicit purposes; nor knowingly permit persons of bad character, prostitutes, gamblers, procurers or intoxicated persons to frequent such agency.

(7) Compel any person to enter such agency for any purpose by the use of force.

(8) Engage in any business on the premises of the employment agency other than the business of operating an employment agency, except as owner, manager, employee or agent, the business of furnishing services to employers through the employment of temporary employees.

(9) Receive or accept any valuable thing or gift as a fee or in lieu thereof, nor divide or share, either directly or indirectly, the fees herein allowed, with contractors, subcontractors, employers or their agents, foremen or any one in their employ, or if the contractors, subcontractors or employers be a corporation, any of the officers, directors or employees of the same to whom applicants for employment are sent.

(10) Require applicants for employees or employment to subscribe to any publication or incidental service or contribute to the cost of advertising.

(11) Make or cause to be made or use any name, sign or advertising device bearing a name which may be similar to or may reasonably be confused with the name of a federal, state, city, county or other government agency.

(12) Refuse to return on demand of an applicant any baggage or personal property belonging to such applicant.

(13) Charge an applicant any fee for a placement in a job which the agency advertised or represented to the job applicant to be a fee-paid job.

(14) Refer an applicant to a specified bank or credit organization for purposes of obtaining a loan.

N.Y. Gen. Bus. Law § 189. Enforcement

1. This article and sections 37.01, 37.03 and 37.05 of the arts and cultural affairs law shall be enforced by the commissioner of labor, except that in the city of New York this article and such sections shall be enforced by the commissioner of consumer affairs of such city.

2. To effectuate the purposes of this article and sections 37.01, 37.03 and 37.05 of the arts and cultural affairs law, the commissioner or any duly authorized agent or inspector designated by such commissioner, shall have authority to inspect

the premises, registers, contract forms, receipt books, application forms, referral forms, reference forms, reference reports and financial records of fees charged and refunds made of each employment agency, which are essential to the operation of such agency, and of each applicant for an employment agency license, as frequently as necessary to insure compliance with this article and such sections; but in no event shall any employment agency be inspected less frequently than once every eighteen months. The commissioner shall also have authority to subpoena records and witnesses or otherwise to conduct investigations of any employer or other person where he has reasonable grounds for believing that such employer or person is violating or has conspired or is conspiring with an employment agency to violate this article or such sections.

3. To effectuate the purposes of this article, the commissioner may make reasonable administrative rules within the standards set in this article. Before such rules shall be issued, the commissioner shall conduct a public hearing, giving due notice thereof to all interested parties. No rule shall become effective until fifteen days after it has been filed in the office of the department of state, if it is a rule of the industrial commissioner, or in the office of the clerk of the city of New York, if it is a rule of the commissioner of licenses of such city, and copies thereof shall be furnished to all employment agencies affected at least fifteen days prior to the effective date of such rule.

4. Complaints against any such licensed person shall be made orally or in writing to the commissioner, or be sent in an affidavit form without appearing in person, and may be made by recognized employment agencies, trade associations, or others. The commissioner may hold a hearing on a complaint with the powers provided by section one hundred seventy-four of this article. If a hearing is held, reasonable notice thereof, not less than five days, shall be given in writing to said licensed person by serving upon the licensed person either personally, by mail, or by leaving the same with the person in charge of his office, a concise statement of the facts constituting the complaint, and the hearing shall commence before the commissioner with reasonable speed but in no event later than two weeks from the date of the filing of the complaint. The commissioner when investigating any matters pertaining to the granting, issuing, transferring, renewing, revoking, suspending or canceling of any license is authorized in his discretion to take such testimony as may be necessary on which to base official action. When taking such testimony he may subpoena witnesses and also direct the production before him of necessary and material books and papers. A daily calendar of all hearings shall be kept by the commissioner and shall be posted in a conspicuous place in his public office for at least one day before the date of such hearings. The commissioner shall render his decision within thirty days from the time the matter is finally submitted to him. The commissioner shall keep a record of all such complaints and hearings.

5. Following such hearing if it has been shown that the licensed person or his agent, employee or anyone acting on his behalf is guilty of violating any

provision of this article or is not a person of good character and responsibility, the commissioner may suspend or revoke the license of such licensed person and/or levy a fine against such licensed person for each violation not to exceed five hundred dollars. Whenever such commissioner shall suspend or revoke the license of any employment agency, or shall levy a fine against such agency, said determination shall be subject to judicial review in proceedings brought pursuant to article seventy-eight of the civil practice law and rules. Whenever such license is revoked, another license or agency manager permit shall not be issued within three years from the date of such revocation to said licensed person or his agency manager or to any person with whom the licensee has been associated in the business of furnishing employment or engagements. Deputy commissioners, or other officials designated to act on behalf of the commissioner, may conduct hearings and act upon applications for licenses, and revoke or suspend such licenses, or levy fines.

N.Y. Gen. Bus. Law § 360-1. Injury to business reputation; dilution

Likelihood of injury to business reputation or of dilution of the distinctive quality of a mark or trade name shall be a ground for injunctive relief in cases of infringement of a mark registered or not registered or in cases of unfair competition, notwithstanding the absence of competition between the parties or the absence of confusion as to the source of goods or services.

TENNESSEE STATUTES

Tenn. Code Ann. § 47-25-1101. Personal Rights Protection Act of 1984

This part shall be known and may be cited as the "Personal Rights Protection Act of 1984."

Tenn. Code Ann. § 47-25-1102. Definitions

As used in this part, unless the context otherwise requires:

(1) "Definable group" means an assemblage of individuals existing or brought together with or without interrelation, orderly form, or arrangement, including, but not limited to, a crowd at any sporting event, a crowd in any street or public building, the audience at any theatrical or stage production, a glee club, or a baseball team;

(2) "Individual" means human being, living or dead;

(3) "Likeness" means the use of an image of an individual for commercial purposes;

(4) "Person" means any firm, association, partnership, corporation, joint stock company, syndicate, receiver, common law trust, conservator, statutory trust, or any other concern by whatever name known or however organized, formed, or created, and includes not-for-profit corporations, associations, educational and religious institutions, political parties, community, civic, or other organizations; and

(5) "Photograph" means any photograph or photographic reproduction, still or moving, or any videotape or live television transmission, of any individual, so that the individual is readily identifiable.

Tenn. Code Ann. § 47-25-1103. Property right in use of name, photograph, likeness

(a) Every individual has a property right in the use of that person's name, photograph, or likeness in any medium in any manner.

(b) The individual rights provided for in subsection (a) constitute property rights and are freely assignable and licensable, and do not expire upon the death of the individual so protected, whether or not such rights were commercially exploited by the individual during the individual's lifetime, but shall be descendible to the executors, assigns, heirs, or devisees of the individual so protected by this part.

Tenn. Code Ann. § 47-25-1104. Exclusivity and duration of right

(a) The rights provided for in this part shall be deemed exclusive to the individual, subject to the assignment or licensing of such rights as provided in § 47-25-1103, during such individual's lifetime and to the executors, heirs, assigns, or devisees for a period of ten (10) years after the death of the individual.

(b) (1) Commercial exploitation of the property right by any executor, assignee, heir, or devisee if the individual is deceased shall maintain the right as the exclusive property of the executor, assignee, heir, or devisee until such right is terminated as provided in this subsection (b).

(2) The exclusive right to commercial exploitation of the property rights is terminated by proof of the non-use of the name, likeness, or image of any individual for commercial purposes by an executor, assignee, heir, or devisee to such use for a period of two (2) years subsequent to the initial ten (10) year period following the individual's death.

Tenn. Code Ann. § 47-25-1105. Unauthorized use prohibited

(a) Any person who knowingly uses or infringes upon the use of another individual's name, photograph, or likeness in any medium, in any manner directed to any person other than such individual, as an item of commerce for purposes of advertising products, merchandise, goods, or services, or for purposes of fund raising, solicitation of donations, purchases of products, merchandise, goods, or services, without such individual's prior consent, or, in the case of a minor, the prior consent of such minor's parent or legal guardian, or in the case of a deceased individual, the consent of the executor or administrator, heirs, or devisees of such deceased individual, shall be liable to a civil action.

(b) In addition to the civil action authorized by this section and the remedies set out in § 47-25-1106, any person who commits unauthorized use as defined in subsection (a) commits a Class C misdemeanor.

(c) It is no defense to the unauthorized use defined in subsection (a) that the photograph includes more than one (1) individual so identifiable; provided, that the individual or individuals complaining of the use shall be represented as individuals per se rather than solely as members of a definable group represented in the photograph.

(d) If an unauthorized use as defined in subsection (a) is by means of products, merchandise, goods or other tangible personal property, all such property is declared contraband and subject to seizure by, and forfeiture to, the state in the same manner as is provided by law for the seizure and forfeiture of other contraband items.

Tenn. Code Ann. § 47-25-1106. Remedies

(a) The chancery and circuit court having jurisdiction for any action arising pursuant to this part may grant injunctions on such terms as it may deem reasonable to prevent or restrain the unauthorized use of an individual's name, photograph, or likeness.

(b) At any time while an action under this part is pending, the court may order the impounding, on such terms as it may deem reasonable, of all materials or any part thereof claimed to have been made or used in violation of the individual's rights, and such court may enjoin the use of all plates, molds, matrices, masters, tapes, film negatives, or other articles by means of which such materials may be reproduced.

(c) As part of a final judgment or decree, the court may order the destruction or other reasonable disposition of all materials found to have been made or used in violation of the individual's rights, and of all plates, molds, matrices, masters, tapes, film negatives, or other articles by means of which such materials may be reproduced.

(d) An individual is entitled to recover the actual damages suffered as a result of the knowing use or infringement of such individual's rights and any profits that are attributable to such use or infringement which are not taken into account in computing the actual damages. Profit or lack thereof by the unauthorized use or infringement of an individual's rights shall not be a criteria of determining liability.

(e) The remedies provided for in this section are cumulative and shall be in addition to any others provided for by law.

Tenn. Code Ann. § 47-25-1107. Exemptions

(a) It is deemed a fair use and no violation of an individual's rights shall be found, for purposes of this part, if the use of a name, photograph, or likeness is in connection with any news, public affairs, or sports broadcast or account.

(b) The use of a name, photograph, or likeness in a commercial medium does not constitute a use for purposes of advertising or solicitation solely because the material containing such use is commercially sponsored or contains paid advertising. Rather it shall be a question of fact whether or not the use of the complainant individual's name, photograph, or likeness was so directly connected with the commercial sponsorship or with the paid advertising as to constitute a use for purposes of advertising or solicitation.

(c) Nothing in this section applies to the owners or employees of any medium used for advertising, including, but not limited to, newspapers, magazines, radio and television stations, billboards, and transit ads, who have published or disseminated any advertisement or solicitation in violation of this part, unless it is established that such owners or employees had knowledge of the unauthorized use of the individual's name, photograph, or likeness as prohibited by this section.

INDEX

[References are to pages.]

[References are to pages.]

[References are to pages.]

[References are to pages.]